FEATURES AND BENEFITS

Pre-Algebra, An Accelerated Course

Comprehensive content includes all standard topics of junior high school mathematics. This course enables the most capable students to make the transition from elementary school mathematics to algebra in one year. It emphasizes pre-algebra skills and concepts, such as variables, equation solving, and problem solving. The full range of topics needed for the successful study of algebra is presented. See the Table of Contents.

Class Exercises, Written Exercises, and **Review Exercises** often develop the theory behind lesson concepts as well as basic pre-algebra skills. See pages 111, 112, 132, 133, and 313–315.

Precision in the use of **mathematical terminology** and **concepts** is emphasized in lesson narratives and in special features like **Reading Mathematics.** See pages 2, 3 and 173–175.

Review and testing features at the ends of lessons and chapters measure student progress, reinforce basic skills, and aid retention of frequently used fundamental concepts. See pages 363, 385, and 388–391.

A unique collection of **supplementary materials** accompanies a **comprehensive teacher's edition** that features side-column notes along with annotated versions of the student book pages, teaching commentary, chalkboard examples, additional exercises, and quick quizzes. The supplementary materials consist of the following:

> **Solution Key** (includes worked-out solutions to all exercises)
>
> **Resource Book** (includes extra testing, practice, enrichment, and review sheets; on blackline copying masters)
>
> **Tests** (different from Resource Book tests; on duplicating masters)
>
> **Practice Masters** (different from Resource Book practice sheets; on duplicating masters)
>
> **Computer Activities** (diskettes are available to accompany this item; on duplicating masters)

In addition to the **Computer Activities** on duplicating masters described above, short features in the student book called **Calculator Key-In** and **Computer Byte** extend and apply pre-algebra concepts by means of calculators and computers. See references under *Calculator* and *Computer* in the Index.

Teacher's Edition

PRE-ALGEBRA

An Accelerated Course

Mary P. Dolciani

Robert H. Sorgenfrey

John A. Graham

Editorial Advisers

Richard G. Brown

Robert B. Kane

HOUGHTON MIFFLIN COMPANY · Boston

Atlanta   Dallas   Geneva, Ill.   Palo Alto   Princeton   Toronto

AUTHORS

Mary P. Dolciani formerly Professor of Mathematical Sciences, Hunter College of the City University of New York

Robert H. Sorgenfrey Professor of Mathematics, University of California, Los Angeles

John A. Graham Mathematics Teacher, Buckingham Browne and Nichols School, Cambridge, Massachusetts

Editorial Advisers

Richard G. Brown Mathematics Teacher, Phillips Exeter Academy, Exeter, New Hampshire

Robert B. Kane Dean of the School of Education and Professor of Mathematics Education, Purdue University, Lafayette, Indiana

Teacher Consultants

John E. Mosby Instructional Coordinator, Dixon School, Chicago, Illinois

William Voligny Mathematics Teacher, Olympia Junior High School, Auburn, Washington

Contents

TEACHING THE COURSE

The Teacher's Edition, Resource Book, and Solution Key are designed to help teach the course. For each chapter the Teacher's Edition provides Lesson Commentary and slightly reduced reproductions of student pages with answer annotations. The Lesson Commentary precedes the student pages for each chapter and includes Teaching Suggestions, designed to help in lesson planning, and Related Activities, which can be used to add variety to the presentation. The Lesson Commentary also includes reduced facsimiles of the appropriate Resource Book pages with answer annotations.

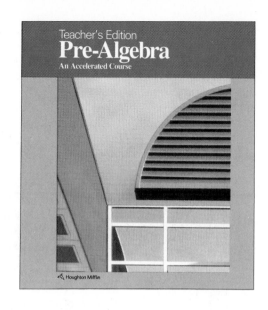

The Resource Book is a book of blackline masters that includes quizzes, tests, reviews, problem solving, enrichment, practice, and calculator or computer pages for each chapter. Four cumulative tests and some teaching aids are also provided. Answers to exercises are printed at the back of the book, as well as in the Teacher's Edition.

The Solution Key provides worked-out solutions and all necessary artwork for the exercises in the student book.

SUPPLEMENTARY MATERIALS

The supplementary materials on duplicating masters include Tests, Practice Masters, and Computer Activities. Each set of masters is keyed to the student textbook and has a separate answer key with answers annotated on facsimiles of the masters.

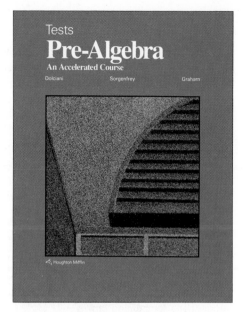

The Tests offer a simple way to measure achievement and keep track of progress.

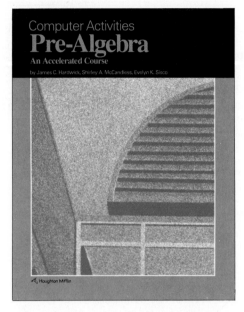

The Computer Activities consist of twenty-four activities in the BASIC computer language. They explore related mathematical topics and are designed to be used independently by the student. Diskettes for the TRS-80 (Model III and Model IV) and Apple II microcomputers are available to be used with the activities. They save students' time by making it unnecessary to type in the programs.

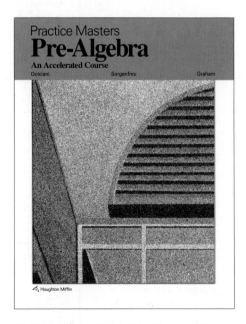

The Practice Masters offer additional practice on the material presented in the student textbook.

This teacher's edition shows nearly full-sized student textbook pages annotated with answers. Time-saving suggestions and additional materials appear in the adjacent margins, where they will be most useful. Sample teacher's edition pages are shown here to explain the material in the side columns. (These are not actual pages.)

Featured are references to the Teaching Suggestions and Related Activities that appear in the Teaching Commentary prior to each chapter.

Reading Mathematics lists vocabulary words and gives suggestions for helping students read and study mathematics.

Chalkboard Examples illustrate each lesson.

Additional Answers supplement the annotations.

Reviews for Retention keep previously learned material alive in students minds.

Teaching Suggestions
p. 393a

Related Activities p. 393a

Reading Mathematics
Students will learn the meaning of the following mathematical terms in this lesson: *square root, perfect square.*

Chalkboard Examples
If the given symbol names an integer, state the integer. If not, name the two consecutive integers between which the number lies.
1. $\sqrt{20}$ 4 and 5
2. $-\sqrt{64}$ -8
3. $\sqrt{121}$ 11
4. $\sqrt{56}$ 7 and 8

Additional Answers
Class Exercises
1. "The positive square root of 7"
2. "3 times the positive square root of 10"
3. "The negative square root of 81"
4. "The positive square root of 64"
5. "2 times the positive square root of 14"

Review for Retention
Solve.
1. $9a - 6a = 39$ 13
2. $-3b - (-2b) = -7$ 7
3. $3(2c - 4) = 12$ 4
4. $2(d - 5) = 4d + 6$ -8
5. $\frac{5}{8}e - 1 = -1$ 0
6. $-2f \le 2$ All the numbers greater than or equal to -1
7. $21 \ge g - 4$ All the numbers less than or equal to 25

394

11-1 Square Roots

Recall that we can write $b \times b$ as b^2 and call it the *square* of b. The factor b is a **square root** of b^2. A given number a has b as a square root if

$$b^2 = a.$$

Thus 9 has 3 as a square root because $3^2 = 9$.

Every positive number has two square roots, and these are opposites of each other. For example, the square roots of 25 are 5 and -5 because

$$5^2 = 5 \times 5 = 25 \quad \text{and} \quad (-5)^2 = (-5) \times (-5) = 25.$$

The only square root of 0 is 0 because $b \times b = 0$ only when $b = 0$.

In this chapter we will work mostly with positive square roots. We use $\sqrt{a}$ to denote the *positive* square root of a. Thus $\sqrt{25} = 5$, not -5. A symbol such as $2\sqrt{25}$ means *2 times the positive square root of 25.* The negative square root of 25 is $-\sqrt{25}$, or -5.

Negative numbers have no real-number square roots because no real number has a square that is negative.

If $\sqrt{a}$ is an integer, we call a a **perfect square.** For example, 36 is a perfect square because $\sqrt{36}$ is the integer 6. Also, 144 is a perfect square because $\sqrt{144} = 12$.

If a is not a perfect square, we can estimate $\sqrt{a}$ by finding the two consecutive integers between which the square root lies. In the process, we use the fact that the smaller of two positive numbers has the smaller positive square root.

EXAMPLE   Between which two consecutive integers does $\sqrt{40}$ lie?

Solution   40 lies between the consecutive perfect squares 36 and 49.

$$36 < 40 < 49$$
$$\sqrt{36} < \sqrt{40} < \sqrt{49}$$
$$\text{Thus} \quad 6 < \sqrt{40} < 7.$$

Class Exercises

Read each symbol.

1. $\sqrt{7}$ 2. $3\sqrt{10}$ 3. $-\sqrt{81}$ 4. $\sqrt{64}$ 5. $2\sqrt{14}$

394   *Chapter 11*

If the given symbol names an integer, state the integer. If not, name the two consecutive integers between which the number lies.

6. $\sqrt{16}$ **7.** $-\sqrt{36}$ **8.** $\sqrt{21}$ **9.** $\sqrt{70}$ **10.** $\sqrt{50}$

11. $-\sqrt{49}$ **12.** $\sqrt{81}$ **13.** $\sqrt{69}$ **14.** $-\sqrt{144}$ **15.** $\sqrt{169}$

Written Exercises

If the given symbol names an integer, state the integer. If not, name the two consecutive integers between which the number lies.

A   **1.** $\sqrt{43}$ **2.** $\sqrt{64}$ **3.** $-\sqrt{16}$ **4.** $\sqrt{24}$ **5.** $\sqrt{1}$

     6. $\sqrt{0}$ **7.** $-\sqrt{6^2}$ **8.** $\sqrt{13}$ **9.** $\sqrt{54}$ **10.** $\sqrt{9}$

     11. $\sqrt{30}$ **12.** $\sqrt{48}$ **13.** $\sqrt{15}$ **14.** $\sqrt{8^2}$ **15.** $\sqrt{2}$

     16. $\sqrt{25} + \sqrt{16}$ **17.** $\sqrt{100} - \sqrt{49}$ **18.** $\sqrt{144} + \sqrt{25}$

     19. $\sqrt{79 - 61}$ **20.** $-\sqrt{66 - 2}$ **21.** $\sqrt{100 - 19}$

Replace the $\underline{\ ?\ }$ with $<$, $>$, or $=$ to make a true statement.

EXAMPLE $\sqrt{9} + \sqrt{25} \underline{\ ?\ } \sqrt{9 + 25}$

Solution $\sqrt{9} + \sqrt{25} = 3 + 5 = 8;\ \sqrt{9 + 25} = \sqrt{34} < 8.$
         Thus $\sqrt{9} + \sqrt{25} > \sqrt{9 + 25}.$

B   **22.** $\sqrt{9} + \sqrt{16} \underline{\ ?\ } \sqrt{9 + 16}$ **23.** $\sqrt{16} + \sqrt{4} \underline{\ ?\ } \sqrt{16 + 4}$

     24. $\sqrt{16} - \sqrt{9} \underline{\ ?\ } \sqrt{16 - 9}$ **25.** $\sqrt{25} - \sqrt{9} \underline{\ ?\ } \sqrt{25 - 9}$

     26. $\sqrt{4} \times \sqrt{9} \underline{\ ?\ } \sqrt{4 \times 9}$ **27.** $\sqrt{25} \times \sqrt{4} \underline{\ ?\ } \sqrt{25 \times 4}$

     28. $2\sqrt{2} \underline{\ ?\ } \sqrt{2 \times 2}$ **29.** $3\sqrt{12} \underline{\ ?\ } \sqrt{3 \times 12}$

Evaluate the expression.

C   **30.** $(\sqrt{25})^2$ **31.** $(\sqrt{81})^2$ **32.** $(\sqrt{49})^2$ **33.** $(\sqrt{11})^2$ **34.** $(\sqrt{2})^2$

Review Exercises

Divide. Round the answer to the nearest hundredth.

1. $44 \div 6.7$ **2.** $35 \div 5.9$ **3.** $72 \div 8.3$ **4.** $96 \div 9.5$

5. $147 \div 12.3$ **6.** $230 \div 14.7$ **7.** $0.0165 \div 0.13$ **8.** $0.68 \div 0.81$

Applying Algebra to Right Triangles   **395**

Assignment Guide/ Management System

To make your planning easier, the following table outlines suggested schedules for core and enriched courses. The core course provides greater review and more drill; the enriched course provides more challenging work and less drill. You can adapt the two courses to the needs of your students.

Key

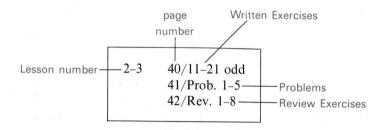

Suggested Time Schedule

Chapter	1	2	3	4	5	6	7	8	9	10	11	12
Core	13	12	13	14	14	14	14	12	12	16	12	14
Enriched	12	10	12	12	10	14	13	14	14	16	16	17

Trimester Semester Trimester

Day	Core Course		Enriched Course	
1	**1-1**	4/1–28; 37, 38 4/Rev. 1–8	**1-1**	4/9–38
2	**1-2**	7/1–24; 29, 31, 33 8/34, 35, 37, 39 8/Calculator Key-In	**1-2**	7/1–23 odd; 25–33 8/34–39 8/Calculator Key-In
3	**1-3**	11/1–15 odd 12/17–49 odd 12/Rev. 1–8	**1-3**	11/9–15 odd 12/25–55 odd; 57–68

Day	Core Course		Enriched Course	
4	**1-4**	16/2–46 even 17/47–54; 60–64 17/Rev. 1–8	**1-4**	2–46 even 17/48–58 even; 59–65 17/Rev. 1–8 17/Challenge
5	**1-5**	21/1–28	**1-5**	21/14–28 even 22/29–38 22/Self-Test A
6	**1-5**	22/29–36 22/Self-Test A	**1-6**	24/1–11 odd 25/19–35 odd; 37–48
7	**1-6**	24/1–11 odd 25/13–37 odd 25/Rev. 1–5	**1-7**	28/29–36; 38–60 even
8	**1-7**	28/2–24 even; 37–45	**1-8**	31/Prob. 1, 3, 5 32/Prob. 8–12 32/Rev. 1–8
9	**1-8**	31/Prob. 1–6 32/Prob. 7–9 32/Rev. 1–8	**1-9**	35/Prob. 2, 4 36/Prob. 5–12
10	**1-9**	35/Prob. 1–4 36/Prob. 5–10	**1-9**	37/Prob. 13–15 37/Self-Test B
11	**1-9**	36/Prob. 11 37/Prob. 13, 15 37/Self-Test B		Prepare for Chapter Test 38–39/Enrichment 40/Chapter Review
12		Prepare for Chapter Test 38–39/Enrichment 40/Chapter Review		Administer Chapter 1 Test Resource Book pp. 15–16 42–43/Cumulative Review
13		Administer Chapter 1 Test 42–43/Cumulative Review Resource Book pp. 15–16	**2-1**	48/23–28 49/30–62 even; 63–65 49/Rev. 6–10
14	**2-1**	48/1–9 odd; 20–28 49/29–51 odd; 63–65 49/Rev. 1–10	**2-2**	52/19–33 odd 53/35–53 odd 53/Rev. 1–9
15	**2-2**	52/2–8 even; 14–32 even 53/36–46 even 53/Rev. 1–9	**2-3**	57/14–42 even, 43 58/Prob. 3–5
16	**2-3**	57/1–37 odd 58/Prob. 1–3	**2-4**	60/9–37 odd 61/51–63 odd 61/Prob. 1–5 62/Prob. 6–9 Self-Test A

Day	Core Course		Enriched Course	
17	**2-4**	60/1–37 odd 61/39–63 odd 61/Prob. 1–5	**2-5**	65/29–38 66/39–55 odd 66/Calculator Key-In 66/Challenge
18	**2-4**	62/Prob. 6–9 62/Self-Test A	**2-6**	68/25–36; 38–50 even 69/52; Rev. 1–8 69/Calculator Key-In
19	**2-5**	65/10–38 even 66/40–50 even 66/Rev. 3–6	**2-7**	72/20–48 72/Calculator Key-In
20	**2-6**	68/1–29 odd; 41–49 odd 69/Rev. 1–5 69/Calculator Key-In	**2-8**	74/7–47 odd 75/Self-Test B 75/Challenge
21	**2-7**	71/2–16 even 72/18–40 even, 47 72/Rev. 2–8 even		Prepare for Chapter Test 76–77/Enrichment 78/Chapter Review
22	**2-8**	44/2–22 even; 23–34		Administer Chapter 2 Test Resource Book pp. 27–28 80–81/Cumulative Review
23	**2-8**	74/39–43 75/Self-Test B	**3-1**	88/11–19 odd; 21–36
24		Prepare for Chapter Test 76–77/Enrichment 78/Chapter Review	**3-2**	91/7–12; 25–38
25		Administer Chapter 2 Test Resource Book pp. 27–28 80–81/Cumulative Review	**3-3**	94/5–11 95/25–43
26	**3-1**	87/6–10 88/11–19 odd; 21–33 88/Rev. 1–7 odd	**3-4**	99/17–35 odd; 40–51
27	**3-2**	91/2–30 even; 31–34 91/Rev. 2–8 even	**3-5**	101/21–32 102/33–39 102/Self-Test A
28	**3-3**	94/1–11 odd 95/17–22; 23–37 odd 95/Rev. 3–6	**3-6**	105/13–31 105/Challenge
29	**3-4**	99/6–38 even; 44–46 99/Rev. 2–8 even	**3-7**	107/21–30 108/31–36; Prob. 4–7
30	**3-5**	101/1–31 odd 102/Self-Test A	**3-8**	112/17–44

Day	Core Course			Enriched Course		
31	**3-6**	104/2–12 even 105/14–26 even, 30 105/Rev. 1–8		**3-9**	115/2–16 even; 20–25 116/Prob. 7–12	
32	**3-7**	107/1–29 odd 108/Prob. 1–5 108/Rev. 1–9		**3-10**	120/19–24; 35–39 120/44–58 even 121/Self-Test B 121/Computer Byte	
33	**3-8**	111/2–16 even 112/18–38 even, 43 112/Rev. 1–8		Prepare for Chapter Test 122–123/Enrichment 124/Chapter Review		
34	**3-9**	115/1–25 odd 116/Prob. 3–9 odd 116/Rev. 1–4		Administer Chapter 3 Test Resource Book pp. 39–40 126–127/Cumulative Review		
35	**3-10**	120/2–50 even		**4-1**	133/2–38 even 133/Rev. 1–6	
36	**3-10**	120/55–60 121/Self-Test B 121/Computer Byte		**4-2**	135/21–38 135/Rev. 1–6	
37	Prepare for Chapter Test 122–123/Enrichment 124/Chapter Review			**4-3**	138/13–20; 22–42 even 138/Calculator Key-In	
38	Administer Chapter 3 Test Resource Book pp. 39–40 126–127 Cumulative Review			**4-4**	141/7–39 odd	
39	**4-1**	133/1–12; 13–27 odd 133/Rev. 1–6		**4-4**	142/40–42 142/Self-Test A 142/Calculator Key-In	
40	**4-2**	135/2–32 even 135/Rev. 1–6		**4-5**	145/15–24 146/27–36 146/Challenge	
41	**4-3**	138/1–33 odd 138/Calculator Key-In		**4-6**	148/1–16	
42	**4-4**	141/2–32 even		**4-7**	150/Prob. 5–10 151/Prob. 11–16 151/Challenge	
43	**4-4**	142/40–42 142/Self-Test A 142/Calculator Key-In		**4-8**	154/Prob. 3–9	
44	**4-5**	145/1–24		**4-8**	155/Prob. 10-11 155/Self-Test B	

Day	Core Course		Enriched Course	
45	**4-5**	146/25–35 146/Rev. 1-8 146/Challenge	Prepare for Chapter Test 156–157/Enrichment 158/Chapter Review	
46	**4-6**	148/1–14 148/Rev. 1-8	Administer Chapter 4 Test 160–161/Cumulative Review Resource Book pp. 53–54	
47	**4-7**	150/Prob. 1–10	**5-1**	168/21–35 168/Rev. 1–8
48	**4-7**	151/Prob. 11–15 151/Rev. 1-6	**5-2**	171/4–6 172/10–20 even; 21–32 172/Rev. 5–9
49	**4-8**	154/Prob. 1–8	**5-3**	176/19–28 177/29, 30 177/Self-Test A
50	**4-8**	154/Prob. 10, 11 154/Self-Test B	**5-4**	181/13–18 182/19–30
51	Prepare for Chapter Test 158/Chapter Review		**5-5**	186/10–20 even; 22–24 187/25–31
52	Administer Chapter 4 Test Resource Book, pp. 53–54 160–161/Cumulative Review		**5-6**	190/19–23 191/24–34
53	**5-1**	167/7–19 odd 168/21–30 168/Rev. 1–8	**5-7**	196/5–8 197/9–15 197/Calculator Key-In
54	**5-2**	171/1–8 172/10–28 even 172/Rev. 1–5	**5-8**	200/8–13 201/15 201/Self-Test B 201/Challenge
55	**5-3**	175/2, 4, 6 176/8–14 even; 19–26	Prepare for Chapter Test 202–203/Enrichment 204/Chapter Review	
56	**5-3**	177/29, 30 177/Self-Test A	Administer Chapter 5 Test Resource Book pp. 65–66 206–207/Cumulative Review	
57	**5-4**	181/2–12 even; 13–18 182/20–26 even 182/Rev. 1–6	**6-1**	211/5–10 212/11–18
58	**5-5**	185/1–8 186/11–21	**6-1**	213/Prob. 4–11 213/Rev. 5–8

Day	Core Course		Enriched Course	
59	**5-5**	186/22–24 187/25–30 187/Rev. 2–8 even	**6-2**	215/Prob. 2–12 even 216/Prob. 13–17
60	**5-6**	190/1–17 odd; 19–22	**6-3**	219/1–33 odd
61	**5-6**	191/24–34 191/Rev. 1–8	**6-4**	221/Prob. 2, 4, 6 222/Prob. 8–14 even; 15–19
62	**5-7**	196/1–8 197/9–12 197/1–8	**6-4**	223/Prob. 20–24 223/Rev. 1–8 223/Calculator Key-In
63	**5-8**	200/1–11	**6-5**	226/7–17 226/Self-Test A
64	**5-8**	200/12, 13 201/Self-Test B 201/Challenge	**6-8**	1–31 odd; 33–36
65	Prepare for Chapter Test 202–203/Enrichment 204/Chapter Review		**6-6**	230/Prob. 2–9 230/Rev. 1–10
66	Administer Chapter 5 Test Resource Book pp. 65–66 206–207/Cumulative Review		**6-7**	233/2–24 even; 29–41
67	**6-1**	211/2–10 213/11–17 odd	**6-8**	235/1–15 odd 236/17–23; Prob. 4–7
68	**6-1**	212/Prob. 1–3 213/Prob. 4–9 213/Rev. 1–6	**6-8**	237/Prob. 8–11 237/Self-Test B
69	**6-2**	215/Prob. 1–12 216/Prob. 15 216/Rev. 1–9 odd	Prepare for Chapter Test 238–239/Enrichment 240/Chapter Review	
70	**6-3**	219/1–29 odd 219/Rev. 1–6	Administer Chapter 6 Test Resource Book pp. 77–78 242–243/Cumulative Review (Mid-Year Test, pp. 43–46)	
71	**6-4**	221/Prob. 3–7 222/Prob. 8–14	**7-1**	247/2–12 even 248/14–20 even; 21–30
72	**6-4**	222/Prob. 15–19 odd 223/Prob. 20, 21 223/Rev. 1–8 223/Calculator Key-In	**7-1**	249/Prob. 3–11 249/Rev. 1–9 odd

Day	Core Course			Enriched Course		
73	**6-5**	225/1–3		**7-2**	252/Prob. 2, 4, 6	
		226/7–14			253/Prob. 9–15	
		226/Self-Test A				
74	**6-6**	229/2–32 even; 33, 34		**7-3**	255/Prob. 1, 3	
					256/Prob. 5–13	
75	**6-6**	230/Prob. 1–7		**7-4**	259/4–6; Prob. 2, 4	
		230/Rev. 1–10			260/Prob. 6–10	
76	**6-7**	233/1–31 odd; 37, 38		**7-4**	261/Prob. 11, 13	
		233/Rev. 1–6			261/Self-Test A	
77	**6-8**	235/1–16		**7-5**	1–15 odd	
		236/Prob. 1–4			265/17–24; Prob. 2	
78	**6-8**	236/5, 7		**7-5**	266/Prob. 3–8	
		237/9			266/Rev. 2–8 even	
		237/Self-Test B			266/Calculator Key-In	
79	Prepare for Chapter Test			**7-6**	268/1–7 odd	
	240/Chapter Review				269/9–15 odd	
					269/Prob. 1, 3, 5	
80	Administer Chapter 6 Test			**7-7**	272/Prob. 3–9	
	242–243/Cumulative Review					
	Resource Book pp. 77–78					
	(Mid-Year Test, pp. 43–46)					
81	**7-1**	247/1–11 odd		**7-7**	273/Prob. 10, 11	
		248/13–24, 27			273/Self-Test B	
82	**7-1**	248/Prob. 1, 2		Prepare for Chapter Test		
		249/Prob. 3–6; 8, 10		274–275/Enrichment		
		249/Rev. 1–7		276/Chapter Review		
83	**7-2**	252/Prob. 1–7		Administer Chapter 7 Test		
		253/Prob. 9, 11, 13		Resource Book pp. 91–92		
				278–279/Cumulative Review		
84	**7-3**	255/Prob. 1–3		**8-1**	283/7–12	
		256/Prob. 4–8, 11			284/25–36	
		256/Rev. 1–8				
85	**7-4**	259/1–6; Prob. 1–4		**8-1**	284/37–48	
		260/Prob. 5–7			284/Challenge	
86	**7-4**	260/Prob. 9, 10		**8-2**	286/17–34	
		261/Prob. 11				
		261/Self-Test A				
87	**7-5**	264/3–16		**8-3**	289/Prob. 5–14	
		265/17–21 odd				

Day	Core Course			Enriched Course		
88	**7-5**	265/Prob. 1, 2 266/Prob. 3–5 266/Rev. 1–9 odd 266/Calculator Key-In		**8-3**	290/Self-Test A 290/Challenge	
89	**7-6**	268/1–8 269/9, 10		**8-4**	291/1–6 292/7–23	
90	**7-6**	269/11–13, 15 269/Prob. 1–4		**8-5**	296/19–34	
91	**7-7**	271/Prob. 1, 2 272/Prob. 3–7		**8-5**	296/35–52	
92	**7-7**	272/Prob. 8, 9 273/Self-Test B		**8-6**	299/2–26 even 300/27–29	
93	Prepare for Chapter Test 274–275/Enrichment 276/Chapter Review			**8-6**	300/30–40 300/Challenge	
94	Administer Chapter 7 Test Resource Book pp. 91–92 278–279/Cumulative Review			**8-7**	302/Prob. 3–9 303/Prob.	
95	**8-1**	283/1–11 odd 284/13–35 odd 284/Rev. 1–4		**8-7**	303/Self-Test B 303/Challenge	
96	**8-2**	286/2–30 even 286/Rev. 2–8 even		Prepare for Chapter Test 304–305/Enrichment 306/Chapter Review		
97	**8-3**	288/Prob. 1, 2 289/Prob. 3–10		Administer Chapter 8 Test Resource Book pp. 103–104 308–309/Cumulative Review		
98	**8-3**	290/Self-Test A 290/Challenge		**9-1**	314/1–17 odd; 19–22 315/23, 24	
99	**8-4**	291/1–6 292/7–18 292/Rev. 1–7 odd		**9-1**	315/25–28; Rev. 1–8 315/Challenge	
100	**8-5**	295/1–17 odd 296/19–33 odd 296/Rev. 1–4		**9-2**	318/10–22 even 319/25–34	
101	**8-6**	299/1–16		**9-2**	319/35–47; Rev. 1–9 odd	
102	**8-6**	299/17–26 300/27–30 300/Rev. 1–8		**9-3**	322/13–39 odd, 40	

Day	Core Course		Enriched Course	
103	**8-7**	302/Prob. 1–8	**9-3**	323/41–47 odd 323/Self-Test A
104	**8-7**	303/Self-Test B 303/Challenge 1, 2	**9-4**	326/1, 3, 5 327/10–15
105	Prepare for Chapter Test 304–305/Enrichment 306/Chapter Review		**9-4**	327/16–20 327/Calculator Key-In
106	Administer Chapter 8 Test Resource Book pp. 103–104 308–309/Cumulative Review		**9-5**	331/Prob. 2 332/Prob. 3–7
107	**9-1**	314/1–22 315/Rev. 1–6	**9-5**	332/8 333/9–11; Rev. 2–8 even 333/Calculator Key-In
108	**9-2**	318/1–23 odd 319/25–30; 35, 36	**9-6**	336/1–23 odd; 25–27
109	**9-3**	321/1–9 odd 322/11–25 odd	**9-6**	337/28–30 337/Self-Test B
110	**9-3**	322/32–35, 40 323/Self-Test A	Prepare for Chapter Test 338–339/Enrichment 340/Chapter Review	
111	**9-4**	326/1–6 327/10–12	Administer Chapter 9 Test Resource Book pp. 115–116 342–343/Cumulative Review	
112	**9-4**	327/14, 15, 20 327/Rev. 1–8 327/Calculator Key-In	**10-1**	349/10–20 even; 21–26 350/Prob. 4–8 350/Rev. 2–8 even
113	**9-5**	331/Prob. 1, 2 332/Prob. 3, 4	**10-2**	354/1–17 odd 355/20–23; Rev. 1–9 odd 355/Challenge
114	**9-5**	332/Prob. 5–7 333/Rev. 1–9	**10-3**	358/2–12 even; 14–19 359/20; Prob. 3–6
115	**9-6**	336/2–22 even; 26, 27	**10-4**	362/3–5; 8–12 363/13
116	**9-6**	337/28, 29 337/Self-Test B	**10-4**	363/14–16 363/Self-Test A
117	Prepare for Chapter Test 340/Chapter Review		**10-5**	366/4, 5, 6 367/7–17 odd; 19–22

Day	Core Course		Enriched Course	
118		Administer Chapter 9 Test Resource Book pp. 115–116 342–343/Cumulative Review	**10-5**	368/23, 24; Prob. 1–5 368/Rev. 1–8
119	**10-1**	348/1, 3 349/5–25 odd 350/Prob. 1–4 350/Rev. 1–7 odd	**10-6**	371/1–15 odd 372/18, 20–22; Prob. 2–4 372/Rev. 1–6
120	**10-2**	354/1–15, 17 355/22; Rev. 1–9	**10-7**	375/3, 4; 7–10 376/11–15
121	**10-3**	358/1–14; 18 359/Prob. 1–4	**10-7**	376/16–19 377/20; Challenge
122	**10-4**	362/1–9	**10-8**	379/2, 4, 6 380/9–18
123	**10-4**	362/10–12 363/Self-Test A	**10-8**	380/19, 20 381/21, 22; Rev. 1–8 381/Calculator Key-In
124	**10-5**	366/1–6 367/7–13, 15	**10-9**	383/1–11 odd 384/13–18; Prob. 2–4
125	**10-5**	367/19–21 368/Prob. 1–3 368/Rev. 1–8	**10-9**	384/Prob. 5 385/Prob. 6 385/Self-Test B
126	**10-6**	371/1–6; 7–15 odd 372/17, 19; Prob. 1, 2 372/Rev. 1–6		Prepare for Chapter Test 386–387/Enrichment 388/Chapter Review
127	**10-7**	375/1–10 376/11		Administer Chapter 10 Test Resource Book pp. 129–130 390–391/Cumulative Review
128	**10-7**	376/12–17 377/Rev. 1–4	**11-1**	395/12–34 395/Rev. 1–7 odd
129	**10-8**	379/1–6 380/7–13	**11-2**	398/5–19 odd; 21–28
130	**10-8**	380/17–19 381/Rev. 1–8 381/Calculator Key-In	**11-2**	398/31–36 398/Rev. 1–8 398/Calculator Key-In
131	**10-9**	383/1–9 384/13–18	**11-3**	400/1–21 odd; 23–30
132	**10-9**	384/Prob. 2, 3 385/Self-Test B	**11-3**	401/32–36; Prob. 3–8 401/Rev. 2-8 even

Day	Core Course		Enriched Course	
133	Prepare for Chapter Test 386–387/Enrichment 388/Chapter Review		**11-4**	404/4–12 even; 14–23 405/Prob. 3–6
134	Administer Chapter 10 Test Resource Book pp. 129–130 390–391/Cumulative Review		**11-4**	405/Prob. 7, 8 405/Self-Test A
135	**11-1**	395/1–25 395/Rev. 1–7 odd	**11-5**	409/6–10; 13–16 410/18–25
136	**11-2**	398/2–28 even 398/Rev. 2–8 even 398/Calculator Key-In	**11-6**	413/1–11 odd 414/13–24
137	**11-3**	400/2–20 even; 22–26 401/Prob. 1–4 401/Rev. 1–5	**11-6**	415/Prob. 4–12 415/Rev. 2–8 even
138	**11-4**	404/1–13; 14–22 even 404/Prob. 1	**11-7**	418/2, 4; 6–10 419/11–14
139	**11-4**	405/Prob. 2–5 405/Self-Test A	**11-7**	419/15–17 419/Rev. 1–8 419/Challenge
140	**11-5**	409/1–14 410/17, 19	**11-8**	422/25–40 423/Prob. 5–8 424/Prob. 10
141	**11-6**	413/1–11 odd 414/13–19 odd; Prob. 1–3 415/Prob. 5, 6 415/Rev. 1–4	**11-8**	424/Self-Test B 425/Computer Byte 425/Challenge
142	**11-7**	418/1–7, 9 419/12, 14 419/Rev. 1–8	Prepare for Chapter Test 426–427/Enrichment 428/Chapter Review	
143	**11-8**	422/2–34 even 423/Prob. 1–7 odd	Administer Chapter 11 Test Resource Book pp. 141–142 430–431/Cumulative Review	
144	**11-8**	424/Self-Test B 425/Computer Byte	**12-1**	436/1, 3, 5 437/9–12 437/Rev. 2–8 even
145	Prepare for Chapter Test 428/Chapter Review		**12-2**	441/2, 4; 8–10
146	Administer Chapter 11 Test Resource Book pp. 141–142 430–431/Cumulative Review		**12-2**	442/12–16 442/Rev. 1–4

Day	Core Course			Enriched Course		
147	**12-1**	436/1–6		**12-3**	444/6–14 even	
		437/8–10			445/15–22	
		437/Rev. 2–8 even			445/Challenge	
148	**12-2**	441/2–10 even		**12-4**	447/2, 4, 6	
		442/Rev. 1–4			448/8–14	
					449/Computer Byte	
149	**12-3**	444/1–13		**12-5**	451/1–9	
		445/Rev. 1–6			452/12, 14, 16	
150	**12-4**	447/1–6		**12-5**	452/17	
		448/7, 9, 11			452/Self-Test A	
		449/Computer Byte				
151	**12-5**	451/1–10		**12-6**	455/2–12 even	
		452/11, 12			456/Prob. 6, 8, 10; 11–1	
152	**12-5**	452/14		**12-6**	457/Prob. 18–20	
		452/Self-Test A			457/Rev. 4–8	
					457/Challenge	
153	**12-6**	455/2–12 even; Prob. 1–4		**12-7**	459/Prob. 3	
		456/Prob. 5–13 odd			460/Prob. 4–12	
		457/Rev. 4–8				
154	**12-7**	459/Prob. 1–3		**12-8**	464/8–28 even; 29–36	
		460/Prob. 4–10 even			465/38, 39	
		460/Rev. 1–8			465/Rev. 1–4	
155	**12-8**	464/1–35 odd		**12-9**	468/1–21 odd; 22–27	
		465/37				
		465/Rev. 1–4				
156	**12-9**	468/1–23		**12-9**	469/28, 29	
		469/Rev. 2–8 even			469/Rev. 3–8	
		469/Computer Byte			46R/Computer Byte	
157	**12-10**	471/1–10		**12-10**	471/2–10 even	
		472/11–16			472/12, 14; 16–23	
158	**12-10**	472/18, 20		**12-10**	473/Challenge	
		473/Self-Test B			473/Self-Test B	
159	Prepare for Chapter Test			Prepare for Chapter Test		
	476/Chapter Review			474–475/Enrichment		
				476/Chapter Review		
160	Administer Chapter 12 Test			Administer Chapter 12 Test		
	Resource Book pp. 153–154			Resource Book pp. 153–154		
	478–479/Cumulative Review			478–479 Cumulative Review		

Supplementary Materials Guide

For use after Lesson	Resource Book page	Practice Masters page	Tests	Computer Activities
(Diagnostic Tests)	1–6	1–2	Diagnostic Test	
1–1		3		
1–2	7	3		1
1–3	8	4		
1–4		4		2
1–5	9	4	1A	
1–6	10	5		
1–7		5		
1–8	11–12	6		
1–9	13	6	1B	
Chapter 1	14–16		Chapter 1 Test	
Cumulative Review	17–18			
2–1	19	7		
2–2		7		
2–3		8		
2–4	20–21	8	2A	
2–5		9		3, 4
2–6		9		
2–7		10		
2–8	22–25	10	2B	
Chapter 2	26–28		Chapter 2 Test	
Cumulative Review	29–30			

For use after Lesson	Resource Book page	Practice Masters page	Tests	Computer Activities
3–1		11		
3–2		11		5
3–3	31	12		
3–4		12		
3–5	32	12	3A	
3–6		13		
3–7	33	13		
3–8	34	13		
3–9	35	14		
3–10	36–37	14	3B	6
Chapter 3	38–40		Chapter 3 Test	
Cumulative Review	41–44	15–16	Cumulative Test	
4–1	45–46	17		
4–2		17		
4–3		18		
4–4	47–48	18	4A	7
4–5		19		
4–6	49–50	19		
4–7		20		
4–8	51	20	4B	8
Chapter 4	52–54		Chapter 4 Test	
Cumulative Review	55–56			

For use after Lesson	Resource Book page	Practice Masters page	Tests	Computer Activities
5–1	57	21		
5–2		21		
5–3	58	22	5A	
5–4		23		9
5–5	59–60	23		10
5–6	61	23		
5–7		24		
5–8	62–63	24	5B	
Chapter 5	64–66		Chapter 5 Test	
Cumulative Review	67–68			
6–1	69	25		
6–2		25		
6–3		25		11
6–4		26		
6–5	70–71	26	6A	12
6–6		27		
6–7		27		
6–8	72–75	28	6B	
Chapter 6	76–78		Chapter 6 Test	
Cumulative Review	79–82	29–30	Cumulative Test	
Mid-Year			Chapters 1–6	
7–1	83	31		13
7–2	84	31		
7–3	85	32		14
7–4	86	32	7A	

For use after Lesson	Resource Book page	Practice Masters page	Tests	Computer Activities
7–5	87–88	33		
7–6		33		
7–7	89	34	7B	
Chapter 7	90–92		Chapter 7 Test	
Cumulative Review	93–94			
8–1	95	35		
8–2		35		
8–3	96–98	36	8A	15
8–4		37		16
8–5		37		
8–6	99	38		
8–7	100–101	38	8B	
Chapter 8	102–104		Chapter 8 Test	
Cumulative Review	105–106			
9–1	107–108	39		
9–2		39		
9–3	109–110	40	9A	17
9–4		41		
9–5	111–112	42		
9–6	113	42	9B	18
Chapter 9	114–116		Chapter 9 Test	
Cumulative Review	117–120	43–44	Cumulative Test	
10–1		45		
10–2		45		19

For use after Lesson	Resource Book page	Practice Masters page	Tests	Computer Activities
10–3	121	46		
10–4	122–123	46	10A	
10–5		47		20
10–6		47		
10–7		48		
10–8	124–126	48		
10–9	127	48	10B	
Chapter 10	128–130		Chapter 10 Test	
Cumulative Review	131–132			
11–1	133–134	49		21
11–2		49		
11–3		50		
11–4	135–136	50	11A	22
11–5		51		
11–6		51		
11–7		52		
11–8	137–139	52	11B	

For use after Lesson	Resource Book page	Practice Masters page	Tests	Computer Activities
Chapter 11	140–142		Chapter 11 Test	
Cumulative Review	143–144			
12–1	145–146	53		
12–2		53		
12–3		54		
12–4		54		
12–5	147	54	12A	23
12–6	148	55		
12–7		55		24
12–8	149–150	56		
12–9		56		
12–10	151	56	12B	
Chapter 12	152–154		Chapter 12 Test	
Cumulative Review	155–158	57–58	Cumulative Test	
Final			Chapters 7–12	

PRE-ALGEBRA

An Accelerated Course

Mary P. Dolciani
Robert H. Sorgenfrey
John A. Graham

Editorial Advisers

Richard G. Brown
Robert B. Kane

HOUGHTON MIFFLIN COMPANY · Boston
Atlanta Dallas Geneva, Ill. Palo Alto Princeton Toronto

AUTHORS

Mary P. Dolciani formerly Professor of Mathematical Sciences, Hunter College of the City University of New York

Robert H. Sorgenfrey Professor of Mathematics, University of California, Los Angeles

John A. Graham Mathematics Teacher, Buckingham Browne and Nichols School, Cambridge, Massachusetts

Editorial Advisers

Richard G. Brown Mathematics Teacher, Phillips Exeter Academy, Exeter, New Hampshire

Robert B. Kane Dean of the School of Education and Professor of Mathematics Education, Purdue University, Lafayette, Indiana

Teacher Consultants

John E. Mosby Instructional Coordinator, Dixon School, Chicago, Illinois

William Voligny Mathematics Teacher, Olympia Junior High School, Auburn, Washington

ISBN: 0-395-59123-6

Contents

iii

iv

Reading Mathematics

This page shows many of the metric measures and symbols that are used in this book. Use this page as a reference when you read the book.

Symbols

		Page			Page
·	times	3	AB	the length of $\overline{AB}$	169
$\approx$	is approximately equal to	14	$\cong$	is congruent to	169
$^-1$	negative one	46	$\angle$	angle	173
$|{^-3}|$	absolute value of $^-3$	46	$60°$	sixty degrees	173
$>$	is greater than	47	$m\angle A$	measure of angle A	173
$<$	is less than	47	$\perp$	is perpendicular to	173
$\neq$	is not equal to	47	$\triangle ABC$	triangle ABC	178
$\geq$	is greater than or equal to	47	π	pi	188
$\leq$	is less than or equal to	47	$1:5$	1 to 5	210
$-b$	the opposite of b	59	$\%$	percent	227
$0.4\overline{36}$	36 repeats without end	117	$(5, 4)$	ordered pair 5, 4	312
$\overleftrightarrow{PQ}$	line PQ	164	$\sqrt{a}$	positive square root of a	394
$\overrightarrow{BA}$	ray BA	164	$\sim$	is similar to	406
$\overline{PQ}$	segment PQ	164	$3!$	3 factorial	453
$\parallel$	is parallel to	165	$P(E)$	probability of event E	461

Metric Measures

Prefixes

Prefix	kilo	centi	milli
Factor	1000	0.01	0.001
Symbol	k	c	m

Base Units

Length: **meter** (m)

Mass: **kilogram** (kg)

Capacity: **liter** (L)

Temperature **Degree Celsius** (°C)

Length	1 mm = 0.001 m	1 cm = 0.01 m	1 km = 1000 m
	1 m = 1000 mm	1 m = 100 cm	1 cm = 10 mm
Mass	1 kg = 1000 g	1 mg = 0.001 g	1 g = 0.001 kg
Capacity	1 mL = 0.001 L	1 L = 1000 mL	1 L = 1000 cm^3
Time	60 s = 1 min	60 min = 1 h	3600 s = 1 h

Examples of compound units   kilometers per hour: km/h

square centimeters: cm^2 cubic meters: m^3

vii

Review of Whole Number and Decimal Skills

OVERVIEW

The Diagnostic Test of Whole Number and Decimal Skills appears on pages viii–ix of the student textbook. Answers appear on pages T32 and T33. This test is designed to help you gauge your students' knowledge of whole number and decimal arithmetic skills before starting the course. Students who need extensive review or reteaching may belong in a less demanding program. For students who need moderate review, pages 480–483 provide additional practice in the four basic skills.

An alternate version of the Diagnostic Test is in the Resource Book. It is shown below. You may wish to use it for retesting after any necessary review. The Resource Book also contains four more pages of practice exercises; these are shown at the right on page T31.

Resource Book: Pages 1–2

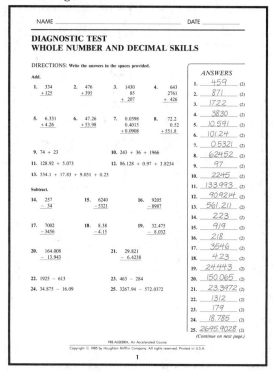

NAME _____ DATE _____

SKILL REVIEW — *Addition*

Add.

```
  7
 34
143
+81
265
```

```
 32.75
  5.093
+531.758
569.601
```

1. 62 +14 = *76*
2. 87 +39 = *126*
3. 536 +47 = *583*
4. 354 +123 = *477*

5. 813 +150 = *963*
6. 672 +129 = *801*
7. 4186 +3645 = *7831*
8. 5643 +2757 = *8400*

9. 9.8 +1.6 = *11.4*
10. 1.27 +4.62 = *5.89*
11. 17.2 +248.83 = *266.03*
12. 532.801 +38.9497 = *571.7507*

13. 3.2 / 142.94 / 3.806 / +29.4 = *179.346*
14. 5.87 / 3.002 / 17.3 / +4.931 = *31.103*
15. 18.6 / 9.82 / 43.1 / +5.007 = *76.527*
16. 503.8 / 7.902 / 83.41 / +7.03 = *602.142*

17. 816 + 162 = *978*
18. 472 + 375 = *847*
19. 346 + 254 = *600*
20. 54.3 + 9.1 = *63.4*
21. 30.5 + 23.81 = *54.31*
22. 12.9 + 8.43 = *21.33*
23. 198 + 272 + 56 = *526*
24. 3.5 + 18.21 + 302.4 = *324.11*
25. 19.2 + 2.438 + 17 + 2.5 = *41.138*
26. 40 + 2.9 + 5.38 + 4.075 = *52.355*
27. 36 + 416 + 8 + 73 = *533*
28. 72 + 413 + 81 + 121 = *687*
29. 18.9 + 31 + 2.87 + 0.08 = *52.85*
30. 32.5 + 1.84 + 219 + 4.07 = *257.41*
31. 964 + 32 + 687 + 41 = *1724*
32. 23 + 487 + 136 + 92 = *738*
33. 6.982 + 5 + 17.3 + 42.81 = *72.092*
34. 0.281 + 39.6 + 5.83 + 7 = *52.711*
35. 312 + 216 + 471 + 1062 = *2061*
36. 410 + 6314 + 293 + 57 = *7074*
37. 0.18 + 5.3 + 7.932 + 4.9 = *18.312*
38. 6.9708 + 21.4 + 0.05 = *31.4208*

3

NAME _____ DATE _____

SKILL REVIEW — *Subtraction*

Subtract.

```
 842
-669
 173
```

```
507.830
-29.007
478.823
```

1. 46 -13 = *33*
2. 87 -62 = *25*
3. 74 -60 = *14*

4. 94 -12 = *82*
5. 649 -125 = *524*
6. 891 -620 = *271*

7. 486 -121 = *365*
8. 895 -214 = *681*
9. 14.932 -4.521 = *10.411*

10. 47.9 -12.6 = *35.3*
11. 79.885 -18.73 = *61.155*
12. 645.9267 -23.005 = *622.9217*

13. 65.27 -53.88 = *11.39*
14. 84.71 -32.65 = *52.06*
15. 93.42 -5.8 = *87.62*

16. 793.84 -69.25 = *724.59*
17. 792 -18.37 = *773.63*
18. 217.008 -64.32 = *152.688*

19. 19.436 -7.524 = *11.912*
20. 3247.93 -658.97 = *2588.96*

21. 49 - 14 = *35*
22. 38 - 15 = *23*
23. 68 - 52 = *16*
24. 96 - 22 = *74*
25. 92 - 46 = *46*
26. 61 - 49 = *12*
27. 379.5 - 85.9 = *293.6*
28. 823.64 - 35.96 = *787.68*
29. 1964 - 792 = *1172*
30. 7421 - 2738 = *4683*
31. 61.0532 - 7.326 = *53.7272*
32. 5421.92 - 735.8 = *4686.12*
33. 3879 - 2904 = *975*
34. 5004 - 1703 = *3301*
35. 16.7 - 3.923 = *12.777*
36. 3.78 - 0.1254 = *3.6546*
37. 0.075 - 0.006 = *0.069*
38. 0.047 - 0.009 = *0.038*
39. 86,000 - 30,346 = *55,654*
40. 76,721 - 14,961 = *61,760*
41. 321.8 - 76.562 = *245.238*
42. 643.1 - 0.016 = *643.084*

4

NAME _____ DATE _____

SKILL REVIEW — *Multiplication*

Multiply.

```
  752
 × 49
 6768
3008
36848
```

```
 43.8    1 place
×0.36    2 places
 2628
1314
15.768   3 places
```

1. 62 ×2 = *124*
2. 82 ×4 = *328*
3. 52 ×3 = *156*
4. 51 ×9 = *459*

5. 32 ×6 = *192*
6. 26 ×4 = *104*
7. 84 ×5 = *420*
8. 59 ×2 = *118*

9. 84 ×96 = *8064*
10. 37 ×81 = *2997*
11. 45 ×27 = *1215*
12. 26 ×53 = *1378*

13. 64 ×1.3 = *83.2*
14. 31.46 ×5 = *157.3*
15. 634 ×3.2 = *2028.8*
16. 18.7 ×6.2 = *115.94*

17. 31.07 ×4.2 = *130.494*
18. 50.7 ×0.84 = *42.588*
19. 28.5 ×5.16 = *147.06*
20. 29.05 ×8.37 = *243.1485*

21. 40 × 70 = *2800*
22. 80 × 20 = *1600*
23. 300 × 60 = *18,000*
24. 50 × 900 = *45,000*
25. 260 × 400 = *104,000*
26. 200 × 5900 = *1,180,000*
27. 13 × 712 = *9256*
28. 186 × 42 = *7812*
29. 28 × 873 = *24,444*
30. 149 × 89 = *13,261*
31. 63.7 × 0.23 = *14.651*
32. 18.7 × 0.37 = *6.919*
33. 16.7 × 0.04 = *0.668*
34. 23.25 × 16.2 = *376.65*
35. 0.083 × 0.06 = *0.00498*
36. 0.0503 × 0.08 = *0.004024*
37. 73.92 × 5.16 = *381.4272*
38. 131.27 × 0.95 = *124.7065*
39. 0.003 × 0.207 = *0.000621*
40. 0.0006 × 0.0134 = *0.00000804*
41. 43.872 × 4.31 = *189.08832*
42. 2346.8 × 7.52 = *17,647.936*

5

NAME _____ DATE _____

SKILL REVIEW — *Division*

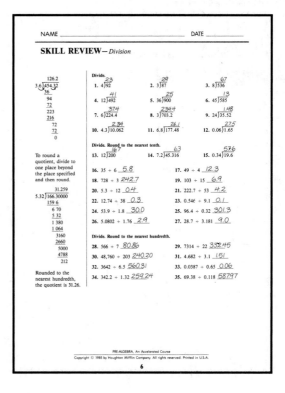

```
      126.2
3.6)454.32
    36
    94
    72
    223
    216
     72
     72
      0
```

To round a quotient, divide to one place beyond the place specified and then round.

```
       31.259
5.32)166.30000
     159 6
       6 70
       5 32
       1 380
       1 064
         3160
         2660
         5000
         4788
          212
```

Rounded to the nearest hundredth, the quotient is 31.26.

Divide.

1. 4)92 = *23*
2. 3)87 = *29*
3. 8)536 = *67*
4. 12)492 = *41*
5. 36)900 = *25*
6. 45)585 = *13*
7. 6)224.4 = *37.4*
8. 3)703.2 = *234.4*
9. 24)35.52 = *1.48*
10. 4.3)10.062 = *2.34*
11. 6.8)177.48 = *26.1*
12. 0.06)1.65 = *27.5*

Divide. Round to the nearest tenth.

13. 12)200 = *16.7*
14. 7.2)45.316 = *6.3*
15. 0.34)19.6 = *57.6*

16. 35 ÷ 6 = *5.8*
17. 49 ÷ 4 = *12.3*
18. 728 ÷ 3 = *242.7*
19. 103 ÷ 15 = *6.9*
20. 5.3 ÷ 12 = *0.4*
21. 222.7 ÷ 53 = *4.2*
22. 12.74 ÷ 38 = *0.3*
23. 0.54 ÷ 9.1 = *0.1*
24. 53.9 ÷ 1.8 = *30.0*
25. 96.4 ÷ 0.32 = *301.3*
26. 5.0802 ÷ 1.76 = *2.9*
27. 28.7 ÷ 3.181 = *9.0*

Divide. Round to the nearest hundredth.

28. 566 ÷ 7 = *80.86*
29. 7314 ÷ 22 = *332.45*
30. 48,760 ÷ 203 = *240.20*
31. 4.682 ÷ 3.1 = *1.51*
32. 3642 ÷ 6.5 = *560.31*
33. 0.0387 ÷ 0.65 = *0.06*
34. 342.2 ÷ 1.32 = *259.24*
35. 69.38 ÷ 0.118 = *587.97*

6

Diagnostic Test of Whole Number and Decimal Skills

This test reviews the skills of addition, subtraction, multiplication, and division necessary to begin Chapter 1. More practice of these skills can be found on pages 480–483.

Addition

Add.

1.
$$142 + 237$$

2.
$$374 + 213$$

3.
$$103 + 19 + 42$$

4.
$$1007 + 285 + 59$$

5.
$$246 + 9 + 1064 + 842 + 83$$

6.
$$5.246 + 6.38$$

7.
$$16.439 + 28.32$$

8.
$$3.84 + 2.07 + 9.39$$

9.
$$72.8 + 6.349 + 0.76$$

10.
$$0.16 + 54.3 + 119.057 + 2.0918$$

11. $32 + 56$

12. $693 + 105$

13. $34 + 17 + 25$

14. $2306 + 19 + 429 + 1443$

15. $18.7 + 5.394$

16. $0.06 + 19.803$

17. $11.882 + 6.49 + 0.083$

18. $583.117 + 72.5 + 3.76824$

19. $35.402 + 17.6 + 5.28 + 0.314$

20. $3.4289 + 5.005 + 31 + 8.57$

Subtraction

Subtract.

1.
$$864 - 231$$

2.
$$9748 - 2635$$

3.
$$4693 - 2758$$

4.
$$801 - 543$$

5.
$$3004 - 2567$$

6.
$$6.75 - 3.81$$

7.
$$14.90 - 7.88$$

8.
$$388.6 - 97.86$$

9.
$$705.56 - 314.6$$

10.
$$0.986 - 0.097$$

11. $768 - 654$

12. $925 - 713$

13. $853 - 432$

14. $2670 - 357$

15. $5323 - 789$

16. $4803 - 567$

viii

Subtract.

17. 9.5 − 4.8   **18.** 46.71 − 22.52   **19.** 0.039 − 0.0271

20. 0.8743 − 0.33591   **21.** 0.039 − 0.0271   **22.** 5.04876 − 229

Multiplication

Multiply.

1. 63 × 21   **2.** 42 × 34   **3.** 131 × 25   **4.** 214 × 37   **5.** 381 × 206

6. 473 × 0.3   **7.** 846 × 2.5   **8.** 127.3 × 6.6   **9.** 67.05 × 2.39   **10.** 99.7 × 10.06

11. 51 × 73   **12.** 92 × 34   **13.** 732 × 24

14. 947 × 62   **15.** 4023 × 570   **16.** 9108 × 6027

17. 18.7 × 16   **18.** 0.08 × 58.6   **19.** 0.75 × 0.69

20. 27.9 × 33.3   **21.** 6.0810 × 148.3   **22.** 5.62 × 83.109

Division

Divide.

1. 7$\overline{)91}$ **2.** 4$\overline{)64}$ **3.** 8$\overline{)296}$

4. 29$\overline{)522}$ **5.** 74$\overline{)3478}$ **6.** 607$\overline{)6677}$

7. 5$\overline{)37.60}$ **8.** 81$\overline{)108.54}$ **9.** 5.4$\overline{)3348}$

10. 1.6$\overline{)99.68}$ **11.** 2.86$\overline{)247.39}$ **12.** 1.13$\overline{)1006.83}$

Divide. Round to the nearest tenth.

13. 56 ÷ 3   **14.** 49 ÷ 8   **15.** 319 ÷ 15

16. 628 ÷ 20   **17.** 948 ÷ 48   **18.** 9963 ÷ 542

19. 0.851 ÷ 0.33   **20.** 0.909 ÷ 1.35   **21.** 0.284 ÷ 7.31

22. 486 ÷ 0.391   **23.** 5.005 ÷ 0.095   **24.** 43.761 ÷ 27.515

ix

T33

1

Introduction to Algebra

All of the many pieces of information handled by computers are stored and processed by means of tiny microchips, such as the one shown at the right. Each microchip is about 2 mm square and is made up of thin layers of silicon crystals. Each layer is treated chemically and etched photographically with different patterns containing tens of thousands of microscopic switches. Information on the microchip is represented by a code made up of a series of "on" or "off" switches.

Although we use words and numbers to communicate with a computer, the machine does not work directly with those words and numbers. A program within the computer automatically translates the information that we use into the special code that the machine understands. In a similar way, when we work with algebra, we translate our words and ideas into the language of mathematics. In this chapter, you will learn many of the symbols that we use to express mathematical ideas.

Career Note

Consider how intricate the design of a single microchip is. Electrical engineers are involved in designing and testing new electrical equipment such as the microchip. Electrical engineers must therefore be qualified in both mathematics and science. Most, in fact, specialize in a major field such as communications, industrial equipment, or computers.

Lesson Commentary
Chapter 1   Introduction to Algebra

Overview

As it should, the first chapter sets a pace and tone for the entire book. A groundwork is established for future work in algebra, both in this course and in any later study of algebra. The concept of variable is introduced in the first lesson. Variables are used in applying the order of operations and in general statements of the properties of whole numbers and decimals.

The second part of the chapter begins with an approach to equations that is more intuitive than rigorous; rigor will come in later chapters. The approach is, however, mathematically correct and will have students solving equations early. The equation-solving skills presented are based on inverse operations, and build on students' background in arithmetic.

Next, students are given a plan for solving word problems. Students are provided with a systematic approach to problem solving based on a set of questions that students are encouraged to ask about each problem. Although the problems in this chapter are often simple enough to be worked without a formal strategy, they illustrate the basic skills that are needed in later lessons.

USING VARIABLES

1-1 Mathematical Expressions

Objective for pages 2–4

■ To evaluate a variable expression for given values of the variables.

Teaching Suggestions

The expressions used here each contain only one operation, because an order of operations rule has yet to be adopted. Students should have no difficulty with the material, finding it very natural to substitute a value for each variable. The only real prerequisite for success here is a good grasp of arithmetic.

Emphasize that if an expression contains several variables, as in $3abc$, we need a value for each one. If the same variable is used more than once, as in $a + a + 2$, the same value must be used each time that variable occurs.

Some students may be so accustomed to working with expressions in vertical form that they are confused by an expression such as $a - b$. Show them that $a - b$ is equivalent to

$$\begin{array}{c} a \\ -b, \end{array} \qquad \text{not} \qquad \begin{array}{c} b \\ -a. \end{array}$$

Similarly, $a \div b$ is equivalent to $b\overline{)a}$, not $a\overline{)b}$.

Related Activities

To reinforce understanding of variable expressions, reverse the usual process. Give the value of the expression, and ask what value of the variable will produce this value.

1. If the value of $100 - x$ is 36, then $x = \underline{\quad?\quad}$. 64
2. If the value of $3 \times c \times c$ is 147, then $c = \underline{\quad?\quad}$. 7
3. If the value of $7 \times a \times b$ is 154 and $b = 2$, then $a = \underline{\quad?\quad}$. 11

To prepare for later work with equations, have students find values of the variables so that the two expressions have the same value.

4. $3h, h + 12$ 6
5. $j - 4, j \div 2$ 8
6. $4d, d + 9$ 3
7. $k - 8, k \div 5$ 10

1-2 Order of Operations

Objective for pages 5–8

■ To use the order of operations to evaluate variable expressions.

Teaching Suggestions

In mathematics, more than in some other forms of written expressions, ambiguity must be eliminated. Otherwise, different people may ascribe different meanings to the same symbols, and communication is faulty. Ambiguity is eliminated using grouping symbols and the order of operations rule. To show that expressions would be ambiguous without grouping symbols and rules, present the expression below and ask students to insert parentheses to make as many different values as possible.

$$4 \times 8 - 6 \div 2 + 1$$

Some possible values are:

$$29 = (4 \times 8) - (6 - 2) + 1$$
$$29 = (4 \times 8) - (6 - (2 + 1))$$
$$7 = ((4 \times (8 - 6)) - 2) + 1$$
$$17 = (4 \times (8 - (6 - 2))) + 1$$
$$12 = 4 \times (8 - ((6 - 2) + 1))$$

To provide a note of humor, write on the board the following statement:

SLOW CHILDREN PLAYING.

This is a common warning sign along streets. Ask if students can explain why the sign is ambiguous. Do the same with

SAVE RAGS AND WASTE PAPER,

a sign that might be found in a factory.

Related Activities

To provide practice in a different way, let students play "Four Fours." Using the symbols $+$, $-$, $\times$, and $\div$, and four fours, write expressions for as many different integers as possible. Insert parentheses as needed. Possible expressions include:

$$\frac{4 \times 4}{4 + 4} = 2$$

$$\frac{(4 \times 4) + 4}{4} = 5$$

To increase awareness of ambiguity in expression, have students find examples of ambiguous expressions in advertising, news reporting, and so on.

Resource Book: Page 7 (Use After Page 8)

NAME _____ DATE _____

CALCULATOR—For use after Lesson 1-2
Calculator Messages

You can use a calculator to write coded messages. When you hold a calculator right side up, you see numbers. But when you hold the calculator upside-down, you can see letters.

number	0	1	2	3	4	5	7	8	9
letter	O	l	Z	E	h	S	L	B	G

EXAMPLE Write a mathematical expression for the code word SIZE.

SOLUTION The code number for SIZE is 3215.
3215 = 5(8 × 80 + 3)

Write a mathematical expression for each code word. *Other answers are possible.*

1. HIS $2(5 \times 50 + 7)$
2. BIG $9 \times 2 \times 17 \times 3$
3. LOG $100 \times 27 - 3 + 7$
4. GOSH $(1000 - 4 + 251) \times 9$
5. GIBE $366 - 6 + 89 \times 42 + 20$
6. ZOOS $2 + (20 \times 20 + 100) \times 10$
7. LIEGE $1709 \times 23 + 10$
8. BEZEL $54 \times 82 \times 16 + 478 \times 5$
9. SHELL $(2209 \times 7 + 6) \times 5$
10. GHILLIE $4068 \times 781 + 41$

Write 5 other code words. Then write a mathematical expression for each. Use a dictionary to find the words. *answers will vary.*

11. _____   _____
12. _____   _____
13. _____   _____
14. _____   _____
15. _____   _____

PRE-ALGEBRA, An Accelerated Course
Copyright © 1985 by Houghton Mifflin Company. All rights reserved. Printed in U.S.A.

7

1-3 Exponents and Powers of Ten

Objective for pages 9–12

■ To evaluate expressions involving powers.

Teaching Suggestions

Emphasize that a power of a number indicates the number of times that number is used as a factor, not the number of multiplications. A common error is for students to think of 3^5 as "3 multiplied by itself 5 times" instead of as "3 is a factor 5 times."

$$3^5 = \underbrace{3 \times 3 \times 3 \times 3 \times 3}_{5 \text{ factors}}$$

You may like to point out that the number of multiplications, 4, is one less than the exponent.

In Example 4 on page 10 you may want to point out that 100×1000 can be written as $10^2 \times 10^3$ and simplified as 10^{2+3} or 10^5. You can use the Related Activities below to help students discover the general rule for multiplying powers of a number.

Students may ask about the value of 0^0. Since $a^0 = 1$ ($a \neq 0$) and $0^b = 0$ ($b \neq 0$), the value is ambiguous. Therefore 0^0 is not defined.

Related Activities

To challenge students, ask them to evaluate the expressions below and to write their answers as powers of ten. Ask students to look for a pattern.

1. $10^2 \times 10^3$ 10^5 **2.** $10^3 \times 10^5$ 10^8
3. $10^2 \times 10^4$ 10^6 **4.** $10^6 \times 10^1$ 10^7
5. $10^8 \times 10^3$ 10^{11} **6.** $10^6 \times 10^3$ 10^9

Challenge students to write a general rule for finding $10^a \times 10^b$ and to explain why it works. Then ask them if the same rule applies when the base, 10, is replaced with another number; for example, $5^a \times 5^b$.

$10^a \times 10^b = 10^{a+b}$. The number of zeros in the product of powers of 10 is the sum of the numbers of zeros in the factors. The exponent in a power of 10 is the same as the number of zeros when the number is written out. Also, $5^a \times 5^b = 5^{a+b}$. Students may discover the general rule, $n^a \times n^b = n^{a+b}$.

Resource Book: Page 8 (Use After Page 12)

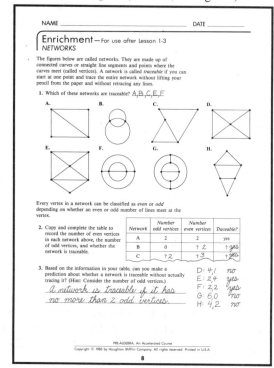

1-4 The Decimal System

Objectives for pages 13–17

■ To read, write, and round decimal numbers.
■ To use rounding of decimal numbers to estimate answers.

Teaching Suggestions

Explain to students that our numbers are called decimal numbers because they are based on powers of ten and not because they have a decimal point. For example, 342 is a decimal number even though the decimal point is not shown.

Students have probably learned rounding in an earlier grade. If they have not mastered the skill completely you may want to present more examples. For example, round 14.862 to the nearest:

ten	tenth	hundredth
14.862	14.862	14.862
^	^	^
10	14.9	14.86
$14.862 \approx 10$	$14.862 \approx 14.9$	$14.862 \approx 14.86$

Be sure that students focus on the digit immediately to the right of the place to which they are rounding. When rounding to the nearest tenth, for example, students often round 0.749 incorrectly to 0.8 instead of 0.7 because they round 0.749 to 0.75 and then to 0.8.

Rounding or approximating numbers is a valuable skill to use when checking computations in everyday problem solving, particularly when placement of decimal points is a problem for students. For example, is the product of 6.82×4.7: 3205.4? 320.54? 32.054? Since $6.82 \approx 7$ and $4.7 \approx 5$, 6.82×4.7 must be approximately 7×5 or 35. Thus, 32.054 is the most reasonable answer.

Related Activities

To help students prepare for standardized tests, show how rounding can speed their work. For example:

Multiply: 12.2×6.21
a. 7.5762   **b.** 75.762   **c.** 757.62

Approximation would show the correct choice, 75.762, without actual evaluation of the product.

1-5 Basic Properties

Objective *for pages 18–22*

■ To use the properties of addition and multiplication.

Teaching Suggestions

To help students understand the words *commutative*, *associative*, and *distributive*, ask students what it means to "commute to work or school." What does it mean to belong to an "association" or to "associate with certain people"? Point out that when you ask a student to "distribute worksheets," this means the student is to give a worksheet to *each* student in the room.

Once students learn that multiplication distributes over addition and subtraction, they often fall into the trap of hasty generalization and try to apply the distributive property in cases where it cannot be used. Caution students that statements such as "$(2 + 3)^2 = 2^2 + 3^2$" are incorrect, because exponentiation does not distribute over addition.

Students may ask about $0 \div 0$. Explain that $0 \div 0$ is an undefined expression because the sentence

$$0 \times \underline{\ ?\ } = 0$$

has infinitely many solutions.

Related Activities

To relate mathematics to students' lives, show how they can use the distributive property to do calculations in their heads. For example, "if one pen costs 89¢, how much do six cost?" This problem is easier if you think,

$$89 = 90 - 1.$$

Then,
$$\begin{aligned}
6 \times 89 &= 6(90 - 1) \\
&= (6 \times 90) - (6 \times 1) \\
&= 540 - 6, \text{ or } 534
\end{aligned}$$

Six pens cost $5.34.

To add an historical note, you can tell students about the famous mathematician Carl Friedrich Gauss. As a student, he amazed a teacher by finding the sum of all the numbers from 1 to 100 in a very short time. Have your students use the associative and commutative properties to see how rapidly they can find this sum.

Some students will discover that

$$\underbrace{(1 + 100) + (2 + 99) + \cdots + (50 + 51)}_{50 \text{ terms}}$$
$$= 50 \times 101 = 5050.$$

Resource Book: Page 9 (Use After Page 22)

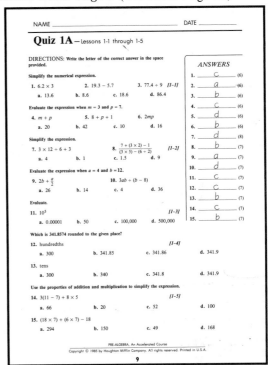

FINDING SOLUTIONS

1-6 Equations

Objective *for pages 23–25*

■ To find the solution of an equation in one variable whose replacement set is given.

Teaching Suggestions

The structure of mathematical expression has some notable parallels in language and grammar. For example, the expression $x + 5$ can be considered a phrase. Add a verb, and it can become a sentence: $x + 5 = 16$. This is an open sentence, because it contains the variable x.

Point out that variables have a role similar to that of pronouns. That is, a sentence with a pronoun, such as "She was awarded the Nobel Prize," is open; it is neither true nor false. When a noun is "substituted" for the pronoun, the sentence is then true or false. Similarly, for mathematical open sentences, when a number is substituted for the variable, the sentence is then true or false.

It may be worthwhile to show that a sentence may have different solutions for different replacement sets. For example, if the replacement set is $\{1, 2, 3, 4\}$, then the sentence "$3x$ is divisible by 6" has solutions 2 and 4. For the same sentence, if the replacement set is $\{1, 3, 5, 7, 9\}$, then there are no solutions at all.

Related Activities

To enhance understanding of open sentences and solutions, have students write open sentences having the following solutions.

1. George Washington
2. Clara Barton
3. Florida, Alabama, Mississippi, Louisiana, and Texas

Resource Book: Page 10 (Use After Page 25)

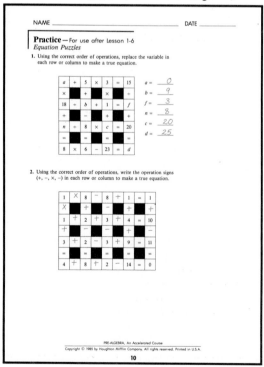

1-7 Inverse Operations

Objective *for pages 26–28*

■ To use the inverse relationship between addition and subtraction and between multiplication and division to solve equations.

Teaching Suggestions

The concept of inverse operations is not new to students. First review the use of inverse operations in basic facts. Then write the same facts with a variable for one addend or factor, as shown below.

$$3 + 5 = 8 \qquad\qquad n + 5 = 8$$
$$3 = 8 - 5 \qquad\qquad n = 8 - 5 = 3$$

$$8 \times 2 = 16 \qquad\qquad 8 \times m = 16$$
$$2 = 16 \div 8 \qquad\qquad m = 16 \div 8 = 2$$

The approach taken here is almost an intuitive one, based on the inverse relationship between addition and subtraction and the inverse relationship between multiplication and division. A more technical approach will be presented in Chapter 4. Remind students to check solutions in the original equation.

In solving equations containing two operations, be sure that students eliminate the added or subtracted term first. Then, they should use the inverse operation of multiplication or division. For example, to solve $3x - 5 = 7$, we write

$$3x = 7 + 5$$
$$3x = 12$$
$$x = 12 \div 3$$
$$x = 4$$

Students who begin by writing

$$3x - 5 = 7$$
$$x - 5 = 7 \div 3$$

will not obtain the correct solution.

Related Activities

To enhance understanding of solving an open sentence, ask students to write open sentences that are true

(a) for no real number;   (b) for all real numbers.

There should be great variety in their answers.

1-8 A Plan for Solving Problems

Objective *for pages 29–32*

■ To use a five-step plan to solve word problems involving one or more operations.

Teaching Suggestions

Here we outline a very broad framework that can be applied to a variety of problem settings. To the dismay of many a student, there is no single "formula" that can be followed to solve any given problem. The five-step plan should help students to focus their thinking and to keep the elements of a problem organized.

As you present Example 1, have the students read the problem several times to make sure that they understand it. You may want to list the facts on the chalkboard, ask whether enough facts are given (yes), and cross out the unnecessary fact (the time). Draw a diagram like the one on page 30 and show how to use it to solve the problem. Emphasize the importance of checking the calculations and making sure you have answered the question.

To show how important it is to read a problem carefully, you may want to have students suggest other questions that could have been asked about the facts in Example 1. One possibility is, "Where did the Nizels stop for lunch?" For this question students could use the diagram to show that the stop was between Harbor Bluffs and Newton.

Another possible question is, "What was the average speed on the trip from Topsfield to Harbor Bluffs?" In this case the trip time would be a necessary fact. Students would need to supply the fact that there are 60 minutes in an hour in order to calculate the average speed, 47.4 mi/h.

Some students may become impatient with the five-step plan. Point out that even with a problem so simple that they can solve it almost intuitively, they are using these steps in a quick and informal way. They should learn to apply the plan consciously so that they can use it to solve the difficult problems that they will encounter later on.

NAME _____ DATE _____

Problem Solving—For use after Lesson 1-8
Using a Table or Chart

Sometimes the facts needed to solve a problem are in a table or chart. At the right is a chart giving the price list for school photos. Select the information you need to solve each problem.

Package Contents	Traditional (matte finish)	Reflection (glossy finish)
Selection 1 1 10 x 13 2 8 x 10 2 5 x 7 2 3 x 5 4 gift size 8 wallets 1 class picture	$23.30	$26.85
Selection 2 1 8 x 10 2 5 x 7 2 3 x 5 10 gift size 8 wallets 1 class picture	$15.40	$18.95
Selection 3 with 10 x 13	$21.90	$25.45
Selection 4 1 8 x 10 1 5 x 7 2 3 x 5 2 gift size 8 wallets 1 class picture	$11.00	$14.55
Selection 5 with 10 x 13	$17.50	$21.05
Selection 6 1 5 x 7 1 3 x 5 2 gift size 4 wallets 1 class picture	$7.65	$11.20
Selection 7 with 10 x 13	$14.15	$17.70

1. The Nortons have two boys in the same class so they want only one class picture. Is there a selection they can make without a class picture? *no*

2. Which selection would be the least costly for the Nortons if they want a 10 x 13 portrait but do not care about the number of other pictures? *Selection 7*

3. How much more does any selection including a 10 x 13 portrait cost than the same selection without the 10 x 13 portrait? *$6.50*

4. Which selection gives you the most individual pictures regardless of size? *Selection 3*

5. Melissa wants as many wallet-size photos as she can get in order to exchange them with her friends. Since her family does not give out too many gift photos, the best choice would be *Selection 4*

6. Roberto likes the Reflection Photos. He does not need a 10 x 13 portrait but would like the maximum number of gift-size photos. How much will the package cost? *$18.95*

PRE-ALGEBRA, An Accelerated Course

11

NAME _____ DATE _____

Problem Solving—For use after Lesson 1-8
Conditions that Affect Solutions

When solving a problem, you need to be aware of the conditions that could affect the solution.

In the schedule of bus fares at the right, how much could you save by buying a monthly bus pass?

The problem cannot be solved unless you know these conditions:

(1) To which zone are you traveling?

(2) Are you disabled, a student, a senior citizen, and so on?

(3) How many trips do you take each month?

Schedule of Fares Effective August 20

	Zone 1	Zone 2	Zone 3	Zone 4	Zone 5
CHILDREN — up to 4 years of age	Free	Free	Free	Free	Free
DISABLED PERSONS Attendant may ride free (one-way fares)	$0.35	$0.50	$0.70	$0.85	$1.05
SENIOR CITIZEN 65 years (one-way fares)	$0.35	$0.50	$0.70	$0.85	$1.05
STUDENT – K through 12 (one-way fare)	$0.50	$0.75	$1.15	$1.50	$1.90
ALL OTHER PASSENGERS (one-way fare)	$0.75	$1.15	$1.50	$1.90	$2.25
MONTHLY BUS PASSES (round-trip fares)	$29	$44	$57	$72	$86

Use the bus-fare schedule to solve the following problems.

1. You are a 35-year-old nondisabled woman who rides to work and back 22 times each month. How much will you save by buying a monthly pass rather than by buying one-way fares?

    Condition I: if you work in Zone 1? *$4.00*   Condition II: if you work in Zone 2? *$6.60*

2. A 29-year-old father is riding with his 5-year-old kindergarten child. How much will it cost to ride

    Condition I: to Zone 5? *$4.15*   Condition II: to Zone 4? *$3.40*

3. A disabled adult is riding to Zone 3 and back. What is the total bus fare

    Condition I: if she is riding with one attendant? *$1.40*

    Condition II: if she is riding with her 50-year-old nondisabled sister and an attendant? *$4.40*

PRE-ALGEBRA, An Accelerated Course

12

1f

Related Activities

To emphasize the connection between algebra and problem solving, provide equations and have each student choose one. Have them write a story containing a problem situation that can be described by that equation. Encourage stories with missing facts or unnecessary facts. Have students exchange stories, write the equation, and try to solve the problem. For example, for the equation $185 - 3x = 170$, a student might write this story: "Marty weighs 185 lb. Two years ago he weighed 160 lb. He would like to weigh 170 lb. He plans to lose the same amount each week for three weeks. How much should he lose each week?" (Answer: 5 lb)

1-9 Solving and Checking Problems

Objective *for pages 33–37*

■ To solve and check a word problem.

Teaching Suggestions

This lesson expands on the problem solving skills taught in the preceding lesson. It shows methods that can be used to check answers to problems. Emphasize that the checking of the answer to a problem is an integral part of its solution. Students often neglect this important step of the process.

Some students will ask for clarification of the value of estimating by rounding to check an answer. Point out that estimating does not suffice to check an answer exactly. It only indicates whether an answer is reasonably close to the exact answer.

Ask which basic property is used in Example 1, Method 2. (It is the distributive property.) Ask which method students prefer. Emphasize that there may be more than one "right way" to solve a problem.

Related Activities

To relate mathematics to students' lives, have each student write five practical problems that use decimals. Let each student choose one to illustrate, with the solution on the reverse side of the paper. Post these on the bulletin board for other students to see and work.

NAME _____ DATE _____

Quiz 1B — Lessons 1-6 through 1-9

DIRECTIONS: Write the letter of the correct answer in the space provided.

Solve for the given replacement set. *[1-6]*

1. $54 - a = 36$ {16, 17, 18}
   a. 15   b. 16   c. 17   d. 18

2. $5m + 16 = 96$ {15, 16, 17}
   a. 15   b. 16   c. 17   d. 18

3. $3(r + 9) = 63$ {12, 14, 16}
   a. 12   b. 14   c. 15   d. 16

4. $(f - 7) \div 2 = 4$ {14, 15, 16}
   a. 12   b. 14   c. 15   d. 16

Use the inverse operation to solve.

5. $h + 16 = 34$
   a. 2   b. 48   c. 50   d. 18

6. $h - 23 = 25$ *[1-7]*

Solve, using the five-step plan.

7. Mark bought 5 lb of flour for $1.29, 3 lb of apples for 49¢ a pound, and a muffin tin for $3.65. How much change did he receive after paying with a ten-dollar bill? *[1-8]*
   a. $6.41   b. $4.57   c. $3.59   d. $5.43

8. Tickets to a baseball game cost $4.00 for adults, $2.00 for children under 12, and $1.50 for senior citizens. If 450 adults, 60 senior citizens, and 125 children attended the ball game, what was the total amount of ticket money collected?
   a. $2107.50   b. $750   c. $635   d. $2140

9. Brenda's checkbook shows that she has a balance of $82. *[1-9]* She has to write checks for $14.50 and for $29.60. She also has a $35 paycheck to deposit. What will her new balance be?
   a. $91.10   b. $72.90   c. $62.90   d. $37.90

10. The school store received a shipment of notebooks and pens. There were 7 cartons of notebooks and 12 boxes of pens. Each carton of notebooks had 24 notebooks in it and each box of pens had 36 pens in it. How many pens did the school store receive?
    a. 168   b. 432   c. 600   d. 684

ANSWERS
1. _d_ (10)
2. _b_ (10)
3. _a_ (10)
4. _c_ (10)
5. _d_ (10)
6. _b_ (10)
7. _c_ (10)
8. _d_ (10)
9. _b_ (10)
10. _b_ (10)

13

NAME _____ DATE _____

Review — Chapter 1

Simplify the numerical expression.

1. $2.3 + 8.79$ _11.09_
2. $33.6 \div 4$ _8.4_
3. 5.2×3.8 _19.76_ *[1-1]*

Evaluate the expression when $f = 7$ and $g = 5$.

4. $f - 6$ _1_
5. $g + 6 - f$ _4_
6. $6fg$ _210_

Simplify the expression. *[1-2]*

7. $6 + 15 \div 3$ _11_
8. $12 - 10 \div 2 + 3$ _10_
9. $(20 \div 4) \times (13 - 7)$ _30_

Evaluate the expression when $a = 3$ and $b = 8$.

10. $(b + 6) \div 14$ _1_
11. $36 \div (5a - 3)$ _3_
12. $9 \times \frac{3b}{a}$ _72_

Simplify the expression.

13. 5^4 _625_
14. $3^2 + 4^3$ _73_
15. $(3 \times 2)^2$ _36_ *[1-3]*

Round to the place specified.

16. hundreds: 746.368 _700_
17. tenths: 37.947 _37.9_
18. tens: 35.753 _40_
19. thousandths: 3.45795 _3.458_ *[1-4]*

Use the properties of addition and multiplication to simplify the expression.

20. $(25 \times 6) + (25 \times 14)$ _500_
21. $(3 + 7)5 + (6 + 9)8$ _170_ *[1-5]*
22. $6(64 \div 4) + 6(56 \div 4)$ _180_
23. $[(76 \div 4) + 2]5$ _110_

Solve for the given replacement set.

24. $47 - m = 19$; {18, 28, 36} _28_
25. $h + 114 = 205$; {91, 121, 319} _91_ *[1-6]*
26. $3(c + 5) = 48$; {11, 13, 15} _11_
27. $64 \div (m - 7) = 4$; {23, 24, 25} _23_

Use the inverse operation to write a related equation and solve for the variable.

28. $w - 26 = 39$ _$w = 39 + 26$; 65_
29. $13 + n = 17$ _$n = 17 - 13$; 4_ *[1-7]*

Solve, using the five-step plan.

30. Jan purchased 5 yards of fabric costing $2.79 a yard, 2 spools of thread priced at 53¢ a spool, and a pattern costing $1.75. What was the total amount of the purchases? _$16.76_ *[1-8]*

31. Matthew Gold enlarges his garden so that its new dimensions are three times its original dimensions. If the new dimensions are 176.4 cm by 240.6 cm, what were the original dimensions? _58.8 cm × 80.2 cm_ *[1-9]*

14

1g

NAME _____ DATE _____

Test—Chapter 1

DIRECTIONS: Write the correct answer in the space provided.

Simplify the numerical expression. *[1-1]*

1. 76.3×9 2. $34.77 \div 3$ 3. $0.3 + 1.72$

Evaluate the expression when $r = 8$ and $s = 10$.

4. $27 + s$ 5. $r - 8 + 12$ 6. $5rs - 3$

Simplify the expression.

7. $5 + 20 \div 5$ 8. $(8 \times 3) - (12 \div 3)$ *[1-2]*

Evaluate the expression when $j = 16$ and $k = 20$.

9. $4 + k \div 2$ 10. $(j + k - 10)(k \div 2)$

Evaluate.

11. 12^2 12. 10^7 *[1-3]*

Round to the place specified.

13. hundreds: 3742.876   14. tenths: 724.463   *[1-4]*

What value of the variable makes the statement true?   *[1-5]*

15. $17p = 17$

16. $6(8 + 3) = (k \times 8) + (k \times 3)$

17. $4(10.2 + 25) = 40.8 + x$

Solve for the given replacement set.   *[1-6]*

18. $b - 19 = 47$; {28, 66, 88}   19. $15r - 2 = 73$; {3, 4, 5}

Use the inverse operation to write a related equation and solve for the variable.

20. $47 + g = 69$ 21. $(p + 5) + 7 = 17$ *[1-7]*

Solve, using the five-step plan.

22. Barry Baker deposits $15.50 in his bank account each   *[1-8]* month. If his bank account had a balance of $120 at the beginning of the year, what was the amount in his bank account at the end of 1 year?

23. Ralph bought a sandwich for $1.50 and a carton of milk   *[1-9]* for 40¢. How much change did he get from a five-dollar bill?

ANSWERS
1. 686.7 (4)
2. 1159 (4)
3. 2.02 (4)
4. 37 (4)
5. 12 (4)
6. 397 (4)
7. 9 (4)
8. 20 (4)
9. 14 (4)
10. 260 (4)
11. 144 (4)
12. 10,000,000 (4)
13. 3700 (4)
14. 724.5 (4)
15. 1 (4)
16. 6 (4)
17. 100 (4)
18. 66 (4)
19. 5 (4)
20. $g = 69 - 47; 22$ (6)
21. $p + 5 = 17 - 7; 50$ (6)
22. $306 (6)
23. $3.10 (6)

15

NAME _____ DATE _____

Make-up Test—Chapter 1

DIRECTIONS: Write the correct answer in the space provided.

Simplify the numerical expression.   *[1-1]*

1. 11×3.3 2. $43.1 + 0.69$ 3. $14.3 - 5.02$

Evaluate the expression when $e = 5$ and $f = 9$.

4. $f - 4$ 5. $13 + e$ 6. $7ef - 2$

Simplify the expression.

7. $12 - 6 \div 3$ 8. $(15 - 7) \times (3 + 5)$ *[1-2]*

Evaluate the expression when $l = 15$ and $m = 25$.

9. $10 + m \div 5$ 10. $2l \div (m - 10)$

Evaluate.

11. 6^3 12. 10^6 *[1-3]*

Round to the place specified.

13. tens: 734.872   14. hundredths: 365.283   *[1-4]*

What value of the variable makes the statement true?   *[1-5]*

15. $(3.2 + 5) + 9.8 = 13 + d$ 16. $14r = 14$

17. $(2 + 7)3 = (2 \times f) + (7 \times f)$ 18. $(3.87 + 7.43)1 = w$

Find the solution of the equation for the given replacement set.   *[1-6]*

19. $8a = 96$; {10, 12, 14}   20. $3x + 5 = 113$; {32, 34, 36}

Use the inverse operation to write a related equation and solve for the variable.   *[1-7]*

21. $18p = 252$ 22. $f - 17 = 34$ 23. $6r + 5 = 47$

Solve, using the five-step plan.

24. Arthur earns $8.00 for mowing a lawn and $4.50 for   *[1-8]* edging a lawn. One week, he edged 5 lawns. If he earned a total of $134.50 for mowing and edging, how many lawns did he mow that week?

25. Wanda Brown bought a used car for $3750. License and   *[1-9]* insurance cost her another $475. How much money was left in her savings account if she had $5460?

ANSWERS
1. 36.3 (4)
2. 43.79 (4)
3. 9.28 (4)
4. 5 (4)
5. 18 (4)
6. 313 (4)
7. 9 (4)
8. 64 (4)
9. 15 (4)
10. 45 (4)
11. 216 (4)
12. 1,000,000 (4)
13. 730 (4)
14. 365.28 (4)
15. 5 (4)
16. 1 (4)
17. 3 (4)
18. 11.3 (4)
19. 12 (4)
20. 36 (4)
21. $p = 252 \div 18; 14$ (4)
22. $f = 34 + 17; 51$ (4)
23. $6r = 47 - 5; 7$ (4)
24. 14 lawns (4)
25. $1235 (4)

16

NAME _____ DATE _____

CUMULATIVE REVIEW—Chapter 1
Exercises

Simplify.

1. $69 + 543$ 612   2. $337 - 65.4$ 271.6   3. $47.6 \div 14$ 3.4

4. 3.7×1.82 6.734   5. 0.6×0.035 0.021   6. $(12 + 4) \div 4$ 4

7. $27 - 3 \times 5 - 2$ 10   8. $(3 + 9) \times (6 - 3)$ 36   9. $(22 + 3) \div (39 - 14)$ 1

Evaluate the expression when $a = 6$ and $b = 4$.

10. $2a + 18$ 30   11. $3b - 7$ 5   12. $b + 5 + a$ 15

13. $30 - ab$ 6   14. $(a - b) \div 2$ 1   15. $b(16 - 9)a$ 168

Evaluate the expression if $r = 2$, $s = 7$, and $t = 4$.

16. $3s^2$ 147   17. $(5r)^3$ 1000   18. t^r 16

Select the most reasonable estimated answer.

19. $37.4 - 8.73$ a. 14   b. 33   c. 28   c

20. 76.74×9.6 a. 770   b. 700   c. 680   a

21. $12.3 + 17.8 + 7.93$ a. 45   b. 30   c. 37   c

True or false?

22. $(54 - 45) = (45 - 54)$ F   23. $47.5 \times 1 = 47.5$ T

24. $63.7 \times 0 = 63.7$ F   25. $15(3 + 6) = 15 \times 3 + 15 \times 2$ F

Find the solution of the equation with the given replacement set.

26. $m + 13 = 21$; {7, 8, 9} 8   27. $36 - f = 19$; {15, 16, 17} 17

28. $5r - 3 = 32$; {5, 7, 9} 7   29. $7(w - 1) = 42$; {5, 6, 7} 7

30. $2n + 6 = 16$; {4, 6, 8} no solution   31. $4(a - 4) = 12$; {5, 6, 7} 7

Use inverse operations to write a related equation and solve for the variable.

32. $f - 11 = 43$ $f = 43 + 11; 54$ 33. $d \div 6 = 12$ $d = 12 \times 6; 72$

34. $3m + 7 = 31$ $3m = 31 - 7; 8$ 35. $8r - 3 = 69$ $8r = 69 + 3; 9$

17

NAME _____ DATE _____

CUMULATIVE REVIEW—Chapter 1 (continued)
Problems

Problem Solving Reminders
Here are some reminders that may help you solve some of the problems on this page.
- Determine which facts are necessary to solve the problem.
- Supply additional information if needed.
- Consider whether drawing a sketch will help.

Solve.

1. A microwave oven uses 1.5 kW·h of electricity in 15 min. How much electricity does it use in 2 h?   12 kW·h

2. Lexington High School plans to buy 3 kilns for each of its 5 art rooms. The cost of each kiln is $342. What will the total cost be? $5130

3. Marie bought a blanket for $16.78, 2 pillows for $6.98 each, and 2 sheets costing $8.50 each. How much change did she get from a fifty-dollar bill? $2.26

4. The Net Tennis Club has 12 tennis courts and 6 racquetball courts. Each court can be rented for $16 an hour. One hour, 3 tennis courts and 1 racquetball court were not used. How much money was collected for that hour? $224

5. A movie theater has 24 rows with 20 seats each. The admission charge is $4.00 for adults and $1.50 for children. If 300 adults and their children fill the movie theater one afternoon, what is the total amount paid for admission? $1470

6. Grapefruit usually sell for 39¢ each. This week, they are on sale for 3 for 89¢. How much money is saved by buying 1 dozen grapefruit this week? $1.12

7. Lenny Costa ordered 3 photo packages for $3.99 each by mail. Each photo package would contain 2 8 x 10 photos and 20 wallet-sized photos. He had to add 84¢ for postage and handling. He had 2 credit coupons for 60¢ each, which he could deduct from his order. How much will Lenny pay for his order? $11.61

8. Max bought a head of lettuce for 89¢, 2 lb of tomatoes costing 69¢ a lb, 2 packages of carrots at 33¢ each, and a package of celery at 69¢. What was the cost of his vegetables? $3.62

18

1h

Teaching Suggestions p. 1a

Related Activities p. 1a

Reading Mathematics

Students will learn the meaning of the following mathematical terms in this lesson: *numerical expression, simplify a numerical expression, variable, value of a variable, variable expression, terms, numerical coefficient.*

Mathematics has its own vocabulary. Some everyday words, such as *expression*, have different meanings in mathematics. Encourage students to pinpoint each key term and learn its meaning. Otherwise, they will not use or understand algebra terminology correctly. Important new terms are printed in boldface type to help students spot them easily.

1-1 Mathematical Expressions

A **numerical expression** is simply a name for a number. For example,

$$4 + 6 \text{ is a numerical expression for the number } 10.$$

Since $4 + 6$ and 10 name the same number, we can use the equals sign, $=$, and write

$$4 + 6 = 10.$$

We **simplify the numerical expression** $4 + 6$ when we replace it with its simplest name, 10.

EXAMPLE 1 Simplify each numerical expression.

        a. 400×4 **b.** $37 - 19$ **c.** $5.1 \div 3$

Solution   **a.** $400 \times 4 = 1600$ **b.** $37 - 19 = 18$ **c.** $5.1 \div 3 = 1.7$

If a computer can do 100 million arithmetic computations in one second, the table below shows how many million computations the computer can do in two, three, and four seconds.

Number of Seconds	Millions of Computations
1	100×1
2	100×2
3	100×3
4	100×4

Each of the numerical expressions 100×1, 100×2, 100×3, and 100×4 fits the pattern

$$100 \times n$$

where n stands for 1, 2, 3, or 4. A letter, such as n, that is used to represent one or more numbers is called a **variable.** The numbers are called the **values of the variable.**

An expression, such as $100 \times n$, that contains a variable is called a **variable expression.** When we write a product that contains a variable, we usually omit the multiplication sign.

$$100 \times n \text{ may be written } 100n.$$

$$x \times y \text{ may be written } xy.$$

In a numerical expression for a product, such as 100×4, we must use a multiplication sign to avoid confusion.

2 *Chapter 1*

A raised dot is also a multiplication sign.

$$100 \times 4 \text{ may be written } 100 \cdot 4.$$

When we replace each variable in a variable expression by one of its values and simplify the resulting numerical expression, we say that we are **evaluating the expression** or **finding the value of the expression.**

When the value of n is 4, the value of $100n$ is 400.

EXAMPLE 2   Evaluate each expression when $a = 6$ and $b = 2$.
   a. $9 + a$ **b.** $a \div b$ **c.** $3ab$

Solution   **a.** Substitute 6 for a. $9 + a = 9 + 6 = 15$
   b. Substitute 6 for a and 2 for b. $a \div b = 6 \div 2 = 3$
   c. Substitute 6 for a and 2 for b. $3ab = 3 \times 6 \times 2 = 36$

In the expression $9 + a$, 9 and a are called the **terms** of the expression because they are the parts that are separated by the $+$. In an expression such as $3ab$, the number 3 is called the **numerical coefficient** of ab.

Reading Mathematics: *Vocabulary*
Look back at this first lesson. Notice the words in heavier type throughout the text. They are important new words and ideas, such as the following:

   numerical expression   simplify a numerical expression
   variable   value of a variable
   variable expression   evaluate a variable expression
   terms   numerical coefficient

When you see a word in heavier type, look near it for an explanation or example to help you understand the new word. For an unusual new word, look up the definition in the glossary to help you understand and remember it.

Class Exercises

Simplify the numerical expression.

1. $24 + 18 + 32$ _74_   **2.** $125 \div 5$ _25_   **3.** $3.6 + 5.1$ _8.7_   **4.** 0.25×10 _2.5_

Evaluate the variable expression when $x = 4$.

5. $x + 7$ _11_   **6.** $5x$ _20_   **7.** $28 \div x$ _7_   **8.** $13 - x$ _9_

9. What is another way to write $17 \times x$?

10. In the variable expression $12a$, the numerical coefficient is __?__ _12_ and the variable is __?__. _a_

Introduction to Algebra   **3**

Chalkboard Examples
Simplify the numerical expression.

1. 12×38 456

2. $18.7 \div 17$ 1.1

Evaluate the expression when $n = 8$.

3. $75 - n$ 67

4. $1000 \div n$ 125

Evaluate the expression when $m = 5$ and $n = 7$.

5. $4mn$ 140

6. $m + 5 + n + 3$ 20

7. What value of a makes the expression $3 \times a \times a$ have the value 48? 4

Additional A Exercises

Simplify the numerical expression.

1. $1212 \div 6$ **202**

2. 17×0.25 **4.25**

3. $3.087 - 1.29$ **1.797**

Evaluate the expression when $c = 3$.

4. $c \times c \times c$ **27**

5. $18 - c$ **15**

6. $51 \div c$ **17**

7. $c - c$ **0**

8. $c \times 4$ **12**

Suggested Assignments

Core
   4/1–28; 37, 38
   4/Rev. 1–8
Enriched
   4/9–38

Supplementary Materials

Practice Masters, p. 3

Written Exercises

Simplify the numerical expression.

A **1.** $16 \cdot 3$ 48   **2.** $37 + 12$ 49   **3.** $114 - 9$ 105   **4.** $918 \div 6$ 153

5. $1.65 + 12.5$ 14.15   **6.** $1.05 + 9.7$ 10.75   **7.** 0.5×9 4.5   **8.** $2.53 \div 11$ 0.23

Evaluate the expression when $y = 2$.

9. $y + 23$ 25   **10.** $6y$ 12   **11.** $8 \div y$ 4   **12.** $4 + y + 7$ 13

Evaluate the expression when $q = 3$.

13. $36 \div q$ 12   **14.** $q \div 3$ 1   **15.** $q \times 9$ 27   **16.** $q - q$ 0

Evaluate the expression when $a = 5$.

17. $a - 3$ 2   **18.** $a \times a$ 25   **19.** $42 + a$ 47   **20.** $a + a$ 10

Evaluate the expression when $m = 8$.

21. $6 + 9 + 3 + m$ 26   **22.** $m \times 3$ 24   **23.** $m \times m \times m$ 512   **24.** $m \div m$ 1

Evaluate the expression when $x = 8$ and $y = 1$.

B **25.** $x + y$ 9   **26.** $x - y - 2$ 5   **27.** $3x$ 24   **28.** $x \div y$ 8

Evaluate the expression when $c = 7.5$ and $d = 3$.

29. $c \div d$ 2.5   **30.** $c + d + 20$ 30.5 **31.** $c \times 15$ 112.5   **32.** $4cd$ 90

Evaluate the expression when $s = 12.3$ and $t = 6.15$.

33. $9st$ 680.805   **34.** $s \div t$ 2   **35.** $s - t - 3$ 3.15   **36.** $73.8 \div s$ 6

C **37.** Find the value of a for which the expressions $2a$ and $2 + a$ have the same value. 2

38. Find a value of x for which $x \div 7$ and $7 \div x$ are equal. 7

Review Exercises

Perform the indicated operation.

1. $43.8 + 8.07$ 51.87 **2.** 51×3.4 173.4   **3.** $80.47 - 34.54$ 45.93 **4.** $6.29 + 0.124$ 6.414

5. $11.61 \div 43$ 0.27 **6.** 6.328×0.729 **7.** $32.004 \div 5.08$ 6.3 **8.** $2403 - 976.8$
                                4.613112   1426.2

4   Chapter 1

4

1-2 Order of Operations

The expression

$$2 + (6 \times 3)$$

involves both addition and multiplication. The parentheses indicate that the multiplication is to be done first.

$$2 + (6 \times 3) = 2 + 18 = 20$$

For the expression

$$(2 + 6) \times 3$$

the parentheses indicate that the addition is to be done first.

$$(2 + 6) \times 3 = 8 \times 3 = 24$$

Parentheses used to indicate the order of the arithmetic operations are called **grouping symbols.** Operations within grouping symbols are to be done first.

We usually write a product such as $4 \times (3 + 5)$ without the multiplication symbol as $4(3 + 5)$. We may also use parentheses in any one of the following ways to indicate a product such as 4×8:

$$4(8) \quad \text{or} \quad (4)8 \quad \text{or} \quad (4)(8).$$

A fraction bar is both a division symbol and a grouping symbol. Recall that $18 \div 2$ may be written as $\frac{18}{2}$. When operation symbols appear above or below the fraction bar, those operations are to be done before the division. For example, to simplify

$$\frac{6 + 15}{3},$$

we add first:

$$\frac{6 + 15}{3} = \frac{21}{3} = 7.$$

EXAMPLE 1 Evaluate each expression when $n = 8$.

    a. $4(n - 3)$ **b.** $\dfrac{45 - 15}{n + 7}$

Solution Substitute 8 for n in each expression.

    a. $4(n - 3) = 4(8 - 3) = 4(5) = 20$

    b. $\dfrac{45 - 15}{n + 7} = \dfrac{45 - 15}{8 + 7} = \dfrac{30}{15} = 2$

Introduction to Algebra   **5**

Teaching Suggestions p. 1b

Related Activities p. 1b

Reading Mathematics

Students will learn the meaning of the following mathematical terms in this lesson: *grouping symbols, order of operations.*

Many students have never thought of a fraction bar as a grouping symbol. Some may not even realize that a fraction bar indicates division. They may still think of fractions exclusively in terms of parts of a whole. Clarify the uses of the fraction bar, advocating use of a horizontal bar rather than a diagonal slash. This will be important when they write fractions such as $\frac{1}{x + 2}$. Students who use a diagonal slash may write $1/x + 2$, which is not the same expression. Using parentheses, as in $1/(x + 2)$, is not incorrect but $\frac{1}{x + 2}$ is easier to read.

If there are no grouping symbols in an expression, we agree to perform the operations in the following order.

Rule for Order of Operations

When there are no grouping symbols:

1. Perform all multiplications and divisions in order from left to right.

2. Perform all additions and subtractions in order from left to right.

EXAMPLE 2   Simplify $392 + 637 \div 49$.

Solution

$$392 + \underbrace{637 \div 49}$$

$$\underbrace{392 + \quad 13}$$

$$405$$

When a product of two numbers or of a number and a variable is written without a multiplication symbol, as in 5(7) or 4*n*, we perform the multiplication before the other operations.

EXAMPLE 3   Evaluate the expression when $x = 6$.

a. $27 \div 2x$ **b.** $\dfrac{3x - 2}{4}$

Solution   Substitute 6 for x in each expression.

a. $27 \div 2x = 27 \div 2(6) = 27 \div 12 = 2.25$

b. $\dfrac{3x - 2}{4} = \dfrac{3(6) - 2}{4} = \dfrac{18 - 2}{4} = \dfrac{16}{4} = 4$

Class Exercises

Tell in which order the operations should be performed to simplify the expression.

1. $6 + 14 \times 3$

2. $(6 + 14)3$

3. $18 - 12 \div 3 + 1$

4. $18 - 12 \div (3 + 1)$

5. $23 - 9 \div 5 + 2$

6. $(9 + 16) \div (4 + 1)$

Evaluate the expression when _m_ = 4.

7. $(m + 6)2$ 20

8. $5m + 8$ 28

9. $3(m - 1)$ 9

10. $8 \div m + 7$ 9

11. $m(2 + m)$ 24

12. $\dfrac{3m}{18 - 6}$ 1

Written Exercises

Simplify the expression.

A **1.** $35 - 14 \div 2 + 64$ 92 **2.** $54 \div 6 + 18 \times 2$ 45 **3.** $44 + 17 - 5 \times 2$ 51

4. $(45 - 19)(8 + 7)$ 390 **5.** $(12 + 18) \div (19 - 4)$ 2 **6.** $\dfrac{9 + (4 \times 3)}{7}$ 3

Evaluate the expression when _n_ = 7.

7. $(14 + n)6$ 126

8. $36 \div (n - 3)$ 9

9. $(n + 28) \div 5$ 7

10. $(27 - n)3$ 60

11. $12(n - 4)$ 36

12. $\dfrac{94 - 38}{n}$ 8

Evaluate the expression when _t_ = 10.

13. $5t \div (14 - 9)$ 10

14. $\dfrac{25 - t}{10 - 5}$ 3

15. $(t + 6 - 9)t$ 70

16. $2(t + 5) - t$ 20

17. $(t - 4)(t - 4)$ 36

18. $50 \div (t + 15) + t$ 12

Evaluate the expression when _s_ = 16.

19. $7(s + 12)$ 196

20. $5(s - 4)$ 60

21. $(s + 32) \div s$ 3

22. $(3s - 6) \div 7$ 6

23. $18(6s - 12)$ 1512

24. $4s \div (s - 8)$ 8

Evaluate the expression when _b_ = 6 and _c_ = 7.

B **25.** $(b + c)c$ 91

26. $3c \div (b - 4)$ 10.5

27. $2bc \div (c - b)$ 84

Evaluate the expression when _m_ = 4 and _n_ = 9.

28. $5n \div (m + 5)$ 5

29. $(n + m) \div (35 - n)$ 0.5

30. $m(n - m) \div 8$ 2.5

Evaluate the expression when _a_ = 3.6 and _b_ = 8.2.

31. $ab \div 2a$ 4.1

32. $(b - a)(3a + 6)$ 77.28

33. $7ab(3b + a)$ 5827.248

Introduction to Algebra **7**

Additional A Exercises

Simplify the expression.

1. $18 - 3 \times 4 \div 6$ 16

2. $(22 - 7)(5 + 3)$ 120

Evaluate the expression when $c = 11$.

3. $3c - 5$ 28

4. $(c - 3)(c + 3)$ 112

5. $(42 - c)c$ 341

6. $(2c - 4) \div 9$ 2

Suggested Assignments

Core
  7/1–24; 29, 31, 33
  8/34, 35, 37, 39
  8/Calculator Key-In

Enriched
  7/1–23 odd; 25–33
  8/34–39
  8/Calculator Key-In

Supplementary Materials

Practice Masters, p. 3
Computer Activity 1

Evaluate the expression when $e = 5$, $f = 8$, and $g = 13$.

34. $(e + f)(g + e)$ 234   **35.** $f \div (g - f) + g$ 14.6   **36.** $f(e + g) - e$ 139

Copy the expression as shown. Add grouping symbols so that the value of the expression is 24 when $x = 3$, $y = 7$, and $z = 21$.

C **37.** $2x \times y - 4 + 2x$ **38.** $y + z \div 4 \times x + x$ **39.** $x \times y + z \div 3 + 1 - z$
　　 or $2x \times y - (4 + 2)x$

Review Exercises

Evaluate the expression when $x = 2$, $y = 1$, and $z = 4$.

1. $2x + y$ 5   **2.** $3z - 3x$ 6   **3.** $5xy - z$ 6   **4.** $4xyz - xz$ 24

5. $6yz \div 4x$ 3   **6.** $12z \times 3y$ 144   **7.** $7z \times 3x$ 168   **8.** $8xy \div z$ 4

▪▪▪▪ Calculator Key-In

To use your calculator to simplify an expression with more than one operation, you must keep in mind the order in which you want the operations to be performed. Try to simplify $2(6 + 4)$ by entering the following on your calculator exactly as it is shown.

$$\boxed{2} \ \boxed{\times} \ \boxed{6} \ \boxed{+} \ \boxed{4} \ \boxed{=}$$

Although the correct answer is 20, your calculator will perform the operations in the order in which you entered them and will display 16 for the answer.

To obtain the correct answer, you must enter the expressions in the order in which you want them to be performed. Enter the following exactly as it is shown.

$$\boxed{6} \ \boxed{+} \ \boxed{4} \ \boxed{=} \ \boxed{\times} \ \boxed{2} \ \boxed{=}$$

Now your calculator should display the correct answer, 20. By entering $=$ after entering the expression in parentheses, you complete the operation inside the parentheses before doing the next operation. Some calculators will complete the operation for you even if you do not enter $=$ between operations. Check to see if your calculator will.

Use your calculator to simplify the expression.

1. $12(15 + 9)$ 288   **2.** $57 \div (36 - 17)$ 3   **3.** $(437 + 322) \div 46$ 16.5

4. $(108 + 63) \div (9 - 6)$ 57   **5.** $(55 + 8) \times (2 + 94)$ 6048   **6.** $(56 - 32) \div (4 + 16) \times 5$ 6

8   *Chapter 1*

1-3 Exponents and Powers of Ten

When two or more numbers are multiplied together, each of the numbers is called a **factor** of the product. For example, in the multiplication

$$3 \times 5 = 15,$$

3 and 5 are the factors of 15.

A product in which each factor is the same is called a **power** of that factor. For example, since

$$2 \times 2 \times 2 \times 2 = 16,$$

16 is called the *fourth power* of 2. We can write this as

$$2^4 = 16.$$

The small numeral 4 is called an **exponent** and represents the number of times 2 is a factor of 16. The number 2 is called the **base**.

EXAMPLE 1 Simplify 4^3.

Solution $4^3 = 4 \times 4 \times 4 = 16 \times 4 = 64$

The second and third powers of a number have special names. The second power is called the **square** of the number and the third power is called the **cube.**

EXAMPLE 2 Read, then simplify.

      a. 12^2 **b.** 9^3

Solution   **a.** 12^2 is read "twelve squared."
              $12^2 = 12 \times 12 = 144$

         b. 9^3 is read "nine cubed."
              $9^3 = 9 \times 9 \times 9 = 81 \times 9 = 729$

Powers of 10 are important in our number system. Here is a list of the first five powers of 10.

First power: 10^1 (exponent usually not written) $= 10$
Second power: $10^2 = 10 \times 10$ $= 100$
Third power: $10^3 = 10 \times 10 \times 10$ $= 1000$
Fourth power: $10^4 = 10 \times 10 \times 10 \times 10$ $= 10{,}000$
Fifth power: $10^5 = 10 \times 10 \times 10 \times 10 \times 10$ $= 100{,}000$

Introduction to Algebra **9**

Reading Mathematics

Students will learn the meaning of the following mathematical terms in this lesson: *factor, power, exponent, base, square, cube.*

Use exponents to write each
of the following expressions.

1. $3 \times 3 \times 3 \times 3$ 3^4

2. $2 \times 2 \times 2 \times 2$ 2^4

3. 20×20 20^2

4. $10 \times 10 \times 10 \times 10 \times 10$
   10^5

Simplify.

5. 9^3 729

6. 1^0 1

7. 12^2 144

8. 3^6 729

If you study the preceding list carefully, you can see that the general rules below apply.

> ### Rules
>
> 1. The exponent in a power of 10 is the same as the number of zeros when the number is written out.
> 2. The number of zeros in the product of powers of 10 is the sum of the numbers of zeros in the factors.

EXAMPLE 3   Write 10,000 as a power of 10.

Solution   Because there are 4 zeros in 10,000, the exponent is 4.

$$10{,}000 = 10^4$$

EXAMPLE 4   Multiply 100×1000.

Solution   Since there are 2 zeros in 100 and 3 zeros in 1000, the product will have $2 + 3$, or 5, zeros.

$$100 \times 1000 = 100{,}000$$

Can we give an expression such as 7^0 a meaning? When the powers of any base are listed in order, we may recognize a pattern. Study the example below.

$$7^4 = 7 \times 7 \times 7 \times 7 = 2401$$
$$7^3 = 7 \times 7 \times 7 = 343$$
$$7^2 = 7 \times 7 = 49$$
$$7^1 = 7$$

Notice that in increasing order each power of 7 is seven times the preceding power. Conversely, in decreasing order, each power of 7 is the quotient of the preceding power divided by a factor of 7. That is, $7^3 = 7^4 \div 7$, $7^2 = 7^3 \div 7$, and so on. This decreasing pattern suggests that 7^0 (read *7 to the zero power*) is $7^1 \div 7$. Study the example below to verify that the expression $7^0 = 1$.

$$7^0 = 7^1 \div 7 = 7 \div 7 = 1$$

10   *Chapter 1*

In general,

> ### *Definition*
> For every number a ($a \neq 0$), $a^0 = 1$.

Class Exercises

Name the exponent and the base.

1. 8^3 3; 8   **2.** 9^7 7; 9   **3.** 3^5 5; 3   **4.** 6^4 4; 6

Write as a power of 10.

5. 1000 10^3 **6.** 100 10^2 **7.** 100,000 10^5 **8.** 100,000,000 10^8

Tell the number of zeros in the number or product.

9. 10^4 4   **10.** 10^8 8   **11.** 1000 × 1000 6   **12.** 100 × 1,000,000 8

Read the following, then simplify each.

13. 7^2 **14.** 9^2 **15.** 13^0 **16.** 6^2

17. 4^3 **18.** 8^0 **19.** 2^7 **20.** 13^2

Written Exercises

Use exponents to write each of the following expressions.

A **1.** $5 \times 5 \times 5 \times 5 \times 5 \times 5$ 5^6 **2.** $12 \times 12 \times 12 \times 12$ 12^4

3. $8 \times 8 \times 8 \times 8 \times 8 \times 8 \times 8 \times 8 \times 8$ 8^9 **4.** $20 \times 20 \times 20 \times 20 \times 20$ 20^5

5. $7 \times 7 \times 7 \times 7 \times 7 \times 7 \times 7$ 7^7 **6.** $9 \times 9 \times 9 \times 9$ 9^4

7. $4 \times 4 \times 4 \times 4 \times 4 \times 4$ 4^6 **8.** $3 \times 3 \times 3 \times 3 \times 3$ 3^5

Write as a power of 10.

9. 10 10^1 **10.** 10,000,000 10^7 **11.** 1,000,000 10^6 **12.** 1,000,000,000 10^9

Multiply.

13. 1000 × 1000 1,000,000   **14.** 10 × 10,000 100,000   **15.** 100 × 100 10,000   **16.** 100 × 100,000 10,000,000

Introduction to Algebra **11**

Suggested Assignments

Core
  11/1–15 odd
  12/17–49 odd
  12/Rev. 1–8

Enriched
  11/9–15 odd
  12/25–55 odd; 57–68

Supplementary Materials

Practice Masters, p. 4

Simplify.

17. 4^2 16

18. 11^3 1331

19. 16^2 256

20. 15^2 225

21. 20^2 400

22. 5^4 625

23. 15^3 3375

24. 2^5 32

25. 80^2 6400

26. 40^3 64,000

27. 2^8 256

28. 12^3 1728

29. 6^4 1296

30. 5^5 3125

31. 16^3 4096

32. 3^5 243

33. 5^3 125

34. 4^6 4096

35. 13^2 169

36. 11^2 121

Multiply.

EXAMPLE $3^4 \times 2^3$

Solution
$$3^4 \times 2^3 = (3 \times 3 \times 3 \times 3) \times (2 \times 2 \times 2)$$
$$= 81 \times 8$$
$$= 648$$

B **37.** $2^4 \times 5^2$ 400

38. $1^3 \times 16^2$ 256

39. $70^2 \times 7^3$ 1,680,700

40. $3^4 \times 10^5$ 8,100,000

41. $0^4 \times 15^8$ 0

42. $15^2 \times 10^3$ 225,000

43. $31^2 \times 1^5$ 961

44. $20^5 \times 3^2$ 28,800,000

45. $2^8 \times 1^5$ 256

46. $5^3 \times 3^4$ 10,125

47. $12^3 \times 2^2$ 6912

48. $200^3 \times 3^2$ 72,000,000

49. $2^3 \times 3^2 \times 10^3$ 72,000

50. $8^2 \times 5^3 \times 1^4$ 8000

51. $119^2 \times 2^5 \times 0^8$ 0

52. $50^4 \times 2 \times 1^5$ 12,500,000

53. $3^3 \times 2^0$ 27

54. $2^5 \times 3^2$ 288

55. $3^2 \times 10^4$ 90,000

56. $10^5 \times 11^0$ 100,000

Evaluate when $a = 3$ and $b = 5$.

C **57.** a^3 27

58. b^3 125

59. $a^5 - b^2$ 218

60. $a^3 + b^2$ 52

61. $50 - b^2$ 25

62. $20a^2$ 180

63. $(ab)^2$ 225

64. a^2b^3 1125

65. a^3b^3 3375

66. $(ab)^3$ 3375

67. $b^2 - a^2$ 16

68. $(a - b)^2$ 4

Review Exercises

Simplify the expression.

1. $48 + 20 \div 4 + 7$ 60

2. $72 \div 9 + 3 \times 8$ 32

3. $50 + 35 \div 7 + 2$ 57

4. $105 - 30 \times 2 \div 5$ 93

5. $36 - 24 \div (3 + 1)$ 30

6. $60 + 40 \div (2 + 8)$ 64

7. $\frac{28 + 20}{4} + 12$ 24

8. $\frac{78 - 18 \div 3}{4} - 8$ 10

12   *Chapter 1*

1-4 The Decimal System

Our number system uses the powers of 10 to express all numbers. This system is called the **decimal system** (from the Latin word *decem,* meaning *ten*). Using the digits 0, 1, 2, . . . , 9, we can write any number. The **value** of each digit depends on the position of the digit in the number. For example, the 2 in 312 means 2 ones, but the 2 in 298 means 2 hundreds. The decimal system is a system with **place value.**

The chart below shows place values for some of the digits of a **decimal number,** or **decimal.**

Place-Value Chart

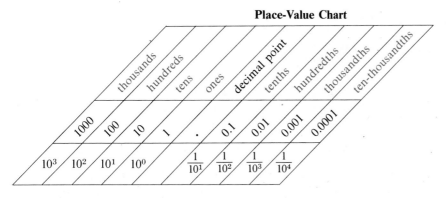

Moving left to right, place values decrease. As illustrated below, each place value is one tenth, or 0.1, of the place value to its left.

$$1000 \times 0.1 = 100 \qquad 10 \times 0.1 = 1 \qquad 0.01 \times 0.1 = 0.001$$

We can see from the place-value chart that values to the left of the decimal point are greater than or equal to 1, while values to the right are less than 1. If a digit is zero, then the product is zero and is usually not written.

When a decimal number is written, the value of the number is the sum of the values of the digits. To illustrate this, we can write decimal numbers in **expanded form,** that is, as a sum of products of each digit and its place value.

EXAMPLE 1   Write the decimal in expanded form.

       a. 3053   **b.** 16.9   **c.** 0.074

Solution   **a.** $3053 = (3 \times 1000) + (5 \times 10) + 3$

              b. $16.9 = (1 \times 10) + 6 + (9 \times 0.1)$

              c. $0.074 = (7 \times 0.01) + (4 \times 0.001)$

Introduction to Algebra   **13**

Teaching Suggestions p. 1c

Related Activities p. 1c

Reading Mathematics

Students will learn the meaning of the following mathematical terms in this lesson: *decimal system, value, place value, decimal number, decimal, expanded form, graph, coordinate, origin, rounding, estimate.*

Chalkboard Examples

Read the number.

1. 472.34
   Four hundred seventy-two and thirty-four hundredths

2. 0.0452
   Four hundred fifty-two ten-thousandths

Write in expanded form.

3. 490 (4 × 100) + (9 × 10)

4. 5.623 5 + (6 × 0.1) + (2 × 0.01) + (3 × 0.001)

Write as a decimal.

5. Eighty-three and fourteen hundredths 83.14

6. Nine hundred thirty-four thousandths 0.934

7. (6 × 100) + 3 + (2 × 0.1) + (1 × 0.001) 603.201

Round to the place indicated.

8. 4̲9.92 50

9. 49.9̲2 49.9

10. 3.9̲85 3.99

Find an estimated answer for each operation.

11. 6.7 + 5.2 12

12. 51.723 − 29.518 22

13. 4.87 × 25.1 125

14. 276 ÷ 19 14

Decimals and whole numbers can be pictured on a number line. The **graph** of a number is the point paired with the number on the number line. The number paired with a point is called the **coordinate** of the point. The graphs of the whole numbers 0 through 8 are shown on the number line below. The coordinates of the points shown are 0, 1, 2, 3, 4, 5, 6, 7, and 8.

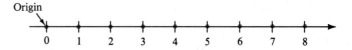

Starting with the graph of 0, which is called the **origin,** the graphs of the whole numbers are equally spaced. The greater a number is, the farther to the right its graph is.

The number line can be used to develop a method for **rounding** numbers. For example, we can see that 6.7 is closer to 7 than to 6 by graphing 6.7 on the number line. First we divide the portion of the number line between 6 and 7 into ten equal parts. Then we graph 6.7 on the number line as shown.

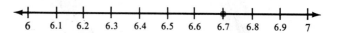

Because 6.7 is closer to 7 than to 6, we say that 6.7 rounded to the nearest whole number is 7. We write 6.7 ≈ 7. The symbol ≈ means *is approximately equal to.*

The rule for rounding decimal numbers can be stated as follows:

Rule

1. Find the decimal place to which you wish to round, and mark it with a caret (‸). Look at the digit to the right.

2. If the digit to the right is 5 or greater, add 1 to the marked digit. If the digit to the right is less than 5, leave the marked digit unchanged.

3. If the marked digit is to the left of the decimal point, replace each digit to the right of the marked place with "0," and drop all digits to the right of the decimal point.
   If the marked digit is to the right of the decimal point, drop all digits to the right of the marked place.

EXAMPLE 2 Round 16.0973 to the nearest

	a. ten	**b.** tenth	**c.** hundredth

Solution

a. 16.0973
$\wedge$
20

$16.0973 \approx 20$

b. 16.0973
$\wedge$
16.1

$16.0973 \approx 16.1$

c. 16.0973
$\wedge$
16.10

$16.0973 \approx 16.10$

Rounding is often used as a quick check on calculations. In general, we **estimate** by rounding to the highest place value of the smaller number for all operations. As a result, our estimated answer should be reasonably close to the exact answer.

EXAMPLE 3 Find an estimated answer for each operation.

a.   386
$+ \ 54$

b.   2.849
$- 0.154$

c.   32.9
$\times 8.7$

d. $12\overline{)253}$

Solution

a.   386 $\longrightarrow$ 390
$+ \ 54$ $\qquad + \ 50$
$\qquad\qquad\qquad\quad 440$

b.   2.849 $\longrightarrow$ 2.8
$- 0.154$ $\qquad - 0.2$
$\qquad\qquad\qquad\quad 2.6$

c.   32.9 $\longrightarrow$ 33
$\times 8.7$ $\qquad \times 9$
$\qquad\qquad\qquad\ 297$

d. $12\overline{)253}$ $\longrightarrow$ $10\overline{)250}$ (25)

Class Exercises

Read the number.

1. 5496   **2.** 0.51   **3.** 28.7   **4.** 0.0317   **5.** 8.026

Give the value of the digit 6 in the number.

6. 657.3 600   **7.** 0.062 0.06   **8.** 8.1416 0.0006   **9.** 6.023 6   **10.** 408.6 0.6

Round to the place underlined.

11. 8.0<u>3</u>9 8.04   **12.** 2<u>9</u>4.65 290   **13.** 7<u>5</u>.452 75   **14.** 1<u>0</u>.988 11

15. 0.9<u>9</u>6 1.00   **16.** 1.35<u>4</u>7 1.355   **17.** <u>3</u>19.84 300   **18.** 0.<u>3</u>828 0.4

Introduction to Algebra   **15**

Round to the highest place value.

19. 43 40

20. 127.14 100

21. 0.036 0.04

22. 0.8981 0.9

23. 1986 2000

24. 532.3 500

25. 0.073 0.07

26. 0.0249 0.02

Written Exercises

Write the decimal in expanded form.

A

1. 38

2. 256

3. 8091

4. 5

5. 0.47

6. 28.4

7. 0.063

8. 9.070

9. 0.187

10. 5.5

Write as a decimal.

11. (5 × 10) + 4 + (5 × 0.1) + (7 × 0.01) 54.57

12. (4 × 100) + (7 × 0.01) + (3 × 0.001) + (2 × 0.0001) 400.0732

13. (9 × 1000) + 2 + (1 × 0.1) + (4 × 0.01) + (6 × 0.001) 9002.146

14. (1 × 100) + (9 × 10) + 3 + (2 × 0.01) + (3 × 0.001) 193.023

Write as a decimal.

15. 7 and 43 hundredths 7.43

16. 11 and 4 tenths 11.4

17. 19 and 5 thousandths 19.005

18. 37 ten-thousandths 0.0037

19. 48 ten-thousandths 0.0048

20. 5 and 6 hundredths 5.06

21. 6 and 25 thousandths 6.025

22. 94 and 7 ten-thousandths 94.0007

Round to the nearest ten.

23. 27.5149 30

24. 82.604 80

25. 293.4 290

26. 70.76 70

27. 648.01 650

28. 108.3 110

29. 159.62344 160

30. 97.23 100

Round to the nearest hundredth.

31. 72.459 72.46

32. 26.804 26.80

33. 0.0643 0.06

34. 12.395 12.40

35. 0.0103 0.01

36. 8.142 8.14

37. 18.1657 18.17

38. 0.70605 0.71

Round to the nearest thousandth.

39. 0.0006 0.001

40. 12.3568 12.357

41. 401.0904 401.090

42. 30.0317 30.032

43. 250.3407 250.341

44. 7.0063 7.006

45. 8.0995 8.100

46. 0.9996 1.000

Write in expanded form using exponents by writing each number as a sum of multiples of powers of 10.

EXAMPLE   367.04

Solution $(3 \times 10^2) + (6 \times 10^1) + (7 \times 10^0) + \left(4 \times \frac{1}{10^2}\right)$

47. 5280 **48.** 64.7 **49.** 183.08 **50.** 0.043

51. 0.091 **52.** 12.931 **53.** 7.482 **54.** 0.806

55. 204.5 **56.** 0.306 **57.** 38.003 **58.** 10.009

Select the most reasonable estimated answer.

B **59.** $89.6 + 13.5$ b   **a.** 90   **b.** 100   **c.** 70

60. $35 + 12 + 26 + 11$ c   **a.** 70   **b.** 110   **c.** 90

61. $65.43 - 8.92$ a   **a.** 56   **b.** 60   **c.** 90

62. $2196 - 924$ a   **a.** 1300   **b.** 1000   **c.** 3100

63. 6.82×4.7 b   **a.** 24   **b.** 35   **c.** 28

64. $54 \div 2.5$ c   **a.** 30   **b.** 20   **c.** 18

65. $36\overline{)283}$ c   **a.** 10   **b.** 3   **c.** 7

Review Exercises

Simplify.

1. $5.7 + (1.3 + 2.4)$ 9.4

2. $(5.7 + 1.3) + 2.4$ 9.4

3. $12 \times (10 \times 8)$ 960

4. $(12 \times 10) \times 8$ 960

5. $6 \times (4.7 + 5.3)$ 60

6. $(6 \times 4.7) + (6 \times 5.3)$ 60

7. $3.7 \times (7.9 - 3.9)$ 14.8

8. $(3.7 \times 7.9) - (3.7 \times 3.9)$ 14.8

▮▮▮ **Challenge**

Write 100 using four 5's and any operation symbols you need. $(5 + 5)(5 + 5)$

Write 100 using the numbers 1 through 9 and any operation symbols you need. $98 - 76 + 45 + 32 + 1$

Write 100 using four 9's and any operation symbols you need. $99 + 9 \div 9$

Other answers are possible.

Introduction to Algebra   **17**

Teaching Suggestions p. 1d

Related Activities p. 1d

Reading Mathematics

Students will learn the meaning of the following mathematical terms in this lesson: *commutative property, associative property, identity element, distributive property.*

1-5 Basic Properties

Decimals and whole numbers share a number of properties which are used frequently in algebra.

Changing the order of the addends in a sum or the factors in a product does not change the sum or product. For example,

$$9.2 + 4.7 = 4.7 + 9.2 \qquad 3.5 \times 8.4 = 8.4 \times 3.5$$

Commutative Property

For all numbers a and b,

$$a + b = b + a \qquad \text{and} \qquad a \times b = b \times a$$

Changing the grouping of addends in a sum or of factors in a product does not change the sum or product. For example,

$5.6 + 0.8 + 11.2$	$4.1 \times 2.3 \times 7.2$
$(5.6 + 0.8) + 11.2 = 17.6$	$(4.1 \times 2.3) \times 7.2 = 67.896$
$5.6 + (0.8 + 11.2) = 17.6$	$4.1 \times (2.3 \times 7.2) = 67.896$

Associative Property

For all numbers a, b, and c,

$$(a + b) + c = a + (b + c)$$

$$\text{and} \qquad (a \times b) \times c = a \times (b \times c)$$

We can use these properties to find the easiest way to add or multiply a long list of numbers.

EXAMPLE 1 Use the properties to simplify the expression.

    a. $4.8 + 1.1 + 0.2 + 3.9 + 7$ **b.** $2 \times 6 \times 5 \times 3$

Solution   One possible way to rearrange the numbers is shown.

    a. $4.8 + 1.1 + 0.2 + 3.9 + 7$ **b.** $2 \times 6 \times 5 \times 3$

        $(4.8 + 0.2) + (1.1 + 3.9) + 7$ $(2 \times 5) \times (6 \times 3)$

                $5 + 5 + 7$ 10×18

                    $10 + 7$ 180

                      17

18   *Chapter 1*

The numbers 0 and 1 are called the **identity elements** for addition and multiplication respectively. The word *identity* comes from the Latin word *idem,* which means *the same.* The result of adding 0 to a number or subtracting 0 from a number is the same as the original number. The result of multiplying a number by 1 or dividing a number by 1 is the same as the original number. Study the following examples.

$$4.53 + 0 = 4.53 \qquad 29.7 \times 1 = 29.7$$

$$4.53 - 0 = 4.53 \qquad 29.7 \div 1 = 29.7$$

Addition and Subtraction Properties of Zero

For every number a,
$$a + 0 = a \qquad a - 0 = a$$
$$0 + a = a \qquad a - a = 0$$

Multiplication and Division Properties of One

For every number a,
$$a \times 1 = a \qquad a \div 1 = a$$
$$1 \times a = a \qquad a \div a = 1$$

The product of any number and 0 is 0. Similarly, 0 divided by any number is 0.

$$3.784 \times 0 = 0 \qquad 0 \div 3.784 = 0$$

Can we divide by 0? Recall that multiplication and division are inverse operations. Thus, if we were to divide 3.784 by 0, we would have the following.

$$3.784 \div 0 = x \qquad 3.784 = x \times 0$$

We cannot accept the equation at the right because any number times 0 is 0. So it makes no sense to divide by 0.

Multiplication and Division Properties of Zero

For every number a,
$$a \times 0 = 0 \qquad \text{and} \qquad 0 \times a = 0$$
For every number a, $a \neq 0$,
$$0 \div a = 0$$

Name the property illustrated.

1. $3.2 + 6.5 = 6.5 + 3.2$
   Commutative Property

2. $(4 + 7.3) + 2.1 = 4 + (7.3 + 2.1)$
   Associative Property

3. $6.4 \times 4.5 = 4.5 \times 6.4$
   Commutative Property

4. $2.6 + 0 = 2.6$ Addition Property of Zero

5. $(12.7 + 4) \times 3 = (12.7 \times 3) + (4 \times 3)$
   Distributive Property

6. $(7.8 \times 2) + (4.2 \times 2) = (7.8 + 4.2) \times 2$
   Distributive Property

Use the properties to simplify the expression. Name the property or properties used.

7. $12.8 \times 2 \times 50$ 1280; Associative Property

8. $5.1 + 6.3 + 4.9$ 16.3; Commutative Property, Associative Property

9. $37.5 \times 84.2 \times 0$ 0 Multiplication Property of Zero

10. $(4.3 \times 3.7) + (4.3 \times 6.3)$ 43; Distributive Property

What value of the variable makes the statement true?

11. $8 + 4 = r + 8$ 4

12. $2.9 \times 5 = 5g$ 2.9

13. $9(3 + 7) = 27 + t$ 63

Additional Answers
Class Exercises

7. 0; multiplication property of 0

8. 30.2; associative property

9. 12.87; multiplication property of 1

10. 18; commutative and associative properties

11. 160; distributive property

12. 0; multiplication property of 0

The distributive property is different from the other properties because it involves two operations. The example below illustrates how we may distribute a multiplier over each term in an addition expression.

$$7 \times (8.2 + 1.8) \qquad\qquad (7 \times 8.2) + (7 \times 1.8)$$
$$7 \times 10 \qquad\qquad\qquad\qquad 57.4 + 12.6$$
$$70 \qquad\qquad\qquad\qquad\qquad 70$$

Therefore $7 \times (8.2 + 1.8) = (7 \times 8.2) + (7 \times 1.8)$.

We may also distribute a multiplier over each term in a subtraction expression.

Distributive Property

For all numbers a, b, and c,

$$a \times (b + c) = (a \times b) + (a \times c)$$
$$a \times (b - c) = (a \times b) - (a \times c)$$

EXAMPLE 2 Use the distributive property to simplify the expression.
   a. $(4 + 6.2)5$ **b.** $(13 \times 2.7) - (13 \times 1.3)$

Solution **a.** $(4 + 6.2)5 = (4 \times 5) + (6.2 \times 5) = 20 + 31 = 51$

      b. $(13 \times 2.7) - (13 \times 1.3) = 13(2.7 - 1.3) = 13(1.4) = 18.2$

EXAMPLE 3 What value of the variable makes the statement true?
   a. $6 + 5 = 5 + m$ **b.** $3.7 \times 4 = 4t$ **c.** $3(14 + 20) = 42 + b$

Solution **a.** $6 + 5 = 5 + m$ **b.** $3.7 \times 4 = 4t$
          $6 + 5 = 5 + 6$, so $m = 6$ $3.7 \times 4 = 4 \times 3.7$, so $t = 3.7$

      c. $3(14 + 20) = 42 + b$
          $3(14 + 20) = (3 \times 14) + (3 \times 20) = 42 + 60$, so $b = 60$

Class Exercises

Name the property illustrated.

1. $7.6 + 0 = 0 + 7.6$
   Commutative Property
3. $11.9 \times 1 = 11.9$
   Multiplication Property of 1
5. $138.6 \times 7.4 = 7.4 \times 138.6$
   Commutative Property

2. $(19 \times 3)6.2 = 19(3 \times 6.2)$
   Associative Property
4. $5(9 + 8.2) = (5 \times 9) + (5 \times 8.2)$
   Distributive Property
6. $6(1.2 + 0.8) = (1.2 + 0.8)6$
   Commutative Property

20   *Chapter 1*

Use the properties of addition and multiplication to simplify the expression. Name the property or properties used.

7. 0.4×0 **8.** $3.02 \times 5 \times 2$ **9.** 1×12.87

10. $2.4 + 13 + 2.6$ **11.** $(8 \times 13) + (8 \times 7)$ **12.** 5.93×0

What value of the variable makes the statement true?

13. $25 + 37 = m + 25$ $m = 37$ **14.** $(7 \times 6) + (5 \times 6) = (7 + 5)q$ $q = 6$

15. $(17 + 12) + 8 = b + (12 + 8)$ $b = 17$ **16.** $9(w - 20) = (9 \times 35) - (9 \times 20)$
$$w = 35$$

Written Exercises

Use the properties to simplify the expression. Name the property or properties used.

A **1.** $2.6 + 11.5 + 0.5$ 14.6; Associative   **2.** 0×23.15 0; Multiplication Property of 0

3. $4(2.5 + 1.06)$ 14.24; Distributive   **4.** $8(40 - 12)$ 224; Distributive

5. $7.24 + 8.97 + 2.76$ 18.97; Commutative and Associative   **6.** $(22 \times 8) + (22 \times 2)$ 220; Distributive

7. $0.5 \times 2.1 \times 0.2$ 0.21; Commutative and Associative   **8.** $11.5 + 2.6 + 0.5 + 0.4$ 15; Commutative and Associative

True or false?

9. $7.386 + 0 = 0$ False   **10.** $(3 + 12)6 = (3 \times 6) + (12 \times 6)$ True

11. $(19.7 + 36 + 41.5)0 = 0$ True   **12.** $15(2 + 7.4) = (15 + 2) \times (15 + 7.4)$
False

What value of the variable makes the statement true?

13. $6 + n = 6$ $n = 0$ **14.** $7.02 \times 23 = t \times 7.02$ $t = 23$

15. $6.4 + t = 3.2 + 6.4$ $t = 3.2$ **16.** $3r = 3$ $r = 1$

17. $5w = w$ $w = 0$ **18.** $2.43 \times 0 = f$ $f = 0$

19. $(15.9 \times 3)4.2 = g(3 \times 4.2)$ $g = 15.9$ **20.** $(13 - 11.7)8 = (13 \times 8) - (r \times 8)$ $r = 11.7$

21. $(2 + 4.8)3 = (2n) + (4.8n)$ $n = 3$ **22.** $(3.02 + 4.9)1 = b$ $b = 7.92$

23. $5(11.7 + 313) = 58.5 + d$ $d = 1565$ **24.** $(7 \times 1.2) + (7 \times 3.8) = 7m$ $m = 5$

25. $(8.31 + 2.73)t = t$ $t = 0$ **26.** $2.59 + 7.03 + 18.61 + 3.97 = a + 11$
$a = 21.2$

Use the properties to simplify the expression.

B **27.** $116 \times 3.7 \times 0 \times 4.93 \times 1.47 + 3.88$ 3.88

28. $(78 \times 1) + (1.36 \times 0) + (92 + 0)$ 170

Introduction to Algebra **21**

Evaluate the expression when $t = 6$ and $s = 4$.

1. $72 \div t$ 12

2. $\frac{s}{4} + t$ 7

3. $5 + s - 3$ 6

4. $2t + s$ 16

Simplify.

5. 9^4 6561

6. $10^3 \times 10^5$ 100,000,000

Round to the place specified.

7. hundreds: 485.16 500

8. hundredths: 61.584 61.58

Use the properties of addition and multiplication to simplify.

9. $(50 \times 4) + 5 + (50 \times 4)$ 405

10. $(16 + 48) + (4 + 12) + 10$ 90

Suggested Assignments

Core
Day 1: 21/1–28
Day 2: 22/29–36
22/Self-Test A

Enriched
21/14–28 even
22/29–38
22/Self-Test A

Supplementary Materials

Practice Masters, p. 4
Test 1A, pp. 3–4

29. $(18 + 46) + (12 + 4) + (8 \times 17) + (23 \times 8)$ 400

30. $(12 \times 7) + (56 \div 8) + (13 \times 12)$ 247

31. $5(81 \div 3) + 5(63 \div 1) + 450$ 900

32. $(18 + 9)4 + (12 + 11)4$ 200

33. $6(13 + 3) - 4(13 + 3)$ 32

34. $1.4(2.61 + 7.39)$ 14

Find values for a, b, and c that show that the equation is not true for all numbers. Answers will vary. An example is supplied.

C 35. $(a \times b) + (b \times c) = b(a \times c)$ $a = 2, b = 3, c = 4$; $(2 \times 3) + (3 \times 4) \neq 3(2 \times 4)$

36. $(a + b)(b + c) = b(a + c)$ $a = 1, b = 2, c = 3$; $(1 + 2)(2 + 3) \neq 2(1 + 3)$

37. $(b + c)(a + c) = c(b \times a)$ $a = 2, b = 4, c = 6$; $(4 + 6)(2 + 6) \neq 6(4 + 2)$

38. $a + (b \times c) = (a + b) \times (a + c)$ $a = 2, b = 4, c = 5$; $2 + (4 \times 5) \neq (2 + 4) \times (2 + 5)$

Self-Test A

Evaluate the expression when $k = 4$ and $m = 6$.

1. $184 \div k$ 46   2. $8 + m + 1$ 15   3. $7km$ 168   [1-1]

Evaluate the expression when $s = 12$ and $t = 18$.

4. $\frac{s}{4} + 6$ 9   5. $(t + 2) \div 5$ 4   6. $2s - t$ 6   [1-2]

Simplify.

7. 2^4 16   8. 8^3 512   9. 9^1 9   10. 1000×100 100,000   11. $10 \times 10,000$ 100,000   [1-3]

Round to the place specified.

12. tens: 84.307 80   13. hundredths: 3.176 3.18   14. hundreds: 293.84 300   [1-4]

Use the properties of addition and multiplication to simplify the expression. Name the property used.

15. $12(15 - 8) + 6 \times 3$ 102; Distributive   16. $(31 \times 4) + (15 \times 4) - 91$ 93; Distributive   [1-5]

17. $7(56 \div 8) - 7(24 \div 6)$ 21; Distributive   18. $9(0.36 \times 4) + 55$ 67.96; Associative

Self-Test answers and Extra Practice are at the back of the book.

1-6 Equations

A **number sentence** indicates a relationship between two mathematical expressions. A sentence, such as the one below, that indicates that two expressions name the same number is called an **equation.**

$$4 \times 3 = 12$$

The expressions to the left and to the right of the equals sign are called the **sides** of the equation. In the example above, 4×3 is the left side of the equation, and 12 is the right side of the equation.

A number sentence may be *true* or *false*. For example, $3 + 9 = 12$ is a true equation, but $3 + 9 = 13$ is a false equation.

A number sentence that contains one or more variables is called an **open number sentence,** or simply an **open sentence.** Frequently a set of intended values, called the **replacement set,** for a variable is specified. An open sentence may be true or false when each variable is replaced by one of the values in its replacement set.

When a value of the variable makes an open sentence a true statement, we say that the value is a **solution** of, or **satisfies,** the sentence. We can **solve** an open sentence in one variable by finding all the solutions of the sentence. An open sentence may have one solution, several solutions, or no solutions.

Reading Mathematics

Students will learn the meaning of the following mathematical terms in this lesson: *number sentence, equation, sides, open sentence, replacement set, solution, satisfy, solve.*

Notice the statement, "A number sentence may be true or false." Here we have *or* used in the exclusive sense, meaning "true or false but not both." Most mathematical usage uses an inclusive *or,* meaning the first, or the second, or both.

EXAMPLE 1 Solve $x + 6 = 13$ for the replacement set $\{5, 6, 7\}$.

Solution Substitute each value in the replacement set for the variable x.

$5 + 6 = 13$	$6 + 6 = 13$	$7 + 6 = 13$
$11 = 13$	$12 = 13$	$13 = 13$
false	false	true

The solution of the equation is 7.

EXAMPLE 2 Solve $a - 1.2 = 0.7$ for the replacement set $\{1.8, 1.9, 2.0\}$.

Solution Substitute each value in the replacement set for the variable a.

$1.8 - 1.2 = 0.7$	$1.9 - 1.2 = 0.7$	$2.0 - 1.2 = 0.7$
$0.6 = 0.7$	$0.7 = 0.7$	$0.8 = 0.7$
false	true	false

The solution of the equation is 1.9.

Introduction to Algebra **23**

The replacement set for x is $\{8, 9, 10, 11\}$. Find all solutions of the equation.

1. $3x = 33$ **11**
2. $x + 5 = 23 - x$ **9**
3. $13 - x = 1$ **No solution**
4. $x(x - 3) = 70$ **10**
5. $x + 1 = x + 2$ **No solution**
6. $2x = x + x$ **8, 9, 10, 11**

EXAMPLE 3   The replacement set for q is the set of whole numbers. Find all solutions of

$$2q = 9.$$

Solution   The replacement set for q is $\{0, 1, 2, 3, \ldots\}$, so $2q$ must be one of the numbers $2 \times 0, 2 \times 1, 2 \times 2, 2 \times 3, \ldots$, or $0, 2, 4, 6, \ldots$. Because 9 is not one of these numbers, the equation $2q = 9$ has no solution in the given replacement set.

Notice that in the solution to Example 2, we used three dots, read *and so on,* to indicate that the list of numbers continues without end.

Class Exercises

Tell whether the equation is true or false for the given value of the variable.

1. $20 - y = 17$; $y = 3$ True
2. $n \times 7 = 42$; $n = 8$ False
3. $144 \div r = 46$; $r = 3$ False
4. $156 + q = 179$; $q = 23$ True
5. $13.56 + p = 21.87$; $p = 6.31$ False
6. $8.91 \div c = 2.97$; $c = 3$ True

Solve the equation for the given replacement set.

7. $m + 6 = 72$; $\{50, 60, 70, 80\}$ No solution
8. $x \div 12 = 7$; $\{81, 82, 83, 84\}$ 84
9. $r - 23 = 19$; $\{40, 41, 42, 43\}$ 42
10. $b \times 8 = 64$; $\{2, 4, 6, 8\}$ 8
11. $3.69 - n = 1.31$; $\{2.36, 2.37, 2.38\}$ 2.38
12. $1.91 \times z = 9.55$; $\{4, 5, 6\}$ 5

Additional A Exercises

Tell whether the equation is true or false for the given value of the variable.

1. $\frac{36 + t}{9} = 4$; $t = 1$ **False**
2. $50 - s = 36$; $s = 14$ **True**

Solve the equation for the given replacement set.

3. $c + 12 = 20$; $\{6, 7, 8\}$ **8**
4. $34 - n = 17$; $\{15, 17, 19\}$ **17**
5. $120 \div a = 20$; $\{3, 4, 8\}$ **No solution**
6. $23t = 322$; $\{10, 12, 14\}$ **14**
7. $1.6 + x = 7.2$; $\{4.5, 5.6, 6.7\}$ **5.6**

Written Exercises

Tell whether the equation is true or false for the given value of the variable.

A

1. $x + 9 = 35$; $x = 26$ True
2. $r - 15 = 40$; $r = 55$ True
3. $10m = 130$; $m = 10$ False
4. $9 + y = 100$; $y = 91$ True
5. $44 - q = 11$; $q = 55$ False
6. $t \times 7 = 84$; $t = 91$ False
7. $n \div 8 = 104$; $n = 832$ True
8. $26 \div d = 2$; $d = 52$ False
9. $x + 6.71 = 10.82$; $x = 4.11$ True
10. $4.16a = 29.12$; $a = 8$ False
11. $m - 26 = 59$; $m = 85$ True
12. $q + 113 = 789$; $q = 901$ False

24   *Chapter 1*

Solve the equation for the given replacement set.

13. $5d = 145$; $\{29, 30, 31\}$ 29

14. $t - 53 = 67$; $\{13, 14, 15\}$ No solution

15. $b \times 14 = 112$; $\{6, 8, 10\}$ 8

16. $c \div 12 = 228$; $\{17, 19, 21\}$ No solution

17. $98 - h = 21$; $\{75, 80, 85\}$ No solution

18. $38f = 912$; $\{24, 25, 26\}$ 24

19. $e \div 19 = 152$; $\{8, 18, 28\}$ No solution

20. $46 + n = 99$; $\{50, 52, 54\}$ No solution

21. $q \div 23 = 66$; $\{1516, 1517, 1518\}$ 1518

22. $b \div 41 = 77$; $\{287, 288, 289\}$ No solution

23. $t + 1.21 = 2.47$; $\{1.25, 1.26, 1.27\}$ 1.26

24. $y \div 1.2 = 3$; $\{3.3, 3.6, 3.9\}$ 3.6

B **25.** $4n + 7 = 51$; $\{10, 11, 12\}$ 11

26. $58 - 3a = 10$; $\{16, 17, 18\}$ 16

27. $4(b - 5) = 28$; $\{10, 11, 12\}$ 12

28. $17(k + 4) = 170$; $\{4, 6, 8\}$ 6

29. $(t + 18) \div 3 = 9$; $\{9, 10, 11\}$ 9

30. $56 \div (d + 8) = 4$; $\{5, 6, 7\}$ 6

31. $5(2c - 4) = 0$; $\{0, 1, 2\}$ 2

32. $(3f + 7) \div 4 = 4$; $\{3, 4, 5\}$ 3

Solve the equation. The replacement set is all even whole numbers.

33. $x + 1 = 10$ No solution

34. $5x = 35$ No solution

35. $4x = 16$ 4

36. $x - 1 = 20$ No solution

Write an equation with the given solution if the replacement set is all whole numbers. Answers will vary for 37–40. An example is supplied.

C **37.** 10 $3x + 5 = 35$

38. 15 $2x \div 6 = 5$

39. 100 $2x - 50 = 150$

40. Write an equation with no solution if the replacement set is all whole numbers. $4x + 13 = 5$

Replace $\underline{\ ?\ }$ with $+$, $-$, $\times$, or $\div$ so the equation has the given solution.

41. $x \underline{\ ?\ }^{+} 17 \underline{\ ?\ }^{-} 13 = 24$; 20

42. $n \underline{\ ?\ }^{\div} 12 \underline{\ ?\ }^{+} 8 = 11$; 36

43. $14 \underline{\ ?\ }^{+} t \underline{\ ?\ }^{\div} 9 = 17$; 27

44. $y \underline{\ ?\ }^{+} 12 \underline{\ ?\ }^{\div} 6 = 10$; 8

45. $d \underline{\ ?\ } (16 \underline{\ ?\ } 4) \underline{\ ?\ } 8 = 8$; 12

46. $27 \underline{\ ?\ }^{\div} (q \underline{\ ?\ }^{-} 9) \underline{\ ?\ }^{\times} 15 = 45$; 18

47. $21 \underline{\ ?\ }^{-} (19 \underline{\ ?\ }^{+} 8) \underline{\ ?\ }^{\div} b = 12$; 3

48. $11 \underline{\ ?\ }^{\times} (16 \underline{\ ?\ }^{-} a) \underline{\ ?\ }^{+} 4 = 59$; 11

45. $-$, $-$, $+$; or $+$, $\div$, $-$; or $\div$, $-$, $\times$

Review Exercises

Perform the indicated operation.

1. $7.81 + 3.86$ 11.67 **2.** $11.65 - 8.58$ 3.07 **3.** 1.18×23 27.14 **4.** $16.74 \div 2.79$ 6

5. 2.53×2.9 7.337 **6.** $10.49 + 9.52$ 20.01 **7.** $13.27 - 10.43$ 2.84 **8.** $24.84 - 4.14$ 20.7

Introduction to Algebra **25**

Suggested Assignments

Core
  24/1–11 odd
  25/13–37 odd
  25/Rev. 1–4

Enriched
  24/1–11 odd
  25/19–35 odd; 37–48

Supplementary Materials

Practice Masters, p. 5

Reading Mathematics

Students will learn the meaning of the following mathematical term in this lesson: *inverse operations.*
    The word *inverse* is used in several different ways in mathematics. For example, reciprocals are called multiplicative inverses; opposites are called additive inverses; certain functions have inverses; and there are inverse proportions. The context in which the word is used reveals which meaning is intended.

1-7 Inverse Operations

Addition and subtraction are related operations, as shown by the following facts.

$$5 + 6 = 11$$
$$5 = 11 - 6$$

We say that adding a number and subtracting the same number are **inverse operations.**
    The relationship between addition and subtraction holds when we work with variables, as well. Thus we can write the following related equations.

$$n + 6 = 11$$
$$n = 11 - 6$$

We can use this relationship to solve equations that involve addition or subtraction. Throughout the rest of the chapter if no replacement set is given for an open sentence, assume that the solution can be any number.

EXAMPLE 1 Use the inverse operation to write a related equation and solve for the variable.

a. $x + 9 = 35$ **b.** $y - 12 = 18$

Solution   **a.** $x = 35 - 9$ **b.** $y = 18 + 12$
                        $x = 26$ $y = 30$
          The solution is 26.   The solution is 30.

To check each solution, substitute the value of the variable in the original equation.

a. $x + 9 = 35$ **b.** $y - 12 = 18$
    $26 + 9 = 35$ $\checkmark$ $30 - 12 = 18$ $\checkmark$

Multiplying by a number and dividing by the same number are inverse operations.

$$4 \times 6 = 24$$
$$6 = 24 \div 4$$

We can use this relationship to help solve equations that involve multiplication and division.

EXAMPLE 2 Use the inverse operation to write a related equation and solve for the variable.

a. $6r = 30$ **b.** $x \div 7 = 12$

26 *Chapter 1*

Solution   **a.** Recall that $6r$ means $6 \times r$.   **b.** $x \div 7 = 12$

$$6 \times r = 30$$
$$r = 30 \div 6$$
$$r = 5$$

The solution is 5.

Check: $6 \times 5 = 30$ $\checkmark$

b. $x \div 7 = 12$
$$x = 12 \times 7$$
$$x = 84$$
The solution is 84.

Check: $84 \div 7 = 12$ $\checkmark$

EXAMPLE 3   Use inverse operations to write a related equation and solve for the variable.

a. $x + 8.21 = 12.64$ **b.** $2.47a = 12.35$

Solution   **a.** $x = 12.64 - 8.21$ **b.** $a = 12.35 \div 2.47$
$$x = 4.43$$
The solution is 4.43.

Check: $4.43 + 8.21 = 12.64$ $\checkmark$

$$a = 5$$
The solution is 5.

Check: $(2.47)(5) = 12.35$ $\checkmark$

We can use inverse operations to solve equations that contain two operations.

EXAMPLE 4   Use inverse operations to solve the equation

$$3n + 25 = 61.$$

Solution   First write the related subtraction equation to find the value of $3n$.

$$3n = 61 - 25$$
$$3n = 36$$

Then write the related division equation to find the value of n.

$$n = 36 \div 3$$
$$n = 12$$

The solution is 12.

Check: $3(12) + 25 = 61$
$$36 + 25 = 61 \checkmark$$

Class Exercises

Use the inverse operation to state a related equation and solve for t.

$t = 15 - 6;\ 9$
1. $t + 6 = 15$

$t = 7 + 4;\ 11$
2. $t - 4 = 7$

$t = 48 \div 6;\ 8$
3. $6t = 48$

$t = 7 \times 8;\ 56$
4. $t \div 8 = 7$

$t = 60 - 24;\ 36$
5. $t + 24 = 60$

$t = 78 \div 13;\ 6$
6. $13t = 78$

$t = 59 + 26;\ 85$
7. $t - 26 = 59$

$t = 8 \times 32;\ 256$
8. $t \div 32 = 8$

$t = 5.26 - 3.19;\ 2.07$
9. $t + 3.19 = 5.26$

10. $t - 21.06 = 31.14$
$t = 31.14 + 21.06;\ 52.2$

$t = 12.56 \div 3.14;\ 4$
11. $3.14t = 12.56$

12. $t \div 1.16 = 12$
$t = 12 \times 1.16;\ 13.92$

Introduction to Algebra   **27**

Chalkboard Examples

Use the appropriate inverse operation to write a related equation and solve for the variable.

1. $x + 21 = 35$
    $x = 35 - 21;\ 14$

2. $y \div 3 = 12$
    $y = 12 \times 3;\ 36$

3. $p - 16 = 30$
    $p = 30 + 16;\ 46$

4. $15t = 45$
    $t = 45 \div 15;\ 3$

Is the solution correct for the given equation?

5. $a - 9 = 22;\ 13$ No

6. $c \div 2 = 8;\ 16$ Yes

7. $3d = 21;\ 63$ No

8. $k + 11 = 11;\ 0$ Yes

Additional A Exercises

Use the appropriate inverse
operation to write a related
equation and solve for the
variable.

1. $x + 3 = 12$
  $x = 12 - 3; 9$

2. $x - 12 = 18$
  $x = 18 + 12; 30$

3. $x \div 12 = 5$
  $x = 5 \times 12; 60$

4. $5x = 50$
  $x = 50 \div 5; 10$

5. $17 + n = 22$
  $n = 22 - 17; 5$

6. $42m = 42$
  $m = 42 \div 42; 1$

**Additional Answers
Written Exercises**

 1. $x = 15 - 8; 7$

 2. $a = 11 - 6; 5$

 3. $f = 74 - 38; 36$

 4. $t = 91 - 46; 45$

 5. $y = 14 + 9; 23$

 6. $n = 9 + 7; 16$

 7. $b = 32 + 25; 57$

 8. $r = 87 + 55; 142$

 9. $c = 27 \div 3; 9$

 10. $g = 45 \div 5; 9$

 11. $m = 108 \div 9; 12$

 12. $d = 88 \div 4; 22$

 13. $n = 9 \times 6; 54$

 14. $s = 4 \times 8; 32$

(cont. on page 29)

Suggested Assignments

Core
  28/1–24 even; 37–45
Enriched
  28/29–36; 38–60 even

Supplementary Materials

Practice Masters, p. 5

28

Written Exercises

Use the inverse operation to write a related equation and solve for the variable.

A **1.** $x + 8 = 15$ **2.** $a + 6 = 11$ **3.** $f + 38 = 74$ **4.** $t + 46 = 91$

  5. $y - 9 = 14$ **6.** $n - 7 = 9$ **7.** $b - 25 = 32$ **8.** $r - 55 = 87$

  9. $3c = 27$ **10.** $5g = 45$ **11.** $9m = 108$ **12.** $4d = 88$

  13. $n \div 6 = 9$ **14.** $s \div 8 = 4$ **15.** $g \div 16 = 7$ **16.** $w \div 9 = 14$

  17. $a + 17 = 17$ **18.** $j - 54 = 61$ **19.** $14n = 42$ **20.** $e + 26 = 61$

  21. $h \div 11 = 297$ **22.** $b + 45 = 256$ **23.** $d - 87 = 110$ **24.** $18b = 18$

  25. $31q = 465$ **26.** $k \div 17 = 527$ **27.** $p + 208 = 358$ **28.** $f - 11 = 523$

  29. $c + 511 = 536$ **30.** $18r = 414$ **31.** $g - 19 = 401$ **32.** $m \div 4 = 216$

  33. $x + 1.6 = 31.9$ **34.** $p - 1.9 = 18.4$ **35.** $1.6c = 2.56$ **36.** $m \div 3.27 = 6$

Use inverse operations to solve.

B **37.** $3q + 9 = 27$ 6   **38.** $4a + 19 = 39$ 5   **39.** $7d - 12 = 37$ 7

  40. $5b - 16 = 39$ 11   **41.** $3r + 24 = 63$ 13   **42.** $2s - 30 = 62$ 46

  43. $9x - 84 = 69$ 17   **44.** $6w + 81 = 486$ 67.5   **45.** $(z \div 3) + 22 = 30$ 24

  46. $(l \div 7) - 4 = 4$ 56   **47.** $(c \div 5) - 13 = 11$ 120   **48.** $(v \div 3) + 15 = 36$ 63

  49. $4s + 7.41 = 9.57$ 0.54   **50.** $6c + 3.60 = 9.72$ 1.02   **51.** $7t - 8.43 = 14.67$ 3.3

  52. $9c - 8.32 = 7.61$ 1.77   **53.** $(x \div 3.21) + 9 = 13$ 12.84   **54.** $(y \div 1.67) + 5 = 12$ 11.69

Replace __?__ with $+$, $-$, $\times$, or $\div$ so the equation has the given solution.

C **55.** $4 \underline{\ ?\ }^{\times} a \underline{\ ?\ }^{+} 5 = 25; 5$ **56.** $7 \underline{\ ?\ }^{\times} n \underline{\ ?\ }^{\div} 4 = 14; 8$

  57. $3 \underline{\ ?\ }^{\times} c \underline{\ ?\ }^{-} 11 = 22; 11$ **58.** $5 \underline{\ ?\ }^{\times} y \underline{\ ?\ }^{-} 3 = 7; 2$

  59. $24 \underline{\ ?\ }^{\div} x \underline{\ ?\ }^{+} 15 = 18; 8$ **60.** $60 \underline{\ ?\ }^{\div} m \underline{\ ?\ }^{\div} 2 = 15; 2$

Review Exercises

Evaluate the expression when $m = 2$, $n = 1$, and $p = 4$.

  1. $2n^2$ 1   **2.** $(m + n)^0$ 1   **3.** $3p^2 + m^2$ 52   **4.** $n^2 + m^3$ 9

  5. $p^3 - (mn)^2$ 60   **6.** $2p^2 - n^0$ 31   **7.** $4m^3 - n^3$ 31   **8.** $(2mn^2)^0$ 1

28 *Chapter 1*

1-8 A Plan for Solving Problems

What we know about mathematics enables us to solve many problems. Problems, however, are not usually as neatly organized as the information in the expressions with which we have been working. We must sort out and organize the facts of a problem before we begin to solve. A plan such as the one below can be useful in solving many kinds of problems.

Plan for Solving Word Problems

1. Read the problem carefully. Make sure that you understand what it says. You may need to read it more than once.

2. Use questions like these in planning the solution:
   What is asked for?
   What facts are given?
   Are enough facts given? If not, what else is needed?
   Are unnecessary facts given? If so, what are they?
   Will a sketch or diagram help?

3. Determine which operation or operations can be used to solve the problem.

4. Carry out the operations carefully.

5. Check your results with the facts given in the problem. Give the answer.

EXAMPLE 1 On Saturday, the Nizel family drove 17 mi from Topsfield to Newton and 22.5 mi from Newton to Harbor Bluffs. The trip took 50 min. On the way back, the Nizels took the same route, but they stopped for lunch after driving 9.5 mi. If they continue on the same route after lunch, how much farther will they have to drive to return to Topsfield?

Solution • The problem asks for the number of miles to return to Topsfield.

• The following facts are given in the problem:
   17 mi from Topsfield to Newton
   22.5 mi from Newton to Harbor Bluffs
   drove 9.5 mi back toward Topsfield

(The solution is continued on the next page.)

Introduction to Algebra **29**

Teaching Suggestions p. 1f

Related Activities p. 1g

Reading Mathematics

Students need to read a problem several times to understand the facts and relationships involved. They should read with pencil and paper at hand, to note the symbolic representation of what they read.

Additional Answers (p. 28)
Written Exercises

15. $g = 7 \times 16$; 112
16. $w = 14 \times 9$; 126
17. $a = 17 - 17$; 0
18. $j = 61 + 54$; 115
19. $n = 42 \div 14$; 3
20. $e = 61 - 26$; 35
21. $h = 297 \times 11$; 3267
22. $b = 256 - 45$; 211
23. $d = 110 + 87$; 197
24. $b = 18 \div 18$; 1
25. $q = 465 \div 31$; 15
26. $k = 527 \times 17$; 8959
27. $p = 358 - 208$; 150
28. $f = 523 + 11$; 534
29. $c = 536 - 511$; 25
30. $r = 414 \div 18$; 23
31. $g = 401 + 19$; 420
32. $m = 216 \times 4$; 864
33. $x = 31.9 - 1.6$; 30.3
34. $p = 18.4 + 1.9$; 20.3
35. $c = 2.56 \div 1.6$; 1.6
36. $m = 6 \times 3.27$; 19.62

1. Martha walked 4 mi on the Ridge Trail, from the Bluffs to Long View, and then 7 mi farther, from Long View to the Knob. How far must she walk to return to the Bluffs? **11 mi**

2. Frank has $2.00 in nickels. How many nickels does he have? **40**

3. What must three grades total, if the average is 90? **270**

• We have enough facts to solve the problem since we know the distance between the cities and the distance driven toward Topsfield.

• We do not need to know that the trip took 50 min.

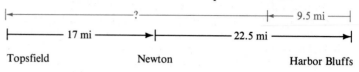

• The sketch shows that we subtract the distance driven back toward Topsfield from the distance between Topsfield and Harbor Bluffs.

$$(17 + 22.5) - 9.5 = 30$$

• Check: If they drive 9.5 mi and 30 mi farther, will the Nizels have driven the distance from Harbor Bluffs to Topsfield?

$$9.5 + 30 = 17 + 22.5 \ \sqrt{}$$

The Nizels must drive 30 mi to return to Topsfield.

EXAMPLE 2 Records at the Howard City Weather Bureau show that it rained on a total of 17 days during the months of July through September and on twice as many days during the months of October through December. During October through December, how many days did not have rain?

Solution • The problem asks for the number of days without rain during October, November, and December.

• Given facts: 17 days of rain in July through September
twice as many days of rain in October through December

• We need to supply these facts:
31 days in October, 30 days in November, 31 days in December

• To find the number of days without rain, subtract the number of days that did have rain from the total number of days.
$$(31 + 30 + 31) - (2 \times 17) = 92 - 34 = 58$$

• Check: Are 34 days twice as many as 17? $34 \div 2 = 17 \ \sqrt{}$
Do 58 days without rain and 34 days with rain total the number of days in the three months?
$$58 + 34 = 31 + 30 + 31 \ \sqrt{}$$

During October through December, 58 days did not have rain.

30 *Chapter 1*

Class Exercises

For each problem, answer the following questions.
a. What number or numbers does the problem ask for?
b. Are enough facts given? If not, what else is needed?
c. Are unneeded facts given? If so, what are they?
d. What operation or operations would you use to find the answer?

1. Kevin completed the bicycle race in 2 h 24 min, Lori completed the race in 2 h 13 min, and Helen completed the race in 2 h 54 min. How much faster than Kevin's time was Lori's time?

2. Steve bought 1 lb of Swiss cheese, 12 oz of mild cheddar cheese, and 6 oz of sharp cheddar cheese. How much cheese did he buy in all?

3. Elise bought a record for $5.69, another record for $4.88, and a record cleaning kit for $12.75. How much more than the cost of the records was the cost of the kit?

4. The eighth-grade classes are holding a hobbies and crafts fair on Saturday. Maurice plans to help out at the stamp-collecting booth from 9 A.M. to 11 A.M. and at the model-airplane booth from 2 P.M. to 5 P.M. How many hours does he plan to spend helping?

Problems

Solve, using the five-step plan.

A 1. Mimi is buying weather-stripping tape for some windows. How much should she buy for a window that needs 4.85 m, a window that needs 4.25 m, and a window that needs 2.55 m? 11.65 m

2. Irene Lanata pays $235.40 each month to repay her automobile loan. How much will she pay in one year? $2824.80

3. Hill School plans to buy 4 computers for each of 12 classrooms. The cost of each computer is $865. What will the total cost be? $41,520

4. An 8 mm camera shoots 24 frames of film each second. How many frames will it shoot in 5 min? 7200 frames

5. A package of 2 paintbrushes is on sale for $2.40. How much will 3 packages cost? $7.20

6. Roy paid $81.88 for a new jacket and sweater. He then exchanged the sweater, which cost $23.00, for another sweater that cost $19.99. What was the final cost for Roy's jacket and sweater? $78.87

Introduction to Algebra **31**

Solve, using the five-step plan.

7. There are 38 rows with 2 dozen seats each in the Little Theater. An additional 24 people are allowed to stand during a performance. What is the total number of people that can attend a performance? **936 people**

8. Yesterday it took Jeff Holland 1 h to get to work. This morning, Jeff drove to the train station in 20 min, waited for the train for 7 min, rode the train for 12 min, and then walked for 15 min to get to work. How long did it take Jeff to get to work this morning? **54 min**

B 9. Tickets for the drama club's performance last weekend cost $2.50 for adults and $2.00 for students. Four hundred twenty adults attended the performance, and 273 students attended. What was the total amount of money collected from tickets for the performance last weekend? **$1596**

10. Sarah Holness had her car tuned up for $60 and she purchased 4 new tires for $37 each. She gave the cashier 11 twenty-dollar bills. How much change did Sarah receive? **$12**

C 11. Joy and David Kramer had $30 to spend on dinner, a movie, and parking. Dinner cost $15.50 and parking cost $4. The Kramers had $2 left after paying for everything. What was the cost of one movie ticket? **$4.25**

12. The museum charges $4.50 per person for a 2 h tour with fewer than 20 people. If 20 or more people take the tour, the charge is $3.75 per person. Of the 23 people in today's tour, 17 had paid $4.50 in advance. How much money will the museum return as a refund? **$12.75**

Review Exercises

Estimate the answer using rounding.

1. $267 + 73$ 340   **2.** $941 - 189$ 750   **3.** $82.7 + 91.8$ 175   **4.** $261.6 - 131.9$ 130   600

5. 24×18 500   **6.** 36×41 1600   **7.** 21.3×19.6 400   **8.** 18.7×29.3

1-9 Solving and Checking Problems

The five-step plan shown in the preceding lesson can be used to solve many problems. It is also useful to have methods for checking answers to problems. For example, when planning your solution to a problem, you may find that there is more than one way to proceed. When there is more than one method for solving a problem, you may find it helpful to use one method to obtain an answer and to use the other method to check your results. Study the following example.

EXAMPLE 1 The Treble Clef celebrated Heritage Day with a two-week sale on the Flexwood turntables. Twelve turntables were sold during the first week of the sale and 17 were sold during the second week of the sale. The sale price for each turntable was $74.90. How much money did the Treble Clef receive for the turntables sold?

Solution
- The problem asks for the amount of money received from the sale of the turntables.

- Given facts: 12 turntables sold the first week
  17 more sold the second week
  $74.90 received for each turntable

- There are two ways to solve this problem.

  Method 1
  First multiply the sale price by the number sold each week to find the amount of money received each week.

  $$12 \times 74.90 = 898.80 \qquad 17 \times 74.90 = 1273.30$$

  Then add the amounts of money received to find the total amount of money received from the sale of the turntables.

  $$898.80 + 1273.30 = 2172.10$$

  Method 2
  First add to find the total number of turntables sold during the sale.

  $$12 + 17 = 29$$

  Then multiply the sale price by the total number sold to find the amount of money received from the sale of the turntables.

  $$29 \times 74.90 = 2172.10$$

- By either method, the Treble Clef received $2172.10 from the sale of the turntables.

Introduction to Algebra **33**

Teaching Suggestions p. 1g

Related Activities p. 1g

Reading Mathematics

As you explain the examples, review and list key mathematical words to look for in solving problems. In Example 1, relate *money received* to total income. In Example 2, *distance traveled* also means total distance.

Solve.

1. Five items cost $4.83, $1.23, $8.57, $3.20, and $12.20. What is the total cost? **$30.03**

2. Rachel bought 25 books for $2.89 each. How much did she pay for them? **$72.25**

3. Clark wants to divide a cost of $74.80 equally among 20 people. How much should each person pay? **$3.74**

4. Find the total cost of 20 batteries at $1.75 each and 7 flashlights at $4.20 each. **$64.40**

Another way to check an answer is to use rounding to find an estimated answer. If the answer and the estimate are close, then the estimate leads us to accept our answer.

EXAMPLE 2 Last summer Elka and David drove from Los Angeles to Boston. Along the way they stopped in Albuquerque, Kansas City, Atlanta, and Washington, D.C. They recorded the distance they traveled, as shown below.

Los Angeles–Albuquerque	806 mi
Albuquerque–Kansas City	790 mi
Kansas City–Atlanta	810 mi
Atlanta–Washington, D.C.	630 mi
Washington, D.C.–Boston	437 mi

How many miles did Elka and David travel?

Solution
- The problem asks for the total distance traveled.

- Given facts: traveled 806 mi, 790 mi, 810 mi, 630 mi, 437 mi

- To find the total distance traveled, we add.

$$806 + 790 + 810 + 630 + 437 = 3473$$

- Elka and David traveled 3473 miles on their trip.

To check the answer, we round the distances and add. In this case, round to the nearest hundred miles.

$$800 + 800 + 800 + 600 + 400 = 3400$$

The estimate, 3400 mi, and the answer, 3473 mi, are quite close, so the actual answer seems reasonable.

Class Exercises

State the operations you would use to solve the problem and the order in which you would use them.

1. The Dreyer Trucking Company moved 453 cartons one day, and then 485 the next day. On the third day they moved twice as many as on the first two days. What is the total number of cartons moved during those three days? addition; multiplication; addition

2. In January, Judy made the following deposits to her savings account: $107.50, $29.35, and $43.20. In February, she deposited twice as much money as in January. How much money did she deposit each month? addition; multiplication

State two methods that you could use to solve the problem.

3. Three friends went out to dinner. The bill was $41.10, and they left a $6.15 tip. If they divide the total three ways, how much did each person pay? addition; division

4. Jay Elder took some clothes to Spotless Drycleaning. He was charged $4.00 for a jacket, $2.50 for a sweater, and $2.25 for a pair of slacks. Jay had coupons that allowed him to deduct $.50 from each item. How much will Jay pay for his drycleaning?
addition; multiplication; subtraction

Estimate the answer to the problem.

5. Frank is in the check-out line at the grocery store. He has a gallon of milk ($1.83), a bag of flour ($2.15), a box of oatmeal ($1.15), a package of cheese ($1.57), and a dozen eggs ($1.05). How much is the bill? $7.50

6. Breda wants to buy a four-door sedan that has a base price of $5624.95, factory-installed options totalling $1213.50, and a destination charge of $183.00. How much does the car cost? $7000

Problems

Solve. Check to be sure you have answered the question.

A
1. The August electric bill for $75.80 was twice as much as the July bill. What was the total cost of electricity for July and August? $113.70

2. Alvin has $1863.50 in his savings account. His sister Alvis has $756 more in her account. Geoffrey borrowed $257 from each person. How much money do Alvin and Alvis have left in each of their accounts after making the loans? Alvin: $1606.50; Alvis: $2362.50

3. Gregory ordered the following items from the Huntington Gardens catalog: a watering can for $15.80, a trowel for $4.49, and 6 packages of seeds for $.75 each. What is the total cost of the items? $24.79

4. Nancy's mobile needs 3 separate pieces of wire that measure 8 cm, 11 cm, and 15 cm. Nina's mobile needs two times the length of wire that Nancy's mobile needs. How much wire is needed for each mobile? Nancy's mobile: 34 cm; Nina's mobile: 68 cm

Introduction to Algebra **35**

Additional A Problems

Solve.

1. Kristin bicycled 249.7 miles in 11 days. How many miles did she average per day? 22.7 mi/d

2. Lee is going to plant 7 rows of pepper plants with 18 plants in each row. If he plants one pepper plant in 0.5 min, how long will it take him to do the job? 63 min

3. The Central Gas Company charges $0.7989 per cubic foot for the first 10 cubic feet of gas and $0.7213 per cubic foot for the next 140 cubic feet. If the Arnold family uses 15.8 cubic feet of gas, calculate their gas bill to the nearest cent. $12.17

4. What is the value, in dollars, of 22 quarters and 89 nickels? $9.95

Solve. Check by using an alternate method.

5. Each member of the Best Buy Book Club receives 2 bonus points for every book ordered through the club. So far Chris has ordered 3 books in March, 2 in April, and 6 in May. How many bonus points has Chris accumulated so far? 22 bonus points

6. The admission ticket to Tyler Amusement Park is $1.25 per person. A total of 815 tickets were sold on Saturday. The attendance decreased by 96 on Sunday. How much money did the park receive from ticket sales in all? $1917.50

Solve. Check by estimating the answer to the problem.

7. Bonnema Brothers recently purchased four beach front lots of land. The areas of the two smaller lots are 2015 ft² and 2248 ft². The areas of the two larger lots are 8730 ft² and 7890 ft². What is the total area of the two smaller lots and the total area of the two larger lots? smaller lot: 4263 ft²; larger lot: 16,620 ft²

8. Lake Tana in Africa has an elevation of 1829 m. Lake Tangra Tso in Tibet is situated 4724 m above sea level. In Europe, Lake Sevan has an elevation of 1915 m. What is the total height of the three lakes? 8468 m

9. During one game at a bowling tournament the five-member Bright Team scored the following points: 169, 152, 187, 174, and 193. What is the difference between the highest and the lowest scores? 41 points

10. Jackie is taking an inventory of the furniture going on sale next week.

sofas, 128	platform beds, 250
love seats, 105	stereo cabinets, 83
lamps, 216	bookcases, 45

How many items are going on sale? 827 items

Solve.

B 11. The Hillview School Band held a car wash on Friday and Saturday. The charge was $2.25 per car on Friday and $2.50 per car on Saturday. On Friday, 87 cars were washed. On Saturday, 117 cars were washed. What was the total amount of money collected? $488.25

12. A photograph is enlarged so that its new dimensions are four times its original dimensions. If the new dimensions are 19.2 cm by 25.6 cm, what were the original dimensions? 4.8 cm by 6.4 cm

36 *Chapter 1*

13. Today the firm of Beckman and Beckman bought three types of stocks: 4780 shares of utility stocks, 1389 shares of commodity stocks, and 3542 shares of energy-related stocks. This is exactly three times the number of shares the firm bought yesterday. How many shares of stock did the firm buy in the past two days? 12,948 shares

14. Yukio bought traveler's checks in the following denominations: five $50 checks, thirty $20 checks, five $10 checks, and twenty $5 checks. What is the total value of the checks bought? $1000

15. A direct dial call from Boston to Australia costs $3.17 for the first minute and $1.19 for each additional minute. A station-to-station operator-assisted call costs $9.45 for the first 3 minutes and $1.19 for each additional minute. How much money would you save by dialing direct for a 5-minute call? $3.90

Self-Test B

Solve for the given replacement set.

1. $72 - m = 43$; {19, 29, 31} 29   2. $6r = 48$; {6, 7, 8} 8   [1-6]

3. $t \div 12 = 11$; {23, 24, 25} No solution   4. $4d + 16 = 28$; {3, 4, 5} 3

Use inverse operations to solve.

5. $g - 32 = 12$ 44   6. $7d = 112$ 16   7. $5a + 4 = 49$ 9   [1-7]

Solve, using the five-step plan.

8. Laura bought a hammer for $12.95, 5 lb of nails for $5.20, and 8 sheets of plywood for $12 each. What was her total bill? $114.15   [1-8]

9. Between the hours of 6 A.M. and 9 P.M., 8 buses that were filled to capacity left the terminal. If the capacity of each bus is the same and 392 tickets were sold, how many passengers were on each bus?
49 passengers

Solve. Check by estimating.

10. Jeremy and his roommate share the monthly utility bills evenly. For November the cost of electricity was $87.90, gas was $24.35, heating fuel was $215.80, and water was $36.43. How much did each person pay that month? $182.24   [1-9]

Self-Test answers and Extra Practice are at the back of the book.

Introduction to Algebra **37**

The Development of Computers

The development of the modern computer began in 1946 with the completion of the ENIAC computer. It weighed 30 tons, contained 18,000 vacuum tubes and 6000 switches, and filled a room 30 feet by 50 feet. Since that time computers have become steadily more compact, powerful, and inexpensive.

Today's large computer systems, called **mainframes,** can process large amounts of data at very fast speeds. **Minicomputers** are smaller and somewhat slower, meeting the needs of colleges and small businesses at lower cost. The smallest of today's computers, such as the computer shown in the photo above, are the **microcomputers.** These computers are often called personal computers because they are inexpensive enough and small enough to go into classrooms and homes. The processing unit of these small computers is the **microprocessor,** a one-quarter-inch-square integrated circuit chip. This tiny chip is more powerful than the ENIAC with its 18,000 vacuum tubes.

The microprocessor controls the microcomputer and performs arithmetic operations. But other parts are needed to make the computer a useful tool. The computer has two kinds of **memory. ROM** (read only memory) permanently stores information needed for the computer to work properly. It cannot be changed by the user. **RAM** (random access memory) is available to the user and can store the user's programs and data. Memory size is measured in **bytes** or K. One K is about 1000 bytes. Each byte can store one character (letter or digit), so an 8K memory can store about 8000 typed characters.

The **keyboard** is used to input programs and data, and the **CRT** screen displays input, results, and graphics. A **disk drive** can be used to read programs and data into the computer from a disk, or to save programs on disk. A **printer** will save output in printed form. A **modem** can connect you to a network of other computers over your telephone line.

As computers have evolved, people have invented programming languages to help users program the computer to solve problems. Some of the more common languages are **BASIC,** which is available on almost all microcomputers, **FORTRAN,** often used for scientific problem solving, and **COBOL,** a business-oriented language. **Pascal** and **Logo** are two languages finding increasing application in education.

The development of computers has opened many new careers. Systems analysts use computers to analyze and solve problems for business and government. Programmers write the programs, or software, that help users apply the computer to their needs. Installation and maintenance of a computer's physical components, or hardware, are done by field engineers.

1. The fastest modern computers can do 100 million arithmetic operations in a second. Estimate how long it would take you to do this many additions. Suppose you are adding two four-digit numbers each time. **Answers will vary.**

2. Each byte of memory will hold one typed character. About how many K of memory would it take to store these two pages? A disk for a microcomputer holds 160 K. About how many pages of this book could you store on one disk? **3K; 107 pages**

3. Ask your librarian to help you find out about the Mark I, IBM 360, and UNIVAC 1 computers. Find out about the size of each computer, the number of its components, its purpose, its inventors.

4. The computer language ADA was named after Ada Byron Lovelace (1815–1852). See what you can find out about Ada Lovelace and the computer language.

Career Activity

Look in the Help Wanted section of a newspaper and make a list of the job openings for systems analysts and programmers. Include in your list education requirements, what computers or computer languages the candidate should be familiar with, and the salary range.

Introduction to Algebra **39**

In Exercise 1 on page 39, the speed mentioned, 100 million arithmetic operations in a second, is the same as 10 nanoseconds per operation. To give some meaning to these time units, give the following comparisons.

1. A millisecond is to a second as a penny is to a $10 bill.
2. A microsecond is to a second as half an hour is to an average human life.
3. A nanosecond is to a second as $1\frac{1}{2}$ inches are to the distance around Earth at the equator.
4. A picosecond is to a second as a $1 bill is to the annual U.S. gross national product.

If students are familiar with binary numbers, you might point out that a byte, typically, is an eight-digit binary number. There are 256 possible combinations of eight 0's and 1's, so 256 distinct bytes are possible. Each of these 256 combinations can represent a letter of the alphabet or other character.

Chapter Review

Match.

1. 22×8 F   2. $52.6 - 9.95$ C   **A.** 32   **B.** 10^8 [1–1]

3. $9 \times (3 + 1) - 4$ A   4. $\dfrac{4 + (6 \times 2 \times 5)}{(14 - 12)5}$ E **C.** 42.65   **D.** 64   [1–2]

5. 4^3 D   6. $100,000,000$ B   **E.** 6.4   **F.** 176   [1–3]

True or false?

7. 21.09 to the nearest whole number is 20. False   [1–4]

8. 124.4 to the nearest hundred is 100. True

9. 83.415 to the nearest hundredth is 83.42. True

10. 0.959 to the nearest tenth is 1.0. True

11. $(17.2 + 1.8)4 = (1.8 + 17.2)4$ illustrates the commutative property. True   [1–5]

12. $(8 + 7.9)2.3 = (8 \times 2.3) + (7.9 \times 2.3)$ illustrates the distributive property of multiplication with respect to subtraction. False

13. $1.3(7 + 4) = (7 + 4)1.3$ illustrates the associative property. False

Is the equation true or false for the given value of the variable?

14. $9y = 108$; $y = 12$ True   15. $k \div 4 = 28$; $k = 7$ False   [1–6]

True or false?

16. If $k + 5 = 140$, $k = 140 - 5$. True   17. If $p \div 21 = 14$, $p = 21 - 14$. False   [1–7]

18. If $9b = 162$, $b = 162 \div 9$. True   19. If $t - 87 = 87$, $t = 87 - 87$. False

Write the letter of the correct answer.

20. Julia Carmona hired 3 people to landscape her yard. They each received the same hourly rate and it took them 5 h to do the job. If her bill was $60, how much did each person earn an hour? d   [1–8]
    a. $6   **b.** $12   **c.** $3   **d.** $4

21. To raise money for a local charity, the 26 students of the eighth-grade class participated in a bike-a-thon. Each of the sponsors agreed to pay the students $.35 for each mile they rode their bicycles. If 20 students ride 20 mi each and the rest of the students ride 30 mi each, for how many miles will the students be paid? d   [1–9]
    a. $203   **b.** 50 mi   **c.** $17.50   **d.** 580 mi

40   *Chapter 1*

Chapter Test

Evaluate the expression when $a = 4$ and $b = 12$.

1. $91 + a$ 95   **2.** $27 - b - a$ 11 **3.** $5b$ 60   **4.** $36 \div a$ 9   [1-1]

Evaluate the expression when $m = 14$ and $n = 16$.

5. $n - 4 \times 3$ 4   **6.** $3 \times \frac{m}{7}$ 6   **7.** $2mn - 9$ 439 **8.** $(m + n) \div 3$ 10   [1-2]

Evaluate.

9. 3^4 81   **10.** 10^3 1000   **11.** 2^5 32   [1-3]

Write as a single power of 10.

12. $10^4 \times 10^7$ 10^{11} **13.** $10^6 \times 10^6$ 10^{12} **14.** 10,000 10^4

Round to the place specified.

15. tenths: 7.49 7.5   **16.** tens: 423.6 420   **17.** hundredths: 4.283 4.28   [1-4]

What value of the variable makes the statement true?

$r = 7.8$
18. $2.4 + (r + 9.5) = 2.4 + (9.5 + 7.8)$ **19.** $19.2k = k$ $k = 0$ [1-5]

20. $62d - 19d = (62 - 19)4$ $d = 4$ **21.** $1(3.4 + 1.3) = a$ $a = 4.7$

Solve for the given replacement set.

22. $d - 9 = 27$; $\{3, 18, 35\}$ No solution   **23.** $14r = 70$; $\{3, 4, 5\}$ 5   [1-6]

24. $9(x + 4) = 63$; $\{1, 2, 3\}$ 3   **25.** $3k + 1 = 13$; $\{4, 5, 6\}$ 4

Use inverse operations to solve.

26. $6g = 72$ 12   **27.** $b \div 9 = 44$ 396   **28.** $3f - 1 = 53$ 18   [1-7]

Solve, using the five-step plan.

29. The tickets for the theater cost $7.50 each. Miles bought 4 of them   [1-8]
and gave the cashier a fifty dollar bill. What was the cost of the
tickets? $30

Solve and check your answer.

30. For the trip, Kari bought 3 stocking caps for $6.75 each and 3 scarfs   [1-9]
for $8.50 each. How much money did she spend? $45.75

Introduction to Algebra **41**

Cumulative Review

Exercises

Simplify.

1. $28 + 781$ 809
2. $630 - 52.1$ 577.9
3. $65.1 \div 21$ 3.1
4. 1.2×3.64 4.368
5. $48 + 303.9$ 351.9
6. 0.042×0.8 0.0336
7. $3(14 - 5)$ 27
8. $(6 + 3) \div 9$ 1
9. $4 \times 5 + 5$ 25
10. $16 - 2 \times 3 - 1$ 9
11. $(8 + 2) \div (12 - 7)$ 2
12. $(14 + 36) \times (54 - 8)$ 2300

Evaluate the expression when $a = 2$, $b = 5$, and $c = 3$.

13. $5b + 18$ 43
14. $9c - 12$ 15
15. $3b + c \div 2$ 16.5
16. $4ab - 8$ 32
17. $30 \div (a + c)$ 6
18. $a(12 - c)b$ 90

Simplify.

19. 3^3 27
20. 4^3 64
21. 2^6 64
22. 6^4 1296
23. 5^6 15,625
24. 11^4 14,641

Select the most reasonable estimated answer.

25. $43.6 - 2.79$ a   **a.** 41   **b.** 20   **c.** 45
26. 9.6×53.66 c   **a.** 500   **b.** 450   **c.** 540
27. $22.7 + 18.9 + 7.38$ a   **a.** 49   **b.** 37   **c.** 110
28. $165.7 + 38.21 + 6.44$ b   **a.** 1300   **b.** 210   **c.** 246

True or false?

29. $16 \div 8 + 2 = 16 \div (8 + 2)$ False   30. $99.5 - (6 + 7) = (99.5 - 6) + 7$ False
31. $(43 \times 0) + (43 \times 1) = 0$ False   32. $11.89 + (426 \div 2) = (11.89 + 426) \div 2$
False

Find the solution of the equation for the given replacement set.

33. $k + 16 = 23$; $\{5, 6, 7\}$ 7
34. $58 - d = 31$; $\{39, 38, 37\}$ No solution
35. $7x - 1 = 20$; $\{1, 2, 3\}$ 3
36. $8(y - 3) = 32$; $\{7, 8, 9\}$ 7
37. $5a = 2a + 57$; $\{19, 20, 21\}$ 19
38. $(c + 6) \div 6 = 1$; $\{0, 1, 2\}$ 0

Use inverse operations to solve.

39. $18 + g = 20$ 2
40. $a \div 9 = 18$ 162
41. $5z = 65$ 13
42. $20d + 8 = 68$ 3
43. $7f - 1 = 13$ 2
44. $3h + 2 = 26$
8

Problems

Solve.

1. Merry and Sandy rented an apartment for $645 each month and shared the rent equally. After 4 months, Tess moved in and the rent was divided three ways. How much was Merry's rent for the year? $3010

2. Hungarian paprika costs $1.30 for 2 oz, $4.00 for $\frac{1}{2}$ lb, and $6.00 for a pound. What is the cost of each ounce if you buy a pound? How much do you save per ounce if you buy a pound? 37.5 cents; 27.5 cents

3. Mal ordered a set of 6 steak knives for $35.00. Additional costs included $4.95 for shipping, $1.25 for a gift box, and $1.75 for tax. What was the total cost of the order? $42.95

4. "I can save $19.50 if I buy a half dozen glasses on sale," said Ellis. How much is saved on each glass? If Ellis pays $30.00 for 6 glasses on sale, what was the original price of each glass? $3.25; $8.25

5. House numerals that are 4 in. high cost $4.00 each. Numerals that are 7 in. high cost $10.00 each. How much will it cost to buy numerals that are 4 in. high for your house if your address is 16332 Long Meadow Road? $20

6. In 1918, a sheet of 100 airmail stamps was mistakenly printed with an airplane upside down. A stamp collector bought the sheet for $.24 per stamp and later sold the sheet for $15,000. How much did the collector make on his lucky buy? $14,976

7. A membership to the Science Center costs $53 per year and includes a subscription to a monthly magazine. If the magazine costs $3 per issue, what are the annual dues for membership alone? $17

8. Dale took advantage of the gas company's offer to make average monthly payments. The payments were based on the average of the two highest and the two lowest bills for the past 12 months. If these bills were $135.50, $142.71, $68.29, and $56.30, what is Dale's average monthly payment? $100.70

Introduction to Algebra **43**

2

Positive and Negative Numbers

Lightning, as seen in the photograph, is a dramatic, electrical reaction that is usually associated with thunderclouds. It occurs as a result of a sudden, powerful exchange between the positive and negative centers within a cloud, between several clouds, or between a cloud, the air, and the ground. The long flash of light we see is part of the interaction. The positive and negative charges move through the atmosphere so rapidly that a tremendous amount of heat is generated, which warms up the surrounding air so quickly that a thunderous explosion results.

In this chapter you will study operations with positive and negative numbers.

Career Note

Earthquakes are similar to lightning in that they are sudden, dramatic natural events. Geologists study earthquakes as part of their study of the earth. By studying the structure and history of the rocks beneath the earth's surface, geologists may be able to predict future earthquakes. Geologists can also specialize in locating oil and other raw materials.

44

Lesson Commentary
Chapter 2   Positive and Negative Numbers

Overview

This chapter begins with definitions important to the integers and expands these definitions to include positive and negative decimal numbers. The topics in this chapter include positive and negative numbers; opposites; absolute value; order; rules governing the four basic operations of addition, subtraction, multiplication, and division; and positive and negative exponents. Chapter 3, which covers the rational numbers, is dependent on the understanding of these topics.

The statement $a < b$ can be interpreted as meaning that b is to the right of a on the number line. Point out that $a < b$ and $b > a$ are equivalent statements. This gives us a way to convert any "greater than" statement to a "less than" statement and vice versa. For example, we can replace the statement $5 < x$ with $x > 5$, which students find much easier to understand and graph.

Students may enjoy learning of two more inequality symbols, formed by negating the $>$ and $<$ symbols. Point out that $a \not> 2$ is equivalent to $a \le 2$, and $c \not< 9$ is equivalent to $c \ge 9$.

SUMS AND DIFFERENCES

2-1 The Integers

Objectives *for pages 46–49*

■ To represent positive and negative integers on a number line.
■ To compare and order positive and negative integers.

Teaching Suggestions

Discuss ways positive and negative numbers are used. Use examples such as those in the first two paragraphs on page 46. The scale of a thermometer can be thought of as a vertical number line. Ask students to give other examples of number lines, such as highways with mileposts or depth markings in swimming pools.

Emphasize that zero is neither positive nor negative. On a number line, positive numbers are to the *right* of zero. Negative numbers are to the *left* of zero.

Insist that students space the markings on their number lines equally. Then the number lines can more accurately show opposites, absolute value, and order.

For any two real numbers a and b one and only one of the following is true:

$$a < b \qquad a = b \qquad a > b$$

Resource Book: Page 19 (Use After Page 49)

Related Activities

To enhance students' understanding of the integers, ask them to solve these equations:

$x = 5$ 5	$x = 0$ 0	$x = {}^-4$ $^-4$
$^-x = 5$ $^-5$	$^-x = 0$ 0	$^-x = {}^-4$ 4
$|x| = 5$ 5, $^-5$	$|x| = 0$ 0	$|x| = {}^-4$ **No solution**

Explain that most of these equations have only one solution. But the equation $|x| = 5$ has two solutions, 5 and $^-5$, and the equation $|x| = {}^-4$ has no solution.

An inequality such as $|x| > 0$ has infinitely many solutions: 1, 2, 3, 4, . . . and $^-1$, $^-2$, $^-3$, $^-4$, ... Only the number 0 will not satisfy this inequality.

In solving equations students must be cautioned that there may be more than one correct solution. Ask them to think of other equations with more than one solution. (Answers include $x \times 0 = 0$ or $x \times 1 = x$.)

2-2 Decimals on the Number Line

Objectives *for pages 50–53*

■ To represent positive and negative decimals on a number line.
■ To compare positive and negative decimals.

Teaching Suggestions

Spend ample time in this lesson placing decimal numbers correctly on the number line, especially the negative decimal numbers. Stress that $^-2.5$ is between $^-3$ and $^-2$ and *not* to the right of $^-2$. You might also show students that between $^-2.5$ and $^-2$ are other decimals such as $^-2.25$, $^-2.13$, and $^-2.064$.

Just as the integers include all whole numbers, decimal numbers include integers and whole numbers. This may be easier for students to remember if you show them examples such as $2 = 2.0$ and $^-3 = {}^-3.0$.

Related Activities

To relate this work to a familiar topic, ask students to compare the number line to a football field where 0 represents the line of scrimmage and 10 or more would represent a first down. If in a series of three plays, a team gains 3 yd, loses 5 yd, and gains 7 yd, would the team have a first down? Graph the action:

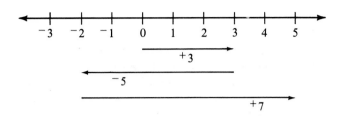

No, the team is 5 yd short of a first down.

2-3 Adding Positive and Negative Numbers

Objective *for pages 54–58*

■ To find the sum of two or more integers.

Teaching Suggestions

Integer addition can be shown concretely by using manipulatives. Give each student several squares of colored paper. Ask them to draw a line dividing a sheet of notebook paper in half. They should label the left side "negative" and the right side "positive."

For $^+2 + {}^+3$, ask students to place 2 squares on the positive side and add 3 squares on the positive side. Ask, "What do you have now?" Answer: 5 squares on the positive side. Thus, $^+2 + {}^+3 = {}^+5$.

For $^-2 + {}^-3$ place 2 squares on the negative side. Add 3 squares on the negative side and the result is 5 squares on the negative side. Thus, $^-2 + {}^-3 = {}^-5$.

For $^+2 + {}^-3$ place 2 squares on the positive side and 3 on the negative side. Explain that any pair consisting of a positive square and a negative square can be canceled out. In this case, one square on the negative side cannot be canceled out. Thus, $^+2 + {}^-3 = {}^-1$.

For $^-2 + {}^+3$ place 2 squares on the negative side and 3 squares on the positive side. Cancel out two negatives with two positives. All that is left is 1 square on the positive side. Thus, $^-2 + {}^+3 = {}^+1$.

Do several examples for integers and develop the rules carefully before using decimals.

Related Activities

To provide practice in a different way, give every student several copies of the triangle below. Fill in integers along the bottom row and have students add upward two at a time to reach the top. Do this as a class activity to encourage speed as well as accuracy.

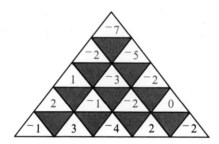

For the integers shown in this triangle, the addition examples include:

$$^-1 + 3 = 2$$
$$^-4 + 2 = ^-2$$
$$3 + ^-4 = ^-1$$
$$2 + ^-2 = 0$$

2-4 Subtracting Positive and Negative Numbers

Objective *for pages 59–62*

■ To find the difference of two integers.

Teaching Suggestions

Emphasize that the rule for subtraction requires that we add the opposite of the *second* number to the first. The first number remains unchanged. Compare this procedure to division of fractions, in which we multiply by the reciprocal of the *second* number and once again the first number remains unchanged.

Point out that when unraised minus signs are used, parentheses must often be used to make the meaning of an expression clear. For example, $12.4 - (-8)$ is clearer than $12.4 - -8$.

Related Activities

To provide mixed practice following this lesson, give students problems that involve a mixture of addition and subtraction. Explain that when students use the rule for subtraction and add the opposite, numbers may be added in any order desired.

1. $-2 + (-3.1) - 6 =$ **−11.1**
2. $4.6 - 2.15 + (-8) =$ **−5.55**
3. $-25 - (-6.3) - 7 =$ **−25.7**
4. $4.9 + (-3.8) - 5.1 =$ **−4**

Resource Book: Page 20 (Use After Page 62)

NAME _____ DATE _____

Quiz 2A — Lessons 2-1 through 2-4

DIRECTIONS: Write the letter of the correct answer in the space provided.

Write the integers in order from least to greatest.

		ANSWERS
1. 0, 7, ⁻5, ⁻6, 1	2. ⁻3, 8, ⁻7, 2 *[2-1]*	1. ___d___ (4)
a. ⁻7, ⁻3, 2, 8	b. ⁻5, ⁻6, 0, 1, 7	2. ___a___ (4)
c. 2, ⁻3, ⁻7, 8	d. ⁻6, ⁻5, 0, 1, 7	3. ___a___ (4)

List the integers that can replace *x* to make the statement true.

4. ___d___ (4)
3. |x| = 3   4. |x| < 4   5. ___d___ (4)
a. 3, ⁻3   b. 3   6. ___C___ (4)
c. 0, 1, 2, 3   d. ⁻3, ⁻2, ⁻1, 0, 1, 2, 3   7. ___C___ (4)

Write the numbers in order from least to greatest.   8. ___d___ (4)
5. ⁻5.11, 1.692, 1.7, ⁻5   6. 3.03, ⁻0.3, 30, ⁻1.3 *[2-2]*   9. ___C___ (4)
a. 1.692, 1.7, ⁻5, ⁻5.11   b. ⁻0.3, ⁻1.3, 3.03, 30   10. ___b___ (4)
c. ⁻1.3, ⁻0.3, 3.03, 30   d. ⁻5.11, ⁻5, 1.692, 1.7   11. ___C___ (5)

List the decimal numbers that can replace *x* to make the statement true.   12. ___b___ (5)
7. |x| = 0.043   8. |x| = |⁻4.3| 13. ___b___ (5)
a. 0.043   b. ⁻4.3   14. ___d___ (5)
c. 0.043, ⁻0.043   d. 4.3, ⁻4.3   15. ___C___ (10)

Find the sum or difference.   16. ___a___ (10)
9. ⁻4.68 + 13.79   10. ⁻13.79 + ⁻4.68 *[2-3]*   17. ___a___ (10)
a. 18.47   b. ⁻18.47   c. 9.11   d. ⁻9.11   18. ___a___ (10)

11. ⁻4.1 + 2.6 + ⁻3.5   12. 0.9 + ⁻3.2 + 7.3
a. ⁻10.2   b. 5.0   c. ⁻5.0   d. ⁻11.4

13. 9 − (−24)   14. −24 − (−9) *[2-4]*
a. −33   b. 33   c. 15   d. −15

Evaluate the expression when *s* = −3.2 and *t* = −4.5.
15. *s* − *t*   16. *s* + *t*   17. *t* − (−*s*)   18. *s* − |*t*|
a. ⁻7.7   b. 7.7   c. 1.3   d. −1.3

PRE-ALGEBRA, An Accelerated Course
Copyright © 1985 by Houghton Mifflin Company. All rights reserved. Printed in U.S.A.

20

Give each student a multiplication table like the one below:

×	3	2	1	0	−1	−2	−3
3	9	6	3	0	−3	−6	−9
2	6	4	2	0	−2	−4	−6
1	3	2	1	0	−1	−2	−3
0	0	0	0	0	0	0	0
−1	−3	−2	−1	0	1	2	3
−2	−6	−4	−2	0	2	4	6
−3	−9	−6	−3	0	3	6	9

Help students to complete the table by beginning in the upper left corner with 3(3), 3(2), 3(1) and 3(0). When students ask about 3(−1), ask them to look for patterns in the products they have already found. In this row products decrease by 3. Continue the pattern for 3(−2) and 3(−3). Use this same approach for multiplying by 2. Complete the next two rows, emphasizing rules for multiplying by 1 and 0.

To multiply −3(3), students may use the commutative property for 3(−3) or they may notice decreasing patterns in the column headed by 3. Complete the entire chart using properties and patterns. Examine the completed chart and notice positive products in the upper left and lower right hand sections. The lower left and upper right sections are negative products.

PRODUCTS AND QUOTIENTS

2-5 Multiplying Positive and Negative Numbers

Objective *for pages 63–66*

■ To find the product of two or more integers.

Teaching Suggestions

There are many examples that could be used as an interpretation for 5(−2). For example, five $2 debts mean that $10 is owed. If the temperature drops 2 degrees per hour for five hours, the final temperature is 10 degrees below the initial temperature. If one brick stretches a spring by 2 cm, then five bricks stretch it by 10 cm. These examples suggest that 5(−2) = −10.

Related Activities

To re-emphasize the Distributive Property, ask students to work these problems using the correct order of operations.

1. a. −6(8) + (−6)(2) **−60**
   b. −6(8 + 2) **−60**
2. a. 3(4.1) − 2(4.1) **4.1**
   b. (3 − 2)(4.1) **4.1**
3. a. 17.9(6.2) − 13.8(6.2) **25.42**
   b. (17.9 − 13.8)(6.2) **25.42**
4. a. −18.3(10) + (−4.5)(10) **−228**
   b. [−18.3 + (−4.5)](10) **−228**

2-6 Dividing Positive and Negative Numbers

Objective for pages 67–69

■ To find the quotient of two integers.

Teaching Suggestions

Remind students that we cannot divide by 0 (page 19). If necessary, review the reason, using the fact that $a \div b = c$ if and only if $b \times c = a$. Thus $0 \div 4 = 0$ since $4 \times 0 = 0$. Explain that $4 \div 0$ is meaningless since there is no number c such that $0 \times c = 4$. Some students have a better understanding of this when asked to answer $0\overline{)4}$. There is no possible quotient which will multiply times the divisor to give 4. When students ask about $0 \div 0$, show that infinitely many numbers can be found rather than a unique result.

Related Activities

To provide mixed practice following the lesson, give students problems that involve several operations.

1. $-42 \div 6 \times (-3)$ **21**
2. $-42 \times 6 \div (-3)$ **84**
3. $-42 + 6 \div (-3)$ **−44**
4. $-42 + 6 - (-3)$ **−33**
5. $-42 - 6 \times (-3)$ **−24**
6. $-42 \div 6 - (-3)$ **−4**

2-7 Using Positive Exponents

Objective for pages 70–72

■ To read, write, and simplify exponential expressions.

Teaching Suggestions

Emphasize that 5^3 means 5 used as a factor three times, *not* 5 multiplied by itself three times. Show that 5^3 actually involves just two multiplications. Also, be certain that students do not think 5^3 means 5×3. The product 5×3 means $5 + 5 + 5$.

Show students that greater numbers like 3^6 can be simplified by reversing the rule $a^m \times a^n = a^{m+n}$ so that $a^{m+n} = a^m \times a^n$ is used.

$$3^6 = 3^3 \times 3^3 = 27 \times 27 = 729$$
$$2^7 = 2^4 \times 2^3 = 16 \times 8 = 128$$

Related Activities

To help students in computations involving exponents, challenge them to memorize the squares and cubes of the whole numbers 2 through 10 and the squares of the whole numbers 11 through 25.

To provide a preview of the use of exponents in algebraic expressions, ask students to find the missing base or bases in problems such as these:

$$a^2 - (7 \times 3^2) = 1 \quad \textbf{8} \qquad b^3 + c^2 = 17 \ \textbf{2, 3; 1, 4; −2, 5}$$

2-8 Negative Integers as Exponents

Objective for pages 73–75

■ To simplify expressions involving negative exponents.

Teaching Suggestions

Your students may find the following informal justification of the rule for defining negative exponents helpful.

The decimal 351.67 can be expanded as shown below (see page 17).

$$351.67 = (3 \times 10^2) + (5 \times 10^1) +$$
$$(1 \times 10^0) + \left(6 \times \frac{1}{10^1}\right) + \left(7 \times \frac{1}{10^2}\right)$$

Point out that the exponents decrease by 1 in the first three terms. For this pattern to continue, the exponents must continue to decrease by 1 in the last two terms. This suggests that the expansion of 351.67 may be written as shown below.

$$351.67 = (3 \times 10^2) + (5 \times 10^1) +$$
$$(1 \times 10^0) + (6 \times 10^{-1}) + (7 \times 10^{-2})$$

Because of this, it is reasonable to define 10^{-1} as $\frac{1}{10^1}$ and 10^{-2} as $\frac{1}{10^2}$. In general,

$$10^{-n} = \frac{1}{10^n}.$$

It may be helpful to review the definition of reciprocals at this time, and to show the relationship between negative exponents and reciprocals. Since $10 \times 0.1 = 1$, 10 and 0.1 are reciprocals. Since $100 \times 0.01 = 1$, 100 and 0.01 are reciprocals. To find 10^{-3} ask for the reciprocal of 10^3. Since $1000 \times 0.001 = 1$, the reciprocal of 10^3 is 0.001. Thus, $10^{-3} = 0.001$.

Related Activities

To relate this material to another subject, have students find examples of the use of negative exponents to represent very small numbers. For instance, the diameter of an atom of silver is 2.5×10^{-8} cm. The diameter of a red blood cell is 7.7×10^{-4} cm, or 0.00077 cm. The speed mentioned in Exercise 1 on page 39, 100 million arithmetic operations in a second, is the same as 10 nanoseconds per operation. A nanosecond is 10^{-9} second, so each operation takes 10^{-8} second.

Resource Book: Pages 23–24 (Use After Page 75)

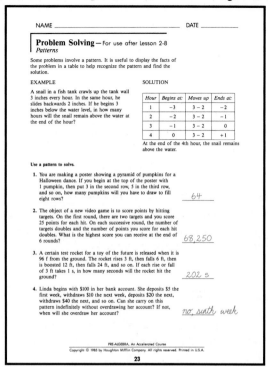

Resource Book: Page 22 (Use After Page 75)

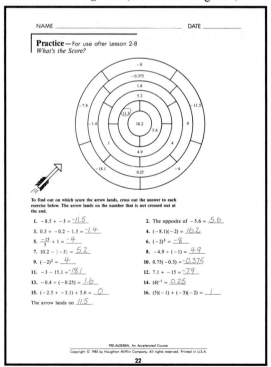

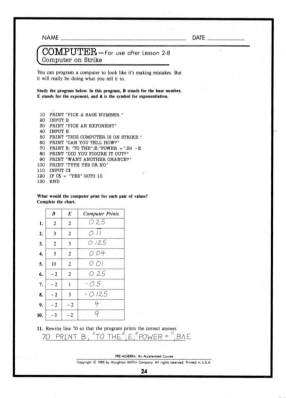

NAME _____ DATE _____

Quiz 2B — Lessons 2-5 through 2-8

DIRECTIONS: Write the letter of the correct answer in the space provided.

Find the product.

1. $-3.2(15.4)$
   a. -33.54 b. 49.28   c. -49.28 d. 33.54   [2-5]

2. $4.3(-2.6)(-3)$
   a. -72 b. 0   c. 144   d. -144

3. $(-4)(3)(-6)(0)(-1)$
   a. -72 b. 0   c. 144   d. -144

4. $(-2)(-3)(6)(4)(-1)$

Find the quotient.

5. $-225 \div (-5)$
   a. -450 b. 450   c. -45 d. 45   [2-6]

6. $270 \div (-0.6)$

7. $0 \div (-1.2)$
   a. -1.2 b. 1.2   c. 0   d. 12

8. $-0.36 \div (-0.3)$

Use inverse operations to solve for the variable.

9. $-8b = 40$
   a. 320   b. -320 c. 5   d. -5

10. $b \div (-8) = -40$

Write as a single power of the given base.

11. $2^4 \times 2 \times 2^5$
   a. 2^{20} b. 2^9 c. 2^{10} d. 2^{18} [2-7]

12. $2^3 \times 2^6 \times 2^0$

Evaluate the expression if $a = 2$, $b = 3$, and $c = 2$.

13. a^2c
   a. 324   b. 36   c. 8   d. 16

14. $(b^2c)^a$

Write the expression without exponents.

15. 3^{-2}
   a. -6 b. $-\frac{1}{9}$ c. $\frac{1}{8}$ d. $\frac{1}{9}$

16. 2^{-3} [2-8]

17. $6^3 \times 6^0 \times 6^{-1}$
   a. 216   b. 0   c. 36   d. -36

18. $(-6)^{-3} \times 6^1 \times (-6)^5$

ANSWERS
1. _c_ (4)
2. _d_ (4)
3. _b_ (4)
4. _d_ (4)
5. _d_ (6)
6. _a_ (6)
7. _c_ (6)
8. _b_ (6)
9. _d_ (6)
10. _a_ (6)
11. _c_ (6)
12. _b_ (6)
13. _c_ (6)
14. _a_ (6)
15. _d_ (6)
16. _d_ (6)
17. _c_ (6)
18. _a_ (6)

25

NAME _____ DATE _____

Review — Chapter 2

Replace _?_ with > or < to make a true statement.   [2-1]

1. -7 _?_ -8 $\underline{>}$ 2. -2 _?_ 0 $\underline{<}$ 3. $|-8|$ _?_ -8 $\underline{>}$

List the integers that can replace x to make the statement true.

4. $|x| = 9$ $\underline{9, -9}$ 5. $|x| < 3$ $\underline{-2, -1, 0, 1, 2}$

Write the numbers in order from least to greatest.

6. $-5.2, 3.8, -7.3, 0$ $\underline{-7.3, -5.2, 0, 3.8}$ 7. $0.4, -0.43, 0.34, -0.2$ $\underline{-0.43, -0.2,}$ [2-2]
   $0.34, 0.4$

List the decimal numbers that can replace x to make the statement true.

8. $|x| = 18.7$ $\underline{18.7, -18.7}$ 9. $|x| = 0$ $\underline{0}$ 10. $|x| = -3.4$ $\underline{3.4, -3.4}$

Find the sum.

11. $-3.2 + 4.9$ $\underline{1.7}$ 12. $-14.4 + -0.78$ $\underline{-15.18}$ [2-3]

13. $-7 + 3 + -8 + 0$ $\underline{-12}$ 14. $-12.6 + 17.2 + -1.8$ $\underline{2.8}$

Solve.

15. One month, the price of a stock went up $4, then down $5, and then up $2.50. What was the net change in the price of the stock that month? $\underline{up\ \$1.50}$

Find the difference.

16. $10 - 19$ $\underline{-9}$ 17. $3.6 - (-5.4)$ $\underline{9}$ [2-4]

18. $42 - (-42)$ $\underline{84}$ 19. $0 - [3.9 - (-5.6)]$ $\underline{-9.5}$

Solve.

20. On a winter day, the temperature dropped from 2°C to –9°C. Find the change in temperature. $\underline{drop\ of\ 11°C}$

Find the product.

21. $-6(-3)(4)$ $\underline{72}$ 22. $(-1.7)(-4)(-0.5)$ $\underline{-3.4}$ [2-5]

Find the quotient.

23. $-14.6 \div (-2)$ $\underline{7.3}$ 24. $24.8 \div 0.01$ $\underline{2480}$ [2-6]

Write the expression without exponents.

25. $2^3 \times 2^5$ $\underline{256}$ 26. $3^0 \times 3^2 \times 3^1$ $\underline{27}$ [2-7]

27. 3^{-3} $\underline{27}$ 28. $(-1)^{-5}$ $\underline{-1}$ [2-8]

29. $6^9 \times 6^{-9}$ $\underline{1}$ 30. $(-2)^3 \times (2)^0 \times (-2)^1$ $\underline{16}$

26

NAME _____ DATE _____

Test — Chapter 2

DIRECTIONS: Write the correct answer in the space provided.

Replace _?_ with =, >, or < to make a true statement.   [2-1]

1. -12 _?_ 14   2. -23 _?_ -25

Express as an integer.

3. $|5|$ 4. $|-13|$

Write the numbers in order from least to greatest.

5. $-4.5, 45, -1.45, 4.54$ [2-2]

6. $-0.78, -7.8, 7.8, -0.87$

Find the sum.   [2-3]

7. $-3 + 22$ 8. $-4.3 + 7.1$

9. $-7.29 + -3.8$ 10. $0 + -3.85$

Find the difference.   [2-4]

11. $13 - 27$ 12. $-5 - (-18)$

13. $28.7 - (-3.5)$ 14. $-0.7 - 3.5$

Evaluate the expression when $r = -6$ and $t = -2.7$.

15. $r - t$ 16. $-r - (-t)$

Find the product.   [2-5]

17. $-7(-9)$ 18. $-2.4(-5.5)$ 19. $-1(23.86)$ 20. $(1.3)(-4)(-3.1)$

Find the quotient.

21. $36 \div (-3)$ 22. $-0.6 \div 2.4$ 23. $-0.08 \div (-0.2)$ 24. $0 \div (-0.3)$ [2-6]

Write the expression without exponents.

25. 2^4 26. 25^0 27. $3^2 \times 3^4$ 28. $7^2 \times 7^0$ [2-7]

29. 3^{-2} 30. $(-2)^{-4}$ 31. $6^2 \times 6^4$ 32. $-2 \times (-2)^{-2}$ [2-8]

ANSWERS
1. $\underline{<}$ (2)   17. $\underline{63}$ (3)
2. $\underline{>}$ (2)   18. $\underline{13.2}$ (3)
3. $\underline{5}$ (2)   19. $\underline{-23.86}$ (3)
4. $\underline{13}$ (2)   20. $\underline{16.12}$ (3)
5. $\underline{-45, -1.45, 4.54, 45}$ (2)   21. $\underline{-12}$ (2)
6. $\underline{-7.8, -0.87, -0.78, 7.8}$ (2)   22. $\underline{-0.25}$ (2)
7. $\underline{19}$ (3)   23. $\underline{0.4}$ (3)
8. $\underline{2.8}$ (3)   24. $\underline{0}$ (3)
9. $\underline{-11.09}$ (3)   25. $\underline{16}$ (4)
10. $\underline{-3.85}$ (3)   26. $\underline{1}$ (4)
11. $\underline{-14}$ (3)   27. $\underline{729}$ (4)
12. $\underline{13}$ (3)   28. $\underline{49}$ (4)
13. $\underline{32.2}$ (3)   29. $\underline{\frac{1}{9}}$ (5)
14. $\underline{-4.2}$ (3)   30. $\underline{\frac{1}{16}}$ (5)
15. $\underline{-3.3}$ (3)   31. $\underline{\frac{1}{36}}$ (5)
16. $\underline{3.3}$ (3)   32. $\underline{-\frac{1}{2}}$ (5)

27

NAME _____ DATE _____

Make-up Test — Chapter 2

DIRECTIONS: Write the correct answer in the space provided.

Replace _?_ with =, >, or < to make a true statement.   [2-1]

1. 16 _?_ -15 2. -5 _?_ -8

Express as an integer.

3. $|-9|$ 4. $|6|$

Write the numbers in order from least to greatest.

5. $8.9, -1.98, 9.8, -1.89$ [2-2]

6. $0.23, -2.3, -2.23, 2$

Find the sum.   [2-3]

7. $-17 + 8$ 8. $-7.4 + -3.9$

9. $-11.5 + 3.8$ 10. $0 + -4.76$

Find the difference.   [2-4]

11. $-3.6 - (-4.2)$ 12. $32.1 - (-32.1)$

Evaluate the expression when $e = -7$ and $f = -2.8$.

13. $-|f|$ 14. $|e + f|$

Find the product.   [2-5]

15. $-8(-7)$ 16. $-3.8(-6.5)$ 17. $-1(72.93)$ 18. $3.2(-5)(-6.1)$

Find the quotient.

19. $64 \div (-4)$ 20. $-0.8 \div 3.2$ 21. $-0.006 \div (-0.3)$ 22. $0 \div (-1.4)$ [2-6]

Write the expression without exponents.

23. 3^3 24. 20^0 25. $2^4 \times 2^2$ 26. $4^3 \times 4^0$ [2-7]

27. 2^{-3} 28. $(-3)^{-3}$ 29. $4^2 \times 4^{-5}$ 30. $-5 \times (-5)^{-3}$ [2-8]

ANSWERS
1. $\underline{>}$ (2)   16. $\underline{24.7}$ (3)
2. $\underline{>}$ (2)   17. $\underline{-72.93}$ (3)
3. $\underline{9}$ (2)   18. $\underline{97.6}$ (3)
4. $\underline{6}$ (2)   19. $\underline{-16}$ (4)
5. $\underline{-1.98, -1.89, 8.9, 9.8}$ (2)   20. $\underline{-0.25}$ (4)
6. $\underline{-2.3, -2.23, 0.23, 2}$ (2)   21. $\underline{0.02}$ (4)
7. $\underline{-9}$ (3)   22. $\underline{0}$ (4)
8. $\underline{-11.3}$ (3)   23. $\underline{27}$ (4)
9. $\underline{-7.7}$ (3)   24. $\underline{1}$ (4)
10. $\underline{-4.76}$ (3)   25. $\underline{64}$ (4)
11. $\underline{0.6}$ (3)   26. $\underline{64}$ (4)
12. $\underline{64.2}$ (3)   27. $\underline{\frac{1}{8}}$ (5)
13. $\underline{-2.8}$ (3)   28. $\underline{-\frac{1}{27}}$ (5)
14. $\underline{9.8}$ (3)   29. $\underline{\frac{1}{64}}$ (5)
15. $\underline{56}$ (3)   30. $\underline{\frac{1}{25}}$ (5)

28

Resource Book: Pages 29-30 (Use After Page 75)

CUMULATIVE REVIEW — Chapters 1-2
Exercises

Evaluate the expression using the given values of the variables.

1. $r + s$; $r = 3.8$, $s = 5.8$ _9.6_   2. $4a - b$; $a = 7.3$, $b = 8$ _21.2_

3. $\frac{c}{d} - 2$; $c = 12$, $d = 0.6$ _18_   4. $\frac{f}{3} + g$; $f = 15$, $g = 1.8$ _6.8_

5. $3k^2 + 7l$; $k = 4$, $l = 1.3$ _57.1_   6. $n \div m$; $n = 28.4$, $m = 4$ _7.1_

Evaluate the expression when $f = 3.8$, $g = 10$, and $h = 5.4$.

7. $fg - h$ _32.6_   8. $gh + f$ _57.8_   9. $2h + 5(g - f)$ _41.8_

10. $(f + h)(g + h)$ _141.68_   11. $3/hg$ _615.6_   12. $5f + 6h$ _51.4_

13. $(h + f) \div g$ _.092_   14. $6(h + 11.6)$ _102_   15. $\frac{24 - h}{f + 2.2}$ _3.1_

Use inverse operations to solve the equation.

16. $r + 14 = 108$ _94_   17. $d - 27 = 85$ _112_   18. $8m + 5 = 61$ _7_

Use $<$ to order the numbers from least to greatest.

19. 7, 15, 11 _7<11<15_   20. 2.3, 1.9, 2.25 _1.9<2.25<2.3_   21. 43, 33, 23 _23<33<43_

22. 3^2, 4^2, 3^3 _$3^2<4^2<3^3$_   23. 2^3, 3^2, 4^0 _$4^0<2^3<3^2$_   24. 5^3, 6^2, 2^5 _$2^5<6^2<5^3$_

Select the most reasonable estimated answer.

25. $19.61 + 8.81$ a. 14   b. 33   c. 28   _c_

26. 85.31×9 a. 770   b. 700   c. 680   _a_

27. $13.1 + 17 + 7.9$ a. 45   b. 30   c. 37   _c_

28. $152.43 - 17.8$ a. 140   b. 134   c. 128   _b_

29. $278.8 \div 19.8$ a. 140   b. 14   c. 20   _b_

True or false?

30. $68 - 21 = 21 - 68$ _F_   31. $16.9 \times 1 = 16.9$ _T_

32. $0 \times 43.5 = 43.5$ _F_   33. $9(3 + 2) = (9 \times 3) \times (9 \times 2)$ _F_

34. $17.4 - (5 + 3) = (17.4 - 5) + 3$ _F_   35. $18 + (10 \div 2) = (18 + 10) \div 2$ _F_

36. $(7 + 6)3 = 7 \times 3 + 6 \times 3$ _T_   37. $(25.3 + 6.25) = (6.25 + 25.3)$ _T_

38. $30 \div 5 + 1 = 30 \div (5 + 1)$ _F_

CUMULATIVE REVIEW — Chapters 1-2 *(continued)*
Problems

Problem Solving Reminders

Here are some reminders that may help you solve some of the problems on this page.
- Determine which facts are necessary to solve the problem.
- Supply additional information if needed.
- Check by using rounding to find an estimated answer.
- If more than one method can be used to solve a problem, use one method to solve and the other to check.

Solve.

1. Carlos and Bill delivered newspapers together, earning a total of $18.00 each week. After sharing their earnings for sixteen weeks, Martin joined them, and the earnings were divided three ways. How much did Carlos earn for 50 weeks? _$348_

2. Pistachio nuts cost $1.80 for 2 oz, $7.00 for $\frac{1}{2}$ lb, and $12.00 for a pound. What is the cost of each ounce if you buy a pound? How much do you save per ounce if you buy a pound? _$.75 save $.15/oz_

3. Hearty Chicken Soup is on sale for 3 cans for $1.10. The regular price is 2 cans for 99¢. How much is saved by buying a dozen cans of soup at the sale price? _$1.54_

4. Bart Kahn ordered a crystal fruit bowl as a gift at a cost of $47.50. The additional costs included $2.85 for tax, $1.25 for a gift box, and $3.95 for shipping. What was the total price of the order? _$55.55_

5. Speedy Cleanser costs 49¢ for an 8-oz can and 89¢ for a 15-oz can. How much change will you receive if you buy 15 larger-size cans of cleanser and pay with a $20 bill? _$6.65_

6. A membership to the Finley Art Museum costs $42 per year and includes a subscription to a monthly magazine. If the magazine costs $2.50 an issue, what are the annual dues for membership alone? _$12_

7. House numerals that are 3 in. high cost $2.00 each. Numerals that are 5 in. high cost $6.00 each. How much will it cost to buy numerals that are 5 in. high for your house if your address is 2742 Colonial Drive? _$24_

8. The February electric bill was $132.40, which was twice as much as the January bill. The March electric bill was $25.00 higher than the January bill. What was the total cost of electricity for January, February, and March? _$289.80_

Related Activities p. 45b

Reading Mathematics

Students will learn the meaning of the following mathematical terms and symbols in this lesson: *positive, negative, opposite, absolute value, integer,* $<$, and $>$.

2-1 The Integers

When we measure temperature, we use a scale that has 0 as a reference point. We use *positive numbers* to indicate temperatures above 0°, and we use *negative numbers* to indicate temperatures below 0°.

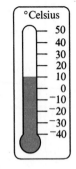

We often have occasion to measure quantities on different sides of a zero reference point, such as distances above and below sea level, time before and after a rocket launch, increases and decreases in stock prices, and deposits and withdrawals in a bank account. Positive and negative numbers help us to measure these quantities.

We may graph both positive and negative numbers on a horizontal number line by extending the number line to the *left* of the origin as shown below. Like the positive whole numbers, the negative whole numbers are equally spaced, but they are positioned to the left of 0.

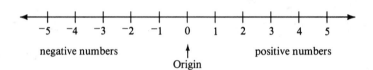

We read $^-1$ as *negative one.* We may read 1 as *positive one,* or simply *one.* For emphasis, we may use the symbol $^+1$ for positive one.

Any pair of numbers, such as 3 and $^-3$, that are the same distance from the origin but in opposite directions are called **opposites.** The opposite of 3 is $^-3$ and the opposite of $^-3$ is 3. The opposite of 0 is 0.

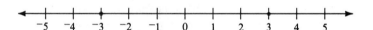

We use the symbol $|^-3|$, read *the absolute value of $^-3$,* to represent the distance between $^-3$ and 0. Because $^-3$ is 3 units from the origin, $|^-3| = 3$. In general, $|n|$ (read *the absolute value of n*) represents the distance between the number *n* and the origin.

The whole numbers, 0, 1, 2, 3, ..., together with their opposites, 0, $^-1$, $^-2$, $^-3$, ..., form the set of numbers called the **integers:**

$$\ldots, \; ^-3, \, ^-2, \, ^-1, 0, 1, 2, 3, \ldots.$$

The **positive integers** are the numbers 1, 2, 3, ..., and the **negative integers** are the numbers $^-1$, $^-2$, $^-3$, ... Although 0 is an integer, it is neither positive nor negative.

46 *Chapter 2*

EXAMPLE 1 Express as an integer.
 a. $|{}^-5|$ **b.** $|0|$

Solution **a.** $|{}^-5|$ represents the distance between 0 and the number $^-5$. Thus $|{}^-5| = 5$.

 b. $|0|$ represents the distance between 0 and 0. Thus $|0| = 0$.

EXAMPLE 2 Arrange $^-3$, 1, $^-4$, 0, $^-1$ in order from least to greatest.

Solution We can graph the numbers on a number line, with 1 at the right of 0.

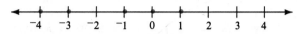

Reading the coordinates of the points from left to right will order the numbers from least to greatest. $^-4, {}^-3, {}^-1, 0, 1$

Positive and negative numbers may be compared using inequality symbols as well as on the number line. The inequality symbols $>$ and $<$ are used to compare mathematical expressions. The use of these symbols in inequalities is shown below.

$8 > 6$ $6 < 8$
Eight is greater than six.   Six is less than eight.

To avoid confusing these symbols, think of them as arrowheads whose small ends point toward the smaller numbers.

We can indicate that one number is between two others by combining two inequalities. We know that $5 < 6$ and $6 < 8$; thus we can write

  $5 < 6 < 8$ or $8 > 6 > 5$.

Other inequality symbols that we use are shown below with their meanings.

  $\neq$ *is not equal to*
  $\geq$ *is greater than or equal to*
  $\leq$ *is less than or equal to*

We can use inequality symbols to write open sentences. The open sentence $n \leq 6$ means $n < 6$ or $n = 6$.

EXAMPLE 3 Replace __?__ with $<$ or $>$.
 a. 14 __?__ 2   **b.** 1 __?__ 11   **c.** 8 __?__ 3 __?__ 0

Solution **a.** $14 > 2$ **b.** $1 < 11$ **c.** $8 > 3 > 0$

Positive and Negative Numbers **47**

Class Exercises

Name an integer that represents each of the following.

1. 15 s before blastoff of a rocket ⁻15

2. A gain of 6 yd in a football play 6

3. A withdrawal of 90 dollars from a bank account ⁻90

4. An elevation of 350 ft below sea level ⁻350

5. The opposite of 80 ⁻80   **6.** The opposite of ⁻2 2

7. The absolute value of ⁻14 14   **8.** The absolute value of 27 27

9. Name two integers, each of which is 12 units from 0. 12, ⁻12

10. If $|n| = 15$, then $n = \underset{15}{\underline{\quad?\quad}}$ or $n = \underset{-15}{\underline{\quad?\quad}}$.   → $|15| = 15$ or $|-15| = 15$

Replace __?__ with > or < to make a true statement.

11. a. ⁻6 $\underset{<}{\underline{\quad?\quad}}$ ⁻2   **b.** $|⁻6|$ $\underset{>}{\underline{\quad?\quad}}$ $|⁻2|$ **12. a.** 4 $\underset{>}{\underline{\quad?\quad}}$ ⁻5   **b.** $|4|$ $\underset{<}{\underline{\quad?\quad}}$ $|⁻5|$

True or false?

13. 7 > 7 False   **14.** 18 ≤ 20 True   **15.** 15 > 5 True

16. 14 > 6 > 2 True   **17.** 20 < 18 < 16 False   **18.** 33 ≥ 24 ≥ 11 True

---

Written Exercises

Graph the integers in each exercise on the same number line. Check students' graphs.

A   **1.** 0, 1, ⁻1, 3, ⁻3   **2.** 0, 2, ⁻2, 5, ⁻5   **3.** 6, 0, ⁻4, ⁻9, 7   **4.** ⁻1, 3, ⁻8, 4, ⁻6

Graph the number and its opposite on the same number line. Check students' graphs.

5. 3   **6.** 10   **7.** ⁻7   **8.** ⁻2   **9.** 0   **10.** ⁻4

Replace __?__ with =, >, or < to make a true statement.

11. 21 __?__ 14 >   **12.** 18 __?__ 35 <   **13.** 76 __?__ 67 >

14. 104 __?__ 104 =   **15.** 265 __?__ 256 >   **16.** 390 __?__ 309 >

17. 17 + 82 __?__ 93 >   **18.** 47 − 31 __?__ 61 <   **19.** 25 ÷ 5 __?__ 10 <

20. 26 × 4 __?__ 52 >   **21.** 19 × 11 __?__ 208 >   **22.** 84 ÷ 3 __?__ 24 >

23. ⁻3 __?__ ⁻4 >   **24.** ⁻2 __?__ 1 <   **25.** 7 __?__ ⁻8 >

26. 0 __?__ ⁻2 >   **27.** ⁻11 __?__ 0 <   **28.** ⁻7 __?__ 10 <

48 *Chapter 2*

Additional A Exercises

Replace __?__ with > or < to make a true statement.

1. ⁻4 $\overset{>}{\underline{\quad?\quad}}$ ⁻5

2. ⁻6 $\overset{>}{\underline{\quad?\quad}}$ ⁻8

3. ⁻4 $\overset{<}{\underline{\quad?\quad}}$ ⁻1

4. Use < to write a true statement about 101, 110, 100.
100 < 101 < 110

Express as an integer.

5. $|⁻20|$ 20

6. $|7|$ 7

7. Write the integers ⁻10, 9, ⁻6, 3, 1 in order from least to greatest. ⁻10, ⁻6, 1, 3, 9

48

Use > or < to write a true statement with the given numbers. $103 < 130 < 310$, or

$18 < 32 < 46$, or $5 < 29 < 31$, or $310 > 130 > 103$

29. 18, 46, 32 $46 > 32 > 18$ **30.** 29, 5, 31 $31 > 29 > 5$ **31.** 103, 130, 310

32. 256, 652, 526

$256 < 526 < 652$, or   **33.** 986, 689, 698   **34.** 717, 177, 771

$652 > 526 > 256$ $689 < 698 < 986$, or $177 < 717 < 771$, or

Express as an integer. $986 > 698 > 689$ $771 > 717 > 177$

35. $|^-3|$ 3   **36.** $|^-6|$ 6   **37.** $|0|$ 0   **38.** $|12|$ 12   **39.** $|9|$ 9   **40.** $|^-7|$ 7   **41.** $|^-8|$ 8   **42.** $|^-1|$

     1

Write the numbers in order from least to greatest.

43. 6, $^-15$, 0, $^-2$ $^-15$, $^-2$, 0, 6   **44.** $^-3$, 1, 0, $^-7$ $^-7$, $^-3$, 0, 1

45. $^-12$, 7, $^-8$, 1, $^-1$ $^-12$, $^-8$, $^-1$, 1, 7   **46.** 0, 2, $^-5$, $^-9$, 10 $^-9$, $^-5$, 0, 2, 10

47. $^-10$, 4, 14, $^-14$, 8 $^-14$, $^-10$, 4, 8, 14   **48.** 3, 9, $^-13$, 11, $^-15$ $^-15$, $^-13$, 3, 9, 11

49. $^-6.4$, 0.6, 3.1, $^-2.7$ $^-6.4$, $^-2.7$, 0.6, 3.1   **50.** 7.1, $^-0.9$, $^-3.6$, $^-9.4$

                                  $^-9.4$, $^-3.6$, $^-0.9$, 7.1

For Exercises 51–62, (a) list the integers that can replace _n_ to make the statement true, and (b) graph the integers on a number line. (b) Check students' graphs

B   **51.** $|n| = 6$ 6, $^-6$ **52.** $|n| = 3$ 3, $^-3$ **53.** $|n| = 4$

                                                                 4, $^-4$

54. $|n| = 5$ 5, $^-5$ **55.** $|n| = 0$ 0   **56.** $|n| = 14$

                         4, 3, 2, 1, 0, $^-1$, $^-2$, $^-3$, $^-4$ 14, $^-14$

57. $|n| < 2$ 1, 0, $^-1$ **58.** $|n| < 5$ **59.** $|n| \le 4$

                                              4, 3, 2, 1, 0, $^-1$, $^-2$, $^-3$, $^-4$

60. $|n| \le 7$ **61.** $2 < |n| < 8$ 7, 6, 5, 4, 3,   **62.** $0 < |n| < 3$

7, 6, 5, . . . $^-5$, $^-6$, $^-7$ $^-3$, $^-4$, $^-5$, $^-6$, $^-7$ 2, 1, $^-1$, $^-2$

Complete with the word _positive_ or _negative_.

C   **63.** If an integer is equal to its absolute value, then the integer must be

      a ___?___ integer or 0. positive

64. If an integer is equal to the opposite of its absolute value, then the

      integer must be a ___?___ integer or 0. negative

65. Explain why there is no number that can replace _n_ to make the

      equation $|n| = {}^-3$ true. $|n|$ represents the distance _n_ from the

                      origin. Distance cannot be negative.

Review Exercises

Graph the number on a number line. Check students' graphs.

1. 4   **2.** 6   **3.** 3   **4.** 0   **5.** 2.4

6. 1.3   **7.** $3\frac{1}{2}$ **8.** $1\frac{1}{3}$ **9.** 3.7   **10.** 4.5

Positive and Negative Numbers   **49**

Suggested Assignments

Core

48/1–9 odd; 20–28

49/29–51 odd; 63–65

49/Rev. 1–10

Enriched

48/23–28

49/30–62 even; 63–65

49/Rev. 1–10

Supplementary Materials

Practice Masters, p. 7

Teaching Suggestions p. 45b

Related Activities p. 45b

Reading Mathematics

Students will learn the meaning of the following mathematical terms in this lesson: *positive decimal, negative decimal, decimal number.*

2-2 Decimals on the Number Line

The graphs of the *positive decimal* 2.5 and its opposite, the *negative decimal* ⁻2.5, are shown on the number line below. We graph 2.5 by locating the point that is 2.5 units to the *right* of 0, and we graph ⁻2.5 by locating the point that is 2.5 units to the *left* of 0.

The positive decimals together with the negative decimals and 0 form the set of *decimal numbers*. The set of decimal numbers includes all of the whole numbers and all of the integers.

EXAMPLE 1   Write the following numbers in order from least to greatest.

$$^-2, 4.1, 0.2, ^-2.6, ^-1.34$$

Solution   We can graph the given numbers on a number line.

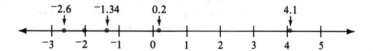

Reading the coordinates from left to right will give the numbers in order from least to greatest.

$$^-2.6, ^-2, ^-1.34, 0.2, 4.1$$

We have been representing decimals by their graphs, that is, by dots on a number line. We can also use directed line segments or arrows to illustrate decimals. Arrows that point to the *left* (the negative direction) represent negative numbers. Arrows that point to the *right* (the positive direction) represent positive numbers.

Notice in the diagram above that both the arrow representing ⁻2.5 and the arrow representing 2.5 have length 2.5.

50   *Chapter 2*

An arrow representing a number may have any point on the number line as its starting point, as long as it has length and direction indicated by that number. The length of the arrow is the absolute value of the number that the arrow represents. The direction of the arrow is determined by the sign of the number.

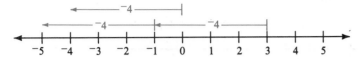

On the number line above, each arrow represents the decimal number ⁻4, for each has length 4 and points to the left.

EXAMPLE 2   What number is represented by the arrow above the number line below?

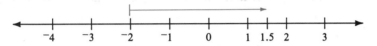

Solution   The starting point of the arrow is ⁻2 and the endpoint is 1.5. The arrow points to the right and is 3.5 units long. Thus, the arrow represents the positive decimal number 3.5.

EXAMPLE 3   An arrow representing the number ⁻7 has starting point 3. What is its endpoint?

Solution   Draw a number line. Starting at 3, draw an arrow 7 units long in the negative direction (left). The endpoint of the arrow is ⁻4.

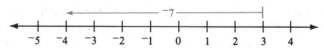

Class Exercises

Name a decimal number that represents each of the following.

1. The opposite of 8.71 ⁻8.71
2. The opposite of ⁻10.16 10.16
3. A discount of fifty-nine cents ⁻0.59
4. A rise in body temperature of 0.6°C   0.6
5. The absolute value of ⁻67.5 67.5
6. The absolute value of 9.07 9.07

Positive and Negative Numbers   **51**

1. 2.7

2. ⁻1.01

3. 0.6

4. ⁻2.7

5. ⁻3.5

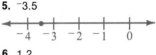

6. 1.2

7. Name the letter written above the graph of the given number.

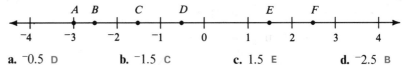

a. ⁻0.5 D   **b.** ⁻1.5 C   **c.** 1.5 E   **d.** ⁻2.5 B

8. State the numbers in Exercise 7 in order from least to greatest.
⁻2.5, ⁻1.5, ⁻0.5, 1.5

Name the number represented by each arrow described below.

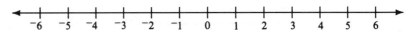

9. Starting point at 0, endpoint at ⁻2.5
⁻2.5

10. Starting point at ⁻1, endpoint at 3
4

11. Starting point at 2, endpoint at ⁻4
⁻6

12. Starting point at ⁻0.5, endpoint at 5
5.5

Written Exercises

Graph the numbers in each exercise on the same number line. Check students' graphs.

A

1. ⁻2, ⁻3.5, 0   **2.** 3.2, ⁻4, ⁻3.2   **3.** ⁻1.5, ⁻7, ⁻3.25   **4.** ⁻0.9, ⁻1, ⁻4.1

Graph the number and its opposite on the same number line. Check students' graphs.

5. 2.25   **6.** 1.9   **7.** ⁻0.5   **8.** ⁻3.1

9. ⁻4.2   **10.** 0.75   **11.** 0.3   **12.** 5.5

Write the decimal number that is equal to each of the following.

13. |⁻2.36| **14.** |1.921| **15.** |⁻16| **16.** |⁻100| **17.** |3.03| **18.** |⁻0.2|
 2.36   1.921   16   100   3.03   0.2

Replace __?__ with < or > to make a true statement.

19. ⁻2.93 _?_ 1.1 <   **20.** 4 _?_ ⁻0.5 >   **21.** ⁻8.1 _?_ 2.3 <

22. ⁻1.95 _?_ ⁻1.96 >   **23.** ⁻5.01 _?_ ⁻4.99 <   **24.** ⁻2.99 _?_ ⁻2.98 <

25. 0.1 _?_ ⁻18.25 >   **26.** 12.2 _?_ ⁻13.3 >   **27.** ⁻3.7 _?_ 3.07 <

Write the numbers in order from least to greatest.

28. ⁻2.72, ⁻3, 0.03, ⁻3.5, 0.2
⁻3.5, ⁻3, ⁻2.72, 0.03, 0.2

29. 6.3, ⁻8, ⁻7.6, ⁻1.75, 6.03
⁻8, ⁻7.6, ⁻1.75, 6.03, 6.3

30. 0, 2.99, ⁻10, ⁻0.1, ⁻0.01
⁻10, ⁻0.1, ⁻0.01, 0, 2.99

31. ⁻100.5, ⁻2, 3.11, ⁻2.1, ⁻46.8
⁻100.5, ⁻46.8, ⁻2.1, ⁻2, 3.11

32. ⁻0.5, ⁻0.05, ⁻5, ⁻50, 500
⁻50, ⁻5, ⁻0.5, ⁻0.05, 500

33. ⁻0.3, 30.3, ⁻0.33, ⁻3.3, 33
⁻3.3, ⁻0.33, ⁻0.3, 30.3, 33

52   *Chapter 2*

Additional A Exercises

Replace __?__ with < or > to make true statements.

1. ⁻0.3 _?_ ⁻0.33
>

2. ⁻8 _?_ ⁻7.3
<

3. 2.1 _?_ 2.01
>

4. ⁻4 _?_ ⁻40
>

Write in order from least to greatest.

5. ⁻3.4, ⁻2.1, ⁻5
⁻5, ⁻3.4, ⁻2.1

6. 0, 0.3, ⁻0.4
⁻0.4, 0, 0.3

Draw an arrow to represent each decimal number described below.

Check students' graphs.

34. The number 3, with starting point ⁻1

35. The number 2.5, with starting point ⁻0.5

36. The number ⁻5, with starting point 1.5

37. The number ⁻3, with starting point ⁻0.5

38. The number 5.5, with starting point ⁻3

39. The number ⁻4, with endpoint ⁻2

40. The number ⁻2, with endpoint 5

List the decimal numbers that can replace *x* to make the statement true.

26.3, ⁻26.3

B **41.** $|x| = 4.1$ 4.1, ⁻4.1   **42.** $|x| = 0.001$ 0.001, ⁻0.001   **43.** $|x| = 26.3$

2.2, ⁻2.2

44. $|x| = 0$ 0   **45.** $|x| = |{-}1.19|$ 1.19, ⁻1.19   **46.** $|x| = |{-}2.2|$

Copy and complete the chart so that the two arrows represent the same decimal number.

	Arrow 1		Arrow 2	
	Starting Point	**Endpoint**	**Starting Point**	**Endpoint**
47.	⁻2.5	⁻7	0	? ⁻4.5
48.	? 7	4	1.5	⁻1.5
49.	⁻0.5	8.5	? ⁻12	⁻3
50.	4	⁻6.25	? 8.25	⁻2

For Exercises 51–54, (a) list the *integers* that can replace *n* to make the statement true, and (b) show their graphs on a number line. (b) Check students' graphs.

51. $|n| < 4.3$ **52.** $|n| < 2.99$ **53.** $|n| \leq 5.001$ **54.** $|n| \leq 0.08$

4, 3, 2, . . . ⁻2, ⁻3, ⁻4   2, 1, 0, ⁻1, ⁻2   5, 4, 3, . . . ⁻3, ⁻4, ⁻5   0

Review Exercises

Use the properties to simplify the expression. Name the property or properties used.

1. $2(4.5 + 1.07)$
11.14; Distributive

2. $3.7 + 12.5 + 0.5$
16.7; Associative

3. 1×27.18 27.18;
Multiplication Prop. of One

4. $8.69 + 4.78 + 2.31$
15.78; Comm. and Asso.

5. $7(30 - 11.1)$
132.3; Distributive

6. $(44 \times 0.3) + (44 \times 0.7)$
44; Distributive and Mult. Prop. of

7. $6.25 \times 43 \times 4$
1075; Comm. and Asso.

8. $0.2 \times 3.7 \times 0.5$
0.37; Comm. and Asso.

9. $17.6 \times 283 \times 0$ One
0; Multiplication Prop. of Zero

Positive and Negative Numbers **53**

Suggested Assignments

Core
  52/2–8 even; 14–32 even
  53/36–46 even
  53/Rev. 1–9

Enriched
  52/19–33 odd
  53/35–53 odd
  53/Rev. 1–9

Supplementary Materials

Practice Masters, p. 7

Reading Mathematics

Students will learn the meaning of the following mathematical terms in this lesson: *addend, sum.*

2-3 Adding Positive and Negative Numbers

We can use arrows on the number line, as shown below, to add two positive numbers or to add two negative numbers. We draw a solid arrow with starting point 0 to represent the first addend. We draw another solid arrow with *starting point at the endpoint of the first arrow* to represent the second addend. To represent the sum, we draw a dashed arrow from the starting point of the first arrow to the endpoint of the second arrow.

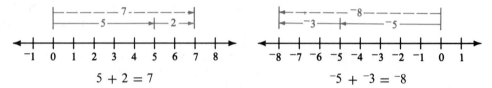

$$5 + 2 = 7 \qquad\qquad -5 + -3 = -8$$

In each case, if we add the absolute values of the addends, we obtain the absolute value of the sum. The sum has the same sign as the addends.

> ## Rules
>
> The sum of two positive numbers is positive.
>
> The sum of two negative numbers is negative.

EXAMPLE 1 Find the sum. **a.** $2.5 + 4.3$ **b.** $^-7 + ^-1.5$

Solution **a.** Since the addends are positive, the sum is positive.
$$2.5 + 4.3 = 6.8$$

b. Since the addends are negative, the sum is negative.
$$^-7 + ^-1.5 = ^-8.5$$

We can also use arrows on the number line to add a positive and a negative number. The sum of a positive and a negative number may be positive, negative, or zero, as shown in the following illustrations.

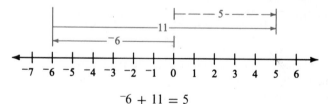

The positive number 11 has greater absolute value than the negative number $^-6$. Thus the sum is positive.

$$^-6 + 11 = 5$$

54 *Chapter 2*

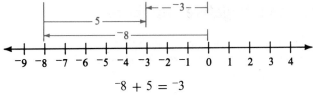

$$-8 + 5 = -3$$

$$7 + {}^-7 = 0$$

The negative number $^-8$ has greater absolute value than the positive number 5. Thus the sum is negative.

The positive number 7 and the negative number $^-7$ are opposites and thus have the same absolute value. The sum is zero.

Notice that, in each case, the absolute value of the sum is the *difference* of the absolute values of the addends. The sum has the same sign as the addend with the greater absolute value.

Rules

The sum of a positive number and a negative number is

1. positive if the positive number has the greater absolute value.
2. negative if the negative number has the greater absolute value.
3. zero if the numbers have the same absolute value.

EXAMPLE 2   Find the sum.

    a. $3.5 + {}^-10.5$ **b.** $^-7.6 + 12.2$ **c.** $^-4.8 + 0$ **d.** $^-6.7 + 6.7$

Solution

    a. The negative addend has the greater absolute value, so the sum is negative.

$$3.5 + {}^-10.5 = {}^-7$$

    b. The positive addend has the greater absolute value, so the sum is positive.

$$^-7.6 + 12.2 = 4.6$$

    c. Think of adding 0 as *moving no units* on the number line. Thus, $^-4.8 + 0 = {}^-4.8$.

    d. The numbers have the same absolute value, so the sum is zero.

$$^-6.7 + 6.7 = 0$$

As shown in Example 2, part (c), the addition property of zero holds for the positive and negative decimals. All of the properties for positive decimals hold for negative decimals as well.

Positive and Negative Numbers   **55**

EXAMPLE 3   Sally Wright bought some stock in ABC Computer Company. The stock went down $2.50 per share in the first week, went up $3.00 in the second week, and went down $1.25 in the third week. If Sally paid $30.50 per share for the stock, did she gain or lose money?

Solution

- The question asks if Sally gained or lost money.

- Given information: Sally paid $30.50 per share
  price went down $2.50, went up $3.00, went down $1.25

- First, find the new price per share. Express the given information as a sum of positive and negative decimals.
$$30.50 + {}^-2.50 + 3 + {}^-1.25 = (30.50 + 3) + ({}^-2.50 + {}^-1.25)$$
$$= 33.50 + {}^-3.75$$
$$= 29.75$$
To find whether Sally gained or lost money, compare the new price per share to the price paid per share.
$$29.75 < 30.50$$

- Because the new price per share is less than the price paid per share, Sally lost money.

Problem Solving Reminder

Many problems involve *more than one step,* but the steps may not always involve operations. In Example 3, we used addition in the first step, but in the second step we compared the answer to the first step with an amount given in the problem.

Class Exercises

State the addition fact illustrated by the diagram.

1.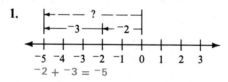

$${}^-2 + {}^-3 = {}^-5$$

2.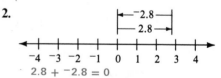

$$2.8 + {}^-2.8 = 0$$

3.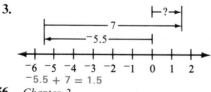

$${}^-5.5 + 7 = 1.5$$

4.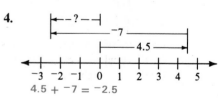

$$4.5 + {}^-7 = {}^-2.5$$

Without computing the exact sum, state whether the sum is positive, negative, or 0.

5. $-3.4 + {}^-2.6$
Negative

6. $25.7 + {}^-8.6 + {}^-25.7$
Negative

7. $2.37 + {}^-9.99$
Negative

8. ${}^-6.8 + 11.5$
Positive

Additional A Exercises
Find the sum.

1. $13 + {}^-9$ 4
2. ${}^-11 + {}^-17$ ${}^-28$
3. ${}^-4 + 3$ ${}^-1$
4. ${}^-15.2 + 3.8$ ${}^-11.4$
5. $6.7 + {}^-4.9$ 1.8
6. $4 + {}^-5.1 + {}^-3.2$ ${}^-4.3$

Written Exercises

Find the sum by using arrows on a number line. Check students' graphs.

A 1. ${}^-3 + {}^-8$ 2. $10.7 + {}^-10.7$ 3. ${}^-12.5 + 22$ 4. $2.9 + {}^-6.9$

Find the sum.

5. ${}^-2 + {}^-17$ ${}^-19$ 6. ${}^-8 + {}^-9$ ${}^-17$ 7. $8.3 + {}^-21.3$ ${}^-13$ 8. ${}^-4.6 + 38.6$ 34

9. ${}^-0.1 + {}^-0.2$ ${}^-0.3$ 10. ${}^-1.82 + {}^-3.68$ ${}^-5.5$ 11. $16.5 + {}^-16.5$ 0   12. ${}^-8.7 + 3.4$ ${}^-5.3$

13. $16.9 + {}^-0.7$ 16.2   14. ${}^-51.3 + 51.3$ 0   15. $12.37 + {}^-8.2$ 4.17   16. ${}^-85 + {}^-41$ ${}^-126$

17. $81.9 + {}^-81.9$ 0   18. $32.8 + {}^-36$ ${}^-3.2$ 19. $0 + {}^-0.12$ ${}^-0.12$ 20. ${}^-7.9 + 0$ ${}^-7.9$

21. ${}^-4.2 + {}^-6.5 + 17$ 6.3   22. $7.1 + {}^-9 + 2.3$ 0.4   23. $5 + {}^-16.9 + 1.1$ ${}^-10.8$

24. ${}^-8.6 + {}^-17.1 + {}^-4.3$ ${}^-30$ 25. ${}^-3.3 + {}^-7.25 + 3.3$ ${}^-7.25$ 26. $0.98 + {}^-13.4 + {}^-0.98$ ${}^-13.4$

What value of the variable makes the statement true?

27. ${}^-8 + x = 4$ 12   28. $x + 4 = {}^-9$ ${}^-13$ 29. ${}^-41 + x = {}^-53$ ${}^-12$

30. ${}^-19 + x = 0$ 19   31. $18.5 + x = 0$ ${}^-18.5$ 32. ${}^-6 + x = {}^-1$ 5

B 33. ${}^-4.3 + x = {}^-6.7$ ${}^-2.4$ 34. $x + {}^-5.6 = {}^-37$ ${}^-31.4$ 35. $x + 18.6 = {}^-1.2$ ${}^-19.8$

36. ${}^-0.66 + x = 0.10$ 0.76   37. $12.9 + x = {}^-13$ ${}^-25.9$ 38. $x + 20.2 = {}^-5.1$ ${}^-25.3$

Replace ? with =, >, or < to make a true statement.

39. $({}^-25.3 + {}^-8.8)$? $({}^-12.4 + {}^-19.7)$ $<$ 40. $(6.24 + {}^-15.9)$? $({}^-6.24 + 15.9)$ $<$

41. $({}^-34.9 + 27.5)$? $(9.7 + {}^-18.4)$ $>$ 42. $(14.4 + {}^-18.6)$? $({}^-3.2 + {}^-0.98)$ $<$

C 43. a. $|{}^-3 + {}^-19|$? $|{}^-3| + |{}^-19|$ $=$ b. $|{}^-4.6 + 4.6|$? $|{}^-4.6| + |4.6|$ $<$

c. $|{}^-8.7 + 12.6|$? $|{}^-8.7| + |12.6|$ $<$ d. $|{}^-18.6 + 4.9|$? $|{}^-18.6| + |4.9|$ $<$

e. $|53.5 + 3.7|$? $|53.5| + |3.7|$ $=$ f. $|{}^-4 + 13.75|$? $|{}^-4| + |13.75|$ $<$

g. On the basis of your answers to parts (a)–(f), write a general rule
for $|x + y|$? $|x| + |y|$ that holds for all numbers x and y.
Explain why this rule is true. $|x + y| \le |x| + |y|$

Positive and Negative Numbers **57**

Suggested Assignments

Core
  57/1–37 odd
  58/Prob. 1–3

Enriched
  57/14–42 even; 43
  58/Prob. 3–5

Supplementary Materials

Practice Masters, p. 8

Problems

Solve Problems 1–3 by first expressing the given data as a sum of positive and negative numbers. Then, compute the sum of the numbers and answer the questions.

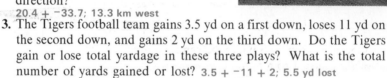

A 1. The temperature in Lynn at 7:00 A.M. was ⁻7°C. By 12:00 noon, the temperature had increased by 13°C, but it then decreased by 3°C between noon and 5:00 P.M. What was the temperature reading at 5:00 P.M.?
  ⁻7 + 13 + ⁻3; 3°C

  2. From the Andersons' farm, Bonnie drove 20.4 km due east to Fairvale. From Fairvale, she drove 33.7 km due west to Ward City. How far was she then from the farm and in what direction?
  20.4 + ⁻33.7; 13.3 km west

  3. The Tigers football team gains 3.5 yd on a first down, loses 11 yd on the second down, and gains 2 yd on the third down. Do the Tigers gain or lose total yardage in these three plays? What is the total number of yards gained or lost? 3.5 + ⁻11 + 2; 5.5 yd lost

B 4. For a summer job, Tom plans to clean the Wilsons' house. He estimates that each week he will spend $1.25 and $3.80 on cleaning supplies. How much should he charge the Wilsons if he wishes to make a profit of $6.50 each week? 1.25 + 3.80 + 6.50; $11.55

  5. Carl purchased stock in the Dependable Equipment Company. The price per share of the stock fell by $4.30 in the first month, rose by $2.50 in the second month, and rose by $2.60 in the third month. Carl sold the stock for $22.00 per share at the end of the third month. Did he gain or lose money? ⁻4.30 + 2.50 + 2.60; gain

Review Exercises

Evaluate the expression when $s = 2.7$ and $t = 8.4$.

1. $(25 - s)7$ 156.1

2. $102 \div (t + 12)$ 5

3. $11(7s - 13)$ 64.9

4. $(t + 6 - 4.4)t$ 84

5. $(s + 4)(s + 4)$ 44.89

6. $10st \div (t - 4.2)$ 54

7. $st \div 2s$ 4.2

8. $(s + t) \div (t + 13.8)$ 0.5

9. $(t - s)(5t + 8)$ 285

58 *Chapter 2*

2-4 Subtracting Positive and Negative Numbers

You know that $7.5 - 3 = 4.5$. In the preceding lesson, you learned that $7.5 + {}^-3 = 4.5$. Thus, $7.5 - 3 = 7.5 + {}^-3$. This example suggests the following general rule.

Rule

For any numbers a and b,

$$a - b = a + \text{(the opposite of } b)$$

or

$$a - b = a + (-b)$$

Note the lowered position of the minus sign in the expression $(-b)$, above. We use an *unraised* minus sign to mean *the opposite of*. For example,

$-3 = {}^-3$, read *the opposite of three equals negative three*

$-({}^-5) = 5$, read *the opposite of negative five equals five*

Because the numerals -3 and ${}^-3$ name the same number, one may be used in place of the other. From now on, we will use an unraised minus sign to denote subtraction, a negative number, and the opposite of a number.

EXAMPLE 1 Find the difference.

 a. $5 - 13$ b. $12.4 - (-8)$ c. $-10.9 - (-3.4)$

Solution

 a. $5 - 13 = 5 + (-13) = -8$

 b. $12.4 - (-8) = 12.4 + 8 = 20.4$

 c. $-10.9 - (-3.4) = -10.9 + 3.4 = -7.5$

It is important to read a variable expression such as $-n$ as *the opposite of n* because n may denote a negative number, a positive number, or 0.

EXAMPLE 2 Evaluate the expression when $m = -5.2$.

 a. $m - 14$ b. $-m - 14$

Solution

 a. $m - 14 = -5.2 - 14 = -5.2 + (-14) = -19.2$

 b. $-m - 14 = -(-5.2) - 14 = 5.2 - 14 = 5.2 + (-14) = -8.8$

Positive and Negative Numbers **59**

Teaching Suggestions p. 45c

Related Activities p. 45c

Reading Mathematics

Students will learn the meaning of the following mathematical terms in this lesson: *opposite, difference*.

Chalkboard Examples

Find the difference.

1. $5 - (-2)$ **7**

2. $-5 - 2$ **−7**

3. $-5 - (-2)$ **−3**

4. $7.8 - 9.3$ **−1.5**

5. $-12 - 4.7$ **−16.7**

6. $0 - 9.1$ **−9.1**

7. $(-1.5 - 7.1) - (-11.4)$ **2.8**

8. $5 - [4.6 - (-1.1)]$ **−0.7**

Reading Mathematics: *Using Examples*

The worked-out examples in each lesson show you how the general statements in the lesson can be applied to specific situations. If you need help as you work on the exercises, look back at the examples for models to follow or for ideas on how to begin your solutions.

Class Exercises

Complete.

1. $6 - 12 = 6 + \underline{\ ?\ }$ **-12**   **2.** $-10 - 8 = -10 + \underline{\ ?\ }$ **-8**

3. $6.7 - (-1.5) = 6.7 + \underline{\ ?\ }$ **1.5**   **4.** $-26.01 - (-8.2) = -26.01 + \underline{\ ?\ }$
8.2

Without computing the exact difference, state whether the difference is positive, negative, or 0.

5. $-4.2 - 4.2$
Negative

6. $4.2 - (-4.2)$
Positive

7. $4.2 - 4.2$
0

8. $-4.2 - (-4.2)$
0

Find the difference.

9. $3 - (-6)$ **9**   **10.** $-2 - (-3.5)$ **1.5**   **11.** $-1.8 - 5.8$ **-7.6** **12.** $2.25 - 4$ **-1.75**

Written Exercises

Write the difference as a sum.

A **1.** $7 - 19$
$7 + (-19)$

2. $-21 - 42$
$-21 + (-42)$

3. $6.2 - (-8.3)$
$6.2 + 8.3$

4. $-2.9 - (-11.6)$
$-2.9 + 11.6$

5–8. Find each difference in Exercises 1–4 above.
5. -12 **6.** -63 **7.** 14.5   **8.** 8.7

Find the difference.

9. $4 - 10$ **-6**   **10.** $25 - 34$ **-9**   **11.** $-3 - 24$ **-27**   **12.** $-12 - 5$ **-17**

13. $9 - (-33)$ **42**   **14.** $14 - (-46)$ **60**   **15.** $-2 - (-17)$ **15**   **16.** $-6 - (-5)$ **-1**

17. $0 - 43$ **-43**   **18.** $0 - 101$ **-101**   **19.** $0 - (-20)$ **20**   **20.** $0 - (-14)$ **14**

21. $44 - 0$ **44**   **22.** $-16 - 0$ **-16**   **23.** $6.9 - 8$ **-1.1**   **24.** $12 - 20.5$ **-8.5**

25. $4.3 - 2.1$ **2.2**   **26.** $23.4 - 6.8$ **16.6**   **27.** $-16.1 - 8.5$
-24.6

28. $-0.4 - 8.9$
-9.3

29. $-19 - 5.6$
-24.6

30. $-41.1 - 2.9$ **-44** **31.** $0 - (-3.37)$ **3.37** **32.** $0 - 12.8$ **-12.8**

33. $12.4 - (-12.4)$ **24.8**   **34.** $-18.1 - (-25)$ **6.9**   **35.** $-52.9 - (-11.6)$
-41.3

36. $(6 - 9.7) - 8.8$ **-12.5** **37.** $(-2.5 - 8.1) - (-12.4)$ **1.8** **38.** $(0 - 8.3) - (-24.1)$
15.8

60   *Chapter 2*

Evaluate the expression when $a = -4.5$ and $b = -6.2$.

39. $-a$ 4.5   **40.** $-b$ 6.2   **41.** $-|b|$ −6.2   **42.** $-|a|$ −4.5

43. $a - b$ 1.7   **44.** $b - a$ −1.7   **45.** $-a - b$ 10.7   **46.** $-b - a$ 10.7

47. $a - (-b)$ −10.7   **48.** $b - (-a)$ −10.7   **49.** $-b - (-a)$ 1.7   **50.** $-a - (-b)$ −1.7

What value of the variable makes the statement true?

B **51.** $2 - d = -6$ 8   **52.** $d - 5 = -13$ −8   **53.** $-3 - d = -11$ 8

54. $8 - d = 13$ −5   **55.** $-7 - d = 12$ −19   **56.** $d - (-6) = -7$ −13

57. $-d - 4 = 14$ −18   **58.** $-d - 5 = -9$ 4   **59.** $7 - (-d) = 14$ 7

60. $d - (-8) = 17$ 9   **61.** $-8 - (-d) = -16$ −8   **62.** $-4 - (-d) = 10$ 14

C **63.** Replace __?__ with $=$, $>$, or $<$ to make a true statement.
   a. $|13.6 - 8.9|$ __?__ $|13.6| - |8.9| =$ **b.** $|-8.9 - (-13.6)|$ __?__ $|-8.9| - |-13.6|$ >
   c. $|8.9 - 13.6|$ __?__ $|8.9| - |13.6|$ >   **d.** $|-8.9 - 13.6|$ __?__ $|-8.9| - |13.6|$ >
   e. Based on your answers to parts (a)–(d), write a general rule for
   $|x - y|$ __?__ $|x| - |y|$, where x and y are any decimal numbers.
   $$|x - y| \geq |x| - |y|$$

Problems

Solve Problems 1–7 by first expressing the given data as a difference of positive and negative numbers. Then, compute the difference of the numbers and answer the question.

A **1.** On a winter day, the temperature dropped from $-3°C$ to $-11°C$. Find the change in temperature. −3 − (−11); 8°C

2. Find the difference in the ages of two people if one was born in 27 B.C. and the other was born in 16 A.D. 16 − (−27); 43 yrs

3. The elevation of the highest point in a region is 1226 m above sea level. If the difference between the highest point and lowest point in the region is 1455 m, find the elevation of the lowest point.
1226 − 1455; −229 m

4. Two stages of a rocket burn for a total of 114.5 s. If the first stage burns for 86.8 s, how long does the second stage burn?
114.5 − 86.8; 27.7 s

5. Jan Miller purchased 140 shares of stock in the ABC Company at a price of $18.75 per share. During the next three days, the value declined by $1.00, $1.75, and $1.50. What was the value of a share of ABC stock at the end of three days?
18.75 − 1 − 1.75 − 1.5; $14.50

Positive and Negative Numbers **61**

Suggested Assignments

Core
Day 1: 60/1–37 odd
61/39–63 odd
61/Prob. 1–5
Day 2: 62/Prob. 6–9
62/Self-Test A

Enriched
60/9–37 odd
61/51–63 odd; Prob. 1–5
62/Prob. 6–9; Self-Test A

Supplementary Materials

Practice Masters, p. 8
Test 2A, pp. 9–10

1. 2 $\overset{<}{\underline{\ ?\ }}$ 3

2. $^-6$ $\overset{<}{\underline{\ ?\ }}$ 0

3. $^-5$ $\overset{<}{\underline{\ ?\ }}$ 4

4. $|^-6|$ $\overset{=}{\underline{\ ?\ }}$ 6

5. $|5|$ $\overset{>}{\underline{\ ?\ }}$ $^-5$

6. $|^-3|$ $\overset{>}{\underline{\ ?\ }}$ $^-3$

Write the numbers in order from least to greatest.

7. 0, 5.6, $^-3.8$, $^-12$, 14
   $^-12$, $^-3.8$, 0, 5.6, 14

8. $^-4.7$, $^-47$, $^-0.47$, $^-4.77$
   $^-47$, $^-4.77$, $^-4.7$, $^-0.47$

9. $^-8.3$, 8.3, $^-8$, 0
   $^-8.3$, $^-8$, 0, 8.3

10. 0.12, 1.2, $^-2.1$, $^-4.2$
    $^-4.2$, $^-2.1$, 0.12, 1.2

Find the sum or difference.

11. $^-16.2 + 9$ $^-7.2$

12. $^-8.3 + ^-5.7$ $^-14$

13. $14.9 + ^-0.83$ 14.07

14. $0 + ^-4.5$ $^-4.5$

15. $^-12.3 + 4.6 + 7.4$ $^-0.3$

(continued on page 63)

6. A parachutist jumped from an airplane flying at an altitude of 1100 m, dropped 200 m in the first 25 s, and then dropped 350 m in the next 35 s. What was the altitude of the parachutist 60 s after jumping?
   $1100 - 200 - 350;$ 550 m

7. In Summit City, 78 cm of snow fell on Sunday. The snow melted approximately 5.8 cm on Monday, approximately 7.5 cm on Tuesday, and approximately 12 cm on Wednesday. Approximately how much snow remained?
   $78 - 5.8 - 7.5 - 12;$ 52.7 cm

B 8. Donna receives an allowance every 2 weeks that includes $20 for school lunches. During the past 4 weeks, she spent $7.50, $8.25, $5.25, and $8.75 on lunches. How much did Donna have left from the money allowed for lunches for the 4 weeks?
   $40 - 7.50 - 8.25 - 5.25 - 8.75;$ $10.25

9. Eric Chung had $65.10 in his checking account on June 1. He wrote two checks in June, one for $42.99. Eric forgot to write down the amount of the other check. At the end of the month, he received a notice that his account was overdrawn by $22.11. What was the amount of Eric's second check? $65.10 - 42.99 + 22.11;$ $44.22

Self-Test A

Replace __?__ with $=$, $>$, or $<$ to make a true statement.

1. 4 __?__ 7 $<$ 2. 2 __?__ 1 $>$ 3. $^-8$ __?__ 9 $<$ 4. $|^-7|$ __?__ 7 $=$ 5. $|0|$ __?__ 0 $=$ [2-1]

Write the numbers in order from least to greatest.

6. 0, 5.4, $^-4.52$, $^-0.25$, $^-54$ 7. $^-3.79$, 37, $^-7.3$, $^-0.37$, $^-0.09$ [2-2]
   $^-54$, $^-4.52$, $^-0.25$, 0, 5.4 $^-7.3$, $^-3.79$, $^-0.37$, $^-0.09$, 37

Find the sum or difference.

8. $^-9.3 + 42.3$ 33   9. $17.8 + ^-17.8$ 0   10. $8.76 + ^-10.2$ $_{-1.44}$ [2-3]

11. $8 - (-27)$ 35   12. $-5.1 - (-5.1)$ 0   13. $0 - 36$ $_{-36}$ [2-4]

Evaluate the expression when $a = -6.4$ and $b = -5.2$.

14. $-b - a$ 11.6   15. $a - (-b)$ $_{-11.6}$ 16. $b - |a|$ $_{-11.6}$

Self-Test answers and Extra Practice are at the back of the book.

62 *Chapter 2*

Teaching Suggestions p. 45d

Related Activities p. 45d

2-5 Multiplying Positive and Negative Numbers

Reading Mathematics

Students will learn the meaning of the following mathematical terms in this lesson: *product, factor.*

To find a product such as $5(-2)$, we can think of the product as the sum of five identical addends.

$$5(-2) = -2 + (-2) + (-2) + (-2) + (-2)$$

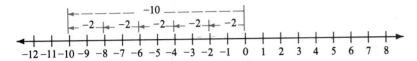

The diagram shows that $-2 + (-2) + (-2) + (-2) + (-2) = -10$. Thus $5(-2) = -10$.

To find the product $-7(2)$, we may use the commutative property of multiplication to write

$$-7(2) = 2(-7).$$

We know that $2(-7) = -7 + (-7) = -14$, so $-7(2) = -14$.

Notice that in the two examples above, the product is the opposite of the product of the absolute values of the numbers. The examples suggest the following rule.

> ### Rule
> The product of a positive number and a negative number is a negative number.

We may use other properties that we have learned for addition and multiplication of positive decimals to determine what a product of negative numbers, such as $-5(-3)$, must be. The multiplication property of zero states that the product of any number and 0 is 0. Thus,

$$-5(0) = 0.$$

Since we know that $3 + (-3) = 0$, we may write

$$-5[3 + (-3)] = 0.$$

By the distributive property, we may write the following.

$$-5(3) + (-5)(-3) = 0$$
$$-15 + (-5)(-3) = 0$$

But we know that $-15 + 15 = 0$, so $-5(-3)$ must equal 15.

Positive and Negative Numbers **63**

Chalkboard Examples

Multiply.

1. 7(−7) **−49**

2. −1.6(8) **−12.8**

3. 1(−8)(2)(−4) **64**

4. −6(2.3)(−1.7) **23.46**

5. 100(−2.33) **−233**

6. 72(−7.2)(0) **0**

Notice that the product of $-5(-3)$ is the product of the absolute values of the factors. The example suggests the following rule.

> ### Rule
> The product of two negative numbers is a positive number.

EXAMPLE 1 Find the product.

a. $-4.5(8.6)$ b. $5.32(-1)$ c. $-1(-14.7)$ d. $-9.2(-3.1)$

Solution

a. One number is negative and one number is positive, so the product is negative.
$$-4.5(8.6) = -38.7$$

b. One number is positive and one number is negative, so the product is negative.
$$5.32(-1) = -5.32$$

c. Both numbers are negative, so the product is positive.
$$-1(-14.7) = 14.7$$

d. Both numbers are negative, so the product is positive.
$$-9.2(-3.1) = 28.52$$

Notice in Example 1, parts (b) and (c), that when one of the factors is -1, the product is the opposite of the other factor.

> ### Rule
> The product of -1 and any number equals the opposite of that number.

We may use the rules for products of positive and negative numbers to multiply any number of positive and negative numbers.

EXAMPLE 2 Find the product.

a. $-3.7(2.5)(-4.8)$ b. $-11.1(-7)(6.5)(-3.2)$

Solution

a. $-3.7(2.5)(-4.8) = [-3.7(2.5)](-4.8) = (-9.25)(-4.8) = 44.4$

b. $-11.1(-7)(6.5)(-3.2) = [-11.1(-7)][(6.5)(-3.2)]$
$$= 77.7(-20.8) = -1616.16$$

64   Chapter 2

Example 2, on the preceding page, illustrates the following rules.

> ### Rules
>
> For a product with no zero factors:
> 1. if the number of negative factors is odd, the product is negative.
> 2. if the number of negative factors is even, the product is positive.

Class Exercises

Without computing the exact product, state whether the product is positive, negative, or 0.

1. $-3(-4.2)$
positive

2. $2.1(-0.8)$
negative

3. $-5(1.6)(-7)$
positive

4. $-4.5(3.7)(0)$
zero

Find the product.

5. $3(-16)$ -48

6. $-7(-12)$ 84

7. $13(-1)(-5)$ 65

8. $-2(-8)(-5)(0)$ 0

Written Exercises

Find the product.

A

1. $-3(-9)$ 27

2. $4(-6)$ -24

3. $-8(7)$ -56

4. $-7(-11)$ 77

5. $2(-8)(-6)$ 96

6. $-3(5)(-6)$ 90

7. $-2(0)(-12)$ 0

8. $14(-1)(0)$ 0

9. $-1.5(8)$ -12

10. $0.6(-9)$ -5.4

11. $-3.4(-1.5)$ 5.1

12. $-0.4(-0.7)$ 0.28

13. $2.9(-1)$ -2.9

14. $-1(7.84)$ -7.84

15. $-8.8(-1.75)$ 15.4

16. $-1.11(70)$ -77.7

17. $-20(0.25)$ -5

18. $12(-1.2)$ -14.4

19. $-15(-30.6)$ 459

20. $0.24(-100)$ -24

21. $3.9(-17.1)$
-66.69

22. $-5.6(80.1)$
-448.56

23. $-13.7(0)$ 0

24. $16.7(0)$ 0

25. $-1.8(-1.9)$
3.42

26. $-0.125(-8.1)$
1.0125

27. $-5.4(20.6)$
-111.24

28. $-8.9(30.9)$
-275.01

29. $10.1(3.75)$
37.875

30. $4.25(20.4)$
86.7

31. $-3.72(-16.5)$
61.38

32. $0.78(-42)$
-32.76

33. $-1.7(-0.2)(-3.1)$
-1.054

34. $-9(-2.7)(-80)$
-1944

35. $3.25(-17)(0)$ 0

36. $-1.21(0)(-1.1)$
0

37. $9.4(-3.5)(-11)$
361.9

38. $18(-5.75)(6.2)$
-641.7

Positive and Negative Numbers **65**

Additional A Exercises

Find the product.

1. $17.9(-3.4)$ -60.86

2. $-1.5(4.5)$ -6.75

3. $-2.8(-2.8)$ 7.84

4. $3(0.26)$ 0.78

5. $4.7(-1.1)(-8.8)$
45.496

6. $7.9(9.9)(0)(-1.6)$ 0

Suggested Assignments

Core
65/10–38 even
66/40–50 even
66/Rev. 3–6

Enriched
65/29–38
66/39–55 odd
66/Calculator Key-In
66/Challenge

Supplementary Materials

Practice Masters, p. 9
Computer Activities 3 and 4

Simplify the expression.

B **39.** $(-1.2 - 6.5)(-1.2 + 6.5)$ -40.81 **40.** $18 + 3 - (-12 - 7)$ 40

41. $(-7)(2.4)(0)(-9.3)(-1) + (-8.2)$ -8.2 **42.** $(14.4 - 200)(14.4 + 200)$ $-39,792.64$

43. $-4[27 - (-9)] + (-4)(-2 - 9)$ -100 **44.** $(-20 + 12)7 + (-2 + 20)7$ 70

Find the integer n that will make the statement true.

45. $-3(n) = 6$ -2 **46.** $4(n) = -28$ -7 **47.** $-9(-n) = -18$ -2

48. $3(n) = 6(-3)$ -6 **49.** $-n(-7) = -14(0)$ 0 **50.** $-5(n) = 25(2)$ -10

C **51.** $-3(-1.5)(-n) = -18(-1)(-0.5)$ 2 **52.** $-1.2(30)(-n) = -9(-0.4)(-100)$ -10

53. $-1.5(n)(-0.8) = -12(-1.5)(-2)$ -30 **54.** $-0.6(-n)(-1.9) = -18(-1.3)(0)$ 0

55. $n(-3.7 + 61.4) = 0$ 0 **56.** $-n(-1.1 - 30.6) = 0$ 0

Review Exercises

Use the inverse operation to solve for the variable.

1. $f + 27 = 83$ 56 **2.** $n - 13 = 54$ 67 **3.** $g + 364 = 518$ 154 **4.** $w - 216 = 435$ 651

5. $6c = 78$ 13 **6.** $x \div 17 = 6$ 102 **7.** $14j = 364$ 26 **8.** $y \div 37 = 142$ 5254

Calculator Key-In

Use your calculator to solve this problem: One day you tell a secret to a friend. The next day your friend tells your secret to two other friends. On the third day, each of the friends who was told your secret the day before tells it to two other friends. If this pattern continues from day to day, how many people will be told your secret on the fourteenth day?

8192

Challenge

Using the first nine counting numbers, fill in the boxes so you get the same sum when you add vertically, horizontally, or diagonally. Can you do this with any nine consecutive counting numbers? yes

66 *Chapter 2*

2-6 Dividing Positive and Negative Numbers

Teaching Suggestions p. 45e

Related Activities p. 45e

Reading Mathematics

Students will learn the meaning of the following mathematical term in this lesson: *quotient*.

Recall that multiplication and division are inverse operations for positive numbers. For example, because we know that $4 \times 8 = 32$, we also know that $8 = 32 \div 4$. We can use the relationship between multiplication and division to find quotients of positive and negative numbers. Consider the following examples.

$$4 \times (-8) = -32 \qquad -8 = -32 \div 4$$
$$-4 \times 8 = -32 \qquad 8 = -32 \div -4$$
$$-4 \times (-8) = 32 \qquad -8 = 32 \div -4$$

Notice that in the examples above, the quotient of two numbers with differing signs is the opposite of the quotient of the absolute values of the numbers. The quotient of two numbers with the same sign is the quotient of the absolute values of the numbers.

The examples suggest the following rules for dividing positive and negative numbers.

Chalkboard Examples

Find the quotient.

1. $7 \div 7$ **1**

2. $24 \div (-12)$ **−2**

3. $-132 \div 3$ **−44**

4. $-13.32 \div 0.9$ **−14.8**

5. $-4.42 \div (-0.26)$ **17**

6. $1108.89 \div (-33.3)$
−33.3

Rules

The quotient of two positive or two negative numbers is positive.

The quotient of a positive number and a negative number is negative.

By the multiplication property of zero, we know that $-4 \times 0 = 0$ and thus $0 = 0 \div (-4)$. Remember that we cannot divide by 0.

EXAMPLE Find the quotient.
   a. $-3.06 \div 0.9$ **b.** $36.8 \div (-2.3)$ **c.** $-4.046 \div (-1.7)$

Solution **a.** Since -3.06 is negative and 0.9 is positive, the quotient will be negative.
$$-3.06 \div 0.9 = -3.4$$

b. Since 36.8 is positive and -2.3 is negative, the quotient will be negative.
$$36.8 \div -2.3 = -16$$

c. Since -4.046 and -1.7 are both negative, the quotient will be positive.
$$-4.046 \div (-1.7) = 2.38$$

Positive and Negative Numbers **67**

Additional A Exercises

Find the quotient.

1. $0 \div 32$ 0

2. $0.92 \div (-0.368)$ -2.5

3. $-22.4 \div (-5.6)$ 4

4. $-7.54 \div 5.8$ -1.3

5. $2.3 \div (-100)$ -0.023

6. $-10 \div 2.5$ -4

Evaluate the expression when $a = -3$ and $b = 1.5$.

7. $a \div b$ -2

8. $b \div a$ -0.5

9. $-2a \div (-b)$ -4

10. $b \div (-2a)$ -0.25

Class Exercises

Without computing the exact quotient, state whether the quotient is positive, negative, or 0.

1. $-3.6 \div (-40)$
positive

2. $-0.216 \div 400$
negative

3. $0 \div (-17.5)$
0

4. $850 \div (-0.05)$
negative

Find the quotient.

5. $-28 \div 7$ -4

6. $33 \div (-1)$ -33

7. $0 \div -50$ 0

8. $-51 \div (-3)$ 17

9. $-22 \div 4$ -5.5

10. $-75 \div 15$ -5

Written Exercises

Find the quotient.

A

1. $-18 \div 3$ -6

2. $25 \div (-5)$ -5

3. $-21 \div (-7)$ 3

4. $-54 \div (-18)$ 3

5. $0 \div (-7)$ 0

6. $0 \div (-24)$ 0

7. $144 \div (-12)$ -12

8. $-100 \div 25$ -4

9. $22.5 \div (-3)$ -7.5

10. $-42 \div 4$ -10.5

11. $-3.6 \div (-1)$ 3.6

12. $-1.01 \div (-1)$ 1.01

13. $-1.75 \div 0.05$ -35

14. $-69.3 \div 3.3$ -21

15. $-32.86 \div 6.2$ -5.3

16. $-17.05 \div (-1.1)$ 15.5

17. $-0.48 \div (-0.06)$ 8

18. $0.06 \div (-0.3)$ -0.2

19. $0 \div (-14.7)$ 0

20. $0 \div (-0.25)$ 0

21. $-0.9 \div 1.8$ -0.5

22. $-0.042 \div (-0.6)$ 0.07

23. $-38 \div 4$ -9.5

24. $-45 \div (-6)$ 7.5

25. $9.9 \div (-4.5)$ -2.2

26. $46.2 \div (-6)$ -7.7

27. $-13.8 \div (-1)$ 13.8

28. $0.003 \div (-1)$ -0.003

29. $-9.27 \div (-60)$ 0.1545

30. $0.25 \div (-40)$ -0.00625

31. $13.23 \div (-2.1)$ -6.3

32. $-2.6 \div 0.52$ -5

33. $-14.57 \div (-3.1)$ 4.7

34. $-0.53 \div (-0.1)$ 5.3

35. $-18.5 \div 10$ -1.85

36. $3.84 \div (-9.6)$ -0.4

Evaluate the expression when $a = -8$ and $b = 2.5$.

37. $a \div b$ -3.2

38. $b \div a$ -0.3125

39. $2b \div (-a)$ 0.625

40. $-3a \div b$ 9.6

41. $(a - b) \div b$ -4.2

42. $2ab \div a$ 5

43. $-9a \div 3ab$ -1.2

44. $-5b \div (-2a)$ -0.78125

Use inverse operations to solve for the variable.

B

45. $-3n = 6$ -2

46. $d \div 5 = -7$ -35

47. $b \div (-8) = 9$ -72

48. $-15x = -30$ 2

49. $-2y - 8 = 8$ -8

50. $4c + 12 = -36$ -12

68 *Chapter 2*

C **51.** Explain why $\left|\dfrac{x}{y}\right| = \dfrac{|x|}{|y|}$ for all decimal numbers for which it is possi-

ble to find the quotient $\dfrac{x}{y}$. $|x|$ and $|y|$ are both positive.
Therefore, their quotient is positive.

52. Replace __?__ with $=$, $>$, or $<$ to make a true statement.

a. $0.10 \underline{?} 2.5$ $<$ **b.** $-0.21 \underline{?} 0$ $<$ **c.** $-3.6 \underline{?} -1.5$ $<$

$\dfrac{0.10}{0.5} \underline{?} \dfrac{2.5}{0.5}$ $<$ $\dfrac{-0.21}{70} \underline{?} \dfrac{0}{70}$ $<$ $\dfrac{-3.6}{3} \underline{?} \dfrac{-1.5}{3}$ $>$

$\dfrac{0.10}{-0.5} \underline{?} \dfrac{2.5}{-0.5}$ $>$ $\dfrac{-0.21}{-70} \underline{?} \dfrac{0}{-70}$ $>$ $\dfrac{-3.6}{-3} \underline{?} \dfrac{-1.5}{-3}$

Use your answers to parts (a)–(c) to answer parts (d) and (e).

d. If $x < y$ and if k is a positive number, then $\dfrac{x}{k} \underline{?} \dfrac{y}{k}$. $<$

e. If $x < y$ and if j is a negative number, then $\dfrac{x}{j} \underline{?} \dfrac{y}{j}$. $>$

Write examples similar to those in parts (a)–(c) to answer parts (f) and (g). Check students' examples.

f. If $x > y$ and if k is a positive number, then $\dfrac{x}{k} \underline{?} \dfrac{y}{k}$. $>$

g. If $x > y$ and if j is a negative number, then $\dfrac{x}{j} \underline{?} \dfrac{y}{j}$. $<$

Suggested Assignments

Core
68/1–29 odd; 41–49 odd
69/Rev. 1–5
69/Calculator Key-In

Enriched
68/25–36; 38–50 even
69/52; Rev. 1–8
69/Calculator Key-In

Supplementary Materials

Practice Masters, p. 9

Review Exercises

Evaluate the expression when $x = 3$, $y = 7$, and $z = 4$.

1. y^2 49   **2.** $5x^2$ 45   **3.** $(7z)^2$ 784   **4.** z^0 1   **5.** $7z^2$ 112

6. $(6x)^2$ 324   **7.** $(yz)^0$ 1   **8.** xy^0 3   **9.** $z^3 - x^3$ 37   **10.** $8x^3y$ 1512

$(6 \cdot 3)^2 = 324$

■■■ **Calculator Key-In**

Does your calculator have a change-sign key? The key may look like this: $\boxed{+/-}$. If you press this key after entering a number or doing a calculation, the sign of the number displayed on your calculator will change. For example, if you enter 116 $\boxed{+/-}$, your calculator will change 116 to -116.

Solve with a calculator that has a change-sign key, if possible.

1. $20.7 + (-19.6)$ 1.1   **2.** $-55.59 + 438.2$ 382.61   **3.** $-0.86 + (-27.341)$ -28.201

4. $-426.38 - (-25.004)$ -401.376 **5.** $-83.5(-61.09)$ 5101.015   **6.** $6.8(-4.17)(-1.61)$ 45.65316

Positive and Negative Numbers **69**

Reading Mathematics

Students may need a little help reading expressions like a^m and a^{m+n}. Tell students that a^m is read "a to the mth power." Then ask them to read the rule on page 70 aloud.

2-7 Using Positive Exponents

In Chapter 1, exponents were introduced. Recall that in the expression 3^5 (called a *power*), 3 is called the *base* and 5 is called the *exponent*.

If a product contains powers of the same base, the product may be written as a single power of that base. For example, $13^2 \times 13^3$ can be written as a single power of 13.

$$13^2 \times 13^3 = (13 \times 13) \times (13 \times 13 \times 13)$$
$$= 13 \times 13 \times 13 \times 13 \times 13$$
$$= 13^5$$

Notice that the exponent in the product is the sum of the exponents in the factors, that is, $2 + 3 = 5$.

In general,

Rule

For every number a ($a \neq 0$) and all whole numbers m and n,

$$a^m \times a^n = a^{m+n}$$

Notice that the bases must be the same.

EXAMPLE 1 Write $15^3 \times 15^4$ as a single power of 15.

Solution $15^3 \times 15^4 = 15^{3+4} = 15^7$

EXAMPLE 2 Evaluate the expression if $n = 3$.

a. n^2 **b.** $4n^2$ **c.** $(4n)^2$ **d.** $n^2 \times n^2$

Solution Replace n with 3 in each expression and simplify.

a. $n^2 = 3^2 = 3 \times 3 = 9$

b. $4n^2 = 4(3^2) = 4 \times 9 = 36$

c. $(4n)^2 = (4 \times 3)^2 = 12^2 = 12 \times 12 = 144$

d. $n^2 \times n^2 = n^{2+2} = n^4 = 3^4 = 3 \times 3 \times 3 \times 3 = 81$

70 Chapter 2

Chalkboard Examples

Simplify.

1. 3^3 27

2. 2^4 16

3. $3^2 \times 2^4$ 144

4. $3^2 + 2^4$ 25

5. Write $9^4 \times 9^3$ as a single power of 9. 9^7

6. Evaluate $3m^2n$ if $m = 2$ and $n = 5$. 60

Notice in parts (b) and (c) of Example 2 how grouping symbols change the values of expressions that have the same numbers.

Reading Mathematics: *Study Helps*
Look back at this lesson. Notice that the information in the blue box on page 70 summarizes important ideas from the lesson. The box gives a definition that is applied in the examples. Throughout the book, boxes are used to help you identify important definitions, rules, properties, facts, and formulas. Use them as reminders when you do the exercises and when you review the lesson.

Class Exercises

Read each expression.

1. 4^5 **2.** 9^1 **3.** 15^2 **4.** 3^7 **5.** 10^3 **6.** 2^8

Write using exponents.

7. 9 to the third power 9^3 **8.** 15 cubed 15^3 **9.** 4 squared 4^2

10. 6 to the fifth power 6^5 **11.** 216 is the third power of 6. $216 = 6^3$

Express the number as a power of 3.

12. 9 3^2 **13.** 27 3^3 **14.** 3 3^1 **15.** 243 3^5 **16.** 1 3^0

Simplify the expression.

17. 8^2 64   **18.** 2^3 8   **19.** 1^{11} 1   **20.** 18^0 1   **21.** 83^1 83

Written Exercises

Simplify the expression.

A   **1.** 2^6 64   **2.** 5^4 625   **3.** 10^2 100   **4.** 6^3 216   **5.** 14^1 14

6. $3^2 + 5^2$ 34   **7.** $(3 \times 5)^2$ 225   **8.** $2^4 + 3^2$ 25   **9.** $(5 + 12)^0$ 1   **10.** $(5 + 12)^1$ 17

Which is greater?

11. 2^3 or 3^2 3^2 **12.** 5^2 or 2^5 2^5 **13.** 9×2 or 9^2 9^2

14. 3×10 or 10^3 10^3 **15.** $(16 \times 4)^2$ or $2 \times 16 \times 4$ $(16 \times 4)^2$ **16.** $(10 + 2)^0$ or $10 + 2$ $10 + 2$

Positive and Negative Numbers   **71**

Write as a single power of the given base.

17. $2^3 \times 2^4$ 2^7　**18.** $3^2 \times 3^5$ 3^7　**19.** 10×10^4 10^5　**20.** $5^5 \times 5^6$ 5^{11}　**21.** $n^3 \times n^8$ n^{11}

Evaluate the expression when $m = 5$, $n = 3$, and $p = 2$.

22. p^2 4　　**23.** $4m^2$ 100　　**24.** $(9n)^2$ 729　**25.** $9n^2$ 81　　**26.** n^0 1

27. $(8n)^2$ 576　**28.** np^0 3　　　**29.** $(mn)^0$ 1　　**30.** $m^3 - n^3$ 98　**31.** $5m^3n$
1875

B　**32.** $(7n)^n$ 9261　**33.** $(3m)^p$ 225　　**34.** $6^2 \times 6^n$ 7776　**35.** $(8 + m)^{n-3}$ 1　**36.** $(15^n)^{p-1}$
　　　　　　　　　　　　　　　　　　　　　　　　　　　　　　　　　3375

37. $p^n m^n$ 1000　**38.** $(7 + n)^n$ 1000　**39.** np^m 96　　**40.** $(p^m p^n) + 4$ 260　**41.** $m^p + n^n$
　　　　　　　　　　　　　　　　　　　　　　　　　　　　　　　　　　　　　　　52

42. $(m^p)^n$　　**43.** $(m - n)^p$ 4　**44.** $\dfrac{m^n}{m^p}$ 5　　**45.** $\dfrac{3p^n}{6p^m}$ $\dfrac{1}{8}$　　**46.** $\dfrac{(m-1)^{n+1}}{p}$
$15{,}625$
　　128

C　**47.** Find a value of n such that $(5 + 2)^n = 5^n + 2^n$. $n = 1$

48. Is the equation true?

　　a. $4^4 \div 4^3 = 4^1$ yes　　　　**b.** $5^3 \div 5^1 = 5^2$ yes　　　　**c.** $2^7 \div 2^4 = 2^3$ yes

　　d. Using your answers from parts (a)–(c), state a general rule to
　　describe what appears to be true for division of powers of the
　　same base. $a^x \div a^y = a^{x-y}$

Review Exercises

Solve using inverse operations.

1. $8 + x = 6$ -2　　**2.** $y + 4 = 1$ -3　　**3.** $n + 6 = 8$ 2　　**4.** $y + 10 = 6$ -4

5. $-7 + a = 5$ 12　**6.** $t + 3 = -8$ -11　**7.** $-2 + c = -1$ 1　**8.** $-13 + x = 0$
　　　　　　　　　　　　　　　　　　　　　　　　　　　　　　　　　　　　13

■■■ **Calculator Key-In**

Use a calculator to simplify the expressions.

1. $15^2 - 13^2$　and　$(15 + 13)(15 - 13)$ $56,\ 56$

2. $47^2 - 21^2$　and　$(47 + 21)(47 - 21)$ $1768,\ 1768$

3. $82^2 - 59^2$　and　$(82 + 59)(82 - 59)$ $3243,\ 3243$

4. $104^2 - 76^2$　and　$(104 + 76)(104 - 76)$ $5040,\ 5040$

Do you recognize a pattern?
Write two expressions that will result in the same pattern. $a^2 - b^2,\ (a + b)(a - b)$

72　*Chapter 2*

2-8 Negative Integers as Exponents

You know by the rule of exponents that you learned for multiplying powers of the same base that

$$10^1 \times 10^2 = 10^{1+2} = 10^3.$$

Since we want to apply the same rule to negative exponents, we must have

$$10^1 \times 10^{-1} = 10^{1+(-1)} = 10^0 = 1$$
$$10^2 \times 10^{-2} = 10^{2+(-2)} = 10^0 = 1$$

and so on. We know that

$$10^1 \times \frac{1}{10} = 10 \times 0.1 = 1 \text{ and } 10^2 \times \frac{1}{10^2} = 100 \times 0.01 = 1,$$

so 10^{-1} should equal $\frac{1}{10}$ and 10^{-2} should equal $\frac{1}{10^2}$. These examples suggest the following general rule.

> ### Rule
> For all numbers $a(a \neq 0)$, m, and n,
> $$a^{-m} = \frac{1}{a^m}$$

EXAMPLE Write the expression without exponents.
  a. 5^{-2} **b.** $(-3)^{-2}$ **c.** $(-4)^{-1}(-4)^{-2}$

Solution   **a.** $5^{-2} = \frac{1}{5^2} = \frac{1}{5 \times 5} = \frac{1}{25}$

   b. $(-3)^{-2} = \frac{1}{(-3)^2} = \frac{1}{(-3)(-3)} = \frac{1}{9}$

   c. $(-4)^{-1} \times (-4)^{-2} = (-4)^{-1+(-2)} = (-4)^{-3}$
$$= \frac{1}{(-4)^3} = \frac{1}{(-4)(-4)(-4)} = \frac{1}{-64}$$

Class Exercises

Use the rules for exponents to state the expression without exponents.

1. 3^{-4} $\frac{1}{81}$ **2.** $(-6)^{-2}$ $\frac{1}{36}$ **3.** $10^4 \times 10^{-4}$ 1   **4.** $3^5 \times 3^{-7}$ $\frac{1}{9}$ **5.** $(-2)^3(-2)^{-1}$ 4

Teaching Suggestions p. 45e

Related Activities p. 45f

Reading Mathematics

Students will learn the meaning of the following mathematical term in this lesson: *negative exponent*.

Chalkboard Examples

Write the expression without exponents.

1. 2^{-4} $\frac{1}{16}$

2. 3^{-1} $\frac{1}{3}$

3. 17^0 1

4. $(-2)^{-2}$ $\frac{1}{4}$

5. $(-1)^{-7}$ -1

6. $(-4)^{-3}$ $\frac{1}{-64}$

7. $(-5)^{-1} \times (-5)^{-2}$ $\frac{1}{-125}$

8. $8^2 \times 8^0 \times 8^{-4}$ $\frac{1}{64}$

Write the expression without exponents.

1. $(-7)^{-2}$ $\frac{1}{49}$

2. 8^{-3} $\frac{1}{512}$

3. $2^{-1} \times 2^{-1}$ $\frac{1}{4}$

4. $12^{-2} \times 12^2$ 1

5. $32^{-1} \times 32^0$ $\frac{1}{32}$

6. $8^{-3} \times 8^{-1} \times 8^5$ 8

What value of the variable makes the sentence true?

7. $6^n = \frac{1}{216}$ -3

8. $5^{-n} = \frac{1}{625}$ 4

Suggested Assignments

Core
Day 1: 74/2–22 even; 23–34
Day 2: 74/39–43
    75/Self-Test B
    75/Challenge

Enriched
    74/7–47 odd
    75/Self-Test B
    75/Challenge

Supplementary Materials

Practice Masters, p. 10
Test 2B, pp. 11–12

Use exponents to state as a power of 2.

6. 8 2^3 **7.** $\frac{1}{8}$ 2^{-3} **8.** 64 2^6 **9.** $\frac{1}{64}$ 2^{-6} **10.** $\frac{1}{512}$ 2^{-9}

Written Exercises

Write the expression without exponents.

A   **1.** $(-2)^{-5}$ $\frac{1}{-32}$ **2.** 3^{-3} $\frac{1}{27}$ **3.** 10^{-3} $\frac{1}{1000}$ **4.** $(-3)^{-5}$ $\frac{1}{-243}$ **5.** 1^{-4} 1

6. $(-1)^{-6}$ 1   **7.** $(-5)^{-2}$ $\frac{1}{25}$ **8.** 4^{-5} $\frac{1}{1024}$ **9.** 2^{-6} $\frac{1}{64}$ **10.** $(-4)^{-2}$ $\frac{1}{16}$

11. $7^4 \times 7^{-6}$ $\frac{1}{49}$ **12.** $10^3 \times 10^{-2}$ 10   **13.** $5^{10} \times 5^{-10}$ 1

14. $6^{-23} \times 6^{23}$ 1   **15.** $3^{-3} \times 3^0$ $\frac{1}{27}$ **16.** $2^{-3} \times 2^{-4}$ $\frac{1}{128}$

17. $(-4)^{-2} \times (-4)^{-2}$ $\frac{1}{256}$ **18.** $(-7)^{-1} \times (-7)^{-1}$ $\frac{1}{49}$ **19.** $(-2)^{-6} \times (-2)^3$ 1

20. $(-8)^{-2} \times (-8)^0$ $\frac{1}{64}$ **21.** $6^{-1} \times 6^3 \times 6^{-2}$ 1   **22.** $9^{-5} \times 9^{-1} \times 9^7$ $\frac{9}{-8}$

What value of the variable makes the statement true?

23. $5^n = \frac{1}{125}$ -3 **24.** $4^{-n} = \frac{1}{256}$ 4   **25.** $3^{-n} = \frac{1}{243}$ 5

26. $4^2 \times 4^{-2} = 4^n$ 0   **27.** $7^3 \times 7^{-5} = 7^n$ -2 **28.** $9^{-4} \times 9^3 = \frac{1}{9^n}$ 1

B   **29.** $3^7 \times 3^n = 3^5$ -2 **30.** $2^{-3} \times 2^n = 2^{-11}$ -8

31. $(2)^{-5} \times (2)^n = 8$ 8   **32.** $(-10)^3 \times (-10)^{-n} = -10$ 2

33. $144 \times 12^{-2} = 12^n$ 0   **34.** $5^{-3} \times 25 = 5^{-n}$ 1

35. $4^n \times 4^{-3} = \frac{1}{16}$ 1   **36.** $6^{-n} \times 6^3 = \frac{1}{216}$ 6

37. $9^{-7} \times 9^{-n} = \frac{1}{729}$ -4 **38.** $8^{-4} \times 8^{-n} = \frac{1}{64}$ -2

39. $(-5)^{-n} \times (-5)^{-3} = 1$ -3 **40.** $(-3)^{-n} \times (-3)^{-8} = \frac{1}{-243}$ -3

Simplify. Write the expression with nonnegative exponents.

41. x^{-5} $\frac{1}{x^5}$ **42.** n^{-9} $\frac{1}{n^9}$ **43.** $a^{-3} \times a^{-2}$ $\frac{1}{a^5}$

44. $b^7 \times b^{-7}$ b^0, or 1   **45.** $w^{-10} \times w^3 \times w^{-1}$ $\frac{1}{w^8}$ **46.** $v^4 \times v^{-12} \times v^3$ $\frac{1}{v^5}$

C   **47.** Explain why $a^m = (-a)^m$ if m is any even integer.
If the number of negative factors is even, the product is positive.
48. Explain why $(-a)^n = -1(a)^n$ if n is any odd integer.
If the number of negative factors is odd, the product is negative.

Self-Test B

Simplify.

1. $4.2(-11.3)$ −47.46
2. $-6.7(20.4)$ −136.68
3. $7.5(-4.2)(-12)$ 378 [2-5]

4. $121 \div (-11)$ −11
5. $-68.2 \div 2.2$ −31
6. $-0.56 \div (-0.07)$ 8 [2-6]

Evaluate the expression when $a = 2$, $b = 5$, and $c = 3$.

7. a^3 8
8. $(bc)^2$ 225
9. $(2c)^4$ 1296 [2-7]

Write the expression without exponents.

10. 4^{-2} $\frac{1}{16}$
11. $(-6)^{-3}$ $\frac{1}{-216}$
12. $7^5 \times 7^{-8}$ $\frac{1}{343}$
13. $(-9)^{-2} \times (-9)^0$ $\frac{1}{81}$ [2-8]

Self-Test answers and Extra Practice are at the back of the book.

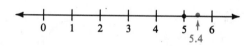

Challenge

We use the symbol $[x]$ (read *the greatest integer in x*) to represent the greatest integer less than or equal to x.

EXAMPLE   **a.** $[5.4]$ **b.** $[^-3.2]$

Solution   **a.** There is no integer equal to 5.4, so we must find the greatest integer that is less than 5.4.

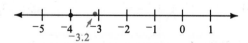

As shown on the number line, the greatest integer that is less than 5.4 is 5. Thus the greatest integer in 5.4 is 5.

b. There is no integer equal to $^-3.2$, so we must find the greatest integer that is less than $^-3.2$.

As shown on the number line, the greatest integer that is less than $^-3.2$ is $^-4$. Thus the greatest integer in $^-3.2$ is $^-4$.

Find the value.

1. $[6.2]$ 6
2. $[1.23]$ 1
3. $[3]$ 3
4. $[45]$ 45

5. $[^-12]$ −12
6. $[^-1]$ −1
7. $[^-4.89]$ −5
8. $[^-0.36]$ −1

Positive and Negative Numbers **75**

Enrichment Note

Understanding exponents and particularly powers of 10 is mandatory for this enrichment feature. Be certain students have grasped the concepts presented in Lesson 2-8 before attempting scientific notation.

Not only is scientific notation convenient for expressing very large and very small numbers, it is also a useful means of multiplying or dividing such numbers by simplifying and shortening computations. It makes numbers having a large number of zeros much more manageable. Calculators and computers always express very large or very small results using scientific notation. Show students how to find the product of 4,400,000 and 1,200,000 by using scientific notation and check the product on a calculator or computer.

$$(4.4 \times 10^6) \times (1.2 \times 10^6)$$
$$= (4.4 \times 1.2) \times (10^6 \times 10^6)$$
$$= \quad 5.28 \quad \times 10^{12}$$
$$= \quad 5,280,000,000,000$$

Scientific Notation

Scientists frequently deal with data that range from very small to very large magnitudes. For example, when Saturn is closest to Earth, it is about 1,630,000,000 km away. The diameter of a hydrogen atom is approximately $\frac{1}{100,000,000}$ cm. To cope with numbers such as these, a method for writing numbers, called **scientific notation,** has been adopted.

Scientific notation makes use of positive exponents to write large numbers and negative exponents to write small numbers. For example,

$$4800 = 4.8 \times 1000 = 4.8 \times 10^3$$

$$0.000507 = 5.07 \times \frac{1}{10,000} = 5.07 \times 10^{-4}$$

Rule

To express any positive number in scientific notation, write it as the product of a power of ten and a number between 1 and 10.

In addition to being a convenient method for expressing very large or very small numbers, scientific notation provides an exact gauge of the precision of a measurement, based on the smallest unit of calibration on the measuring instrument. Each digit in a number that specifies the degree of precision of measurement is called a **significant digit.**

76   *Chapter 2*

Zeros that appear to the right of nonzero digits, and to the right of the decimal point, are significant. For example,

$$0.50 \text{ has two significant digits,}$$

$$40,521 \text{ has five significant digits.}$$

The zeros in a measurement such as 41,500 km, however, may be misleading since it is unclear whether the number is rounded to the nearest hundred or is an exact measurement. Scientific notation provides a means of avoiding this confusion. For example, when we write 40,500 as 4.05×10^4, it means that the measurement is precise to three significant digits. When we write 40,500 as 4.050×10^4, it means that the measurement is precise to four significant digits.

In general, to write a number in scientific notation, shift the decimal point to just after the first nonzero digit. Then multiply by 10^n, when n is the number of places the decimal point was shifted. As an example,

$$3165 = 3.165 \times 10^3.$$

Note that 7.46 is written as 7.46 since $10^0 = 1$. Also, 1,000,000 is usually written simply as 10^6 rather than 1×10^6.

Write the number in scientific notation.

Write the number in scientific notation.

1. 5798 5.798×10^3 **2.** 30,090 3.009×10^4 **3.** 8,915,673 8.915673×10^6 **4.** 2,175,000,000 2.175×10^9

5. 1.75 1.75 **6.** 0.003 3×10^{-3} **7.** 0.0501 5.01×10^{-2} **8.** 0.0333 3.33×10^{-2}

Write the number in decimal form.

9. 3.79×10^3 3790 **10.** 4.86×10^4 $48,600$ **11.** 3.01×10^5 $301,000$ **12.** 6×10^9 $6,000,000,000$

13. 5.6×10^{-2} 0.056 **14.** 7.09×10^{-3} 0.00709 **15.** 3.99×10^{-8} 0.0000000399 **16.** 2.0111×10^{-6} 0.0000020111

17. The diameter of a red blood cell is about 0.00074 cm. Write this number in scientific notation with two significant digits. 7.4×10^{-4}

18. An atom of gold is about 0.0000000025 m in diameter. Write this number in scientific notation with two significant digits. 2.5×10^{-9}

19. The radius of Earth's orbit is 150,000,000,000 m. Write this number in scientific notation with two significant digits. 1.5×10^{11}

20. A communications satellite was orbited at an altitude of 625,000 m. Write this number in scientific notation with three significant digits. 625×10^5

Positive and Negative Numbers **77**

Show students how numbers in scientific notation are expressed on a calculator and on a computer. For example, here are three numbers in scientific notation.

$$4.7 \times 10^5$$
$$8.3 \times 10^{25}$$
$$7.1 \times 10^{-9}$$

On a calculator these would be expressed as

4.7	05
8.3	25
7.1 −	09

A computer using BASIC would express them as

4.7E + 5
8.3E + 25
7.1E − 9

Chapter Review

Complete. Use =, >, or < to make a true statement.

1. $2 \underline{\ ?\ } 11$ <
2. $5 \underline{\ ?\ } 3$ >
3. $3 \underline{\ ?\ } {}^-4$ >   [2-1]
4. $0 \underline{\ ?\ } {}^-1$ >
5. $|{}^-9| \underline{\ ?\ } 9$ =
6. $|2| \underline{\ ?\ } {}^-2$ >
7. ${}^-8.7 \underline{\ ?\ } {}^-0.87$ <
8. ${}^-42 \underline{\ ?\ } 2.4$ <
9. $3.05 \underline{\ ?\ } -3.55$ >   [2-2]
10. $0.4 \underline{\ ?\ } {}^-4.3$ >
11. $|{}^-5.6| \underline{\ ?\ } {}^-5.6$ >
12. $|4.93| \underline{\ ?\ } |{}^-4.93|$ =

True or false?

13. $0 + {}^-14.2 = 0$ False
14. $16.8 + {}^-16.8 = 33.6$ False   [2-3]
15. ${}^-13.2 + {}^-7.8 = {}^-21$ True
16. $7.6 + {}^-10.5 = 2.9$ False
17. ${}^-33 + 20.2 = {}^-12.8$ True
18. $19.5 + {}^-14.3 = {}^-5.2$ False
19. $37.2 - (-9.6) = 25.6$ False
20. $-5.8 - (-5.8) = 11.6$ False   [2-4]
21. $-12.2 - 13.1 = -25.3$ True
22. $0 - (-0.5) = -0.05$ False
23. If $a = -7$, $-a = -7$ False
24. If $b = -2.4$, $-|b| = -2.4$ True
25. $-40(0.33) = -1.42$ False
26. $1.2(-6.2) = -7.4$ False   [2-5]
27. $-17(-24.2) = 411.4$ True
28. $7(-8.3)0 = -58.1$ False
29. $-5(2.8)(-20) = 280$ True
30. $-12(-1)(-8.6) = 103.2$ False
31. $75.5 \div (-5) = -15.1$ True
32. $-0.006 \div (-1) = 0.006$ True   [2-6]
33. $-115.2 \div (-2.4) = 48$ True
34. $-5.04 \div 3.6 = 1.4$ False
35. $0 \div (-19.8) = 0$ True
36. $-6.21 \div (-0.23) = -27$ False

What value of the variable makes the statement true? Write the letter of the correct answer.

37. $2^n = 32$ c   **a.** 16   **b.** -5 **c.** 5   **d.** 30   [2-7]
38. $5^6 \times 5^2 = 5^n$ b   **a.** 4   **b.** 8   **c.** 12   **d.** 36
39. $7^n = 1$ d   **a.** 7   **b.** -6 **c.** 6   **d.** 0
40. $3^n = \frac{1}{81}$ c   **a.** 4   **b.** 81   **c.** -4 **d.** 9   [2-8]
41. $4^{-n} = \frac{1}{64}$ d   **a.** 16   **b.** -16 **c.** 4   **d.** 3
42. $7^{-6} \times 7^6 = 7^n$ b   **a.** -36 **b.** 0   **c.** 12   **d.** -12

78   *Chapter 2*

Chapter Test

Replace __?__ with =, >, or < to make a true statement.

1. 7 _?_ 10 <   **2.** 6 _?_ 1 >   **3.** 0 _?_ ⁻6 >   **4.** ⁻2 _?_ ⁻3 >   [2-1]

Express as an integer.

5. |⁻3| 3   **6.** |7| 7   **7.** |⁻12| 12   **8.** |0| 0

Write the numbers in order from least to greatest.

9. ⁻6.5, ⁻56, 6.05, ⁻556, ⁻0.6   **10.** 3.02, ⁻3.2, ⁻23, 0.32, ⁻333   [2-2]
⁻556, ⁻56, ⁻6.5, ⁻0.6, 6.05   ⁻333, ⁻23, ⁻3.2, 0.32, 3.02

Find the sum.

11. ⁻8.4 + 36.8 28.4   **12.** ⁻6.3 + ⁻0.12 ⁻6.42   **13.** 13.2 + ⁻13.2 0   [2-3]

14. 14.6 + 23.1 37.7   **15.** 0 + ⁻11.5 ⁻11.5   **16.** 0.89 + ⁻16.1 + ⁻0.94 ⁻16.15

Find the difference.

17. 26.5 − 8.3 18.2   **18.** −4.3 − 20.6 −24.9   **19.** 0 − 13.6 ⁻13.6   [2-4]

20. −14.2 − (−9.5) −4.7   **21.** 41 − (−11.67) 52.67   **22.** −6.4 − (−6.4) 0

Evaluate the expression when $a = -5$ and $b = -3.6$.

23. $-a - b$ 8.6   **24.** $-a - (-b)$ 1.4   **25.** $-|b|$ −3.6

$-(-5) - (-3.6)$
$= +5 + 3.6 = 8.6$

$-(-5) - (-[-3.6])$
$= +5 + (-3.6)$
$= +5 - 3.6 = 1.4$

Find the product.

26. 12(−6.37) −76.44   **27.** −30(0.45) −13.5   **28.** −0.37(−20.8) 7.696   [2-5]

29. −1(−14.27) 14.27   **30.** 5.4(−8.2)(−3) 132.84   **31.** −6.11(−9)(−5.5) −302.445

Find the quotient.

32. 69.3 ÷ (−3) −23.1   **33.** −18 ÷ (−2.5) 7.2   **34.** −19.2 ÷ 10 −1.92   [2-6]

35. −0.004 ÷ (−1) 0.004   **36.** 0 ÷ (−15) 0   **37.** −0.08 ÷ (−0.2) 0.4

Write the expression without exponents.

38. 5^3 125   **39.** 20^0 1   **40.** $4^2 \times 4^3$ 1024 (4×4)×(4×4×4)   **41.** 2^6 64   [2-7]

42. 6^{-2} $\frac{1}{36}$ **43.** $(-5)^{-3}$ $\frac{1}{-125}$ **44.** $8^{-9} \times 8^7$ $\frac{1}{64}$ **45.** $(-3) \times (-3)^{-2}$ $\frac{1}{-3}$ [2-8]

$-9 + 7$ *Positive and Negative Numbers* **79**
$= -2$

$8^{-2} = \frac{1}{64}$ $(-3)^{-1} = \frac{1}{-3}$

0 power = 1
EX: $395^0 = 1$

$20^1 = 20$

Evaluate the expression when $a = 3$ and $b = 13$.

1. $68 + a$ 71

2. $54 - b - a$ 38

3. $4b$ 52

4. $27 \div a \times b$ 117

Evaluate the expression when $m = 15$ and $n = 18$.

5. $n - 3 \times 5$ 3

6. $2 \times \frac{m}{3}$ 10

7. $mn - 70$ 200

8. $(m + n) \div 11$ 3

Evaluate.

9. 4^3 64

10. 10^4 10,000

11. 2^6 64

Write as a power of 10.

12. $10^6 \times 10^3$ 10^9

13. $10^7 \times 10^7$ 10^{14}

14. 100,000 10^5

Write the decimal in expanded form.

15. 144
$(1 \times 100) + (4 \times 10) + 4$

16. 60.05
$(6 \times 10) + (5 \times 0.01)$

17. 2.302
$2 + (3 \times 0.1) + (2 \times 0.001)$

18. 7.9
$7 + (9 \times 0.1)$

Round to the place specified.

19. tenths: 16.59 16.6

20. tens: 324.6 320

21. hundredths: 6.285 6.29

(continued on next page)

Cumulative Review (Chapters 1 and 2)
Exercises

Use inverse operations to solve.

1. $9x = 54$ 6

2. $17 + a = 20$ 3

3. $a \div 6 = 30$ 180

4. $35 - b = 7$ 28

5. $15z = 45$ 3

6. $w \div 12 = 96$ 1152

7. $18 + p = 35$ 17

8. $n - 5 = 19$ 24

True or false?

9. $46.7 \times 1.0 = 46.7$ True

10. $87.91 \times 0 = 87.91$ False

11. $4(8 + 2) = 4 \times 8 + 4 \times 2$ True

12. $9 \times 7 - 9 \times 3 = 9 \times (7 - 3)$ True

13. $84 - (2 + 3) = (84 - 2) + 3$ False

14. $63 \times (9 \times 0) = (63 \times 9) \times 0$ True

15. $21(6 \times 3) = (21 \times 6) + (21 \times 3)$ False

16. $(68 - 7) = (7 - 68)$ False

17. $(658 + 15)7 = (7 \times 658) + (7 \times 15)$ True

Find the sum.

18. $^-8 + 4$ $^-4$

19. $^-3.21 + ^-2.97$ $^-6.18$

20. $^-4.1 + 6.6 + ^-1.9$ 0.6

Find the difference.

21. $6 - 14$ $^-8$

22. $11 - (-13)$ 24

23. $1.6 - (-2.7)$ 4.3

Find the product.

24. $-7(-11)$ 77

25. $-0.2(0.6)$ -0.12

26. $3.7(-2.4)$ -8.88

Find the quotient.

27. $-27 \div 3$ -9

28. $-66.3 \div (-3)$ 22.1

29. $-0.96 \div 0.6$ -1.6

Round to the place specified.

30. tenths: 68.461 68.5

31. thousandths: 4.00891 4.009

32. tens: 188.72 190

33. hundreds: 7740.68 7700

34. hundredths: 37.5505 37.55

35. tenths: 909.09 909.1

Simplify the expression.

36. $75.8 + (6.7 + 3.3)^2$ 175.8

37. $100.6 + (3^3 \div 9)$ 103.6

38. $(4^3 - 6) \times (81 - 5^2)$ 3248

39. $10^3 \times 10^7$ 10,000,000,000

40. $2^4 \times 3^2$ 144

41. $(2^2)^3$ 64

$(4)^3 = 64$

Express as an integer.

42. $|-2|$ 2

43. $|6|$ 6

44. $|0|$ 0

45. $|-100|$ 100

46. $|-15|$ 15

Write the integers in order from least to greatest.

47. 12, 15, 0, −7, 6, −20
−20, −7, 0, 6, 12, 15

48. 0, −5, 6, −6, 5
−6, −5, 0, 5, 6

49. 7, 9, −3, −5, 0, 1
−5, −3, 0, 1, 7, 9

Problems

Problem Solving Reminders

Here are some reminders that may help you solve some of the problems on this page.
- Determine which facts are necessary to solve the problem.
- Determine which operations are needed to solve the problem.
- Supply additional information if necessary.

Solve.

1. At Angler's Supply Company, deluxe waders cost $69.95 a pair. A similar product can be purchased for $10.49 less at Go Fish Discount. What is the price at Go Fish Discount? $59.46

2. Alice's Mountain Goat Cheese is currently being promoted through supermarket taste demonstrations. An average of 200 samples are distributed between 11:00 A.M. and 5:00 P.M. each day. To the nearest whole number, find the average number of samples given out each hour. If the daily cost of samples averages $50, what is the average cost per sample? 33 samples/hr; $0.25/sample

3. Cabin Fever Ski Area runs a mountain slide ride during the summer months. A single ride costs $3.75 and a day's pass costs $14.00. How many times would you have to ride the slide to make it less expensive to buy a day's pass? 4 times

4. Approximately 3.3 Calories are burned per hour per kilogram of body mass by walking. If a student with mass 58 kg takes 20 min to walk to school, how many Calories are burned? 63.8 Calories

5. The Gourmet Luncheonette is giving out coupons that let customers buy one large roast beef sandwich at the regular price of $2.45 and receive one free. Deli Delights is giving out coupons that let customers deduct $.75 from the regular price of $1.95 for every large roast beef sandwich. Is it less expensive to buy two large roast beef sandwiches at The Gourmet Luncheonette or at Deli Delights?
Deli Delights

6. Because of a grain shortage, the price of a loaf of bread increased by 2 cents. When grain again became plentiful, the price decreased by 4 cents, but later it again rose by 5 cents because of inflation. If the original price was 86 cents per loaf, what was the final price?
89 cents/loaf

Positive and Negative Numbers **81**

What value of the variable makes the statement true?

22. $5(2.8 + 1.6) = 5t + 8$ **2.8**

23. $(2.4 + x) + 9.6 = 2.4 + (1.6 + 9.6)$ **1.6**

24. $75.3q = 0$ **0**

25. $2.56 + 0.59 = 0.59 + j$
2.56

Solve the equation for the given replacement set.

26. $k − 8 = 25$;
$\{17, 27, 33\}$ **33**

27. $15p = 90$; $\{5, 7, 9\}$ **No solution**

28. $4(x + 9) = 52$; $\{0, 4, 8\}$
4

29. $3w − 1 = 14$; $\{5, 6, 7\}$ **5**

Use the inverse operation to write a related equation and solve for the variable.

30. $3x = 36$ $x = 36 ÷ 3$;
12

31. $y + 7 = 15$
$y = 15 − 7$; **8**

32. $z ÷ 5 = 10$
$z = 10 × 5$; **50**

33. $v − 2 = 19$
$v = 19 + 2$; **21**

81

3

Rational Numbers

Hummingbirds, like the Violet-Capped Woodnymph Hummingbird shown at the right, can fly forward, vertically, and even backward. Perhaps their most unusual feat is their ability to hover apparently motionless in the air while sipping nectar from a flower. This ability comes from their specialized wing structure and its unique movement. The hummingbird pictured lives in the forests of Brazil. It is only $4\frac{1}{2}$ in. long and has a wing beat of 33 beats per second. To photograph the hummingbird so that its wings appear motionless, an electronic flash time of about $\frac{1}{1000}$ of a second was used. Exposure times of $\frac{1}{100,000}$ of a second have been used to study the precise motion of some hummingbirds' wings and to learn exactly how the wings enable hummingbirds to remain at a fixed point with great ease. In this chapter on rational numbers, you will learn about fractions and decimals and their relationship to each other.

Career Note

Understanding the relationship between animals and their environments is the job of the ecologist. Ecologists study the influence that factors such as temperature, humidity, rainfall, and altitude have on the environment. They monitor levels of pollutants and predict their long term effects on the life cycles of plants and animals.

83

Lesson Commentary
Chapter 3 Rational Numbers

Overview

In the first section of this chapter, students will review the number theory topics necessary for an understanding of fractions. Fraction concepts are extended to include negative fractions, and rational numbers are defined. Students may be interested in learning that the theory of numbers is historically significant as one of the oldest branches of mathematics, dating back to Pythagoras (569–500 B.C.). The famous mathematician Karl Friedrich Gauss called the theory of numbers "the queen of mathematics." It is the foundation upon which mathematics is built.

In the second section of this chapter, students learn the four basic operations with rational numbers. Emphasis is placed on the justification for the procedures we use. Students also learn in this section about the relationship between rational numbers and decimals. In so doing, they learn that the set of real numbers consists of the rational numbers and the irrational numbers.

NUMBER THEORY AND FRACTIONS

3-1 Factors and Divisibility

Objectives *for pages 84–88*

- To find the whole-number factors and multiples of a given whole number.
- To find and use tests for divisibility.

Teaching Suggestions

The word *factor* is derived from the Latin word for "maker," the same root as for *factory* and *manufacture*. When multiplied together, factors "make" a number: factor × factor = product. You may wish to explain to students that the word *factor* is usually used to mean "whole-number factor." Thus, we say "3 is not a factor

of 8" because there is no whole number whose product with 3 is 8. However, the word *factor* is sometimes used to refer to any multiplier. For example, in the product $3 \times \frac{8}{3} = 8$, we sometimes say that the factors of 8 are 3 and $\frac{8}{3}$. Unless otherwise indicated, the word *factor* in this book will always mean "whole-number factor."

Example 2 on page 84 shows that factors of a number are usually found in pairs. The divisibility tests of this lesson can be used to identify one factor of a number. The second factor can then be found by dividing the number by the known factor.

You may wish to ask students the following questions concerning the properties of 0 and 1:

1. What number is a factor of every number? **1**
2. Is every number a factor of itself? **Yes**
3. What are the only multiples of 0? **0**
4. How many numbers have 0 as a factor?
   Only one number, 0

Related Activities

To develop in students an awareness of number patterns and their applications, ask students to examine the last digits of the multiples of 1 through 10. Then ask questions like those below. Encourage students to explain their answers.

1. If the last digit of a number is 3, can the number be a multiple of 8? **No**
2. If the last digit of a number is 6, could 8 be a factor? **Yes**
3. If the last digit of a number is 7, how can you find all factors less than 10 by doing no more than 3 divisions?
   Divide by 3 and 7. If 3 is a factor, divide by 9.
4. If the last digit of a number is 5, can the number be a multiple of 14? **No**
5. If the last digit of a number is 6, could the number be a multiple of 18? **Yes**

To help students discover patterns of divisibility, have students do each exercise below three or four times, each time with a different choice of numbers. Encourage students to state the patterns they notice in general terms.

6. Choose two numbers, a and b, less than 10. List all the numbers less than 100 that are divisible by both a and b. Which of these numbers are also divisible by ab? **Answers will vary. For example, if a = 6 and b = 9, then 18, 36, 54, 72, and 90 are divisible by a and by b, but only 54 is divisible by ab, or 6 × 9.**

7. Choose two numbers less than 100 that are divisible by 9. Are their sum and difference also divisible by 9? Repeat, using 5 instead of 9. **If a and b are divisible by c, then a + b and a − b are divisible by c.**

3-2 Prime Numbers and Composite Numbers

Objectives *for pages 89–91*

■ To determine whether or not a given whole number greater than 1 is prime or composite.
■ To write the prime factorization of a number.

Teaching Suggestions

Students may wonder why prime numbers are defined in such a way as to exclude 1. There are several reasons. First, it is possible to write a number as the product of prime numbers without using 1 as a factor. Secondly, since 1 is a factor of every number, knowing that 1 is a factor says nothing about the number. Also, the restriction that prime numbers not include 1 makes it possible to state the Fundamental Theorem of Arithmetic, for then each number has a unique prime factorization. Students should realize that the number 1 is crossed out on the Sieve of Eratosthenes because it is not prime.

Be sure students understand that changing the order of the factors does not give a different factorization. For example, 28 may be factored as $2^2 \cdot 7$, or as $2 \cdot 7 \cdot 2$, or as $7 \cdot 2^2$; these are three ways of writing the same prime factors. You may wish to suggest the use of divisibility tests as an aid in writing the prime factorization of a number.

Students should realize that the final quotient in a short division is part of the final factorization; it must be a prime number, or else the prime factorization is not complete. Also, each branch of a factor tree must end with a prime number.

Related Activities

To reinforce the concept of prime numbers, tell students about Goldbach's conjecture. In 1742 the mathematician Christian Goldbach stated that every even number greater than 2 can be written as the sum of two prime numbers. For example, $14 = 3 + 11$ and $18 = 5 + 13$. To this day, no one knows whether or not he was right. Nevertheless, no one has found an even number greater than 2 that cannot be written this way. Ask students to test Goldbach's conjecture with each number.

1. 6   2. 16   3. 22
   3 + 3   3 + 13 or 5 + 11   3 + 19 or 5 + 17

3-3 Positive and Negative Fractions

Objective *for pages 92–95*

■ To use terms and properties concerning positive and negative fractions.

Teaching Suggestions

Emphasize the relationship between fractions and division. Since $\frac{3}{5}$ means $3 \div 5$, we will be able to find decimal and percent equivalents for fractions. This also explains why some decimals and percents are themselves rational numbers.

Stress that $\frac{3}{5}$ means $\frac{1}{5} + \frac{1}{5} + \frac{1}{5}$ as well as $3 \times \frac{1}{5}$. Then $-\frac{3}{5}$, written as $\frac{-3}{5}$, becomes $3 \times (-\frac{1}{5})$ or $(-\frac{1}{5}) + (-\frac{1}{5}) + (-\frac{1}{5})$.

It is necessary that students understand that $-\frac{3}{5} = \frac{-3}{5} = \frac{3}{-5}$ but not $\frac{-3}{-5}$, which equals $+\frac{3}{5}$. Remind students that a negative number divided by a negative number equals a positive number.

Point out that the properties of whole numbers and decimals (Chapter 1) also apply to positive and negative fractions.

Related Activities

To relate this topic to students' lives, ask them to watch and listen for frequently used fractions. List these on a poster and discuss which numbers are most frequently used in denominators.

To develop an awareness of the history and uses of mathematics, have students investigate when, where, and why fractions were first used.

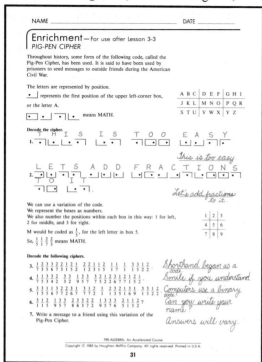

Students should be familiar with common factors and the greatest common factor (GCF) from earlier courses, but a brief review may be useful. For example, ask for the GCF of 16 and 12. The factors of 16 are 1, 2, 4, 8, and 16. The factors of 12 are 1, 2, 3, 4, 6, and 12. The common factors of 16 and 12 are 1, 2, and 4. The GCF is 4.

Related Activities

To relate this lesson to the daily lives of your students, you can draw on their familiarity with money and their understanding of the following relationships:

$$1 \text{ cent} = \frac{1}{100} \text{ dollar} \qquad 1 \text{ nickel} = \frac{1}{20} \text{ dollar}$$

$$1 \text{ dime} = \frac{1}{10} \text{ dollar} \qquad 1 \text{ quarter} = \frac{1}{4} \text{ dollar}$$

Use these relationships to complete and to explain the equivalence of each pair of fractions.

1. $\frac{20}{100} = \frac{?}{10}$ 2

    20 cents = 2 dimes

2. $\frac{2}{4} = \frac{5}{?}$ 10

    2 quarters = 5 dimes

3. $\frac{6}{20} = \frac{?}{100}$ 30

    6 nickels = 30 cents

4. $\frac{75}{100} = \frac{?}{20}$ 15

    75 cents = 15 nickels

Similarly, students can use the relationship of 1 min = $\frac{1}{60}$ h to write and explain equivalent fractions for $\frac{1}{4}$, $\frac{1}{2}$, and $\frac{3}{4}$. Ask students if they can think of other such relationships in their daily lives.

3-4 Equivalent Fractions

Objectives for pages 96–99

■ To write proper and improper fractions as equivalent fractions or mixed numbers in lowest terms.
■ To write mixed numbers as improper fractions.

Teaching Suggestions

The number line using halves and fourths presents an opportunity to review markings on a ruler. Show that most inch rulers are divided into sixteenths of an inch. Two sixteenths, $\frac{2}{16}$, is usually read *one eighth*, $\frac{1}{8}$. Four sixteenths, $\frac{4}{16}$, is usually read *one fourth*, $\frac{1}{4}$, and so on. Use a different number line to show fifths and tenths or thirds and sixths.

When you present the Rule on page 96, you could point out that multiplying both the numerator and the denominator of a fraction by c is equivalent to multiplying the fraction by $\frac{c}{c}$, or 1.

3-5 Least Common Denominator

Objective for pages 100–102

■ To write two or more fractions as equivalent fractions with the least common denominator.

Teaching Suggestions

If students are concerned about finding the least common denominator, assure them that any common denominator can be used for calculations and comparisons involving fractions. A common denominator can always be found by multiplying the denominators of the fractions. For example:

$$\frac{3}{20} + \frac{4}{25} = \frac{75}{500} + \frac{80}{500} = \frac{155}{500} = \frac{31}{100}$$

However, it is more efficient to use the LCD:

$$\frac{3}{20} + \frac{4}{25} = \frac{15}{100} + \frac{16}{100} = \frac{31}{100}$$

Listing all multiples is a valid way to find the LCM, but time-consuming. For Example 1, this would mean listing

Multiples of 48 = 48, 96, 144, 192, 240, . . .
Multiples of 120 = 120, 240, . . .

before the LCM, 240, is found.

Prime factorization is helpful in finding the equivalent fraction. You may want to use this method with your students.

$$\frac{5}{48} = \frac{5}{2^4 \times 3} = \frac{5 \times 5}{2^4 \times 3 \times 5} = \frac{25}{240}$$

$$\frac{11}{120} = \frac{11}{2^3 \times 3 \times 5} = \frac{11 \times 2}{2^3 \times 3 \times 5 \times 2} = \frac{22}{240}$$

Encourage students to use mental arithmetic as much as possible in finding least common denominators.

Resource Book: Page 32 (Use After Page 102)

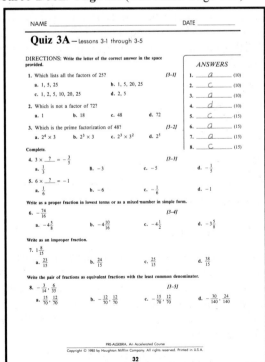

Related Activities

To develop a greater understanding of factorization, have students look for generalizations and clues for finding the LCD. One is that if the denominators have no common factors, the LCD is their product. For example, the denominators may both be prime numbers: The LCD of $\frac{1}{3}$ and $\frac{1}{7}$ is $3 \times 7 = 21$. The denominators may be consecutive numbers: the LCD of $\frac{1}{8}$ and $\frac{1}{9}$ is $8 \times 9 = 72$. Challenge students to look for other clues.

OPERATIONS WITH FRACTIONS

3-6 Adding and Subtracting Common Fractions

Objective *for pages 103–105*

■ To add and subtract common fractions.

Teaching Suggestions

Most of your students already know how to add and to subtract fractions. You may wish to use this opportunity to prepare students for algebra while you review the content. You can call attention to the use of variables to state the rules on page 103. Have students choose values for *a*, *b*, and *c* and explain the rule by substituting the values in the two equations. Be sure that students do not overlook the restrictions for *a*, *b*, and *c* stated in the first line of the rule. To encourage students to think about the reasons for these restrictions, ask students why the condition $c \neq 0$ is necessary. In the rule for subtraction, have students choose a value for *a* that is greater than *b* so that $a - b$ will be positive. The rule is stated here in its most general form because it applies to negative as well as to positive numbers.

Students usually find addition and subtraction exercises involving fractions much easier to understand if they are written in vertical form. As a preparation for algebra, however, be sure your students become familiar with exercises in a horizontal format.

Prior to calculating sums and differences with fractions, have the students complete some addition and subtraction exercises with integers. Remind them that we subtract by adding the opposite. It may be necessary to review the methods for finding a common denominator, stressing the computational advantage of using the LCD.

Related Activities

To provide a change of pace, have students use the map below to locate the buried treasure. Tell them to add the fractions on each segment. The treasure is buried at the point of intersection of the two line segments whose sums are equal. "X" marks the spot where the treasure is buried.

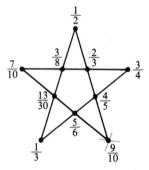

If one number is negative and one is positive, it is often easier to write both numbers as improper fractions, as in Example 2a, than it is to regroup or "borrow." Nevertheless, some students may prefer to solve Example 2a as follows:

$$
\begin{array}{rcl}
5\frac{1}{4} & = & 5\frac{3}{12} & = & 4\frac{15}{12} \\
+\left(-2\frac{1}{3}\right) & = & +\left(-2\frac{4}{12}\right) & = & +\left(-2\frac{4}{12}\right) \\
\hline
& & & & 2\frac{11}{12}
\end{array}
$$

Caution students who wish to use this method that $-2\frac{1}{3} = -2 + (-\frac{1}{3}) = -2 - \frac{1}{3}$, not $-2 + \frac{1}{3}$. Some students may incorrectly add $4\frac{15}{12}$ and $(-2\frac{4}{12})$ above to obtain $2\frac{19}{12}$, or $3\frac{7}{12}$.

3-7 Adding and Subtracting Mixed Numbers

Objective *for pages 106–108*

■ To add and subtract mixed numbers.

Teaching Suggestions

The method shown in the lesson is to convert the mixed numbers to improper fractions having a common denominator before adding or subtracting.

Some students may have learned in previous courses to add mixed numbers by adding the whole number parts and then adding the fractional parts. This is a valid method, and is often convenient if both numbers are positive or if both numbers are negative. Example 1a can be solved as follows:

$$
\begin{array}{r}
3\frac{7}{8} \\
+2\frac{3}{8} \\
\hline
5\frac{10}{8} = 6\frac{2}{8} = 6\frac{1}{4}
\end{array}
$$

Resource Book: Page 33 (Use After Page 108)

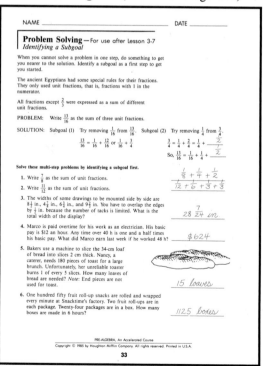

NAME _____ DATE _____

Problem Solving—For use after Lesson 3-7
Reasonable Results

Use estimation to check for the reasonableness of your results. When working with fractions, you might round to the nearest whole number or to the nearest half to make an estimate.

EXAMPLE 1

You are going to triple a soup recipe that requires $1\frac{1}{2}$ qt of chicken stock. How much stock will you need?

ESTIMATED SOLUTION

$1\frac{1}{2}$ is between 1 and 2.

$3 \times 1 = 3 \qquad 3 \times 2 = 6$

You will need between 3 to 6 qt of stock.

EXACT SOLUTION

$3 \times 1\frac{1}{2} = 3 \times \frac{3}{2}$
$= \frac{9}{2}$
$= 4\frac{1}{2}$

You will need $4\frac{1}{2}$ qt. This checks with the estimate.

EXAMPLE 2

A carpenter needs boards that measure $3\frac{5}{8}$ ft, $4\frac{7}{8}$ ft, and $2\frac{1}{3}$ ft. What length lumber should he buy?

ESTIMATED SOLUTION

$3\frac{5}{8}$ is about equal to $3\frac{1}{2}$.

$4\frac{7}{8}$ is about equal to 5.

$2\frac{1}{3}$ is about equal to $2\frac{1}{2}$.

11 ft is a good estimate.

$3\frac{5}{8} + 4\frac{7}{8} + 2\frac{1}{3} =$
$3\frac{15}{24} + 4\frac{21}{24} + 2\frac{8}{24} = 10\frac{5}{6}$

You will need $10\frac{5}{6}$ ft. This checks with the estimate.

Solve. Use estimation to check the reasonableness of your results.

1. A bedroom measures 12 ft 3 in. by 15 ft 9 in. How many square feet of carpeting is needed?

   192.94 ft² (*estimate: 192*)

2. A toy-company stock had the following gains and losses over a 5-day period. What was the overall gain or loss for that period? $+1\frac{1}{8}, -2\frac{1}{4}, +1\frac{1}{8}, -\frac{1}{8}, +1\frac{1}{8}$.

   +1 23/24 (estimate: +2)

3. A recipe requires $\frac{1}{4}$ tsp nutmeg, $\frac{1}{2}$ tsp salt, $\frac{1}{4}$ tsp dried mustard, and $1\frac{1}{2}$ tsp dried parsley. How many teaspoons of dry ingredients are there in 4 times the recipe?

   9½ tsp (estimate: 10 tsp)

4. Mr. Jackowski is making draperies that are $81\frac{7}{16}$ in. long with a bottom hem of $4\frac{1}{8}$ in. He needs twice the length of material for both panels. Is 5 yd of material enough?

   yes · 4 yd 2 ft 4⅝ in. (estimate: 4 yd)

5. A glass of orange juice at Mrs. Breakfast's Family Restaurant is $3\frac{7}{8}$ oz. How many servings will a 64-oz bottle of juice make?

   16.52 (estimate: 16)

PRE-ALGEBRA, An Accelerated Course

34

Related Activities

To challenge students, have them complete the magic square below by finding the values of the variables in order from *a* to *f*. The sums in all directions (horizontal, vertical, and diagonal) are equal.

$1\frac{1}{3}$	$\frac{1}{4}$	$-\frac{2}{3}$	$1\frac{1}{12}$
$-\frac{5}{12}$	b	a	$\frac{2}{3}$
d	c	$\frac{7}{12}$	1
e	$1\frac{1}{4}$	$1\frac{1}{6}$	f

$a = \frac{11}{12}$; $b = \frac{5}{6}$;

$c = -\frac{1}{3}$; $d = \frac{3}{4}$;

$e = \frac{1}{3}$; $f = -\frac{3}{4}$

3-8 Multiplying Fractions

Objective *for pages 109–112*

■ To multiply fractions and mixed numbers.

Teaching Suggestions

The rule for multiplying any two fractions, given on page 110, suggests that you do not need a common denominator to multiply fractions. Emphasize this fact to your students. If students ask what happens in a multiplication when you use common denominators, demonstrate that you get the correct answer but do a great deal more work. Example 1 on page 110 would be done as follows:

$$-\frac{4}{12} \times \frac{3}{12} = -\frac{4 \times 3}{12 \times 12} = -\frac{12}{144} = -\frac{1}{12}$$

Example 3 illustrates how the multiplication of two fractions can be simplified by dividing either of the numerators and either of the denominators by a common factor. Be sure that students understand that this procedure can be used only when multiplying fractions. Warn them against trying to simplify additions and subtractions in this way.

Related Activities

To relate this lesson to earlier work, you may wish to show students how to use the distributive property to multiply a whole number and a mixed number:

$$4 \times 3\frac{1}{3} = 4 \times \left(3 + \frac{1}{3}\right) = 4 \times 3 + 4 \times \frac{1}{3}$$
$$= 12 + 1\frac{1}{3} = 13\frac{1}{3}$$

3-9 Dividing Fractions

Objective *for pages 113–116*

■ To divide fractions and mixed numbers.

Teaching Suggestions

In this lesson students will learn that to divide by a fraction means to multiply by the reciprocal of the divisor, the second fraction. Compare this to the subtraction of negative numbers, in which we add the opposite of the second number.

Help students to develop general rules about the signs of reciprocals by reminding them that the product of any number and its reciprocal must be $+1$. Therefore, the reciprocal of a positive fraction is a positive fraction, and the reciprocal of a negative fraction is a negative fraction. Mixed numbers should be changed to improper fractions before calculations begin.

Related Activities

To provide a challenge, introduce students to complex fractions by showing that

$$\frac{3}{5} \div \frac{1}{4} = \frac{\frac{3}{5}}{\frac{1}{4}}$$

Ask students to simplify the following complex fractions.

1. $\dfrac{\frac{4}{9}}{\frac{2}{9}}$ $\dfrac{2}{9}$

2. $\dfrac{7 + 3\frac{1}{3}}{\frac{1}{4}}$ $41\frac{1}{3}$

3. $\dfrac{\frac{3}{8} + \frac{1}{3}}{4\frac{1}{5} + 2\frac{1}{2}}$ $\dfrac{85}{804}$

Resource Book: Page 35 (Use After Page 116)

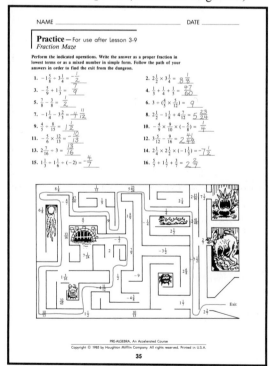

3-10 Fractions and Decimals

Objectives *for pages 117–121*

■ To write fractions and mixed numbers as equivalent terminating or repeating decimals.
■ To write terminating or repeating decimals as equivalent fractions or mixed numbers.

Teaching Suggestions

Review the meaning of $\frac{a}{b}$, emphasized on page 92 as $a \div b$. For students who think that $\frac{3}{5}$ means $3\overline{)5}$ instead of $5\overline{)3.0}$, point out that $\frac{3}{5}$ is less than $\frac{5}{5}$ or 1, so $3 \div 5$ must also be less than 1.

Explain that every rational number can be written as a terminating or repeating decimal. Demonstrate this on the chalkboard by using a fraction that can be written as a repeating decimal, such as

$$\frac{5}{7} = 0.\overline{714285}.$$

As you do the division, $7\overline{)5}$, ask students if they see a relationship between the remainder and the divisor. Ask questions such as:

1. What are the possible remainders?
   0, 1, 2, 3, 4, 5, 6
2. How many digits are in the repeating block? **6**
3. What is the maximum number of digits possible in a repeating block? **A number one less than the divisor (denominator)**
4. How can we tell that this is a repeating decimal? **We get a remainder that we have had before.**
5. How would we know if this were a terminating decimal? **At some point we would get a remainder of 0.**

Have students read decimal numbers orally before they write the fractional equivalent. For example, 0.37 is read thirty-seven hundredths, so $0.37 = \frac{37}{100}$. This helps students use the correct denominator.

Give some examples of irrational numbers. For example, the ratio of the circumference of a circle to its diameter is π. The length of the diagonal of a square with sides of length 1 is $\sqrt{2}$. These numbers can be shown to be irrational using advanced methods.

In Exercise 44, students may be confused to learn that

$5.\overline{9}$ is equal to 6. You can point out that $5.\overline{9}$ is equivalent to the series

$$5.0 + 0.9 + 0.09 + 0.009 + 0.0009 + \ldots$$

As each term is added to the previous sum, the sum comes closer and closer to 6. In Algebra 2 students will learn that 6 is the sum of this series. For now, tell them that they have learned another decimal name for 6. They may enjoy finding other similar repeating decimals, for example, $0.\overline{9}$, which equals 1.

Related Activities

To help students memorize fractional equivalents, have them complete a chart similar to the one below:

$\frac{1}{2} = 0.5$	$\frac{1}{3} = 0.\overline{3}$	$\frac{1}{4} = 0.25$	$\frac{1}{5} = 0.2$	$\frac{1}{6} = 0.1\overline{6}$	$\frac{1}{8} = 0.125$
	$\frac{2}{3} = 0.\overline{6}$	$\frac{2}{4} = 0.5$	$\frac{2}{5} = 0.4$	$\frac{2}{6} = 0.\overline{3}$	$\frac{2}{8} = 0.25$
		$\frac{3}{4} = 0.75$	$\frac{3}{5} = 0.6$	$\frac{3}{6} = 0.5$	$\frac{3}{8} = 0.375$
			$\frac{4}{5} = 0.8$	$\frac{4}{6} = 0.\overline{6}$	$\frac{4}{8} = 0.5$
				$\frac{5}{6} = 0.83\overline{3}$	$\frac{5}{8} = 0.625$
					$\frac{6}{8} = 0.75$
					$\frac{7}{8} = 0.875$

Some students will ask why the sevenths and ninths were left out. Explain that these are less-used fractional equivalents but nevertheless very interesting. Encourage students to investigate them. The elevenths also produce an interesting pattern.

To emphasize that many problems can be solved in more than one way, provide students with problems involving fractions and decimals. Allow them to work each problem in the most convenient way. Examples:

1. $3\frac{1}{8} + 4.75$ **7.875**

2. $5\frac{1}{3} - 2.5$ **2.8$\overline{3}$** or **2$\frac{5}{6}$**

3. $-2\frac{1}{7} \times (-5.6)$ **12**

4. $-4\frac{1}{5} \times 2.75$ **−11.55**

Resource Book: Page 36 (Use After Page 121)

NAME _____ DATE _____

CALCULATOR — For use after Lesson 3-10
Equivalent Fractions and Decimals

Play this game with a friend. Each player lists ten fractions. Independently, each player estimates the decimal equivalent to the nearest thousandth for all ten fractions. Then use your calculator to find the actual decimal equivalent to the nearest thousandth. Find the difference between each actual and estimated decimal. Add the ten differences. The player with the lowest sum wins that round. *Answers will vary.*

	Round I					Round II		
	Decimal Equivalent					**Decimal Equivalent**		
Fraction	Estimated	Actual	Difference		Fraction	Estimated	Actual	Difference
Sum of differences					Sum of differences			

NAME _____ DATE _____

Quiz 3B — Lessons 3-6 through 3-10

DIRECTIONS: Write the letter of the correct answer in the space provided.

Add or subtract. Write the answer as a proper fraction in lowest terms or as a mixed number in simple form.

1. $\frac{7}{10} - \frac{3}{4}$ [3-6]

   a. $-\frac{1}{20}$ b. $\frac{1}{20}$ c. $\frac{4}{6}$ d. $\frac{2}{3}$

2. $2\frac{1}{3} - (-3\frac{3}{4})$ [3-7]

   a. $-1\frac{5}{12}$ b. $-6\frac{7}{12}$ c. $6\frac{1}{12}$ d. $1\frac{5}{12}$

Multiply. Show the answer as a proper fraction in lowest terms or as a mixed number in simple form.

3. $-\frac{3}{8} \times (-\frac{20}{27})$ [3-8]

   a. $\frac{10}{36}$ b. $-\frac{10}{36}$ c. $\frac{5}{18}$ d. $3\frac{3}{5}$

4. $5\frac{5}{8} \times \frac{2}{9}$

   a. $\frac{5}{18}$ b. $-\frac{5}{4}$ c. $1\frac{18}{72}$ d. $1\frac{1}{4}$

Divide. Show the answer as a proper fraction in lowest terms or as a mixed number in simple form.

5. $\frac{2}{7} \div (-\frac{16}{21})$ [3-9]

   a. $2\frac{2}{3}$ b. $-\frac{3}{8}$ c. $-2\frac{2}{3}$ d. $\frac{3}{8}$

6. $-4 \div (\frac{15}{4} \times \frac{2}{5})$

   a. 6 b. -6 c. $-2\frac{2}{3}$ d. $\frac{8}{3}$

Show as a terminating or repeating decimal. Use a bar to show the repetend.

7. $\frac{3}{8}$ [3-10]

   a. 0.38   b. 0.375   c. 0.385   d. $0.\overline{3}$

Show as a proper fraction in lowest terms or as a mixed number in simple form.

8. $0.\overline{36}$

   a. $\frac{36}{100}$ b. $\frac{9}{25}$ c. $-\frac{12}{33}$ d. $\frac{4}{11}$

ANSWERS

1. _a_ (15)
2. _c_ (15)
3. _c_ (15)
4. _d_ (15)
5. _b_ (10)
6. _c_ (10)
7. _b_ (10)
8. _d_ (10)

37

NAME _____ DATE _____

Review — Chapter 3

List all the factors of each number.

1. 84 _1, 2, 3, 4, 6, 7, 12, 14, 21, 28, 42, 84_   [3-1]

2. 165 _1, 3, 5, 11, 15, 33, 55, 165_

State which of the numbers 2, 3, 4, 5, 9, and 10 are factors of each number. Use the tests of divisibility.

3. 135 _3, 5, 9_   4. 264 _2, 3, 4_   5. 240 _2, 3, 4, 5, 10_

Find out whether each number is prime or composite. If it is composite, give its prime factorization.

6. 48 _$2^4 \times 3$_   7. 71 _prime_   8. 270 _$2 \times 3^3 \times 5$_ [3-2]

Complete.

9. $\frac{?}{7} \times 6 = \frac{6}{7}$ 10. $9 \times \frac{-1}{9} = -1$ 11. $-\frac{5}{8} \times \frac{8}{5} = -1$ [3-3]

Write as a proper fraction in lowest terms or as a mixed number in simple form.

12. $\frac{16}{9}$ _$\frac{4}{9}$_   13. $-\frac{92}{7}$ _$-13\frac{1}{7}$_   14. $-\frac{116}{348}$ _$-\frac{1}{3}$_   [3-4]

Write as an improper fraction.

15. $3\frac{3}{8}$ _$\frac{27}{8}$_   16. $-7\frac{4}{9}$ _$-\frac{67}{9}$_   17. $1\frac{7}{15}$ _$\frac{22}{15}$_

Write each pair of fractions as equivalent fractions with the least common denominator.

18. $\frac{2}{5}, \frac{7}{15}$ _$\frac{6}{15}, \frac{7}{15}$_   19. $\frac{5}{8}, \frac{13}{20}$ _$\frac{25}{40}, \frac{26}{40}$_   20. $\frac{5}{x}, \frac{8}{y}$ _$\frac{5y}{xy}, \frac{8x}{xy}$_   [3-5]

Perform the indicated operation. Write the answer as a proper fraction or as a mixed number in simple form.

21. $\frac{4}{5} + \frac{1}{3}$ _$1\frac{2}{15}$_   22. $-\frac{7}{4} + \frac{1}{8}$ _$-\frac{5}{8}$_   23. $\frac{1}{3} - \frac{7}{8}$ _$-\frac{13}{24}$_   [3-6]

24. $2\frac{4}{5} + (-6\frac{1}{2})$ _$-4\frac{3}{10}$_   25. $3\frac{3}{5} - 4\frac{1}{2}$ _$-\frac{5}{6}$_   26. $7\frac{1}{4} - \frac{7}{8}$ _$6\frac{3}{8}$_   [3-7]

27. $\frac{3}{5} \times (-\frac{20}{30})$ _$-\frac{2}{5}$_   28. $-4\frac{1}{2} \times 2\frac{2}{9}$ _-10_   29. $-6\frac{2}{3} \times (-7) \times 1\frac{1}{5}$ _$\frac{[3-8]}{56}$_

30. $2\frac{9}{10} \div 1\frac{3}{5}$ _$1\frac{13}{16}$_   31. $2\frac{4}{7} \div (-\frac{9}{4})$ _$-1\frac{1}{7}$_   32. $2 \div (-\frac{3}{4})$ _$-2\frac{2}{3}$_   [3-9]

Write as a terminating or repeating decimal. Use a bar to show a repetend.

33. $\frac{8}{25}$ _0.32_   34. $3\frac{7}{8}$ _3.875_   35. $\frac{8}{15}$ _$0.5\overline{3}$_   [3-10]

38

NAME _____ DATE _____

Test — Chapter 3

DIRECTIONS: Write the answers in the spaces provided.

List all the factors.

1. 18   2. 46   3. 220   [3-1]

State which of the numbers 2, 3, 4, 5, 9, and 10 are factors of each number. Use divisibility tests.

4. 312   5. 600   6. 540

Find out whether each number is prime or composite. If it is composite, give its prime factorization.

7. 45   8. 29   [3-2]

Complete.

9. $9 \times \frac{?}{} = \frac{9}{14}$ 10. $\frac{1}{5} \times 5 = \underline{\ ?\ }$ [3-3]

Show as a proper fraction in lowest terms or as a mixed number in simple form.

11. $\frac{42}{48}$ 12. $\frac{18}{8}$ 13. $-\frac{68}{5}$ [3-4]

Show each pair of fractions as equivalent fractions with the least common denominator.

14. $\frac{2}{3}, \frac{5}{12}$ 15. $\frac{7}{12}, \frac{11}{30}$ 16. $\frac{x}{5}, \frac{y}{3}$ [3-5]

Perform the indicated operation. Write the answer as a proper fraction or as a mixed number in simple form.

17. $\frac{7}{8} + \frac{1}{16}$ 18. $-\frac{2}{3} + (-\frac{1}{4})$ [3-6]

19. $3\frac{5}{6} + 2\frac{3}{4}$ 20. $2\frac{1}{3} - (-2\frac{1}{4})$ [3-7]

21. $\frac{5}{9} \times (-\frac{18}{80})$ 22. $10\frac{1}{8} \times 4\frac{2}{3}$ [3-8]

23. $\frac{9}{10} \div 1\frac{3}{5}$ 24. $\frac{4}{5} \div (-\frac{6}{20})$ [3-9]

Write as a terminating or repeating decimal. Use a bar to show a repetend.

25. $-4\frac{5}{8}$ 26. $\frac{4}{33}$ [3-10]

ANSWERS

1. _1, 2, 3, 6, 9, 18_ (4)
2. _1, 2, 23, 46_ (4)
3. _1, 2, 4, 5, 10, 11, 20, 22, 44, 55, 110, 220_ (4)
4. _2, 3, 4_ (2)
5. _2, 3, 4, 5, 10_ (2)
6. _2, 3, 4, 5, 9, 10_ (4)
7. _$3^2 \times 5$_ (4)
8. _prime_ (4)
9. _$\frac{1}{14}$_ (4)
10. _$\frac{7}{8}$_ (4)
11. _$\frac{7}{8}$_ (4)
12. _$2\frac{1}{4}$_ (4)
13. _$-13\frac{3}{5}$_ (4)
14. _$\frac{8}{12}, \frac{5}{12}$_ (4)
15. _$\frac{35}{60}, \frac{22}{60}$_ (4)
16. _$\frac{3x}{15}, \frac{5y}{15}$_ (4)
17. _$\frac{15}{16}$_ (4)
18. _$-\frac{11}{12}$_ (4)
19. _$6\frac{7}{12}$_ (4)
20. _$4\frac{7}{30}$_ (4)
21. _$-\frac{9}{8}$_ (4)
22. _$47\frac{1}{4}$_ (4)
23. _$\frac{9}{16}$_ (4)
24. _-2_ (4)
25. _-4.625_ (4)
26. _$0.\overline{12}$_ (4)

39

NAME _____ DATE _____

Make-up Test — Chapter 3

DIRECTIONS: Write the answers in the spaces provided.

Find all the factors of each number.

1. 30   2. 58   3. 125   [3-1]

State which of the numbers 2, 3, 4, 5, 9, and 10 are factors of each number. Use divisibility tests.

4. 50   5. 342   6. 360

Find out whether each number is prime or composite. If it is composite, give its prime factorization.

7. 31   8. 75   [3-2]

Complete.

9. $6 \times \frac{?}{} = \frac{6}{11}$ 10. $\frac{1}{3} \times 3 = \underline{\ ?\ }$ [3-3]

Write as a proper fraction in lowest terms or as a mixed number in simple form.

11. $\frac{28}{36}$ 12. $\frac{18}{10}$ 13. $-\frac{74}{8}$ [3-4]

Write each pair of fractions as equivalent fractions with the least common denominator.

14. $\frac{1}{2}, \frac{3}{10}$ 15. $\frac{5}{9}, \frac{7}{30}$ 16. $\frac{a}{9}, \frac{b}{5}$ [3-5]

Perform the indicated operation. Write the answer as a proper fraction or as a mixed number in simple form.

17. $\frac{3}{5} + \frac{1}{2}$ 18. $\frac{2}{3} - (-\frac{1}{5})$ [3-6]

19. $2\frac{1}{4} + 3\frac{2}{3}$ 20. $-4\frac{1}{10} + (-2\frac{1}{4})$ [3-7]

21. $3\frac{1}{3} \times \frac{1}{2}$ 22. $\frac{3}{4} \times \frac{10}{21}$ [3-8]

23. $\frac{2}{3} \div \frac{7}{15}$ 24. $1\frac{1}{3} \div \frac{4}{7}$ [3-9]

Write as a terminating or repeating decimal. Use a bar to show a repetend.

25. $-3\frac{7}{8}$ 26. $\frac{5}{33}$ 27. $\frac{5}{6}$ [3-10]

ANSWERS

1. _1, 2, 3, 5, 6, 10, 15, 30_ (2)
2. _1, 2, 29, 58_ (2)
3. _1, 5, 25, 125_ (2)
4. _2, 5, 10_ (2)
5. _2, 3, 9_ (3)
6. _2, 3, 4, 5, 9, 10_ (4)
7. _prime_ (4)
8. _3×5^2_ (4)
9. _$\frac{1}{11}$_ (4)
10. _1_ (4)
11. _$\frac{7}{9}$_ (4)
12. _$1\frac{4}{5}$_ (4)
13. _$-9\frac{1}{4}$_ (4)
14. _$\frac{5}{10}, \frac{3}{10}$_ (4)
15. _$\frac{50}{90}, \frac{21}{90}$_ (4)
16. _$\frac{4a}{12}, \frac{9b}{12}$_ (4)
17. _$1\frac{1}{10}$_ (4)
18. _$\frac{13}{21}$_ (4)
19. _$5\frac{11}{12}$_ (4)
20. _$-6\frac{7}{20}$_ (4)
21. _$1\frac{2}{3}$_ (4)
22. _$\frac{5}{14}$_ (4)
23. _$\frac{5}{7}$_ (4)
24. _$2\frac{1}{3}$_ (4)
25. _-3.875_ (4)
26. _$0.\overline{15}$_ (4)
27. _$0.8\overline{3}$_ (4)

40

Page 41

NAME _____ DATE _____

CUMULATIVE REVIEW — Chapters 1–3
Exercises

Give the solution or solutions of the equation with the given replacement set.

1. $r + 17 = 43$; {26, 36, 60} *26*
2. $15p = 180$; {10, 12, 14} *12*
3. $6(4 + z) = 72$; {6, 7, 8} *8*
4. $4d + 7 = 9$; $\{1\frac{1}{2}, \frac{1}{3}, \frac{1}{4}\}$ *$\frac{1}{2}$*
5. $(t + 3) + (5 - t) = 3$; {2, 3, 4} *3*
6. $3a + a^2 = 28$; {2, 3, 4} *4*

Evaluate the expression if $r = 2$, $s = 6$, and $t = 0.4$.

7. sr^2 *24*
8. rs^2 *72*
9. $3t^2$ *0.48*
10. $(r + s)^2$ *64*
11. r^3s^2 *288*
12. $\frac{(10)^2}{r}$ *8*

Use the symbol $>$ to order the numbers from greatest to least.

13. 3.42, 34.2, 3.24 *$34.2 > 3.42 > 3.24$*
14. 0.07, 0.70, 0.76 *$0.76 > 0.70 > 0.07$*
15. 5×3.4, 7×2.6 *$7 \times 2.6 > 5 \times 3.4 > 16$*
16. $12 \div 3$, 2.5×2, $9 \div 2$ *$2.5 \times 2 > 9 \div 2 > 12 \div 3$*

List the integers that can replace x to make the statement true.

17. $|x| = 5$ *$-5, 5$*
18. $|x| \le 3$ *$-3, -2, -1, 0, 1, 2, 3$*
19. $|x| < 2.7$ *$-2, -1, 0, 1, 2$*
20. $7 < |x| < 9$ *$-8, 8$*
21. $3 > |x| > 0$ *$-2, -1, 1, 2$*
22. $12 \le |x| \le 14$ *$-14, -13, -12, 12, 13, 14$*

What value of the variable makes the statement true?

23. $a + 19 = -4$ *-23*
24. $-8 + r = 14$ *22*
25. $6(-p) = 54$ *-9*
26. $-d + 12 = 4$ *-48*
27. $17 - a = 11$ *6*
28. $-8(-b) = 56$ *7*
29. $64 + f = 42$ *-22*
30. $5v = -105$ *-21*
31. $-7s = 49$ *-7*

Evaluate the expression when $a = 3$, $b = -6$, and $c = -2$.

32. $\frac{a+b}{b}$ *$\frac{1}{2}$*
33. $\frac{b+3c}{a}$ *-4*
34. $\frac{bc}{a}$ *4*
35. $a^2 + c^2$ *13*
36. $\frac{b}{2} + \frac{c}{2}$ *-4*
37. $\frac{abc}{-4}$ *-9*

Solve. Write the answer as a proper fraction in lowest terms or as a mixed number in simple form.

38. $3 \times (\frac{5}{8} + \frac{15}{16})$ *6*
39. $3\frac{1}{8} - [2\frac{1}{2}(-3\frac{1}{5})]$ *$11\frac{1}{8}$*

41

Page 42

NAME _____ DATE _____

CUMULATIVE REVIEW — Chapters 1–3 (continued)
Problems

Problem Solving Reminders
Here are some reminders that may help you solve some of the problems on this page.
• You may need to supply additional information.
• Some steps in your plan may not involve operations.
• Reread the question to be sure you have answered with the information requested.

Solve.

1. The Ardsley Business Club is sponsoring a dinner party for its 75 members. The cost is $18.50 per person and a deposit of $\frac{1}{3}$ of the total bill must be paid to the restaurant in advance. How much is the advance payment? *$462.50*

2. A carpenter estimates the cost of building wood decks at $9.50 per square foot. Will Millie Young pay less than $2500 to have a deck built that is 278 square feet? *no*

3. Carolyn Mercer is a temporary typist registered with Archer Employment Agency. The fees include $5.25 an hour for the typist and $1.50 an hour for the agency. How much will a company pay to hire a typist for 7 h? *$47.25*

4. Jim Marshall bought 150 shares of Medcall stock for $10,275. When the price of the stock went up, he sold it for $108 a share. What was his total profit on the stock? *$5925*

5. The admission price to a concert is $5.75 per adult and $2.50 per child. One evening, 250 adults and 75 children attended the concert. What was the total admission fee collected? *$1625*

6. Storm-window insulating tape costs $3.00 per foot. What is the cost of 5 yards of tape? *$45*

7. Mrs. Jamison found that the dry-cleaning costs for her family for a three-month period totaled $78.50. Based on this total, what would she expect to pay for dry cleaning for the entire year? *$314*

8. Daniel purchased 2 sweaters costing $22.50 each, 3 ties for $7.50 each, and a pair of slacks for $25.95. If he paid with a $100 bill, how much change did he receive? *$6.55*

42

Page 43

NAME _____ DATE _____

CUMULATIVE TEST — Chapters 1–3

DIRECTIONS: Write the answer in the space provided.

Chapter 1

Evaluate the expression when $e = 6$ and $f = 14$.

1. $e + f$
2. $f - e \times 2$
3. $42 \div \frac{f}{2}$
4. $2f - e$

Which is greater?

5. 2^3 or 3^2
6. $3^2 \times 3^5$ or $4^3 \times 4^4$
7. $(3 + 2)^3$ or 10^2
8. 10^2 or $5^2 \times 2$

Round to the place specified.

9. hundredths: 132.3998
10. tens: 385.045

Use the inverse operation to write a related equation and solve for the variable.

11. $9r = 126$
12. $m \div 3 = 12$
13. $2b + 6 = 28$
14. $s + 9 = 15$

Solve, using the five-step plan.

15. Adam purchased a fishing rod for $19.98, a package of six hooks for $2.00, a roll of 200 ft of fishing line costing $3.75, three lures costing 92¢ each, and a tackle box costing $5.83. How much change did he get after paying with a $50 bill?

Chapter 2

Replace __?__ with =, >, or < to make a true statement.

16. -3 __?__ -5
17. $|6|$ __?__ $|-7|$
18. $.12$ __?__ -13
19. -8 __?__ 3

Find the sum or difference.

20. $-16.3 + 24.1$
21. $-8.2 + (-0.36)$
22. $-7 + 5 + (-11)$
23. $46.9 - (-12.3)$
24. $-8.3 - (-8.3)$
25. $0 - 54.7$

ANSWERS

1. *20* (1)
2. *2* (1)
3. *6* (1)
4. *22* (1)
5. *3^2* (2)
6. *$4^3 \times 4^4$* (2)
7. *$(3+2)^3$* (2)
8. *10^2* (2)
9. *132.40* (2)
10. *390* (2)
11. *$r = 126 \div 9; 14$* (2)
12. *$m = 12 \times 3; 36$* (2)
13. *$2b = 28 - 6; 11$* (2)
14. *$s = 15 - 9; 6$* (2)
15. *$15.68* (2)
16. *>* (2)
17. *<* (2)
18. *>* (2)
19. *<* (2)
20. *7.8* (2)
21. *-8.56* (2)
22. *-13* (2)
23. *59.2* (2)
24. *0* (2)
25. *-54.7* (2)

43

Page 44

NAME _____ DATE _____

CUMULATIVE TEST — Chapters 1–3 (continued)

Find the product or quotient.

26. $-5.2(-14.3)$
27. $-3(-2)(-5)(-10)$
28. $-0.06 \div 0.2$
29. $-8(3.06)$

Evaluate the expression when $r = -2.4$ and $s = -5.6$.

30. $r + s$
31. $10rs$

Write the expression without exponents.

32. 4^{-2}
33. $5^{-7} \times 5^6$
34. $(-2)^3 \times (-2)^{-2}$
35. 3×10^{-4}

Chapter 3

36. Find all the factors of 24.
37. Which of the numbers 2, 3, 4, 5, 9, and 10 are factors of 240?
38. Write the prime factorization of 50.

Write as a proper fraction in lowest terms or as a mixed number in simple form.

39. $\frac{16}{56}$
40. $-\frac{135}{180}$
41. $\frac{-72}{20}$

Add or subtract. Write the answer as a proper fraction in lowest terms or as a mixed number in simple form.

42. $\frac{3}{4} + \frac{7}{10}$
43. $-\frac{5}{8} + \frac{11}{12}$
44. $1\frac{2}{3} - (-3\frac{5}{6})$
45. $-1\frac{1}{2} - \frac{1}{2}$

Multiply or divide. Write the answer as a proper fraction in lowest terms or as a mixed number in simple form.

46. $\frac{3}{8} \times (-\frac{24}{27})$
47. $-6\frac{2}{7} \times (-1\frac{3}{11})$
48. $5\frac{1}{9} \div 1\frac{1}{3}$
49. $3\frac{1}{3} \div (-2\frac{1}{2})$

Write as a terminating or repeating decimal. Use a bar to show a repetend.

50. $\frac{8}{25}$
51. $\frac{7}{8}$
52. $\frac{5}{12}$

ANSWERS

26. *74.36* (2)
27. *300* (2)
28. *-0.3* (2)
29. *-24.48* (2)
30. *-8* (2)
31. *1344* (2)
32. *$\frac{1}{16}$* (2)
33. *$\frac{1}{5}$* (2)
34. *-2* (2)
35. *0.0003* (2)
36. *1, 2, 3, 4, 6, 8, 12, 24* (2)
37. *2, 3, 4, 5, 10* (2)
38. *2×5^2* (2)
39. *$\frac{2}{7}$* (2)
40. *$-\frac{3}{4}$* (2)
41. *$-3\frac{3}{5}$* (2)
42. *$1\frac{9}{20}$* (2)
43. *$\frac{7}{24}$* (2)
44. *$5\frac{1}{2}$* (2)
45. *-2* (2)
46. *$-\frac{1}{3}$* (2)
47. *8* (2)
48. *$3\frac{5}{6}$* (2)
49. *$-1\frac{1}{3}$* (2)
50. *0.32* (2)
51. *0.875* (2)
52. *$0.41\overline{6}$* (2)

44

Reading Mathematics

Students will learn the meaning of the following mathematical terms in this lesson: *multiple, even number, odd number, factor, divisible.*

3-1 Factors and Divisibility

A **multiple** of a whole number is the product of that number and any whole number. You can find the multiples of a given whole number by multiplying that number by 0, 1, 2, 3, 4, and so on. For example, the first four multiples of 7 are 0, 7, 14, and 21, since:

$$0 \cdot 7 = 0 \qquad 1 \cdot 7 = 7 \qquad 2 \cdot 7 = 14 \qquad 3 \cdot 7 = 21$$

Any multiple of 2 is called an **even number.** A whole number that is not an even number is called an **odd number.** Notice that since

$$0 = 0 \cdot 2,$$

0 is a multiple of 2 and is therefore an even number.

In general, any number is a multiple of each of its factors. For example, 21 is a multiple of 7 and of 3.

You know that 60 can be written as the product of 5 and 12. Whenever a number, such as 60, can be written as the product of two whole numbers, such as 5 and 12, these two numbers are called **whole number factors** of the first number. A number is said to be **divisible** by its whole number factors. Thus, 60 is divisible by the factors 5 and 12.

To find out if a smaller whole number is a factor of a larger whole number, we divide the larger number by the smaller. If the remainder is 0, then the smaller number is a factor of the larger number. If the remainder is *not* 0, then the smaller number is *not* a factor of the larger number.

EXAMPLE 1 State whether or not the smaller number is a factor of the larger.

　　　　　　　a. 6; 138 　　　　　　　　　　　**b.** 8; 154

Solution 　**a.** Divide 138 by 6. 　　　　　　**b.** Divide 154 by 8.

　　　　　　　　$138 \div 6 = 23 \text{ R } 0$ 　　　　　　　$154 \div 8 = 19 \text{ R } 2$

　　　　　　　　Since the remainder is 0, 　　　　Since the remainder is not 0,
　　　　　　　　6 is a factor of 138. 　　　　　　8 is not a factor of 154.

EXAMPLE 2 Find all the factors of 24.

Solution 　Try each whole number as a divisor, starting with 1.

　　　　　　　　$24 \div 1 = 24$ 　　　　Thus, 1 and 24 are factors.
　　　　　　　　$24 \div 2 = 12$ 　　　　Thus, 2 and 12 are factors.
　　　　　　　　$24 \div 3 = 8$ 　　　　Thus, 3 and 8 are factors.

84　　*Chapter 3*

$24 \div 4 = 6$ Thus, 4 and 6 are factors.
$24 \div 5 = 4 \text{ R } 4$ Thus, 5 is not a factor.

Since $24 \div 6 = 4$, the factors begin to repeat, and we do not have to try any whole number greater than 5 as a divisor. Thus, the factors of 24 are 1, 2, 3, 4, 6, 8, 12, and 24.

Sometimes it may be possible to find the factors of a number by an inspection of the digits of the number. For example, let us

consider multiples of 2: 0, 2, 4, 6, 8, 10, 12, 14, 16, . . .
consider multiples of 5: 0, 5, 10, 15, 20, . . .
consider multiples of 10: 0, 10, 20, 30, 40, . . .

From the patterns we see in the last digits of the sets of multiples above, we can devise the following tests for divisibility.

> Divisibility by 2: A whole number has 2 as a factor if its last digit has 2 as a factor.
>
> Divisibility by 5: A whole number has 5 as a factor if its last digit is 5 or 0.
>
> Divisibility by 10: A whole number has 10 as a factor if its last digit is 0.

Suppose we want to check whether a number, such as 712, is divisible by 4. Since any multiple of 100 is divisible by 4, we know that 700 is divisible by 4. To test 712, then, we simply look at the last two digits. Since 12 is a multiple of 4, the number 712 is also a multiple of 4 ($712 \div 4 = 178$). A similar inspection shows that 950 is not a multiple of 4, since the number represented by the last two digits, 50, is not a multiple of 4 ($950 \div 4$ gives 237 R 2). This suggests the following test for divisibility.

> Divisibility by 4: A whole number has 4 as a factor if its last two digits represent a multiple of 4.

Rational Numbers **85**

EXAMPLE 3 Test each number for divisibility by 2, 4, 5, and 10.

        a. 35   **b.** 150   **c.** 7736   **d.** 920

Solution

a. 35: Since the last digit is 5 and is odd, 2 and 10 are not factors. Since 35 is not a multiple of 4, 4 is not a factor. Since the last digit is 5, 5 is a factor.

b. 150: Since 0 is the last digit, 2, 5, and 10 are factors. 4 is not a factor, since 50 is not a multiple of 4.

c. 7736: 2 is a factor, since the last digit, 6, is even. 4 is a factor, since 36 is a multiple of 4. 5 and 10 are not factors, since the last digit is not 5 or 0.

d. 920: 2, 5, and 10 are all factors, since the last digit is 0. 4 is a factor, since the last two digits, 20, represent a multiple of 4.

Rules for recognizing numbers divisible by 3 or 9 are a bit more difficult to discover. The rules relate to the sum of the digits of the number. Study the following numbers.

	Divisible by 3	**Divisible by 9**	**Sum of digits**
393	yes $393 \div 3 = 131$	no $393 \div 9$ gives 43 R 6	15
394	no $394 \div 3$ gives 131 R 1	no $394 \div 9$ gives 43 R 7	16
395	no $395 \div 3$ gives 131 R 2	no $395 \div 9$ gives 43 R 8	17
396	yes $396 \div 3 = 132$	yes $396 \div 9 = 44$	18

Notice that when the sum of the digits of the number is divisible by 3 (15 or 18), the number (393 or 396) is divisible by 3. Notice also that when the sum of the digits is divisible by 9 (18), the number (396) is divisible by 9. This illustrates the following tests.

> Divisibility by 3: A whole number has 3 as a factor if the sum of the digits of the number is a multiple of 3.
>
> Divisibility by 9: A whole number has 9 as a factor if the sum of the digits of the number is a multiple of 9.

86 *Chapter 3*

EXAMPLE 4 Test each number for divisibility by 3 and 9.

        a. 714   **b.** 6291   **c.** 4813

Solution   **a.** $7 + 1 + 4 = 12$. Since 12 is a multiple of 3 but not a multiple of 9, 714 is divisible by 3, but not by 9.

          b. $6 + 2 + 9 + 1 = 18$. Since 18 is a multiple of 3 and of 9, 6291 is divisible by 3 and by 9.

          c. $4 + 8 + 1 + 3 = 16$. Since 16 is not a multiple of 3 or of 9, 4813 is not divisible by 3 or by 9.

Class Exercises

State all the factors of each number.

5. 1, 2, 3, 5, 6, 10, 15, 30

1. 6 1, 2, 3, 6   **2.** 10 1, 2, 5, 10   **3.** 20 1, 2, 4, 5, 10, 20   **4.** 18   **5.** 30

1, 2, 3, 6, 9, 18

6. What number is a factor of every whole number? 1

Write the first five multiples of each number.

10. 0, 18, 36, 54, 72

7. 9 0, 9, 18, 27, 36   **8.** 14 0, 14, 28, 42, 56   **9.** 15 0, 15, 30, 45, 60   **10.** 18

Test each number for divisibility by 2.

                                                                 yes

11. 130 yes   **12.** 4681 no   **13.** 105 no   **14.** 3576

Test each number for divisibility by 4.

                                                                 yes

15. 8310 no   **16.** 712 yes   **17.** 86,222 no   **18.** 5732

Test each number for divisibility by 5 and 10.

                                                            yes; no

19. 8325 yes; no   **20.** 7602 no; no   **21.** 870 yes; yes   **22.** 6395

Test each number for divisibility by 3 and 9.

                                                            yes; yes

23. 175 no; no   **24.** 288 yes; yes   **25.** 651 yes; no   **26.** 8766

Written Exercises

List all the factors of each number.

A   **1.** 42   **2.** 45   **3.** 32   **4.** 40   **5.** 56

      6. 31   **7.** 84   **8.** 51   **9.** 41   **10.** 112

Rational Numbers **87**

Additional Answers
Written Exercises

1. 1, 2, 3, 6, 7, 14, 21, 42
2. 1, 3, 5, 9, 15, 45
3. 1, 2, 4, 8, 16, 32
4. 1, 2, 4, 5, 8, 10, 20, 40
5. 1, 2, 4, 7, 8, 14, 28, 56
6. 1, 31
7. 1, 2, 3, 4, 6, 7, 12, 14, 21, 28, 42, 84
8. 1, 3, 17, 51
9. 1, 41
10. 1, 2, 4, 7, 8, 14, 16, 28, 56, 112

State which of the numbers 2, 3, 4, 5, 9, and 10 are factors of the given number. Use the tests for divisibility.

11. 132   2, 3, 4   12. 150   2, 3, 5, 10   13. 195   3, 5   14. 4280   2, 4, 5, 10   15. 567   3, 9

16. 8155   5   17. 43,260   2, 3, 4, 5, 10   18. 720   2, 3, 4, 5, 9, 10   19. 1147   none   20. 78,921   3, 9

For each number, determine whether (a) 2 is a factor, (b) 3 is a factor, and (c) 6 is a factor. What appears to be true in order for 6 to be a factor?

21. 1316   yes; no; no   22. 2,817,000   yes; yes; yes   23. 31,027,302   yes; yes; yes

24. 1224   yes; yes; yes   25. 2,147,640   yes; yes; yes   26. 36,111,114   yes; yes; yes
A number has 6 as a factor if it has 2 and 3 as a factor.

Supply the missing digit of the first number if it is known to have the other two numbers as factors.

B   27. 35?; 2, 3   4   28. 876?; 2, 5   0   29. 910?; 3, 5   5

30. 472?; 3, 4   8   31. 61?2; 4, 9   9   32. 47?2; 4, 9   5

33. Any multiple of 1000 is divisible by 8. Use this fact to devise a test for divisibility by 8.

34. The total number of pages in a book must be a multiple of 32. If the book consists of 10 chapters, each 24 pages long, and 8 pages of introductory material, how many blank pages will be left?   8 pages

C   35. Devise a test for divisibility by 25.

36. A **perfect number** is one that is the sum of all of its factors except itself. The smallest perfect number is 6, since 6 = 1 + 2 + 3. Find the next perfect number.   28

Review Exercises

Complete with <, >, or =.

1. 80 __?__ 800   <   2. 136 __?__ 119   >   3. 21.6 __?__ 2.29   >   4. 0.87 __?__ 0.0941   >

5. 3.081 __?__ 3.101   <   6. 48.88 __?__ 49.17   <   7. 3^3 __?__ $(2 + 1)^2$ >   8. $2^3 + 1$ __?__ $(2 + 1)^3$ <

3-2 Prime Numbers and Composite Numbers

Teaching Suggestions p. 83b

Related Activities p. 83b

Reading Mathematics

Students will learn the meaning of the following mathematical terms in this lesson: *prime number, composite number, Sieve of Eratosthenes, factor tree, prime factorization, Fundamental Theorem of Arithmetic.*

The word *prime* is sometimes used as a noun to mean "prime number."

Consider the list of counting numbers and their factors given at the right. Notice that each of the numbers 2, 3, 5, 7, and 11 has *exactly* two factors: 1 and the number itself. A number with this property is called a **prime number.** A counting number that has more than two factors is called a **composite number.** In the list 4, 6, 8, 9, 10, and 12 are all composite numbers. Since 1 has exactly one factor, it is neither prime nor composite.

Number	Factors
1	1
2	1, 2
3	1, 3
4	1, 2, 4
5	1, 5
6	1, 2, 3, 6
7	1, 7
8	1, 2, 4, 8
9	1, 3, 9
10	1, 2, 5, 10
11	1, 11
12	1, 2, 3, 4, 6, 12

About 230 B.C. Eratosthenes, a Greek mathematician, suggested a way to find prime numbers in a list of all the counting numbers up to a certain number. Eratosthenes first crossed out all multiples of 2, except 2 itself. Next he crossed out all multiples of the next remaining number, 3, except 3 itself. He continued crossing out multiples of each successive remaining number except the number itself. The numbers remaining at the end of this process are the primes.

```
     1    2    3    4    5    6    7    8    9
10   11   12   13   14   15   16   17   18   19
20   21   22   23   24   25   26   27   28   29
30   31   32   33   34   35   36   37   . . .
```

The method just described is called the **Sieve of Eratosthenes,** because it picks out the prime numbers as a strainer, or sieve, picks out solid particles from a liquid.

Every counting number greater than 1 has at least one prime factor, which may be the number itself. You can factor a number into prime factors by using either of the following methods.

Inverted short division

```
2)42
3)21
   7
```

Factor tree

```
    42
   /  \
  2    21
      /  \
     3    7
```

Rational Numbers **89**

State the prime factorization of the given number.

1. 6 2 · 3

2. 16 2⁴

3. 40 2³ · 5

4. 108 2² · 3³

Use a factor tree to find the prime factorization of each number.

5. 172

172 = 2² · 43

6. 165

165 = 3 · 5 · 11

Give the prime factorization of each number.

1. 64 2⁶

2. 96 2⁵ · 3

3. 18 2 · 3²

4. 72 2³ · 3²

5. 120 2³ · 3 · 5

6. 123 3 · 41

Another factor tree for the number 42 is shown at the right. Notice that the prime factors of 42 are the same in either factor tree except for their order. Every whole number is similar to 42 in this respect. This fact is expressed in the following theorem.

42
/ \
3   14
    / \
   7   2

Fundamental Theorem of Arithmetic

Every whole number greater than 1 can be written as a product of prime factors in exactly one way, except for the order of the factors.

When we write 42 as 2 · 3 · 7, this product of prime factors is called the **prime factorization** of 42.

EXAMPLE Give the prime factorization of 60.

Solution

Method 1

$2)\overline{60}$
$2)\overline{30}$
$3)\overline{15}$
$\quad 5$

Method 2

60
/ \
2   30
    / \
   2   15
       / \
      3   5

Using either method, we find that the prime factorization of 60 is 2 · 2 · 3 · 5, or 2² · 3 · 5.

Class Exercises

State whether each number is prime or composite.

1. 7 prime **2.** 9 composite **3.** 15 composite **4.** 23 prime **5.** 22 composite **6.** 19 prime

Name the prime factors of each number.

7. 21 3, 7 **8.** 10 2, 5 **9.** 18 2, 3 **10.** 26 2, 13 **11.** 30 2, 3, 5 **12.** 70 2, 5, 7

Name the number whose prime factorization is given.

13. 3² · 5 45 **14.** 2² · 3² 36 **15.** 2³ · 3 24

16. 2 · 7² 98 **17.** 3² · 11 99 **18.** 2² · 5² 100

90 *Chapter 3*

Written Exercises

State whether each number is prime or composite.

A
1. 39 *composite*   2. 41 *prime*   3. 51 *composite*   4. 111 *composite*   5. 124 *composite*   6. 321 *composite*

7. 641 *prime*   8. 753 *composite*   9. 894 *composite*   10. 1164 *composite*   11. 2061 *composite*   12. 3001 *prime*

Give the prime factorization of each whole number.

13. 12 $2^2 \cdot 3$ 14. 50 $2 \cdot 5^2$ 15. 24 $2^3 \cdot 3$ 16. 28 $2^2 \cdot 7$ 17. 39 $3 \cdot 13$ 18. 56 $2^3 \cdot 7$

19. 66 $2 \cdot 3 \cdot 11$ 20. 51 $3 \cdot 17$ 21. 54 $2 \cdot 3^3$ 22. 63 $3^2 \cdot 7$ 23. 84 $2^2 \cdot 3 \cdot 7$ 24. 90 $2 \cdot 3^2 \cdot 5$

25. 196 $2^2 \cdot 7^2$ 26. 360 $2^3 \cdot 3^2 \cdot 5$ 27. 308 $2^2 \cdot 7 \cdot 11$ 28. 693 $3^2 \cdot 7 \cdot 11$ 29. 114 $2 \cdot 3 \cdot 19$ 30. 1150 $2 \cdot 5^2 \cdot 23$

B 31. Explain why 2 is the only even prime number.

32. Write the prime factorizations of the square numbers 16, 36, 81, and 144 by using exponents. What do you think must be true of the exponents in the prime factorization of a square number?

33. Explain why the sum of two prime numbers greater than 2 can never be a prime number.

34. Explain how you know that each of the following numbers must be composite: 111; 111,111; 111,111,111; ...

35. List all the possible digits that can be the last digit of a prime number that is greater than 10. *1, 3, 7, 9*

C 36. Choose a six-digit number, such as 652,652, the last three digits of which are a repeat of the first three digits. Show that 7, 11, and 13 are all factors of the number you chose.

37. Since 7, 11, and 13 are factors of any number of the type defined in Exercise 36, what is the largest composite number that is always a factor of such a number? What is the other factor?

38. Give an example to show that the Fundamental Theorem of Arithmetic would be false if 1 were defined to be a prime number.
Answers will vary. For example, $6 = 1 \cdot 2 \cdot 3 = 2 \cdot 3$.

Review Exercises

Simplify.

1. $-4 + 6$ *2*   2. $8 + (-12)$ *−4*   3. $3 - 4$ *−1*   4. $10 - (-15)$ *25*

5. $-12 \cdot (-20)$ *240*   6. $7 \cdot (-3)$ *−21*   7. $-48 \div (-24)$ *2*   8. $-72 \div 8$ *−9*

Rational Numbers **91**

Reading Mathematics

Students will learn the meaning of the following mathematical terms in this lesson: *numerator, denominator, opposite, rational number.*

3-3 Positive and Negative Fractions

In any fraction the number above the fraction bar is called the **numerator** and the number below the bar is called the **denominator.** Since the fraction bar indicates division,

$$\frac{3}{5} \text{ means } 3 \div 5.$$

   A study of fractions on a number line shows some important properties of fractions.

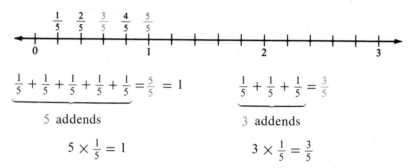

$$\underbrace{\frac{1}{5} + \frac{1}{5} + \frac{1}{5} + \frac{1}{5} + \frac{1}{5}}_{5 \text{ addends}} = \frac{5}{5} = 1 \qquad \underbrace{\frac{1}{5} + \frac{1}{5} + \frac{1}{5}}_{3 \text{ addends}} = \frac{3}{5}$$

$$5 \times \frac{1}{5} = 1 \qquad\qquad 3 \times \frac{1}{5} = \frac{3}{5}$$

We can state these properties in general terms that apply to all positive fractions.

> ## *Properties*
>
> For all whole numbers a and b ($a > 0, b > 0$),
>
> $$\underbrace{\frac{1}{b} + \frac{1}{b} + \cdots + \frac{1}{b}}_{b \text{ addends}} = \frac{b}{b} = 1 \qquad \underbrace{\frac{1}{b} + \frac{1}{b} + \cdots + \frac{1}{b}}_{a \text{ addends}} = \frac{a}{b}$$
>
> $$b \times \frac{1}{b} = 1 \qquad\qquad a \times \frac{1}{b} = \frac{a}{b}$$
>
> $$1 \div b = \frac{1}{b} \qquad\qquad a \div b = \frac{a}{b}$$

   Just as the negative integers are the opposites of the positive integers, the negative fractions are the opposites of the positive fractions. For every fraction $\frac{a}{b}$ there is a fraction denoted by $-\frac{a}{b}$ that is said to be

92   *Chapter 3*

the **opposite** of $\frac{a}{b}$. On the number line the graphs of $\frac{a}{b}$ and $-\frac{a}{b}$ are on opposite sides of 0 and at equal distances from 0. For example, $\frac{3}{5}$ and $-\frac{3}{5}$ are opposites. They are shown on the number line below.

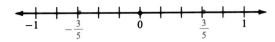

Properties similar to those for positive fractions apply to negative fractions.

$$-\frac{1}{5} + \left(-\frac{1}{5}\right) + \left(-\frac{1}{5}\right) + \left(-\frac{1}{5}\right) + \left(-\frac{1}{5}\right) = -1 \qquad -\frac{1}{5} + \left(-\frac{1}{5}\right) + \left(-\frac{1}{5}\right) = -\frac{3}{5}$$

$$\underbrace{\phantom{-\frac{1}{5} + \left(-\frac{1}{5}\right) + \left(-\frac{1}{5}\right) + \left(-\frac{1}{5}\right) + \left(-\frac{1}{5}\right)}}_{\text{5 addends}} \qquad \underbrace{\phantom{-\frac{1}{5} + \left(-\frac{1}{5}\right) + \left(-\frac{1}{5}\right)}}_{\text{3 addends}}$$

$$5 \times \left(-\frac{1}{5}\right) = -1 \qquad\qquad 3 \times \left(-\frac{1}{5}\right) = -\frac{3}{5}$$

In an earlier section you learned that the quotient of two numbers of opposite sign is negative. Using this rule we can write the following:

$$1 \div (-4) = \frac{1}{-4} = -\frac{1}{4} \qquad\qquad (-1) \div 4 = \frac{-1}{4} = -\frac{1}{4}$$

Therefore, we can write the opposite of $\frac{1}{4}$ as $-\frac{1}{4}$, or as $\frac{-1}{4}$, or as $\frac{1}{-4}$. In general, for $b \neq 0$, $-\frac{a}{b} = \frac{-a}{b} = \frac{a}{-b}$.

EXAMPLE 1 Express $-\frac{3}{8}$ in two other ways.

Solution $\qquad -\frac{3}{8} = \frac{-3}{8} = \frac{3}{-8}$

EXAMPLE 2 Complete.

a. $\left(-\frac{1}{3}\right) + \left(-\frac{1}{3}\right) + \left(-\frac{1}{3}\right) = \underline{}$ \qquad b. $3 \times \underline{} = -1$

c. $2 \times \left(-\frac{1}{5}\right) = \underline{}$ \qquad d. $-\frac{2}{5} = \underline{} \div 5$

Solution a. $\left(-\frac{1}{3}\right) + \left(-\frac{1}{3}\right) + \left(-\frac{1}{3}\right) = -1$ \qquad b. $3 \times \left(-\frac{1}{3}\right) = -1$

c. $2 \times \left(-\frac{1}{5}\right) = -\frac{2}{5}$ \qquad d. $-\frac{2}{5} = \frac{-2}{5} = -2 \div 5$

Rational Numbers **93**

1. Explain the meaning of $\frac{3}{8}$.

$3 \div 8$

2. Express $-\frac{5}{6}$ in two other ways. $\frac{-5}{6}, \frac{5}{-6}$

3. What is $4 \div 7$? $\frac{4}{7}$

Complete.

4. $-\frac{2}{3} = \underline{} \div 3$ -2

5. $2 \times \left(-\frac{1}{3}\right) = \underline{}$ $-\frac{2}{3}$

6. $\frac{1}{4} + \frac{1}{4} + \frac{1}{4} = \underline{}$ $\frac{3}{4}$

7. $5 \times \underline{} = -\frac{5}{9}$ $-\frac{1}{9}$

When we work with fractions having numerators and denominators that are integers, we are working with a new set of numbers called *rational numbers.* Any number that can be represented by a fraction $\frac{a}{b}$, where a and b are integers and b is not 0, is a **rational number.** Notice that the integers themselves are rational numbers. For example, -9 can be written as $\frac{-9}{1}$, 0 as $\frac{0}{1}$, and 26 as $\frac{26}{1}$.

Class Exercises

Name the rational numbers whose graphs are shown.

1.

2.

$A: -\frac{4}{5}; B: -\frac{3}{5};$
$C: -\frac{2}{5}; D: -\frac{1}{5}.$

3.

4.

Complete.

5. $\frac{1}{7} + \frac{1}{7} = \underline{\ ?\ } \quad \frac{2}{7}$

6. $2 \times \frac{1}{7} = \underline{\ ?\ } \quad \frac{2}{7}$

7. $2 \div 7 = \underline{\ ?\ } \quad \frac{2}{7}$

8. $\left(-\frac{1}{8}\right) + \left(-\frac{1}{8}\right) + \left(-\frac{1}{8}\right) = \underline{\ ?\ } \quad -\frac{3}{8}$

9. $3 \times \left(-\frac{1}{8}\right) = \underline{\ ?\ } \quad -\frac{3}{8}$

10. $3 \div (-8) = \underline{\ ?\ } \quad -\frac{3}{8}$

11. $4 \times \underline{\ ?\ } = -1 - \frac{1}{4}$

12. $5 \times \underline{\ ?\ } = -\frac{5}{8} \quad -\frac{1}{8}$

13. $\frac{2}{9} = 2 \div \underline{\ ?\ } \quad 9$

Written Exercises

Graph each set of rational numbers on a number line. Check students' graphs.

A

1. $-1, -\frac{1}{3}, 0, \frac{1}{3}, 1$

2. $-1, -\frac{1}{4}, 0, \frac{1}{4}, 1$

3. $0, \frac{1}{5}, \frac{5}{5}, \frac{6}{5}$

4. $-\frac{4}{3}, -\frac{3}{3}, -\frac{2}{3}, 0$

5. $-\frac{5}{4}, -\frac{3}{4}, \frac{3}{4}, \frac{5}{4}$

6. $-\frac{5}{3}, -\frac{4}{3}, \frac{4}{3}, \frac{5}{3}$

Express in two other ways.

7. $-\frac{1}{2} \quad \frac{-1}{2}, \frac{1}{-2}$

8. $\frac{-1}{3} \quad -\frac{1}{3}, \frac{1}{-3}$

9. $\frac{-1}{11} \quad -\frac{1}{11}, \frac{1}{-11}$

10. $\frac{-1}{6} \quad -\frac{1}{6}, \frac{1}{-6}$

11. $\frac{2}{-9} \quad -\frac{2}{9}, \frac{-2}{9}$

12. $\frac{-9}{10} \quad -\frac{9}{10}, \frac{9}{-10}$

13. $-\frac{13}{6} \quad \frac{-13}{6}, \frac{13}{-6}$

14. $\frac{5}{-8} \quad -\frac{5}{8}, \frac{-5}{8}$

15. $-\frac{3}{4} \quad \frac{-3}{4}, \frac{3}{-4}$

16. $\frac{5}{-9} \quad -\frac{5}{9}, \frac{-5}{9}$

94   *Chapter 3*

Additional A Exercises

Express in two other ways.

1. $-\frac{1}{5} \quad \frac{-1}{5}, \frac{1}{-5}$

2. $\frac{-12}{7} \quad \frac{12}{-7}, -\frac{12}{7}$

3. $\frac{4}{-9} \quad \frac{-4}{9}, -\frac{4}{9}$

Complete.

4. $\underline{\ ?\ } \times \left(-\frac{4}{3}\right) = -4 \quad 3$

5. $1 \div 2 = \underline{\ ?\ } \quad \frac{1}{2}$

6. $5 \times \underline{\ ?\ } = \frac{5}{7} \quad \frac{1}{7}$

Complete.

17. $\underline{\ \ ?\ \ } \times \left(-\frac{1}{6}\right) = -16$

18. $4 \times \underline{\ \ ?\ \ } = \frac{4}{7}\ \frac{1}{7}$

19. $3 \times \underline{\ \ ?\ \ } = \frac{3}{4}\ \frac{1}{4}$

20. $5 \div 6 = \underline{\ \ ?\ \ }\ \frac{5}{6}$

21. $2 \div \underline{\ \ ?\ \ } = \frac{2}{3}\ 3$

22. $4 \times \underline{\ \ ?\ \ } = -\frac{4}{9}$

$-\frac{1}{9}$

Evaluate the expression when $a = 4$, $b = -3$, and $c = 5$.

B 23. $\frac{a+c}{b}\ -3$
24. $\frac{a-c}{a}\ -\frac{1}{4}$
25. $\frac{2b-1}{8}\ -\frac{7}{8}$
26. $\frac{2c-b}{a}\ \frac{13}{4}$
27. $\frac{a^2-c^2}{a+c}$

-1

What value of the variable makes the statement true?

28. $x \times \frac{1}{5} = 1\ 5$

29. $3y = -1\ -\frac{1}{3}$

30. $\frac{1}{b} = -\frac{1}{8}\ -8$

31. $-\frac{3}{4} = \frac{c}{4}\ -3$

32. $-\frac{3}{5} = d \div 5\ -3$

33. $\frac{-5}{9} = \frac{5}{m}\ -9$

Write the expression as a positive or a negative fraction.

EXAMPLE   **a.** $3(7)^{-1}$ **b.** $(-5)^{-1}$

Solution   **a.** $3(7)^{-1} = 3 \times \frac{1}{7} = \frac{3}{7}$ **b.** $(-5)^{-1} = \frac{1}{-5} = -\frac{1}{5}$

$\frac{3}{7}$

C 34. $2(3)^{-1}\ \frac{2}{3}$ **35.** $7(6)^{-1}\ \frac{7}{6}$ **36.** $5^{-1} + 5^{-1}\ \frac{2}{5}$ **37.** $7^{-1} + 7^{-1} + 7^{-1}$

38. $(-2)^{-1}\ -\frac{1}{2}$ **39.** $(-9)^{-1}\ -\frac{1}{9}$ **40.** $3(-5)^{-1}\ -\frac{3}{5}$ **41.** $2(-7)^{-1}\ -\frac{2}{7}$

42. $(-3)^{-1} + (-3)^{-1}\ -\frac{2}{3}$ **43.** $(-8)^{-1} + (-8)^{-1} + (-8)^{-1}\ -\frac{3}{8}$

Review Exercises

Complete.

1. Factors of 72: 1, 2, $\underline{\ ?\ 3}$, $\underline{\ ?\ 4}$, 6, $\underline{\ ?\ 8}$, 9, 12, $\underline{\ ?18}$, 24, $\underline{\ ?36}$, 72

2. What is the prime factorization of 72? $2^3 \cdot 3^2$

3. Factors of 90: $\underline{\ ?\ 1}$, 2, 3, $\underline{\ ?\ 5}$, $\underline{\ ?\ 6}$, 9, $\underline{\ ?10}$, $\underline{\ ?15}$, 18, $\underline{\ ?30}$, $\underline{\ ?45}$, 90

4. What is the prime factorization of 90? $2 \cdot 3^2 \cdot 5$

5. $18x^2y = 3 \times \underline{\ ?\ 6} \times x \times \underline{\ ?\ x} \times y$

6. $24ab^3 = 4 \times \underline{\ ?\ 6} \times \underline{\ ?\ a} \times \underline{\ ?\ b} \times b \times b$

Rational Numbers   **95**

Suggested Assignments

Core
  94/1–11 odd
  95/17–22; 23–37 odd
  95/Rev. 1–6

Enriched
  94/5–11
  95/25–43

Supplementary Materials

Practice Masters, p. 12

Reading Mathematics

Students will learn the meaning of the following mathematical terms in this lesson: *equivalent fractions, lowest terms, greatest common factor (GCF), relatively prime, common fraction, proper fraction, improper fraction, mixed number, simple form.*

3-4 Equivalent Fractions

The number line shows the graphs of several fractions.

Since $-\frac{1}{2}$ and $-\frac{2}{4}$ have the same graph, they are two names for the same number. Fractions that represent the same number are called **equivalent** fractions. Thus,

$$-\frac{3}{2} \text{ is equivalent to } -\frac{6}{4}; \quad \frac{3}{2} \text{ is equivalent to } \frac{6}{4}.$$

Notice that $\frac{3}{2} = \frac{3 \times 2}{2 \times 2} = \frac{6}{4}$ and $\frac{6}{4} = \frac{6 \div 2}{4 \div 2} = \frac{3}{2}$.

We may state the following general rule.

Rule

For all numbers a, b, and c ($b \neq 0, c \neq 0$),

$$\frac{a}{b} = \frac{a \times c}{b \times c} \qquad \text{and} \qquad \frac{a}{b} = \frac{a \div c}{b \div c}$$

EXAMPLE 1 Write as an equivalent fraction with a denominator of 12.

    a. $\frac{5}{6}$ **b.** $-\frac{32}{48}$

Solution   **a.** Since $6 \times 2 = 12$, we write $\frac{5}{6} = \frac{5 \times 2}{6 \times 2} = \frac{10}{12}$.

    b. *Method 1*
       Since $48 \div 4 = 12$, we write

$$-\frac{32}{48} = \frac{-32}{48} = \frac{-32 \div 4}{48 \div 4} = \frac{-8}{12}, \text{ or } -\frac{8}{12}.$$

       Method 2
$$-\frac{32}{48} = -\frac{32 \div 4}{48 \div 4} = -\frac{8}{12}$$

Notice that we usually write our answers with the minus sign in front of the fraction.

96   *Chapter 3*

Sometimes we simply show the results of dividing a numerator and denominator by the same number. In Example 1, we can think of dividing by 4 as we write

$$-\frac{\overset{8}{\cancel{32}}}{\underset{12}{\cancel{48}}} = -\frac{8}{12}.$$

A fraction is in **lowest terms** when the numerator and denominator have no common factor other than 1. To write a fraction in lowest terms, we can divide numerator and denominator by a common factor as many times as needed until they have no common factor other than 1.

$$\frac{45}{75} = \frac{45 \div 5}{75 \div 5} = \frac{9 \div 3}{15 \div 3} = \frac{3}{5}$$

Another way to write a fraction in lowest terms is to use the greatest common factor method. The **greatest common factor** (GCF) of two numbers is the greatest whole number that is a factor of each number. To find the GCF of two numbers, we write the prime factorizations of the two numbers, and find the greatest power of each prime factor that occurs in *both* factorizations. The product of these powers is the GCF.

EXAMPLE 2   Find the GCF of 84 and 120.

Solution
$$84 = 2 \times 2 \times 3 \times 7 = 2^2 \times 3 \times 7$$
$$120 = 2 \times 2 \times 2 \times 3 \times 5 = 2^3 \times 3 \times 5$$
$$GCF = 2^2 \times 3 = 12$$

To write a fraction in lowest terms, we divide the numerator and the denominator by their GCF.

EXAMPLE 3   Write $\frac{72}{80}$ in lowest terms.

Solution
$$72 = 2 \times 2 \times 2 \times 3 \times 3 = 2^3 \times 3^2$$
$$80 = 2 \times 2 \times 2 \times 2 \times 5 = 2^4 \times 5$$
$$GCF = 2^3 = 8$$

$$\frac{72}{80} = \frac{72 \div 8}{80 \div 8} = \frac{9}{10}$$

When two numbers have no common factor other than 1, they are said to be **relatively prime.** For example, 9 and 10 are relatively prime. A fraction is in lowest terms when its numerator and denominator are relatively prime.

Rational Numbers   **97**

State an equivalent fraction in lowest terms.

1. $\frac{12}{36}$ $\frac{1}{3}$

2. $\frac{60}{132}$ $\frac{5}{11}$

3. $-\frac{30}{45}$ $-\frac{2}{3}$

4. $\frac{14}{63}$ $\frac{2}{9}$

Write as a mixed number in simple form.

5. $\frac{23}{5}$ $4\frac{3}{5}$

6. $\frac{16}{3}$ $5\frac{1}{3}$

7. $-\frac{49}{14}$ $-3\frac{1}{2}$

8. $-\frac{402}{20}$ $-20\frac{1}{10}$

Write as an improper fraction.

9. $3\frac{2}{3}$ $\frac{11}{3}$

10. $1\frac{5}{9}$ $\frac{14}{9}$

11. $-4\frac{1}{5}$ $-\frac{21}{5}$

12. $-1\frac{7}{10}$ $-\frac{17}{10}$

A **common fraction** is a fraction whose numerator and denominator are both integers; for example, $\frac{2}{5}$ or $-\frac{12}{7}$. A **proper fraction** is a positive fraction whose numerator is less than its denominator, or the opposite of such a fraction; for example, $\frac{3}{8}$ or $-\frac{7}{9}$. A fraction that is not a proper fraction, such as $\frac{9}{4}$ or $-\frac{9}{4}$, is called an **improper fraction.** A number, such as $1\frac{1}{4}$, consisting of a whole number plus a fraction, is called a **mixed number.** Mixed numbers may be written as improper fractions, and improper fractions may be written as mixed numbers. A mixed number is in simple form if the fractional part is in lowest terms.

$$7\frac{15}{27} \text{ in simple form is } 7\frac{5}{9}.$$

EXAMPLE 4   Write as a mixed number in simple form.

   a. $\frac{12}{8}$ **b.** $-\frac{12}{8}$

Solution   **a.** $\frac{12}{8} = 12 \div 8$, which gives 1 R4.

   Therefore $\frac{12}{8} = 1\frac{4}{8} = 1\frac{1}{2}$.

   b. $-\frac{12}{8}$ is *the opposite of* $\frac{12}{8}$, so $-\frac{12}{8} = -1\frac{1}{2}$.

EXAMPLE 5   Write $7\frac{2}{5}$ as an improper fraction.

Solution $7\frac{2}{5} = \frac{7}{1} + \frac{2}{5} = \frac{7 \times 5}{1 \times 5} + \frac{2}{5} = \frac{(7 \times 5) + 2}{5} = \frac{37}{5}$

Class Exercises

For each fraction, state the GCF of the numerator and denominator. Then state an equivalent fraction in lowest terms.

1. $\frac{4}{24}$ 4; $\frac{1}{6}$ 2. $\frac{5}{20}$ 5; $\frac{1}{4}$ 3. $\frac{-12}{16}$ 4; $-\frac{3}{4}$ 4. $-\frac{8}{12}$ 4; $-\frac{2}{3}$ 5. $\frac{-9}{12}$ 3; $\frac{-3}{4}$

State an equivalent improper fraction.

6. $3\frac{2}{5}$ $\frac{17}{5}$ 7. $-4\frac{1}{8}$ $-\frac{33}{8}$ 8. $-7\frac{2}{3}$ $-\frac{23}{3}$ 9. $9\frac{3}{4}$ $\frac{39}{4}$ 10. $-5\frac{1}{6}$ $-\frac{31}{6}$

State an equivalent mixed number in simple form.

11. $\frac{13}{5}$ $2\frac{3}{5}$ 12. $-\frac{14}{4}$ $-3\frac{1}{2}$ 13. $\frac{-24}{5}$ $-4\frac{4}{5}$ 14. $\frac{19}{3}$ $6\frac{1}{3}$ 15. $\frac{-32}{10}$ $-3\frac{1}{5}$

Written Exercises

Complete.

A **1.** $\dfrac{2}{3}=\dfrac{?}{6}$ 4 **2.** $\dfrac{5}{7}=\dfrac{?}{21}$ 15 **3.** $1=\dfrac{5}{?}$ 5 **4.** $4=\dfrac{?}{2}$ 8 **5.** $-\dfrac{14}{32}=-\dfrac{?}{16}$ 7

6. $\dfrac{42}{-54}=\dfrac{?}{-9}$ 7 **7.** $\dfrac{18}{27}=\dfrac{2}{?}$ 3 **8.** $-7=-\dfrac{?}{3}$ 21 **9.** $\dfrac{-7}{25}=\dfrac{-35}{?}$ 125 **10.** $-\dfrac{3}{4}=-\dfrac{?}{16}$ 12

Write as a proper fraction in lowest terms or as a mixed number in simple form.

11. $\dfrac{21}{35}$ $\dfrac{3}{5}$ **12.** $\dfrac{24}{40}$ $\dfrac{3}{5}$ **13.** $\dfrac{11}{4}$ $2\dfrac{3}{4}$ **14.** $\dfrac{25}{7}$ $3\dfrac{4}{7}$ **15.** $-\dfrac{9}{81}$ $-\dfrac{1}{9}$

16. $\dfrac{54}{81}$ $\dfrac{2}{3}$ **17.** $-\dfrac{17}{3}$ $-5\dfrac{2}{3}$ **18.** $-\dfrac{56}{72}$ $-\dfrac{7}{9}$ **19.** $\dfrac{-34}{85}$ $\dfrac{-2}{5}$ **20.** $-\dfrac{29}{5}$ $-5\dfrac{4}{5}$

21. $\dfrac{125}{12}$ $10\dfrac{5}{12}$ **22.** $\dfrac{49}{63}$ $\dfrac{7}{9}$ **23.** $-\dfrac{79}{13}$ $-6\dfrac{1}{13}$ **24.** $\dfrac{32}{10}$ $3\dfrac{1}{5}$ **25.** $\dfrac{-300}{7}$ $-42\dfrac{6}{7}$

Write as an improper fraction.

26. $3\dfrac{1}{4}$ $\dfrac{13}{4}$ **27.** $2\dfrac{1}{8}$ $\dfrac{17}{8}$ **28.** $5\dfrac{3}{7}$ $\dfrac{38}{7}$ **29.** $6\dfrac{3}{16}$ $\dfrac{99}{16}$ **30.** $5\dfrac{3}{8}$ $\dfrac{43}{8}$

31. $-4\dfrac{3}{8}$ $-\dfrac{35}{8}$ **32.** $-3\dfrac{7}{8}$ $-\dfrac{31}{8}$ **33.** $-16\dfrac{1}{3}$ $-\dfrac{49}{3}$ **34.** $-7\dfrac{2}{9}$ $-\dfrac{65}{9}$ **35.** $-8\dfrac{3}{10}$ $-\dfrac{83}{10}$

What value of the variable makes the statement true?

B **36.** $\dfrac{b}{4}=\dfrac{6}{12}$ 2 **37.** $\dfrac{x}{16}=\dfrac{9}{48}$ 3 **38.** $\dfrac{a}{6}=\dfrac{10}{60}$ 1 **39.** $\dfrac{d}{5}=\dfrac{-3}{15}$ -1

40. $\dfrac{1}{x}=\dfrac{4}{16}$ 4 **41.** $\dfrac{0}{6}=\dfrac{n}{12}$ 0 **42.** $\dfrac{5}{-1}=\dfrac{20}{n}$ -4 **43.** $\dfrac{1}{3}=\dfrac{8}{n}$ 24

Simplify by writing an equivalent fraction in which the numerator and denominator have no common factors.

EXAMPLE $\dfrac{15x^2y}{20xy^2}=\dfrac{3\times\cancel{5}\times\cancel{x}\times x\times\cancel{y}}{4\times\cancel{5}\times\cancel{x}\times\cancel{y}\times y}=\dfrac{3x}{4y}$

44. $\dfrac{2a}{6a}$ $\dfrac{1}{3}$ **45.** $\dfrac{4b}{20}$ $\dfrac{b}{5}$ **46.** $\dfrac{c}{c^2}$ $\dfrac{1}{c}$ **47.** $\dfrac{d^2e}{de^2}$ $\dfrac{d}{e}$

48. $\dfrac{3x}{15y}$ $\dfrac{x}{5y}$ **49.** $\dfrac{6n^2}{18n}$ $\dfrac{n}{3}$ **50.** $\dfrac{4h\cdot}{6hk}$ $\dfrac{2}{3k}$ **51.** $\dfrac{uv^2}{3u^2v}$ $\dfrac{v}{3u}$

Review Exercises

Simplify.

1. 7^2 49 **2.** 11^3 1331 **3.** 6^4 1296 **4.** 2^8 256 **5.** 1^5 1

6. $5^2\times3^2$ 225 **7.** $4^3\times9^2$ 5184 **8.** $2^4\times6^2$ 576 **9.** $3^3\times3^2$ 243 **10.** $8^2\times2^4$ 1024

Rational Numbers **99**

3-5 Least Common Denominator

In calculations and comparisons, we work with more than one fraction.
It is sometimes necessary to replace fractions with equivalent fractions
so that all have the same denominator, called a *common denominator*.
For example, in the addition $\frac{1}{6} + \frac{3}{4}$ we may write $\frac{1}{6}$ as $\frac{2}{12}$ and $\frac{3}{4}$ as $\frac{9}{12}$,
using 12 as a common denominator. We may also use 24, 36, 48, or any
other multiple of both denominators as a common denominator.

The **least common denominator** (LCD) is the most convenient denominator to use. The LCD is the least common multiple (LCM) of the
denominators. The LCD is found using the prime factorizations of the
denominators. For each prime factor of any of the denominators, find
the highest power of that factor that occurs in *any* prime factorization.
The product of these powers is the LCD.

EXAMPLE 1   Write equivalent fractions with the LCD: $\frac{5}{48}$, $\frac{11}{120}$.

Solution   The LCD is the least common multiple of 48 and 120. Use prime
factorization to find the LCM.

Prime factorization of 48: $2 \times 2 \times 2 \times 2 \times 3$, or $2^4 \times 3$
Prime factorization of 120: $2 \times 2 \times 2 \times 3 \times 5$, or $2^3 \times 3 \times 5$

The LCM is the product of the highest powers of each factor. The
LCM $= 2^4 \times 3 \times 5 = 240$, so the LCD $= 240$.

$$\frac{5}{48} = \frac{5 \times 5}{48 \times 5} = \frac{25}{240} \qquad\qquad \frac{11}{120} = \frac{11 \times 2}{120 \times 2} = \frac{22}{240}$$

EXAMPLE 2   Replace _?_ with $<$, $>$, or $=$ to make a true statement.

a. $\frac{5}{6}$ _?_ $\frac{6}{7}$ **b.** $-\frac{5}{8}$ _?_ $-\frac{9}{14}$

Solution   First rewrite each pair of fractions as equivalent fractions with the
LCD. Then compare the fractions.

a. The LCD is the LCM of 6 and 7, or 42.

$$\frac{5}{6} = \frac{5 \times 7}{6 \times 7} = \frac{35}{42} \qquad\qquad \frac{6}{7} = \frac{6 \times 6}{7 \times 6} = \frac{36}{42}$$

$$\frac{35}{42} < \frac{36}{42}, \text{ so } \frac{5}{6} < \frac{6}{7}.$$

b. The LCD is the LCM of 8 and 14, or 56.

$$-\frac{5}{8} = -\frac{5 \times 7}{8 \times 7} = -\frac{35}{56} \qquad\qquad -\frac{9}{14} = -\frac{9 \times 4}{14 \times 4} = -\frac{36}{56}$$

$$-\frac{35}{56} > -\frac{36}{56}, \text{ so } -\frac{5}{8} > -\frac{9}{14}.$$

100   *Chapter 3*

When fractions have variables in their denominators, we may obtain a common denominator by finding a common multiple of the denominators.

EXAMPLE 3   Write as equivalent fractions with a common denominator: $\frac{2}{a}, \frac{3}{b}$.

Solution $\frac{2}{a} = \frac{2 \times b}{a \times b} = \frac{2b}{ab}$ $\frac{3}{b} = \frac{3 \times a}{b \times a} = \frac{3a}{ab}$

Class Exercises

State the LCM of the pair of numbers.

1. 6, 18 18   **2.** 11, 4 44   **3.** 10, 8 40   **4.** 15, 12 60   **5.** 32, 48 96

State the LCD of the pair of fractions.

6. $\frac{1}{2}, \frac{3}{4}$ 4   **7.** $\frac{5}{6}, \frac{1}{2}$ 6   **8.** $\frac{3}{4}, -\frac{1}{3}$ 12   **9.** $-\frac{2}{9}, \frac{1}{6}$ 18   **10.** $\frac{1}{16}, \frac{5}{12}$ 48

Written Exercises

Write the fractions as equivalent fractions with the least common denominator (LCD).

A

1. $\frac{1}{3}, \frac{1}{12}$ $\frac{4}{12}, \frac{1}{12}$ **2.** $\frac{1}{4}, \frac{1}{12}$ $\frac{3}{12}, \frac{1}{12}$ **3.** $\frac{3}{4}, \frac{5}{8}$ $\frac{6}{8}, \frac{5}{8}$ **4.** $\frac{3}{8}, \frac{3}{16}$ $\frac{6}{16}, \frac{3}{16}$

5. $\frac{2}{9}, -\frac{1}{27}$ $\frac{6}{27}, -\frac{1}{27}$ **6.** $-\frac{1}{7}, \frac{1}{49}$ $-\frac{7}{49}, \frac{1}{49}$ **7.** $\frac{10}{21}, \frac{2}{49}$ $\frac{70}{147}, \frac{6}{147}$ **8.** $\frac{7}{18}, \frac{5}{36}$ $\frac{14}{36}, \frac{5}{36}$

9. $-\frac{2}{3}, \frac{7}{30}$ $-\frac{20}{30}, \frac{7}{30}$ **10.** $\frac{5}{12}, -\frac{6}{11}$ $\frac{55}{132}, -\frac{72}{132}$ **11.** $\frac{4}{75}, \frac{7}{100}$ $\frac{16}{300}, \frac{21}{300}$ **12.** $\frac{9}{56}, \frac{4}{63}$ $\frac{81}{504}, \frac{32}{504}$

13. $-\frac{3}{7}, -\frac{7}{112}$ **14.** $-\frac{4}{17}, -\frac{9}{16}$ $\frac{132}{}$ **15.** $\frac{5}{42}, \frac{5}{49}$ **16.** $\frac{5}{84}, \frac{7}{12}$ $\frac{5}{84}, \frac{49}{84}$

B **17.** $\frac{7}{8}, \frac{5}{16}, \frac{21}{40}$ **18.** $\frac{1}{4}, \frac{1}{9}, \frac{1}{5}$ **19.** $\frac{3}{7}, \frac{7}{4}, \frac{4}{9}$ **20.** $\frac{11}{18}, \frac{1}{54}, \frac{2}{27}$

21. $\frac{1}{65}, \frac{3}{5}, \frac{9}{26}$ **22.** $-\frac{7}{8}, \frac{9}{28}, \frac{2}{49}$ **23.** $-\frac{5}{6}, \frac{2}{9}, -\frac{7}{8}$ **24.** $\frac{11}{12}, \frac{1}{72}, -\frac{7}{8}$

25. $\frac{a}{3}, \frac{b}{6}$ $\frac{2a}{6}, \frac{b}{6}$ **26.** $\frac{m}{25}, \frac{n}{15}$ $\frac{3m}{75}, \frac{5n}{75}$ **27.** $\frac{h}{25}, \frac{h}{100}, \frac{h}{125}$ **28.** $\frac{a}{2}, \frac{b}{3}, \frac{c}{4}$

Write the fractions as equivalent fractions with a common denominator.

29. $\frac{1}{c}, \frac{2}{3c}$ $\frac{3}{3c}, \frac{2}{3c}$ **30.** $\frac{1}{x}, \frac{1}{y}$ $\frac{y}{xy}, \frac{x}{xy}$ **31.** $\frac{3}{x}, \frac{1}{y}, \frac{5}{z}$ **32.** $\frac{-1}{r}, \frac{2}{rs}, \frac{r}{s}$

Rational Numbers **101**

Additional A Exercises

Write the fractions as equivalent fractions with the least common denominator (LCD).

1. $\frac{2}{3}, \frac{5}{9}$ $\frac{6}{9}, \frac{5}{9}$

2. $\frac{7}{3}, \frac{3}{4}$ $\frac{28}{12}, \frac{9}{12}$

3. $-\frac{3}{5}, \frac{7}{20}$ $-\frac{12}{20}, \frac{7}{20}$

4. $-\frac{5}{17}, -\frac{12}{7}$
$-\frac{35}{119}, -\frac{204}{119}$

5. $\frac{5}{12}, \frac{7}{24}$ $\frac{10}{24}, \frac{7}{24}$

Additional Answers Written Exercises

13. $-\frac{48}{112}, -\frac{7}{112}$

14. $-\frac{64}{272}, -\frac{153}{272}$

15. $\frac{35}{294}, \frac{30}{294}$

17. $\frac{70}{80}, \frac{25}{80}, \frac{42}{80}$

18. $\frac{45}{180}, \frac{20}{180}, \frac{36}{180}$

19. $\frac{108}{252}, \frac{441}{252}, \frac{112}{252}$

20. $\frac{33}{54}, \frac{1}{54}, \frac{4}{54}$

21. $\frac{2}{130}, \frac{78}{130}, \frac{45}{130}$

22. $-\frac{343}{392}, \frac{126}{392}, \frac{16}{392}$

23. $-\frac{60}{72}, \frac{16}{72}, -\frac{63}{72}$

24. $\frac{66}{72}, \frac{1}{72}, \frac{63}{72}$

27. $\frac{20h}{500}, \frac{5h}{500}, \frac{4h}{500}$

28. $\frac{6a}{12}, \frac{4b}{12}, \frac{3c}{12}$

31. $\frac{3yz}{xyz}, \frac{xz}{xyz}, \frac{5xy}{xyz}$

32. $-\frac{s}{rs}, \frac{2}{rs}, \frac{r^2}{rs}$

Suggested Assignments

Core
   101/1–31 odd
   102/Self-Test A
Enriched
   101/21–32
   102/33–39
   102/Self-Test A

Supplementary Materials

Practice Masters, p. 12
Test 3A, pp. 15–16

Quick Quiz A

State which of the numbers
2, 3, 4, 5, 9, and 10 are factors of the given number.
Use the tests of divisibility.

1. 356 2, 4

2. 8172 2, 3, 4, 9

3. 31,410 2, 3, 5, 9, 10

4. 44,347 None

Find out whether each number is prime or composite. If
it is composite, give its prime
factorization.

5. 137 prime

6. 35 composite, $5 \cdot 7$

7. 144 composite, $2^4 \cdot 3^2$

8. 210 composite,
    $2 \cdot 3 \cdot 5 \cdot 7$

Complete.

9. $7 \times \underline{\ \ ?\ \ } = -\frac{7}{8}$ $-\frac{1}{8}$

10. $2 \times \underline{\ \ ?\ \ } = 1\frac{1}{2}$

11. $3 \div 6 = \underline{\ \ ?\ \ }$ $\frac{3}{6}$

12. $-\frac{5}{3} = \frac{5}{-3} = \underline{\ \ ?\ \ }$ $\frac{-5}{3}$

(continued on next page)

102

Replace $\underline{\ \ ?\ \ }$ with $<$, $>$, or $=$ to make a true statement.

33. $\frac{1}{3}\ \underline{\ ?\ }\ \frac{3}{6}$ **34.** $\frac{3}{4}\ \underline{\ ?\ }\ \frac{5}{8}$ **35.** $-\frac{2}{3}\ \underline{\ ?\ }\ -\frac{7}{12}$

36. $-\frac{5}{8}\ \underline{\ ?\ }\ -\frac{5}{16}$ **37.** $-\frac{3}{5}\ \underline{\ ?\ }\ -\frac{5}{7}$ **38.** $-\frac{2}{4}\ \underline{\ ?\ }\ -\frac{3}{5}$.

C   **39.** Let $\frac{a}{b}$ and $\frac{c}{d}$ be fractions with $b > 0$ and $d > 0$. Write $\frac{a}{b}$ and $\frac{c}{d}$ as equivalent fractions with a common denominator. How do $\frac{a}{b}$ and $\frac{c}{d}$ compare when $ad < bc$? when $ad = bc$? when $ad > bc$? Give two examples to illustrate each of your conclusions.

Self-Test A

State which of the numbers 2, 3, 4, 5, 9, and 10 are factors of the given number. Use the tests for divisibility.

1. 756   **2.** 7821   **3.** 11,340   **4.** 34,447   [3–1]

Find out whether each number is prime or composite. If it is composite, give its prime factorization.

5. 108   **6.** 79   **7.** 87   **8.** 109   [3–2]

Complete.

9. $3 \times \underline{\ \ ?\ \ } = -1$ **10.** $7 \div 9 = \underline{\ \ ?\ \ }$ **11.** $-\frac{2}{3} = \frac{-2}{3} = \underline{\ \ ?\ \ }$ [3–3]

Write as a proper fraction in lowest terms or as a mixed number in simple form.

12. $\frac{16}{64}$ **13.** $-\frac{72}{30}$ **14.** $\frac{32}{42}$ **15.** $\frac{-71}{48}$ **16.** $\frac{68}{16}$ [3–4]

Write as an improper fraction.

17. $2\frac{1}{5}$ **18.** $-3\frac{2}{3}$ **19.** $6\frac{4}{15}$ **20.** $1\frac{7}{12}$ **21.** $-8\frac{5}{8}$

Write as equivalent fractions with the least common denominator.

22. $\frac{7}{10}, \frac{7}{8}$ **23.** $-\frac{10}{49}, \frac{2}{21}$ **24.** $\frac{3}{50}, \frac{6}{225}$ **25.** $-\frac{8}{15}, \frac{-1}{30}$ [3–5]

Self-Test answers and Extra Practice are at the back of the book.

102   *Chapter 3*

Teaching Suggestions p. 83d

Related Activities p. 83e

3-6 Adding and Subtracting Common Fractions

You have added fractions having a common denominator by adding the numerators and writing the result with the same denominator. We can illustrate the reasoning for this rule using the sum $\frac{2}{13} + \frac{5}{13}$. The reason for each statement at left below is given on the same line at right. All of the properties for addition, subtraction, multiplication, and division of positive and negative numbers hold for the rational numbers.

$$\frac{2}{13} + \frac{5}{13} = \left(2 \times \frac{1}{13}\right) \times \left(5 \times \frac{1}{13}\right) \qquad \text{By the rule } \frac{a}{b} = a \times \frac{1}{b}$$

$$= (2 + 5) \times \frac{1}{13} \qquad \text{By the distributive property}$$

$$= (7) \times \frac{1}{13} \qquad \text{Substitution of 7 for } 2 + 5$$

$$= \frac{7}{13} \qquad \text{By the rule } a \times \frac{1}{b} = \frac{a}{b}$$

The methods for adding and subtracting positive fractions apply as well to adding and subtracting negative fractions.

Rules

For all numbers a, b, and $c(c \neq 0)$,

$$\frac{a}{c} + \frac{b}{c} = \frac{a+b}{c} \quad \text{and} \quad \frac{a}{c} - \frac{b}{c} = \frac{a-b}{c}$$

EXAMPLE 1   Add or subtract. Write the answers in lowest terms.

    a. $-\frac{3}{8} + \frac{1}{8}$ **b.** $\frac{23}{60} - \left(-\frac{17}{60}\right)$

Solution   **a.** $-\frac{3}{8} + \frac{1}{8} = \frac{-3}{8} + \frac{1}{8}$ **b.** $\frac{23}{60} - \left(-\frac{17}{60}\right) = \frac{23}{60} + \frac{17}{60}$

$$= \frac{-3+1}{8} \qquad\qquad\qquad\qquad = \frac{23+17}{60}$$

$$= \frac{-2}{8} \qquad\qquad\qquad\qquad\qquad = \frac{40}{60}$$

$$= \frac{-1}{4}, \text{ or } -\frac{1}{4} \qquad\qquad\qquad = \frac{2}{3}$$

Rational Numbers   **103**

Quick Quiz A
(continued from page 102)

Write as a proper fraction in lowest terms or as a mixed number in simple form.

13. $\frac{21}{70}$ $\frac{3}{10}$

14. $-\frac{13}{4}$ $-3\frac{1}{4}$

15. $-\frac{32}{128}$ $-\frac{1}{4}$

16. $-\frac{100}{3}$ $-33\frac{1}{3}$

17. $\frac{56}{64}$ $\frac{7}{8}$

Write as an improper fraction.

18. $2\frac{1}{4}$ $\frac{9}{4}$

19. $-5\frac{3}{5}$ $-\frac{28}{5}$

20. $4\frac{5}{7}$ $\frac{33}{7}$

21. $-6\frac{9}{10}$ $-\frac{69}{10}$

22. $1\frac{15}{16}$ $\frac{31}{16}$

Write as equivalent fractions with the least common denominator.

23. $\frac{1}{3}, \frac{3}{7}$ $\frac{7}{21}, \frac{9}{21}$

24. $-\frac{11}{24}, \frac{3}{32}$ $-\frac{44}{96}, \frac{9}{96}$

25. $\frac{5}{11}, \frac{10}{13}$ $\frac{65}{143}, \frac{110}{143}$

26. $-\frac{5}{12}, \frac{49}{100}$ $-\frac{125}{300},$ $-\frac{147}{300}$

Chalkboard Examples

Add or subtract. Write the answer as a whole number or as a common fraction in lowest terms.

1. $\frac{3}{11} + \frac{8}{11}$ 1

2. $-\frac{2}{3} + \frac{3}{7}$ $-\frac{5}{21}$

3. $-\frac{4}{5} + \frac{3}{4}$ $-\frac{1}{20}$

4. $\frac{5}{9} - \frac{2}{3}$ $-\frac{1}{9}$

5. $-\frac{1}{6} - \left(-\frac{2}{9}\right)$ $\frac{1}{18}$

6. $\frac{6}{7} - \frac{3}{4}$ $\frac{3}{28}$

When two fractions have different denominators, write the fractions as equivalent fractions with a common denominator before adding or subtracting.

EXAMPLE 2 Add or subtract. Write the answer in lowest terms.

a. $\frac{1}{4} - \frac{7}{12}$ 　　　　　　b. $-\frac{1}{10} + \left(-\frac{5}{6}\right)$

Solution　　a. $\frac{1}{4} - \frac{7}{12} = \frac{3}{12} - \frac{7}{12}$ 　b. $-\frac{1}{10} + \left(-\frac{5}{6}\right) = -\frac{3}{30} + \left(-\frac{25}{30}\right)$

$$= \frac{3-7}{12} \qquad\qquad\qquad = \frac{-3}{30} + \frac{-25}{30}$$

$$= \frac{-4}{12} \qquad\qquad\qquad = \frac{-3+(-25)}{30}$$

$$= \frac{-1}{3}, \text{ or } -\frac{1}{3} \qquad\quad = \frac{-28}{30}$$

$$\qquad\qquad\qquad\qquad\qquad = \frac{-14}{15}, \text{ or } -\frac{14}{15}$$

Class Exercises

Add or subtract. Write the answer as a whole number or as a common fraction in lowest terms.

1. $\frac{3}{16} + \frac{8}{16}$ $\frac{11}{16}$ 　　2. $\frac{7}{10} - \frac{3}{10}$ $\frac{2}{5}$ 　　3. $\frac{7}{11} + \frac{8}{11}$ $\frac{15}{11}$ 　　4. $\frac{4}{6} - \frac{11}{6}$ $-\frac{7}{6}$

5. $-\frac{8}{5} + \frac{4}{5}$ $-\frac{4}{5}$ 　　6. $\frac{12}{5} - \frac{16}{5}$ $-\frac{4}{5}$ 　　7. $-\frac{14}{3} + \frac{20}{3}$ 2 　　8. $-\frac{9}{4} - \frac{13}{4}$ $-\frac{11}{2}$

9. $-\frac{1}{7} + \left(-\frac{3}{7}\right)$ $-\frac{4}{7}$ 　10. $\frac{11}{15} - \left(-\frac{2}{15}\right)$ $\frac{13}{15}$ 　11. $-\frac{4}{21} - \left(-\frac{2}{21}\right)$ $-\frac{2}{21}$ 　12. $-\frac{7}{10} - \left(-\frac{3}{10}\right)$ $-\frac{2}{5}$

Written Exercises

Additional A Exercises

Add or subtract. Write the answer as a whole number or as a common fraction in lowest terms.

1. $\frac{6}{13} + \frac{7}{13}$ 1

2. $\frac{3}{4} - \frac{3}{4}$ 0

3. $-\frac{5}{8} + \frac{2}{5}$ $-\frac{9}{40}$

4. $-\frac{5}{9} - \frac{1}{4}$ $-\frac{29}{36}$

5. $\frac{17}{36} - \frac{3}{18}$ $\frac{11}{36}$

6. $-\frac{17}{24} - \left(-\frac{5}{6}\right)$ $\frac{1}{8}$

Add or subtract. Write the answer as a whole number or as a common fraction in lowest terms.

A　1. $\frac{2}{15} + \frac{8}{15}$ $\frac{2}{3}$ 　　2. $\frac{9}{20} - \frac{7}{20}$ $\frac{1}{10}$ 　　3. $-\frac{8}{17} + \frac{4}{17} - \frac{4}{17}$ 　　4. $\frac{17}{8} - \frac{9}{8}$ 1

5. $\frac{3}{4} + \left(-\frac{3}{4}\right)$ 0 　　6. $-\frac{11}{15} - \frac{16}{15}$ $-\frac{9}{5}$ 　　7. $-\frac{9}{10} + \left(-\frac{13}{10}\right) - \frac{11}{5}$ 　8. $-\frac{7}{16} - \left(-\frac{23}{16}\right)$

9. $\frac{3}{7} + \frac{1}{3}$ $\frac{16}{21}$ 　　10. $\frac{5}{4} - \frac{1}{2}$ $\frac{3}{4}$ 　　11. $-\frac{7}{6} + \frac{14}{3}$ $\frac{7}{2}$ 　　12. $-\frac{17}{7} - \frac{7}{3}$

1

$-\frac{100}{21}$

13. $\frac{15}{4} + \left(-\frac{33}{8}\right) - \frac{3}{8}$ 14. $-\frac{17}{5} - \frac{11}{3}$ 15. $-\frac{23}{10} + \left(-\frac{14}{5}\right)$ 16. $-\frac{21}{4} - \left(-\frac{32}{5}\right)$

17. $\frac{11}{12} + \frac{12}{13}$ $\frac{287}{156}$ 18. $-\frac{5}{6} + \frac{7}{20} - \frac{29}{60}$ 19. $-\frac{5}{8} + \frac{1}{18} - \frac{41}{72}$ 20. $-\frac{2}{15} + \frac{6}{21}$ $\frac{16}{105}$

31. $\frac{a}{c} - \frac{b}{c}$

$= \left(a \times \frac{1}{c}\right) - \left(b \times \frac{1}{c}\right)$

$\left(\text{because } a \times \frac{1}{b} = \frac{a}{b}\right)$

$= (a - b) \times \frac{1}{c}$

(by the Distributive
Property)

$= \frac{a - b}{c}$

$\left(\text{because } a \times \frac{1}{b} = \frac{a}{b}\right)$

B 21. $\frac{1}{3} + \frac{1}{6} + \frac{1}{12}$ $\frac{7}{12}$ 22. $\frac{2}{15} + \frac{1}{5} + \frac{2}{3}$ 1   23. $\frac{7}{10} + \left(-\frac{1}{2}\right) + \frac{2}{5}$ $\frac{3}{5}$

24. $\frac{11}{12} + \frac{2}{7} + \left(-\frac{1}{2}\right)$ $\frac{59}{84}$ 25. $-\frac{5}{6} + \frac{2}{9} + \left(-\frac{1}{3}\right)$ $-\frac{17}{18}$ 26. $\frac{8}{14} - \left(-\frac{1}{7}\right) + \frac{3}{2}$ $\frac{31}{14}$

27. $\frac{3}{2} + \frac{7}{4} + \left(-\frac{5}{3}\right)$ $\frac{19}{12}$ 28. $-\frac{7}{3} + \frac{2}{3} + \frac{9}{5}$ $\frac{2}{15}$ 29. $\frac{9}{15} + \left(-\frac{2}{3}\right) - \left(-\frac{1}{6}\right)$

$\frac{1}{10}$

C 30. Show that $\frac{a}{c} + \frac{b}{c} = \frac{a+b}{c}$ $(c \neq 0)$ by applying the rule or property
that justifies each statement.

$\frac{a}{b} + \frac{b}{c} = \left(a \times \frac{1}{c}\right) + \left(b \times \frac{1}{c}\right)$ Why? $a \times \frac{1}{b} = \frac{a}{b}$

$= (a + b) \times \frac{1}{c}$ Why? **Distributive Property**

$= \frac{a + b}{c}$ Why? $a \times \frac{1}{b} = \frac{a}{b}$

31. As in Exercise 30, show that $\frac{a}{c} - \frac{b}{c} = \frac{a-b}{c}$ $(c \neq 0)$.

Review Exercises

Write each fraction as a mixed number.

$5\frac{1}{6}$

1. $\frac{11}{8}$ $1\frac{3}{8}$ 2. $\frac{15}{11}$ $1\frac{4}{11}$ 3. $\frac{23}{7}$ $3\frac{2}{7}$ 4. $\frac{31}{6}$

5. $\frac{71}{12}$ $5\frac{11}{12}$ 6. $\frac{83}{9}$ $9\frac{2}{9}$ 7. $\frac{121}{13}$ $9\frac{4}{13}$ 8. $\frac{169}{16}$

$10\frac{9}{16}$

▍▍▍ **Challenge**

Many answers are possible.
Write a fraction whose value is between the given fractions. Sample answers are given.

1. $\frac{2}{5} < \underline{\ ?\ } < \frac{3}{5}$ $\frac{1}{2}$ 2. $-\frac{2}{3} < \underline{\ ?\ } < -\frac{1}{3}$ $-\frac{1}{2}$ 3. $\frac{1}{8} < \underline{\ ?\ } < \frac{1}{4}$ $\frac{3}{16}$

4. $-\frac{2}{7} < \underline{\ ?\ } < -\frac{3}{14}$ $-\frac{1}{4}$ 5. $\frac{1}{6} < \underline{\ ?\ } < \frac{1}{4}$ $\frac{5}{24}$ 6. $-\frac{5}{6} < \underline{\ ?\ } < -\frac{7}{9}$

$-\frac{29}{36}$

Rational Numbers **105**

Suggested Assignments

Core
104/2–12 even
105/14–26 even, 30
105/Rev. 1–8

Enriched
105/13–31
105/Challenge

Supplementary Materials

Practice Masters, p. 13

105

3-7 Adding and Subtracting Mixed Numbers

The rules for adding and subtracting fractions also apply to mixed numbers. Before mixed numbers are added or subtracted, convert them to improper fractions.

EXAMPLE 1 Add or subtract. Write the answer as a proper fraction in lowest terms or as a mixed number in simple form.

   a. $3\frac{7}{8} + 2\frac{3}{8}$ b. $2\frac{3}{5} - 1\frac{4}{5}$

Solution   a. $3\frac{7}{8} + 2\frac{3}{8} = \frac{31}{8} + \frac{19}{8}$ b. $2\frac{3}{5} - 1\frac{4}{5} = \frac{13}{5} - \frac{9}{5}$

$= \frac{50}{8}$ $= \frac{4}{5}$

$= 6\frac{2}{8} = 6\frac{1}{4}$

It is sometimes necessary to write mixed numbers as improper fractions having a common denominator before adding or subtracting.

EXAMPLE 2 Add or subtract. Write the answer as a proper fraction in lowest terms or as a mixed number in simple form.

   a. $5\frac{1}{4} + \left(-2\frac{1}{3}\right)$ b. $\frac{5}{6} - 2\frac{3}{8}$

Solution   a. $5\frac{1}{4} + \left(-2\frac{1}{3}\right) = \frac{21}{4} + \left(-\frac{7}{3}\right)$ b. $\frac{5}{6} - 2\frac{3}{8} = \frac{5}{6} - \frac{19}{8}$

$= \frac{63}{12} + \left(-\frac{28}{12}\right)$ $= \frac{20}{24} - \frac{57}{24}$

$= \frac{35}{12}$ $= -\frac{37}{24}$

$= 2\frac{11}{12}$ $= -1\frac{13}{24}$

Mixed numbers can be added or subtracted using a vertical format.

EXAMPLE 3 Add or subtract. Write the answer as a proper fraction in lowest terms or as a mixed number in simple form.

   a. $2\frac{3}{10} + 4\frac{1}{10}$ b. $4\frac{7}{8} - 2\frac{1}{5}$

106 *Chapter 3*

Solution

a. $2\frac{3}{10}$

$+4\frac{1}{10}$

$6\frac{4}{10} = 6\frac{2}{5}$

b. $4\frac{7}{8} = 4\frac{35}{40}$

$-2\frac{1}{5} = -2\frac{8}{40}$

$2\frac{27}{40}$

Class Exercises

Add or subtract. Write the answer as a proper fraction in lowest terms or as a mixed number in simple form.

1. $1\frac{1}{3} + 3\frac{1}{3}$ $4\frac{2}{3}$ 2. $2\frac{7}{10} - 1\frac{5}{10}$ $1\frac{1}{5}$ 3. $4\frac{13}{15} + 5\frac{4}{15}$ $10\frac{2}{15}$ 4. $5\frac{5}{12} - 4\frac{7}{12}$ $\frac{5}{6}$

5. $-6\frac{1}{4} + 2\frac{3}{4}$ $-3\frac{1}{2}$ 6. $5\frac{3}{8} - 6\frac{7}{8}$ $-1\frac{1}{2}$ 7. $-8\frac{7}{11} + 9\frac{8}{11}$ $1\frac{1}{11}$ 8. $-6\frac{3}{5} - 8\frac{4}{5}$ $-15\frac{2}{5}$

9. $-1\frac{5}{6} + \left(-3\frac{1}{6}\right)$ -5 10. $2\frac{4}{7} - \left(-7\frac{6}{7}\right)$ $10\frac{3}{7}$ 11. $-10\frac{1}{9} - \left(-8\frac{7}{9}\right)$ $-1\frac{1}{3}$ 12. $-3\frac{7}{10} - \left(-1\frac{3}{10}\right)$ $-2\frac{2}{5}$

Written Exercises

Add or subtract. Write the answer as a proper fraction in lowest terms or as a mixed number in simple form.

A 1. $5\frac{2}{5} + 3\frac{2}{5}$ $8\frac{4}{5}$ 2. $9\frac{7}{10} - 6\frac{3}{10}$ $3\frac{2}{5}$ 3. $-6\frac{4}{11} + 7\frac{3}{11}$ $\frac{10}{11}$ 4. $-8\frac{3}{4} - 4\frac{1}{4}$ -13

5. $1\frac{5}{6} + 4\frac{5}{6}$ $6\frac{2}{3}$ 6. $-3\frac{3}{8} - 9\frac{5}{8}$ -13 7. $-10\frac{3}{7} + \left(-9\frac{5}{7}\right)$ $-20\frac{1}{7}$ 8. $-2\frac{4}{15} - \left(-7\frac{7}{15}\right)$ $5\frac{1}{5}$

9. $2\frac{1}{2} + 1\frac{1}{3}$ $3\frac{5}{6}$ 10. $5\frac{3}{5} - 2\frac{1}{4}$ $3\frac{7}{20}$ 11. $-2\frac{1}{6} + 4\frac{2}{3}$ $2\frac{1}{2}$ 12. $-5\frac{3}{7} - 2\frac{1}{3}$ $-7\frac{16}{21}$

13. $10\frac{3}{8} + \left(-12\frac{7}{12}\right)$ $-2\frac{5}{24}$ 14. $-5\frac{2}{5} - 6\frac{5}{6}$ $-12\frac{7}{30}$ 15. $-1\frac{9}{10} + \left(-1\frac{2}{3}\right)$ $-3\frac{17}{30}$ 16. $-3\frac{7}{9} - \left(-5\frac{11}{15}\right)$ $1\frac{43}{45}$

17. $5 + \frac{3}{4}$ $5\frac{3}{4}$ 18. $7 - \frac{1}{5}$ $6\frac{4}{5}$ 19. $-3 - \frac{7}{8}$ $-3\frac{7}{8}$ 20. $-2 - \frac{7}{10}$ $-2\frac{7}{10}$

21. $5\frac{2}{3} + 6$ $11\frac{2}{3}$ 22. $3\frac{9}{10} - 7$ $-3\frac{1}{10}$ 23. $-10\frac{1}{5} + (-9)$ $-19\frac{1}{5}$ 24. $-7 - \left(-8\frac{1}{9}\right)$ $1\frac{1}{9}$

B 25. $3\frac{1}{2} + 2\frac{1}{3} + 4\frac{1}{12}$ $9\frac{11}{12}$ 26. $8\frac{3}{5} + 2\frac{1}{2} - 11\frac{1}{10}$ 0 27. $-4\frac{1}{3} + 2\frac{1}{4} - 6\frac{1}{6}$ $-8\frac{1}{4}$

28. $10\frac{1}{8} + \left(-6\frac{3}{4}\right) - 9\frac{11}{24}$ $-6\frac{1}{12}$ 29. $-4\frac{1}{7} + 3\frac{1}{2} + \left(-7\frac{9}{14}\right)$ $-8\frac{2}{7}$ 30. $-8\frac{9}{10} + 6\frac{2}{5} - 3\frac{1}{2}$ -6

Rational Numbers **107**

31. $-1\frac{2}{3} - \left(-2\frac{1}{5}\right) + 3\frac{7}{15}$ **32.** $-6\frac{7}{10} - \left(-3\frac{2}{5}\right) - \left(-3\frac{3}{10}\right)$ **33.** $3 + 2\frac{1}{3} - 5\frac{1}{5}$ $\quad\frac{2}{15}$

4

34. $4\frac{7}{8} + (-3) - 2\frac{1}{4}$ $\quad-\frac{3}{8}$ **35.** $1\frac{1}{5} + \frac{3}{10} - 1\frac{1}{4}$ $\quad\frac{1}{4}$ $\qquad 0$ **36.** $-4\frac{9}{16} + \frac{3}{32} + \frac{1}{2}$

$-3\frac{31}{32}$

Problems

Solve.

A 1. Joan Kent bought $15\frac{3}{4}$ yd of drapery material for $63 at a sale. If she used all except $1\frac{1}{16}$ yd, how much material did she actually use? $\quad 14\frac{11}{16}$ yd

2. Carl is 6 ft tall. If he grew $1\frac{1}{8}$ in. during the past year and $\frac{3}{4}$ in.. the year before, how tall was he one year ago? $\quad$ 5 ft $10\frac{7}{8}$ in.

3. On Monday Kim jogged $1\frac{1}{2}$ mi in $\frac{1}{4}$ h. On Wednesday she jogged $2\frac{1}{3}$ mi in $\frac{1}{3}$ h. How much farther did Kim jog on Wednesday? $\quad\frac{5}{6}$ mi

4. The gas tank of a popular compact car holds $15\frac{2}{5}$ gal of gasoline. How much gas has been used if $10\frac{1}{3}$ gal remain in the tank? $\quad 5\frac{1}{15}$ gal

B 5. Last year, total rainfall for April and May was $7\frac{1}{4}$ in. This year 3 in. of rain fell in April and $2\frac{5}{8}$ in. fell in May. How much less rain fell this year than last year during April and May? $\quad 1\frac{5}{8}$ in.

6. Each share of stock in Unified Electronics had a value of $34\frac{3}{4}$ on Monday. The value of the stock declined by $1\frac{5}{8}$ on Tuesday and by $\frac{7}{8}$ on Wednesday. What was the value of the stock after Wednesday? $32\frac{1}{4}

7. A 512-page book has pages that are 7 in. wide and 9 in. high. The printed area measures $5\frac{3}{8}$ in. by $7\frac{3}{4}$ in. The left margin is $\frac{5}{16}$ in. and the top margin is $\frac{9}{16}$ in. How wide are the margins at the right and at the bottom of the page? right: $1\frac{5}{16}$ in.; bottom: $\frac{11}{16}$ in.

Review Exercises

Complete.

1. $-\frac{2}{7} = \frac{-2}{7} = \frac{?}{-7}$ $\quad\frac{2}{-7}$ **2.** $-\frac{4}{11} = \frac{4}{-11} = \frac{?}{11}$ $\quad\frac{-4}{11}$ **3.** $-\frac{5}{9} = \frac{-5}{9} = \frac{5}{?}$ $\quad\frac{5}{-9}$

4. $\frac{7}{-20} = -\frac{7}{20} = \frac{?}{20}$ $\quad\frac{-7}{20}$ **5.** $7 \times \underline{} = -1\frac{1}{7}$ **6.** $6 \times \left(-\frac{1}{7}\right) = \frac{-6}{?}$ $\quad\frac{-6}{7}$

7. $-\frac{4}{11} = \underline{} \div (-11)$ 4 **8.** $\frac{-1}{4} = 1 \div \underline{}$ -4 **9.** $3 \div \underline{} = 1$ 3

3-8 Multiplying Fractions

To develop a method for multiplying fractions, we begin by showing that $\frac{7}{3} \times 3 = 7$.

$$\frac{7}{3} \times 3 = \left(7 \times \frac{1}{3}\right) \times 3 \qquad \text{By the rule: } \frac{a}{b} = a \times \frac{1}{b}$$

$$= 7 \times \left(\frac{1}{3} \times 3\right) \qquad \text{By the associative property}$$

$$= 7 \times \left(3 \times \frac{1}{3}\right) \qquad \text{By the commutative property}$$

$$= 7 \times 1 \qquad \text{By the rule: } b \times \frac{1}{b} = 1$$

$$= 7 \qquad \text{By the multiplication property of one}$$

In a similar way, it can be shown that $-\frac{7}{3} \times 3 = -7$. It is possible to prove the following general rule for all fractions.

. *Rule*

For all numbers a and b ($b \neq 0$),

$$\frac{a}{b} \times b = a$$

The rule tells us how to find the product of a fraction and a whole number. Using the rule on page 92, we can arrive at another rule for finding the product of two fractions such as $\frac{1}{5} \times \frac{1}{2}$. We begin by showing that $10 \times (\frac{1}{5} \times \frac{1}{2}) = 1$.

$$10 \times \left(\frac{1}{5} \times \frac{1}{2}\right) = (2 \times 5) \times \left(\frac{1}{5} \times \frac{1}{2}\right) \qquad \text{Substitution of } 2 \times 5 \text{ for } 10$$

$$= \left(2 \times \frac{1}{2}\right) \times \left(5 \times \frac{1}{5}\right) \qquad \text{By the associative and commutative properties}$$

$$= 1 \times 1 \qquad \text{By the rule: } b \times \frac{1}{b} = 1$$

$$= 1 \qquad \text{By the multiplication property of one}$$

We have shown that $10 \times (\frac{1}{5} \times \frac{1}{2}) = 1$ and we know that $10 \times \frac{1}{10} = 1$, so we conclude that $\frac{1}{5} \times \frac{1}{2} = \frac{1}{10}$. Similarly, we may prove the general rule shown on the following page.

Rational Numbers **109**

Teaching Suggestions p. 83f

Related Activities p. 83f

Reading Mathematics

The Reading Mathematics feature on page 111 is intended to call students' attention to the importance of directionality in mathematical symbols. This will become even more important as students deal with more complex algebraic expressions. Remind them of the use of directionality in distinguishing between:

57	and	75
x^3	and	$3x$
$2\overline{)4}$	and	$4\overline{)2}$

If students have difficulty reading fractions or other expressions, try writing an expression on the chalkboard and reading it aloud, pointing to each symbol in order. Note any possible alternative readings.

Chalkboard Examples

Multiply. Write the answer as a proper fraction in lowest terms or as a mixed number in simple form.

1. $-\frac{3}{4} \times \frac{4}{5}$ $-\frac{3}{5}$

2. $-\frac{9}{14} \times \frac{18}{45}$ $-\frac{9}{35}$

3. $-2\frac{5}{8} \times \left(-\frac{16}{19}\right)$ $2\frac{4}{19}$

4. $8 \times \left(-\frac{3}{4}\right) \times \left(-3\frac{1}{4}\right)$ $19\frac{1}{2}$

5. $6\frac{3}{4} \times (-10) \times \left(-1\frac{1}{3}\right)$ 90

6. $-4\frac{1}{3} \times \frac{3}{13}$ -1

> ### Rule
>
> For all numbers a and b ($a \neq 0$, $b \neq 0$),
> $$\frac{1}{a} \times \frac{1}{b} = \frac{1}{ab}$$

EXAMPLE 1   Multiply $\frac{1}{-3} \times \frac{1}{4}$.

Solution $\frac{1}{-3} \times \frac{1}{4} = \frac{1}{-3 \times 4} = \frac{1}{-12}$, or $-\frac{1}{12}$

The preceding rules are used to prove the following rule for multiplying two fractions.

> ### Rule
>
> For all numbers a, b, c, and d ($b \neq 0$, $d \neq 0$),
> $$\frac{a}{b} \times \frac{c}{d} = \frac{ac}{bd}$$

EXAMPLE 2   Multiply. Write the answers to parts (a) and (b) as proper fractions in lowest terms or as mixed numbers in simple form.

   a. $\frac{5}{6} \times \frac{7}{3}$ **b.** $\frac{3}{2} \times \left(-\frac{5}{7}\right)$ **c.** $-\frac{7}{a} \times \left(-\frac{4}{b}\right)$

Solution   **a.** $\frac{5}{6} \times \frac{7}{3} = \frac{5 \times 7}{6 \times 3} = \frac{35}{18}$, or $1\frac{17}{18}$

b. $\frac{3}{2} \times \left(-\frac{5}{7}\right) = \frac{3}{2} \times \frac{-5}{7} = \frac{3 \times (-5)}{2 \times 7} = \frac{-15}{14}$, or $-1\frac{1}{14}$

c. $-\frac{7}{a} \times \left(-\frac{4}{b}\right) = \frac{-7}{a} \times \frac{-4}{b} = \frac{-7 \times (-4)}{a \times b} = \frac{28}{ab}$

Sometimes it is easier to divide by common factors of the numerator and denominator before multiplying.

EXAMPLE 3   Multiply $\frac{-3}{5} \times \frac{15}{16} \times \frac{-2}{3}$.

Solution $\frac{-3}{5} \times \frac{15}{16} \times \frac{-2}{3} = \frac{\overset{-1}{\cancel{-3}}}{\underset{1}{\cancel{5}}} \times \frac{\overset{3}{\cancel{15}}}{\underset{8}{\cancel{16}}} \times \frac{\overset{-1}{\cancel{-2}}}{\underset{1}{\cancel{3}}} = \frac{-1 \times 3 \times (-1)}{1 \times 8 \times 1} = \frac{3}{8}$

110   *Chapter 3*

Reading Mathematics: *Reading Fractions*

Usually you read across a line from left to right, and you read a page from top to bottom. You have learned many special ways to read things in mathematics. For example, you read a fraction from top to bottom. You read first the numerator and then the denominator of each fraction before continuing to the next word or symbol.

To multiply mixed numbers, first write each mixed number as an improper fraction.

EXAMPLE 4   Multiply. Write the answer as a proper fraction in lowest terms or as a mixed number in simple form.

a. $3\frac{1}{2} \times \left(-\frac{1}{4}\right)$ b. $5\frac{1}{4} \times 1\frac{3}{7}$

Solution   a. $3\frac{1}{2} \times \left(-\frac{1}{4}\right) = \frac{7}{2} \times \frac{-1}{4} = \frac{-7}{8}$, or $-\frac{7}{8}$

b. $5\frac{1}{4} \times 1\frac{3}{7} = \frac{\overset{3}{\cancel{21}}}{\underset{2}{\cancel{4}}} \times \frac{\overset{5}{\cancel{10}}}{\underset{1}{\cancel{7}}} = \frac{15}{2}$, or $7\frac{1}{2}$

Class Exercises

Multiply.

1. $\frac{5}{6} \times 6$ 5

2. $-\frac{3}{5} \times (-5)$ 3

3. $-4 \times \frac{7}{4}$ −7

4. $9 \times \left(-\frac{8}{9}\right)$ −8 $\frac{1}{100}$

5. $\frac{1}{8} \times \frac{1}{3}$ $\frac{1}{24}$

6. $-\frac{1}{4} \times \frac{1}{5}$ $-\frac{1}{20}$

7. $\frac{1}{15} \times \left(-\frac{1}{2}\right)$ $-\frac{1}{30}$

8. $-\frac{1}{10} \times \left(-\frac{1}{10}\right)$

9. $\frac{5}{8} \times \frac{3}{11}$ $\frac{15}{88}$

10. $\frac{2}{5} \times \left(-\frac{3}{7}\right)$ $-\frac{6}{35}$

11. $1\frac{1}{2} \times 2$ 3

12. $-3 \times 1\frac{1}{5}$ $-3\frac{3}{5}$

Written Exercises

Multiply. Write the answer as a proper fraction in lowest terms or as a mixed number in simple form.

A   1. $\frac{7}{12} \times 12$ 7

2. $-6 \times \frac{3}{6}$ −3

3. $3 \times \left(-\frac{2}{3}\right)$ −2

4. $-14 \times \left(-\frac{5}{14}\right)$ 5

5. $-\frac{1}{4} \times \left(-\frac{1}{7}\right)$ $\frac{1}{28}$

6. $\frac{1}{8} \times \left(-\frac{1}{20}\right)$ $-\frac{1}{160}$

7. $-\frac{1}{10} \times \frac{1}{6}$ $-\frac{1}{60}$

8. $-\frac{1}{15} \times \frac{1}{2}$ $-\frac{1}{30}$

9. $\frac{2}{3} \times \frac{5}{9}$ $\frac{10}{27}$

10. $\frac{6}{7} \times \frac{2}{5}$ $\frac{12}{35}$

11. $\frac{3}{8} \times \left(-\frac{2}{3}\right)$ $-\frac{1}{4}$

12. $\frac{5}{6} \times \left(-\frac{2}{5}\right)$ $-\frac{1}{3}$

13. $-\frac{1}{3} \times \frac{2}{9}$ $-\frac{2}{27}$

14. $-\frac{3}{8} \times \frac{2}{9}$ $-\frac{1}{12}$

15. $\frac{-5}{8} \times (-1)$ $\frac{5}{8}$

16. $\frac{-2}{5} \times \left(-\frac{15}{16}\right)$ $\frac{3}{8}$

Rational Numbers   **111**

Additional A Exercises

Multiply. Write the answer as a proper fraction in lowest terms or as a mixed number in simple form.

1. $-\frac{5}{8} \times (-4)$ $2\frac{1}{2}$

2. $-\frac{1}{3} \times \left(-\frac{2}{5}\right)$ $\frac{2}{15}$

3. $\frac{24}{25} \times \left(-\frac{35}{16}\right)$ $-2\frac{1}{10}$

4. $-\frac{3}{8} \times \frac{4}{9}$ $-\frac{1}{6}$

5. $-\frac{4}{5} \times 0$ 0

6. $-\frac{12}{17} \times \left(-\frac{34}{63}\right)$ $\frac{8}{21}$

111

Multiply.

17. $-\frac{1}{4} \times 0$ 0

18. $-\frac{3}{4} \times 0$ 0

19. $\frac{5}{16} \times \frac{30}{40}$ $\frac{15}{64}$

20. $\frac{9}{8} \times \frac{24}{27}$ 1

B **21.** $3\frac{1}{4} \times \frac{4}{13}$ 1

22. $5\frac{2}{5} \times \frac{5}{9}$ 3

23. $4\frac{1}{4} \times 10\frac{1}{3}$ $43\frac{11}{12}$

24. $10\frac{1}{2} \times 2\frac{3}{4}$ $28\frac{7}{8}$

25. $-4\frac{2}{7} \times 5\frac{1}{6}$ $-22\frac{1}{7}$

26. $3\frac{1}{8} \times \left(-4\frac{1}{5}\right)$ $-13\frac{1}{8}$

27. $-2\frac{1}{3} \times \left(-1\frac{4}{9}\right)$ $3\frac{10}{27}$

28. $-6\frac{1}{4} \times \left(-5\frac{2}{5}\right)$ $33\frac{3}{4}$

29. $\frac{1}{4} \times \frac{1}{3} \times \frac{1}{2}$ $\frac{1}{24}$

30. $\frac{5}{16} \times \frac{1}{2} \times \frac{1}{5}$ $\frac{1}{32}$

31. $\frac{3}{4} \times \frac{1}{6} \times \frac{1}{9}$ $\frac{1}{72}$

32. $-\frac{5}{8} \times \left(-\frac{3}{25}\right) \times \left(-\frac{1}{9}\right)$ $-\frac{1}{120}$

33. $-2\frac{1}{4} \times 6\frac{1}{2} \times \frac{12}{39}$ $-4\frac{1}{2}$

34. $-5\frac{1}{8} \times \frac{24}{25} \times 10\frac{1}{2}$ $-51\frac{33}{50}$

Multiply. Simplify the answer.

EXAMPLE $\frac{3}{5} \times 15a = \frac{3}{\cancel{5}_1} \times \frac{\overset{3a}{\cancel{15a}}}{1} = \frac{3 \times 3a}{1 \times 1} = 9a$

35. $\frac{2}{3} \times 9n$ $6n$

36. $5 \times \frac{3x}{10}$ $\frac{3x}{2}$

37. $-3 \times \frac{y}{6}$ $-\frac{y}{2}$

38. $-5 \times \left(\frac{-7a}{10}\right)$ $\frac{7a}{2}$

39. $\frac{2r}{5} \times \frac{1}{r}$ $\frac{2}{5}$

40. $\frac{-6}{s} \times \frac{s}{2}$ -3

41. $\frac{3c}{5} \times \frac{5}{c}$ 3

42. $\frac{2m}{7} \times \frac{14}{m}$ 4

C **43.** Let $\frac{a}{b}$ be any fraction ($b \neq 0$). Show that $\frac{a}{b} \times b = a$ by supplying the rule or property that justifies each statement.

$\frac{a}{b} \times b = \left(a \times \frac{1}{b}\right) \times b$ Why? $\frac{a}{b} = a \times \frac{1}{b}$

$\quad\quad = a \times \left(\frac{1}{b} \times b\right)$ Why? Associative Property

$\quad\quad = a \times \left(b \times \frac{1}{b}\right)$ Why? Commutative Property

$\quad\quad = a \times 1$ Why? $b \times \frac{1}{b} = 1$

$\quad\quad = a$ Why? Multiplication Property of 1

44. Let $\frac{a}{b}$ and $\frac{c}{d}$ represent any two fractions ($b \neq 0, d \neq 0$). Show as in Exercise 43 that $\frac{a}{b} \times \frac{c}{d} = \frac{ac}{bd}$.

Review Exercises

Evaluate the expression when $x = -8$ and $y = 12$.

1. $5 \times y$ 60

2. $7x \div 4$ -14

3. $3x - y$ -36

4. $x + 8y$ 88

5. $2(x + y)$ 8

6. $x \div (y - 6)$ $-1\frac{1}{3}$

7. $(2y + 4) \div (x - 1)$ $-3\frac{1}{9}$

8. $(x \div 4) \times (y \div 3)$ -8

3-9 Dividing Fractions

Teaching Suggestions p. 83f

Related Activities p. 83g

Reading Mathematics

Students will learn the meaning of the following mathematical term in this lesson: *reciprocal.*

To develop a method for dividing fractions, recall that multiplication and division are inverse operations. If $2 \times n = 10$, then $n = 10 \div 2$. Similarly, if $\frac{7}{5} \times x = \frac{2}{3}$, then $x = \frac{2}{3} \div \frac{7}{5}$. We can show by substitution that the multiplication equation is true when the value of x is $(\frac{2}{3} \times \frac{5}{7})$.

$$\frac{7}{5} \times \left(\frac{2}{3} \times \frac{5}{7}\right) = \frac{\cancel{7} \times 2 \times \cancel{5}}{\cancel{5} \times 3 \times \cancel{7}} = \frac{2}{3}$$

Therefore, the related division equation must also be true when the value of x is $(\frac{2}{3} \times \frac{5}{7})$. That is,

$$\frac{2}{3} \times \frac{5}{7} = \frac{2}{3} \div \frac{7}{5}.$$

Two numbers, like $\frac{5}{7}$ and $\frac{7}{5}$, whose product is 1 are called **reciprocals.** The reciprocal of $\frac{c}{d}$ is $\frac{d}{c}$ because $\frac{c}{d} \times \frac{d}{c} = 1$. Every nonzero rational number has exactly one reciprocal.

We may state the following general rule.

Rule

For all numbers a, b, c, and d ($b \neq 0, c \neq 0, d \neq 0$),

$$\frac{a}{b} \div \frac{c}{d} = \frac{a}{b} \times \frac{d}{c}$$

To divide by a fraction, multiply by its reciprocal.

EXAMPLE 1   Name the reciprocal, if any.

    a. $\frac{2}{3}$ **b.** $-\frac{5}{8}$ **c.** 2   **d.** 0

Solution

    a. The reciprocal of $\frac{2}{3}$ is $\frac{3}{2}$ since $\frac{2}{3} \times \frac{3}{2} = 1$.

    b. The reciprocal of $-\frac{5}{8}$ is $-\frac{8}{5}$ since $-\frac{5}{8} \times \left(-\frac{8}{5}\right) = 1$.

    c. The reciprocal of 2 is $\frac{1}{2}$ since $2 \times \frac{1}{2} = 1$.

    d. The equation $0 \times n = 1$ has no solution since 0 times any number is 0. Therefore, 0 has no reciprocal.

Rational Numbers **113**

State the reciprocal of:

1. $-4 \quad -\frac{1}{4}$

2. $\frac{4}{9} \quad \frac{9}{4}$

3. $\frac{1}{2} \quad 2$

Divide. Write the answer as a proper fraction in lowest terms or as a mixed number in simple form.

4. $\frac{7}{12} \div \left(-\frac{5}{6}\right) \quad -\frac{7}{10}$

5. $-3\frac{1}{6} \div \frac{1}{4} \quad -12\frac{2}{3}$

6. $-5\frac{1}{4} \div \left(-3\frac{3}{8}\right) \quad 1\frac{5}{9}$

EXAMPLE 2 Divide. Write the answer as a proper fraction in lowest terms or as a mixed number in simple form.

a. $-\frac{4}{3} \div \frac{5}{8}$ b. $2\frac{1}{3} \div 1\frac{3}{8}$ c. $\frac{\frac{2}{5}}{\frac{1}{4}}$

Solution   a. $-\frac{4}{3} \div \frac{5}{8} = -\frac{4}{3} \times \frac{8}{5} = -\frac{32}{15}$, or $-2\frac{2}{15}$

b. $2\frac{1}{3} \div 1\frac{3}{8} = \frac{7}{3} \div \frac{11}{8} = \frac{7}{3} \times \frac{8}{11} = \frac{56}{33}$, or $1\frac{23}{33}$

c. $\frac{\frac{2}{5}}{\frac{1}{4}} = \frac{2}{5} \div \frac{1}{4} = \frac{2}{5} \times \frac{4}{1} = \frac{8}{5}$, or $1\frac{3}{5}$

EXAMPLE 3 Ann bought 2 packages of ground beef. One package was $2\frac{1}{2}$ lb, and the other package was $3\frac{1}{8}$ lb. Ann divided the total amount of beef into 5 equal packages for the freezer. How many pounds were in each package?

Solution   • The problem asks for the number of pounds in each of the 5 packages.

• Given facts: $2\frac{1}{2}$ lb and $3\frac{1}{8}$ lb of beef
                 total divided into 5 equal packages

• To solve, first add to find the total amount of beef, and then divide to find the amount in each package.

$$2\frac{1}{2} + 3\frac{1}{8} = 2\frac{4}{8} + 3\frac{1}{8} = 5\frac{5}{8}$$

$$5\frac{5}{8} \div 5 = \overset{9}{\cancel{45}} \times \frac{1}{\underset{1}{\cancel{5}}} = \frac{9 \times 1}{8 \times 1} = \frac{9}{8}, \text{ or } 1\frac{1}{8}$$

Each package contained $1\frac{1}{8}$ lb of beef.

Problem Solving Reminder
When solving a problem, *review the problem solving strategies and tips* that you have learned. As you work through the problems in the lesson, remember that you may need to supply additional information, eliminate extra information, or plan more than one step. Remember to reread the problem to be sure your answer is complete.

114 *Chapter 3*

Class Exercises

State the reciprocal.

1. $4\frac{1}{4}$ **2.** -5 $-\frac{1}{5}$ **3.** $\frac{3}{4}$ $\frac{4}{3}$ **4.** $-\frac{5}{8}$ $-\frac{8}{5}$ **5.** $\frac{2}{7}$ $\frac{7}{2}$ **6.** $\frac{11}{3}$ $\frac{3}{11}$

7. $-\frac{2}{3}$ $-\frac{3}{2}$ **8.** $-\frac{6}{5}$ $-\frac{5}{6}$ **9.** $\frac{11}{12}$ $\frac{12}{11}$ **10.** $\frac{3}{16}$ $\frac{16}{3}$ **11.** $-\frac{4}{7}$ $-\frac{7}{4}$ **12.** $\frac{14}{5}$ $\frac{5}{14}$

Complete.

13. $\frac{2}{3} \div 5 = \frac{2}{3} \times \underline{\ ?\ }$ $\frac{1}{5}$ **14.** $\frac{2}{3} \div \frac{1}{5} = \frac{2}{3} \times \underline{\ ?\ }$ 5

15. $\frac{6}{5} \div (-10) = \underline{\ ?\ } \times \left(-\frac{1}{10}\right)$ $\frac{6}{5}$ **16.** $-\frac{3}{4} \div \frac{3}{10} = \underline{\ ?\ } \times \underline{\ ?\ }$ $-\frac{3}{4} \times \frac{10}{3}$

Written Exercises

Divide. Write the answer as a proper fraction in lowest terms or as a mixed number in simple form.

A   **1.** $\frac{2}{5} \div \frac{3}{5}$ $\frac{2}{3}$ **2.** $\frac{7}{8} \div \frac{3}{8}$ $2\frac{1}{3}$ **3.** $5 \div \frac{1}{5}$ 25 **4.** $10 \div \frac{1}{2}$ 20

    5. $\frac{5}{8} \div \frac{9}{5}$ $\frac{25}{72}$ **6.** $\frac{3}{4} \div \frac{7}{8}$ $\frac{6}{7}$ **7.** $\frac{\frac{5}{9}}{\frac{1}{7}}$ $3\frac{8}{9}$ **8.** $\frac{\frac{2}{3}}{\frac{3}{8}}$ $1\frac{7}{9}$

    9. $-\frac{21}{4} \div \left(-\frac{7}{8}\right)$ 6 **10.** $-\frac{4}{5} \div \left(-\frac{36}{25}\right)$ $\frac{5}{9}$ **11.** $3\frac{1}{4} \div \frac{5}{8}$ $5\frac{1}{5}$ **12.** $10\frac{1}{2} \div \frac{8}{9}$ $11\frac{13}{16}$

    13. $-5\frac{5}{8} \div 10$ $-\frac{9}{16}$ **14.** $11\frac{1}{9} \div 100$ $\frac{1}{9}$ **15.** $-6\frac{1}{3} \div \left(-\frac{19}{21}\right)$ 7 **16.** $-10\frac{1}{3} \div \left(-\frac{31}{33}\right)$ 11

B   **17.** $6\frac{1}{8} \div \left(\frac{8}{3} \times \frac{3}{7}\right)$ $5\frac{23}{64}$ **18.** $-7 \div \left(\frac{21}{4} \times \frac{3}{7}\right)$ $-3\frac{1}{9}$ **19.** $\left(-1\frac{2}{3} \times \frac{18}{5}\right) \div 3$ -2

    20. $-\left(\frac{35}{4} \times \frac{2}{7}\right) \div \left(-\frac{4}{3}\right)$ $1\frac{7}{8}$ **21.** $-\left(3\frac{1}{5} \times \frac{5}{2}\right) \div \frac{8}{9}$ -9 **22.** $\left(-2\frac{1}{6} \div \frac{1}{9}\right) \times \frac{1}{13}$ $-1\frac{1}{2}$

    23. $-\left(4\frac{1}{6} \div 5\right) \times \left(-\frac{2}{5}\right)$ $\frac{1}{3}$ **24.** $-3\frac{1}{8} \div 4 \div \left(-\frac{5}{4}\right)$ $\frac{5}{8}$ **25.** $5\frac{1}{3} \div 2\frac{2}{3} \div (-4)$ $-\frac{1}{2}$

Problems

Solve.

A   **1.** To the nearest million, the number of households in the United States having television sets was 4 million in 1950 and 76 million in 1980. Express the first number as a fraction of the second. $\frac{1}{19}$

    2. A gasoline tank with a capacity of 15 gal is $\frac{3}{4}$ full. How many gallons will it take to fill the tank? $3\frac{3}{4}$ gal

Rational Numbers   **115**

Additional A Exercises

Divide. Write the answer as a proper fraction in lowest terms or as a mixed number in simple form.

1. $4 \div 2\frac{2}{5}$ $1\frac{2}{3}$

2. $\frac{4}{7} \div \frac{9}{20}$ $1\frac{17}{63}$

3. $-16 \div 2\frac{10}{11}$ $-5\frac{1}{2}$

4. $-\frac{3}{4} \div \left(-\frac{5}{12}\right)$ $1\frac{4}{5}$

5. $\frac{5}{6} \div \left(-4\frac{1}{2}\right)$ $-\frac{5}{27}$

6. $1\frac{1}{2} \div \frac{3}{8}$ 4

Suggested Assignments

Core
115/1–25 odd
116/Prob. 3–9 odd
116/Rev. 1–4

Enriched
115/2–16 even; 20–25
116/Prob. 7–12

Supplementary Materials

Practice Masters, p. 14

3. A town has raised $\frac{3}{8}$ of the $12,000 it needs to furnish its new library. How much more is it hoping to raise? $7500

4. How many packages will $5\frac{1}{2}$ lb of raisins fill if each package holds 9 oz? $9\frac{7}{9}$ packages

5. Karen Northrup worked $12\frac{1}{2}$ h last week and earned $50. What was her hourly rate of pay? $4/hr

6. A television station released 300 balloons at an outdoor celebration. Of these, $\frac{3}{4}$ were orange. How many were orange? 225

7. Leo Delray earns $2 an hour for babysitting. If he works $3\frac{1}{4}$ h one evening, how much does he earn? $6.50

8. In a recent year there were 32,000 persons in the United States who had celebrated their 100th birthday. Of these, $\frac{3}{4}$ were women. How many were men? 8000

B 9. One half of the class voted to have a picnic. One third of the class voted to hold a dinner instead. What fraction of the class wanted neither a picnic nor a dinner? $\frac{1}{6}$ of the class

10. A picture measures $8\frac{3}{4}$ in. by 8 in. When framed it measures $10\frac{3}{4}$ in. by 10 in. How wide is each side of the frame? 1 in.

C 11. Only $\frac{1}{5}$ of the downtown workers drive to work. Of those who do not drive, $\frac{3}{16}$ ride bicycles to work. What fraction of the workers ride bicycles to work? $\frac{3}{20}$ of the workers

12. Kevin's regular rate of pay is $4 per hour. When he works overtime, he earns $1\frac{1}{2}$ times as much per hour. How much will Kevin earn for $5\frac{1}{2}$ h of overtime work? $33

**Additional Answers
Review Exercises**

1. $n = 240 - 135$; 105

2. $x = 52 + 45$; 97

3. $y = 156 \div 4$; 39

4. $t = 504 \div 9$; 56

5. $x = 432 \div 12$; 36

6. $r = 27 \times 17$; 459

7. $m \doteq 418 \div 38$; 11

8. $a = 33 \times 22$; 726

Review Exercises

Use the inverse operation to write a related equation. Solve for the variable.

1. $n + 135 = 240$ 2. $x - 45 = 52$ 3. $4y = 156$ 4. $9t = 504$

5. $12x = 432$ 6. $r \div 17 = 27$ 7. $38m = 418$ 8. $a \div 22 = 33$

116   *Chapter 3*

3-10 Fractions and Decimals

Any fraction can be represented as a decimal. You may recall that a fraction such as $\frac{3}{4}$ can be easily written as an equivalent fraction whose denominator is a power of 10, and then as a decimal. To represent $\frac{3}{4}$ as a decimal, we first write it as an equivalent fraction with denominator 100.

$$\frac{3}{4} = \frac{3 \times 25}{4 \times 25} = \frac{75}{100} = 0.75$$

For most fractions, however, we use the fact that $\frac{a}{b} = a \div b$ and divide numerator by denominator.

EXAMPLE 1   Write as a decimal: **a.** $-\frac{5}{16}$ **b.** $\frac{24}{55}$

Solution   **a.** First find $5 \div 16$.

$$
\begin{array}{r}
0.3125 \\
16\overline{)5.0000} \\
\underline{4\ 8} \\
20 \\
\underline{16} \\
40 \\
\underline{32} \\
80 \\
\underline{80} \\
0
\end{array}
$$

Therefore, $-\frac{5}{16} = -0.3125$.

The decimal -0.3125 is called a **terminating decimal** because the final remainder is 0 and the division ends.

b. Find $24 \div 55$.

$$
\begin{array}{r}
0.43636 \\
55\overline{)24.00000} \\
\underline{22\ 0} \\
2\ 00 \\
\underline{1\ 65} \\
350 \\
\underline{330} \\
200 \\
\underline{165} \\
350 \\
\underline{330} \\
20
\end{array}
$$

Therefore, $\frac{24}{55} = 0.43636\ldots$.

The digits 36 continue to repeat without end. The decimal $0.43636\ldots$ is called a **repeating decimal.** We often write $0.43636\ldots$ as $0.4\overline{36}$, with a bar over the block of digits that repeats.

Rational Numbers   **117**

Reading Mathematics

Students will learn the meaning of the following mathematical terms in this lesson: *terminating decimal, repeating decimal, irrational number, real number, real number line.*

    Although there is no formal convention for reading a repeating decimal such as $0.4\overline{36}$, you will probably wish to distinguish $0.4\overline{36}$ from 0.436 or $0.43\overline{6}$ when you or your students read aloud. Here are some ways of doing this: You can read $0.4\overline{36}$ as "zero, point, four, three, six; the three, six repeats," or "zero, point, four, three, six, three, six, three, six, etc," or "zero, point, four, three, six, with a bar over three, six." Whichever choice is made, the decimal $0.4\overline{36}$ must be distinguished from 0.436.

Write as a proper fraction in lowest terms or as a mixed number in simple form.

1. 2.8 $2\frac{4}{5}$

2. -5.25 $-5\frac{1}{4}$

3. $-21.\overline{33}$ $-21\frac{1}{3}$

4. $4.\overline{72}$ $4\frac{8}{11}$

Write as a terminating or repeating decimal.

5. $-\frac{7}{8}$ -0.875

6. $\frac{1}{5}$ 0.2

7. $3\frac{1}{8}$ 3.125

8. $-2\frac{5}{12}$ $-2.41\overline{6}$

To say that $\frac{24}{55} = 0.43636\ldots$ means that the successive decimals 0.436, 0.4363, 0.43636, and so on, will come closer and closer to the value $\frac{24}{55}$.

We can predict when a fraction will result in a terminating decimal because the fraction in lowest terms has a denominator with no prime factors other than 2 and 5. Thus, the fraction $\frac{24}{55}$ does not result in a terminating decimal because its denominator has 11 as a prime factor.

When working with a mixed number, such as $-1\frac{5}{16}$ or $1\frac{24}{25}$, we may consider the mixed number as a sum of a whole number and a fraction, or we may rewrite the mixed number as an improper fraction and then divide.

If a and b are integers and $b \neq 0$, the quotient $a \div b$ is either a terminating decimal or a repeating decimal. The reason for this is that, for any divisor, the number of possible remainders at each step of the division is limited to the whole numbers less than the divisor. Sooner or later, either the remainder is 0 and the division ends, as in part (a) of Example 1, or one of the remainders reappears in the division as in part (b) of Example 1. Then the same block of digits will reappear in the quotient.

Property

Every rational number can be represented by either a terminating decimal or a repeating decimal.

You already know how to write a terminating decimal as a fraction. Rewrite the decimal as a fraction whose denominator is a power of 10.

EXAMPLE 2 Write -0.625 as a fraction in lowest terms.

Solution $-0.625 = -\dfrac{625}{1000} = -\dfrac{625 \div 125}{1000 \div 125} = -\dfrac{5}{8}$

The next example shows a method for writing a repeating decimal as a fraction.

EXAMPLE 3 Write $-1.\overline{21}$ as a fraction in lowest terms.

Solution Let $n = 1.\overline{21}$.

Multiply both sides of the equation by a power of 10 determined by the number of digits in the block of repeating digits. Since there are

118 *Chapter 3*

^{2} digits that repeat in the number $1.\overline{21}$, we multiply by 10^2, or 100.

$$100n = 121.\overline{21}$$

Subtract: $\quad\quad \dfrac{n = \quad 1.\overline{21}}{99n = 120}$

$$n = \frac{120}{99} = \frac{40}{33}$$

Thus, $-1.\overline{21} = -\dfrac{40}{33}$, or $-1\dfrac{7}{33}$.

Property

Every terminating or repeating decimal represents a rational number.

Some decimals, such as those below, neither terminate nor repeat.

$0.01001000100001\ldots$ $\quad\quad\quad$ $1.234567891011121314\ldots$

The two decimals shown follow patterns, but they are not repeating patterns. The decimal on the right is made up of consecutive whole numbers beginning with 1.

Decimals that neither terminate nor repeat represent **irrational numbers.** Together, the rational numbers and the irrational numbers make up the set of **real numbers.** The number line that you have studied is sometimes called the **real number line.** For every point on the line, there is exactly one real number and for every real number there is exactly one point on the number line.

Class Exercises

Tell whether the decimal for the fraction is terminating or repeating. If the decimal is terminating, state the decimal.

1. $\dfrac{1}{4}$ **2.** $\dfrac{5}{6}$ **3.** $2\dfrac{2}{5}$ **4.** $-\dfrac{9}{10}$ **5.** $-1\dfrac{1}{2}$ **6.** $\dfrac{13}{30}$

State as a fraction in which the numerator is an integer and the denominator is a power of 10.

7. 0.13 $\dfrac{13}{100}$ **8.** -0.9 $-\dfrac{9}{10}$ **9.** 1.4 $\dfrac{14}{10}$ **10.** -0.007 $\dfrac{-7}{1000}$ **11.** 3.03 $\dfrac{303}{100}$ **12.** -5.001 $\dfrac{-5001}{1000}$

Rational Numbers **119**

Additional A Exercises

Write as a terminating or repeating decimal.

1. $-\dfrac{9}{20}$ -0.45

2. $\dfrac{5}{9}$ $0.\overline{5}$

3. $5\dfrac{3}{8}$ 5.375

4. $\dfrac{5}{11}$ $0.\overline{45}$

Write as a fraction in lowest terms or as a mixed number in simple form.

5. $-0.\overline{66}$ $-\dfrac{2}{3}$

6. 3.05 $3\dfrac{1}{20}$

7. -11.9 $-11\dfrac{9}{10}$

8. $7.\overline{7}$ $7\dfrac{7}{9}$

Quick Quiz B

Perform the indicated operation. Write the answer as a proper fraction in lowest terms or as a mixed number in simple form.

1. $\dfrac{1}{3} + \dfrac{1}{6}$ $\dfrac{1}{2}$

2. $-\dfrac{17}{18} + \dfrac{5}{12}$ $-\dfrac{19}{36}$

3. $7\dfrac{1}{4} + 3\dfrac{2}{7}$ $10\dfrac{15}{28}$

4. $-5\dfrac{2}{3} - 2\dfrac{3}{8}$ $-8\dfrac{1}{24}$

5. $13\dfrac{7}{8} - \left(-\dfrac{5}{6}\right)$ $14\dfrac{17}{24}$

6. $\dfrac{1}{7} - \dfrac{1}{3}$ $-\dfrac{4}{21}$

7. $\dfrac{21}{56} \times \dfrac{22}{25}$ $\dfrac{33}{100}$

8. $4\dfrac{2}{7} \times 2\dfrac{1}{4}$ $9\dfrac{9}{14}$

9. $-3\dfrac{1}{4} \times \left(-2\dfrac{2}{3}\right)$ $8\dfrac{2}{3}$

(continued on next page)

120

State the repeating digit(s) for each decimal.

13. $6.666\ldots$ 6 **14.** $0.0444\ldots$ 4 **15.** $6.050505\ldots$ 05 **16.** $0.1666\ldots$ 6

17. $5.1\overline{5}$ 5 **18.** $0.\overline{422}$ 422 **19.** $1.0\overline{6}$ 6 **20.** $0.3\overline{64}$ 64

Written Exercises

Write as a terminating or repeating decimal. Use a bar to show repeating digits.

A **1.** $\dfrac{1}{4}$ 0.25 **2.** $\dfrac{1}{5}$ 0.2 **3.** $\dfrac{2}{9}$ $0.\overline{2}$ **4.** $\dfrac{3}{16}$ 0.1875 **5.** $\dfrac{9}{10}$ 0.9 **6.** $-\dfrac{1}{18}$ $-0.05\overline{5}$

7. $-\dfrac{2}{3}$ $-0.\overline{6}$ **8.** $\dfrac{4}{9}$ $0.\overline{4}$ **9.** $-\dfrac{3}{8}$ -0.375 **10.** $\dfrac{3}{5}$ 0.6 **11.** $-\dfrac{3}{25}$ -0.12 **12.** $\dfrac{7}{15}$ $0.4\overline{6}$

13. $1\dfrac{1}{10}$ 1.1 **14.** $5\dfrac{2}{5}$ 5.4 **15.** $\dfrac{7}{12}$ $0.58\overline{3}$ **16.** $-\dfrac{3}{11}$ $-0.\overline{27}$ **17.** $\dfrac{4}{15}$ $0.2\overline{6}$ **18.** $-4\dfrac{7}{8}$ -4.875

19. $-1\dfrac{7}{18}$ $-1.38\overline{8}$ **20.** $2\dfrac{1}{9}$ $2.\overline{1}$ **21.** $\dfrac{3}{20}$ 0.15 **22.** $\dfrac{17}{36}$ $0.47\overline{2}$ **23.** $3\dfrac{2}{7}$ $3.\overline{285714}$ **24.** $\dfrac{5}{13}$ $0.\overline{384615}$

Write as a proper fraction in lowest terms or as a mixed number in simple form.

25. 0.05 $\dfrac{1}{20}$ **26.** 0.005 $\dfrac{1}{200}$ **27.** -0.6 $-\dfrac{3}{5}$ **28.** -2.1 $-2\dfrac{1}{10}$ **29.** 2.07 $2\dfrac{7}{100}$

30. -0.62 $-\dfrac{31}{50}$ **31.** 5.125 $5\dfrac{1}{8}$ **32.** 4.3 $4\dfrac{3}{10}$ **33.** -1.375 $-1\dfrac{3}{8}$ **34.** -10.001 $-10\dfrac{1}{1000}$

35. 12.625 $12\dfrac{5}{8}$ **36.** 10.3 $10\dfrac{3}{10}$ **37.** 0.225 $\dfrac{9}{40}$ **38.** 0.8375 $\dfrac{67}{80}$ **39.** -1.826 $-1\dfrac{413}{500}$

B **40.** $0.444\ldots$ $\dfrac{4}{9}$ **41.** $-0.555\ldots$ $-\dfrac{5}{9}$ **42.** $0.0\overline{3}$ $\dfrac{1}{30}$ **43.** $-1.0\overline{1}$ $-1\dfrac{1}{90}$ **44.** $5.\overline{9}$ 6

45. $0.1515\ldots$ $\dfrac{5}{33}$ **46.** $-1.\overline{20}$ $-1\dfrac{20}{99}$ **47.** $0.\overline{35}$ $\dfrac{35}{99}$ **48.** $0.\overline{72}$ $\dfrac{8}{11}$ **49.** $-1.\overline{12}$ $-1\dfrac{4}{33}$

50. $1.3\overline{62}$ $1\dfrac{359}{990}$ **51.** $2.13\overline{4}$ $2\dfrac{121}{900}$ **52.** $-8.0\overline{16}$ $-8\dfrac{8}{495}$ **53.** $0.\overline{123}$ $\dfrac{41}{333}$ **54.** $-5.\overline{862}$ $-5\dfrac{862}{999}$

Tell whether the number is rational or irrational.

55. $\dfrac{-13}{17}$ rational **56.** $1.515151\ldots$ rational **57.** -3.72 rational **58.** $2.121121112\ldots$ irrational

Arrange the numbers in order from least to greatest.

59. $3.0,\ 3.\overline{09},\ 3.00\overline{9},\ 3.1$ $3.0, 3.009, 3.09, 3.1$ **60.** $0.182,\ 0.182\overline{5},\ 0.18\overline{2},\ 0.1\overline{8}$ $0.182, 0.18\overline{2}, 0.1825, 0.1\overline{8}$

a. Express the first number as a fraction or mixed number.
b. Compare the first number with the second.

C **61.** $0.\overline{9};\ 11;\ =$ **62.** $0.4\overline{9};\ \dfrac{1}{2}$ $\dfrac{1}{2};\ =$ **63.** $-1.24\overline{9};\ -\dfrac{5}{4}$ $-1\dfrac{1}{4};\ =$ **64.** $2.3\overline{9};\ 2\dfrac{2}{5}$ $2\dfrac{2}{5};\ =$

120 *Chapter 3*

Self-Test B

Perform the indicated operation. Write the answer as a proper fraction in lowest terms or as a mixed number in simple form.

1. $\frac{1}{3} + \frac{1}{4}$ $\frac{7}{12}$

2. $\frac{2}{15} + \left(-\frac{5}{6}\right)$ $-\frac{7}{10}$

3. $\frac{1}{5} - \frac{1}{3}$ $-\frac{2}{15}$ **[3-6]**

4. $17\frac{1}{3} + 5\frac{1}{9}$ $22\frac{4}{9}$

5. $-6\frac{3}{8} - 3\frac{2}{3}$ $-10\frac{1}{24}$

6. $16\frac{5}{8} - \left(-\frac{3}{4}\right)$ $17\frac{3}{8}$ **[3-7]**

7. $\frac{3}{4} \times 5$ $3\frac{3}{4}$

8. $\frac{1}{8} \times \left(-\frac{1}{3}\right)$ $-\frac{1}{24}$

9. $-2\frac{4}{7} \times 3\frac{1}{6}$ $-8\frac{1}{7}$ **[3-8]**

10. $\frac{5}{8} \div \frac{10}{24}$ $1\frac{1}{2}$

11. $-\frac{11}{16} \div \frac{44}{8}$ $-\frac{1}{8}$

12. $4\frac{1}{3} \div \left(-\frac{26}{27}\right)$ $-4\frac{1}{2}$ **[3-9]**

Write as a decimal. Use a bar to show repeating digits.

13. $\frac{5}{8}$ 0.625

14. $\frac{2}{11}$ $0.1\overline{8}$

15. $-\frac{1}{80}$ -0.0125

16. $\frac{7}{6}$ $1.1\overline{6}$ **[3-10]**

Write as a proper fraction in lowest terms or as a mixed number in simple form.

17. 0.875 $\frac{7}{8}$

18. $1.\overline{6}$ $1\frac{2}{3}$

19. -2.213 $-2\frac{213}{1000}$

20. $0.2\overline{3}$ $\frac{7}{30}$

Self-Test answers and Extra Practice are at the back of the book.

▋▋▋ Computer Byte

The following program will find the least common multiple of two numbers.

```
10   PRINT "TO FIND LCM:"
20   PRINT "INPUT A, B";
30   INPUT A,B
40   FOR X = 1 TO B
50   LET A1 = A * X
60   LET Q = A1 / B
70   IF Q = INT (Q) THEN 90
80   NEXT X
90   PRINT "LCM(";A;",";B;") = ";A1
100  END
```

RUN the program to find the least common multiple of the following.

1. 12, 25 300
2. 72, 84 504
3. 34, 60 1020
4. 45, 80 720
5. 110, 240 2640
6. 235, 180 8460

Rational Numbers **121**

Suggested Assignments

Core
Day 1: 120/2–50 even
Day 2: 120/55–60
        121/Self-Test B
        121/Computer Byte

Enriched
  120/19–24; 35–39
  120/44–58 even
  121/Self-Test B
  121/Computer Byte

Supplementary Materials

Practice Masters, p. 14

Test 3B, pp. 17–18

Computer Activity 6

Quick Quiz B

(continued from page 120)

10. $\frac{3}{7} \div 2\frac{4}{9}$ $\frac{27}{154}$

11. $-1\frac{2}{3} \div 2\frac{2}{9}$ $-\frac{3}{4}$

12. $4\frac{3}{11} \div \left(-\frac{47}{11}\right)$ -1

Write as a decimal. Use a bar to show repeating digits.

13. $\frac{3}{8}$ 0.375

14. $\frac{7}{9}$ $0.\overline{7}$

15. $-\frac{1}{20}$ -0.05

16. $\frac{4}{11}$ $0.\overline{36}$

Write as a proper fraction in lowest terms or as a mixed number in simple form.

17. 0.4 $\frac{2}{5}$

18. $2.\overline{6}$ $2\frac{2}{3}$

19. -4.44 $-4\frac{11}{25}$

20. $0.\overline{23}$ $\frac{23}{99}$

BASIC, A Computer Language

Computers are very powerful tools, but issuing an order such as "Do problem 12 on page 46 of my math book" will produce no results at all. There are many things computers can do more quickly and efficiently than people, but we need to communicate with computers in a special way to get them to work for us.

To tell a computer what to do, we write a set of instructions, called a *program,* using a *programming language.* Since most microcomputers use some version of BASIC (with slight differences), that is the language that we will use in this book. A BASIC program is made up of a set of *numbered lines* that provide step-by-step instructions for the computer. We can use any numbers from 1 to 99999 for line numbers, but we often use numbers in intervals of 10 so that we can insert other lines later if we need to.

A *statement* that tells the computer what to do follows each line number in a program. In the BASIC language, we use the symbols shown below to tell the computer to perform arithmetic operations.

+	addition	−	subtraction
*	multiplication	/	division

The symbol ↑ (or some similar symbol) is used to indicate exponentiation. Thus $3 \uparrow 6$ means 3^6. When a statement contains more than one operation, the computer will perform all operations in parentheses first and will follow the order of operations that you learned in Chapters 1 and 2.

We use a **PRINT** statement to tell the computer to perform the operations listed in a statement and to print the result. We use an **END**

122 *Chapter 3*

statement to tell the computer that the program is over. The program shown below tells the computer to simplify the numerical expression and print the answer.

```
10   PRINT 5↑3 * (16 - 8 / 2)
20   END
```

After you have typed in this program (press RETURN or ENTER after each line), you type the *command* **RUN** to tell the computer to run (or *execute*) the program. The result, or *output,* is 1500.

A computer handles variables much as we do. We can ask it, for example, to give us the value of a variable expression when we give it a value of the variable in it. One way of doing this is to use an **INPUT** statement. This causes the computer to print a question mark and wait for the value to be typed in. Here is a simple program with a RUN shown at the right below.

```
10   INPUT X                    RUN
20   PRINT X↑2 + 2 * X + 4      ?10
30   END                        124
```

As you can see, we need some statement to tell the person using this program what is expected after the question mark. We do this by enclosing a descriptive expression in quotation marks in a PRINT statement, as in line 5 below. The semicolon at the end of line 5 will cause the question mark from line 10 to be printed right after the quoted expression. We have also inserted lines 12 and 15. After typing lines 5, 12, and 15, we can type the command **LIST** to see the revised program. A RUN is shown at the right below.

```
5    PRINT "WHAT IS YOUR VALUE OF X";
10   INPUT X                           RUN
12   PRINT "FOR X = ";X                WHAT IS YOUR VALUE OF X?10
15   PRINT "X↑2 + 2X + 4 = ";          FOR X = 10
20   PRINT X↑2 + 2 * X + 4             X↑2 + 2X + 4 = 124
30   END
```

1. Change lines 15 and 20 in the program above to evaluate another variable expression, with x as the variable, that involves the operation or operations listed.
   a. subtraction **b.** multiplication
   c. division **d.** multiplication and addition
   e. division and subtraction

2. Change the program above to evaluate a variable expression using m as the variable.

Rational Numbers **123**

Discuss the strengths and limitations of computers. Emphasize that, although a computer can do calculations very rapidly, it is not intelligent. For example, if a programmer makes a minor typing error, the computer may be unable to interpret or execute a command. Complex instructions are needed to teach a computer tasks that a human infant can do, such as recognizing an object or understanding a voice. Students can probably give many examples of tasks that computers do well, from monitoring earthquake activity to producing special effects for movies.

Additional Answers

Answers will vary. Examples are given.

1. **a.** 15 PRINT "X - 5 = ";
   20 PRINT X - 5
   b. 15 PRINT "3 * X = ";
   20 PRINT 3 * X
   c. 15 PRINT "X/7 = ";
   20 PRINT X/7
   d. 15 PRINT "2 * X + 1 = ";
   20 PRINT 2 * X + 1
   e. 15 PRINT "X/4 - 1 = ";
   20 PRINT X/4 - 1

2. 5 PRINT "WHAT IS
   YOUR VALUE OF M";
   10 INPUT M
   12 PRINT "FOR M = ";M
   15 PRINT "M↑2 - M = ";
   20 PRINT M↑2 - M
   30 END

Chapter Review

Complete.

1. 1, 2, 3, _?4_, _?6_, _?8_, _?12_, and _?24_ are factors of 24.   [3–1]

2. 40 is divisible by _?1_, _?2_, _?4_, _?5_, _?8_, _?10_, _?20_, and _?40_.

Write the letter of the correct answer.

3. What is the next prime number after 47? c   [3–2]

    a. 49   **b.** 51   **c.** 53   **d.** 57

4. What is the prime factorization of 72? c

    a. $1 \cdot 72$ **b.** $6^2 \cdot 2$ **c.** $2^3 \cdot 3^2$ **d.** $3^3 \cdot 2^2$

True or false?

5. $8 \times \frac{1}{9} = \frac{9}{8}$ False   **6.** $4 \times \left(-\frac{1}{5}\right) = -\frac{4}{5}$ True   **7.** $\frac{-7}{11} = -\frac{7}{11}$ True   [3–3]

8. $-\frac{24}{148}$ in lowest terms is $-\frac{12}{74}$. False   **9.** $7\frac{3}{8} = \frac{29}{8}$ False   [3–4]

10. The LCD of $\frac{2}{3}$ and $\frac{5}{11}$ is 33. True   **11.** The LCD of $\frac{7}{30}$ and $-\frac{3}{35}$ is 150. False   [3–5]

Match.

12. $\frac{5}{12} + \frac{11}{18}$ C   **13.** $\frac{1}{8} - \frac{3}{8}$ F   **A.** $-2\frac{11}{18}$ **B.** $-8\frac{17}{18}$ [3–6]

14. $-\frac{9}{16} - \left(-\frac{3}{4}\right)$ D   **15.** $\frac{2}{5} + \frac{3}{10}$ G   **C.** $\frac{37}{36}$ **D.** $\frac{3}{16}$

16. $-2\frac{1}{6} + \left(-\frac{4}{9}\right)$ A   **17.** $1\frac{3}{7} - \frac{5}{8}$ K   **E.** $\frac{27}{28}$ **F.** $-\frac{1}{4}$ [3–7]

18. $\frac{1}{4} \times \frac{1}{9}$ H   **19.** $\frac{4}{5} \times \frac{3}{8}$ L   **G.** $\frac{7}{10}$ **H.** $\frac{1}{36}$ [3–8]

20. $-7\frac{2}{3} \times 1\frac{1}{6}$ B   **21.** $\frac{2}{3} \times 5$ I   **I.** $3\frac{1}{3}$ **J.** $-1\frac{19}{30}$ [3–9]

22. $\frac{3}{14} \div \frac{2}{9}$ E   **23.** $1\frac{2}{5} \div \left(-\frac{6}{7}\right)$ J   **K.** $\frac{45}{56}$ **L.** $\frac{3}{10}$

Complete. Use a bar to show repeating digits.

24. $\frac{4}{3}$ written as a decimal is ___?___. $1.\overline{3}$ [3–10]

124 *Chapter 3*

Chapter Test

Supplementary Materials

Chapter 3 Test, pp. 19–20

State which of the numbers **2, 3, 4, 5, 9**, and **10** are factors of each number. Use the tests for divisibility.

1. 822   2, 3   **2.** 410   2, 5, 10   **3.** 315   3, 5, 9   2, 3, 4, 5, 10   **4.** 660   **[3–1]**

Give the prime factorization of each number.

5. 168 $2^3 \cdot 3 \cdot 7$ **6.** 96 $2^5 \cdot 3$ **7.** 53 $1 \cdot 53$ $3 \cdot 37$ **8.** 111   **[3–2]**

Complete.

9. $5 \times \underline{\ ?\ } = \frac{5}{7}$ $\frac{1}{7}$ **10.** $6 \times \frac{1}{6} = \underline{\ ?\ }$ 1   **11.** $\frac{-1}{4} = \frac{1}{-4} = \underline{\ ?\ }$ $-\frac{1}{4}$ **[3–3]**

Write as a fraction in lowest terms or as a mixed number in simple form.

12. $\frac{14}{40}$ $\frac{7}{20}$ **13.** $-\frac{26}{52}$ $-\frac{1}{2}$ **14.** $-\frac{136}{160}$ $-\frac{17}{20}$ **15.** $\frac{15}{4}$ $3\frac{3}{4}$ **16.** $\frac{-83}{9}$ $-9\frac{2}{9}$ **[3–4]**

Write each pair of fractions as equivalent fractions with the least common denominator.

17. $\frac{3}{7}, \frac{5}{14}$ $\frac{6}{14}, \frac{5}{14}$ **18.** $\frac{1}{9}, \frac{6}{11}$ $\frac{11}{99}, \frac{54}{99}$ **19.** $\frac{5}{8}, \frac{13}{36}$ $\frac{45}{72}, \frac{26}{72}$ $\frac{14}{24}, \frac{5}{24}$ **20.** $\frac{7}{12}, \frac{5}{24}$ **[3–5]**

Perform the indicated operations. Write the answer as a proper fraction in lowest terms or as a mixed number in simple form.

21. $\frac{3}{8} + \frac{1}{7}$ $\frac{29}{56}$ **22.** $-\frac{3}{10} + \left(-\frac{1}{4}\right)$ $-\frac{11}{20}$ **23.** $\frac{1}{2} - \frac{5}{12}$ $\frac{1}{12}$ **[3–6]**

24. $1\frac{3}{4} + \left(-2\frac{1}{2}\right)$ $-\frac{3}{4}$ **25.** $1\frac{1}{3} - \left(-2\frac{3}{4}\right)$ $4\frac{1}{12}$ **26.** $-2\frac{7}{10} - \left(4\frac{9}{11}\right)$ $-7\frac{57}{110}$ **[3–7]**

27. $\frac{4}{7} \times \left(-\frac{4}{11}\right)$ $-\frac{16}{77}$ **28.** $8\frac{1}{8} \times 2\frac{3}{5}$ $21\frac{1}{8}$ **29.** $-\frac{1}{4} \times \left(-\frac{1}{6}\right)$ $\frac{1}{24}$ **[3–8]**

30. $\frac{2}{3} \div \frac{7}{9}$ $\frac{6}{7}$ **31.** $-\frac{6}{19} \div \frac{9}{38}$ $-1\frac{1}{3}$ **32.** $-1\frac{1}{6} \div \left(-4\frac{2}{3}\right)$ $\frac{1}{4}$ **[3–9]**

Write as a decimal. Use a bar to show repeating digits.

33. $\frac{6}{25}$ 0.24   **34.** $\frac{5}{33}$ $0.\overline{15}$ **35.** $\frac{9}{16}$ 0.5625   **36.** $\frac{4}{9}$ $0.\overline{4}$ **[3–10]**

Write as a fraction in lowest terms or as a mixed number in simple form.

37. 0.04 $\frac{1}{25}$ **38.** -0.375 $-\frac{3}{8}$ **39.** 6.125 $6\frac{1}{8}$ **40.** $0.\overline{7}$ $\frac{7}{9}$

Rational Numbers   **125**

Review for Retention

Replace __?__ with =, >, or < to make a true statement.

1. 8 __?__ 11 <
2. 4 __?__ −6 >
3. −10 __?__ 0 <
4. −1 __?__ −4 >

Express as an integer.

5. |−9| 9
6. |3| 3
7. |−19| 19
8. |11| 11

Write the numbers in order from least to greatest.

9. −5.4, −45, 5.04, −445, −0.5 **−445, −45, −5.04, −0.5, 5.04**
10. 2.01, −2.1, −222, −12, 0.21 **−222, −12, −2.1, 0.21, 2.01**

Find the sum.

11. −7.3 + 25.7 **18.4**
12. −0.09 + −5.2 **−5.29**
13. 43.1 + 41.6 **84.7**
14. 4.32 + −4.32 **0**
15. −23.3 + 0 **−23.3**
16. 0.98 + −15.2 + −0.49 **−14.71**

Find the difference.

17. 62.4 − 3.8 **58.6**
18. −3.4 − 18.7 **−22.1**
19. 0 − 6.31 **−6.31**
20. −41.3 − (−5.9) **−35.4**
21. 32 − (−2.67) **34.67**
22. −4.6 − (−4.6) **0**

Cumulative Review (Chapters 1–3)

Exercises

Give the solution of the equation for the given replacement set.

1. $x - 12 = 46$; {58, 59, 60} 58
2. $8d = 2$; $\left\{\frac{1}{3}, \frac{1}{4}, \frac{1}{5}\right\}$ $\frac{1}{4}$
3. $3(6 + y) = 39$; {7, 14, 21} 7
4. $(5 - a) \div (a + 7) = \frac{1}{5}$; {1, 2, 3} 3
5. $16r - 11 = 69$; {0, 5, 10} 5
6. $m^2(7 + m) = 176$; {3, 4, 5} 4

Evaluate the expression if $a = 3$, $b = 2$, and $c = 5$.

7. ab^2 12
8. $a^2 + b^2$ 13
9. a^2c^2 225
10. bc^2 50
11. $2b^2$ 8
12. a^2b^3 72
13. $(a + b)^2$ 25
14. $c(a^2 + b)$ 55
15. bc^3 250
16. $\frac{10b^2}{c^2}$ $1\frac{3}{5}$

Use the symbol > to order the numbers from greatest to least.

17. 75.70, 75.40, 75.06
   75.70 > 75.40 > 75.06
18. 19.05, 19.18, 19.50
   19.50 > 19.18 > 19.05
19. 0.03, 0.30, 0.33
   0.33 > 0.30 > 0.03
20. 105.07, 10.507, 1050.7
   1050.7 > 105.07 > 10.507

List the integers that can replace x to make the statement true.

21. $|x| = 7$ 7, −7
22. $|x| = 18$ 18, −18
23. $|x| \geq 5$ . . . −7, −6, −5, 5, 6, 7, . . .
24. $|x| < 7.3$ −7, −6, −5, . . . 5, 6, 7
25. $4 < |x| < 6$ 5, −5
26. $6 > |x| > 0$ −5, −4, −3, −2, −1, 1, 2, 3, 4, 5
27. $31 < |x| < 40$ −39, −38, −37, . . . −32, 32, 33, 34, . . . 39
28. $17 \leq |x| \leq 25$ −25, −24, −23, . . . −17, 17, 18, 19, . . . 25

What value of the variable makes the statement true?

29. $-7 + y = 11$ 18
30. $-3n = 51$ −17
31. $-6(-b) = 72$ 12
32. $17 - x = -5$ 22
33. $8(-n) = 32$ −4
34. $-a \div 15 = 3$ −45

Evaluate the expression when $x = 5$, $y = -7$, and $z = -5$.

35. $\frac{y + 3}{x} - \frac{4}{5}$ $-1\frac{3}{7}$
36. $\frac{xy}{z}$ 7
37. $\frac{x + y}{z}$ $\frac{2}{5}$
38. $\frac{yz}{x}$ 7
39. $\frac{x - z}{y}$
40. $\frac{x^2 + y^2}{z^2}$ $2\frac{24}{25}$
41. $\frac{x}{7} + \frac{y}{7}$ $-\frac{2}{7}$
42. $\frac{2x}{15} + \frac{z}{3}$ −1
43. $\frac{-y + z}{x}$ $\frac{2}{5}$
44. $\frac{-z - x}{-y}$ 0

Solve. Write the answer as a proper fraction in lowest terms or as a mixed number in simple form.

45. $-5 \times \left(\frac{3}{8} \div \frac{1}{3}\right)$ $-5\frac{5}{8}$
46. $2\frac{1}{2} \div \left(\frac{5}{8} \times 1\frac{3}{4}\right)$ $2\frac{2}{7}$
47. $7\frac{3}{8} + \left[-4\frac{1}{2} \div \left(-5\frac{2}{3}\right)\right]$ $8\frac{23}{136}$

126 *Chapter 3*

Problems

> **Problem Solving Reminders**
>
> Here are some reminders that may help you solve some of the problems on this page.
> - You may need to supply additional information.
> - Some steps in your plan may not involve operations.
> - Reread the question to be sure you have answered with the information requested.

Solve.

1. The Maxwell children have hired a caterer to provide food for an anniversary party for their parents. The caterer has quoted a price of $15.75 per person and is asking for an advance payment of $\frac{1}{4}$ of the total bill. If the estimated number of guests is 50, how much is the advance payment? $196.88

2. The Clean-as-a-Whistle Company provides a matching service for people looking for home cleaners and people wishing to clean homes. The fees include $6.50 per hour for the cleaner, plus $1.50 per hour for the agency. If you hire a cleaner from the company for 5 h, how much will you pay? $40

3. As a general rule for brick work, masons estimate 6.5 bricks per square foot. Based on this estimate, will 2500 bricks be enough for a patio that is 396 ft²? No

4. The controller of a hospital found that laundry fees for a four-month period totaled $8755. Based on this total, what would be the estimated fee for an entire year? $26,265

5. Store owners at the Wagon Wheel Mall pay a monthly rental fee plus a maintenance fee. The maintenance fee is determined by the number of square feet occupied by the shop. The entire mall is 200,000 ft² and the annual fee for the entire mall is $63,000. What is the annual share of the maintenance fee for a store that occupies 2500 ft²? $787.50

6. An investor bought 12 acres of land for $70,000. She later subdivided the land into 22 lots that she sold for $4500 apiece. What was her profit on the sale? $29,000

7. Douglas bought 75 shares of Health Care Company (HCC) stock and 150 shares of Bowwow Brands (BWB) stock. Last year HCC paid a dividend of $1.85 per share and BWB paid a dividend of $2.04 per share. What was the total of the dividends that Douglas received? $444.75

Rational Numbers **127**

Evaluate the expression when $a = -4$ and $b = -2.6$.

23. $-a + b$ **1.4**

24. $-a - b$ **6.6**

25. $-|a|$ **−4**

Find the product.

26. $13(-7.38)$ **−95.94**

27. $-40(0.57)$ **−22.8**

28. $-0.27(-19.8)$ **5.346**

29. $-1(-1.59)$ **1.59**

30. $4.5(-6.8)(-5)$ **153**

31. $-5.22(-8)(-2.2)$ **−91.872**

Find the quotient.

32. $85.2 \div (-4)$ **−21.3**

33. $-63 \div (-2.8)$ **22.5**

34. $-29.3 \div 10$ **−2.93**

35. $-0.012 \div (-1)$ **0.012**

36. $0 \div (-25)$ **0**

37. $-0.09 \div (-0.3)$ **0.3**

Write the expression without exponents.

38. 3^4 **81**

39. 11^0 **1**

40. $2^3 \times 2^2$ **32**

41. 4^3 **64**

42. 5^{-1} $\frac{1}{5}$

43. $(-2)^{-4}$ $\frac{1}{16}$

44. $9^{-8} \times 9^6$ $\frac{1}{81}$

45. $(-6) \times (-6)^{-2}$ $-\frac{1}{6}$

4

Solving Equations

NASA (National Aeronautics and Space Administration) is the government agency responsible for space exploration and experiments. The photograph shows a rocket about to be fired into space. It is carrying the space shuttle Columbia.

Aboard the shuttle is the Spacelab research station, where astronauts and other scientists will conduct in-flight scientific experiments. Much of the research will take months to analyze, but we know from earlier flights that the results will be of enormous importance in many fields, such as astronomy and medicine. For example, many of the experiments concern the effect of weightlessness on the human body.

Career Note

Space scientists require a strong background in mathematics, physics, and related sciences. The work is demanding but exciting. The men and women who perform experiments in the Spacelab are selected because of their specialized knowledge in various fields, for example, in biology, chemistry, or medicine.

Lesson Commentary
Chapter 4   Solving Equations

Overview

In Chapter 1 students learned to solve equations using inverse operations; in this chapter students learn to solve equations using transformations. Students will find the latter method much more efficient.

The second part of the chapter emphasizes using equations to solve problems. Lessons 4-6 and 4-7 require only that students select or write an equation for a problem. This allows students to focus on the method of solving the problem, rather than on finding an answer. In Lesson 4-8, students will write equations for problems and solve them. The gradual development of this sequence of lessons is designed to give students a firm foundation for beginning algebra.

The purpose of the study of algebra is to be able to solve problems. The ability to organize a problem and to reduce it to a concise mathematical statement is the basis of applied mathematics. In this chapter, students begin to use their algebra skills to translate problems into open sentences and to solve them. This emphasizes the connection between abstract mathematics and the concrete "real" world.

USING TRANSFORMATIONS

4-1 Equations: Addition and Subtraction

Objective *for pages 130–133*

■ To solve equations involving addition and subtraction.

Teaching Suggestions

Students have an intuitive understanding of the following two principles of equality:

(1) If equals are added to equals, the sums are equal.
(2) If equals are subtracted from equals, the differences are equal.

These two principles are the basis of transformation of an equation by addition or subtraction. You may wish to use a diagram of a set of balance scales to illustrate these two principles. For example, the diagram that follows can be used to illustrate the statement:

If $x - 7 = 12$, then $x - 7 + 7 = 12 + 7$.

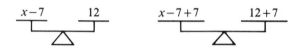

Students should understand that applying transformations to an equation results in a sequence of equations that are equivalent to the first, that is, equations that have the same solution. The ultimate goal in using transformations to solve an equation is to arrive at the "world's easiest equation," one of the form $x = c$ where c is a constant.

If your students are ready for a small note of rigor, start them off on the right foot by insisting that they state the solution of an equation as a number, rather than as another equation. For example, the solution of $x - 2 = 8$ is the number 10, not the equation $x = 10$.

To avoid negative numbers in an equation like $34 - x = 27$ in Example 5, tell students to begin by adding x to each side first.

Some students prefer that the variable always be on the left side of an equation. You can tell students that another valid transformation is exchanging the two sides of an equation. The equation

$$17 = 12 + x$$

is equivalent to the equation

$$12 + x = 17.$$

Related Activities

To help students understand why a replacement set is defined for a variable in an equation, have students consider which replacements for a variable make sense in each situation. Ask them to state which of the numbers listed are sensible replacements for the variable. Then define an appropriate replacement set.

1. Let x represent the number of passengers on a 50-passenger bus. Can x be 20? $6\frac{1}{2}$? π? 1028? 0?

   yes, no, no, no, yes; {whole numbers less than or equal to 50}

2. Let y represent the house numbers of houses on the same side of Walnut Street as number 23. Can y be 48? 0? 21? 96? **no, no, yes, no; {odd counting numbers}**

3. Let d represent the number of dimes in a bank. Can d be 61? 0? $57\frac{1}{2}$? π? **yes, yes, no, no; {whole numbers}**

4. Let a represent the area of a circle in square centimeters. Can a be 32? $5\frac{1}{2}$? π? 115? 0? **yes, yes, yes, yes, no; {all numbers greater than 0}**

Resource Book: Page 45 (Use After Page 133)

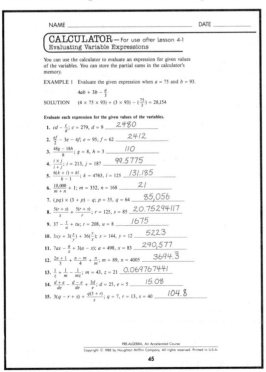

Resource Book: Page 46 (Use After Page 133)

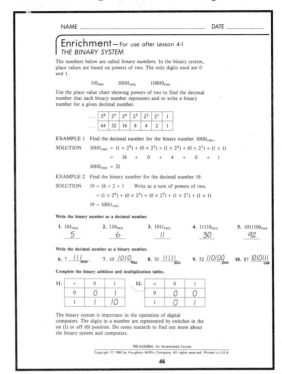

4-2 Equations: Multiplication and Division

Objective for pages 134–135

■ To solve equations involving multiplication and division.

Teaching Suggestions

The parallels between this lesson and the preceding one will be fairly obvious to students. Multiplication and division have the same inverse relationship that addition and subtraction do. Also, by choosing carefully we apply the multiplication and division properties of equality to produce an equation of the form $x = c$ ("the world's easiest equation") to solve, as we did before by applying the addition and subtraction properties.

Before solving equations, it would probably be helpful to remind students that

$$\frac{ab}{a} = b \quad \text{and} \quad \frac{b}{a} \times a = b \quad (a \neq 0).$$

Practice using these identities to simplify expressions.

129b

When students first learn to solve equations by using transformations, they sometimes fail to perform the *same* operation on both sides. For example, if $4x = 9$, some students may incorrectly conclude that $x = 5$.

Discuss with students why the rule for transformation by multiplication specifies that both sides be multiplied by the same *nonzero* number. If both sides of an equation of the form $ax = b$ are multiplied by zero, the result is $ax \times 0 = b \times 0$, or the identity $0 = 0$. Ask students why it is important to use only a *nonzero* number in the transformation by division. They should be able to reply that division by zero is impossible.

Related Activities

To help students develop their abilities to think in abstract terms, have them solve these equations.

1. Solve $A = bh$ for h. $h = \dfrac{A}{b}$

2. Solve $P = 4s$ for s. $s = \dfrac{P}{4}$

3. Solve $C = 2\pi r$ for r. $r = \dfrac{C}{2\pi}$

4-3 Equations: Decimals and Fractions

Objective *for pages 136–138*

■ To solve equations involving fractions and decimals.

Teaching Suggestions

Before you teach the rule in the box at the bottom of page 136, you may want to show students an alternate method of solving some simple equations. To solve an equation like $5x = 55$, we can either divide both sides by 5 or multiply both sides by $\frac{1}{5}$, the reciprocal of 5. To solve an equation like $\frac{1}{3}y = 6$ or $\frac{z}{3} = 9$, we multiply both sides by 3, the reciprocal of $\frac{1}{3}$.

Remind students that the product of a number and its reciprocal is 1. The objective in applying transformations to an equation is to obtain an equivalent equation of the form $x = c$ where c is a constant. Write the equation $\frac{2}{3}x = 6$ on the board. Then ask students by what number they must multiply both sides to obtain an equation of the form $x = c$. Remind them that the understood coefficient of x in the equation $x = c$ is 1.

$$\frac{2}{3}x = 6$$
$$\frac{3}{2}\left(\frac{2}{3}x\right) = \frac{3}{2} \times 6$$
$$\left(\frac{3}{2} \times \frac{2}{3}\right)x = 9$$
$$(1)x = 9$$
$$x = 9$$

Explain that this procedure is the one that is summarized in the box on page 136.

Related Activities

To provide additional practice, have students solve the equations and list the variables in order from the one with the least value to the one with the greatest value. Doing so will spell the name of the first large-scale electronic computer. ENIAC

$\frac{7}{8}N = 1\frac{2}{5}$ $1\frac{3}{5}$

$\frac{12}{5}A = 98$ $40\frac{5}{6}$

$\frac{C}{6.3} = 13$ 81.9

$2.8I = 9.8$ 3.5

$24E = 15$ $\frac{5}{8}$

4-4 Combined Operations

Objective *for pages 139–142*

■ To solve equations using more than one transformation.

Teaching Suggestions

The procedure outlined in the box on page 139 can be used to solve any equation that can be written in the form $ax + b = c$. The steps listed reverse the order of operations that students learned in Lesson 1-2. You can explain that to solve an equation, they can think of "undoing" the operations in reverse order.

In Example 3 on page 140, some students may want to begin by subtracting 40 from both sides of the equation; the result is the equation $-\frac{5}{3}n = -25$. Then they could multiply both sides of the equation by $-\frac{3}{5}$; the result is $n = 15$. You may want to show more than one way to solve some other equations. Then discuss the order of the transformations and try to determine which way, if any, was the faster way.

Related Activities

To expand on the idea that there is often more than one way to solve an equation, show students how Example 2 can be solved using the following steps.

1. First, multiply both sides by 2. Notice that the resulting equation has no fractions. Remind students to use the distributive property on the left side.

$$\frac{3}{2}n + 7 = -8$$

$$2\left(\frac{3}{2}n + 7\right) = 2 \times -8$$

$$3n + 14 = -16$$

2. Next, subtract 14 from both sides.

$$3n + 14 - 14 = -16 - 14$$
$$3n = -30$$

3. Finally, divide both sides by 3.

$$\frac{3n}{3} = \frac{-30}{3}$$

$$n = -10$$

The solution is -10.

Have students solve each equation below twice: (1) using the sequence of steps on page 139, and (2) following the steps listed. The solutions should be the same for both methods.

1. $3r - 18 = 24$
Divide both sides by 3; then add 6 to both sides. **14**

2. $\frac{3}{8}a - \frac{3}{4} = \frac{7}{8}$
Multiply both sides by 8; add 6 to both sides; divide both sides by 3. $4\frac{1}{3}$

To show that operations cannot be done in just any order, ask what operations (ordinary actions), in what order, are needed to solve each of the following problems.

1. A person wearing shoes and socks wants to go barefoot.

2. A package of frozen fish is to be broiled for dinner.

Resource Book: Pages 47–48 (Use After Page 142)

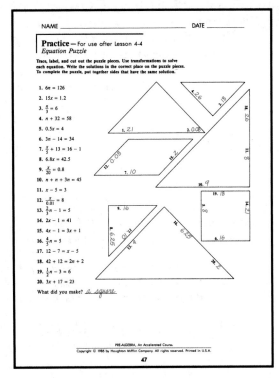

129d

WORD PROBLEMS

4-5 Writing Expressions for Word Phrases

Objective *for pages 143–146*

■ To translate word phrases describing numerical operations into variable expressions.

Teaching Suggestions

A major reason for studying mathematics is to be able to use mathematical models to represent situations in the real world. The real world does not usually present a problem tidily wrapped up as an equation. Thus, it is essential that we be able to translate from ordinary language into mathematical terms, as taught in this lesson. Once this is done, we can use all our knowledge of mathematics to solve the problem.

You may wish to mention that the equation $a + a = a \times a$ shown in the Challenge can also be written $2a = a^2$. Explain to your students that they will learn standard techniques for solving such equations when they study Algebra 1.

Related Activities

To broaden understanding of the relationship between word phrases and the corresponding mathematical expression, show how seemingly very different situations can be described by the same variable expression. Ask students to write a variable expression for each word phrase.

1. Mary's age, if she is 25 years older than Harry, who is x years old.
2. The amount of money, if there were x cents before and a quarter was deposited.
3. The length of a board that is 25 cm longer than a board x cm long.
4. Your speed, if you were going x miles per hour over the speed limit in a 25-miles-per-hour zone.
5. Gary's weight, if he weighed x pounds last year and has since gained 25 pounds.

Each of these situations can be represented by the expression $x + 25$.

4-6 Word Sentences and Equations

Objective *for pages 147–148*

■ To translate word sentences involving numerical operations into equations.

Teaching Suggestions

A difficulty in teaching students to solve word problems is that students seem to expect to see the solution virtually instantly, with little real grappling with the problem. In most cases they cannot, so they need to be cautioned frequently to slow down and to move ahead a step at a time.

As an example of writing an open sentence a step at a time, consider writing an equation for the sentence: "The product of six and a number, increased by two, is equal to fifteen." Show how each part of the sentence is represented by an algebraic term or expression.

product of six and a number: $6x$
increased by two: $+ 2$
is equal to fifteen: $= 15$

$$6x + 2 = 15$$

Students will see that this lesson simply carries the previous lesson one step further. The comments for Lesson 1-6 about algebra as a language, in which sentences must have verbs, apply here too.

Related Activities

To provide a challenge, ask students to write an equation for the famous algebra problem concerning the life of the ancient Greek mathematician Diophantus:

Diophantus's youth was $\frac{1}{6}$ of his life. After $\frac{1}{12}$ more of his life he grew a beard. After $\frac{1}{7}$ more he married. Five years later he had a son. The son lived half as long as Diophantus, who died four years after his son.

Students may need hints, one being that all the parts must add up to Diophantus's age when he died.

$$x = \frac{x}{6} + \frac{x}{12} + \frac{x}{7} + 5 + \frac{x}{2} + 4$$

4-7 Writing Equations for Word Problems

Objective *for pages 149–151*

■ To relate word problems and equations.

Teaching Suggestions

Emphasize that the first step in writing an equation is to identify the unknown and to select a variable to represent it. For example, for Problem 1 a student could begin by saying,

"Let $m =$ the number of miles per day."

The next step is to write two equal expressions, using the variable in at least one of the two expressions.

Related Activities

Ask students to determine whether the equation given represents the word problem. If it doesn't, have them write the correct equation.

1. The square of a number (n) is 4 less than twice the number.
$n^2 = 4 - 2n$ No; $n^2 = 2n - 4$

2. Three times the sum of 14 and the product of a number (x) and a number (y) is 62.
$3(14 + xy) = 62$ Yes

3. Thirteen less than the product of 4 and n is the same as the sum of 130 and twice the number (n).
$4n - 13 = 2(130 + n)$ No; $4n - 13 = 130 + 2n$

4. The sum of five times a number (x) and 3 times the square of the number is 58 more than two times the number.
$5x + 3x^2 = 58(2x)$ No; $5x + 3x^2 = 2x + 58$

As a challenge, have students write equations for some difficult problems.

5. The sum of 3 times a number (n) and the square of the number is 30 more than twice the number.
$3n + n^2 = 30 + 2n$

6. The product of 4 and the square of a number (n) is 3 less than twice the number. $4n^2 = 2n - 3$

7. Seventy-two less than 36 times a number (n) is 4 more than the number divided by 6.
$36n - 72 = 4 + \frac{n}{6}$

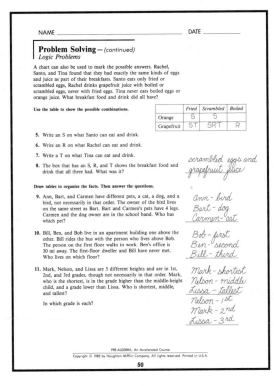

8. The product of two consecutive whole numbers is 38 less than 40 times the smaller number.

$n(n + 1) = 40n - 38$

4-8 Solving Word Problems

Objective *for pages 152–155*

■ To use equations to solve word problems.

Teaching Suggestions

The method for solving word problems given on page 152 is similar to the method outlined on page 29 of Lesson 1-8; the difference between the two is that the method of page 152 focuses on using an equation, whereas the one on page 29 is more general.

In Step 1, students sometimes discount the importance of reading a problem more than once. You may want to encourage students to read each problem at least twice before proceeding to Step 2. Suggest that on the second reading, they draw a sketch if appropriate. Doing so will help them draw the essential information from the problem, work through some of the steps with simple numbers, and provide an extra check on the validity of the solution.

Emphasize the importance, in Step 5, of checking the results with the words of the original problem. If the solution is checked only in the equation, there is still the possibility that the equation itself is incorrect.

Apply the plan to a few examples. If a student is experiencing difficulties, try to determine whether the fault lies in the lack of reading ability, weakness of interpretation, computational deficiencies, or simply a lack of confidence.

Related Activities

To stimulate interest and provide additional practice, have students use newspapers, magazines, or a book to find a fact that involves a number. Tell them to write an equation that has the number as a solution; then, use the equation to write a word problem. For example,

Fact: 1620 homes were sold in Milville last year.

Equation: $3(1620) = 4860$ $3h = 4860$

Problem: Three times the number of homes sold in Milville last year is 4860. How many homes were sold in Milville last year?

129g

Resource Book: Pages 51–52 (Use After Page 155)

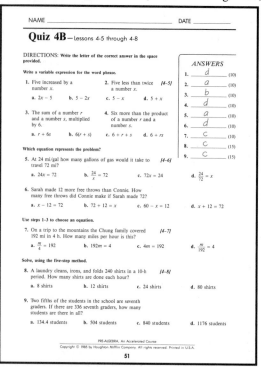

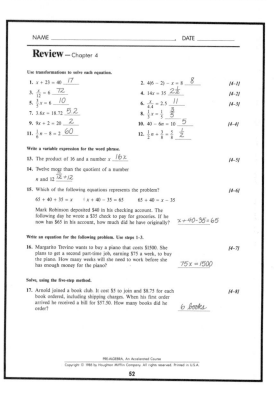

Resource Book: Pages 53–56 (Use After Page 155)

Test — Chapter 4

DIRECTIONS: Write the answers in the spaces provided.

Use transformations to solve each equation. *[4-1]*

1. $16 - x = 7$
2. $5(7 - 2) + x = 32$
3. $-7 + y = 64$
4. $6n = 2$
5. $\frac{n}{6} = 15$
6. $9n = 12$ *[4-2]*
7. $\frac{3}{8} x = 6$
8. $0.36x = 18$
9. $\frac{n}{1.2} = 4.3$ *[4-3]*
10. $2x + 8 = 28$
11. $\frac{2}{3} n + 10 = 20$ *[4-4]*
12. $12 - \frac{1}{2} n = 7$
13. $\frac{4}{3} y + 3 = 11$

Write a variable expression for the word phrase.

14. The product of 14 and a number n. *[4-5]*

15. Sixteen added to the quotient of a number p and six.

16. Which of the following equations represents the problem? *[4-6]*

$2n + 2 = 16$ $2n = 16 + 2$ $16 - 2 = n + 2$

Susan is 2 years more than twice her brother's age. If she is 16, how old is her brother?

Write an equation for the problem. Use steps 1-3.

17. After Ari withdrew $200 from his bank account, he had $1600 left. How much money was in the account before the withdrawal? *[4-7]*

Solve, using the five-step method.

18. Max walked 2.4 mi to the shopping center in 1.2 h. If he walks at the same speed, how far can he walk in 2 h? *[4-8]*

19. In the recent municipal election, $\frac{17}{20}$ of a town's eligible voters cast ballots. If there are 2500 eligible voters, how many of them actually voted?

ANSWERS	
1.	9 (5)
2.	7 (5)
3.	71 (5)
4.	$\frac{1}{3}$ (5)
5.	90 (5)
6.	$1\frac{1}{3}$ (5)
7.	16 (5)
8.	50 (5)
9.	5.16 (5)
10.	10 (5)
11.	25 (5)
12.	10 (5)
13.	10 (5)
14.	$14n$ (5)
15.	$16 + \frac{p}{6}$ (5)
16.	$2n + 2 = 16$ (5)
17.	$1600 = x - 200$ (5)
18.	$4 mi$ (5)
19.	2125 voters (10)

Make-up Test — Chapter 4

DIRECTIONS: Write the answers in the spaces provided.

Use transformations to solve each equation. *[4-1]*

1. $18 - x = 15$
2. $4(6 + 2) + x = 36$
3. $-5 + y = -4$
4. $4n = 2$
5. $\frac{n}{8} = 12$
6. $12n = 20$ *[4-2]*
7. $\frac{3}{5} x = 12$
8. $0.24x = 12$
9. $\frac{x}{1.4} = 6.2$ *[4-3]*
10. $3x + 6 = 36$
11. $\frac{5}{8} n + 6 = 31$
12. $10 - \frac{1}{3} n = 5$ *[4-4]*

Write a variable expression for each word phrase.

13. A number a minus 6 *[4-5]*

14. Forty-three times a number b

15. A number c increased by 8

16. Which of the following equations represents the problem? *[4-6]*

$3x - 8.5 = 46$ $3x = 46 + 8.5$ $3x + 8.5 = 46$

George bought three shirts and a tie. If the tie cost $8.50 and the total bill was $46, how much did one shirt cost?

Write an equation for the problem. Use steps 1-3.

17. When a number is subtracted from one hundred forty-three the difference is ninety-six. Find the number. *[4-7]*

Solve, using the five-step method.

18. Mary White's car gets 22 mi/gal. She plans to drive 550 mi on her vacation. If gas cost $1.15 per gallon, how much would she expect to pay for gas? *[4-8]*

19. Edwardo Hernandez has $10.16 in nickels and pennies. If he has 41 pennies, how many nickels does he have?

ANSWERS	
1.	3 (5)
2.	4 (5)
3.	1 (5)
4.	$\frac{1}{2}$ (5)
5.	96 (5)
6.	$1\frac{2}{3}$ (5)
7.	20 (5)
8.	50 (5)
9.	8.68 (5)
10.	10 (5)
11.	40 (5)
12.	15 (5)
13.	$a - 6$ (5)
14.	$43b$ (5)
15.	$c + 8$ (5)
16.	$3x + 8.5 = 46$ (5)
17.	$143 - x = 96$ (5)
18.	$28.75 (5)
19.	195 nickels (10)

CUMULATIVE REVIEW — Chapters 1–4
Exercises

Replace the variable with the given value and tell whether the resulting statement is true or false.

1. $r - 7 = 12$; 18 F
2. $2d + 3 = 37$; 17 T
3. $3s - 1 = 8$; $2\frac{1}{2}$ F
4. $t + 9 = 4 - t$; -3 F
5. $5a + 7 = 2a - 5$; -4 T
6. $\frac{n}{9} - 4 = 5$; 1 F

Use the symbol < to order the numbers from least to greatest.

7. 5, 3.4, -1.0, -2.8, 1.0 $-2.8 < -1.0 < 1.0 < 3.4 < 5$
8. 3.2, -2.3, 0.32, -1.02 $-2.3 < -1.02 < 0.32 < 3.2$
9. 5, 9, -3, 2, -8, -7 $-8 < -7 < -3 < 2 < 5 < 9$
10. -5.1, 3.8, 2.1, -5.19, -2 $-5.19 < -5.1 < -2 < 2.1 < 3.8$

Write the fractions as equal fractions having the least common denominator (LCD).

11. $\frac{1}{3}$, $\frac{2}{9}$ $\frac{3}{9}$, $\frac{2}{9}$
12. $\frac{5}{6}$, $\frac{1}{2}$ $\frac{5}{6}$, $\frac{3}{6}$
13. $\frac{2}{3}$, $\frac{3}{5}$ $\frac{10}{15}$, $\frac{9}{15}$
14. $\frac{1}{4}$, $-\frac{2}{7}$ $\frac{7}{28}$, $-\frac{8}{28}$
15. $-\frac{3}{10}$, $\frac{4}{15}$ $-\frac{9}{30}$, $\frac{8}{30}$
16. $-\frac{3}{4}$, $-\frac{1}{10}$ $-\frac{15}{20}$, $-\frac{2}{20}$

Perform the indicated operation.

17. $17.43 + (-38.29)$ -20.86
18. $-24.2 + 0.16$ -51.25
19. $-3\frac{5}{6} + 1\frac{1}{3}$ $-2\frac{3}{10}$
20. $-12.864 - 0.907$ -13.771

Express as a fraction or mixed number in lowest terms.

21. 0.6 $\frac{3}{5}$
22. 2.25 $2\frac{1}{4}$
23. 18.45 $18\frac{9}{20}$
24. 9.64 $9\frac{16}{25}$
25. 0.08 $\frac{2}{25}$
26. 6.002 $6\frac{1}{500}$
27. 0.475 $\frac{19}{40}$
28. 98.05 $98\frac{1}{20}$

Round to the place specified.

29. tenths: 67.345   67.3
30. hundreds: 6249.036   6200
31. thousandths: 3.0749   3.075
32. hundredths: 29.4073   29.41

Solve.

33. $v - 29 = 108$ 137
34. $7n + 11 = 88$ 11
35. $9p - 6 = -42$ -4
36. $20d \div 2 = 80$ 8
37. $16 - 4x = 24$ -2
38. $19r + 8 = 27$ 1
39. $5 + 3a + 6 = 102$ $30\frac{1}{3}$
40. $3 - 7f = -39$ 6
41. $-6m + 3 = 9$ -1

CUMULATIVE REVIEW — Chapters 1–4 (continued)
Problems

Problem Solving Reminders

Here are some problem solving reminders that may help you solve some of the problems on this page.
- Determine which facts are necessary to solve the problem.
- Check your answer by using rounding to find an estimated answer.
- Supply additional information if necessary.

Solve.

1. Bread is on sale for 2 loaves for $1.19. How much will one dozen loaves cost? $7.14

2. Jason earned twice as much as Larry did shoveling snow. Together they earned $85.50. How much did Jason earn? $57

3. An election survey showed that 2.3 million people voted in the state election. Approximately $\frac{1}{4}$ of them were under 25 years old. About how many voters were under 25?   575,000

4. ABC Sportswear is having a sale where $\frac{1}{3}$ of the original price is deducted from the cost. What is the sale price of a suit that originally sold for $188.70? $125.80

5. The Ross family planned to spend $2000 on their vacation. They spent the following amounts:

   Food: $436.75   Admission Fees: $185.50
   Room: $425.00   Souvenirs: $43.60
   Transportation: $785.85

   Did they stay within their budget?   yes

6. Gwen is 3 years older than Sara and Janet is twice as old as Sara. If the sum of their ages is 51, how old is Janet?   24 y

7. Martin Downs earns $498.60 per week. Pat O'Connor earns $75 more per week than Martin. If Bob Rebern earns $\frac{6}{7}$ as much as Pat does, how much does Bob earn? $501.90

8. The school soccer team won $\frac{3}{4}$ of its games. The school football team won $\frac{1}{5}$ of its games. The two teams played the same number of games and together won a total of 55 games. How many games did the football team win?   25 games

9. William's recipe for carrot pudding calls for $3\frac{1}{4}$ cups of flour and $2\frac{1}{2}$ cups of sugar. He plans to make $\frac{8}{15}$ of the amount of the recipe. How much sugar should he use? $1\frac{2}{3}$ c

4-1 Equations: Addition and Subtraction

You have learned that an *equation* is a sentence that states that two expressions name the same number. A *replacement set*, consisting of values which may be substituted for the variable, is always stated or understood. For example, the equation

$$2x + 9 = 15$$

may have the replacement set $\{1, 3, 5\}$.

When a number from the replacement set makes an equation a true statement, it is called a *solution* of the equation. To determine whether a value in the replacement set $\{1, 3, 5\}$ is a solution of $2x + 9 = 15$, substitute it into the equation.

$2x + 9 = 15$	$2x + 9 = 15$	$2x + 9 = 15$
$2(1) + 9 = 15$	$2(3) + 9 = 15$	$2(5) + 9 = 15$
$2 + 9 = 15$	$6 + 9 = 15$	$10 + 9 = 15$
$11 = 15$	$15 = 15$	$19 = 15$
false	true	false

Thus, 3 is a solution of the equation $2x + 9 = 15$.

If the replacement set for an equation is the set of whole numbers, it is not practical to use substitution to solve the equation. Instead, we **transform,** or change, the given equation into a simpler, **equivalent equation,** that is, one that has the same solution. When we transform the given equation, our goal is to arrive at an equivalent equation of the form

$$\text{variable} = \text{number.}$$

For example:

$$n = 5$$

The number, 5, is then the solution of the original equation. The following transformations can be used to solve equations.

> Simplify numerical expressions and variable expressions.
>
> *Transformation by addition:* Add the same number to both sides.
>
> *Transformation by subtraction:* Subtract the same number from both sides.

EXAMPLE 1 Solve $x = 3 + 5$.

Solution Simplify the numerical expression $3 + 5$.

$$x = 3 + 5$$
$$x = 8$$

The solution is 8.

EXAMPLE 2 Solve $x - 2 = 8$.

Solution Our goal is to find an equivalent equation of the form

$$x = \text{a number.}$$

The left side of the given equation is $x - 2$. Recall that addition and subtraction are inverse operations. If we add 2 to both sides, the left side simplifies to x.

$$x - 2 = 8$$
$$x - 2 + 2 = 8 + 2$$
$$x = 10$$

The solution is 10.

EXAMPLE 3 Solve $x + 6 = -8$.

Solution Subtract 6 from both sides of the equation to get an equivalent equation of the form $x = $ a number.

$$x + 6 = -8$$
$$x + 6 - 6 = -8 - 6$$
$$x = -14$$
The solution is -14.

In equations involving a number of steps, it is a good idea to check your answer. This can be done quite easily by substituting the answer in the original equation. Checking is illustrated in Example 4.

EXAMPLE 4 Solve $5 + x + 4 = 17$.

Solution

$$5 + x + 4 = 17$$
$$5 + 4 + x = 17$$
$$9 + x = 17$$
$$9 + x - 9 = 17 - 9$$
$$x = 8$$

Check: $5 + x + 4 = 17$
$5 + 8 + 4 \overset{?}{=} 17$
$13 + 4 = 17$ ✓

The solution is 8.

Solving Equations **131**

Complete each equation. State which transformation is used.

1. $15 + 9 = r$
$\underline{\quad ? \quad} = r$
24; simplify left side

2. $a - 8 = 12$
$a - 8 + 8 = 12 + \underline{\quad ? \quad}$
$a = \underline{\quad ? \quad}$
8; transformation by addition. 20; simplify both sides.

3. $8 + r = 45$
$8 + r - 8 = 45 - \underline{\quad ? \quad}$
$r = \underline{\quad ? \quad}$
8; transformation by subtraction. 37; simplify both sides.

4. $12 + b = 6(9 - 2)$
$12 + b = \underline{\quad ? \quad}$
$12 + b - 12 = 42 - \underline{\quad ? \quad}$
$b = \underline{\quad ? \quad}$
42; simplify right side. 12; transformation by subtraction. 30; simplify both sides.

The following example shows how to solve an equation, such as $34 - x = 27$, in which the variable is being subtracted.

EXAMPLE 5   Solve $34 - x = 27$.

Solution   Add x to both sides.
$$34 - x = 27$$
$$34 - x + x = 27 + x$$
$$34 = 27 + x$$

Subtract 27 from both sides.
$$34 - 27 = 27 + x - 27$$
$$7 = x$$

The solution is 7.

Reading Mathematics: *Study Skills*

Review the worked-out examples if you need help in solving any of the exercises. When doing so, be certain to read carefully and to make sure that you understand what is happening in each step.

You may be able to solve some of the equations in the exercises without pencil and paper. Nevertheless, it is important to show all the steps in your work and to make sure you can tell which transformation you are using in each step.

Throughout the rest of this chapter, if no replacement set is given for an equation, you should assume that the replacement set is the set of all numbers in our decimal system.

Class Exercises

State which transformation was used to transform the first equation into the second.

1. $x - 3 = 5$
$x - 3 + 3 = 5 + 3$

2. $x = 8 + 7$
$x = 15$

3. $-3 - 1 = 3 - x$
$-4 = 3 - x$

4. $x - 5 = 9$
$x - 5 + 5 = 9 + 5$

Complete each equation. State which transformation has been used.

5. $x = 11 + 17$
$x = \underline{\ ?\ }$

6. $x - 11 = 12$
$x - 11 + 11 = 12 + \underline{\ ?\ }$

7. $x + 7 = 13$
$x + 7 - 7 = 13 \underline{\ ?\ } 7$

8. $4 - x = -2$
$4 - x + x = -2 \underline{\ ?\ } x$

Written Exercises

Use transformations to solve each equation. Write down all the steps.

A   **1.** $x + 15 = 27$ 12

3. $x - 6 = -7$ −1

5. $8 + (-12) = x$ −4

7. $x = 38 - 15$ 23

9. $x + 7 = 3(6 + 2)$ 17

11. $23 = 30 - x$ 7

2. $x - 8 = 21$ 29

4. $19 + x = 35$ 16

6. $3 + 16 = x$ 19

8. $x = -24 + 15$ −9

10. $34 = 4(3 - 1) + x$ 26

12. $42 - x = -4$ 46

B   **13.** $5(2 + 7) - x = 33$ 12

15. $9 + 12 = (3 \times 5) + x$ 6

17. $4(10 - 7) = x + 4$ 8

19. $-\frac{3}{5} + n = -1$ $-\frac{2}{5}$

21. $5 = 8\frac{2}{3} - a$ $3\frac{2}{3}$

23. $n - 0.76 = 0.34$ 1.1

25. $0.894 - y = 0.641$ 0.253

27. $x - 0.323 = 0.873$ 1.196

29. $3\frac{1}{2} + 5\frac{1}{4} = n - 1$ $9\frac{3}{4}$

31. $n + 3\frac{1}{6} + 4\frac{1}{4} = 10$ $2\frac{7}{12}$

33. $n + 0.813 - 0.529 = 0.642$ 0.358

14. $6(8 - 3) = 48 - x$ 18

16. $3(72 \div 12) - x = 5$ 13

18. $22 + x = 4(39 \div 3)$ 30

20. $n - \frac{3}{4} = 3$ $3\frac{3}{4}$

22. $-4\frac{1}{5} + c = -2$ $2\frac{1}{5}$

24. $n + 0.519 = 0.597$ 0.078

26. $0.321 + r = 0.58$ 0.259

28. $-0.187 + t = 0.67$ 0.857

30. $4\frac{1}{3} - 1\frac{5}{6} = b + 1$ $1\frac{1}{2}$

32. $n + 5\frac{7}{8} - 1\frac{1}{6} = 7$ $2\frac{7}{24}$

34. $a + 0.952 - 0.751 = 0.7$ 0.499

C   **35.** $8\left(4\frac{1}{10} - 3\frac{1}{4}\right) = y + 3$ $3\frac{4}{5}$

37. $7(0.34 - 0.21) = b - 0.82$ 1.73

36. $3\left(2\frac{1}{9} + 4\frac{5}{6}\right) = 25 - c$ $4\frac{1}{6}$

38. $4(0.641 + 0.222) = n + 0.357$ 3.095

Review Exercises

Complete.

1. $5x \div \underline{\ \ ?\ \ } = x$ 5

2. $y \times 8 \div 8 = \underline{\ \ ?\ \ }$ y

3. $3z \div \underline{\ \ ?\ \ } = z$ 3

4. $\frac{x}{4} \times \underline{\ \ ?\ \ } = x$ 4

5. $\frac{x}{9} \times \underline{\ \ ?\ \ } = x$ 9

6. $\frac{z}{7} \times 7 = \underline{\ \ ?\ \ }$ z

Solving Equations   **133**

Chalkboard Examples

Complete each equation.
State which transformation is
used.

1. $3r = 57$

$\frac{3r}{3} = \frac{57}{?}$

$r = \underline{\quad ? \quad}$

3; transformation by di-
vision. 19; simplify both
sides.

2. $714 = 7t$

$\frac{?}{?} = \frac{7t}{7}$

$\underline{\quad ? \quad} = t$

$\frac{714}{7}$; transformation by
division. 102; simplify
both sides.

3. $\frac{m}{9} = 30$

$\frac{m}{9} \times 9 = 30 \times \underline{\quad ? \quad}$

$m = \underline{\quad ? \quad}$

9; transformation by
multiplication. 270; sim-
plify both sides.

4. $\frac{1}{12}t = 10$

$\frac{1}{12}t \times 12 = 10 \times \underline{\quad ? \quad}$

$t = \underline{\quad ? \quad}$

12; transformation by
multiplication. 120; sim-
plify both sides.

Suggested Assignments

Core
  135/2–32 even
  135/Rev. 1–6
Enriched
  135/21–38
  135/Rev. 1–6

Supplementary Materials

Practice Masters, p. 17

4-2 Equations: Multiplication and Division

If an equation involves multiplication or division, the following transformations are used to solve the equation.

> *Transformation by multiplication:* Multiply both sides of the
> equation by the same nonzero number.
>
> *Transformation by division:* Divide both sides of the equation
> by the same nonzero number.

EXAMPLE 1 Solve $3n = 24$.

Solution Our goal is to find an equivalent equation of the form
$$n = \text{a number.}$$
Use the fact that multiplication and division are inverse operations
and that $3n \div 3 = n$.
$$3n = 24$$
$$\frac{3n}{3} = \frac{24}{3}$$
$$n = 8$$

The solution is 8.

EXAMPLE 2 Solve $-5x = 53$.

Solution Divide both sides by 5.
$$-5x = 53$$
$$\frac{-5x}{-5} = \frac{53}{-5}$$
$$x = -10\frac{3}{5}$$

The solution is $-10\frac{3}{5}$.

EXAMPLE 3 Solve $\frac{n}{4} = 7$.

Solution Multiply both sides by 4.
$$\frac{n}{4} = 7$$
$$\frac{n}{4} \times 4 = 7 \times 4$$
$$n = 28$$
The solution is 28.

134 *Chapter 4*

Class Exercises

a. State the transformation you would use to solve each equation.
b. Solve the equation.

1. $2n = 26$ **2.** $\frac{n}{2} = -5$ **3.** $\frac{n}{3} = 12$ **4.** $-3n = 12$

5. $5n = 35$ **6.** $33 = 11n$ **7.** $-7 = \frac{n}{4}$ **8.** $\frac{n}{5} = 20$

9. $4 + x = 7$ **10.** $4x = -24$ **11.** $28 = \frac{x}{7}$ **12.** $-11 = x - 2$

Written Exercises

Use the transformations given in this chapter to solve each equation.
Show all steps. Check your solution.

A **1.** $5n = 75$ 15 **2.** $-87 = 3n$ −29 **3.** $\frac{n}{3} = 6$ 18 **4.** $-3n = 15$ $^{-5}$

5. $7n = 42$ 6 **6.** $\frac{n}{4} = -8$ −32 **7.** $\frac{n}{6} = 9$ 54 **8.** $-\frac{n}{5} = 6$ −30

9. $\frac{n}{4} = -21$ −84 **10.** $10 = \frac{n}{6}$ 60 **11.** $4 = \frac{n}{7}$ 28 **12.** $5n = 55$ 11

13. $9n = 45$ 5 **14.** $\frac{n}{8} = 9$ 72 **15.** $11n = -110$ −10 **16.** $8n = 96$ 12

17. $\frac{n}{13} = 7$ 91 **18.** $\frac{n}{16} = -6$ −96 **19.** $12n = 132$ 11 **20.** $17n = -289$ $^{-17}$

B **21.** $6x = 45$ $7\frac{1}{2}$ **22.** $18x = 12$ $\frac{2}{3}$ **23.** $\frac{x}{17} = -13$ −221 **24.** $\frac{x}{15} = 11$ 165

25. $-\frac{x}{21} = 12$ −252 **26.** $\frac{x}{27} = 23$ 621 **27.** $24x = -20$ $-\frac{5}{6}$ **28.** $12x = 76$ $6\frac{1}{3}$

29. $9x = 80 + 7$ $9\frac{2}{3}$ **30.** $-64x = 100 - 48$ $-\frac{13}{16}$ **31.** $\frac{x}{26} = 2(3 + 4)$ 364

32. $42 + x = 179$ 137 **33.** $x - 193 = 54$ 247 **34.** $296 - x = -51$ 347

C **35.** $7x = \frac{14}{19}$ $\frac{2}{19}$ **36.** $11x = \frac{13}{20}$ $\frac{13}{220}$ **37.** $\frac{x}{16} = \frac{21}{32}$ $10\frac{1}{2}$ **38.** $\frac{x}{9} = \frac{13}{84}$ $1\frac{11}{28}$

Review Exercises

Multiply or divide.

1. $\frac{5}{8} \times \frac{12}{35}$ $\frac{3}{14}$ **2.** $\frac{14}{30} \div \frac{2}{15}$ $3\frac{1}{2}$ **3.** $\frac{17}{9} \times \frac{6}{85}$ $\frac{2}{15}$

4. $3\frac{2}{3} \times 5\frac{9}{11}$ $21\frac{1}{3}$ **5.** $3\frac{5}{8} \div 1\frac{3}{16}$ $3\frac{1}{19}$ **6.** 0.09×3.74 0.3360

Solving Equations **135**

Additional A Exercises

Use the transformations given in this chapter to solve each equation. Show all steps. Check your solution.

1. $\frac{1}{7}u = 18$ 126

2. $7t = 91$ 13

3. $5 = \frac{1}{21}x$ 105

4. $\frac{1}{9}s = 23$ 207

5. $8p = 112$ 14

6. $\frac{1}{25}x = 25$ 625

7. $5v = 555$ 111

8. $\frac{1}{5}r = 555$ 2775

135

4-3 Equations: Decimals and Fractions

Sometimes the variable expression in an equation may involve a decimal. When this occurs, you can use the transformations that you have learned in the previous lessons.

EXAMPLE 1 Solve the equation $0.42x = 1.05$.

Solution Divide both sides by 0.42.

$$0.42x = 1.05$$

$$\frac{0.42x}{0.42} = \frac{1.05}{0.42}$$

$$x = 2.5$$

The solution is 2.5.

EXAMPLE 2 Solve the equation $\frac{n}{0.15} = 92$.

Solution Multiply both sides by 0.15.

$$\frac{n}{0.15} = 92$$

$$0.15 \times \frac{n}{0.15} = 0.15 \times 92$$

$$n = 13.80$$

The solution is 13.80.

The variable expression in an equation may also involve a fraction. To see how to solve an equation such as $\frac{2}{3}x = 6$, think how you would solve an equation such as $2x = 6$. (You would divide both sides by 2, getting $x = 3$.) Thus, to solve $\frac{2}{3}x = 6$, you would divide both sides by $\frac{2}{3}$. This is the same as multiplying by the reciprocal of $\frac{2}{3}$, or $\frac{3}{2}$. Therefore, we solve equations involving fractions in the following way.

If an equation has the form

$$\frac{a}{b}x = c,$$

where both a and b are nonzero,

multiply both sides by $\frac{b}{a}$, the reciprocal of $\frac{a}{b}$.

136 *Chapter 4*

EXAMPLE 3 Solve the equation $\frac{1}{3}y = 18$.

Solution Multiply both sides by 3, the reciprocal of $\frac{1}{3}$.

$$\frac{1}{3}y = 18$$

$$3 \times \frac{1}{3}y = 3 \times 18$$

$$y = 3 \times 18$$

$$y = 54$$

The solution is 54.

EXAMPLE 4 Solve the equation $\frac{6}{7}n = 8$. Check.

Solution Multiply both sides by $\frac{7}{6}$, the reciprocal of $\frac{6}{7}$.

$$\frac{6}{7}n = 8 \qquad \text{Check:} \qquad \frac{6}{7}n = 8$$

$$\frac{7}{6} \times \frac{6}{7}n = \frac{7}{6} \times 8 \qquad\qquad \frac{6}{7} \times \frac{28}{3} \overset{?}{=} 8$$

$$n = \frac{7}{\overset{}{\underset{3}{6}}} \times \overset{4}{8} \qquad\qquad \frac{\overset{2}{6}}{\overset{}{\underset{1}{7}}} \times \frac{\overset{4}{28}}{\overset{}{\underset{1}{3}}} \overset{?}{=} 8$$

$$n = \frac{28}{3} \qquad\qquad \frac{2}{1} \times \frac{4}{1} = 8$$

The solution is $\frac{28}{3}$, or $9\frac{1}{3}$.

Class Exercises

a. **State what number you would multiply or divide both sides of each equation by in order to solve it.**

b. **Solve the equation.**

1. $\frac{3}{4}x = 15$ **2.** $0.2x = 6$ **3.** $\frac{x}{0.4} = 1.7$ **4.** $\frac{x}{1.3} = 2.4$

5. $\frac{1}{8}x = 7$ **6.** $\frac{17}{12}x = 34$ **7.** $\frac{8}{3}x = 24$ **8.** $\frac{1}{9}x = 14$

9. $\frac{x}{1.8} = 2.9$ **10.** $\frac{x}{2.3} = 5$ **11.** $0.35x = 10.5$ **12.** $0.55x = 2.20$

13. $0.28x = 2.24$ **14.** $0.67x = 6.03$ **15.** $\frac{x}{2.6} = 3.7$ **16.** $\frac{x}{5.9} = 14.2$

Solving Equations **137**

Additional A Exercises

Solve each equation.

1. $\frac{1}{9}p = 33$ 297

2. $\frac{b}{3.2} = -2$ −6.4

3. $-\frac{2}{7}h = 8$ −28

4. $\frac{3}{20}w = -72$ −480

5. $1.8u = 5.76$ 3.2

6. $-3.4a = 3.74$ −1.1

Written Exercises

Solve each equation.

A

1. $\frac{1}{8}x = 11$ 88   **2.** $-\frac{1}{3}x = 13$ −39   **3.** $0.4x = 8$ 20   **4.** $0.6x = 24$ 40

5. $\frac{x}{0.3} = -5$ −1.5   **6.** $\frac{x}{0.7} = 4$ 2.8   **7.** $-\frac{2}{3}x = 16$ −24   **8.** $\frac{3}{4}x = 21$ 28

9. $0.25x = 15$ 60   **10.** $0.44x = -22$ −50   **11.** $\frac{x}{1.5} = 13$ 19.5   **12.** $-\frac{x}{2.2} = 22$ −48.4

13. $\frac{3}{2}x = 27$ 18   **14.** $\frac{5}{9}x = -65$ −117   **15.** $\frac{12}{5}x = 48$ 20   **16.** $\frac{12}{7}x = 60$ 35

17. $-1.3x = 39$ −30   **18.** $3.2x = 128$ 40   **19.** $\frac{x}{4.5} = -11$ −49.5   **20.** $\frac{x}{6.2} = 17$ 105.4

B

21. $\frac{4}{3}n = 18$ $13\frac{1}{2}$ **22.** $-\frac{6}{5}n = 20$ $-16\frac{2}{3}$ **23.** $\frac{8}{3}n = 28$ $10\frac{1}{2}$ **24.** $\frac{6}{7}n = -21$ $-24\frac{1}{2}$

25. $3.9 = 0.6n$ 6.5   **26.** $3.6 = 1.6n$ 2.25   **27.** $-1.5n = 1.2$ −0.8   **28.** $1.25n = 3.5$ 2.8

29. $\left(2\frac{2}{5}\right)n = \frac{-4}{15}$ $-\frac{1}{9}$ **30.** $\frac{3}{11} = \frac{9}{5}n$ $\frac{5}{33}$ **31.** $-\frac{7}{9} = \frac{14}{15}n$ $-\frac{5}{6}$ **32.** $1\frac{5}{7}n = \frac{16}{35}$ $\frac{4}{15}$

33. $\frac{n}{2.45} = 3.1$ 7.595   **34.** $\frac{n}{6.31} = -2.12$ −13.3772   **35.** $\frac{n}{5.37} = 0.004$ 0.02148   **36.** $-\frac{n}{0.09} = 2.79$ −0.2511

C

37. $\frac{2}{3}x = 3.8$ 5.7   **38.** $\frac{3}{4}x = -6.93$ −9.24   **39.** $\frac{3}{5}x = 9.36$ 15.6

40. $\frac{x}{6.4} = \frac{5}{8}$ 4   **41.** $\frac{x}{2.7} = \frac{11}{9}$ 3.3   **42.** $\frac{x}{4.2} = \frac{17}{6}$ 11.9

Review Exercises

Solve.

1. $x + 17 = 47$ 30   **2.** $55 + x = 75$ 20   **3.** $96 - x = 41$ 55

4. $82 - x = 37$ 45   **5.** $x - 45 = 58$ 103   **6.** $5x = 95$ 19

7. $3x = 51$ 17   **8.** $7x = 91$ 13   **9.** $4x = 76$ 19

▮▮▮ Calculator Key-In

Using a calculator can greatly simplify the computations involved in solving an equation with decimals. Use a calculator to solve the following equations.

1. $0.32x = 0.096$ 0.3   **2.** $3.02x = 1.84$ 0.6092715   **3.** $2.11x = 5.74$ 2.7203791

4. $\frac{x}{0.79} = 1.08$ 0.8532   **5.** $\frac{x}{1.91} = 1.77$ 3.3807   **6.** $\frac{x}{4.002} = 0.107$ 0.428214

Suggested Assignments

Core
138/1–33 odd
138/Calculator Key-In

Enriched
138/13–20; 22–42 even
138/Calculator Key-In

Supplementary Materials

Practice Masters, p. 18

4-4 Combined Operations

Teaching Suggestions
p. 129c

Related Activities p. 129d

Many equations may be written in the form

$$ax + b = c,$$

where a, b, and c are given numbers and x is a variable. To solve such an equation, it is necessary to use more than one transformation.

EXAMPLE 1 Solve the equation $3n - 5 = 10 + 6$.

Solution Simplify the numerical expression.

$$3n - 5 = 10 + 6$$
$$3n - 5 = 16$$

Add 5 to both sides.

$$3n - 5 + 5 = 16 + 5$$
$$3n = 21$$

Divide both sides by 3.

$$\frac{3n}{3} = \frac{21}{3}$$
$$n = 7$$

The solution is 7.

Example 1 suggests the following general procedure for solving equations.

1. Simplify each side of the equation.

2. If there are still indicated additions or subtractions, use the inverse operations to undo them.

3. If there are indicated multiplications or divisions involving the variable, use the inverse operations to undo them.

It is important to remember that in using the procedure outlined above you must *always perform the same operation on both sides of the equation*. Also, you must use the steps in the procedure in the order indicated. That is, you first simplify each side of the equation, then undo additions and subtractions, and then undo multiplications and divisions.

Solving Equations **139**

139

Solve each equation.

1. $5a - 4 = 56$ 12

2. $6 - 1.5b = 3$ 2

3. $\frac{3}{2}c - 8 = 22$ 20

4. $46 + 12d = 10$ -3

5. $12 - 3e = 9$ 1

6. $81 + \frac{2}{3}f = 21$ -90

EXAMPLE 2   Solve the equation $\frac{3}{2}n + 7 = -8$.

Solution   Subtract 7 from both sides.

$$\frac{3}{2}n + 7 = -8$$

$$\frac{3}{2}n + 7 - 7 = -8 - 7$$

$$\frac{3}{2}n = -15$$

Multiply both sides by $\frac{2}{3}$, the reciprocal of $\frac{3}{2}$.

$$\frac{2}{3} \times \frac{3}{2}n = \frac{2}{3} \times (-15)$$

$$n = \frac{2}{\overset{3}{1}} \times (-\overset{5}{15})$$

$$n = -10$$

The solution is -10.

EXAMPLE 3   Solve the equation $40 - \frac{5}{3}n = 15$.

Solution   Add $\frac{5}{3}n$ to both sides.

$$40 - \frac{5}{3}n = 15$$

$$40 - \frac{5}{3}n + \frac{5}{3}n = 15 + \frac{5}{3}n$$

$$40 = 15 + \frac{5}{3}n$$

Subtract 15 from both sides.

$$40 - 15 = 15 + \frac{5}{3}n - 15$$

$$25 = \frac{5}{3}n$$

Multiply both sides by $\frac{3}{5}$.

$$\frac{3}{5} \times 25 = \frac{3}{5} \times \frac{5}{3}n$$

$$\frac{3}{\overset{\,}{5}} \times \overset{5}{25} = n$$

$$15 = n$$

The solution is 15.

140   *Chapter 4*

Class Exercises

State the two transformations you would use to find the solution of each equation. Be sure to specify which transformation you would use first.

1. $3n + 2 = -10$

2. $4n - 1 = 19$

3. $\frac{1}{2}n - 6 = 1$

4. $\frac{1}{3}n + 5 = 7$

5. $\frac{2}{3}n - 6 = -12$

6. $\frac{5}{2}n + 2 = 13$

7. $3n - 6 = 15$

8. $7n + 21 = -63$

9. $\frac{3}{4}n - 8 = 12$

10. $\frac{1}{2}n + 2 = -5$

11. $2\frac{1}{3}n - 2 = 8$

12. $1\frac{2}{3}n + 15 = -21$

Written Exercises

Solve each equation.

A

1. $2n - 5 = 17$ 11

2. $3n + 6 = -24$ −10

3. $5n + 6 = 41$ 7

4. $4n - 15 = 9$ 6

5. $6n + 11 = 77$ 11

6. $8n - 13 = 51$ 8

7. $50 - 3n = 20$ 10

8. $42 - 5n = 7$ 7

9. $29 - 6n = 11$ 3

10. $-79 - 8n = -15$ −8

11. $\frac{1}{4}n + 5 = 25$ 80

12. $\frac{1}{8}n - 11 = 21$ 256

13. $\frac{1}{2}n + 3 = 18$ 30

14. $\frac{1}{3}n - 7 = -11$ −12

15. $\frac{1}{5}n - 2 = 9$ 55

16. $\frac{1}{4}n + 3 = 8$ 20

17. $\frac{2}{3}n + 12 = 28$ 24

18. $\frac{3}{5}n + 11 = -7$ −30

19. $6n - 7 = 19$ $4\frac{1}{3}$

20. $10n - 6 = -39$ $-3\frac{3}{10}$

21. $\frac{6}{5}n - 7 = 20$ $22\frac{1}{2}$

22. $\frac{15}{4}n + 7 = -68$ −20

23. $2\frac{2}{5}n + 5 = 23$ $7\frac{1}{2}$

24. $1\frac{1}{7}n - 9 = 27$ $31\frac{1}{2}$

B

25. $\frac{3}{5}n + \frac{2}{3} = \frac{8}{3}$ $3\frac{1}{3}$

26. $\frac{2}{3}n - \frac{5}{6} = -\frac{1}{8}$ $1\frac{1}{16}$

27. $\frac{3}{4}n - \frac{11}{15} = \frac{3}{5}$ $1\frac{7}{9}$

28. $\frac{5}{6}n + \frac{1}{10} = \frac{29}{30}$ $1\frac{1}{25}$

29. $\frac{7}{8}n - \frac{5}{6} = \frac{3}{4}$ $1\frac{17}{21}$

30. $\frac{1}{3}n - \frac{11}{25} = \frac{3}{10}$ $2\frac{11}{50}$

31. $\frac{2}{5}n + \frac{3}{7} = \frac{11}{5}$ $4\frac{3}{7}$

32. $\frac{1}{6}n + \frac{3}{5} = \frac{7}{11}$ $\frac{12}{55}$

33. $1\frac{1}{3}n + \frac{5}{12} = \frac{3}{4}$ $\frac{1}{4}$

34. $2\frac{2}{3}n - \frac{4}{7} = \frac{8}{9}$ $\frac{23}{42}$

35. $\frac{11}{3}n - \frac{5}{9} = \frac{5}{6}$ $\frac{25}{66}$

36. $\frac{7}{2}n - \frac{11}{12} = \frac{5}{9}$ $\frac{53}{126}$

37. $1\frac{3}{8}n + \frac{1}{4} = \frac{7}{8}$ $\frac{5}{11}$

38. $\frac{3}{4}n - \frac{1}{12} = \frac{7}{3}$ $3\frac{2}{9}$

39. $\frac{3}{7}n + \frac{4}{5} = \frac{6}{7}$ $\frac{2}{15}$

Use transformations to solve each equation.

1. $x - 5 = 42 - 40$ 7
2. $45 - x = 13$ 32
3. $14x = 266$ 19
4. $\frac{m}{11} = 6$ 66
5. $\frac{t}{4} = 23$ 92
6. $\frac{15}{11}h = 1\frac{1}{2}$ $1\frac{1}{10}$
7. $45a = 202.5$ 4.5
8. $\frac{m}{2.5} = 25$ 62.5
9. $14n - 66 = 900$ 69
10. $19 - 2j = 10$ $4\frac{1}{2}$
11. $-\frac{x}{2} = 15$ -30
12. $0.25k = -4$ -16
13. $\frac{2}{5}n + 1 = -11$ -30
14. $6(8 - 5) = 12 - 2x$ -3
15. $6 - x = 6$ 0
16. $\frac{1}{7}y - 5 = -7$ -14

Suggested Assignments

Core
Day 1: 141/2–32 even
Day 2: 142/40–42
    142/Self-Test A
    142/Calculator Key-In

Enriched
Day 1: 141/7–39 odd
Day 2: 142/40–42
    142/Self-Test A
    142/Calculator Key-In

Supplementary Materials

Practice Masters, p. 18
Computer Activity 7
Test 4A, pp. 23–24

C **40.** Solve $C = 2\pi r$ for r if $C = 220$ and $\pi \approx \frac{22}{7}$. 35

41. Solve $P = 2l + 2w$ for w if $P = 64$ and $l = 5$. 27

42. Solve $d = rt$ for r if $d = 308$ and $t = 3.5$. 88

Self-Test A

Use transformations to solve each equation.

1. $y + 7 = -17$ -24
2. $x - 6 = 4$ 10 [4-1]
3. $x + 6 = 27 - 12$ 9
4. $5(7 + 2) = x - 11$ 56
5. $7a = -91$ -13
6. $-\frac{c}{4} = 17$ -68 [4-2]
7. $-4t = -68$ 17
8. $\frac{p}{3} = -11$ -33
9. $\frac{1}{6}z = 25$ 150
10. $-\frac{13}{3}y = 10$ $-2\frac{4}{13}$ [4-3]
11. $0.35a = -28$ -80
12. $\frac{x}{0.03} = -58$ -1.74
13. $8n - 40 = 180$ $27\frac{1}{2}$
14. $\frac{2}{3}n + 18 = 98$ 120 [4-4]
15. $\frac{1}{3}x + 4 = 6$ 6
16. $5x - 2 = -17$ -3

Self-Test answers and Extra Practice are at the back of the book.

Calculator Key-In

Do the following on your calculator.

1. Press any 3 digits.	852
2. Repeat the digits.	852,852
3. Divide by 7.	? 121,836
4. Divide by 11.	? 11,076
5. Divide by 13.	? 852

What is your answer? Now multiply your answer by 1001. Try again using three different digits. Explain your results.

4-5 Writing Expressions for Word Phrases

In mathematics we often use symbols to translate word phrases into mathematical expressions. The same mathematical expression can be used to translate many different word expressions. Consider the phrases below.

Three more than a number *n*   The sum of three and a number *n*

Written as a variable expression, each of the phrases becomes

$$3 + n.$$

Notice that both the phrase *more than* and the phrase *the sum of* indicate addition.

The following are some of the word phrases that we associate with each of the four operations.

+	−	×	÷
add	subtract	multiply	divide
sum	difference	product	quotient
plus	minus	times	
total	remainder		
more than	less than		
increased by	decreased by		

Reading Mathematics

There is often some confusion in students' minds over expressions like "three more than *x*" and "three is more than *x*." The usual error encountered the use of $3 > x$ as a translation of the first phrase, instead of the proper $x + 3$. The same is true, of course, about "five less than *x*" and "five is less than *x*." Another common error is to use $4 - x$ rather than $x - 4$ for "four less than *x*."

EXAMPLE 1   Write a variable expression for the word phrase.
   a. A number *t* increased by nine   **b.** Sixteen less than a number *q*
   c. A number *x* decreased by twelve, divided by forty
   d. The product of sixteen and the sum of five and a number *r*

Solution   **a.** In this expression, the phrase *increased by* indicates that the operation is addition. $t + 9$

   b. In this expression, the phrase *less than* indicates that the operation is subtraction. $q - 16$

   c. In this expression, the phrases *decreased by* and *divided by* indicate that two operations, subtraction and division, are involved. $(x - 12) \div 40$

   d. In this expression, the words *product* and *sum* indicate that multiplication and addition are involved.
   $16 \times (5 + r)$,   or $16(5 + r)$

Solving Equations   **143**

Write a variable expression for the word phrase.

1. A number eleven more than a number t $t + 11$

2. Twice the sum of a number a and twelve

   $2(a + 12)$

3. Six more than twice a number x $2x + 6$

4. The sum of two consecutive whole numbers if the first is n $n + (n + 1)$, or $2n + 1$

5. The difference between twenty and the product of four and a number c

   $20 - 4c$

Reading Mathematics: *Attention to Order*

Often a word expression contains more than one phrase that indicates an operation. Notice in Example 1 parts (c) and (d), on page 143 how parentheses were needed to represent the word phrase accurately. When translating from words to symbols, be sure to include grouping symbols if they are needed to make the meaning of an expression clear.

Many words that we use in everyday speech indicate operations or relationships between numbers. *Twice* and *doubled*, for example, indicate multiplication by 2. *Consecutive* whole numbers are whole numbers that differ by 1. The *preceding* whole number is the whole number *before* a particular number, and the *next* whole number is the whole number *after* a particular number.

EXAMPLE 2 If $2n$ is a whole number, represent (a) the preceding whole number and (b) the next four consecutive whole numbers.

Solution

a. The preceding whole number is 1 less than $2n$, or $2n - 1$.

b. Each of the next whole numbers is 1 more than the whole number before.

$$2n + 1, \ 2n + 2, \ 2n + 3, \ 2n + 4$$

Class Exercises

Match.

1. A number x multiplied by fourteen I

2. The quotient of fourteen and a number x E

3. Fourteen less than a number x G

4. Seven increased by a number x H

5. A number x subtracted from fourteen A

6. Fourteen more than a number x J

7. Seven more than the product of fourteen and a number x D

8. Twice the sum of a number x and seven B

9. The product of seven and the sum of fourteen and a number x F

10. Fourteen divided by the difference between seven and x C

A. $14 - x$

B. $2(x + 7)$

C. $14 \div (7 - x)$

D. $7 + 14x$

E. $14 \div x$

F. $7(14 + x)$

G. $x - 14$

H. $7 + x$

I. $14x$

J. $x + 14$

Written Exercises

Write a variable expression for the word phrase.

A 1. The product of eight and a number b $8b$

2. A number q divided by sixteen $q \div 16$

3. A number d subtracted from fifty-three $53 - d$

4. Four less than a number f $f - 4$

5. Thirty increased by a number t $30 + t$

6. Five times a number c $5c$

7. The sum of a number g and nine $g + 9$

8. A number k minus twenty-seven $k - 27$

9. Seventy-eight decreased by a number m $78 - m$

10. A number y added to ninety $y + 90$

11. Nineteen more than a number n $n + 19$

12. Sixty-two plus a number h $62 + h$

13. The quotient when a number d is divided by eleven $d \div 11$

14. The difference when a number a is subtracted from a number b $b - a$

15. The remainder when a number z is subtracted from twelve $12 - z$

16. The total of a number x, a number y, and thirteen $x + y + 13$

17. Fifteen more than the product of a number t and eleven $11t + 15$

18. The quotient when a number b is divided by nine, decreased by seven $(b \div 9) - 7$

19. The sum of a number m and a number n, multiplied by ninety-one $91(m + n)$

20. Forty-one times the difference when six is subtracted from a number a $41(a - 6)$

21. A number r divided by the difference between eighty-three and ten $r \div (83 - 10)$

22. The total of a number p and twelve, divided by eighteen $(p + 12) \div 18$

23. The product of a number c and three more than the sum of nine and twelve $c[(9 + 12) + 3]$

24. The sum of a number y and ten, divided by the difference when a number x is decreased by five $(y + 10) \div (x - 5)$

Solving Equations **145**

Additional A Exercises

Write a variable expression for the word phrase.

1. The sum of thirty and a number m $30 + m$

2. The product of twelve and a number x $12x$

3. A number n divided by fourteen $n \div 14$

4. The sum of nine and the product of seven and a number w $9 + 7w$

5. The remainder when the quotient of six and a number z is subtracted from a number x $x - \dfrac{6}{z}$

Suggested Assignments

Core
Day 1: 145/1–24
Day 2: 146/25–35
        146/Rev. 1–8
        146/Challenge
Enriched
    145/15–24
    146/27–36
    146/Challenge

Supplementary Materials

Practice Masters, p. 19

25. The total of sixty, forty, and ten, divided by a number d $(60 + 40 + 10) \div d$

26. The product of eighteen less than a number b and the sum of twenty-two and forty-five $(b - 18)(22 + 45)$

B **27.** The greatest of four consecutive whole numbers, the smallest of which is b $b + 3$

28. The smallest of three consecutive whole numbers, the greatest of which is q $q - 2$

29. The greatest of three consecutive even numbers following the even number x $x + 4$

30. The greatest of three consecutive odd numbers following the odd number y $y + 4$

31. The value in cents of q quarters $25q$

32. The number of inches in f feet $12f$

33. The number of hours in x minutes $x \div 60$

34. The number of dollars in y cents $y \div 100$

C **35.** The difference between two numbers is ten. The greater number is x. Write a variable expression for the smaller number. $x - 10$

36. One number is six times another. The greater number is a. Write a variable expression for the smaller number. $a \div 6$

Review Exercises

Use the inverse operation to solve for the variable.

1. $x + 32 = 59$ 27 **2.** $2y = 68$ 34 **3.** $a \div 8 = 72$ 576 **4.** $q - 14 = -23$

5. $-7c = 105$ -15 **6.** $y - 11 = 21$ 32 **7.** $n - 6 = 13$ 19 **8.** $p + 3 = -39$ $^{-9}$
                                                                                                    -42

Challenge

In the set of whole numbers, there are two different values for a for which this equation is true.

$$a + a = a \times a$$

What are they? $0, 2$

4-6 Word Sentences and Equations

Just as word phrases can be translated into mathematical expressions, word sentences can be translated into equations.

EXAMPLE 1 Write an equation for the word sentence.

a. Twice a number x is equal to 14.
b. Thirty-five is sixteen more than a number t.

Solution

a. First, write the phrase *twice a number* x as the variable expression $2x$. Use the symbol $=$ to translate *is equal to*.

$$2x = 14$$

b. Use the equals sign to translate *is*. Write *sixteen more than a number* as $t + 16$.

$$35 = t + 16$$

A word sentence may involve an unknown number without specifying a variable. When translating such a sentence into an equation, we may use any letter to represent the unknown number.

EXAMPLE 2 Write an equation for the word sentence.
a. The sum of a number and seven is thirteen.
b. A number increased by six is equal to three times the number.

Solution

a. Let n stand for the unknown number. $n + 7 = 13$
b. Let x stand for the unknown number. $x + 6 = 3x$

Class Exercises

Write a problem that each equation could represent. Use the words in parentheses as the subject of the problem. Answers will vary.

1. $x + 16 = 180$ (number of students in the eighth grade)

2. $0.59x = 2.36$ (buying groceries)

3. $48x = 630$ (traveling in a car)

4. $x - 25 = 175$ (number of cars in a parking lot)

5. $256 - x = 219$ (price reduction in a department store)

6. $10x = 26$ (running race)

7. $25x = 175$ (fuel economy in a car)

Solving Equations **147**

Teaching Suggestions
p. 129d

Related Activities p. 129d

Chalkboard Examples

Match each problem with one of the equations below.

a. $12x = 42$ **b.** $12 + x = 42$
c. $x - 12 = 42$

1. Peter has $12. If he needs $42 in all to buy a tape recorder, how much more money does Peter need? **b**

2. If 12 tickets to a play cost $42, how much does one ticket cost? **a**

3. Paula's bike cost $12 less than Carla's. If Paula paid $42 for her bike, how much did Carla pay? **c**

4. There are 12 more students in the Pep Club than in the French Club. If there are 42 students in the Pep Club, how many are in the French Club? **b**

Write an equation for the word sentence.

5. Eight less than the product of a number x and five equals ten. $5x - 8 = 10$

6. A number decreased by seven equals nine. $n - 7 = 9$

7. The difference when a number y is subtracted from eighteen is four. $18 - y = 4$

8. Four times a number, divided by five, is twenty. $\frac{4n}{5} = 20$

Additional Answers
Class Exercises

Answers will vary. Examples are given.

1. The students in the eighth grade went to the science museum with 16 adults. If 180 people went to the science museum in all, how many students are in the eighth grade?

(Continue on page 151)

Write an equation for the word sentence.

1. Six times a number m is equal to thirty-six.
$6m = 36$

2. Thirteen equals a number divided by eight.
$13 = n \div 8$

3. The sum of a number and six is equal to twelve.
$n + 6 = 12$

4. A number k increased by twenty-five is seventy.
$k + 25 = 70$

5. Nine divided by the product of five and a number q is equal to thirty.
$9 \div 5q = 30$

6. The product of six and a number, decreased by two, is equal to ten.
$6x - 2 = 10$

Written Exercises

Write an equation for the word sentence.

A — 1. Five times a number d is equal to twenty. $5d = 20$

2. A number t increased by thirty-five is sixty. $t + 35 = 60$

3. Seven less than the product of a number w and three equals eight.
$3w - 7 = 8$

4. The difference when a number z is subtracted from sixteen is two.
$16 - z = 2$

5. Five divided by a number r equals forty-two. $5 \div r = 42$

6. The sum of a number and seven is equal to nine. $n + 7 = 9$

7. A number decreased by one equals five. $n - 1 = 5$

8. Twelve equals a number divided by four. $12 = n \div 4$

9. Twice a number, divided by three, is fifteen. $2n \div 3 = 15$

10. The product of a number and eight, decreased by three, is equal to nine. $8n - 3 = 9$

B 11. The quotient when the sum of four and x is divided by two is thirty-four. $(4 + x) \div 2 = 34$

12. The sum of n and twenty-two, multiplied by three, is seventy-eight.
$3(n + 22) = 78$

13. Fifty-nine minus x equals the sum of three and twice x.
$59 - x = 3 + 2x$

14. Two increased by eight times c is equal to c divided by five.
$2 + 8c = c \div 5$

C 15. The quotient when the difference between x and 5 is divided by three is 2. $(x - 5) \div 3 = 2$

16. Twice a number is equal to the product when the sum of the number and four is multiplied by eight. $2n = 8(n + 4)$

Review Exercises

Write a mathematical expression for each word phrase.

1. Four less than a number $n - 4$

2. Five times a number $5n$

3. A number divided by seven $n \div 7$

4. Ten more than a number $n + 10$

5. Forty minus a number $40 - n$

6. Twelve plus a number $12 + n$

7. A number times two $2n$

8. Ninety divided by a number $90 \div n$

Suggested Assignments

Core
148/1–14
148/Rev. 1–8

Enriched
148/1–16

Supplementary Materials

Practice Masters, p. 19

4-7 Writing Equations for Word Problems

In order to represent a word problem by an equation, we first read the problem carefully.

Next, we decide what numbers are being asked for. We then choose a variable and use it with the given conditions of the problem to represent the number or numbers asked for.

Now, we write an equation based on the given conditions of the problem. To do this, we write an expression involving the variable and set it equal to another variable expression or a number given in the problem that represents the same quantity.

The following example illustrates this procedure.

EXAMPLE 1   Write an equation for the following word problem.

Fran spent 3 times as long on her homework for English class as on her science homework. If she spent a total of 60 min on homework, how long did she spend on her science homework?

Solution
- The problem asks how long Fran spent on her science homework.

- Let t = time spent on science. Since Fran spent 3 times as long on her English homework, she spent $3t$ on English. Therefore, the expression $t + 3t$ represents the amount of time spent on the two assignments. We are given that the total amount of time was 60 min.

- An equation that represents the conditions is

$$t + 3t = 60$$

Class Exercises

a. Name the quantity you would represent by a variable.
b. State an equation that expresses the conditions of the word problem.

1. Jennifer bought 5 lb of apples for $3.45. What was the price per pound?

2. After Henry withdrew $350 from his account, he had $1150 left. How much money was in his account before this withdrawal?

3. A road that is 8.5 m wide is to be extended to 10.6 m wide. What is the width of the new paving?

4. In the seventh grade, 86 students made the honor roll. This is $\frac{2}{5}$ of the entire class. How many students are in the seventh grade?

Solving Equations   **149**

Teaching Suggestions
p. 129f

Related Activities p. 129f

Chalkboard Examples

a. Name the quantity you would represent by a variable.
b. State an equation that expresses the conditions of the word problem.

1. Jan swam 12 yd farther than Joan. If Jan swam 109 yd, how far did Joan swim? **Distance Joan swam;** $n + 12 = 109$

2. Kim wants to delete 19 programs from a computer's memory. How many programs are in memory now, if there will be 91 programs after the deletions? **Number of programs in memory now;** $n - 19 = 91$

3. A pet store sold $\frac{2}{5}$ as many pets in January as it did in December. If it sold 88 pets in January, how many pets were sold in December? **Number of pets sold in December;** $\frac{2}{5}n = 88$

4. Mario is 5 years older than twice his brother's age. If Mario is 27, how old is his brother? **Mario's brother's age;** $2n + 5 = 27$

Additional Answers
Class Exercises

1. Price per pound; $5n = 3.45$

2. Original amount; $n - 350 = 1150$

3. Width of new paving; $8.5 + n = 10.6$

4. Number of students in seventh grade; $\frac{2}{5}n = 86$

a. **Name the quantity you would represent by a variable.**
b. **State an equation that expresses the conditions of the word problem.**

5. A 25-floor building is 105 m tall. What is the height of each floor if they are all of equal height?

6. A 150 L tank in a chemical factory can be filled by a pipe in 60 s. At how many liters per second does the liquid enter the tank?

Problems

Choose a variable and write an equation for each problem.

A 1. On one portion of a trip across the country, the Oates family covered 1170 miles in 9 days. How many miles per day is this? $9n = 1170$

2. Carey's car went 224 km on 28 L of gas. How many kilometers per liter is this? $28n = 224$

3. Marge has purchased 18 subway tokens at a total cost of $13.50. What is the cost per token? $18n = 13.50$

4. After $525 was spent on the class trip, there was $325 left in the class treasury. How much was in the treasury before the trip? $n - 525 = 325$

5. By the end of one month a hardware store had 116 socket wrench sets left out of a shipment of 144. How many sets were sold during the month? $144 - n = 116$

6. After depositing his tax refund of $350, Manuel Ruiz had $1580 in his bank account. How much money was in the account before the deposit? $1580 - n = 350$

7. If Mary Ling follows her usual route to work, she travels 12 km on one road and 18 km on another. If she takes a short cut her total distance to work is 19 km. How many kilometers does she save by taking the short cut? $n = (12 + 18) - 19$

8. A department store's total receipts from a sale on pillowcases were $251.64. If 36 pillowcases were sold, what was the price of each?
   $36n = 251.64$

9. An investor has deposited $2000 into a special savings account. Two years later, the balance in the account is $2650. How much interest has been earned? $2000 + n = 2650$

10. Deane's account in the company credit union had a balance of $3155. After she made a withdrawal to pay for car repairs, her balance was $2855. How much money did Deane withdraw?
    $3155 - n = 2855$

150 *Chapter 4*

B 11. In a school election $\frac{4}{5}$ of the students voted. There were 180 ballots. How many students are in the school?

12. In a heat-loss survey it was found that $\frac{3}{10}$ of the total wall area of the Gables' house consists of windows. The combined area of the windows is 240 ft². What is the total wall area of the house? $\frac{3}{10}n = 240$

13. The difference between twice a number and thirty is 20. What is the number? $2n - 30 = 20$

14. A bookstore received a shipment of books. Twenty were sold and $\frac{2}{5}$ of those remaining were returned to the publisher. If 48 books were returned, how many books were in the original shipment? $\frac{2}{5}(n - 20) = 48$

C 15. By mass, $\frac{1}{9}$ of any quantity of water consists of hydrogen. What quantity of water contains 5 g of hydrogen? $\frac{1}{9}n = 5$

16. The balance in Peter Flynn's savings account is \$6800. A withdrawal of \$1000 is made, and the balance is to be withdrawn in 40 equal installments. What is the amount of each installment?
$6800 - 1000 = 40n$

11. $\frac{4}{5}n = 180$

Review Exercises

Write an equation for each word sentence.

1. Eight less than a number is forty-three. $n - 8 = 43$

2. Twelve times a number is one hundred eight. $12n = 108$

3. Fourteen more than a number is seventy. $n + 14 = 70$

4. A number divided by nine is twenty-two. $n \div 9 = 22$

5. A number minus seventeen is thirty-four. $n - 17 = 34$

6. Five times a number is sixty-five. $5n = 65$

Challenge

A thoroughbred is 80 m ahead of a quarter horse, and is running at the rate of 27 m/s. The quarter horse is following at the rate of 31 m/s. In how many seconds will the quarter horse overtake the thoroughbred? 20 s

Solving Equations **151**

Additional Answers
Class Exercises (p. 147)

2. If apples cost \$.59 per pound and you buy a bag of apples that costs \$2.36, how many pounds of apples are you buying?

3. How long will it take you to drive a distance of 630 mi at 48 mi/h?

4. A parking lot is filled to capacity at noon. If 25 cars leave the lot between noon and 1 P.M., and 175 cars remain in the lot, how many cars were parked in the lot at noon?

5. A \$256 television is on sale for \$219. By how much has the price been reduced?

6. Jack ran 26 km in 10 h. How far did Jack run in 1 h?

7. Marie can drive her car 25 mi on 1 gal of gas. How many gallons does she need to go 175 mi?

Suggested Assignments

Core
Day 1: 150/Prob. 1–10
Day 2: 151/Prob. 11–15
    151/Rev. 1–6

Enriched
    150/Prob. 5–10
    151/Prob. 11–16
    151/Challenge

Supplementary Materials

Practice Masters, p. 20

4-8 Solving Word Problems

The following five-step method will be helpful in solving word problems using an equation.

> ## Solving a Word Problem Using an Equation
>
> **Step 1** Read the problem carefully. Make sure that you understand what it says. You may need to read it more than once.
>
> **Step 2** Decide what numbers are asked for. Choose a variable and use it with the given conditions of the problem to represent the number(s) asked for.
>
> **Step 3** Write an equation based on the given conditions.
>
> **Step 4** Solve the equation and find the required numbers.
>
> **Step 5** Check your results with the words of the problem. Give the answer.

EXAMPLE 1 An evergreen in Sam's yard is now 78 in. tall. If it grows 6 in. each year, how many years will it take to grow to a height of 105 in.?

Solution

- The problem says
  present tree height, 78 in.
  tree growth per year, 6 in.
  future tree height, 105 in.

- The problem asks for
  number of years for tree to grow to 105 in.

  Let n = number of years for tree to grow to 105 in.

  Since the tree grows 6 in. per year:
  height after 1 year, $78 + 6$
  height after 2 years, $78 + (6 \times 2)$
  height after 3 years, $78 + (6 \times 3)$
  height after n years, $78 + 6n$

- We now have two expressions for the height of the tree after n years. We set them equal to each other.

  $$78 + 6n = 105$$

- Solve.
$$78 + 6n = 105$$
$$78 + 6n - 78 = 105 - 78$$
$$6n = 27$$
$$\frac{6n}{6} = \frac{27}{6}$$
$$n = 4\frac{1}{2}$$

- Check: If the tree grows 6 in. each year, in $4\frac{1}{2}$ years it will grow $4\frac{1}{2} \times 6$, or 27 in. The tree is now 78 in. tall. $78 + 27 = 105$. The result checks.

In $4\frac{1}{2}$ years the tree will grow to 105 in.

EXAMPLE 2 Two fifths of the members of the Riverview Sailing Club have signed up in advance for a club-wide race. On the day of the race, seven more members sign up, bringing the total of 41. How many members does the club have?

Solution

- The problem says
  two fifths of the members have signed up in advance
  the sum of this number and 7 is 41

- The problem asks for
  number of members in the club.

  Let n = number of members in the club.
  Two fifths of the members, or $\frac{2}{5}n$, have signed up in advance.
  The sum of this number and 7, or $\frac{2}{5}n + 7$, is 41.

- We now have two expressions for the same number. We set them equal to each other.

$$\frac{2}{5}n + 7 = 41$$

- Solve.
$$\frac{2}{5}n + 7 = 41$$
$$\frac{2}{5}n + 7 - 7 = 41 - 7$$
$$\frac{2}{5}n = 34$$
$$\frac{5}{2} \times \frac{2}{5}n = \frac{5}{2} \times 34$$
$$n = 85$$

- Check: Two fifths of 85 is 34, and $34 + 7 = 41$. The result checks.

The club has 85 members.

Solving Equations **153**

Additional A Problems

Solve each problem using the five-step method.

1. Karen types 15 words/min faster than Kim. If Karen types 75 words/min, how fast does Kim type?
   60 words/min

2. Jerry is 3 years older than Sal. If Jerry is 19, how old is Sal? **16 years old**

3. The sum when 51 is added to a number is 80. Find the number. **29**

4. Three fifths of the tickets for the theater are sold. This amounts to 270 tickets sold. How many tickets are there in all?
   450 tickets

Suggested Assignments

Core
Day 1: 154/Prob. 1–8
Day 2: 154/Prob. 10, 11
     154/Self-Test B

Enriched
Day 1: 154/Prob. 3–9
Day 2: 155/Prob. 10, 11
     155/Self-Test B

Supplementary Materials

Practice Masters, p. 20
Test 4B, pp. 25–26
Computer Activity 8

Problems

Solve each problem using the five-step method.

A

1. A mineralogist has learned that $\frac{2}{5}$ of a certain ore is pure copper. If a quantity of this ore yields 100 lb of pure copper, how large is the quantity? **250 lb**

2. Three tenths of the seats in a college's football stadium are reserved for alumni on Homecoming Weekend. This amounts to 4800 seats. What is the capacity of the stadium? **16,000 seats**

3. Three fourths of all the books in a school library are nonfiction. There are 360 nonfiction books. How many books are in the school library altogether? **480 books**

4. Charles has $800 in a savings account. If he decides to deposit $40 into the account each week, how many weeks will it take for the account balance to reach $2000?
   30 weeks

5. A department store received five cartons of shirts. One week later 25 shirts had been sold and 95 shirts were left in stock. How many shirts came in each carton? **24 shirts**

6. The four walls in Fran's room have equal areas. The combined area of the doors and windows of the room is 12 m². If the total wall area (including doors and windows) is 68 m², what is the area of one wall? **14 m²**

B

7. Three fifths of those attending a club picnic decided to play touch football. After one more person decided to play, there were 16 players. How many people attended the picnic? **25 people**

8. Four fifths of the athletic club treasury was to be spent on an awards banquet. After $450 was paid for food, there was $150 left out of the funds designated for the banquet. How much money had been in the treasury originally? **$750**

9. After using $\frac{2}{3}$ of a bag of fertilizer on his garden, Kent gave 8 lb to a neighbor. If Kent had 42 lb left, how much had been in the full bag? **150 lb**

154 *Chapter 4*

10. Marcie biked to a point 5 km from her home. After a short rest, she then biked to a point 55 km from her home along the same road. If the second part of her trip took 4 hours, what was Marcie's speed, assuming her speed was constant? 12.5 km/h

- C 11. When the gas gauge on her car was on the $\frac{3}{8}$ mark, Karen pumped 15 gal of gas into the tank in order to fill it. How many gallons of gas does the tank in Karen's car hold? 24 gal

Self-Test B

Write a variable expression for the word phrase.

1. The product of twelve and a number x 12x [4-5]

2. A number d subtracted from sixty 60 − d

Match each problem with one of the following equations.

a. $x - 18 = 72$ **b.** $18x = 72$ **c.** $x + 18 = 72$ **d.** $72x = 18$

3. At 72 km/h how many hours would it take a car to travel 18 km? d [4-6]

4. Seth bought 18 more model cars for his collection. If he now has 72 cars, how many did he have before? c

5. After the first day, 18 people were eliminated from the tournament. If 72 people were still playing, how many people started the tournament? a

Choose a variable and write an equation for each problem.

6. Luann's car gets 21 miles per gallon. How many gallons of gasoline will Luann use to drive 189 miles? 21n = 189 [4-7]

7. John Silver made a withdrawal of $450 from his bank account. If there is $1845 left in the account, how much did he have in the bank before the withdrawal? n − 450 = 1845

Solve.

8. At a recent tennis tournament, $\frac{3}{4}$ of the new balls were used. If 309 balls were used, how many new balls were there at the start of the tournament? 412 tennis balls [4-8]

Self-Test answers and Extra Practice are at the back of the book.

Write a variable expression for the word phrase.

1. Twelve less than a number m m − 12

2. The product of five and a number g 5g

Match each problem with one of the following equations.

a. $x - 12 = 46$ **b.** $12x = 46$
c. $x + 12 = 46$ **d.** $46x = 12$

3. At 46 km/h, how many hours would it take a car to travel 12 km? d

4. If 46 yd of material are to be cut into 12 equal lengths, how long will each length be? b

5. Ryan wrote out 46 birthday invitations and sent 12 of them. How many more does he have to send? c

Choose a variable and write an equation for each problem.

6. Carol bought some 12-cent stamps and twenty-four 20-cent stamps. If she spent $8.64, how many 12-cent stamps did she buy? Let x = number of 12-cent stamps; 12x + 24(20) = 864

7. On Monday Hal worked on 14 computer problems, and on Tuesday he worked on 6 fewer problems. How many problems did he work on altogether?

Let x = number of problems altogether; x − 14 = 14 − 6

Solve each problem using the five-step method.

8. Mel's motorcycle gets 55 miles per gallon. How many gallons of gasoline will Mel use to drive 385 miles? 7 gal

Balancing Equations in Chemistry

The basic chemical substances that make up the universe are called **elements.** Scientists often use standard symbols for the names of elements. Some of these symbols are given in the table below.

Element	Symbol	Element	Symbol	Element	Symbol
Hydrogen	H	Helium	He	Carbon	C
Nitrogen	N	Oxygen	O	Sodium	Na
Aluminum	Al	Sulfur	S	Potassium	K
Chlorine	Cl	Copper	Cu	Iron	Fe

The smallest particle of an element is called an **atom.** A pure substance made of atoms of two or more different elements is called a **compound.** In a compound the numbers of atoms of the elements always occur in a definite proportion. The formula for a compound shows this proportion. For example, the formula for water, H_2O, shows that in any sample of water there are twice as many hydrogen atoms as oxygen atoms.

In some elements and compounds, the atoms group together into **molecules.** The formula for a molecule is the same as the formula for the compound. The formula for oxygen is O_2 because a molecule of oxygen is made of two oxygen atoms. A molecule of water is made of two hydrogen atoms and one oxygen atom, so its formula is H_2O.

When compounds change chemically in a chemical reaction, we can describe this change by means of what chemists call an equation, although the equals sign is replaced by an arrow. An example of such a chemical equation is the following.

$$N_2 \quad + \quad 3\,H_2 \quad \longrightarrow \quad 2\,NH_3$$

nitrogen   hydrogen   ammonia

This equation indicates that a molecule of nitrogen (2 atoms) can combine with 3 molecules of hydrogen (2 atoms each) producing 2 molecules of ammonia.

Notice in the example that each side of the equation accounts for

$$\text{2 atoms of nitrogen: } N_2 \ldots \quad \longrightarrow \quad 2\,N \ldots$$

and   6 atoms of hydrogen: $\ldots 3\,H_2 \longrightarrow 2 \ldots H_3$

A chemical equation in which the same number of atoms of each element appears on both sides is said to be **balanced**. What number should replace the __?__ in order to balance the following equation?

$$S \quad + \quad 2\,H_2SO_4 \quad \longrightarrow \quad ?\,SO_2 \quad + \quad 2\,H_2O$$

sulfur   sulfuric   sulfur   water
                acid   dioxide

To answer this question, let n represent the unknown number. Then by equating the number of oxygen atoms on each side, we have

$$2 \times 4 = (n \times 2) + (2 \times 1)$$

or $8 = 2n + 2$.

Solving for n, we find that $n = 3$.

Replace each __?__ with a whole number to produce a balanced equation.

1. __?__ NO_2 **3** $+$ H_2O $\longrightarrow$ $2\,HNO_3$ $+$ NO
   nitric oxide   water   nitric acid   nitrous acid

2. $4\,FeS_2$ $+$ **11** __?__ O_2 $\longrightarrow$ $2\,Fe_2O_3$ $+$ $8\,SO_2$
   iron sulfide   oxygen   iron oxide   sulfur dioxide

3. $Al(OH)_3$ $+$ $3\,HCl$ $\longrightarrow$ $AlCl_3$ $+$ **3** __?__ H_2O
   aluminum   hydrochloric   aluminum   water
   hydroxide   acid   chloride

4. C_2H_5OH $+$ **3** __?__ O_2 $\longrightarrow$ $2\,CO_2$ $+$ $3\,H_2O$
   ethanol   oxygen   carbon dioxide   water

5. __?__ C_2H_6 **2** $+$ **7** __?__ O_2 $\longrightarrow$ $4\,CO_2$ $+$ $6\,H_2O$
   ethane   oxygen   carbon dioxide   water

Solving Equations **157**

Similarities between chemical equations and algebraic equations exist in the use of coefficients and parentheses.

Chemistry	Algebra
$2NH_3$	$2(N + 3H)$
	$2N + 6H$

That is, for 2 molecules of ammonia (NH_3), 2 atoms of nitrogen (N) and 6 atoms of hydrogen (H) are required. A resemblance to the distributive property of algebra is also seen in chemistry.

Chemistry	Algebra
$4Al(OH)_3$	$4[Al + 3(O + H)]$
	$4[Al + 3O + 3H]$
	$4Al + 12O + 12H$

That is, $4Al(OH)_3$ represents 4 atoms of aluminum (Al), 12 atoms of oxygen (O), and 12 atoms of hydrogen (H).

Ask students to use this method to explain how many atoms of each element are required for $2H_2SO_4$ (sulfuric acid).

Chapter Review

Complete.

1. An equivalent equation for $2x - 4 = 16$ is $2x = \underline{\ ?\ }$. 20   [4–1]

2. The solution to $5(11 - 3 + 12) = 2x$ is $\underline{\ ?\ }$. 50

3. To solve $4x = 82$, you would $\underline{\ \ ?\ \ }$ both sides by 4. divide   [4–2]

4. The solution to $\frac{n}{9} = 27$ is $\underline{\ ?\ }$. 243

Write the letter of the correct answer.

5. Solve $\frac{4}{3}x = 60$. a   6. Solve $\frac{n}{0.15} = 15$. b   [4–3]

   a. 45   **b.** 80   **c.** $60\frac{3}{4}$ **a.** 1   **b.** 2.25   **c.** 22.5

7. Solve $\frac{3}{2}n - 5 = 70$. c   8. Solve $\frac{n}{6} + 9 = 10.5$. a   [4–4]

   a. 40   **b.** $112\frac{1}{2}$ **c.** 50   **a.** 9   **b.** 120   **c.** 96

9. Which expression represents the word phrase "the difference be-   [4–5]
tween seven and a number n"? b
   a. $n - 7$ **b.** $7 - n$ **c.** $7n - 7$ **d.** $7 + n$

10. Which equation represents the problem?   [4–6]

   Luis bought 3 records on sale. The original cost of the records had
been $29.85, but Luis paid only $23.25 for all three. How much did
Luis save on each record? c
   a. $29.85 + 3x = 23.25$ **b.** $23.25 - 3x = 29.85$ **c.** $29.85 - 3x = 23.25$

11. Write an equation for the following problem.   [4–7]

   A rectangle has a perimeter of 84 cm. Find the length if the width is
15 cm. b
   a. $2l + 2w = 84$ **b.** $2l + 30 = 84$ **c.** $2l + 15 = 84$ **d.** $2l = 99$

12. Use the five-step method to solve the following problem.   [4–8]

   Tanya and Sara went biking. When they returned, they found that
they had gone 18 km in 0.75 h. What was their speed on the trip? d
   a. 13.5 km/h   **b.** 32 km/h   **c.** 12 km/h   **d.** 24 km/h

Chapter Test

Supplementary Materials

Chapter 4 Test, pp. 27–28

Use transformations to solve each equation.

1. $x - 18 = 11$ **29**

2. $3(7 - 2) + x = 19$ **4**

[4–1]

3. $9n = 1$ $\frac{1}{9}$

4. $\frac{n}{11} = 13$ **143**

5. $15n = 12$ $\frac{4}{5}$

[4–2]

6. $\frac{2}{3}x = 24$ **36**

7. $0.55x = 11$ **20**

8. $\frac{x}{1.2} = 8.6$ **10.32**

[4–3]

9. $4n - 16 = 32$ **12**

10. $\frac{3}{4}n + 18 = 51$ **44**

11. $30 - \frac{1}{2}n = 11$ **38**

[4–4]

Write an expression for each word phrase.

12. The product of a number n and twenty-one **21n**

[4–5]

13. Nine times the quotient of a number n and 3 $9\left(\frac{n}{3}\right)$

Which equation represents the problem?

14. Toby Baylor wrote a check for $12 to pay a bill. Two days later he deposited $20 in his checking account. If Toby had $88 in his account after these transactions, how much did he have originally? **b**

[4–6]

a. $20x - 12 = 88$ **b.** $x - 12 + 20 = 88$ **c.** $x - 88 = 12 + 20$

Write an equation for the following problem.

15. Annette Loo's car gets 23 miles per gallon. She is planning a trip to San Diego. If Annette lives 345 miles from San Diego, how many gallons of gasoline will she use driving to San Diego? **23x = 345**

[4–7]

Solve the following problem by the five-step method.

16. Bill and Roberta are shipping boxes to their new house. It costs $35 to ship each box and there is also a charge of $50 for the entire shipment. If the cost of shipping the boxes, including the $50 charge, comes to $610, how many boxes are being shipped?
16 boxes

[4–8]

Review for Retention

Evaluate the expression when $a = 2$ and $b = 10$.

1. $6a$ 12

2. $5(b \div a)$ 25

3. Evaluate 7^3. 343

4. Write $10^2 \times 10^5$ as a single power of 10. . 10^7

5. What value of the variable makes $p = 1.3p$ true? 0

Find the solution or solutions for the given replacement set.

6. $5 - m = 3$; $\{0, 2, 4\}$ 2

7. $3(k + 2) = 21$; $\{1, 3, 5\}$ 5

Use the inverse operation to solve for the variable.

8. $5z = 60$ 12

9. $4y - 2 = 42$ 11

Write an equation for the word sentence.

10. Six more than the product of a number w and two equals ten.
$2w + 6 = 10$

List all the factors of each number.

11. 84 1, 2, 3, 4, 6, 14, 21, 28, 42, 84

12. 112 1, 2, 4, 7, 8, 14, 16, 28, 56, 112

Cumulative Review (Chapters 1–4)

Exercises

Evaluate the expression when $x = 2$, $y = 4$, and $z = 1$.

1. $x + y - z$ 5

2. $6(x + y) - 5z$ 31

3. $10y \div (3x + 2z)$ 5

4. $-x - y$ −6

5. $-y - (-3z)$ −1

6. $y + 5z - (-2x)$ 13

7. x^5 32

8. $3y^3$ 192

9. y^x 16

Replace __?__ with =, >, or < to make a true statement.

10. $31 \underline{\ ?\ } 24$ >

11. $206 \underline{\ ?\ } 260$ <

12. $581 \underline{\ ?\ } 519$ >

13. $-4.68 \underline{\ ?\ } 3.2$ <

14. $0.6 \underline{\ ?\ } -15.23$ >

15. $-8.99 \underline{\ ?\ } -8.98$ <

16. $\frac{1}{2} \underline{\ ?\ } \frac{4}{6}$ <

17. $-\frac{3}{7} \underline{\ ?\ } -\frac{4}{9}$ >

18. $\frac{11}{35} \underline{\ ?\ } -\frac{9}{40}$ >

What value of the variable makes the statement true?

19. $-6 + x = 2$ 8

20. $x + 5 = -3$ −8

21. $-11 + x = -31$ −20

22. $-5.1 + x = -7.4$ −2.3

23. $17.5 + x = -1$ −18.5

24. $x + 28.3 = -4.7$ −33

25. $3 - x = -2$ 5

26. $x - 7 = -11$ −4

27. $x - (-9) = -3$ −12

Simplify.

28. $\frac{2}{3} + \left(-\frac{1}{6}\right)$ $\frac{1}{2}$

29. $-1\frac{1}{4} + \left(-2\frac{1}{3}\right)$ $-3\frac{7}{12}$

30. $\frac{5}{8} + (-6)$ $-5\frac{3}{8}$

31. $\frac{11}{8} - \frac{11}{4}$ $-1\frac{3}{8}$

32. $-2\frac{2}{3} - 1\frac{1}{5}$ $-3\frac{13}{15}$

33. $-11\frac{3}{4} - \left(-12\frac{9}{10}\right)$ $1\frac{3}{20}$

34. $\frac{1}{7} \times \left(-\frac{1}{12}\right)$ $-\frac{1}{84}$

35. $-12 \times 1\frac{3}{4}$ −21

36. $-\frac{11}{16} \times \left(\frac{-9}{20}\right)$ $\frac{99}{320}$

37. $-11\frac{1}{9} \div 100$ $-\frac{1}{9}$

38. $2\frac{1}{3} \div \left(-\frac{3}{7}\right)$ $-5\frac{4}{9}$

39. $-10\frac{1}{3} \div \left(-3\frac{1}{5}\right)$ $3\frac{11}{48}$

Use transformations to solve each equation.

40. $y + 11 = 31$ 20

41. $n - 8 = 12$ 20

42. $29 = 5(6 - 3) + x$ 14

43. $\frac{2}{3}x = 16$ 24

44. $36 = 9y$ 4

45. $-13n = 182$ −14

46. $\frac{4}{3}t = -40$ −30

47. $1.6c = 1.2$ 0.75

48. $-1.5x = -22.5$ 15

49. $4p - 7 = 37$ 11

50. $\frac{1}{6}y - 7 = 14$ 126

51. $\frac{-2}{3}n - 11 = -7$ −6

Problems

> **Problem Solving Reminders**
>
> Here are some problem solving reminders that may help you solve some of the problems on this page.
> - Determine which facts are necessary to solve the problem.
> - Check your answer by using rounding to find an estimated answer.
> - Supply additional information if necessary.

Solve.

1. Calculator batteries are being sold at 2 for 99¢. How much will 6 batteries cost? **$2.97**

2. "My new camera cost a fortune," boasted Frank. "Mine cost twice as much as yours," returned Eddie. If together the two cameras cost $545.25, how much did Frank's camera cost? **$181.75**

3. A newspaper with a circulation of 1.1 million readers estimates $\frac{1}{5}$ of its readers have subscriptions. About how many readers have subscriptions? **220,000 readers**

4. Amos Ellingsworth earns $455 per week. About $\frac{1}{4}$ of his pay is deducted for taxes, insurance, and Social Security. To the nearest dollar, how much does Amos take home each week? **$341**

5. Sally Gray takes home $378.50 per week. She will get a $50 per week raise in her next weekly check. If Sally takes home $\frac{4}{5}$ of her raise, what will be her new take-home pay? **$418.50**

6. The population of Elmwood was 26,547 in 1950, 31,068 in 1960, 30,327 in 1970, and 29,598 in 1980. What was the total increase in population between 1950 and 1980? **3051**

7. The Carpenters make annual mortgage payments of $6430.56 and property tax payments of $1446.00. What are the combined monthly payments for mortgage and taxes? **$656.38**

8. Cormo Corporation stock sells for $13\frac{5}{8}$ dollars a share. If Lorraine has $327, how many shares can she buy? **24 shares**

9. At a recent job fair, there were $\frac{2}{3}$ as many inquiries about jobs in health care as in electronics. A reported 250 inquires were made about both fields. How many inquiries were made about health care? **100 inquiries**

State which of the numbers 2, 3, 4, 5, 9, and 10 are factors of each number. Use the tests for divisibility.

13. 282   **2, 3**

14. 513   **3, 9**

Add or subtract. Write the answer as a proper fraction in lowest terms or as a mixed number in simple form.

15. $\frac{5}{8} + \frac{3}{7}$ $1\frac{3}{56}$

16. $-\frac{7}{10} + \frac{1}{2}$ $-\frac{1}{5}$

17. $\frac{3}{5} - \frac{7}{8}$ $-\frac{11}{40}$

18. $2\frac{2}{3} - \left(-2\frac{1}{3}\right)$ 5

Multiply or divide. Write the answer as a proper fraction in lowest terms or as a mixed number in simple form.

19. $\frac{7}{2} \times \left(-\frac{14}{15}\right)$ $-3\frac{4}{15}$

20. $-3\frac{1}{2} \times \left(-2\frac{3}{4}\right)$ $9\frac{5}{8}$

21. $-\frac{9}{38} \div \left(-\frac{6}{19}\right)$ $\frac{3}{4}$

22. $2\frac{1}{2} \div (-5)$ $-\frac{1}{2}$

23. Write $\frac{10}{11}$ as a repeating decimal. $0.\overline{90}$

24. Write -2.875 as a mixed number in simple form.
$-2\frac{7}{8}$

5

Geometric Figures

The three fields shown in the center of the photograph are irrigated using the center-pivot irrigation system. Long arms, or booms, revolve around center pivots and distribute water over circular areas of land, such as those visible in the photograph. Although the booms miss the corners of the fields, traveling sprinklers would be much more expensive to use. The booms have the advantage of being able to control the amounts of water delivered with a minimum of labor.

Farmers have used irrigation for centuries, at least as far back as the Egyptians in 5000 B.C. Today we could not hope to feed the huge world population without the extension of water supplies by irrigation. According to a recent estimate, there are about 155,700,000 hectares of land under irrigation.

Career Note

The demand for a greater variety of farm products, for improved farming methods and machinery, and for more careful environmental planning has led to an increase in the demand for agricultural engineers. Manufacturers of farm equipment look for engineers to design systems and machinery. Engineers also participate in research, production, sales, and management.

Lesson Commentary
Chapter 5   Geometric Figures

Overview

In this chapter, students will review fundamental concepts of geometry and its language and notation to help prepare them for a formal course in geometry in the future.

The chapter begins with a discussion of points, lines, and planes and includes an introduction to geometric notation. A discussion of measurement introduces the concepts of length and congruence of segments, degree measure, and congruence of angles. For your convenience, the Resource Book provides protractors and centimeter rulers on black-line masters on page 161.

In the second part of the chapter students learn properties of triangles and use the idea of congruence to classify triangles by sides and angles. Lessons on polygons and circles are followed by a lesson on congruent figures. A formal introduction to congruent figures is followed by a discussion of rigid motions to help students visualize the implications of congruence. A lesson on geometric constructions concludes the chapter.

BASIC FIGURES

5-1 Points, Lines, Planes

Objectives *for pages 164–168*

- To name points, segments, rays, lines and planes.
- To identify intersecting and parallel lines and planes.

Teaching Suggestions

Vocabulary is such an important part of this chapter that you should have your students plan now to make a list of key words and symbols. Ask them to alert you to any terms which are entirely new to them. Spend additional time explaining these new concepts. To help students learn the vocabulary, have them prepare from their lists fill-in-the-blank sentences and True-False questions to use for brief discussions.

Point, line, and *plane* are undefined terms. The concept of undefined terms, although important, is difficult for many students and need not be emphasized.

Students probably have an intuitive understanding of the terms *point* and *line*. Build on this understanding by drawing representations of points and lines. Explain that although a dot drawn with chalk or pencil must have size in order to be seen, the point it represents has no size. Likewise a line has no thickness. Emphasize that a line in geometry is straight.

The concept of a plane is probably familiar. (Students may have learned about plains in social studies. Both *plain* and *plane* come from the Latin word *planus,* meaning "flat.") Use the walls, floor, and ceiling of the classroom as examples. Remind students that a plane extends infinitely in all directions and has no thickness.

Emphasize the use of capital letters to name points. Point out that the letter is best placed above or below the dot representing a point and not covering the dot. A dot representing a point on a line should be drawn far enough from the arrow to be clearly distinguished. Explain that even though any two points are used to name a line, segment, or ray, each such figure is composed of infinitely many points yet unnamed or not yet designated in the drawing.

You may wish to discuss the meaning of the phrases "exactly one" and "one and only one" by using equivalent sentences. "There is exactly one line through two points P and Q" is equivalent to the combination of the two sentences "There is a line through P and Q" and "There is only one line through P and Q." That is, a line through P and Q exists, and that line is unique.

Related Activities

To provide a challenge and a change of pace, ask your students if they can trace over the lines of the figures on the next page without lifting their pencils and without going over the same line twice. If they can do this, the figure is said to be *unicursal.*

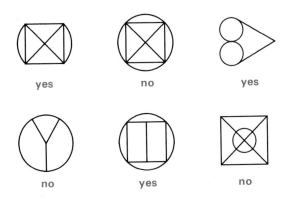

| yes | no | yes |
| no | yes | no |

Resource Book: Page 57 (Use After Page 168)

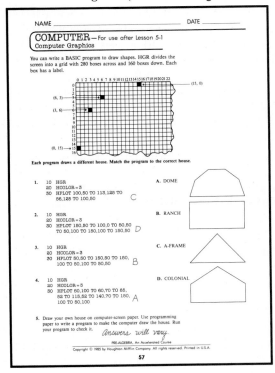

5-2 Measuring Segments

Objective *for pages 169–172*

■ To measure segments and determine congruent segments.

Teaching Suggestions

One way to provide students with practice in taking measurements is to measure objects in the school.

Students should differentiate between a segment and its measure. A segment is a set of points, whereas its measure is a number. We say the measures of two segments are equal, and write $AB = CD$, or we say that the segments are congruent and write $\overline{AB} \cong \overline{CD}$.

If time permits, you might discuss how every measurement of a segment is really an approximation. The degree of precision used in measuring depends on the application. A part for a fine surgical instrument may be measured to the nearest 0.1 mm, but the distance between two cities to the nearest meter. Because measurements are never exact, we can never determine that two segments are congruent by measuring them.

Related Activities

To provide another approach to the idea of congruent segments, you may wish to begin instruction in the use of compass and straightedge at this time instead of waiting until Lesson 5-8. Students can copy segments or construct a segment with a given endpoint that is congruent to a given segment.

It may be helpful to observe in this context that the construction of congruent segments does not rely on a standard unit of measurement. You can construct a segment equal in length to another segment without measuring.

5-3 Angles and Angle Measure

Objective *for pages 173–177*

■ To measure angles and identify types of angles.

Teaching Suggestions

To many students the most confusing aspect of using a protractor is knowing whether to use the inside or outside scale. It may be helpful to begin this section by showing students that they can use the corner of a piece of paper to determine if an angle is less than or greater than 90°. Some students may find it helpful to compare acute angles to a 45° angle, which can be obtained by folding a piece of paper so that two adjacent sides coincide. Although such estimations are very rough, they should make using a protractor much easier for students.

163b

To measure an angle accurately, it is important that students always extend the sides of the angle beyond the protractor scale. Emphasize that they should never guess where the side may meet the protractor. Be sure they realize that extending the sides does not affect the size of the angle.

As with line segments and their measures, students should also distinguish between an angle and its measure. An angle consists of two rays with a common endpoint, whereas the measure of an angle is a number. We say that the measures of two angles are equal and we write $m \angle A = m \angle B$, or we say that the angles are congruent and write $\angle A \cong \angle B$.

Related Activities

To encourage students to question the reasonableness of their measurements, help students develop their estimation skills. Have students draw angles of various sizes, estimate their measures, then measure using a protractor. Students can then exchange papers and repeat the estimation and measurement.

Resource Book: Page 58 (Use After Page 177)

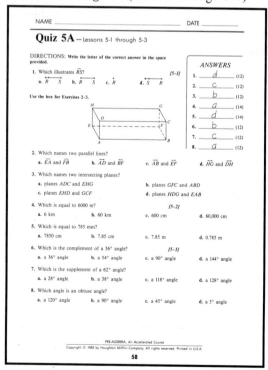

FIGURES IN THE PLANE

5-4 Triangles

Objective *for pages 178–182*

■ To classify triangles.

Teaching Suggestions

Students know intuitively that the shortest path between two points is the line segment joining them. Any other path is longer. Students can give concrete examples to justify this principle. For example, when a baseball is thrown from the pitcher's mound (P) to first base (F) to home plate (H), the ball travels farther than if it is thrown directly from the pitcher's mound to home plate. In geometry the shortest distance from P to H is PH. That is, $PF + FH$ is greater than PH. The sum of the lengths of any two sides of a triangle is greater than the length of the third side.

Exercises 30 and 31 provide a challenge. Although students have not yet learned to bisect angles and segments, they can do these exercises by measurement. In Lesson 5-8, when they have learned the necessary vocabulary and techniques, they can solve the same problems by geometric construction (page 200, Exercises 8 and 13).

The point found in Exercise 30, the intersection of the bisectors of the angles of a triangle, is called the **incenter.** It is the center of a circle inscribed in the triangle.

Exercise 31 defines the medians of a triangle. The point where the medians intersect is called the **centroid.** It is two-thirds of the distance from a vertex to the opposite side. The centroid is also called the point of balance. A cardboard triangle should balance at its centroid.

Related Activities

To demonstrate that the sum of the measures of the angles of a triangle is 180°, use a large paper triangle. Tear off the corners and fit them together as shown in the lesson. Have students repeat the demonstration with right triangles and obtuse triangles. The result is guaranteed to convince the most hardened skeptic!

5-5 Polygons

Objective *for pages 183–187*

■ To identify polygons and find their perimeters.

Teaching Suggestions

Draw on the chalkboard some polygons and some figures that are not polygons.

Of the figures above, *B*, *D*, and *F* are not polygons. *C* is a concave polygon.

The following diagram is often very useful when presenting special quadrilaterals.

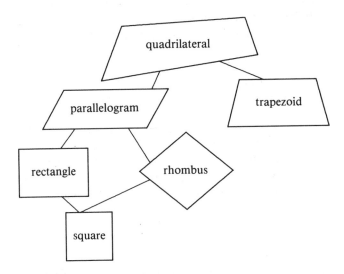

You can use this diagram not only to help students classify quadrilaterals, but also to help them distinguish the meanings of the quantifiers *some, all, every, each,* and *no.* For example, you can ask students to tell whether each sentence below is true or false and to use the diagram to explain the reasons for their answers.

All trapezoids are quadrilaterals. (True)
Every rhombus is a square. (False)
No rectangle is a rhombus. (False)
Some rectangles are squares. (True)
Every rectangle is a parallelogram. (True)
All quadrilaterals are trapezoids. (False)
Each square is a parallelogram. (True)

You may wish to show students how to mark congruent sides and congruent angles on their sketches with tick marks and curves, respectively. The marks on the parallelogram below indicate that

$$\overline{AB} \cong \overline{DC},$$
$$\overline{BC} \cong \overline{AD},$$
$$\angle A \cong \angle C,$$
and $\angle B \cong \angle D.$

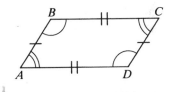

Related Activities

To provide an opportunity for a more thorough investigation of parallelograms, have students draw diagonals and complete a table like this one.

Property	Parallel-ogram	Rec-tangle	Rhombus	Square
Diagonal forms two congruent triangles	√	√	√	√
Diagonals bisect each other	√	√	√	√
Diagonals are congruent		√		√
Diagonals are perpendicular			√	√
Diagonals bisect opposite angles			√	√

163d

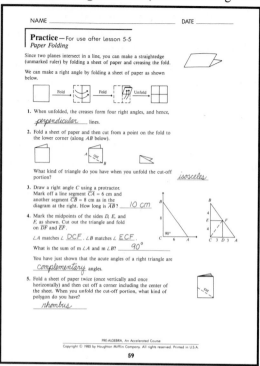

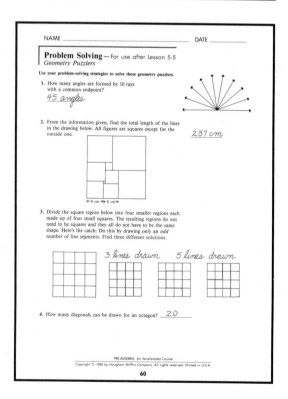

5-6 Circles

Objective *for pages 188–191*

■ To identify parts of a circle and find its circumference.

Teaching Suggestions

As a demonstration of the definition of *circle*, draw a point on the chalkboard and ask students to place points 20 cm from the given point. You may want to ask what would happen if we did not specify that the points be in a plane; in that case a sphere would be produced.

Students know that two points determine a line and that three noncollinear points determine a triangle. Although at this time you cannot prove that three noncollinear points determine a circle, you can show intuitively that this is true. Show a variety of triangles inscribed in circles and explain that triangles have a special property, namely that it is possible to draw a circle through each of the vertices.

Then show that not all polygons have this property by drawing polygons with circles that do not pass through all of the vertices.

Students may want to try drawing sketches of other polygons that cannot be inscribed in a circle. If some students draw a rectangle inscribed in a circle, you can explain that while it is possible to inscribe some quadrilaterals, you cannot inscribe all quadrilaterals in a circle.

Later, if you wish, after completing Lesson 5–8, you can use the perpendicular bisector construction to demonstrate that a circle can be drawn that passes through the three vertices of any triangle. To do this, construct the perpendicular bisectors of two sides of the triangle. Using the point of intersection of the perpendicular bisectors as the center and the distance from the center to one of the vertices as the radius, construct the circle that passes through all three vertices of the triangle.

You may wish to emphasize that 3.14 is only an approximation for π and that all calculations using 3.14 for π are also approximations. The results of these calculations can be no more exact than the approximations used. In this book all calculations using 3.14 for π are rounded to three digits. You may wish to caution students that, if they use the value of π on their calculators, their answers will probably differ from those given.

Resource Book: Page 61 (Use After Page 191)

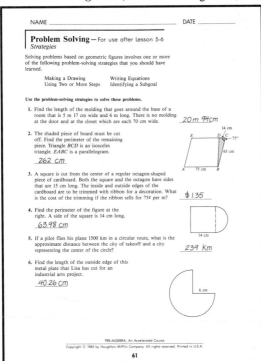

Related Activities

To reinforce the fact that the ratio of the circumference of a circle to its diameter is the same for any circle, you can use a variety of circular objects. With string and ruler, measure the circumference and diameter of each object. In each case divide the circumference by the diameter and record the results. Notice how many are *near* 3.14!

To provide a challenge, present the following problem. "If you tied a rope firmly around Earth's equator, lengthened it by 10 ft, and supported it so that it was the same height above the surface all the way around, how high would it be?" Students may be surprised when they calculate that the height would be 3.18 ft. This height is $10 \div \pi$ and is independent of the diameter of the sphere; students may want to prove this algebraically.

5-7 Congruent Figures

Objective for pages 192–197

■ To identify congruent figures and their corresponding parts.

Teaching Suggestions

Before teaching this lesson it may be helpful to review the definitions of congruent segments and congruent angles. If two angles have equal measures, they are congruent; and if two segments have equal measures, they are congruent.

When you present the tests for congruence, you could have the students experiment with possible tests. To demonstrate the side-angle-side test, for example, have one student draw a triangle with $AB = 5$ cm, $m \angle B = 30°$, and $BC = 7$ cm. Another student, before looking at $\triangle ABC$, can draw $\triangle XYZ$ with $XY = 7$ cm, $m < Y = 30°$, and $YZ = 5$ cm. Compare the triangles and show that

$$\triangle ABC \cong \triangle ZYX.$$

When you demonstrate the side-side-side test, be sure that the lengths you assign will form a triangle.

Not every set of three congruent parts will establish that two triangles are congruent. If the three angles of one triangle are congruent to the three angles of another triangle, the triangles may still be of different sizes.

The terms *translation, rotation,* and *reflection* are introduced because it is natural to test for congruency by imagining one figure being lifted up and set down on the other. However, students who have difficulty with spatial relations may need help visualizing the three kinds of rigid motions. You may wish to illustrate each by tracing a concrete object, such as a protractor, and then moving it physically through each of the three kinds of rigid motions.

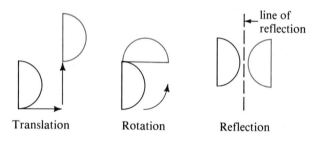

Translation   Rotation   Reflection

Some students can visualize reflections best by imagining that they are folding the paper along an imaginary line called a line of reflection. Congruent figures will coincide. The line of reflection for Example 2 is shown below.

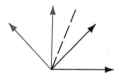

Related Activities

To provide a change of pace, challenge students to form four congruent equilateral triangles using nine congruent lengths (toothpicks). Then challenge successful students to form four congruent equilateral triangles using six congruent lengths.

5-8 Geometric Constructions

Objective *for pages 198–201*

■ To construct geometric figures.

Teaching Suggestions

As you begin this lesson, a few helpful hints and a demonstration on the use of a compass and straightedge can spare your students some frustration. If they use rulers as straightedges, you may want to have them put masking tape over the markings to remind them that the straightedge is not used to measure lengths. Suggest that they place a second sheet of paper or cardboard under the paper they are using. This helps to anchor the compass, preventing it from sliding on the hard desk surface, and also protects the desk top. Show students how to hold a compass and how to draw arcs using only the thumb and forefinger of one hand. Caution them against applying inward pressure to the pencil of the compass as doing so will change the radius and give unsatisfactory results.

Encourage students to make large constructions because the compass is usually easier to use with a radius greater than 1 in. Students who are learning to use a compass for the first time will benefit from practice in making random arcs and circles and constructing congruent segments before trying the constructions of this lesson.

Throughout this section keep emphasizing the need for large drawings. It will be almost impossible to do Exercises 7–9 if a student begins with a small triangle.

In Exercise 9, students find that the perpendicular bisectors of the sides of a triangle are concurrent. The point where the bisectors meet is called the **circumcenter** of the triangle. The distance from this point to each vertex is the same and would be the radius of a circle circumscribed around the triangle.

Related Activities

To provide a challenge for students, explain that, although it is impossible to trisect an angle using only straightedge and compass, it is fairly easy to approximate a trisecting line, using these steps:

1. Given $\angle XOY$, construct bisector $\overrightarrow{OA}$.

2. Construct the bisector of $\angle XOA$; label the bisector $\overrightarrow{OB}$.

3. Construct $\overrightarrow{OC}$, the bisector of the angle formed by $\overrightarrow{OA}$ and $\overrightarrow{OB}$.

4. Construct $\overrightarrow{OD}$, the bisector of the angle formed by $\overrightarrow{OB}$ and $\overrightarrow{OC}$.

5. Continue in this manner.

The bisectors will approach a line that divides the original angle in the ratio of two to one.

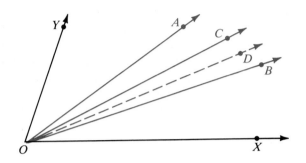

Resource Book: Page 62 (Use After Page 201)

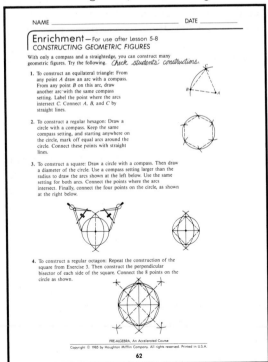

Resource Book: Pages 63-64 (Use After Page 201)

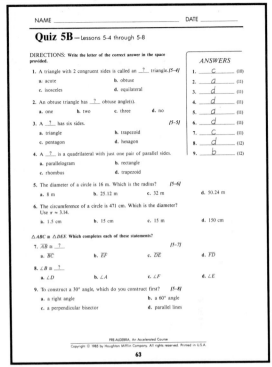

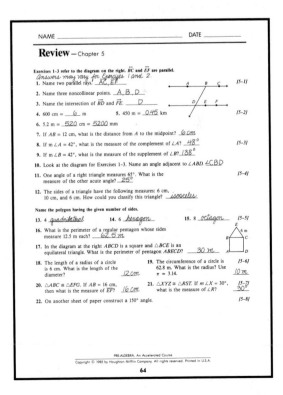

Panel 1 (page 65)

NAME _____ DATE _____

Test — Chapter 5

DIRECTIONS: **Write the answers in the spaces provided.**

Exercises 1–3 refer to the diagram at the right.

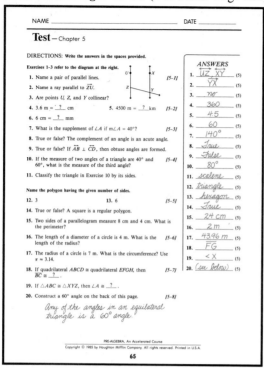

1. Name a pair of parallel lines. [5-1]
2. Name a ray parallel to $\overleftrightarrow{ZU}$.
3. Are points U, Z, and Y collinear?
4. 3.6 m = __?__ cm   5. 4500 m = __?__ km [5-2]
6. 6 cm = __?__ mm
7. What is the supplement of $\angle A$ if $m\angle A = 40°$? [5-3]
8. True or false? The complement of an angle is an acute angle.
9. True or false? If $\overleftrightarrow{AB} \perp \overleftrightarrow{CD}$, then obtuse angles are formed.
10. If the measure of two angles of a triangle are 40° and [5-4] 60°, what is the measure of the third angle?
11. Classify the triangle in Exercise 10 by its sides.

Name the polygon having the given number of sides.

12. 3   13. 6 [5-5]
14. True or false? A square is a regular polygon.
15. Two sides of a parallelogram measure 8 cm and 4 cm. What is the perimeter?
16. The length of a diameter of a circle is 4 m. What is the [5-6] length of the radius?
17. The radius of a circle is 7 m. What is the circumference? Use $\pi = 3.14$.
18. If quadrilateral $ABCD \cong$ quadrilateral $EFGH$, then [5-7] $\overline{BC} \cong$ __?__.
19. If $\triangle ABC \cong \triangle XYZ$, then $\angle A \cong$ __?__.
20. Construct a 60° angle on the back of this page. [5-8]

Any of the angles in an equilateral triangle is a 60° angle.

ANSWERS	
1. $\overleftrightarrow{UZ}, \overleftrightarrow{XY}$	(5)
2. $\overrightarrow{YX}$	(5)
3. no	(5)
4. 360	(5)
5. 4.5	(5)
6. 60	(5)
7. 140°	(5)
8. True	(5)
9. False	(5)
10. 80°	(5)
11. scalene	(5)
12. triangle	(5)
13. hexagon	(5)
14. True	(5)
15. 24 cm	(5)
16. 2 m	(5)
17. 43.96 m	(5)
18. $\overline{FG}$	(5)
19. $\angle X$	(5)
20. (see below)	(5)

65

Panel 2 (page 66)

NAME _____ DATE _____

Make-up Test — Chapter 5

DIRECTIONS: **Write the answers in the spaces provided.**

Exercises 1–3 refer to the diagram at the right.

1. Name three rays with the endpoint B. [5-1]
2. Name two lines that intersect.
3. Are points D, B, C noncollinear?
4. 450 cm = __?__ m   5. 7.6 km = __?__ m [5-2]
6. 14 mm = __?__ cm
7. What is the complement of $\angle A$ if $m\angle A = 30°$? [5-3]
8. True or false? The supplement of an angle cannot be an obtuse angle.
9. True or false? If $\overleftrightarrow{AB} \perp \overleftrightarrow{CD}$, then right angles are formed.
10. Two angles of a triangle measure 20° each. What is the [5-4] measure of the third angle?
11. Classify the triangle in Exercise 10 by its angles.

Name the polygon having the given number of sides.

12. 5   13. 8 [5-5]
14. True or false? A rhombus is a regular polygon.
15. One side of a regular hexagon measures 12 cm. What is the perimeter?
16. The length of a radius of a circle is 4 cm. What is the [5-6] length of the diameter?
17. The radius of a circle is 6 m. What is the length of the circumference? Use $\pi = 3.14$.
18. If $\triangle ABC \cong \triangle XYZ$, then $\overline{BC} \cong$ __?__. [5-7]
19. If quadrilateral $ABCD \cong$ quadrilateral $WXYZ$, then $\angle B \cong$ __?__.
20. Construct a 45° angle on the back of this page. [5-8]

Construct a 90° angle. Then construct its bisector.

ANSWERS	
1. $\overrightarrow{BA}, \overrightarrow{BD}, \overrightarrow{BC}$	(5)
2. $\overleftrightarrow{AB}, \overleftrightarrow{BC}$	(5)
3. yes	(5)
4. 4.5	(5)
5. 7600	(5)
6. 1.4	(5)
7. 60°	(5)
8. False	(5)
9. True	(5)
10. 140°	(5)
11. obtuse	(5)
12. pentagon	(5)
13. octagon	(5)
14. False	(5)
15. 72 cm	(5)
16. 8 cm	(5)
17. 37.68 m	(5)
18. $\overline{YZ}$	(5)
19. $\angle X$	(5)
20. (see below)	(5)

66

Panel 3 (page 67)

NAME _____ DATE _____

CUMULATIVE REVIEW — Chapters 1-5
Exercises

Evaluate the expression when $a = 2$ and $b = 4$.

1. $2a + b$ 8
2. $-5a + b$ -6
3. $a + 9b$ 38
4. $b - a + 5$ 7
5. a^3 8
6. $(ab)^2$ 64
7. $a^2 b^2$ 64
8. $a^2 b$ 16
9. $(2a)^3$ 64

Solve using transformations.

10. $y + 12 = 60$ 48
11. $c - 31 = -10$ 21
12. $6x = 72$ 12
13. $-5a = 120$ -24
14. $\frac{n}{4} = 12$ 48
15. $-\frac{2a}{3} = 6$ -9
16. $\frac{5}{6}y = 30$ 36
17. $0.2c = 6$ 30
18. $-0.4a = -10$ 25

Perform the indicated operation.

19. $\frac{1}{4} + \frac{5}{8}$ $\frac{7}{8}$
20. $-\frac{6}{7} - \frac{1}{5}$ $-1\frac{4}{21}$
21. $\frac{2}{15} + \frac{1}{5} + \frac{1}{3}$ $\frac{2}{3}$
22. $2\frac{1}{5} + 3\frac{3}{10}$ $5\frac{1}{2}$
23. $-6\frac{2}{11} + 5\frac{7}{11}$ $-\frac{6}{11}$
24. $\frac{9}{10} \times 20$ 18
25. $\frac{5}{6} \times \left(-\frac{4}{5}\right)$ $-\frac{2}{3}$
26. $\frac{9}{10} \div \frac{3}{20}$ 6
27. $\frac{5}{9} \div \frac{10}{21}$ $1\frac{1}{6}$

Express as a decimal. Use a bar to indicate repeating digits.

28. $\frac{3}{4}$ 0.75
29. $\frac{1}{3}$ $0.\overline{3}$
30. $\frac{2}{3}$ $0.\overline{6}$
31. $\frac{9}{10}$ 0.9
32. $\frac{4}{7}$ $0.\overline{571428}$
33. $\frac{14}{11}$ $1.\overline{27}$

Complete.

34. Lines in the same plane that do not intersect are called   parallel
35. Two intersecting lines which form right angles are called   perpendicular
36. In a   scalene   triangle, no two sides are congruent.
37. The   parallelogram   is a type of quadrilateral in which opposite sides are parallel and equal.

67

Panel 4 (page 68)

NAME _____ DATE _____

CUMULATIVE REVIEW — Chapters 1-5 *(continued)*
Problems

Problem Solving Reminders
Here are some reminders that may help you solve some of the problems on this page.
• Consider whether drawing a sketch will help.
• Check by using rounding to find an estimated answer.
• Reread the question to be sure that you have answered with the information requested.

Solve.

1. The Wilsons budget $140 per month for clothing. Last month they went shopping for clothes three times spending $29.83, $79.42, and $21.09. Did they exceed their budget? If so, by how much?   no

2. The Potters make annual mortgage payments of $9460.38 and property tax payments of $1856.82. What are the combined monthly payments for mortgage and taxes? $943.10

3. Joan Levenberg is an interviewer for a consumer research company. She must interview eight people in the next hour. If each interview requires 3 min of set-up time, how long can each interview last? $4\frac{1}{2}$ min

4. One morning, the temperature at 4:00 A.M. was 3° below zero. By 5:00 A.M., the temperature had fallen 4°. By 7:00 A.M., the temperature rose 5°. What was the temperature then?   -2°

5. The basketball coach ordered new towels for the team in packages of 6. The volleyball coach ordered new towels in packages of 12. The tennis coach also ordered towels but in packages of 8. If they each ordered the same number of towels, what is the smallest number of towels that could have been ordered in all?   72 towels

6. Eight students have been asked to decorate one bulletin board each to promote the school carnival. There are 44 large sheets of art paper left in the supply room. How many sheets will each student receive, if they are shared evenly? $5\frac{1}{2}$ sheets

7. The perimeter of a rectangle is 82 cm. The length of the rectangle is 34 cm. What is the width of the rectangle?   7 cm

68

LOGIC PROBLEMS

To challenge students to use their power of logical reasoning, you can use the problems that follow. These problems do not require the use of any specific mathematical skills; they are, therefore, suitable for use at any time throughout the year.

1. A man standing in front of a portrait says the following verse about the portrait: "Brothers and sisters I have none, but this man's father is my father's son." Who is the man in the portrait?

   The speaker's father's son must be himself. Therefore the man in the portrait is the speaker's son.

2. Linda, Dawn, and Ken have formed a rock band. One person plays lead guitar, one plays the drums, and one plays bass guitar. Only one of the following statements is true. Who plays what instrument?
   (a) Linda plays the bass guitar.
   (b) Linda does not play the drums.
   (c) Ken does not play lead guitar.
   (d) Ken does not play the drums.

   If (a) was the only true statement, that would mean that Ken would play the drums as well as lead guitar. Since each person plays one instrument, this must be false. Similarly, (b) must be false. If (c) was true, then Linda and Ken would both play the drums. Statement (d) must be the true statement. This means Linda plays the drums, Ken plays lead guitar, and Dawn plays bass guitar.

3. There are five teams in a local basketball league. From the following clues, can you tell the order that the teams finished in last year's season?
   (a) Cairo finished ahead of Acton.
   (b) Belmont finished ahead of Elwood and Dennis.
   (c) Acton finished between Dennis and Belmont.

   Since Acton finished between Dennis and Belmont, Cairo finished ahead of Acton, and Elwood finished after Acton, Acton had to finish third. It follows that Cairo finished first. Belmont finished second, Dennis finished fourth, and Elwood fifth.

4. Four neighbors have painted their houses, each a different color from the following choices; red, blue, white, and yellow. Determine from the clues the color selected by each neighbor.
   (a) Mickey didn't paint his house blue or white.
   (b) Mickey and Steve live across the street from Nancy and Miles.
   (c) All four neighbors started painting at the same time and the yellow house was the first one completed.
   (d) Steve bought all the paint for his house as well as a can of blue paint for one of his neighbors.
   (e) Steve's house took the longest to paint. The house next to Miles took the least time to paint.

   The person living next to Miles is Nancy. Since she was the first one done, her house must be yellow. Because Mickey didn't use blue or white, his house is red. Steve bought a can of blue paint for his neighbor, so his house must be white. Miles painted his house blue.

5. Two pairs of twins work in the same office. They live in four separate communities. From the information below, can you determine the names of each pair of twins?
   (a) Janet drives to work with Diane. Terry and Kim each commute alone.
   (b) Diane is the only person who can open the office.
   (c) Kim is always the last person to arrive at the office.
   (d) Janet's sister walks to work. Each morning she is waiting at the office to be let in.

   Because Kim is the last to arrive at work and since Diane commutes with Janet, Terry must be Janet's twin. Diane and Kim are twins.

6. Four trains, each from a different side of a city, are heading for the central terminal. From the following clues, determine which side of the city each train is from and the name of the town where each train started.
   (a) The train from the east was the first to arrive at the terminal. The train from Dover was the next to arrive.
   (b) The train from Harwich is not from the east or west side of town.
   (c) The train from Lakeville was the last to arrive, just after the train from the north.
   (d) Dover and Littleton are on opposite sides of the city.

   The train from the east, which arrived first, is not from Dover, Harwich, or Lakeville, so it is from Littleton. Therefore the train from Dover is from the opposite direction, west. The train from the north, which arrived third, was not from Dover, Littleton, or Lakeville, so it is from Harwich. Therefore the train from the south is from Lakeville.

Teaching Suggestions
p. 163a

Related Activities p. 163a

Reading Mathematics

Students will learn the meaning of the following mathematical terms in this lesson: *point, line, collinear points, noncollinear points, ray, endpoint, segment, plane, parallel lines, intersecting lines, parallel planes, intersecting planes, skew lines.*

The words *point, line,* and *plane* are undefined words in geometry; we can only describe them, not define them. Nevertheless, these words are used to define *line segment, ray, parallel lines, intersecting lines,* and *skew lines.* Using words like *costar* and *nonstop,* explain the meanings of the prefixes *co* and *non.* Then help students use their knowledge of these prefixes to define the words *collinear, noncollinear, coplanar, nonparallel,* and *nonintersecting.*

5-1 Points, Lines, Planes

All of the figures that we study in geometry are made up of **points.** We usually picture a single point by making a dot and labeling it with a capital letter.

P Q

Point P Point Q

Among the most important geometric figures that we study are straight lines, or simply **lines.** You probably know this important fact about lines:

Two points determine exactly one line.

This means that through two points P and Q we can draw one line, and only one line, which we denote by $\overleftrightarrow{PQ}$ (or $\overleftrightarrow{QP}$).

Line PQ: $\overleftrightarrow{PQ}$, or $\overleftrightarrow{QP}$

Notice the use of arrowheads to show that a line extends without end in either direction.

Three points may or may not lie on the same line. Three or more points that do lie on the same line are called **collinear.** Points not on the same line are called **noncollinear.**

If we take a point P on a line and all the points on the line that lie on one side of P, we have a **ray** with **endpoint** P. We name a ray by naming first its endpoint and then any other point on it.

Ray PQ: $\overrightarrow{PQ}$ Ray BA: $\overrightarrow{BA}$

It is important to remember that the endpoint is always named first. $\overrightarrow{AB}$ is *not* the same ray as $\overrightarrow{BA}$.

If we take two points P and Q on a line and all the points that lie between P and Q, we have a **segment** denoted by $\overline{PQ}$ (or $\overline{QP}$). The points P and Q are called the **endpoints** of $\overline{PQ}$.

Segment PQ: $\overline{PQ}$, or $\overline{QP}$

164 *Chapter 5*

EXAMPLE 1 Name (a) one line, (b) two rays, (c) three segments, (d) three collinear points, and (e) three noncollinear points in the given diagram. (Various answers are possible.)

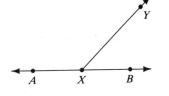

Solution   **a.** $\overleftrightarrow{AB}$ **b.** $\overrightarrow{XY}, \overrightarrow{AB}$ **c.** $\overline{AX}, \overline{XB}, \overline{XY}$ **d.** A, X, B **e.** A, Y, B

Just as two points determine a line, three noncollinear points in space determine a flat surface called a **plane.** We can name a plane by naming any three noncollinear points on it. Because a plane extends without limit in all directions of the surface, we can show only part of it, as in the figure below.

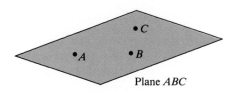

Plane ABC

Lines in the same plane that do not intersect are called **parallel lines.** Two segments or rays are parallel if they are parts of parallel lines. "$\overleftrightarrow{AB}$ is parallel to $\overleftrightarrow{CD}$" may be written as $\overleftrightarrow{AB} \parallel \overleftrightarrow{CD}$.

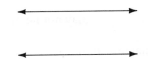

Intersecting lines intersect in a point.

Parallel lines do not intersect.

Planes that do not intersect are called **parallel planes.**

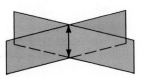

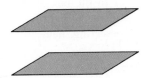

Intersecting planes intersect in a line.

Parallel planes do not intersect.

Geometric Figures   **165**

Chalkboard Examples

Draw and label noncollinear points *A*, *B*, and *C*. Draw the figure specified.

Check students' drawings.
1. $\overline{AB}$ **2.** $\overrightarrow{BC}$ **3.** $\overleftrightarrow{AC}$
4. $\overleftrightarrow{BD}$ parallel to $\overleftrightarrow{AC}$

Copy the figure. Name the points.

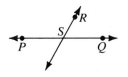

5. 3 collinear points
   P, S, Q

6. 3 noncollinear points
   P, S, R or *Q, S, R* or *P, R, Q*

7. The intersection of $\overrightarrow{PQ}$ and $\overrightarrow{SR}$ *S*

165

EXAMPLE 2 Use the box to name (a) two parallel lines, (b) two parallel planes, (c) two intersecting lines, (d) two intersecting planes, and (e) two nonparallel lines that do not intersect. (Various answers are possible.)

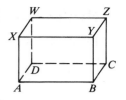

Solution

a. $\overleftrightarrow{AX}$ and $\overleftrightarrow{BY}$

b. plane ABC and plane XYZ

c. $\overleftrightarrow{AB}$ and $\overleftrightarrow{AX}$

d. plane ABC and plane ABY

e. $\overleftrightarrow{AD}$ and $\overleftrightarrow{BY}$

Two nonparallel lines that do not intersect, such as $\overleftrightarrow{AD}$ and $\overleftrightarrow{BY}$ in Example 2, are called **skew lines**.

Class Exercises

Tell how many endpoints each figure has.

1. a segment two

2. a line none

3. a plane none

4. a ray one

Exercises 5–9 refer to the diagram at the right in which $\overleftrightarrow{AB}$ and $\overleftrightarrow{CD}$ are parallel lines. Answers may vary.

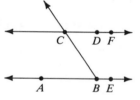

5. Name three collinear points. C, D, F or A, B, E

6. Name two parallel rays. $\overrightarrow{CD}$, $\overrightarrow{BE}$, or $\overrightarrow{DC}$, $\overrightarrow{BA}$

7. Name two parallel segments. $\overline{CD}$, $\overline{AB}$

8. Name two segments that are not parallel. $\overline{CB}$, $\overline{CD}$

9. Name two rays that are not parallel. $\overrightarrow{BC}$, $\overrightarrow{BA}$

Exercises 10–14 refer to the box at the right. Classify each pair of planes as parallel or intersecting. If the planes are intersecting, name the line of intersection.

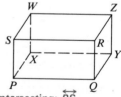

10. planes QRY and WSP parallel

11. planes PQR and $\overleftrightarrow{PSW}$ intersecting; $\overleftrightarrow{PS}$

12. planes SPW and XYQ intersecting; $\overleftrightarrow{XP}$

13. planes PQR and WXY parallel

14. In the box are $\overleftrightarrow{WX}$ and $\overleftrightarrow{RS}$ parallel, intersecting, or skew? skew

Written Exercises

In Exercises 1–4, give another name for the indicated figure.

A **1.** $\overline{XY}$
$\overline{YX}$

2. $\overleftrightarrow{BC}$ $\overleftrightarrow{AB}$ or $\overleftrightarrow{AC}$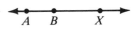

3. $\overrightarrow{PR}$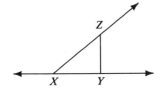
$\overrightarrow{PQ}$

4. $\overrightarrow{VU}$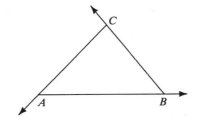
$\overrightarrow{UT}$

5. Name one line and three rays in the diagram below.
$\overleftrightarrow{XY}$, $\overrightarrow{XZ}$, $\overrightarrow{XY}$, $\overrightarrow{YX}$

6. Name three rays and three segments in the diagram below.
$\overrightarrow{CA}$, $\overrightarrow{AB}$, $\overrightarrow{BC}$, $\overline{CA}$, $\overline{AB}$, $\overline{BC}$

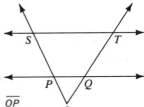

Exercises 7–20 refer to the diagram at the right. $\overleftrightarrow{PQ}$ and $\overleftrightarrow{ST}$ are parallel. (There may be several correct answers to each exercise.) Answers may vary.

7. Name three collinear points. S, P, O or T, Q, O

8. Name three noncollinear points. S, T, P or S, P, Q

9. Name three segments that intersect at P. $\overline{SP}$, $\overline{QP}$, $\overline{OP}$

10. Name two parallel rays. $\overrightarrow{ST}$ and $\overrightarrow{PQ}$

11. Name two parallel segments. $\overline{ST}$ and $\overline{PQ}$

12. Name two nonparallel segments that do not intersect. $\overline{SP}$ and $\overline{OQ}$

13. Name two nonparallel rays that do not intersect. $\overrightarrow{QT}$ and $\overrightarrow{PS}$

14. Name two segments that intersect in exactly one point. $\overline{SO}$ and $\overline{TO}$

15. Name two rays that intersect in exactly one point. $\overrightarrow{OS}$ and $\overrightarrow{OT}$

16. Name a ray that is contained in $\overrightarrow{OT}$. $\overrightarrow{QT}$

17. Name a ray that contains $\overline{SP}$. $\overrightarrow{OS}$

18. Name the segment that is in $\overrightarrow{PQ}$ and $\overrightarrow{QP}$. $\overline{PQ}$

19. Name four segments that contain O. $\overline{OP}$, $\overline{OS}$, $\overline{OQ}$, $\overline{OT}$

20. Name two rays that intersect in more than one point. $\overrightarrow{OQ}$, $\overrightarrow{OT}$

Geometric Figures **167**

Exercises 21–24 refer to the box at the right. (There may be several correct answers to each exercise.)

Answers may vary.

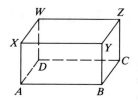

21. Name two intersecting lines and their point of intersection. $\overleftrightarrow{AX}$ and $\overleftrightarrow{XY}$; X

22. Name two intersecting planes and their line of intersection. plane BYC and plane WZD; $\overleftrightarrow{ZC}$

23. Name two parallel lines and the plane that contains them both.

24. Name two skew lines. $\overleftrightarrow{XW}$ and $\overleftrightarrow{YB}$ $\overleftrightarrow{XY}$ and $\overleftrightarrow{AB}$; plane XYB

In Exercises 25–32, tell whether the statement is true or false.

B **25.** Two lines cannot intersect in more than one point. True

26. Two rays cannot intersect in more than one point. False

27. Two segments cannot intersect in more than one point. False

28. If two rays are parallel, they do not intersect. True

29. If two rays do not intersect, they are parallel. False

30. If two points of a segment are contained in a line, then the whole segment is contained in the line. True

31. If two points of a ray are contained in a line, then the whole ray is contained in the line. True

32. If two points of a segment are contained in a ray, then the whole segment is contained in the ray. True

C **33.** Draw $\overleftrightarrow{AB}$ and a point P not on $\overleftrightarrow{AB}$. Now draw a line through P parallel to $\overleftrightarrow{AB}$. How many such lines can be drawn? One

34. Draw four points A, B, C, and D so that $\overline{AB}$ is parallel to $\overline{CD}$ and $\overline{AD}$ is parallel to $\overline{BC}$. Do you think that $\overline{AC}$ and $\overline{BD}$ must intersect?
yes

35. We know that two points determine a line. Explain what we mean by saying that two nonparallel lines in a plane determine a point.
Two nonparallel lines in a plane must intersect in a point.

Review Exercises

Round to the nearest tenth.

1. 2.87 2.9   **2.** 6.32 6.3   **3.** 4.56 4.6   **4.** 7.08 7.1

5. 2.98 3.0   **6.** 11.753 11.8   **7.** 9.347 9.3   **8.** 6.482 6.5

168 *Chapter 5*

5-2 Measuring Segments

In Washington, D.C., Jill estimated the length of a jet to be about 165 feet. When the plane landed in Paris, Jacques guessed the jet's length to be about 50 meters. Although the numbers 165 and 50 are quite different, the two estimates are about the same. This is so because of the difference in the units of measurement used.

The metric system of measurement uses the **meter (m)** as its basic unit of length. For smaller measurements we divide the meter into 100 equal parts called **centimeters (cm).**

We can measure a length to the nearest centimeter by using a ruler marked off in centimeters, as illustrated below.

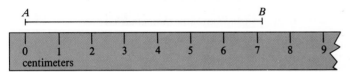

We see that the length of $\overline{AB}$ is closer to 7 cm than to 8 cm. The length of $\overline{AB}$ is written AB. The symbol $\approx$ means *is approximately equal to*. Therefore, $AB \approx 7$ cm.

The drawing at the right shows that the length of $\overline{XY}$ is about 3 cm.

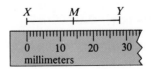

$$XY \approx 3 \text{ cm}$$

Measurements made with small units are more precise than those made with larger units. We can measure lengths more precisely by using a ruler on which each centimeter has been divided into ten equal parts called **millimeters (mm).** We see that to the nearest millimeter the length of $\overline{AB}$ is 73 mm.

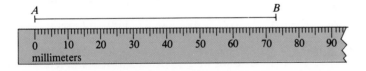

The drawing at the right shows that the length of $\overline{XY}$ is 28 mm and the lengths of $\overline{XM}$ and $\overline{MY}$ are 14 mm each. A point, such as M, that divides a segment into two other segments of equal length is called the **midpoint** of the segment. Thus, M is the midpoint of $\overline{XY}$. Segments of equal length are called **congruent segments.** The symbol $\cong$ means *is congruent to*. Since $XM = MY$, $\overline{XM} \cong \overline{MY}$.

Geometric Figures **169**

Teaching Suggestions
p. 163b

Related Activities p. 163b

Reading Mathematics

Students will learn the meaning of the following mathematical terms in this lesson: *meter (m), centimeter (cm), millimeter (mm), midpoint, congruent segments, kilometer (km).*

When reading geometry, it is important that, from the beginning, students develop the habit of reading each symbol correctly. The symbol $\overline{AB}$ is read "segment AB," and $\overleftrightarrow{AB}$ is read "line AB."

1. Name two objects in the classroom that you would measure in meters.
Answers will vary.

2. Name two objects in the classroom that you would measure in millimeters.
Answers will vary.

3. Name a distance that would normally be measured in kilometers.
Answers will vary.

Name all the pairs of congruent line segments.

4. Q is the midpoint of $\overline{PR}$.
$\overline{PQ} \cong \overline{QR}$.

5. X is the midpoint of $\overline{YZ}$.
$\overline{YX} \cong \overline{XZ}$.

6. A, B, C, and D are points on a line. B is the midpoint of $\overline{AC}$, and C is the midpoint of $\overline{BD}$.
$\overline{AB} \cong \overline{BC}$;
$\overline{BC} \cong \overline{CD}$;
$\overline{AB} \cong \overline{CD}$;
$\overline{AC} \cong \overline{BD}$.

Usually centimeters and millimeters are marked on the same ruler, as shown below.

To measure longer lengths, such as distances between cities, we use **kilometers (km).** A kilometer is 1000 meters.

> 1 m = 100 cm = 1000 mm   1 cm = 10 mm
>
> 1 cm = 0.01 m   (*centi* means *hundredths*)
>
> 1 mm = 0.001 m   (*milli* means *thousandths*)
>
> 1 km = 1000 m   (*kilo* means *thousand*)

Never mix metric units of length. For example, do not write 3 m 18 cm; write 3.18 m or 318 cm instead.

Class Exercises

Copy and complete these tables.

	1.	2.	3.	4.
Number of meters	4	? 0.6	? 0.52	? 0.036
Number of centimeters	? 400	60	52	? 3.6
Number of millimeters	? 4000	? 600	? 520	36

	5.	6.	7.	8.
Number of meters	3500	? 4200	475	? 34
Number of kilometers	? 3.5	4.2	? 0.475	0.034

9. Estimate the length and width of your desk top to the nearest centimeter. Answers will vary.

10. Estimate the length and width of this book to the nearest centimeter. 24 cm × 19 cm

11. Estimate the height of the classroom door to the nearest centimeter.
Answers will vary.

12. Estimate your height to the nearest centimeter. Answers will vary.

170 *Chapter 5*

13. Estimate the thickness of your pencil to the nearest millimeter.
Answers will vary.
14. Estimate the distance from your home to school in meters and in
kilometers. Answers will vary.

**In Exercises 15 and 16, *M* is the midpoint of $\overline{AB}$. Draw a sketch to help
you complete these sentences.**

15. If $AB = 18$ cm, then $AM = \underline{\ ?\ }^9$ cm and $MB = \underline{\ ?\ }^9$ cm.

16. If $AM = 4$ mm, then $MB = \underline{\ ?\ }^4$ mm and $AB = \underline{\ ?\ }^8$ mm.

**In Exercises 17 and 18, *P* is a point of $\overline{XY}$. Draw a sketch to help you
complete these sentences.**

17. If $XP = YP$, then $\overline{XP}$ is $\underline{\ ?\ }$ to $\overline{YP}$. congruent

18. If $\overline{XP} \cong \overline{YP}$, then P is the $\underline{\ ?\ }$ of $\overline{XY}$. midpoint

---

Written Exercises

**Measure each segment (a) to the nearest centimeter and (b) to the near-
est millimeter. (If you do not have a metric ruler, mark each segment on
the edge of a piece of paper and use the ruler pictured earlier.)**

A **1.** $\overline{AE}$ 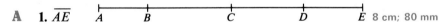 8 cm; 80 mm

2. $\overline{VZ}$ 4 cm; 40 mm

3. $\overline{MQ}$ 9 cm; 92 mm

4. $\overline{GJ}$ 4 cm; 38 mm

5. $\overline{PT}$ 8 cm; 82 mm

12 cm; 120 cm

6. $\overline{NX}$

7. In Exercises 1–6, which pairs of the segments $\overline{AE}$, $\overline{VZ}$, $\overline{MQ}$, $\overline{GJ}$, $\overline{PT}$,
and $\overline{NX}$ are approximately equal in length? $\overline{AE}$ and $\overline{PT}$; $\overline{VZ}$ and $\overline{GJ}$

8. In Exercises 1–6, name the midpoints of $\overline{AE}$, $\overline{VZ}$, $\overline{MQ}$, $\overline{GJ}$, $\overline{PT}$, and
$\overline{NX}$ given that the midpoint is named in each diagram. *C, X, O, I, R, A*

Geometric Figures **171**

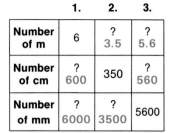

Suggested Assignments

Core
171/1–8
172/10–28 even
172/Rev. 1–5

Enriched
171/4–6
172/10–20 even; 21–32
172/Rev. 5–9

Supplementary Materials

Practice Masters, p. 21

Copy and complete these tables.

	9.	10.	11.	12.	13.	14.
Number of meters	4.5	1.63	? 2.5	? 0.826	? 60	? 0.368
Number of centimeters	? 450	? 163	250	82.6	? 6000	? 36.8
Number of millimeters	? 4500	? 1630	? 2500	? 826	60,000	368

	15.	16.	17.	18.	19.	20.
Number of meters	2000	20	625	? 3000	? 4500	? 250
Number of kilometers	? 2	? 0.02	? 0.625	3	4.5	0.25

Small units are often used to avoid decimals. However, it is sometimes easier to think about lengths given in meters. Change the following dimensions to meters.

B **21.** 374 cm by 520 cm 3.74 m by 5.2 m   **22.** 425 cm by 650 cm 4.25 m by 6.5 m

23. 4675 mm by 7050 mm
  4.675 m by 7.05 m   **24.** 5925 mm by 8275 mm
  5.925 m by 8.275 m

Rewrite each measurement using a unit that will avoid decimals.

25. 2.7 cm 27 mm   **26.** 4.32 km 4320 m   **27.** 0.65 m 65 cm   **28.** 10.6 cm 106 mm

For Exercises 29–32 use the following diagram and information.

C is the midpoint of $\overline{AB}$; D is the midpoint of $\overline{AC}$;
E is the midpoint of $\overline{AD}$; F is the midpoint of $\overline{AE}$;
G is the midpoint of $\overline{AF}$; H is the midpoint of $\overline{AG}$.

C **29.** If $AB = 140$ mm, $AH = \underline{\quad?\quad}$ mm. 2.1875   **30.** If $BC = 70$ mm, $AF = \underline{\quad?\quad}$ mm. 8.75

31. If $AG = 4.375$ mm, $AD = \underline{\quad?\quad}$ mm. 35   **32.** If $FE = 8.75$ mm, $DC = \underline{\quad?\quad}$ mm. 35

Review Exercises

Solve.

1. $x + 90 = 180$ 90   **2.** $x + 20 = 90$ 70   **3.** $x + 35 = 75$ 40

4. $100 - x = 45$ 55   **5.** $180 - x = 40$ 140   **6.** $90 - x = 30$ 60

7. $75 + x = 180$ 105   **8.** $180 - x = 115$ 65   **9.** $25 + x = 90$ 65

172 *Chapter 5*

5-3 Angles and Angle Measure

An **angle** is a figure formed by two rays with the same endpoint. The common endpoint is called the **vertex,** and the rays are called the **sides.**

We may name an angle by giving its vertex letter if this is the only angle with that vertex, or by listing letters for points on the two sides with the vertex letter in the middle. We use the symbol $\angle$ for *angle*. The diagram at the right shows several ways of naming an angle.

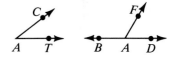

Angle *A*, angle *BAC*, or angle *CAB*
$\angle A$, $\angle BAC$,   or $\angle CAB$

To measure segments we used a ruler marked off in unit lengths. To measure angles, we use a **protractor** that is marked off in units of angle measure, called **degrees.** To use a protractor, place its center point at the vertex of the angle to be measured and one of its zero points on a side. In the drawing at the left below we use the outer scale and read the measure of $\angle E$ to be 60 degrees (60°). We write m $\angle E = 60°$.

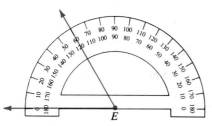
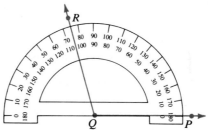

In the drawing on the right above the inner scale shows that m$\angle PQR = 105°$.

We often label angles with their measures, as shown in the figures. Since $\angle A$ and $\angle B$ have equal measures we can write m$\angle A = $ m$\angle B$. We say that $\angle A$ and $\angle B$ are **congruent angles** and we write $\angle A \cong \angle B$.

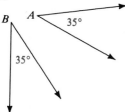

If two lines intersect so that the angles they form are all congruent, the lines are **perpendicular.** We use the symbol $\perp$ to mean *is perpendicular to*. In the figure $\overline{WY} \perp \overline{XZ}$.

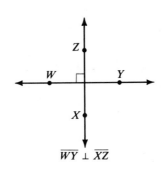

$\overline{WY} \perp \overline{XZ}$

Geometric Figures **173**

Teaching Suggestions p. 163b

Related Activities p. 163c

Reading Mathematics

Students will learn the meaning of the following mathematical terms in this lesson: *angle, vertex, side, protractor, degree, congruent angles, perpendicular lines, right angle, acute angle, obtuse angle, complementary angles, supplementary angles, complement, supplement, adjacent angles.*

It is acceptable to refer to the angle on the left as $\angle A$. In the figure on the right, however, three letters are needed to name an angle to avoid ambiguity.

An angle is the "complement" of another angle if the two angles are complementary. Likewise, an angle is the "supplement" of another angle if the two angles are supplementary.

Angles formed by perpendicular lines each have measure 90°. A 90° angle is called a **right angle.** A small square is often used to indicate a right angle in a diagram.

An **acute angle** is an angle with measure less than 90°. An **obtuse angle** has measure between 90° and 180°.

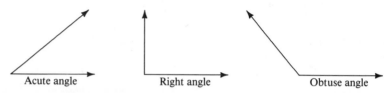

Acute angle   Right angle   Obtuse angle

Two angles are **complementary** if the sum of their measures is 90°. Two angles are **supplementary** if the sum of their measures is 180°.

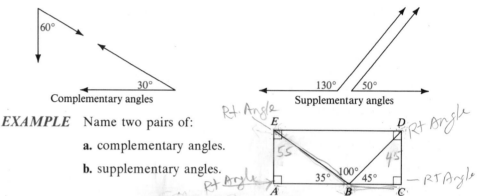

Complementary angles   Supplementary angles

EXAMPLE   Name two pairs of:

   a. complementary angles.

   b. supplementary angles.

Solution   **a.** Since ∠AEB and ∠BED form a right angle, they are complementary. Similarly, ∠CDB and ∠BDE are complementary.

   b. Since the sum of m∠ABE and m∠EBC is 180°, they are supplementary. Similarly, ∠ABD and ∠DBC are supplementary.

Although the sides of angles are rays, we often show the sides as segments, as in the figure for the example.

Reading Mathematics: *Symbols*

When you read a mathematical sentence, be sure to give each symbol its complete meaning. For example:

$\overleftrightarrow{AB} \perp \overleftrightarrow{CD}$ is read as *line AB is perpendicular to line CD.*

$\overline{AB} \cong \overline{CD}$ is read as *segment AB is congruent to segment CD.*

$AB \approx 6$ cm is read as *the length of $\overline{AB}$ is approximately equal to six centimeters.*

m∠A = 10° is read as *the measure of angle A is equal to ten degrees.*

174   *Chapter 5*

Class Exercises

1. If an angle is named $\angle EFG$, its vertex is __?__. *F*

2. If an angle is named $\angle GEF$, its vertex is __?__. *E*

Give three names for each angle.

3. Any 3 of:
$\angle Q$, $\angle PQR$, $\angle PQS$,
$\angle SQP$, $\angle RQP$

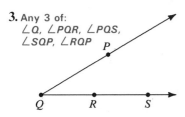

4. $\angle V$, $\angle UVW$, $\angle WVU$

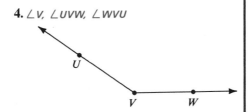

5. Use a protractor to find the measures of the angles in Exercises 3 and 4. $m\angle Q = 30°$, $m\angle V = 145°$

Exercises 6–9 refer to the diagram at the right.

6. Name five acute angles and one obtuse angle.

7. Name a pair of perpendicular segments. $\overline{AB}$ and $\overline{BC}$

8. Name a pair of complementary angles.
$\angle ABD$ and $\angle DBC$ or $\angle CAB$ and $\angle ACB$

9. Name a pair of supplementary angles.
$\angle ADB$ and $\angle BDC$

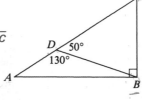

State the measures of the complement and supplement of each angle.

10. $m\angle F = 70°$
20°; 110°

11. $m\angle G = 15°$
75°; 165°

12. $m\angle H = 45°$
45°; 135°

13. $m\angle J = 60°$
30°; 120°

Written Exercises

Use a protractor to draw an angle having the given measure. Check students' papers.

A **1.** 75° **2.** 20° **3.** 120° **4.** 155°

Use a protractor to measure the given angle. State whether the angle is acute or obtuse.

5. 50°; acute

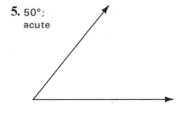

6. 30°; acute

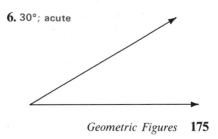

Geometric Figures **175**

Additional A Exercises

Refer to the diagram below to answer questions 1–4.

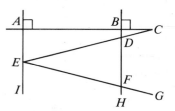

Answers will vary.

1. Name two right angles.
$\angle EAC$; $\angle DBC$

2. Name two acute angles.
For example, $\angle ACD$;
$\angle BDC$

3. Name two obtuse angles.
For example, $\angle AEG$;
$\angle IEC$

4. Name a supplement of
$\angle BDE$. $\angle BDC$ or $\angle EDF$

a. State the measure of the supplement of each angle.

b. State the measure of the complement of each angle.

5. $m\angle A = 31°$ 149°; 59°

6. $m\angle B = 62°$ 118°; 28°

7. $m\angle C = 83°$ 97°; 7°

Measure the given angle. Is the angle acute or obtuse?

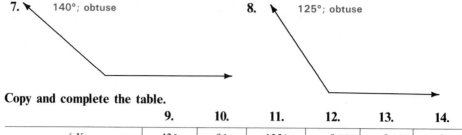

7. 140°; obtuse

8. 125°; obtuse

Copy and complete the table.

	9.	**10.**	**11.**	**12.**	**13.**	**14.**
$\angle X$	43°	9°	135°	? 78°	? 19°	? 30°
Complement of $\angle X$	? 47°	?81°		12°	71°	? 60°
Supplement of $\angle X$	? 137°	?171°	? 45°	? 102°	? 161°	150°

Use a protractor to draw an angle congruent to the angle in each given exercise.
Check students' papers.

15. Exercise 5   **16.** Exercise 6   **17.** Exercise 7   **18.** Exercise 8

Exercises 19–22 refer to the diagram at the right.

19. Name two pairs of perpendicular lines.

20. Name two pairs of complementary angles.

21. Name two pairs of supplementary angles.

22. What is the sum of the measures of the four angles having vertex E? 360°

Angles that share a common vertex and a common side, but with no common points in their interiors, are called *adjacent angles.*

B 23. Draw two adjacent complementary angles, one of which has measure 65°.
Check students' papers.

24. Draw two adjacent supplementary angles, one of which has measure 105°.
Check students' papers.

25. Draw two congruent adjacent supplementary angles. What is the measure of each? 90°

26. Draw two congruent adjacent complementary angles. What is the measure of each? 45°

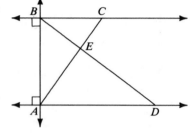

$\angle FEG$ is adjacent to $\angle GEH$
$\angle FEG$ is *not* adjacent to $\angle FEH$

True or false?

27. The supplement of an obtuse angle is acute. True

28. The complement of an acute angle is obtuse. False

176   *Chapter 5*

C 29. Measure the angles labeled 1, 2, 3, and 4. What general fact do your results suggest about angles formed by intersecting lines?

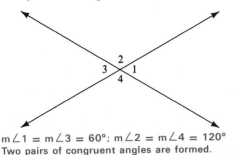

$m\angle 1 = m\angle 3 = 60°$; $m\angle 2 = m\angle 4 = 120°$
Two pairs of congruent angles are formed.

30. Measure the angles labeled 1, 2, 3, and 4. What general facts do your results suggest about two parallel lines intersected by a third line?

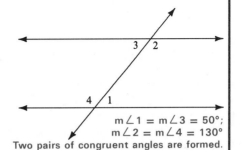

$m\angle 1 = m\angle 3 = 50°$;
$m\angle 2 = m\angle 4 = 130°$
Two pairs of congruent angles are formed.

Self-Test A

Draw a sketch to illustrate each of the following.

1. $\overline{CD}$ **2.** $\overleftrightarrow{AX}$ **3.** $\overrightarrow{RS}$ [5-1]

Exercises 4–7 refer to the diagram below. Answers may vary.

4. Name two parallel lines. $\overleftrightarrow{XW}$ and $\overleftrightarrow{YZ}$

5. Name two parallel planes.
plane *WXY* and plane *DAB*

6. Name two intersecting lines. $\overleftrightarrow{BC}$ and $\overleftrightarrow{ZC}$

7. Name two intersecting planes.
plane *DCB* and plane *ZCD*

Complete each statement.

8. 4000 m = __?__ km   4   **9.** 87 cm = __?__ m   0.87   [5-2]

10. 785 mm = __?__ m   0.785   **11.** 109 mm = __?__ cm   10.9

12. If M is the midpoint of $\overline{AB}$, then $AM =$ __?__ and $\overline{AM} \cong$ __?__.   MB, $\overline{MB}$

13. A right angle has measure __?__.   90°   [5-3]

14. Two angles with the same measures are __?__.   congruent

15. $\perp$ is the symbol for __?__.   is perpendicular to

16. A 37° angle is a(n) __?__ angle.   acute

17. The complement of a 42° angle has measure __?__°.   48

18. The supplement of a 107° angle has measure __?__°.   73

Self-Test answers and Extra Practice are at the back of the book.

Geometric Figures **177**

Complete each statement.

8. 6000 m = __?__ km   6

9. 42 cm = __?__ m   0.42

10. 232 mm = __?__ cm   23.2

11. 153 mm = __?__ m   0.153

12. If X is the midpoint of $\overline{PQ}$, then $\overline{PX} \cong$ __?__ and $PX =$ __?__.   XQ; XQ

13. The measure of an acute angle is __?__ 90°.   less than

14. Two angles whose measures have a sum is 90° are __?__ angles.   complementary

15. $\cong$ is the symbol for __?__.   is congruent to

16. A 125° angle is a(n) __?__ angle.   obtuse

17. The complement of a 23° angle has measure __?__.   67°

18. The supplement of a 122° angle has measure __?__.   58°

Suggested Assignments

Core
Day 1: 175/2, 4, 6
    176/8–14 even;
        19–26
Day 2: 177/29, 30
    177/Self-Test A

Enriched
  176/19–28
  177/29, 30
  177/Self-Test A

Supplementary Materials

Practice Masters, p. 22
Test 5A, pp. 29–30

Teaching Suggestions
p. 163c

Related Activities p. 163c

Reading Mathematics

Students will learn the meaning of the following mathematical terms in this lesson: *triangle, side of a triangle, angle of a triangle, vertex of a triangle* (plural, *vertices*), *acute triangle, right triangle, obtuse triangle, scalene triangle, isosceles triangle, equilateral triangle, median of a triangle.*

Encourage students to draw sketches when they read mathematics. A sketch should be of the most general case described. For example, a sketch of an "isosceles triangle" should be an acute triangle rather than a right triangle. You may wish to have students practice drawing triangles that you describe. For example, "obtuse triangle," "isosceles right triangle," and so on.

5-4 Triangles

A **triangle** is the figure formed when three points not on a line are joined by segments. The drawing at the right shows triangle *ABC*, written △*ABC*, having the segments $\overline{AB}$, $\overline{BC}$, and $\overline{CA}$ as its **sides**. Each of the points *A*, *B*, and *C* is called a **vertex** (plural: *vertices*) of △*ABC*. Each of the angles ∠*A*, ∠*B*, and ∠*C* is called an **angle** of △*ABC*.

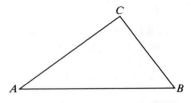

Suppose *A*, *B*, and *C* in the triangle above represent three points on a map. Do you think it is farther to travel from *A* to *B* and then to *C* or to travel directly from *A* to *C*? Measure to check. This illustrates the first fact about triangles stated below.

> In any triangle:
>
> **1.** The sum of the lengths of any two sides is greater than the length of the third side.
>
> **2.** The sum of the measures of the angles is 180°.

You can verify the second fact by tearing off the corners of any paper triangle and fitting them together as shown at the right.

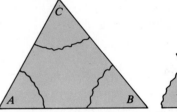
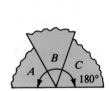

EXAMPLE 1   One angle of a triangle measures 40° and the other two angles have equal measures. Find the measures of the congruent angles.

Solution   The sum of the measures of the angles of a triangle is 180°. The sum of the measures of the congruent angles must be 180° − 40°, or 140°. Therefore each of the two congruent angles has measure 70°.

Problem Solving Reminder

Some problems do not give enough information. Sometimes you must *supply previously learned facts.* In the example above, you need to supply the additional information about the sum of the measures of the angles of a triangle.

178   *Chapter 5*

There are several ways to name triangles. One way is by angles.

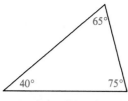

Acute Triangle
Three acute angles

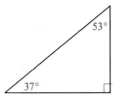

Right Triangle
One right angle

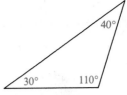

Obtuse Triangle
One obtuse angle

Triangles can also be classified by their sides.

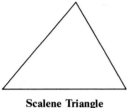

Scalene Triangle
No two sides
congruent

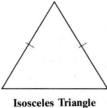

Isosceles Triangle
At least two sides
congruent

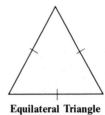

Equilateral Triangle
All three sides
congruent

As you might expect, the longest side of a triangle is opposite the largest angle, and the shortest side is opposite the smallest angle. Two angles are congruent if and only if the sides opposite them are congruent.

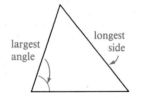

EXAMPLE 2   Classify each triangle by sides and by angles.

a.
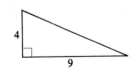

b.
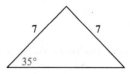

Solution

a. No two sides are congruent; the triangle is scalene.
There is one right angle; the triangle is a right triangle.
Scalene right triangle

b. Two sides are congruent; the triangle is isosceles.
The angles opposite the congruent sides are congruent; thus, the third angle has a measure of 110°; the triangle is obtuse.
Isosceles obtuse triangle

Geometric Figures   **179**

Is an angle with the given measure acute, right, or obtuse?

1. 88°
acute

2. 45°
acute

3. 90°
right

4. 94°
obtuse

Draw the figure. Use a protractor and a ruler if necessary. Check students' drawings.

5. An acute triangle

6. A right triangle

7. A scalene triangle

8. An obtuse triangle

What is the measure of the third angle?

9. 50°

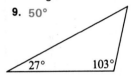

10. 80°

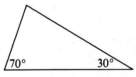

11. Draw an equilateral triangle. Check students' drawings.

12. Draw an obtuse scalene triangle. Check students' drawings.

Class Exercises

How do you know, without measuring, that these triangles are labeled incorrectly?

1. $5 + 2 \not> 8$

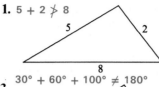

2. $7 + 7 \not> 14$

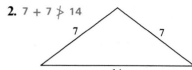

3. $30° + 60° + 100° \neq 180°$

4. $40° + 40° + 90° \neq 180°$

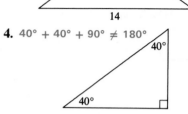

Exercises 5 and 6 refer to the triangles below.

a.   b. c. d.

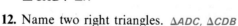

5. Classify each triangle by sides. scalene, equilateral, isosceles, isosceles

6. Classify each triangle by angles. right, acute, obtuse, right

7. Explain how you know that a triangle with two congruent angles is isosceles.

8. Explain how you know that a triangle with three congruent angles is equilateral.

Exercises 9–13 refer to the diagram at the right.

9. What segment is a common side of △ADC and △BCD? $\overline{CD}$

10. What segment is a common side of △ABC and △BCD? $\overline{CB}$

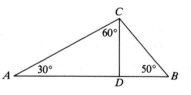

11. What angle is common to △ABC and △CAD? ∠A

12. Name two right triangles. △ADC, △CDB

13. Name an obtuse triangle. △ACB

180 *Chapter 5*

Written Exercises

The measures of two angles of a triangle are given. Find the measure of the third angle.

A **1.** 40°, 60° 80°   **2.** 15°, 105° 60°   **3.** 35°, 55° 90°   **4.** 160°, 10° 10°

Classify each triangle by its sides.

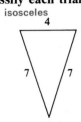
5. isosceles

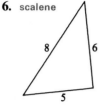
6. scalene

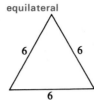
7. equilateral

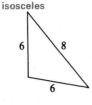
8. isosceles

Classify each triangle by its sides and by its angles.

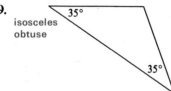
9. isosceles obtuse

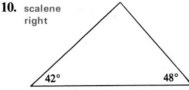
10. scalene right

11. scalene acute

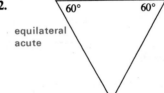
12. equilateral acute

Exercises 13–16 refer to the diagram at the right.

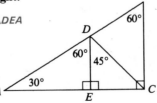

13. Name three right triangles. △BCA, △DEC, △DEA

14. Name an isosceles triangle. △DEC

15. Name an acute scalene triangle. △BDC

16. Name an obtuse triangle. △ADC

17. Use a ruler and a protractor to draw (a) a scalene acute triangle and (b) an isosceles obtuse triangle. Check students' papers.

18. Use a ruler and a protractor to draw (a) a scalene obtuse triangle and (b) an isosceles acute triangle. Check students' papers.

Geometric Figures **181**

B 19. What measures do the angles of an equilateral triangle have? 60°

20. One of the congruent angles of an isosceles triangle has measure 40°.
What measures do the other angles have? 40°, 100°

21. One of the acute angles of a right triangle measures 75°. What
measure does the other acute angle have? 15°

22. What measures do the angles of an isosceles right triangle have?
45°, 45°, 90°

23. An isosceles triangle has a 96° angle. What are the measures of its
other angles? 42°, 42°

24. An isosceles triangle has a 60° angle. What are the measures of its
other angles? 60°, 60°

25. One acute angle of a right triangle is 45°. What relationship, if any,
is there between the two shorter sides? They are congruent.

26. Why is it not possible to have an equilateral right triangle?

C 27. In $\triangle ABC$, $AB = 8$ and $BC = 5$. Then (a) $AC < \underline{\ ?\ }$, and
(b) $AC > \underline{\ ?\ }$. 13; 3

28. In $\triangle PQR$, $PR = 10$ and $RQ = 7$. Then (a) $PQ < \underline{\ ?\ }$, and
(b) $PQ > \underline{\ ?\ }$. 17; 3

29. Explain why in any triangle the difference of the lengths of any two
sides cannot be greater than the length of the third side.

30. Draw a triangle. Draw rays that divide each of its angles into two
congruent angles. Do this for several triangles of different shapes.
What seems always to be true of the three rays? The angle
bisectors intersect in one point.

31. Draw a triangle. Then draw segments joining each vertex to the
midpoint of the opposite side. (These segments are called **medians**
of the triangle.) Do this for several triangles of different shapes.
What seems always to be true? The medians intersect in one point.

Review Exercises

Add.

15.52
1. $3.75 + 4.92 + 6.41$ 15.08   2. $7.83 + 6.91 + 5.29$ 20.03 3. $8.36 + 4.95 + 2.21$

4. $5.3 + 6.21 + 7.3$ 18.81   5. $8.02 + 5.1 + 7.21$ 20.33 6. $3.07 + 4 + 5.93$ 13

7. $11.27 + 6.513 + 4.09$ 8. $10.03 + 5.7 + 4.93$ 20.66 9. $12.004 + 4.9 + 7.864$
21.873   24.768

5-5 Polygons

A **polygon** is a closed figure formed by joining segments (**sides** of the polygon) at their endpoints (**vertices** of the polygon). We name polygons according to the number of sides they have.

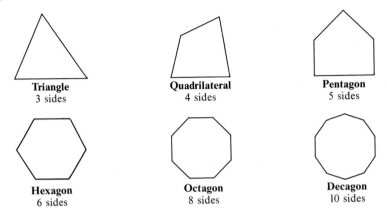

Triangle 3 sides	**Quadrilateral** 4 sides	**Pentagon** 5 sides
Hexagon 6 sides	**Octagon** 8 sides	**Decagon** 10 sides

A polygon is **regular** if all its sides are congruent and all its angles are congruent. As drawn above, the hexagon, the octagon, and the decagon are regular while the triangle, the quadrilateral, and the pentagon are not.

To name a polygon, we name its consecutive vertices in order. The quadrilateral shown at the right may be named quadrilateral *PQRS*.

A **diagonal** of a polygon is a segment joining two nonconsecutive vertices. Thus, $\overline{PR}$ and $\overline{QS}$ are the diagonals of quadrilateral *PQRS*.

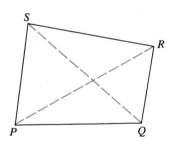

Certain quadrilaterals have special names.

A **parallelogram** has its opposite sides parallel and congruent.

A **trapezoid** has just one pair of parallel sides.

Geometric Figures **183**

Teaching Suggestions
p. 163d

Related Activities p. 163d

Reading Mathematics
Students will learn the meaning of the following mathematical terms in this lesson: *polygon, side of a polygon, vertex of a polygon* (plural *vertices*), *quadrilateral, pentagon, hexagon, octagon, decagon, regular polygon, diagonal, parallelogram, trapezoid, rhombus, square, rectangle, perimeter.*

It is a common mistake for students to overlook the order of the vertices when naming polygons. A suggestion to avoid such confusion is to have students imagine that they are actually drawing the polygon as they name it.

State the number of sides for the polygon.

1. pentagon 5

2. octagon 8

Complete.

3. A quadrilateral with only two parallel sides is called a __?__. trapezoid

4. Find the perimeter of a polygon whose sides have the lengths 6 cm, 12.4 cm, 14.6 cm, 21 cm. 54 cm

5. Find the perimeter of a regular pentagon whose sides are all 18 cm long. 90 cm

6. The perimeter of an equilateral triangle is 60 cm. How long is one of its sides? 20 cm

Certain parallelograms also have special names.

   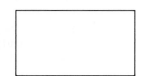

A **rhombus** has all its sides congruent.
A **square** has congruent sides and congruent angles.
A **rectangle** has all its angles congruent.

Reading Mathematics: *Vocabulary*

Many terms in mathematics have definitions with more than one condition. Be certain to read and learn the full definition. For example, a polygon is regular if (1) all its sides are congruent and (2) all its angles are congruent. Because the rhombus shown above does not meet condition 2, it is not a regular polygon. The square meets both conditions, so it is regular.

The **perimeter** of a figure is the distance around it. Thus, the perimeter of a polygon is the sum of the lengths of its sides.

EXAMPLE   Find the perimeter of each polygon.

a.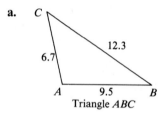
Triangle *ABC*

b.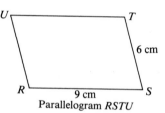
Parallelogram *RSTU*

Solution   **a.** Perimeter $= 9.5 + 12.3 + 6.7 = 28.5$

b. Because opposite sides of a parallelogram are congruent, the unlabeled sides have lengths 9 cm and 6 cm. Therefore:
$$\text{Perimeter} = (9 + 6 + 9 + 6) \text{ cm} = 30 \text{ cm}$$

Class Exercises

Name each polygon according to the number of sides.

1. 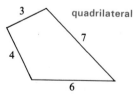 quadrilateral

2. hexagon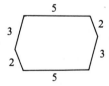

Name each polygon according to the number of sides.

3. 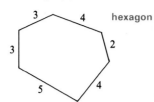 hexagon   **4.** octagon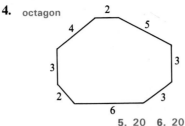

5–8. Find the perimeter of each polygon in Exercises 1–4.   **5.** 20   **6.** 20
                                                     7. 21   **8.** 28

9–12. State the number of diagonals that can be drawn from any one vertex of each figure in Exercises 1–4.   **9.** 1   **10.** 3   **11.** 3   **12.** 5

Give the most special name for each quadrilateral.

13.

Four congruent sides
Four congruent angles
square

14.

Four congruent angles
rectangle

15.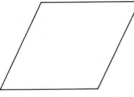

Opposite sides parallel
and congruent
parallelogram

16.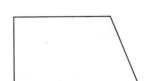

One pair of parallel sides
trapezoid

Written Exercises

Name the polygon having the given number of sides.

A   **1.** 5   pentagon   **2.** 4   **3.** 6   hexagon   **4.** 10   decagon   **5.** 3   triangle   **6.** 8
                              quadrilateral   octagon

7. What is another name for a regular quadrilateral?   square

8. What is another name for a regular triangle?   equilateral triangle

Geometric Figures   **185**

Find the perimeter of each pentagon.

9. 14.1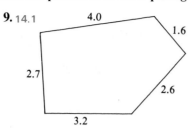

10. 14.7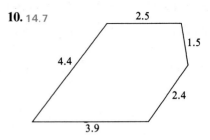

Find the perimeter of a regular polygon whose sides have the given length.

11. Hexagon, 52 cm 312 cm

12. Pentagon, 43 mm 215 mm

13. Triangle, 24.2 mm 72.6 mm

14. Quadrilateral, 16.5 m 66 m

15. Decagon, 135.6 m 1356 m

16. Octagon, 4.25 m 34 m

17. The sum of the measures of the angles of a pentagon is 540°. Find the measure of each angle of a regular pentagon. 108°

18. The sum of the measures of the angles of a hexagon is 720°. Find the measure of each angle of a regular hexagon. 120°

19. A STOP sign is a regular octagon 32 cm on a side. Express its perimeter in meters. 2.56 m

20. The Pentagon building in Washington, D.C., is in the form of a regular pentagon 276 m on a side. Express its perimeter in kilometers. 1.38 km

21. The perimeter of a regular pentagon is 60 m. How long is each side? 12 m

Exercises 22–24 refer to the hexagon at the right. The shorter sides are half as long as the longer sides.

22. Each shorter side is 3.2 cm long. What is the perimeter? 25.6 cm

23. How many diagonals can be drawn from vertex *A*? 3

B 24. How many diagonals are there in all? 9

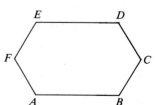

186 *Chapter 5*

Use a protractor and a ruler for Exercises 25 and 26. The sum of the measures of the angles of a hexagon is 720°.

25. Draw a hexagon that is not regular, but has all its angles congruent. Check students' papers.

26. Draw a hexagon that is not regular, but has all its sides congruent. Check students' papers.

27. In the diagram below, *ABDE* is a rhombus and $\angle DBC \cong \angle DCB$. Find the perimeter of trapezoid *ACDE*. 22

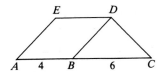

For Exercises 28 and 29 draw several polygons with different numbers of sides. Pick a vertex and draw all the diagonals from this vertex.

28. Count the number of triangles formed by the diagonals. How does the number of triangles compare to the number of sides of each polygon? The number of triangles is two less than the number of sides.

29. If the sum of the measures of the angles of the triangles formed equals the sum of the measures of the angles of the polygon, find the sum of the measures of the angles of the following.
a. quadrilateral 360° **b.** decagon 1440° **c.** trapezoid 360° **d.** octagon 1080°

C **30.** Write a general formula for the sum of the measures of the angles of any polygon with *n* sides. (*Hint:* See Exercises 28 and 29.)
$S = (n - 2) \cdot 180°$

31. Every pentagon has the same number of diagonals. How many? (*Hint:* First decide how many diagonals can be drawn from one vertex.) 5

32. Every octagon has the same number of diagonals. How many? (See the hint for Exercise 31.) 20

Review Exercises

Evaluate if *a* = 7, *b* = 3.2, and *c* = 5.45.

1. *ab* 22.4 **2.** *ac* 38.15 **3.** a^2 49 **4.** 15*b* 48

5. 2*c* 10.9 **6.** 2*bc* 34.88 **7.** 2*ab* 44.8 **8.** *abc* 122.08

Geometric Figures **187**

Suggested Assignments
Core
Day 1: 185/1–8
186/11–21
Day 2: 186/22–24
187/25–30
187/Rev. 2–8 even
Enriched
186/10–20 even; 22–24
187/25–31

Supplementary Materials
Practice Masters, p. 23
Computer Activity 10

Reading Mathematics

Students will learn the meaning of the following mathematical terms in this lesson: *circle, center, compass, radius, (plural radii), chord, diameter, semicircle, circumference, pi (π), inscribed polygon.*

Students sometimes mistakenly think of points inside a circle as part of the circle. It may help to mention that a circle with center O and radius *r* consists of all points in the plane whose distance from O is exactly equal to *r*. Points in the plane whose distance from O is less than *r* are *inside* the circle, and those whose distance from O is greater than *r* are *outside* the circle.

Similarly, because a semicircle is one-half of a circle, the semicircle does not include the diameter. You may wish to remind students of this fact before they do Exercises 30 and 31.

5-6 Circles

A **circle** is the set of all points in a plane at a given distance from a given point O called the **center.** The drawing at the right shows how to use a **compass** to draw a circle with center O.

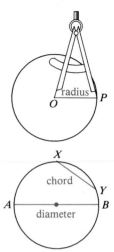

A segment, such as $\overline{OP}$, joining the center to a point on the circle is called a **radius** (plural: *radii*) of the circle. All radii of a given circle have the same length, and this length is called **the radius** of the circle.

A segment, such as $\overline{XY}$, joining two points on a circle is called a **chord,** and a chord passing through the center is a **diameter** of the circle. The ends of a diameter divide the circle into two **semicircles.** The length of a diameter is called **the diameter** of the circle.

The perimeter of a circle is called the **circumference.** The quotient

$$\text{circumference} \div \text{diameter}$$

can be shown to be the same for all circles, regardless of their size. This quotient is denoted by the Greek letter π (pronounced "pie"). No decimal gives π exactly, but a fairly good approximation is 3.14.

If we denote the circumference by C and the diameter by d, we can write

$$C \div d = \pi.$$

This formula can be put into several useful forms.

Formulas

Let C = circumference, d = diameter, and r = radius $(d = 2r)$. Then:

$$C = \pi d$$
$$C = 2\pi r$$

EXAMPLE 1 The diameter of a circle is 6 cm. Find the circumference.

Solution We are given d and asked to find C. We use the formula $C = \pi d$.

$$C = \pi d$$
$$C \approx 3.14 \times 6 = 18.84$$
$$C \approx 18.8 \text{ cm, or } 188 \text{ mm}$$

188 *Chapter 5*

When using the approximation $\pi \approx 3.14$, give your answer to only three digits (as in Example 1) because the approximation is good only to three digits. That is, we round to the place occupied by the third digit from the left.

EXAMPLE 2 The circumference of a circle is 20. Find the radius.

Solution To find the radius, use the formula $C = 2\pi r$.

$$C = 2\pi r$$
$$20 \approx (2 \times 3.14)r$$
$$20 \approx 6.28r$$
$$\frac{20}{6.28} \approx r$$
$$3.1847 \approx r$$

Since the third digit from the left is in the hundredths' place, round to the nearest hundredth. Thus, $r \approx 3.18$.

A polygon is **inscribed** in a circle if all of its vertices are on the circle. The diagram at the right shows a triangle inscribed in a circle.

It can be shown that three points *not on a line* determine a circle. This means that there is one circle, and only one circle, that passes through the three given points.

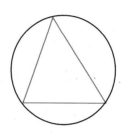

Class Exercises

Exercises 1–5 refer to the diagram below. *B* is the center of the circle. Name each of the following.

1. a diameter $\overline{AC}$

2. three radii $\overline{BA}, \overline{BC}, \overline{BE}$

3. five chords $\overline{AD}, \overline{AC}, \overline{AE}, \overline{EC}, \overline{DC}$

4. two inscribed triangles $\triangle ADC, \triangle AEC$

5. two isosceles triangles $\triangle EBC, \triangle ABE$

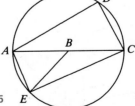

Exercises 6–8 refer to the diagram above.

6. If $BE = 8$, find AC. 16

7. If $AC = 10$, find AB. 5

8. If $BC = 20$, find the circumference of the circle. 126

Draw a circle and an inscribed polygon of the specified kind. Check students' papers.

9. a pentagon

10. a hexagon

11. an octagon

Geometric Figures **189**

Written Exercises

Use $\pi \approx 3.14$ and round to three digits unless otherwise specified.

Find the circumference of each circle with the given diameter or radius.

A 1. diameter = 8 cm 25.1 cm

2. diameter = 20 km 62.8 km

3. radius = 450 mm 2830 mm

4. radius = 16 cm 100 cm

5. diameter = 42.6 m 134 m

6. radius = 278 mm 1750 mm

Find the diameter of each circle.

7. circumference = 283 m 90.1 m

8. circumference = 175 cm 55.7 cm

9. circumference = 450 km 143 km

10. circumference = 468 mm 149 mm

11. circumference = 625 m 199 m

12. circumference = 180 km 573 km

Find the radius of each circle.

13. circumference = 10 mm 1.59 mm

14. circumference = 20 m 3.18 m

15. circumference = 23.5 km 3.74 km

16. circumference = 33.3 km 5.30 km

17. circumference = 17.5 cm 2.79 cm

18. circumference = 27.2 m 4.33 m

19. The equator of Earth is approximately a circle of radius 6378 km. What is the circumference of Earth at the equator? Use the approximation $\pi \approx 3.1416$ and give your answer to five digits. 40,074 km

20. A park near Cristi's home contains a circular pool with a fountain at the center. Cristi paced off the distance around the pool and found it to be 220 m. What is the radius of the pool? 35.0 m

21. The diameter of a circular lake is measured and found to be 15 km. What is the circumference of the lake? 47.1 km

22. It is 45 m from the center of a circular field to the inside edge of the track surrounding it. The distance from the center of the field to the outside edge is 55 m. Find the circumference of each edge. 283 m, 345 m

B 23. One circle has a radius of 15 m and a second has a radius of 30 m. How much larger is the circumference of the larger circle? 94.2 m

190 *Chapter 5*

The curves in the diagrams below are parts of circles, and the angles are right angles. Find the perimeter of each figure.

24. 20.6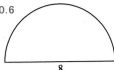

8

25. 35.7

10

26. 28.6

4

4

27. 41.4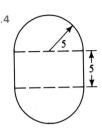

5

5

28. 40.3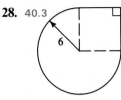

6

29. 22.7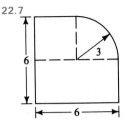

6

3

6

30. Find a formula that expresses the length, S, of a semicircle in terms of the radius, r. $S = \pi r$

31. Find a formula that expresses the length, S, of a semicircle in terms of the diameter, d. $S = \frac{1}{2}\pi d$

In Exercises 32 and 33 use the fact that three points not on a line determine a circle.

32. Every triangle can be inscribed in some circle. Explain why this is so.

33. Explain how to draw a quadrilateral that cannot be inscribed in any circle.

C **34.** What is the radius of the semicircle that forms the curve of a 400 meter track if each straightaway is 116 m long? 26.8 m

35. Draw a circle and one of its diameters, $\overline{AB}$. Then draw and measure $\angle APB$, where P is a point on the circle. Repeat this for several positions of P. What does this experiment suggest? $\angle APB$ is a right angle.
An angle inscribed in a semicircle is a right angle.

Review Exercises

Simplify.

1. $6 + 4 \times 3$ 18　　**2.** $16 \div 2 + 2$ 10　**3.** $3(4 + 5)$ 27　　　**4.** $8(7 - 3)$ 32

5. $64 \div (2 + 6)$ 8　**6.** $(18 + 3)2$ 42　**7.** $14 + 3 \times 2 - 6$ 14　**8.** $52 - 18 \div 3 + 16$
62

Geometric Figures **191**

Additional Answers Written Exercises

32. The vertices of a triangle are three noncollinear points. Any three non-collinear points deter-mine a circle.

33. Draw a circle and label three points, *A*, *B*, and *C* on the circle. Let Point *D* be any point not on the circle. Quadrilateral *ABCD* cannot be in-scribed in a circle.

Suggested Assignments

Core
Day 1: 190/1–17 odd; 19–22
Day 2: 191/24–34
　　　191/Rev. 1–8
Enriched
　190/19–23
　191/24–34

Supplementary Materials

Practice Masters, p. 23

Related Activities p. 163g

Reading Mathematics

Students will learn the meaning of the following mathematical terms in this lesson: *congruent figures, corresponding vertices, corresponding angles, corresponding sides, side-angle-side test, SAS, angle-side-angle test, ASA, side-side-side test, SSS, rigid motion, translation, rotation, reflection.*
   You will probably want to emphasize the importance of naming the vertices of congruent polygons in corresponding order. The statement △*KMP* ≅ △*STV* is equivalent to the statement △*MPK* ≅ △*TVS*.

5-7 Congruent Figures

Two figures are **congruent** if they have the same size and shape. Triangles *ABC* and *XYZ* shown below are congruent.

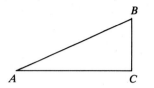 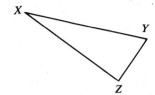

   If we could lift △*ABC* and place it on △*XYZ, A* would fall on *X, B* on *Y,* and *C* on *Z.* These matching vertices are called **corresponding vertices.** Angles at corresponding vertices are **corresponding angles,** and the sides joining corresponding vertices are **corresponding sides.**

> Corresponding angles of congruent figures are congruent.
>
> Corresponding sides of congruent figures are congruent.

   When we name two congruent figures, we list corresponding vertices in the same order. Thus, when we see

$$\triangle ABC \cong \triangle XYZ \quad \text{or} \quad \triangle CAB \cong \triangle ZXY,$$

we know that:

$$\angle A \cong \angle X, \qquad \angle B \cong \angle Y, \qquad \angle C \cong \angle Z$$
$$\overline{AB} \cong \overline{XY}, \qquad \overline{BC} \cong \overline{YZ}, \qquad \overline{CA} \cong \overline{ZX}$$

EXAMPLE 1   pentagon *PQUVW* ≅ pentagon *LMHKT*

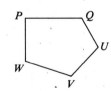 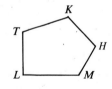

Complete these statements:

$$\angle W \cong \angle \underline{\,?\,} \qquad \overline{QU} \cong \underline{\,?\,} \qquad \angle H \cong \angle \underline{\,?\,} \qquad \overline{TL} \cong \underline{\,?\,}$$

Solution $\angle W \cong \angle T$ $\qquad \overline{QU} \cong \overline{MH}$ $\qquad \angle H \cong \angle U$ $\qquad \overline{TL} \cong \overline{WP}$

192   *Chapter 5*

If two figures are congruent, we can make them coincide (occupy the same place) by using one or more of these basic **rigid motions:**

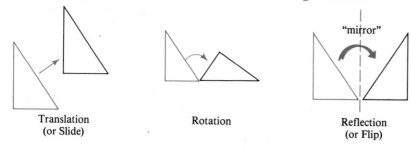

Translation (or Slide)   Rotation   "mirror"   Reflection (or Flip)

Consider the congruent trapezoids in panel (1) below. We can make *ABCD* coincide with *PQRS* by first reflecting *ABCD* in the line $\overleftrightarrow{BC}$ as in panel (2), and then translating this reflection as shown in panel (3).

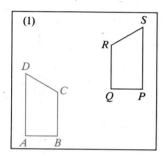
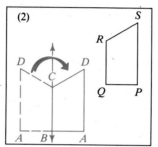
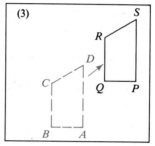

EXAMPLE 2   What type of rigid motion would make the red figure coincide with the black one?

a.
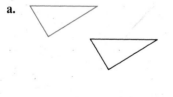

b.
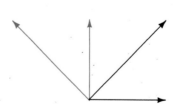

Solution   **a.** a translation: sliding the red triangle down and to the right would make it coincide with the black triangle

b. a rotation or a reflection: rotating the red angle around the vertex would make it coincide with the black angle; flipping the red angle over a line passing through the vertex would also make it coincide with the black angle

Geometric Figures   **193**

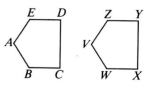

When working with triangles, we do not need to check all sides and all angles to establish congruence. Suppose that in the two triangles below, the sides and the angles marked alike are congruent.

If we were to match the congruent parts by using translation, we would find that all other corresponding sides and angles are congruent also. Thus we can use the following method to establish congruence in two triangles.

The side-angle-side (SAS) test for congruence
If two sides of one triangle and the angle they form (the *included angle*) are congruent to two sides and the included angle of another triangle, then the two triangles are congruent.

Two other methods that we can use to establish congruence in triangles are:

The angle-side-angle (ASA) test for congruence
If two angles and the side between them (the *included side*) are congruent to two angles and the included side of another triangle, then the two triangles are congruent.

The side-side-side (SSS) test for congruence
If three sides of one triangle are congruent to the three sides of another triangle, then the two triangles are congruent.

EXAMPLE 3 In the diagram, triangle ABC is isosceles, with $\overline{AB} \cong \overline{CB}$. $\overline{BD}$ bisects $\angle ABC$. Explain why $\triangle ABD \cong \triangle CBD$.

Solution We know that $\overline{AB} \cong \overline{CB}$.
Since $\overline{BD}$ bisects $\angle ABC$, $\angle 1 \cong \angle 2$.
Also, $\overline{BD}$ is a side of both triangles.
Therefore, by the SAS test,
$\triangle ABD \cong \triangle CBD$.

194   *Chapter 5*

Class Exercises

Each figure in Exercises 1–8 is congruent to one of the figures $A - E$.
State which one.

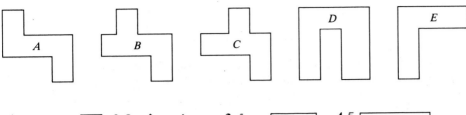

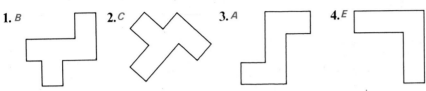

1. B 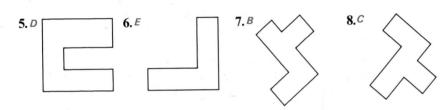 **2.** C **3.** A **4.** E

5. D 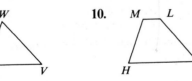 **6.** E 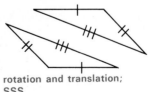 **7.** B  **8.** C

Complete the statements about each pair of congruent figures.

9.

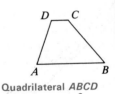

a. $\triangle MNO \cong$ __?__ $\triangle UVW$
b. $\angle N \cong$ __?__ $\angle V$
c. $\overline{MO} \cong$ __?__ $\overline{UW}$

10.

Quadrilateral *ABCD*

a. Quadrilateral $HKLM \cong$ __?__
b. $\angle B \cong$ __?__ $\angle K$
c. $\overline{HM} \cong$ __?__ $\overline{AD}$

State which of the rigid motions is needed to match the vertices of the
triangles in each pair and give a reason why the triangles are congruent.

11.

translation; SAS

12.

reflection and
translation; ASA

13.

rotation and translation;
SSS

Geometric Figures **195**

195

Additional A Exercises

Complete the statement.

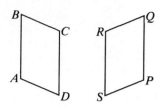

Polygon *ABCD* ≅ Polygon
PQRS.

1. Polygon *BCDA* ≅ polygon
 ___?___ . *QRSP*

2. $\overline{AB}$ ≅ ___?___ $\overline{PQ}$

3. $\overline{DC}$ ≅ ___?___ $\overline{SR}$

4. $\overline{AD}$ ≅ ___?___ $\overline{PS}$

5. ∠*ABC* ≅ ___?___ ∠*PQR*

6. ∠*RSP* ≅ ___?___ ∠*CDA*

Written Exercises

Which statement is correct?

A **1.** c

 a. △*BCA* ≅ △*GEF*
 b. △*ABC* ≅ △*EGF*
 c. △*BCA* ≅ △*FGE*

2. b

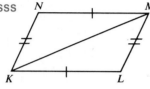

 a. △*PQR* ≅ △*XYZ*
 b. △*QRP* ≅ △*XZY*
 c. △*PQR* ≅ △*XZY*

Explain why the triangles in each pair are congruent.

3. SSS

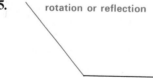

△*KLM* ≅ △*MNK*

4. ASA or SAS

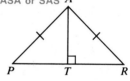

△*PAT* ≅ △*RAT*

What type of rigid motion would make the red figure coincide with the black one?

5. rotation or reflection

6. translation

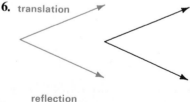

7. rotation, two reflections, or translation and reflection

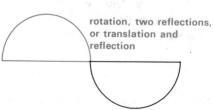

8. reflection

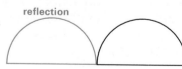

Name a pair of congruent triangles and explain why they are congruent.

B **9.**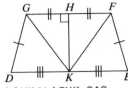

$\triangle GHK \cong \triangle FHK$; SAS

10.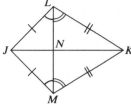

$\triangle JLK \cong \triangle JMK$; SAS or SSS

Complete each statement.

11. $\triangle XRL \cong \triangle NYS$
   a. $\angle X \cong$ __?__ $\angle N$ **b.** $\angle R \cong$ __?__ $\angle Y$ **c.** $\overline{XL} \cong$ __?__ $\overline{NS}$ **d.** $\overline{YS} \cong$ __?__ $\overline{RL}$

12. $PQTV \cong HJKM$
   a. $\angle Q \cong$ __?__ $\angle J$ **b.** $\angle M \cong$ __?__ $\angle V$ **c.** $\overline{VP} \cong$ __?__ $\overline{MH}$ **d.** $\overline{JK} \cong$ __?__ $\overline{QT}$

13. $ABCD \cong EFGH$
   a. $\overline{BC} \cong$ __?__ $\overline{FG}$ **b.** $\overline{AD} \cong$ __?__ $\overline{EH}$ **c.** $\angle ABC \cong$ __?__ $\angle EFG$ **d.** $\overline{GH} \cong$ __?__ $\overline{CD}$

C **14.** *ABCDEF* is a regular hexagon. If all the diagonals from *F* are drawn, name the following.
   a. all pairs of congruent triangles   **b.** a pair of congruent quadrilaterals
   c. a pair of congruent pentagons

15. Let $\overline{AB}$ and $\overline{PQ}$ be corresponding sides of two congruent polygons. If one polygon is moved so that $\overline{AB}$ falls on $\overline{PQ}$, must the two polygons coincide? No

Review Exercises

Solve.

1. $6x = 42$ 7   **2.** $5x = 50$ 10   **3.** $y \times 4 = 44$ 11   **4.** $y \times 7 = 56$ 8

5. $x \div 9 = 8$ 72   **6.** $x \div 11 = 6$ 66   **7.** $84 \div y = 21$ 4   **8.** $65 \div y = 13$ 5

▌▌▌ Calculator Key-In

Many ancient civilizations used approximations for π. Use a calculator to determine the following approximations for π as decimals. Which approximation is closest to the modern approximation of 3.14159265358?

1. Egyptian: $\frac{256}{81}$ 3.1604938   **2.** Greek: $\frac{223}{71}$ 3.140845   **3.** Roman: $\frac{377}{120}$ 3.141$\overline{6}$

4. Chinese: $\frac{355}{113}$ 3.1415929   **5.** Hindu: $\frac{3927}{1250}$ 3.1416   **6.** Babylonian: $\frac{25}{8}$ 3.125

Geometric Figures **197**

Reading Mathematics

Students will learn the meaning of the following mathematical terms in this lesson: *geometric construction, bisect, arc, perpendicular bisector, angle bisector, concurrent lines, altitude of a triangle, median of a triangle.*
  Before students begin the exercises, you may wish to discuss and illustrate several terms that are defined in the exercises. *Concurrent lines* (Exercises 8, 9, 12 and 13) are two or more lines that intersect in a single point. An *altitude* (Exercise 12) of a triangle is a line segment from a vertex perpendicular to the line that contains the opposite side. A *median* (Exercise 13) of a triangle is a line segment from a vertex to the midpoint of the opposite side.

5-8 Geometric Constructions

There is a difference between making a drawing and a **geometric construction.** For drawings, we may measure segments and angles; that is, we may use a ruler and a protractor to draw the figures. For geometric constructions, however, we may use only a compass and a straightedge. (We may use a ruler, but we must ignore the markings.)

  Here are some important constructions. Construction I and Construction II involve dividing a segment or angle into two congruent parts. This process is called **bisecting** the segment or the angle.

Construction I: To bisect a segment $\overline{AB}$.

Use the compass to draw an arc (part of a circle) with center A and radius greater than $\frac{1}{2}AB$. Using the same radius but with center B, draw another arc. Call the points of intersection X and Y. $\overleftrightarrow{XY}$ is the **perpendicular bisector** of $\overline{AB}$ because it is perpendicular to $\overline{AB}$ and divides $\overline{AB}$ into two congruent segments.

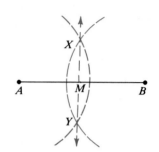

Construction II: To bisect an angle BAC.

Draw an arc with center A. Let X and Y be the points where the arc intersects the sides of the angle. Draw arcs of equal radii with centers X and Y. Call the point of intersection Z. $\overrightarrow{AZ}$ is the **angle bisector** of $\angle BAC$, and $\angle CAZ \cong \angle ZAB$.

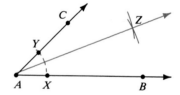

Construction III: To construct an angle congruent to a given angle Y.

Draw $\overrightarrow{MN}$. Draw an arc on $\angle Y$ with center Y. Let X and Z be the points where the arc intersects the sides of the angle. Draw an arc with center M and the same radius as arc XZ. Let S be the point where this arc intersects $\overrightarrow{MN}$. Call the other end of the arc R. With S as center draw an arc with radius equal to XZ. Let Q be the point where this arc intersects arc RS. Draw $\overrightarrow{MQ}$. $\angle NMQ \cong \angle Y$.

original angle   new angle

198   *Chapter 5*

EXAMPLE 1 Construct a line that is perpendicular to $\overleftrightarrow{AB}$ and contains A.

Solution

1. Place the compass at point A and draw an arc intersecting $\overleftrightarrow{AB}$ at two points. Call these two points X and Y, respectively. A is now the midpoint of $\overline{XY}$.

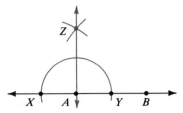

2. Place the compass at X and, as in Construction I, draw an arc with radius greater than $\overline{YA}$. Keeping the same radius, place the compass at Y and draw a second arc that intersects the first arc. Call the point of intersection of the two arcs Z.

3. Draw $\overleftrightarrow{AZ}$. Since $\overleftrightarrow{AZ}$ is the perpendicular bisector of $\overline{XY}$, and thus perpendicular to $\overleftrightarrow{AB}$, it is the required line.

EXAMPLE 2 Construct a 60° angle.

Solution

1. Draw a ray with endpoint A.

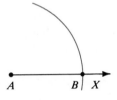

2. Draw an arc, with center A and any radius, intersecting the ray at B.

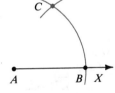

3. Draw an arc, with center B and the same radius as in step 2, intersecting the first arc at C.

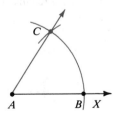

4. Draw $\overrightarrow{AC}$. Since $\triangle ABC$ is equilateral, $m\angle BAC = 60°$.

Geometric Figures **199**

Construct an angle with the measure specified.

Check students' papers.

1. 90°   **2.** 11.25°   **3.** 150°

4. Draw $\overleftrightarrow{HK}$ with M on $\overleftrightarrow{HK}$. Construct a line that is perpendicular to $\overleftrightarrow{HK}$ and contains M.

5. Draw a large acute triangle ABC. Draw $\overleftrightarrow{PR}$ with Q on $\overleftrightarrow{PR}$.

  a. Construct $\angle PQS$ with measure equal to $m\angle A + m\angle B$.

  b. Construct $\angle SQV \cong \angle C$. What happens? $\overrightarrow{QV}$ appears to coincide with $\overrightarrow{QR}$.

  c. Repeat using an obtuse triangle for $\angle ABC$. What appears to be true? $m\angle PQS + m\angle SQV = 180°$; $m\angle A + m\angle B + m\angle C = 180°$

Suggested Assignments

Core
Day 1: 200/1–11
Day 2: 200/12, 13
      201/Self-Test B
      201/Challenge

Enriched
  200/8–13
  201/15
  201/Self-Test B
  201/Challenge

Supplementary Materials

Practice Masters, p. 24
Test 5B, pp. 31–32

Written Exercises

In this exercise set use a compass and straightedge as your only construction tools. Check students' papers.

A   **1.** Construct a 45° angle. (Method: Construct a right angle as in Example 1 and then bisect it.)

  2. Construct a 30° angle. (Method: Construct a 60° angle as in Example 2 and then bisect it.)

  3. Construct a 22.5° angle. (Use Exercise 1.)

  4. Construct a 15° angle. (Use Exercise 2.)

  5. Use a protractor to draw an angle with measure 75°. Construct an angle congruent to this angle.

  6. Use a protractor to draw an angle with measure 130°. Construct an angle congruent to this angle.

  7. Draw a large isosceles triangle. Using this triangle, construct the perpendicular bisector of the base. Through what point does the perpendicular bisector appear to pass? the vertex of the angle formed by the two congruent sides

  8. Draw a large scalene triangle. Bisect its three angles. Are the angle bisectors **concurrent;** that is, do all three have a point in common? yes

  9. Draw a large scalene triangle. Construct the perpendicular bisectors of its sides. Are these bisectors concurrent? yes

In Exercises 10 and 11, draw $\overleftrightarrow{ST}$ and a point P not on $\overleftrightarrow{ST}$.

B   **10.** Construct a line through P perpendicular to $\overleftrightarrow{ST}$. (Method: Draw an arc with center P to intersect $\overleftrightarrow{ST}$ in two points, A and B. Construct the perpendicular bisector of $\overline{AB}$.)

  11. Construct a line through P parallel to $\overleftrightarrow{ST}$. (Method: 1. Construct $\overleftrightarrow{PQ}$ perpendicular to $\overleftrightarrow{ST}$ as in Exercise 10. 2. Construct $\overleftrightarrow{PR}$ perpendicular to $\overleftrightarrow{PQ}$ as in Example 1.)

  12. Draw a large scalene triangle. A line through a vertex that is perpendicular to the opposite side is called an **altitude** of the triangle. Construct the three altitudes of the triangle (see Exercise 10). Are they concurrent? yes

  13. Draw a large scalene triangle. A line through a vertex and the midpoint of the side opposite the vertex is called a **median** of the triangle. Construct the three medians (see Construction I). Are they concurrent? yes

200   *Chapter 5*

C **14.** Draw three noncollinear points, *A*, *B*, and *C*. Construct the circle that passes through these points. (*Hint:* The perpendicular bisectors of $\overline{AB}$ and $\overline{BC}$ both pass through the center of the circle.)

15. Use a compass to construct a regular hexagon. (*Hint:* The length of each side of a regular hexagon inscribed in a circle equals the radius of the circle.)

Self-Test B

Complete each statement.

1. A triangle with three congruent sides is ___?___. **equilateral** [5-4]

2. The sum of the measures of the angles of a triangle is __?__°. **180**

3. An acute triangle has ___?___ acute angle(s). **3**

4. A(n) ___?___ has eight sides. **octagon** [5-5]

5. A ___?___ has its opposite sides parallel and congruent. **parallelogram**

6. A trapezoid has sides of 7 cm, 5 cm, 7 cm, and 14 cm. Find its perimeter. **33 cm**

7. The radius of a circle is 16 cm. Find its circumference. Use $\pi \approx 3.14$ and round to three digits. **100 cm** [5-6]

True or false?

8. A diameter cuts a circle into two semicircles. **True**

9. A radius is a chord. **False**

10. Pentagon *ABCDE* $\cong$ Pentagon *FGHIJ*. Complete each statement. [5-7]
a. $\overline{AB} \cong$ ___?___ **FG**   **b.** $\angle E \cong \angle$ ___?___ **J**   **c.** $\angle DEA \cong \angle$ ___?___ **IJF**

11. Construct an isosceles right triangle. **Check students' papers.** [5-8]

12. Construct an equilateral triangle. **Check students' papers.**

Self-Test answers and Extra Practice are at the back of the book.

▮▮▮ Challenge

You have your choice of your height in nickels that are stacked or in quarters that are laid side by side. Which would you choose?

Geometric Figures **201**

More Programming in BASIC

In Chapter 3 we learned that to enter different values of a variable in BASIC we can use the INPUT statement.

To assign a value to a variable that will be repeated over and over again, we use the **LET** statement. For example, the statement

$$20 \quad \text{LET K} = 4037$$

assigns the value 4037 to the variable K. This statement tells the computer to store 4037 in its memory at location K. The value of a variable can be changed by assigning a new value. When we write

$$20 \quad \text{LET K} = 0.025$$

the original value, 4037, is replaced by the new value, 0.025.

The program below converts miles to kilometers by using the fact that 1 mi = 1.61 km.

```
10   PRINT "FROM MILES TO KILOMETERS"
20   PRINT "DISTANCE IN MILES";
30   INPUT X
40   LET A = 1.61
50   PRINT X;" MI = ";A*X;" KM"
60   END
```

Let us use the program to convert the approximate distance in miles from the planet Saturn to the Sun. That is, convert 887,000,000 mi to kilometers.

```
RUN
FROM MILES TO KILOMETERS
DISTANCE IN MILES? 887000000   ←——— do not use commas
887000000 MI = 1428070000 KM          to enter the distance
```

202   *Chapter 5*

Use the program on the previous page to complete the table.

	Planet	Distance (in mi) from the Sun	Distance (in km) from the Sun
1.	Mercury	36,000,000	? 57,960,000
2.	Venus	67,000,000	? 107,570,000
3.	Earth	93,000,000	? 149,730,000

Instead of running the program three times, we can modify it to repeat lines 20 through 50 so that all three distances are converted in one RUN. To do this, we use the **FOR** and **NEXT** statements to create a *loop*. The loop starts with the FOR statement, and ends with the NEXT statement. These two statements tell the computer how many times to repeat a group of statements located between them. The program below is now modified to repeat the loop three times. The output for Exercises 1–3 is shown at the right.

```
10   PRINT "FROM MILES TO KILOMETERS"       RUN
15   FOR I = 1 TO 3                         FROM MILES TO KILOMETERS
20   PRINT "DISTANCE IN MILES";             DISTANCE IN MILES? 36000000
30   INPUT X                                36000000 MI = 57960000 KM
40   LET A = 1.61                           DISTANCE IN MILES? 67000000
50   PRINT X;" MI = ";A*X;" KM"             67000000 MI = 107870000 KM
55   NEXT I                                 DISTANCE IN MILES? 93000000
60   END                                    93000000 MI = 149730000 KM
```

Depending on the computer you are using, the output displayed for the conversions above may be expressed in *scientific notation*. That is, a number such as 376770000 may be expressed as

$$3.7677E+08.$$

The code E+08 means "times 10 raised to the power of 8." Therefore

$$3.7677E+08 \text{ means } 3.7677 \times 10^8, \text{ or } 376770000.$$

Complete.

4. $37{,}492{,}000{,}000 = 3.7492E + \underline{}$ 10

5. $5{,}491{,}000{,}000{,}000 = 5.491E + \underline{}$ 12

6. $9.4678E+07 = \underline{}$ 94678000

7. $3.2186E+10 = \underline{}$ 32186000000

8. Write a program to print out the multiples of 2 from one to ten.

9. Write a program to print out the distance traveled at a constant rate of 760 mi/h for 15, 27, 31, 40, and 55 hours. Use the formula $d = rt$.

Geometric Figures **203**

To do a simple calculation such as converting one distance, there is little point in using a computer. However, using a FOR-NEXT loop, you could have the computer convert hundreds of distances, and it would never complain of being tired or bored.

Have students think of monotonous and repetitive tasks in industry for which computers are being used.

For solving more complex equations, the use of computers can be valuable and efficient. The volume and surface area formulas in Chapter 10—particularly for the cylinder, cone, and sphere—are sufficiently complex to provide a challenge to a programmer.

Additional Answers
Enrichment

8.
```
10   FOR I = 1 TO 5
20   PRINT I * 2
30   NEXT I
40   END
```

9.
```
10   PRINT "DISTANCE
     TRAVELED"
20   FOR I = 1 TO 5
30   PRINT "HOW
     MANY HOURS";
40   INPUT T
50   LET R = 760
60   PRINT
     "DISTANCE = ";
     R * T; "MILES"
70   NEXT I
80   END
```

Chapter Review

Complete.

1. Points on the same line are called ___?___. collinear points   [5-1]

2. A ___?___ has one endpoint. ray

3. Z divides $\overline{XY}$ into two congruent segments. Z is called the ___?___   [5-2]
   of $\overline{XY}$. midpoint

4. 927 mm = _?_ cm = _?_ m 92.7; 0.927

True or false?

5. A right angle is obtuse. False   [5-3]

6. In $\angle ABC$, A is the vertex. False

7. The supplement of a 40° angle has measure 140°. True

8. A triangle that has three sides of different lengths is called scalene. True   [5-4]

9. In a triangle, the longest side is opposite the smallest angle. False

10. All quadrilaterals are parallelograms. False   [5-5]

Write the letter of the correct answer.

11. A hexagon is regular. One side has length 8 cm. What is the perimeter? d
    a. 40 cm   **b.** 64 cm   **c.** 80 cm   **d.** 48 cm

12. Name the segment joining the center of a circle to a point on the   [5-6]
    circle. c
    a. diameter   **b.** chord   **c.** radius   **d.** circumference

13. A circle has diameter 16 cm. Use $\pi \approx 3.14$ to find the circumference and round to three digits. c
    a. 50.24 cm   **b.** 50.3 cm   **c.** 50.2 cm   **d.** 50 cm

14. Which is the symbol for congruence? a   [5-7]
    a. $\cong$ **b.** $\perp$ **c.** $\angle$ **d.** $\triangle$

15. Construct a 120° angle. Check students' papers.   [5-8]

16. Construct a right triangle. Check students' papers.

Chapter Test

Exercises 1–3 refer to the diagram at the right.

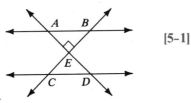

1. Name a pair of perpendicular lines. $\overleftrightarrow{AE}$, $\overleftrightarrow{BE}$ [5-1]

2. Name two rays that are not parallel, but do not intersect. $\overrightarrow{EA}$, $\overrightarrow{CD}$

3. Name three collinear points. *A, E, D* or *B, E, C*

Complete.

4. 27 m = ? cm 2700   5. 3.6 km = ? m 3600   [5-2]

6. 5000 cm = ? km 0.05   7. 4 mm = ? m 0.004

8. Give the measures of the complement and the supplement of $\angle A$ if $m\angle A = 27°$. 63°; 153°   [5-3]

9. If $\angle X \cong \angle Y$, then $m\angle X = $? . $m\angle Y$

10. True or false? The sides of a right angle are perpendicular. True

11. One angle of an isosceles triangle has measure 98°. Find the measures of the two congruent angles. 41°; 41°   [5-4]

12. An obtuse triangle has how many obtuse angles? one

13. True or false? A square is a rhombus. True   [5-5]

14. A quadrilateral has sides of length 8 cm, 13 cm, 9 cm, and 16 cm. Find the perimeter. 46 cm

15. A regular hexagon has perimeter 84 mm. Find the length of each side. 14 mm

16. The diameter of a circle is 18 cm. Find the radius. 9 cm   [5-6]

17. A circle has radius 50 mm. Find the circumference. Use $\pi \approx 3.14$. 314 mm

18. True or false? Every triangle can be inscribed in a circle. True

19. If quadrilateral *ABCD* $\cong$ quadrilateral *WXYZ*, then $\overline{AD} \cong$? . $\overline{WZ}$ [5-7]

20. Draw a segment. Construct the perpendicular bisector. Then construct the bisector of one of the right angles. Check students' papers.   [5-8]

Geometric Figures **205**

Express as an integer.

1. |13| 13

2. |−13| 13

Write the numbers in order from least to greatest.

3. −0.7, −667, 7.06, −67, −7.6 **−667, −67, −7.6, −0.7, 7.06**

4. 4.03, −4.3, −43, 0.43, −444 **−444, −43, −4.3, 0.43, 4.03**

Find the sum or difference.

5. 26.8 + −9.4 **17.4**

6. −6.3 + −30.6 **−36.9**

7. 0.98 + −17.2 + −0.49 **−16.71**

8. 37.7 − 9.4 **28.3**

9. −5.3 − 30.5 **−35.8**

10. −16.5 − (−8.7) **−7.8**

11. 52 − (−13.31) **65.31**

Find the product or quotient.

12. 11(−5.6) **−61.6**

13. −0.29(−3.5) **1.015**

14. 6.5(−4.9)(−5) **159.25**

15. 84.4 ÷ (−4) **−21.1**

16. −12.96 ÷ (−3.6) **3.6**

17. −0.06 ÷ (0.2) **−0.3**

Evaluate the expression when $a = -6$ and $b = -2.9$.

18. $-a - b$ **8.9**

19. $-|a|$ **−6**

Write the expression without exponents.

20. 6^3 **216**

21. 5^{-1} $\frac{1}{5}$

22. $2^4 \times 2^2$ **64**

23. $(-4) \times (-4)^{-3}$ $\frac{1}{16}$

Cumulative Review (Chapters 1–5)

Exercises

Evaluate the expression if $x = 3$ and $y = 5$.

1. $x + y$ 8

2. $2x + y$ 11

3. $2y - x$ 7

4. $x + 6y$ 33

5. $y + x + 4$ 12

6. $-x - y$ −8

7. $-3x - 2y$ −19

8. $5x + (-y) - 7$ 3

9. x^2 9

10. xy^2 75

11. $(-x)^2y$ 45

12. $-(xy)^2$ −225

Solve using transformations.

13. $x + 36 = 50$ 14

14. $x - 11 = -4$ 7

15. $-4x = 75$ $-18\frac{3}{4}$

16. $-7x = -105$ 15

17. $\frac{x}{8} = 9$ 72

18. $\frac{x}{7} = -8$ −56

19. $\frac{2}{3}x = 16$ 24

20. $-\frac{5}{6}x = 25$ −30

21. $0.45x = 13.5$ 30

22. $\frac{x}{1.8} = 2.7$ 4.86

23. $\frac{4}{5}x + 8 = 20$ 15

24. $\frac{15}{4}x + 6 = -4$ $-2\frac{2}{3}$

Write in lowest terms.

25. $\frac{32}{40}$ $\frac{4}{5}$

26. $\frac{56}{80}$ $\frac{7}{10}$

27. $-\frac{12}{108}$ $-\frac{1}{9}$

28. $-\frac{13}{182}$ $-\frac{1}{14}$

29. $\frac{98}{147}$ $\frac{2}{3}$

30. $\frac{72}{96}$ $\frac{3}{4}$

Write as a terminating or repeating decimal. Use a bar to indicate repeating digits.

31. $\frac{2}{5}$ 0.4

32. $\frac{3}{4}$ 0.75

33. $\frac{7}{16}$ 0.4375

34. $\frac{3}{10}$ 0.3

35. $-\frac{5}{18}$ $-0.2\overline{7}$

36. $-\frac{2}{3}$ $-0.\overline{6}$

Write as a proper fraction in lowest terms or as a mixed number in simple form.

37. 0.07 $\frac{7}{100}$

38. 0.007 $\frac{7}{1000}$

39. $1.\overline{9}$ 2

40. $4.\overline{20}$ $4\frac{20}{99}$

41. $-1.\overline{24}$ $-1\frac{8}{33}$

42. $-4.\overline{862}$ $-4\frac{862}{999}$

True or false?

43. An equilateral triangle is acute. True

44. A diameter is a chord. True

206 *Chapter 5*

Problems

Problem Solving Reminders
Here are some reminders that may help you solve some of the problems on this page.
- Determine which facts are necessary to solve the problem.
- Determine whether more than one operation is needed.
- Estimate to check your answers.

Solve.

1. Susan purchased the following items for the school dance: streamers, $2.89; tape, $4.59; bunting, $8.88; paper decorations, $14.75. How much did Susan spend? $31.11

2. Fred's Fish Farm started the week with 2078 fish. On Monday Fred sold 473 fish, on Tuesday he sold 509 fish, and on Wednesday 617 fish were sold. Fred bought 675 fish on Thursday and sold 349 on Friday. How many fish did Fred have at the end of the week? 805 fish

3. Mr. Chou was putting a certain amount into his savings account each month. Last month he increased the amount by $38. If Mr. Chou deposited $162 into his savings account last month, how much was he putting in before the increase? $124

4. Yonora bought 7 gallons of paint at $16.95 a gallon, 3 brushes at $6.99 each, 4 rollers at $2.95 each, and a dropcloth for $7.88. How much did Yonora spend on painting supplies? $159.30

5. A side of a square is 13 m long. Find the perimeter. 52 m

6. If a number is multiplied by 3, the result is 51. Find the number. 17

7. The seventh grade sold greeting cards to raise money for a trip. There were 12 cards and 12 envelopes in each box. If the class sold 1524 cards with envelopes, how many boxes did they sell? 127 boxes

8. Elgin had $150 in his checking account. He wrote checks for $17.95, $23.98, $45.17, and $31.26. How much does Elgin have left in his account? $31.64

9. Becky bought a round pool that is 7 m in diameter. What is the circumference of the pool to the nearest meter? 22 m

10. Juanita is 7 years older than her brother Carlos, who is 3 years older than their sister Maria. If Carlos is 6 years old, how old are Juanita and Maria? Juanita: 13; Maria: 3

Geometric Figures **207**

Use transformations to solve each equation.

24. $x - 17 = 12$ 29

25. $2(5 - 3) + y = 11$ 7

26. $8z = 3$ $\frac{3}{8}$

27. $\frac{x}{9} = -12$ -108

28. $18y = 14$ $\frac{7}{9}$

29. $\frac{3}{4}z = -27$ -36

30. $\frac{x}{1.4} = 5.2$ 7.28

31. $3y - 8 = -5$ 1

32. $\frac{5}{6}z + 15 = -15$ -36

33. $60 - \frac{1}{5}x = 25$ 175

6

Ratio, Proportion, and Percent

Before the invention of the microscope, objects appeared to consist only of those materials seen with the unaided eye. Today the ability to magnify objects, such as the salt crystals shown at the right, has enabled scientists to understand the structures of various compounds in detail. The most advanced microscopes in use at the present time are electron microscopes. Electron microscopes can magnify objects hundreds of thousands of times by using beams of focused electrons.

The visibility of fine detail in a magnification depends on several factors, including the light and the magnifying power of the microscope. For a simple microscope, the magnifying power can be expressed as this ratio:

$$\frac{\text{size of the image on the viewer's eye}}{\text{size of the object seen without a microscope}}.$$

In this chapter, you will learn how scales and ratios are used.

Career Note

When you think of photography, you probably think of it as a means of portraying people and places. When used in conjunction with a microscope (photomicrography), or with infrared or ultraviolet light, photography can become an important research tool. Scientific photographers must have a knowledge of film, filters, lenses, illuminators, and all other types of camera equipment. They must also have a thorough understanding of scale and proportion in order to find the best composition for a particular photograph.

Lesson Commentary
Chapter 6   Ratio, Proportion, and Percent

Overview

In the first part of this chapter students will study ratios and proportions and their applications. A solid foundation in using proportions is essential for understanding percents in the second part of this chapter and probability in Chapter 12. For this reason it is advisable to spend extra time on these lessons, if necessary, to make certain that students have mastered them.

In the last three lessons of the chapter students will gain a working knowledge of percents. This knowledge will be applied in the first part of Chapter 7.

RATIO AND PROPORTION

6-1 Ratios

Objective *for pages 210–213*

■ To express ratios in lowest terms.

Teaching Suggestions

Ratio is an important concept because of its widespread applications. The students can easily find examples of ratios in newspapers and magazines. You might point out that although we can write a ratio in several ways, it is usually easier to work with a ratio written in the form of a fraction in lowest terms. Stress that when forming a ratio of quantities of the same kind, the same unit of measure for each quantity must be used when writing the ratio in lowest terms. A ratio can be written as an improper fraction, such as $\frac{4}{3}$, but not as a mixed number or as a whole number.

Related Activities

Have the students find other examples of ratio. They might concentrate their search in the sports and financial sections in newspapers. Data can also be in the form of school activities, events, attendance, or enrollment. Students should write several problems about their ratios and exchange them with a classmate for solution.

Resource Book: Page 69 (Use After Page 213)

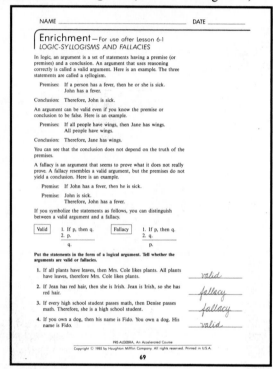

6-2 Rates

Objective *for pages 214–216*

■ To express rates in per unit form.

Teaching Suggestions

Students are already familiar with many rates, such as miles per hour, miles per gallon, and dollars per pound.

Point out that rates are used in many familiar situations. Ask for other rates and suggest a few, such as students per class, points per game, seats per row, days per week, and pencils per package. Students may think that only a speed is a rate; assure them that all of these examples are rates.

Some students may be curious about the difference between ratio and rate. A simple way to explain the difference is to tell them that rate is a ratio in which the units are different. You can also point out that since rates are usually expressed as whole numbers or decimals, they are written in the form 5.5 km/h, for example, which actually means the same as $\frac{5.5 \text{ km}}{1 \text{ h}}$.

When calculating a rate, students sometimes have difficulty deciding which number is to be the numerator and which is to be the denominator. The word *per* is often a clue that the next quantity is the denominator. For example, a typist who types 290 words in 5 min types at a rate of 58 words *per* minute, or 58 words/min.

$$\frac{290 \text{ words}}{5 \text{ min}} = \frac{58 \text{ words}}{1 \text{ min}}$$

Related Activities

To give students experience with an application of rates, discuss the use of unit pricing in supermarkets. Unit prices are rates in per unit form. The unit may be 1 lb for meat or cheese, 1 oz for many canned goods, or 100 ft^2 for paper products. Unit prices enable consumers to compare values more easily. Determine the unit price for each item. The desired units is specified in parentheses. Which item in each pair is the better value? Round answers to the nearest cent.

1. All Clear Dishwasher Detergent (1 oz)
   a. 50 oz for $3.19 $.06/oz; better value
   b. 20 oz for $1.44 $.07/oz
2. Sea Chicken Tuna (1 oz)
   a. 3 oz for $.42 $.14/oz
   b. 7 oz for $.89 $.13/oz; better value
3. Clear Vu Sandwich Bags (100 bags)
   a. 200 bags for $1.09 $.55/hundred; better value
   b. 75 bags for $.60 $.80/hundred
4. Crafty Cheddar Cheese (1 lb)
   a. 8 oz for $1.59 $3.18/lb; better value
   b. 12 oz for $2.43 $3.24/lb

6-3 Proportions

Objective for pages 217–219

■ To solve proportions.

Teaching Suggestions

Before you begin to teach this lesson, you may want to review how to solve equations using related multiplication and division facts (Lesson 4-2). Point out that it is no more difficult (assuming students can divide) to solve an equation like $160n = 1920$ than it is to solve $3n = 6$.

Students sometimes learn to solve a proportion by cross-multiplying without learning why the procedure works. Learning from the start why the procedure works helps students avoid using the procedure inappropriately. Stress that cross-multiplying may be used to solve proportions only; it does not work for equations that are not proportions, for example $x + \frac{1}{2} = \frac{7}{8}$. Review fractions (Chapter 3) if needed.

Show that more than one set of ratios can be set up for a situation. For the proportion on page 217 we could write

$$\frac{10 \text{ teachers}}{160 \text{ students}} = \frac{9 \text{ teachers}}{144 \text{ students}} \quad \text{or} \quad \frac{160 \text{ students}}{10 \text{ teachers}} = \frac{144 \text{ students}}{9 \text{ teachers}}$$

or even

$$\frac{160 \text{ students}}{144 \text{ students}} = \frac{10 \text{ teachers}}{9 \text{ teachers}} \quad \text{or} \quad \frac{144 \text{ students}}{160 \text{ students}} = \frac{9 \text{ teachers}}{10 \text{ teachers}}$$

If a student suggests values of a, b, c, and d that demonstrate that the implication in Exercise 32 is true, you might take some time to discuss the power of a counterexample. If a particular choice of values for the variables results in a false conclusion, that suffices to prove the statement false. However, if certain values for the variables result in a true conclusion, all we know is that the statement is true *for that choice of values;* it does *not* prove that the statement is true in general. To emphasize this point, you can use the equation $x^2 = x$. If the values of 0 or 1 are chosen for x, the statement *appears* to be true. However, if we choose to replace x with 2, we see clearly that $x^2 = x$ is not generally true because $2^2 \neq 2$.

Related Activities

To help students develop their powers of abstract reasoning, you can show in general terms the reasons for the property stated on page 218. If $\frac{a}{b} = \frac{c}{d}$ with $b \neq 0$

and $d \neq 0$, we can write each of the ratios with the common denominator bd.

$$\frac{a}{b} = \frac{c}{d}$$

$$\frac{a \times d}{b \times d} = \frac{b \times c}{b \times d}$$

Because the two ratios are equal and they also have the same denominator, the numerators must be equal as well. Therefore,

$$a \times d = b \times c.$$

6-4 Solving Problems with Proportions

Objective *for pages 220–223*

■ To use proportions to solve problems.

Teaching Suggestions

You may wish to give students some guidelines they can use to determine when it is appropriate to use a proportion to solve a word problem. Suggest that they ask the following questions:
(1) If one quantity increases, does the other quantity also increase? (If one quantity decreases, does the other quantity also decrease?) In the Example on page 220, when the number of tires is increased, the cost is also increased.
(2) Does the amount of change (increase or decrease) of one quantity *depend upon* the amount of change (increase or decrease) of the other quantity? In the Example, the amount of increase in the cost depends upon the number of additional tires bought.
(3) Does one quantity equal some known number times the other quantity? In the Example, the total cost equals the cost of one tire times the number of tires. The cost of one tire is constant.
If the answers to all the questions above is "yes," then it is appropriate to use a proportion. By solving the problems in Lessons 6-4 and 6-5 students will develop a sense of the kind of problems that can be solved using proportions.

Students sometimes have difficulty using the information in a problem to write a proportion. You might suggest that they try organizing the information in a table. The following table can be used to help solve the problem in the Example on page 220.

Number of Tires	Cost
4	$264
5	c

Using the Example on page 220 and the table above, you can show that any of the following proportions can be used to solve the problem.

$$\frac{4}{5} = \frac{264}{c}$$

$$\frac{5}{4} = \frac{c}{264}$$

$$\frac{4}{264} = \frac{5}{c}$$

$$\frac{264}{4} = \frac{c}{5}$$

All of the above proportions result in the same equation:

$$4c = 5 \times 264$$

Although problems in this lesson may be solved without using proportions, you may want to insist that students write a proportion for each problem. Students can then check their work by another method.

Related Activities

To help students better understand when to use a proportion to solve a problem, have them use the questions listed in the Teaching Suggestions on this page to determine if the quantities below are proportional.

1. The cost of a tank of gasoline; the price per gallon
   yes
2. The number of Calories in a glass of milk; the size of the glass yes
3. The number of hours a student spends studying; the student's height no
4. The amount of time it takes to drive 50 mi; the rate at which the distance is driven no

Have students list other quantities that are proportional.

6-5 Scale Drawing

Objective *for pages 224–226*

■ To use scale drawings.

Teaching Suggestions

This lesson gives students experience with a practical application of proportions. You can introduce this lesson by showing students examples of scale drawings such as road maps, house plans, or diagrams in books. Ask students to name some instruments that are used to enlarge or reduce images, for example, telescopes, microscopes, binoculars, and so on.

Student book pages are reduced in this teacher's edition to 90% of the original. Therefore, measurements on drawings and maps in this teacher's edition are 90% of the corresponding measurements in the books that your students are using. You may wish to use your own book as an example of a reduction. The scale of the reduced facsimile pages is 0.9 cm : 1 cm.

To help students distinguish between the scale for an enlargement and the scale for a reduction, tell them that the first number usually represents measurements in the drawing. Thus a scale of 1 cm : 3 cm describes a reduction to $\frac{1}{3}$ of the original size: but a scale of 3 cm : 1 cm describes an enlargement to 3 times that of the original size.

Related Activities

To provide additional practice with scale drawings have students use graph paper to make their own scale drawings.

1. Draw a small design, a star, for example, on a piece of graph paper within a 5×5 unit square. Then draw an enlargement whose dimensions are 4 times the size of the original.
2. Draw a design in a 20×20 unit square (a house, for example). Then draw a reduction whose dimensions are $\frac{1}{2}$ of the dimensions of the original.

Point out that enlarging the dimensions of a design to 4 times the dimensions of the original has the effect of multiplying the area by 16. Reducing the dimensions to $\frac{1}{2}$ their original size has the effect of reducing the area to $\frac{1}{4}$ that of the original design.

209d

PERCENTS

6-6 Percents and Fractions

Objective *for pages 227–230*

■ To change fractions to percents and percents to fractions.

Teaching Suggestions

Test scores provide an easy introduction to percents. Most students know that if they answer 94 questions correctly out of 100 on a test, their grade will be 94%. That is, $\frac{94}{100} = 94\%$. Many will also reason that if they answer 18 questions correctly out of 20, then each question has a value of $100\% \div 20$, or 5%; therefore, 18 questions have a value of $18 \times 5\%$, or 90%. You can build on students' understanding by showing that they are, in fact, writing the ratio $\frac{18}{20}$ as an equivalent ratio with a denominator of 100.

$$\frac{18}{20} = \frac{n}{100}; \qquad \frac{18}{20} = \frac{90}{100} = 90\%$$

You may wish to remind students that proportions as in Example 1 may be solved by cross multiplying.

Related Activities

To help students visualize percents, have them compare percents with familiar representations of fractions. Doing so will later help them approximate percentages to determine the reasonableness of their answers. For example, 30% is almost $33\frac{1}{3}\%$, or $\frac{1}{3}$. So, 30% of a number will be slightly less than $\frac{1}{3}$ of that number.

Select the diagram that gives the closest approximation of each percent.

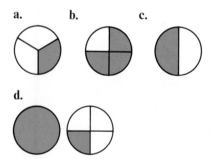

a.   b.   c.

d.

1. 45% c   **2.** 78% b   **3.** 120% d   **4.** 35% a

6-7 Percents and Decimals

Objective *for pages 231–233*

■ To change decimals to percents and percents to decimals.

Teaching Suggestions

Remind students that to divide a number by 100, it is convenient to think of moving the decimal point two places to the left. To write a decimal as a percent, we must reverse the above procedure, or multiply by 100. Thus we move the decimal point two places to the right.

$$0.86 = 86\% \qquad 1.32 = 132\%$$

When expressing a decimal such as 3.06 as a percent some students may have a tendency to write 3.06% as an answer because of the hundredths' place in the decimal.

$$3.06 = 306\%$$

Be sure students understand the two rules on page 231. The decimal point must be moved when expressing decimals as percents or percents as decimals.

Related Activities

To provide additional practice writing fractions as percents, you can use the familiar application of test scores. You may wish to allow students to use calculators.

Write each test score as a fraction. Then calculate the grade to the nearest whole percent.

1. 18 questions right out of 30 60%
2. 12 questions right; 3 wrong 80%
3. 7 questions right out of 8 88%
4. 10 questions right out of 12 83%
5. 13 questions right; 2 wrong 87%

6-8 Computing with Percents

Objective *for pages 234–237*

■ To compute with percents.

Teaching Suggestions

You may want to point out that all three types of percent problems use the same formula. In the sentence "20% of 300 is 60" the percent, 20%, is called the rate; 300 is the base; 60 is the percentage. Thus the general formula is *percentage = rate × base*, or *p = rb*. In Example 1 we use it in this form to solve for *p*. In Example 2 we solve for *r*, *r = p ÷ b*. In Example 3 we solve for *b*, *b = p ÷ r*.

Students often misplace decimal points in percent problems. Remind them to check their results. Estimation is a useful skill. Have students practice doing problems involving 1%, 10%, and 50% so that they become able to recognize a reasonable answer.

Related Activities

To extend the lesson, have students examine the effect of taking successive percents of a number. Let *n* = 100.

1. **a.** What is 12% of *n*? **12**
   b. What is 40% of the answer in part a? **4.8**
2. **a.** What is 40% of *n*? **40**
   b. What is 12% of the answer in part a? **4.8**
3. **a.** What is 20% of 60% of *n*? **12**
   b. What is 60% of 20% of *n*? **12**
4-6. Repeat Exercises 1–3 with *n* = 240.
   4. 28.8; 11.52   **5.** 96; 11.52   **6.** 28.8; 28.8

Resource Book: Pages 72–74 (Use After Page 237)

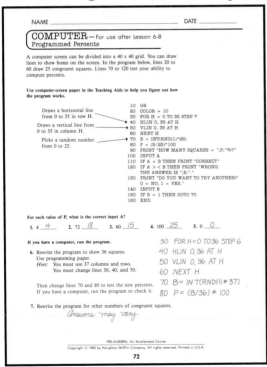

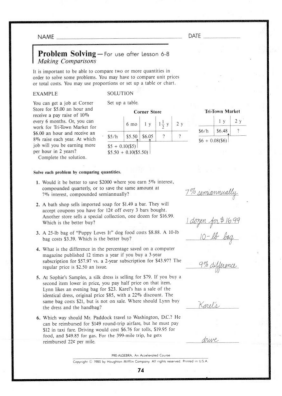

209f

NAME _____ DATE _____

Quiz 6B — Lessons 6-6 through 6-8

DIRECTIONS: Write the letter of the correct answer in the space provided.

1. Which is the fraction in lowest terms for 22%?   *[6-6]*

   a. $\frac{1}{5}$ b. $\frac{2}{5}$ c. $\frac{11}{25}$ d. $\frac{11}{50}$

2. Which is the percent for $2\frac{3}{4}$?

   a. 27.5%   b. 2.34%   c. 2.75%   d. 275%

3. Which is the fraction for $33\frac{1}{3}$%?

   a. $\frac{2}{3}$ b. $\frac{1}{3}$ c. $\frac{1}{6}$ d. $\frac{3}{10}$

4. Which is the decimal for 0.7%?   *[6-7]*

   a. 0.007   b. 0.07   c. 7   d. 70

5. Which is the percent for 0.84?

   a. 0.0084%   b. 0.84%   c. 84%   d. 840%

6. Which is the percent for $\frac{8}{9}$?

   a. $89\frac{8}{9}$%   b. 80%   c. $88\frac{8}{9}$%   d. 89%

7. What percent of 64 is 32?   *[6-8]*

   a. 200%   b. 50%   c. 5%   d. 0.5%

8. What is 5% of 75?

   a. 3.75   b. $37\frac{1}{2}$ c. 375   d. 1500

9. 22 is what percent of 55?

   a. $\frac{2}{5}$%   b. 0.4%   c. 40%   d. 250%

10. What percent of 120 is 80?

    a. 150%   b. 67%   c. 80%   d. $66\frac{2}{3}$%

ANSWERS	
1. _d_	(10)
2. _d_	(10)
3. _b_	(10)
4. _a_	(10)
5. _c_	(10)
6. _c_	(10)
7. _b_	(10)
8. _a_	(10)
9. _c_	(10)
10. _d_	(10)

75

NAME _____ DATE _____

Test — Chapter 6

DIRECTIONS: Write the answers in the spaces provided.

Express each ratio in lowest terms.

1. 32 cm : 4 m   2. 4 h : 45 min   *[6-1]*

Give the unit price of each item.   *[6-2]*

3. 2 radial tires for $96.12   4. 12 picture frames for $138

Solve.

5. $\frac{n}{28} = \frac{3}{4}$ 6. $\frac{32}{6} = \frac{x}{12}$ 7. $\frac{5}{17} = \frac{15}{a}$ *[6-3]*

8. A car can travel 155 mi on 5 gal of gas. How many   *[6-4]*
   gallons of gas are needed for a trip of 248 mi?

9. On a map 2 cm represents 5 km. If the actual distance   *[6-5]*
   across a lake is 45 km, how far would it be on the map?

Express as a fraction in lowest terms or as a mixed number in simple form.

10. 27%   11. 62%   12. 225%   *[6-6]*

Express as a percent.

13. $\frac{9}{10}$ 14. $\frac{16}{25}$ 15. $2\frac{1}{5}$

Express as a decimal.

16. 43%   17. 132%   18. 0.6%   *[6-7]*

Express as a percent.

19. 0.56   20. 0.064   21. 3.4

22. What is 20% of 80?   *[6-8]*

23. 30 is what percent of 150?

24. 24 is 60% of what number?

ANSWERS	
1. _2:25_	(4)
2. _16:3_	(4)
3. _$48.06/tire_	(4)
4. _$11.50/frame_	(4)
5. _21_	(4)
6. _64_	(4)
7. _51_	(4)
8. _8 gal_	(4)
9. _18 cm_	(6)
10. _$\frac{27}{100}$_	(4)
11. _$\frac{31}{50}$_	(4)
12. _$2\frac{1}{4}$_	(4)
13. _90%_	(4)
14. _64%_	(4)
15. _220%_	(4)
16. _0.43_	(4)
17. _1.32_	(4)
18. _0.006_	(4)
19. _56%_	(4)
20. _6.4%_	(4)
21. _340%_	(4)
22. _16_	(4)
23. _20%_	(4)
24. _40_	(4)

77

NAME _____ DATE _____

Review — Chapter 6

Express each ratio in lowest terms.

1. 6:15   _2:5_   2. 2 h to 10 min   _12:1_   3. 20 cm to 1 m   _1:5_   *[6-1]*

Solve.

4. What is the cost of gasoline in dollars per gallon if 4.2 gal of   _$1.07/gal_   *[6-2]*
   gasoline cost $4.49? Round to the nearest cent.

5. A local streetcar travels a distance of 45 mi in 2 h. What is the   _22.5 mi/h_
   streetcar's average speed?

6. $\frac{1}{4} = \frac{32}{n}$ _128_   7. $\frac{11}{n} = \frac{66}{30}$ _5_   8. $\frac{4}{7} = \frac{n}{105}$ _60_   *[6-3]*

9. If it requires $1\frac{1}{4}$ c of powdered milk to make 1 qt of milk,   _10 c_   *[6-4]*
   how much is needed for 2 gal?

10. A 40-acre field yields 600 bushels of wheat. How many bushels   _1125 bushels_
    of wheat will a 75-acre field yield?

11. A $6\frac{1}{2}$-ounce can of Sea View Tuna costs 91¢. Three 2-pound   _Ocean Blue (12¢ per_
    cans of Ocean Blue Tuna cost $11.52. Based on unit price alone,   _ounce is less than 14¢_
    which brand is the better buy? Why?   _per ounce)_

12. A map uses the scale 1 cm:20 km. If the distance between two   _8.5 cm_   *[6-5]*
    cities is 170 km, what is the difference on the map?

Express as a fraction in lowest terms or as a mixed number in simple form.

13. 52%   _$\frac{13}{25}$_   14. 2%   _$\frac{1}{50}$_   15. 350%   _$3\frac{1}{2}$_   16. 155%   _$1\frac{11}{20}$_   *[6-6]*

Solve.

17. In a public opinion poll 750 questionnaires were sent out; 225
    questionnaires were returned. What percent were returned?   _30%_

Express as a decimal.

18. 87%   _0.87_   19. 12%   _0.12_   20. 145%   _1.45_   21. 3.4%   _0.034_   *[6-7]*

Solve.

22. The choir needs to replace 0.7 of its robes. What percent is this?   _70%_

23. What percent of 85 is 17?   _20%_   *[6-8]*

24. What is 15% of 50?   _75_

76

NAME _____ DATE _____

Make-up Test — Chapter 6

DIRECTIONS: Write the answers in the spaces provided.

Express each ratio in lowest terms.

1. 30 s : 4 min   2. 3 ft : 6 in.   *[6-1]*

Give the unit price of each item.

3. 6 lb of coffee for $14.94   4. 12 gal for $11.64   *[6-2]*

Solve.

5. $\frac{n}{24} = \frac{5}{6}$ 6. $\frac{30}{8} = \frac{x}{24}$ 7. $\frac{4}{13} = \frac{12}{a}$ *[6-3]*

8. A car traveled 196 mi in 4 h. How many hours would it   *[6-4]*
   take to travel 294 mi?

9. On a model plane a 2-in. propeller blade represents a 3-   *[6-5]*
   ft blade. If the wing on the model is 18 in., how long is
   the actual wing?

Express as a fraction in lowest terms or as a mixed number in simple form.

10. 81%   11. 14%   12. 320%   *[6-6]*

Express as a percent.

13. $\frac{7}{10}$ 14. $\frac{9}{20}$ 15. $1\frac{1}{4}$

Express as a decimal.

16. 67%   17. 318%   18. 0.4%   *[6-7]*

Express as a percent.

19. 0.59   20. 0.042   21. 2.5

22. What is 40% of 60?   *[6-8]*

23. 48 is what percent of 160?

24. 40 is 80% of what number?

ANSWERS	
1. _1:8_	(4)
2. _6:1_	(4)
3. _$2.49/lb_	(4)
4. _$.97/gal_	(4)
5. _20_	(4)
6. _90_	(4)
7. _39_	(4)
8. _6 h_	(6)
9. _27 ft_	(6)
10. _$\frac{81}{100}$_	(4)
11. _$\frac{7}{50}$_	(4)
12. _$3\frac{1}{5}$_	(4)
13. _70%_	(4)
14. _45%_	(4)
15. _125%_	(4)
16. _0.67_	(4)
17. _3.18_	(4)
18. _0.004_	(4)
19. _59%_	(4)
20. _4.2%_	(4)
21. _250%_	(4)
22. _24_	(4)
23. _30%_	(4)
24. _50_	(4)

78

209g

Resource Book: Pages 79-82 (Use After Page 237)

CUMULATIVE REVIEW — Chapters 1-6
Exercises

Evaluate the expression if $f = 7$ **and** $g = 4$.

1. $f + g$ *11*
2. $2f - g$ *10*
3. $-g - f$ *−11*
4. $f^2 g$ *196*
5. $3f + 2g$ *29*
6. $g - f - 5$ *−8*

Write the numbers in order from least to greatest.

7. $5.2, 3.1, -4.9, -0.8, 0$ *−4.9, −0.8, 0, 3.1, 5.2*
8. $-26, -2.6, 2.5, 0.26$ *−26, −2.6, 0.26, 2.5*

Tell whether the statement is true or false for the given value of the variable.

9. $18 - 2m = 42; 12$ *F*
10. $6d \le 2; \frac{1}{4}$ *T*
11. $t < -3t + 8; -2$ *T*
12. $\frac{w}{-3} > 12; 39$ *F*
13. $9 + 5x = x + 13; 1$ *T*
14. $2s \div 4 = 20; 2\frac{1}{2}$ *F*

Write the fractions as equal fractions having the least common denominator (LCD).

15. $\frac{3}{5}, \frac{5}{8}$ *$\frac{24}{40}, \frac{25}{40}$*
16. $-\frac{1}{3}, \frac{4}{9}$ *$-\frac{3}{9}, \frac{4}{9}$*
17. $\frac{5}{6}, -\frac{3}{4}$ *$\frac{10}{12}, -\frac{9}{12}$*

Solve the equation.

18. $6p - 18 = 15$ *$5\frac{1}{2}$*
19. $-8m = -24$ *3*
20. $-5f + 17 = 32$ *−3*

Complete.

21. 158% of 75 is *118.5* .
22. 15 is 30% of *50* .
23. 24 is *60* % of 40.
24. *5.98* is 6.5% of 92.

Solve each proportion.

25. $\frac{3}{16} = \frac{x}{80}$ *15*
26. $\frac{4.2}{d} = \frac{21}{15}$ *3*
27. $\frac{18}{6} = \frac{72}{m}$ *24*

Write a variable expression for the word phrase.

28. The product of a number r and sixty-five   *65r*
29. The sum of five times a number d and eighteen   *5d + 18*
30. The difference between forty and a number t *40 − t*

True or false?

31. In a triangle, the shortest side is adjacent to the smallest angle.   *F*
32. A radius of a circle is a line segment joining the center of the circle to a point on the circle.   *T*

CUMULATIVE REVIEW — Chapters 1-6 (continued)
Problems

Problem Solving Reminders

Here are some reminders that may help you solve some of the problems on this page.
- Determine which facts are necessary to solve the problem.
- Determine whether more than one operation is needed.
- Consider whether drawing a sketch will help.
- Estimate to check the reasonableness of your results.

1. An order of 192 baseballs was shipped in 16 cartons weighing 10 lb each. If each carton had an equal number of baseballs, how many baseballs were in each carton?   *12 baseballs*

2. Each side of a regular pentagon is 54.9 cm long. What is the perimeter of the pentagon?   *274.5 cm*

3. In Carver Park there is a circular sidewalk around a 20-ft flag pole. The flag pole is 9 ft from the outer edge of the sidewalk. What is the distance around the outer edge of the sidewalk?   *56.52 ft*

4. Linda Brown spends 15 h out of a 40-h work week looking for new customers. John Williams spends 13 h out of a 36-h work week searching for new customers. Who spends a greater fraction of his or her time looking for new customers?   *Linda*

5. Erin travels 40 min each way to get back and forth from school. She spends 6 h attending classes, 35 min for lunch, and 45 min participating in student activities. If she leaves home at 7:15 A.M., what time does she arrive home?   *3:35 P.M.*

6. What is the total grocery bill for 2 gal of milk at $1.89 each, 1 lb of butter at $2.36, 6 oranges at 15¢ each, and 3 lb of fish at $2.69 per pound?   *$15.11*

7. A glove factory makes 2 different kinds of gloves each day. Ladies' leather gloves are made every 6 days and kids' ski gloves are made every 15 days. If both gloves are being made today, how many days will it be before both are made on the same day again?   *30 days*

8. Mr. Wong's car gets 26 mi per gallon in town and 5 mi more per gallon on the highway. His next trip will be all highway driving for 744 mi. How much gas will he need?   *24 gal*

CUMULATIVE TEST — Chapters 4-6

DIRECTIONS: **Write the answer in the space provided.**

Chapter 4

Use transformations to solve each equation.

1. $16 + x = 42$
2. $\frac{n}{7} = 15$
3. $-5n = 65$
4. $y - 21 = -33$
5. $0.36y = 0.936$
6. $13 - \frac{1}{4}n = 10$
7. $\frac{2}{3}x = -\frac{1}{2}$
8. $-1.5a = -4.5$

Write a variable expression for the word phrase.

9. The product of a number n and seven.
10. Nine more than the sum of a number c and three.

Write an equation for the problem. Use Steps 1-3.

11. Pat is 2 years less than three times her sister's age. If Pat is 13, how old is his sister?

Solve, using the five-step method.

12. One third of the student body is taking a music class. If 540 students are taking a music class, how many students are there in all?

Chapter 5

Exercises 1-2 refer to the diagram at the right.

13. Name two lines that intersect.
14. Name a ray with the endpoint C.
15. 850 cm = __?__ m
16. 3.6 km = __?__ m
17. What is the supplement of $\angle A$ if m $\angle A = 30°$?
18. True or false? If $\overline{WX} \perp \overline{YZ}$, then 90° angles are formed.

ANSWERS	
1. *26*	(2)
2. *105*	(2)
3. *−13*	(2)
4. *−12*	(2)
5. *2.6*	(2)
6. *12*	(2)
7. *$-\frac{3}{4}$*	(2)
8. *3*	(2)
9. *7n*	(2)
10. *(c+3)+9*	(2)
11. *3n−2=13*	(2)
12. *1620*	(3)
13. *$\overleftrightarrow{AC}, \overleftrightarrow{AB}$*	(3)
14. *$\overrightarrow{CD}$ or $\overrightarrow{CA}$*	(3)
15. *8.5*	(3)
16. *3600*	(3)
17. *150°*	(3)
18. *T*	(3)

CUMULATIVE TEST — Chapters 4-6 (continued)

19. How many equal sides does an isosceles triangle have?
20. If two angles of a triangle measure 30° and 40°, what is the measure of the third angle?
21. Name the polygon with 6 sides.
22. One side of a rhombus measures 13 cm. What is the perimeter?
23. The length of the radius of a circle is 6 m. What is the length of the circumference? Use $\pi \approx 3.14$.
24. If $\triangle ABC \cong \triangle XYZ$, then $\overline{BC} \cong$ __?__ .
25. On another sheet of paper construct perpendicular lines.

Chapter 6

26. Write the ratio 8 in. : 2 ft in lowest terms.

Solve.

27. $\frac{n}{32} = \frac{3}{4}$
28. $\frac{4}{15} = \frac{16}{n}$
29. A car traveled 396 mi on 16 gal of gasoline. How far could it travel on 8 gal of gasoline?
30. What is the scale of a drawing in which a 4-ft wide doorway is drawn 2 in. wide?
31. Express 40% as a fraction in lowest terms.
32. Express $1\frac{1}{2}$ as a percent.
33. Express 33% as a decimal.
34. Express 0.043 as a percent.
35. What is 30% of 60?
36. 48 is what percent of 240?
37. 16 is 40% of what number?

ANSWERS	
19. *2*	(3)
20. *110°*	(3)
21. *hexagon*	(3)
22. *52 cm*	(3)
23. *37.68 m*	(3)
24. *YZ*	(3)
25. *check construction*	(3)
26. *1:3*	(3)
27. *24*	(3)
28. *60*	(3)
29. *198 mi*	(3)
30. *1 in : 2 ft*	(3)
31. *$\frac{2}{5}$*	(3)
32. *150%*	(3)
33. *0.33*	(3)
34. *4.3%*	(3)
35. *18*	(3)
36. *20%*	(3)
37. *40*	(3)

209h

Teaching Suggestions
p. 209a

Related Activities p. 209a

Reading Mathematics

Students will learn the meaning of the following mathematical terms in this lesson: *ratio, lowest terms*.

6-1 Ratios

At Fair Oaks Junior High School there are 35 teachers and 525 students. We can compare the number of teachers to the number of students by writing a quotient.

$$\frac{\text{number of teachers}}{\text{number of students}} = \frac{35}{525}, \text{ or } \frac{1}{15}$$

The indicated quotient of one number divided by a second number is called the **ratio** of the first number to the second number. We can write the ratio above in the following ways.

$$\frac{1}{15} \qquad 1:15 \qquad 1 \text{ to } 15$$

All of these expressions are read *one to fifteen*. If the colon notation is used, the first number is divided by the second. A ratio is said to be in **lowest terms** if the two numbers are relatively prime. You do not change an improper fraction to a mixed number if the improper fraction represents a ratio.

EXAMPLE 1 There are 9 players on a baseball team. Four of these are infielders and 3 are outfielders. Find each ratio in lowest terms.

a. infielders to outfielders

b. outfielders to total players

Solution **a.** $\dfrac{\text{infielders}}{\text{outfielders}} = \dfrac{4}{3}$, or $4:3$, or 4 to 3

b. $\dfrac{\text{outfielders}}{\text{total players}} = \dfrac{3}{9} = \dfrac{1}{3}$, or $1:3$, or 1 to 3

Some ratios compare measurements. In these cases, we must be sure that the measurements are expressed in the same unit.

EXAMPLE 2 It takes Herb 4 min to mix some paint. Herb can paint a room in 3 h. What is the ratio of the time it takes Herb to mix the paint to the time it takes Herb to paint the room?

Solution Use minutes as a common unit for measuring time.

$$3 \text{ h} = 3 \times 60 \text{ min} = 180 \text{ min}$$

The ratio is $\dfrac{\text{min to mix}}{\text{min to paint}} = \dfrac{4}{180} = \dfrac{1}{45}$, or $1:45$.

210 *Chapter 6*

Chalkboard Examples

Express each ratio as a fraction in lowest terms.

1. $24:60$ $\dfrac{2}{5}$

2. $\dfrac{12 \text{ mm}}{5 \text{ cm}}$ $\dfrac{6}{25}$

3. $\dfrac{\$5}{25\cancel{c}}$ $\dfrac{20}{1}$

4. $\dfrac{40 \text{ min}}{2 \text{ h}}$ $\dfrac{1}{3}$

Solve.

5. A hockey player scored 3 goals in 12 attempts. What is the player's ratio of successes to failures? $\dfrac{1}{3}$

Problem Solving Reminder

There is *not enough information* given in some problems. To solve such problems, you must recall facts that are part of your general knowledge. In Example 2, you must recall that 1 h = 60 min.

Class Exercises

Express each ratio as a fraction in lowest terms.

1. 5 to 7 $\frac{5}{7}$ **2.** 11 to 6 $\frac{11}{6}$ **3.** 10:30 $\frac{1}{3}$ **4.** 12:24 $\frac{1}{2}$

5. 8 to 2 $\frac{4}{1}$ **6.** 32 to 4 $\frac{8}{1}$ **7.** 68:17 $\frac{4}{1}$ **8.** 45:18 $\frac{5}{2}$

Rewrite each ratio so that the numerator and denominator are expressed in the same unit of measure. Answers may vary.

9. $\frac{2 \text{ dollars}}{50 \text{ cents}}$ $\frac{200 \text{ cents}}{50 \text{ cents}}$ **10.** $\frac{5 \text{ months}}{2 \text{ years}}$ $\frac{5 \text{ months}}{24 \text{ months}}$ **11.** $\frac{35 \text{ cm}}{1 \text{ m}}$ $\frac{35 \text{ cm}}{100 \text{ cm}}$ **12.** $\frac{12 \text{ min}}{2 \text{ h}}$ $\frac{12 \text{ min}}{120 \text{ min}}$

Written Exercises

For each diagram below, name each ratio as a fraction in lowest terms.
a. The number of shaded squares to the number of unshaded squares
b. The number of shaded squares to the total number of squares
c. The total number of squares to the number of unshaded squares

A **1.**

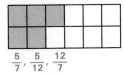

$\frac{5}{7}, \frac{5}{12}, \frac{12}{7}$

2.

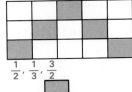

$\frac{1}{2}, \frac{1}{3}, \frac{3}{2}$

3.

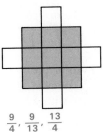

$\frac{9}{4}, \frac{9}{13}, \frac{13}{4}$

4.

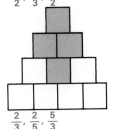

$\frac{2}{3}, \frac{2}{5}, \frac{5}{3}$

Express each ratio as a fraction in lowest terms.

5. 18 hours to 2 days $\frac{3}{8}$ **6.** 25 cm to 3 m $\frac{1}{12}$ **7.** 4 days:2 weeks $\frac{2}{7}$

8. 48 s:5 min $\frac{4}{25}$ **9.** 3 kg:800 g $\frac{15}{4}$ **10.** 6 lb:24 oz $\frac{4}{1}$

Ratio, Proportion, and Percent **211**

Express each ratio as a fraction in lowest terms.

1. 18 h to 3 days $\frac{1}{4}$

2. 18 cm to 3 m $\frac{3}{50}$

3. 40 g to 40 kg $\frac{1}{1000}$

4. 5 quarts to 12 gallons $\frac{5}{48}$

5. In an equilateral triangle, what is the ratio of the length of one side to the perimeter? $\frac{1}{3}$

6. The front wheel of a tricycle has a circumference of 1.2 m and one of the rear wheels has a circumference of 60 cm. What is the ratio of the circumference of the front wheel to that of the rear wheel? $\frac{2}{1}$

Find each ratio as a fraction in lowest terms.

B **11. a.** The number of vowels to the number of consonants in the alphabet (consider y a consonant) $\frac{5}{21}$

    b. The number of consonants to the total number of letters $\frac{21}{26}$

    c. The total number of letters to the number of vowels $\frac{26}{5}$

12. a. The number of weekdays to the number of weekend days (Saturdays and Sundays) in the month of February (not in a leap year) $\frac{5}{2}$

    b. The number of weekdays in the month of February (not a leap year) to the number of days in February $\frac{5}{7}$

    c. The number of days to the number of Sundays in the month of February (not a leap year) $\frac{7}{1}$

13. a. The number of diagonals drawn in the figure at the right to the total number of segments $\frac{1}{3}$

    b. The number of sides of the figure to the number of diagonals $\frac{2}{1}$

    c. The total number of segments to the number of sides $\frac{3}{2}$

14. a. The number of prime numbers between 10 and 25 to the number of whole numbers between 10 and 25 $\frac{5}{14}$

    b. The number of prime numbers between 10 and 25 to the number of composite numbers between 10 and 25 $\frac{5}{9}$

    c. The number of whole numbers between 10 and 25 to the number of composite numbers between 10 and 25 $\frac{14}{9}$

In Exercises 15–18, $AB = 7\frac{1}{5}$, $CD = 10\frac{1}{2}$, $EF = 12$, and $GH = 6\frac{3}{4}$. Express each ratio in lowest terms.

C **15.** $\frac{AB}{EF}$ $\frac{3}{5}$ **16.** $\frac{EF}{GH}$ $\frac{16}{9}$ **17.** $\frac{CD}{GH}$ $\frac{14}{9}$ **18.** $\frac{GH}{AB}$ $\frac{15}{16}$

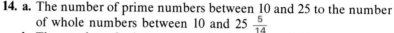

Problems

Solve.

A **1.** The *mechanical advantage* of a simple machine is the ratio of the weight lifted by the machine to the force necessary to lift it. What is the mechanical advantage of a jack that lifts a 3200-lb car with a force of 120 lb? $\frac{80}{3}$

2. The *C*-string of a cello vibrates 654 times in 5 seconds. How many vibrations per second is this? $130\frac{4}{5}$ vibrations per second

3. At sea level, 4 ft³ of water weighs 250 lb. What is the density of water in pounds per cubic foot? $62\frac{1}{2}$ lb/ft³

212 *Chapter 6*

4. The *index of refraction* of a transparent substance is the ratio of the speed of light in space to the speed of light in the substance. Using the table, find the index of refraction of
a. glass. $\frac{3}{2}$ **b.** water. $\frac{4}{3}$

Substance	Speed of Light (in km/s)
space	300,000
glass	200,000
water	225,000

5. A share of stock that cost $88 earned $16 last year. What was the price-to-earnings ratio of this stock? $\frac{11}{2}$

In Exercises 6 and 7, find the ratio in lowest terms.

B   **6. a.** $\dfrac{AB}{DE}$ $\dfrac{3}{2}$

    b. $\dfrac{\text{Perimeter of } \triangle ABC}{\text{Perimeter of } \triangle DEF}$ $\dfrac{3}{2}$

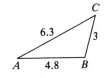

7. a. $PQ:TU$ $\dfrac{2}{5}$
    b. $QR:UV$ $\dfrac{2}{5}$
    c. $\dfrac{\text{Perimeter of } PQRS}{\text{Perimeter of } TUVW}$ $\dfrac{2}{5}$

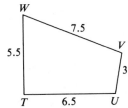

For Exercises 8–11, refer to the table to find the ratios in lowest terms.

8. The population of Centerville in 1980 to its population in 1970 $\dfrac{11}{9}$

9. The growth in the population of Easton to its 1980 population $\dfrac{3}{7}$

	Population (in thousands)	
Town	**1970**	**1980**
Centerville	36	44
Easton	16	28

10. The total population of both towns in 1970 to their total population in 1980 $\dfrac{13}{18}$

11. The total growth in the population of both towns to their total 1980 population $\dfrac{5}{18}$

Review Exercises

Solve.

1. $6x = 54$ 9
2. $11x = 99$ 9
3. $5x = 45$ 9
4. $3x = 39$ 13
5. $20x = 100$ 5
6. $10x = 80$ 8
7. $12x = 144$ 12
8. $9x = 72$ 8

Ratio, Proportion, and Percent **213**

Suggested Assignments

Core
Day 1: 211/2–10
    212/11–17 odd
Day 2: 212/Prob. 1–3
    213/Prob. 4–9
    213/Rev. 1–6

Enriched
Day 1: 211/5–10
    212/11–18
Day 2: 213/Prob. 4–11
    213/Rev. 5–8

Supplementary Materials

Practice Masters, p. 25

Teaching Suggestions
p. 209a

Related Activities p. 209b

Reading Mathematics

Students will learn the meaning of the following mathematical term in this lesson: *rate*. When a rate is expressed in a per unit form, such a rate is often called a *unit rate*.

Chalkboard Examples

Express each rate in per unit form.

1. $\frac{522 \text{ words}}{9 \text{ min}}$ 58 words/min

2. $\frac{125 \text{ mi}}{2 \text{ h}}$ $62\frac{1}{2}$ mi/h

3. $\frac{16 \text{ g}}{20 \text{ cm}^3}$ 0.8 g/cm³

4. $\frac{630 \text{ mi}}{30 \text{ gal}}$ 21 mi/gal

Solve.

5. A snail traveled 10 cm in 2 h. What was the snail's average speed in cm/h?
   5 cm/h

6-2 Rates

Some ratios are of the form

40 miles per hour   or   5 for a dollar.

These ratios involve quantities of different kinds and are called **rates.** Rates may be expressed as decimals or mixed numbers. Rates should be simplified to a *per unit* form.

EXAMPLE 1   Alice's car went 258 mi on 12 gal of gasoline. Express the rate of fuel consumption in miles per gallon.

Solution   The rate of fuel consumption is

$$\frac{258}{12} = \frac{43}{2} = 21\frac{1}{2} \text{ miles per gallon.}$$

Alice's car consumes 1 gal of gasoline every $21\frac{1}{2}$ mi.

Some of the units in which rates are given are:

mi/gal (or mpg)	miles per gallon	km/L	kilometers per liter
mi/h (or mph)	miles per hour	km/h	kilometers per hour

If a rate is the price of one item, it is called the **unit price.** For example, if 2 peaches sell for 78¢, the unit price is $\frac{78}{2}$, or 39, cents per peach.

EXAMPLE 2   If 5 oranges sell for 95¢, what is the cost of 12 oranges?

Solution   You can plan to find the price of one orange and then multiply by 12 to answer the question in the problem.

$$\text{unit price} = \frac{95}{5} = 19 \text{ (cents per orange)}$$

$$\text{cost of 12 oranges} = 12 \times 19 = 228 \text{ (cents)}$$

The cost of 12 oranges is 228¢, or $2.28.

Class Exercises

Express each rate in per unit form.

1. 120 km in 3 h 40 km/h

2. 70 mi on 5 gal of gasoline 14 mi/gal

3. $1000 in 4 months $250/month

4. 30 km on 3 L of gasoline 10 km/L

5. Three melons for $1.59

6. Two cans of tennis balls for $5.88

7. Six cans of water per 2 cans of juice

8. 28 bicycles sold in 7 days

9. 192.5 km in 3.5 h

10. A dozen eggs for $1.08

11. Ten oranges for $1.65

12. 225 m in 25 s

13. 28 teachers per 56 students

14. 18°F in 2 hours

15. 11 tickets for $30.80

16. Seven days for $399

Problems

Give the unit price of each item.

A

1. 7 oz of crackers for $1.19 17¢

2. 14 oz of cottage cheese for $1.19 8.5¢

3. 5 yd of upholstery fabric for $80 $16

4. 16 boxes of raisins for $5.60 35¢

Solve.

5. A certain kind of lumber costs $3.00 for 8 ft. At this rate, how much does a piece that is 14 ft long cost? $5.25

6. A package of 3 lb of ground beef costs $5.10. How much ground beef could you buy for $3.40 at this rate? 2 lb

7. A car travels for 3 h at an average speed of 65 km/h. How far does the car travel? 195 km

8. A boat covers 48 km in 2 h. What is the boat's average speed? 24 km/hr

9. A homing pigeon flies 180 km in 3 h. At this average speed, how far could the pigeon travel in 4 h? 240 km

10. A bicyclist travels for 2 h at an average speed of 12 km/h. How far does the bicyclist travel? At this speed, how long will it take the bicyclist to travel 54 km? 24 km; 4.5 h

Determine the better buy based on unit price alone.

B

11. A can of 35 oz of Best Brand Pear Tomatoes is on sale for 69¢. A can of 4 lb of Sun Ripe Pear Tomatoes costs $1.88. Which brand is the better buy? Best Brand Pear Tomatoes

12. A can of Favorite Beef Dog Food holds $14\frac{1}{2}$ oz. Four cans cost $1.00. Three cans of Delight Beef Dog Food, each containing 12 oz, cost $.58. Which is the better buy? Delight Beef Dog Food

Ratio, Proportion, and Percent **215**

Suggested Assignments

Core
215/Prob. 1–12
216/Prob. 15
216/Rev. 1–9 odd

Enriched
215/Prob. 2–12 even
216/Prob. 13–17

Supplementary Materials

Practice Masters, p. 25

13. Three bottles of Bright Shine Window Cleaner, each containing 15 oz, cost $2.75. Two bottles of Sparkle Window Cleaner, each containing 18.75 oz, can be purchased for $1.98. Which is the better buy? Sparkle Window Cleaner

14. A bottle of Harvest Time Apple Juice contains 64 oz and costs 99¢. Farm Fresh Juice is available in bottles that contain 1 gal for $1.88 each. Which is the better buy? Farm Fresh Juice

Solve.

15. A car uses 3 gal of gasoline every 117 mi. During the first part of a trip, the car traveled 130 mi in 4 h. If the car continues to travel at the same average speed and the trip takes a total of 6 h, how many gallons of gasoline will be consumed? 5 gal

16. Emily Depietro purchased 3 trays of strawberry plants for $16.47. Emily also purchased 10 trays of ivy plants. If the ratio of the price per tray of strawberry plants to the price per tray of ivy plants is 3 to 2, what is the total cost of the plants? $53.07

C 17. In the time that it takes one car to travel 93 km, a second car travels 111 km. If the average speed of the second car is 12 km/h faster than the speed of the first car, what is the speed of each car? 62 km/h; 74 km/h

Review Exercises

Find the perimeter of a regular polygon whose sides have the given length.

1. pentagon, 4 cm 20 cm

2. square, 6.2 m 24.8 m

3. octagon, 10.5 cm 84 cm

4. triangle, 8.9 m 26.7 m

5. rhombus, 35.6 m 142.4 m

6. hexagon, 21.75 cm 130.5 cm

7. quadrilateral, 14.35 m 57.4 m

8. decagon, 64.87 cm 648.7 cm

9. rhombus, 12.36 cm 49.44 cm

6-3 Proportions

The seventh grade at Madison Junior High School has 160 students and 10 teachers. The seventh grade at Jefferson Junior High School has 144 students and 9 teachers. Let us compare the two teacher-student ratios.

$$\frac{10}{160} = \frac{1}{16} \qquad \frac{9}{144} = \frac{1}{16}$$

Thus, the two ratios are equal.

$$\frac{10}{160} = \frac{9}{144}$$

An equation that states that two ratios are equal is called a **proportion.** The proportion above may be read as

10 is to 160 as 9 is to 144.

The numbers 10, 160, 9, and 144 are called the **terms** of the proportion.

Sometimes one of the terms of a proportion is a variable. If, for example, 192 students will be in the seventh grade at Madison Junior High next year, how many teachers will be needed if the teacher-student ratio is to remain the same?

Let n be the number of teachers needed next year. Then, if the teacher-student ratio is to be the same, we must have

$$\frac{n}{192} = \frac{10}{160}.$$

To **solve** this proportion, we find the value of the variable that makes the equation true. This can be done by finding equivalent fractions with a common denominator. For example:

$$\frac{160 \times n}{160 \times 192} = \frac{10 \times 192}{160 \times 192}$$

Since the denominators are equal, the numerators also must be equal.

$$160 \times n = 10 \times 192$$

Notice that this result could also be obtained by **cross-multiplying** in the original proportion.

$$\frac{n}{192} \diagdown\!\!\!\!\!\diagup \frac{10}{160}$$

$$160 \times n = 10 \times 192$$
$$160n = 1920$$
$$n = 1920 \div 160 = 12$$

Therefore, the seventh grade will need 12 teachers next year.

Ratio, Proportion, and Percent **217**

Teaching Suggestions
p. 209b

Related Activities p. 209b

Reading Mathematics

Students will learn the meaning of the following mathematical terms in this lesson: *proportion, terms of a proportion, cross-multiplying.*

To help students become familiar with the way we read proportions, have students read aloud the proportions in Exercises 1–4 and then state the required equation. For example, in Exercise 1, have students say "n is to 3 as 12 is to 9; so, $9n = 36$."

Solve and check.

1. $\frac{n}{5} = \frac{3}{15}$ 1

2. $\frac{1}{n} = \frac{15}{45}$ 3

3. $\frac{36}{11} = \frac{9}{n}$ $2\frac{3}{4}$

4. $\frac{n}{75} = \frac{3}{10}$ $22\frac{1}{2}$

Solve.

5. If 5 apples cost 90¢, how many apples can be bought for $2.00?
11 apples

The example on the previous page illustrates the following property of proportions.

> ## *Property*
>
> If $\frac{a}{b} = \frac{c}{d}$, with $b \neq 0$ and $d \neq 0$, then $ad = bc$.

In the proportion $\qquad \frac{a}{b} = \frac{c}{d}$

the terms a and d are called the **extremes,** and the terms b and c are called the **means.** The property above can therefore be stated:

The product of the means equals the product of the extremes.

EXAMPLE   Solve $\frac{3}{8} = \frac{12}{n}$.

Solution
$$\frac{3}{8} = \frac{12}{n}$$
$$3 \times n = 8 \times 12$$
$$3n = 96$$
$$n = 96 \div 3 = 32$$

It is a simple matter to check your answer when solving a proportion. You merely substitute your answer for the variable and cross-multiply. For instance, in the example above:

$$\frac{3}{8} \overset{?}{=} \frac{12}{32}$$
$$3 \times 32 \overset{?}{=} 8 \times 12$$
$$96 = 96$$

Class Exercises

Cross-multiply and state an equation that does not involve fractions.

1. $\frac{n}{9} = \frac{2}{3}$ $3n = 18$

2. $\frac{3}{5} = \frac{n}{20}$ $5n = 60$

3. $\frac{2}{7} = \frac{6}{n}$ $2n = 42$

4. $\frac{3}{n} = \frac{6}{10}$ $6n = 30$

5. $\frac{12}{15} = \frac{n}{5}$ $15n = 60$

6. $\frac{2}{n} = \frac{3}{9}$ $3n = 18$

7. $\frac{n}{16} = \frac{3}{4}$ $4n = 48$

8. $\frac{8}{3} = \frac{24}{n}$ $8n = 72$

218   *Chapter 6*

Written Exercises

Solve and check.

A **1.** $\frac{n}{3} = \frac{12}{9}$ 4

2. $\frac{7}{2} = \frac{x}{10}$ 35

3. $\frac{21}{r} = \frac{3}{8}$ 56

50 **4.** $\frac{3}{75} = \frac{2}{m}$

5. $\frac{8}{5} = \frac{56}{u}$ 35

6. $\frac{14}{n} = \frac{7}{9}$ 18

7. $\frac{80}{c} = \frac{4}{3}$ 60

40 **8.** $\frac{b}{24} = \frac{15}{9}$

9. $\frac{8}{7} = \frac{x}{63}$ 72

10. $\frac{d}{20} = \frac{14}{8}$ 35

11. $\frac{15}{11} = \frac{n}{33}$ 45

22 **12.** $\frac{13}{11} = \frac{26}{m}$

13. $\frac{5}{r} = \frac{2}{3}$ $7\frac{1}{2}$

14. $\frac{4}{3} = \frac{n}{7}$ $9\frac{1}{3}$

15. $\frac{17}{20} = \frac{v}{10}$ $8\frac{1}{2}$

$\frac{2}{3}$ **16.** $\frac{c}{2} = \frac{6}{18}$

B **17.** $\frac{x}{5} = \frac{20}{10}$ 10

18. $\frac{3}{m} = \frac{9}{27}$ 9

19. $\frac{4}{n} = \frac{12}{36}$ 12

8 **20.** $\frac{a}{16} = \frac{4}{8}$

21. $\frac{20}{25} = \frac{16}{y}$ 20

22. $\frac{v}{50} = \frac{18}{30}$ 30

23. $\frac{25}{x} = \frac{15}{9}$ 15

$12\frac{1}{4}$ **24.** $\frac{49}{16} = \frac{n}{4}$

25. $\frac{n}{8} = \frac{7}{10}$ $5\frac{3}{5}$

26. $\frac{15}{4} = \frac{9}{r}$ $2\frac{2}{5}$

27. $\frac{9}{10} = \frac{b}{5}$ $4\frac{1}{2}$

$4\frac{1}{5}$ **28.** $\frac{9}{n} = \frac{15}{7}$

29. If $\frac{x}{7} = \frac{3}{21}$, what is the ratio of x to 3? $\frac{1}{3}$

30. If $\frac{27}{m} = \frac{9}{2}$, what is the ratio of m to 27? $\frac{2}{9}$

31. If $\frac{3}{5} = \frac{12}{n}$, what is the ratio of n to 5? $\frac{4}{1}$

C **32.** Choose nonzero whole numbers a, b, c, d, x, and y such that $\frac{a}{b} = \frac{x}{y}$ and $\frac{c}{d} = \frac{x}{y}$. Use these numbers to check whether $\frac{a+c}{b+d} = \frac{x}{y}$.

33. Find nonzero whole numbers a, b, c, and d to show that if $\frac{a+c}{b+d} = \frac{x}{y}$, it may not be true that $\frac{a}{b} = \frac{x}{y}$ and $\frac{c}{d} = \frac{x}{y}$.

Review Exercises

Multiply.

1. $2\frac{2}{3} \times 5$ $13\frac{1}{3}$

2. $3\frac{5}{8} \times 6$ $21\frac{3}{4}$

3. $5 \times 4\frac{5}{9}$ $22\frac{7}{9}$

4. $7 \times 6\frac{3}{4}$ $47\frac{1}{4}$

5. $3\frac{4}{9} \times 2\frac{1}{2}$ $8\frac{11}{18}$

6. $4\frac{1}{3} \times 5\frac{1}{4}$ $22\frac{3}{4}$

7. $6 \times 7\frac{1}{4}$ $43\frac{1}{2}$

8. $5 \times 8\frac{3}{5}$ 43

9. $9 \times 6\frac{7}{10}$ $60\frac{3}{10}$

Ratio, Proportion, and Percent **219**

Additional A Exercises

Solve and check.

1. $\frac{10}{2} = \frac{x}{3}$ 15

2. $\frac{5}{4} = \frac{x}{10}$ $12\frac{1}{2}$

3. $\frac{3}{2} = \frac{x}{120}$ 180

4. $\frac{6}{5} = \frac{4}{x}$ $3\frac{1}{3}$

5. $\frac{2}{30} = \frac{x}{12}$ $\frac{4}{5}$

6. $\frac{8}{5} = \frac{3}{x}$ $1\frac{7}{8}$

7. $\frac{2}{x} = \frac{14}{13}$ $1\frac{6}{7}$

8. $\frac{x}{12} = \frac{13}{14}$ $11\frac{1}{7}$

Additional Answers
Written Exercises

32. Answers will vary. One possible set of values is $a = 6$, $b = 9$, $c = 8$, $d = 12$, $x = 2$, and $y = 3$:
$\frac{6}{9} = \frac{2}{3}$ and $\frac{8}{12} = \frac{2}{3}$; $\frac{6+8}{9+12} = \frac{14}{21} = \frac{2}{3}$.

33. Answers will vary. One possible set of values is $a = 1$, $b = 3$, $c = 2$, $d = 4$, $x = 3$, and $y = 7$: $\frac{1+2}{3+4} = \frac{3}{7}$, $\frac{1}{3} \neq \frac{3}{7}$ and $\frac{2}{4} \neq \frac{3}{7}$.

Suggested Assignments

Core
 219/1–29 odd
 219/Rev. 1–6

Enriched
 219/1–33 odd

Supplementary Materials

Practice Masters, p. 25
Computer Activity 11

Related Activities p. 209c

Chalkboard Examples

Use a proportion to solve each problem.

1. If 2 tires cost $74, how much will 4 tires cost? **$148**

2. A car uses 5 gal of gasoline to travel 150 mi. How much gasoline will it use to travel 5 mi? $\frac{1}{6}$ **gal**

3. For every 5 sailboats in a harbor there are 3 motorboats. If there are 30 sailboats in the harbor, how many motorboats are there? **18 motorboats**

4. A horse eats 8 lb of grain and 12 lb of hay. If the amount of grain is increased by 2 lb, how much hay should be given to the horse if the ratio of grain to hay is to remain the same? **15 lb**

6-4 Solving Problems with Proportions

Proportions can be used to solve problems. The following steps are helpful in solving problems using proportions.

1. Decide which quantity is to be found and represent it by a variable.
2. Determine whether the quantities involved can be compared using ratios (rates).
3. Equate the ratios in a proportion.
4. Solve the proportion.

EXAMPLE Linda Chu bought 4 tires for her car at a total cost of $264. How much would 5 tires cost at the same rate?

Solution Let c = the cost of 5 tires. Set up a proportion.

$$\frac{4}{264} = \frac{5}{c} \qquad \longleftarrow \text{ number of tires} \\ \longleftarrow \text{ cost}$$

Solve the proportion.

$$\frac{4}{264} = \frac{5}{c}$$
$$4c = 5 \times 264$$
$$4c = 1320$$
$$c = 330$$

Therefore, 5 tires would cost $330.

Notice that the proportion in the Example could also be written as:

$$\frac{264}{4} = \frac{c}{5} \qquad \longleftarrow \text{ cost} \\ \longleftarrow \text{ number of tires}$$

Class Exercises

State a proportion you could use to solve each problem.

1. If 4 bars of soap cost $1.50, how much would 8 bars cost? $\frac{4}{1.50} = \frac{8}{x}$

2. If you can buy 4 containers of cottage cheese for $4.20, how many could you buy for $9.45? $\frac{4}{4.20} = \frac{x}{9.45}$

3. If a satellite travels 19,500 km in 3 h, how far does it travel in 7 h? $\frac{19,500}{3} = \frac{x}{7}$

4. If a car uses 5 gal of gasoline to travel 160 mi, how many gallons would the car use in traveling 96 mi? $\frac{5}{160} = \frac{x}{96}$

220   *Chapter 6*

5. A recipe for 20 rolls calls for 5 tablespoons of butter. How many tablespoons are needed for 30 rolls? $\frac{20}{5} = \frac{30}{x}$

6. If 9 kg of fertilizer will feed 300 m² of grass, how much fertilizer would be required to feed 500 m²? $\frac{9}{300} = \frac{x}{500}$

7. If 2 cans of paint will cover a wall measuring 900 ft², what area will 3 cans cover? $\frac{2}{900} = \frac{3}{x}$

Problems

Solve.

A
1. A train traveled 720 km in 9 h.
   a. How far would it travel in 11 h?
   b. How long would it take to go 1120 km? **a. 880 km   b. 14 h**

2. Five pounds of apples cost $3.70.
   a. How many pounds could you buy for $5.92? **8 lb**
   b. How much would 9 lb cost? **$6.66**

3. Eight oranges cost $1.50.   **$3.75**
   a. How much would 20 oranges cost?
   b. How many oranges could you buy for $5.25? **28 oranges**

4. Due to Earth's rotation, a point on the equator travels about 40,000 km every 24 h.
   a. How far does a point on the equator travel in 33 h? **55,000 km**
   b. How long does it take a point on the equator to travel 95,000 km? **57 h**

5. Seventy-five cubic centimeters of maple sap can be boiled down to make 2 cm³ of maple syrup.
   a. How much maple syrup would 200 cm³ of sap make? **5.$\overline{3}$ cm³**
   b. How much sap would be needed to make 9 cm³ of syrup? **337.5 cm³**

6. A long-playing record revolves 100 times every 3 min.
   a. How many revolutions does it make in 2.25 min? **75 revolutions**
   b. How long does it take for 275 revolutions? **8.25 min**

7. Three and a half pounds of peaches cost $1.68. How much would $2\frac{1}{2}$ lb of peaches cost? **$1.20**

Ratio, Proportion, and Percent **221**

Solve.

8. A type of steel used for bicycle frames contains 5 g of manganese in every 400 g of steel. How much manganese would a 2200 g bicycle frame contain? 27.5 g

9. Five cans of paint will cover 130 m² of wall space. How many cans will be needed to cover 208 m²? 8 cans

10. To obtain the correct strength of a medicine, 5 cm³ of distilled water is added to 12 cm³ of an antibiotic. How much water should be added to 30 cm³ of the antibiotic? 12.5 cm³

11. A receipe that serves 8 calls for 15 oz of cooked tomatoes. How many ounces of tomatoes will be needed if the recipe is reduced to serve 6 people? How many servings can be made with 20 oz of cooked tomatoes? $11\frac{1}{4}$ oz; $10\frac{2}{3}$ servings

12. A geologist found that silt was deposited on a river bed at the rate of 4 cm every 170 years. How long would it take for 5 cm of silt to be deposited? How much silt would be deposited in 225 years? $212\frac{1}{2}$ yr, $5\frac{5}{17}$ cm

13. A printing press can print 350 sheets in 4 min. How long would it take to print 525 sheets? 6 min

14. A pharmacist combines 5 g of a powder with 45 cm³ of water to make a prescription medicine. How much powder should she mix with 81 cm³ of water to make a larger amount of the same medicine? 9 g

B 15. A baseball team has won 8 games and lost 6. If the team continues to have the same ratio of wins to losses, how many wins will the team have after playing 21 games? 12 wins

16. The ratio of cars to trucks passing a certain intersection is found to be 7:2. If 63 vehicles (cars and trucks) pass the intersection, how many might be trucks? 14 trucks

17. Five vests can be made from $2\frac{1}{2}$ yd of fabric. How many vests can be made from 6 yd of fabric? 12 vests

18. A fruit punch recipe calls for 3 parts of apple juice to 4 parts of cranberry juice. How many liters of cranberry juice should be added to 4.5 L of apple juice? 6 L

19. A 3 lb bag of Fairlawn's Number 25 grass seed covers a 4000 ft² area. How great an area will 16 oz of the Number 25 grass seed cover? $1333\frac{1}{3}$ ft²

20. A wall hanging requires 54 cm of braided trim. How many wall hangings can be completed if 3 m of braided trim is available?

5 wall hangings

C **21.** In a recent election, the ratio of votes *for* a particular proposal to votes *against* the proposal was 5 to 2. There were 4173 more votes for the proposal than against the proposal. How many votes were for and how many votes were against the proposal? 6955 votes for, 2782 votes against

22. A certain soil mixture calls for 8 parts of potting soil to 3 parts of sand. To make the correct mixture, Vern used 0.672 kg of sand and 2 bags of potting soil. How much potting soil was in each bag?

0.896 kg

23. In the third century B.C., the Greek mathematician Eratosthenes calculated that an angle of $7\frac{1}{2}°$ at Earth's center cuts off an arc of about 1600 km on Earth's surface. From this information compute the circumference of Earth. 76,800 km

24. In the diagram $\overline{PQ}$ is perpendicular to $\overline{MN}$. It can be shown that $\frac{a}{x} = \frac{x}{b}$. If $a = 50$ and $b = 2$, find x. 10

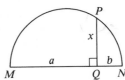

Suggested Assignments

Core
Day 1: 221/Prob. 3–7
　　　　222/Prob. 8–14
Day 2: 222/Prob. 15–19 odd
　　　　223/Prob. 20, 21
　　　　223/Rev. 1–8
　　　　223/Calculator Key-In

Enriched
Day 1: 221/Prob. 2, 4, 6
　　　　222/Prob. 8–14 even;
　　　　　　　15–19
Day 2: 223/Prob. 20–24
　　　　223/Rev. 1–8
　　　　223/Calculator Key-In

Supplementary Materials

Practice Masters, p. 26

Review Exercises

Rewrite each ratio so that the numerator and denominator are expressed in the same unit of measure. Answers may vary.

1. $\frac{2 \text{ m}}{15 \text{ cm}}$　$\frac{200 \text{ cm}}{15 \text{ cm}}$

2. $\frac{20 \text{ mm}}{7 \text{ cm}}$　$\frac{2 \text{ cm}}{7 \text{ cm}}$

3. $\frac{10 \text{ yd}}{5 \text{ ft}}$　$\frac{30 \text{ ft}}{5 \text{ ft}}$

4. $\frac{8 \text{ in.}}{3 \text{ ft}}$　$\frac{8 \text{ in.}}{36 \text{ in.}}$　$\frac{8 \text{ in.}}{3 \text{ ft}}$

5. $\frac{2 \text{ km}}{450 \text{ m}}$　$\frac{2000 \text{ m}}{450 \text{ m}}$

6. $\frac{85 \text{ cm}}{4 \text{ m}}$　$\frac{85 \text{ cm}}{400 \text{ cm}}$

7. $\frac{1 \text{ yd}}{20 \text{ in.}}$　$\frac{36 \text{ in.}}{20 \text{ in.}}$

8. $\frac{310 \text{ m}}{3 \text{ km}}$　$\frac{310 \text{ m}}{3000 \text{ m}}$

▮▮▮ Calculator Key-In

It is fairly simple to find the reciprocal of a fraction or a whole number. It is harder to find the reciprocal of a decimal. However, many calculators have a reciprocal key to carry out this procedure.

Use a calculator with a reciprocal key to find each reciprocal.

1. 0.67　　**2.** 0.579　　**3.** 0.2539　　**4.** 1.564　　**5.** 4.7851
　1.4925373　　1.7271157　　3.9385584　　0.6393861　　0.208982

Ratio, Proportion, and Percent **223**

Teaching Suggestions
p. 209d

Related Activities p. 209d

Reading Mathematics

Students will learn the meaning of the following mathematical terms in this lesson:
scale drawing, scale.

Chalkboard Examples

Give the actual dimension
corresponding to each scale
dimension given:

1. Scale: 1 cm:5 m
   a. 4 cm 20 m
   b. 6 cm 30 m
   c. 10.5 cm 52.5 m

2. Scale: 4 cm:10 km
   a. 1 cm 2.5 km
   b. 6 cm 15 km
   c. 1.2 cm 3 km

3. Scale: 15 mm:1 cm
   a. 1.5 mm 0.1 cm
   b. 21 mm 1.4 cm
   c. 105 mm 7 cm

6-5 Scale Drawing

In the drawing of the house the actual height of 9 m is represented by a length of 3 cm, and the actual length of 21 m is represented by a length of 7 cm. This means that 1 cm in the drawing rep- resents 3 m in the actual building. Such a drawing in which all lengths are in the same ratio to actual

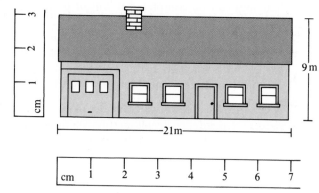

lengths is called a **scale drawing.** The relationship of length in the drawing to actual length is called the **scale.** In the drawing of the house the scale is 1 cm:3 m.

We can express the scale as a ratio, called the scale ratio, if a common unit of measure is used. Since 3 m equals 300 cm, the scale ratio above is $\frac{1}{300}$.

EXAMPLE Find the length and width of the room shown if the scale of the drawing is 1 cm:1.5 m.

Solution Measuring the drawing, we find that it has length 4 cm and width 3 cm.

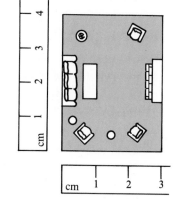

Method 1 Write a proportion for the length.

$\frac{1}{1.5} = \frac{4}{l}$ ← unit lengths in the drawing
 ← actual length

$l = 1.5 \times 4 = 6$
The room is 6 m long.

Write a proportion for the width. $\frac{1}{1.5} = \frac{3}{w}$

$w = 1.5 \times 3 = 4.5$ The room is 4.5 m wide.

Method 2 Use the scale ratio: $\frac{1\,cm}{1.5\,m} = \frac{1\,cm}{150\,cm} = \frac{1}{150}$

The actual length is 150 times the length in the drawing.

$l = 150 \times 4 = 600\,cm = 6\,m$ $w = 150 \times 3 = 450\,cm = 4.5\,m$

224 *Chapter 6*

Class Exercises

A drawing of a bureau is to be made with a scale of 1 cm to 10 cm. Find the dimension on the drawing if the actual dimension is given.

1. Height of bureau (70 cm) 7 cm

2. Width of bureau (80 cm) 8 cm

3. Height of legs (17.5 cm) 1.75 cm

4. Width of top (75 cm) 7.5 cm

5. Height of top drawer (10 cm) 1 cm

6. Height of second drawer (12.5 cm) 1.25 cm

7. Height of third drawer (15 cm) 1.5 cm

8. Width of drawer (72.5 cm) 7.25 cm

Written Exercises

An O-gauge model railroad has a scale of 1 in.: 48 in. Find the actual length of each railroad car, given the scale dimension.

A

1. Flat car: 23 in. 1104 in. 2. Freight car: 11 in. 528 in.   3. Tank car: 12 in. 576 in.

4. Caboose: 9 in. 432 in. 5. Passenger car: 20 in. 960 in. 6. Refrigerator car: 15 in. 720 in.

Exercises 7–14, on the next page, refer to the map below.
a. Measure each distance in the map shown to the nearest 0.5 cm.
b. Compute the actual distance to the nearest 100 km.

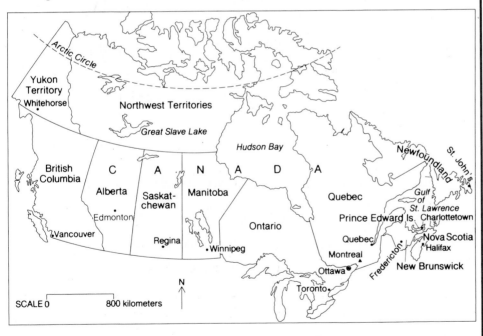

1. A picture shows a computer chip to be a square 8 cm by 8 cm. If the length in the picture is 10 times actual size, what are the dimensions of the chip? **8 mm by 8 mm**

2. The scale on a map is 1 cm to 240 m.
   a. The distance from Michael's house to his school is 10 cm on the map. What is the actual distance? **2400 m, or 2.4 km**

   b. The actual distance from the intersection of Linden Street and 3rd Street to Michael's house is 2.4 km. What is this distance on the map? **10 cm**

3. The actual distance from Cate's camp to the river is 1.2 km. The distance on a map is 2.4 cm. What is the scale of the map? **1 cm : 0.5 km**

4. A picture of an insect has a scale of 7 to 1. The length of the insect in the picture is 5.6 cm. What is the actual length of the insect? **0.8 cm, or 8 mm**

5. A house plan shows a scale $\frac{1}{4}$ in. = 1 ft. What is the actual length of a wall that measures $3\frac{5}{16}$ in. on the drawing? **$13\frac{1}{4}$ ft**

Express each ratio as a fraction in lowest terms.

1. 21:33 $\frac{7}{11}$

2. 32 to 56 $\frac{4}{7}$

3. 99 to 121 $\frac{9}{11}$

Give the unit price of each item.

4. 8 gal of paint for $102 $12.75/gal

5. 9 lb of ground beef for $14.31 $1.59/lb

Solve.

6. $\frac{2}{5} = \frac{12}{x}$ 30

7. $\frac{13}{15} = \frac{x}{25}$ $21\frac{2}{3}$

8. $\frac{11}{x} = \frac{121}{2}$ $\frac{2}{11}$

9. A $12\frac{1}{2}$-oz can of peas costs $.50. What is the cost per ounce? $.04

10. If 25 sheets of photographic paper cost $12.50, how much do 10 sheets cost? $5.00

11. On a map 1 cm represents 1.2 m. What is the actual distance if a measurement on the map is 16 cm?   19.2 m

12. In an archaeological drawing a meter is represented by 2 cm. What is the scale of the drawing?   1 cm : 0.5 m

Suggested Assignments

Core
  225/1–3
  226/7–14
  226/Self-Test A
Enriched
  226/7–17
  226/Self-Test A

Supplementary Materials

Practice Masters, p. 26
Computer Activity 12
Test 6A, pp. 35–36

---

7. Vancouver to Edmonton   2 cm; 800 km   **8.** Toronto to Winnipeg   4 cm; 1600 km

9. Whitehorse to Montreal   105 cm; 4200 km   **10.** Ottawa to Charlottetown   2.5 cm; 1000 km

11. Toronto to Halifax   3 cm; 1200 km   **12.** Fredericton to St. John's   2.5 cm; 1000 km

B 13. By how many kilometers would an airplane route from Winnipeg to Montreal be extended if the plane went by way of Toronto?   400 km

14. How much farther is it by air from Vancouver to Edmonton to Whitehorse than it is from Vancouver directly to Whitehorse?   800 km

If Earth had the diameter of a peppercorn (5 mm), the sun would have the diameter of a large beach ball (54.5 cm) and it would be about the length of two basketball courts (58.75 m) away. Assuming that the diameter of Earth is about 12,700 km, compute each measurement.

15. The actual diameter of the sun   1,384,300 km

16. The distance from Earth to the sun   149,225,000 km

17. In the scale described above, the diameter of the planet Jupiter would be 55 mm. What is the actual diameter of Jupiter?   139,700 km

---

Self-Test A

Express each ratio as a fraction in lowest terms.

1. 12:8 $\frac{3}{2}$ **2.** 51 to 27 $\frac{17}{9}$ **3.** $\frac{18}{99}$ $\frac{2}{11}$ [6–1]

Give the unit price of each item.

4. 8 gal of gasoline for $9.20 $1.15   **5.** 11 cans of pet food for $6.72 $.61   [6–2]

Solve.

6. $\frac{x}{3} = \frac{8}{12}$ 2   **7.** $\frac{12}{9} = \frac{n}{3}$ 4   **8.** $\frac{180}{n} = \frac{4}{3}$ 135   [6–3]

9. Find the price per gram of a metal that costs $154.10 for 230 g. $.67   [6–4]

10. A company paid a dividend of $30 on 12 shares of stock. How much will it pay on 44 shares? $110

11. On a map, 3 in. represents 16 ft. What length represents $5\frac{1}{3}$ ft?   1 in.   [6–5]

12. What is the scale in a drawing in which a vase 28 cm tall is drawn 1.75 cm high?   1 cm : 16 cm

---

Self-Test answers and Extra Practice are at the back of the book.

226   *Chapter 6*

6-6 Percents and Fractions

During basketball season, Alice made 17 out of 25 free throws, while Nina made 7 out of 10. To see who did better, we compare the fractions representing each girl's successful free throws:

$$\frac{17}{25} \quad \text{and} \quad \frac{7}{10}$$

In comparing fractions it is often convenient to use the common denominator 100, even if 100 is not the LCD of the fractions.

$$\frac{17}{25} = \frac{17 \times 4}{25 \times 4} = \frac{68}{100} \qquad \frac{7}{10} = \frac{7 \times 10}{10 \times 10} = \frac{70}{100}$$

Since Alice makes 68 free throws per hundred and Nina makes 70 per hundred, Nina is the better free-throw shooter.

The ratio of a number to 100 is called a **percent.** We write percents by using the symbol %. For example,

$$\frac{17}{25} = \frac{68}{100} = 68\% \qquad \text{and} \qquad \frac{7}{10} = \frac{70}{100} = 70\%.$$

Rule

To express the fraction $\frac{a}{b}$ as a percent, solve the equation

$\frac{n}{100} = \frac{a}{b}$ for the variable n and write $n\%$.

EXAMPLE 1   Express $\frac{17}{40}$ as a percent.

Solution $\frac{n}{100} = \frac{17}{40}$

Cross-multiply.

$40 \times n = 17 \times 100$

$$n = \frac{17}{40} \times 100 = \frac{17}{40} \times \overset{5}{100} = \frac{85}{2} = 42\frac{1}{2}$$

Therefore, $\frac{17}{40} = 42\frac{1}{2}\%$, or 42.5%.

Ratio, Proportion, and Percent   **227**

Teaching Suggestions
p. 209e

Related Activities p. 209e

Reading Mathematics

Students will learn the meaning of the following mathematical term in this lesson: *percent.*

Be sure that when students read a percent, they read both the number and the percent symbol, that is 12% is read "12 percent." Emphasize that 12 and 12% are very different.

You may wish to relate the meaning of the word *percent* to other words that are familiar to your students. A century is 100 years; that is, 1 year is $\frac{1}{100}$ of a century. A cent is $\frac{1}{100}$ of a dollar, or $.01. The word *percent* is derived from the Latin *per centum,* meaning "per hundred" or "out of one hundred"; thus, 12% means 12 out of 100, or $\frac{12}{100}$.

Express as a fraction in lowest terms or as a mixed number in simple form.

1. 20% $\frac{1}{5}$

2. 58% $\frac{29}{50}$

3. 77% $\frac{77}{100}$

4. 400% 4

5. 325% $3\frac{1}{4}$

6. $9\frac{2}{5}$% $\frac{47}{500}$

Express as a percent.

7. $\frac{3}{50}$ 6%

8. $\frac{7}{20}$ 35%

9. $\frac{6}{25}$ 24%

10. 7 700%

11. $4\frac{17}{20}$ 485%

12. $3\frac{9}{50}$ 318%

> ### Rule
> To express $n\%$ as a fraction, write the fraction
> $$\frac{n}{100}$$
> in lowest terms.

EXAMPLE 2 Express $7\frac{1}{2}\%$ as a fraction in lowest terms.

Solution $7\frac{1}{2}\% = 7.5\% = \frac{7.5}{100} = \frac{7.5 \times 10}{100 \times 10} = \frac{75}{1000} = \frac{3}{40}$

Since a percent is the ratio of a number to 100, we can have percents that are greater than or equal to 100%. For example,

$$\frac{100}{100} = 100\% \qquad \text{and} \qquad \frac{165}{100} = 165\%.$$

EXAMPLE 3 Write 250% as a mixed number in simple form.

Solution $250\% = \frac{250}{100}$

$= 2\frac{50}{100} = 2\frac{1}{2}$

EXAMPLE 4 A certain town spends 42% of its budget on education. What percent is used for other purposes?

Solution The whole budget is represented by 100%. Therefore, the part used for other purposes is

$$100 - 42, \text{ or } 58\%.$$

Class Exercises

Express as a fraction in lowest terms or as a mixed number in simple form.

1. 17% $\frac{17}{100}$ **2.** 90% $\frac{9}{10}$ **3.** 50% $\frac{1}{2}$ $\frac{1}{4}$ **4.** 25%

5. 20% $\frac{1}{5}$ **6.** 100% 1   **7.** 4% $\frac{1}{25}$ $1\frac{1}{2}$ **8.** 150%

9. 300% 3   **10.** 30% $\frac{3}{10}$ **11.** 35% $\frac{7}{20}$ $2\frac{1}{10}$ **12.** 210%

228 *Chapter 6*

Express as a percent.

13. $\frac{1}{50}$ 2% 14. $\frac{1}{10}$ 10% 15. $\frac{7}{10}$ 70% 100% 16. 1

17. 2 200% 18. $\frac{1}{20}$ 5% 19. $3\frac{1}{2}$ 350% 90% 20. $\frac{9}{10}$

21. $\frac{3}{4}$ 75% 22. $4\frac{1}{2}$ 450% 23. $\frac{2}{25}$ 8% 15% 24. $\frac{3}{20}$

Written Exercises

Express as a fraction in lowest terms or as a mixed number in simple form.

A 1. 75% $\frac{3}{4}$ 2. 60% $\frac{3}{5}$ 3. 45% $\frac{9}{20}$ $\frac{19}{20}$ 4. 95%

5. 12% $\frac{3}{25}$ 6. 76% $\frac{19}{25}$ 7. 125% $1\frac{1}{4}$ $2\frac{1}{5}$ 8. 220%

9. $15\frac{1}{2}$% $\frac{31}{200}$ 10. $8\frac{4}{5}$% $\frac{11}{125}$ 11. $10\frac{3}{4}$% $\frac{43}{400}$ $\frac{43}{800}$ 12. $5\frac{3}{8}$%

Express as a percent.

13. $\frac{4}{5}$ 80% 14. $\frac{1}{4}$ 25% 15. $\frac{3}{10}$ 30% 4% 16. $\frac{1}{25}$

17. $\frac{12}{25}$ 48% 18. $\frac{17}{20}$ 85% 19. $\frac{31}{50}$ 62% 175% 20. $1\frac{3}{4}$

21. $2\frac{1}{5}$ 220% 22. $3\frac{11}{25}$ 344% 23. $\frac{51}{50}$ 102% 124% 24. $\frac{31}{25}$

B 25. $\frac{7}{8}$ 87.5% 26. $\frac{7}{40}$ 17.5% 27. $\frac{1}{200}$ 0.5% 9.6% 28. $\frac{12}{125}$

29. $\frac{3}{400}$ 0.75% 30. $\frac{9}{250}$ 3.6% 31. $\frac{121}{40}$ 302.5% 32. $\frac{25}{8}$
312.5%

EXAMPLE Express $33\frac{1}{3}$% as a fraction in lowest terms.

Solution $33\frac{1}{3}\% = \frac{33\frac{1}{3}}{100} = 33\frac{1}{3} \div 100$

$= \frac{100}{3} \times \frac{1}{100} = \frac{1}{3}$

Express each percent as a fraction in lowest terms.

C 33. $16\frac{2}{3}$% $\frac{1}{6}$ 34. $66\frac{2}{3}$% $\frac{2}{3}$ 35. $41\frac{2}{3}$% $\frac{5}{12}$ $\frac{5}{6}$ 36. $83\frac{1}{3}$%

Ratio, Proportion, and Percent **229**

Suggested Assignments

Core
Day 1: 229/2–32 even; 33, 34
Day 2: 230/Prob. 1–7
        230/Rev. 1–10

Enriched
Day 1: 229/1–31 odd; 33–36
Day 2: 230/Prob. 2–9
        230/Rev. 1–10

Supplementary Materials

Practice Masters, p. 27

Problems

A 1. In a public opinion poll 62% of the questionnaires sent out were returned. What percent were not returned? 38%

2. The efficiency of a machine is the percent of energy going into the machine that does useful work. A turbine in a hydroelectric plant is 92% efficient. What percent of the energy is wasted? 8%

3. Of the 300 acres on Swanson's farm, 180 acres are used to grow wheat. What percent of the land is used to grow wheat? 60%

4. Of the selling price of a pair of gloves, 42% pays the wholesale cost of the gloves, 33% pays store expenses, and the rest is profit. What percent is profit? 25%

B 5. In a 500 kg metal bar, 475 kg is iron and the remainder is impurities. What percent of the bar is impurities? 5%

6. A baseball team won 42 games out of its first 80. What percent of the games did the team win? $52\frac{1}{2}$%

7. One year the Caterpillars lost 5 games out of 16. If the Caterpillars also tied 1 game, what percent of their games did they win? $62\frac{1}{2}$%

C 8. The Bears won 40 games and lost 24, while the Bulls won 32 games and lost 18. Which team had the higher percent of wins? Bulls

9. At a company sales conference there were 4 executives, 28 salespeople, and 8 marketing consultants. What percent of the people were executives? Salespeople? Not marketing consultants?
10%; 70%; 80%

Review Exercises

Change each fraction to a decimal.

1. $\frac{9}{20}$ 0.45 2. $\frac{19}{25}$ 0.76 3. $\frac{11}{40}$ 0.275 4. $\frac{17}{80}$ 0.2125 5. $\frac{1}{25}$ 0.04

6. $\frac{13}{30}$ 0.4$\overline{3}$ 7. $\frac{8}{11}$ 0.$\overline{72}$ 8. $\frac{19}{22}$ 0.86$\overline{3}$ 9. $\frac{43}{75}$ 0.573$\overline{3}$ 10. $\frac{83}{90}$ 0.9$\overline{2}$

230 *Chapter 6*

230

6-7 Percents and Decimals

By looking at the following examples, you may be able to see a general relationship between decimals and percents.

$$57\% = \frac{57}{100} = 0.57 \qquad\qquad 0.79 = \frac{79}{100} = 79\%$$

$$113\% = \frac{113}{100} = 1\frac{13}{100} = 1.13 \qquad 0.06 = \frac{6}{100} = 6\%$$

These examples suggest the following rules.

Rules

1. To express a percent as a decimal, move the decimal point two places to the left and remove the percent sign.

$$57\% = 0.57 \qquad 113\% = 1.13$$

2. To express a decimal as a percent, move the decimal point two places to the right and add a percent sign.

$$0.79 = 79\% \qquad 0.06 = 6\%$$

EXAMPLE 1 Express each percent as a decimal.
  a. 83.5%   **b.** 450%   **c.** 0.25%

Solution **a.** $83.5\% = 0.835$

  b. $450\% = 4.50 = 4.5$

  c. $0.25\% = 0.0025$

EXAMPLE 2 Express each decimal as a percent.
  a. 10.5   **b.** 0.0062   **c.** 0.574

Solution **a.** $10.5 = 1050\%$

  b. $0.0062 = 00.62\%$

  c. $0.574 = 57.4\%$

   In the previous lesson you learned one method of changing a fraction to a percent. The ease of changing a decimal to a percent suggests the alternative method shown on the following page.

Ratio, Proportion, and Percent   **231**

Teaching Suggestions p. 209e

Related Activities p. 209e

Chalkboard Examples

Express as a decimal.
1. 47% 0.47
2. 8% 0.08
3. 55.3% 0.553
4. 0.9% 0.009

Express as a percent.
5. 0.48 48%
6. 0.94 94%
7. 1.06 106%
8. 0.025 2.5%

Express first as a decimal and then as a percent.
9. $\frac{3}{20}$ 0.15; 15%
10. $\frac{9}{50}$ 0.18; 18%
11. $1\frac{1}{4}$ 1.25; 125%
12. $\frac{13}{20}$ 0.65; 65%

Rule

To express a fraction as a percent, first express the fraction as a decimal and then as a percent.

EXAMPLE 3 Express $\frac{7}{8}$ as a percent.

Solution Divide 7 by 8.

$$8\overline{)7.000} \quad \begin{array}{r} 0.875 \\ \hline \end{array}$$

$$\begin{array}{r} 6\,4 \\ \hline 60 \\ 56 \\ \hline 40 \\ 40 \\ \hline 0 \end{array}$$

$$\frac{7}{8} = 0.875 = 87.5\%$$

EXAMPLE 4 Express $\frac{1}{3}$ as a percent. Round to the nearest tenth of a percent.

Solution Divide 1 by 3 to the ten-thousandths' place.

Round the quotient to the nearest thousandth.

$$0.3333 \approx 0.333$$

Express the decimal as a percent.

$$0.333 = 33.3\%$$

$$3\overline{)1.0000} \quad \begin{array}{r} 0.3333 \\ \hline \end{array}$$

$$\begin{array}{r} 9 \\ \hline 10 \\ 9 \\ \hline 10 \\ 9 \\ \hline 10 \\ 9 \\ \hline 1 \end{array}$$

To the nearest tenth of a percent, $\frac{1}{3} = 33.3\%$.

Class Exercises

Express each percent as a decimal.

1. 39% 0.39   **2.** 4% 0.04   **3.** 150% 1.5   **4.** 0.8% 0.008   **5.** 1080% 10.80   **6.** 1% 0.01

Express each decimal as a percent.

7. 0.56 56%   **8.** 0.005 0.5%   **9.** 0.07 7%   **10.** 1.6 160%   **11.** 5.3 530%   **12.** 0.0001 0.01%

Express each of the following first as a decimal and then as a percent.

13. $\frac{1}{2}$ **14.** $\frac{1}{4}$ **15.** $\frac{3}{5}$ **16.** $2\frac{1}{2}$ **17.** $\frac{1}{1000}$ **18.** $\frac{23}{1000}$

232 *Chapter 6*

Written Exercises

Express each percent as a decimal.

A **1.** 93% 0.93 **2.** 46% 0.46 **3.** 114% 1.14 1.75 **4.** 175%

5. 260% 2.6 **6.** 1150% 11.5 **7.** 49.5% 0.495 0.782 **8.** 78.2%

9. 0.6% 0.006 **10.** 99.44% 0.9944 **11.** 0.05% 0.0005 **12.** 0.032%
0.00032

Express each decimal as a percent.

13. 0.59 59% **14.** 0.87 87% **15.** 0.09 9% 7.5% **16.** 0.075

17. 2.6 260% **18.** 10.6 1060% **19.** 12.83 1283% 501% **20.** 5.01

21. 0.007 0.7% **22.** 0.033 3.3% **23.** 0.0867 8.67% **24.** 0.0026
0.26%

Express each fraction as a decimal and then as a percent. Round to the nearest tenth of a percent if necessary.

B **25.** $\frac{3}{8}$ **26.** $\frac{9}{125}$ **27.** $\frac{3}{500}$ **28.** $\frac{27}{40}$

29. $1\frac{5}{8}$ **30.** $2\frac{37}{40}$ **31.** $\frac{47}{80}$ **32.** $\frac{7}{11}$

33. $\frac{17}{24}$ **34.** $\frac{19}{12}$ **35.** $\frac{2}{7}$ **36.** $\frac{16}{9}$

Express each fraction as an exact percent.

EXAMPLE $\frac{1}{3}$

Solution Divide 1 by 3 to the $1 \div 3 = 0.33$ R 1, or $0.33\frac{1}{3}$
hundredths' place:

Express the quotient as a percent: $0.33\frac{1}{3} = 33\frac{1}{3}\%$

Thus, as a percent, $\frac{1}{3} = 33\frac{1}{3}\%$.

C **37.** $\frac{1}{6}$ $16\frac{2}{3}\%$ **38.** $\frac{2}{3}$ $66\frac{2}{3}\%$ **39.** $\frac{8}{9}$ $88\frac{8}{9}\%$ **40.** $\frac{1}{15}$ $6\frac{2}{3}\%$ **41.** $\frac{5}{6}$
$83\frac{1}{3}\%$

Review Exercises

Solve.
15.438
1. $x + 2.47 = 5.42$ 2.95 **2.** $x - 3.43 = 1.91$ 5.34 **3.** $x \div 3.72 = 4.15$

4. $2.48x = 8.1096$ 3.27 **5.** $x \div 4.03 = 5.92$ 23.8576 **6.** $1.37x = 11.4806$
8.38

Ratio, Proportion, and Percent **233**

Reading Mathematics

You may wish to discuss with students the various uses of the word *of* in mathematics. The word *of* often indicates multiplication as in "One-half of the 20 students are boys" and "Forty percent of 12,000 registered voters went to the polls." Students should be cautioned, however, that the word *of* does have other uses. For example, "8 students out of a class of 27 received honor grades" indicates the ratio $\frac{8}{27}$.

Chalkboard Examples

Solve.

1. What percent of 30 is 27? **90%**

2. What percent of 45 is 72? **160%**

3. What is 25% of 60? **15**

4. What is 68% of 145? **98.6**

5. 80 is 40% of what number? **200**

6-8 Computing with Percents

The statement 20% of 300 is 60 can be translated into the equations

$$\frac{20}{100} \times 300 = 60 \quad \text{and} \quad 0.20 \times 300 = 60.$$

Notice the following relationship between the words and the symbols.

| 20% | of | 300 | is | 60 |

$$\left.\begin{array}{c} \frac{20}{100} \\ \\ 0.20 \end{array}\right\} \quad \times \quad 300 \quad = \quad 60$$

A similar relationship occurs whenever a statement or a question involves a number that is a percent of another number.

EXAMPLE 1   What number is 8% of 75?

Solution   Let n represent the number asked for.

| What number | is | 8% of 75? |

$$n \qquad = 0.08 \times 75$$

6 is 8% of 75.

EXAMPLE 2   What percent of 40 is 6?

Solution   Let $n\%$ represent the percent asked for. We can translate the question into an equation as follows.

| What percent | of | 40 | is | 6? |

$$n\% \qquad \times \quad 40 \quad = \quad 6$$

$$n\% \times 40 = 6$$

$$n\% = \frac{6}{40}$$

$$\frac{n}{100} = \frac{3}{20}$$

$$n = \frac{3}{20} \times 100 = 15$$

15% of 40 is 6.

234   *Chapter 6*

EXAMPLE 3   140 is 35% of what number?

Solution   Let n represent the number asked for.

140 $\quad$ is $\quad$ 35% $\quad$ of $\quad$ what number?

140 $\quad\quad = 0.35 \quad \times \quad n$

$$140 = 0.35n$$
$$140 \div 0.35 = 0.35n \div 0.35$$
$$140 \div 0.35 = n$$
$$400 = n$$

140 is 35% of 400

Class Exercises

State an equation involving a variable that expresses the conditions of the question.

1. What number is 10% of 920?
$$n = 0.10 \times 920$$
3. 28 is 80% of what number?
$$28 = 0.80 \times n$$
5. 40% of 25 is what number?
$$0.40 \times 25 = n$$
7. 60 is 75% of what number?
$$60 = 0.75 \times n$$

2. What percent of 650 is 130?
$$n\% \times 650 = 130$$
4. 120 is what percent of 150?
$$120 = n\% \times 150$$
6. What percent of 80 is 100?
$$n\% \times 80 = 100$$
8. What number is 125% of 160?
$$n = 1.25 \times 160$$

Written Exercises

Answer each question by writing an equation and solving it. Round your answer to the nearest tenth of a percent if necessary.

A 1. What percent of 225 is 90? 40%

2. What number is 76% of 350? 266

3. 45% of 600 is what number? 270

4. What percent of 150 is 48? 32%

5. 52 is 4% of what number? 1300

6. 56 is 4% of what number? 1400

7. What number is 36% of 15? 5.4

8. 96% of 85 is what number? 81.6

9. What percent of 36 is 30? 83.3%

10. 48 is what percent of 72? 66.7%

B 11. What is 110% of 95? 104.5

12. 0.5% of what number is 15? 3000

13. 116% of 75 is what number? 87

14. What percent of 40 is 86? 215%

15. What is 0.35% of 256? 0.896

16. 12 is 150% of what number? 8

Ratio, Proportion, and Percent **235**

Additional A Exercises

Answer each question by writing an equation and solving it. Round your answer to the nearest tenth of a percent if necessary.

1. What is 22% of 56? 12.32

2. What is 120% of 16? 19.2

3. 50 is what percent of 72? 69.4%

4. 22 is what percent of 21? 104.8%

5. What percent of 120 is 40? 33.3%

6. What percent of 85 is 51? 60%

7. If 150 invitations were mailed and 90 people replied, what percent of the people replied? 60%

Answer each question by writing an equation and solving it. Round your answer to the nearest tenth of a percent if necessary.

17. What percent of 21 is 24? 114.3%   **18.** What is 81% of 60? 48.6

19. 12.5% of what number is 28? 224   **20.** What percent of 45 is 600? 1333.3%

C 21. 18 is $33\frac{1}{3}$% of what number? 54

(*Hint:* Write the percent as a fraction in lowest terms.)

22. What is $41\frac{2}{3}$% of 300? 125   **23.** 231 is $91\frac{2}{3}$% of what number? 252

Problems

Solve.

A 1. Lisa earns $250 a week and lives in a state that taxes income at 5%. How much does Lisa pay in state tax each week? $12.50

2. A baseball park has 40,000 seats of which 13,040 are box seats and 18,200 are reserved seats. What percent of the seats are box seats? Reserved seats? 32.6%; 45.5%

3. A basketball player made 62 out of 80 free-throw shots. What percent of the free throws did she make? 77.5%

4. A sweater is 65% wool by weight. If the sweater weighs 12.4 ounces, how much wool is in the sweater? 8.06 oz

B 5. In a class of 40 students, 36 received passing grades on a geography test. What percent of the students in the class did not receive passing grades? 10%

6. A service contract offered by a washing machine manufacturer can be purchased for 9% of the price of a washing machine. If a certain washer costs $580, what is the price of the service contract? $52.20

7. Of the 427 people responding to a public opinion poll, 224 answered *Yes* to a certain question and 154 answered *No*. What percent of those corresponding were undecided? Give your answer to the nearest tenth of a percent. 11.5%

236   *Chapter 6*

8. In 1979 the United States produced 3112 million barrels of oil. This was 13.7% of the world oil output. What was the world oil output to the nearest million barrels? **22,715 million barrels**

9. It is estimated that 60% of the people of the world live in Asia. If there are 2.4 billion people living in Asia, what is the population of the world? **4 billion**

C 10. In a recent election, 45% of the eligible voters actually voted. Of these, 55% voted for the winner.
   a. What percent of eligible voters voted for the winning candidate? **24.75%**
   b. Suppose 495 people voted for the winner. How many eligible voters were there? **2000**

11. Of a city's 180,000 workers, 25% use the subway system. Of these, 18,000 use the subway between 7 A.M. and 9:30 A.M.
   a. What percent of the city's total number of workers ride the subway between 7 A.M. and 9:30 A.M.? **10%**
   b. What percent of the total number of subway riders use the subway between 7 A.M. and 9:30 A.M.? **40%**

Self-Test B

Express as a fraction in lowest terms or as a mixed number in simple form.

1. 27% $\frac{27}{100}$
2. 83% $\frac{83}{100}$
3. 164% $1\frac{16}{25}$
4. 290% $2\frac{9}{10}$ [6-6]

Express as a percent.

5. $\frac{1}{20}$ 5%
6. $\frac{3}{8}$ 37.5%
7. 4 400%
8. $3\frac{1}{4}$ 325%

Express as a decimal.

9. 45% 0.45
10. 78% 0.78
11. 348% 3.48
12. 0.8% 0.008 [6-7]

Express as a percent.

13. 0.64 64%
14. 0.81 81%
15. 7.85 785%
16. 0.068 6.8%

17. What percent of 56 is 14? 25%
18. 82 is what percent of 40? 205% [6-8]
19. What is 44% of 25? 11
20. 70% of what number is 84? 120

Self-Test answers and Extra Practice are at the back of the book.

Ratio, Proportion, and Percent **237**

Enrichment Note

For further understanding of the Golden Ratio, have students draw a square 1 by 1, add another square 1 by 1, add another square 2 by 2, another 3 by 3, another 5 by 5, and so on. The side of each new square should be the next number in the Fibonacci sequence.

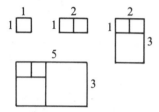

Point out that each side of each rectangle is a number in the Fibonacci sequence. After the first few rectangles, the shapes change very little as the sizes increase.

If the ratio of length to width of a rectangle is the Golden Ratio, the rectangle is called a **golden rectangle.** Have students calculate the ratios of length to width for several rectangular objects such as books, pictures, desks, index cards, and food packages. Many of these ratios will be close to the Golden Ratio.

Golden rectangles have been used in art and architecture for thousands of years. Interested students might want to calculate the ratio of length to width for paintings and the facades of buildings. (The front of the Parthenon is a classic example.) By drawing golden rectangles of various sizes on clear plastic or tracing paper, and placing one over a painting, students may discover that the artist arranged the subjects in a golden rectangle.

Fibonacci Numbers

In the thirteenth century, an Italian mathematician named Leonardo of Pisa, nicknamed Fibonacci, discovered a sequence of numbers that has many interesting mathematical properties, as well as applications to biology, art, and architecture. Fibonacci defined the sequence as the number of pairs of rabbits you would have, starting with one pair, if each pair produced a new pair after two months and another new pair every month thereafter.

The diagram below illustrates the process that Fibonacci described for the first six months:

Months		Number of Pairs
1		1
2		1
3		2
4		3
5		5
6		8

The sequence formed by the numbers of pairs is called the **Fibonacci sequence.** Note that any number in the sequence is the sum of the two numbers that precede it (for example, $2 + 3 = 5, 3 + 5 = 8$). Thus the sequence would continue:

1, 1, 2, 3, 5, 8, 13, 21, 34, 55, 89, 144, 233, 377, 610, . . .

To see one of the many mathematical properties of this sequence, study the sums of the squares of some pairs of consecutive Fibonacci numbers:

$$2^2 + 3^2 = 4 + 9 = 13$$
$$5^2 + 8^2 = 25 + 64 = 89$$
$$13^2 + 21^2 = 169 + 441 = 610$$

Note that in each case the sum is another number in the sequence.

238 *Chapter 6*

The Fibonacci sequence also relates to a historically important number called the **Golden Ratio,** or the **Golden Mean.** The Golden Ratio is the ratio of the length to the width of a "perfect" rectangle. A rectangle was considered to be "perfect" if the ratio of its length to its width was the same as the ratio of their sum to its length, as written in the proportion at the right. If we let the width of the rectangle be 1, the length is the nonterminating, nonrepeating decimal 1.61828 . . . . Thus, the Golden Ratio is the ratio 1.61828 . . . to 1.

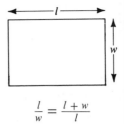

$$\frac{l}{w} = \frac{l + w}{l}$$

It is remarkable that the ratios of successive terms of the Fibonacci sequence get closer and closer to this number. For example,

$\frac{8}{5} = 1.6$ $\qquad$ $\frac{13}{8} = 1.625$ $\qquad$ $\frac{21}{13} = 1.615384\ldots$

$\frac{34}{21} = 1.61904\ldots$ $\qquad$ $\frac{55}{34} = 1.61764\ldots$ $\qquad$ $\frac{89}{55} = 1.61818\ldots$

1. Examine the fourth, eighth, twelfth, and sixteenth terms of the Fibonacci sequence. What do these numbers have in common? Try the fifth, tenth, and fifteenth terms.

Find some other numerical patterns by performing these calculations with the numbers in the Fibonacci sequence listed on the previous page. Tell what you notice about each new pattern.

2. Find the difference of two numbers that are two places apart in the sequence (the first and the third terms, the second and the fourth terms, the third and the fifth terms, and so on).

3. Subtract the squares of two numbers that are two places apart (as in Exercise 2).

4. Multiply two consecutive numbers (the first and second terms), multiply the next two consecutive numbers (the second and third terms), and then add the products.

5. Multiply two numbers that are two places apart (begin with the second and fourth terms), multiply two other numbers that "straddle" one of these (the first and third terms), and then add the products.

Career Activity Botanists have discovered that Fibonacci numbers occur naturally in many plant forms. For example, a pine cone is made up of 8 spirals swirling upward in one direction and 13 spirals swirling upward in the opposite direction. Find some other instances of Fibonacci numbers that botanists have found in nature.

Ratio, Proportion, and Percent **239**

If students draw a golden rectangle *ABCD* and mark off a square *ABEF*, the rectangle *CDFE* is also a golden rectangle.

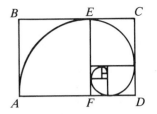

If students continue this process and draw a circular arc in each square as shown, the curve is approximately a logarithmic spiral, similar to a snail shell. Students may want to investigate the kinds of spirals.

The golden ratio has many other names. Students who want to read more about it should also look up *golden mean, golden section, golden proportion,* and *divine proportion.*

Additional Answers

1. 3, 21, 144, and 987 are divisible by 3; 5, 55, and 610 are divisible by 5.

2. The Fibonacci sequence

3. Every other member of the Fibonacci sequence, starting with 3.

4. Every other member of the Fibonacci sequence, starting with 3.

5. Every other member of the Fibonacci sequence, starting with 5.

Chapter Review

Match.

1. 2 min to 90 sec a **2.** 1 lb : 8 oz c   **a.** 4 : 3   **b.** 22 mi/gal   [6–1]

3. 682 mi on 31 gal b **4.** 40 km in 30 min **c.** 2 : 1   **d.** $1\frac{1}{3}$ km/min [6–2]
                                   d

Write the letter of the correct answer.

5. Solve $\frac{6}{x} = \frac{9}{75}$. c   [6–3]

  a. 450   **b.** 54   **c.** 50   **d.** 37.5

6. A bicyclist went 7 mi in 30 min. How far would the cyclist go in [6–4]
45 min? c

  a. 4.2 mi   **b.** 14 mi   **c.** $10\frac{1}{2}$ mi **d.** $\frac{14}{3}$ mi

7. Three cans of paint will cover 80 m² of wall. What area will 5 cans
cover? a

  a. $133\frac{1}{3}$ m²   **b.** 48 m²   **c.** 1200 m² **d.** 400 m²

8. A model truck has a scale of 1 cm : 25 cm. The model is 14 cm high. [6–5]
How high is the actual truck? d
  a. 60 cm   **b.** 160 cm   **c.** 24 cm   **d.** 350 cm

9. On an engineering diagram the scale is 5 mm : 1 mm. A circuit
measures 4 mm across. What is the length of the circuit in the
drawing? b
  a. 0.8 mm   **b.** 20 mm   **c.** 1.25 mm **d.** 4 cm

Match.

10. 75% f   **11.** $\frac{13}{20}$ c   **a.** 600%   **b.** 7.5%   [6–6]

12. 6 a   **13.** 0.6% e   **c.** 65%   **d.** 60%

14. $\frac{3}{5}$ d   **15.** 0.075 b   **e.** 0.006   **f.** $\frac{3}{4}$ [6–7]

Write the letter of the correct answer.

16. What is 65% of 140? d   [6–8]
  a. 215   **b.** 9100   **c.** 0.46   **d.** 91

17. 18 is what percent of 40? c
  a. 222%   **b.** 0.45   **c.** 45%   **d.** 7.2%

240   *Chapter 6*

Chapter Test

Express each ratio as a fraction in lowest terms.

1. 35 min : 3 h $\frac{7}{36}$

2. 2 m to 85 cm $\frac{40}{17}$

[6-1]

Give the unit price of each item.

3. 5 basketballs for $59.75 **$11.95**

4. 12 oz of cereal for $1.32 **11¢**

[6-2]

Solve.

5. $\frac{n}{40} = \frac{3}{8}$ **15**

6. $\frac{24}{5} = \frac{x}{10}$ **48**

7. $\frac{5}{11} = \frac{20}{a}$ **44**

[6-3]

8. A car traveled 162 mi in 3 h. How many hours would it take to travel 351 mi? **6.5 h**

[6-4]

9. On a map, 2 in. represents 300 mi. If two points are separated by 5 in. on the map, what is the actual distance between them? **750 mi**

[6-5]

Express as a fraction in lowest terms or as a mixed number in simple form.

10. 48% $\frac{12}{25}$

11. 6% $\frac{3}{50}$

12. 215% $2\frac{3}{20}$

13. 190% $1\frac{9}{10}$

[6-6]

Express as a percent.

14. $\frac{11}{20}$ **55%**

15. $\frac{5}{8}$ **62.5%**

16. 3 **300%**

17. $2\frac{1}{8}$ **212.5%**

Express as a decimal.

18. 93% **0.93**

19. 42% **0.42**

20. 259% **2.59**

21. 0.86% **0.0086**

[6-7]

Express as a percent.

22. 0.81 **81%**

23. 0.07 **7%**

24. 2.91 **291%**

25. 1.01 **101%**

Solve.

26. What percent of 85 is 51? **60%**

[6-8]

27. 27 is what percent of 60? **45%**

28. What is 30% of 80? **24**

29. 20% of what number is 25? **125**

Ratio, Proportion, and Percent **241**

Supplementary Materials

Practice Masters, pp. 29–30
Cumulative Test, pp. 41–42
Mid-Year Test, pp. 43–46

Cumulative Review (Chapters 1–6)

Exercises

Evaluate the expression when $x = 2$, $y = 3$, and $z = -2$.

1. $5y - 10$ 5

2. $6x + 3y$ 21

3. $2z + 6$ 2

4. $8 - z$ 10

5. $4xy \div (-2z)$ 6

6. $3x + 3y \div z$ $1\frac{1}{2}$

7. $5y \div (2 + y)$ 3

8. $10x - (3y + 1)$ 10

9. x^x 4

10. $2y^2$ 18

11. $(2y)^2$ 36

12. $(3x)^{-2}$ $\frac{1}{36}$

True or false?

13. $2.1(3 \times 4.7) = (2.1 \times 3)(2.1 \times 4.7)$ False

14. $9.51 + (-6.21) = (-6.21) + 9.51$ True

15. $1(-10.3) = 10.3$ False

16. $7.4 \times 0 = 0$ True

Write as equivalent fractions using the LCD.

17. $\frac{2}{3}, \frac{1}{5}$ $\frac{10}{15}, \frac{3}{15}$

18. $\frac{3}{4}, \frac{6}{7}$ $\frac{21}{28}, \frac{24}{28}$

19. $-\frac{1}{8}, \frac{1}{3}$ $-\frac{3}{24}, \frac{8}{24}$

20. $\frac{7}{10}, -\frac{4}{9}$ $\frac{63}{90}, -\frac{40}{90}$

21. $\frac{2}{5}, \frac{1}{6}, \frac{1}{4}$ $\frac{24}{60}, \frac{10}{60}, \frac{15}{60}$

22. $\frac{3}{11}, \frac{1}{2}, \frac{3}{4}$ $\frac{12}{44}, \frac{22}{44}, \frac{33}{44}$

Use transformations to solve each equation.

23. $x + 7 = 12$ 5

24. $x - 3 = -6$ −3

25. $6x = 18$ 3

26. $-9x = 27$ −3

27. $\frac{3}{4}x = 12$ 16

28. $2x + 9 = 27$ 9

Solve.

29. $\frac{x}{4} = \frac{2}{8}$ 1

30. $\frac{x}{7} = \frac{9}{21}$ 3

31. $\frac{3}{8} = \frac{24}{x}$ 64

32. $\frac{48}{176} = \frac{8}{x}$ $29\frac{1}{3}$

33. $\frac{13}{11} = \frac{3}{x}$ $2\frac{7}{13}$

34. $\frac{148}{4} = \frac{x}{5}$ 185

Complete.

35. A _?_ is a parallelogram with four equal sides. rhombus

36. If two lines are _?_ , they form four right angles. perpendicular

37. A _?_ is a chord of a circle which is twice as long as the radius. diameter

38. To the nearest hundredth, the ratio of the circumference of a circle to its diameter is _?_. 3.14

242 *Chapter 6*

Problems

Problem Solving Reminders

Here are some reminders that may help you solve some of the problems on this page.
- Consider whether a chart will help to organize information.
- Supply additional information if needed.
- Reread the problem to be sure that your answer is complete.

Solve.

1. Donald bought a pair of hiking boots for $35.83, a sweater for $24.65, and a backpack for $18. The tax on his purchase was $.90. How much did Donald spend? **$79.38**

2. This week, Marisa worked $1\frac{1}{2}$ h on Monday, $2\frac{1}{4}$ h on Tuesday, $1\frac{1}{3}$ h on Wednesday, and $7\frac{1}{2}$ h on Saturday. How many hours did she work this week? **$12\frac{7}{12}$ h**

3. An airplane flying at an altitude of 25,000 ft dropped 4000 ft in the first 25 s and rose 2500 ft in the next 15 s. What was the altitude of the airplane after 40 s? **23,500 ft**

4. Carolyn Cramer spent 3 h 15 min mowing and raking her lawn. She spent twice as long raking as she did mowing. How long did she spend on each task? **raking: 2 h 10 min; mowing: 1 h 5 min**

5. At a milk processing plant 100 lb of farm milk are needed to make 8.13 lb of nonfat dry milk. To the nearest pound, how many pounds of farm milk are needed to produce 100 lb of nonfat dry milk? **1230 lb**

6. A highway noise barrier that is 120 m long is constructed in two pieces. One piece is 45 m longer than the other. Find the length of each piece. **37.5 m; 825 m**

7. The perimeter of a rectangle is 40 m. The length of the rectangle is 10 m greater than the width. Find the length and the width. **15 m; 5 m**

8. Oak Hill School, Longview School, and Peabody School participated in a clean-up campaign to collect scrap aluminum. Oak Hill School collected 40% more scrap aluminum than Longview School. Longview School collected 25% more than Peabody School. If the total collected by the 3 schools was 560 kg, how much did Oak Hill School collect? **245 kg**

9. Eladio invested $200 at 6% annual interest and $350 at 5.75% annual interest, both compounded annually. If he makes no deposits or withdrawals, how much will he have after two years? **$616.13**

Ratio, Proportion, and Percent **243**

Exercises 13 and 14 refer to the diagram.

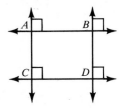

13. Name the perpendicular lines that intersect at B. **$\overleftrightarrow{AB}$, $\overleftrightarrow{BD}$**

14. Name four segments. **$\overline{AB}$, $\overline{BD}$, $\overline{DC}$, $\overline{CA}$**

Complete.

15. 19 m = __?__ cm **1900**

16. 650 cm = __?__ km **0.00065**

17. Give the measures of the complement and the supplement of $\angle A$ if m$\angle A$ = 59°. **31°; 121°**

18. A right triangle has how many right angles? **1**

19. A quadrilateral has sides of length 6 m, 11 m, 7 m, and 14 m. Find the perimeter. **38 m**

20. A circle has radius 15 cm. Find the circumference. Use $\pi \approx 3.14$. **94.2 cm**

21. A regular pentagon has perimeter 60 mm. Find the length of each side. **12 mm**

22. If $\triangle ABC \cong \triangle DBE$, then $\angle C \cong$ __?__. **$\angle E$**

23. True or false? All triangles are quadrilaterals. **False**

24. Construct a 45° angle. **Check students' papers.**

7

Percents and Problem Solving

The photograph shows a strand of DNA, or deoxyribonucleic acid, as seen through the center of the strand. In 1953 James Watson and Francis Crick developed a model for the DNA. They called it the double helix. In 1962 Watson and Crick were awarded the Nobel Prize in Medicine for their work with the double helix model.

According to the model, a strand of DNA is built much like a spiral staircase with phosphates and sugars forming the frame of the staircase. The four bases, adenine, guanine, thymine, and cytosine, form the steps. In analysis of DNA obtained from different organisms, it can be shown that the percentages of the four bases vary considerably. Thus, the sequence of the four bases are thought to determine individual heredity.

In this chapter, you will learn some interesting applications of percents to business, consumer, and financial situations.

Career Note

Chemists analyze the structure, composition, and nature of matter. They can specialize in a variety of fields from developing new products to organic analysis of moon rocks. Their work involves quantitative and qualitative analyses, as well as practical applications of basic research. A strong background in science and mathematics and an inquisitive mind are essential for this career.

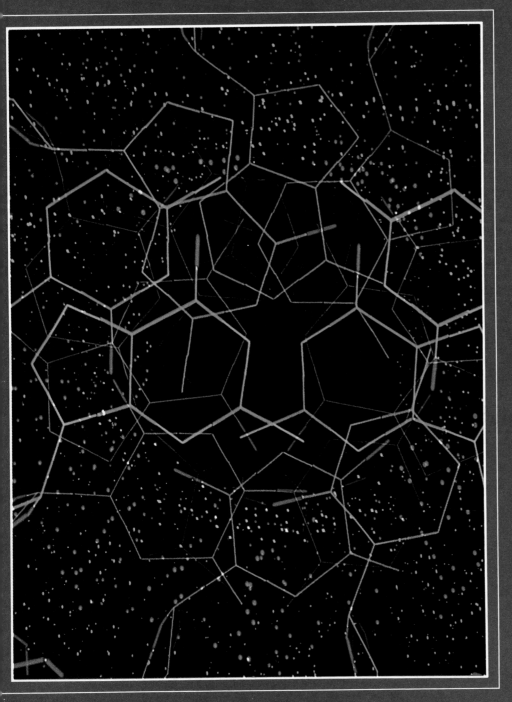

Lesson Commentary
Chapter 7 Percents and Problem Solving

Overview

This chapter presents topics that will enable students to apply percents to business, consumer, banking, and investment problems. Because many business, consumer, banking, and investment issues require an understanding of percents, it is essential that students develop a thorough understanding of their meaning and use.

Lesson 7-1 introduces the concept of percent of increase or decrease. In Lessons 7-2 through 7-7, students will apply what they have learned about percent of increase or decrease in such relevant areas as discount and markup, commission and profit, and both simple and compound interest.

Related Activities

To emphasize the distinction between amount of change and percent of change, have your students compare the percent of increase for each pair of numbers. If necessary they can round their answers to the nearest tenth. Instruct them to replace the ? with $<$, $>$, or $=$. The correct answers will surprise many of your students.

1. 5 to 6 ? 4 to 5 $<$
2. 16 to 18 ? 21 to 23 $>$
3. 14 to 17 ? 29 to 31 $>$
4. 20 to 45 ? 3 to 9 $<$
5. 4 to 6 ? 40 to 60 $=$
6. 5 to 6 ? 10 to 12 $=$

BUSINESS AND CONSUMER PROBLEMS

7-1 Percent of Increase or Decrease

Objective *for pages 246–249*

■ To find the percent and amount of change.

Teaching Suggestions

Your students will find the material in this lesson easy to understand if they remember that the denominator of the fraction showing the percent of change must be the original amount, not the new amount. Caution students to avoid using the new amount for the denominator.

You may wish to discuss with your students another approach they can use to find a new number after an increase or decrease. If a number is increased by 25% of itself, the new number will be 100% + 25%, or 125% of the original number. For example, if the number 40 is increased by 25%, the new number is 125% of 40: $1.25 \times 40 = 50$. Similarly, if a number is decreased by 20% of itself, the new number is 100% − 20%, or 80% of the original number. If the number 60 is decreased by 20%, the new number is 80% × 60; $0.80 \times 60 = 48$.

Resource Book: Page 83 (Use After Page 249)

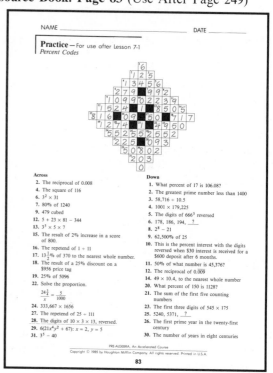

NAME _____ DATE _____

Practice—For use after Lesson 7-1
Percent Codes

Across
2. The reciprocal of 0.008
4. The square of 116
6. $3^2 \times 31$
7. 80% of 1240
9. 479 cubed
12. $5 + 23 \times 81 - 344$
13. $3^5 \times 5 \times 7$
15. The result of 2% increase in a score of 800.
16. The repetend of $1 \div 11$
17. $13\frac{1}{2}$% of 370 to the nearest whole number.
18. The result of a 25% discount on a $956 price tag
19. 25% of 5096
22. Solve the proportion.
$$\frac{24\frac{1}{4}}{x} = \frac{5}{1000}$$
24. 333,667 × 1656
27. The repetend of 25 ÷ 111
28. The digits of 10 × 3 × 13, reversed.
29. $6(21x^4y^2 + 67); x = 2, y = 5$
31. $3^5 - 40$

Down
1. What percent of 17 is 106.08?
2. The greatest prime number less than 1400
3. 58,716 ÷ 10.5
4. 1001 × 179,225
5. The digits of 666^3 reversed
6. 178, 186, 194, __?__
8. $2^8 - 21$
9. 62,500% of 25
10. This is the percent interest with the digits reversed when $30 interest is received for a $600 deposit after 6 months.
11. 50% of what number is 45,376?
12. The reciprocal of $0.\overline{009}$
14. 49 × 10.4, to the nearest whole number
20. What percent of 150 is 1128?
21. The sum of the first five counting numbers
23. The first three digits of 545 × 175
25. 5240, 5371, __?__
26. The first prime year in the twenty-first century
30. The number of years in eight centuries

83

7-2 Discount and Markup

Objective *for pages 250–253*

■ To solve problems involving discount and markup.

Teaching Suggestions

Students at this level sometimes have difficulty with the topics of discount and markup. You may wish to begin the lesson with a brief discussion of a few of the reasons businesses use discounts and markups. For example, a store may give a discount to attract new customers, or to sell seasonal items quickly. A store owner adds a markup to the cost of an item to pay for expenses, such as salaries, rent, and heat, and to realize a profit.

A discount is a decrease in price; a markup is an increase in price. Each is an amount of change that is usually calculated as a percent of an original price. That is, discount and markup are both applications of percent of change discussed in Lesson 7-1. The new price is given by

$$\text{new price} = \text{original price} - \text{discount}$$

or

$$\text{new price} = \text{original price} + \text{markup}$$

To help students absorb this much information, you may wish to guide students through Method 1 of Examples 1 and 2. It may then be helpful to do the odd-numbered Class Exercises using Method 1.

After students have had some practice using Method 1, you can show them how Method 2 is a shortened form of Method 1. For example, if the original price of an item is p and a 12% discount is taken, the new price is given by

$$p - 0.12p,$$
$$\text{or } 1.00p - 0.12p.$$

Using the distributive property,

$$\text{new price} = (1.00 - 0.12)p$$
$$= 0.88p.$$

This last equation is the basis for Method 2. You can follow this discussion by using Method 2 to do the even-numbered Class Exercises.

Related Activities

To give some practice on percent of increase and percent of decrease and to dispel a common misconception, have your students do the following exercises.

1. Increase 12 by 5%, then decrease the result by 5%. Is the final amount equal to 12? **11.97; no**
2. Increase 40 by 25%, then decrease the result by 25%. Is the final amount equal to 40? **37.5; no**
3. Decrease 100 by 40%, then increase the result by 40%. Is the final amount equal to 100? **84; no**
4. Decrease 20 by 10%, then increase the result by 10%. Is the final amount equal to 20? **19.8; no**
5. If Tom gets a 10% decrease in his pay then a 10% increase in his pay, is the final amount equal to the original amount? **no**
6. If the price of a jacket is increased by 20% then decreased by 20%, is the final amount equal to the original amount? **no**

Resource Book: Page 84 (Use After Page 253)

7-3 Commission and Profit

Objective *for pages 254–256*

■ To solve problems involving commission and profit.

Teaching Suggestions

To help students understand commission and profit, it may be helpful to relate these topics to percent of change learned in Lesson 7-1. The concepts presented in Lessons 7-1, 7-2, and 7-3 are very much alike. To illustrate the similarity, you can have students compare the following problems and their solutions.

1. A plant grew from 50 cm to 80 cm. Find the percent of increase in its height. (Lesson 7-1)
2. A jewelry store marked up the price of a ring from $50 to $80. Find the percent of markup. (Lesson 7-2)
3. Alan bought a baseball glove for $50 and sold it for $80. What was his percent of profit? (Lesson 7-3)

The solutions of all the above problems are identical.

$$\text{percent of change} = \frac{\text{amount of change}}{\text{original amount}}$$

$$= \frac{80 - 50}{50} = \frac{30}{50}, \text{ or } 60\%$$

Related Activities

To give students another way of solving problems involving commissions, tell them that they can think of a percent of a commission as a percent of change in which the original amount is the total sales. That is,

$$\frac{\text{amount of commission}}{\text{total sales}} = \text{percent of commission}$$

Using this method, we can solve Example 1 as follows:

$$\frac{a}{42,000} = 0.03$$

$$a = 0.03 \times 42,000, \text{ or } \$1260$$

Use this method to find the amount of commission.

	Total sales	Percent of commission
1.	$1280	6% $76.80
2.	$2400	8% $192

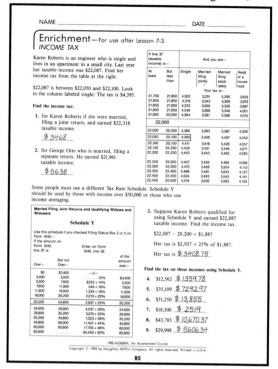
7-4 Percents and Proportions

Objective *for pages 257–261*

■ To use proportions to solve problems involving percents.

Teaching Suggestions

Word problems involving percent can be confusing to students when problems of different types are mixed. Encourage students to spend time understanding the problem before deciding what operation or proportion to use. The proportion method unifies the three types of percent problems to the single task of finding the missing term of a proportion. The definition of a percent as a ratio is the key to setting up the proportion. Notice that in each example the percent ratio is considered first before the proportion is written.

In Example 3, note that the first step of the computation is finding 25% of $59. This problem could also be solved by subtracting 25% from 100% and finding 75% of $59.

245c

Related Activities

To relate this topic to personal finances, have students list how much money they spend each week and find the percent spent on each category (clothing, snacks, etc.). Then have them make a budget with percent goals (making sure the total is 100%) and calculate the dollar amount they could spend on each category.

Resource Book: Page 86 (Use After Page 261)

NAME _____ DATE _____

Quiz 7A — Lessons 7-1 through 7-4

DIRECTIONS: Write the letter of the correct answer in the space provided.

1. What is the percent increase from 40 to 50? *[7-1]*
   a. 20%   b. 25%   c. 80%   d. 125%

2. What is the percent decrease from 54 to 18?
   a. $33\frac{1}{3}$%   b. $66\frac{2}{3}$%   c. 200%   d. 300%

3. What is 90 decreased by 30%?
   a. 2700   b. 27   c. 63   d. 73

4. A $250 bike is on sale for $200. What is the percent of discount? *[7-2]*
   a. 20%   b. 25%   c. 50%   d. 80%

5. Because of an increase of 6% in wholesale prices of plants, a florist had to mark up new stock by the same percent. What was the new price of a jade plant that had sold for $15.50?
   a. $.93   b. $14.57   c. $16.43   d. $17.43

6. Su Lee earns a 5% commission on her sales of merchandise at Taylor Department Store. One week her sales totaled $9650. What was her commission for the week? *[7-3]*
   a. $48.25   b. $482.50   c. $9698.25   d. $10,132.50

7. Edwardo Salazar appliance store had sales of $27,000 last month. The store's profits were $4050. What was the percent of profit?
   a. 12%   b. 13%   c. 14%   d. 15%

8. Last year, 75% of the students attended the school play. If 285 students attended the school play, how many students were in the school? Which proportion would solve this problem? *[7-4]*
   a. $\frac{75}{285} = \frac{n}{100}$ b. $\frac{210}{b} = \frac{75}{100}$ c. $\frac{285}{b} = \frac{75}{100}$ d. $\frac{285}{360} = \frac{n}{100}$

9. The Lions have won 12 of the 15 games they have played this season. What percent of this season's games have the Lions lost? Use a proportion to solve.
   a. 80%   b. 8%   c. 2%   d. 20%

ANSWERS
1. _b_ (11)
2. _b_ (11)
3. _c_ (11)
4. _a_ (11)
5. _c_ (11)
6. _b_ (11)
7. _d_ (11)
8. _c_ (12)
9. _d_ (12)

PRE-ALGEBRA, An Accelerated Course
Copyright © 1985 by Houghton Mifflin Company. All rights reserved. Printed in U.S.A.

86

INVESTMENT AND APPLICATION PROBLEMS

7-5 Simple Interest

Objective *for pages 262–266*

■ To solve problems involving simple interest.

Teaching Suggestions

Most students at this level have had very limited experience with borrowing and lending money. On the other hand, many of your students may be aware that banks pay interest on savings accounts. Before beginning this lesson on simple interest, you may wish to discuss the concept of interest, and why it is paid.

Interest is money that a borrower pays to a lender for the use of money. If you are the borrower, you pay interest; if you are the lender, you receive interest. Students may not understand why banks pay interest on deposits. Tell them that they can think of a deposit as a loan to a bank. The bank makes loans to individuals and businesses who in turn pay interest to the bank. The bank then pays its depositors part of the interest it receives from its borrowers.

Before students begin the Problems on page 265, you may wish to discuss the practice of repaying loans in installments and of receiving interest on investments semiannually or monthly. The Related Activities below may help students understand the idea of installment payments. Simple interest is paid when a borrower repays a loan in a single lump-sum payment after a specified period of time. When a loan is repaid in installments, the law requires that interest be changed only on the outstanding balance. Because these calculations are very involved, banks use tables and computers to calculate the interest. The annual rate is the equivalent simple interest rate that will yield the same amount of interest.

Because the annual rate is calculated as simple interest, it provides an easy way to compare various loan charges and investment returns. The law requires that the annual percentage rate (APR) be declared on all loans and investments.

Related Activities

To help students understand the concept of equal installment payments, explain that many loans are repaid in equal monthly payments. To find out how much a monthly payment is, your students can use the following equation. (Round to the nearest cent.)

Monthly payment =
(Interest + Principal) ÷ (12 × no. of years)

Find the monthly payment on each loan.

1. $9000 for 10 years at an annual rate of 18%
   $210

2. $500 for 2 years at an annual rate of 15%
$27.08

3. $1000 for 6 months at an annual rate of 20%
$183.33

4. $3500 for 3 years at an annual rate of 15%
$140.97

Resource Book: Page 87 (Use After Page 266)

then in 2.5 years interest is paid after each of 4 × 2.5, or 10, quarters. It is important that students understand that the amount at the end of one period (quarter, month, half-year) becomes the principal at the beginning of the next period (quarter, month, half-year).

To avoid confusion, you might emphasize the importance of arranging the work systematically and of labeling each step. An alternative to the system shown in the Example on page 267 is a chart like the one shown below.

Quarter	Beginning Principal	Interest	Amount at end of quarter
1	$500	$10	$510
2	$510	$10.20	$520.20
3	$520.20	$10.40	$530.60
4	$530.60	$10.61	$541.21

You may wish to allow students to use calculators for the exercises of this lesson.

Related Activities

To help students simplify their calculations, you may wish to explain that, in the Example on page 267, an 8% annual rate is equivalent to 8% ÷ 4, or 2%, each quarter. The amount at the end of the quarter equals 100% of the principal (p) at the beginning of the quarter plus the interest for that quarter, $0.02p$. That is, the amount at the end of the quarter is $1.00p + 0.02p$, or $1.02p$. Using this method, the solution of the Example is greatly simplified. The amount after four quarters is given by $500 \times 1.02 \times 1.02 \times 1.02 \times 1.02$, or $500 \times (1.02)^4$.

Have students use this method to find the amount of each investment.

Answers may vary slightly due to rounding.

1. $3000 for 2 years compounded semiannually at 10% $3646.52

2. $8000 for 1.5 years compounded quarterly at 8% $9009.30

3. $1500 for 6 months compounded monthly at 12% $1592.28

7-6 Compound Interest

Objective *for pages 267–269*

■ To solve problems involving compound interest.

Teaching Suggestions

Compound interest is difficult for some students to understand, mainly because of the many steps involved in the solutions to compound interest problems. The first step is to determine the total number of periods (quarters, months, or half-years) for which the interest is to be compounded. For example, if interest is paid quarterly,

245e

7-7 Percents and Problem Solving

Objective *for pages 270–273*

■ To solve mixed problems involving percent.

Teaching Suggestions

Students learned in Lessons 7-1 through 7-6 to solve problems involving percents in various business and consumer settings. In this lesson these problems are extended.

Many of the ideas and terms in this lesson will be new to most students, and thus will appear more difficult than they really are. You will need to discuss the meaning of the following terms: social security, property taxes, combined amount, assessed value of property, market value, per kW·h, total finance charge, annual dividend, certificate of deposit, royalty, bonds, and savings certificate.

You may wish to review the five-step plan for problem solving suggested on page 29. Strongly urge the students to read each problem very carefully.

Related Activities

To demonstrate the range of services offered by financial instructions, make a display of pamphlets, advertisements, and other materials.

To provide a challenge for the computer programmers in your class, suggest that they write a program to calculate compound interest.

Resource Book: Page 88 (Use After Page 273)

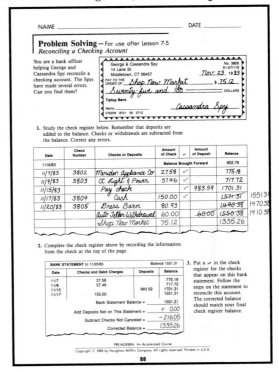

Resource Book: Pages 89–92 (Use After Page 273)

Quiz 7B — Lessons 7-5 through 7-7

NAME _____ DATE _____

DIRECTIONS: Write the letter of the correct answer in the space provided.

1. What is the simple interest on a $12,000 loan at 18% for 6 months? *[7-5]*

   a. $1296   b. $1080   c. $2160   d. $14,160

2. What is the annual rate of interest for a $1500 loan that has $270 due in simple interest after $1\frac{1}{2}$ yr?

   a. 9%   b. 10%   c. 12%   d. 18%

3. How much will $2400 amount to in 1 yr if it earns 8% interest, compounded semiannually? *[7-6]*

   a. $2496   b. $2499.84   c. $2592   d. $2595.84

4. You open a savings account with $600. The bank pays $5\frac{1}{2}$% interest, compounded quarterly. If you make no other deposits or withdrawals, how much is in your account at the end of nine months?

   a. $616.61   b. $625.09   c. $633.00   d. $624.75

5. After a 12% decrease, the price of a bicycle is $122.32. What was the old price of the bicycle?

   a. $110.32   b. $139.00   c. $107.64   d. $140.25

6. A sweater that usually sells for $34.60 is discounted 15%. How much is saved by buying the sweater at the sale price? *[7-7]*

   a. $29.41   b. $19.60   c. $5.19   d. $517.50

7. A real estate agent earns a 6% commission for selling houses. If her commission last week was $8520, what was the total value of her sales?

   a. $51,120   b. $14,200   c. $51,000   d. $142,000

ANSWERS

1. __b__ (12)
2. __c__ (12)
3. __d__ (12)
4. __b__ (12)
5. __b__ (12)
6. __c__ (20)
7. __d__ (20)

Review — Chapter 7

NAME _____ DATE _____

State the percent of increase or decrease from the first number to the second.

1. 50 to 20 __60%__   2. 40 to 45 __12.5%__   3. 75 to 24 __68%__ *[7-1]*

Solve.

4. Jason Bloom's salary increased $25 a week to $525. What was the percent of increase? __5%__

5. The price of a new boat model was marked up 8% over the previous year's model. If the new boat cost $6750, what was last year's price? __6250__ *[7-2]*

6. Crystal's Fish Market sold $4200 worth of fish last week. If Crystal's costs were $3696, what was her percent of profit? __12%__ *[7-3]*

7. When a salesman sold a vacuum cleaner for $165, he received a commission of $13.20. What was the rate of commission? __8%__ *[7-4]*

8. Mary Karp bought a car for $8200. By the end of the year, the value of the car had decreased $2706. By what percent had the car decreased in value? Use a proportion to solve. __33%__

9. How much simple interest is due on a $5000 loan at 18% after $1\frac{1}{2}$ years? __$1350__ *[7-5]*

10. How much will $6400 amount to after 2 years compounded annually at 6%? __$7191.04__ *[7-6]*

11. There were 132 planes on an airfield. If 75% of the planes took off for a flight, how many planes were left at the airfield? __33__ *[7-7]*

12. After a 24% increase, the price of a tennis racquet was $37.82. What was the old price of the racquet? __$30.50__

13. A sales representative sold eight copies of a new book to a small bookstore. The price per copy was $16.50. If the representative earned a 6% commission, how much did she earn? __$9.90__

14. Jack Stanford deposited $280 in a Holiday Club savings account which pays $6\frac{1}{4}$% interest, compounded semiannually. If Jack makes no additional deposits, how much will be in his account at the end of a year? __$298.50__

Test — Chapter 7

NAME _____ DATE _____

DIRECTIONS: Write the answers in the spaces provided.

Solve.

1. What is the percent decrease from 50 to 40? *[7-1]*

2. A television that sells for $425 is on sale at a 15% discount. What is the sale price? *[7-2]*

3. The Up-Down Company total sales last month were $75,000. If its costs were $67,950, what was the percent of profit? *[7-3]*

Use a proportion to solve Exercises 4 and 5.

4. 32,850 parts were made in a factory. When they were tested, 2% were found to be defective. How many parts were good? *[7-4]*

5. In a school, 60 students participate in the Bowling Club. If this is 12% of the student body, how many students are in the school?

6. Maria Sanchez borrowed $1500 for $1\frac{1}{2}$ yr at 12% simple interest. How much must she repay when the loan is due? *[7-5]*

7. Easystreet Bank pays 9.5% interest compounded semiannually. How much will $2000 amount to in 18 mo? *[7-6]*

8. If Marie deposits $320 in a bank account at $5\frac{1}{2}$% per year, how much simple interest will she earn after 2 years? *[7-7]*

9. Victor opens a savings account with $750. The account pays 6% interest, compounded quarterly. If he makes no other deposits or withdrawals, how much will Victor have in his account after 9 months?

ANSWERS

1. __20%__ (10)
2. __$361.25__ (10)
3. __10%__ (10)
4. __32,193__ (10)
5. __500__ (10)
6. __$1770__ (10)
7. __$2298.75__ (10)
8. __$33.60__ (15)
9. __$784.26__ (15)

Make-up Test — Chapter 7

NAME _____ DATE _____

DIRECTIONS: Write the answers in the spaces provided.

Solve.

1. What is the percent increase from 40 to 50? *[7-1]*

2. A pair of jeans that regularly sell for $22 is on sale for $17.60. What is the percent of discount? *[7-2]*

3. The Right-Left Company makes a 15% profit. If its sales last quarter were $55,200, what were its profits? *[7-3]*

4. A football team won 9 games, which was 60% of the games it played. How many games did the team play? Solve using a proportion. *[7-4]*

5. Max Barker bought a suit for $185 and paid $12.95 as a sales tax. What percent was the tax? Solve using a proportion.

6. Mark Whitehawk borrowed $3000 for $1\frac{1}{2}$ yr at 18% simple interest. How much must he repay when the loan is due? *[7-5]*

7. Easymoney Bank pays 8.5% interest compounded quarterly. How much will $4000 amount to in 9 mo? *[7-6]*

8. A van is discounted 28% of the original price. What is the sale price if the original price was $16,400? *[7-7]*

9. How much simple interest would be earned on a savings account of $450 at $6\frac{1}{4}$% interest per year after 2 years?

10. Jackson deposited $180 into a special savings account that pays 7% interest, compounded semiannually. If he makes no other deposits or withdrawals, how much will be in his account after 18 mo?

ANSWERS

1. __25%__ (10)
2. __20%__ (10)
3. __$8280__ (10)
4. __15__ (10)
5. __7%__ (10)
6. __$3810__ (10)
7. __$4260.46__ (10)
8. __$11,808__ (10)
9. __$56.25__ (10)
10. __$199.57__ (10)

Resource Book: Pages 93-94 (Use After Page 273)

CUMULATIVE REVIEW—Chapters 1-7
Exercises

Evaluate the following for $x = 0.4$, $y = 1.2$, and $z = 2$.

1. $xy + yz$ *2.88*

2. x^2yz *0.384*

3. $5x + 2xy$ *2.96*

4. $z^2 + zx + x^2$ *4.96*

Arrange in order from least to greatest.

5. 7.14, 7.41, 7.04 *7.04, 7.14, 7.41*

6. 0.67, 0.67, 0.6 *0.6, 0.67, 0.67*

Perform the indicated operation.

7. $\frac{2}{3} + \frac{1}{2}$ *$1\frac{1}{6}$*

8. $1\frac{1}{3} - \frac{3}{4}$ *$\frac{7}{12}$*

9. $3\frac{1}{3} + 2\frac{1}{5}$ *$5\frac{8}{15}$*

10. $\frac{9}{10} \times \frac{13}{27}$ *$\frac{13}{30}$*

11. $2\frac{1}{3} \times \frac{5}{14}$ *$\frac{5}{6}$*

12. $\frac{10}{13} \div \frac{5}{26}$ *4*

Find the perimeter or circumference. Use $\pi \approx 3.14$ when necessary.

13. square
side: 9 in. *36 in.*

14. circle
radius: 4 ft *25.12 ft*

15. circle
diameter: 5 m *15.7 m*

16. regular
hexagon
side: 12 m *72 m*

17. rectangle
width: 4 ft
length: 6 ft *20 ft*

18. equilateral
triangle
side: 9 cm *27 cm*

Solve.

19. $\frac{x}{4} = \frac{12}{16}$ *3*

20. $\frac{19}{x} = \frac{38}{102}$ *51*

21. $\frac{2}{5} = \frac{18}{y}$ *45*

22. $3x = 15$ *5*

23. $\frac{1}{2}y = 6$ *12*

24. $\frac{n}{7} = 3$ *21*

25. $x + 14 = 37$ *23*

26. $28 - n = 9$ *19*

27. $\frac{1}{4}y + 19 = 23$ *16*

28. $\frac{1}{2}x - 16 = 4$ *40*

29. $30 - 0.5n = 21$ *18*

30. $\frac{x}{4.5} - 2 = 0$ *9*

31. 24 is 32% of what number? *75*

32. What is $20\frac{1}{2}$% of 620? *127.1*

33. 30.69 is what percent of 68.2? *45%*

34. 91 is 140% of what number? *65*

CUMULATIVE REVIEW—Chapters 1-7 (continued)
Problems

Problem Solving Reminders
Here are some reminders that may help you solve some of the problems
on this page.
• Determine whether a formula applies.
• Supply additional information, if needed.
• Determine whether there are unnecessary facts given.

Solve.

1. The Clark family took a 2-wk vacation and drove through the
Rocky Mountains. If they drove 200 mi each day, how many
miles did they drive during their vacation? *2800 mi*

2. The Blue Sox scored 24 points. This was three times as many
points as the Green Sox. How many points did the Green Sox
score? *8 points*

3. Matthew has saved $42 for a new bike that costs $106. He earns
$2 an hour baby-sitting. How many hours will he have to work
to have the $64 he needs for the new bike? *32 h*

4. The Old Time Shoe Store had $3600 in sales last week. If their
costs were $3420, what was the percent of profit? *5%*

5. How many feet of braid are needed to go around the edge of a
circular frame with a 9-in. radius? *56.52 in.*

6. Ruth and Michelle are running for president of their sports club.
Ruth received 36 votes and Michelle received 54 votes. What
fraction of the total votes did Ruth get? *$\frac{2}{5}$*

7. Due to Earth's rotation, a point on the equator travels about
40,000 km every 24 h. How far does a point on the equator
travel in $1\frac{1}{2}$ d? *60,000 km*

8. Tony took $50 to the supermarket. He bought a $2.49 package
of ground beef, 3 loaves of bread for 89¢ each, and a box of
detergent for $4.89. How much did he spend at the
supermarket? *$10.05*

Teaching Suggestions
p. 245a

Related Activities p. 245a

Reading Mathematics

Students will learn the meaning of the following mathematical terms in this lesson: *amount of change, percent of change, increase, decrease.*

When we read that a quantity is increased by 20% it is implied that the increase is 20% of some base amount, for 20% cannot stand alone as a measure. Encourage students to ask questions like "20% of what?" whenever they read a statement that includes a percent.

7-1 Percent of Increase or Decrease

A department store has a sale on audio equipment. An amplifier that originally sold for $260 is selling for $208. To find the **amount of change** in the price, we subtract the sale price from the original price.

$$\$260 - \$208 = \$52$$

To find the **percent of change** in the price we divide the amount of change by the original price and express the result as a percent.

$$\frac{52}{260} = 0.20 = 20\%$$

Formula

$$\text{percent of change} = \frac{\text{amount of change}}{\text{original amount}}$$

The denominator in the formula above is always the *original* amount, whether smaller or larger than the new amount.

EXAMPLE 1 Find the percent of increase from 20 to 24.

Solution amount of change $= 24 - 20 = 4$

percent of change $= \frac{\text{amount of change}}{\text{original amount}} = \frac{4}{20} = 0.2 = 20\%$

The formula above can be rewritten to find the amount of change when the original amount and the percent of change are known.

Formula

$$\text{amount of change} = \text{percent of change} \times \text{original amount}$$

EXAMPLE 2 Find the new number when 75 is decreased by 26%.

Solution First find the amount of change.

amount of change $=$ percent of change $\times$ original amount
$$= \quad 26\% \quad \times \quad 75$$
$$= 0.26 \times 75 = 19.5$$

Since the original number is being decreased, we subtract to find the new number. $75 - 19.5 = 55.5$

EXAMPLE 3 The population of Eastown grew from 25,000 to 28,000 in 3 years. What was the percent of increase for this period?

Solution   The problem asks for the percent of increase.

amount of change $= 28,000 - 25,000 = 3000$

$$\text{percent of change} = \frac{\text{amount of change}}{\text{original amount}}$$

$$= \frac{3000}{25,000} = \frac{3}{25} = 0.12 = 12\%$$

The percent of increase was 12%.

Problem Solving Reminder

Sometimes *extra information* is given in a problem. The time period, 3 years, is not needed for the solution of the problem in Example 3.

Chalkboard Examples

a. State the amount of increase or decrease from the first number to the second.

b. State the percent of increase or decrease from the first number to the second.

1. 10 to 15 5 increase; 50%

2. 200 to 100
   100 decrease; 50%

3. 100 to 110
   10 increase; 10%

4. 25 to 20
   5 decrease; 20%

5. 50 to 40
   10 decrease; 20%

6. 10 to 9 1 decrease; 10%

7. 1000 to 2500
   1500 increase; 150%

8. 1 to 10
   9 increase; 900%

Class Exercises

a. State the amount of change from the first number to the second.
b. State the percent of increase or decrease from the first number to the second.

1. 10 to 12 2; 20%   2. 4 to 3 1; 25%   3. 12 to 6 6; 50%   4. 6 to 12 6; 100%

5. 2 to 5 3; 150%   6. 5 to 7 2; 40%   7. 25 to 4 21; 84%   8. 1 to 4 3; 300%

9. 4 to 7 3; 75%   10. 100 to 55 45; 45%   11. 100 to 160 60; 60%   12. 125 to 100 25; 20%

Find the new number produced when the given number is increased or decreased by the given percent.

13. 120; 20% decrease 96   14. 30; 10% decrease 27

15. 48; 50% increase 72   16. 24; 25% increase 30

Written Exercises

Find the percent of increase or decrease from the first number to the second. **Round to the nearest tenth of a percent if necessary.**

A   1. 20 to 17 15%   2. 25 to 12 52%   3. 70 to 98 40%   4. 16 to 10 37.5%

5. 40 to 73 82.5%   6. 63 to 79 25.4%   7. 32 to 17 46.9%   8. 8 to 19 137.5%

9. 125 to 124 0.8%   10. 160 to 380 137.5%   11. 12 to 8.7 27.5%   12. 240 to 245.5 2.3%

Percents and Problem Solving   **247**

Find the percent of increase
or decrease from the first
number to the second.
Round to the nearest tenth
of a percent if necessary.

1. 20 to 16 **20% decrease**

2. 40 to 55
   37.5% increase

3. 120 to 130
   8.3% increase

4. 130 to 120
   7.7% decrease

Find the new number pro-
duced when the given num-
ber is increased or de-
creased by the given
percent.

5. 45; 20% increase **54**

6. 240; 40% decrease **144**

7. 12; 2% decrease **11.76**

8. 12; 2% increase **12.24**

Solve. Round to the nearest
tenth of a percent if necessary.

9. The number of students
   at Coopersville Junior
   High School in 1980 was
   980, and this year it is
   1220. What is the per-
   cent of increase? **24.5%**

10. Fido's weight decreased
    5% last month. If he
    weighed 30 lb on the first
    of the month, what did
    he weigh at the end of
    the month? **28.5 lb**

Find the new number produced when the given number is increased or decreased by the given percent.

13. 165; 20% decrease 132

14. 76; 25% increase 95

15. 65; 12% decrease 57.2

16. 250; 63% decrease 92.5

17. 84; 145% increase 205.8

18. 260; 105% increase 533

19. 125; 0.4% decrease 124.5

20. 1950; 0.8% increase 1965.6

Find the new number produced when the given number is changed by the first percent, and then the resulting number is changed by the second percent.

B 21. 80; increase by 50%; decrease by 50% 60

22. 128; decrease by 25% increase by 25% 120

23. 150; increase by 40%; increase by 60% 336

24. 480; decrease by 35%; decrease by 65% 109.2

25. 350; increase by 76%; decrease by 45% 338.8

26. 136; decrease by 85%; increase by 175% 56.1

Find the original number if the given number is the result of increasing or decreasing the original number by the given percent.

C 27. 80; original number increased by 25% 64

28. 63; original number increased by 75% 36

29. 78; original number decreased by 35% 120

30. 30; original number decreased by 85% 200

Problems

Solve. Round to the nearest tenth of a percent if necessary.

A 1. The number of employees at a factory was increased by 5% from its original total of 1080 workers. What was the new number of employees? 1134 employees

2. The cost of a basket of groceries at the Shopfast Supermarket was $62.50 in April. In May the cost of the same groceries had risen by 0.8%. What was the cost in May? $63

248 *Chapter 7*

3. The attendance at a baseball stadium went from 1,440,000 one year to 1,800,000 the next year. What was the percent of increase? **25%**

4. The number of registered motor vehicles in Smalltown dropped from 350 in 1978 to 329 in 1979. What percent of decrease is this? **6%**

5. The new Maple City Library budget will enable the library to increase its collection of books by 3.6%. If the library now has 7250 books, how many will it have after the increase? **7511 books**

B **6.** The number of students at Center State University is 22,540. Ten years ago there were only 7000 students. What is the percent of increase? **222%**

7. The annual budget of Brictown was $9,000,000 last year. Currently, the budget is only $7,500,000. Find the percent of decrease. **16.7%**

8. Last year the population of Spoon Forks grew from 1250 to 1300. If the population of the town grows by the same percent this year, what will the population be? **1352**

9. This year, Village Realty sold 289 homes. Last year the realty sold 340 homes. If sales decrease by the same percent next year, how many homes can Village Realty expect to sell? **246 homes**

C **10.** Contributions to the annual Grayson School fund raising campaign were 10% greater in 1984 than they were in 1983. In 1983, contributions were 15% greater than they were in 1982. If contributions for 1984 total $8855, what was the total in 1982? **$7000**

11. In July the price of a gallon of gasoline at Quick Sale Service Station rose 12%. In August it fell 15% of its final July price, ending the month at $1.19. What was its price at the beginning of July? **$1.25**

Review Exercises

Solve.

1. $p = 0.36 \times 27$ **9.72**

2. $1.89 = r \times 7$ **0.27**

3. $144.5 = 8.5n$ **17**

4. $21.65 \times 0.7 = m$ **15.155**

5. $156 = 0.3q$ **520**

6. $a \times 0.15 = 4.125$ **27.5**

7. $\frac{x}{21} = 10.5$ **220.5**

8. $91.53 \times 0.4 = t$ **36.612**

9. $\frac{324}{y} = 8100$ **0.04**

Percents and Problem Solving **249**

Suggested Assignments

Core
Day 1: 247/1–11 odd
248/13–24, 27
Day 2: 248/Prob. 1, 2
249/Prob. 3–6, 8, 10
249/Rev. 1–7

Enriched
Day 1: 247/2–12 even
248/14–20 even; 21–30
Day 2: 249/Prob. 3–11
249/Rev. 1–9 odd

Supplementary Materials

Practice Masters, p. 31
Computer Activity 13

Teaching Suggestions
p. 245b

Related Activities p. 245b

Reading Mathematics

Students will learn the meaning of the following mathematical terms in this lesson:
discount, markup.

7-2 Discount and Markup

A **discount** is a decrease in the price of an item. A **markup** is an increase in the price of an item. Both of these changes can be expressed as an amount of money or as a percent of the original price of the item. For example, a store may announce a discount of $3 off the original price of a $30 basketball, or a discount of 10%.

EXAMPLE 1   A warm-up suit that sold for $42.50 is on sale at a 12% discount. What is the sale price?

Solution   *Method 1* Use the formula:

amount of change = percent of change × original amount
= 12% × 42.50
Therefore, the discount is 0.12 × 42.50, or $5.10.

The amount of the discount is $5.10.
The sale price is 42.50 − 5.10, or $37.40.

Method 2 Since the discount is 12%, the sale price is 100% − 12%, or 88%, of the original price. The sale price is 0.88 × 42.50, or $37.40.

As shown in the solutions to Example 1, when you know the amount of discount you subtract to find the new price. When dealing with a markup, you add to find the new price.

EXAMPLE 2   The price of a new car model was marked up 6% over the previous year's model. If the previous year's model sold for $7800, what is the cost of the new car?

Solution   *Method 1* Use the formula:

amount of change = percent of change × original amount
= 6% × 7800
Therefore, the markup is 0.06 × 7800, or $468.

The amount of the markup is $468.
The new price is 7800 + 468, or $8268.

Method 2 Since the markup is 6%, the new price is 100% + 6%, or 106%, of the original price. The new price is 1.06 × 7800, or $8268.

A method similar to the second method of the previous examples can be used to solve problems like the one in the next example.

250   *Chapter 7*

EXAMPLE 3 This year a pair of ice skates sells for $46 after a 15% markup over last year's price. What was last year's price?

Solution This year's price is $100 + 15$, or 115%, of last year's price. Let n represent last year's price.

$$46 = \frac{115}{100} \times n$$
$$46 = 1.15 \times n$$
$$\frac{46}{1.15} = n$$
$$40 = n$$

The price of the skates last year was $40.

Example 4 illustrates how to find the original price if you know the discounted price.

EXAMPLE 4 A department store advertised electric shavers at a sale price of $36. If this is a 20% discount, what was the original price?

Solution The sale price is $100 - 20$, or 80%, of the original price. Let n represent the original price.

$$36 = \frac{80}{100} \times n$$
$$36 = 0.8 \times n$$
$$36 \div 0.8 = n$$
$$45 = n$$

The original price was $45.

Problem Solving Reminder

Be sure that your *answers are reasonable*. In Example 3, last year's price should be less than this year's marked-up price. In Example 4, the original price should be greater than the sale price.

We can use the following formula to find the percent of discount or the percent of markup.

$$\text{percent of change} = \frac{\text{amount of change}}{\text{original amount}}$$

For example, if the original price of an item was $25 and the new price is $20, the amount of discount is $5 and the percent of discount is $5 \div 25 = 0.2$, or 20%.

Percents and Problem Solving **251**

Solve.

1. The XT-100 computer is offered at a 24% discount. If the original price is $560, what is the sale price? **$425.60**

2. A store offers a $\frac{1}{4}$ off sale. What is the percent of discount? **25%**

3. A service station gives cash customers a 5% discount on the price of gasoline. If gasoline regularly sells for $1.20 a gallon, what is the discounted price? **$1.14**

4. A store marks up the price of a $5 item to $12. What is the percent of markup? **140%**

5. A bicycle has been marked down from $90 to $81. Find the percent of discount. **10%**

6. Computer software is bought by a store for $270 and is sold for $729. Find the percent of markup. **170%**

Class Exercises

Copy and complete the following table.

	Old price	Percent of change	Amount of change	New price
1.	$12	25% discount	?**$3 discount**	? **$9**
2.	$60	10% markup	?**$6 markup**	? **$66**
3.	$50	20% ? markup	?**$10 markup**	$60
4.	$120	100%? markup	?**$120 markup**	$240
5.	$200	15% ? markup	$30 markup	? **$230**
6.	$250	40% ? discount	$100 discount	? **$150**
7.	? **$400**	12% discount	$48 discount	? **$352**
8.	? **$50**	5% markup	$2.50 markup	? **$52.50**
9.	? **$200**	20% discount	?**$40 discount**	$160
10.	? **$20**	150% markup	?**$30 markup**	$50

Problems

Solve.

A

1. A basketball backboard set that sold for $79 is discounted 15%. What is the new price? **$67.15**

2. A parka that sold for $65 is marked up to $70.20. What is the percent of markup? **8%**

3. A stereo tape deck that sold for $235 was on sale for $202.10. What was the percent of discount? **14%**

4. At the end-of-summer sale, an air conditioner that sold for $310 was discounted 21%. What was the sale price? **$244.90**

5. Because of an increase of 8% in wholesale prices, a shoe store had to mark up its new stock by the same percent. What was the new price of a pair of shoes that had sold for $24.50? **$26.46**

6. A department store has a sale on gloves. The sale price is 18% less than the original price, resulting in a saving of $2.97. What was the original price of the gloves? What is the sale price? **$16.50; $1353**

7. A coat that originally cost $40 was marked up 50%. During a sale the coat was discounted 50%. What was the sale price? **$30**

252 *Chapter 7*

8. A 7% sales tax added $3.15 to the selling price of a pair of ski boots. What was the selling price of the boots? What was the total price including the tax? $45; $48.15

B **9.** A tape recorder that cost $50 was discounted 20% for a sale. It was then returned to its original price. What percent of markup was the original price over the sale price? 25%

10. At an end-of-season sale a power lawnmower was on sale for $168. A sign advertised that this was 20% off the original price. What was the original price? $210

11. At a paint sale a gallon can of latex was discounted 24%. If the sale price of a gallon is $9.50, what was the original price? $12.50

12. The cost of a record album was $10.53, including an 8% sales tax. What was the price of the album without the tax? $9.75

C **13.** An item is discounted 20%. Then another 10% discount is given on the new price. What percent of the original price is the final price? 72%

14. An item is marked up 20% and then discounted 15% based on the new price. What percent of the original price is the final price? 102%

15. Which of the following situations will produce a lower final price on a given item?
a. The item is marked up 30% and then discounted 30% of the new price.
b. The item is discounted 30% and then marked up 30% of the new price.
The final prices are the same.

Review Exercises

Complete.

1. circumference = $2\pi \times$ __?__ radius

2. amount of change = __?__ $\times$ original amount percent of change

3. circumference = $\pi \times$ __?__ diameter

4. percent of change = $\dfrac{?}{\text{original amount}}$ amount of change

Percents and Problem Solving **253**

Suggested Assignments

Core
252/Prob. 1–7
253/Prob. 9, 11, 13
Enriched
252/Prob. 2, 4, 6
253/Prob. 9–15

Supplementary Materials
Practice Masters, p. 31

7-3 Commission and Profit

In addition to a salary, many salespeople are paid a percent of the price of the products they sell. This payment is called a **commission.** Like a discount, a commission can be expressed as a percent or as an amount of money. The following formula applies to commissions.

> ## Formula
> amount of commission = percent of commission $\times$ total sales

EXAMPLE 1 Maria Bertram sold $42,000 worth of insurance in January. If her commission is 3% of the total sales, what was the amount of her commission in January?

Solution amount of commission = percent $\times$ total sales
$$= 0.03 \times 42{,}000 = 1260$$

Her commission was $1260.

Profit is the difference between total income and total operating costs.

> ## Formula
> profit = total income − total costs

The **percent of profit** is the percent of total income that is profit.

> ## Formula
> percent of profit $= \dfrac{\text{profit}}{\text{total income}}$

EXAMPLE 2 In April, a shoe store had an income of $8600 and operating costs of $7310. What percent of the store's income was profit?

Solution profit = total income − total costs = 8600 − 7310 = 1290

percent of profit $= \dfrac{\text{profit}}{\text{total income}} = \dfrac{1290}{8600} = 0.15$

The percent of profit was 15%.

Class Exercises

Copy and complete the following table.

	Total sales	Percent of commission	Amount of commission
1.	$3250	10%	? $325
2.	$680	20%	? $136
3.	$900	? 25%	$225
4.	$2500	? 5%	$125
5.	? $2000	15%	$300
6.	? $145	10%	$14.50

a. State the amount of profit.
b. Give an equation that could be used to find the percent of profit.
c. Find the percent of profit.

7. Income $12,000; costs $9000

8. Income $10,000; costs $8700

9. Income $14,000; costs $12,600

10. Income $3000; costs $2850

11. Income $5000; costs $4950

12. Income $24,000; costs $16,800

13. Income $12,300; costs $9840

14. Income $105,360; costs $63,216

Problems

Solve.

A **1.** Esther Simpson receives a 15% commission on magazine subscriptions. One week her sales totaled $860. What was her commission for the week? $129

2. The Greenwood Lumber Company had an income of $7680 for one week in May. If the company's profit for this period was 15% of its income, what were its costs for the week? $6528

3. Margaret DeRosa's day-care service makes a profit of $222 per week. What are her costs if this profit is 18.5% of her total income? $978

Percents and Problem Solving **255**

3. John earned $12 for selling $240 worth of car care products. What percent of commission did he earn? **5%**

4. Susan received $250 for helping to sell a $1250 horse. What percent of commission did she earn? **20%**

5. The French Club made a profit of $27 running a car wash. They earned a total of $90. What was their percent of profit? **30%**

6. Discount City needs to make a profit of 10% on each item sold. If they buy toothbrushes for $1.00 each, find the selling price for each toothbrush. **$1.10**

4. Harvey Williams sold new insurance policies worth $5120 in August. If he receives a 4.5% commission on new policies, how much did he earn in commissions in August? **$230.40**

B **5.** Sole Mates Shoes has expenses of $9592 per month. What must the store's total income be if it is to make a 12% profit? **$10,900**

6. The Top Drawer Furniture Company made a profit of $4360 in one month. What were its operating costs if this profit was 16% of its total income? **$22,890**

Nina Perez is a real estate agent who receives a commission of 6% of the selling price of each house she sells. The seller of the house pays Nina's commission out of the selling price and keeps the remainder. What should be the selling price of each house if the seller wants to keep the amount indicated below?

7. $61,000. **$64,893.62**   **8.** $66,000 **$70,212.77**   **9.** $55,000 **$58,510.64**   **10.** $70,500 **$75,000**

C **11.** In May Sal's Bakery had operating costs of $6630 and made a profit of $1170. In June the operating costs are expected to be $6273. What must the bakery's income be if its profit is to remain the same percent of its income? **$7380**

12. Each month Fran Parks receives a 6% commission on all her sales of barber supplies up to $15,000. She receives 8% commission on the portion of her sales that are above $15,000. Her commission for March was $1260. What were her sales? **$19,500**

13. Mildred Hofstadter receives a 5% commission on her sales of exercise equipment and a 6% commission on her sales of weight-training equipment. One month she sold $7900 worth of exercise equipment and made a total of $650 in commissions. How much were her sales of weight-training equipment that month? **$4250**

14. Norman's Natural Foods has weekly expenses of $1075 and makes a profit of 14% of sales. If his weekly expenses increase to $1225 and he wants to make the same dollar profit as before, what percent of sales will this profit represent? **12.5%**

Review Exercises

Evaluate if $w = 8$, $x = 0.25$, $y = 0.8$, and $z = 5$.

1. wxz 10   **2.** xyz 1   **3.** $wx + yz$ 6   **4.** $wy - xz$ 5.15

5. $(wyz) \div x$ 128   **6.** $(wy) \div (xz)$ 5.12   **7.** $0.2wx$ 0.4   **8.** $1.3wyz$ 41.6

256   *Chapter 7*

Suggested Assignments

Core
  255/Prob. 1–3
  256/Prob. 4–8, 11
  256/Rev. 1–8

Enriched
  255/Prob. 1–3
  256/Prob. 5–13

Supplementary Materials

Practice Masters, p. 32
Computer Activity 14

7-4 Percents and Proportions

Teaching Suggestions
p. 245c

Related Activities p. 245d

In Chapter 6, you learned how to use a proportion to write a fraction as a percent. You can also use proportions to solve problems involving percents. The following discussion shows how we may write a proportion that relates percentage, rate, and base.

The statement *9 is 15% of 60* can be written as $9 = 15\% \times 60$. Because a percent is an amount *per hundred,* we can think of 15% as 15 per hundred, or the ratio of 15 to 100, $\frac{15}{100}$. Substituting, we can write the original statement as

$$9 = \frac{15}{100} \times 60.$$

Dividing both sides of the equation by 60, we obtain the proportion

$$\frac{9}{60} = \frac{15}{100},$$

or 9 is to 60 as 15 is to 100.

Note that $\frac{9}{60}$ is the ratio of the percentage (p) to the base (b).

Percentage, base, and rate are related as shown in the following proportion:

$$\frac{p}{b} = \frac{n}{100},$$

where $\frac{n}{100}$ is the rate expressed as an amount per hundred.

EXAMPLE 1   143 is 65% of what number?

Solution   The rate, 65%, expressed in the form $\frac{n}{100}$, is $\frac{65}{100}$.

The percentage, p, is 143. Write a proportion to find the base, b.

$$\frac{p}{b} = \frac{n}{100}$$

$$\frac{143}{b} = \frac{65}{100}$$

$$65b = 100 \times 143$$

$$b = \frac{14{,}300}{65} = 220$$

Percents and Problem Solving   **257**

Set up a proportion and use it to solve the problem.

1. Shirts are on sale for 15% off. How much is saved on a shirt that is regularly $20?

$\frac{15}{100} = \frac{n}{20}$, $n = 3$, $3

2. A color TV, regularly $450, is on sale for $405. What is the rate of discount?

$\frac{45}{450} = \frac{n}{100}$, $n = 10$, 10%

3. Alex saves 30% of what he earns working part time. Last month he earned $65. How much did he save?

$\frac{30}{100} = \frac{n}{65}$, $n = 19.50$, $19.50

EXAMPLE 2 In a recent survey, 38 of 120 people preferred the Bright Light disposable flashlight to other flashlights. What percent of the people surveyed preferred Bright Light?

Solution The question asks what percent, or how many people per hundred, prefer Bright Light.

Let n equal the number per hundred.
You know that p is 38 and b is 120.
Set up a proportion and then solve for n.

$$\frac{p}{b} = \frac{n}{100}$$

$$\frac{38}{120} = \frac{n}{100}$$

$$38 \times 100 = 120n$$

$$\frac{3800}{120} = n$$

$$n = 31\frac{2}{3}$$

In the survey, $31\frac{2}{3}\%$ of the people preferred Bright Light.

EXAMPLE 3 The price of a pocket cassette player has been discounted 25%. The original price was $59. What is the sale price?

Solution The question asks you to find the sale price.

First find the amount of the discount.
p is to be found, b is 59, and n is 25.
Set up a proportion and then solve for p.

$$\frac{p}{b} = \frac{n}{100}$$

$$\frac{p}{59} = \frac{25}{100}$$

$$100p = 59 \times 25$$

$$p = \frac{1475}{100} = 14.75$$

The amount of the discount is $14.75.

Next find the sale price.

$$59 - 14.75 = 44.25$$

The sale price is $44.25.

258 *Chapter 7*

Class Exercises

For each exercise, set up a proportion to find the number or percent. Do not solve the proportion.

1. What percent of 32 is 20? $\dfrac{20}{32} = \dfrac{n}{100}$

2. 14 is 25% of what number? $\dfrac{14}{n} = \dfrac{25}{100}$

3. What is 58% of 24? $\dfrac{n}{24} = \dfrac{58}{100}$

4. A digital clock is selling at a discount of 15%. The original price was $8.98. How much money will you save by buying the clock at the sale price? $\dfrac{15}{100} = \dfrac{n}{8.98}$

5. Catherine answered 95% of the test questions correctly. If she answered 38 questions correctly, how many questions were on the test? $\dfrac{95}{100} = \dfrac{38}{n}$

6. This year, 360 people ran in the town marathon. Only 315 people finished the race. What percent of the people finished the race? $\dfrac{315}{360} = \dfrac{n}{100}$

Written Exercises

Use a proportion to solve.

A 1. What is 16% of 32? 5.12

2. 306 is 51% of what number? 600

3. What percent of 20 is 16? 80%

4. What is 104% of 85? 88.4

5. 15 is 37.5% of what number? 40

6. What percent of 72 is 18? 25%

Problems

Use a proportion to solve.

A 1. The Plantery received a shipment of 40 plants on Wednesday. By Friday, 33 of the plants had been sold. What percent of the plants were sold? 82.5%

2. The Eagles have won 6 of the 8 games they have played this season. What percent of this season's games have the Eagles won? 75%

3. The library ordered 56 new books. 87.5% of the books are nonfiction. How many books are nonfiction? 49 books

4. This year 18.75% more students have joined the Long Hill High School Drama Club. The records show that 6 new students have joined. How many students were members last year? 32 students

Additional A Exercises

Use a proportion to solve.

1. What is 98% of 44? 43.12

2. What percent of 48 is 16?
   $33\dfrac{1}{3}\%$

3. 250 is 125% of what number? 200

4. Ann made 8 out of 15 field goal attempts in a basketball game. What percent did she make?
   $53\dfrac{1}{3}\%$

Suggested Assignments

Core
Day 1: 259/1–6; Prob. 1–4
260/Prob. 5–7
Day 2: 260/Prob. 9, 10
261/Prob. 11
261/Self-Test A

Enriched
Day 1: 259/4–6; Prob. 2, 4
260/Prob. 6–10
Day 2: 261/Prob. 11, 13
261/Self-Test A

Supplementary Materials

Practice Masters, p. 32
Test 7A, pp. 47–48

5. A water purifier is discounted 20% of the original price for a saving of $6.96. What is the original price of the water purifier? What is the sale price? $34.80; $27.84

6. The original price of a Sportsmaster 300 fishing pole was $37.80. The price has now been discounted 15%. What is the amount of the discount? What is the sale price? $5.67; $32.13

B **7.** Steve recently received a raise of 6% of his salary at his part-time job. He now earns $38.69 per week. How much did he earn per week before his raise? $36.50

8. Since the beginning of the year, the number of subscriptions to *New Tech Magazine* has increased by 180%. The number of subscriptions is now 140,000. What was the number of subscriptions at the beginning of the year? 50,000 subscriptions

EXAMPLE This **pie chart,** or **circle graph,** shows the distribution of the Valley Springs annual budget. Use a proportion to find the measure of the angle for the wedge for education.

VALLEY SPRINGS BUDGET
$12 MILLION

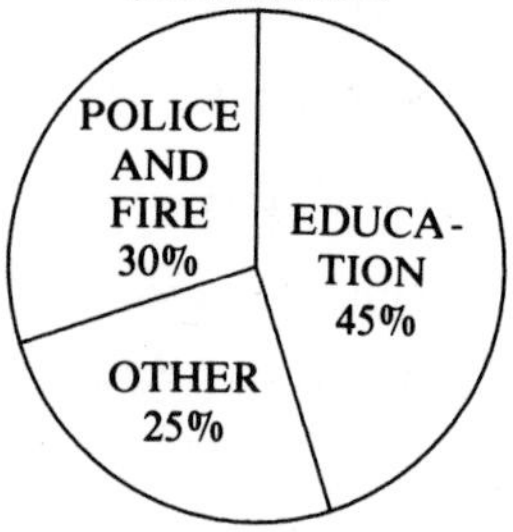

POLICE AND FIRE 30%

EDUCATION 45%

OTHER 25%

Solution The number of degrees in a circle is 360°. The circle represents the total budget. 45% of the total budget is for education. Therefore,

$$\frac{45}{100} = \frac{n}{360}$$

$$100n = 45 \times 360$$

$$n = \frac{16{,}200}{100}$$

$$n = 162$$

There are 162° in the wedge for education.

Use proportions to answer these questions about the pie chart above.

9. a. What is the measure of the angle for the wedge for police and fire expenses? 108°
b. How much money is budgeted for police and fire expenses? $3.6 million

10. a. What is the measure of the angle for the wedge for other expenses? 90°
b. How much money is budgeted for other expenses? $3 million

260 *Chapter 7*

For Exercises 11-13, (a) use a compass and protractor to draw a pie chart to represent the budget, and (b) use proportions to find the dollar value of each expense. Check students' drawings.

C 11. The monthly budget of the Miller family allows for spending 25% on food, 15% on clothing, 30% on housing expenses, 10% on medical expenses, and 20% on other expenses. Their total budget is $1800 per month.

12. The total weekly expenses of Daisy's Diner average $8400. Of this total, 20% is spent for employee's salaries, 60% is spent on food, 5% is spent on advertising, 10% is spent on rent, and 5% is used for other expenses.

13. The Chimney Hill school budget allows 72% for salaries, 8% for maintenance and repair, and 5% for books and supplies. The remainder is divided equally among recreation, after-school programs, and teacher training. The budget totals $680,000.

Self-Test A

Find the percent of increase or decrease.

1. 12 to 15 25%   2. 20 to 13 35%   3. 200 to 246 23%   [7-1]

4. A sleeping bag that cost $85 is marked up 22%. What is the new price? $103.70   [7-2]

5. A toy that had sold for $16.50 was on sale for $11.55. What was the percent of discount? 30%

6. A real estate agency charges a commission of 6% on sales. How much is the commission on a house that sells for $106,000? $6360   [7-3]

7. In August, Middle Mountain Mines had an income of $82,600. If profit for August was 12% of income, what were the company's costs that month? $72,688

Use a proportion to solve.

8. What is 81% of 540? 437.4   9. 64 is what percent of 80? 80%   [7-4]

10. Of the traffic violations cited by Officer Huang, 64% were for speeding. If Officer Huang cited 48 motorists for speeding, how many violations were there altogether? 75 violations

Self-Test answers and Extra Practice are at the end of the book.

Percents and Problem Solving **261**

Quick Quiz A

Find the percent of increase or decrease. Round to the nearest tenth if necessary.

1. 12 to 20 $66\frac{2}{3}$%

2. 30 to 18 40%

3. 200 to 425 $112\frac{1}{2}$%

4. A record album that sold for $9 is on sale at a 15% discount. What is the sale price? $7.65

5. A towel that had sold for $20 was on sale for $18. What was the percent of discount? 10%

6. Jim Smith receives a 16% commission on magazine subscriptions. One month his sales totaled $2500. What was his commission for the month? $400

7. Amy Brown's stained glass business makes a profit of $250 per week. What are her costs if this profit is 15% of her total income? $1666.67

Use a proportion to solve.

8. What is 72% of 550? 396

9. 74 is what percent of 111? $66\frac{2}{3}$%

10. The Falcons have won 5 of the 8 games they have played this season. What percent of this season's games have the Falcons lost? 37.5%

7-5 Simple Interest

Teaching Suggestions
p. 245d

Related Activities p. 245d

Reading Mathematics

Students will learn the meaning of the following mathematical terms in this lesson: *interest, annual rate, simple interest, installments, principal.*

Students should understand that interest is an amount of money whereas the annual rate of interest is a percent. In everyday speech, however, people sometimes use the word "interest" when they mean "rate of interest."

When you lease a car or an apartment, you pay the owner rent for the use of the car or the apartment. When you borrow money, you pay the lender **interest** for the use of the money. The amount of interest you pay is usually a percent of the amount borrowed figured on a yearly basis. This percent is called the **annual rate.** For example, if you borrow $150 at an annual rate of 12%, you pay:

$$\$150 \times 0.12 = \$18 \text{ interest for one year}$$
$$\$150 \times 0.12 \times 2 = \$36 \text{ interest for two years}$$
$$\$150 \times 0.12 \times 3 = \$54 \text{ interest for three years}$$

When interest is computed year by year in this manner we call it **simple interest.** The example above illustrates the following formula.

Formula

Let I = simple interest charged

P = amount borrowed, or **principal**

r = annual rate

t = time in years for which the amount is borrowed

Then, interest = principal $\times$ rate $\times$ time, or $I = Prt$.

EXAMPLE 1 How much simple interest do you pay if you borrow $640 for 3 years at an annual rate of 15%?

Solution Use the formula: $I = Prt$
$$I = 640 \times 0.15 \times 3 = 288$$

The interest is $288.

EXAMPLE 2 Sarah Sachs borrowed $3650 for 4 years at an annual rate of 16%. How much money must she repay in all?

Solution Use the formula: $I = Prt$
$$I = 3650 \times 0.16 \times 4 = 2336$$

The interest is $2336.
The total to be repaid is the principal plus the interest: 3650 + 2336, or $5986.

262 *Chapter 7*

Problem Solving Reminder

When solving a problem, be certain to *answer the question asked.* In Example 2, you are asked to find the total amount to be repaid, not just the interest. To get the total amount to be repaid, you must add the interest to the amount borrowed.

EXAMPLE 3   Renny Soloman paid $375 simple interest on a loan of $1500 at 12.5%. What was the length of time for the loan?

Solution   Let t = time.

Use the formula: $I = Prt$
$$375 = 1500 \times 0.125 \times t$$
$$375 = 187.5t$$
$$\frac{375}{187.5} = t$$
$$t = 2$$

The loan was for 2 years.

EXAMPLE 4   George Landon paid $585 simple interest on a loan of $6500 for 6 months. What was the annual rate?

Solution   Let r = annual rate.

Use the formula: $I = Prt$
$$585 = 6500 \times r \times \frac{1}{2}$$
$$585 = 3250r$$
$$r = \frac{585}{3250} = 0.18$$

The annual rate was 18%.

In Example 4 notice that the time, 6 months, is expressed as $\frac{1}{2}$ year, since the rate of interest in the formula is the *annual or yearly rate.*

Chalkboard Examples

A bank will pay simple interest at an annual rate of 5% per year. Find the interest paid on each of the following deposits.

1. $200 for 1 year $10

2. $4000 for 2 years $400

3. $1500 for 3 years $225

4. $300 for 6 months $7.50

A bank charges an annual rate of 16% on loans. Find the interest charged on each of the following loans.

5. $2000 for 1 year $320

6. $8000 for 3 years $3840

7. $1400 for 6 months $112

8. $2400 for 18 months $576

Class Exercises

Give the simple interest on each loan at the given annual rate for 1 year, 3 years, and 6 months.

1. $100 at 8% $8; $24; $4

2. $200 at 12% $24; $72; $12

3. $5000 at 10% $500; $1500; $250

4. $400 at 5% $20; $60; $10

5. $1500 at 6% $90; $270; $45

6. $100 at 8.4% $8.40; $25.20; $4.20

Percents and Problem Solving   **263**

	1.	2.
Principal	$2000	$600
Annual Rate	12%	18%
Time	3 y	6 mo

$720 $54

Find the annual rate of interest for each loan.

	3.	4.
Principal	$6000	$1500
Time	2 y	6 mo
Interest	$1200	$90

10%   12%

Find the length of time for each loan.

	5.	6.
Principal	$4000	$1800
Annual Rate	15%	16%
Interest	$1800	$432

3 y   1.5 y

Find the annual rate of interest for each loan.

7. principal: $1100, time: 2 years, simple interest: $220   10%

8. principal: $1600, time: $1\frac{1}{2}$ years, simple interest: $120   5%

Find the length of time for each loan.

9. principal: $1200, interest rate: 6%, simple interest: $144   2 years

10. principal: $500, interest rate: 8%, simple interest: $30   9 months

Find the total amount that must be repaid on each loan.

11. principal: $200, interest rate: 15%, time: 2 years $260

12. principal: $600, interest rate: 9%, time: 3 years $762

Written Exercises

Find the simple interest on each loan and the total amount to be repaid.

A   1. $1280 at 15% for 2 years

2. $4250 at 12% for 3 years

3. $2760 at 18% for 1 year, 6 months

4. $3500 at 16% for 9 months

5. $5640 at 7.5% for 4 years

6. $7250 at 12.8% for $2\frac{1}{2}$ years

7. $6380 at 14.5% for 6 years

8. $14,650 at 16.4% for $3\frac{1}{2}$ years

Find the annual rate of interest for each loan.

9. $4360 for 2 years, 6 months; simple interest: $1526   14%

10. $1240 for 3 years, 6 months; simple interest: $651   15%

11. $2600 for 4 years; total to be repaid: $3484   8.5%

12. $5760 for 2 years, 9 months; total to be repaid: $8532   17.5%

13. $6520 for 3 years, 3 months; simple interest: $3390.40   16%

14. $3980 for $4\frac{1}{2}$ years; total to be repaid: $7024.70   17%

Find the length of time for each loan.

15. $3775 at 12%; simple interest: $226.50   6 months

16. $7850 at 6.5%; simple interest: $510.25   1 year

264   *Chapter 7*

Find the original amount (principal) of the given loan.

EXAMPLE   9% for 4 years; total to be repaid: $7140

Solution   Let P = the original amount of the loan.

$$\text{amount to be repaid} = P + Prt$$
$$= P + P \times 0.09 \times 4$$
$$= P + 0.36P$$
$$= P(1 + 0.36)$$
$$7140 = 1.36P$$
$$P = \frac{7140}{1.36} = 5250$$

The original amount of the loan was $5250.

B 17. 8% for $4\frac{1}{2}$ years; total to be repaid: $6052 **$4450**

18. 13.5% for 5 years; total to be repaid: $3417 **$2040**

19. 16% for 2 years, 3 months; total to be repaid: $9139.20 **$6720**

20. 12.4% for 3 years, 6 months; total to be repaid: $2222.70 ~~$1530~~ 1550

21. 9.6% for 4 years; total to be repaid: $2560.40 **$1850**

22. 10.8% for 2 years, 9 months; total to be repaid: $4734.05 **$3650**

Solve.

C 23. If the simple interest on $250 for 1 year, 8 months is $30, how much is the interest on $425.50 for 3 years, 4 months? **$102.02**

24. If $150 earns $28.75 simple interest in 1 year and 8 months, what principal is required to earn $747.50 interest in 2 years, 6 months? **$2600**

Problems

Solve.

A 1. Lois Pocket owns bonds worth $10,500 that pay 11% annual interest. The interest is paid semiannually in two equal amounts. How much is each payment? **$577.50**

2. A car loan of $4650 at an annual rate of 16% for 2 years is to be repaid in 24 equal monthly payments, including principal and interest. How much is each of these payments? **$255.75**

Percents and Problem Solving **265**

Suggested Assignments

Core
Day 1: 264/3–16
        265/17–21 odd
Day 2: 265/Prob. 1, 2
        266/Prob. 3–5
        266/Rev. 1–9 odd
        266/Calculator
              Key-In

Enriched
Day 1: 264/1–15 odd
        265/17–24
Day 2: 266/Prob. 3–8
        266/Rev. 2–8 even
        266/Calculator
              Key-In

Supplementary Materials

Practice Masters, p. 33

3. Gilbert White wants to borrow $2250 for 3 years to remodel his garage. The annual rate is 18%. If the principal and interest are repaid in equal monthly installments, how much will each installment be? $96.25

4. Fernando Lopez can borrow $5640 at 12.5% for 4 years, or he can borrow the same amount for 3 years at 15%. Find the total amount to be repaid on each loan. Which amount is smaller?
        $8460 at 12.5%; $8178 at 15%; the 15% loan

B 5. An education loan of $8400 for ten years is to be repaid in monthly installments of $122.50. What is the annual rate of this loan, computed as simple interest? 7.5%

6. Will Darcy's three-year home improvement loan is to be repaid in monthly installments of $375.90 each. If the annual rate (as simple interest) is 14.4%, what is the principal of the loan? $9450

C 7. In how many years would the amount to be repaid on a loan at 12.5% simple interest be double the principal of the loan? 8 years

8. At what rate of simple interest would the amount to be repaid on a loan be triple the principal of the loan after 25 years? 8%

Review Exercises

Multiply. Round to the nearest thousandth if necessary.

1. $\frac{1}{2} \times 0.75$ 0.375   2. $\frac{1}{4} \times 0.3$ 0.075   3. $\frac{1}{5} \times 0.25$ 0.05

4. $\frac{3}{4} \times 0.61$ 0.458   5. $\frac{4}{5} \times 1.87$ 1.496   6. $\frac{3}{10} \times 2.03$ 0.609

7. $\frac{2}{3} \times 1.25$ 0.833   8. $\frac{7}{9} \times 2.375$ 1.847   9. $\frac{5}{6} \times 2.875$ 2.396

▮▮▮ Calculator Key-In

Some calculators have a percent key. Use a calculator with a percent key to do the following exercises.

1. What is 8% of 200? 16   2. 35 is 20% of what number? 175

3. What percent of 75 is 36? 48%   4. Express $\frac{17}{20}$ as a percent. 85%

5. Express $\frac{13}{15}$ as a percent. $86.\overline{6}\%$ 6. Express $\frac{7}{11}$ as a percent. $63.\overline{63}\%$

266 *Chapter 7*

266

7-6 Compound Interest

If you deposited $100 in an account that paid 10% interest, you would have $10 interest after one year for a total of $110. You could then withdraw the $10 interest or leave it in the account. By withdrawing the interest, your principal would remain $100, and you would again receive simple interest. If, however, you left the $10 interest in the account, your principal would become $110, and you would accumulate **compound interest,** that is, interest on principal plus interest. The following chart illustrates these alternatives.

	Simple Interest		Compound Interest	
After	Interest	Principal	Interest	Principal
0 years	0	$100	0	$100
1 year	10% of $100 = $10	$100	10% of $100 = $10	$100 + $10 = $110
2 years	10% of $100 = $10	$100	10% of $110 = $11	$110 + $11 = $121
3 years	10% of $100 = $10	$100	10% of $121 = $12.10	$121 + $12.10 = $133.10
	Total interest: $30		Total interest: $33.10	

Notice that because the principal increases as interest is compounded, the total amount of interest paid on $100 after 3 years is greater than what is paid at the same rate of simple interest.

Interest is often compounded in one of the following manners.

monthly: 12 times a year
quarterly: 4 times a year
semiannually: 2 times a year

EXAMPLE If $500 is deposited in an account paying 8% interest compounded quarterly, how much will the principal amount to after 1 year?

Solution Use the formula $I = Prt$.

After 1 quarter:
$I = 500 \times 0.08 \times \frac{1}{4} = 10 $P = 500 + 10 = 510

After 2 quarters:
$I = 510 \times 0.08 \times \frac{1}{4} = 10.20 $P = 510 + 10.20 = 520.20

After 3 quarters:
$I = 520.20 \times 0.08 \times \frac{1}{4} \approx 10.40 $P = 520.20 + 10.40 = 530.60

After 4 quarters:
$I = 530.60 \times 0.08 \times \frac{1}{4} \approx 10.61 $P = 530.60 + 10.61 = 541.21

Percents and Problem Solving **267**

Teaching Suggestions
p. 245e

Related Activities p. 245e

Reading Mathematics

Students will learn the meaning of the following mathematical terms in this lesson: *compound interest, maturity, monthly, quarterly, semiannually.*

Some students may not be familiar with the use of the word "quarter" to refer to one-fourth of a year, or 3 months. You can avoid a possible source of confusion by briefly reviewing the meaning of the words *semiannually, quarterly,* and *monthly.*

You may wish to explain that a certificate is "mature" when the time limit has expired. After the amount of time specified on the certificate has elapsed, the full amount, principal plus interest, is due. For example, in Problem 1 the certificate reaches maturity after 18 months. That is, after 18 months the value of the certificate equals the principal, $1600, plus the interest that has accrued.

Chalkboard Examples

How much will a principal of $500 amount to after 2 years under the following conditions?

Answers may vary slightly due to rounding.

1. 12% per year compounded annually.
   $627.20

2. 12% per year compounded semiannually.
   $631.24

3. 12% per year compounded quarterly.
   $633.39

How much will the principal amount to under the following conditions? Round answers to the nearest cent.

1. $1000 after 2 years, at 10% per year compounded annually. $1210.00

2. $1000 after 1.5 years, at 12% per year compounded semiannually. $1191.02

3. $5000 after 6 months at 8% per year compounded quarterly. $5202.00

Solve.

4. The Allen Bank pays 6% per year compounded monthly. How much will $350 amount to after 2 months? $353.51

Reading Mathematics: *Study Skills*

After you read an interest problem, ask yourself the following questions:
  What is asked for, simple interest or compound interest?
  What is the time period? For example, is it 3 months or 3 years?
  Is the answer to be the interest, the new principal, or the total amount to be repaid?

Class Exercises

$8000 is deposited in a bank that compounds interest annually at 5%. Find the following.

1. The interest paid at the end of the first year $400

2. The new principal at the beginning of the second year $8400

3. The interest paid at the end of the second year $420

4. The new principal at the beginning of the third year $8820

5. The interest paid at the end of the third year $441

$1000 is invested at 12%, compounded quarterly. Find the following.

6. The interest paid after 3 months $30   7. The new principal after 3 months $1030

8. The interest paid after 6 months $30.90 9. The new principal after 6 months $1060.90

Written Exercises

How much will each principal amount to if it is deposited for the given time at the given rate? (If you do not have a calculator, round to the nearest penny at each step.)

A
1. $6400 for 2 years at 5%, compounded annually $7056

2. $500 for 1 year at 8%, compounded semiannually $540.80

3. $1500 for 6 months at 8%, compounded quarterly $1560.60

4. $8000 for 2 months at 6%, compounded monthly $8080.20

5. $2500 for 18 months at 16%, compounded semiannually $3149.28

6. $1280 for 9 months at 10%, compounded quarterly $1378.42

7. $1800 for 1 year, 3 months at 14%, compounded quarterly $2137.84

8. $3475 for $2\frac{1}{2}$ years at 6%, compounded semiannually $4028.48

268   *Chapter 7*

How much will each principal amount to if it is deposited for the given time at the given rate? (If you do not have a calculator, round to the nearest penny at each step.) Answers may vary slightly due to rounding.

B   **9.** $3200 for 3 years at 7.5%, compounded annually $3975.35

   10. $3125 for 3 months at 9.6%, compounded monthly $3200.60

   11. $8000 for 2 years at 10%, compounded semiannually $9724.05

   12. $6250 for 1 year at 16%, compounded quarterly $7311.62

   13. What is the difference between the simple and compound (compounded semiannually) interest on $250 in 2 years at 14% per year? $7.71

   14. What is the difference between the interest on $800 in 1 year at 8% per year compounded semiannually and compounded quarterly? $.67

C   **15.** How long would it take $2560 to grow to $2756.84 at 10% compounded quarterly? 9 mo

   16. What principal will grow to $1367.10 after 1 year at 10% compounded semiannually? $1240

Problems

Solve. (If you do not have a calculator, round to the nearest penny at each step.) Answers may vary slightly due to rounding.

A   **1.** The River Bank and Trust Company pays 10%, compounded semiannually, on their 18-month certificates. How much would a certificate for $1600 be worth at maturity? $1852.20

   2. Mike Estrada invested $1250 at 9.6%, compounded monthly. How much was his investment worth at the end of 3 months? $1280.24

B   **3.** Jennifer Thornton can invest $3200 at 12% simple interest or at 10% interest compounded quarterly. Which investment will earn more in 9 months? 12% simple interest

   4. Which is a better way to invest $6400 for $1\frac{1}{2}$ years: 16% simple interest or 15% compounded semiannually? 15% compounded semiannually

C   **5.** A money market fund pays 12.8% per year, compounded semiannually. For a deposit of $5000, this compound interest rate is equivalent to what simple interest rate for 1 year? Give your answer to the nearest tenth of a percent. 13.2%

Percents and Problem Solving **269**

Teaching Suggestions
p. 245f

Related Activities, p. 245f

Reading Mathematics

Students will learn the meaning of the following mathematical terms in this lesson:
social security, property
taxes, combined amount,
assessed value of property,
market value, per kW·h, total
finance charge, annual dividend, certificate of deposit,
royalty, bonds, and savings
certificate.

7-7 Percents and Problem Solving

Percents are used frequently to express facts about situations we encounter. The skills acquired earlier for working with percents can be
used to solve problems that are involved in these situations.

EXAMPLE 1 Eve Malik has a yearly salary of $27,600. She is paid in equal
amounts twice a month. She and her employer each pay 6.7% of her
salary to her social security account. What is the combined amount
paid to social security for Eve each pay period?

Solution The problem asks for the combined amount paid to social security.
Given facts: yearly salary $27,600
                2 paychecks a month
                6.7% each for social security

2 payments a month for 12 months: $2 \times 12 = 24$ payments
$27,600 \div 24 = \$1150$, salary per payment
social security paid by each is 6.7% of $1150

$$0.067 \times 1150 = \$77.05$$

Combined amount paid to social security is $2 \times \$77.05$, or $154.10.

EXAMPLE 2 Property taxes in Jackson County are $1.42 per $100 of assessed
value of the property. Assessed value is 60% of the actual market
value. If taxes on a home are $681.60, what is the market value of
the property?

Solution The problem asks for the market value.
Given facts: Taxes are $681.60
                Tax rate is $1.42 per $100 of assessed value.
                Assessed value is 60% of market value.

Divide $681.60 by $1.42 to find how many $100's are in the assessed
value: $681.60 \div 1.42 = 480$
Assessed value is $480 \times 100 = 48,000$
Assessed value is 60% ($= 0.6$) of market value.

$$48,000 = 0.6 \times m$$

$$\frac{48,000}{0.6} = m$$

$$80,000 = m$$

The market value is $80,000.

270   *Chapter 7*

EXAMPLE 3   Central Electric Co. charges $.055 per kW·h for the first 500 kW·h and $.05 per kW·h for the next 2000 kW·h. There is a discount of 2% for paying bills promptly. In March the Gronskis used 1450 kW·h. How much did they pay if they paid in time to receive the discount for prompt payment?

Solution   The problem asks how much the Gronskis paid.

Given facts: Cost is $.55 per kW·h for the first 500 kW·h,
$.05 per kW·h for the next 2000 kW·h.
1450 kW·h were used.
Discount is 2%.

First find the total charge.
500 kW·h at $.055 each: $500 \times 0.055 = \$27.50$
$1450 - 500 = 950$
950 kW·h at $.05 each: $950 \times 0.05 = \$47.50$
Total charge: $\$27.50 + \$47.50 = \$75.00$

Since the discount is 2%, they only paid 100% − 2%, or 98%, of the actual charge.

$$75 \times 0.98 = 73.50$$

The Gronskis paid $73.50.

Problem Solving Reminder

In some problems, it is necessary to use several operations. Notice that Example 3 above required that the charge for the first 500 kW·h and the charge for the next 950 kW·h be found separately and then added to find the total charge. Finally, the discounted price was calculated.

Problems

Solve.

A   **1.** Jim Damato charged $86.50 on his FasterCharge card and got a cash advance of $120. There is a finance charge of 1.5% on purchases and 1% on cash advances. How much was his total finance charge? $2.50

2. Esther Upperman invested $1250 in 50 shares of BU + U stock, which pays an annual dividend of $1.90 per share. Which investment gives a greater yield, the BU + U shares or a certificate of deposit that pays 7% interest? BU + U shares

Percents and Problem Solving **271**

Solve. Round to the nearest cent.

1. The creator of a new game receives a royalty of 8% of the selling price of each game sold. The company that produces the game receives the remaining amount. If the company receives $10.10 per game, what is the selling price of the game? $10.98

2. Jim Bacon invested $1400 in 45 shares of TMC stock, which pays an annual dividend of $2.30 per share. Which investment gives a greater yield, the TMC shares or a certificate of deposit that pays 8%? certificate

3. Emily Katz charged $98.50 on her Faster-Charge card, and got a cash advance of $175. There is a finance charge of 1.5% on purchases and 1% on cash advances. How much was her total finance charge? $3.23

Solve. Round to the nearest cent.

1. Property taxes in Carver are $15 per $1000 of assessed value of the property. Assessed value is 75% of the actual market value. If taxes on a home are $1125, what is the market value of the property? **$100,000**

2. A rock singer earns a royalty of 18% of the selling price of an audio-cassette tape. If she earns $1.44 on each tape sold, what is the selling price of the tape? **$8**

3. Ron Swanson has a yearly salary of $25,400. He is paid in equal amounts weekly. He and his employer each pay 6.7% of his salary to his social security account. How much is paid to social security for Ron each pay period? **$65.45**

4. At a summer sale, a snow blower was discounted 28%. The snow blower sold for $650, including a sales tax of 5% of the sale price. What was the original price of the snow blower? **$859.79**

272

3. A guitarist is to be paid a royalty of 6% of the selling price of a new album. If 46,000 copies of the album were sold at $7.95 each, how much should the guitarist be paid? **$21,942**

4. The publisher of *Lost in the Jungle* receives $12.60 from each copy sold. The remaining portion of the $15 selling price goes to the author. What royalty rate does the author earn? **16%**

5. At a clearance sale, a gas-powered lawn mower was discounted 32%. The lawn mower was sold for $117.81, including a sales tax of 5% of the sale price. What was the original price of the mower? **$165**

6. The Ransoms intend to reduce their electricity use by 15% in September. In August they used 2200 kW·h. Their electric company charges $0.062 per kW·h for the first 1000 kW·h, $0.055 per kW·h for the next 1000 kW·h, and $0.05 per kW·h for any additional use. How much can the Ransoms expect to save? **$17.15**

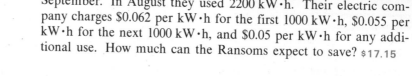

B 7. Anita Ramirez owns two bonds, one paying 8.5% interest and the other paying 9% interest. Every six months Anita receives a total of $485 in interest from both bonds. If the 8.5% bond is worth $4000, how much is the 9% bond worth? **$7000**

8. Mike Robarts owns two bonds, one worth $3000, the other worth $5000. The $3000 bond pays 12% interest. Every 6 months, Mike receives a total of $530 interest from both bonds. What is the annual rate of the $5000 bond? **14%**

C 9. The property tax rate in Glendale is $2.15 per $100 of assessed value. Assessed value is 60% of market value. This year the Prestons' tax bill was $129 more than last year, when the market value of their house was $84,000. What is the present assessed value of their house? **$56,400**

10. In the primary election, 56% of eligible voters voted. Smith received 65% of the votes, Jones got 30%, and 5% of the voters chose other candidates. Smith won by a margin of 5488 votes over Jones. How many eligible voters are there? **28,000**

11. David Cho deposited $10,000 in a six-month savings certificate that paid simple interest at an annual rate of 12%. After 6 months, David deposited the total value of his investment in another six-month savings certificate. David made no other deposits or withdrawals. After 6 months, David's investment was worth $11,130. What was the annual simple interest rate of the second certificate? **10%**

12. A savings account pays 5% interest, compounded annually. Show that if $1000 is deposited in the account, the account will contain

1000×1.05 dollars after 1 year.
$1000 \times (1.05)^2$ dollars after 2 years.
$1000 \times (1.05)^3$ dollars after 3 years, and so on.

Self-Test B

Solve.

1. A loan of $6400 at 12.5% simple interest is to be repaid in $4\frac{1}{2}$ years. What is the total amount to be repaid? **$10,000** [7–5]

2. A $6500 automobile loan is to be repaid in 3 years. The total amount to be repaid is $9230. If the interest were simple interest, what would be the annual rate? **14%**

3. You borrow $2500 at 16% interest, compounded semiannually. No interest is due until you repay the loan. If you repay the loan at the end of 18 months, how much will you pay? **$3149.28** [7–6]

4. Julian Dolby invested $5000 in a special savings account that pays 8% interest, compounded quarterly. How long must Julian keep his money in the account to earn at least $250 in interest? **9 mo**

5. Mary Barnes earns $9.00 an hour. In 1984 she worked an average of 38 h a week. She pays 5% of her wages to a pension plan, and her employer pays an additional 7.2% of her wages to the same plan. How much was paid to the plan for Mary in 1984? **$2169.65** [7–7]

Self-Test answers and Extra Practice are at the back of the book.

12. After 1 year:
    $1000 + 1000(0.05)$
    $= 1000(1.05)$.
    After 2 years:
$1000(1.05) + 1000(1.05)(0.05)$
    $= 1000(1.05)(1.05)$
    $= 1000(1.05)^2$,
    and so on.

Quick Quiz B

Solve. Round to the nearest cent.

1. A loan of $6000 at 12.5% simple interest is to be repaid in $3\frac{1}{2}$ years. What is the total amount to be repaid? **$8625**

2. A $8500 automobile loan is to be repaid in 4 years. The total amount to be repaid is $12,070. If the interest were simple interest, what would be the annual rate? **10.5%**

3. You borrow $2400 at 15% interest compounded semiannually. No interest is due until you repay the loan. If you repay the loan at the end of 2 years, how much will you pay? **$3205.13**

4. You invest $2000 in a special savings account the pays 10% interest, compounded quarterly. How long must you keep your money in the account to earn at least $158.78 in interest? **9 months**

5. Jim Barnes earns $8.00 an hour. In 1984 he worked an average of 35 h a week. He pays 5% of his wages to a pension plan, and his employer pays an additional 7.2% of his wages to the same plan. How much was paid to the plan for Jim in 1984? **$1776.32**

Credit Balances

Before stores or banks issue credit cards, they do a complete credit check of the prospective charge customer. Why? Because issuing credit is actually lending money. When customers use credit cards they are getting instant loans. For credit loans, interest, in the form of a *finance charge,* is paid for the favor of the loan.

To keep track of charge account activity, monthly statements are prepared. The sample statement below is a typical summary of activity.

Customer's Statement Account Number 35–0119–4G				Billing Cycle Closing Date 9/22 Payment Due Date 10/17			
Date	**Dept. No.**		**Description**	**Purchases & Charges**		**Payments & Credits**	
9/3 9/14 9/17	753 212		TOYS HOUSEWARES PAYMENT	30.00 12.50		 20.00	
Previous Balance	**Payments & Credits**	**Unpaid Balance**	**Finance Charge**	**Purchases & Charges**	**New Balance**	**Minimum Payment**	
40.99	20.00	20.99	.61	42.50	64.10	20.00	

Statements usually show any finance charges and a complete list of transactions completed during the billing cycle. Finance charges are determined in a variety of ways. One common method is to compute the amount of the unpaid balance and make a charge based on that amount. Then new purchases are added to compute the new balance on which a minimum payment is due.

To manage the masses of data generated by a credit system, many merchants use computerized cash registers. The cash registers work in the following way. When a customer asks to have a purchase charged, the salesperson enters the amount of the purchase and the customer's credit card number into the computer. The computer then retrieves the

274 *Chapter 7*

account balance from memory, adds in the new purchase, and compares the total to the limit allowed for the account. If the account limit has not been reached, the transaction is completed and the amount of the new purchase is stored in memory. At the end of the billing cycle, the computer totals the costs of the new purchases, deducts payments or credits, adds any applicable finance charges, and prints out a detailed statement.

Copy and complete. Use the chart below to find the minimum payment.

	Previous Balance	Payments and Credits	Unpaid Balance	Finance Charge	Purchases and Charges	New Balance	Minimum Payment
1.	175.86	50.00	?	1.89	35.00	?	?
2.	20.00	20.00	?	0	30.00	?	?
3.	289.75	40.00	?	5.25	68.80	?	?
4.	580.00	52.00	?	8.00	189.65	?	?
5.	775.61	110.00	?	10.48	0	?	?

Solve.

6. Debra Dinardo is comparing her sales receipts to her charge account statement for the month. The billing cycle closing date for the statement is 4/18. Debra has sales receipts for the following dates and amounts.

3/30 $17.60   4/8 $21.54
4/16 $33.12   4/26 $9.75

On April 14, Debra paid the balance on her last statement with a check for $139.80. Her statement shows the information below. Is the statement correct? Explain. **yes**

New Balance	Minimum Payment
Up to $20.00	New Balance
$ 20.01 to $200.00	$20.00
$200.01 to $250.00	$25.00
$250.01 to $300.00	$30.00
$300.01 to $350.00	$35.00
$350.01 to $400.00	$40.00
$400.01 to $450.00	$45.00
$450.01 to $500.00	$50.00
Over $500.00	$50.00 plus $10.00 for each $50.00 (or fraction thereof) of New Balance over $500

Previous Balance	Payments & Credits	Unpaid Balance	Finance Charge	Purchases & Charges	New Balance	Minimum Payment
139.80	139.80	0	0	72.26	72.26	20.00

Research Activity   Find out why stores and banks are willing to extend credit. How are the expenses of running the credit department paid for? Why do some stores offer discounts to customers who pay cash?

Chapter Review

Complete each statement.

1. The percent of increase from 24 to 30 is __?__.   25%   [7-1]

2. The percent of decrease from 50 to 37 is __?__.   26%

3. The percent of increase from 76 to __?__ is 25%.   95

Write the letter of the correct answer.

4. A pair of shoes that regularly sells for $32 is on sale for $24. What is   [7-2]
the percent of discount?   b

    a. $33\frac{1}{3}\%$ **b.** 25%   **c.** 8%   **d.** 125%

5. The Vico Manufacturing Company makes a 12% profit. If the com-   [7-3]
pany sold $15,250 worth of goods in April, what was its profit?   c
    a. $13,420   **b.** $15,250   **c.** $1830   **d.** $18,300

6. The Ski Club has 50 members. If 36 members attend the ski trip,   [7-4]
what percent attends the ski trip? Which of the following proportions could be used to solve this problem?   b

    a. $\dfrac{36}{100} = \dfrac{n}{50}$ **b.** $\dfrac{n}{100} = \dfrac{36}{50}$

True or false?

7. If George's aunt gives him a loan of $650 for one year at 12% simple   [7-5]
interest, George will owe $728 at the end of the year.   True

8. An investment of $500 for 2 years at 12% simple interest will pay
more than one of $500 at $8\frac{1}{2}\%$ for 30 months.   True

Write the letter of the correct answer.

9. Lorraine Eldar invested $6000 at 8% interest compounded semian-   [7-6]
nually. How long will it take her investment to exceed $7000?   c

    a. 1 year   **b.** $1\frac{1}{2}$ years   **c.** 2 years   **d.** $2\frac{1}{2}$ years

10. Anita Ramirez owns two bonds, one paying 8.5% interest and the   [7-7]
other paying 9% interest. Every six months Anita receives a total of
$485 in interest from both bonds. If the 8.5% bond is worth $4000,
how much is the 9% bond worth?   a
    a. $7000   **b.** $4000   **c.** $1611.11   **d.** $10,777.78

276   *Chapter 7*

Chapter Test

Solve.

1. Sam Golden's salary increased $30 a week. If his salary was $400 a week before the raise, by what percent did his salary increase? **7.5%**   [7-1]

2. A clock ratio that sells for $30 is on sale at a 20% discount. What is the sale price? **$24**   [7-2]

3. Edna's Autos sold $24,000 worth of cars last week. If Edna's costs were $16,800, how much profit did Edna make and what was the percent of profit? **$7200; 30%**   [7-3]

4. Computer Village had sales of $16,000 for December. The store's profits were $2880. What was the percent of profit? **18%**

Use proportions to solve Exercises 5 and 6.

5. The Pro Shop sold 6 of 20 tennis rackets in May. What percent of the tennis rackets were sold? **30%**   [7-4]

6. This term, 36% of the students in one class are on the honor roll. If 9 students are on the honor roll, how many students are in the class? **25 students**

Solve.

7. John Anthony borrowed $1200 for $1\frac{1}{2}$ years at 13% simple interest. How much must he repay when the loan is due? **$1434**   [7-5]

8. Joan Wu invested $5000 in an account that pays 13% simple interest. If the interest is paid 4 times a year, how much is each payment? **$162.50**

9. Billtown Bank pays 8% interest compounded quarterly. To the nearest penny, how much will $2500 earn in one year? **$2706.08**   [7-6]

10. You deposit money in a savings account and make no other deposits or withdrawals. How much is in the account at the end of three months if you deposit $350 at 6% interest, compounded monthly? **$355.28**

11. A major credit card charges a 1.5% interest rate each month on unpaid balances. If you were charged $8.50 in interest in June, what was your balance? **$566.67**   [7-7]

Use transformations to solve each equation.

1. $k - 25 = -15$ 10
2. $x + 2(7 - 3) = 13$ 5
3. $-8m = 7$ $-\frac{7}{8}$
4. $\frac{z}{9} = -13$ -117
5. $-14n = -42$ 3
6. $\frac{2}{3}y = -1$ $-\frac{3}{2}$
7. $0.25x = 11$ 44
8. $3p - 11 = -47$ -12
9. $\frac{4}{7}w + 15 = 15$ 0
10. $-12 - \frac{1}{4}t = -10$ -8

Solve.

11. $\frac{x}{30} = \frac{5}{6}$ 25
12. $\frac{27}{8} = \frac{x}{16}$ 54

Additional Answers

13. $-7, -2.5, -2.2, 0, 3,$ 6.4

14. $-7.3, -6.2, 0, 2.5, 3.5, 4$

15. $-8.4, -3, -1.6, -1.0,$ 0.5

16. $-11.9, -4.7, -0.6, 0.7,$ 1, 3.8

37. rotation and translation; ASA

38. rotation and translation, or reflection and translation; SAS

39. rotation and translation; SSS

Cumulative Review (Chapters 1–7)

Exercises

Evaluate the expression if $x = 3$ and $y = 5$.

1. $x + y$ 8
2. $2x + y$ 11
3. $2y - x$ 7
4. $x + 6y$ 33
5. $y + x + 4$ 12
6. $-x - y$ -8
7. $-3x - 2y$ -19
8. $5x + (-y) - 7$ 3
9. x^2 9
10. xy^2 75
11. $(-x)^2y$ 45
12. $-(xy)^2$ -225

Write the numbers in order from least to greatest.

13. $3, -2.5, 0, -7, 6.4, -2.2$
14. $4, -6.2, -7.3, 0, 3.5, 2.5$
15. $-1.6, -8.4, -3, -1.0, 0.5$
16. $-4.7, -11.9, 1, 3.8, 0.7, -0.6$

Tell whether the statement is true or false for the given value of the variable.

17. $t - 3 \le -6$; -4 True
18. $-m - 3 > 0$; -3 False
19. $2b < 3$; 1   True
20. $3 - x = 2$; 5   False
21. $n + 1 \ge -7$; -6 True
22. $r < -2r - 4$; -2 True

Write the fractions as equivalent fractions having the least common denominator (LCD).

23. $\frac{2}{3}, \frac{5}{9}$ $\frac{6}{9}, \frac{5}{9}$
24. $-\frac{3}{5}, \frac{7}{20}$ $-\frac{12}{20}, \frac{7}{20}$
25. $-\frac{8}{3}, \frac{9}{11}$ $-\frac{88}{33}, \frac{27}{33}$
26. $-\frac{5}{7}, -\frac{12}{17}$ $-\frac{85}{119}, -\frac{84}{119}$
27. $\frac{7}{3}, \frac{3}{4}$ $\frac{28}{12}, \frac{9}{12}$
28. $\frac{8}{45}, \frac{11}{75}$ $\frac{40}{225}, \frac{33}{225}$
29. $\frac{17}{32}, -\frac{3}{128}$ $\frac{68}{128}, -\frac{3}{128}$
30. $\frac{3}{34}, \frac{5}{39}$ $\frac{117}{1326}, \frac{170}{1326}$

Solve.

31. $\frac{n}{4} = \frac{36}{12}$ 12
32. $\frac{5}{n} = \frac{60}{12}$ 1
33. $\frac{90}{n} = \frac{4}{8}$ 180
34. $\frac{4}{6} = \frac{n}{30}$ 20
35. $\frac{21}{28} = \frac{n}{84}$ 63
36. $\frac{20}{10} = \frac{10}{n}$ 5

State which of the rigid motions are needed to match the vertices of the triangles and explain why the triangles are congruent.

37.

38.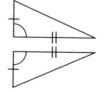

39.

278   *Chapter 7*

Problems

Problem Solving Reminders

Here are some reminders that may help you solve some of the problems on this page.

- Consider whether drawing a sketch will help.
- Check by using rounding to find an estimated answer.
- Reread the question to be sure that you have answered with the information requested.

Solve.

1. The perimeter of an equilateral triangle is 45 cm. What is the length of each side? **15 cm**

2. A photographer works 35 h a week and earns $295. What is the hourly rate to the nearest cent? **$8.43**

3. Elena commutes to work. She travels 2.6 km by subway and 1.8 km by bus. How far is that in all? **4.4 km**

4. The temperature at 11:30 P.M. was 7° below zero. By the next morning, the temperature had fallen 6°. What was the temperature then? **13° below zero**

5. During one week, the stock of DataTech Corporation had the following daily changes in price: Monday, up $1\frac{1}{2}$ points; Tuesday, down 2 points; Wednesday, down $\frac{3}{4}$ of a point; Thursday, up $3\frac{1}{8}$ points; Friday, up $2\frac{3}{4}$ points. What was the change in the price of the stock for the week? **up $4\frac{5}{8}$ points**

6. A rope 25 m long is cut into 2 pieces so that one piece is 9 m shorter than the other. Find the length of each piece. **17 m, 8 m**

7. A water purification device can purify 15.5 L of water in one hour. How many liters can it purify in $3\frac{3}{4}$ hours? **58.125 L**

8. The Onagas have a wall at the back of their property. They want to fence off a rectangular garden using 7 m of the existing wall for the back part of the fence. If they have 15 m of fencing, what will be the length of each of the shorter sides? **4 m**

9. Maria Sanchez gave 8% of her mathematics students a grade of A. If she had 125 students in her 4 classes, how many of these students received an A? **10 students**

Express as a fraction in lowest terms or as a mixed number in simple form.

13. 59% $\frac{59}{100}$

14. 2% $\frac{1}{50}$

15. 310% $3\frac{1}{10}$

16. 500%   5

Express as a percent.

17. $\frac{2}{20}$ 10%

18. $\frac{3}{4}$ 75%

19. 4   400%

20. $3\frac{7}{8}$ 387.5%

Express as a decimal.

21. 39%   0.39

22. 113%   1.13

23. 9.3%   0.093

24. 0.16%   0.0016

Express as a percent.

25. 0.99   99%

26. 0.04   4%

27. What percent of 75 is 15?   20%

28. 54 is what percent of 120?   45%

29. What is 3.5% of 60?   2.1

30. 60% of what number is 51?   85

Give the unit price of each item.

31. 6 oz of fruit salad for $.96 $.16/oz

32. 4 tires for $356 $89/tire

Percents and Problem Solving   **279**

8

Equations and Inequalities

The trains pictured at the right were introduced in France. They can travel at speeds of up to 160 km/h on conventional tracks and nearly triple that on their own continuously welded tracks. The speed of a train on an actual trip depends, of course, on the number of curves and the type of track. A trip of 425 km from Paris to Lyon that takes about 4 h in a conventional train, for instance, can be completed in about 2.5 h in one of these trains.

The time it takes a train to complete a trip depends on the speed of the train and the distance traveled. Some relationships, such as the relationship between time, rate, and distance, can be expressed as equations. Other relationships can be expressed as inequalities. You will learn more about equations and inequalities and methods to solve both in this chapter. You will also learn how to use equations to help solve problems.

Career Note

Reporters representing newspapers, magazines, and radio and television stations often attend newsworthy events such as the introduction of new trains. Reporters need a wide educational background. They must report facts, not their own opinions. They must be willing to meet deadlines and often to work at irregular hours.

281

Lesson Commentary
Chapter 8   Equations and Inequalities

Overview

The transformations used to solve equations in Chapter 4 are extended in the first section of this chapter to solve more difficult equations that involve combining like terms, eliminating parentheses, and having the variable on both sides of the equation. The remainder of this section focuses on solving word problems using the five-step plan.

The second part of the chapter moves logically into the transformational approach to solving inequalities and the utilization of graphs to show solution sets. The chapter concludes with solving word problems requiring the solution of inequalities.

dure must be followed in the order shown.

Many students wonder which transformation must be done first in an equation such as $3x - 12 = 6$. It is possible to divide by 3 first and then add. However, the division by 3 must be distributed over all terms, and students often forget to do this. Students tend to do better if they add 12 first. Both methods work, and both are mathematically correct, but for most students the latter approach is safer.

In Example 3, emphasize the importance of first simplifying the left-hand side of the equation by eliminating the parentheses and combining like terms prior to performing any transformations. Some students will want to use transformations before simplifying. Discourage this practice.

ADVANCED EQUATION SOLVING

8-1 Equations: Variable on One Side

Objectives for pages 282–284

- To simplify variable expressions that involve parentheses and combining like terms.
- To solve equations when the variable appears on one side.

Teaching Suggestions

Equations that require more than one transformation do not require any new theoretical tools for their solution, but students must use transformations carefully. Remind them to choose the transformation properly, so that they are not adding when they should be multiplying, for example. Also remind them to perform any given operation on both sides, using the same operation. Students sometimes get so indoctrinated by our left-to-right bias that they feel they must always get the variable on the left side. Advise them that this is not necessary; $a = x$ is just as acceptable as $x = a$.

Review the general procedure for solving equations shown on page 139. Stress that the steps in the proce-

Resource Book: Page 95 (Use After Page 284)

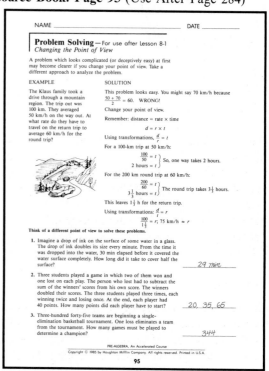

Related Activities

To emphasize the necessity of doing the operations in the proper order when solving equations, ask what operations (ordinary actions), in what order, are needed to solve each of the following problems.

1. A person wearing shoes and socks wants to go barefoot.
2. A package of frozen fish is to be broiled for dinner.
3. A table is set with dishes and a tablecloth. You wish to clear the table completely.

8-2 Equations: Variable on Both Sides

Objective *for pages 285–286*

■ To solve equations when the variable appears on both sides.

Teaching Suggestions

Use a diagram of a balance scale to begin the lesson.

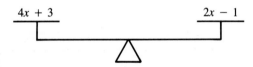

Solicit suggestions from students as to how to solve this "balance problem." Here are two possible steps: (a) Subtract 3 from both sides, or (b) Subtract $2x$ from both sides.
If (a) is the first step, then (b) is the second.
If (b) is the first step, then (a) is the second.

After the balance problem is solved, review it using the equation $4x + 3 = 2x - 1$. After steps (a) and (b) are completed, you will have $2x = -4$. Use the division or multiplication transformation to obtain the result $x = -2$.

Then have students solve equations which have various patterns of signs, like $3x - 4 = x + 4$ and $3x + 4 = 8 - x$.

Related Activities

To reinforce the proper use of the distributive property, have students cut graph paper into rectangles with dimensions such as 5×8, 5×4, and 4×3. These can be assembled into larger rectangles by joining them along sides of the same length. For example, 5×8 and 5×4

pieces can be combined into a 5×12 rectangle. By considering areas, lead students to make statements such as:

$$5 \times 8 + 5 \times 4 = 5(8 + 4)$$
$$= 5 \times 12$$

8-3 Equations in Problem Solving

Objective *for pages 287–290*

■ To use an equation to solve a word problem.

Teaching Suggestions

This will be a challenging section for many students. Encourage them to build up equations a bit at a time as they read and understand the parts of a problem. Also encourage them to use the plan and to write equations. Unfortunately, students tend to view word problems as arithmetic. Urge them to write and solve equations in the easy problems so they will be prepared for the later problems for which a strictly arithmetic approach is too limiting.

Write the following sentence. Jeff has 5 more albums than Corey. Ask students to write an expression for this relationship.

Let a = number of albums Corey has
Then $a + 5$ = number of albums Jeff has

Then write "Jeff has 12 albums." Have students write an equation using the expression they just wrote. Finally, write "How many albums does Corey have?" Point out where in the equation $a + 5 = 12$ they can find the number of albums Corey has. Ask the class to solve the equation.

Perform several simple problems of this type. Then, have your students each write a word problem. Review some of these and have hour students solve them using the model above.

Related Activities

To provide a challenge ask students to write word problems for more complicated equations such as those they studied in Lesson 8-2. Students may want to write their best problems and the related equations on separate pieces of paper and set up a large matching exercise on the bulletin board.

NAME _____ DATE _____

Enrichment—For use after Lesson 8-3
MODULAR ARITHMETIC

While studying questions about prime numbers and divisibility, mathematicians invented modular arithmetic to avoid dealing with very large numbers.

If any whole number is divided by any other whole number, a remainder of 0 or more will result.

EXAMPLE $17 \div 5$ $5\overline{)17}$ with quotient 3, $\frac{15}{2}$ 17 has a remainder of 2 when divided by 5.

The remainder can be thought of as the number "left over" when the largest multiple of 5 has been subtracted from 17. We say that "17 is congruent to 2 modulo 5," and we write $17 \equiv 2 \pmod 5$.

$32 \div 5$ $5\overline{)32}$ with quotient 6, $\frac{30}{2}$ 32 has a remainder of 2 when divided by 5. We write $32 \equiv 2 \pmod 5$.

Numbers like 17 and 32 that have identical remainders when divided by the same whole number are said to be *congruent* relative to the *divisor*.

Write true or false.

1. $16 \equiv 1 \pmod 5$ *True*
2. $45 \equiv 4 \pmod 3$ *False*
3. $27 \equiv 0 \pmod 3$ *True*
4. $60 \equiv 5 \pmod{12}$ *False*

5. Find three more numbers congruent to 2 (mod 5). 27, 42, 92, etc.
6. Find three numbers congruent to 3 (mod 5). 13, 18, 38, etc.
7. Find three numbers congruent to 1 (mod 5). 8, 15, 22, etc.
8. Find three numbers congruent to 4 (mod 5). 14, 19, 24, etc.

9. If a, b, p, and q are whole numbers, find an example which demonstrates that if $a \equiv p \pmod 5$ and $b \equiv q \pmod 5$ then $a + b \equiv p + q \pmod 5$. $13 \equiv 3 \pmod 5$, $14 \equiv 4 \pmod 5$, and $27 \equiv 7 \pmod 5$. (Hint: Use answers from Ex. 6 and from Ex. 9 to show it.)

10. Find an example which demonstrates that if $a \equiv p \pmod n$ and $b \equiv q \pmod n$, then $a \times b \equiv p \times q \pmod n$. $17 \equiv 2 \pmod 5$, $18 \equiv 3 \pmod 5$, and $306 \equiv 6 \pmod 5$.

11. A French mathematician, Pierre Fermat, proved a theorem that if p is a prime number, then for any number b, $b^p \equiv b \pmod p$ if $p > b$. Choose some numbers and test the theorem. $2^7 = 128$; $128 \div 7 = 18$ R 2; $2^7 \equiv 2 \pmod 7$.

PRE-ALGEBRA, An Accelerated Course
Copyright © 1985 by Houghton Mifflin Company. All rights reserved. Printed in U.S.A.

96

NAME _____ DATE _____

Quiz 8A—Lessons 8-1 through 8-3

DIRECTIONS: Write the letter of the correct answer in the space provided.

Solve.

	ANSWERS
1.	c (10)
2.	b (10)
3.	d (10)
4.	a (10)
5.	c (15)
6.	a (15)
7.	a (15)
8.	c (15)

1. $6y + 14y = 50$ [8-1]
   a. $6\frac{1}{4}$ b. 3   c. $2\frac{1}{2}$ d. $1\frac{1}{2}$

2. $4a - a = 3$
   a. 3   b. 1   c. 2   d. -1

3. $3(a - 2) = 21$
   a. 2   b. 8   c. -5 d. 9

4. $4c = 2c + 10$ [8-2]
   a. 5   b. 10   c. -5 d. $1\frac{2}{3}$

5. $5t + 4 = 7t + 3$
   a. 2   b. $\frac{1}{12}$ c. $\frac{1}{2}$ d. $\frac{7}{12}$

6. $2(d - 1) + 4d = 3d + 2$
   a. $1\frac{1}{3}$ b. 0   c. 4   d. 3

7. A 51 ft long piece of wire is cut into two pieces, one twice as long as the other. How long is the shorter piece?   [8-3]
   a. 17 ft   b. 34 ft   c. 16 ft   d. 51 ft

8. The sum of two consecutive integers is 121. Find the two integers.
   a. 59, 60   b. 58, 63   c. 60, 61   d. 61, 62

PRE-ALGEBRA, An Accelerated Course
Copyright © 1985 by Houghton Mifflin Company. All rights reserved. Printed in U.S.A.

98

NAME _____ DATE _____

Problem Solving—For use after Lesson 8-3
Two-Step Equations

Solving two-step problems often involves writing an equation with more than one operation.

EXAMPLE Heather's mother is 42 years old. She is 10 years older than 4 times Heather's age. How old is Heather?

SOLUTION Choose the variable ⟶ Let a = Heather's age
First operation ⟶ $4a$ = 4 times Heather's age
Second operation ⟶ $4a + 10$ = mother's age
Write the equation ⟶ $4a + 10 = 42$
Solve ⟶ $4a = 32$
$a = 8$

Heather is 8 years old.

Write and solve two-step equations for the following problems.

1. A number is multiplied by 3. Then 8 is added to the product. The result is 50. What is the number? $3n + 8 = 50$; 14

2. If you add 120 to last year's enrollment at Dixville Elementary School, you have twice last year's enrollment. Find last year's enrollment. $n + 120 = 2n$; 120

3. Carla began with 12 yd² of material. She made 3 pairs of curtains and had 5 yd² left over. How much material did she use for each pair of curtains? $12 - 3n = 5$; $2\frac{1}{3}$ yd²

4. The product of a number and 5 decreased by 17 is 138. Find the number. $5n - 17 = 138$; 31

5. A family spends $169 a month on heating. They use 20 50-lb bags of coal and $85 worth of oil. How much does a 50-lb bag of coal cost? $20n + 85 = 169$; $4.20

6. Lou owes Rick $62. This is half the cost of a stereo they bought less $5 that Rick owed Lou. How much did the stereo cost? $\frac{1}{2}n - 5 = 62$; $134

PRE-ALGEBRA, An Accelerated Course
Copyright © 1985 by Houghton Mifflin Company. All rights reserved. Printed in U.S.A.

97

INEQUALITIES

8-4 Writing Inequalities

Objectives *for pages 291–292*

■ To express the relationship between two numbers by using inequality symbols.
■ To write inequalities for word sentences.

Teaching Suggestions

Tell students that an inequality is another kind of mathematical sentence. An equation states that the numbers named by two expressions are equal. An inequality states that the number named by one expression is less than or greater than another. Students should understand that the following inequalities are equivalent:

$$2 < 5$$
$$5 > 2$$

In this lesson the new material for many students will be the use of variables in an inequality. Students will readily think of the numbers . . . , $-2, -1, 0, 1, 2, 3$ as solutions to $n < 4$. You may wish to tell students that values such as -3.2, $-1\frac{1}{2}$, $\frac{1}{3}$ or 2.025 also make the inequality true.

In preparation for Written Exercises 7–10, you may remind students that two consecutive integers may be expressed as $n, n + 1$; and three consecutive integers as $n, n + 1$, and $n + 2$. You can point out that, even though a specific value for n is not known, it is still possible to show the relative positions of the graphs of n, $n + 1$, and $n + 2$ on a number line.

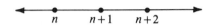

Related Activities

To provide additional practice in a recreational format, have students copy the number line shown and solve the following puzzle.

The letters A, F, H, I, M, N, S, T, and U represent whole numbers that are to be graphed on the number line. Using the clues given, arrange the letters on the number line to spell a message.

1. M represents the least number and N represents the greatest.
2. $M + 4$ is not graphed.
3. $M + 4$, I, S, and $S + 1$ represent four consecutive whole numbers and $I < S$.
4. $S + 1$ is not graphed.
5. $A < T$ and $T + 1 = H$.
6. U is between S and N.
7. $S < F < U$

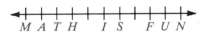

8-5 Equivalent Inequalities

Objective for pages 293–296

■ To solve an inequality in one variable that involves addition, subtraction, multiplication, or division.

Teaching Suggestions

Many students are relieved to find that there is little difference between techniques for solving equations and inequalities. They are prepared to have to learn a whole new set of skills, but find that the only significant difference is the need to reverse inequality signs when multiplying or dividing by a negative number.

Remind students that solving an open sentence means finding all numbers that satisfy the sentence. They may also need to be reminded of the existence of nonintegral numbers. Otherwise, when considering an inequality such as $x > 2\frac{1}{2}$, they may want to say that the solution is $\{3, 4, 5, \ldots\}$, which is not correct. The solution is actually all numbers greater than $2\frac{1}{2}$. Note that the solution of an inequality is typically an infinite set; this is another major difference compared to equations.

Trying to proceed by rote, students may have difficulty with inequalities like $2 > x$. They can become so determined that this is a "greater than" inequality that they give the solution as all numbers greater than 2. Suggest that they rewrite such inequalities, using $x > a$ for $a < x$ and $x < a$ for $a > x$. Most people are more comfortable with inequalities in which the variable is on the left and the constant is on the right.

Related Activities

To emphasize the reversal involved when multiplying by a negative number, have students draw nomographs as follows. To make a "$\times 3$" nomograph, draw two number lines, with arrows from numbers on one line to the products by 3 on the other.

Now draw a "$\times(-2)$" nomograph. This time draw arrows from numbers to their products by -2. The difference will be apparent. In a "multiplication by a negative number" nomograph, the reversal is given a visual interpretation. The nomographs are shown on the following page.

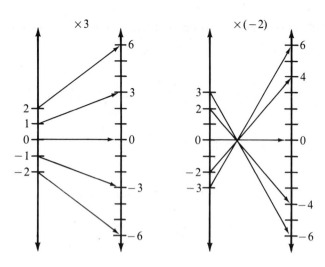

Have students construct nomographs for:

1. $\times 1$ **2.** $\times(-1)$

3. $\times \frac{1}{2}$ **4.** $\times(-3)$

5. $\times 0$ **6.** $\times\left(-\frac{1}{2}\right)$

8-6 Solving Inequalities by Several Transformations

Objective *for pages 297–300*

■ To use several transformations to solve an inequality in one variable.

Teaching Suggestions

An earlier warning can be repeated here. Just because an inequality contains a "greater than" symbol does not guarantee that the graph is an arrow pointing to the right. For example, the graph of $-3 > x$ is

Students may have great difficulty when an inequality simplifies to one like $-x > 2$. Frequently they proceed as if this says $x > 2$ and graph it incorrectly. Remind them that the procedure we use requires us to have the variable only, alone on one side. Thus $-x > 2$ must be transformed:

$$-x > 2$$
$$-1(-x) < -1(2)$$
$$x < -2$$

Have students describe some of the solution sets in their own words so that you know they understand which numbers are solutions. Ask them to give some specific solutions and prove that they work. Discuss carefully the correct use of arrows and open and solid circles in graphing sets of numbers on a number line.

Resource Book: Page 99 (Use After Page 300)

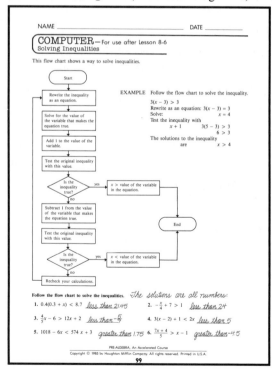

Resource Book: Page 100 (Use After Page 300)

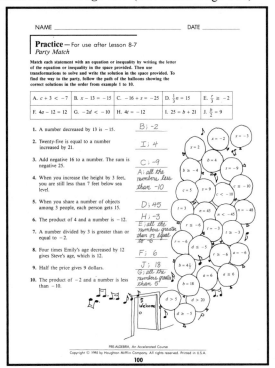

Related Activities

To reverse the usual process, give students the graph, and ask them to give an inequality for that graph.

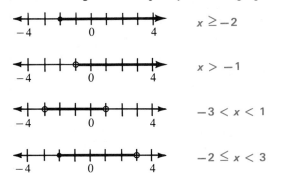

$x \geq -2$

$x > -1$

$-3 < x < 1$

$-2 \leq x < 3$

To review absolute values and strengthen skill in graphing inequalities, have students give an inequality of the form $|x| > a$, $|x| \geq a$, $|x| < a$, or $|x| \leq a$.

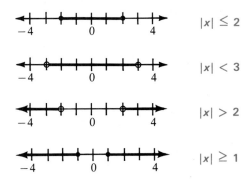

$|x| \leq 2$

$|x| < 3$

$|x| > 2$

$|x| \geq 1$

8-7 Inequalities in Problem Solving

Objective *for pages 301–303*

■ To use an inequality to solve a word problem.

Teaching Suggestions

Remind your students of the plan for solving word problems. Before assigning any of the exercises in this section, give your students practice in translating word sentences into inequalities.

Related Activities

Give the class various solution sets. Ask them to create inequalities to fit the solution sets. For example, if you give them {all positive integers greater than or equal to 2}, they might write: $x \geq 2, 2x \geq 4, 3x + 2 \geq 8$, and so forth.

NAME _____ DATE _____

Quiz 8B — Lessons 8-4 through 8-7

DIRECTIONS: Write the letter of the correct answer in the space provided.

Which inequality represents the word sentence?

1. A number x is less than 10 times a number y. *[8-4]*

   a. $10y < x$ b. $10x < y$ c. $x < 10y$ d. $10x > y$

2. On a number line, fifteen is between two numbers x and y.

   a. $y < 15 > x$ b. $x < 15 < y$

   c. $x \le 15 < y$ d. $y \le 15 \le x$

Select the equivalent inequality.

3. $3 + z < 7$ *[8-5]*

   a. $z < -4$ b. $z \le 4$ c. $z < 2\frac{1}{3}$ d. $z < 4$

4. $-8 \le -\frac{y}{6}$

   a. $y \ge 48$ b. $y \le 48$ c. $y \ge -48$ d. $y \le -48$

5. $-2r > 16.6$

   a. $r < 8.2$ b. $r > 8.3$ c. $r < -8.3$ d. $r \le 8.3$

6. $3a + 3 \ge 12$ *[8-6]*

   a. $a \ge 9$ b. $a \ge 3$ c. $a \ge 5$ d. $a < 3$

7. $19 < 6c + 1$

   a. $c \ge 3$ b. $c < 3$ c. $c < 3\frac{1}{3}$ d. $c > -3$

8. $2n + 5n \le 49$

   a. $n \le 14$ b. $n \ge 7$ c. $n < 7$ d. $n \le 7$

Solve.

9. The sum of two consecutive integers is less than 50. Find the greatest pair of integers having this property. *[8-7]*

   a. 24, 26   b. 23, 24   c. 24, 25   d. 25, 26

ANSWERS

1. _c_ (10)
2. _b_ (10)
3. _d_ (10)
4. _b_ (10)
5. _c_ (10)
6. _b_ (10)
7. _a_ (10)
8. _d_ (15)
9. _c_ (15)

101

NAME _____ DATE _____

Review — Chapter 8

Solve.

1. $7y + 5y = 6$ $\frac{1}{2}$ 2. $-3x + 9x = 30$ 5 *[8-1]*
3. $2a + 5 + a = 15$ $3\frac{1}{3}$ 4. $2(t-3) = 8$ 7
5. $10z + 9 = 4z$ $-1\frac{1}{2}$ 6. $15 + 8y = 3y$ -3 *[8-2]*
7. $6n + 4 = 3n + 12$ $2\frac{2}{3}$ 8. $3y - 4 = 4(y-5)$ 16

9. The sum of two numbers is 200. One number is 50 less than the other number. What is the smaller number? 75 *[8-3]*

10. The perimeter of an isosceles triangle is 80 mm. The congruent sides of the triangle are each twice as long as the remaining side. What is the length of the shortest side? $16mm$

Write an inequality for each word sentence.

11. Sixteen is greater than or equal to a number t. $16 \ge t$ *[8-4]*

12. A number x is between fourteen and twenty. $14 < x < 20$

13. Twenty is less than or equal to a number z. $20 \le z$

Solve. *The solutions are all the numbers:*

14. $c - 13 \ge 50$ *greater than or equal to 63*   15. $-5x < 40$ *greater than -8*   *[8-5]*
16. $t + 4 \le 10$ *less than or equal to 6*   17. $-10y > 30$ *less than -3*
18. $-50 \ge -2n$ *greater than or equal to 25*   19. $x - 31 \ge -35$ *greater than or equal to -4*
20. $6x > 48$ *greater than 8*   21. $\frac{x}{6} + 1 > 7$ *greater than 36*   *[8-6]*
22. $2y + 4 \ge 5$ *greater than or equal to $\frac{1}{2}$*   23. $x + 1 \ge 2x$ *less than or equal to 1*
24. $2q - 4 > 7$ *greater than $5\frac{1}{2}$*   25. $-3p + 6 \le -6$ *greater than or equal to 4*   *[8-7]*

26. Of all pairs of consecutive integers whose sum is greater than 120, find the pair whose sum is least. $60, 61$

102

NAME _____ DATE _____

Test — Chapter 8

DIRECTIONS: Write the correct answer in the space provided.

Solve.

1. $4n + 8n = 48$ 2. $7x - 12x = -10$ *[8-1]*
3. $6a - 3a = 2$ 4. $15 = 3z + 4 + 8z$
5. $2(x-3) = 4$ 6. $-12 = 4(a+1)$
7. $2x - 9 = -x$ 8. $33 + 10y = -y$ *[8-2]*
9. $m + 5 = 6m - 15$ 10. $10t - 3 = 6 + t$
11. $-2(a-3) = 4a + 2$ 12. $3(y+2) = 2(y+4)$

13. Find two consecutive integers whose sum is 219.   *[8-3]*

14. A collection of rare coins includes two pennies, one 60 years old and the other 15 years old. In how many years will the older penny be twice as old as the newer penny?

Write an inequality for each word sentence.

15. A number c is greater than fourteen.   *[8-4]*

16. On a number line, sixty is between fifty and a number y.

Solve.

17. $t - 9 \le 31$ 18. $-3c < 30$ *[8-5]*
19. $-5x \ge -50$ 20. $3 \le z \le -3$
21. $2x - 3 < 43$ 22. $-25 < 2x + 5 + 3x$ *[8-6]*

23. Two cars start from the same point and travel in opposite directions, one at a speed of 45 mi/h and the other at a speed of 55 mi/h. At least how long must they travel to be 250 mi apart?   *[8-7]*

All the numbers
17. less than or equal to 40
18. greater than -10
19. less than or equal to 10
20. less than or equal to -6
21. less than 23
22. greater than -6

ANSWERS

1. _4_ (4)
2. _$\frac{2}{3}$_ (4)
3. _$\frac{2}{3}$_ (4)
4. _1_ (4)
5. _5_ (4)
6. _-4_ (4)
7. _3_ (4)
8. _-3_ (4)
9. _4_ (4)
10. _1_ (4)
11. _$\frac{2}{3}$_ (4)
12. _2_ (4)
13. _109, 110_ (6)
14. _30y_ (6)
15. _$c > 14$_ (4)
16. _$50 < 60 < y$_ (see below for 17-22) (4)
17. _____ (4)
18. _____ (4)
19. _____ (4)
20. _____ (4)
21. _____ (4)
22. _____ (6)
23. _2.5 h_ (6)

103

NAME _____ DATE _____

Make-up Test — Chapter 8

DIRECTIONS: Write the correct answer in the space provided.

Solve.

1. $2y + 6y = 24$ 2. $-5x + 6x = -3$ *[8-1]*
3. $9z - 12z = -6$ 4. $4 = 3t - 1 + 6t$
5. $4(t+3) = 6$ 6. $-9 = 3(n+1)$
7. $-3t = t + 4$ 8. $21 - 6x = -x$ *[8-2]*
9. $2c - 6 = 3c + 2$ 10. $12a - 8 = 4 + 6a$
11. $2(t-4) = 6r$ 12. $-4(n-3) = 10n$

13. Find three consecutive integers whose sum is 138.   *[8-3]*

14. A piece of wire needed in a construction project is 80 ft long. It is cut into two pieces, one four times as long as the other. How long is the shorter piece of wire?

Write an inequality for each sentence.

15. Thirty-nine is less than a number x.   *[8-4]*

16. On a number line, forty is between a number x and seventy.

Solve.

17. $x + 7 \ge 10$ 18. $-2y > -42$ *[8-5]*
19. $-x + 2 > 7$ 20. $3x \le 12$
21. $3t - 5 < 30$ 22. $-21 \le -7z + 14$ *[8-6]*

23. Phil is three quarters as old as Teresa. Four years from now, he will be at least four fifths as old as Teresa. At least how old is Phil now?   *[8-7]*

All the numbers
17. greater than or equal to 3
18. less than 21
19. less than -5
20. less than or equal to 4
21. less than $11\frac{2}{3}$
22. less than or equal to 5

ANSWERS

1. _3_ (4)
2. _-3_ (4)
3. _2_ (4)
4. _$\frac{5}{9}$_ (4)
5. _$-1\frac{1}{2}$_ (4)
6. _2_ (4)
7. _-1_ (4)
8. _3_ (4)
9. _-8_ (4)
10. _2_ (4)
11. _$\frac{-2}{7}$_ (4)
12. _$\frac{6}{7}$_ (4)
13. _45, 46, 47_ (6)
14. _16 ft_ (6)
15. _$39 < x$_ (4)
16. _$x < 40 < 70$_ (see below for 17-22) (4)
17. _____ (4)
18. _____ (4)
19. _____ (4)
20. _____ (4)
21. _____ (4)
22. _____ (6)
23. _12y_ (6)

104

Resource Book: Pages 105–106 (Use After Page 303)

CUMULATIVE REVIEW—Chapters 1-8
Exercises

Complete.

1. The measure of a(n) *obtuse* angle is between 90° and 180°.

2. A(n) *equilateral* triangle has all sides congruent.

3. If the circumference of a circle is 12π, the radius of the circle measures ___6___.

4. If the sum of the measures of two angles is ___180°___, the angles are supplementary.

Round to the nearest hundredth.

5. 32.329 ___32.33___   6. 148.096 ___148.10___   7. 0.8949 ___0.89___

Perform the indicated operation.

8. $-13.7421 - 27.399$ ___-41.1411___   9. $144.9 \div -4.2$ ___-34.5___

10. $-2\frac{2}{5} + 1\frac{5}{8} - 2\frac{3}{4}$ ___$-3\frac{21}{40}$___   11. $\frac{3}{14} \div -\frac{6}{21}$ ___$-\frac{3}{4}$___

12. -7.65×-3.08 ___23.562___   13. $-5\frac{3}{5} \times 1\frac{1}{14}$ ___-6___

Write an equation or inequality for the word sentence and solve.

14. The product of t and 9 is seventy-two. $9t = 72; 8$

15. The product of negative twelve and m is twenty-four. $-12m = 24; -2$

16. The sum of x and six is greater than the product of x and 3. $x + 6 > 3x;$ all the numbers less than 3

Solve the proportion.

17. $\frac{x}{9.6} = \frac{0.3}{2.4}$ ___1.2___   18. $\frac{16}{n} = \frac{80}{5}$ ___1___   19. $\frac{23}{69} = \frac{t}{4.2}$ ___1.4___

Find the percent of increase or decrease.

20. 20 to 25 ___25%___   21. 30 to 18 ___40%___

22. 1 to 2 ___100%___   23. 6 to 4.5 ___25%___

CUMULATIVE REVIEW—Chapters 1-8 *(continued)*
Problems

Problem Solving Reminders
Here are some reminders that may help you solve some of the problems on this page.
• Consider whether a chart will help to organize information.
• Supply additional information if needed.
• Reread the problem to be sure that your answer is complete.

Solve.

1. This week, Ira jogged $1\frac{1}{4}$ h on Monday, $1\frac{1}{3}$ h on Wednesday, $1\frac{5}{6}$ h on Friday, and $2\frac{1}{2}$ h on Saturday. How many hours did he jog this week? $7\frac{1}{12}$ h

2. Barry spent 3 h and 20 min writing a book report and playing the trumpet. He spent three times as long writing the book report as he did practicing. How long did he spend on the book report?   2 h 30 min

3. Camera film is selling at the rate of 3 rolls for $7.47. How many rolls can you buy for $19.92?   8 rolls

4. Marsha bought a coat for $109.80, a hat for $5.95, and a scarf for $7.25. The tax on her purchase was $11.07. What percent of the total purchase was the tax?   9%

5. A savings account was opened with $3000. The bank pays $5\frac{1}{2}$% interest, compounded monthly. How much money is in the account after 3 months? $3041.43

6. The side of a square is the same length as the radius of a circle with circumference 44 m. Find the perimeter of the square. Use $\pi \approx \frac{22}{7}$.   28 m

7. Mary Foster earns $3.25 an hour working as a hospital aide. Last week she worked from 10:00 A.M. to 2:30 P.M. on Monday, Tuesday, and Wednesday. How much did she earn? $43.88

8. The publisher of *Swimming Today* receives $9.30 from each copy sold. The remaining portion of the $12 selling price goes to the author. What percent does the author earn?   22.5%

9. Each of the two equal sides of an isosceles triangle is 16 cm longer than the third side. If the perimeter of the triangle is 89 cm, find the lengths of the sides.   19 cm, 35 cm, 35 cm

8-1 Equations: Variable on One Side

In Chapter 4, you learned the transformations that are used in solving equations. In this chapter, you will learn how these transformations can be used to solve more difficult equations.

Two terms are called **like terms** if their variable parts are the same. For example, x and $11x$ are like terms, as are $-4y$ and $7y$. Because their variable parts are different, $4x$, $3x^2$, and $6xy$ are not like terms.

We can use the properties of addition and multiplication to simplify expressions with like terms. To simplify $3a + 11 + 4a$, we use the commutative and distributive properties.

$$3a + 11 + 4a = (3a + 4a) + 11$$
$$= (3 + 4)a + 11$$
$$= 7a + 11$$

The terms $7a$ and 11 cannot be combined because they are not like terms. When an expression is in *simplest form,* it contains no like terms.

We can use the distributive property $a(b + c) = ab + ac$ to simplify certain variable expressions that involve parentheses.

EXAMPLE 1 Simplify $-2(x - 6) + 8x$.

Solution
$$-2(x - 6) + 8x = -2x + 12 + 8x$$
$$= -2x + 8x + 12$$
$$= 6x + 12$$

These procedures may be used when solving an equation.

EXAMPLE 2 Solve $2x + 15 + 8x = 20$.

Solution
$$2x + 15 + 8x = 20$$
$$2x + 8x + 15 = 20$$
$$10x + 15 = 20$$
$$10x + 15 - 15 = 20 - 15$$
$$10x = 5$$
$$\frac{10x}{10} = \frac{5}{10}$$
$$x = \frac{1}{2}$$

The solution is $\frac{1}{2}$.

282 *Chapter 8*

EXAMPLE 3   Solve $3(x + 3) + 6x = 12$.

Solution
$$3(x + 3) + 6x = 12$$
$$3x + 9 + 6x = 12$$
$$3x + 6x + 9 = 12$$
$$9x + 9 = 12$$
$$9x + 9 - 9 = 12 - 9$$
$$9x = 3$$
$$\frac{9x}{9} = \frac{3}{9}$$
$$x = \frac{1}{3}$$

The solution is $\frac{1}{3}$.

Class Exercises

Which pairs of terms are like terms? 1, 2, 5

1. $7a$, $12a$ **2.** $4x$, $-6x$ **3.** $3r$, $4rs$ **4.** $6a$, $6b$

5. $-8y$, y **6.** -11, $-11x$ **7.** a^2, $7a$ **8.** $3a^2$, $3a$

Simplify.

9. $4c + 7c$ 11c   **10.** $13y - 8y$ 5y   **11.** $z - 7z$ $-6z$

12. $2t + t + 4t$ 7t   **13.** $-5x + 6x - x$ 0   **14.** $4p - p + 5p$ 8p

15. $2(b + 5)$ 2b + 10   **16.** $-3(x + 7)$ $-3x - 21$ **17.** $9(c - 4)$ 9c − 36

18. $4(n + 4) + 3$ 4n + 19   **19.** $-5(x - 1) - 6$ $-5x - 1$ **20.** $3(y + 4) + 2y$ 5y + 12

21. $12(d - 4) - 10d$ 2d − 48   **22.** $-10(p - 3) + 6p$ $-4p + 30$ **23.** $15(y + 1) + 10(y - 2)$ 25y − 5

Written Exercises

Simplify.

A   **1.** $10m - 8m$ 2m   **2.** $-3a + 11a$ 8a   **3.** $-8c + c$ $-7c$

4. $-3n + 8 + 8n$ 5n + 8   **5.** $-5 + 6c - 5c$ c − 5   **6.** $12 + 10z - 12z$ 12 − 2z

7. $-7(y - 11)$ $-7y + 77$ **8.** $6(n + 3) + 2n$ 8n + 18   **9.** $-10(a + 3) + 6a$ $-4a - 30$

10. $8(p + 4) + 6(p - 3)$ **11.** $4(x - 3) + 2(x - 1)$ **12.** $-5(n - 5) + 7(n + 1)$

Equations and Inequalities   **283**

Suggested Assignments

Core
283/1–11 odd
284/13–35 odd
284/Rev. 1–4

Enriched
Day 1: 283/7–12
284/25–36
Day 2: 284/37–48
284/Challenge

Supplementary Materials

Practice Masters, p. 35

Solve.

13. $4x + 8x = 6$ $\frac{1}{2}$ 14. $5z - 7z = -4$ 2   15. $-2y + 6y = 36$ 9

16. $p - 10p = -27$ 3   17. $-7c - 9c = 20$ $-1\frac{1}{4}$ 18. $-z - 10z = -3$ $\frac{3}{11}$

19. $3n + 2n - 8 = 17$ 5   20. $-6a + 7a - 3 = 8$ 11 21. $-x + 9 - 5x = 12$ $-\frac{1}{2}$

22. $4t - 8 + 8t = 32$ $3\frac{1}{3}$ 23. $5 - 4y - 7y = 16$ -1 24. $-7 + 3n + 9n = 29$ 3

25. $12 = 8y + 16y$ $\frac{1}{2}$ 26. $-9 = 3y - 9y$ $1\frac{1}{2}$ 27. $15 = x + 6 - 10x$ -1

28. $-4 = 3z - 10 + 4z$ $\frac{6}{7}$ 29. $-14 = 6 + z - 9z$ $2\frac{1}{2}$ 30. $3 = t - 4t + 15$ 4

B 31. $2(x + 1) = 4$ 1   32. $-3(y + 4) = -6$ -2 33. $8(t - 1) = -16$ -1

34. $-7(c - 3) = 35$ -2 35. $3(7 - p) = 3$ 6   36. $-6(4 - z) = 20$ $7\frac{1}{3}$

37. $2(n + 4) + 6n = 2$ $-\frac{3}{4}$ 38. $6(c - 2) + 4c = 8$ 2 39. $-5(d + 3) - 7d = 5$ $-1\frac{2}{3}$

40. $-4(x - 5) - 16x = 10$ $\frac{1}{2}$ 41. $2(3 - y) + 6y = 12$ $1\frac{1}{2}$ 42. $-3(2 - z) - 8z = 15$ $-4\frac{1}{5}$

C 43. $3(a + 2) - (a - 1) = 17$ 5   44. $5(c - 3) - (5 - c) = 0$ $3\frac{1}{3}$

45. $4(p + 2) - 2(1 - p) - 4p = 0$ -3 46. $5(v - 2) - 2(v + 4) = 6$ 8

47. $2(y - 5) + 7 = 4(y + 7) - 3$ -14 48. $-3(x + 2) + 3 = 5(x - 1) + 10$ -1

Review Exercises

Solve.

1. $\frac{n}{4} = \frac{8}{32}$ 1   2. $\frac{n}{48} = \frac{5}{6}$ 40   3. $\frac{6}{n} = \frac{24}{60}$ 15

4. $\frac{50}{n} = \frac{5}{15}$ 150   5. $\frac{2}{11} = \frac{n}{66}$ 12   6. $\frac{1}{6} = \frac{n}{18}$ 3

7. $\frac{2}{3} = \frac{7}{n}$ $10\frac{1}{2}$ 8. $\frac{12}{84} = \frac{1}{n}$ 7   9. $\frac{36}{n} = \frac{72}{8}$ 4

Challenge

Fill in the blanks.

1. 6, 10, 15, 21, __?__, 36, 45 28   2. 103, __?__, 305, 406, 507 204

3. 5, 3, 4, 2, __?__, 1, 2 3   4. 132, 243, 354, 465, __?__ 576

5. 17, 16, 18, __?__, 19, 14, 20, 13 15   6. 6, 11, 21, 41, __?__ 81

8-2 Equations: Variable on Both Sides

Teaching Suggestions
p. 281b

Related Activities p. 281b

Chalkboard Examples
Solve.

1. $-x - 25 = 4x$ -5

2. $34 - 7y = 2y + 6 + 5y$ 2

3. $3z + 5 - z = 5 - 2z$ 0

4. $7n - 11 + n =$
         $8(n + 3) - n$ 35

Some equations have variables on each side. To solve such an equation, add a variable expression to each side, or subtract a variable expression from each side.

EXAMPLE 1   Solve $8c = c + 14$.

Solution   Subtract c from both sides.

$$8c = c + 14$$
$$8c - c = c + 14 - c$$
$$7c = 14$$
$$\frac{7c}{7} = \frac{14}{7}$$
$$c = 2$$

The solution is 2.

EXAMPLE 2   Solve $7c = 3 - 2c$.

Solution   Add $2c$ to both sides.

$$7c = 3 - 2c$$
$$7c + 2c = 3 - 2c + 2c$$
$$9c = 3$$
$$\frac{9c}{9} = \frac{3}{9}$$
$$c = \frac{1}{3}$$

The solution is $\frac{1}{3}$.

EXAMPLE 3   Solve $2(a - 3) = 5(a + 3)$.

Solution
$$2(a - 3) = 5(a + 3)$$
$$2a - 6 = 5a + 15$$
$$2a - 6 + 6 = 5a + 15 + 6$$
$$2a = 5a + 21$$
$$2a - 5a = 5a + 21 - 5a$$
$$-3a = 21$$
$$\frac{-3a}{-3} = \frac{21}{-3}$$
$$a = -7$$

The solution is -7.

Equations and Inequalities   **285**

Solve.

1. $8x = 10x - 3$ $1\frac{1}{2}$

2. $-6y = 3y + 3$ $-\frac{1}{3}$

3. $8z - 45 = 17z$ -5

4. $2m - 7 = 8 - 3m$ 3

5. $-4n - 8 = 6n + 12$ -2

6. $2k + 4 + 5k = 6k + 4$ 0

Suggested Assignments

Core
  286/2–30 even
  286/Rev. 2–8 even

Enriched
  286/17–34

Supplementary Materials

Practice Masters, p. 35

Class Exercises

Solve.

1. $2y = y + 1$ 1　　**2.** $t + 3 = 2t$ 3　　**3.** $4a + 2 = 5a$ 2　　**4.** $3n + 5 = 4n$ 5

5. $a - 1 = 2a$ -1　　**6.** $6p = 5p - 4$ -4　　**7.** $2a - 7 = 3a$ -7　　**8.** $6t + 1 = 7t$ 1

Written Exercises

Solve.

A **1.** $6c = 4c + 10$ 5　　　**2.** $13z = 15 + 8z$ 3　　　**3.** $49 + a = 8a$ 7

4. $8x + 16 = 4x$ -4　　**5.** $7y = 5y - 12$ -6　　**6.** $17t = 8t - 36$ -4

7. $32y = 24y - 4$ $-\frac{1}{2}$　　**8.** $17z = 15z - 3$ $-1\frac{1}{2}$　　**9.** $3s = -6s - 36$ -4

10. $-14p = 6p + 10$ $-\frac{1}{2}$　　**11.** $11n + 9 = -4n - \frac{3}{5}$　　**12.** $-4x + 6 = -2x$ 3

13. $2c + 6 = 5c - 6$ 4　　**14.** $6y + 3 = 8y + 2\frac{1}{2}$　　**15.** $-3d - 8 = 7d + 17$ $-2\frac{1}{2}$

16. $10a - 1 = 2a - (-5)$ $\frac{3}{4}$　**17.** $15 - 7x = 8x - 30$ 3　**18.** $y - 11 = 24 - 9y$ $3\frac{1}{2}$

B **19.** $2(x + 1) = 4x$ 1　　　　**20.** $-3(y + 4) = -6y$ 4　**21.** $8(t - 1) = -16t$ $\frac{1}{3}$

22. $-5(d + 3) = 7d + 5$ $-1\frac{2}{3}$ **23.** $6(c - 2) + 4c = 8c$ 6　**24.** $-4(x - 5) = 16x + 10$ $\frac{1}{2}$

25. $6(d + 1) = 4(d + 2)$ 1　　　　　　**26.** $8(p + 4) = 6(p - 2)$ -22

27. $-2(c - 3) = 4(c + 6)$ -3　　　　　**28.** $-2(x - 4) = 5(x - 2)$ $2\frac{4}{7}$

29. $10(y + 2) + 4 = 6(y - 3) + 8$ $-8\frac{1}{2}$　**30.** $-12(x + 3) + 2 = 6(x - 1) + 8$ -2

C **31.** $\frac{1}{2}(x + 4) = \frac{1}{4}(x - 8)$ -16　　　**32.** $\frac{1}{3}(y - 6) = \frac{2}{9}(y + 18)$ 54

33. $\frac{2}{5}(a + 10) = \frac{1}{4}(a + 20)$ $6\frac{2}{3}$　　　**34.** $\frac{5}{8}(t - 24) = \frac{1}{4}(t + 12)$ 48

35. $\frac{9}{10}(n - 30) = \frac{1}{2}(n + 10)$ 80　　　**36.** $\frac{1}{3}(p + 21) = \frac{1}{6}(p - 9)$ -51

Review Exercises

Use inverse operations to solve.

1. $x + 8 = 12$ 4　　**2.** $x + (-5) = -3$ 2　　**3.** $x - 5 = 1$ 6　　**4.** $x - (-3) = 4$ 1

5. $6x = 72$ 12　　**6.** $-9x = 81$ -9　　**7.** $\frac{x}{4} = 6$ 24　　**8.** $-\frac{x}{7} = 11$ -77

286 *Chapter 8*

8-3 Equations in Problem Solving

The five-step method that was shown in Chapter 4 may be applied with the procedures shown in this chapter.

> ## *Solving a Word Problem Using an Equation*
>
> **Step 1** Read the problem carefully. Make sure that you understand what it says. You may need to read it more than once.
>
> **Step 2** Decide what numbers are asked for. Choose a variable and use it to represent the number(s) asked for.
>
> **Step 3** Write an equation based on the given conditions.
>
> **Step 4** Solve the equation and find the required number(s).
>
> **Step 5** Check your results with the words of the problem. Give the answer.

EXAMPLE 1 An electrician has a length of wire that is 120 m long. The wire is cut into two pieces, one 30 m longer than the other. Find the lengths of the two pieces of wire.

Solution

- The problem says: length of wire is 120 m, one piece is 30 m longer than the other

- The problem asks for: the lengths of the two pieces of wire
  Let $l =$ the length of shorter piece of wire.
  The length of the other piece of wire $= l + 30$.

- We set the sum of the lengths $(l + l + 30)$ equal to 120.

$$l + l + 30 = 120$$

- Solve.
$$l + l + 30 = 120$$
$$2l + 30 = 120$$
$$2l + 30 - 30 = 120 - 30$$
$$2l = 90$$
$$\frac{2l}{2} = \frac{90}{2}$$
$$l = 45, \quad l + 30 = 75$$

- Check: $45 + 75 = 120$, and $75 - 45 = 30$. The result checks.

The lengths are 45 m and 75 m.

Equations and Inequalities **287**

Teaching Suggestions p. 281b

Related Activities p. 281b

Chalkboard Examples

Solve.

1. The perimeter of a triangle is 60 mm. One side is 4 times as long as the shortest side and the other side is 6 mm longer than the shortest side. Find the length of the longest side. **36 mm**

2. A tape cassette and a record album cost $16 altogether. The cassette costs $5 less than twice as much as the album. How much does the cassette cost? **$9**

1. The sum of two numbers is 19. Five times the lesser number is four more than twice the greater. What are the numbers? **6, 13**

2. The perimeter of a rectangle is 40 cm. Four times the length is 3 cm more than seven times the width. Find the length of the rectangle. **13 cm**

EXAMPLE 2   The sum of two consecutive integers is 137. Name the larger integer.

Solution

• The problem says: the sum of two consecutive integers is 137

• The problem asks for: the larger of the two integers

Let n = the smaller integer.
Then the larger integer = $n + 1$.
The sum of the two integers is $n + n + 1$.
The sum of the two integers is 137.

• We set the expression for the sum of the two integers ($n + n + 1$) equal to 137.

$$n + n + 1 = 137$$

• Solve.

$$n + n + 1 = 137$$
$$2n + 1 = 137$$
$$2n + 1 - 1 = 137 - 1$$
$$2n = 136$$
$$\frac{2n}{2} = \frac{136}{2}$$
$$n = 68$$
$$n + 1 = 69$$

• Check: $68 + 69 = 137$.

The larger integer is 69.

Reading Mathematics: Study Skills
When you find a reference in the text to material you learned earlier, reread the material in the earlier lesson to help you understand the new lesson. For example, page 287 includes a reference to the five-step method learned in Chapter 4. Turn back to Chapter 4 to review how the five-step method was used.

Problems

Solve.

A   1. A 40 ft board is cut into two pieces so that one piece is 8 ft longer than the other piece. Find the lengths of the two pieces. **16 ft, 24 ft**

2. The sum of two numbers is 60. One number is 16 less than the other number. What is the larger number? **38**

288   *Chapter 8*

3. Marisa Gonzalez is training for a cross-country race. Yesterday, it took her 80 minutes to jog to the reservoir and back. The return trip took 10 minutes longer than the trip to the reservoir. How long did it take her each way? 35 min; 45 min

4. Mark Johnson's weight is 18 kg greater than his sister's. If they weigh a total of 110 kg, what are their weights? 46 kg, 64 kg

5. The perimeter of an isosceles triangle is 50 cm. If the congruent sides of the triangle are each twice as long as the remaining side, what is the length of each side of the triangle? 10 cm, 20 cm, 20 cm

6. Find two consecutive integers whose sum is 115. 57, 58

7. West High School defeated Central High by eleven points in the city championship basketball game. If a total of 159 points were scored in the game, how many points did Central High score? 74

8. Together, a table and a set of four chairs cost $499. If the table costs $35 more than the set of chairs, what is the cost of the table? $267

B 9. A 50 ft rope is cut into two pieces. One piece is 2 ft longer than twice the length of the other. Find the length of the longer piece. 34 ft

10. Twice the sum of two consecutive integers is 42. What are the two integers? 10, 11

11. A collection of jewelry includes two rings, one 18 years old and the other 46 years old. In how many years will the older ring be twice as old as the newer ring? 10 yr

12. Neil is 4 years older than Andrea. If Neil was twice as old as Andrea four years ago, how old was Andrea? 4 yr

C 13. A sailing race takes place on a 3000 m course. The second leg of the course is 100 m longer than the first, and the third leg is 100 m longer than the second. How long is the second leg? 1000 m

14. A teller's supply of dimes and nickels totals $3.60. If the teller's supply of dimes numbers one more than three times the number of nickels, how many dimes are there? 31 dimes

Equations and Inequalities **289**

Solve.

1. $4t + 3t = 84$ **12**

2. $7h - 11h = 2$ $-\frac{1}{2}$

3. $-x + 3 - 3x = 7$ **−1**

4. $5 - g - 5g = -4$ $1\frac{1}{2}$

5. $-30 = 2(y - 10)$ **−5**

6. $-2(3 - u) - 2u = u - 6$
   0

7. $9d = d - 8$ **−1**

8. $7e = 10e - 1$ $\frac{1}{3}$

9. $5f - 1 = 10f + 14$ **−3**

10. $3(m + 4) =$
    $1 - 2m + 1$ **−2**

11. $5(n + 1) = -2(n + 1)$
    −1

12. $-3(w + 2) = -5(w - 2)$
    8

13. Find a number whose product with 6 is the same as its sum with 60. **12**

14. The difference of two numbers is 16. Four times the lesser number is thirteen less than three times the greater. Find the numbers. **35, 51**

Self-Test A

Solve.

1. $3x + 9x = 48$ **4**

2. $2a - 4a = 1$ $-\frac{1}{2}$ **[8-1]**

3. $-y + 6 - 5y = 18$ **−2**

4. $6 - z - 4z = -4$ **2**

5. $5(y - 6) = -60$ **−6**

6. $-4(x - 3) - 6x = 10$ $\frac{1}{5}$

7. $2(z - 4) - z = 8$ **16**

8. $-4(n + 3) + 2n = 6$ **−9**

9. $3c = c + 10$ **5**

10. $9t = 4t - 20$ **−4** **[8-2]**

11. $3p - 1 = 8p + 9$ **−2**

12. $3(a + 1) = 19 - 5a$ **2**

13. $2(p - 1) = 5(p + 2)$ **−4**

14. $-4(t + 2) = 5(t - 3)$ $\frac{7}{9}$

15. $3(c + 4) + c = 2(c - 5)$ **−11**

16. $5(x - 3) = 3(x + 5) - 2x$ $7\frac{1}{2}$

17. A 60 ft long piece of chain link fence is cut into two pieces, one twice as long as the other. What is the length of the shorter piece? **20 ft** **[8-3]**

18. The sum of two consecutive integers is 211. What is the larger integer? **106**

Self-Test answers and Extra Practice are at the back of the book.

Challenge

Flanders, Fulton, and Farnsworth teach two subjects each in a small junior high school. The courses are mathematics, science, carpentry, music, social studies, and English.

1. The carpentry and music teachers are next-door neighbors.

2. The science teacher is older than the mathematics teacher.

3. The teachers ride together going to school and coming home. Farnsworth, the science teacher, and the music teacher each drive one week out of three.

4. Flanders is the youngest.

5. When they can find another player, the English teacher, the mathematics teacher, and Flanders spend their lunch period playing bridge.

What subjects does each teach? Flanders: social studies, music;
Farnsworth: math, carpentry;
Fulton: science, English

8-4 Writing Inequalities

In previous chapters, you have learned how to use the *inequality symbols* $<$ (less than) and $>$ (greater than). Sentences written using these symbols are called **inequalities.**

EXAMPLE Write an inequality for each word sentence.

a. Two is less than ten.
b. A number $2 + x$ is greater than a number t.
c. A number n is between 6 and 12.

Solution **a.** $2 < 10$
b. $2 + x > t$
c. $6 < n < 12$, or $12 > n > 6$

Related Activities p. 281d

Reading Mathematics

Students will learn the meaning of the following mathematical term in this lesson: *inequalities.*

Chalkboard Examples

Write an inequality for each word sentence.

1. Twelve is less than twenty.
$12 < 20$

2. Nine is greater than three.
$9 > 3$

3. On a number line six is between zero and eleven.
$0 < 6 < 11$

4. Thirty is greater than a number x. $30 > x$

Class Exercises

Suppose the numbers given in Exercises 1–6 have been graphed on a number line. Replace the first __?__ with "left" or "right." Replace the second __?__ with $<$ or $>$.

1. The graph of 9 is to the __?__ (right) of the graph of 2. $9 \underset{<}{\overset{>}{\underline{}}} 2$

2. The graph of 4 is to the __?__ (left) of the graph of 7. $4 \underset{<}{\underline{}} 7$

3. The graph of 3 is to the __?__ (left) of the graph of 8. $3 \overset{>}{\underline{}} 8$

4. The graph of 10 is to the __?__ (right) of the graph of 0. $10 \underset{<}{\underline{}} 0$

5. The graph of 0 is to the __?__ (left) of the graph of 5. $0 \overset{>}{\underline{}} 5$

6. The graph of 6 is to the __?__ (right) of the graph of 1. $6 \underline{} 1$

Written Exercises

Write an inequality for each word sentence. Accept equivalent inequalities.

A **1.** Twelve is less than twenty-two. $12 < 22$ **2.** Nineteen is greater than nine. $19 > 9$

3. Six is greater than zero. $6 > 0$ **4.** Twenty-two is less than thirty-three. $22 < 23$

5. On a number line eight is between zero and ten. $0 < 8 < 10$

B **6.** On a number line twenty-five is between fifty-two and five. $5 < 25 < 52$

Equations and Inequalities **291**

Write an inequality for each word sentence.

1. Seventeen is less than twenty. $17 < 20$

2. Fifteen is greater than ten. $15 > 10$

3. On a number line five is between three and eight. $3 < 5 < 8$

4. On a number line fifty is between forty and seventy. $40 < 50 < 70$

Suggested Assignments

Core
291/1–6
292/7–18
292/Rev. 1–7 odd

Enriched
291/1–6
292/7–23

Supplementary Materials

Practice Masters, p. 37
Computer Activity 16

Pictured below is a portion of a number line showing the graph of a whole number *m*. Copy this number line and graph each of the following numbers. Check students' graphs.

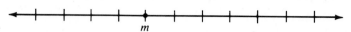

7. $m + 1$

8. $m - 2$

9. $m + 2 - 3$

10. $m - 2 + 3$

Write an inequality for each word sentence.

11. Six is greater than a number *t*. $6 > t$

12. Twenty-seven is less than a number $3m$. $27 < 3m$

13. A number *p* is greater than a number *q*. $p > q$

14. A number *a* is less than a number *b*. $a < b$

15. The value in cents of *d* dimes is less than the value in cents of *n* nickels. $10d < 5n$

16. The value in cents of *m* pennies is greater than the value in cents of *y* quarters. $m > 25y$

17. On a number line a number $2n$ is between 6 and 8. $6 < 2n < 8$

18. On a number line a number $r + 1$ is between 10 and 4. $4 < r + 1 < 10$

19. On a number line a number *a* is between a number *x* and a number *y*, where $x < y$. $x < a < y$

20. On a number line a number $4x$ is between a number *m* and a number *n*, where $m > n$. $n < 4x < m$

C **21.** On a number line 6 is between 2 and 10, and 20 is between 10 and 50. $2 < 6 < 10 < 20 < 50$

22. On a number line a number *x* is between 0 and 10, and a number *y* is between 10 and 14. $0 < x < 10 < y < 14$

23. On a number line 5 is between a number *a* and a number *b*, where $a < b$, and 8 is also between *a* and *b*. $a < 5 < 8 < b$

Review Exercises

Solve using transformations.

1. $x + 4 = 9$ 5

2. $x + 11 = 14$ 3

3. $x - 3 = 2$ 5

4. $x - 6 = -4$ 2

5. $4x = 36$ 9

6. $-5x = 70$ −14

7. $\frac{x}{7} = 11$ 77

8. $-\frac{x}{5} = 6$ −30

292   *Chapter 8*

8-5 Equivalent Inequalities

To solve an inequality, we transform the inequality into an **equivalent inequality.** The transformations that we use are similar to those we use to solve equations.

> Simplify numerical expressions and variable expressions.
>
> Add the same number to, or subtract the same number from, both sides of the inequality.
>
> Multiply or divide both sides of the inequality by the same *positive* number.
>
> Multiply or divide both sides of the inequality by the same *negative number and reverse the inequality sign.*

Notice that we do not multiply the sides of an inequality by 0.

It is easy to see that when the inequality $-6 < 5$ is multiplied by 2, the inequality sign does not change. The following shows why we must reverse the inequality sign when multiplying or dividing by a negative number.

$$-6 < 5$$
$$-2(-6) \ ? \ -2(5)$$
$$12 > -10$$

EXAMPLE 1   Solve each inequality.

a. $x + 7 \leq -18$ **b.** $y - 4.5 > 32$

Solution

a. Subtract 7 from both sides of the inequality.

$$x + 7 \leq -18$$
$$x + 7 - 7 \leq -18 - 7$$
$$x \leq -25$$

The solutions are all the numbers less than or equal to -25.

b. Add 4.5 to both sides of the inequality.

$$y - 4.5 > 32$$
$$y - 4.5 + 4.5 > 32 + 4.5$$
$$y > 36.5$$

The solutions are all the numbers greater than 36.5.

Equations and Inequalities   **293**

Teaching Suggestions
p. 281d

Related Activities p. 281d

Reading Mathematics

Students will learn the meaning of the following mathematical term in this lesson: *equivalent inequality.*

Chalkboard Examples

Complete the inequality to form a true statement.

1. If $a > 2$, then $a + 6 \underline{\ ? \ } 8$.
   >

2. If $c < 5$, then $c - 4 \underline{\ ? \ } 1$.
   <

3. If $x < -2$, then $4x \underline{\ ? \ } -8$.
   <

4. If $y > -4$, then $-3y \underline{\ ? \ } 12$.
   <

5. If $-5 < t$, then $t \underline{\ ? \ } -5$.
   >

6. If $\frac{x}{6} > 4$, then $x \underline{\ ? \ } 24$. >

Solve.

7. $a + 5 < 2$. All the numbers less than -3

8. $-2b > 10$ All the numbers less than -5

9. $\frac{c}{-4} \leq 5$ All the numbers greater than or equal to -20

10. $d - 4 \geq 2$ All the numbers greater than or equal to 6

Use transformations to solve the inequality.

1. $h + 4 > 18$ **All the numbers greater than 14**

2. $x - 7 \leq -10$ **All the numbers less than or equal to −3**

3. $3c > -42$ **All the numbers greater than −14**

4. $6 < w - 16$ **All the numbers greater than 22**

5. $\frac{v}{-6} \geq 4$ **All the numbers less than or equal to −24**

6. $-7m < -98$ **All the numbers greater than 14**

EXAMPLE 2 Solve $2\frac{1}{4} - \frac{1}{2} \geq n$.

Solution We may exchange the sides of the inequality and *reverse the inequality sign* before we simplify the numerical expression.

$$2\frac{1}{4} - \frac{1}{2} \geq n$$
$$n \leq 2\frac{1}{4} - \frac{1}{2}$$
$$n \leq \frac{7}{4}, \text{ or } 1\frac{3}{4}$$

The solutions are all the numbers less than or equal to $\frac{7}{4}$.

EXAMPLE 3 Solve each inequality.

a. $7a < 91$ **b.** $-3x \geq 18$ **c.** $26 \leq \frac{y}{4}$ **d.** $\frac{d}{-9} > -108$

Solution **a.** Divide both sides by 7.
$$7a < 91$$
$$\frac{7a}{7} < \frac{91}{7}$$
$$a < 13$$
The solutions are all the numbers less than 13.

b. Divide both sides by −3 and *reverse the inequality sign*.
$$-3x \geq 18$$
$$\frac{-3x}{-3} \leq \frac{18}{-3}$$
$$x \leq -6$$
The solutions are all the numbers less than or equal to −6.

c. Multiply both sides by 4.
$$26 \leq \frac{y}{4}$$
$$4 \times 26 \leq 4 \times \frac{y}{4}$$
$$104 \leq y$$
The solutions are all the numbers greater than or equal to 104.

d. Multiply both sides by −9 and *reverse the inequality sign*.
$$\frac{d}{-9} > -108$$
$$-9 \times \frac{d}{-9} < -9 \times (-108)$$
$$d < 972$$
The solutions are all the numbers less than 972.

294 *Chapter 8*

Class Exercises

Identify the transformation used to transform the first inequality into the second.

1. $e + 5 > 8$ subtraction
$e + 5 - 5 > 8 - 5$

2. $q - 3 < 7$ addition
$q - 3 + 3 < 7 + 3$

3. $\frac{1}{2}k < 4$ multiplication
$2 \times \frac{1}{2}k < 2 \times 4$

4. $6a > 12$ division
$\frac{6a}{6} > \frac{12}{6}$

5. $-\frac{1}{4}u > 3$ multiplication
$-4 \times -\frac{1}{4}u < -4 \times 3$

6. $-9m < 27$ division
$\frac{-9m}{-9} > \frac{27}{-9}$

Identify each transformation and complete the equivalent inequality.

7. $n - 6 > 9$ addition
$n - 6 + 6 \underset{>}{\overset{?}{\quad}} 9 + 6$

8. $d + 4 < -3$ subtraction
$d + 4 - 4 \underset{<}{\overset{?}{\quad}} -3 - 4$

9. $3r < 15$ division
$\frac{3r}{3} \underset{<}{\overset{?}{\quad}} \frac{15}{3}$

10. $\frac{1}{5}v > 6$ multiplication
$5 \times \frac{1}{5}v \underset{>}{\overset{?}{\quad}} 5 \times 6$

11. $-4z > 32.8$ division
$\frac{-4z}{-4} \underset{<}{\overset{?}{\quad}} \frac{32.8}{-4}$

12. $-\frac{1}{3}s < 2\frac{1}{3}$ multiplication
$-3 \times -\frac{1}{3}s \underset{>}{\overset{?}{\quad}} -3 \times \frac{7}{3}$

Written Exercises

Use transformations to solve the inequality. Write down all the steps.

A

1. $-4 + 16 > k$
2. $g < -18 - 9$
3. $(17 + 4)2 < j$
4. $f \geq 7(23 - 9)$
5. $a + 7 < 10$
6. $c + 8 > 13$
7. $e - 11 \geq 9$
8. $m - 5 \leq 15$
9. $-16 > n + 2$
10. $-13 < q - 6$
11. $8w < 56$
12. $7y > 42$
13. $-5t > 35$
14. $-6a < 18$
15. $-48 \leq -4b$
16. $-49 \geq -7m$
17. $\frac{u}{3} \leq 5$
18. $\frac{w}{4} \geq 9$

Equations and Inequalities **295**

**Additional Answers
Written Exercises**

The solutions are all the numbers:

1. less than 12.
2. less than -27.
3. greater than 42.
4. greater than or equal to 98.
5. less than 3.
6. greater than 5.
7. greater than or equal to 20.
8. less than or equal to 20.
9. less than -18.
10. greater than -7.
11. less than 7.
12. greater than 6.
13. less than -7.
14. greater than -3.
15. less than or equal to 12.
16. greater than or equal to 7.
17. less than or equal to 15.
18. greater than or equal to 36.
19. less than -26.
20. greater than -60.
21. less than or equal to 60.
22. less than or equal to -36.
23. less than or equal to -11.
24. less than 4.
25. less than -168.
26. greater than or equal to 16.27.
27. greater than 21.3.
28. less than or equal to 79.
29. less than $5\frac{3}{7}$.
30. greater than $-13\frac{1}{4}$.
31. less than or equal to -3.87.
32. less than 44.4.
33. less than or equal to 47.

296

Use transformations to solve the inequality. Write down all the steps.

19. $\dfrac{f}{-2} > 13$

20. $\dfrac{n}{-5} < 12$

21. $-10 \leq \dfrac{y}{-6}$

22. $-9 \geq \dfrac{d}{4}$

23. $\dfrac{4h - 2h}{2} \leq -6 - 5$

24. $\dfrac{16}{4} > \dfrac{7n - 2n}{5}$

B **25.** $-8(13.4 + 7.6) > a$

26. $12 \leq p - 4.27$

27. $3r > 63.9$

28. $10\left(3\frac{1}{2} + 4\frac{2}{5}\right) \geq g$

29. $j + 3\frac{4}{7} < 9$

30. $d + 5\frac{1}{4} > -8$

31. $-10 \geq n - 6.13$

32. $c < (18.7 - 7.6)4$

33. $e \leq \left(5\frac{1}{3} + 2\frac{1}{2}\right)6$

34. $42.4 < 4t$

35. $\dfrac{d}{0.6} \leq -18$

36. $\dfrac{1}{5}w \geq \dfrac{2}{5}$

37. $\dfrac{3}{4} \leq \dfrac{1}{4}n$

38. $\dfrac{m}{3.1} \geq 12$

39. $-7 > -\dfrac{1}{3}d$

40. $-\dfrac{1}{2}f \leq -13$

41. $-6y < 24.6$

42. $42.5 > -5b$

43. $\dfrac{a}{-13.2} \geq 7$

44. $\dfrac{x}{-0.3} < -9$

45. $h - 10\frac{2}{3} > 12\frac{1}{5}$

46. $-8.27 \leq k + 17.41$

47. $22.5 \geq -2.5m$

48. $3.2u \geq 25.6$

C **49.** $\dfrac{3}{4}n + \dfrac{1}{2}n > \dfrac{2}{3} \times \dfrac{3}{8}$

50. $\dfrac{-5}{8}p - \dfrac{1}{8}p > \dfrac{1}{4} \div 7$

51. $3.4(21.2 - 18.9) < 4.6(-3b + 2b)$

52. $\dfrac{5(-1.6t)}{2} < -14.3 - 9.7$

Review Exercises

Write the numbers in order from least to greatest.

$-2.6, -1.4, 1.2, 3.2$
1. $-1.4, 1.2, -2.6, 3.2$

$-4.1, -3.07, 3, 3.7, 4.02$
2. $3.7, 4.02, -3.07, -4.1, 3$

$-12.2, -12.09, -11.2, 12, 112$
3. $12, -12.2, -12.09, 112, -11.2$

$-9, -8.09, -0.98, 0.89, 9.8$
4. $9.8, -8.09, 0.89, -0.98, -9$

$-30.05, -5.3, -5.03, 0.35, 3.05$
5. $-5.03, 3.05, -30.05, 0.35, -5.3$

$-20, -2, -0.2, -0.02, 200$
6. $-0.2, -0.02, -2, -20, 200$

$-2.89, -2.8, 2.089, 2.89, 28.9$
7. $2.89, 2.089, -2.8, 28.9, -2.89$

$-76.0, -7.6, -7.06, -0.76, -0.076$
8. $-7.6, -0.76, -7.06, -0.076, -76.0$

8-6 Solving Inequalities by Several Transformations

We may need to use more than one transformation to solve some inequalities. It is helpful to follow the same steps that we use for solving equations.

> 1. Simplify each side of the inequality.
>
> 2. Use the inverse operations to undo any indicated additions or subtractions.
>
> 3. Use the inverse operations to undo any indicated multiplications or divisions.

EXAMPLE 1   Solve $-4r + 6 + 2r - 18 < -8$.

Solution   Simplify the left side.
$$-4r + 6 + 2r - 18 < -8$$
$$-2r - 12 < -8$$

Add 12 to both sides.
$$-2r - 12 + 12 < -8 + 12$$
$$-2r < 4$$

Divide both sides by -2 and reverse the inequality sign.
$$\frac{-2r}{-2} > \frac{4}{-2}$$
$$r > -2$$

The solutions are all the numbers greater than -2.

The solutions to the inequality in Example 1 include all numbers greater than -2. We show the graph of the solutions on the number line in the following way.

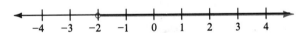

The open dot at -2 indicates that -2 is not on the graph of the solutions of the inequality.

We use a solid dot to show that a number is on the graph of the solutions. We graph the solutions of $r \geq -2$ in the following way.

Equations and Inequalities   **297**

Teaching Suggestions
p. 281e

Related Activities p. 281f

Reading Mathematics

Some students use the terms *empty* and *filled* for *open* and *solid*, respectively, when referring to dots on a number line. Reassure students that using the correct terms is not as important as distinguishing between points whose coordinates do satisfy the condition (solid dots) and those that do not (open dots).

Match the correct inequality with the graph.

A. $a \leq -2$ **B.** $b \leq 1$
C. $c > -2$ **D.** $d < 1$

1.   D

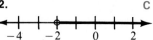

2.   C

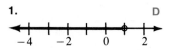

3.   A

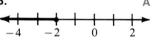

4.   B

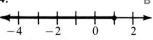

Complete each inequality so that it is equivalent to the preceding one.

5. $8 - 3x < -4$
$-3x < \underline{\ ?\ } \ -12$
$x > \underline{\ ?\ } \ 4$

6. $6 - 2x \geq 11 + 3x$
$6 \geq 11 + \underline{\ ?\ } \ 5x$
$-5 \underline{\ ?\ } 5x \geq$
$5x \underline{\ ?\ } -5 \leq$
$x \leq \underline{\ ?\ } \ -1$

Solve.

7. $7 - 3m < -9 + m$
All the numbers greater than 4

8. $\frac{1}{3}(3x - 9) \geq 2x + 1$
All the numbers less than or equal to −4

Suggested Assignments

Core
Day 1: 299/1–16
Day 2: 299/17–26
     300/27–30
     300/Rev. 1–8

Enriched
Day 1: 299/2–26 even
     300/27–29
Day 2: 300/30–40
     300/Challenge

Supplementary Materials

Practice Masters, p. 38

298

EXAMPLE 2 Solve $3(5 + x) \leq -3$ and graph the solutions.

Solution Simplify the left side.

$$3(5 + x) \leq -3$$
$$3(5) + 3x \leq -3$$
$$15 + 3x \leq -3$$

Subtract 15 from both sides.

$$15 + 3x - 15 \leq -3 - 15$$
$$3x \leq -18$$

Divide both sides by 3.

$$\frac{3x}{3} \leq \frac{-18}{3}$$
$$x \leq -6$$

The solutions are all the numbers less than or equal to -6.

Because -6 is on the graph, we used a solid dot to graph the solutions of the inequality.

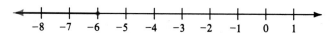

Like equations, inequalities may have variables on both sides. We may add a variable expression to both sides or subtract a variable expression from both sides to obtain an equivalent inequality.

EXAMPLE 3 Solve $-z + 7 \leq 3z - 18$.

Solution Add z to both sides.

$$-z + 7 \leq 3z - 18$$
$$z + (-z) + 7 \leq z + 3z - 18$$
$$7 \leq 4z - 18$$

Add 18 to both sides.

$$7 + 18 \leq 4z - 18 + 18$$
$$25 \leq 4z$$

Divide both sides by 4.

$$\frac{25}{4} \leq \frac{4z}{4}$$
$$6.25 \leq z$$

The solutions are all the numbers greater than or equal to 6.25.

Class Exercises

State which transformations you would use to solve the inequality. State them in the order in which you would use them.

1. $8x + 7 - 5x + 2 \leq 30$

2. $-29 > 5 - 2y - 10 - 4y$

3. $7 \geq \frac{-4}{5}m + 6 + \frac{3}{5}m - 4$

4. $\frac{6}{7}k - 8 - \frac{5}{7}k + 3 < -3$

5. $4(h - 3) > 16$

6. $-4 \geq \frac{1}{2}(w + 12)$

7. $2 < (k + 45)\frac{-1}{5}$

8. $(3 - s)7 \leq 42$

9. $-u + 8 \geq 4u - 10$

10. $a - 6 < -5a - 18$

Written Exercises

Solve and graph the solutions. Check students' graphs.

A **1.** $3q + 5 < -13$

2. $-7 + 5m > 28$

3. $30 \geq -4b - 6$

4. $-57 \leq -8z - 9$

5. $-\frac{w}{2} + 8 > 23$

6. $-\frac{c}{3} + 7 < -18$

7. $-12 \leq -5 + \frac{r}{6}$

8. $13 \geq 6 + \frac{e}{4}$

Solve.

9. $3v + 11 - 8v - 5 < -21$

10. $9 - 12u + 4 + 6u > -5$

11. $12 \geq \frac{3}{5}f + 6 - \frac{4}{5}f + 4$

12. $19 \leq 7 + \frac{1}{3}k + 2 - \frac{2}{3}k$

13. $h > -5h + 18 - 6$

14. $t < 17 - 4t - 2$

15. $38 - 8 - 7n \leq 3n$

16. $-9q + 18 - 3 \geq 6q$

17. $\frac{1}{4}(20 - x) < 6$

18. $\frac{1}{6}(42 - p) > 12$

19. $21 \geq 7(m - 2)$

20. $-25 \leq 5(w + 3)$

21. $j + 8 > 4j - 16$

22. $-6f + 7 < 2f - 9$

23. $10 + \frac{3}{4}a \leq \frac{-7}{8}a + 5$

24. $\frac{5}{6}g - 4 \geq \frac{2}{3}g + 6$

B **25.** $-12.8c + 8 + 7.8c - 6 \geq 17$

26. $4 + 7.5y - 9 + 2.5y > 25$

Equations and Inequalities **299**

Solve.

27. $1\frac{4}{5} < 8m + 4\frac{1}{5} - 3m - 7\frac{2}{5}$

28. $-2\frac{2}{3} \le 5\frac{2}{3} - 9u + 4\frac{2}{3} + 3u$

29. $0.2(40k + 62.5) \le -3.5$

30. $-0.5(12v - 18.6) < 21.3$

31. $-2\frac{7}{8} > \left(\frac{5}{8} - t\right)\frac{1}{5}$

32. $5\frac{3}{4} \le \frac{1}{3}\left(x - \frac{3}{4}\right)$

33. $2.7e + 8.2 < -9.3e + 32.2$

34. $5.4 - 10.9w \ge 9.1w - 14.6$

35. $\frac{5}{6}f - 2\frac{4}{5} > 1\frac{1}{5} + \frac{2}{3}f$

36. $-2\frac{1}{9}d + \frac{3}{5} \le -3\frac{2}{9}d - 4\frac{2}{5}$

C 37. $0.11(360 + 25n) < (1.86n \div 6) - 3.06n$

38. $\frac{1}{5}\left(w - 5\frac{5}{9}\right) + \frac{2}{9} + \frac{3}{4}w \ge \frac{1}{8}w - 1 + \frac{5}{8}w$

39. $[(250.25x - 10.5) \div -5] - 14.6 \le -0.05x + 502.5$

40. $9\frac{4}{5} + \frac{2}{7}k - 7\frac{3}{5} > -\frac{11}{12} + \left[\left(\frac{4}{7}k + 2\frac{1}{3}\right) \div \frac{4}{5}\right]$

Review Exercises

Use n to write a variable expression for the word phrase.

1. A number increased by nine $n + 9$

2. Twice a number $2n$

3. Sixteen less than a number $n - 16$

4. Half of a number $\frac{n}{2}$, or $\frac{1}{2}n$

5. The sum of a number and three $n + 3$

6. Six more than a number $6 + n$

7. A number divided by five $\frac{n}{5}$

8. Eight times a number $8n$

▌▌▌ Challenge

Each letter in each exercise stands for a digit from 0 through 9. Find the value of each letter to make the computation correct. (There may be more than one correct answer.) Answers may vary.

1.	2.	3.
H O W	T I M E	M A T H
+ A R E	+ S U R E	− I S
Y O U	F L I E S	F U N

8-7 Inequalities in Problem Solving

The five-step method is also helpful in solving problems that require inequalities.

EXAMPLE The sum of two consecutive integers is less than 40. What pair of integers with this property has the greatest sum?

Chalkboard Examples

Use the variable provided to translate the word sentence into an inequality.

Solution
- The problem says:
  the sum of two consecutive integers is less than 40

- The problem asks for:
  the greatest pair of integers whose sum is less than 40
  Let n = the smaller of the two integers.
  Then the other integer = $n + 1$.
  The sum of the two integers is $n + n + 1$.
  The sum of the two integers is less than 40.

- We now have enough information to write an inequality.

$$n + n + 1 < 40$$

- Solve.

$$n + n + 1 < 40$$
$$2n + 1 < 40$$
$$2n + 1 - 1 < 40 - 1$$
$$2n < 39$$
$$\frac{2n}{2} < \frac{39}{2}$$
$$n < 19.5$$
$$n = 19$$
$$n + 1 = 20$$

- Check: $19 + 20 = 39$, $39 < 40$. The result checks.

  The two integers are 19 and 20.

1. The temperature (t) today is at least 20°C. $t \geq 20$

2. Joan's blouse (b) cost no more than $24.95. $b \leq 24.95$

3. The cost of the trip (c) is more than $500. $c > 500$

Solve.

4. Find three consecutive positive odd integers whose sum is less than twice the greatest integer.
   1, 3, 5

5. A triangle has two equal sides each of which is 5 cm longer than one third of the remaining side. If the lengths of the sides of the triangle must be integers, find the longest sides possible if the perimeter is less than 16.
   3 cm, 6 cm, 6 cm

Additional Answers
(p. 300)
Written Exercises

The solutions are all the numbers:

32. greater than or equal to 18.

33. less than 2.

34. less than or equal to 1.

35. greater than 24.

36. less than or equal to $-4\frac{1}{2}$.

37. less than -7.2.

38. greater than or equal to $-\frac{5}{9}$.

39. greater than or equal to -10.3.

40. less than $\frac{7}{15}$.

Class Exercises

Using x as the variable, write an inequality based on the given information. Do not solve.

1. A used-car dealer has sold 30 of his compact cars and now has fewer than 70 left. $x - 30 < 70$

2. Alejandro Mendoza, who had more than 60 base hits during his school team's baseball season, had 25 more hits than his teammate Peter Evans. $x + 25 > 60$

Additional A Exercises

Solve.

1. The sum of three consecutive integers is less than 54. Find the greatest possible values for the integers. **16, 17, 18**

2. Of all pairs of consecutive odd integers whose sum is greater than 45, find the pair whose sum is the least. **23, 25**

3. Jenny is two thirds as old as Lynn. Four years from now she will be at most five sevenths as old as Lynn. At least how old is Jenny? **16 y**

Suggested Assignments

Core
Day 1: 302/Prob. 1–8
Day 2: 303/Self-Test A
  303/Challenge

Enriched
Day 1: 302/Prob. 3–9
  303/Prob. 10, 11
Day 2: 303/Self-Test A
  303/Challenge

Supplementary Materials

Practice Masters, p. 38
Test 8B pp. 55–56

Quick Quiz B

Write an inequality for each word sentence.

1. Twenty-one is less than a number x. **$21 < x$**

2. A number y is greater than a number z. **$y > z$**

3. Eighteen is less than a number $2w$. **$18 < 2w$**

Use transformations to solve the inequality.

4. $a - 6 \leq 10$ **All the numbers less than or equal to 16**

5. $b + 5 > 7$ **All the numbers greater than 2**

6. $c + 9 \geq 12$ **All the numbers greater than or equal to 3**

---

3. Deborah's bowling score was 8 less than half of Lydia's score. Deborah's score was less than 95. **$\frac{1}{2}x - 8 < 95$**

4. A house and lot together cost more than $120,000. The cost of the house was $2000 more than six times the cost of the lot.
$6x + 2000 + x > 120,000$

5. The number of students at Ivytown High School who study computer science is twice the number who study home economics. The total number of students enrolled in these courses exceeds 600. **$2x + x > 600$**

6. The sum of two consecutive integers is greater than 30. **$x + x + 1 > 30$**

Problems

Solve.

A 1. The sum of two consecutive integers is less than 75. Find the pair of integers with the greatest sum. **36, 37**

2. Of all pairs of consecutive integers whose sum is greater than 100, find the pair whose sum is the least. **50, 51**

3. Two trucks start from the same point traveling in different directions. One truck travels at a speed of 54 mi/h, the other at 48 mi/h. How long must they travel to be at least 408 mi apart? **4 h**

4. A purse contains 30 coins, all either quarters or dimes. The total value of the coins is greater than $5.20. At least how many of the coins are quarters? At most how many are dimes? **15 quarters; 15 dimes**

5. A home and adjoining lot cost more than $160,000 together. The cost of the house was $1000 more than six times the cost of the lot. What is the smallest possible cost of the lot? **$22,714.29**

6. Paul is two fifths as old as Janet. Five years from now, he will be at least half as old as Janet. At most how old is Paul now? **10 yr**

B 7. The sum of three consecutive integers, decreased by five, is greater than twice the smallest of the integers. What are the three least positive integers with this property? **3, 4, 5**

8. A pair of consecutive integers has the property that five times the smaller is less than four times the greater. Find the greatest pair of integers with this property. **3, 4**

9. The number of Software Services employees who use public transportation to commute to work is 200 more than twice the number who drive their own cars. If there are 1400 employees, how many drive their own cars? **400 employees**

C **10.** Bonanza Rent-A-Car rents cars for $40 per day and 10¢ for every mile driven. Autos Unlimited rents cars for $50 per day with no extra charge for mileage. How many miles per day can you drive a Bonanza car if it is to cost you less than an Auto Unlimited car? 100 mi

11. A bank offers two types of checking accounts. Account A has a $4 maintenance fee each month and charges 10¢ for each check cashed. Account B has a $6 maintenance fee and charges 6¢ for each check. What is the least number of checks that can be written each month for the "A" account to be more expensive? 51 checks

Self-Test B

Write an inequality for each word sentence.

1. A number a is less than a number b. $a < b$ [8-4]

2. Thirty-five is greater than a number $4z$. $35 > 4z$

Use transformations to solve the inequality.

3. $m - 8 \leq 20$ **4.** $t + 3 > 6$ **5.** $c + 7 \geq 14$ [8-5]

6. $9p > 42$ **7.** $-4b < 56$ **8.** $-7x < -35$

Solve.

9. $2x + 4 + 6x - 2 < 18$ **10.** $12 - 6u + 4 + 8u > 20$ [8-6]

11. $\frac{1}{2}(30 - 6y) \geq 15$ **12.** $-30 \leq 6(t + 1)$

13. The sum of two consecutive integers is less than 150. Find the greatest pair of integers with this property. 74, 75   [8-7]

 Challenge

Using each of the digits 1, 3, 5, 7, and 9 exactly once, create a three-digit integer and a two-digit integer. The integers may be either positive or negative.

1. What is the greatest possible sum of the two integers? the least possible sum? 953 + 71 = 1024; −953 + (−71) = −1024, or
973 + 51 = 1024; −973 + (−51) = −1024

2. What is the greatest possible difference between the two integers? the least possible difference? 953 − (−71) = 1024; −953 − 71 = −1024

3. What is the greatest possible product of the two integers? the least possible product? 751 × 93 = 69,843; −751 × 93 = 751 × (−93) = −69,843

Equations and Inequalities **303**

People in Mathematics

Archimedes (287–212 B.C.)

Archimedes is considered to be one of the greatest mathematicians of all time. He was a native of the Greek city of Syracuse, although he did spend some time at the University of Alexandria in Egypt.

Archimedes is the subject of many stories and legends. The most famous story about Archimedes is that of King Hieron's crown. The crown was supposedly all gold, but the king suspected that it contained silver and he asked Archimedes to determine whether it was pure gold. Archimedes hit upon the solution, while bathing, by discovering the first law of hydrostatics. The story relates that he jumped from the bath and ran through the streets shouting "Eureka."

Archimedes discovered many important mathematical facts. He found formulas for the volumes and surface areas of many geometric solids. He invented a method for approximating π and studied spirals, one of which bears his name. His work, as shown by a paper not found until 1906, even contained the beginning of calculus, a branch of mathematics not developed until the seventeenth century.

Sonya Kovaleski (1850–1891)

Sonya Kovaleski was one of the great mathematicians of the nineteenth century. Her work includes papers on such diverse topics as partial differential equations (a theorem is named in her honor), Abelian integrals, and the rings of Saturn. Her other work included research in the topics of analysis and physics. In 1888 her research paper entitled *On the Rotation of a Solid Body about a Fixed Point* was awarded the Prix Bordin of the French Academy of Sciences. It was considered so outstanding that the prize of 3000 francs was doubled.

304 *Chapter 8*

Kovaleski's rise to prominence was far from easy. In order to leave Russia to study at a foreign university, she had to arrange a marriage, at age eighteen, to Vladimir Kovaleski. In 1868 they went to Heidelberg where she studied with Kirchhoff and Helmholtz, two famous physicists. In 1871 she went to Berlin to study with Karl Weierstrass. Since women were not admitted to university lectures, all her studying was done privately. Finally, in 1874, the University of Gottingen awarded her a doctorate *in absentia*. However, she was unable to find an academic position for ten years despite strong letters of recommendation from Weierstrass. Finally, in 1884, she was appointed as a lecturer at the University of Stockholm where she was made a full professor five years later.

Emmy Noether (1882–1935)

Emmy Noether is considered one of the brilliant mathematicians of the twentieth century. Her most important work was done in the field of advanced algebra, a branch of mathematics that deals with structures called "groups" and "rings." An important theorem in advanced algebra is called the Noether-Lasker Decomposition Theorem. Noether is also known for work she did on Einstein's theory of relativity.

Although her father was a mathematician, Noether faced many of the same obstacles as Sonya Kovaleski. She sat in on courses at the University of Erlangen (shown in the photograph) and the University of Gottingen from 1900 to 1903, but was not allowed to officially enroll until 1904 when Erlangen changed its policy toward women. She received her doctorate in 1907.

In 1915 Noether was invited to Gottingen by David Hilbert. There, she worked with Hilbert and Felix Klein, two prominent mathematicians, although she was not appointed to the faculty until 1922. She left Gottingen in 1933 and took a professorship at Bryn Mawr College in Pennsylvania.

Research Activities

1. Look up the statement of the law of physics known as Archimedes' principle. Using a measuring cup, devise a simple experiment to verify this law.

2. Archimedes discovered a way to calculate the number π very accurately. Look up the history of π in an encyclopedia. Find what values ancient civilizations thought it had.

3. Two other people considered important in the history of mathematics are Hypatia and Maria Agnesi. Find out about the lives and work of these mathematicians.

Equations and Inequalities **305**

Students may be interested to learn that over the centuries there have been many famous women mathematicians. This is in spite of the fact that in the past much less emphasis was placed on the education of women than of men.

Chapter Review

True or false?

1. If $2y + 8y = -20$, $y = 2$. False

2. If $p + 6 - 6p = -8$, $p = -3$. False **[8–1]**

3. If $4(n - 3) = 6$, $n = 4\frac{1}{2}$. True

4. If $-4(a + 3) = 15$, $a = \frac{3}{4}$. False

5. If $5z + 4 = 3z + 6$, $z = 1$. True

6. If $6x - 11 = 12x - 7$, $x = 4$. False **[8–2]**

7. If $2(x - 4) = 5(x + 3)$, $x = 20$. False

8. If $4(y + 7) = 3(y - 6)$, $y = -2$. False

Write the letter of the correct answer.

9. The perimeter of an isosceles triangle is 63 cm. If the congruent sides of the triangle are each three times as long as the remaining side, how long are the congruent sides? b **[8–3]**
   a. 7 cm   b. 27 cm   c. 9 cm   d. 18 cm

10. A 60 ft board with a thickness of 1 in. is to be cut into two pieces, one three times as long as the other. Find the lengths of the two pieces. c
    a. 30 ft, 30 ft   b. 40 ft, 20 ft   c. 45 ft, 15 ft   d. 48 ft, 12 ft

11. Which inequality represents the word sentence? Thirty is greater than a number x. c **[8–4]**
    a. $30 < x$ b. $30 \leq x$ c. $30 > x$ d. $30 \geq x$

Match the equivalent inequalities.

12. $-8 + 12 < x$ C   13. $6x > 54$ D   A. $x \leq 8$ B. $x > 8$ **[8–5]**

14. $-64 \leq -8x$ A   15. $2x < 8$ B   C. $x > 4$ D. $x > 9$

16. $\frac{1}{2}x + 6 < 26$ F   17. $\frac{x}{-5} + 5 \geq 10$ E   E. $x \leq -25$ F. $x < 40$ **[8–6]**

18. $-17 \leq -5 + \frac{x}{3}$ H   19. $-\frac{x}{6} + 5 > -3$ G   G. $x < 48$ H. $x \geq -36$

Write the letter of the correct answer.

20. The sum of two consecutive integers is greater than 60. Find the least pair of integers having this property. c **[8–7]**
    a. 29, 30   b. 20, 21   c. 30, 31   d. 31, 32

21. NewBank offers two checking accounts. Account A has a monthly fee of $2 and charges 15¢ for each check cashed. Account B has a monthly fee of $5 and charges 10¢ for each check cashed. What is the greatest number of checks that can be cashed for Account A to be less expensive than Account B? b
    a. 60   b. 59   c. 61   d. 20

306   *Chapter 8*

Chapter Test

Supplementary Materials

Chapter 8 Test, pp. 57–58

Solve.

1. $9a + 6a = 120$ **8**

2. $-6z - (-4z) = -5$ **2$\frac{1}{2}$** [8-1]

3. $4 + (-4a) + 20 = 16$ **2**

4. $-7n - 6 + 8n = -6$ **0**

5. $4(x - 5) = 10$ **7$\frac{1}{2}$**

6. $8(y + 5) = -20$ **−7$\frac{1}{2}$**

7. $5y + 4 = 6y - 3$ **7**

8. $6(x + 4) = -2x$ **−3** [8-2]

9. $-3(a + 1) = 6a + 12$ **−1$\frac{2}{3}$**

10. $6(p + 1) = 4(p + 2)$ **1**

11. $-3(n - 3) = 2n + 5$ **$\frac{4}{5}$**

12. $4(y + 2) = -6y + 8$ **0**

Use an equation to solve.

13. The sum of two numbers is 100. One number is 24 less than the other number. What is the larger number? **62** [8-3]

Write an inequality for each word sentence. Accept equivalent inequalities.

14. Sixty-eight is less than eighty. **68 < 80** [8-4]

15. Nineteen is between fourteen and thirty. **14 < 19 < 30**

16. Zero is less than a number y. **0 < y**

17. A number z is greater than a number r. **z > r**

Solve.

18. $a + 12 < 19$

19. $\frac{m}{4} > -8$

20. $-3y \leq 42$ [8-5]

21. $\frac{w}{-6} \geq 9$

22. $75 < 5p$

23. $27 \geq n - 16$

Solve and graph the solutions.

24. $\frac{1}{4}d - 2 \leq 18$

25. $-35 \leq -5(r + 8)$ [8-6]

26. $\frac{a}{9} + 17 \geq 20$

27. $8x - 4 < 5x + 23$

Solve.

28. Two trucks start from the same point traveling in opposite directions. One truck travels at a speed of 50 mi/h, the other travels at a speed of 45 mi/h. How long must they travel to be 380 mi apart? [8-7]

Equations and Inequalities **307**

**Additional Answers
Chapter Test**

The solutions are all the numbers:

18. less than 7.

19. greater than −32.

20. greater than or equal to −14.

21. less than or equal to −54.

22. greater than 15.

23. less than or equal to 43.

24. less than 80.

25. less than or equal to −1.

26. greater than or equal to 27.

27. less than 9.

1. Evaluate 10^6. **1,000,000**

2. Write $10^4 \times 10^5$ as a single power of 10. **10^9**

3. Round 26.379 to the nearest hundredth. **23.38**

4. Find the solution of $2k + 1 = 7$ if the replacement set is $\{1, 3, 9\}$. **3**

5. One angle of an isosceles triangle has a measure 56°. Find the measures of the two congruent angles. **62°, 62°**

6. A regular pentagon has perimeter 65 cm. Find the length of each side. **13 cm**

7. A circle has radius 20 mm. Find the circumference. Use $\pi \approx 3.14$. **125.6 mm**

8. George Thornton's salary increased $50 a week. If his salary was $200 a week before the raise, by what percent did his salary increase? **25%**

9. Paper Moon Gifts had sales of $8000 for September. The store's profits were $4500. What was the percent of profit? **56.25%**

Cumulative Review (Chapters 1–8)

Exercises

Evaluate the expression when $a = 2$, $b = -4$, and $c = 3$.

1. $a + b - c$ **-5**

2. $c - b + a$ **9**

3. $3ac$ **18**

4. $-2b$ **8**

5. $4c - 5a$ **2**

6. $10a - 3b$ **32**

7. $8c \div (-3b)$ **2**

8. $50 \div (a + c)$ **10**

9. a^2 **4**

10. b^2 **16**

11. $(-b)^3$ **64**

12. $(ab)^2$ **64**

Solve.

13. $x + 9 = 12$ **3**

14. $x - 4 = -11$ **-7**

15. $2x = 14$ **7**

16. $-5x = 35$ **-7**

17. $3x + 7 = 22$ **5**

18. $-7x + 3 = -32$ **5**

19. $2x + 3x = 20$ **4**

20. $10x - 18x = 4$ **$-\frac{1}{2}$**

21. $-7x - 9x + 7 = 11$ **$-\frac{1}{4}$**

22. $5x = 30 - 10x$ **2**

23. $7x - 3 = 3x + 9$ **3**

24. $x - 14 = 26 - 9x$ **4**

Write as equivalent fractions using the LCD.

25. $\frac{1}{2}, \frac{7}{8}$ **$\frac{4}{8}, \frac{7}{8}$**

26. $\frac{3}{5}, \frac{9}{20}$ **$\frac{12}{20}, \frac{9}{20}$**

27. $\frac{1}{5}, \frac{3}{4}$ **$\frac{4}{20}, \frac{15}{20}$**

28. $\frac{2}{7}, \frac{5}{9}$ **$\frac{18}{63}, \frac{35}{63}$**

29. $\frac{2}{3}, \frac{1}{4}, \frac{5}{12}$ **$\frac{8}{12}, \frac{3}{12}, \frac{5}{12}$**

30. $\frac{21}{24}, \frac{5}{8}, \frac{7}{9}$ **$\frac{63}{72}, \frac{45}{72}, \frac{56}{72}$**

Complete.

31. Two nonparallel lines that do not intersect are called ___?___ lines. **skew**

32. In a ___?___ triangle, no two sides are congruent. **scalene**

33. The number π is the ratio of the circumference of a circle to its ___?___. **diameter**

34. The ___?___ of a figure is the distance around it. **perimeter**

35. The common endpoint of the two rays of an angle is called the ___?___. **vertex**

36. A ___?___ of a polygon is a segment joining two nonconsecutive vertices. **diagonal**

Solve.

37. What percent of 60 is 55? **$91\frac{2}{3}\%$**

38. What is 81% of 120? **97.2**

39. 30 is 15% of what number? **200**

40. What percent of 100 is 49? **49%**

308 *Chapter 8*

Problems

Problem Solving Reminders

Here are some reminders that may help you solve some of the problems on this page.
- Consider whether a chart will help to organize information.
- Supply additional information if needed.
- Reread the problem to be sure that your answer is complete.

Solve.

1. Donald bought a pair of hiking boots for $35.83, a sweater for $24.65, and a backpack for $18. The tax on his purchase was $.90. How much did Donald spend? $79.38

2. This week, Marisa worked $1\frac{1}{2}$ h on Monday, $2\frac{1}{4}$ h on Tuesday, $1\frac{1}{3}$ h on Wednesday, and $7\frac{1}{2}$ h on Saturday. How many hours did she work this week? $12\frac{7}{12}$ h

3. An airplane flying at an altitude of 25,000 ft dropped 4000 ft in the first 25 s and rose 2500 ft in the next 15 s. What was the altitude of the airplane after 40 s? 23,500 ft

4. The difference between twice a number and 50 is 10. What is the number? 30

5. At a milk processing plant 100 lb of farm milk are needed to make 8.13 lb of nonfat dry milk. To the nearest pound, how many pounds of farm milk are needed to produce 100 lb of nonfat dry milk? 1230 lb

6. A highway noise barrier that is 120 m long is constructed in two pieces. One piece is 45 m longer than the other. Find the length of each piece. 37.5 m, 82.5 m

7. A side of a square is 13 cm long. What is the perimeter of the square? 52 cm

8. Oak Hill School, Longview School, and Peabody School participated in a clean-up campaign to collect scrap aluminum. Oak Hill School collected 40% more scrap aluminum than Longview School. Longview School collected 25% more than Peabody School. If the total collected by the 3 schools was 560 kg, how much did Oak Hill School collect? 245 kg

9. Eladio invested $200 at 6% annual interest and $350 at 5.75% annual interest, both compounded annually. If he makes no deposits or withdrawals, how much will he have after two years? $616.13

10. A television that sells for $400 is on sale at a 15% discount. What is the sale price? $340

11. The Golf Shop sold 8 of 25 sets of clubs in April. What percent of the sales of clubs were sold? 32%

12. Althea Maxwell borrowed $1500 for $1\frac{1}{4}$ years at 13% simple interest. How much must she repay when the loan is due? $1743.75

Equations and Inequalities **309**

9

The Coordinate Plane

One of the most fascinating aspects of computer science is the field of computer-aided design (C.A.D.). Computers are used to design a wide variety of goods ranging from televisions and cars to skyscrapers, airplanes, and spacecraft. Computers are also used to generate designs for decorative purposes, such as the rug pattern shown at the right. A particular advantage of using the computer is the ease with which the design can be prepared and modified. The designer may use a light pen to create the design on the computer screen and may type in commands to tell the computer to enlarge, reduce, or rotate the design. Although the actual programs for computer graphics are often complicated, the underlying idea is based on establishing a grid with labeled reference points. The grid is actually an application of the coordinate plane that is presented in this chapter.

Career Note

If you enjoy working with fabrics and drawing your own patterns, you might consider a career as a textile designer. Textile designers create the graphic designs printed or woven on all kinds of fabrics. In addition to having a good understanding of graphics, textile designers must possess a knowledge of textile production. Another important part of textile design is the ability to appeal to current tastes.

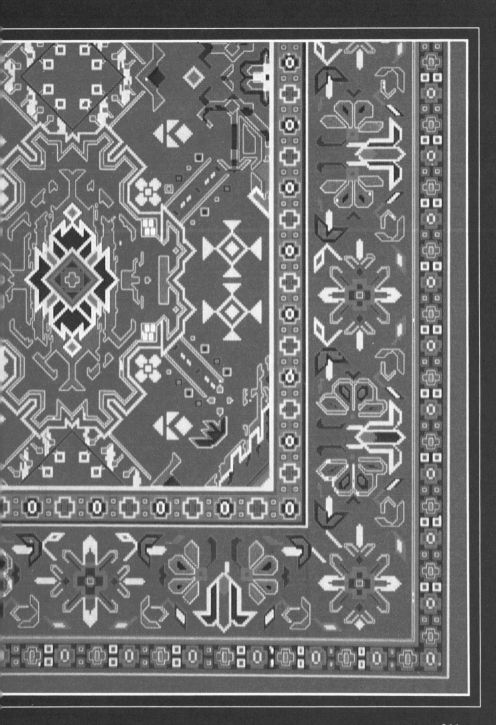

Lesson Commentary
Chapter 9 The Coordinate Plane

Overview

The coordinate, or Cartesian, plane makes it possible to unify numerical and algebraic concepts with geometric and visual concepts. By now students are prepared to deal with positive and negative coordinates, to evaluate expressions for given values of the variable, and to convert equations into forms easier to graph.

Once the basic skills of graphing equations are established, it is possible to move on to consider more advanced concepts, though at an elementary level. When equations can be graphed, there is no real difficulty in finding the intersection of two graphs, or in extending the idea of a graph to include that of an inequality.

It may be satisfying for students to realize that the concepts and skills that they acquire now will be useful and important in all further study of mathematics, as well as in science, economics, and wherever else it is necessary to represent information in graphs.

EQUATIONS AND THE COORDINATE PLANE

9-1 The Coordinate Plane

Objectives for pages 312–315

- To assign coordinates to a point in the plane.
- To graph an ordered pair of numbers in the coordinate plane.

Teaching Suggestions

Students generally consider this material to be straightforward. Conceptually, it will be important to develop the idea of one-to-one correspondence between points in the plane and pairs of real numbers. You might mention the arbitrary decisions that have been made, such as the names of the axes, positive and negative directions, and the order of the coordinates in a number pair.

To clarify the meaning of *order* in the term *ordered pair*, graph pairs such as $(-6, 3)$ and $(3, -6)$, showing that they are not the same. It may be necessary to give special attention to points on the axes. Students are tempted to give only one coordinate for such points, rather than a pair of coordinates.

For your convenience, coordinate systems are provided in the Resource Book, pages 164–165.

Related Activities

As an example of using ordered pairs to locate points, bring in a map with an index. Show how to find, for example, a town located at C-5. A map of a city with numbered streets and avenues is also useful.

To provide a living example of a coordinate grid, assign seats one day by giving each student an ordered pair of numbers. Establish an origin and axes, and have the students seat themselves accordingly.

Resource Book: Page 107 (Use After Page 315)

NAME _____ DATE _____

Practice — For use after Lesson 9-1
Pictures in the Plane

Graph the given ordered pairs on a coordinate plane. (Use the grid paper in the teaching aids at the back of the book.) Connect each set of points in the order listed by drawing line segments. What have you drawn?

FIGURE A	FIGURE B	FIGURE C	FIGURE D
1. (−3, 4)	1. (9, 1)	1. (−5, 10)	1. (1, −6)
2. (4, 4)	2. (5, 1)	2. (−5, 9)	2. (2, −6)
3. (−3, 11)	3. (8, 8)	3. (−7, 9)	3. (3, −7)
4. (−3, 3)	4. (11, 8)	4. (−7, 10)	4. (3, −8)
5. (−8, 3)	5. (14, 1)	5. (−12, 10)	5. (2, −9)
6. (−7, 1)	6. (10, 1)	6. (−11, 11)	6. (1, −9)
7. (4, 1)	7. (10, −6)	7. (−7, 13)	7. (0, −8)
8. (5, 3)	8. (12, −6)	8. (−4, 14)	8. (0, −7)
9. (−3, 3)	9. (12, −7)	9. (1, 14)	9. (1, −6)
sailboat	10. (7, −7)	10. (4, 13)	10. (1½, −4)
	11. (7, −6)	11. (6, 14)	11. (2, −6)
	12. (9, −6)	12. (7, 12)	12. (4, −5)
	13. (9, 1)	13. (6, 12)	13. (3, −7)
	lamp	14. (7, 11)	14. (5, −7½)
		15. (5, 11)	15. (3, −8)
		16. (3, 10)	16. (4, −10)
		17. (3, 9)	17. (2, −9)
		18. (1, 9)	18. (1½, −11)
		19. (1, 10)	19. (1, −9)
		20. (−5, 10)	20. (−1, −10)
		turtle	21. (0, −8)
			22. (−2, −7½)
			23. (0, −7)
			24. (−1, −5)
			25. (1, −6)
			sun

Without drawing the figure, write the ordered pairs for moving Figure A down 5 spaces. Then test your answers by drawing the picture.

FIGURE E

1. (−3, −1)	*See answer key*
2. (4, −1)	*for drawings.*
3. (−3, 6)	
4. (−3, −2)	
5. (−8, −2)	
6. (−7, −4)	
7. (4, −4)	
8. (5, −2)	
9. (3, −2)	

PRE-ALGEBRA, An Accelerated Course
Copyright © 1985 by Houghton Mifflin Company. All rights reserved. Printed in U.S.A.

108

9-2 Equations in Two Variables

Objective *for pages 316–319*

■ To find solutions for an equation in two variables.

Teaching Suggestions

By this time students find it quite natural to substitute for variables. They need to be reminded, however, that we have agreed to the convention that ordered pairs are (x, y) pairs. Thus, when we find in Example 1 that $2(4) + (−1) = 7$ we see that $(4, −1)$ is a solution of $2x + y = 7$. This does not mean that $(4, −1)$ is a solution of $2y + x = 7$. Conversely, students should be warned to substitute correctly when checking a given number pair in an equation. In Example 1, $(4, −1)$ is a solution but $(−1, 4)$ is not because $2(−1) + 4 \neq 7$.

Although it is not necessary to point this out to students, it is worth noting that all the equations in this section are linear. Therefore they are also one-to-one functions on the real numbers; this guarantees that it is all right to substitute any value whatsoever for x (or y) and that there will be exactly one corresponding value for y (or x).

Students are sometimes reluctant to solve an equation for a variable. Treating the equation as if it were a formula can help here. In the equation $A = lw$, we may be given A and w, and need to solve for l.

After showing how to solve for y (Example 3), point out that often certain values of x are easier to use than others. For example, in $y = 3 − \frac{3}{5}x$ it is especially easy to use 0 and multiples of 5 for x.

The definition of a function is a very precise one. Illustrate what kinds of sets are not functions. The equation $x = y^2$ is not a function of x because the number pairs $(4, 2)$ and $(4, −2)$ both satisfy the equation. Graphically, the definition requires that a function can not cross any vertical line more than once; this requirement is sometimes called the vertical line test.

You may want to remind students that if the same variable occurs more than once in an equation, then the same value must be substituted for each occurrence of that variable.

Related Activities

To extend the concept of ordered pairs as solutions of equations in two variables, ask students to find ordered triples that are solutions of equations in three variables. For example, find solutions of the equation $2x + 3y − z = 1$. Also, determine whether a given triple is a solution of a given equation. For example, is $(−2, 3, −1)$ a solution of $3x − y − z + 8 = 0$? (It is, since $3(−2) − 3 − (−1) + 8 = −6 − 3 + 1 + 8 = 0$.)

To reinforce their understanding of number properties, have students look for solutions to equations that are true for all x and y, such as $x + y = y + x$, $(x + 6) + y = (x + y) + 6$, and $x(3 + y) = 3x + xy$. Also, ask them to consider solutions of equations representing special situations. For example, $x + y = y$ is true for any pair $(0, y)$, regardless of the value of y; $x + y = 0$ is true for all number pairs such that the numbers are opposites; $xy = x$ is true for any pair $(0, y)$ or $(x, 1)$.

Show the utility of the ideas in this section by presenting examples of equantities that are related to each other by linear equations. Use $D = 55T$ (distance traveled at 55 mi/h) and $A = 100(1 + r)$ (value of $100 original deposit after receiving r% simple interest) as examples.

9-3 Graphing Equations in the Coordinate Plane

Objective *for pages 320–323*

■ To graph a linear equation in two variables.

Teaching Suggestions

When students are told that the set of pairs satisfying a linear equation is infinite they sometimes respond by saying, "Then you can use anything!" This is not the case. For the equation $y = 2x$, the solution set is an infinite set of number pairs, but we must have, nevertheless, only pairs where the second number is twice the first.

Encourage students to extend the lines they graph, so they do not appear to lie in only a limited part of the plane. Students typically prefer to work with positive numbers and may draw lines in only the first quadrant. You could point out that, except for vertical and horizontal lines and lines through the origin, all line pass through three of the four quadrants.

Before working with intercepts, you may want to demonstrate that the equations of the x- and y-axes are $y = 0$ and $x = 0$ respectively. This may help when it becomes necessary to substitute 0 for y in order to find the x-intercept and vice versa.

Related Activities

To make the idea of the graph of a linear equation more concrete, number the rows and columns of your seating arrangement. Then have students stand if their coordinates satisfy a given requirement.

1. "Everyone whose column number is 2." (a vertical line)
2. "Everyone whose row number is 1." (a horizontal line)
3. "Everyone whose row number is the same as the column number." (a diagonal line bisecting the first quadrant)

You can anticipate graphs of inequalities by using requirements as follows:

4. "Everyone whose column number is more than 2." (all points to the right of the second column)
5. "Everyone whose row number is less than 3." (all points forward of the third row)

311c

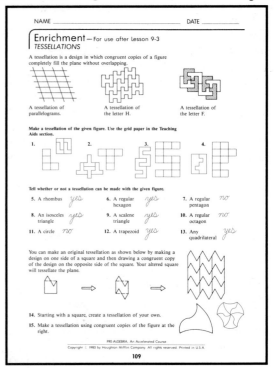

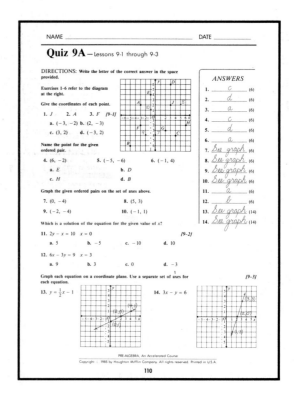

To enhance understanding of intercepts, use situations where the intercepts have a specific meaning.

1. Car rental. If it costs $20 plus 10¢ per mile to rent a car, then $20 is the y-intercept, when x represents mileage and y is total cost.
2. Price vs. quantity. If we graph a relationship between the price of a product and the number of units sold, we generally have the kind of graph shown. Here the x-intercept is a price so high that no sales are made. The y-intercept would represent the number of items people would want if the product were free.

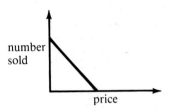

As a challenge for better students, show the graph of a line on an overhead transparency or a chalkboard coordinate grid. Have students determine an equation of the line. Remind them to check by taking two points of the line and substituting the coordinates in the equation they think is correct.

GRAPHING SYSTEMS IN THE COORDINATE PLANE

9-4 Graphing a System of Equations

Objective *for pages 324–327*

■ To solve systems of equations using graphs.

Teaching Suggestions

If students mastered the technique for graphing a linear equation in Section 9-3, they will have no trouble here. No new graphing skills are needed. The new skill is primarily that of locating a point of intersection of two lines and determining its coordinates.

Remind students of the ways two lines in a plane may be related. They may be parallel, they may intersect in only one point, or they may coincide. Be prepared for some debate over whether coincident lines are two lines

or one. Most people feel that there is only one line. The important point is that the same line may have any number of equations, so it is possible to have seemingly different equations whose graphs are the same line.

To strengthen students' understanding of linear equations, you might point out that not all equations are linear. Consequently it is conceivable that the graphs of two equations might intersect in more than two points, even though they do not coincide.

This is an opportunity to emphasize the importance of checking solutions. Reading solutions from a graph is a matter of approximation. You may get lucky and happen onto an exact solution, but there is no guarantee of this. Thus, after using graphs to "find" a solution, it is absolutely essential to substitute both values in both equations to verify the solution.

To demonstrate the importance of checking solutions, graph a system whose solution is not integral, such as $4x - y = 5$, $y - x = 2$. The exact solution is $(2\frac{1}{3}, 4\frac{1}{3})$. Working from the graphs, students can make a reasonable approximation such as $(2.3, 4.5)$. By substituting these coordinates in the equations, they will learn that this is not the exact solution.

Related Activities

To extend the concept of intersecting sets of points, have students consider intersections of a line and a circle and of two circles. Have them determine the possible numbers of intersections. For a line and a circle, there can be 0, 1, or 2 intersections. For two circles, there can be 0, 1, 2, or infinitely many intersections.

To provide a preview of future algebra courses, show that the system of linear equations below can be solved by using substitution.

$$(1)\ 2x + y = 5 \qquad (2)\ x - y = 4$$

a. Express (2) in terms of x.	$y = x - 4$
b. Substitute into (1).	$2x + x - 4 = 5$
c. Simplify.	$3x - 4 = 5$
d. Solve for x.	$3x = 9$
	$x = 3$
e. Substitute and solve for y.	$y = x - 4$
	$= 3 - 4 = -1$
f. The solution of the system:	$(3, -1)$

Have the students use substitution to solve Exercises 1–18 on pages 326–327.

To provide a challenge, have students think about the intersections of figures in space. They may want to use or visualize models, such as an orange cut in two (intersection of a plane and a sphere), a wall and a ceiling (intersection of two planes), and so on.

9-5 Using Graphs to Solve Problems

Objective *for pages 328–333*

■ To solve problems using graphs.

Teaching Suggestions

To help students prepare for calculating slopes, have them practice reading coordinates directly from the graph of a line. Show a graph and ask students to find the *y*-coordinate for a given *x*-coordinate and vice versa. For example, ask them to find the *y*-coordinate corresponding to an *x*-coordinate of −2, and the *x*-coordinate for a point with a *y*-coordinate of −2. This helps prepare for the work on slopes, and strengthens students' ability to read the kinds of graphs found in other courses and in magazine and newspaper articles.

Resource Book: Page 111 (Use After Page 333)

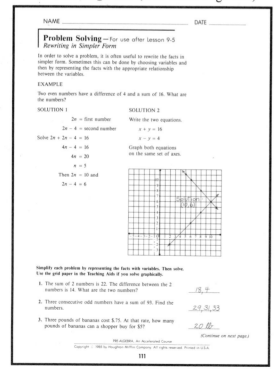

Resource Book: Page 112 (Use After Page 333)

NAME _____ DATE _____

Problem Solving—For use after Lesson 9-5 (continued)
Rewriting in Simpler Form

4. Boys and girls in a fitness class began with 15 jumping jacks. Each week, 20 more were added. How many jumping jacks will the class be doing in the sixth week? *115*

5. Jean Kroll has $176.18 in her checking account at the beginning of the third week of a month. She began the month with twice that much. If she spends an equal amount each week for expenses, how much will she have left in her account at the beginning of the 4th week? *$88.09*

6. A garden is enclosed by a quadrilateral. The fencing is 107 feet long. How long is each side if one side is twice the length of the first, another side is three times the length of the first increased by 1 ft, and the fourth side is three times the first decreased by 2 ft? *12 ft, 24 ft 37 ft, 34 ft*

7. On June 1, the water temperature in a small lake was 59°F. On June 15, it was 62°F. If the temperature continues to rise at a constant rate, what will be the water temperature on July 20? *69°*

8. Fast Manufacturing can produce 128 machine parts in 4 h. Speedy Tool Shop can produce 112 parts in 4 h. How long will it take both shops working together to produce 1260 parts? *21 h*

9. The second year at work, Jack earned $12,950. The fifth year, his salary was up to $15,800. He earned the same dollar amount in raise each year.

   a. What was his starting salary? *$12,000*

   b. How much was he earning in his eighth year with the company? *$18,650*

10. Five cooks worked 3 days to make 1500 loaves of bread for a convention. How many loaves can 20 cooks make in 5 days? *10,000*

11. A truck ran out of gas and is slowing down at a constant rate. Fifty feet after running out of gas, the truck was traveling at 20 mi/h. In 25 more feet, it was going only 10 mi/h.

    a. What was the truck's rate of speed when it first ran out of gas? *40 mi/h*

    b. What is the total distance it rolls to a stop after running out of gas? *100 ft*

Related Activities

To enhance the understanding of slope, graph several parallel lines on the same set of axes. Have students determine two points on each line and calculate the slope. Ask them what seems to be true about slopes of parallel lines. **They are equal.**

9-6 Graphing Inequalities

Objective *for pages 334–337*

■ To graph a linear inequality.

Teaching Suggestions

To convince students that the graph of an inequality should be a half-plane, consider the inequality $y \geq x + 1$ (page 334). Ask students to find solutions of the form $(2, y)$. They will readily see that they can use any value of y such that $y \geq 3$. Do the same for pairs $(-3, y)$, where y must satisfy $y \geq -2$.

If these points are graphed, it soon becomes clear that we are graphing the points on and above the line $y = x + 1$.

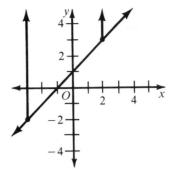

Students often make the mistake of assuming that any inequality with the symbol $>$ is an upper half-plane, and one with $<$ is always a lower half-plane. This is not true, as the inequality $2x - y < 3$ shows. Encourage students to test points above or below the line in the inequality. The points that satisfy the inequality will be in the half-plane to be shaded.

Students may find it amusing to note that in the graph at the right, A is above the line and B is below the line, even though A is below B.

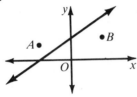

Related Activities

To provide a challenge for your abler students, introduce **linear programming,** a method used by economists to find the best combination of quantities. We need to find the maximum or minimum value of an expression on the points in a region on the coordinate plane. The region is usually defined by several inequalities. If the expression has a maximum or minimum value, it will occur at one of the corner points (the points of intersection). The ordered pair that produces the desired extreme is the solution.

Example: We intend to plant strawberries and raspberries. We want to know how many acres of each to plant in order to earn the most money. The constraints are represented by inequalities in which x represents the number of acres of strawberries, and y the number of acres of raspberries.

1. We can plant at most 2 acres of strawberries and 3 acres of raspberries. $x \le 2, y \le 3$
2. It will take 2 weeks to prepare and plant each acre of strawberries, and 1 week for each acre of raspberries. We have at most 5 weeks to do this work. $2x + y \le 5$

On the graph, the shaded region represents the intersection of the three inequalities. The corner points are $(0, 3)$, $(1, 3)$, $(2, 1)$, $(2, 0)$, and $(0, 0)$.

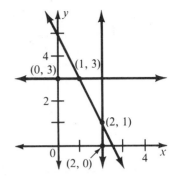

When we sell the fruit, we expect to receive $5000 per acre of strawberries, and $4000 per acre of raspberries. We want to maximize the equation $5000x + 4000y = E$, in which E represents our earnings. Substituting the coordinates of the corner points, we get: $(0, 3)$: 12,000; $(1, 3)$: 17,000; $(2, 1)$: 14,000; $(2, 0)$: 10,000. Planting 1 acre of strawberries and 3 acres of raspberries will earn the most money, $17,000.

Present the following problem: You run a factory that makes toasters and irons. You want to know how many hours per day to produce each product in order to earn the most money. Let x represent the number of hours toasters are produced, and y the number of hours irons are produced.

1. The machinery that produces toasters can be run 6 h per day. The machinery that produces irons can be run 8 h per day. Write inequalities representing these statements. $x \le 6; y \le 8$
2. The toaster machinery produces 4 toasters per hour. The iron machinery produces 2 irons per hour. The factory can produce at most 32 appliances per day. Write an inequality for the number of toasters and irons that can be produced per day. $4x + 2y \le 32$
3. Graph the three inequalities. What are the corner points? $(0, 8); (4, 8); (6, 4); (6, 0); (0, 0)$
4. You can sell each toaster for $20 and each iron for $15. How much do you earn per hour making toasters? making irons? Write an equation for your earnings. $80; $30; 80x + 30y = E$
5. Substitute the coordinates of the corner points into the equation. What are the earnings? $240; $560; $600; $480; $0
6. What is the maximum earnings? How many hours per day should you produce toasters? How many hours per day should you produce irons? $600, 6 h; 4 h

311f

Resource Book: Pages 113–116 (Use After Page 337)

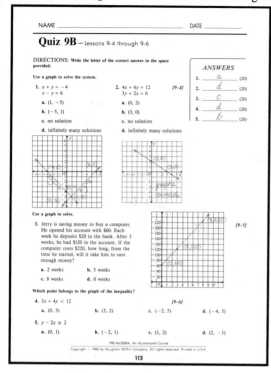

NAME _____ DATE _____

Quiz 9B — Lessons 9-4 through 9-6

DIRECTIONS: Write the letter of the correct answer in the space provided.

Use a graph to solve the system.

1. $x + y = -4$
   $x - y = 6$ *[9-4]*
   a. $(1, -5)$
   b. $(-5, 1)$
   c. no solution
   d. infinitely many solutions

2. $4x + 6y = 12$
   $3y + 2x = 6$
   a. $(0, 2)$
   b. $(3, 0)$
   c. no solution
   d. infinitely many solutions

ANSWERS
1. _*a*_ (20)
2. _*d*_ (20)
3. _*c*_ (20)
4. _*d*_ (20)
5. _*b*_ (20)

Use a graph to solve.

3. Jerry is saving money to buy a computer. He opened his account with $60. Each week he deposits $20 in the bank. After 3 weeks, he had $120 in the account. If the computer costs $220, how long, from the time he started, will it take him to save enough money?   *[9-5]*
   a. 2 weeks   b. 3 weeks
   c. 8 weeks   d. 0 weeks

Which point belongs to the graph of the inequality?

4. $3x + 4y < 12$ *[9-6]*
   a. $(0, 3)$ b. $(3, 2)$ c. $(-2, 5)$ d. $(-4, 5)$

5. $y - 2x \geq 2$
   a. $(0, 1)$ b. $(-2, 1)$ c. $(1, 2)$ d. $(2, -1)$

113

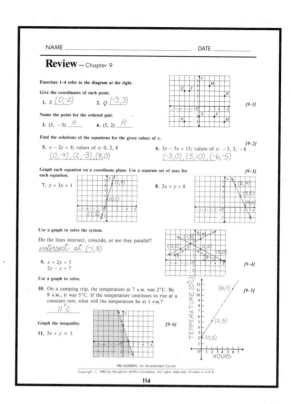

NAME _____ DATE _____

Review — Chapter 9

Exercises 1–4 refer to the diagram at the right.

Give the coordinates of each point.

1. S _(0,-2)_   2. Q _(-3,3)_   *[9-1]*

Name the point for the ordered pair.

3. $(5, -3)$ _H_   4. $(5, 2)$ _R_

Find the solutions of the equations for the given values of x.   *[9-2]*

5. $x - 2y = 8$; values of x: 0, 2, 8
   _(0,-4), (2,-3), (8,0)_

6. $3y - 5x = 15$; values of x: -3, 3, -6
   _(-3,0), (3,10), (-6,-5)_

Graph each equation on a coordinate plane. Use a separate set of axes for each equation.   *[9-3]*

7. $y = 3x + 1$ 8. $2x + y = 8$

Use a graph to solve the system.

Do the lines intersect, coincide, or are they parallel?
intersect at (-1,3)

9. $x + 2y = 5$
   $2y - x = 7$ *[9-4]*

Use a graph to solve.

10. On a camping trip, the temperature at 7 A.M. was 2°C. By 9 A.M., it was 5°C. If the temperature continues to rise at a constant rate, what will the temperature be at 1 P.M.?   *[9-5]*
    _11°C_

Graph the inequality.

11. $3x + y < 3$

114

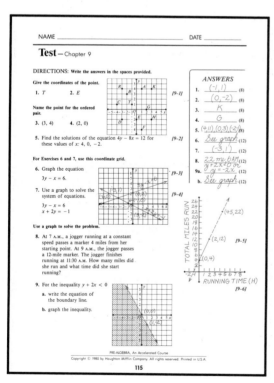

NAME _____ DATE _____

Test — Chapter 9

DIRECTIONS: Write the answers in the spaces provided.

Give the coordinates of the point.

1. T 2. E *[9-1]*

Name the point for the ordered pair.

3. $(3, 4)$ 4. $(2, 0)$

ANSWERS
1. _(-1, 1)_ (8)
2. _(0, -2)_ (8)
3. _K_ (8)
4. _G_ (8)
5. _(4,11),(0,3),(-2,-1)_ (12)
6. _See graph_ (12)
7. _(-3, 1)_ (12)
8. _22 mi, 6AM_ (12)
9a. _y + 2x = 0 or y = -2x_ (12)
9b. _See graph_ (12)

5. Find the solutions of the equation $4y - 8x = 12$ for these values of x: 4, 0, -2.   *[9-2]*

For Exercises 6 and 7, use this coordinate grid.

6. Graph the equation
   $3y - x = 6$.   *[9-3]*

7. Use a graph to solve the system of equations.   *[9-4]*
   $3y - x = 6$
   $x + 2y = -1$

Use a graph to solve the problem.

8. At 7 A.M., a jogger running at a constant speed passes a marker 4 miles from her starting point. At 9 A.M., the jogger passes a 12-mile marker. The jogger finishes running at 11:30 A.M. How many miles did she run and what time did she start running?   *[9-5]*

9. For the inequality $y + 2x < 0$ *[9-6]*
   a. write the equation of the boundary line.
   b. graph the inequality.

115

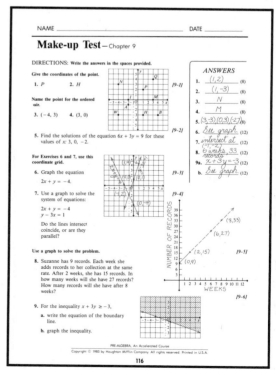

NAME _____ DATE _____

Make-up Test — Chapter 9

DIRECTIONS: Write the answers in the spaces provided.

Give the coordinates of the point.

1. P 2. H *[9-1]*

Name the point for the ordered pair.

3. $(-4, 3)$ 4. $(3, 0)$

ANSWERS
1. _(1, 2)_ (8)
2. _(1, -3)_ (8)
3. _N_ (8)
4. _M_ (8)
5. _(3,-3),(0,3),(-2,7)_ (8)
6. _See graph_ (12)
7. _intersect at (-1,-2)_ (12)
8. _6 weeks, 33 records_ (12)
9a. _x + 3y = -3_ (12)
9b. _See graph_ (12)

5. Find the solutions of the equation $6x + 3y = 9$ for these values of x: 3, 0, -2.   *[9-2]*

For Exercises 6 and 7, use this coordinate grid.

6. Graph the equation
   $2x + y = -4$.   *[9-3]*

7. Use a graph to solve the system of equations: *[9-4]*
   $2x + y = -4$
   $y - 3x = 1$
   Do the lines intersect coincide, or are they parallel?

Use a graph to solve the problem.

8. Suzanne has 9 records. Each week she adds records to her collection at the same rate. After 2 weeks, she has 15 records. In how many weeks will she have 27 records? How many records will she have after 8 weeks?   *[9-5]*

9. For the inequality $x + 3y \geq -3$,   *[9-6]*
   a. write the equation of the boundary line.
   b. graph the inequality.

116

311g

NAME _____ DATE _____

CUMULATIVE REVIEW — Chapters 1-9
Exercises

Simplify.

1. $7(4+5) + 20 - 2 + 3$ ___76___
2. $3(x+2) + x - 8$ ___$4x - 2$___
3. $(3^3 - 5) \times (23 - 4^2)$ ___154___
4. $4x + 3y - x + 2y - 2x$ ___$x + 5y$___
5. $40.2 + (4^3 - 16)$ ___442___
6. $3^2 + 18 \div 3$ ___15___

Write an equation or inequality for the word sentence.

7. Three less than five times a number t is thirty-seven. ___$5t - 3 = 37$___
8. Thirteen increased by the product of v and nine is greater than forty-eight. ___$13 - 9v > 48$___
9. The quotient when a number q is divided by four is equal to the sum of the number and six. ___$\frac{q}{4} > q + 6$___

Complete. Use $\pi \approx \frac{22}{7}$ if necessary.

10. If the circumference of a circle is 308, the radius is ___49___.
11. If the area of a square is 144 m², a side of the square is ___$12\,m$___.
12. If the diameter of a circle is 14, the area is ___154___.

Solve.

13. $5x + 9 = 8x + 12$ ___-1___
14. $t + \frac{2}{3} > 2\frac{3}{4}$ *all numbers greater than 2$\frac{1}{12}$*
15. $18 - 3x < 0$ *all numbers greater than 6*
16. What is 132% of 70? ___92.4___
17. What percent of 40 is 26? ___65%___
18. 48 is 75% of what number? ___64___
19. What is $\frac{1}{2}$% of 8? ___.25___

Write the fraction in lowest terms.

20. $\frac{18}{216}$ ___$\frac{1}{12}$___
21. $-\frac{32}{128}$ ___$-\frac{1}{4}$___
22. $\frac{13}{260}$ ___$\frac{1}{20}$___
23. $-\frac{45}{60}$ ___$-\frac{3}{4}$___

Match each equation with the ordered pair that satisfies the equation.

24. $3x + 2y = 6$ ___D___
25. $y = -2x + 7$ ___B___
26. $-2x + 6y = 0$ ___A___
27. $y - x = 1$ ___C___

A. (3, 1)
B. (−6, −7)
C. (7, 8)
D. (4, −3)

NAME _____ DATE _____

CUMULATIVE REVIEW — Chapters 1-9
Problems

Problem Solving Reminders
Here are some reminders that may help you solve some of the problems on this page.
• Determine whether a formula applies.
• Determine whether an equation can be used.
• Determine whether drawing a sketch will help.

1. The attendance at the second track meet of the season was 500 less than the 2500 that attended the first track meet. What was the percent of decrease in attendance? ___20%___
2. A jacket cost $12 less than twice the cost of a skirt. If a jacket cost $65, what was the cost of a skirt? ___$38.50___
3. A circle has a circumference of 11 m. What is the diameter? Use $\pi \approx \frac{22}{7}$. ___$3\frac{1}{2}\,m$___
4. Mark received 352 of the votes cast for president of the student body. His opponent received 448 votes. What fraction of the votes cast did Mark receive? ___$\frac{11}{25}$___
5. If two kinds of bricks have heights of 15 cm and 20 cm respectively, what is the least number of rows of each kind that will have the same height? *4 rows of 15 cm bricks; 3 rows of 20 cm bricks*
6. When the stock market opened at 10 A.M., HMC Corporation stock was priced at $56\frac{1}{2}$. After 2 h the stock had risen $3\frac{1}{4}$ points. In the next hour it fell $2\frac{3}{4}$ points. At closing it had fallen another point. What was the price at closing? ___$56___
7. Sara Sahekawa bought a new house for $84,000. Peter Smith bought a new condominium. If the new house cost 20% more than the condominium, what did the condominium cost? ___$70,000___
8. One fourth of those attending a concert left before intermission. When five more people left during intermission, 350 people had left. How many people attended the concert? ___1380___
9. A realtor is expecting an average price increase of 4% on homes this year. If a certain house sold for $80,000 last year, how much would it be expected to sell for this year? ___$83,200___

NAME _____ DATE _____

CUMULATIVE TEST — Chapters 7-9

DIRECTIONS: Write the answer in the space provided.

Chapter 7

1. What is the percent decrease from 35 to 28?
2. What is the percent increase from 60 to 180?
3. A sweater that regularly sells for $25 is on sale for $20. What is the percent discount?
4. At an end-of-season sale a lawnmower sells for $250. Two months later, the price is changed to $300. What is the percent of markup?
5. Mary Stuart earns a 6% commission on her net sales of merchandise at Riches Department Store. Her commission for last week was $555. What were her sales for the week?
6. James Tisdale sold software worth $18,000 between June 1 and September 1. If his commission was $3600, what was his percent of commission?
7. What is the simple interest on a $2000 loan for 2 yr at 18%?
8. A bank pays 9% interest compounded quarterly. How much will $3000 amount to after 6 mo?

Chapter 8

Solve.

9. $-3y + 7y = 36$
10. $z - 8z = -49$
11. $7 = 4x + 10x$
12. $3(t - 3) = 6$
13. $2(n - 3) + n = 12$
14. $-4(a - 3) + 2a = 20$

ANSWERS

1. ___20%___ (3)
2. ___200%___ (3)
3. ___20%___ (3)
4. ___20%___ (3)
5. ___$9250___ (3)
6. ___20%___ (3)
7. ___$720___ (3)
8. ___$3276.07___ (3)
9. ___9___ (3)
10. ___7___ (3)
11. ___$\frac{1}{2}$___ (3)
12. ___5___ (3)
13. ___6___ (3)
14. ___-4___ (3)

NAME _____ DATE _____

CUMULATIVE TEST — Chapters 7-9 (continued)

15. $2a = 4a - 2$
16. $36 + c = 9c$
17. $24y = 16y - 2$
18. $-7x + 5 = 3x$
19. $6(y - 3) = 2y + 12$
20. $-3(n + 4) + 5n = 12$
21. Find two consecutive integers whose sum is 43.

Solve.

22. $-6 + 12 > t$
23. $3v + 11 \le 4v - 21$
24. $2y + 6 \ge -4y$
25. $-6x + 2 + 3x - 3 \le -5x$

Chapter 9

Tell whether the ordered pair is a solution of the given equation.

$x - 4y = 2$

26. (0, −2)
27. (2, 0)
28. (−2, −1)

Solve the equation for y in terms of x.

29. $\frac{2}{3}x - y = 6$
30. $3x + 4y = 12$
31. $2y - 8x = 6$

Complete.

32. To find the solution of a system of equations, find the point of ___?___ of the graphs of the two equations.
33. If the graphs of two linear equations coincide, this system has ___?___ solution(s).

Is the ordered pair a solution of the system of equations?

34. (4, −2) $\begin{array}{l} x + y = 2 \\ x - y = 6 \end{array}$
35. (2, −6) $\begin{array}{l} 2x + y = -3 \\ x - y = 9 \end{array}$

Complete.

36. A basic property of a straight line graph is that its slope remains ___?___.
37. The boundary line for the graph $y > x + 5$ is shown as a ___?___ line.

ANSWERS

15. ___1___ (3)
16. ___$4\frac{1}{2}$___ (3)
17. ___$-\frac{1}{4}$___ (3)
18. ___$\frac{1}{2}$___ (3)
19. ___$7\frac{1}{2}$___ (3)
20. ___12___ (3)
21. ___21, 22___ (3)
22. *all the numbers less than 6* (3)
23. *all numbers greater than or equal to 32* (3)
24. *all numbers greater than or equal to −1* (3)
25. *all numbers less than or equal to $\frac{1}{2}$* (3)
26. ___no___ (2)
27. ___yes___ (2)
28. ___yes___ (2)
29. ___$y = \frac{2}{3}x - 6$___ (2)
30. ___$y = 3 - \frac{3}{4}x$___ (2)
31. ___$y = 4x + 3$___ (2)
32. ___intersection___ (2)
33. ___infinitely many___ (2)
34. ___yes___ (2)
35. ___no___ (2)
36. ___constant___ (2)
37. ___broken___ (2)

Teaching Suggestions
p. 311a

Related Activities p. 311a

Reading Mathematics

Students will learn the meaning of the following mathematical terms in this lesson:
*rectangular coordinate sys-
tem, origin, x-axis, y-axis,
coordinate plane, x-coordinate, abscissa, y-coordinate,
ordinate, ordered pair of
numbers, quadrant.*
    Point out the importance
of looking carefully at the
diagrams in this chapter. Students may not have much
experience with textbooks in
which diagrams are an integral part of the exposition.

Chalkboard Examples

Give the coordinates of the
point.

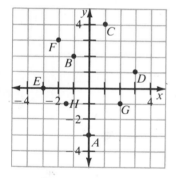

1. *A* (0, −3)
2. *F* (−2, 3)
3. *H* (−1.5, −1)
4. *D* (3, 1)

Name the point for the ordered pair.
5. (2, −1) *G*
6. (−1, 2) *B*
7. (−3, 0) *E*
8. (1, 4) *C*

Name the quadrant containing the point.
9. *B* II   10. *H* III
11. *D* I   12. *G* IV

312

9-1 The Coordinate Plane

We describe the position of a point on a number line by stating its
coordinate. Similarly, we can describe the position of a point in a plane
by stating a pair of coordinates that locate it in a **rectangular coordinate
system.** This system consists of two number lines perpendicular to each
other at point *O*, called the **origin.** The horizontal line is called the
x-axis, and the vertical line is called the **y-axis.** The positive direction is
to the right of the origin on the *x*-axis and upward on the *y*-axis. The
negative direction is to the left of the origin and downward.

Reading Mathematics: *Diagrams*
As you read text that is next to a diagram, stop after each sentence and relate
what you have read to what you see in the diagram. For example, as you
read the first paragraph next to the diagram below, locate point *M* on the
graph, and find the vertical line from *M* to the *x*-axis.

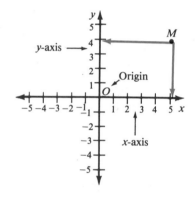

To assign a pair of coordinates to point *M* located in the **coordinate plane,** first draw a vertical
line from *M* to the *x*-axis. The point of intersection
on the *x*-axis is called the **x-coordinate,** or **abscissa.** The abscissa of *M* is 5.
    Next draw a horizontal line from *M* to the *y*-
axis. The point of intersection on the *y*-axis is
called the **y-coordinate,** or **ordinate.** The ordinate
of *M* is 4.
    Together, the abscissa and ordinate form an
ordered pair of numbers that are the coordinates of
a point. The coordinates of *M* are (5, 4).

EXAMPLE 1 Give the coordinates of each point.
    a. *F*   **b.** *S*   **c.** *P*   **d.** *T*

Solution   **a.** Point *F* has *x*-coordinate 4
                and *y*-coordinate −3.
                F has coordinates (4, −3).

            Similarly,

            b. *S* has coordinates (0, 2).

            c. *P* has coordinates (−3, 4).

            d. *T* has coordinates (−5, −5).

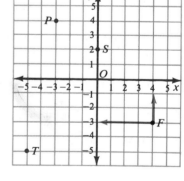

Notice that $(4, -3)$ and $(-3, 4)$ are coordinates of different points. In an ordered pair of numbers the x-coordinate is listed first, followed by the y-coordinate, in the form **(x, y).**

Just as each point in the plane is associated with exactly one ordered pair, each ordered pair of numbers determines exactly one point in the plane.

EXAMPLE 2 Graph these ordered pairs: $(-6, 5)$, $(5, -4)$, $(0, 3)$, $(-3, -2)$, and $\left(2\frac{1}{2}, 1\right)$.

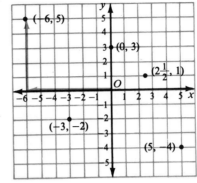

Solution First locate the x-coordinate on the x-axis. Then move up or down to locate the y-coordinate.

The x- and y-axes divide the coordinate plane into **Quadrants I, II, III,** and **IV.** The ranges of values for the x-coordinate and y-coordinate of any point in each quadrant are shown at the right.

II
$x < 0$
$y > 0$

I
$x > 0$
$y > 0$

III
$x < 0$
$y < 0$

IV
$x > 0$
$y < 0$

Class Exercises

Give the coordinates of the point.

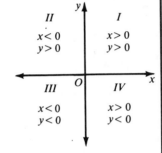

1. A (2, 1)   **2.** K (5, −1)   **3.** E (0, −3)

4. J (−2, −5)   **5.** L (3, 5)   **6.** F (−1, 3)

Name the point for the ordered pair.

7. $(5, 2)$ H   **8.** $(-6, 0)$ I

9. $(4, -5)$ D   **10.** $(-4, -2)$ G

11. $(-3, 5)$ C   **12.** $(-6, 3)$ B

Name the quadrant containing the point.

13. F II   **14.** D IV   **15.** H I   **16.** J III   **17.** K IV

The Coordinate Plane **313**

Give the coordinates of the point.

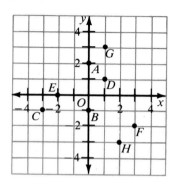

1. A (0, 2)

2. C (−3, −1)

3. E (−2, 0)

4. G (1, 3)

Name the point for the ordered pair.

5. (3, −2) F

6. (0, −1) B

7. (1, 1) D

8. (2, −3) H

Written Exercises

For Exercises 1–18, use the graph at the right.

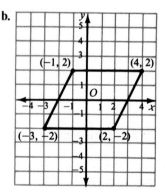

Give the coordinates of the point.

A   **1.** N   **2.** $\left(2\frac{1}{2}, -3\right)$ $\left(\frac{1}{P2}, -3\right)$ **3.** T   **4.** R

5. Q (−5, −5)   **6.** M   **7.** S (5, 1)   **8.** V (0, 3)

(−3, −2)   (0, −6)   (−1, 4)   (−5, 1)

Name the point for the ordered pair.

9. (4, −5) I

10. (−3, −2) Q

11. (−5, 1) V

12. $\left(\frac{5}{2}, -3\right)$ P

13. $\left(-\frac{7}{2}, 3\right)$ D

14. (1, −2) H

15. $\left(\frac{3}{2}, 1\right)$ W

16. (−1, 4) S

17. (0, −6) M

18. (0, 3) R

a. Graph the given ordered pairs on a coordinate plane.

b. Draw line segments to connect the points in the order listed and to connect the first and last points. Check students' graphs.

c. Name the closed figure as specifically as you can.

EXAMPLE   (−3, −2), (−1, 2), (4, 2), (2, −2)

Solution   a.

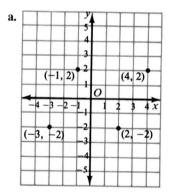

c. parallelogram

B **19.** (1, −2), (3, −2), (3, 4), (1, 4) rectangle

20. (0, 1), (3, −2), (6, 1), (3, 4) square

21. (0, −5), (0, 2), (−3, 6), (−3, −1) parallelogram

22. (−5, 0), (−1, 2), (1, 6), (−3, 4) rhombus

314   *Chapter 9*

We can translate a figure on a coordinate plane by changing the ordered pairs. We can reflect a figure on a coordinate plane by changing the signs of the ordered pairs.

a. Graph the given ordered pairs on a coordinate plane, connect the points in the order listed, and connect the first and last points.
b. Change the values of the coordinates as directed.
c. Graph and connect all the new points to form a second figure.
d. Identify the change as translation or reflection.

Check students' graphs.

C **23.** $(-5, 4)$, $(-2, 1)$, $(2, 1)$, $(2, 4)$
Decrease all y-coordinates by 3.
(*Hint:* $(-5, 4)$ becomes $(-5, 1)$)

24. $(1, 5)$, $(1, 1)$, $(5, 3)$
Decrease all x-coordinates by 2.

25. $(-2, -2)$, $(2, -2)$, $(4, -4)$, $(4, -6)$, $(1, -4)$, $(-1, -4)$, $(-4, -6)$, $(-4, -4)$
Increase all y-coordinates by 5.

26. $(-8, 4)$, $(-4, 4)$, $(-4, 5)$, $(-1, 3)$, $(-4, 1)$, $(-4, 2)$, $(-8, 2)$
Increase all x-coordinates by 9.

27. $(6, 5)$, $(2, 1)$, $(9, 3)$
Multiply all x-coordinates by -1.

28. $(1, 7)$, $(4, 2)$, $(7, 3)$, $(4, 8)$
Multiply all y-coordinates by -1.

Review Exercises

Complete.

1. If $x + 5 = 13$, then $x = \underline{\ ?\ }$. 8

2. If $8 + x = -1$, then $x = \underline{\ ?\ }$. -9

3. If $9x = 243$, then $x = \underline{\ ?\ }$. 27

4. If $-4x = 52$, then $x = \underline{\ ?\ }$. -13

5. If $2x + 11 = 1$, then $x = \underline{\ ?\ }$. -5

6. If $99 - 9x = 18$, then $x = \underline{\ ?\ }$. 9

7. If $-\frac{4}{5}x = 12$, then $x = \underline{\ ?\ }$. -15

8. If $9 + \frac{2}{3}x = 15$, then $x = \underline{\ ?\ }$. 9

▌▌▌ Challenge

Set up a pair of coordinate axes on graph paper. Connect the following points in the order given:

$$(-9, 3),\ (-4, 3),\ (-1.5, 1),\ (2, -1),$$
$$(2, -4),(8.5, -5),\ (9.5, -1),\ (2, -1)$$

Do you recognize the figure? (*Hint:* It is a well-known group of stars that is part of the constellation *Ursa Major*.) The Big Dipper

The Coordinate Plane **315**

Reading Mathematics

Students will learn the meaning of the following mathematical term in this lesson: *function*.

The word *solution* is by now familiar. Point out that the same word may be used in slightly different ways as one progresses through mathematics. Here, a solution is a number pair, not a single number.

9-2 Equations in Two Variables

The equation

$$x + y = 5$$

has two variables, x and y. A solution to this equation consists of two numbers, one for each variable. The solution can be expressed as an ordered pair of numbers, (x, y). There are many ordered pairs that satisfy this equation. Some solutions are

$$(-3, 8), (5, 0), (4, 1), (0, 5), (11, -6).$$

In fact, there are *infinitely* many ordered pairs that satisfy this equation.

EXAMPLE 1 Tell whether each ordered pair is a solution of the equation $2x + y = 7$.

    a. $(4, -1)$ **b.** $(-4, 1)$

Solution Substitute the given values of x and y in the equation.

  a. $2x + y = 7$ **b.** $2x + y = 7$

        $2(4) + (-1) \stackrel{?}{=} 7$ $2(-4) + 1 \stackrel{?}{=} 7$

               $8 - 1 \stackrel{?}{=} 7$ $-8 + 1 \stackrel{?}{=} 7$

                    $7 = 7$ $-7 \neq 7$

    $(4, -1)$ is a solution. $(-4, 1)$ is not a solution.

An equation in the two variables x and y establishes a correspondence between values of x and values of y. To find a solution of a given equation in x and y, we can choose any value for x, substitute it in the equation, and solve for the corresponding value for y.

EXAMPLE 2 Give one solution of the equation $x - 3y = 2$.

Solution Choose any value for x. For example, if $x = 14$:

$$x - 3y = 2$$
$$14 - 3y = 2$$
$$-3y = 2 - 14$$
$$y = \frac{-12}{-3} = 4$$

The values $x = 14$ and $y = 4$ correspond.

$(14, 4)$ is one solution of the equation.

To find the value of y corresponding to any given value of x, we could substitute the value of x into a given equation and solve for y, as in Example 2. An easier method is to solve for y in terms of x first, and then substitute, as in Example 3.

EXAMPLE 3 Find the solutions for $2x + 3y = 6$ for the following values of x: $-9, -3, 0, 3, 6$.

Solution First solve for y in terms of x by writing an equation with y on one side and x on the other.

$$2x + 3y = 6$$
$$3y = 6 - 2x$$
$$y = 2 - \frac{2}{3}x$$

Then substitute the values of x in the new equation and solve for the corresponding values of y.

x	$y = 2 - \frac{2}{3}x$	(x, y)
-9	$2 - \frac{2}{3}(-9) = 8$	$(-9, 8)$
-3	$2 - \frac{2}{3}(-3) = 4$	$(-3, 4)$
0	$2 - \frac{2}{3}(0) = 2$	$(0, 2)$
3	$2 - \frac{2}{3}(3) = 0$	$(3, 0)$
6	$2 - \frac{2}{3}(6) = -2$	$(6, -2)$

Thus $(-9, 8)$, $(-3, 4)$, $(0, 2)$, $(3, 0)$, and $(6, -2)$ are solutions of the equation for the given values of x.

Notice in the table above that each given value of x corresponds to exactly one value of y. In general, any set of ordered pairs such that no two different ordered pairs have the same x-coordinate is called a **function**. An equation, as the one above, that produces such a set of ordered pairs defines a function.

The Coordinate Plane **317**

Tell whether the ordered pair is a solution of the equation.

1. $2x - y = 5$; $(4, 3)$ **Yes**

2. $3y + x = 10$; $(3, 1)$ **No**

Solve the equation for y in terms of x.

3. $4x + 2y = 5$

  $y = 2\frac{1}{2} - 2x$

4. $3x - 4y = 12$

  $y = \frac{3}{4}x - 3$

If $2y - x - 6 = 0$, give the value of y such that the ordered pair is a solution of the equation.

5. $x = 1$ $3\frac{1}{2}$

6. $x = -2$ 2

7. $x = 0$ 3

8. $x = -6$ 0

Tell whether the ordered pair is a solution of the equation.

1. $-x + y = 5$
   a. $(0, 5)$ Yes
   b. $(5, 0)$ No
   c. $(-3, 2)$ Yes
   d. $(4, 1)$ No

2. $2x - 5y = -4$
   a. $(-2, 0)$ Yes
   b. $(3, 2)$ Yes
   c. $(0, 1)$ No
   d. $(8, 4)$ Yes

Solve the equation for y in terms of x.

3. $3x - y = 10$
   $y = 3x - 10$

4. $6x + 3y = 5$
   $y = -2x + \frac{5}{3}$

23. a. $y = x + 7$
    b. $(2, 9), (-5, 2), (7, 14)$

24. a. $y = -x - 1$
    b. $(3, -4), (1, -2),$
    $(-2, 1)$

Class Exercises

Tell whether the ordered pair is a solution of the given equation.

$2x + y = 7$

1. $(2, 3)$ yes   2. $(1, 5)$ yes   3. $(7, 0)$ no   4. $(0, 7)$ yes

$x - 3y = 1$

5. $(2, 1)$ no   6. $(4, 1)$ yes   7. $(7, 2)$ yes   8. $(-2, 1)$ no

Solve the equation for y in terms of x.

9. $x - y = 5$ $y = x - 5$ 10. $x - y = 9$ $y = x - 9$ 11. $-3x + y = 7$
$y = 3x + 7$

If $y = x - 12$, give the value of y such that the ordered pair is a solution of the equation.

12. $(9, ?)$ -3 13. $(-4, ?)$ -16 14. $(0, ?)$ -12 15. $(-6, ?)$ -18

Written Exercises

Tell whether the ordered pair is a solution of the given equation.

A $-x + 3y = 15$

1. $(0, 5)$ yes   2. $(6, -7)$ no   3. $(6, 7)$ yes   4. $(-3, 6)$ no

$x - 4y = 12$

5. $(4, 2)$ no   6. $(-6, -12)$ no   7. $(0, 3)$ no   8. $\left(13, \frac{1}{4}\right)$ yes

$3x - 2y = 8$

9. $(1, 6)$ no   10. $(0, 4)$ no   11. $(4, 0)$ no   12. $\left(3, \frac{1}{2}\right)$ yes

$-5x - 2y = 18$

13. $(-2, -4)$ yes   14. $(-4, 1)$ yes   15. $\left(1, -\frac{23}{2}\right)$ yes   16. $(0, 0)$ no

Solve the equation for y in terms of x.

17. $2x + y = 7$ $y = -2x + 7$ 18. $-8x + 5y = 10$ $y = \frac{8}{5}x + 2$ 19. $-12x + 3y = 48$
$y = 4x + 16$

20. $4x - 9y = 36$ $y = \frac{4}{9}x - 4$ 21. $x - \frac{3}{2}y = 3$ $y = \frac{2}{3}x - 2$ 22. $5x - 4y = 20$
$y = \frac{5}{4}x - 5$

a. **Solve the equation for y in terms of x.**
b. **Find the solutions of the equation for the given values of x.**

23. $y - x = 7$
    values of x: $2, -5, 7$

24. $x + y = -1$
    values of x: $3, 1, -2$

318   *Chapter 9*

25. $-x + 2y = 10$
values of x: 4, 0, 6

26. $x - 3y = 12$
values of x: -3, 6, 12

27. $x + 4y = 20$
values of x: 4, -8, 0

28. $-x - 2y = 8$
values of x: -6, -2, 10

B **29.** $3x - 2y = 6$
values of x: 4, -2, -8

30. $-2x + 3y = 12$
values of x: 3, -3, -12

31. $2y - x = 5$
values of x: 3, 5, -1

32. $-3y + x = 7$
values of x: 1, 7, -5

33. $2y - 5x = 6$
values of x: 2, 1, -3

34. $4y - 3x = 1$
values of x: 9, -1, -5

Give any three ordered pairs that are solutions of the equation. Answers may vary.

35. $y + x = -1$
(0, -1), (1, -2), (2, -3)

36. $x - y = 6$
(0, -6), (1, -5), (2, -4)

37. $x + y = 0$
(0, 0), (1, -1), (2, -2)

38. $4y - x = 7$
$\left(0, 1\frac{3}{4}\right)$, (1, 2), ($-3$, 1)

39. $5x - y = -5$
(0, 5), (1, 10), (-1, 0)

40. $-3x - 2y = 0$
(0, 0), (2, -3), (-2, 3)

41. $2x - 3y = 12$
(0, -4), (3, -2), (-3, -6)

42. $-\frac{1}{4}y - x = 0$
(0, 0), (1, -4), (2, -8)

43. $-x + \frac{1}{2}y = 3$
(0, 6), (1, 8), (2, 10)

Write an equation that expresses a relationship between the coordinates of each ordered pair. Answers may vary.

EXAMPLE   (1, 4), (2, 3), (5, 0), (-1, 6)

Solution   Notice that all the coordinates share a common property: the sum of the coordinates in each pair is 5. You can express this relationship by the equation $x + y = 5$.

C **44.** (7, 6), (11, 10), (4, 3) $x - y = 1$

45. (3, -3), (6, -6), (-4, 4) $x + y = 0$

46. (-2, -4), (-3, -5), (4, 2) $x - y = 2$

47. (3, -6), (-3, 0), (6, -9)
$x + y = -3$

Review Exercises

Solve.

1. $8a = 24$ 3

2. $6 - 5m = 11$ -1

3. $6t - 31 = 137$ 28

4. $-7x + 4 = -10$ 2

5. $9c = 18 + 3c$ 3

6. $\frac{4}{5}y = 16$ 20

7. $2 + \frac{7}{8}d = -47$ -56

8. $-10 - \frac{2}{3}f = 12$ -33

9. $5(8 + 2h) = 0$ -4

The Coordinate Plane   **319**

Reading Mathematics

Students will learn the meaning of the following mathematical terms in this lesson: *table of values, graph of an equation, y-intercept, x-intercept, linear equation in two variables.*

9-3 Graphing Equations in the Coordinate Plane

The equation in two variables

$$x + 2y = 6$$

has infinitely many solutions. The **table of values** below lists some of the solutions. When we graph the solutions on a coordinate plane, we find that they all lie on a straight line.

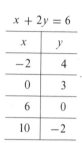

$x + 2y = 6$

x	y
-2	4
0	3
6	0
10	-2

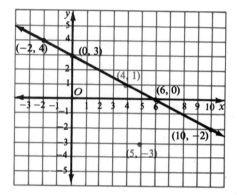

If we choose any other point on this line, we will find that the coordinates also satisfy the equation. For example, the ordered pair $(4, 1)$ is a solution:

$$x + 2y = 6$$
$$4 + 2(1) = 6$$

If we choose a point *not* on this line, such as the graph of $(5, -3)$, we find that its coordinates *do not* satisfy the equation:

$$x + 2y = 6$$
$$5 + 2(-3) \neq 6$$

The graph of an ordered pair is on the line if and only if it is a solution of the equation. The set of all points that are the graphs of solutions of a given equation is called the **graph of the equation.**

Note that the graph of $x + 2y = 6$ crosses the y-axis at $(0, 3)$. The y-coordinate of a point where a graph crosses the y-axis is called the **y-intercept** of the graph. In this case, the y-intercept is 3. Since the graph also crosses the x-axis at $(6, 0)$, the **x-intercept** of the graph is 6.

In general, any equation that can be written in the form

$$ax + by = c$$

where x and y are variables and a, b, and c are numbers (with a and b

320   *Chapter 9*

not both zero), is called a **linear equation in two variables** because its graph is always a straight line in the plane.

In order to graph a linear equation, we need to graph only two points whose coordinates satisfy the equation and then join them by means of a line. It is wise, however, to graph a third point as a check.

EXAMPLE Graph the equation $x + 3y = 6$.

Solution First find three points whose coordinates satisfy the equation. It is usually easier to start with the y-intercept and the x-intercept, that is, $(0, y)$ and $(x, 0)$.

If $x = 0$: $\quad 0 + 3y = 6$ $\qquad\qquad$ If $y = 0$: $\quad x + 3(0) = 6$
$\qquad\qquad\qquad\quad 3y = 6$ $\qquad\qquad\qquad\qquad\qquad\qquad x = 6$
$\qquad\qquad\qquad\qquad y = 2$

As a check, if $x = 3$: $\quad 3 + 3y = 6$
$\qquad\qquad\qquad\qquad\qquad\quad 3y = 3$
$\qquad\qquad\qquad\qquad\qquad\quad\; y = 1$

$x + 3y = 6$

x	y
0	2
6	0
3	1

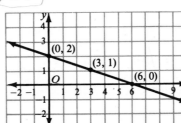

Class Exercises

Find three solutions of the linear equation. Include those that are in the form $(0, y)$ and $(x, 0)$. Answers may vary.

1. $x - y = 7$ $\qquad\qquad$ **2.** $y + x = -4$ $\qquad\qquad$ **3.** $-x - 2y = 8$

4. $3y - x = 9$ $\qquad\qquad$ **5.** $2x + y = 10$ $\qquad\qquad$ **6.** $3x - 2y = 3$

7. $y = x$ $\qquad\qquad\qquad$ **8.** $y = 3x$ $\qquad\qquad\qquad$ **9.** $y = \frac{1}{2}x$

Written Exercises

A 1–9. Graph each equation in Class Exercises 1–9. Use a separate set of coordinate axes for each equation. Check students' graphs.

The Coordinate Plane **321**

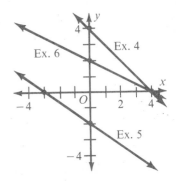

Give the coordinates of each point.

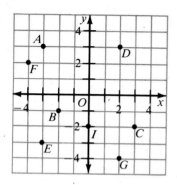

1. D (2, 3)
2. B (−2, −1)
3. I (0, −2)
4. A (−3, 3)

Name the point for the given ordered pair.

5. (−4, 2) F
6. (2, −4) G
7. (−3, −3) E
8. (3, −2) C

Graph the ordered pairs on one set of axes.

9. (−2, −1) 10. (4, −4)
11. (−1, 3)   12. (1, 2)
13. (−4, 1)   14. (0, −3)

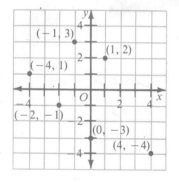

Graph the equation on a coordinate plane. Use a separate set of axes for each equation. Check students' graphs.

10. $x + y = 5$

11. $x - 6 = y$

12. $y - x = 4$

13. $y + x = -3$

14. $2x - y = 10$

15. $8x + 2y = 8$

16. $3y + x = 0$

17. $3x - y = -6$

18. $-2x + 3y = 12$

19. $2y - \frac{1}{2}x = 4$

20. $\frac{1}{3}y + 2x = 3$

21. $4y - 3x = 12$

22. $4x - 3y = 6$

23. $-2x + 5y = 5$

24. $\frac{1}{2}y + 2x = 3$

B 25. $\frac{x + y}{3} = 2$

26. $\frac{x - y}{4} = -1$

27. $\frac{3x - y}{2} = 3$

28. $\frac{2x + y}{3} = 1$

29. $\frac{x - 2y}{3} = -4$

30. $\frac{x + 3}{4} = y$

31. $\frac{3x - 1}{2} = y$

32. $\frac{-3y + 2x}{4} = -2$

33. $\frac{-4x + 3y}{6} = -4$

Graph the equation. Use a separate set of axes for each equation.
Check students' graphs.

EXAMPLE $y = 6$

Solution   Rewrite the equation in the form

$$y = 0x + 6.$$

Find three solutions.

If $x = -1$: $y = 0(-1) + 6 = 6$

If $x = 2$: $y = 0(2) + 6 = 6$

If $x = 3$: $y = 0(3) + 6 = 6$

Three solutions are (−1, 6), (2, 6), and (3, 6). Graph these points and draw the line.

The graph of $y = 6$ is a horizontal line.

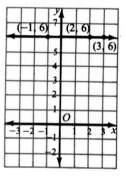

34. $y = 2$

35. $x = -4$

36. $y = 0$

37. $y = -3$

38. $x = 6$

39. $y = \frac{3}{2}$

C 40. Graph the equation $y = x^2$ by graphing the points with x-coordinates −3, −2, −1, 0, 1, 2, and 3. Join the points by means of a curved line. (This curve is called a **parabola**.) Check students' graphs.

322   *Chapter 9*

41. Graph the equation $xy = 12$ by graphing the points with x-coordinates 1, 3, 6, and 12. Join the points by means of a curved line. On the same set of axes, graph the points with x-coordinates -1, -3, -6, and -12. Join the points by means of a curved line. (This two-branched curve is called a **hyperbola**.) Check students' graphs.

Graph the equation using the following values of x: -5, -2, 0, 2, 5. Join the points by means of a straight line. Check students' graphs.

42. $y = |x|$ **43.** $y = -|x|$ **44.** $y = |x - 2|$ **45.** $y - 4 = |x|$

For what value of k is the graph of the given ordered pair in the graph of the given equation?

46. $(3, -2);\ 2y + kx = 14$ 6   **47.** $(-5, 4);\ 3x - ky = -12$ $-\frac{3}{4}$

Self-Test A

Exercises 1–6 refer to the diagram. Give the coordinates of each point.

1. M $(-3, 6)$ **2.** Z $(4, -4)$ **3.** L $(6, 6)$

Name the point for the given ordered pair.

4. $(-6, -3)$ C **5.** $(2, 2)$ T **6.** $(-5, 3)$ P

[9-1]

Graph the given ordered pairs on one set of axes. Check students' graphs.

7. $(-3, 5)$ **8.** $(9, 7)$ **9.** $(-4, -8)$

10. $(11, -10)$ **11.** $(0, -2)$ **12.** $(-4, 2)$

Find the solutions of the equation for the given values of x.

13. $4y - x = 2$
values of x: 0, -4, 9
$\left(0, \frac{1}{2}\right), \left(-4, -\frac{1}{2}\right), \left(9, 2\frac{3}{4}\right)$

14. $y + 2x = 6$
values of x: -3, $\frac{1}{2}$, 11
$(-3, 12), \left(\frac{1}{2}, 5\right), (11, -16)$

[9-2]

Graph each equation on a coordinate plane. Use a separate set of axes for each equation. Check students' graphs.

15. $y = x - 1$ **16.** $y = 2x$ **17.** $4x - y = 9$ **18.** $x = 7$ [9-3]

Self-Test answers and Extra Practice are at the back of the book.

Find the solutions of the equation for the given values of x.

15. $3x - y = 5$
values of x:
0, 2, -3, -5, 4
-5, 1, -14, -20, 7

16. $-x + 2y = -3$
values of x:
3, -3, -1, 0, 7
0, -3, -2, $-1\frac{1}{2}$, 2

Graph each equation on a coordinate plane. Use a separate set of axes for each equation.

17. $y = x + 3$

18. $y = 2x - 2$

19. $3x + y = 3$

20. $y = -3$

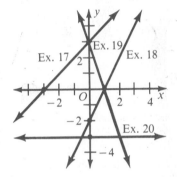

9-4 Graphing a System of Equations

Two equations in the same variables are called a **system of equations.** If the graphs of two linear equations in a system have a point in common, the coordinates of that point must be a solution of both equations. We can find a solution of a system of equations such as

$$x - y = 2$$
$$x + 2y = 5$$

by finding the *point of intersection* of the graphs of the two equations.

The graphs of the two equations above are shown on the same set of axes. The point with coordinates $(3, 1)$ appears to be the point of intersection of the graphs. To check whether $(3, 1)$ satisfies the given system, we substitute its coordinates in both equations:

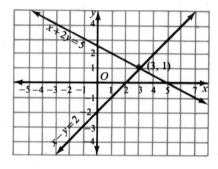

$$x - y = 2 \qquad x + 2y = 5$$
$$3 - 1 = 2 \qquad 3 + 2(1) = 5$$

Since the coordinates satisfy both equations, $(3, 1)$ is the solution of the given system of equations.

EXAMPLE 1 Use a graph to solve the system of equations:

$$y - x = 4$$
$$3y + x = 8$$

Solution First make a table of values for each equation, then graph both equations on one set of axes.

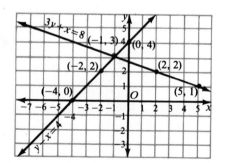

$y - x = 4$		$3y + x = 8$	
x	y	x	y
0	4	-1	3
-4	0	5	1
-2	2	2	2

The point of intersection appears to be $(-1, 3)$.

324 *Chapter 9*

To check, substitute the coordinates $(-1, 3)$ in both equations:

$$y - x = 4 \qquad\qquad 3y + x = 8$$
$$3 - (-1) \overset{?}{=} 4 \qquad\quad 3(3) + (-1) \overset{?}{=} 8$$
$$3 + 1 = 4 \checkmark \qquad\qquad 9 - 1 = 8 \checkmark$$

The solution for the given system is $(-1, 3)$.

EXAMPLE 2 Use a graph to solve the system of equations: $2y - x = 2$
$$2y - x = -4$$

Solution Make a table of values for each equation and graph both equations on one set of axes.

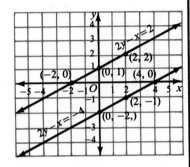

2y − x = 2			2y − x = −4	
x	y		x	y
0	1		0	−2
−2	0		4	0
2	2		2	−1

The graphs do not intersect; they are **parallel lines.** Thus, the system has *no solution.*

A system may have infinitely many solutions, as the following example illustrates.

EXAMPLE 3 Use a graph to solve the system of equations: $6x + 3y = 18$
$$2x + y = 6$$

Solution Make a table of values for each equation and graph both equations on one set of axes.

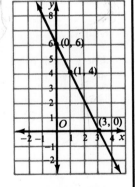

6x + 3y = 18			2x + y = 6	
x	y		x	y
0	6		0	6
3	0		3	0
1	4		1	4

The graphs *coincide.* The coordinates of all points on the line satisfy both equations. This system has *infinitely many solutions.*

The Coordinate Plane **325**

To solve a system of equations, first graph the equations on one set of axes. Then consider:

If the graphs intersect, the system has one solution. The coordinates of the point of intersection form the solution.

If the graphs are parallel, the system has no solution.

If the graphs coincide, the system has infinitely many solutions.

Class Exercises

Is the ordered pair a solution of the system of equations?

1. $(4, -1)$ $x + y = 3$ yes
$x - y = 5$

2. $(5, -1)$ $x + y = -6$ no
$x - y = 4$

3. $(3, 1)$ $x + 2y = 5$ yes
$x - y = 2$

4. $(-4, -4)$ $2x + y = -12$ yes
$x - y = 0$

5. A system of two linear equations has no solution. What does the graph of this system look like? parallel lines

6. The coordinates $(-3, -1)$, $(0, 0)$, and $(3, 1)$ are solutions of a system of two linear equations. What does the graph of this system look like? a single line through the origin

7. The graphs of two equations appear to intersect at $(-4, 5)$. How can you check to see whether $(-4, 5)$ satisfies the system? Substitute $(-4, 5)$ in both equations.

Written Exercises

Use a graph to solve the system. Do the lines intersect or coincide, or are they parallel?

A **1.** $x + y = 6$ (3, 3);
$x - y = 0$ intersect

2. $x + y = 5$ infinitely many solutions; coincide
$3y + 3x = 15$

3. $x - y = -3$ no solution; parallel
$x - y = 2$

4. $x - y = 4$ (2, −2);
$x + y = 0$ intersect

5. $-2y - 2x = -6$
$x + y = 3$ infinitely many solutions; coincide

6. $2x - y = 4$
$y + 2x = 2$
$\left(1\frac{1}{2}, -1\right)$; intersect

326 *Chapter 9*

7. $x - 2y = 8$ no solution;
$2y - x = 4$ parallel

8. $6y + 4x = 24$ infinitely many
$2x + 3y = 12$ solutions;
coincide

9. $3x - y = -6$
$y - x = 6$

10. $x - 2y = -8$ $(-2, 3)$;
$2y - 3x = 12$ intersect

11. $7x - 14y = 70$ infinitely many
$x - 2y = 10$ solutions;
coincide

12. $3x + 2y = 6$
$3x + 2y = 12$

B **13.** $2x + \frac{3}{2}y = 2$ $(-2, 4)$;
intersect
$x + 2y = 6$

14. $x + 3y = 2$ $(-1, 1)$;
intersect
$2x + 5y = 3$

15. $\frac{2}{3}x - y = 2$
$6y - 4x = 18$

16. $3x - 5y = 9$ $(-2, -3)$;
intersect
$\frac{1}{2}x - 2y = 5$

17. $\frac{3}{2}x + 2y = 4$ $(4, -1)$;
intersect
$2x + 5y = 3$

18. $-7x - 2y = 7$
$-\frac{7}{2}x - y = 1$

C **19.** Find the value of k in the equations

$$6x - 4y = 12$$
$$3x - ky = 6 \quad 2$$

such that the system has infinitely many solutions.

20. Find the value of k in the equations

$$5x - 3y = 15$$
$$kx - 9y = 30 \quad 15$$

such that the system has no solution.

Review Exercises

Write in lowest terms.

1. $\frac{18}{16}$ $1\frac{1}{8}$

2. $\frac{12}{27}$ $\frac{4}{9}$

3. $\frac{49}{56}$ $\frac{7}{8}$

4. $\frac{18}{81}$ $\frac{2}{9}$

5. $\frac{24}{30}$ $\frac{4}{5}$

6. $\frac{48}{144}$ $\frac{1}{3}$

7. $\frac{13}{169}$ $\frac{1}{13}$

8. $\frac{17}{101}$ $\frac{17}{101}$

▌▌▌ **Calculator Key-In**

On Roger's first birthday he received a dime from his parents. For each
birthday after that, they doubled the money. How much will Roger
receive for his eighteenth birthday? $13,107.20

The Coordinate Plane **327**

Reading Mathematics

Students will learn the meaning of the following mathematical term in this lesson: *slope of a line*.

Many students have never dealt with problems that require this degree of analysis and persistence through several stages. You will be doing them a favor if you can encourage them to read, and re-read, problems carefully and to build up their solutions step by step.

9-5 Using Graphs to Solve Problems

In the drawing at the left below, the slope of the hill changes. It becomes steeper partway up, and then flattens out near the top.

 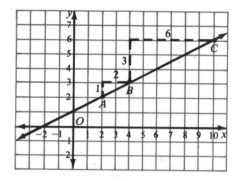

On the other hand, the slope of the straight line shown in the graph above does not change. It remains constant. The **slope of a line** is the ratio of the change in the y-coordinate to the change in the x-coordinate when moving from one point on the line to another.

Moving from A to B: slope $= \dfrac{\text{change in } y}{\text{change in } x} = \dfrac{1}{2}$

Moving from B to C: slope $= \dfrac{\text{change in } y}{\text{change in } x} = \dfrac{3}{6} = \dfrac{1}{2}$

A basic property of a straight line is that its slope is constant.

A straight-line graph sometimes expresses the relationship between two physical quantities. For example, such a graph can represent the conditions of temperature falling at a constant rate or of a hiker walking at a steady pace. If we can locate two points of a graph that is known to be a straight line, then we can extend the graph and get more information about the relationship.

EXAMPLE 1   The temperature at 8 A.M. was 3°C. At 10 A.M. it was 7°C. If the temperature climbed at a constant rate from 6 A.M. to 12 noon, what was it at 6 A.M.? What was it at 12 noon?

Solution   Set up a pair of axes.

Let the coordinates on the horizontal axis represent the hours after 6 A.M.

Let the vertical axis represent the temperature.

328   *Chapter 9*

Use the information given to plot the points.

At 8 A.M., or 2 h after 6 A.M., the temperature was 3°C.
This gives us the point (2, 3).

At 10 A.M., or 4 h after 6 A.M., the temperature was 7°C.
This gives us the point (4, 7).

Since we know that the temperature climbed at a constant rate, we can first graph the two points and then draw a straight line through them.

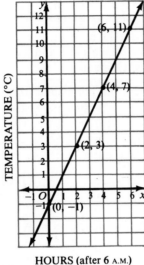

HOURS (after 6 A.M.)

We can see that the line crosses the vertical axis at −1. Therefore, at 6 A.M., or 0 h after 6 A.M., the temperature was −1°C. At 12 noon, or 6 h after 6 A.M., the temperature was 11°C.

Sometimes we are given information about the relationship between two quantities. We can use the information to write and graph an equation. We can then read additional information from the graph.

EXAMPLE 2 Maryanne uses 15 Cal of energy in stretching before she runs and 10 Cal for every minute of running time. Write an equation that relates the total number of Calories (y) that she uses when she stretches and goes for a run to the number of minutes (x) that she spends running. Graph this equation. From your graph, determine how long Maryanne must run after stretching to use a total of 55 Cal.

(The solution is on the next page.)

The Coordinate Plane **329**

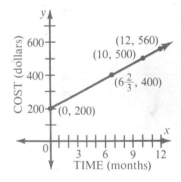

Solution   Consider the facts given:
15 Cal used in stretching
10 Cal/min used in running

Use the variables suggested.
If x = running time in minutes, then $10x$ = Cal used in running for x min.
If y = Cal used in stretching *and* running for x min, then $y = 15 + 10x$.

Make a table of values to locate two points. Because the number of Calories is large compared with the number of minutes, mark the vertical axis in intervals of 5 and the horizontal axis in intervals of 1.

$y = 15 + 10x$

x	y
0	15
2	35

Plot the points and draw the graph.

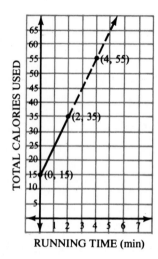

From the graph, you can see that Maryanne must run 4 min after stretching to use a total of 55 Cal.

Problem Solving Reminder

To help identify the conditions of a problem, it may be useful strategy to *rewrite the facts in simpler form.* In Example 2, we list the given facts before writing an equation based on the conditions of the problem.

Class Exercises

Complete for each graph.

1. change in $y = \underline{}$ 2
change in $x = \underline{}$ 4
slope $= \underline{}$ $\frac{1}{2}$

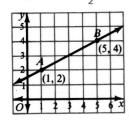

2. change in $y = \underline{}$ 3
change in $x = \underline{}$ 1
slope $= \underline{}$ 3

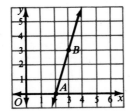

3. change in $y = \underline{2}$
change in $x = \underline{5}$
slope $= \underline{}$ $\frac{2}{5}$

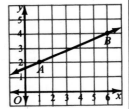

Use a straight-line graph to complete the ordered pairs, then find the slope.

4. $A(1, 3)$, $B(5, 5)$, $C(9, ?)$, $D(?, -1)$ 7; -7; $\frac{1}{2}$

5. $A(0, -3)$, $B(2, 2)$, $C(4, ?)$, $D(?, -8)$ 7; -2; $\frac{5}{2}$

6. $A(8, 4)$, $B(-1, -8)$, $C(5, ?)$, $D(?, -4)$ 0; 2; $\frac{4}{3}$

7. $A(0, 1)$, $B(2, 3)$, $C(-2, ?)$, $D(?, 0)$ -1; -1; 1

8. $A(-1, 6)$, $B(0, 4)$, $C(2, ?)$, $D(?, -4)$ 0; 4; -2

Problems

Solve. Use the same intervals for both axes.

A   **1.** A pack of greeting cards costs $1.50. Five packs will cost $7.50. Draw a straight-line graph to show the relationship between the number of packs and the cost. Let the x-axis represent the number of packs and the y-axis represent the cost in dollars. What is the slope of the line? $\frac{3}{2}$

2. An object of 2 g suspended from a spring stretches the spring to a length of 6 cm. An object of 5 g stretches the spring to a length of 11 cm. Draw a straight-line graph to show the relationship between the number of grams of the object and the length of the stretched spring. Let the x-axis represent grams, and the y-axis represent centimeters. What is the slope of the line? $\frac{5}{3}$

The Coordinate Plane   **331**

Additional A Problem

Solve. Use the same intervals for both axes.

A tree was 2 m tall when it was 3 years old, and 3.5 m tall when it was 6 years old. Draw a straight-line graph to show the relationship between the age of the tree and the height. Let the x-axis represent the age of the tree and the y-axis represent the height in meters. What is the slope of the line? $\frac{1}{2}$

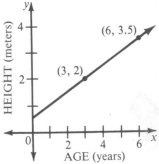

Use a graph to solve the problem.

B   **3.** At 1 A.M. the temperature was −6°C. At 5 A.M. it was −1°C. If the temperature continues to rise steadily, what will the temperature be at 9 A.M.? 4°C

4. Hernando is saving money for a camping trip. Each week he deposits $5 in the bank. He had $25 to start the account. In 3 weeks he had $40 in the account.
   a. How much money will Hernando have by the seventh week? $60
   b. If the trip costs $85, how long will it take him to save enough money? 12 weeks

5. At 9 A.M. a test car driving at a constant speed passes a marker 50 mi from its starting point. At noon the car is about 130 mi from the marker. If the test drive ends at 1:30 P.M., how far will the car be from its starting point? 245 mi

6. Between 1970 and 1980, the Rockfort Corporation used a 10-year expansion plan to increase its annual earnings steadily. The corporation had earnings of $3.6 million in 1975 and $6 million in 1977.
   a. About how much were the corporation's annual earnings in 1972? 0
   b. About how much did it earn by the end of the 10-year plan?
   $9.6 million

a. Write an equation relating the quantity labeled y to the quantity labeled x.

b. Graph the equation. Check students' graphs.

c. Use the graph to answer the question.

C   **7.** A butcher charges $4.50 a pound for the best cut of beef. For an additional $2.00, any order will be delivered. Relate the total cost (y) to the amount of beef (x) ordered and delivered. How many pounds of beef can be ordered and delivered for $33.50?
$y = 4.5x + 2$; 7 lb

8. It takes a work crew 15 min to set up its equipment, and 3 min to paint each square meter of a wall. Relate the number of minutes (y) it takes to complete a job to the number of square meters (x) to be painted. If it took the crew 33 hours to complete the job, about how many square meters was the wall? $y = 3x + 15$; 655 m²

332   *Chapter 9*

9. A word processor can store documents in its memory. It takes about 10 s to get the information, and about 35 s to print each page of it. Therefore, in about 360 s, or 6 min, the processor can complete a 10-page document. Relate the time (y) in minutes it takes to complete a document to the number of pages (x) to be typed. How many minutes will it take to complete an 18-page document? $y = \frac{7}{12}x + \frac{1}{6}$; $10\frac{2}{3}$ min

10. Shaoli Hyatt earns a salary of $215 a week, plus a $15 commission for each encyclopedia she sells. Relate her total pay for one week (y) to the number of encyclopedias she sells during the week (x). How many encyclopedias must she sell to receive $350 for one week? $y = 15x + 215$; 9 encyclopedias

Use a graph to solve.

11. The velocity of a model rocket is 3 km/min at 1 s after takeoff. The velocity decreases to 2 km/min at 2.5 s after takeoff. When the rocket reaches its maximum height, the velocity will be 0. Assume that the decrease in velocity is constant. How long will it take the rocket to reach its maximum height? 5.5 s

Review Exercises

Solve.

1. $3x + 4 > 8$

2. $5y - 10 < 0$

3. $7 + 3y \geq -4y$

4. $2(8x + 3) < -2$

5. $6(2y + 7) \leq 42$

6. $-3\left(9x - \frac{2}{3}\right) > -7$

7. $4(9x + 10) \geq 4$

8. $5(4y + 9) \leq 15$

9. $12\left(\frac{x}{6} - \frac{5}{6}\right) > 72$

▌▌▌ Calculator Key-In

Use a calculator to find the product.

$$11,111^2 = 123454321$$
$$111,111^2 = 12345654321$$
$$1,111,111^2 = 1234567654321$$
$$11,111,111^2 = 123456787654321$$
$$111,111,111^2 = 12345678987654321$$

$1^2 = \underline{}$ 1
$11^2 = \underline{}$ 121
$111^2 = \underline{}$ 12321
$1111^2 = \underline{}$ 1234321

Use the pattern to predict the products $11,111^2$, $111,111^2$, $1,111,111^2$, $11,111,111^2$, and $111,111,111^2$.

The Coordinate Plane **333**

Additional Answers
Review Exercises

The solutions are all the numbers:

1. greater than $1\frac{1}{3}$.

2. less than 2.

3. greater than or equal to -1.

4. less than $-\frac{1}{2}$.

5. less than or equal to 0.

6. less than $\frac{1}{3}$.

7. greater than or equal to -1.

8. less than or equal to $-1\frac{1}{2}$.

9. greater than 41.

Suggested Assignments

Core
Day 1: 331/Prob. 1, 2
      332/Prob. 3, 4
Day 2: 332/Prob. 5–7
      333/Rev. 1–9

Enriched
Day 1: 331/Prob. 1, 2
      332/Prob. 3–7
Day 2: 332/8
      333/9–11
      333/Rev. 2–8 even
      333/Calculator Key-In

Supplementary Materials

Practice Masters, p. 42

Reading Mathematics

Students will learn the meaning of the following mathematical terms in this lesson: *boundary line, relation.*

Chalkboard Examples

Transform the inequality into an equivalent inequality with y alone on one side. State the equation of the boundary line.

1. $x + y \leq 4$
   $y \leq -x + 4$;
   $y = -x + 4$

2. $x - 2y > 6$
   $y < \frac{1}{2}x - 3$;
   $y = \frac{1}{2}x - 3$

3. $2y - 3x < 0$
   $y < \frac{3}{2}x$; $y = \frac{3}{2}x$

4. $3x - y > 6$
   $y < 3x - 6$; $y = 3x - 6$

State whether each point belongs to the graph of the inequality $y < x + 2$.

5. (2, 3) yes

6. (−2, 3) no

7. (0, 0) yes

9-6 Graphing Inequalities

When we graph a linear equation such as

$$y = x + 1$$

we see that the graph separates the coordinate plane into three sets of points:

(1) those above the line, such as (−4, 5),

(2) those below the line, such as (3, 1), and

(3) those on the line, such as (2, 3).

The region *above* the line is the graph of the set of solutions of the inequality

$$y > x + 1.$$

The region *below* the line is the graph of the set of solutions of the inequality

$$y < x + 1.$$

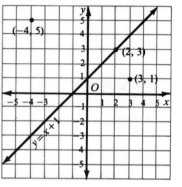

The line $y = x + 1$ forms the **boundary line** of the graphs of the inequalities $y > x + 1$ and $y < x + 1$. For any inequality we can get the boundary line by replacing the inequality symbol with the "equals" symbol.

Since the graph of an inequality consists of all the points above or below a boundary line, we use shading to indicate the region. If the boundary line is part of the graph, it is drawn with a solid line. If the boundary line is not part of the graph, use a dashed line.

$y > x + 1$	$y \geq x + 1$	$y < x + 1$	$y \leq x + 1$
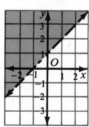	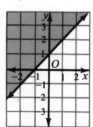	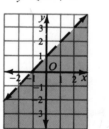	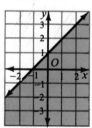

To check whether the shading is correct, choose a point in the shaded region. Then substitute its coordinates for x and y in the inequality. If the coordinates satisfy the inequality, then the shading is correct.

Any set of ordered pairs is a **relation.** Each of the open sentences

334 *Chapter 9*

$y = x + 1, y > x + 1, y \geq x + 1, y < x + 1,$ and $y \leq x + 1$ defines a relation. The equation $y = x + 1$ is a special kind of relation because it defines a function. Not all relations are functions. Recall that for a function, every value of x has only one corresponding value of y. Notice in the shaded region of each graph above, more than one value of y may be associated with each value of x. For example, the following ordered pairs all satisfy the inequalities $y > x + 1$ and $y \geq x + 1$:

$$(-2, 0), (-2, 1), (-2, 2), (-2, 3)$$

Therefore, the relation defined by the inequalities $y > x + 1$ and $y \geq x + 1$ is not a function.

EXAMPLE 1 Graph $y - x < 4$.

Solution First transform $y - x < 4$ into an equivalent inequality with y alone on one side.

$$y < 4 + x$$

Then locate the boundary line by graphing

$$y = 4 + x.$$

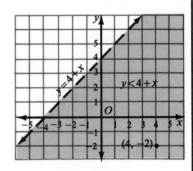

Use a dashed line to draw the boundary line, and shade the region below.

Check: Use $(4, -2)$.
$$y - x \overset{<}{} 4$$
$$-2 - 4 \overset{?}{<} 4$$
$$-6 < 4 \quad \sqrt{}$$

EXAMPLE 2 Graph $x \geq -7$.

Solution Locate the boundary line by graphing

$$x = -7.$$

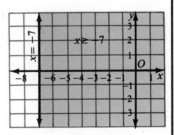

Use a solid line to draw the boundary. Shade the region to the right since all values of x greater than -7 lie to the right of the boundary line.

The Coordinate Plane **335**

Additional A Exercises

State the equation of the boundary line.

1. $2x - 5 \geq -3y$

$y = -\frac{2}{3}x + \frac{5}{3}$

2. $x - y < 5$ $y = x - 5$

Graph the inequality.

3. $y < x - 2$

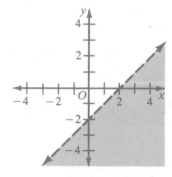

4. $2x + y \geq 4$

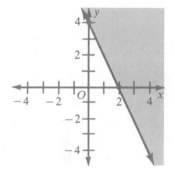

Suggested Assignments

Core
Day 1: 336/2–22 even; 26, 27
Day 2: 337/28, 29
337/Self-Test B

Enriched
Day 1: 336/1–23 odd; 25–27
Day 2: 337/28–30
337/Self-Test B

Supplementary Materials

Practice Masters, p. 42
Computer Activity 18
Test 9B, pp. 61–62

335

Use a graph to solve the system. State whether the lines intersect, coincide, or are parallel.

1. $y - x = -3$
$y + x = 3$
intersect

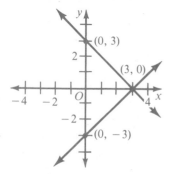

2. $2x - y = 5$
$3x + y = 5$
intersect

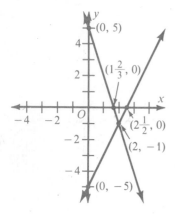

3. $2x + y = 1$
$-y - 2x = 1$
parallel

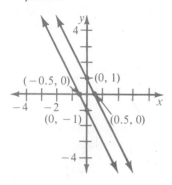

Class Exercises

Transform the inequality into an equivalent inequality with y alone on one side. State the equation of the boundary line. $y > -\frac{1}{2}x + \frac{5}{2}$
$y = -\frac{1}{2}x + \frac{5}{2}$

1. $4x + y < 8$ $\quad y < -4x + 8$
$y = -4x + 8$

2. $y - 9x < 2$ $\quad y < 9x + 2$
$y = 9x + 2$

3. $4y + 2x > 10$

4. $6x - y > 0$ $\quad y < 6x$
$y = 6x$

5. $3 \leq 5x + y$ $\quad y \geq -5x + 3$
$y = -5x + 3$

6. $9y \geq 18$ $\quad y \geq 2$
$y = 2$

State whether each point belongs to the graph of the given inequality.

7. $y \leq x + 2$ $\quad (0, 1), (3, 6)$ $\quad$ yes; no

8. $-x + 2y \geq 0$ $\quad (4, 4), (-2, 1)$ $\quad$ yes; yes

9. $x \leq -7$ $\quad (-4, -10), (-8, 0)$ $\quad$ no; yes

10. $5 \leq -x + y$ $\quad (-6, -5), (2, 7)$ $\quad$ no; yes

11. $0 \geq x + y - 5$ $\quad (2, 1), (4, 1)$ $\quad$ yes; yes

12. $y \geq 3$ $\quad (9, 4), (0, 8)$ $\quad$ yes; yes

Written Exercises

State the equation of the boundary line.

A **1.** $3x + y > -6$
$y = -3x - 6$

2. $x + y \geq 2$
$y = 2 - x$

3. $x - y \leq 2$
$y = x - 2$

4. $2y - 4 > 0$
$y = 2$

5. $-x \geq y - 3$
$y = 3 - x$

6. $2y - 6x < 0$
$y = 3x$

Graph the inequality. $\quad$ Check students' graphs.

7. $x + y \geq 9$

8. $y > -3x + 3$

9. $-2x + y \geq 2$

10. $x + 6y \leq -5$

11. $4x + 2y \geq 8$

12. $3y - x < -3$

13. $y \geq 2x + 5$

14. $x + 2y \leq 6$

15. $3y - 4 > 2x - 5$

B **16.** $3(x - y) > 6$

17. $y \leq 8$

18. $6x + 2y + 3 < 2x - 1$

19. $4x + 3y \leq x - 3$

20. $3y - 6 > 0$

21. $x \leq -3$

22. $y > 0$

23. $2(x + y) < 6x + 10$

24. $3y - 6 \geq 3(x + 2y)$

Write an inequality for the graph shown.

25.

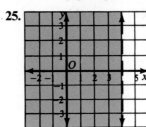

$x < 4$

26.

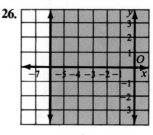

$x \geq -6$

27.

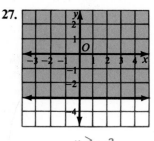

$y \geq -3$

Graph the solutions of each system of inequalities. Check students' graphs.

EXAMPLE $y \geq -3 + x$
$y \leq 2 - x$

Solution First graph $y \geq -3 + x$. Use blue to shade the region. Then graph $y \leq 2 - x$. Use gray to shade the region.

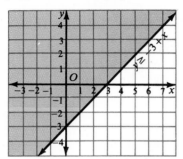 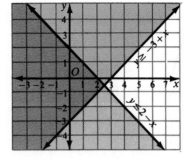

The graph of the solutions of the system is the region where the blue and gray shading overlap.

C **28.** $y \geq -4$
$x \leq 2$

29. $y > 5 - x$
$y \geq x + 5$

30. $x \leq 9 - y$
$y < x + 3$

31. $x \geq -6$
$x < 3$

Self-Test B

Use a graph to solve the system. Do the lines intersect or coincide, or are they parallel?

infinitely many solutions;

1. $x + y = 6$ intersect;
$y - x = -2$ (4, 2)

2. $x + 2y = 6$ coincide
$6y + 3x = 18$

3. $2x + y = 3$
$-2x - y = 2$
no solution; parallel

[9-4]

Use a graph to solve.

4. When Fritz enrolled in a speed-reading class, he read about 250 words per minute. Two weeks later, his reading speed was about 750 words per minute. If his reading speed increases steadily, how many weeks after enrollment will it take Fritz to read about 1250 words per minute? 4 weeks

[9-5]

Graph each inequality. Check students' graphs.

5. $x + y \leq 10$

6. $3y - x > 9$

7. $x - 5y \geq 5$

[9-6]

Self-Test answers and Extra Practice are at the back of the book.

The Coordinate Plane **337**

Use a graph to solve.

4. When Kim began training with the swimming team, she could swim the length of the pool in 37 s. Four weeks later it took 35 s. If her time improves steadily, how many weeks after starting to train will she reach her goal of 34 s?
6 weeks

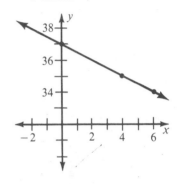

Graph each inequality.

5. $x - y \geq 4$

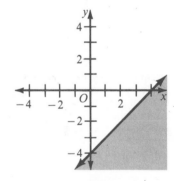

6. $y - 2x > -3$

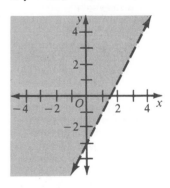

This is a very valuable and versatile activity. It helps students gain experience with the computer while dealing with a genuinely practical application of elementary mathematics.

Many real-world relationships are linear, or nearly so. These can be modeled using linear equations. Although you need not use the words, notice that the models derived here, which are linear equations, are used to *interpolate*, as in Exercises 4 and 5a, and to *extrapolate*, as in Exercises 3, 5b, 6, and 7.

In cases in which the data are quite linear and there are not too many points, many people can approximate a well-fitting line by eye and draw it. The program uses a statistical technique known as the least-squares method. Basically, we obtain a line so that the points deviate from this line, altogether, as little at possible. The equation is given in slope-intercept form. If *m* is the slope of the line and the *y*-intercept is *b*, the equation is $y = mx + b$.

You might want to point out that even if the data under consideration are not very linear, the program still computes the best-fitting line for the given points.

This would be a good place to discuss how one provides data to the computer when running programs in BASIC. The READ and DATA statements are very useful for this purpose. For new data, it is a simple matter to enter a new DATA statement. A new statement given line number 40 will supersede the original line 40. Note that, since we have READ X, Y in line 60, the data will be taken two at a time, one value for X and

The Computer and Linear Equations

For a science project, Nina watered 6 identical lima bean gardens by different amounts. The crop yields were as recorded below.

Water applied daily in cm (x)	0.5	1.0	1.5	2.0	2.5	3.0
Yield of lima beans in kg (y)	1.6	1.8	2.0	2.4	2.6	2.8

Can Nina use these data to predict crop yields for other amounts of daily watering? If we plot her findings as shown on the graph at the right, we see that the points are very nearly on a line.

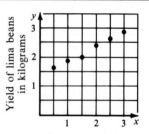

Water applied daily in centimeters

The computer program below gives the equation of the line that best fits the points on the graph. This line is often called the **line of best fit.** The instruction in line 40 provides the program with all the coordinates of the points. Compare the numbers in line 40 to the numbers in the chart.

```
10   DIM L(50)
20   PRINT "NUMBER OF POINTS ON GRAPH IS";
30   INPUT N
40   DATA .5,1.6,1,1.8,1.5,2,2,2.4,2.5,2.6,3,2.8
50   FOR I = 1 TO N
60   READ X,Y
70   LET A = A + X
80   LET B = B + Y
90   LET C = C + X * X
100  LET D = D + X * Y
110  NEXT I
120  LET Q = N * C - A * A
130  LET R =  INT (100 * (N * D - A * B) / Q + .5) / 100
140  LET S =  INT (100 * (B * C - A * D) / Q + .5) / 100
145  PRINT
150  PRINT "EQUATION OF BEST FITTING LINE IS"
155  PRINT " Y = ";R;"X";
160  IF S >  = 0 THEN 190
170  PRINT S
180  STOP
190  PRINT " ";"+ ";S
200  END
```

1. RUN the program to find the equation of the best fitting line for Nina's data. $y = 0.5x + 1.32$

2. Draw the graph of the equation. Check students' graphs. Answers may vary for 3–7.

3. Use the graph to predict the yield (y) if Nina applied 3.3 cm of water daily (x). 2.97 kg

Use the computer program to find the equation of the line of best fit for the data given in each chart. Graph each equation and use the equation to answer each question.

4. The chart below shows the distance a spring stretches when different masses are hung from it. $y = 5.39x + 0.97$

Mass in kg	0.3	0.6	0.9	1.2	1.5	1.8
Stretch in cm	2.1	4.9	6.0	7.1	8.9	10.8

About how much stretch would a 1 kg mass produce? 6.36 cm

5. The chart below shows temperature changes as a cold front approached. $y = -3.3x + 20.8$

Time in hours from 1st reading	0	1	2	3	4
Temperature in °C	21	17	14	12	7

a. Estimate the temperature 1.5 hours from the first reading. 15.85°C

b. If the temperature continues to decrease steadily, about how many hours will it take to reach 0°C? 6.3 h

6. The chart below shows the profit earned by a bookstore on the sale of a bestseller. $y = 4.5x$

No. sold	3	4	7	9	11
Profit	$13.50	$18.00	$31.50	$40.50	$49.50

How many sales will it take to earn a profit of at least $80? 18

7. The chart below shows the cost of college education for the past 5 years. $y = 0.59x + 7.39$

Year	1	2	3	4	5
Cost (in thousands)	$7.8	$8.6	$9.4	$9.9	$10.1

Predict the cost of college education for the next two years.
$10,930; $11,520

The Coordinate Plane **339**

one for Y. Therefore the programmer must type a value of X, then a value of Y, then X, then Y, and so on.

Some students may wonder why INPUT is not used in the program. Point out that when all data values are known ahead, it is more efficient to use DATA statements. We could use INPUT, but there is no real need for the interactive mode employed in using INPUT.

Point out that the computer prints all numerical values as decimals. Students may not be accustomed to linear equations being written with decimal constants, but this should present no real difficulty.

In Problem 7, point out that Year 5 is this year, Year 4 is last year, and so on.

Chapter Review

True or false?

1. The coordinates of point G are $(3, 2)$. False

2. The abscissa of point W is 2. True

3. The ordinate of point T is 1. True

4. Point B is associated with the ordered pair $(2, -3)$. False

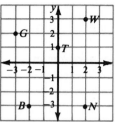

[9-1]

Match each equation with an ordered pair that satisfies the equation.

5. $2y - 7x = 4$ C   **A.** $(-18, 1)$

6. $10x + \frac{5}{9}y = 0$ D   **B.** $(9, 2)$

7. $-2x + 9y = 0$ B   **C.** $(2, 9)$

8. $y - \frac{1}{3}x = 7$ A   **D.** $(1, -18)$

[9-2]

Graph the equation on a coordinate plane. Use a separate set of axes for each equation. Check students' graphs.

9. $x + y = 0$ 10. $2y - 3x = -6$ 11. $y - 2x = 2$

[9-3]

Use a graph to solve the system of equations. Match the system with the word that describes its graphs.

12. $y + x = -3$ A   13. $y - 3x = -6$ C   14. $5y - 2x = 4$ B
   $2y - 3x = 4$ $y - 3x = 3$ $15y - 6x = 12$

[9-4]

A. intersect   **B.** coincide   **C.** parallel

Complete.

15. A basic property of a straight line is that its slope remains _?_. constant

[9-5]

16. The slope of a line is the ratio of the change in the _?_ ᵧ-coordinate to the change in the _?_ ˣ-coordinate when moving from one point on the line to another.

17. The boundary line for the graph of $y > x + 6$ is a _?_ dashed line.

[9-6]

18. If the boundary line is part of the graph of an inequality, it is drawn with a _?_ line. solid

340   *Chapter 9*

Chapter Test

Give the coordinates of the point.

1. I **2.** M **3.** E **4.** R [9–1]
(5, −2)   (−5, 3)   (−3, −5)   (3, 4)

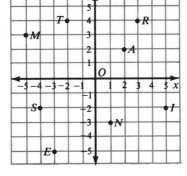

Name the point for the ordered pair.

5. (−2, 4) T **6.** (1, −3) N

7. (−4, −2) S **8.** (5, −2) I

a. Solve the equation for y in terms of x.
b. Find solutions of the equation for the given values of x: **−3, 0, 4.**

9. $y + 7x = 23$ **10.** $2y - 4x = 1$ **11.** $3y - 6x = 0$ [9–2]

Graph the equation on a coordinate plane. Use a separate set of axes for each equation. Check students' graphs.

12. $y - 3x = 7$ **13.** $4y - x = 8$ **14.** $2y + x = -10$ [9–3]

Use a graph to solve the system. Do the lines intersect or coincide, or are they parallel?

15. $x - 2y = 0$ (2, 1);   **16.** $3x - y = -4$ **17.** $5x + y = 2$ [9–4]
     $2x + y = 5$ intersect $3x - y = 3$ no solution; $10x + 2y = 4$
                          parallel   infinitely
                                    many solutions;
Use a graph to solve the problem.   parallel

18. One hour after the start of an experiment, the temperature of a   [9–5]
solution was $-15°C$. Three hours later it was $-6°C$. If the temperature continues to rise steadily, about how many hours will it take for the temperature to reach $0°C$? two more hours

19. It takes the window washers 24 min to get ready and 4 min to wash a 6 m by 6 m window.
    a. Write an equation relating the total time (y) required on the job to the number of windows (x) to be washed. $y = 4x + 24$
    b. Graph the equation. Check students' graphs.
    c. About how many 6 m by 6 m windows can they wash in 2 h?
                                             24 windows

a. State the equation of the boundary line.
b. Graph the inequality. Check students' graphs.
    $y = 2x + 1$ $y = -x - 4$ $y = 3x$
20. $y \geq 2x + 1$ **21.** $x + y > -4$ **22.** $y - 3x < 0$ [9–6]

The Coordinate Plane **341**

Additional Answers

9. $y = -7x + 23$; $(-3, 44)$, $(0, 23)$, $(4, -5)$

10. $y = 2x + \frac{1}{2}$; $\left(-3, -5\frac{1}{2}\right)$, $\left(0, \frac{1}{2}\right)$, $\left(4, 8\frac{1}{2}\right)$

11. $y = 2x$; $(-3, -6)$, $(0, 0)$, $(4, 8)$

Review for Retention

Perform the indicated operation.

1. $-6.5 + 3.9$ **−2.6**

2. $17.4 - 21.6$ **−4.2**

3. $-5 - (-3.4)$ **−1.6**

4. $(-1.6)(0.7)$ **−1.12**

5. $-2.5(-2.5)$ **6.25**

6. $-18.2 \div 0.2$ **−91**

Write the expression without exponents.

7. 11^2 **121**

8. 11^{-2} $\frac{1}{121}$

9. $(-2)^{-6}$ $\frac{1}{64}$

Solve.

10. $\frac{x}{35} = \frac{9}{7}$ **45**

11. $\frac{5}{16} = \frac{10}{x}$ **32**

Express as a percent.

12. $\frac{13}{20}$ **65%**

13. $\frac{1}{6}$ $16\frac{2}{3}\%$

14. 0.31 **31%**

15. 1.03 **103%**

Cumulative Review (Chapters 1–9)

Exercises

Write a variable expression for the word phrase.

1. The product of b and five **5b**

2. Eight times a number x **8x**

3. Twelve less than the sum of y and z $y + z - 12$

4. A number q divided by seven $\frac{q}{7}$

5. The sum of three times a number p and seven $3p + 7$

Round to the nearest hundredth.

6. 46.871 **46.87**   **7.** 288.005 **288.01**   **8.** 0.7826 **0.78**   **9.** 100.758 **100.76**   **10.** 33.663 **33.66**

Perform the indicated operation.

11. $-8.709 + 13.6001$ **4.8911**   **12.** $7615.7 - 333.61$ **7282.09**   **13.** $606.08 + (-51.99)$ **554.09**

14. $272.65 - (-0.88)$ **273.53**   **15.** 37.61×0.08 **3.0088**   **16.** $1.5798 \div 0.03$ **52.66**

17. -11.56×36.77 **−425.0612** **18.** $72.5 \div 5$ **14.5**   **19.** $6.7 \times (-1.22)$ **−8.174**

20. $-\frac{1}{3} + \frac{4}{5}$ $\frac{7}{15}$

21. $\frac{4}{7} \times \left(-\frac{3}{8}\right) - \frac{3}{14}$

22. $6\frac{1}{2} \div \left(-2\frac{1}{2}\right) - 2\frac{3}{5}$

23. $\frac{7}{8} - \left(-\frac{1}{4}\right)$ $1\frac{1}{8}$

24. $3\frac{1}{2} - 1\frac{7}{8}$ $1\frac{5}{8}$

25. $-3\frac{4}{5} \times 1\frac{3}{10}$ $-4\frac{47}{50}$

Write an equation or inequality for the word sentence and solve.

26. The sum of x and three is seven. $x + 3 = 7$; **4**

27. A number t is the product of negative three fourths and one fifth. $t = \left(-\frac{3}{4}\right)\left(\frac{1}{5}\right)$; $-\frac{3}{20}$

28. The quotient of negative eight divided by w is seven. $\frac{-8}{w} = 7$; $-1\frac{1}{7}$

29. The sum of x and twelve is greater than the product of x and 2. $x + 12 > 2x$; all the numbers less than 12

Find the circumference of the circle described. Use $\pi \approx 3.14$.

30. diameter $= 28$ cm **87.9 cm**   **31.** radius $= 3.3$ m **20.7 m**   **32.** diameter $= 88.5$ km **278 km**

Solve the proportion.

33. $\frac{n}{4.8} = \frac{0.4}{1.2}$ **1.6**   **34.** $\frac{1.5}{n} = \frac{1}{4}$ **6**   **35.** $\frac{13}{14} = \frac{39}{n}$ **42**   **36.** $\frac{1.2}{2.0} = \frac{n}{3.0}$ **1.8**

Tell whether the ordered pair is a solution of the given equation.

$2x + y = 15$ **37.** $(0, 12)$ **no**   **38.** $(-5, 25)$ **yes**   **39.** $(5, 5)$ **yes**   **40.** $(4, 13)$ **no**

342   *Chapter 9*

Problems

Problem Solving Reminders

Here are some reminders that may help you solve some of the problems on this page.
- Sometimes more than one method can be used to solve.
- Consider whether making a sketch will help.
- When rounding an answer to division, consider whether it is reasonable to round up or round down.

Solve.

1. Bill Murphy earns $4.85 an hour working in a day care center. Last week he worked from 1:00 P.M. to 4:30 P.M. on Monday through Friday. How much did he earn? $84.88

2. "I feel like I ran a mile," gasped Marge. If Marge ran 5 times around a circular track with a diameter of 210 ft, did she really run a mile? (*Hint:* 5280 ft = 1 mi) No

3. Light travels at a speed of 297,600 km/s. If the circumference of Earth is about 39,800 km, about how many times could light travel around Earth in 1 s? 7.5 times

4. Michael Woolsey bought $5671 worth of stock. The commission rate was $28 plus 0.6% of the dollar amount. How much was the commission? $62.03

5. A car dealer is expecting a price increase of between $2\frac{1}{2}$% and 5% over the price of last year's models. If a certain car sold for $9560 last year, what is the least it can be expected to sell for this year? the most? $9799; $10,038

6. Myra Daley was given an advance of $18,000 on royalties expected from a book she wrote. If the selling price of the book is $15.95 and her royalty rate is 5%, how many books must be sold before her royalties exceed her advance? 22,571 books

7. A baby that weighed 7 lb 6 oz at birth weighed 10 lb 10 oz at 6 weeks of age. To the nearest tenth of a percent, what was the percent of increase? 44.1%

8. It took Thomas 25 min longer to do his math homework than to do his French homework. He spent a total of 2.25 h on both subjects. How much time did he spend on math? 1 h 20 min

9. If a microwave oven uses 1.5 kilowatt hours (kW·h) of electricity in 15 min, how much electricity does it use in 5 min? 0.5 kW·h

16. What percent of 60 is 40? $66\frac{2}{3}$%

17. 21 is what percent of 35? 60%

18. What is 125% of 30? 37.5

19. $33\frac{1}{3}$% of what number is 22? 66

20. Give the unit price if 3 grapefruit cost $1.47. $.49/grapefruit

Solve.

21. $7a + 5a = -96$ -8

22. $3(b - 1) = 12 - 2b$ 3

23. $9 - c < 7$ All the numbers greater than 2.

24. $\frac{d}{3} \geq -4$ All the numbers greater than or equal to -12.

25. $36 \leq e - 7$ All the numbers greater than or equal to 43.

The Coordinate Plane **343**

10

Areas and Volumes

Pyramids are one type of space figure in geometry. The bottom, or base, of a pyramid is in the shape of a polygon and the sides are always triangular. When your study of measurement is extended to include area, volume, and capacity, you can then describe the pyramid shown in the photograph in more mathematical terms.

The pyramid in the photograph is one of the pyramids built by the Egyptian kings, or Pharaohs, as a monumental tomb. The largest is the Great Pyramid, built by Pharaoh Khufu around 2600 B.C. The Great Pyramid has a square base measuring about 230 m on a side and originally rose to an approximate height of 150 m. When built, it contained about 2,300,000 stone blocks, each having a mass of nearly 2.5 t.

Career Note

Architects are responsible for the design and visual appearance of buildings. Good architectural designs are appealing, safe, and functional. Architects must combine technical skills with a strong sense of style. Course work in mathematics, engineering, and art provide the necessary background for this profession.

344

345

Lesson Commentary
Chapter 10   Areas and Volumes

Overview

In this chapter, students will learn how to find the areas of various plane figures and the volumes, lateral areas, and total areas of right prisms and cylinders. This chapter builds upon the fundamental concepts of geometry presented in Chapter 5. The vocabulary, formulas, and methods presented will provide a solid foundation for future study in mathematics and science.

Initially, students learn to find the areas of various polygons and polygonal regions. Later, they learn how to find areas of circles and circular regions. Lesson 10-4 introduces using the concept of symmetry to find the areas of figures that are symmetric with respect to a point or a line and requires students to use the area formulas presented earlier in the chapter.

In the second part of the chapter students use the basic formulas for plane figures to find the volumes and surface areas of geometric solids. Careful attention will be given to understanding what volume is as well as how it is calculated using a formula. The same is true of surface area. A lesson is also included on finding the mass of an object of a given density.

AREAS

10-1 Areas of Rectangles and Parallelograms

Objective for pages 346–350

■ To find the areas of rectangles and parallelograms.

Teaching Suggestions

To introduce this lesson, you may wish to ask your students for some real-life situations in which they would find perimeter, such as determining how much binding is needed to finish a quilt, and for situations in which they would find area, like determining how much paint is needed to paint a room, so that the difference between the two concepts is clearly established.

Encourage students to use sketches in their work.

To review the characteristics of parallelograms, rectangles, and squares, you can ask a series of true-false questions, such as:

Every parallelogram is a rectangle.
False
Every parallelogram is a square.
False
Every square is a parallelogram.
True
Every square is a rectangle.
True
Every rectangle is a square.
False

This type of questioning gets the students interested and reinforces their knowledge of these polygons.

Even though many of your students understand what a square unit is, it may be worthwhile to draw a segment one unit long on the chalkboard and a square one square unit in area next to it to demonstrate the difference between one unit and one square unit.

Note that the label cm^2 is really $cm \times cm$. If your students forget to label the answer to a problem involving area or label it incorrectly, suggest that they think of multiplying the labels along with the numbers. Remind them how different a unit and a square unit look.

The formula for the area of a rectangle will be familiar, but the formula for the area of a parallelogram may be new for some of your students. To demonstrate the latter formula you could take a cardboard parallelogram, cut off one end and fit it on the other end as shown on page 351. It may also be worthwhile to show, by measuring, that the area is the same no matter which base and corresponding height is used.

Related Activities

To give an interesting application of area, have your students find the "population density," or the number of people per unit area, of the regions listed in the table below. Have students round their answers to three digits, if necessary.

	Region	Population	Area (Square Miles)
1.	Colorado	2,889,000	104,000
2.	Greenland	50,000	840,000
3.	Hong Kong	4,525,000	400
4.	Rhode Island	947,000	1000
5.	Texas	11,197,000	267,000

1. 27.8 people per square mile
2. 0.060 people per square mile
3. 11,300 people per square mile
4. 947 people per square mile
5. 41.9 people per square mile

You can place two congruent trapezoids cut from cardboard together, as shown on page 352, to demonstrate that the area of one of the trapezoids is half of the area of the parallelogram formed. Since the quantity $\frac{1}{2}(b_1 + b_2)$ is the average of the quantities b_1 and b_2, students can think of the area of a trapezoid as the height times the average of the two bases.

Related Activities

To provide your students with additional practice finding the areas of trapezoids, have your students find the area of the polygon below.

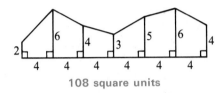

108 square units

10-2 Areas of Triangles and Trapezoids

Objective for pages 351–355

■ To find the areas of triangles and trapezoids.

Teaching Suggestions

This lesson completes our presentation of formulas for finding the areas of polygons.

To show that the area of a triangle is half the area of a rectangle, cut two congruent triangles from cardboard and put them together to form a parallelogram as illustrated on page 351. This demonstration should help your students remember the formula for finding the area of a triangle.

By measuring one of these cardboard triangles, you can show your students that the area of the triangle is the same no matter which of the three sides is chosen as a base. Stress that when a different side is chosen as the base, the height to that base is used. As you go over part (b) of Example 1 on page 351, you should point out that the height of a right triangle can be one of the sides. When going over part (c) of Example 1, emphasize that although it may be necessary to extend the base of an obtuse triangle, the height is measured to the line containing the side.

10-3 Areas of Circles

Objective for pages 356–359

■ To find areas of circles and of regions involving circles.

Teaching Suggestions

You may wish to introduce this lesson by cutting a cardboard circle into pieces as shown on page 357. This demonstration will make it easier for your students to accept the plausibility of the formula for finding the area of a circle.

Remind students that $2r = d$; $r^2 \neq d$. To find the area of a circle using the formula $A = \pi r^2$, we use the radius. If we are given the diameter, we must find the radius as a preliminary step. Be sure students understand that to calculate the area, they must, first, square the radius, then multiply by π.

To help your students avoid confusing the formula for finding the circumference of a circle with the formula for finding the area of a circle, tell them to associate the area, which is measured in square units, with r^2.

Note that we round areas found using $\pi \approx 3.14$ to three digits whenever the answer contains more than three digits. If your students have calculators you may want them to use their calculators and give your own instructions regarding rounding. Because a calculator with a π key stores a more exact approximation for π than 3.14, students using this key may obtain answers that differ from those we give.

If you feel that your students might have difficulty finding the area of a circle using $\frac{22}{7}$ for π, be sure to work such an example with them.

When approximations for π are used, be sure that students are reading the answers: "The area is approximately equal to . . . ." They should not say "The area is . . ." or "The area is equal to . . . ."

Related Activities

To stimulate interest in areas of circles, ask students to determine the maximum number of regions into which a circle can be divided by four straight lines.

11 regions

Resource Book: Page 121 (Use After Page 359)

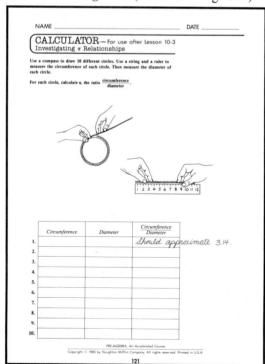

10-4 Using Symmetry to Find Areas

Objectives for pages 360–363

■ To show the lines or points of symmetry of symmetric figures.
■ To find areas using symmetry.

Teaching Suggestions

Before working the examples in this section, it might be beneficial to ask students for the area formulas presented thus far and to write them on the chalkboard. It is easier to note differences in the formulas and to study them when they are grouped together.

Designs, including designs made of students' names, and figures symmetric with respect to a line can easily be drawn as follows. Have students place a sheet of carbon paper on top of a sheet of paper with the carbon side towards the paper. Have them fold once and draw whatever design they wish.

To draw a figure symmetric with respect to a point, have students fold the paper and carbon paper together in quarters and draw a pattern. When the paper is opened, the two pairs of figures lying in diagonally opposite quarters are symmetric with respect to the point where the two perpendicular fold lines intersect.

Related Activities

To help students understand the concept of symmetry, have them draw the figures described below.
Answers may vary. An example is given.

1. a figure that has exactly one line of symmetry
   an isosceles triangle
2. a figure that has exactly one point of symmetry
   a circle
3. a figure that has both a line and a point of symmetry **a rectangle**
4. a figure that has exactly two lines of symmetry
   a rectangle
5. a figure that has exactly three lines of symmetry
   an equilateral triangle
6. a figure that is symmetric with respect to every line through its point of symmetry **a circle**
7. a figure that has neither a line of symmetry nor a point of symmetry **a scalene triangle**

NAME _____ DATE _____

Quiz 10A — Lessons 10-1 through 10-4

DIRECTIONS: Write the letter of the correct answer in the space provided.

Find the area.

1. rectangle: 14 cm by 2 cm   **[10-1]**

    a. 14 cm²   b. 16 cm²   c. 28 cm²   d. 32 cm²

2. parallelogram
base: 4 m   height: 3 m

    a. 6 m²   b. 7 m²   c. 12 m²   d. 14 m²

3. triangle   **[10-2]**
base: 14   height: 6

    a. 84 square units   b. 42 square units

    c. 40 square units   d. 20 square units

4. trapezoid
bases: 5 m and 3 m   height: 6 m

    a. 20 m²   b. 24 m²   c. 48 m²   d. 45 m²

5. circle: Use $\pi \approx 3.14$.   **[10-3]**
diameter: 1.2 m

    a. 1.13 m²   b. 1.88 m²   c. 3.77 m²   d. 4.52 m²

6. circle: Use $\pi \approx \frac{22}{7}$.
radius: $1\frac{1}{2}$ cm

    a. $4\frac{5}{7}$ cm²   b. $7\frac{1}{14}$ cm²   c. $9\frac{3}{7}$ cm²   d. $28\frac{2}{7}$ cm²

Use the figure at the right to answer Exercises 7–8.

7. How many lines of symmetry does the figure have?   **[10-4]**

    a. 1   b. 2   c. 4   d. 6

8. Find the area of the symmetric figure.

    a. 230 m²   b. 460 m²   c. 1380 m²   d. 2760 m²

ANSWERS	
1. _c_	(12)
2. _c_	(12)
3. _b_	(12)
4. _b_	(12)
5. _a_	(12)
6. _b_	(12)
7. _d_	(12)
8. _c_	(16)

PRE-ALGEBRA, An Accelerated Course
Copyright © 1985 by Houghton Mifflin Company. All rights reserved. Printed in U.S.A.
122

NAME _____ DATE _____

Enrichment — For use after Lesson 10-4
TILING FLOORS

It is easy to tile a floor using square tiles. The floor can be completely covered by placing tiles end to end.

Different patterns result when other shapes are used. Tiles shaped like equilateral triangles must be placed in different orientations in order to cover a floor completely. Some are "upside-down!"

Rhombus-shaped tiles result in one pattern when the tiles are placed in the same way, but in a different pattern when successive rows are reversed.

or

Trace the shapes below and cut out a few models of each shape. Then experiment to answer these questions.

A. isosceles triangle   B. scalene triangle   C. octagon   D. hexagon

E. isosceles trapezoid   F. irregular quadrilateral   G. parallelogram

1. Will the isosceles triangle, shape A, result in one or more patterns in tiling a floor?   _one_

2. Can you completely cover a floor using only a scalene triangle like shape B?   _no_

3. Can you tile a floor using a hexagonal tile like shape D?   _yes_

4. Can you tile a floor using any regular polygon? (Hint: Try shape C).   _no_

5. Can you make more than one pattern of tiles for shape E? for shape G?   _yes, yes_

6. Can you completely cover a floor using only shape F?   _no_

7. Use an isosceles trapezoid like shape E and an isosceles triangle to tile a floor. Draw a picture of your pattern.   _answers may vary_

8. How many degrees the sum of the corner angles in order for tiles to fit together?   _360°_

PRE-ALGEBRA, An Accelerated Course
Copyright © 1985 by Houghton Mifflin Company. All rights reserved. Printed in U.S.A.
123

VOLUMES AND AREAS OF SOLIDS

10-5 Volumes of Prisms and Cylinders

Objective for pages 364–368

■ To find the volumes and capacities of prisms and cylinders.

Teaching Suggestions

Divide the class into groups of two or three students and provide each group with a rectangular box and a can. Have students measure the length, width, and height of the box to the nearest centimeter and calculate the volume using $V = l \times w \times h$. Remind them that the symbol for cubic centimeter is cm³. Give each group at least one cubic-centimeter model to remind them of its size.

For the can, have students measure the diameter of the bottom and the height. Ask them to calculate the volume by using $V = \pi r^2 h$.

Provide some rice or sand and a graduated liter beaker for each group to check the accuracy of their measurements and calculations using the important metric relationship that one liter contains 1000 cm³. Show that this relationship is factual by pouring a liter of rice or sand into a cube 10 cm by 10 cm by 10 cm.

The formulas for finding volumes are very straightforward. You might review the formulas for finding the areas of polygons, as this is usually where errors occur.

Related Activities

To emphasize the practical importance of this material, give students problems like those below and have them write some of their own.

1. Find the volume of a cylindrical oil tank if the diameter of the base is 3 m and the height is 4 m. Use $\pi \approx 3.14$.
28.3 m³

2. A fish tank in the form of a rectangular prism is 50 cm by 40 cm by 36 cm. Find the number of liters of water it will hold.
72 L

10-6 Volumes of Pyramids and Cones

Objective *for pages 369–372*

■ To find the volumes and capacities of pyramids and cones.

Teaching Suggestions

Have available several examples of prisms and pyramids with the same base and height, and cylinders and cones of the same base and height. Demonstrate again the relationship $V = \frac{1}{3}Bh$ by pouring rice or sand into the models as explained in the teaching suggestions for Lesson 10-5.

Be sure students understand that the height of a pyramid or a cone is the perpendicular distance from its vertex to its base, not the slant height.

Related Activities

To provide a change of pace, supply patterns for the geometric solids such as the tetrahedron, octahedron, dodecahedron, and icosahedron and have students make attractive mobiles using these patterns. Through research on Archimedes and Plato students can discover historical meanings and uses of these solid shapes.

10-7 Surface Areas of Prisms and Cylinders

Objective *for pages 373–377*

■ To find the surface areas of prisms and cylinders.

Teaching Suggestions

Visualization is very important when discussing this section. Begin by cutting a rectangular box open and laying it flat as in Written Exercise 12 to show students the six rectangles that make up the box. Cover the flattened box with a transparent centimeter grid to show the number of square centimeters in each rectangle. Students will notice three pairs of two identical rectangles, the top and bottom, the back and front, and the two sides.

Also take an empty juice can or an oatmeal box and cut the lateral surface perpendicular to the bases to produce the flattened figure shown on page 373. A biscuit can opens "naturally" into a parallelogram and two cir-

cles. This is another excellent model to use while explaining the formulas.

Understanding the concept of surface area is more important than memorizing the formulas in this lesson. Students who understand surface area can use easier formulas for plane figures to develop the formulas for solid figures.

Point out that the lateral surface of a prism is all the lateral faces. A triangular prism such as the one on page 373 has three lateral faces.

Related Activities

To expand on this topic, have students develop a formula for the surface area of a pyramid. Suggest that one important measurement is the slant height of a lateral face. (For a regular pyramid, if the slant height is h, the length of one side of the base is a, and the number of sides is n, the lateral area is $\frac{1}{2}nah$.)

To provide a challenge, suggest that students write computer programs to calculate the volumes and surface areas of prisms and cylinders, and the volumes of pyramids and cones.

10-8 Volumes and Surface Areas of Spheres

Objective *for pages 378–381*

■ To find the surface areas and volumes of spheres.

Teaching Suggestions

Draw a sphere that fits snugly into a cylinder as shown. (If students have trouble visualizing this, demonstrate with a balloon and an oatmeal box.) If the radius of the sphere is r, then the height of the cylinder is $2r$. Thus the volume of the cylinder is $\pi r^2 h = \pi r^2(2r) = 2\pi r^3$.

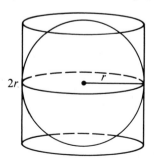

The volume of the sphere is less than the volume of the cylinder. As shown on page 378, it is $\frac{4}{3}\pi r^3$, which is two-thirds of $2\pi r^3$.

The surface area of a sphere is four times the area of the great circle (the circle whose radius is the same as the radius of the sphere) or $4\pi r^2$.

Remind students of the order of operations requirement for doing exponents before multiplication. To simplify calculations of volume, suggest that if the radius or height is not divisible by 3, then all computations should be done before the division by 3.

If students do the Calculator Key-In on page 381, note that on some calculators the exponent entry key is marked EE rather than EXP. The display will vary depending on the type of calculator used.

Related Activities

To relate mathematics to other subjects and provide practice using scientific notation, have students calculate the surface areas of Earth and the other planets. These areas can be used for other calculations, such as dividing the area of Earth by the human population.

Resource Book: Page 124 (Use After Page 381)

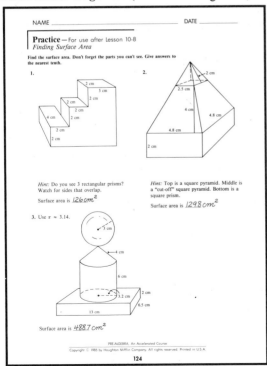

Resource Book: Pages 125–126 (Use After Page 381)

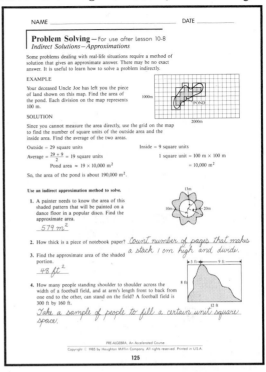

10-9 Mass and Density

Objective *for pages 382–385*

■ To find the mass of an object of a given density.

Teaching Suggestions

Most students have some idea of the meaning of *mass,* but may confuse it with *weight.* Explain to students that weight depends on the amount of gravitational pull on an object. As the force of gravity on an object decreases, the weight of an object decreases. Mass, however, remains constant and is the measure of the amount of matter an object contains. A rock will weigh less on the moon than on Earth because the gravity on the moon is less. The mass of the rock is the same whether it is on Earth, on the moon, or in space.

Demonstrate why the multiplier in Table 1 is 1,000,000:

$$1 \text{ m}^3 = (100 \text{ cm})^3 = 1,000,000 \text{ cm}^3$$
$$1 \text{ t} = 1000 \text{ kg} = 1000(1000 \text{ g}) = 1,000,000 \text{ g}$$

Related Activities

To relate mathematics to social studies, have students find out what units of measurement and measuring instruments have been used in the past and in various parts of the world. They could also find out the standards for the units of measurement that are used now.

To provide experience in measuring, have students measure the masses and volumes of objects. (If they are studying physical science, they may already have done this.) A spring scale may be marked in grams, but it actually measures the weight of an object; its reading would be less on the moon. A pan balance measures may be comparing the weight of an object with the weights of standard masses; its reading would be the same on the moon. To find the volume of a block of wood, students can measure the dimensions and multiply. To find the volume of an irregular object, read the water level in a graduated container, drop the object in, read the water level again, and subtract. When students calculate the density of an object, ask whether it would float in water and let them test the prediction. You might have other liquids available, such as vegetable oil (density about 0.9 g/cm³) or concentrated sugar solution (density about 1.2 g/cm³).

345g

Page 129

NAME _____ DATE _____

Test — Chapter 10

DIRECTIONS: Write the answers in the spaces provided.

Find the area of each figure described.

1. rectangle
   length: 10 mm
   width: 4 mm

2. parallelogram *[10-1]*
   base: 8 m
   height: 3 m

3. triangle
   base: 8 cm
   height: 5 cm

4. trapezoid *[10-2]*
   bases: 3 m and 7 m
   height: 7 m

5. circle: Use $\pi \approx 3.14$.
   radius: 9 cm

6. circle: Use $\pi \approx 3\frac{1}{7}$. *[10-3]*
   diameter: 14 m

7. Draw any lines or points of symmetry. *[10-4]*

8. Find the area of the symmetric figure.

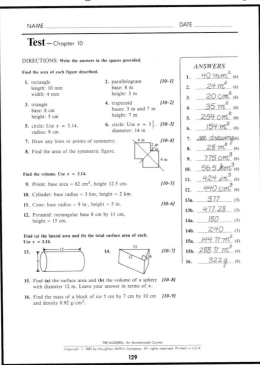

Find the volume. Use $\pi \approx 3.14$.

9. Prism: base area = 62 cm², height 12.5 cm. *[10-5]*

10. Cylinder: base radius = 3 km, height = 2 km.

11. Cone: base radius = 9 in., height = 5 in. *[10-6]*

12. Pyramid: rectangular base 8 cm by 11 cm,
    height = 15 cm.

Find (a) the lateral area and (b) the total surface area of each.
Use $\pi \approx 3.14$.

13.   14. *[10-7]*

15. Find (a) the surface area and (b) the volume of a sphere *[10-8]*
    with diameter 12 m. Leave your answer in terms of π.

16. Find the mass of a block of ice 5 cm by 7 cm by 10 cm *[10-9]*
    and density 0.92 g/cm³.

ANSWERS	
1.	$40\ mm^2$ (6)
2.	$24\ m^2$ (6)
3.	$20\ cm^2$ (6)
4.	$35\ m^2$ (6)
5.	$254\ cm^2$ (6)
6.	$154\ m^2$ (6)
7.	see drawing (6)
8.	$28\ m^2$ (6)
9.	$775\ cm^3$ (6)
10.	$56.5\ km^3$ (6)
11.	$424\ in.^3$ (6)
12.	$440\ cm^3$ (6)
13a.	377 (3)
13b.	477.28 (3)
14a.	180 (3)
14b.	240 (3)
15a.	$144\,\pi\ m^2$ (4)
15b.	$288\,\pi\ m^3$ (4)
16.	$322\ g$ (8)

129

Page 130

NAME _____ DATE _____

Make-up Test — Chapter 10

DIRECTIONS: Write the answers in the spaces provided.

Find the area of each figure described.

1. rectangle
   length: 12 cm
   width: 3 cm

2. parallelogram *[10-1]*
   base: 10 m
   height: 6 m

3. triangle
   base: 6 m
   height: 7 m

4. trapezoid *[10-2]*
   bases: 4 cm and 8 cm
   height: 5 cm

5. circle: Use $\pi \approx 3.14$.
   radius: 8 m

6. circle: Use $\pi \approx \frac{22}{7}$. *[10-3]*
   diameter: 28 cm

7. Draw any lines or points of symmetry. *[10-4]*

8. Find the area of the symmetric figure.

Find the volume. Use $\pi \approx 3.14$.

9. Prism: base area = 48.5 cm², height = 16 cm. *[10-5]*

10. Cylinder: base radius = 10 ft, height = 2.6 ft.

11. Pyramid: square base 14 cm high = 21 cm. *[10-6]*

12. Cone: base diameter = 5 m, height = 12 m.

Find (a) the lateral area and (b) the total surface area of each.
Use $\pi \approx 3.14$.

13.   14. *[10-7]*

15. Find (a) the surface area and (b) the volume of a sphere *[10-8]*
    with diameter 18 cm. Leave your answer in terms of π.

16. Find the mass of a block of wood 4 cm by 9 cm by *[10-9]*
    12 cm having density 0.85 g/cm³.

ANSWERS	
1.	$36\ cm^2$ (6)
2.	$60\ m^2$ (6)
3.	$21\ m^2$ (6)
4.	$30\ cm^2$ (6)
5.	$201\ m^2$ (6)
6.	$616\ cm^2$ (6)
7.	see drawing (6)
8.	$120\ m^2$ (6)
9.	$776\ cm^3$ (6)
10.	$816\ ft^3$ (6)
11.	$1372\ cm^3$ (6)
12.	$78.5\ m^3$ (6)
13a.	251 (3)
13b.	879 (3)
14a.	480 (3)
14b.	600 (3)
15a.	$324\,\pi\ cm^2$ (4)
15b.	$972\,\pi\ cm^3$ (4)
16.	$367\ g$ (8)

130

Page 131

NAME _____ DATE _____

CUMULATIVE REVIEW — Chapters 1–10
Exercises

Evaluate the expression if $p = 4$, $q = 0.5$, and $r = 12$.

1. $pq + r$ 14
2. pqr 24
3. $3r - 8p$ 4
4. $r^2 + p^3$ 208
5. pq^2 1
6. $10q - r$ -7

Solve.

7. $46 > 3x - 17$ all the numbers less than 21
8. $3r + 23 = 68$ 15
9. $\frac{d}{4} \le 12$ all the numbers less than or equal to 48
10. $4r + 9 = 8$ 18
11. $7 - 2w < 15$ all the numbers greater than -4
12. $2m + 12 = 5m - 15$ 9

Complete.

13. The area of a trapezoid having bases 14 and 24 and height 8 is 152.

14. The area of a circle with a diameter 8 m is 16 π.

15. The volume of a pyramid of height 16 cm having a 6-cm by
    10-cm rectangle as a base is $320\ cm^3$.

16. A cylinder with base radius 3 and height 8 has a lateral area of 48 π
    and a surface area of 66 π.

17. 24 is 32% of what number? 75
18. What is $20\frac{1}{2}$% of 620? 127.1
19. 30.69 is what percent of 68.2? 45%
20. 91 is 140% of what number? 65

Solve the equation for y in terms of x.

21. $3x + y = 15$ $y = 15 - 3x$
22. $xy = 42$ $y = \frac{42}{x}$
23. $\frac{x}{3} + y = 12$ $y = 12 - \frac{x}{3}$
24. $2x + 2y = 10$ $y = 5 - x$
25. $y - x^2 = 49$ $y = 49 + x^2$
26. $3y - x = 5x$ $y = 2x$

Find the area of the figure described. Leave your answer in terms of π
if necessary.

27. Circle with radius 5 cm. $25\,\pi\ cm^2$
28. Triangle with height 7 m and base 12 m. $42\ m^2$
29. Parallelogram with height 5 in. and base 16 in. $80\ in.^2$
30. Circle with diameter 34 cm. $289\,\pi\ cm^2$

131

Page 132

NAME _____ DATE _____

CUMULATIVE REVIEW — Chapters 1–10 *(continued)*
Problems

Problem Solving Reminders
Here are some reminders that may help you solve some of the problems
on this page.
• Determine what information is necessary to solve the problem.
• Consider whether drawing a sketch will help.
• If more than one method can be used to solve a problem, use one
  method to solve and one to check.

Solve.

1. A cylindrical storage tank 6 m in diameter is 4 m high. What is
   the volume of the tank? Use $\pi \approx 3.14$. $113.04\ m^3$

2. An insurance agent earns a commission of $3\frac{1}{2}$% of the first
   $8000 of insurance she sells each week and 5% of the value in
   excess of $8000. One week she sold $17,540 of insurance. How
   much did she earn? 757

3. After a 12% increase, the price of a warm-up suit was $43.40.
   What was the old price of the suit? $38.75

4. Mark's living room measures 14 ft by 18 ft. How much will it
   cost to carpet the room if carpet costs $15.95 per square yard,
   padding costs $2.50 per square yard, and installation is $3.00 per
   square yard? (Hint: 9 ft² = 1 yd²) $600.60

5. Amy purchased soccer cleats costing $14.95, shin guards costing
   $10.50, and two pair of soccer socks costing $2.75 each. There
   was a 6% tax on her purchases. How much did she get after
   paying with two twenty-dollar bills? $7.19

6. Jack Nissen purchased a piece of wood that he cut into two
   sections for shelving. One section was 5 in. longer than twice
   the length of the other. If the piece of wood measured 2 ft 8 in.,
   how long was each section? 9 in., 23 in.

7. The cost of piano sheet music rose from $1.95 to $2.60 in three
   years. What was the percent of increase? $33\frac{1}{3}\%$

132

345h

Reading Mathematics

Students will learn the meaning of the following mathematical terms in this lesson: *area of a polygon, length of a rectangle, width of a rectangle, dimensions of a rectangle, base of a parallelogram, height of a parallelogram, unit area, square centimeter (cm²), square kilometer (km²), square meter (m²), square millimeter (mm²), square unit.*

10-1 Areas of Rectangles and Parallelograms

Earlier we measured lengths of segments and found perimeters of polygons. Now we will measure the part of the plane enclosed by a polygon. We call this measure the **area** of the polygon.

Just as we needed a unit length to measure segments, we now need a unit area. In the metric system a unit area often used is the **square centimeter (cm²).**

The rectangular regions shown in the diagrams have been divided into square centimeters to show the areas of the rectangles.

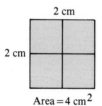

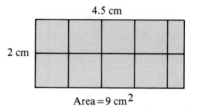

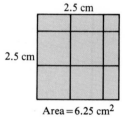

Notice that the area of each rectangle is the product of the lengths of two consecutive sides. These sides are called the **length** and the **width** of the rectangle. The length names the longer side and the width names the shorter side. We have the following formula for any rectangle.

Formula

Area of rectangle = length × width

$$A = lw$$

The length and width of a rectangle are called its **dimensions.**

In the case of a parallelogram, we may consider either pair of parallel sides to be the **bases.** (The word *base* is also used to denote the length of the base.) The **height** is the perpendicular distance between the bases.

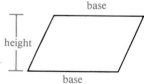

The colored region in the figure at the top of the next page can be moved to the right, as shown in the second figure, to form a rectangle having dimensions *b* and *h*. Thus, the area of the parallelogram is the same as the area of the rectangle, *bh*.

346 *Chapter 10*

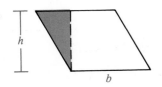
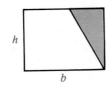

The area of any parallelogram can be found by using the following formula.

> ## Formula
>
> Area of parallelogram = base × height
>
> $$A = bh$$

EXAMPLE 1 Find the area of each parallelogram.

a.
25 m, 30 m

b.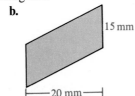
15 mm, 20 mm

Solution

a. $A = bh$
$= 25 \times 30 = 750$
The area is 750 m².

b. $A = bh$
$= 15 \times 20 = 300$
The area is 300 mm².

EXAMPLE 2 A parallelogram has an area of 375 cm² and a height of 15 cm. Find the length of the base.

Solution

$A = bh$

$375 = b \times 15$

$\dfrac{375}{15} = b$

$25 = b$

The length of the base is 25 cm.

The unit areas used in the examples are **square meters (m²), square millimeters (mm²),** and **square centimeters (cm²).** For very large regions, such as states or countries, we could use **square kilometers (km²).**

Areas and Volumes **347**

Sometimes we may work with an unspecified unit of length. Then the unit of area is simply called a **square unit.** Thus, the area of the rectangle shown at the right is 250 square units.

Class Exercises

Find the area of each shaded region.

1.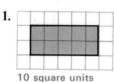
10 square units

2.
9 square units

3.
6 square units

4.
8 square units

5. Find the perimeters of the regions in Exercises 1 and 2. 14 units; 12 units

6. Find the area of a square with sides 4 cm long. 16 cm²

Complete.

7. 1 cm = ? mm 10

1 cm² = ? mm² 100

8. 1 m = ? cm 100

1 m² = ? cm² 10,000

9. 1 km = ? m 1000

1 km² = ? m² 1,000,000

10. Explain why the blue parallelogram and the gray one have equal areas. They have the same base and height.

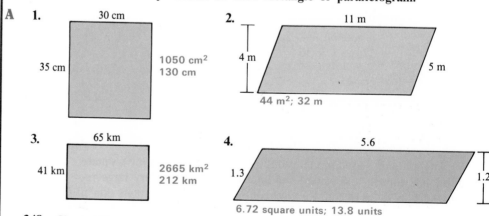

Written Exercises

Find the area and the perimeter of each rectangle or parallelogram.

A **1.** 30 cm, 35 cm — 1050 cm² 130 cm

2. 11 m, 4 m, 5 m — 44 m²; 32 m

3. 65 km, 41 km — 2665 km² 212 km

4. 5.6, 1.3, 1.2 — 6.72 square units; 13.8 units

348   *Chapter 10*

Supply the missing information for a rectangle.

1. length: 5, width: 2,
perimeter: ? 14,
area: ? 10

2. length: 2.4,
perimeter: 22.8,
width: ? 9,
area: ? 21.6

3. width: 1.1, perimeter: 5.2,
length: ? 1.5,
area: ? 1.65

4. width: 1, area: 5,
length: ? 5,
perimeter: ? 12

5. length: 34, area: 68,
width: ? 2,
perimeter: ? 72

Supply the missing information for a parallelogram.

6. base: 3, height: 10,
area ? 30

7. height: 12, area: 72,
base: ? 6

Find the area and the perimeter of a rectangle having the given dimensions.

5. 48 mm by 92 mm 4416 mm²; 280 mm

6. 55 cm by 32 cm 1760 cm²; 174 cm

7. 63.7 km by 39.1 km 2490.67 km²; 205.6 km

8. 206.3 m by 33.15 m 6838.845 m² 478.9 m

Copy and complete the tables.

Rectangle	9.	10.	11.	12.	13.	14.
length	12.5	12	? 80	? 6	8.6	? 1
width	7.5	? 5	45	2.5	? 0.4	? 1
perimeter	? 40	? 34	? 250	17.0	18.0	4
area	? 93.75	60	3600	? 15	? 3.44	1

Parallelogram	15.	16.	17.	18.	19.	20.
base	18.5	2.7	? 0.5	14.3	2.9	? 9
height	4.0	? 3	1.6	3.2	? 4	0.4
area	? 74	8.1	0.8	? 45.76	11.6	3.6

Find the area of each region. (*Hint:* Subdivide each region into simpler ones if necessary.)

B 21.

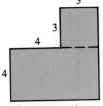

37 square units

22.

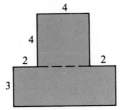

40 square units

23.

30 square units

24.

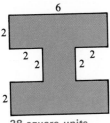

28 square units

25.

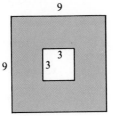

72 square units

26.

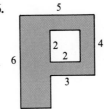

20 square units

Areas and Volumes **349**

Suggested Assignments

Core
348/1, 3
349/5–25 odd
350/Prob. 1–4
350/Rev. 1–7 odd

Enriched
349/10–20 even; 21–26
350/Prob. 4–8
350/Rev. 2–8 even

Supplementary Materials

Practice Masters, p. 45

Problems

Solve.

A **1.** How many square meters of wallpaper are needed to cover a wall 8 m long and 3 m high? 24 m²

2. a. How many square yards of carpeting are needed to cover a floor that measures 8 yd by 5 yd? 40 sq yd
b. How much will the carpeting cost at $24 per square yard? $960

3. a. How many square feet of vinyl floor covering are needed to cover a floor measuring 60 ft by 12 ft? 720 sq ft
b. How much will the floor covering cost at $1.50 per square foot? $1080

4. Jose wishes to line the open box shown at the right using five sheets of plastic. How many square centimeters will he need? 3680 cm²

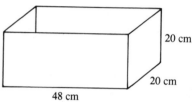
20 cm
20 cm
48 cm

B **5.** Yoneko wishes to obtain 6 m² of plastic from a roll 40 cm wide. How many meters should she unroll? 15 m

6. A square pool 5 m on each side is surrounded by a brick walk 2 m wide. What is the area of the walk? 56 m²

7. A construction site in the shape of a square is surrounded by a wooden wall 2 m high. If the length of one side of the wall is 45 m, find the area of the construction site. 2025 m²

8. A rectangular cow pasture has an area of 1925 m². If the length of one side of the pasture is 55 m, find the lengths of the other sides.
55 m; 35 m; 35 m

Review Exercises

Multiply.

1. $\frac{1}{2} \times 8 \times 7$ 28

2. $\frac{1}{3} \times 11 \times 9$ 33

3. $\frac{1}{2} \times 1.3 \times 1.6$ 1.04

4. $\frac{1}{2}(8 + 9)11$ 93.5

5. $\frac{1}{4}(20 + 12)5$ 40

6. $\frac{1}{2}(0.11 + 0.17)0.6$ 0.084

7. $\frac{1}{3}(0.26 + 0.52)0.3$ 0.078

8. $\frac{1}{4}(1.76 + 2.69)1.94$ 2.15825

350 *Chapter 10*

10-2 Areas of Triangles and Trapezoids

Teaching Suggestions
p. 345b

Related Activities p. 345b

Any side of a triangle can be considered to be the **base**. The **height** is then the perpendicular distance from the opposite vertex to the base line.

Let us find the area of a triangle having base b and height h. The triangle and a congruent copy of it can be put together to form a parallelogram as shown in the diagrams.

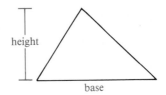

Reading Mathematics

Students will learn the meaning of the following mathematical terms in this lesson: *base of a triangle, height of a triangle, bases of a trapezoid, height of a trapezoid.*

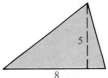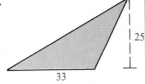

Since the area of the parallelogram is bh and the area of the triangle is half the parallelogram, we have the following formula.

> ### Formula
>
> Area of triangle $= \frac{1}{2} \times$ base $\times$ height
>
> $$A = \frac{1}{2}bh$$

EXAMPLE Find the area of each triangle.

a.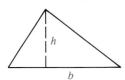

b.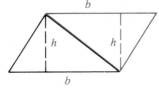

c.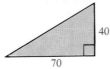

Solution

a. $A = \frac{1}{2}bh$

$\quad = \frac{1}{2} \times 8 \times 5$

$\quad = 20$

$A = 20$ square units

b. $A = \frac{1}{2}bh$

$\quad = \frac{1}{2} \times 70 \times 40$

$\quad = 1400$

$A = 1400$ square units

c. $A = \frac{1}{2}bh$

$\quad = \frac{1}{2} \times 33 \times 25$

$\quad = 4125$

$A = 412.5$ square units

Areas and Volumes **351**

Find the area of each triangle.

1.

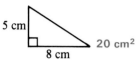

5 cm

8 cm

20 cm²

2.

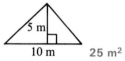

2 cm

2 cm

2 cm²

3.

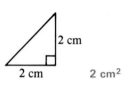

5 m

10 m

25 m²

4.

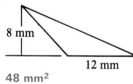

8 mm

12 mm

48 mm²

Note in part (b) of Example 1 that the lengths of the sides of the *right angle* of the triangle were used as the base and the height. This can be done for any *right* triangle, even if the triangle is positioned so that it is "standing" on the side opposite the right angle.

The **height** of a trapezoid is the perpendicular distance between the parallel sides. These parallel sides are called the **bases** of the trapezoid. The method used to find the formula for the area of a triangle can be used to find the formula for the area of a trapezoid having bases b_1 and b_2 and height h. The trapezoid and a congruent copy of it can be put together to form a parallelogram. The area of the parallelogram is $(b_1 + b_2)h$ and the area of the original trapezoid is half of the area of the parallelogram.

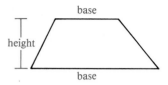

base

height

base

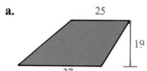

b_2

h

b_1

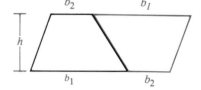

b_2 b_1

h

b_1 b_2

We, therefore, have the following formula.

Formula

Area of trapezoid $= \frac{1}{2} \times$ (sum of bases) $\times$ height

$$A = \frac{1}{2}(b_1 + b_2)h$$

EXAMPLE 2 Find the area of each trapezoid.

a.

25

19

37

b.

5 cm

2 cm

8 cm

Solution

a. $A = \frac{1}{2}(b_1 + b_2)h$

$= \frac{1}{2} \times (37 + 25) \times 19 = 589$

$A = 589$ square units

b. $A = \frac{1}{2}(b_1 + b_2)h$

$= \frac{1}{2} \times (5 + 2) \times 8 = 28$

$A = 28$ m²

352 *Chapter 10*

EXAMPLE 3   A trapezoid has an area of 200 cm² and bases of 15 cm and 25 cm. Find the height.

Solution

$$A = \frac{1}{2}(b_1 + b_2)h$$

$$200 = \frac{1}{2} \times (15 + 25) \times h$$

$$200 = \frac{1}{2} \times 40 \times h$$

$$200 = 20h$$
$$10 = h$$

The height is 10 cm.

Find the area of each trapezoid.

5.

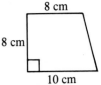

72 cm²

6.

12 km

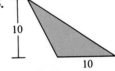

10 km

24 km

180 km²

Class Exercises

Find the area of each polygon.

1.

8

10

40 square units

2.

8

12

48 square units

3.

10

10

50 square units

4.

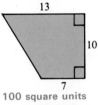

13

10

7

100 square units

5.

4

4

6

20 square units

6.

5

3

6

24 square units

7.

15 square units

8.

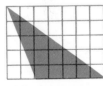

8 square units

9.

28 square units

10.

12.5 square units

11.

12 square units

12.

16 square units

Areas and Volumes   **353**

Additional A Exercises

Find the area of each polygon.

1. triangle: base 12 cm, height 6 cm 36 cm²

2. triangle: base 7 m, height 1.2 m 4.2 m²

3. trapezoid: bases 20 cm and 30 cm, height 40 cm 1000 cm²

4. trapezoid: bases 1 m and 2 m, height 3 m 4.5 m²

Find the height of each polygon.

5. triangle: base 12 cm, area 120 cm² 20 cm

6. trapezoid: bases 3 km and 5 km, area 128 km² 32 km

Written Exercises

Find the area of each polygon.

A **1.** 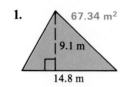 67.34 m²

9.1 m

14.8 m

2. 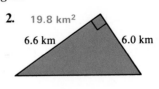 19.8 km² 6.6 km 6.0 km

3. 2127.5 cm² 75 cm 37 cm 40 cm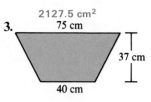

4. 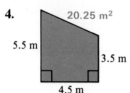 20.25 m² 5.5 m 3.5 m 4.5 m

5. 290 mm² 29 mm 20 mm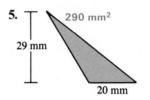

6. 30 cm 810 cm² 54 cm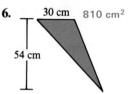

7. Triangle: base 122 km, height 30 km 1830 km²

8. Triangle: base 480 m, height 480 m 115,200 m²

9. Trapezoid: bases 12.3 cm and 6.2 cm, height 4.8 cm 44.4 cm²

10. Trapezoid: bases 14.6 km and 22.4 km, height 14.0 km 259 km²

Copy and complete the tables.

Triangle	11.	12.	13.	14.
base	6 cm	16 mm	? 4 m	? 0.6 m
height	? 24 cm	? 10 mm	2.4 m	1.4 m
area	72 cm²	80 mm²	4.8 m²	0.42 m²

B

Trapezoid	15.	16.	17.	18.
base	0.7 mm	0.8 m	3	2
base	1.7 mm	1.2 m	? 15	? 10
height	? 8 mm	? 1 m	2	3
area	9.6 mm²	1.0 m²	18	18

19. In the figure at the right, $\overline{PQ}$ is parallel to $\overline{RT}$. Explain why triangles PQR, PQS, and PQT all have the same area. The triangles have the same base and height.

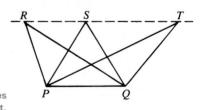

354 *Chapter 10*

In Exercises 20 and 21 find the area of (a) the blue part and (b) the red part of the pennant.

20.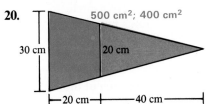
500 cm²; 400 cm²

21.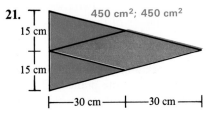
450 cm²; 450 cm²

 30 cm, 20 cm, 20 cm, 40 cm

 15 cm, 15 cm, 30 cm, 30 cm

C **22.** One triangle has a base and a height that are twice as large as the base and the height of another triangle. What is the ratio of their areas? 4 : 1

23. One rectangle has a base and a height that are 3 times the base and the height of another rectangle. What is the ratio of their areas? their perimeters? 9 : 1; 3 : 1

Review Exercises

Simplify.

1. 3×5^2 75

2. 1.2×9^2 97.2

3. 4×1.3^2 6.76

4. $3 \times 7^2 - 2 \times 4^2$ 115

5. $4 \times 5^2 + 3 \times 8^2$ 292

6. $11^2 \times 3 - 6^2 \times 4$ 219

7. $5 \times 1.4^2 - 7 \times 1.1^2$ 1.33

8. $2.5^2 \times 4 + 3.2^2 \times 7$ 96.68

9. $17 \times 14^2 + 6 \times 16^2$ 4868

▌▌▌▌ **Challenge**

The ancient Egyptians worked primarily with fractions with a numerator of 1. They expressed fractions such as $\frac{2}{5}$ as the sum of these fractions: $\frac{2}{5} = \frac{1}{3} + \frac{1}{15}$. These sums were listed in a table. Find the following sums selected from the Egyptian fraction table.

1. $\frac{1}{8} + \frac{1}{52} + \frac{1}{104}$ $\frac{2}{13}$

2. $\frac{1}{12} + \frac{1}{51} + \frac{1}{68}$ $\frac{2}{17}$

3. $\frac{1}{12} + \frac{1}{76} + \frac{1}{114}$ $\frac{2}{19}$

4. $\frac{1}{24} + \frac{1}{58} + \frac{1}{174} + \frac{1}{232}$ $\frac{2}{29}$

5. $\frac{1}{20} + \frac{1}{124} + \frac{1}{155}$ $\frac{2}{31}$

6. $\frac{1}{24} + \frac{1}{111} + \frac{1}{296}$ $\frac{2}{37}$

Areas and Volumes **355**

Suggested Assignments
Core
354/1–15, 17
355/22; Rev. 1–9
Enriched
354/1–19 odd
355/20–23; Rev. 1–9 odd
355/Challenge

Supplementary Materials

Practice Masters, p. 45
Computer Activity 19

Students will learn the meaning of the following mathematical term in this lesson:
area of a circle.
    Diagrams should be large
enough to read and clearly
labeled with all the given information, such as point
names, segment lengths, and
congruent parts. Students
may have to read the problems several times and should
check their diagrams against
the words of the problem to
make sure they have not
omitted any given information. Then they should add
any information to the diagram that they can deduce
from the given facts. They
cannot assume information
based on how a given dia-
gram looks, nor should they
draw a diagram that has special characteristics not given
in the problem.

10-3 Areas of Circles

Recall that there are two formulas for the circumference, C, of a circle. If the diameter of the circle is denoted by d and the radius by r, then

$$C = \pi d \quad \text{and} \quad C = 2\pi r.$$

Two approximations for the number π are 3.14 and $\frac{22}{7}$.
    The part of the plane enclosed by a circle is called the **area of the circle.** This area is given by the following formula.

Formula

Area of circle $= \pi \times (\text{radius})^2$

$$A = \pi r^2$$

EXAMPLE 1 Find the areas of the shaded regions. Use $\pi \approx 3.14$.

a.

7 cm

b.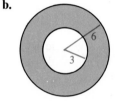

6

3

Solution

a. $A = \pi r^2$
$\approx 3.14 \times 7^2$
$\approx 3.14 \times 49 \approx 153.86$
$A \approx 154 \text{ cm}^2$

b. $A = (\pi \times 6^2) - (\pi \times 3^2)$
$= (\pi \times 36) - (\pi \times 9)$
$= \pi(36 - 9) = \pi \times 27$
$\approx 3.14 \times 27 \approx 84.78$
$A \approx 84.8 \text{ square units}$

Recall that we give answers to only three digits when we use the approximation $\pi \approx 3.14$. Sometimes, to avoid approximations, we give an answer in terms of π.

EXAMPLE 2 Find the area of the shaded region. Leave your answer in terms of π.

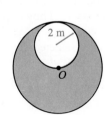

2 m

O

Solution

Area of shaded region
$= (\text{Area of large circle}) -$
$\qquad\qquad (\text{Area of small circle})$
We first find the area of the small circle.

$$A = \pi r^2 = \pi \times 2^2 = 4\pi$$

We then find the area of the large circle.
Since the radius of the large circle is the same as the diameter of the small circle, we know that the radius of the large circle is 4 m.

$$A = \pi r^2 = \pi \times 4^2 = 16\pi$$

Thus, area of shaded region is equal to $16\pi - 4\pi = 12\pi$
The area of the shaded region is 12π m².

To make the formula $A = \pi r^2$ seem reasonable to you, think of the circular region below cut like a pie.

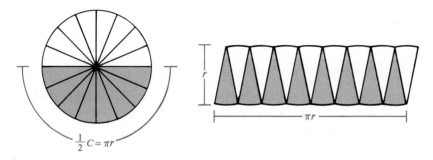

The pieces can be arranged to form a figure rather like a parallelogram with base πr and height r. This suggests that the area is given by

$$\pi r \times r = \pi r^2.$$

Reading Mathematics: *Diagrams*
To read and understand an explanation that is illustrated by a diagram, ask yourself questions about the diagram as you read. In the explanation above, for example, ask yourself, why is the figure "rather like" a parallelogram. How is it different? Why is the measure of the base πr?

Class Exercises

Solve.

1. A circle has radius 10 cm. What is its area? Use $\pi \approx 3.14$. 314 cm²

2. A circle has diameter 14 units. What is its area? Use $\pi \approx \frac{22}{7}$. 154 square units

3. A circle has diameter 6. What is its area? Give your answer in terms of π. 9π square units

4. A circle has radius 5. What is its area? Give your answer in terms of π. 25π square units

Areas and Volumes   **357**

Find the area of the circle. Use $\pi \approx 3.14$ and round answers involving π to three digits.

1. radius $= 9$ cm **254 cm²**

2. diameter $= 0.8$ m
0.502 m²

3. A circle has radius 21. What is its area? Use $\pi \approx \frac{22}{7}$. **1386 square units**

4. A circle has diameter 44 m. What is its area? Leave your answer in terms of π. **484π m²**

5. The area of a circle is 144π m². What is its radius? **12 m**

6. The area of a circle is $\frac{1}{9}\pi$ square units. What is its radius? **$\frac{1}{3}$ unit**

Use $\pi \approx 3.14$.

7. The radius of a circular coin is 1.5 cm. Find the area of one side of the coin. **7.07 cm²**

8. The diameter of the hole in a glass tube is 0.1 mm. Find its area. **0.008 mm²**

5. A circle has area 4π cm². What is its radius? **2 cm**

6. A circle has area 9π. What is its diameter? **6 units**

Written Exercises

Find the area of the circle. Use $\pi \approx 3.14$ and round the answer to three digits.

A **1.** radius $= 5$ km **78.5 km²**   **2.** radius $= 8$ cm **201 cm²**   **3.** diameter $= 0.6$ m **0.283 m²**

Find the area of the circle. Use $\pi \approx \frac{22}{7}$.

4. radius $= 14$ cm **616 cm²**   **5.** diameter $= 3\frac{1}{2}$ **$9\frac{5}{8}$ square units**   **6.** diameter $= 28$ cm **616 cm²**

Find the area of the circle. Leave your answer in terms of π.

7. diameter $= 20$ m **100π m²**   **8.** radius $= 15$ cm **225π cm²**   **9.** circumference $= 4\pi$ **4π square units**

Find the radius of a circle having the given area. Use $\pi \approx 3.14$.

10. $A = 78.5$ cm² **5 cm**   **11.** $A = 314$ m² **10 m**

Find the diameter of a circle having the given area. Use $\pi \approx \frac{22}{7}$.

12. $A = 154$ km² **14 km**   **13.** $A = 3\frac{1}{7}$ cm² **2 cm**

Find the circumference of a circle with the given area in terms of π.

B **14.** $A = 16\pi$ **8π units**   **15.** $A = 4\pi$ **4π units**

Find the area of the shaded region. Leave your answer in terms of π.

16.

10 m
5 m
75π m²

17.

9 cm
12 cm
31.5π cm²

18.

3   3
9π square units

19.

10 m
(25π − 50) m²

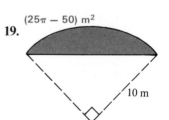

C 20. Find a formula giving the area of a circle in terms of the diameter. $A = \frac{\pi}{4}d^2$

21. Find the formula giving the area of a circle in terms of the circumference. $A = \frac{C^2}{4\pi}$

Problems

Solve. Draw a sketch illustrating the problem if necessary. Use $\pi \approx 3.14$ and round the answer to three digits.

A **1.** A circular lawn 10 m in diameter is to be resodded at a cost of $14 per m². Find the total cost. $1100

2. The Connaught Centre building in Hong Kong has 1748 circular plate glass windows, each 2.4 m in diameter. If glass costs $12 per m², what is the cost of the glass in a single window? $54.30

3. The circumference of a circular pond is 62.8 m. If its diameter is 20 m, find the area. 314 m²

B **4.** A circular pond 20 m in diameter is surrounded by a gravel path 5 m wide. The path is to be replaced by a brick walk costing $30 per square meter. How much will the walk cost? $11,800

5. The inner and outer radii of the grooved part of a phonograph record are 7 cm and 14 cm. What is the area of the grooved part? 462 cm²

Hint for Problems 6 and 7: Let the radius of the circle be 1 unit.

C **6.** A circle is inscribed in a square. What fraction of the area of the square is taken up by the circle? $\frac{\pi}{4}$

7. A square is inscribed in a circle. What fraction of the area of the circle is taken up by the square? $\frac{2}{\pi}$

Review Exercises

Estimate to the nearest whole number.

1. $(3.9)^2$ 16   **2.** $(5.3)^2$ 25   **3.** $(2.72)^2$ 9   **4.** $(6.18)^2$ 36

5. 2.7×6 18   **6.** 3.1×4.9 15   **7.** 3.14×5.3 15   **8.** 4.92×5.13 25

Areas and Volumes **359**

Suggested Assignments

Core
358/1–14, 18
359/Prob. 1–4

Enriched
358/2–12 even; 14–19
359/20; Prob. 3–6

Supplementary Materials

Practice Masters, p. 46

Teaching Suggestions
p. 345c

Related Activities p. 345c

Reading Mathematics

Students will learn the meaning of the following mathematical terms in this lesson: *symmetric with respect to a line*, *line of symmetry*, and *symmetric with respect to a point*.

10-4 Using Symmetry to Find Areas

We say that the figure at the right is **symmetric with respect to a line,** $\overleftrightarrow{AB}$, because if it were folded along $\overleftrightarrow{AB}$, the lower half would fall exactly on the upper half. $\overleftrightarrow{AB}$ is called a **line of symmetry.**

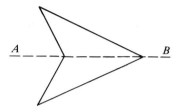

The diagrams below show that figures may have more than one line of symmetry.

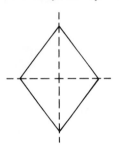 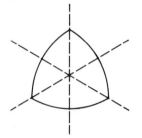 

Symmetry can be helpful in finding areas.

EXAMPLE 1   Find the area of the symmetric figure.

Solution   The symmetry of this figure is such that the four triangles are congruent. Therefore,

$$A = 4 \times \tfrac{1}{2}bh$$

$$= 4 \times \left(\tfrac{1}{2} \times 7 \times 6\right) = 84$$

Thus, the area is 84 square units.

Figures can also be **symmetric with respect to a point.** Although the figure at the right has no line of symmetry, it is symmetric with respect to point *O*. A figure is symmetric with respect to a point, *O*, if for every point *P* on the figure there corresponds an opposite point *Q* on the figure such that *O* is the midpoint of the segment $\overline{PQ}$. Every line through the point of symmetry divides the figure into two congruent figures.

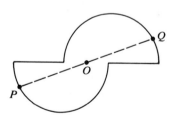

360   *Chapter 10*

EXAMPLE 2 Find the area of the symmetric figure.

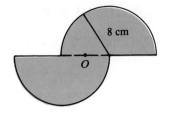

8 cm

O

Solution The dashed line divides the region into two semicircles of radius 8 cm.

$$A = 2 \times \left(\tfrac{1}{2}\pi r^2\right)$$

$$= 2 \times \left(\tfrac{1}{2}\pi \times 8^2\right)$$

$$\approx 3.14 \times 64 = 200.96$$

The area is approximately 201 cm².

Class Exercises

Copy each figure and show on your drawing any lines or points of symmetry.

1.

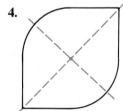

Equilateral
Triangle

2.

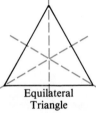

Semicircle

3.

Square

4.

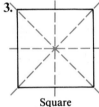

5.

6.

70° | 70°

7.

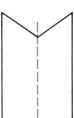

8.

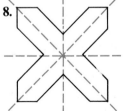

9.

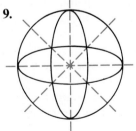

Areas and Volumes **361**

Chalkboard Examples

Identify which of the following figures are symmetric with respect to a line and which are symmetric with respect to a point.

1.

line

2.

point

3.

line

4.

line

5.

point

6.

point

Copy each figure and show on your drawing any lines or points of symmetry.

1.

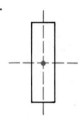

2.

3.

4.

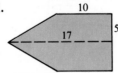

Find the area. Round answers involving π to three digits.

1. rectangle
length: 12 cm
width: 14 cm
168 cm²

2. parallelogram
base: 6 cm
height: 10 cm
60 cm²

Written Exercises

Copy each figure and show on your drawing any lines or points of symmetry.

A 1.

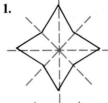

2.

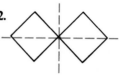

3.

4.

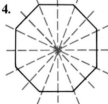

5.

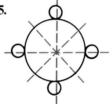

6.

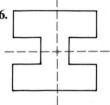

Find the areas of the following symmetric figures. Give your answers in terms of π if necessary.

7.

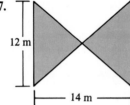

12 m
14 m
84 m²

8.

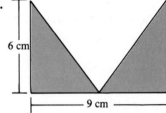

6 cm
9 cm
27 cm²

B 9.

5
50π square units

10.

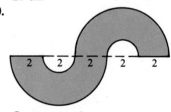

2 2 2 2 2
8π square units

11.

10
17
5
135 square units

12.

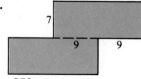

7
9 9
252 square units

13.

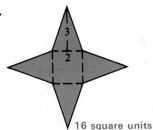

16 square units

14.

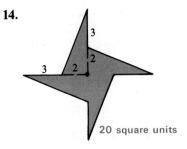

20 square units

15.

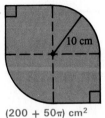

$(200 + 50\pi)$ cm²

16.

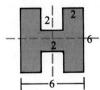

20 cm²

Self-Test A

Find the area. Round the answer to three digits if necessary.

1. rectangle
length: 21 cm
width: 13 cm 273 cm²

2. parallelogram [10–1]
base: 7 m
height: 12 m 84 m²

3. triangle
base: 18 cm
height: 8 cm 72 cm²

4. trapezoid [10–2]
bases: 11 m and 7 m
height: 4 m 36 m²

5. circle: Use $\pi \approx 3.14$.
radius: 15 mm 707 mm²

6. circle: Use $\pi \approx \frac{22}{7}$. [10–3]
diameter: 28 cm 616 cm²

7. Copy the figure and show any lines or points of symmetry. [10–4]

8. Find the area of the symmetric figure.
28 square units

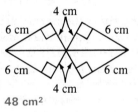

Self-Test answers and Extra Practice are at the back of the book.

Areas and Volumes **363**

---

3. triangle
base: 10 m
height: 11 m
55 m²

4. trapezoid
bases: 4 cm and 10 cm
height: 11 cm
77 cm²

5. circle: Use $\pi \approx 3.14$.
radius: 11 cm
380 cm²

6. circle: Use $\pi \approx \frac{22}{7}$.
diameter: 56 mm
2464 mm²

7. Copy the figure and show any lines or points of symmetry.

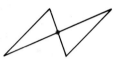

8. Find the area of the symmetric figure.

4 cm

6 cm   6 cm

6 cm   6 cm

4 cm

48 cm²

Suggested Assignments

Core
Day 1: 362/1–9
Day 2: 362/10–12
363/Self-Test A

Enriched
Day 1: 362/3–5; 8–12
363/13
Day 2: 363/14–16
363/Self-Test A

Supplementary Materials

Practice Masters, p. 46
Test 10A, pp. 67–68

Teaching Suggestions
p. 345d

Related Activities p. 345d

Reading Mathematics

Students will learn the meaning of the following mathematical terms in this lesson: *polyhedron, prism, bases, height, solid, volume, cylinder, capacity, liter, milliliter.*

10-5 Volumes of Prisms and Cylinders

A **polyhedron** is a figure formed of polygonal parts of planes, called **faces,** that enclose a region of space. A **prism** is a polyhedron that has two congruent faces, called **bases,** that are parallel. The other faces are regions bounded by parallelograms. The bases may also be parallelograms. Prisms are named according to their bases. Unless otherwise stated, we will only consider prisms whose other faces are rectangles.

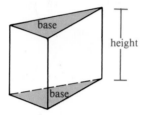

Triangular Prism

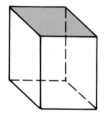

Square Prism

In each figure above, the bases are shaded. The perpendicular distance between the bases is the **height** of the prism.

A polyhedron together with the region inside it is called a **solid.** The measure of the space occupied by a solid is called the **volume** of the solid. The prism at the right, filled with 3 layers of 8 unit cubes, has 24 unit cubes. In this case, each unit cube is a cubic centimeter (cm³). Thus the volume of the cube is 24 cm³.

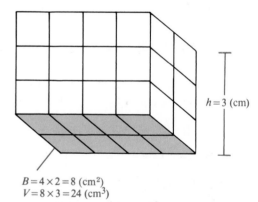

$h = 3$ (cm)

$B = 4 \times 2 = 8$ (cm²)
$V = 8 \times 3 = 24$ (cm³)

This example suggests a formula for finding the volume of any prism.

Formula

Volume of prism = base area × height

$$V = Bh$$

364 *Chapter 10*

EXAMPLE 1 A watering trough is in the form of a trapezoidal prism. Its ends have the dimensions shown. How long is the trough if it holds 12 m³?

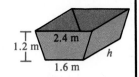

Solution Examine the diagram carefully to determine which regions are the bases. In this diagram, one of the bases is at the front. You know that the volume is 12 m³. Find the area of the base.

$$B = \frac{1}{2}(1.6 + 2.4) \times 1.2 = 2.4 \ (m^2)$$

Then, use the formula.

$$V = Bh$$
$$12 = 2.4h$$
$$5 = h$$

The length of the trough is 5 m.

A **cylinder** is like a prism except that its bases are circles instead of polygons. We will only consider cylinders with congruent bases. The area of the base, B, is πr^2. Thus:

Formula

Volume of cylinder = base area × height

$$V = \pi r^2 h$$

The volume of a container is often called its **capacity.** The capacity of containers of fluids is usually measured in **liters** (L) or **milliliters** (mL).

$$1 \ L = 1000 \ cm^3 \qquad 1 \ mL = 1 \ cm^3$$

It is easy to show that 1 m³ = 1000 L.

EXAMPLE 2 A cylindrical storage tank 1 m in diameter is 1.2 m high. Find its capacity in liters. Use $\pi \approx 3.14$.

Solution Use the formula $V = \pi r^2 h$. The height is 1.2 m and, because the diameter is 1 m, the radius is 0.5 m.

$$V \approx 3.14 \times (0.5)^2 \times 1.2 = 0.942 \ (m^3)$$

Since 1 m³ = 1000 L, 0.942 m³ = 942 L. The capacity of the tank is approximately 942 L.

Areas and Volumes **365**

Chalkboard Examples

Find the volume of the solid. Round to three digits if necessary. Use $\pi \approx 3.14$.

1.
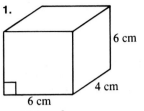

144 cm³

2.

30.6 cm³

3.
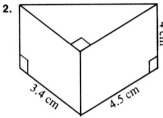

251 cm²

Find the capacity in liters of the prism or cylinder.

4. Prism:
base area = 4.5 m²,
height = 0.8 m **3600 L**

5. Cylinder:
base radius = 15 cm,
height = 20 cm **14.1 L**

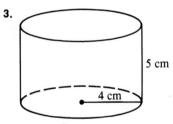

Additional A Exercises

Find the volume of the solid. Round to three digits if necessary. Use $\pi \approx 3.14$.

1.

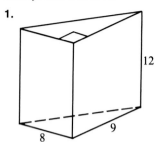

432 cubic units

2.

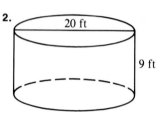

20 ft
9 ft

2830 ft³

3.

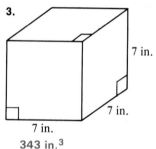

7 in.
7 in.
7 in.

343 in.³

Find the capacity in liters of the prism or cylinder.

4. Prism: base area 120 cm², height 16 cm **1.92 L**

5. Cylinder: base diameter 1 m, height 1.2 m **942 L**

Class Exercises

Find the volume of the solid. In Exercises 5 and 6, leave your answer in terms of π.

1.

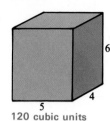

6
5
4

120 cubic units

2.

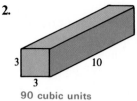

3
3
10

90 cubic units

3.

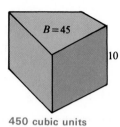

$B=45$
10

450 cubic units

4.

$B=20$
3

60 cubic units

5.

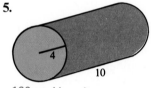

4
10

160π cubic units

6.

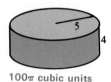

5
4

100π cubic units

7. a. 1 m = ___?___ cm 100
   b. 1 m³ = ___?___ cm³ 1,000,000
   c. 1000 L = ___?___ cm³ 1,000,000

8. a. 1 cm = ___?___ mm 10
   b. 1 cm³ = ___?___ mm³ 1000
   c. 1 mL = ___?___ mm³ 1000

Written Exercises

In this exercise set, use $\pi \approx 3.14$ and round the answer to three digits.

Find the volume of the solid.

A 1.

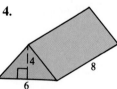

3
5
12

90 cubic units

2.

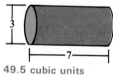

3
7

49.5 cubic units

3.

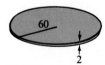

2
3
6
9

108 cubic units

4.

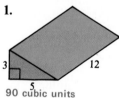

4
6
8

96 cubic units

5.

60
2

22,600 cubic units

6.

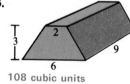

8
4
10
15

900 cubic units

366 *Chapter 10*

7.

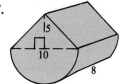

514 cubic units

8.

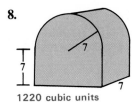

1220 cubic units

Find the capacity in liters of the prism or cylinder.

9. Square prism: 25 cm by 25 cm by 80 cm 50 L

10. Prism: base area = 1.2 m², height = 2.3 m 2760 L

11. Cylinder: base radius = 1.2 m, height = 1.4 m 6330 L

12. Cylinder: base diameter = 1 m, height = 75 cm 589 L

The table below refers to cylinders. Copy and complete it. Leave your answers in terms of π.

B

	13.	14.	15.	16.	17.	18.
volume	12π	150π	100π	20π	18π	100π
base radius	2	5	? 5	? 2	? 3	? 2
base area	? 4π	? 25π	25π	4π	? 9π	? 4π
height	? 3	? 6	? 4	? 5	2	25

Find the volume of the prism if the pattern were folded.

19. 60

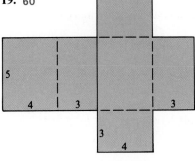

20. 30

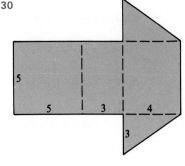

C 21. What happens to the volume of a cylinder if this change is made?
    a. The radius is doubled. quadrupled   **b.** The height is halved. halved
    c. The radius is doubled and the height is halved. doubled

22. What happens to the volume of a cylinder if this change is made?
    a. The radius is halved. quartered   **b.** The height is doubled. doubled
    c. The radius is halved and the height is doubled. halved

Suggested Assignments

Core
Day 1: 366/1–6
        367/7–13, 15
Day 2: 367/19–21
        368/Prob. 1–3
        368/Rev. 1–8

Enriched
Day 1: 366/4, 5, 6
        367/7–17 odd; 19–22
Day 2: 368/23, 24; Prob. 1–5
        368/Rev. 1–8

Supplementary Materials

Practice Masters, p. 47
Computer Activity 20

In an *oblique prism,* the bases are *not* perpendicular to the other faces. The volume formula $V = Bh$ still applies, where h is the perpendicular distance between the bases. Find the volume of each figure shown in red.

23.

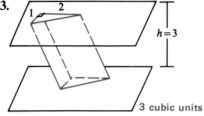

$h = 3$

3 cubic units

24.

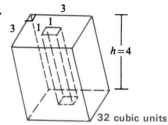

$h = 4$

32 cubic units

Problems

Solve. Use $\pi \approx 3.14$ and round the answer to three digits.

A **1.** Find the capacity in liters of the V-shaped trough shown below.

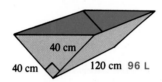

40 cm

40 cm   120 cm 96 L

2. Find the capacity in liters of the half-cylinder trough shown below.

15.7 L

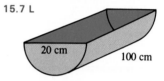

20 cm   100 cm

B **3.** Find the volume of metal in the copper pipe shown below.

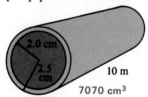

2.0 cm

2.5 cm   10 m

7070 cm³

4. Find the volume of concrete in the construction block shown below.

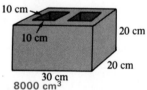

10 cm

10 cm   20 cm

30 cm   20 cm
8000 cm³

C **5.** A cylindrical water bottle is 28 cm in diameter. How many centimeters does the water level drop when one liter is drawn off? 1.62 cm

Review Exercises

Solve for x.

1. $x = \frac{1}{3} \times 6.4 \times 15$ 32   **2.** $x = \frac{1}{2}(7.2) \times 3$ 10.8   **3.** $3.38 = 4x$ 0.845   **4.** $\frac{1}{3}x = 11$ 33

5. $3.14 \times 20^2 = x$ 1256   **6.** $(0.8)^2x = 5.12$ 8   **7.** $314 = 3.14x^2$ 10; −10   **8.** $x^2 = 169$ 13; −13

10-6 Volumes of Pyramids and Cones

If we shrink one base of a prism to a point, we obtain a **pyramid** with that point as its **vertex.** A **cone** is obtained in the same way from a cylinder. In each case, the **height** of the solid is the perpendicular distance from its vertex to its base. As for a prism, the shape of the base of a pyramid determines its name. All other faces of a pyramid are triangles. A cone is like a pyramid except that its base is a circle instead of a polygon.

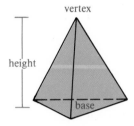

**Triangular Pyramid
or Tetrahedron**

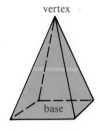

Square Pyramid

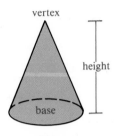

Cone

The volume of a pyramid can be found using this formula:

Formula

Volume of pyramid $= \frac{1}{3} \times$ base area $\times$ height

$$V = \frac{1}{3}Bh$$

EXAMPLE 1 Find the volume of the square pyramid shown at the right.

Solution First find the base area. Since the base is a square,

$$B = 12^2 = 144 \,(\text{cm}^2).$$

Then use the volume formula.

$$V = \frac{1}{3}Bh$$

$$= \frac{1}{3} \times 144 \times 25 = 1200 \,(\text{cm}^3)$$

Areas and Volumes **369**

Teaching Suggestions
p. 345e

Related Activities p. 345e

Reading Mathematics

Students will learn the meaning of the following mathematical terms in this lesson: *pyramid, vertex, cone, height, base, tetrahedron.*

For a cone, the base area is given by the formula $B = \pi r^2$.

Formula

Volume of cone $= \frac{1}{3} \times$ base area $\times$ height

$$V = \frac{1}{3}\pi r^2 h$$

EXAMPLE 2 A conical container is 20 cm across the top and 21 cm deep. Find its capacity in liters. Use $\pi \approx 3.14$ and round to three digits.

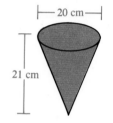

Solution The diameter of the base of the cone is 20 cm, so the radius is 10 cm.

$$V = \frac{1}{3}\pi \times 10^2 \times 21$$

$$\approx \frac{1}{3} \times 3.14 \times 100 \times 21 = 2198$$

Rounding the product to three digits, the volume is approximately 2200 cm³. Because 1000 cm³ equals 1 L, the capacity of the conical container is approximately 2.2 L.

Reading Mathematics: *Vocabulary*

Words that we use in everyday speech may have different meanings in mathematics. For example, the everyday word *base* often refers to the part of an object that it is resting on. The geometrical term *base* refers to a particular face of a figure that may appear at the top, the side, or the end of the figure in a drawing. In Example 2, above, the base appears at the top of the container.

Class Exercises

Find the volume of the solid. In Exercise 3, the base is a square. In Exercise 4, leave your answer in terms of π.

1.
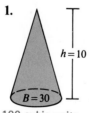
$h = 10$
$B = 30$
100 cubic units

2.
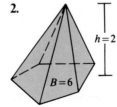
$h = 2$
$B = 6$
4 cubic units

3.
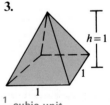
$h = 1$
1
1
$\frac{1}{3}$ cubic unit

4.
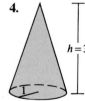
$h = 3$
π cubic units

370 *Chapter 10*

Complete.

5. Except for the base, the shapes of all the faces of a pyramid are __?__. triangles

6. The shapes of all the faces of a tetrahedron are __?__. triangles

7. A cone has base radius 3 and height 6. The volume of the cone is __?__ π. 18

Written Exercises

For Exercises 1–10, use $\pi \approx 3.14$ and round the answer to three digits if necessary.

Find the volume of the solid pictured.

A

1.

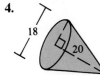

72 cubic units

2.

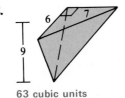

63 cubic units

3.

301 cubic units

4.

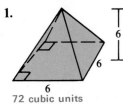

1700 cubic units

5.

56 cubic units

6.

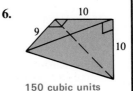

150 cubic units

Find the capacity in liters of the cone or pyramid described.

7. A pyramid of height 12 cm having a 5 cm by 8 cm rectangle as base 0.16 L

8. A pyramid having height 10 m and a square base 15 m on a side 750,000 L

9. A cone having base radius 0.8 m and height 1.5 m 1000 L

10. A cone of height 24 cm and base diameter 11 cm 0.76 L

Copy and complete the table for pyramids.

	11.	12.	13.	14.	15.	16.
base area, *B*	5	33	4	13	? 3	? 4
height, *h*	6	12	? 6	? 3	10	15
volume, *V*	? 10	? 132	8	13	10	20

Supplementary Materials

Practice Masters, p. 47

Copy and complete the table for cones.

B

	17.	18.	19.	20.
radius, r	1	2	? 3	? 1
height, h	? 15	? 9	4	15
volume, V	5π	12π	12π	5π

Complete.

C **21.** A cone has volume 6 cm³. The volume of a cylinder having the same base and same height is __?__ cm³. 18

22. A cylinder of height 2 m has the same base and same volume as a cone. The cone's height is __?__ m. 6

Problems

Solve. Use $\pi \approx 3.14$ and round the answer to three digits.

A **1.** The Great Pyramid in Egypt has a square base approximately 230 m on a side. Its original height was approximately 147 m. What was its approximate volume originally? 2,592,100 m³

2. A volcano is in the form of a cone approximately 1.8 km high and 12 km in diameter. Find its volume. 67.8 km³

B **3.** Find the volume of this buoy.

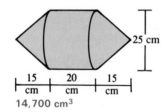

25 cm

15 cm 20 cm 15 cm

14,700 cm³

4. Find the volume of this tent. The floor of the tent is square.

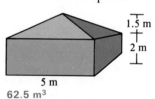

1.5 m

2 m

5 m

62.5 m³

Review Exercises

Find the perimeter of the figure whose sides have the given lengths.

1. rhombus: 9 m per side 36 m

2. trapezoid: 4 cm, 4 cm, 5 cm, 7 cm 20 cm

3. triangle: 35 cm per side 105 cm

4. parallelogram: 15 m, 7 m, 15 m, 7 m 44 m

5. square: 12.8 km per side 51.2 km

6. rectangle: 24.63 km by 37.40 km 124.06 km

7. square: 145.2 km per side 580.8 km

8. triangle: 3.70 m, 12.90 m, 14.85 m 31.45 m

372 *Chapter 10*

10-7 Surface Areas of Prisms and Cylinders

The **surface area** of every prism and cylinder is made up of its two **bases** and its **lateral surface** as illustrated in the figures below. The lateral surface of a prism is made up of its **lateral faces.** Each lateral face is a rectangle.

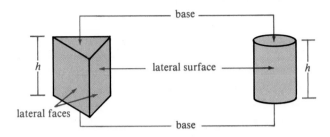

If we were to cut open and flatten out the prism and cylinder shown above, the bases and the lateral surfaces of the figures would look like this:

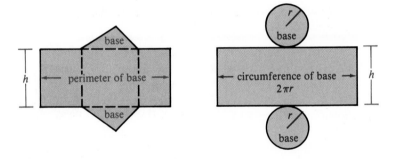

In each of the figures above, the area of the lateral surface, called the **lateral area,** is the product of the perimeter of the base and the height of the figure. To find the **total surface area** of a prism or cylinder, we simply add the area of the two bases to the lateral area of the figure.

Formulas

For a prism or cylinder,

lateral area = perimeter of base × height

total surface area = lateral area + area of bases

Areas and Volumes **373**

Teaching Suggestions
p. 345e

Related Activities p. 345e

Reading Mathematics
Students will learn the meaning of the following mathematical terms in this lesson: *surface area, bases, lateral surface, lateral faces, lateral area, total surface area.*

Find the total surface area of
a rectangular prism having
the given dimensions. Round
to three digits if necessary.

1. 2.7 cm by 4.8 cm by
5.3 cm **105.42 cm²**

2. 10 m by 9 m by 6 m
408 m²

Find the lateral surface area
and the total surface area of
each cylinder. Round to
three digits if necessary.
Use $\pi \approx 3.14$.

3. A cylinder having height
4 m and base radius
1.5 m. **37.7 m², 51.8 m²**

4. A cylinder having base
diameter 10 cm and height
11 cm. **345 cm², 502 cm²**

EXAMPLE 1   Find (a) the lateral area, (b) the
area of the bases, and (c) the total
surface area of the prism shown.

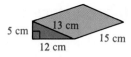

Solution

    a. perimeter of base $= 5 + 12 + 13 = 30$ (cm)
       height $= 15$ cm
       lateral area $= 30 \times 15 = 450$ (cm²)

    b. area of bases $= 2 \times \left(\frac{1}{2} \times 12 \times 5\right) = 60$ (cm²)

    c. total surface area $= 450 + 60 = 510$ (cm²)

    In a cylinder of base radius r, the perimeter (circumference) of the
base is $2\pi r$. Thus:

Formulas

For a cylinder,

    lateral area $= 2\pi rh$

    area of bases $= 2\pi r^2$

    total surface area $= 2\pi rh + 2\pi r^2$

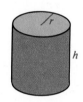

EXAMPLE 2   A can of paint will cover 50 m². How many
cans are necessary to paint the inside (top,
bottom, and sides) of the storage tank
shown? Use $\pi \approx 3.14$.

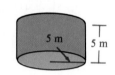

Solution

    Since $r = 5$ and $h = 5$,
    total surface area $= (2\pi \times 5 \times 5) + (2\pi \times 5^2)$
                     $\approx (3.14 \times 50) + (3.14 \times 50) = 314$

The total surface area is approximately 314 m².

The number of cans of paint is $314 \div 50$, or 6.28. Rounding *up* to
the nearest whole number, the answer is 7 cans.

Problem Solving Reminder
For problems whose answers are the result of division, take time to consider
whether it is reasonable *to round up or round down*. In Example 2, the answer
to the division was 6.28 cans of paint. Because paint cannot be purchased in
hundredths of a can, the answer was rounded up to the nearest whole number. If the answer had been rounded down, there would not have been
enough paint to cover the interior of the tank.

374   *Chapter 10*

Class Exercises

1. If a prism has hexagonal bases, how many lateral faces does it have? How many faces does it have in all? 6; 8

Find the lateral area and the total surface area. Use $\pi \approx 3.14$ and round the answer to three digits.

2.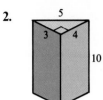

120; 132

3.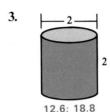

12.6; 18.8

4.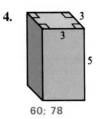

60; 78

5. If each edge of a cube is one unit long, what is the total surface area in square units? 6 square units

Written Exercises

Find the total surface area of a rectangular prism having the given dimensions.

A
1. 45 cm by 30 cm by 20 cm 5700 cm²
2. 5 cm by 18 cm by 25 cm 1330 cm²
3. 2.5 m by 1.6 m by 0.8 m 14.56 m²
4. 1.8 m by 0.6 m by 2.0 m 11.76 m²

Find (a) the lateral area and (b) the total surface area of the cylinder or prism. Use $\pi \approx 3.14$ and round the answer to three digits.

5. A cylinder having base radius 12 cm and height 22 cm 1660 cm²; 2560 cm²

6. A cylinder having base diameter 6 m and height 4.5 m 84.8 m²; 141 m²

7.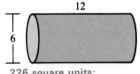

226 square units;
283 square units

8.

25.1 square units;
126 square units

9.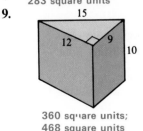

360 square units;
468 square units

10.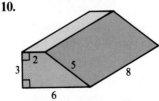

128 square units; 152 square units

Areas and Volumes **375**

If the patterns below were drawn on cardboard, they could be folded along the dotted lines to form prisms. Find (a) the volume and (b) the total surface area of each.

B 11.

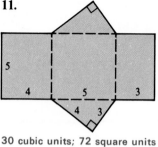

30 cubic units; 72 square units

12.

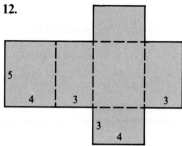

60 cubic units; 94 square units

13. Find the length of the edge of a cube whose total area is 150 cm². 5 cm

14. Three faces of a box have a common vertex and their combined area is 20 cm². What is the total surface area of the box? 40 cm²

15. One can of varnish will cover 64 m² of wood. If you want to put one coat of varnish on each of 24 wooden cubes with the dimensions shown at the right, how many cans of varnish should you buy? 6 cans

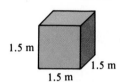

1.5 m
1.5 m
1.5 m

16. You have two cans of red paint, each of which will cover 100 m². Which of the two cylinders pictured below can you paint completely using just the paint that you have? B

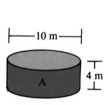

⊢—10 m—⊣

A

4 m

⊢4 m⊣

B

10 m

17. A prism of height 3 m has bases that are right triangles with sides 6 m, 8 m, and 10 m. Find the lateral area and the total surface area. (Be sure to draw and label a sketch.) 72 m²; 120 m²

18. A prism of height 10 cm has bases that are right triangles with sides 5 cm, 12 cm, and 13 cm. Find the lateral area and the surface area. (Be sure to draw and label a sketch.) 300 cm²; 360 cm²

19. If the number of faces of a prism is represented by n, write an algebraic expression to represent the number of lateral faces. $n - 2$

376 *Chapter 10*

C **20.** The lateral surface of a cone is made up of many small wedges like the one shown in color. Thinking of the wedge as a triangle of base b and height s, we see that its area is $\frac{1}{2}bs$. When we add all these areas together, we obtain $\frac{1}{2}(2\pi r)s$, or πrs, because the sum of all the b's is $2\pi r$, the circumference of the base. Thus, for a cone:

$$\text{lateral area} = \pi rs$$

$$\text{area of base} = \pi r^2$$

$$\text{total surface area} = \pi rs + \pi r^2$$

The length s is called the **slant height** of the cone.

Find the total surface area of each figure.

a.

$s = 14$

298 square units

b.

$s = 4$

3

$s = 6$

94.2 square units

c.

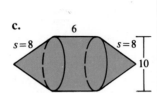

6

$s = 8$ $s = 8$

10

440 square units

Review Exercises

Find the radius of the circle with the given circumference C or diameter d. Use $\pi \approx 3.14$ and round the answer to three digits.

1. $d = 12$ 6   **2.** $C = 62.8$ 10   **3.** $d = 210$ 105   **4.** $C = 83.6$ 13.3

5. $C = 220$ 35   **6.** $d = 25$ 12.5   **7.** $d = 76$ 38   **8.** $C = 2.42$ 0.385

Challenge

1. Copy the square at the right and cut it into four pieces along the dashed lines. Re-form the four pieces into a larger square with a "hollow" square at the center.

2. Repeat step 1 several times, assigning different values to a and b each time. In each case, what is the area of the "hollow" square?

$(b - a)^2$

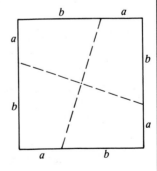

Areas and Volumes   **377**

377

Reading Mathematics

Students will learn the meaning of the following mathematical terms in this lesson: *sphere, radius, center, diameter, hemisphere.*

10-8 Volumes and Surface Areas of Spheres

The **sphere** with **radius** r and **center** at C consists of all points at the distance r from point C. The word *radius* also is used for any segment having C as one endpoint and a point of the sphere as another (for example, $\overline{CP}$ in the figure). The word **diameter** is also used in two ways: for a *segment* through C having its endpoints on the sphere (for example, $\overline{AB}$), and for the *length* of such a segment.

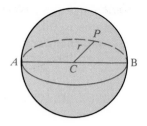

The following formulas for the surface area and volume of a sphere can be proved using higher mathematics.

Formulas

For any sphere of radius r,

Area $= 4\pi \times$ (radius)^2 Volume $= \frac{4}{3}\pi \times$ (radius)^3

$A = 4\pi r^2$ $V = \frac{4}{3}\pi r^3$

The surface area of a sphere is usually referred to simply as the *area* of the sphere.

Reading Mathematics: *Diagrams*

Reading diagrams correctly is an important reading skill in mathematics. When three-dimensional objects are pictured on a two-dimensional page, the lines used to draw congruent segments may be of different lengths. For example, in the drawing above, you understand that all radii of a sphere are congruent and that $CP = CB$. Yet these radii cannot be drawn to be of equal length if the picture is to look realistic.

EXAMPLE 1   Find (a) the surface area and (b) the volume of a sphere having diameter 18. Leave your answer in terms of π.

Solution   The radius equals $\frac{1}{2}$ the diameter, so $r = 9$.

a. $A = 4\pi r^2 = 4\pi \times 9^2 = 4\pi \times 81 = 324\pi$

b. $V = \frac{4}{3}\pi r^3 = \frac{4}{3}\pi \times 9^3 = \frac{4}{3}\pi \times 729 = 972\pi$

378   *Chapter 10*

EXAMPLE 2 The area of a sphere is 1600π cm². What is the radius?

Solution   Substitute 1600π for A in the formula $A = 4\pi r^2$.

$$1600\pi = 4\pi r^2$$

$$\frac{1600\pi}{4\pi} = \frac{4\pi r^2}{4\pi}$$

$$400 = r^2$$

Since $20^2 = 400$, $r = 20$ cm.

Class Exercises

Complete. In Exercises 1 and 2, give your answers in terms of π.

1. The area of a sphere of radius 1 is __?__, and the volume is __?__. $4\pi, \frac{4}{3}\pi$

2. The area of a sphere of radius 2 is __?__, and the volume is __?__. $16\pi, \frac{32}{3}\pi$

3. If the radius of a sphere is doubled, the area is multiplied by __?__. 4

4. If the radius of a sphere is doubled, the volume is multiplied by __?__. 8

5. If $\overline{AB}$ is a diameter of a sphere having center C, then $\overline{AC}$ and $\overline{BC}$ are __?__ of the sphere. radii

Complete the following analogies with choice a, b, c, or d.

6. Sphere: Circle = Cube: __?__ c
   a. Pyramid   b. Prism   c. Square   d. Cylinder

7. Cone: Pyramid = Cylinder: __?__ b
   a. Sphere   b. Prism   c. Circle   d. Triangle

Written Exercises

Copy and complete the table below. Leave your answers in terms of π.

A

	1.	2.	3.	4.	5.	6.
radius of sphere	3	5	6	9	10	12
surface area	? 36π	? 100π	? 144π	? 324π	? 400π	? 576π
volume	? 36π	? $\frac{500}{3}\pi$	? 288π	? 972π	? $\frac{4000}{3}\pi$	? 2304π

Areas and Volumes **379**

Solve. Leave your answers in terms of π. Round to three digits if necessary.

1. Find the surface area and volume of a sphere having radius 6. **144π, 288π**

2. Find the diameter of a sphere whose surface area is 1600π. **40**

3. Find the radius of a sphere whose volume is 2304π. **12**

4. Find the volume of a hemisphere of radius 3. **18π**

Additional A Exercises

Leave your answers in terms of π.

1. Find the surface area and volume of a sphere having radius 9. **324π, 972π**

2. The surface area of a sphere is 100π cm². What is its radius? **5 cm**

3. The volume of a sphere is 36π m³. What is its diameter? **6 m**

4. Find the area of the curved surface of a hemisphere of radius 7. **98π**

Half of a sphere is called a *hemisphere*. **Solve. Leave your answers in terms of π.**

7. Find the volume of a hemisphere of radius 2. $\frac{16}{3}\pi$

8. Find the area of the curved surface of a hemisphere of radius 8. **128π**

9. Find the area of the curved surface of a hemisphere of radius 2.2. **9.68π**

10. Find the volume of a hemisphere of radius 3.3. **23.958π**

Copy and complete the table below. Leave your answers in terms of π.

B

	11.	12.	13.	14.	15.	16.
radius of sphere	3.6	? 4	? 9	4.5	? 8	? 6
surface area	? 51.84π	64π	? 324π	? 81π	256π	? 144π
volume	? 62.208π	? $\frac{256}{3}\pi$	972π	? 121.5π	? $\frac{2048}{3}\pi$	288π

Solve. Leave your answers in terms of π.

17. The observatory building shown at the right consists of a cylinder surmounted by a hemisphere. Find its volume. **324π m³**

18. The water tank at the right consists of a cone surmounted by a cylinder surmounted by a hemisphere. Find its volume. **456π m³**

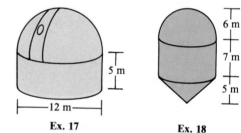

5 m

6 m

7 m

5 m

12 m

Ex. 17 **Ex. 18**

19. Earth's diameter is about $3\frac{2}{3}$ times that of the moon. How do their volumes compare? Earth's volume is about 49.3 times that of the moon.

20. The sun's diameter is about 110 times that of Earth. How do their volumes compare? The sun's volume is about 1,331,000 times that of Earth.

380   *Chapter 10*

If a sphere fits snugly inside a cylinder it is said to be *inscribed* in the cylinder. Use the diagram at the right for Exercises 21 and 22.

C **21. a.** A sphere of radius 4 is inscribed in a cylinder of height 8. What is the ratio of the volume of the sphere to the volume of the cylinder? **2 : 3**

　　b. A sphere of radius 5 is inscribed in a cylinder of height 10. What is the ratio of the volume of the sphere to the volume of the cylinder? **2 : 3**

　　c. A sphere of radius *r* is inscribed in a cylinder. What is the ratio of the volume of the sphere to the volume of the cylinder?
　　　　　　　　　　　　　　　　　　　　　　4r : 3h or 2 : 3

22. a. A sphere of radius 6 is inscribed in a cylinder of height 12. What is the ratio of the surface area of the sphere to the lateral area of the cylinder? **1 : 1**

　　b. A sphere of radius 7 is inscribed in a cylinder of height 14. What is the ratio of the surface area of the sphere to the lateral area of the cylinder? **1 : 1**

　　c. A sphere of radius *r* is inscribed in a cylinder. What is the ratio of the surface area of the sphere to the lateral area of the cylinder?
　　　　　　　　　　　　　　　　　　　　　　　　　1 : 1

Suggested Assignments

Core
Day 1: 379/1–6
　　　380/7–13
Day 2: 380/17–19
　　　381/Rev. 1–8
　　　381/Calculator Key-In

Enriched
Day 1: 379/2, 4, 6
　　　380/9–18
Day 2: 380/19, 20
　　　381/21, 22; Rev. 1–8
　　　381/Calculator Key-In

Supplementary Materials

Practice Masters, p. 48

Review Exercises

Simplify these in your head if you can. Write down the answers.

1. 7×0.3 **2.1**　　**2.** 4×5.1 **20.4**　　**3.** 0.8×0.8 **0.64**　　**4.** 23.3×100 **2330**

5. $3500 \div 1000$ **3.5**　**6.** $10.75 \div 100$ **0.1075** **7.** 300×2.7 **810**　**8.** 0.0004×0.2 **0.00008**

 Calculator Key-In

The surface area of Earth is approximately 510,070,000 km². The surface area of Jupiter is approximately 64,017,000,000 km². About how many times greater than the surface area of Earth is the surface area of Jupiter? **126 times greater**

If you try to enter the numbers as they are shown above on your calculator, you may find it will not accept more than eight digits. Many calculators have a key marked *EXP* that allows you to use scientific notation to express very large (or very small) numbers. For example, you can enter 510,070,000 by thinking of the number as 5.1007×10^8 and entering 5.1007 ┃ EXP ┃ 8. Your calculator may show 5.1007　08.

Try to find a calculator that will accept scientific notation and solve the problem above.

Areas and Volumes **381**

Teaching Suggestions
p. 345g

Related Activities p. 345g

Reading Mathematics

Students will learn the meaning of the following mathematical terms in this lesson: *mass, gram, kilogram, metric ton, weight, density.*

10-9 Mass and Density

The **mass** of an object is a measure of the amount of matter it contains. In the metric system, units of mass are the **gram (g)**, the **kilogram (kg)**, and the **metric ton (t)**.

> 1 g = mass of 1 cm³ of water under standard conditions. (Standard conditions are 4°C at sea-level pressure.)
>
> $$1 \text{ kg} = 1000 \text{ g}$$
>
> $$1 \text{ t} = 1000 \text{ kg}$$

The *weight* of an object is the force of gravity acting on it. While the mass of an object remains constant, its weight would be less on a mountaintop or on the moon than at sea level. In a given region, mass and weight are proportional (so that mass can be found by weighing).

The tables below give the masses of unit volumes (1 cm³) of several substances.

TABLE 1

Substance	Mass of 1 cm³	Mass of 1 m³
Pine	0.56 g	0.56 t
Ice	0.92 g	0.92 t
Water	1.00 g	1.00 t
Aluminum	2.70 g	2.70 t
Steel	7.82 g	7.82 t
Gold	19.3 g	19.3 t

TABLE 2

Substance	Mass of 1 cm³	Mass of 1 L
Helium	0.00018 g	0.00018 kg
Air	0.0012 g	0.0012 kg
Gasoline	0.66 g	0.66 kg
Water	1.00 g	1.00 kg
Milk	1.03 g	1.03 kg
Mercury	13.6 g	13.6 kg

The mass per unit volume of a substance is its **density.** In describing densities we use a slash (/) for the word *per.* For example, the density of gasoline is 0.66 kg/L.

EXAMPLE   Find the mass of a block 3 cm by 5 cm by 10 cm made of wood having density 0.8 g/cm³.

Solution   The volume of the block is 3 × 5 × 10, or 150, cm³.

Since 1 cm³ of the wood has mass 0.8 g, 150 cm³ has mass 0.8 × 150, or 120, g.

The example illustrates the following formula.

Formula
Mass = Density × Volume

In Table 2, the number of grams per cubic centimeter is the same as the number of kilograms per liter. This is because there are 1000 g in a kilogram and 1000 cm^3 in a liter. Similarly in Table 1, the number of grams per cubic centimeter is the same as the number of metric tons per cubic meter.

Class Exercises

Complete.

1. 1 t = __?__ kg **1000**

2. 1 kg = __?__ g **1000**

3. 1 t = __?__ g **1,000,000**

4. 2400 kg = __?__ t **2.4**

5. 0.62 kg = __?__ g **620**

6. 400 g = __?__ kg **0.4**

Use the tables in this lesson to give the mass of the following.

7. 2 L of water **2 kg**

8. 10 cm^3 of gasoline **6.6 g**

9. 100 cm^3 of milk **103 g**

10. 4 L of gasoline **2.64 kg**

11. helium filling a 1000 L tank **0.18 kg**

12. a cube of ice 2 cm on each edge **7.36 g**

13. the block of steel shown **78.2 g**

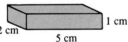

2 cm   5 cm   1 cm

Written Exercises

Complete.

A **1.** 6.3 kg = __?__ g **6300**

2. 2500 kg = __?__ t **2.5**

3. 4.3 t = __?__ kg **4300**

Use the tables in this lesson to find the mass of the following.

4. 50 cm^3 of gold **965 g**

5. 300 cm^3 of aluminum **810 g**

6. 25 L of gasoline **16.5 kg**

7. 2.5 L of mercury **34 kg**

8. 500 m^3 of water **500 t**

9. 500 m^3 of ice **460 t**

10. 1 m^3 of air **1200 g**

11. 1 m^3 of helium **180 g**

12. 4 L of milk **4.12 kg**

Areas and Volumes **383**

In Exercises 13–18, use $\pi \approx 3.14$ and round the answer to three digits.
In Exercises 13–15, the solid pictured is made of the specified material.
Use the tables in this lesson to find the mass of the solid.

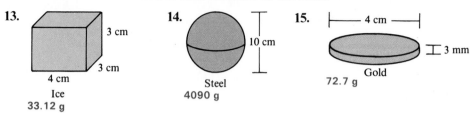

13.

3 cm
3 cm
4 cm
Ice
33.12 g

14.

10 cm
Steel
4090 g

15.

4 cm
3 mm
Gold
72.7 g

In Exercises 16–18, use the tables in this lesson to find the mass of the
named content of the container pictured.

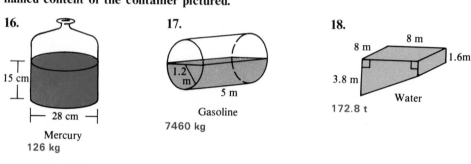

16.

15 cm
28 cm
Mercury
126 kg

17.

1.2 m
5 m
Gasoline
7460 kg

18.

8 m
8 m
1.6m
3.8 m
Water
172.8 t

Problems

Solve. Use the tables in this lesson if no density is given. Use $\pi \approx 3.14$
and round the answer to three digits.

A

1. A solid gold bar has dimensions of approximately 17 cm by 9 cm by 4.5 cm. Find its mass in kilograms.
   13.28805 kg

2. A solid pine board has dimensions of approximately 100 cm by 30 cm by 1.5 cm. Find its mass in grams. **2520 g**

3. The optical prism shown at the right is made of glass having density 4.8 g/cm³. Find its mass. **81.12 g**

4. A piece of ice is in the form of a half-cylinder 5 cm in radius and 3 cm high. What is its mass? **108 g**

B

5. What is the mass in metric tons of the steel I-beam shown at the right? **3.91 t**

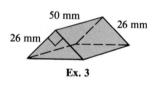

50 mm
26 mm
26 mm
Ex. 3

Ex. 4

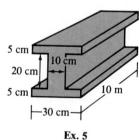

5 cm
10 cm
20 cm
5 cm
10 m
30 cm
Ex. 5

384   *Chapter 10*

6. The drawing at the right shows the cross section of a two-kilometer-long tunnel that is to be dug through a mountain. How many metric tons of earth must be removed if its density is 2.8 t/m³? 253,000 t

Ex. 6

Self-Test B

Use $\pi \approx 3.14$ and round answers involving π to three digits.

Complete.

1. Triangular prism: base area = 7.6 m², height = 5.5 m, volume = __?__ m³ 41.8   [10–5]

2. Cylinder: base diameter = 38 cm, height = 24 cm, volume = __?__ cm³ 27,200

3. Square prism: 17 cm by 17 cm by 32 cm, volume = __?__ cm³, 9248 capacity = __?__ L 9.248

Find the volume of the solid.

4. A cone with base radius 0.5 m and height 1.2 m 0.314 m³   [10–6]

5. A pyramid with base of 180 m² and height 20 m 1200 m³

6. A square pyramid with base 26 cm on a side and height 48 cm 10,816 cm³

Find (a) the lateral area and (b) the total surface area of the solid.

7. A rectangular prism with base 4 by 3 and height 7   [10–7]
98 square units; 122 square units
8. A cylinder with base diameter 10 and height 3
94.2 square units; 251 square units
9. A square prism with height 42 and base 18 per side
3024 square units; 3672 square units

Find (a) the surface area and (b) the volume of a sphere with the given dimensions. Leave your answers in terms of π.

10. radius = 18 cm
1296π cm²; 7776π cm³
    11. diameter = 12 m   [10–8]
144π m²; 288π m³

Find the mass of the solid. 12. 8240 g   13. 181.76 g
12. A sphere of aluminum with diameter 18 cm, density 2.70 g/cm³   [10–9]

13. A 4 cm by 4 cm by 20 cm block of pine, density of 0.568 g/cm³

Self-Test answers and Extra Practice are at the back of the book.

---

2. A cylinder: base diameter = 10 m, height = 6 m, volume = __?__ m³ 471

3. A rectangular prism: 12 cm by 8 cm by 11 cm, volume = __?__ cm³, capacity = __?__ L
1056, 1.056

Find the volume of the solid.

4. A cone with base radius 4 cm and height 7 cm
117 cm³

5. A pyramid with base area 60 cm² and height 7 cm
140 cm³

6. A square pyramid with base 4.5 m on a side and height 5 m 33.75 m³

Find the lateral area and the total surface area of the solid.

7. A rectangular prism with base 6 cm by 2 cm and height 3 cm
48 cm², 72 cm²

8. A cylinder with base diameter 8 cm and height 20 cm
502 cm², 602 cm²

9. A square prism with height 60 cm and base 9 cm per side
2160 cm², 2322 cm²

Find the surface area and the volume of a sphere with the given dimensions. Leave your answers in terms of π.

10. radius = 21 m
1764π m², 12,348π m³

11. diameter = 18 cm
324π cm², 972π cm³

Find the mass of the solid.

12. A 2 cm by 20 cm by 4 cm block of pine, density 0.56 g/cm³ 89.6 g

13. A sphere of aluminum with diameter 10 cm, density 2.70 g/cm³
1.41 kg

Enrichment Note

If possible, use a globe to show students lines of latitude and longitude. Demonstrate that parallels of latitude really are parallel.

Even though latitude is always measured and expressed in degrees, it is easily converted into miles. The distance from the equator to either pole is 6,222 statute (ordinary) miles. Divided by 90, this gives an average of about 69.1 statute miles to each degree of latitude. Minneapolis is located at 45°N, so by multiplying 45 by 69.1 we learn that Minneapolis is about 3100 statute miles north of the equator.

Meridians of longitude are not parallel. They become closer and closer together with increasing distance from the equator. This means that the number of miles in 1° of longitude is different for each latitude.

Students may wonder why the meridians on the map on page 387 are parallel. Explain that it is impossible to make a curved surface flat without stretching or tearing it. As a demonstration, challenge students to flatten the rind of half an orange. The map on page 387 is a Mercator projection, which is stretched near the poles. Interested students can make a display of different projections; they should label each map to show how it is stretched or cut, and what features of the Earth's surface it shows best.

The prime meridian is also the starting point for establishing international time zones. Hourly changes occur approximately every 15° of longitude. P.M. stands for *post meridiem*, a Latin phrase for "after noon." A.M. stands for *ante meridiem*, which means "before noon." Locate maps of time zones to display in the classroom.

Locating Points on Earth

We can think of Earth as a sphere rotating on an axis that is a diameter with endpoints at the North Pole (N) and South Pole (S). A **great circle** on a sphere is the intersection of the sphere with a plane that contains the center of the sphere. The great circle whose plane is perpendicular to Earth's axis is called the **equator.** The equator divides Earth into the Northern and Southern Hemispheres.

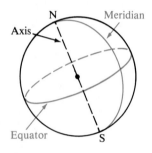

Semicircles with endpoints at the North and South Poles are called **meridians.** The meridian that passes through Greenwich, England, is called the **prime meridian.** The great circle on which the prime meridian lies divides Earth into the Eastern and Western Hemispheres.

The prime meridian and the equator are important parts of a degree-coordinate system that we use to describe the location of points on Earth. A series of circles whose planes are parallel to the equator, called **parallels of latitude,** identify the **latitude** of a point as a number of degrees between 0° and 90° *north* or *south of the equator.* The meridians identify the **longitude** of a point as the number of degrees between 0° and 180° *east* or *west of the prime meridian.*

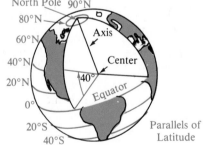

Parallels of Latitude

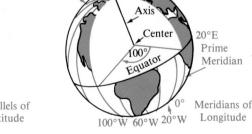

Meridians of Longitude

Thus, each point on the surface of Earth can be assigned an ordered pair of degree-coordinates: (latitude, longitude).

The flat map below, called a **Mercator projection,** shows the meridians and parallels of latitude marked off in 10° intervals as perpendicular lines. Notice that the city of Paris, France, is located at about 48°N, 2°E.

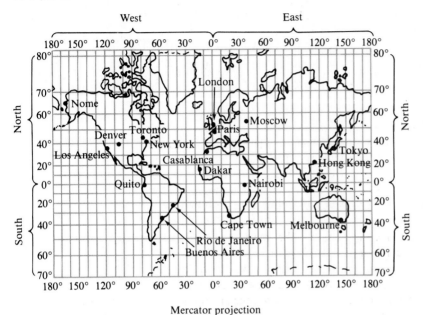

Mercator projection

Use the map above to name the major city at the location specified.

New York	Buenos Aires	Rio de Janeiro	Cape Town
1. 40°N, 74°W	**2.** 34°S, 58°W	**3.** 23°S, 43°W	**4.** 34°S, 18°E

Moscow	Melbourne	Casablanca	Los Angeles
5. 55°N, 37°E	**6.** 37°S, 145°E	**7.** 33°N, 7°W	**8.** 34°N, 118°W

Give the latitude and longitude of the following cities to the nearest 5°.

40°N, 105°W	0°N, 35°E	55°N, 0°	0°, 80°W
9. Denver	**10.** Nairobi	**11.** London	**12.** Quito

15°N, 15°W	45°N, 80°W	65°N, 165°W	20°N, 115°E
13. Dakar	**14.** Toronto	**15.** Nome	**16.** Hong Kong

Career Activity

Ancient navigators determined their position by observing the sun and the stars. Modern navigators use much more sophisticated methods. If you were a navigator today what are some of the instruments and methods you might use?

Chapter Review

Write the letter of the correct answer.

1. Find the area of a rectangle 17 cm long and 5 cm wide. b   [10–1]
   a. 44 cm²   **b.** 85 cm²   **c.** 42.5 cm²   **d.** 22 cm²

2. A parallelogram has a base of 16 m and a height of 4 m. Find the area. d
   a. 32 m²   **b.** 40 m²   **c.** 20 m²   **d.** 64 m²

3. A triangle has a base of 14 m and a height of 10 m. Find the area. c   [10–2]
   a. 140 m²   **b.** 34 m²   **c.** 70 m²   **d.** 35 m²

4. A trapezoid has bases of 9 cm and 15 cm and a height of 6 cm. Find the area. a
   a. 72 cm²   **b.** 144 cm²   **c.** 810 cm²   **d.** 189 cm²

5. A circle has a diameter of 18 cm. Find the area. Use $\pi \approx 3.14$ and round to three digits. d   [10–3]
   a. 28.3 cm²   **b.** 1020 cm²   **c.** 56.5 cm²   **d.** 254 cm²

Complete. Use $\pi \approx 3.14$ and round answers involving π to three digits.

6. Figures may be symmetric with respect to a __?__ line or a __?__ point.   [10–4]

7. A rectangular prism has a base 12 cm by 14 cm and height 23 cm.   [10–5]
   Its volume is __?__. 3864 cm³

8. A cylinder has base radius 4 cm and height 15 cm. Its capacity is __?__ liters. 0.754

9. A cone with base diameter 6 and height 4.8 has volume __?__. 45.2 cubic units   [10–6]

10. A pyramid with base area 160 cm² and height 24 cm has volume __?__. 1280 cm³

11. A cylinder with base radius 7 and height 12 has lateral area __?__ π 168   [10–7]
    and surface area __?__ π. 266

12. A prism has height 16. Its bases are triangles with base 15, height 12, and remaining side 18. Its total surface area is __?__. 900 square units

13. A sphere with radius 24 has surface area __?__ π 2304 and volume __?__ π. 18,432   [10–8]

14. A sphere with radius 32 has surface area __?__ π 4096 and volume __?__ π. 43,690 $\frac{2}{3}$

15. A rectangular storage tank has dimensions 14 m by 6 m by 4 m. It is   [10–9]
    filled with helium of density 0.00018 kg/L. The mass of the helium is __?__. 60.48 kg

388   *Chapter 10*

Chapter Test

Find the area. Use $\pi \approx 3.14$ and round the answer to three digits.

1. rectangle:
length = 14 cm 126 m²
width = 9 m

2. parallelogram: [10-1]
base = 23 cm   253 cm²
height = 11 cm

3. triangle:
base = 9 mm   72 mm²
height = 16 mm

4. trapezoid: [10-2]
bases = 8 m and 14 m 77 m²
height = 7 m

5. circle:
radius = 17 mm 907 mm²

6. circle: [10-3]
diameter = 42 cm 1385 cm²

7. Copy the figure at the right and show any lines or points of symmetry.

8. Find the area of the symmetric figure at the right. 180 square units

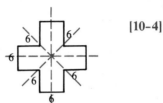

[10-4]

Find the volume. Use $\pi \approx 3.14$ and round the answer to three digits.

9. Cylinder: base radius = 7.2 m, height = 5.8 m 944 m³   [10-5]

10. Prism: base area = 45 cm², height = 33 cm 1485 cm³

11. Cone: base diameter = 6 cm, height = 14 cm 132 cm³   [10-6]

12. Pyramid: square base 17 cm on a side, height = 21 cm 2023 cm³

Find (a) the lateral area and (b) the total surface area of each. Use $\pi \approx 3.14$ and round the answer to three digits.

13.

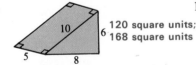

120 square units;
168 square units

14.

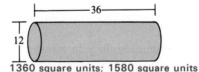

[10-7]

1360 square units; 1580 square units

Find (a) the surface area and (b) the volume of a sphere with the given dimensions. Leave your answer in terms of π.

15. diameter = 18 cm 324π cm²; 972π cm³

16. radius = 45 m 8100π m²; 121,500π m³   [10-8]

17. Find the mass of a sphere with diameter 20 cm and density 8.9 g/cm³. Use $\pi \approx 3.14$ and round the answer to three digits. 37,300 g   [10-9]

18. Find the mass of a cube 9 cm on each edge with density 0.56 g/cm³. 408.24 g

Areas and Volumes **389**

Add or subtract. Simplify.

1. $\frac{7}{8} + \left(-\frac{2}{3}\right)$ $\frac{5}{24}$

2. $-1\frac{3}{4} + 1\frac{1}{6}$ $-\frac{7}{12}$

3. $-\frac{5}{7} - \frac{4}{5}$ $-1\frac{18}{35}$

4. $3\frac{1}{7} - 5\frac{5}{6}$ $-2\frac{29}{42}$

Multiply or divide. Simplify.

5. $\frac{5}{21}\left(-\frac{7}{5}\right)$ $-\frac{1}{3}$

6. $\left(-\frac{3}{11}\right)\left(-\frac{22}{33}\right)(11)$ 2

7. $-\frac{9}{10} \div \left(-\frac{3}{25}\right)$ $7\frac{1}{2}$

8. $-3\frac{2}{5} \div 2\frac{1}{4}$ $-1\frac{23}{45}$

9. Write $\frac{19}{50}$ as a decimal.
0.38

10. Write $\frac{7}{9}$ as a decimal.
$0.\overline{7}$

11. This term, 34% of the students in one class are on the honor roll. If 85 students are on the honor roll, how many students are in class?
250 students

Cumulative Review (Chapters 1–10)

Exercises

Evaluate the expression if $a = 0.5$, $b = 5$, and $c = 2$.

1. abc 5

2. $a + b + c$ 7.5

3. $b \div a$ 10

4. $3a - 3b$ -13.5

5. ab^2 12.5

6. $c^2 + b^3$ 129

7. $6(a^2 - c^2)$ -22.5

8. $10a - \frac{b}{c}$ 2.5

Evaluate the expression if $x = \frac{1}{3}$, $y = 2\frac{3}{4}$, and $z = -\frac{3}{5}$.

9. $x + y$ $3\frac{1}{12}$

10. xz $-\frac{1}{5}$

11. $3x + z$ $\frac{2}{5}$

12. $5z - x$ $-3\frac{1}{3}$

13. $x + 4y - 10z$ $17\frac{1}{3}$

14. $6x + 8y + z$ $23\frac{2}{5}$

15. $20z - (-y)$ $-9\frac{1}{4}$

16. $12x \div z$ $-6\frac{2}{3}$

Solve.

17. $15n + 7 > 52$

18. $6 - 2x < 21$

19. $38 \geq x - 2$

20. $\frac{n}{8} > 3$

21. $27 \leq 3x$

22. $3b + 5 < 56$

23. $4x + 7 = 35$ 7

24. $-y + 10 = 26$ -16

25. $\frac{3w}{7} = 9$ 21

26. Find the measure of each angle of an equilateral triangle. 60°, 60°, 60°

27. The measure of one angle in an isosceles triangle is 90°. Find the measures of the other angles. 45°, 45°

28. An equilateral triangle has perimeter 37.5 cm. Find the length of each side. 12.5 cm, 12.5 cm, 12.5 cm

29. What is 18% of 45? 8.1

30. 8 is what percent of 4000? 0.2%

31. 6.48 is what percent of 27? 24%

32. 105 is 42% of what number? 250

33. 316 is 0.5% of what number? 63,200

34. What is $34\frac{1}{2}$% of 1100? 379.5

Solve the equation for y in terms of x.

35. $4x + y = 18$ $y = 18 - 4x$

36. $x + 2y = 15$ $y = 7\frac{1}{2} - \frac{1}{2}x$

37. $6x - 6y = 50$ $y = x - 8\frac{1}{3}$

38. $\frac{x}{2} + y = 17$ $y = 17 - \frac{x}{2}$

39. $xy = 20$ $y = \frac{20}{x}$

40. $x^2 + y = 100$ $y = 100 - x^2$

Find the area of the circle described. Leave your answer in terms of π.

41. radius 14 cm 196π cm²

42. diameter 46 mm 529π mm²

43. radius 125 km $15,625\pi$ km²

44. diameter 286 m $20,449\pi$ m²

45. radius 1805 cm $3,258,025\pi$ cm²

46. diameter 305.6 m $23,347.84\pi$ m²

390   *Chapter 10*

Find the surface area and volume for the sphere described. Leave your answer in terms of π.

47. radius 8   256π square units; $\frac{2048}{3}\pi$ cubic units

48. radius 15   900π square units; 4500π cubic units

49. radius 36   5184π square units; 62,208π cubic units

Problems

Problem Solving Reminders

Here are some reminders that may help you solve some of the problems on this page.
- Determine what information is necessary to solve the problem.
- Consider whether drawing a sketch will help.
- If more than one method can be used to solve a problem, use one method to solve and one to check.

Solve.

1. The Aleutian Trench in the Pacific Ocean is 8100 m deep. Each story of an average skyscraper is about 4.2 m high. How many stories would a skyscraper as tall as the Aleutian Trench have? Round your answer to the nearest whole number. 1929 stories

2. These announcements were heard at a rocket launch: "Minus 45 seconds and counting," and "We have second-stage ignition at plus 110 seconds." How much time elapsed between the announcements? 155 seconds

3. A rancher bought 15 fence sections at $58 each to complete one side of a corral. If the length of the side is 375 m and each section is the same length, what is the length of a section? 25 m

4. George had 15 flat tires last year. The cost of repairing each tire was $6.35 plus 5% tax. How much did he spend on repairs for the year? $100.05

5. Fred bought a bag of nuts. He gave $\frac{1}{4}$ of it to one brother, $\frac{1}{6}$ to another, $\frac{1}{3}$ to his sister, and kept the rest. How much did he keep? $\frac{1}{4}$

6. Gus is canning tomato sauce. He has 20 jars that have a diameter of 9 cm and height of 9 cm. If he must leave one centimeter of air space at the top of each jar, what volume of sauce can a jar hold? Use $\pi \approx 3.14$ and round the answer to three digits. 509 cm³

7. The cost of an average basket of groceries rose from $78.80 in April to $82.74 in June. What was the percent of increase? 5%

8. A roll of 36-exposure film costs $5.85. Processing for color prints costs $.42 per print. What is the total cost for film and processing of 36 prints? $20.97

Areas and Volumes **391**

12. Mary Murphy borrowed $3000 for 2 years at 14% simple interest. How much must she repay when the loan is due? $3840

13. Millville Bank pays 8% interest compounded quarterly. To the nearest penny, how much will $5000 earn in one year? $412.16

Graph the equation on a coordinate plane. Use a separate set of axes for each equation. Check students' graphs

14. $4x - y = -8$

15. $x = -3$

Use a graph to solve the system. Do the lines intersect or coincide, or are they parallel? Check students' graphs

16. $y = -2x + 3$ no solution; $2x + y = -2$ parallel

17. $2y + x = -7$ $(-3, -2)$; $3 = x - 3y$ intersect

Graph the inequality. Check students' graphs

18. $y \leq 2x - 3$

19. $y - 3x < 1$

11

Applying Algebra to Right Triangles

One of the basic shapes used in building hang-gliders such as the one shown at the right is the triangle. Triangles are especially well-suited for use in building because they are the simplest rigid forms. A rigid form is a figure that preserves its shape under pressure. Because of their rigidity, triangles are used in the construction of many large-scale projects, such as bridges, towers, and statues.

One important type of triangle is the right triangle. The ratios of the lengths of the sides of a right triangle are called trigonometric ratios. In this chapter, you will extend your knowledge of triangles and learn about trigonometric ratios. You will also study some methods for finding angles and lengths where triangles are involved.

Career Note

The job of surveyor is a career in which knowledge of right triangles and trigonometry plays an important role. Surveyors are responsible for establishing legal land boundaries. About half of their time is spent on location measuring sites and collecting data for maps and charts. The remaining part of their time is spent preparing reports, drawing maps, and planning future surveys.

393

Lesson Commentary
Chapter 11   Applying Algebra to Right Triangles

Overview

This chapter unifies virtually all of the major topics that have been presented up to this point. In particular, it builds on the earlier material covering positive and negative numbers, decimals, triangles, and area.

For most students, this will be the first introduction to square roots. They encounter the meaning of the term *square root*, and become familiar with the radical sign. They will learn to evaluate rational square roots. For irrational square roots, students will be able to approximate, using both an arithmetic method and a table of square roots.

Square root concepts and skills lead to the study of right triangles through the Pythagorean theorem. On the formal level, similar triangles will be a new concept for most students, and will require careful development. Similar triangles provide the basis for defining the basic trigonometric ratios. Finally, the process of solving a right triangle brings all the concepts of the chapter together in a single context. Solving a right triangle can involve the Pythagorean theorem, squares and square roots, trigonometric ratios, and the use of tables, all in one problem.

SQUARE ROOTS

11-1 Square Roots

Objective *for pages 394–395*

■ To estimate the positive square root of a positive number by determining the two consecutive integers between which the square root lies.

Teaching Suggestions

It will help to review arithmetic of positive and negative numbers before starting on square roots. This will make it easier to see that every positive number has two square roots, while a negative number has no real-number square root.

As an aid to understanding square roots, point out that, since the number $\sqrt{a}$ is the square root of a ($a \geq 0$), this means that $(\sqrt{a})^2 = a$. This provides a way to test whether $\sqrt{a}$ has a given value.

Students often find it interesting to realize that $\sqrt{a}$, where a is an integer, is rational only when a is the square of an integer. This has a bearing, among other things, on which entries in the square root table are exact and which are approximate. You may wish to point out that the relation between numbers and their square roots is not a linear one. This means that, for example, although 17 is halfway between 9 and 25, $\sqrt{17}$ is not 4, which is halfway between $\sqrt{9}$ and $\sqrt{25}$.

Related Activities

To strengthen understanding of squares and prime numbers, have students find the number of prime factors (page 89) of each integer from 1 to 25. Then have students categorize integers according to the number of prime factors. The only integers with one factor are primes. Have students examine the prime factors of perfect squares such as 9, 3×3, and 16, $2 \times 2 \times 2 \times 2$. They should be able to predict that

$$36 = 2 \times 2 \times 3 \times 3$$

is a perfect square but

$$32 = 2 \times 2 \times 2 \times 2 \times 2$$

is not.

To enhance understanding of the fact that $\sqrt{a^2} = |a|$, have students fill in a chart headed as shown.

a	a^2	$\sqrt{a^2}$	$|a|$
2	4	2	2
−2	4	2	2

Use a variety of both positive and negative numbers for a. Students should notice that when a is positive, $\sqrt{a^2} = a$; when a is negative, $\sqrt{a^2} = -a$. But in all cases, $\sqrt{a^2} = |a|$.

11-2 Approximating Square Roots

Objective *for pages 396–398*

■ To use the "divide-and-average" method to approximate the square root of a number.

Teaching Suggestions

Although the focus here is primarily on the divide-and-average algorithm itself, the concept behind it is one that students readily grasp. In essence, the idea is that if x is an approximation of $\sqrt{a}$, and $y = \frac{a}{x}$, then if $x < \sqrt{a}$, then $y > \sqrt{a}$, and the average of x and y is closer to $\sqrt{a}$ than either x or y is. This gives us a quick and manageable method for approximating $\sqrt{a}$. Moreover, it is a process that can be reiterated any number of times to achieve whatever degree of accuracy is desired for $\sqrt{a}$. In Example 1, point out that to approximate to a particular decimal place, continue the division to one more place than desired in the final answer.

There are, of course, other techniques for approximating square roots. For example, in the "guess-and-correct" method one guesses a value for $\sqrt{a}$, then checks by squaring the guess. If the result is greater than a, the next guess should be lower, and vice versa. Some teachers may have learned a computational algorithm for approximating $\sqrt{a}$, in which digits are marked off in pairs, and so on. This algorithm is no longer encountered very often.

In this lesson we are approximating square roots to the tenths' place, not to the nearest tenth. The answers given are not rounded up, even when the digit in the next place is 5 or greater.

Related Activities

To extend students' understanding of irrational numbers, mention that irrational numbers are those that can be written as nonrepeating, nonterminating decimals. Encourage students to "invent" their own irrational numbers, such as $0.121221222\ldots$ and $1.213141516\ldots$

To provide a challenge, have students prove that $\sqrt{2}$ is irrational. If $\sqrt{2}$ were rational, there would be integers p and q such that $\sqrt{2} = \frac{p}{q}$ where p and q have no common factor. Then $p^2 = 2q^2$. Consider the prime factorization of p^2 and $2q^2$. Since p^2 is a multiple of 2, it is even, and p must also be even. Since p and q have no common

---

Worksheet (Page 133)

NAME _____ DATE _____

Problem Solving — For use after Lesson 11-1
Logic Problems

Some logic problems can be solved using the method of elimination. Each clue eliminates a name or position from consideration. Making a chart can help you organize the facts. In the chart below, an x is drawn whenever a fact eliminates a possibility.

EXAMPLE

Ann Jogger, Claire Bowler, and Ben Swimmer exercise in ways that do *not* match their names. Ben is the jogger's cousin. Who is the swimmer?

SOLUTION

— Cross out the sport that matches each name. These are impossible according to the first sentence in the problem.

— If Ben is the jogger's cousin, then he is not the jogger. Cross out Ben in the jogger column.

— When only one possibility is left in a row or column, put a (✓).

	Jogger	Bowler	Swimmer
Ann	x	✕	✓
Claire	✓	x	✕
Ben	x	✓	x

Who must be the jogger? *Claire*

Who must be the bowler? *Ben*

Who must be the swimmer? *Ann*

Complete the charts to answer each question.

1. Marla, Michelle, and Mike live in three different nearby villages: Eastville, Westtown, and Southbury. Michelle and the person from Eastville are in the same math class. The people from Eastville and Westtown stay for French Club with Mike. Who lives in Westtown?

	Eastville	Westtown	Southbury
Marla	✓		
Michelle	✕	✓	
Mike	✕	✕	✓

Michelle

(Continue on next page.)

PRE-ALGEBRA, An Accelerated Course
Copyright © 1985 by Houghton Mifflin Company. All rights reserved. Printed in U.S.A.

133

Worksheet (Page 134)

NAME _____ DATE _____

Problem Solving — For use after Lesson 11-1 *(continued)*
Logic Problems (continued)

2. Three airline passengers named Barker, Cashman, and Phillips are talking to a flight attendant. The passengers are a teacher, a musician, and a salesperson. Cashman and the musician are from the same city. Barker and the teacher are sitting together on the plane. Both the teacher and Phillips enjoy the musician's albums. Who is the salesperson?

	Teacher	Musician	Salesperson
Barker	✕	✓	
Cashman	✓	✕	
Phillips	✕	✕	✓

Phillips

Make a chart if necessary to help you solve the following logic problems.

3. Peg, John, and Maggie live in a three-story building, but no two on any one floor. Their ages are 5, 7, and 8, although not necessarily in that order. Peg, who is youngest, lives above the seven-year-old and below Maggie. Find the children's ages and on which floor each lives. *Maggie is 8 and lives on the third floor. John is 7 and lives on the first floor. Peg is 5 and lives on the second floor.*

4. Linda, Tim, Karen, and Gary are freshman, sophomore, junior, and senior students who major in chemistry, architecture, mathematics, and business, not necessarily in that order. Pair each person according to major and class. You have the following clues:

   (a) Karen and the sophomore business-major room together.

   (b) Tim will graduate this year.

   (c) Gary had to do a term paper on Egyptian pyramids.

   (d) Linda will graduate the year after Karen and the year before the architecture major.

   (e) The mathematics major graduated from the same high school as Karen and Linda. *Linda – sophomore – business; Tim – senior – mathematics; Karen – junior – chemistry; Gary – freshman – architecture.*

5. One of three identical triplets — Edward, Edwin, or Edmond — was seen leaving the scene of a crime. When questioned, each made the following statements:

   Edward: It wasn't me! Edwin: Edward is lying! Edmond: Edwin is lying!

   Only one of the triplets was lying. Determine who lied. Can you determine who was seen leaving the scene of the crime? *Edwin is lying. Not enough information to determine who was seen leaving the scene of the crime.*

PRE-ALGEBRA, An Accelerated Course
Copyright © 1985 by Houghton Mifflin Company. All rights reserved. Printed in U.S.A.

134

393b

factor, q must be odd. If p is even, $p = 2m$, where m is an integer. Then $p^2 = 4m^2$ and $2q^2 = 4m^2$, so that $q^2 = 2m^2$. Now we have q^2 and therefore q is even, contradicting the earlier conclusion that q is odd. Thus the original supposition that $\sqrt{2}$ is rational is false, and $\sqrt{2}$ is irrational.

11-3 Using a Square Root Table

Objective *for pages 399–401*

■ To use a table or interpolation to find the approximate square root of a number.

Teaching Suggestions

It would be worthwhile to make it clear that every non-negative number has a nonnegative square root. This includes integers that are not perfect squares, as well as decimals and fractions. Some students have difficulty accepting the fact that $\sqrt{78}$, for example, is indeed a real number.

It may heighten understanding of the meaning of a square root to show that the square root table is also a table of squares, that is, if we locate a given number x in the column headed $\sqrt{N}$, then x^2 will be the entry in the N column. Inform students that very few entries in the square root table are exact square roots. In fact, only the square roots of numbers that are squares of integers $(1, 4, 9, 16, 25, \ldots)$ are exact. All other entries in the table are decimal approximations of irrational numbers.

Some students may benefit from organizing interpolation in a tabular format, as in the following determination of $\sqrt{7.3}$.

$$
\begin{array}{ccc}
 & x & \sqrt{x} \\
 & 8 & 2.828 \\
1.0 \left[\begin{array}{c} 0.3 \left[\begin{array}{c} 7.3 \\ 7 \end{array} \right. \end{array} \right. & \begin{array}{c} ? \\ 2.646 \end{array} & \left] d \right] 0.182
\end{array}
$$

$$\frac{0.3}{1.0} = \frac{d}{0.182} \qquad d = 0.3(0.182) = 0.0546$$

$$\sqrt{7.3} \approx 2.646 + d = 2.7006 \approx 2.701$$

Square roots found by interpolation from a table may differ from those given by a calculator. Answers in each section of this chapter reflect the method taught in the lesson.

Related Activities

To put tables into a more general context, bring in a variety of tables for students to practice reading. These could include income tax and sales tax tables, tables of population growth, and so on.

To improve students' graphing skills, have them graph the equation $y = \sqrt{x}$, using the table of square roots to fino the values.

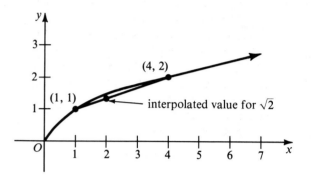

interpolated value for $\sqrt{2}$

The graph is a "smooth" curve. Tell students that a curve shaped like this is said to be concave downward. Ask whether a segment joining two points on the curve will lie below or above the curve. **Below** Then point out that interpolation, basically, approximates a portion of the curve with a segment. Ask how the interpolated square root of a number compares to the actual square root. **The interpolated value is always less.**

11-4 The Pythagorean Theorem

Objective *for pages 402–405*

■ To use the Pythagorean theorem and its converse.

Teaching Suggestions

The Pythagorean theorem is probably the single best-known proposition of mathematics. It is used for such varied purposes as finding the distance between points in the coordinate plane, laying out playing fields, and calculating the lengths of roof rafters.

Demonstrate that the longest side of a triangle is always opposite the largest angle. A right angle in a triangle is always the largest angle, so the hypotenuse is the longest side.

Many students will not be familiar with the term *converse*. The conditional sentence "If p, then q" can be represented as $p \rightarrow q$. For this sentence we have the following related sentences, where $\sim p$ is the negation of p, read "not p."

Converse	$q \rightarrow p$	If q, then p.
Inverse	$\sim p \rightarrow \sim q$	If not p, then not q.
Contrapositive	$\sim q \rightarrow \sim p$	If not q, then not p.

Logically, the contrapositive is equivalent to the original sentence. The sentences $p \rightarrow q$ and $\sim q \rightarrow \sim p$ have the same meaning. If $p \rightarrow q$ is true, then $\sim q \rightarrow \sim p$ must also be true. The converses or inverses of some true sentences are true, but those of some true sentences are false. The Pythagorean theorem happens to be a proposition whose converse is true. The converse is useful for testing the given measures of the sides of a triangle to see if it is a right triangle.

As an example of a true conditional whose converse is not true, consider the statement

$$\text{If } x = 3, \text{ then } x^2 = 9.$$

The converse is

$$\text{If } x^2 = 9, \text{ then } x = 3,$$

which is false because $(-3)^2$ is also 9.

It may be helpful to develop two alternative forms of the Pythagorean theorem. If

$$c^2 = a^2 + b^2,$$

then we can also say

$$a^2 = c^2 - b^2 \quad \text{and} \quad b^2 = c^2 - a^2.$$

These forms of the theorem are suited for use when the objective is to solve for the length of a leg rather than the length of the hypotenuse.

In some of these exercises, such as Written Exercises 18–21 and Problems 1, 3, 4, 6, and 7, students need to find the square roots of numbers greater than 100. If students do not use calculators, refer them to Written Exercises 32–37 on page 401.

The introduction to Written Exercises 22–24 shows how to find Pythagorean Triples. The Computer Byte on page 425 presents a program for producing Pythagorean Triples.

Related Activities

To reinforce the meaning of the converse of the Pythagorean theorem, knot a piece of string 12 ft long to form a loop. Make a mark every foot. Ask one student to hold the string at any mark, another to hold it 3 ft from the first, and another to hold it 4 ft from the second. Have them pull the string until it is taut, and examine the resulting triangle It is a right triangle because $3^2 + 4^2 = 5^2$. It has been said that the ancient Egyptians used such strings to lay out right angles when surveying their fields, although there is some question whether the historic evidence supports this assertion. Students interested in the history of mathematics might want to read Chapter 5 of *The Ascent of Man* by Jacob Bronowski.

To extend the Pythagorean theorem, consider triangles that are not right triangles. If the sides of a triangle have lengths a, b, and c, and the angle opposite the side of length c is obtuse, then $c^2 > a^2 + b^2$; if the angle is acute, then $c^2 < a^2 + b^2$. Determine whether the angle opposite side c is acute, right, or obtuse.

1. $a = 8$, $b = 5$, $c = 10$ obtuse
2. $a = 20$, $b = 21$, $c = 29$ right
3. $a = 7$, $b = 10$, $c = 14$ obtuse
4. $a = 2$, $b = 3$, $c = \sqrt{10}$ acute

Resource Book: Page 135 (Use After Page 405)

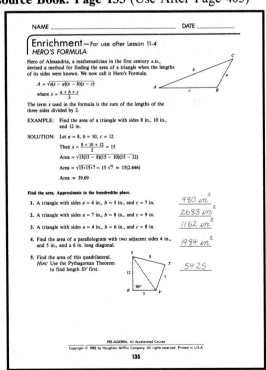

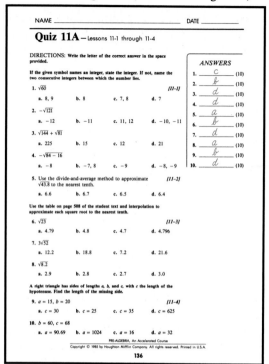

Students are sometimes reluctant to accept that the way similarity is expressed makes a difference. Referring to the triangles in the diagram on page 406, it is certainly true that $\triangle DEF$ can also be called $\triangle DFE$, $\triangle FDE$, and so on. However, if we intend to convey information about correspondence of sides and angles, we are not free to use any name for this triangle once a name has been chosen for the other triangle. We can state any of the following similarities:

$$\triangle ABC \sim \triangle DEF \qquad \triangle ACB \sim \triangle DFE$$
$$\triangle BCA \sim \triangle EFD \qquad \triangle BAC \sim \triangle EDF$$
$$\triangle CAB \sim \triangle FDE \qquad \triangle CBA \sim \triangle FED$$

You may want to show how much information is contained in a statement of similarity even without reference to a diagram. For example, if $\triangle FOR \sim \triangle NXT$, then:

$$\angle F \cong \angle N \qquad \angle O \cong \angle X \qquad \angle R \cong \angle T$$

and $\dfrac{FO}{NX} = \dfrac{OR}{XT} = \dfrac{FR}{NT}$.

Related Activities

To apply similar triangles to a practical problem, use similar triangles for "indirect measurement," that is, to find the heights of objects that cannot actually be measured. At any given time, the triangles determined by objects and their shadows are similar. To find a, the unknown height of object A, use an object B of known height b, such as a meter stick. Measure c, the length of A's shadow, and d, the length of B's shadow. Then since $\dfrac{a}{c} = \dfrac{b}{d}$, we have $a = \dfrac{bc}{d}$ and can readily determine the height a.

To illustrate the idea of similar figures in general, use an opaque projector to project the same picture from several different distances. Trace the image on paper or on the chalkboard. This will give several similar copies of the same original, all of different sizes.

USING RIGHT TRIANGLES

11-5 Similar Triangles

Objective for pages 406–410

■ To apply facts about similar triangles.

Teaching Suggestions

Similarity as a formal concept is not familiar to most students. To give a general flavor, discuss various sized photo enlargements, maps of the same area with different scales, and scale models. These are all examples of similar figures.

Two triangles are similar if they have three pairs of congruent angles. (In fact, if two pairs of angles are congruent, the third pair must be congruent.) Do not imply, however, that pairs of equal angles guarantee similarity for other figures. A square and a rectangle have four pairs of equal angles but may easily not be similar. On the other hand, all squares are similar.

11-6 Special Right Triangles

Objective for pages 411–415

■ To find the lengths of missing sides of a 45° right triangle, and of a 30°-60° right triangle, given the length of one side.

Although the point was made in the last lesson, it would be worth repeating that any two right triangles with one pair of congruent acute angles must be similar to each other. This gives us, in the current section, a property that is true of all 45° right triangles and another that is true of all 30°–60° right triangles. This similarity property is also involved later, when we define trigonometric ratios as functions of angles and not of particular triangles.

For the sake of thoroughness, you might present an example of a 45° right triangle for which the hypotenuse is known and a leg is to be found. Here, since the hypotenuse is $\sqrt{2}$ times the leg, it becomes necessary to divide by $\sqrt{2}$ to find the leg. Similarly, you might give the leg opposite the 60° angle in a 30°–60° right triangle. Then this leg is divided by $\sqrt{3}$ to find the shorter leg, which is in turn doubled to find the hypotenuse.

Students may not realize at first that it matters which leg is involved in a 30°–60° right triangle problem. Emphasize that the hypotenuse is twice the leg opposite the 30° angle, not just any leg. Conversely, the leg opposite the 30° angle is half the hypotenuse.

The rule against radicals in denominators is a convention, an agreement people have made about how something is done. As such it is similar to the order of operations convention and the convention that $-\frac{1}{2}$ is preferred to $\frac{-1}{2}$ or $\frac{1}{-2}$. Do not try to justify the procedure as one that makes calculation easier. With a calculator it is no more difficult to calculate $\frac{6}{\sqrt{3}}$ than $2\sqrt{3}$. The original intent of the rule may have been to make quick decimal approximations easy to find using mental arithmetic. In this case, $2\sqrt{3} \approx 2(1.73) = 3.46$.

When an expression with a radical in the denominator is rewritten, the equivalent expression is often a fraction. For example, $\frac{3}{\sqrt{5}} = \frac{3\sqrt{5}}{5}$.

In Class Exercise 12, most students will use the same procedure as in Example 1: $x = 10\sqrt{2}$; $y = 10\sqrt{2} \div \sqrt{2} = 10$. Some students may realize that each triangle is isosceles, so the length of the unmarked leg of the lower triangle is 10. Since the measure of each unmarked angle is 45°, the quadrilateral is a rectangle; since two consecutive sides are congruent it is a square and $y = 10$. Thus $x = 10\sqrt{2}$.

To give concrete meaning to irrational numbers and increase facility with the Pythagorean theorem, have students use rulers and protractors to construct a spiral as shown.

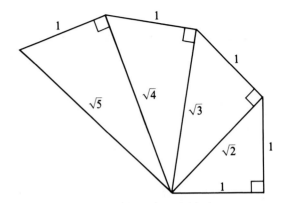

Choose a unit and construct a second leg of the same length perpendicular to it. Then draw the hypotenuse and determine its length using the Pythagorean theorem. Using this hypotenuse as a leg, construct another unit leg, and find the new hypotenuse. This process produces a spiral with a series of hypotenuses of lengths $\sqrt{2}$, $\sqrt{3}$, $\sqrt{4}$, $\sqrt{5}$, ...

11-7 Trigonometric Ratios

Objective *for pages 416–419*

■ To calculate the sine, cosine, and tangent of an acute angle of a right triangle, given the lengths of two sides.

Teaching Suggestions

Students need to realize that a particular side of a right triangle is not always the opposite. For example the leg that is the opposite side for one acute angle is the adjacent side for the other. For this reason we see that if $\angle A$ and $\angle B$ are the acute angles of a right triangle, then $\sin A = \cos B$ and $\cos A = \sin B$. Make sure students realize that our definitions apply only to the acute angles, not the right angle.

Some students assume that sin 30°, cos 45°, and so on are variables. Actually these are numbers. Point out that for any x between 0° and 90° both the cosine and the sine of x are real numbers between 0 and 1. With more able students you might investigate the behavior of tan x near 0° and 90°. Since the tangent is $\frac{\text{opposite}}{\text{adjacent}}$, then as x approaches 90°, tan x approaches infinity. (Opposite becomes larger, adjacent becomes smaller.) Conversely, as x approaches 0°, tan x approaches 0. (Opposite becomes smaller, adjacent becomes larger.)

Remind students that they can use square root tables if necessary to approximate ratios containing radicals. Of course, some students will prefer to use a calculator.

Many students find the mnemonic SOH CAH TOA useful for remembering the definitions: $\sin x = \frac{\text{opposite}}{\text{hypotenuse}}$, $\cos x = \frac{\text{adjacent}}{\text{hypotenuse}}$, $\tan x = \frac{\text{opposite}}{\text{adjacent}}$.

The purpose of Written Exercises 15–17 is to apply the right triangle properties and trigonometric ratios to obtain an unknown value of a trigonometric ratio from one that is known. Answers will vary slightly depending on when students round.

Related Activities

By completing the chart below, students can discover that $\sin^2 A + \cos^2 A = 1$.

A	sin A	cos A	(sin A)²	(cos A)²
30°	0.5	$\frac{\sqrt{3}}{2}$	0.25	0.75
45°	$\frac{\sqrt{2}}{2}$	$\frac{\sqrt{2}}{2}$	0.5	0.5
60°	$\frac{\sqrt{3}}{2}$	0.5	0.75	0.25

To approximate trigonometric functions of angles besides 30°, 45°, and 60°, have students draw x- and y-axes, and a large circle with center at the origin and radius 1. Use a scale so that 10 graph paper squares represent a unit, as shown to the right at the top of the page. To evaluate functions of a given angle A, use a protractor to draw the angle in standard position. Since the radius of the circle is 1, sin A is the y-coordinate of the point where the second ray of the angle crosses the circle. These values can be approximated fairly accurately directly from the graph, and will give students an idea of where the values in trigonometric tables, introduced in the next section, come from.

To provide a challenge, ask students to predict the

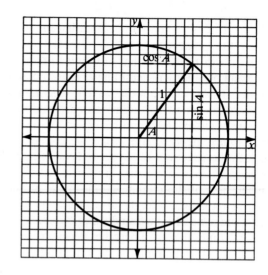

range of values each trigonometric function can have. The sine and cosine must be between 0 and 1 because the hypotenuse is longer than either leg. The tangent can have any value. In later courses students will learn that trigonometric ratios can be applied to angles larger than 90° and to triangles that are in quadrants II, III, and IV of the coordinate plane.

11-8 Solving Right Triangles

Objective for pages 420–425

■ To solve a right triangle by using a trigonometric table.

Teaching Suggestions

A triangle is said to have six "parts": the three angles and the three sides. The parts of $\triangle ABC$ are $\angle A$, $\angle B$, $\angle C$, $\overline{AB}$, $\overline{BC}$, and $\overline{AC}$. Solving a triangle means to find the measures of all of these parts. To solve a right triangle, we must be given at least two parts besides the right angle. In a right triangle we must only account for five of the six parts, since we already know that one angle is a right angle. Emphasize, as suggested earlier, that an expression like sin 75° or tan 25° is a number, or constant, not an unknown, or variable. To solve for a part of a right triangle we must find a relationship involving only one unknown term. For example, we can use $\tan A = \frac{\text{opposite}}{\text{adjacent}}$ when the opposite side is not known but the measures of $\angle A$ and the adjacent side are known.

Examination of the trigonometric table on page 509 can be interesting. Observe that the cosine column is just the reverse of the sine column, and that both vary between 0 and 1. Tangents run from nearly zero to a very large number indeed. The table does not use 0 before decimal points, as the rest of this book does. This is to familiarize students with this type of notation, which is generally used in tables of trigonometric functions.

For the Computer Byte on page 425, refer students back to the definition of Pythagorean Triples on page 404. In Exercise 5 they will discover that the smallest triple is 3, 4, 5.

To provide a challenge, have students use the sine function to derive an area formula for triangles that does not require knowing the altitude. Suppose $\triangle ABC$ is as shown.

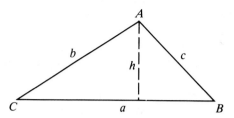

Then $\sin C = \dfrac{h}{b}$, or $h = b \sin C$. Also, area of $\triangle ABC = \frac{1}{2}ah = \frac{1}{2}ab \sin C$. Thus we can find areas of triangles directly from the sides and angles of the triangle, with no need to determine the altitude.

Resource Book: Page 137 (Use After Page 425)

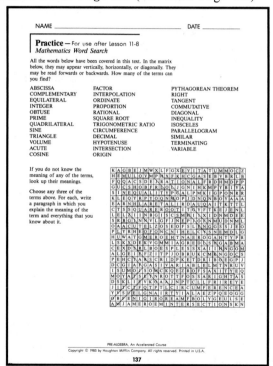

Related Activities

To illustrate the pattern of variation of the sine function, have students graph the sines of angles from 0° to 90°.

Resource Book: Page 138 (Use After Page 425)

Resource Book: Pages 139–142 (Use After Page 425)

NAME _____ DATE _____

Quiz 11B— Lessons 11-5 through 11-8

DIRECTIONS: Write the letter of the correct answer in the space provided.

Exercises 1-4 refer to the diagram below. △QMT ~ △QVR. Complete.

1. $\frac{QT}{QR} = \frac{?}{QV}$ [11-5]
   a. MT   b. QM   c. VR   d. QT

2. $\frac{VR}{?} = \frac{QR}{QT}$
   a. QV   b. QT   c. MT   d. QM

3. QT = ?
   a. 4   b. 10   c. 6   d. 15

4. MV = ?
   a. 6   b. 24   c. 21   d. 15

In Exercises 5 and 6, give answers in terms of radicals with the radical in the numerator.

5. The hypotenuse of an isosceles right triangle is 8.2 in. long. What is the length of each leg?   [11-6]
   a. 16.4   b. 8.2√2   c. 4.1√2   d. (√8.2) (2)

6. A ladder 12 m long that leans against a building makes an angle of 60° with the ground. How far up the wall does it reach?
   a. 6√2 m   b. 12√3 m   c. 6 m   d. 6√3 m

Exercises 7-8 refer to the diagram at the right. Complete.

7. sin M = ?   [11-7]
   a. $\frac{f}{l}$ b. $\frac{m}{l}$ c. $\frac{m}{f}$ d. $\frac{l}{f}$

8. tan F = ?
   a. $\frac{f}{l}$ b. $\frac{l}{m}$ c. $\frac{f}{m}$ d. $\frac{m}{l}$

Find the measure of the angle to the nearest degree and the length to the nearest tenth. Use the table on page 509 of the student text.

9. If l = 9 and m = 7, then f = ? and ∠M = ?   [11-8]
   a. 5.7, 39°   b. 11.4, 51°   c. 11.4, 39°   d. 5.7, 51°

ANSWERS
1. _b_ (10)
2. _c_ (10)
3. _b_ (10)
4. _a_ (10)
5. _c_ (15)
6. _d_ (15)
7. _b_ (10)
8. _c_ (10)
9. _d_ (10)

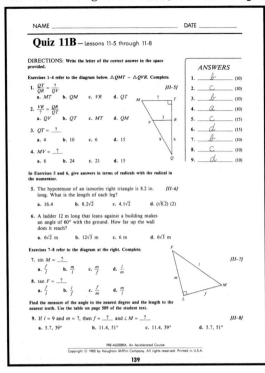

PRE-ALGEBRA, An Accelerated Course
Copyright © 1985 by Houghton Mifflin Company. All rights reserved. Printed in U.S.A.

139

NAME _____ DATE _____

Review — Chapter 11

If the given symbol names an integer, state the integer. If not, name the two consecutive integers between which the number lies.

1. −√169   _-13_   2. √88   _9,10_   3. √100 − 25   _8,9_   [11-1]

4. Use the divide-and-average method to approximate √110 to the nearest tenth.   _10.4_   [11-2]

Use the table on page 508 of the student text and interpolation to approximate each square root to the nearest tenth.

5. 5√29 _26.9_   6. $\frac{1}{10}$√15 _0.4_   7. √14.6 _3.8_   [11-3]

The lengths of the sides of a triangle are given. Is it a right triangle?

8. 8, 20, 25 _no_   9. 24, 45, 51 _yes_   [11-4]

Solve. Give your answer to the nearest tenth.

10. Find the length of a diagonal of a 9-cm by 9-cm square.   _12.7 cm_

Exercises 12-14 refer to the diagram at the right. △ABC ~ △EDC. Complete.

11. $\frac{AC}{EC} = \frac{BC}{?}$ _DC_   [11-5]
12. ED = _15_
13. BD = _48_

Solve.

14. One day, Daniel, who is 160 cm tall, cast a shadow 200 cm long while Bob's shadow was 220 cm long. How tall is Bob? _176 cm_   [11-6]

Exercises 15-18 refer to the diagram at the right. Give all ratios in lowest terms.

15. x = _24_   16. sin T = _$\frac{4}{5}$_   [11-7]
17. cos T = _$\frac{3}{5}$_   18. tan S = _$\frac{3}{4}$_

Exercises 19-22 refer to the diagram at the right. Find the measures of the angles to the nearest degree and the lengths to the nearest tenth. Use the tables on pages 508-509 in the student text.

19. If h = 14 and f = 10, find g. _9.8_   [11-8]
20. If h = 9 and ∠F = 54°, find f. _7.3_
21. If f = 6 and ∠G = 25°, find h. _6.6_
22. If f = 6 and g = 14, find ∠F. _23°_

PRE-ALGEBRA, An Accelerated Course
Copyright © 1985 by Houghton Mifflin Company. All rights reserved. Printed in U.S.A.

140

NAME _____ DATE _____

Test — Chapter 11

DIRECTIONS: Write the correct answer in the space provided.

If the given symbol names an integer, state the integer. If not, name the two consecutive integers between which the number lies.

1. −√441   2. √400 − √144   3. √29 + 43   [11-1]

4. Use the divide-and-average method to approximate √28.6 to the nearest tenth.   [11-2]

Solve. Give your answer to the nearest tenth.

5. Using interpolation and the table on page 508 in the student text, √78.9 ? .   [11-3]

6. The area of a square wall is 90 m². What is the length of one side?

Is the triangle with sides of the given lengths a right triangle?

7. 8, 10, 12   8. 16, 30, 34   9. 5, 12, 14   [11-4]

Exercises 10-13 refer to the diagram at the right. △FGH ~ △NMP.

10. $\frac{FG}{MN} = \frac{HF}{?}$ [11-5]
11. Find the length of $\overline{HF}$.
12. Find the length of $\overline{MP}$.
13. Find the measure of ∠F.

Give answers in terms of radicals with the radical in the numerator.

14. The hypotenuse of an isosceles right triangle has a length of 16. How long is each leg?   [11-6]

15. Find the height of an equilateral triangle with sides 6 cm long.

Exercises 16 to 18 refer to the diagram at the right. Give all ratios in lowest terms.

16. sin P   17. tan R   18. cos R   [11-7]

Each of the equal legs of an isosceles triangle is 30 and the perimeter of the triangle is 128.

19. Find the length of the third leg of the isosceles triangle. [11-8]

ANSWERS
1. _-21_ (5)
2. _8_ (5)
3. _8,9_ (5)
4. _5.3_ (5)
5. _8.9_ (5)
6. _9.5 m_ (5)
7. _no_ (5)
8. _yes_ (5)
9. _no_ (5)
10. _PN_ (5)
11. _9_ (5)
12. _16_ (5)
13. _108°_ (5)
14. _8√2_ (5)
15. _3√3 cm_ (6)
16. _$\frac{5}{13}$_ (6)
17. _$\frac{12}{5}$_ (6)
18. _$\frac{5}{13}$_ (6)
19. _36_ (6)

PRE-ALGEBRA, An Accelerated Course
Copyright © 1985 by Houghton Mifflin Company. All rights reserved. Printed in U.S.A.

141

NAME _____ DATE _____

Make-up Test — Chapter 11

DIRECTIONS: Write the correct answer in the space provided.

If the given symbol names an integer, state the integer. If not, name the two consecutive integers between which the number lies.

1. −√49   2. √900 + √100   3. √170 − 43   [11-1]

4. Use the divide-and-average method to approximate √40.2 to the nearest tenth.   [11-2]

Solve. Give the answer to the nearest tenth.

5. A square floor has an area of 47 m². Find the length of one side.   [11-3]

6. Using interpolation and the table on page 508 in the student text, √56.8 ≈ ?

Is the triangle with sides of the given lengths a right triangle?

7. 6, 9, 12   8. 5, 11, 13   9. 40, 75, 85   [11-4]

Exercises 10-13 refer to the diagram at the right. △ABC ~ △RST.

10. $\frac{AB}{SR} = \frac{?}{TS}$ [11-5]
11. Finish the length of $\overline{TS}$.
12. Find the length of $\overline{AC}$.
13. Find the measure of ∠T.

Give answers in terms of radicals with the radical in the numerator.

14. Find the height of an equilateral triangle with sides 14 cm long.   [11-6]

15. The hypotenuse of a 45° right triangle has a length of 24. How long is each leg?

Exercises 16-18 refer to the diagram at the right. Give all ratios in lowest terms.

16. tan G   17. cos F   18. sin G   [11-7]

Each of the base angles of an isosceles triangle is 37° and each of the equal sides has length 30.

19. Find the perimeter of the isosceles triangle.   [11-8]

20. Find the vertex angle of the isosceles triangle.

ANSWERS
1. _7_ (5)
2. _40_ (5)
3. _11,12_ (5)
4. _6.3_ (5)
5. _6.9 m_ (5)
6. _7.5_ (5)
7. _no_ (5)
8. _no_ (5)
9. _yes_ (5)
10. _BC_ (5)
11. _15_ (5)
12. _6_ (5)
13. _87°_ (5)
14. _7√3_ (5)
15. _$\frac{12\sqrt{2}}{15}$_ (5)
16. _$\frac{8}{15}$_ (5)
17. _$\frac{17}{15}$_ (5)
18. _$\frac{15}{17}$_ (5)
19. _107.9_ (5)
20. _106°_ (5)

PRE-ALGEBRA, An Accelerated Course
Copyright © 1985 by Houghton Mifflin Company. All rights reserved. Printed in U.S.A.

142

393i

NAME _____ DATE _____

CUMULATIVE REVIEW—Chapters 1-11
Exercises

Simplify the expression.

1. $3(6 + 5) \times 8 \div 2 + 5$ _137_

2. $3 \times 7 + 2 \times 8 + 3^2$ _46_

3. $[(5 - 3)(6 \times \frac{1}{2})] - 12 \div 2$ _0_

4. $4(7 - 9) \div (-8 - 4)$ _$\frac{2}{3}$_

Evaluate the expression when $a = 9$, $b = -2$, and $c = \frac{1}{3}$.

5. abc _$-4\frac{2}{3}$_

6. $bc + a$ _$8\frac{1}{3}$_

7. $ab \div c$ _-72_

8. c^2 _$\frac{1}{6}$_

9. $b^2 a$ _36_

10. $-16bc$ _8_

Use >, <, or = to make a true statement.

11. 5.324 _<_ 5.33

12. $\frac{1}{2}$ _=_ $\frac{2}{3} - \frac{1}{6}$

13. $-\frac{2}{5}$ _>_ $-\frac{3}{4}$

Solve the equation.

14. $29 + p = 42$ _13_

15. $17d = -204$ _-12_

16. $\frac{r}{-12} = 3$ _-36_

17. $t + 3.62 = 9.5$ _34.39_ _5.88_

18. $e + \frac{1}{8} = 9\frac{1}{6}$ _$9\frac{1}{24}$_

19. $2w - \frac{2}{5} = 8$ _$4\frac{1}{5}$_

Find the area of the given figure. Use $\pi \approx \frac{22}{7}$, if necessary.

20. square: sides of 1.5 ft _$2.25\,ft^2$_

21. circle: diameter of 14 cm _$154\,cm^2$_

Tell whether the ordered pair is a solution of the given equation.

$3x + 4y = 12$ 22. $(0, 4)$ _no_   23. $(8, -3)$ _yes_   24. $(-4, 6)$ _yes_

$4a - 5b = -10$ 25. $(5, 6)$ _yes_   26. $(0, -2)$ _no_   27. $(-8, -4)$ _no_

Is the triangle with sides of the given lengths a right triangle?

28. 9, 12, 15 _yes_   29. 5, 13, 14 _no_   30. 2, 3, 4 _no_

Rewrite the expression in lowest terms with the radical in the numerator.

31. $\frac{3}{\sqrt{6}}$ _$\frac{\sqrt{6}}{2}$_

32. $\frac{4}{\sqrt{2}}$ _$2\sqrt{2}$_

33. $\frac{3r}{\sqrt{r}}$ _$3\sqrt{r}$_

Express as a fraction or mixed number in lowest terms.

34. 5.06 _$5\frac{3}{50}$_

35. -0.048 _$-\frac{6}{125}$_

36. 12.825 _$12\frac{33}{40}$_

NAME _____ DATE _____

CUMULATIVE REVIEW—Chapters 1-11 *(continued)*
Problems

Problem Solving Reminders
Here are some problem solving reminders that may help you solve some of the problems on this page.
- Sometimes more than one method can be used to solve.
- Supply additional information if necessary.
- Check your results with the facts given in the problem.

Solve.

1. Marie counted the change in her bank and found that she had 4 more quarters than dimes. If she had a total of $2.05 in quarters and dimes, how many quarters did she have? _7 quarters_

2. Erika bought a car for $9600. At the end of a year, the car was worth $6912, due to depreciation. What was the percent of decrease in value? _28%_

3. Each of the equal sides of an isosceles triangle is 8 in. more than 3 times the base. The perimeter of the triangle is 58 in. Find the length of each side of the triangle. _6 in., 26 in., 26 in._

4. John's recipe for a loaf of banana bread calls for $2\frac{3}{4}$ cups of flour and $1\frac{1}{4}$ cups of mashed banana. If John plans to bake 5 loaves, how much flour will he need? _$13\frac{3}{4}$ cups flour_

5. In a school having 756 students, there is a student ratio of 11 boys to 10 girls. How many boys are there? girls? _396 boys, 360 girls_

6. A pair of skis that originally sold for $125.80 was discounted 15% in December. In March, the sales price was discounted 25%. What was the new sales price in March? _$80.20_

7. A regular octagon has a perimeter of 454.4 m. Find the length of each side. _56.8 m_

Teaching Suggestions
p. 393a

Related Activities p. 393a

Reading Mathematics

Students will learn the meaning of the following mathematical terms in this lesson: *square root, perfect square.*

Symbols, like words, require clear definition. This is the case with the symbol $\sqrt{}$. Students sometimes assume that a single radical can have two values, because they mistakenly believe that the radical sign means "square root." You can eliminate this problem by defining $\sqrt{a}$, in the very beginning, to be the principal, or nonnegative, square root of a.

Chalkboard Examples

If the given symbol names an integer, state the integer. If not, name the two consecutive integers between which the number lies.

1. $\sqrt{20}$ 4 and 5
2. $-\sqrt{64}$ −8
3. $\sqrt{121}$ 11
4. $\sqrt{56}$ 7 and 8

Additional Answers
Class Exercises

1. "The positive square root of 7"
2. "3 times the positive square root of 10"
3. "The negative square root of 81"
4. "The positive square root of 64"
5. "2 times the positive square root of 14"

11-1 Square Roots

Recall that we can write $b \times b$ as b^2 and call it the *square* of b. The factor b is a **square root** of b^2. A given number a has b as a square root if

$$b^2 = a.$$

Thus 9 has 3 as a square root because $3^2 = 9$.

Every positive number has two square roots, and these are opposites of each other. For example, the square roots of 25 are 5 and -5 because

$$5^2 = 5 \times 5 = 25 \quad \text{and} \quad (-5)^2 = (-5) \times (-5) = 25.$$

The only square root of 0 is 0 because $b \times b = 0$ only when $b = 0$.

In this chapter we will work mostly with positive square roots. We use $\sqrt{a}$ to denote the *positive* square root of a. Thus $\sqrt{25} = 5$, not -5. A symbol such as $2\sqrt{25}$ means *2 times the positive square root of 25.* The negative square root of 25 is $-\sqrt{25}$, or -5.

Negative numbers have no real-number square roots because no real number has a square that is negative.

If $\sqrt{a}$ is an integer, we call a a **perfect square.** For example, 36 is a perfect square because $\sqrt{36}$ is the integer 6. Also, 144 is a perfect square because $\sqrt{144} = 12$.

If a is not a perfect square, we can estimate $\sqrt{a}$ by finding the two consecutive integers between which the square root lies. In the process, we use the fact that the smaller of two positive numbers has the smaller positive square root.

EXAMPLE Between which two consecutive integers does $\sqrt{40}$ lie?

Solution 40 lies between the consecutive perfect squares 36 and 49.

$$36 < 40 < 49$$
$$\sqrt{36} < \sqrt{40} < \sqrt{49}$$
$$\text{Thus} \quad 6 < \sqrt{40} < 7.$$

Class Exercises

Read each symbol.

1. $\sqrt{7}$ **2.** $3\sqrt{10}$ **3.** $-\sqrt{81}$ **4.** $\sqrt{64}$ **5.** $2\sqrt{14}$

394   *Chapter 11*

If the given symbol names an integer, state the integer. If not, name the
two consecutive integers between which the number lies.

6. $\sqrt{16}$ 4   **7.** $-\sqrt{36}$ −6   **8.** $\sqrt{21}$ 4 and 5   **9.** $\sqrt{70}$ 8 and 9   **10.** $\sqrt{50}$ 7 and 8

11. $-\sqrt{49}$ −7   **12.** $\sqrt{81}$ 9   **13.** $\sqrt{69}$ 8 and 9 **14.** $-\sqrt{144}$ −12 **15.** $\sqrt{169}$ 13

Written Exercises

If the given symbol names an integer, state the integer. If not, name the
two consecutive integers between which the number lies.

A **1.** $\sqrt{43}$ 6 and 7   **2.** $\sqrt{64}$ 8   **3.** $-\sqrt{16}$ −4   **4.** $\sqrt{24}$ 4 and 5   **5.** $\sqrt{1}$ 1

6. $\sqrt{0}$ 0   **7.** $-\sqrt{6^2}$ −6.   **8.** $\sqrt{13}$ 3 and 4   **9.** $\sqrt{54}$ 7 and 8   **10.** $\sqrt{9}$ 3

11. $\sqrt{30}$ 5 and 6 **12.** $\sqrt{48}$ 6 and 7 **13.** $\sqrt{15}$ 3 and 4 **14.** $\sqrt{8^2}$ 8   **15.** $\sqrt{2}$ 1 and 2

16. $\sqrt{25} + \sqrt{16}$ 9   **17.** $\sqrt{100} - \sqrt{49}$ 3   **18.** $\sqrt{144} + \sqrt{25}$ 17

19. $\sqrt{79 - 61}$ 4 and 5   **20.** $-\sqrt{66 - 2}$ −8   **21.** $\sqrt{100 - 19}$ 9

Replace the __?__ with <, >, or = to make a true statement.

EXAMPLE $\sqrt{9} + \sqrt{25}$ __?__ $\sqrt{9 + 25}$

Solution $\sqrt{9} + \sqrt{25} = 3 + 5 = 8;$ $\sqrt{9 + 25} = \sqrt{34} < 8.$
            Thus $\sqrt{9} + \sqrt{25} > \sqrt{9 + 25}.$

B **22.** $\sqrt{9} + \sqrt{16}$ __?__ $\sqrt{9 + 16}$ >   **23.** $\sqrt{16} + \sqrt{4}$ __?__ $\sqrt{16 + 4}$ >

24. $\sqrt{16} - \sqrt{9}$ __?__ $\sqrt{16 - 9}$ <   **25.** $\sqrt{25} - \sqrt{9}$ __?__ $\sqrt{25 - 9}$ <

26. $\sqrt{4} \times \sqrt{9}$ __?__ $\sqrt{4 \times 9}$ =   **27.** $\sqrt{25} \times \sqrt{4}$ __?__ $\sqrt{25 \times 4}$ =

28. $2\sqrt{2}$ __?__ $\sqrt{2 \times 2}$ >   **29.** $3\sqrt{12}$ __?__ $\sqrt{3 \times 12}$ >

Evaluate the expression.

C **30.** $\left(\sqrt{25}\right)^2$ 25   **31.** $\left(\sqrt{81}\right)^2$ 81   **32.** $\left(\sqrt{49}\right)^2$ 49   **33.** $\left(\sqrt{11}\right)^2$ 11   **34.** $\left(\sqrt{2}\right)^2$ 2

Review Exercises

Divide. Round the answer to the nearest hundredth.

1. $44 \div 6.7$ 6.57   **2.** $35 \div 5.9$ 5.93   **3.** $72 \div 8.3$ 8.67   **4.** $96 \div 9.5$ 10.11

5. $147 \div 12.3$ 11.95 **6.** $230 \div 14.7$ 15.65 **7.** $0.0165 \div 0.13$ 0.13   **8.** $0.68 \div 0.81$ 0.84

Applying Algebra to Right Triangles **395**

Additional A Exercises

If the given symbol names an
integer, state the integer. If
not, name the two consecutive integers between which
the number lies.

1. $-\sqrt{100}$ −10
2. $\sqrt{61}$ 7 and 8
3. $\sqrt{6^2}$ 6
4. $\sqrt{18}$ 4 and 5
5. $\sqrt{75}$ 8 and 9
6. $-\sqrt{4}$ −2
7. $\sqrt{90}$ 9 and 10

Suggested Assignments

Core
  395/1–25
  395/Rev. 1–7 odd

Enriched
  395/12–34
  395/Rev. 1–7 odd

Supplementary Materials

Practice Masters, p. 49
Computer Activity 21

Teaching Suggestions
p. 393b

Related Activities p. 393b

Reading Mathematics

Students will learn the meaning of the following mathematical terms in this lesson: *divide and average method, irrational number, real number.*

11-2 Approximating Square Roots

To get a close approximation of a square root, we can use the *divide-and-average* method. This method is based on the fact that

$$\text{if } \sqrt{a} = b, \text{ then } a = b \times b \text{ and } \frac{a}{b} = b.$$

In other words, when we divide a number a by its square root b, the quotient is b. When we use an estimate for b that is *less* than b for a divisor, the quotient is then *greater* than b. The average of the divisor and quotient can be used as a new estimate for b.

EXAMPLE 1   Approximate $\sqrt{55}$ to the tenths' place.

Solution   Step 1   To estimate $\sqrt{55}$, first find the two integers between which $\sqrt{55}$ lies.

$$49 < 55 < 64$$
$$\sqrt{49} < \sqrt{55} < \sqrt{64}$$
$$7 < \sqrt{55} < 8$$

Since 55 is closer to 49 than to 64, you might try 7.3 as an estimate of $\sqrt{55}$.

Step 2   Divide 55 by the estimate, 7.3. Compute to one more place than you want in the final answer.

$$\begin{array}{r} 7.53 \\ 7.3\overline{)55.000} \\ 51\,1 \\ \hline 3\,90 \\ 3\,65 \\ \hline 250 \\ 219 \\ \hline 31 \end{array}$$

Step 3   Average the divisor and quotient.

$$\frac{7.3 + 7.53}{2} \approx 7.42$$

Use the average as the next estimate and repeat Steps 2 and 3 until your divisor and quotient agree in the tenths' place.

In this case, use 7.42 as your next estimate and divide.

$$\begin{array}{r} 7.41 \\ 7.42\overline{)55.0000} \\ 51\,94 \\ \hline 3\,060 \\ 2\,968 \\ \hline 920 \\ 742 \\ \hline 178 \end{array}$$

As you can see, $\sqrt{55} \approx 7.4$ to the tenths' place.

396   *Chapter 11*

We can approximate $\sqrt{55}$ to whatever decimal place we wish by repeating the steps shown in Example 1 on the previous page. Because $\sqrt{55}$ is a nonterminating, nonrepeating decimal, we say that $\sqrt{55}$ is an **irrational number.** Together, irrational and rational numbers form the set of **real numbers.** Other irrational numbers are discussed on page 119.

To find the square root of a number that is not an integer by the divide-and-average method, we use the same steps as in Example 1. The first step, finding the two integers between which a square root lies, is shown below.

EXAMPLE 2 Complete the first step in estimating each square root.

  a. $\sqrt{12.3}$ **b.** $\sqrt{0.7}$

Solution The first step in estimating a square root is to find the two integers between which it lies.

  a. $9 < 12.3 < 16$ **b.** $0 < 0.7 < 1$
       $\sqrt{9} < \sqrt{12.3} < \sqrt{16}$ $\sqrt{0} < \sqrt{0.7} < \sqrt{1}$
       $3 < \sqrt{12.3} < 4$ $0 < \sqrt{0.7} < 1$

Class Exercises

Give the first digit of the square root.

1. $\sqrt{7}$ 2   **2.** $\sqrt{11}$ 3   **3.** $\sqrt{30}$ 5   **4.** $\sqrt{50}$ 7   **5.** $\sqrt{94}$ over which is 9

Give the next estimate for the square root of the dividend.

EXAMPLE $3.8\overline{)15.000}$ with 3.95 above

Solution $\dfrac{3.8 + 3.95}{2} \approx 3.88$

Thus 3.88 is the next estimate.

6. $2\overline{)4.8}$ with 2.4 above 2.2   **7.** $3\overline{)11}$ with 3.7 above 3.35   **8.** $5\overline{)28.5}$ with 5.7 above 5.35   **9.** $4.3\overline{)21.000}$ with 4.59/4.88 above

10. $14\overline{)225}$ with 16 above 15   **11.** $0.7\overline{)0.53}$ with 0.76 above 0.73   **12.** $0.6\overline{)0.3}$ with 0.5 above 0.55   **13.** $0.9\overline{)0.83}$ with 0.92 above 0.91

Applying Algebra to Right Triangles **397**

Written Exercises

Approximate to the tenths' place.

A

1. $\sqrt{11}$ 3.3
2. $\sqrt{13}$ 3.6
3. $\sqrt{33}$ 5.7
4.8 **4.** $\sqrt{23}$

5. $\sqrt{8}$ 2.8
6. $\sqrt{5}$ 2.2
7. $\sqrt{26}$ 5.1
6.4 **8.** $\sqrt{42}$

9. $\sqrt{57}$ 7.5
10. $\sqrt{75}$ 8.6
11. $\sqrt{91}$ 9.5
8.3 **12.** $\sqrt{69}$

13. $\sqrt{5.7}$ 2.3
14. $\sqrt{7.5}$ 2.7
15. $\sqrt{9.1}$ 3.0
2.6 **16.** $\sqrt{6.9}$

17. $\sqrt{8.2}$ 2.8
18. $\sqrt{4.6}$ 2.1
19. $\sqrt{3.5}$ 1.8
1.2 **20.** $\sqrt{1.6}$

B

21. $\sqrt{152}$ 12.3
22. $\sqrt{285}$ 16.8
23. $\sqrt{705}$ 26.5
18.1 **24.** $\sqrt{328}$

25. $\sqrt{15.2}$ 3.9
26. $\sqrt{28.5}$ 5.3
27. $\sqrt{70.5}$ 8.4
5.6 **28.** $\sqrt{32.4}$

29. $\sqrt{0.4}$ 0.6
30. $\sqrt{0.6}$ 0.7
31. $\sqrt{0.05}$ 0.2
0.4 **32.** $\sqrt{0.21}$

Approximate to the hundredths' place.

33. $\sqrt{2}$ 1.41
34. $\sqrt{3}$ 1.73
35. $\sqrt{5}$ 2.23
3.16 **36.** $\sqrt{10}$

Review Exercises

Simplify.

1. $4(11 - 2) + 3(2) + 2(5 + 3)$ 58
2. $5(81 \div 9) - 36 + 11$ 20
3. $7.3 + (9.14 - 6.91) - 2.81$ 6.72
4. $11.32 - 67(8.01 - 7.92)$ 5.29
5. $3.617 + 0.7(5.301 - 4.911)$ 3.89
6. $14.95 + 5(3.2 + 14) - 90.84$ 10.11
7. $(72 - 65) + 11(8.76 - 0.89)$ 93.57
8. $5.143 + 0.3(8.914 - 7.126)$ 5.6794

▮▮▮ Calculator Key-In

On many calculators there is a square-root key. If you have access to such a calculator, use it to find the square roots below.

1. **a.** $\sqrt{1}$ 1   **b.** $\sqrt{100}$ 10   **c.** $\sqrt{10,000}$ 100

2. **a.** $\sqrt{7}$ 2.6457513   **b.** $\sqrt{700}$ 26.457513   **c.** $\sqrt{70,000}$ 264.57513

3. **a.** $\sqrt{70}$ 8.3666002   **b.** $\sqrt{7000}$ 83.666002   **c.** $\sqrt{700,000}$ 836.66002

4. **a.** $\sqrt{0.08}$ 0.2828427   **b.** $\sqrt{8}$ 2.8284271   **c.** $\sqrt{800}$ 28.284271

5. **a.** $\sqrt{0.54}$ 0.7348469   **b.** $\sqrt{54}$ 7.3484692   **c.** $\sqrt{5400}$ 73.484692

11-3 Using a Square-Root Table

Part of the Table of Square Roots on page 508 is shown below. Square roots of integers are given to the nearest thousandth.

Number	Positive Square Root	Number	Positive Square Root	Number	Positive Square Root	Number	Positive Square Root
N	$\sqrt{N}$	N	$\sqrt{N}$	N	$\sqrt{N}$	N	$\sqrt{N}$
1	1	26	5.099	51	7.141	76	8.718
2	1.414	27	5.196	52	7.211	77	8.775
3	1.732	28	5.292	53	7.280	78	8.832
4	2	29	5.385	54	7.348	79	8.888

We can use the table to approximate the square roots of integers from 1 to 100. For example, to find $\sqrt{78}$, first locate 78 under a column headed "Number." Then read off the value beside 78 in the "Square Root" column.

$$\sqrt{78} \approx 8.832$$

Reading Mathematics: *Tables*
Some tables may have many columns of information. When you are reading a table, use a ruler to help guide your eyes across the page or down a column. This way you can be sure to find the correct entry.

To find an approximate square root of a number that lies between two entries in the column headed "Number," we can use a process called **interpolation.** The interpolation process may cause an error in the last digit of the approximation.

EXAMPLE 1   Approximate $\sqrt{3.8}$ to the nearest thousandth by interpolation.

Solution   On a number line $\sqrt{3.8}$ lies between $\sqrt{3}$ and $\sqrt{4}$. We can assume that $\sqrt{3.8}$ is about 0.8 of the distance between $\sqrt{3}$ and $\sqrt{4}$.

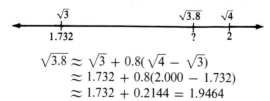

$$\sqrt{3.8} \approx \sqrt{3} + 0.8(\sqrt{4} - \sqrt{3})$$
$$\approx 1.732 + 0.8(2.000 - 1.732)$$
$$\approx 1.732 + 0.2144 = 1.9464$$

Thus, rounded to the thousandths' place, $\sqrt{3.8} = 1.946$.

Applying Algebra to Right Triangles   **399**

Teaching Suggestions p. 393c

Related Activities p. 393c

Reading Mathematics

Students will learn the meaning of the following mathematical term in this lesson: *interpolation*.

Students may not have much experience reading tables. Show them that in this table we look for a number in the N column, then find its square root in the $\sqrt{N}$ column. Encourage students to study the table to see some patterns. As N increases, so does $\sqrt{N}$, but not as rapidly.

Use the table on page 508 to find the approximate square root.

1. $\sqrt{68}$ 8.246

2. $\sqrt{29}$ 5.385

3. $5\sqrt{22}$ 23.45

Find two decimals in the table between which the square root lies.

4. $\sqrt{21.6}$ 4.583, 4.690

5. $\sqrt{73.4}$ 8.544, 8.602

6. The area of a square roof is 89.5 m². Find the length of a side to the nearest hundredth of a meter. 9.46 m

---

EXAMPLE 2   The area of a square display room is 71 m². Find the length of a side to the nearest hundredth of a meter.

Solution   Recall that the formula for the area of a square is $A = s^2$.

$$s^2 = 71$$
$$s = \sqrt{71}$$

Using the table on page 508, we see that $\sqrt{71} = 8.426$. To the nearest hundredth of a meter, the length of a side is 8.43 m.

Class Exercises

Use the table on page 508 to find the approximate square root.

1. $\sqrt{39}$ 6.245   **2.** $\sqrt{83}$ 9.110   **3.** $\sqrt{20}$ 4.472   **4.** $\sqrt{95}$ 9.747   **5.** $\sqrt{34}$ 5.831

6. $\sqrt{49}$ 7   **7.** $\sqrt{11}$ 3.317   **8.** $\sqrt{52}$ 7.211   **9.** $10\sqrt{87}$ 93.27   **10.** $\frac{1}{10}\sqrt{22}$ 0.469

Find two decimals in the table on page 508 between which the square root lies.

11. $\sqrt{54.3}$ **12.** $\sqrt{1.7}$ **13.** $\sqrt{60.7}$ **14.** $\sqrt{4.5}$ **15.** $\sqrt{28.6}$
7.348 and 7.416   1 and 1.414   7.746 and 7.810   2 and 2.236   5.292 and 5.385

Written Exercises

For Exercises 1–37, refer to the table on page 508.

Approximate to the nearest hundredth.

A   **1.** $\sqrt{65}$ 8.06   **2.** $\sqrt{31}$ 5.57   **3.** $\sqrt{56}$ 7.48   **4.** $\sqrt{13}$ 3.61   **5.** $\sqrt{97}$ 9.85 0.49

6. $10\sqrt{37}$ 60.83   **7.** $10\sqrt{41}$ 64.03   **8.** $\frac{1}{10}\sqrt{83}$ 0.91   **9.** $\frac{1}{10}\sqrt{75}$ 0.87   **10.** $\frac{1}{10}\sqrt{24}$ 59.40

11. $3\sqrt{55}$ 22.25   **12.** $2\sqrt{30}$ 10.95   **13.** $6\sqrt{19}$ 26.15   **14.** $4\sqrt{18}$ 16.97   **15.** $7\sqrt{72}$

B   **16.** $\sqrt{39} + \sqrt{16}$ 10.25   **17.** $\sqrt{28} + \sqrt{53}$ 12.57   **18.** $\sqrt{71} - \sqrt{25}$ 3.43

19. $\sqrt{91} - \sqrt{84}$ 0.37   **20.** $2\sqrt{56} - \sqrt{4}$ 12.97   **21.** $\sqrt{37} - 2\sqrt{8}$ 0.43

Approximate to the nearest hundredth by interpolation.

22. $\sqrt{13.2}$ 3.63   **23.** $\sqrt{5.9}$ 2.43   **24.** $\sqrt{14.7}$ 3.83   **25.** $\sqrt{81.6}$ 9.03   **26.** $\sqrt{24.3}$ 4.93

27. $\sqrt{8.7}$ 2.95   **28.** $\sqrt{69.2}$ 8.32   **29.** $\sqrt{50.9}$ 7.13   **30.** $5\sqrt{84.4}$ 45.94   **31.** $3\sqrt{81.9}$ 27.15

400   *Chapter 11*

Use the table on page 508. Approximate the square root to the nearest hundredth.

1. $\sqrt{13}$ 3.61

2. $\sqrt{21}$ 4.58

3. $\sqrt{65}$ 8.06

4. $10\sqrt{50}$ 70.71

5. $5\sqrt{90}$ 47.44

6. $8\sqrt{32}$ 45.26

Approximate to the nearest hundredth.

C **32.** $\sqrt{700}$ (*Hint:* $\sqrt{100 \times 7} = \sqrt{100} \times \sqrt{7} = 10\sqrt{7}$) **33.** $\sqrt{500}$ **34.** $\sqrt{1100}$

     26.46   22.36   33.17

35. $\sqrt{380}$ (*Hint:* $\sqrt{100 \times 3.8} = \sqrt{100} \times \sqrt{3.8} = 10\sqrt{3.8}$) **36.** $\sqrt{420}$ **37.** $\sqrt{3470}$

                                   19.46   20.47   58.91

Problems

Solve.

A **1.** The area of a square is 85 m². Find the length of a side to the nearest hundredth of a meter. **9.22 m**

2. A square floor has an area of 32 m². Find the length of a side to the nearest tenth of a meter. **5.7 m**

3. The area of a square room measures 225 ft². How much will it cost to put molding around the ceiling at \$.35 per foot? **\$21**

B **4.** An isosceles right triangle has an area of 13.5 cm². Find the length of the equal sides to the nearest tenth of a centimeter. **5.2 cm**

5. A circle has an area of 47.1 cm². Find its radius to the nearest hundredth of a centimeter. (Use $\pi \approx 3.14$.) **3.87 cm**

6. The height of a parallelogram is half the length of its base. The parallelogram has an area of 67 cm². Find the height to the nearest tenth of a centimeter. **5.8 cm**

C **7.** The total surface area of a cube is 210 m². Find the length of an edge to the nearest hundredth of a meter. **5.92 m**

8. One base of a trapezoid is three times as long as the other base. The height of the trapezoid is the same as the shorter base. The trapezoid has an area of 83 cm². Find the height to the nearest tenth of a centimeter. **6.4 cm**

Review Exercises

Write the value of the product.

1. 0.9^2 **2.** 0.05^2 **3.** 0.06^2 **4.** 0.7^2 **5.** 3.7^2 **6.** 1.9^2 **7.** 24.3^2 **8.** 5.03^2
  0.81   0.0025   0.0036   0.49   13.69   3.61   590.49 25.3009

Applying Algebra to Right Triangles **401**

Suggested Assignments

Core
    400/2–20 even; 22–26
    401/Prob. 1–4
    401/Rev. 1–5
Enriched
Day 1: 400/1–21 odd; 23–30
Day 2: 401/32–36; Prob. 3–8
       401/Rev. 2–8 even

Supplementary Materials

Practice Masters, p. 50

Teaching Suggestions
p. 393c

Related Activities p. 393d

Reading Mathematics

Students will learn the meaning of the following mathematical terms in this lesson: *hypotenuse, leg, Pythagorean theorem, converse, Pythagorean Triple.*

11-4 The Pythagorean Theorem

The longest side of a right triangle is opposite the right angle and is called the **hypotenuse.** The two shorter sides are called **legs.**

About 2500 years ago, the Greek mathematician Pythagoras proved the following useful fact about right triangles.

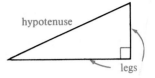

The Pythagorean Theorem

If the hypotenuse of a right triangle has length c, and the legs have lengths a and b, then

$$c^2 = a^2 + b^2.$$

The figure at the right illustrates the Pythagorean theorem. We see that the area of the square on the hypotenuse equals the sum of the areas of the squares on the legs:

$$25 = 9 + 16,$$

$$\text{or } 5^2 = 3^2 + 4^2.$$

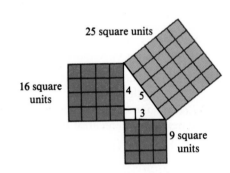

The converse of the Pythagorean theorem is also true. It can be used to test whether a triangle is a right triangle.

Converse of the Pythagorean Theorem

If the sides of a triangle have lengths a, b, and c, such that $c^2 = a^2 + b^2$, then the triangle is a right triangle.

EXAMPLE 1 Is the triangle with sides of the given lengths a right triangle?
        a. 4, 5, 7   **b.** 5, 12, 13

Solution **a.** $4^2 = 16$, $5^2 = 25$, $7^2 = 49$
                No, since $16 + 25 \neq 49$. The triangle with sides of lengths 4, 5, and 7 *cannot* be a right triangle.

402 *Chapter 11*

b. $5^2 = 25$, $12^2 = 144$, $13^2 = 169$

Yes, since $25 + 144 = 169$. The triangle with sides of lengths 5, 12, and 13 is a right triangle.

Sometimes it may be necessary to solve for the length of a missing side of a right triangle. The example below illustrates the steps involved.

EXAMPLE 2 For right triangle ABC, find the length of the missing side to the nearest hundredth. Use the table on page 508.

a. $a = 3$, $b = 7$ 　　　　**b.** $a = 4$, $c = 9$

Solution Using the equation $c^2 = a^2 + b^2$:

a. $c^2 = 3^2 + 7^2$
$= 9 + 49 = 58$
$c = \sqrt{58}$
$c \approx 7.62$

b. $9^2 = 4^2 + b^2$
$9^2 - 4^2 = b^2$
$81 - 16 = b^2$
$65 = b^2$
$\sqrt{65} = b$
$b \approx 8.06$

Class Exercises

Without actually counting them, tell how many unit squares there are in the shaded square.

1.

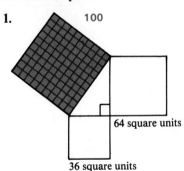

100

64 square units

36 square units

2.

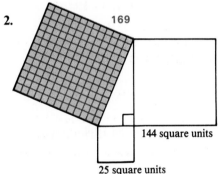

169

144 square units

25 square units

Replace __?__ with $=$ or $\neq$ to make a true statement.

3. 6^2 __?__ $4^2 + 5^2$ $\neq$　　　　**4.** 5^2 __?__ $3^2 + 4^2$ $=$　　　　**5.** 10^2 __?__ $6^2 + 8^2$ $=$

The lengths of the sides of a triangle are given. Is it a right triangle?

6. 3, 4, 5 Yes　　　　**7.** 7, 24, 25 Yes　　　　**8.** 5, 10, 12 No　　　　**9.** 10, 24, 26 Yes

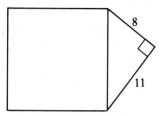

Additional A Exercises

1. Find the area of the square. 185 square units

Is the triangle with sides of the given lengths a right triangle?

2. 2, 3, 4 No
3. 12, 16, 20 Yes
4. 0.1, 0.24, 0.26 Yes
5. 6, 9, 11 No

Written Exercises

Find the area of the square.

A **1.**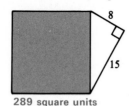

289 square units

2.

169 square units

3.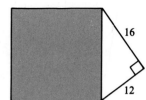

400 square units

Is the triangle with sides of the given lengths a right triangle?

4. 6, 8, 10 Yes   **5.** 8, 15, 17 Yes

6. 16 cm, 30 cm, 34 cm Yes   **7.** 9 m, 12 m, 15 m Yes

8. 1.5 mm, 2.0 mm, 2.5 mm Yes   **9.** 0.6 km, 0.8 km, 1.0 km Yes

10. 9 m, 21 m, 23 m No   **11.** 20 cm, 21 cm, 29 cm Yes

12. 9 km, 40 km, 41 km Yes   **13.** 8 m, 37 m, 39 m No

A right triangle has sides of lengths a, b, and c, with c the length of the hypotenuse. Find the length of the missing side. If necessary, use the table on page 508 for the square-root values and round answers to the nearest hundredth. Answers found by interpolation.

B **14.** $a = 2$, $b = 1$ $c = 2.24$ **15.** $a = 8$, $b = 6$ $c = 10$ **16.** $a = 4$, $c = 9$ $b = 8.06$ **17.** $b = 5$, $c = 6$ $a = 3.32$

18. $a = 5$, $b = 12$ $c = 13$ **19.** $a = 9$, $b = 7$ $c = 11.24$ **20.** $b = 11$, $c = 19$ $a = 15.41$ **21.** $a = 24$, $c = 74$ $b = 70$

A **Pythagorean triple** consists of three positive integers a, b, and c that satisfy the equation $a^2 + b^2 = c^2$. You can find as many Pythagorean triples as you wish by substituting positive integers for m and n (such that $m > n$) in the following expressions for a, b, and c.

$$a = m^2 - n^2 \qquad b = 2mn \qquad c = m^2 + n^2$$

Find Pythagorean triples using the given values of m and n.

C **22.** $m = 5$, $n = 1$
$a = 24$
$b = 10$
$c = 26$

23. $m = 6$, $n = 3$
$a = 27$
$b = 36$
$c = 45$

24. $m = 4$, $n = 2$
$a = 12$
$b = 16$
$c = 20$

Problems In this chapter, answers may vary depending on the method used to find a square root.

Solve. Round your answer to the nearest tenth.

A **1.** A plane flies 90 km due east and then 60 km due north. How far is it then from its starting point? 108.2 km

404   *Chapter 11*

2. The foot of a 6 m ladder is 2.5 m from the base of a wall. How high up the wall does the ladder reach? **5.5 m**

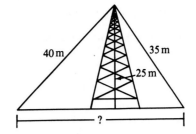

3. The figure shows two cables bracing a television tower. What is the distance between the points where the cables touch the ground? **55.7 m**

4. Find the length of a diagonal of a 10 cm by 10 cm square. **14.1 cm**

B 5. A square has diagonals 10 cm long. Find the length of a side. **7.1 cm**

6. The diagonals of a rhombus are perpendicular and bisect each other. Find the length of a side of a rhombus whose diagonals have lengths 12 m and 18 m. **10.8 m**

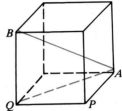

C 7. Find the length of a diagonal of a 10 by 10 by 10 cube. (*Hint:* First find AQ using right triangle PQA. Then find the required length AB using right triangle AQB.) **17.3**

8. Find the length of a diagonal of a box having dimensions 2 by 3 by 6. (See the *Hint* for Problem 7.) **7**

Self-Test A

If the given symbol names an integer, state the integer. If not, name the two consecutive integers between which the number lies.

1. $\sqrt{56}$ **7 and 8** 2. $-\sqrt{81}$ **−9** 3. $\sqrt{9} + \sqrt{25}$ **8** 4. $\sqrt{106 - 57}$ **7** [11-1]

5. Use the divide-and-average method to approximate $\sqrt{86.4}$ to the nearest tenth. **9.3** [11-2]

Use the table on page 508 and interpolation to approximate each square root to the nearest tenth.

6. $\sqrt{18}$ **4.2** 7. $\sqrt{50}$ **7.1** 8. $\sqrt{9.8}$ **3.1** 9. $\sqrt{5.6}$ **2.4** [11-3]

A right triangle has sides of lengths a, b, and c, with c the length of the hypotenuse. Find the length of the missing side.

10. $a = 3, b = 4$ **$c = 5$** 11. $b = 96, c = 100$ **$a = 28$** 12. $c = 20, a = 12$ **$b = 16$** [11-4]

Self-Test answers and Extra Practice are at the back of the book.

Suggested Assignments

Core
Day 1: 404/1–13; 14–22 even
404/Prob. 1
Day 2: 405/Prob. 2–5
405/Self-Test A
Enriched
Day 1: 404/4–12 even; 14–23
405/Prob. 3–6
Day 2: 405/Prob. 7, 8
405/Self-Test A

Supplementary Materials

Practice Masters, p. 50
Computer Activity 22
Test 11A, pp. 73–74

Quick Quiz A

If the given symbol names an integer, state the integer. If not, name the two consecutive integers between which the number lies.

1. $\sqrt{77}$ **8, 9**
2. $-\sqrt{196}$ **−14**
3. $\sqrt{100} + \sqrt{4}$ **12**
4. $\sqrt{107 - 82}$ **5**
5. Use the divide-and-average method to approximate $\sqrt{42.2}$ to the nearest tenth. **6.5**

Use the table on page 508 and interpolation to approximate each square root to the nearest tenth.

6. $\sqrt{52}$ **7.2**
7. $\sqrt{88}$ **9.4**
8. $\sqrt{6.5}$ **2.5**
9. $\sqrt{12.4}$ **3.5**

A right triangle has sides of lengths a, b, and c, with c the length of the hypotenuse. Find the length of the missing side.

10. $a = 50, b = 120$ **$c = 130$**
11. $b = 80, c = 100$ **$a = 60$**
12. $a = 9, c = 15$ **$b = 12$**

405

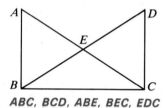
11-5 Similar Triangles

As you know, we say that two figures are congruent when they are identical in both shape and size. When two figures have the same shape, but do not necessarily have the same size, we say that the figures are **similar.**

For two *triangles* to be similar it is enough that the measures of their corresponding angles are equal.

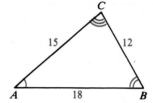 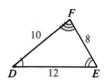

To indicate that the triangles shown above are similar, we can write the following:

$$\triangle ABC \sim \triangle DEF$$

The symbol $\sim$ means *is similar to.* Note that when we write expressions such as the one above, we list corresponding vertices in the same order.

In triangles *ABC* and *DEF*, we see that the lengths of the corresponding sides have the same ratio:

$$\frac{AB}{DE} = \frac{18}{12} = \frac{3}{2} \qquad \frac{BC}{EF} = \frac{12}{8} = \frac{3}{2} \qquad \frac{CA}{FD} = \frac{15}{10} = \frac{3}{2}$$

Therefore,

$$\frac{AB}{DE} = \frac{BC}{EF} = \frac{CA}{FD}.$$

Because the ratios are equal, we say that the lengths of the corresponding sides are *proportional.*

In general, we can say the following:

> For two similar triangles,
>
> corresponding angles are congruent
>
> and
>
> lengths of corresponding sides are proportional.

406   *Chapter 11*

If $\triangle RUN \sim \triangle JOG$, find the lengths marked x and y.

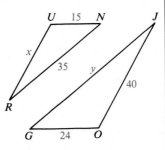

Solution

Since the corresponding vertices are listed in the same order, we know the following.

$$\angle R \cong \angle J$$

$$\angle U \cong \angle O$$

$$\angle N \cong \angle G$$

$$\frac{RU}{JO} = \frac{UN}{OG} = \frac{NR}{GJ}$$

Substituting the values that are given in the diagram, we obtain

$$\frac{x}{40} = \frac{15}{24} = \frac{35}{y}.$$

Therefore, we can set up one proportion involving x and another involving y.

$$\frac{x}{40} = \frac{15}{24} \qquad\qquad \frac{15}{24} = \frac{35}{y}$$

$$24x = 15 \times 40 \qquad\qquad 15y = 35 \times 24$$

$$x = \frac{15 \times 40}{24} \qquad\qquad y = \frac{35 \times 24}{15}$$

$$x = \frac{600}{24} = 25 \qquad\qquad y = \frac{840}{15} = 56$$

The length marked x is 25 and the length marked y is 56.

In the two *right triangles* shown at the right, the measures of two acute angles are equal. Since all right angles have equal measure, 90°, the two remaining acute angles must also have equal measure. (Recall that the sum of the angle measures of any triangle is 180°.) Thus the two right triangles are similar.

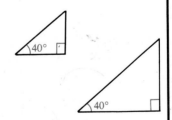

> If an acute angle of one *right* triangle is congruent to an angle of a second *right* triangle, then the triangles are similar.

Chalkboard Examples

1. $\triangle NEV \sim \triangle CAL$.
   Name three pairs of congruent angles.
   $\angle N \cong \angle C$, $\angle E \cong \angle A$, $\angle V \cong \angle L$

2. $\triangle WHO \sim \triangle DUN$.
   $\frac{WO}{DN} = \frac{?}{NU}$ *OH*

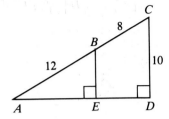

Applying Algebra to Right Triangles **407**

EXAMPLE 2 At the same time a tree on level ground casts a shadow 48 m long, a 2 m pole casts a shadow 5 m long. Find the height, h, of the tree.

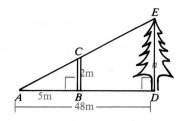

Solution In the diagram, right triangles ABC and ADE share acute $\angle A$ and thus are similar. Since $\frac{AD}{AB} = \frac{DE}{BC} = \frac{EA}{CA}$, we can set up a proportion to solve for h.

$$\frac{h}{2} = \frac{48}{5}$$

$$5h = 48 \times 2$$

$$h = \frac{48 \times 2}{5} = 19.2$$

The height of the tree is 19.2 m.

Reading Mathematics: *Diagrams*

To help you read a diagram that has overlapping triangles, you can redraw the diagram, pulling apart the individual triangles. For example, $\triangle ADE$ above can be separated as shown below.

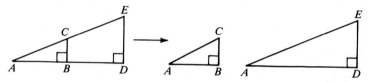

Class Exercises

In Exercises 1–4, $\triangle LOG \sim \triangle RIT$.

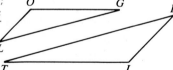

1. Name all pairs of corresponding angles. $\angle L, \angle R;$ $\angle O, \angle I;$ $\angle G, \angle T$

2. Name all pairs of corresponding sides. $\overline{LO}, \overline{RI};$ $\overline{OG}, \overline{IT};$ $\overline{GL}, \overline{TR}$

3. $\frac{OL}{IR} = \frac{OG}{\underset{IT}{?}}$

4. $\frac{LG}{\underset{RT}{?}} = \frac{GO}{TI}$

True or false?

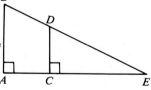

5. $\triangle BAE$ and $\triangle DCE$ are right triangles. True

6. $m \angle ABE = m \angle CDE$ True **7.** $\triangle BAE \sim \triangle DCE$ True

8. $\frac{CE}{AE} = \frac{BA}{DE}$ False   **9.** $\frac{BA}{DC} = \frac{BE}{DE}$ True

408 Chapter 11

Written Exercises

Exercises 1–5 refer to the diagram at the right. $\triangle ABC \sim \triangle PQR$.

A **1.** $\dfrac{PR}{AC} = \dfrac{?}{CB}$ RQ

2. $\dfrac{BA}{?} = \dfrac{CB}{RQ}$ QP

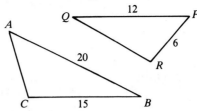

3. Find the length of $\overline{RQ}$. 9

4. Find the length of $\overline{AC}$. 10

5. m $\angle A = 47°$ and m $\angle Q = 29°$,
 m $\angle C = \underline{\ ?\ }°$. 104

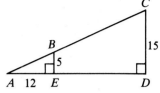

$\triangle BEA \sim \triangle CDA$.

1. The length of $\overline{AD} = \underline{\ ?\ }$
 36

2. The length of $\overline{ED} = \underline{\ ?\ }$
 24

3. The length of $\overline{AB} = \underline{\ ?\ }$
 13

4. The length of $\overline{AC} = \underline{\ ?\ }$
 39

Exercises 6–10 refer to the diagram at the right. $\triangle AED \sim \triangle ACB$.

6. The length of $\overline{AE} = \underline{\ ?\ }$. 48

7. The length of $\overline{AB} = \underline{\ ?\ }$. 25

8. The length of $\overline{AD} = \underline{\ ?\ }$. 50

9. If m $\angle A = 25°$, then m $\angle ABC = \underline{\ ?\ }°$ 65
 and m $\angle ADE = \underline{\ ?\ }°$. 65

10. If $\dfrac{BC}{DE} = \dfrac{1}{2}$, then $\dfrac{AB}{AD} = \underline{\ ?\ }$. $\dfrac{1}{2}$

5. If m $\angle A = 23°$,
 then m $\angle ACD = \underline{\ ?\ }°$ 67

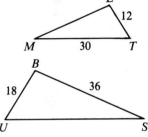

$\triangle MET \sim \triangle SBU$.

6. The length of $\overline{ME} = \underline{\ ?\ }$.
 24

7. The length of $\overline{SU} = \underline{\ ?\ }$.
 45

Find the lengths marked x and y.

11. $\triangle MAB \sim \triangle SRO$

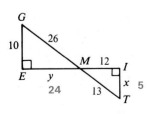

12. $\triangle DIP \sim \triangle MON$

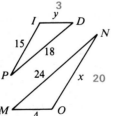

13. $\triangle RST \sim \triangle RUV$

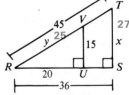

B **14.** $\triangle GEM \sim \triangle TIM$

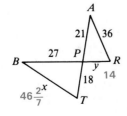

15. $\triangle PAR \sim \triangle PBT$

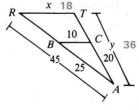

16. $\triangle ART \sim \triangle ABC$

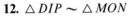

Applying Algebra to Right Triangles **409**

17. One day Jessica, who is 150 cm tall, cast a shadow that was 200 cm long while her father's shadow was 240 cm long. How tall is her father? **180 cm**

18. A person 1.8 m tall standing 7 m from a streetlight casts a shadow 3 m long. How high is the light? **6 m**

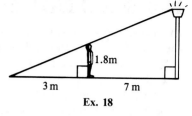

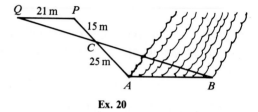

Ex. 18

19. Find (a) the perimeter and (b) the area of the shaded trapezoid in the figure at the left below. **18 units; 18 square units**

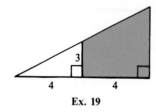

Ex. 19

Ex. 20

20. To find the distance AB across a river, surveyors laid off $\overline{PQ}$ parallel to $\overline{AB}$ and created 2 similar triangles. They made the measurements shown in the figure at the right above. Find the length of $\overline{AB}$.
35 m

Exercises 21–22 refer to the diagram at the right.

C **21.** Explain why $\triangle ADC \sim \triangle ACB$.

22. Explain why $\triangle ADC \sim \triangle CDB$.

23. If $\triangle MNO \sim \triangle PQR$ and $\triangle PQR \sim \triangle STU$, is $\triangle MNO \sim \triangle STU$? Explain your answer.

24. If $\triangle MNO \cong \triangle PQR$, is $\triangle MNO \sim \triangle PQR$? Explain your answer.

25. If $\triangle MNO \sim \triangle PQR$, is $\triangle MNO \cong \triangle PQR$? Explain your answer.

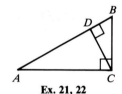

Ex. 21, 22

Review Exercises

Multiply.

1. 300×1.73 **519**

2. 500×3.9 **1950**

3. 7.81×200 **1562**

4. 16.34×120 **1960.8**

5. 2.18×1.03 **2.2454**

6. 3.17×6.01 **19.0517**

7. 54.2×0.09 **4.878**

8. 683×2.48 **1693.84**

9. 71.4×52.4 **3741.36**

410 *Chapter 11*

11-6 Special Right Triangles

In an *isosceles right triangle* the two acute angles are congruent. Since the sum of the measures of these two angles is 90°, each angle measures 45°. For this reason, an isosceles right triangle is often called a **45° right triangle.**

In the diagram each leg is 1 unit long. If the hypotenuse is c units long, by the Pythagorean theorem we know that $c^2 = 1^2 + 1^2 = 2$ and thus

$$c = \sqrt{2}.$$

Every 45° right triangle is similar to the one shown. Since corresponding sides of similar triangles are proportional, we have the following property.

> If each leg of a 45° right triangle is a units long, then the hypotenuse is $a\sqrt{2}$ units long.

EXAMPLE 1 A square park measures 200 m on each edge. Find the length, d, of a path extending diagonally from one corner to the opposite corner. Use $\sqrt{2} \approx 1.414$.

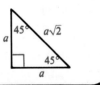

Solution Since the park is square, we can apply the property of 45° right triangles to solve for d. We use the fact that d is the hypotenuse of the right triangle and that each side measures 200 m.

$$d = 200\sqrt{2} \approx 200 \times 1.414 = 282.8$$

Thus the path measures approximately 282.8 m.

A **30°-60° right triangle,** such as $\triangle ACB$, may be thought of as half an equilateral triangle. If hypotenuse $\overline{AB}$ is 2 units long, then the shorter leg $\overline{AC}$ (half of $\overline{AD}$) is 1 unit long. To find BC, we use the Pythagorean theorem:

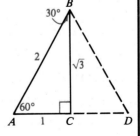

$$(AC)^2 + (BC)^2 = (AB)^2$$
$$1^2 + (BC)^2 = 2^2$$
$$(BC)^2 = 2^2 - 1^2 = 3$$
$$BC = \sqrt{3}$$

Applying Algebra to Right Triangles **411**

Teaching Suggestions p. 393f

Related Activities p. 393f

Reading Mathematics

Students will learn the meaning of the following mathematical terms in this lesson: *45° right triangle, 30°–60° right triangle, radical sign, radical.*

1. Each leg of a 45° right triangle is 3 units long. Find the length of the hypotenuse. $3\sqrt{2}$

2. The hypotenuse of a 45° right triangle is 6 units long. Find the length of each leg. $3\sqrt{2}$

Use the diagram for Exercises 3–5.

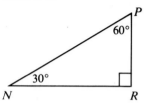

3. If $PR = 4$, then $PN = \underline{\ ?\ }$. 8

4. If $PR = 2$, then $NR = \underline{\ ?\ }$. $2\sqrt{3}$

5. If $PN = 10$, then $RN = \underline{\ ?\ }$. $5\sqrt{3}$

Every 30°–60° right triangle is similar to the one shown on the preceding page, and since corresponding sides of similar triangles are proportional, we have the following property.

> If the shorter leg of a 30°–60° right triangle is a units long, then the longer leg is $a\sqrt{3}$ units long, and the hypotenuse is $2a$ units long.

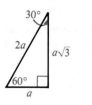

EXAMPLE 2   The hypotenuse of a 30°–60° right triangle is 8 cm long. Find the lengths of the legs.

Solution   Using the 30°–60° right triangle property, we know that
$$2a = 8, \ a = 4, \text{ and } a\sqrt{3} = 4\sqrt{3}.$$
Thus the lengths of the legs are 4 cm and $4\sqrt{3}$ cm.

The symbol $\sqrt{\ }$ is called the **radical sign.** An expression such as $\sqrt{3}$ or $\sqrt{x}$ is called a **radical.** We often leave answers *in terms of radicals* with the radical in the numerator. To rewrite expressions such as $\dfrac{6}{\sqrt{3}}$ so that the radical appears in the numerator, we may use the fact that $\sqrt{x} \times \sqrt{x} = x$.

EXAMPLE 3   Rewrite $\dfrac{6}{\sqrt{3}}$ in lowest terms with the radical in the numerator.

Solution   If we multiply the numerator and denominator by $\sqrt{3}$, we will find an equivalent fraction with the radical in the numerator.

$$\frac{6}{\sqrt{3}} = \frac{6 \times \sqrt{3}}{\sqrt{3} \times \sqrt{3}}$$

$$= \frac{6\sqrt{3}}{3}$$

$$= 2\sqrt{3}$$

Thus, $2\sqrt{3}$ is equivalent to $\dfrac{6}{\sqrt{3}}$ in lowest terms with the radical in the numerator.

Class Exercises

Rewrite the expression in lowest terms with the radical in the numerator.

1. $\dfrac{1}{\sqrt{3}}$ $\dfrac{\sqrt{3}}{3}$ **2.** $\dfrac{2}{\sqrt{3}}$ $\dfrac{2\sqrt{3}}{3}$ **3.** $\dfrac{2}{\sqrt{2}}$ $\sqrt{2}$ **4.** $\dfrac{6}{\sqrt{2}}$ $3\sqrt{2}$ **5.** $\dfrac{1}{\sqrt{x}}$ $\dfrac{\sqrt{x}}{x}$ **6.** $\dfrac{\frac{\sqrt{x}}{x}}{\sqrt{x}}$

Find the lengths marked x and y in the triangle. Give your answer in terms of radicals when radicals occur.

7.
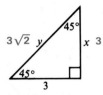

8.
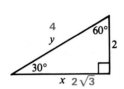

9.
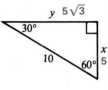

10.

11.
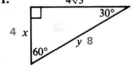

12.
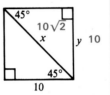

Written Exercises

Rewrite the expression in lowest terms with the radical in the numerator.

A **1.** $\dfrac{6}{\sqrt{10}}$ $\dfrac{3\sqrt{10}}{5}$ **2.** $\dfrac{12}{\sqrt{13}}$ $\dfrac{12\sqrt{13}}{13}$ **3.** $\dfrac{3}{\sqrt{3}}$ $\sqrt{3}$ **4.** $\dfrac{1}{\sqrt{2}}$ $\dfrac{\sqrt{2}}{2}$ **5.** $\dfrac{2}{\sqrt{x}}$ $\dfrac{2\sqrt{x}}{x}$ **6.** $\dfrac{3x}{\sqrt{x}}$ $3\sqrt{x}$

Approximate the lengths marked x and y to the nearest tenth. Use $\sqrt{2} \approx 1.414$ and $\sqrt{3} \approx 1.732$.

7.
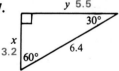

8.

9.
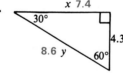

10.
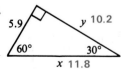

11.
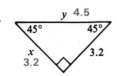

12.
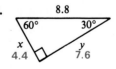

Applying Algebra to Right Triangles **413**

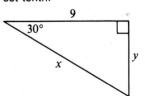

In Exercises 13–16, give answers in terms of radicals with the radical in the numerator.

B **13.** The hypotenuse of an isosceles right triangle has length 4. How long is each leg? $2\sqrt{2}$

14. The hypotenuse of a 45° right triangle has length 10. How long is each leg? $5\sqrt{2}$

15. The longer leg of a 30°–60° right triangle has length 15. How long are the other sides? $5\sqrt{3}$, $10\sqrt{3}$

16. The side opposite the 60° angle of a right triangle has length 3. How long are the other sides? $\sqrt{3}$, $2\sqrt{3}$

In Exercises 17–22, $\angle C$ is a right angle in $\triangle ABC$. Find the length of the missing side to the nearest tenth.

17. $AC = 2$, $BC = 5$ $AB = 5.4$ **18.** $AB = 18$, $AC = 9$ $BC = 15.6$

19. $AB = 6\sqrt{2}$, $AC = 6$ $BC = 6$ **20.** $AC = CB = x$ $AB = 1.4x$

C **21.** $\frac{1}{2}BA = CA = y$ $BC = 1.7y$ **22.** $2BC = BA = z$ $AC = 0.9z$

Approximate the lengths marked x and y to the nearest tenth.

23. 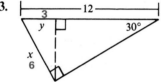   **24.**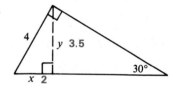

Problems

Solve. Round answers to the nearest tenth.

A **1.** A ladder 10 m long resting against a wall makes a 60° angle with the ground. How far up the wall does it reach? **8.7 m**

2. A baseball diamond is a square 90 ft on each side. How far is it diagonally from home plate to second base? **127.3 ft**

3. A hillside is inclined at an angle of 30° with the horizontal. How much altitude has Mary gained after hiking 40 m up the hill? **20 m**

4. The diagram on the right shows the roof of a house. Find the dimensions marked *x* and *y*.

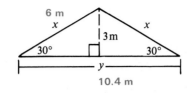

B **5.** A checkerboard has 8 squares on each side. If one side of a square is 5 cm long, how far is it from one corner of the board to the opposite corner? 56.6 cm

6. Find the height of an equilateral triangle with sides 12 cm long. 10.4 cm

7. Find the perimeters of the two squares shown in the diagram. larger: 40; smaller: 28.3

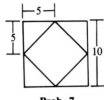

Prob. 7

8. An equilateral triangle has sides 10 units long. Find (a) the height and (b) the area. 8.7 units; 43.3 square units

C **9.** An equilateral triangle has sides *r* units long. Find both (a) the height and (b) the area in terms of *r*. 0.9*r* units; 0.4*r*² square units

10. The area of a square pan is 900 cm². What is the length of a diagonal of the pan? 42.4 cm

11. A 10 m pole is supported in a vertical position by three 6 m guy wires. If one end of each wire is fastened to the ground at a 60° angle, how high on the pole is the other end fastened? 5.2 m

12. A rhombus has angles of 60° and 120°. Each side of the rhombus is 8 cm long. What are the lengths of the diagonals? (*Hint:* The diagonals bisect the angles of the rhombus.) shorter: 8 cm; longer: 13.9 cm

Review Exercises

Write the fraction as a decimal. Use a bar to show a repeating decimal.

$0.\overline{36}$

1. $\frac{5}{4}$ 1.25   **2.** $\frac{3}{5}$ 0.6   **3.** $\frac{2}{9}$ $0.\overline{2}$ **4.** $\frac{7}{12}$ $0.58\overline{3}$ **5.** $\frac{11}{10}$ 1.1   **6.** $\frac{3}{16}$ 0.1875   **7.** $\frac{1}{6}$ $0.1\overline{6}$ **8.** $\frac{4}{11}$

Applying Algebra to Right Triangles   **415**

Suggested Assignments

Core
413/1–11 odd
414/13–19 odd; Prob. 1–3
415/Prob. 5, 6
415/Rev. 1–4

Enriched
Day 1: 413/1–11 odd
414/13–23
Day 2: 415/Prob. 4–12
415/Rev. 2–8 even

Supplementary Materials

Practice Masters, p. 51

Related Activities p. 393g

Reading Mathematics

Students will learn the meaning of the following mathematical terms in this lesson: *trigonometric ratios, sine, sin A, cosine, cos A, tangent, tan A.*

11-7 Trigonometric Ratios

Since each of the three triangles in the diagram below contains $\angle A$ and a right angle, the triangles are *similar* and the lengths of their sides are *proportional*. Thus, the ratios written below for the smallest triangle apply to all three triangles.

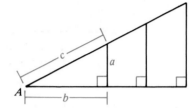

$$\frac{\text{length of side opposite } \angle A}{\text{length of hypotenuse}} = \frac{a}{c}$$

$$\frac{\text{length of side adjacent to } \angle A}{\text{length of hypotenuse}} = \frac{b}{c}$$

$$\frac{\text{length of side opposite } \angle A}{\text{length of side adjacent to } \angle A} = \frac{a}{b}$$

These ratios, called the **trigonometric ratios,** are so useful that each has been given a special name.

$\frac{a}{c}$ is called the **sine** of $\angle A$, or **sin A.**

$\frac{b}{c}$ is called the **cosine** of $\angle A$, or **cos A.**

$\frac{a}{b}$ is called the **tangent** of $\angle A$, or **tan A.**

It is important to understand that each trigonometric ratio depends only on the measure of $\angle A$ and *not* on the size of the right triangle.

The following shortened forms of the definitions may help you remember the trigonometric ratios.

$\sin A = \dfrac{\text{opposite}}{\text{hypotenuse}}$

$\cos A = \dfrac{\text{adjacent}}{\text{hypotenuse}}$

$\tan A = \dfrac{\text{opposite}}{\text{adjacent}}$

EXAMPLE 1   For $\angle A$ find the value of each trigonometric ratio in lowest terms.

a. sin A **b.** cos A **c.** tan A

Solution   To find the value of the trigonometric ratios for $\angle A$, first find the value of x. By the Pythagorean theorem:

$$x^2 + 5^2 = 6^2$$
$$x^2 + 25 = 36$$
$$x^2 = 36 - 25$$
$$x^2 = 11$$
$$x = \sqrt{11}$$

a. $\sin A = \dfrac{\text{opposite}}{\text{hypotenuse}} = \dfrac{5}{6}$

b. $\cos A = \dfrac{\text{adjacent}}{\text{hypotenuse}} = \dfrac{\sqrt{11}}{6}$

c. $\tan A = \dfrac{\text{opposite}}{\text{adjacent}} = \dfrac{5}{\sqrt{11}} = \dfrac{5 \times \sqrt{11}}{\sqrt{11} \times \sqrt{11}} = \dfrac{5\sqrt{11}}{11}$

EXAMPLE 2   Find the sine, cosine, and tangent of a $30°$ angle to the nearest thousandth.

Solution   To find the values of these trigonometric ratios, first draw a $30°$–$60°$ right triangle. Let the shorter leg be 1 unit long and write in the lengths of the other sides according to the property of $30°$–$60°$ triangles that you learned in the previous lesson.

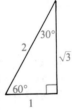

$$\sin 30° = \frac{1}{2} = 0.500$$

$$\cos 30° = \frac{\sqrt{3}}{2} \approx 0.866$$

$$\tan 30° = \frac{1}{\sqrt{3}} = \frac{\sqrt{3}}{3} \approx 0.577$$

Class Exercises

Find the value of the trigonometric ratio.

1. $\sin A$ $\frac{4}{5}$ 2. $\cos A$ $\frac{3}{5}$

3. $\tan A$ $\frac{4}{3}$ 4. $\sin B$ $\frac{3}{5}$

5. $\cos B$ $\frac{4}{5}$ 6. $\tan B$ $\frac{3}{4}$

Applying Algebra to Right Triangles   **417**

Chalkboard Examples

Give each trigonometric ratio as a decimal to the nearest hundredth.

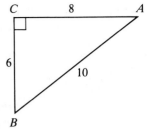

1. $\cos B$ 0.60
2. $\tan A$ 0.75
3. $\sin A$ 0.60
4. $\tan B$ 1.33
5. Evaluate $\cos 60°$ to the nearest hundredth. 0.50
6. Evaluate $\sin 45°$ to the nearest hundredth. 0.71

Find the value of the trigonometric ratio.

7. $\sin P$ $\frac{y}{z}$

8. $\cos P$ $\frac{x}{z}$

9. $\tan P$ $\frac{y}{x}$

10. $\sin R$ $\frac{x}{z}$

11. $\cos R$ $\frac{y}{z}$

12. $\tan R$ $\frac{x}{y}$

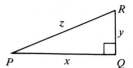

Written Exercises

Give the value of the sine, cosine, and tangent of $\angle A$ and $\angle B$. Give all ratios in lowest terms.

A 1.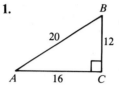

2.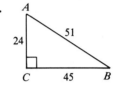

3.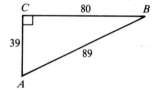

4.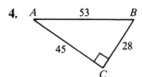

5.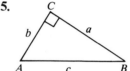

6.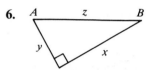

B **In Exercises 7–12, give all ratios in lowest terms and with the radical in the numerator.**

Find the value of x. Then find $\tan A$.

7.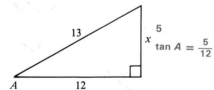

$\tan A = \frac{5}{12}$

8.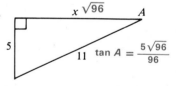

$\tan A = \frac{5\sqrt{96}}{96}$

Find the value of x. Then find $\sin A$.

9.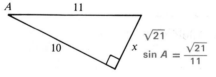

$\sin A = \frac{\sqrt{21}}{11}$

10.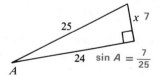

$\sin A = \frac{7}{25}$

Find the value of x. Then find $\cos A$.

11.
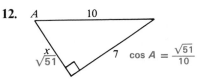
$\cos A = \dfrac{12}{13}$

12.
$\cos A = \dfrac{\sqrt{51}}{10}$

Find the sine, cosine, and tangent. Write the answer both as a fraction and as a decimal to the nearest thousandth. (*Hint:* See Example 2.)

13. **a.** $\sin 60°$ **b.** $\cos 60°$ **c.** $\tan 60°$ 14. **a.** $\sin 45°$ **b.** $\cos 45°$ **c.** $\tan 45°$

Give answers to the nearest tenth. Answers for parts (b) and (c) are found using rounded answer from part (a).

C 15. $\sin 67° = 0.9205$
  a. $x = \underline{\ ?\ }$ 6.4
  b. $y = \underline{\ ?\ }$ 2.8
  c. $\sin 23° = \underline{\ ?\ }$ 0.4

16. $\tan 40° = 0.8391$
  a. $m = \underline{\ ?\ }$ 12.6
  b. $n = \underline{\ ?\ }$ 19.6
  c. $\cos 50° = \underline{\ ?\ }$ 0.6

17. $\cos 65° = 0.4226$
  a. $e = \underline{\ ?\ }$ 3.8
  b. $f = \underline{\ ?\ }$ 8.2
  c. $\tan 25° = \dfrac{\ ?\ }{0.5}$

Review Exercises

Select the number that is closest to the one given.

1. 0.3765 b
  a. 0.3774   **b.** 0.3759

2. 8.1443 b
  a. 8.1430   **b.** 8.1451

3. 0.9004 a
  a. 0.9019   **b.** 0.8954

4. 1.8040 b
  a. 1.829   **b.** 1.788

5. 0.2126 b
  a. 0.2666   **b.** 0.1986

6. 11.4301 a
  a. 12.0801   **b.** 10.6801

7. 0.1758 b
  a. 0.1744   **b.** 0.1764

8. 3.2709 a
  a. 3.2712   **b.** 3.2705

▌▌▌▌ Challenge

Leslie is considering two job offers. Alloid Metals pays an hourly wage of $7.30. Acme Steel Company pays an annual salary of $14,040. Both jobs have a 40-hour work week. Which job offers a better salary? Alloid

Applying Algebra to Right Triangles **419**

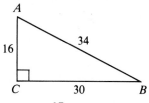
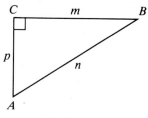

Teaching Suggestions
p. 393g

Related Activities p. 393h

Reading Mathematics

Students will learn the meaning of the following mathematical term in this lesson:
solve a right triangle.

11-8 Solving Right Triangles

The table on page 509 gives approximate values of the sine, the cosine, and the tangent of angles with measure $1°, 2°, 3°, \ldots , 90°$. To find $\sin 45°$, look down the column headed "Angle" to $45°$. To the right of it in the column headed "Sine," you see that $\sin 45° \approx 0.7071$.

The values in the table on page 509 are, in general, accurate to only four decimal places. However, in computational work with sine, cosine, and tangent, it is customary to use $=$ instead of $\approx$. In this lesson, we will write *$\sin 45° = 0.7071$* instead of *$\sin 45° \approx 0.7071$*.

We can use the values in the table to **solve right triangles,** that is, to find approximate measures of all the sides and all the angles of any right triangle.

EXAMPLE 1 Solve $\triangle ABC$ by finding each measure.
  a. c to the nearest tenth
  b. $m \angle A$
  c. $m \angle B$

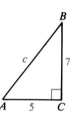

Solution

a. The diagram indicates that $\angle C$ is a right triangle, therefore by the Pythagorean theorem:

$$c^2 = 7^2 + 5^2 = 74$$
$$c = \sqrt{74} = 8.6$$

To the nearest tenth, $c = 8.6$.

b. $\tan A = \dfrac{7}{5} = 1.4$

In the tangent column in the table, the closest entry to 1.4 is 1.3764, for angle measure $54°$. Thus, to the nearest degree, $m \angle A = 54°$.

c. $m \angle A + m \angle B + m \angle C = 180°$
  $54° + m \angle B + 90° = 180°$
  $m \angle B = 180° - 90° - 54°$
  $m \angle B = 36°$

Problem Solving Reminder

To solve some problems, you might need to *use previously obtained solutions* in order to complete the answer. In Example 1, it was convenient to use the $m \angle A$ found in part *b* to solve for the $m \angle B$.

EXAMPLE 2 Solve $\triangle ABC$ by finding each measure.
a. m $\angle B$
b. a to the nearest tenth
c. b to the nearest tenth

Solution

a. m $\angle A$ + m $\angle B$ + m $\angle C$ = 180°
$38° + $ m $\angle B$ + 90° = 180°
m $\angle B$ = 180° − 90° − 38° = 52°

b. $\sin 38° = \dfrac{a}{6.5}$

$a = \sin 38° \times 6.5$
$= 0.6157 \times 6.5 = 4.00205$

To the nearest tenth, $a = 4.0$.

c. $\cos 38° = \dfrac{b}{6.5}$

$b = \cos 38° \times 6.5$
$= 0.7880 \times 6.5 = 5.122$

To the nearest tenth, $b = 5.1$.

Chalkboard Examples

Use the table on page 509 to
find each value.

1. tan 72° **3.0777**

2. sin 17° **0.2924**

3. Find the measure of $\angle A$
to the nearest degree, if
$\cos A = 0.732$. **43°**

Find each measure for
$\triangle ABC$. Round lengths to the
nearest tenth and angle
measures to the nearest degree.

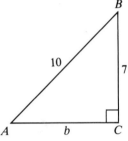

4. b **7.1**

5. m $\angle A$ **44°**

6. m $\angle B$ **46°**

Class Exercises

**State whether you would use the sine, cosine, or tangent ratio to find x
in each diagram.**

1.

x sine

2.
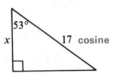
x 17 cosine

3.
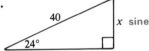
x tangent

4.
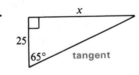
x tangent

For Exercises 5–18, use the table on page 509.

Find a value for the trigonometric ratio.

5. $\cos 8°$ **0.9903**   6. $\sin 67°$ **0.9205**   7. $\tan 36°$ **0.7265**   8. $\tan 82°$ **7.1154**

9. $\sin 15°$ **0.2588**   10. $\cos 75°$ **0.2588**   11. $\cos 20°$ **0.9397**   12. $\sin 70°$ **0.9397**

Applying Algebra to Right Triangles **421**

422

Find the measure of $\angle A$ to the nearest degree.

13. sin A = 0.4   24°

14. tan A = 1.6   58°

15. cos A = 0.85   32°

16. cos A = 0.19   79°

17. tan A = 0.819   39°

18. sin A = 0.208   12°

Written Exercises

For Exercises 1–40, use the tables on page 508 and page 509.

Find sin A, cos A, and tan A for the given measure of $\angle A$.

A

1. 25° **2.** 76° **3.** 88° **4.** 11° **5.** 39° **6.** 42°

7. 74° **8.** 13° **9.** 40° **10.** 52° **11.** 65° **12.** 81°

Find the measure of $\angle A$ to the nearest degree.

13. sin A = 0.9877   81°

14. cos A = 0.9205   23°

15. tan A = 0.0175   1°

16. cos A = 0.8572   31°

17. tan A = 4.0108   76°

18. sin A = 0.2250   13°

Find the measure of the angle to the nearest degree or the length of the side to the nearest whole number.

19. m$\angle A$ 30°

21. m$\angle B$ 60°

23. t 6

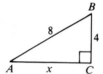

20. x 7

22. m$\angle L$ 35°

24. u 7

Find the measure of $\angle A$ to the nearest degree.

B

25. sin A = 0.8483   58°

26. cos A = 0.2758   74°

27. tan A = 0.4560   25°

28. sin A = 0.6559   41°

29. tan A = 2.7500   70°

30. cos A = 0.5148   59°

Solve $\triangle ABC$. Round angle measures to the nearest degree and lengths to the nearest tenth.

31. a = 5, b = 8

32. a = 4, b = 7

33. m$\angle A$ = 72°, c = 10

34. m$\angle B$ = 26°, c = 8

35. b = 4, c = 9

36. a = 5, c = 7

37. m$\angle B$ = 20°, b = 15

38. m$\angle A$ = 80°, a = 9

39. m$\angle A$ = 58°, b = 12

40. m$\angle B$ = 39°, a = 20

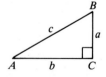

Problems

Give angle measures to the nearest degree and lengths to the nearest tenth.

A **1.** How tall is the tree in the diagram below? **42.0 m**

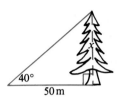

40°
50 m

2. How tall is the flagpole in the diagram below? **16.8 m**

x
35°
24 m

3. In the diagram below, the road rises 20 m for every 100 m traveled horizontally. What angle does it make with the horizontal? **11°**

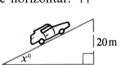

20 m
x°
100 m

4. What angle does the rope make with the horizontal in the diagram below? **63°**

10 m
x°
4.6 m

B **5. a.** How tall is the building in the diagram below? **42.5 m**
   b. How tall is the antenna? **10.7 m**

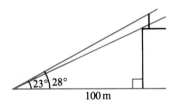

23° 28°
100 m

6. What is the height of the child in the diagram below? **1.3 m**

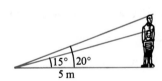

15° 20°
5 m

7. In △ABC, $\overline{AC}$ is 8 cm long. The length of the altitude to $\overline{AB}$ is 5 cm. Find the measure of ∠A. **39°**

8. Triangle MNO is an isosceles triangle with $\overline{MO}$ congruent to $\overline{NO}$. The third side of the triangle, $\overline{MN}$, is 36 cm long. The perimeter of the triangle is 96 cm.
   a. Find the lengths of $\overline{MO}$ and $\overline{NO}$. **30 cm**
   b. The altitude from O to $\overline{MN}$ bisects $\overline{MN}$. Find the measure of ∠OMN. **53°**

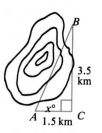

Suggested Assignments

Core
Day 1: 422/2–34 even
       423/Prob. 1–7 odd
Day 2: 424/Self-Test B
       425/Computer Byte

Enriched
Day 1: 422/25–40
       423/Prob. 5–8
       424/Prob. 10
Day 2: 424/Self-Test B
       425/Computer Byte
       425/Challenge

Supplementary Materials

Practice Masters, p. 52
Test 11B, pp. 75–76

Quick Quiz B

Complete.

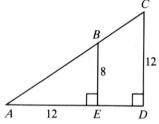

1. △DCA ~ △__?__ *EBA*

2. $\frac{AE}{AD}$ = __?__ *AB*
$\frac{?}{AC}$

3. AD = __?__ 18

4. m∠ACD = m∠__?__
ABE

Give answers in terms of radicals with the radical in the numerator.

5. The hypotenuse of a 45° right triangle is 8 cm long. How long is a leg? $4\sqrt{2}$ cm

(continued on next page)

Additional Answers
Self-Test B

10. m∠P = 60°, p = 5.2,
m∠R = 30°

11. q = 24.1, p = 23.5,
m∠R = 12°

12. m∠P = 67°, r = 3.4,
q = 8.7

13. m∠P = 33°, p = 13.1,
r = 20.1

424

Give angle measures to the nearest degree and lengths to the nearest tenth.

9. A surveyor is determining the direction in which tunnel $\overline{AB}$ is to be dug through a mountain. She locates point C so that ∠C is a right angle, the length of $\overline{AC}$ is 1.5 km, and the length of $\overline{BC}$ is 3.5 km. Find the measure of ∠A. 67°

C **10.** In △RST, the measure of ∠S is 142°. The length of $\overline{RS}$ is 10. Find the length of the altitude from vertex R. 6.2

Self-Test B

Exercises 1–4 refer to the diagram below. Complete.

1. △TOY __?__ △TIN ~   [11-5]

2. $\frac{TI}{TO}$ = $\frac{IN}{OY}$ = $\frac{?}{?}$ $\frac{TN}{TY}$

3. TY = __?__ 7.5

4. m∠TIN __?__ m∠TOY =

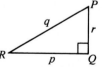

In Exercises 5 and 6, give answers in terms of radicals with the radical in the numerator.

5. The hypotenuse of a 45° right triangle is $6\sqrt{2}$ cm long. What is the length of each leg? 6 cm   [11-6]

6. The longer leg of a 30°–60° right triangle has length 12. What are the lengths of the shorter leg and the hypotenuse? $4\sqrt{3}$, $8\sqrt{3}$

Exercises 7–13 refer to the diagram at the right.

Complete in terms of p, q, and r.

7. sin P = __?__ $\frac{p}{q}$ **8.** cos P = __?__ $\frac{r}{q}$ [11-7]

9. tan P = __?__ $\frac{p}{r}$

Find the measure of the angles to the nearest degree and the lengths to the nearest tenth. Use the tables on page 508 and page 509.

10. r = 3, q = 6   **11.** m∠P = 78°, r = 5   [11-8]

12. m∠R = 23°, p = 8   **13.** m∠R = 57°, q = 24

Self-Test answers and Extra Practice are at the back of the book.

424 *Chapter 11*

Computer Byte

The following program produces a Pythagorean triple using any counting number greater than 2.

```
10   PRINT "INPUT THE DESIRED NUMBER";
20   INPUT N
30   IF N * (N − 1) * (N − 2) < > 0 THEN 60
40   PRINT "THERE IS NO SUCH TRIPLE."
50   GOTO 150
60   IF INT (N / 2) < > N / 2 THEN 120
70   IF N = 4 THEN 110
80   LET N = N / 2
90   LET C = C + 1
100  GOTO 60
110  LET N = 3
120  PRINT "A PYTHAGOREAN TRIPLE IS:"
130  LET B = INT (N ↑ 2 / 2)
140  PRINT 2 ↑ C * N,2 ↑ C * B,2 ↑ C * (B + 1)
150  END
```

4. 6, 8, 10
7, 24, 25
6, 8, 10
11, 60, 61
17, 144, 145
24, 32, 40
101, 5100, 510

1. Use the program to find a triple with the number 3. Does it give
   you the triple you had expected? 3, 4, 5

2. Use the program to find a triple with the number 4. Does it give
   you the triple you had expected? 3, 4, 5

3. Now try 5. Is the output what you had expected? 5, 12, 13

4. Input each of these numbers to produce Pythagorean triples:

   6, 7, 8, 11, 17, 24, 101

   Check three of your answers by multiplying.

5. Try 1 or 2 in the program. Can you explain why this output is true?
   Output: THERE IS NO SUCH TRIPLE. Neither 1^2 nor 2^2
   can equal the difference of the squares of two
   integers.

Challenge

Trace the two squares as they are shown
at the right. Can you draw one line that
will divide each of the squares into two
parts of equal area?
Connect the centers of the squares.

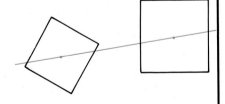

Applying Algebra to Right Triangles **425**

6. The longer leg of a
   30°–60° right triangle is
   15 units long. How long
   is the shorter leg? $5\sqrt{3}$
   units

Complete in terms of r, s,
and t.

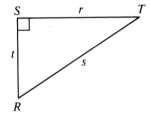

7. tan R $\dfrac{r}{t}$

8. cos T $\dfrac{r}{s}$

9. sin T $\dfrac{t}{s}$

In right triangle *JKL* find
lengths to the nearest tenth
and angles to the nearest
degree.

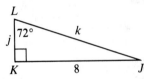

10. m∠J = _?_ 18°

11. j = _?_ 2.6

12. k = _?_ 8.4

Other Roots and Fractions as Exponents

As you learned earlier, $\sqrt{49} = 7$ because $7^2 = 49$. Recall that we chose 7 and not -7 since 7 is the positive square root of 49.

We can extend the idea of square roots to other roots. The fourth root of 16, denoted $\sqrt[4]{16}$, is 2 since $2^4 = 16$. In general,

> For any positive *even* integer n, and positive integer c,
> $$\sqrt[n]{a} = c, \text{ if } c^n = a.$$

The third root, or cube root, of a number may be positive or negative depending on the sign of the number. For example,

$$\sqrt[3]{64} = 4 \text{ because } 4^3 = 64$$

and

$$\sqrt[3]{-27} = -3 \text{ because } (-3)^3 = -27.$$

In general,

> For any positive *odd* integer n, and any integers a and c,
> $$\sqrt[n]{a} = c, \text{ if } c^n = a.$$

The following cases will complete our discussion of roots.

If $a = 0$, then $\sqrt[n]{a} = 0$ because $a^n = 0^n = 0$.

If a is a negative number and n is *even,* there is no real nth root of a.

426 *Chapter 11*

Recall that you add exponents when multiplying powers of the same base.

$$9^1 \times 9^2 = 9^{1+2} = 9^3$$

When this rule is applied to fractional exponents, we have

$$9^{\frac{1}{2}} \times 9^{\frac{1}{2}} = 9^{\frac{1}{2} + \frac{1}{2}} = 9^1 = 9.$$

This example suggests that we define $9^{\frac{1}{2}}$ as $\sqrt{9}$, since $(\sqrt{9})^2 = 9$.

In general,

$$a^{\frac{1}{n}} = \sqrt[n]{a}.$$

Find the root. If the root does not exist, explain why. 7 and 8: No square root because a is negative and n is even.

1. $\sqrt[3]{27}$ 3
2. $\sqrt[6]{0}$ 0
3. $\sqrt[4]{16}$ 2
4. $\sqrt[3]{1000}$ 10

5. $\sqrt[3]{64}$ 4
6. $\sqrt[3]{-27}$ −3
7. $\sqrt{-49}$
8. $\sqrt[4]{-16}$

9. $\sqrt[3]{-1000}$ −10
10. $\sqrt[5]{-32}$ −2
11. $\sqrt[3]{125}$ 5
12. $\sqrt[7]{-1}$ −1

Write the expression without exponents.

13. $36^{\frac{1}{2}}$ 6
14. $27^{\frac{1}{3}}$ 3
15. $64^{\frac{1}{3}}$ 4
16. $64^{\frac{1}{6}}$ 2
17. $16^{\frac{1}{4}}$ 2
18. $1000^{\frac{1}{3}}$ 10
19. $81^{\frac{1}{4}}$ 3

Calculator Activity

Most scientific calculators have a $\boxed{\sqrt[x]{y}}$ key that can be used to approximate roots that are not integers. For example, to obtain $\sqrt[4]{7}$, enter $\boxed{7}$ $\boxed{\sqrt[x]{y}}$ $\boxed{4}$ $\boxed{=}$ to get 1.6265766. On some calculators, the $\boxed{\sqrt[x]{y}}$ key may be a second function. In this case, push the $\boxed{\text{2nd F}}$ key to activate the root function.

Other calculators have a $\boxed{y^x}$ and a $\boxed{1/x}$ key. In this case, we can obtain $\sqrt[4]{7}$ by calculating $7^{\frac{1}{4}}$ in the following way.

$$\boxed{7} \quad \boxed{y^x} \quad \underbrace{\boxed{4} \quad \boxed{1/x}} \quad \boxed{=}$$

This is $\frac{1}{4}$.

Use a calculator to approximate the following.

1. $\sqrt[3]{10}$
2. $\sqrt[3]{4}$
3. $\sqrt[5]{50}$
4. $\sqrt[4]{44}$
5. $5^{\frac{1}{4}}$
6. $11^{\frac{1}{3}}$

2.1544347   1.5874011   2.1867241   2.5755096   1.4953488   2.2239801

7. The volume of a sphere is related to its radius by the formula $V = \frac{4}{3}\pi r^3$. Use the formula to find the radius of a balloon that has a volume of 3500 ft³. Use $\pi \approx 3.14$.   9.4203395 ft

Applying Algebra to Right Triangles   **427**

Chapter Review

Complete.

1. A positive number has exactly __?__ different square root(s). **2** [11–1]

2. $\sqrt{169}$ is 13, therefore 169 is a __?__ square. **perfect**

3. If 5.2 is used as an estimate for $\sqrt{28.6}$ in the divide-and-average method, the next estimate will be __?__. **5.35** [11–2]

4. Using the divide-and-average method, $\sqrt{53} = $ __?__ to the tenths' place. **7.2**

5. In the table on page 508, $\sqrt{24.6}$ lies between __?__ and __?__. **4.899 5** [11–3]

6. Using interpolation and the table on page 498, $\sqrt{5.7} = $ __?__ to the nearest hundredth. **2.39**

True or false?

7. The Pythagorean theorem applies to all triangles. **False** [11–4]

8. The hypotenuse is the longest side of a right triangle and is opposite the right angle. **True**

9. The measure of the diagonal of a 5 cm by 5 cm square is 50 cm. **False**

Exercises 10–12 refer to the diagram below. $\triangle ABC \sim \triangle DEF$. Complete.

10. $\frac{BA}{?} = \frac{AC}{DF}$ **ED**   **11.** $\angle C \cong \angle$ __?__ **D** [11–5]

12. $\overline{BC}$ corresponds to __?__. $\overline{EF}$

13. An isosceles right triangle is also called a __?__ ° right triangle. **45** [11–6]

14. An equilateral triangle with sides 16 cm long has an altitude of __?__ cm. $8\sqrt{3}$

15. The legs of an isosceles right triangle are 7 cm long. The length of the hypotenuse is __?__ cm. $7\sqrt{2}$

Exercises 16–21 refer to the diagram at the right. Match.

16. $\sin F$ **C**   **17.** $\cos F$ **A**   **A.** $\frac{x}{7}$ **B.** $\cos 42° \times 7$ [11–7]

18. $\tan N$ **E**   **19.** y **D**   **C.** $\frac{y}{7}$ **D.** $\sin 42° \times 7$ [11–8]

20. x **B**   **21.** $m \angle N$ **F**   **E.** $\frac{x}{y}$ **F.** $48°$

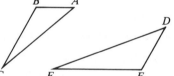

428 *Chapter 11*

Chapter Test

If the given symbol names an integer, state the integer. If not, name the two consecutive integers between which the number lies.

1. $\sqrt{16}$ 4   **2.** $-\sqrt{144}$ −12 **3.** $\sqrt{169} - \sqrt{121}$ 2   **4.** $\sqrt{38 + 43}$ 9   [11-1]

Solve. Round your answer to the nearest tenth.

5. Use the divide-and-average method to approximate $\sqrt{13.7}$. 3.7   [11-2]

6. Using interpolation and the table on page 508, $\sqrt{12.6} \approx \underline{\ ?\ }$. 3.5   [11-3]

7. The area of a square deck is 65.6 m². Find the length of the side. 8.1 m

Is the triangle with sides of the given lengths a right triangle?

8. 6, 8, 10 Yes   **9.** 7, 11, 19 No   **10.** 8, 15, 17 Yes   [11-4]

Exercises 11–13 refer to the diagram at the right.
$\triangle MNO \sim \triangle XYZ.$

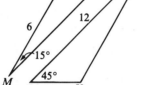

11. If $\dfrac{MN}{XY} = \dfrac{3}{4}$, then $\dfrac{NO}{YZ} = \underline{\ ?\ }$. $\dfrac{3}{4}$ [11-5]

12. Find the length of $\overline{MO}$. 9

13. Find the measure of $\angle N$. 120°

Give answers in terms of radicals with the radical in the numerator.

14. In a 30°–60° right triangle, the shorter leg has length 5. How long is   [11-6]
    (a) the longer leg and (b) the hypotenuse? $5\sqrt{3}$; 10

15. The hypotenuse of a 45° right triangle has a
    length of 36. How long is each leg? $18\sqrt{2}$

Exercises 16–19 refer to the diagram at the right.
Find a value for the trigonometric ratio.

16. $\cos A$ $\dfrac{4}{5}$ **17.** $\tan A$ $\dfrac{3}{4}$ **18.** $\cos B$ $\dfrac{3}{5}$ **19.** $\sin B$ $\dfrac{4}{5}$ [11-7]

$\triangle KLM$ **is an isosceles triangle with** $\overline{KL} \cong \overline{LM}$. **The third side,** $\overline{KM}$, **is 42 cm long. The perimeter of** $\triangle KLM$ **is 112 cm.**

20. Find the lengths of $\overline{KL}$ and $\overline{LM}$.   **21.** Find the height of $\triangle KLM$.   [11-8]
    35 cm   28 cm
22. Find m $\angle K$ and m $\angle M$ to the nearest degree. Use the table on page
    509. 53°, 53°

Applying Algebra to Right Triangles   **429**

Solve.

1. $9a - 6a = 39$ 13
2. $-3b - (-2b) = -7$ 7
3. $3(2c - 4) = 12$ 4
4. $2(d - 5) = 4d + 6$ −8
5. $\frac{5}{8}e - 1 = -1$ 0
6. $-2f \leq 2$ All the numbers greater than or equal to −1
7. $21 \geq g - 4$ All the numbers less than or equal to 25
8. $\frac{3}{4}h - 3 < 9$ All the numbers less than 16
9. $5i - 3 > 3i + 23$ All the numbers greater than 13
10. $\frac{k}{3} + 1 \geq 0$ All the numbers greater than or equal to −3

Find the area. Use $\pi \approx 3.14$ and round the answer to three digits.

11. rectangle: length 13 m, width 8 m 104 m²
12. triangle: base 7 cm, height 8 cm 28 cm²
13. circle: radius 9 mm 254 mm²

Find the surface area. Round answers involving π to three digits.

14. cylinder: diameter of base 6 cm, height 16 cm 358 cm²
15. rectangular prism: length = 1.2 in., width = 3.2 in., height = 4.2 in. 44.64 in.²

Cumulative Review (Chapters 1–11)

Exercises

Simplify the expression.

1. $(8 + 2) \div (3 \times 9)$ $\frac{10}{27}$
2. $15 \div 8 + 7 \div 9$ $2\frac{47}{72}$
3. $[48(2 + 5) - 6] \times 10$ 3300
4. $-26 - 7 + 9 \times 3$ −6
5. $2(10 + 5) \div (-3 - 6)$ $-3\frac{1}{3}$
6. $[(7 - 5)(3 \times 5)] - 5$ 25

Evaluate the expression when $a = 10$, $b = -10$, and $c = 0.5$.

7. ab −100
8. ac 5
9. $a + b$ 0
10. $a - b$ 20
11. $2ab$ −200
12. b^2 100
13. ac^2 2.5
14. a^2c 50
15. $\frac{b}{a}$ −1
16. $\frac{ab}{c}$ −200

Replace ? with <, >, or = to make a true statement.

17. $\frac{1}{2}$ _?_ $\frac{3}{8}$ >
18. $\frac{1}{5}$ _?_ $\frac{2}{8}$ <
19. $-\frac{4}{5}$ _?_ $\frac{3}{4}$ <
20. $-\frac{1}{3}$ _?_ $-\frac{7}{9}$ >

Solve the equation.

21. $12 + a = 50$ 38
22. $x - 27 = 56$ 83
23. $43m = 107.5$ 2.5
24. $\frac{n}{38.6} = 15$ 579
25. $a + \frac{2}{3} = 8$ $7\frac{1}{3}$
26. $w - \frac{1}{5} = 12$ $12\frac{1}{5}$
27. $2x + 4x = 48$ 8
28. $5c - 12c = 35$ −5
29. $3(t - 4) = 24$ 12
30. $6z = 32 + z$ $6\frac{2}{5}$
31. $2 + 5a = 30$ $5\frac{3}{5}$
32. $7(x - 6) = 3x$ $10\frac{1}{2}$

Find the perimeter of the given polygon.

33. square: sides of 2.9 ft 11.6 ft
34. triangle: 7.11 in., 8.11 in., 12.45 in. 27.67 in.

Solve the proportion.

35. $\frac{n}{15} = \frac{12}{45}$ 4
36. $\frac{6}{7} = \frac{n}{35}$ 30
37. $\frac{8}{n} = \frac{32}{40}$ 10
38. $\frac{3}{5} = \frac{24}{n}$ 40

Graph each equation on a separate coordinate plane. Check students' graphs.

39. $x + 2y = 7$
40. $2x + 2y = 9$
41. $x + \frac{1}{5}y = 1$

Find the volume of a cylinder with the given dimensions. Leave your answer in terms of π.

42. radius: 7 height: 12 588π
43. radius: 2.3 height: 10.5 55.545π

430 *Chapter 11*

Rewrite the expression in lowest terms with the radical in the numerator.

44. $\dfrac{4}{\sqrt{10}}$
$\dfrac{2\sqrt{10}}{5}$

45. $\dfrac{5}{\sqrt{2}}$
$\dfrac{5\sqrt{2}}{2}$

46. $\dfrac{18}{\sqrt{37}}$
$\dfrac{18\sqrt{37}}{37}$

47. $\dfrac{2n}{\sqrt{n}}$
$2\sqrt{n}$

48. $\dfrac{6m}{\sqrt{m}}$
$6\sqrt{m}$

Problems

Problem Solving Reminders

Here are some problem solving reminders that may help you solve some of the problems on this page.
- Sometimes more than one method can be used to solve.
- Supply additional information if necessary.
- Check your results with the facts given in the problem.

Solve.

1. Evan is a parking lot attendant at the Lonestar Garage. When counting his tips from Monday he discovered he had 12 more quarters than dimes and 3 fewer nickels than quarters. If Evan earned a total of $19.45 in tips, how many of each type of coin did he have?
40 dimes, 49 nickels, 52 quarters

2. A regular pentagon has a perimeter of 378.5 m. Find the length of each side. **75.7 m**

3. A discount store has an automatic markdown policy. Every 7 days, the price of an item is marked down 25% until the item is sold or 4 weeks have elapsed. If the first price of an item is $40 on September 17, what will the price be on October 1? **$22.50**

4. A window washer uses a vinegar and water solution in the ratio of one-half cup of vinegar to three cups of water. How much vinegar will be in two gallons of solution? $4\frac{4}{7}$ c

5. Lavender soap is sold in boxes of 3 bars for $6.50. To the nearest cent, what is the cost of one bar? **$2.17**

6. Bertha Magnuson had purchased 2500 shares of ABC stock for $3.50 per share. When she sold the stock, its value had gone down to $\frac{5}{8}$ of the total purchase price. How much did Bertha lose? **$3281.25**

7. The area of a square table is 1936 in.². What will be the dimensions of a square tablecloth that drops 4 in. over each side of the table?
52 in. × 52 in.

8. Mary has $300 to spend on new boots and a winter coat. She expects to spend $\frac{2}{5}$ as much for boots as for a coat. What is the most she can spend on boots? **$85.71**

Find the volume. Use $\pi \approx 3.14$ and round the answer to three digits.

16. Cylinder: base radius = 2 m, height = 3.2 m **40.2 m³**

17. Pyramid: square base 3 cm on a side, height = 5 cm **15 cm³**

18. Sphere: diameter = 10 mm **523 mm³**

19. Find the mass of a cube 8.5 cm on each edge with density 0.56 g/cm³. **344 g**

12

Statistics and Probability

For ecological and other reasons, it is sometimes important to determine the size and geographical location of a group of migrating birds such as those shown in the photograph. A total count of a particular kind of bird obviously poses a difficult problem. By using a sample count, however, only a small part of the bird population needs to be counted. The total number of birds in the entire area can then be estimated from the number in the sampled area.

The simplest method of counting birds and studying migration is direct observation. Because of the disadvantages of this method, more sophisticated methods are being developed and used. These include banding, radio tracking, and radar observation. With the help of computers, this data can be quickly collected and examined.

In this chapter, you will learn some methods for gathering and analyzing data.

Career Note

Statisticians collect, analyze, and interpret numerical results of surveys and experiments. They may use the information that is gathered to determine suitable choices, evaluate a report, or redesign an existing program. Statisticians are usually employed in manufacturing, finance, or government positions. A thorough knowledge of mathematics and a background in economics or natural science is needed.

433

433

Lesson Commentary
Chapter 12 Statistics and Probability

Overview

The first section of this chapter is an introduction to statistics. The standard statistical measures are introduced: range, mean, median, and mode. Probability is a subject that most students enjoy. With the increased use of probabilistic models in science, business, and so on, it is a subject receiving considerable attention. The second part of the chapter defines and applies probability and odds and concludes with an introduction to mutually exclusive events.

ANALYZING DATA

12-1 Picturing Numerical Data

Objectives *for pages 434–437*

■ To interpret data from bar graphs and broken-line graphs.
■ To draw bar graphs and broken-line graphs to illustrate data.

Teaching Suggestions

Bar graphs and broken-line graphs illustrate a relationship between two quantities, one represented on a horizontal axis and the other on a vertical axis. You can begin this lesson by having students compare the data in the table on page 434 with the graphs on the same page.

Call the attention of your students to the fact that the vertical scale in each graph on page 434 starts at 0. Tell them that starting a scale at a number other than 0 can be very misleading. Tell students to use these steps to draw a bar graph:

1. Decide which quantity to show on the horizontal axis and which to show on the vertical axis.
2. Choose a data unit and label the scale on each axis.
3. Determine the height of each bar by reading the scale.
4. Draw the bars and give the graph a title.

You may want to give students some guidance on how to choose a data unit. The data unit must be large enough so that differences in the data can be seen and small enough to fit on a piece of paper. Tell students to begin by looking at the largest quantity to be graphed and to use the formula below to test a convenient data unit.

$$\frac{\text{Greatest quantity}}{\text{Data unit}} = \text{Number of units needed}$$

On page 434, the greatest quantity is 8,200,000 cars. If a data unit of 1,000,000 cars is used, then 8.2 units are needed to graph the greatest quantity. For the graphs on page 434, a data unit of 2,000,000 cars was used, requiring 4.1 units to graph the greatest quantity. Either 1,000,000 or 2,000,000 cars is a good choice for a data unit in this example because they both result in a graph whose size is both convenient and easy to read. Ask students why 1000 cars or 5,000,000 cars would not be good choices for a data unit.

Students are sometimes confused about whether a given set of data is best represented by a bar graph or a broken-line graph. Tell them that on a bar graph only one scale need be continuous, whereas on a broken-line graph, intermediate values on both scales should have meaning. For example, in the graph for Class Exercises 6–10, as the population increases, it assumes each of the intermediate values. For Class Exercises 1–5, however, a bar graph rather than a broken-line graph is used to show the elevations of mountain ranges because each of the four mountains on the horizontal axis is unconnected to any of the others.

Related Activities

To impress on students the need to start a scale of a graph at 0, have students use a piece of paper to cover sections of bar graphs in this chapter. For example, on page 434, if the lowest section of the bar graph is covered, the vertical scale starts at 2 million. This creates a false impression; it appears as if car sales in 1930 were more than two times as great as sales in 1920. Students can test other graphs for similar effects when a scale does not start at zero. Tell students to look for examples of this error in newspapers and magazines; ask them to bring one to class if they find one.

12-2 Pictographs and Circle Graphs

Objectives for pages 438-442

■ To interpret data from pictographs and circle graphs.
■ To draw pictographs and circle graphs to illustrate data.

Teaching Suggestions

A graph enables a reader to comprehend a general trend easily. The greater the data unit, the less detail seen on the graph. Ask students what general impression or trend they notice in each of the pictographs on page 438. Use questions like the following:

1. "Has the number of cars sold per year since 1920 generally increased? Or has it decreased?" **Increased**
2. "In the years shown on the graph, which years showed a decrease in sales?" **1960 and 1980**
3. "Between which two years was there the most dramatic increase in books published in the United States?" **1960 to 1970**
4. "Do you really think there were exactly 42,000 books published in the United States in 1980?" **No** "Could the exact number have been 41,556?" **Yes** "45,000?" **No** "40,000?" **No**

You can use this last question to lead into a discussion of the need for rounding data when drawing a graph. Ask students to what place they think the data for each graph on page 438 have been rounded.

Emphasize that, in a circle graph, the whole circle (360°) represents the whole of some quantity and each wedge of the circle represents a part of the whole. The number of degrees in each wedge of the graph (x) is proportional to the size of the part it is depicting:

$$\frac{\text{Part}}{\text{Whole}} = \frac{x}{360°}$$

Point out to students that they can check their work by adding the number of degrees for all the wedges. In Example 2, the sum $93° + 144° + 123°$ equals $360°$.

Mention that degree measures for circle graphs are usually rounded to the nearest degree because we can not measure any more accurately with a protractor. Students will have to round degree measures in the Written Exercises. Because of rounding, the sum of all the angle measures may not be exactly 360°.

Related Activities

To stimulate interest and provide extra practice, survey your class to find each student's most popular musical group from a selection of five. Then have them make a circle graph that shows the results.

12-3 Mean, Median, and Range

Objective for pages 443-445

■ To find the mean, median, and range of a set of data.

Teaching Suggestions

Tell students that the mean, median, and range all describe characteristics of a set of data and show a general tendency.

To help students remember that the median is the middle number in a set of data, you can tell them to think of the median strip that is in the middle of a highway.

It may be worthwhile to discuss with your class the advantages and disadvantages of using the mean and the median to describe data. For example, a group of people may have a median age of 13 and a mean age of 25 if the ages are 12, 13, and 50. The median age, however, is probably more representative for this group.

Students are sometimes perplexed that the mean and median are often not themselves elements of the set of data that they describe. Use the Example on page 443 to point out that this is often the case.

Related Activities

To help students understand how the mean is affected by extreme scores, have them solve the following problems. Suppose that six people took a test and got the following scores: 67, 72, 80, 80, 80, 83.

1. Find the mean and the median of the test scores.
   77, 80

2. Suppose a seventh person was absent when the test was given, takes the test, and gets a score of 0. Find the new mean and median of all the test scores.
66, 80

12-4 Frequency Distributions

Objective for pages 446–449

■ To make and use a frequency table to find statistical measures.

Teaching Suggestions

Students have learned to arrange data in order from least to greatest as an aid to locating the median. By now they can appreciate how tedious and cumbersome this method must be for large sets of data, like a census, for instance. Tell them that a frequency table is a method of organizing data that makes it easier to find the mean and median.

The Example on page 446 shows students how they can use a frequency distribution to find the range, mean, and median. Tell students that the numbers under the head "$x \times f$" in the Example are partial sums of the scores listed above. Students who have calculators can easily verify that the sum of the partial sums under "$x \times f$" is the same as the sum of the individual scores at the top of the page.

The mode of a set of data can be found easily using a frequency table. The item with the greatest frequency is the mode. Caution students that the frequency itself is not the mode. In the Example on page 446, the mode is 7, not its frequency, 12. Tell students that a set of data may have no mode; for example, 1, 2, 3, 4, 5. A set of data may have more than one mode. There are two modes in the following set of data:

$$10, 10, 10, 15, 20, 20, 20$$

The two modes are 10 and 20; both occur with the same frequency.

Before students solve Exercises 7–12, you may want to suggest that they use a tally of the data to help them find the frequency of each item.

Related Activities

To give students experience in collecting data and compiling a frequency distribution, have students find a paragraph in this book having at least three lines and no symbols. Have them count the number of one-letter words, two-letter words, three-letter words, and so on. Then tell the class to summarize these data using a frequency table and find the mean, median, range, and mode. If you wish, as part of the next lesson, you can have students draw a histogram and a frequency polygon for the data.

12-5 Histograms and Frequency Polygons

Objective for pages 450–452

■ To read and draw histograms and frequency polygons.

Teaching Suggestions

This lesson is an extension of the previous lesson. Students may notice that the data in the frequency table on page 450 are the same as those on page 446.

Tell students that a frequency table summarizes a set of data, which in some cases can be very large. Histograms and frequency polygons help us picture the information in a frequency table so that we can more easily see general trends.

In a histogram each rectangle is centered over the corresponding number on the horizontal axis; the sides of the rectangle are halfway between the two data units. No spaces are left between the rectangles.

Related Activities

To extend the lesson, teach students about relative frequency. The frequency of an occurrence can be given as a percent of the total number of data items. For example, the table on page 450 shows that 6 people scored 9 on the quiz. Since 40 people took the quiz, we can say that the part of the class that scored 9 was 6/40, or 0.15, or 15%. This is the relative frequency of the score 9.

The vertical axis of the histogram on page 450 can be relabeled to make a relative frequency histogram. We replace the frequency labels 2, 4, 6, . . . by 0.05, 0.10, 0.15, . . . Thus we can see that 30% of the class had a score of 7.

Have students relabel the vertical axis of the frequency polygon on page 451 to obtain a relative frequency polygon.

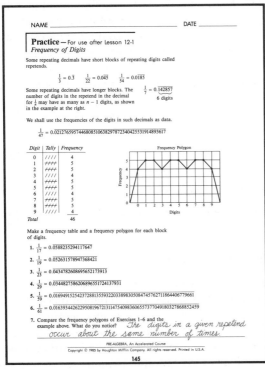

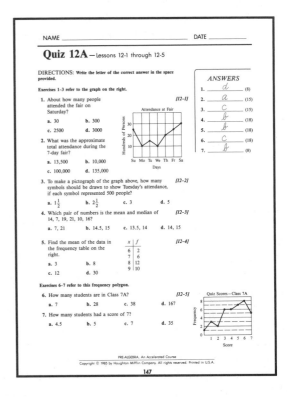

NAME _____ DATE _____

Problem Solving—For use after Lesson 12-1
Venn Diagrams

Diagrams are sometimes useful in problem solving. Venn diagrams show the relationships among groups of objects or numbers.

This Venn diagram shows one circle entirely within the other. From the diagram we can tell that all whales are mammals and that some mammals are not whales. These are *valid* statements. It is *not valid* that all mammals are whales.

When the circles overlap, as in this Venn diagram, some valid statements are "some soccer players are girls" and "some girls are soccer players." To say "all girls are soccer players" is not valid.

Study the Venn diagram. Tell whether the statement is valid or not valid.

1. All piano players are musicians. *valid*
2. All musicians are piano players. *not valid*
3. No musicians are piano players. *not valid*
4. Some girls are wearing sandals. *valid*
5. All girls are wearing faded jeans and sandals. *not valid*
6. Some girls are wearing faded jeans and sandals. *valid*
7. Some people play basketball and baseball. *valid*
8. Some people play football but not baseball. *valid*
9. No people play only football. *not valid*
10. Some people play all three games. *valid*

This Venn diagram shows the number of students enrolled in language classes at Frost School. Use the Venn diagram to answer the questions.

French 25, 11, Spanish 30, 3, German 16

11. How many students take 3 languages? *1*
12. How many take French and Spanish? *12*
13. How many take only German? *16*
14. How many Spanish students are there in all? *47*
15. If the total number of French students is 46, what is the total number of German students? *31*

146

PROBABILITY

12-6 Permutations

Objective for pages 453–457

■ To determine the number of permutations that can be made from a group of objects.

Teaching Suggestions

Although the counting principle may seem obvious and a matter of common sense, it is probable that students have never considered it formally. When presenting examples, it would be a good idea to actually list the possible choices or arrangements of things. It is important to emphasize that, if there are m ways to do one thing and n ways to do another, then there are n ways to do the second thing for each of the m ways of doing the first. If this point is not clarified there will be students who want to add m and n rather than multiplying.

When discussing permutations, make the point that the word *arrangement* is synonymous with *permutation*.

433d

There are many possible permutations of a given set of objects, even though the objects are the same in each case. Students may realize that they can determine the number of permutations of a given set by using the counting principle, and that memorizing the permutations formula may not be mandatory.

Venn diagrams, which are introduced on page 457, can represent collections of data. If you present this material, show that if there were no red sedans the circles would not overlap. Draw a Venn diagram showing the number of students in two school activities.

Resource Book: Page 148 (Use After Page 457)

Related Activities

To provide a challenge, ask students to solve problems such as the following.

1. Find the number of different license plates possible if each plate has three digits followed by three letters. **17,576,000**
2. Find out how many telephone numbers can be made if no number begins with zero and each telephone has a seven-digit number. **9,000,000**

To provide practice with a calculator or computer, have students investigate factorial numbers. Evaluate $n!$ for many values of n. Students are usually impressed to find how quickly these numbers become very large. To display factorials larger than 11! an 8-digit calculator uses scientific notation.

Most calculators cannot go beyond 69!, since 70! exceeds 10^{100} and thus the capacity of the calculator. Students may also notice that each factorial from 5! on ends in zero; this is because 2 and 5 are factors.

12-7 Combinations

Objective for pages 458–460

■ To determine the number of combinations that can be made from a group of objects.

Teaching Suggestions

Emphasize the difference between combinations and permutations. For a given combination there are many permutations. It can be useful to call permutations "arrangements" and combinations "selections." To help illustrate the distinction, discuss electing officers, where order matters, and choosing a committee, where order doesn't matter.

Try to make the need for dividing by $_rP_r$ in the combinations formula as clear as possible. The reason is that otherwise we would be counting many permutations of the same combination. Why, specifically, is it $_rP_r$ that we divide by? Precisely because this is the number of arrangements of any one selection of r objects. In Example 1 on page 458, if we use the permutations formula then we would be counting ABCD, ABDC, ACBD, and so on separately. However, we should count all of these as only one combination. For any such 4-letter combination, there are $_4P_4$, or 24, permutations, so we divide by $_4P_4$ in order to count all of these permutations as only one combination.

Related Activities

To expand this topic, show students how to form Pascal's Triangle. Each entry is the sum of the numbers above and to the left and right. For example, $3 = 2 + 1$.

```
            1
          1   1
        1   2   1
      1   3   3   1
    1   4   6   4   1
```

Ask students to find the number of combinations of four things taken four at a time, three at a time, and so on. Compare the resulting numbers to the fourth row of Pascal's Triangle, which is the same series of numbers. Explain that this is true for each row; the *n*th row of the triangle is the number of combinations of *n* things.

12-8 The Probability of an Event

Objective *for pages 461–465*

■ To determine the probability of an event when the outcomes are equally likely.

Teaching Suggestions

When all possible outcomes are equally likely, we can assign probabilities and use the formula on page 461. Students may ask about experiments for which all outcomes are not equally likely. An example would be a game cube that is "loaded," or a spinner with sectors that are not all the same size.

Point out that the sum of the probability of the possible outcomes must equal 1. In the case of the five cards at the top of page 461,

$$P(\text{heart}) + P(\text{club}) + P(\text{diamond}) + P(\text{spade}) =$$
$$\tfrac{2}{5} + \tfrac{1}{5} + \tfrac{1}{5} + \tfrac{1}{5} = 1.$$

Be sure to take enough time to develop the lattice of points to represent the outcome when rolling two game cubes. Students are generally ready to agree that there are eleven possible sums, but they may not realize that there are 36 possible outcomes until they remember the counting principle in Lesson 12-6.

Related Activities

To simulate probability experiments using random numbers, use a telephone directory. Students might choose the last number on each page. To simulate tossing a game cube, look at the last two digits of each number. Reject any number if the last two digits contain 0, 7, 8, or 9. Record 60 numbers. Find the sum of the two digits of each number. How many sevens are there? The probability of a seven is $\tfrac{1}{6}$.

Resource Book: Pages 149–150 (Use After Page 465)

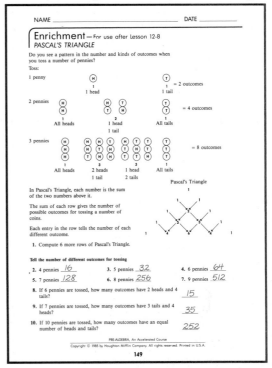

12-9 Odds in Favor and Odds Against

Objective *for pages 466–469*

- To determine the odds in favor of an event and the odds against an event.

Teaching Suggestions

Many students have the mistaken impression that odds and probability are the same concept. Point out that probability is a ratio of *numbers* (whole) of outcomes, but odds are a ratio of *probabilities*. In most cases, to find the odds for or odds against an event happening, we must find the quotient of two fractions. Emphasize that the value of a probability ranges from 0 to 1, whereas the value of odds may be greater than 1.

The sum of the probabilities of all the possible outcomes must be 1; that is, it is certain that the result of an experiment must be one of the possible outcomes. In experiments with n equally likely outcomes the probability of each outcome is $\frac{1}{n}$; there is a sum of $n\left(\frac{1}{n}\right) = 1$ for all n outcomes. A consequence of this is that if $P(A) = p$, then $P(\text{not } A) = 1 - p$, since all outcomes must be in either A or not A.

Odds of 1 to 1 are called even odds. This occurs when $\frac{p}{1-p} = 1$, or $p = 1 - p$. By applying some simple algebra, show your class that $p = 1 - p$ can occur only when $p = \frac{1}{2}$. Thus even, or 1 to 1, odds are the same as a probability of $\frac{1}{2}$, as in flipping a coin. When an event has more than an even chance the odds are greater than 1. If there is less than an even chance the odds are less than 1. Point out that the odds in favor of an event and the odds against the event are reciprocals of each other.

Related Activities

To provide a challenge, ask students to determine which event has the better odds. They will have to devise a method for answering; an example would be to divide b into a, when odds are a to b, and express the odds as a decimal.

	Odds in Favor	
	Event A	Event B
1.	18 to 11 1.63	23 to 14 1.64 B better
2.	7 to 16 0.44	8 to 19 0.42 A better
3.	37 to 48 0.77	40 to 53 0.75 A better

12-10 Mutually Exclusive Events

Objective *for pages 470–473*

- To identify mutually exclusive events and apply the formula for the probability of "A or B" where A and B are mutually exclusive events.

Resource Book: Page 151 (Use After Page 473)

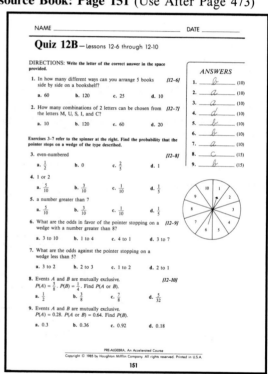

Teaching Suggestions

Be sure that students understand mutually exclusive events. For the pointer shown on page 470, events O and E are mutually exclusive because they cannot both occur at once. Events R and O are not mutually exclusive because they both occur when the pointer stops on a red wedge that is odd-numbered.

The formula for mutually exclusive events on page 470 is actually a special case of the more general formula

$$P(A \text{ or } B) = P(A) + P(B) - P(A \text{ and } B).$$

The general formula applies to any two events A and B. If A and B also happen to be mutually exclusive, then $P(A \text{ and } B) = 0$, and we have the formula for mutually exclusive events.

$$P(A \text{ or } B) = P(A) + P(B).$$

It may seem to students that this should be the general formula. However, A and B have a nonempty intersection when they are not mutually exclusive, so adding $P(A)$ and $P(B)$ would actually count some outcomes twice.

Related Activities

To provide a challenge, present the following problem. A clinic is staffed by doctors and nurses. There are always 1, 2, or 3 doctors and 1, 2, or 3 nurses. The possible combinations are shown in the diagram.

1. Describe in words the event indicated.
   a. A 1 nurse, 1 or 2 doctors
   b. B total staff 3
   c. C 2 nurses
   d. D total staff 4
   e. E 3 nurses or 3 doctors

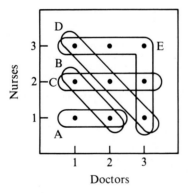

2. Are the following pairs of events mutually exclusive?
   a. A and B No
   b. A and C Yes
   c. B and C No
   d. B and D Yes
   e. B and E Yes
   f. C and D No
   g. C and E No
   h. A and D Yes
   i. A and E Yes

Resource Book: Page 152 (Use After Page 473)

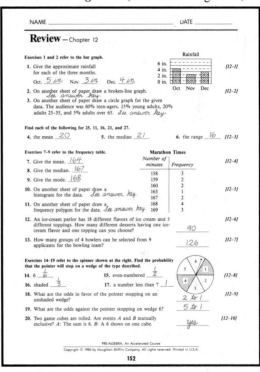

NAME _____ DATE _____

Test—Chapter 12

DIRECTIONS: Write the answers in the spaces provided.

Exercises 1–3 refer to the bar graph.

1. Approximately how many points did Team B score? *[12-1]*

2. Approximately how many points did Team C score?

3. Draw a broken-line graph for the data.

*4. Draw a pictograph for the given data. *[12-2]*

Albums Sold					
Week	1	2	3	4	5
Number Sold	4030	5540	3480	5040	4750

Find each of the following for 24, 10, 15, 20, 26.

5. the mean   6. the median   7. the range *[12-3]*

Exercises 8–10 refer to the frequency table.

Scores on a 6-item Quiz

Score	Frequency
6	7
5	9
4	6
3	3
2	3

8. Give the mean of the data. *[12-4]*

9. Give the median of the data.

10. Draw a frequency polygon for the data. *[12-5]*

11. In how many different ways can you arrange the letters in the word THEORY? *[12-6]*

12. In how many ways can a science student choose 4 experiments to perform out of 7? *[12-7]*

Exercises 13–15 refer to the spinner shown at the right. Find the probability that the pointer will stop on a wedge of the type described.

13. odd-numbered   14. a number less than 9 *[12-8]*

15. What are the odds against the pointer stopping on a wedge with a number less than 6? *[12-9]*

16. Events Q and R are mutually exclusive. $P(R) = 0.34$, $P(Q \text{ or } R) = 0.52$. Find $P(Q)$. *[12-10]*

ANSWERS
1. 80 (5)
2. 75 (5)
3. See answer key (5)
4. See answer key (5)
5. 19 (5)
6. 20 (5)
7. 16 (7)
8. 4.5 (7)
9. 5 (7)
10. See answer key (7)
11. 720 (7)
12. 35 (7)
13. $\frac{5}{2}$ (7)
14. 1 (7)
15. 3 to 5 (7)
16. 0.18 (7)

NAME _____ DATE _____

Make-up Test—Chapter 12

DIRECTIONS: Write the answers in the spaces provided.

Exercises 1–3 refer to the bar graph.

1. Approximately how much money did Class 7B collect? *[12-1]*

2. Approximately how much money did Class 7C collect?

3. Draw a broken-line graph of the data.

4. Draw a pictograph for the given data. *[12-2]*

Number of Books Borrowed				
Week	1	2	3	4
Books	6010	4520	5740	5010

Find each of the following for 30, 16, 21, 26, 32.

5. the mean   6. the median   7. the range *[12-3]*

Exercises 8–10 refer to the frequency table.

Average Daily Temperature

°C	Frequency
18	4
17	3
16	6
15	10
14	8

8. Give the mean of the data. *[12-4]*

9. Give the median of the data.

10. Draw a histogram for the data. *[12-5]*

11. In how many different ways can 5 students be lined up for a group picture? *[12-6]*

12. How many groups of 3 stereo tapes can be selected from 10 tapes? *[12-7]*

Exercises 13–15 refer to the spinner shown at the right. Find the probability that the pointer will stop on a wedge of the type described.

13. even-numbered   14. a number greater than 5 *[12-8]*

15. What are the odds in favor of the pointer stopping on a wedge with a number less than 7? *[12-9]*

16. Events F and G are mutually exclusive. $P(F) = 0.43$, $P(G) = 0.38$. Find $P(F \text{ or } G)$. *[12-10]*

ANSWERS
1. $80 (7)
2. $55 (7)
3. See answer key (7)
4. See answer key (7)
5. 25 (7)
6. 26 (7)
7. 16 (7)
8. 15.5 °C (7)
9. 15 °C (7)
10. See answer key (7)
11. 120 (5)
12. 120 (5)
13. $\frac{2}{3}$ (5)
14. $\frac{3}{8}$ (5)
15. 3 to 1 (5)
16. 0.81 (5)

NAME _____ DATE _____

CUMULATIVE REVIEW—Chapters 1–12
Exercises

Evaluate the expression if $a = 4$, $b = 12$, and $c = \frac{1}{4}$.

1. $a + bc$ 7   2. $-3a + 8c$ -10   3. $a^2 - b$ 4

4. $(-b)^2$ 144   5. $(-ac)^3$ -1   6. $a - b - 3$ -11

Solve for y in terms of x.

7. $3x + y = 7$ $y = 7 - 3x$ 8. $4x + 2y = 10$ $y = 5 - 2x$ 9. $2x - y = 1$ $y = 2x - 1$

Express as a percent.

10. $\frac{1}{5}$ 20%   11. $\frac{5}{8}$ $62\frac{1}{2}$%   12. $\frac{7}{4}$ 175%   13. $\frac{2}{3}$ $66\frac{2}{3}$%

Find the perimeter and area of the polygon described.

14. A square with side 2.5 m. $P = 10\,m$, $A = 6.25\,m^2$

15. A rhombus with base 16 cm and height 12 cm. $P = 64\,cm$, $A = 192\,cm^2$

16. A right triangle with legs 5 in. and 12 in. $P = 30\,in$, $A = 30\,in^2$

Use >, <, or = to make a true statement.

17. 53.465 < 53.47   18. $-3.07 < -2.98$ 19. $-\frac{3}{4} > -\frac{7}{9}$

Round to the place specified.

20. hundreds: 732.894 700   21. tenths: 67.493 67.5

22. thousandths: 3.8995 3.900   23. hundredths: 431.087 431.09

For Exercises 24–27, refer to the table on page 508. Approximate the square root to the nearest hundredth.

24. $\sqrt{45}$ 6.71   25. $\sqrt{60}$ 7.75   26. $\sqrt{10}$ 3.16   27. $3\sqrt{91}$ 28.62

Complete. For Exercises 28–32, refer to the following set of data:
6, 9, 4, 5, 8, 6, 5, 9, 8, 6.

28. The range is 5 .   29. The mean is 6.6 .

30. The median is 6 .   31. The mode is 6 .

32. If you choose a number at random from the given set of data, the probability of picking an 8 is $\frac{1}{5}$.

NAME _____ DATE _____

CUMULATIVE REVIEW—Chapters 1–12 (continued)
Problems

Problem Solving Reminders
Here are some problem solving reminders that may help you solve some of the problems on this page.
• Sometimes more than one method can be used to solve a problem.
• Consider whether drawing a sketch will help.
• When rounding an answer to division, consider whether it is reasonable to round up or round down.

Solve.

1. Sheila has a Happy Time laundry-powder coupon for "buy three, get one free." If she purchases 14 boxes of laundry powder, how many boxes will she receive free?   4 boxes

2. Keith scored 96, 89, 88, 91, and 99 on chemistry tests. What is the least he can score on the next test if he wants to maintain a 92 average?   89

3. Angela has 6 different skirts and 8 different sweaters. How many outfit combinations does she have?   48

4. Mark bought a backyard swing set for $79.95, a sandbox for $39.50, and 8 lb of sand costing $1.45 per pound. There was an assembly charge of $8.00 for the swing set and 6% sales tax on the sand. What was the total cost of Mark's purchases? $139.75

5. Leslie bought 45 packs of baseball cards for 96¢ a pack. Each pack contained 32 cards. He later sold all the cards for $115.20. How much profit did he make per card?   5¢ per card

6. Two game cubes are tossed at the same time. Each cube has sides numbered 1 to 6. What is the probability that the sum of the two sides showing is greater than nine? $\frac{1}{6}$

greater than twelve?   0

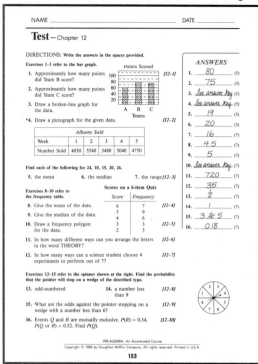

Resource Book: Pages 157–158 (Use After Page 473)

CUMULATIVE TEST—Chapters 10–12

DIRECTIONS: Write the answer in the space provided.

Chapter 10

Find the area of each figure described.

1. parallelogram
base: 12 cm
height: 8 cm

2. triangle
base: 8 m
height: 9 m

3. circle: Use $\pi \approx 3.14$.
diameter: 10 m

4. circle: Use $\pi \approx \frac{22}{7}$.
radius: 3.5 cm

5. Find the area of this symmetric figure. Use $\pi \approx 3.14$.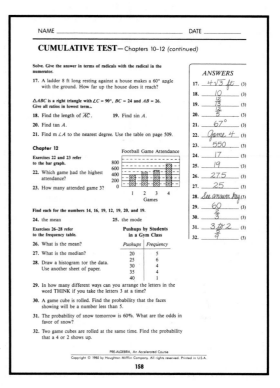

6. Draw the point of symmetry for the diagram in problem 5.

Find the volume. Use $\pi \approx \frac{22}{7}$ if necessary.

7. Prism: base area = 36 cm², height = 8.5 cm.

8. Cone: base diameter = 8 m, height = 3 m.

Solve.

9. A carpet remnant is on sale for $828. If the carpet piece measures 8 ft by 9 ft, what is the cost per square foot?

10. Find the lateral area and the total surface area of a cylinder with a radius of 7 m and a height of 20 m. Use $\pi \approx \frac{22}{7}$.

11. The area of a sphere is 900 π m². What is the diameter?

Chapter 11

Replace the $\underline{\ ?\ }$ with >, <, or = to make a true statement.

12. $-\sqrt{100}\ \underline{\ ?\ }\ \sqrt{64}$

13. $\sqrt{16} + \sqrt{9}\ \underline{\ ?\ }\ \sqrt{16+9}$

14. $\sqrt{4} \times \sqrt{9}\ \underline{\ ?\ }\ \sqrt{4 \times 9}$

Solve. Use interpolation and the table on page 508.

15. A square floor has an area of 68.8 m². Find the length of a side to the nearest tenth of a meter.

16. Find the length of a diagonal of a 15-cm by 15-cm square to the nearest tenth of a centimeter.

ANSWERS

1. 96 cm² (3)
2. 36 m² (3)
3. 78.5 m² (3)
4. 38.5 cm² (3)
5. 84.78 m² (3)
6. See problem (3)
7. 306 cm³ (3)
8. 50.3 m³ (3)
9. $11.50 (3)
10. 880 m², 1188 m² (3)
11. 30 m (3)
12. < (3)
13. > (3)
14. = (3)
15. 8.3 m (5)
16. 21.2 cm (5)

CUMULATIVE TEST—Chapters 10–12 (continued)

Solve. Give the answer in terms of radicals with the radical in the numerator.

17. A ladder 8 ft long resting against a house makes a 60° angle with the ground. How far up the house does it reach?

$\triangle ABC$ is a right triangle with $\angle C = 90°$, $BC = 24$ and $AB = 26$. Give all ratios in lowest term..

18. Find the length of $\overline{AC}$.

19. Find sin A.

20. Find tan A.

21. Find m $\angle A$ to the nearest degree. Use the table on page 509.

Chapter 12

Exercises 22 and 23 refer to the bar graph.

22. Which game had the highest attendance?

23. How many attended game 3?

Football Game Attendance

(bar graph: vertical axis 0, 200, 400, 600, 800; horizontal axis Games 1 2 3 4)

Find each for the numbers 14, 16, 19, 12, 19, 20, and 19.

24. the mean

25. the mode

Exercises 26–28 refer to the frequency table.

26. What is the mean?

27. What is the median?

28. Draw a histogram for the data. Use another sheet of paper.

Pushups by Students in a Gym Class

Pushups	Frequency
20	5
25	6
30	4
35	4
40	1

29. In how many different ways can you arrange the letters in the word THINK if you take the letters 3 at a time?

30. A game cube is rolled. Find the probability that the faces showing will be a number less than 5.

31. The probability of snow tomorrow is 60%. What are the odds in favor of snow?

32. Two game cubes are rolled at the same time. Find the probability that a 4 or 2 shows up.

ANSWERS

17. $4\sqrt{3}$ ft (3)
18. 10 (3)
19. $\frac{12}{13}$ (3)
20. $\frac{12}{5}$ (3)
21. 67° (3)
22. Game 4 (3)
23. 550 (3)
24. 17 (3)
25. 19 (3)
26. 27.5 (3)
27. 25 (3)
28. See answer key (3)
29. 60 (3)
30. $\frac{2}{3}$ (3)
31. 3 or 2 (3)
32. $\frac{3}{9}$ (3)

12-1 Picturing Numerical Data

Many scientific, social, and economic studies produce numerical facts. Such numerical information is called **data.** At the right are some data about the number of automobiles sold in the United States.

These data can be pictured by using a **bar graph** (below left) or a **broken-line graph** (below right). On the bar graph the height of each bar is drawn to the scale marked at the left and so is proportional to the data it represents. All bars have the same width. The broken-line graph can be made by joining the midpoints of the tops of the bars.

We can see from either graph that the most rapid 10-year increase in auto sales occurred between 1940 and 1950.

Car Sales	
Year	**Number Sold (nearest 100,000)**
1920	2,200,000
1930	3,400,000
1940	4,500,000
1950	8,000,000
1960	7,900,000
1970	8,200,000
1980	8,000,000

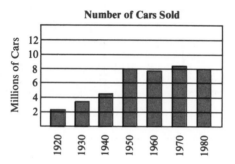

To draw a graph we must choose a **data unit** to mark off one of the axes. If the data are small numbers, the data unit can be a small number, such as 1 or 5. If the data are large numbers, a larger data unit should be chosen so that the graph will be a reasonable size. For example, the data unit in the graphs above is 2,000,000 automobiles.

EXAMPLE The following table gives the average monthly temperatures in Minneapolis, Minnesota. Construct a bar graph to illustrate the data.

Month	J	F	M	A	M	J	J	A	S	O	N	D
°C	−11.1	−8.3	−2.2	7.2	13.9	19.4	22.2	21.1	15.6	10.0	0	−7.2

434 *Chapter 12*

Solution Label the horizontal axis with symbols for the months. Label the vertical axis using a data unit of 5°. Then draw bars of equal widths and proper lengths. Draw the bars downward for negative data. Finally, give the graph a title.

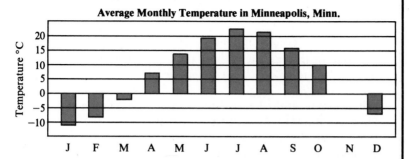

Average Monthly Temperature in Minneapolis, Minn.

Sometimes it is more convenient to arrange the bars in a graph horizontally. In the graph at the right, the data unit for the horizontal axis is 10,000 km² and the vertical axis is labeled with the names of the lakes.

We can estimate data from graphs. For example, we see from the graph that the area of Lake Erie is approximately 25,000 km².

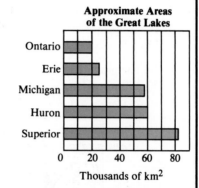

Approximate Areas of the Great Lakes

Thousands of km²

Size of Glass	Number
4 oz	80
5 oz	100
6 oz	25
7 oz	45
8 oz	110
9 oz	15

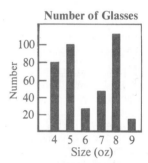

Number of Glasses

Size (oz)

2. Draw a broken-line graph showing the weight of a puppy.

Age (Months)	Weight (Pounds)
0	1.5
3	4.5
6	6.2
9	8.9
12	9.2

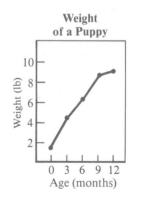

Weight of a Puppy

Age (months)

Class Exercises

Exercises 1–5 refer to the bar graph at the right.

1. What data unit is used on the vertical axis? ten thousand feet

2. Which mountain has the lowest elevation? What is its elevation?
Mt. Kosciusco; 8000 ft

3. Which mountain has the highest elevation? What is its elevation?
Mt. Everest; 28,000 ft

4. Which two mountains have nearly the same elevation? Mt. Vinson and Mt. McKinley

5. Find the ratio of the elevation of Mount Vinson to the elevation of Mount McKinley. approx. 9 : 11

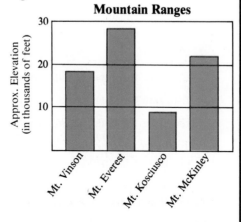

Mountain Ranges

Approx. Elevation (in thousands of feet)

Mt. Vinson Mt. Everest Mt. Kosciusco Mt. McKinley

3. Explain why it is not appropriate to use a broken-line graph for Exercise 1 above and why a broken-line graph is appropriate in Exercise 2 above.

In Exercise 1, there are no glasses whose sizes are between those listed. The number of glasses of one size has no connection with the number for another size. In Exercise 2, the puppy's age and weight both assume all the values between those listed.

Additional A Exercises

1. Draw a bar graph to compare the lengths of the bridges.

Bridge	Length (m)
Golden Gate	1280
Mackinac	1158
Bosporus	1074
Salazar	1013
Kammon	716

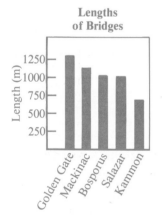

Lengths
of Bridges

Exercises 6-10 refer to the broken-line graph at the right.

6. What data unit is used on the vertical axis?
50 million persons

7. What was the approximate population in 1900? In 1950? 75,000,000; 150,000,000

8. In approximately what year did the population pass 100 million? 150 million? 200 million? 1920; 1950; 1970

9. In which 20-year period did the population increase the most? 1940 to 1960

10. Find the approximate total increase in population during the twentieth century. 175,000,000

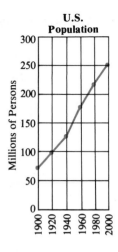

U.S.
Population

Written Exercises

The bar graph below shows the seven nations having populations over 100 million. Use the graph for Exercises 1-6.

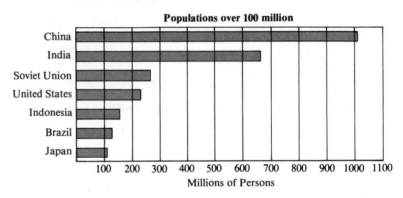

Populations over 100 million

A **1.** What data unit is used on the horizontal axis? 100 million persons

2. Estimate the total population of the three largest nations. 1900 million

3. Estimate the total population of the three smallest nations. 400 million

4. Estimate the total population of the seven nations. 2500 million

5. To the nearest percent, what percent of the world's 4.5 billion people live in China? 22%

6. To the nearest percent, what percent of the world's 4.5 billion people live in the seven nations shown on the graph? 56%

436 *Chapter 12*

In Exercises 7–9, make a bar graph to illustrate the given data.

Check students' graphs.
7. The six longest highway tunnels are: Saint Gotthard, 16.2 km; Arlberg, 14 km; Frejus, 12.8 km; Mont Blanc, 11.7 km; Enasson, 8.5 km; and San Bernadino, 6.6 km.

8. The areas of the world's five largest islands in thousands of square kilometers are: Greenland, 2175; New Guinea, 792; Borneo, 725; Madagascar, 587; and Baffin, 507.

9. The table below gives the length of each continent's longest river.

Continent	River	Length (km)
Africa	Nile	6632
Asia	Yangtze	6342
Australia	Murray-Darling	3693
Europe	Volga	3510
North America	Mississippi-Missouri	5936
South America	Amazon	6400

10. Make a broken-line graph to illustrate the given data.

Number of U.S. High School Graduates (in thousands)

1920	1930	1940	1950	1960	1970	1980
311	667	1221	1200	1864	2896	3078

B 11. Make a bar graph to illustrate the data. Net profits of the XYZ Company in thousands of dollars were: 30 in 1981; −20 (loss) in 1982; −5 (loss) in 1983; 45 in 1984; and 60 in 1985.

12. Make a broken-line graph to illustrate the average monthly temperatures in Minneapolis. (Use the table in the example in this lesson.)

Review Exercises

Perform the indicated operation.

1. $\frac{47}{60} \times 360$ 282

2. $\frac{74}{83} \times 249$ 222

3. $\frac{118}{37} \times 111$ 354

4. $\frac{85}{156} \times 312$ 170

5. 25% of 540 135

6. 47% of 360 169.2

7. 73% of 180 131.4

8. 81% of 360 291.6

Statistics and Probability **437**

2. Draw a broken-line graph showing the change in temperature at a weather station.

Time	Temperature (°F)
6 A.M.	−16°
7 A.M.	−3°
8 A.M.	6°
9 A.M.	8°
10 A.M.	20°
11 A.M.	22°
12 Noon	30°

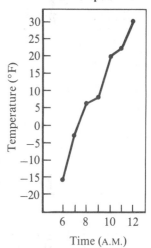

Change in Temperature

Suggested Assignments

Core
436/1–6
437/8–10
437/Rev. 2–8 even

Enriched
436/1, 3, 5
437/9–12
437/Rev. 2–8 even

Supplementary Materials

Practice Masters, p. 53

Teaching Suggestions
p. 433b

Related Activities p. 433b

Reading Mathematics

Students will learn the meaning of the following mathematical terms in this lesson: *pictograph, circle graph.*
   Mention that a pictograph is sometimes called a *pictogram* or a *picture graph,* and a circle graph is sometimes called a *pie graph* or a *pie chart.*

12-2 Pictographs and Circle Graphs

Nontechnical magazines often present data using pictures. These **pictographs** take the form of bar graphs with the bars replaced by rows or columns of symbols. Each symbol represents an assigned quantity. This amount must be clearly indicated on the pictograph. For example, the pictograph below illustrates the data on automobile sales given in the previous lesson.

Number of Cars Sold

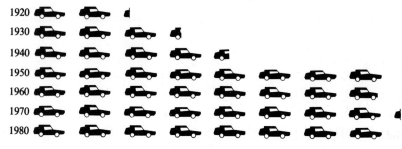

= 1,000,000 cars

EXAMPLE 1   The approximate numbers of different book titles published in the United States in selected years are: 11,000 in 1950; 15,000 in 1960; 36,000 in 1970; and 42,000 in 1980. Illustrate the data with a pictograph.

Solution   Stacks of books are appropriate symbols. We let one thick book represent 5000 titles and one thin book represent 1000 titles.

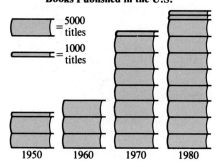

Chalkboard Examples

1. Beckley's Dairy Farm has 75 Holstein cows, 52 Jersey cows, and 73 Guernsey cows. Draw a circle graph to illustrate the data.

Beckley's Dairy Farm

438   *Chapter 12*

The **circle graph** at the right shows how the world's water is distributed. Circle graphs are often more effective than other graphs in picturing how a total amount is divided into parts.

The following example illustrates how to make a circle graph.

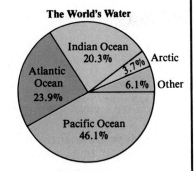

The World's Water

Indian Ocean 20.3%
Arctic 3.7%
Atlantic Ocean 23.9%
Other 6.1%
Pacific Ocean 46.1%

EXAMPLE 2
The seventh-grade class voted to decide where to have their year-end picnic. The results were as follows: Mountain Park, 62 votes; State Beach, 96 votes; City Zoo, 82 votes. Draw a circle graph to illustrate this distribution.

Solution
The whole circle represents the total number of votes. We plan to divide the circle into wedges to represent the distribution of the votes. Since the sum of all the adjacent angles around a point is 360°, the sum of the angle measures of all the wedges is 360°.

First find the total of all votes cast.

$$62 + 96 + 82 = 240$$

Then find the fraction of the vote cast for each place and the corresponding angle measure.

For Mountain Park:

$$\frac{62}{240} \times 360° = 93°$$

For State Beach:

$$\frac{96}{240} \times 360° = 144°$$

For City Zoo:

$$\frac{82}{240} \times 360° = 123°$$

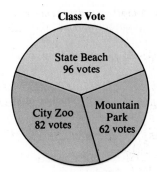

Class Vote

State Beach 96 votes
City Zoo 82 votes
Mountain Park 62 votes

Now use a compass to draw a circle and a protractor to draw three radii forming the angles found above. Finally, label the wedges and give the graph a title.

Statistics and Probability **439**

Chalkboard Examples (Cont.)

2. The Oakes family used their family computer for educational programs 72 hours during the first week, 96 hours the second week, 61 hours the third week, and 58 hours the fourth week. Use a pictograph to illustrate the data.

Computer Usage

= 10 hours of use

First Week   Second Week   Third Week   Fourth Week

439

Illustrate using (a) a circle graph and (b) a pictograph.

1. At lunch today 200 students bought the school lunch with the weekly ticket, 45 bought the lunch with the daily ticket, and 105 brought their lunches from home.

a. **School Lunch**

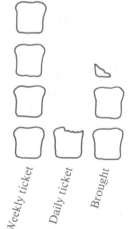

b. **School Lunch**

50 students =

Class Exercises

Check students' drawings.

1. Draw a circle and divide it into 4 equal parts.

2. Draw a circle and divide it into 6 equal parts.

3. Draw a circle and divide it into 9 equal parts.

4. Draw a circle and divide it into 12 equal parts.

The circle graph at the right pictures the distribution of students playing the various instruments in the school orchestra.

Composition of the School Orchestra

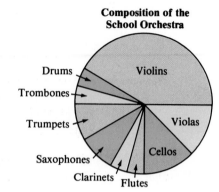

5. Which instrument is played by the greatest number of students in the orchestra? violins

6. How does the number of students playing stringed instruments (violins, violas, and cellos) compare with the number of students playing all the other instruments? about twice as large

7. Which four instruments are played by the fewest students? flutes, clarinets, trombones, drums

8. How does the number of saxophone players compare with the number of trumpet players? about the same

Written Exercises

Complete the following tables and construct a circle graph for each.

A 1. The Junior Athletic Association decided to raise money by selling greeting cards. Orders were obtained for the following kinds of cards.

Kind of Card	Number of Boxes	Fraction of the Whole	Number of Degrees in the Angle
birthday	60	? $\frac{1}{4}$	? 90°
get well	72	? $\frac{3}{10}$	? 108°
friendship	48	? $\frac{1}{5}$	? 72°
thank you	60	? $\frac{1}{4}$	? 90°
Total	? 240	? 1	? 360°

2. The winter issue of the school magazine contained the following kinds of material.

Kind of Material	Number of Pages	Fraction of the Whole	Number of Degrees in the Angle
fiction	32	? $\frac{1}{2}$	? 180°
essays	8	? $\frac{1}{8}$	? 45°
sports	16	? $\frac{1}{4}$	? 90°
advertisements	8	? $\frac{1}{8}$	? 45°
Total	? 64	? 1	? 360°

Illustrate, using a circle graph. Check students' graphs.

3. The surface of Earth is 30% land and 70% water.

4. Earth's atmosphere is 78% nitrogen, 21% oxygen, and 1% other gases.

Illustrate, using a pictograph. The parentheses contain a suggestion as to what symbol to use. Check students' graphs.

5. The XYZ Car Rental Company rented 520 cars in July, 350 cars in August, 350 cars in September, 400 cars in October, and 110 cars in November. (cars)

6. The Meadowbrook School ordered 200 cartons of milk the first week, 220 the second week, 240 the third week, and 180 the fourth week. (milk cartons)

7. The number of fish caught in Clear Lake: 4500 in 1970; 3500 in 1975; 4200 in 1980; 4800 in 1985. (fish)

8. The cost of higher education in the United States in billions of dollars: 1965 — $13; 1970 — $23; 1975 — $39; 1980 — $55. (dollars)

Illustrate, using (a) a circle graph and (b) a pictograph. The parentheses contain a suggestion as to what symbol to use in the pictograph.
Check students' graphs.

B **9.** In the United States about 167 million people live in cities and about 59 million live in rural areas. (people)

10. A fund-raising event made $420 from the sale of antiques, $280 from crafts items, and $240 from food. (dollars)

2. The time spent on a computer was divided among the following tasks.

Word processing: 134 min
Programming: 156 min
Running programs: 70 min

a. Computer Usage

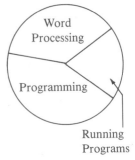

b. **Computer Usage**

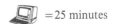 = 25 minutes

Illustrate, using (a) a circle graph and (b) a pictograph. The parentheses contain a suggestion as to what symbol to use in the pictograph.

Check students' graphs.

11. The average seasonal rainfall in Honolulu is 26 cm in winter, 7 cm in spring, 5 cm in summer, and 21 cm in autumn. (raindrops)

12. Of each dollar the United States government takes in, 47¢ comes from individual income taxes, 27¢ from Social Security, 12¢ from corporation taxes, and 14¢ from other sources. (piles of coins)

13. A family spends $440.75 of the monthly budget on food, $530.00 on rent, $617.00 total on clothes, medicine, and other items, and $175.25 on transportation. (dollars)

14. A total of 387 people were polled on Proposition Q, 46% favored it, 33% opposed it, and 21% had no opinion. (people)

15. The library received a $1300 grant. The librarian plans to spend 10% of the grant to extend magazine subscriptions, 35% to buy new books, 15% to repair damaged books, 30% to buy new furniture, and 10% to locate missing books. (books)

C 16. Which pictograph correctly shows that the production of a certain oil field doubled between 1975 and 1985? Explain your answer.

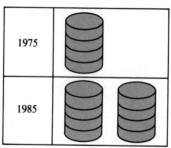

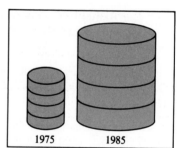

The one on the left. The units used are the same for 1975 and 1985.

Review Exercises

Arrange in order from least to greatest.

1. 4, 2.6, 7, 0.84, 3 0.84, 2.6, 3, 4, 7

2. 4, -8, -3, 1, 10, -5
   -8, -5, -3, 1, 4, 10

3. 7, $3\frac{1}{2}$, -5, $4\frac{1}{4}$, -6 -6, -5, $3\frac{1}{2}$, $4\frac{1}{4}$, 7

4. $\frac{7}{8}$, $\frac{5}{6}$, $\frac{11}{9}$, $\frac{7}{12}$, $\frac{12}{7}$ $\frac{7}{12}$, $\frac{5}{6}$, $\frac{7}{8}$, $\frac{11}{9}$, $\frac{12}{7}$

5. -6, -10, -2, -12, -9
   -12, -10, -9, -6, -2

6. $3\frac{7}{8}$, $2\frac{9}{10}$, $2\frac{8}{9}$, $3\frac{11}{16}$ $2\frac{8}{9}$, $2\frac{9}{10}$, $3\frac{11}{16}$, $3\frac{7}{8}$

7. 1.09, 1.1, 0.9, 0.09
   0.09, 0.9, 1.09, 1.1

8. $\frac{17}{4}$, $\frac{11}{2}$, $\frac{15}{8}$, $\frac{9}{4}$, $\frac{7}{5}$ $\frac{7}{5}$, $\frac{15}{8}$, $\frac{9}{4}$, $\frac{17}{4}$, $\frac{11}{2}$

442 *Chapter 12*

12-3 Mean, Median, and Range

The daytime high temperatures in °C for five days in May were

$$23°, 14°, 18°, 28°, \text{ and } 25°.$$

Here are two ways to summarize this information.

(1) The **mean** of the temperatures is their sum divided by the number of temperatures.

$$\frac{23° + 14° + 18° + 28° + 25°}{5} = \frac{108°}{5} = 21.6°$$

(2) The **median** of the temperatures is the middle temperature when they are arranged in order of size.

$$14°, 18°, 23°, 25°, 28° \qquad \text{Median} = 23°$$

For an even number of data items the median is midway between the two middle numbers.

The **range** of a set of data is the difference between the greatest and least numbers in the set. For example, the range of the above temperatures is $28° - 14°$, or $14°$.

EXAMPLE Find the mean, median, and range of each set of numbers. Round to the nearest tenth.

    a. 11, 19, 7, 45, 22, 38   **b.** 0, 1, 3, −4, 4, −6, 7

Solution   **a.** Mean $= \dfrac{11 + 19 + 7 + 45 + 22 + 38}{6} = \dfrac{142}{6} \approx 23.7$

        Arrange the numbers in order of size: 7, 11, 19, 22, 38, 45

        Median $= \dfrac{19 + 22}{2} = 20.5$ Range $= 45 - 7 = 38$

    b. Mean $= \dfrac{0 + 1 + 3 + (-4) + 4 + (-6) + 7}{7} = \dfrac{5}{7} \approx 0.7$

        Arrange the numbers in order of size: −6, −4, 0, 1, 3, 4, 7

        Median $= 1$ Range $= 7 - (-6) = 13$

In everyday conversation the word *average* is usually used for mean.

Analyzing data as we have been doing is part of the branch of mathematics called **statistics.**

Statistics and Probability   **443**

Find the mean, median, and range of each set of data.

1. −22, −11, 0, 11, 22
0, 0, 44

2. 1, 2, 3, 4, 5, 6
3.5, 3.5, 5

3. 62, 48, 97, 4, 37, 19
44.5, 42.5, 93

4. 8.4, 3.6, 1.2, 0.7, 14.9
5.76, 3.6, 14.2

5. Janet scored 7, 12, 9, 6, and 9 points in 5 games. Find the mean number of points made. 8.6 points

Class Exercises

Find the mean, median, and range of each set of data.

1. 1, 2, 3, 4, 5 3, 3, 4

2. 5, 3, 1 3, 3, 4

3. 10, 10, 6, 2 7, 8, 8

4. 3, 4, 5, 6, 8, 10 6, 5.5, 7

5. −4, −2, 0, 2, 4 0, 0, 8

6. 3, 2, 1, 0, −1, −2, −3 0, 0, 6

7. −3, −1, 0, 4, 5 1, 0, 8

8. 6, 5, 5, 0, −1 3, 5, 7

9. −15, −11, −7, −7, −7, 0, 2, 5, 9, 15, 18, 22 2, 1, 37

10. −37, −28, −15, −15, −6, 1, 13, 26, 34 −3, −6, 71

11. 11, 17, 31, 43, 58, 61, 58, 89, 94, 58, 94, 107, 215 72, 58, 204

Written Exercises

Find the mean, median, and range of each set of data. If necessary, round to the nearest tenth.

A

1. 30, 18, 21, 28, 23 24, 23, 12

2. 42, 58, 55, 61, 39 51, 55, 22

3. 7, 16, 20, 13, 26, 14 16, 15, 19

4. 85, 70, 93, 101, 116, 111 96, 97, 46

5. 47, 61, 53, 69, 45, 58 55.5, 55.5, 24

6. 17, 11, 9, 13, 7, 21, 8, 18 13, 12, 14

7. 3.6, 2.7, 2.9, 3.4, 3.4 3.2, 3.4, 0.9

8. 8.1, 9.2, 6.8, 7.3, 7.9, 6.9 7.7, 7.6, 2.4

B

9. −3, 2, −2, −5, 3 −1, −2, 8

10. 8, −8, −12, 16, −8, 7 0.5, −0.5, 28

11. 1.3, −0.8, −0.1, 0.2, 0.9 0.3, 0.2, 2.1

12. 4.1, −3.2, −0.8, −1.5, 2.7, −0.1
0.2, −0.45, 7.3

13. Low Temperatures in February (°C)
−13° −8° −10° −4° 1° 0° −2°
−5° −7° −12° −8° −7° −5° 0°
−2° −3° −5° 1° 2° 3° 1°
2° 4° 2° 4° 4° 5° 6°
−2°, −1°, 19°

14. Elevations Along the Salton Sea Railway (meters)
6.82 2.55 1.60 −0.21 −1.35
−2.68 −1.95 −2.06 −0.88 −0.02
0.41 1.15 3.15 6.51 5.86
1.26, 0.41, 9.5

444 *Chapter 12*

15. Insert another number in the list 15, 23, 11, 17 in such a way that the median is not changed. 16

16. Replace one of the numbers in the list 15, 23, 11, 17 so that the median becomes 17. Replace 15 with 17, or replace 17 with 19.

Find the value of x such that the mean of the given list is the specified number.

17. 6, 9, 13, x; mean = 11 16

18. 8, 14, 16, 12, x; mean = 15 25

19. Janet's scores on her first four mathematics tests were 98, 78, 84, and 96. What score must she make on the fifth test to have the mean of the five tests equal 90? 94

20. The heights of the starting guards and forwards on the basketball team are 178 cm, 185 cm, 165 cm, and 188 cm. How tall is the center if the mean height of the starting five is 182 cm? 194 cm

C 21. If each number in a list is increased by 5, how is the median affected? It is increased by 5.

22. If each number in a list is increased by 5, how is the mean affected? It is increased by 5.

Review Exercises

Perform the indicated operations. Round to the nearest tenth if necessary.

1. $(4 \times 2 + 7 \times 5 + 6 \times 8) \div 15$ 6.1

2. $(9 \times 4 + 6 \times 7 + 11 \times 5) \div 16$ 8.3

3. $(14 \times 6 + 3 \times 0 + 16 \times 4) \div 10$ 14.8

4. $(12 \times 1 + 8 \times 11 + 5 \times 6) \div 18$ 7.2

5. $(18 \times 3 + 20 \times 5 + 7 \times 6) \div 14$ 14

6. $(7 \times 15 + 4 \times 9 + 7 \times 2) \div 26$ 6.0

7. $(11 \times 3 \times 2 + 8 \times 3 + 9) \div 33$ 3

8. $(12 \times 2 \times 8 + 9 \times 3 \times 4) \div 15$ 20

 Challenge

Cellini and Valdez were each appointed to a new job. Cellini is paid a starting salary of $16,500 a year with a $1000 raise at the end of each year. Valdez is paid a starting salary of $8000 for the first 6 months with a raise of $500 at the end of every 6 months. How much does each make at the end of the first year? The third year? Who has the better pay plan?

Statistics and Probability **445**

Suggested Assignments

Core
444/1–13
445/Rev. 1–6

Enriched
444/6–14 even
445/15–22
445/Challenge

Supplementary Materials
Practice Masters, p. 54

Additional Answers
Challenge

Cellini: year 1: $16,500; year 2: $16,500 + $1000 = $17,500; year 3: $17,500 + $1000 = $18,500. Valdez: year 1: $8000 + $8500 = $16,500; year 2: $9000 + $9500 = $18,500: year 3: $10,000 + $10,500 = $20,500. Valdez has the better plan.

Reading Mathematics

Students will learn the meaning of the following mathematical terms in this lesson:
*frequency table, frequency,
frequency distribution, mode.*
    To help students remem-
ber the meaning of the word
''mode'' and to distinguish it
from other terms learned in
this chapter, remind them
that the word ''mode'' in
everyday speech refers to a
popular fashion. Students
can think of the mode as the
most popular item of data.

Chalkboard Examples

Use the data in the table to
find the statistical measure
specified.

Valley Central High School

Class Size	Frequency
15	3
16	2
19	2
21	11
22	9
25	2
30	1

1. the number of classes 30
2. the range 15
3. the mean 20.8
4. the median 21
5. the mode 21

12-4 Frequency Distributions

Forty students took a quiz and received the following scores.

```
8  7  10  6   8   7  9   7   8  5
9  7   8  8   7   9  3   8   8  6
7  5   6  8  10  10  7  10   8  9
7  7   9  7   8   7  9  10  10  7
```

In order to analyze these data, we can arrange them in a
frequency table as shown at the right. The number of times
a score occurs is its **frequency**. Since a score of 9 was received by 6 students, we can say that the frequency of 9 is
6. The pairing of the scores with their frequencies is called
a **frequency distribution.**

Score	Frequency
3	1
4	0
5	2
6	3
7	12
8	10
9	6
10	6

EXAMPLE Find the range, mean, and median for the data above.

Solution Since the lowest score is 3 and the highest is 10, the range is $10 - 3$,
or 7.

To find the *mean* of the data,
first multiply each possible score by
its frequency. Enter the product in
a third column as shown. The sum
of the numbers in this column
equals the sum of the 40 scores.
Therefore:

$$\text{mean} = \frac{309}{40} = 7.725$$

Score x	Frequency f	$x \times f$
3	1	3
4	0	0
5	2	10
6	3	18
7	12	84
8	10	80
9	6	54
10	6	60
Total	40	309

To find the median, first rearrange the data in order from least to
greatest. Since there are 40 scores, the median is the average of the
twentieth and twenty-first scores, both of which are 8.

$$\text{median} = \frac{8 + 8}{2} = 8$$

Reading Mathematics: *Tables*
As you use a table, reread the headings to remind yourself what each number represents. For example, the frequency table above shows that the *score*
of 8 had a *frequency* of 10; that is, there are 10 scores of 8, not 8 scores of
10.

446   *Chapter 12*

The **mode** of a set of data is the item that occurs with the greatest frequency. In the example on the preceding page, the mode is 7 since it has the greatest frequency, 12. Sometimes there is more than one mode. The mode usually is used with nonnumerical data, such as to determine the popularity of car colors.

Class Exercises

Find the range, the mean, the median, and the mode(s) of each student's test score, x.

1. Evelyn

x	f
70	1
80	4
90	3
100	2

30, 86, 85, 80

2. Bruce

x	f
75	2
85	3
90	1
100	4

25, 89.5, 87.5, 100

3. Shana

x	f
70	4
85	3
95	2
100	1

30, 82.5, 85, 70

4. Elroy

x	f
75	1
80	2
95	3
100	4

25, 92, 95, 100

Written Exercises

In Exercises 1–6, find the range, the mean, the median, and the mode(s) of the data in each frequency table.

A **1.**

x	f
5	2
6	4
7	8
8	5
9	1

4, 6.95, 7, 7

2.

x	f
0	3
1	2
2	7
3	8
4	5

4, 2.4, 3, 3

3.

x	f
25	1
20	0
15	3
10	5
5	6

20, 10, 10, 5

4.

x	f
18	1
15	0
12	3
9	6
6	7
3	1
0	2

18, 7.65, 7.5, 6

5.

x	f
14	2
15	5
16	11
17	11
18	8
19	0
20	3

6, 16.75, 17, 16 and 17

6.

x	f
28	2
27	4
26	11
25	11
24	4
23	2
22	1

6, 25.4, 25, 25 and 26

Statistics and Probability **447**

8.

x	f
25	1
26	3
27	5
28	4
29	2

range, 4 s; mean, 27.2 s;
median, 27 s; mode, 27 s

9.

x	f
14	1
15	1
16	2
17	5
18	8
19	7
20	6

range, 6; mean, 18.1;
median, 18; mode, 18

10.

x	f
14	6
15	7
16	5
17	6
18	4
20	2

range, 6; mean, 16.1;
median, 16; mode, 15

11.

x	f
97	1
99	3
100	9
101	6
102	2
103	2

range, 6; mean, 100.4;
median, 100; mode, 100

12.

x	f
12	2
13	6
14	10
15	10
16	8
17	2
18	2

range, 6; mean, 14.8;
median, 15;
modes, 14 and 15

In Exercises 7–12, make a frequency table for the given data, and then find the range, the mean, the median, and the mode(s) of the data. Round the mean to the nearest tenth if necessary.

B **7.** The number of runs scored by Jan's team in recent softball games:
5, 1, 4, 4, 8, 6, 4, 1, 5, 0, 1, 5, 3, 8, 4, 5, 3, 4

8. Jim's 200 m dash practice times: 28 s, 29 s, 27 s, 27 s, 28 s, 29 s, 28 s, 26 s, 27 s, 26 s, 28 s, 27 s, 27 s, 25 s, 26 s

9.

April in Pleasantville
Average Temperatures (°C)

	16	15	14	16	17
17	18	18	18	19	19	18
17	18	17	18	19	20	20
19	19	18	17	18	19	20
20	20	19	20

10.

Class Test Scores

16	14	20	15	15	17
15	17	17	16	14	18
17	15	14	14	20	15
14	16	15	18	17	16
15	16	18	14	18	17

11.

Samples of Steel Rods (diameters in millimeters)

101	102	100	97	101	103	100	100	101	100	99	100
99	100	101	103	102	100	101	99	100	100	101	

12.

Ages of Members of the Moose Hill Hiking Club

15	14	15	13	16	14	18	16	15	14	14	15	18	15
13	13	14	15	14	16	16	17	14	15	13	12	14	16
14	16	15	13	16	14	15	17	12	13	16	15		

Exercises 13 and 14 refer to a class of 24 boys and 16 girls. (*Hint:* If you know the number of scores and their mean, you can find the sum of the scores.)

C **13.** On test A, the mean of the boys' scores was 70 and the mean of the girls' scores was 75. What was the class mean? 72

14. On test B, the class mean was 75 and the mean of the girls' scores was 72. What was the mean of the boys' scores? 77

Review Exercises

Explain the meaning of each term.

1. mean   **2.** median   **3.** mode   **4.** range

5. odd number   **6.** even number   **7.** prime number   **8.** multiple of 7

448   *Chapter 12*

Computer Byte

The following computer program will find the average, or mean, of several numbers. The program finds the sum of the numbers and then divides this sum by the number of numbers. For example, if you input 2, 4, 7, 8, and 11, the computer would find their sum, 32, and divide it by 5, the number of items, resulting in an answer of 6.4.

```
10   PRINT "TO FIND THE AVERAGE,"
20   PRINT "INPUT THE NUMBERS ONE AT A TIME."
30   PRINT "TYPE -1 AT END OF LIST."
40   PRINT
50   LET N = 0
60   LET S = 0
70   INPUT A
80   IF A = - 1 THEN 120
90   LET N = N + 1
100  LET S = S + A
110  GOTO 70
120  PRINT
130  PRINT "N = ";N
140  PRINT "SUM = ";S
150  PRINT "AVERAGE = ";S/N
160  END
```

Use the program to find the average of the following. Be sure to type −1 at the end of each list.

1. 12, 19, 23, 8, 17, 31 18.$\overline{3}$

2. 57, 3, 86, 79, 101, 9 55.8$\overline{3}$

3. 542, 863, 921, 254, 378, 511 578.1$\overline{6}$

4. 1649, 15,241, 8463, 11,684 9259.25

5. 887, 3105, 6324, 7048, 2103, 1298, 5541, 7201, 4961, 1114, 2260, 1954, 7322, 5665, 5321, 3742, 4457, 8916, 9923, 4309, 2385, 3342, 4187

4494.1304

6.			
21,542	11,372	63,982	14,320
78,864	24,953	21,419	17,160
47,922	72,315	18,560	21,000
91,254	94,456	41,215	35,743
20,964	34,290	38,730	44,287 40,717.4

7.			
502,784	339,065	764,290	274,415
114,902	765,329	314,675	441,823
345,245	465,367	468,901	687,390
113,823	589,001	892,030	389,210
992,084	314,675	440,871	572,903 489,439.2

Statistics and Probability   **449**

**Additional Answers
Review Exercises**

1. The *mean* of a set of data is the sum of the data divided by the number of items.

2. The *median* of a set of data is the middle item when the items are arranged in order of size. In the case of an even number of items, the median is the average of the two middle numbers.

3. The *mode* of a set of data is the item that occurs with the greatest frequency.

4. The *range* of a set of data is the difference between the greatest and the least numbers in the set.

5. An *odd number* is a whole number that is *not* a multiple of 2.

6. An *even number* is a multiple of 2.

7. A *prime number* is a counting number with exactly two factors, 1 and the number itself.

8. A *multiple of 7* is the product of 7 and any whole number.

Suggested Assignments

Core
   447/1–6
   448/7, 9, 11
   449/Computer Byte

Enriched
   447/2, 4, 6
   448/8–14
   449/Computer Byte

Supplementary Materials

Practice Masters, p. 54

Teaching Suggestions
p. 433c

Related Activities p. 433c

Reading Mathematics

Students will learn the meaning of the following mathematical terms in this lesson:
*histogram, frequency poly-
gon.*

Chalkboard Examples

Use the histogram below for
Exercises 1–4. Find the statistical measure specified.

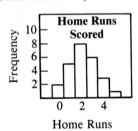

1. range **5**   2. mode **2**
3. median **2**   4. mean
                            2.24

12-5 Histograms and Frequency Polygons

When a bar graph is used to picture a frequency distribution, it is called a **histogram.**
No spaces are left between the bars. The histogram for the quiz-score data of the table is
shown at the left below.

The broken-line graph shown at the right
below is the **frequency polygon** for the same
distribution. The broken-line graph of the frequencies is connected to the horizontal axis at
each end to form a polygon.

We can find the range, the mode, the
mean, and the median from a histogram and
from a frequency polygon.

Score x	Frequency f
3	1
4	0
5	2
6	3
7	12
8	10
9	6
10	6

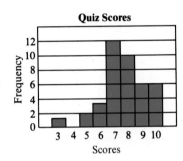

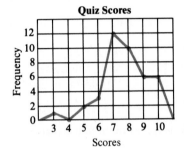

EXAMPLE   Find the range, the mode, the mean, and the median for the data
represented in the graphs above.

Solution   The range is the difference between the least number representing
data on the horizontal axis and the greatest number.

The range is $10 - 3$, or 7.

The tallest bar or highest point represents the mode.

The mode is 7.

To find the mean, we first multiply each data item by its frequency.

$3 \times 1 = 3$ $4 \times 0 = 0$ $5 \times 2 = 10$ $6 \times 3 = 18$
$7 \times 12 = 84$ $8 \times 10 = 80$ $9 \times 6 = 54$ $10 \times 6 = 60$

We then add the products.

$3 + 0 + 10 + 18 + 84 + 80 + 54 + 60 = 309$

450   *Chapter 12*

We then add the frequencies.

$$1 + 0 + 2 + 9 + 12 + 8 + 5 + 3 = 40$$

We then divide the sum of the products by the sum of the frequencies.

$$309 \div 40 = 7.725$$

The mean is 7.725.

Since there are 40 data items, the median is the average of the middle two items, both of which are 8. Thus, their average is 8.

The median is 8.

Class Exercises

Refer to the histogram at the right.

1. What is the mode of the scores? 70

2. What is the range of the scores? 60

3. How many students received scores of 90? 60? 50? 40? 3, 5, 0, 1

4. How many students took the test? 24

5. What is the median score? 70

6. What is the mean of the scores? Round to the nearest tenth. 74.2

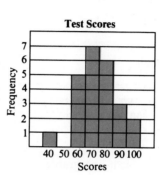

Test Scores

Written Exercises

Exercises 1-10 refer to the frequency polygon below.

A **1.** What is the range of the data? 15   **2.** What is the mode of the data? 35

How many students did the following numbers of pushups?

3. 25   1   **4.** 30   6   **5.** 35   9   **6.** 40   4

7. How many students are in the class? 20

8. What is the median of the data? 35

9. What is the mean of the data? 34

10. Draw a histogram for the data. Check students' papers.

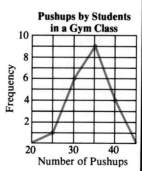

Pushups by Students in a Gym Class

Statistics and Probability   **451**

Additional A Exercises

Exercises 1–4 refer to the histogram below. Find the statistical measure specified.

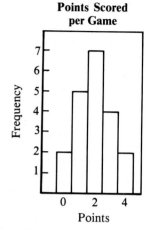

Points Scored per Game

1. range 4   **2.** mode 2

3. median 2   **4.** mean 1.95

Quick Quiz A

Customers at Parks Department Store spent an average of $28 in January; $16 in February; $35 in March; and $41 in April. Use these data for Exercises 1–3 below. Graphs appear on pp. 476–477.

1. Draw a bar graph.

2. Draw a broken-line graph.

3. Draw a pictograph. Use a dollar sign as a symbol.

4. In the Kingswood Basketball League, 20% are 6th graders; 35%, 7th graders; 25%, 8th graders; 15%, 9th graders; and 5%, 10th graders. Draw a circle graph for the given data.

5. Find the mean, the median, and the range of 54 cm, 12 cm, 10 cm, 2 cm, 78 cm, 44 cm, and 3 cm. 29 cm, 12 cm, 76 cm

(continued on next page)

451

6. Make a frequency table
for 12, 11, 11, 10, 10, 10,
9, 8, 8, 7, 6, 6, 6, 5, 5, 4.

x	f
4	1
5	2
6	3
7	1
8	2
9	1
10	3
11	2
12	1

Exercises 7–9 refer to the
histogram.

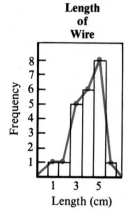

**Length
of
Wire**

Length (cm)

**7. How many samples had
a length of 3 cm? 5**

**8. How many samples were
taken? 22**

**9. Draw a frequency poly-
gon for the data.**
The frequency polygon
is shown in red with
the histogram above.

Suggested Assignments

Core
Day 1: 451/1–10
452/11, 12
Day 2: 452/14
452/Self-Test A

Enriched
Day 1: 451/1–9
452/12, 14, 16
Day 2: 452/17
452/Self-Test A

Supplementary Materials

Practice Masters, p. 54
Computer Activity 23
Test 12A, pp. 79–80

452

**Draw a histogram and a frequency polygon for the data in the following
exercises of Lesson 12–4.** Check students' papers.

B **11.** Exercise 7   **12.** Exercise 8   **13.** Exercise 9

14. Exercise 10   **15.** Exercise 11   **16.** Exercise 12

C **17.** Arrange the data listed below into the following intervals.

10–15, 15–20, 20–25, 25–30, 30–35, 35–40, 40–45

Then draw a histogram for the seven intervals.

23, 43, 27, 41, 12, 13, 19, 32, 43, 22, 36, 28, 44, 29, 31, 24, 34, 44, 37,
23, 17, 14, 23, 32, 36, 33, 43, 28, 39, 19

Self-Test A

**The number of people employed in farming in the United States was:
11,100,000 in 1900; 10,400,000 in 1920; 9,500,000 in 1940; 5,400,000 in
1960; and 3,400,000 in 1980.** Check students' papers.

1. Draw a bar graph.   [12–1]

2. Draw a broken-line graph.

3. Draw a pictograph. Use people as symbols.   [12–2]

4. The sign-up records at the school's computer room showed the following usage: students, 40%; teachers, 30%; administration, 25%;
other, 5%. Draw a circle graph for the given data.

5. Find the mean, median, and range of 13, 6, 20, 20, 9, 15, 11, 10.   [12–3]

6. Make a frequency table for 12, 18, 15, 12, 9, 15, 15, 16, 9, 12, 18, 12. [12–4]

Exercises 7–10 refer to the histogram.

7. How many runners had a time of 16 s? 3   [12–5]

8. How many runners were there in all? 12

9. Draw a frequency polygon for the data.
Check students' papers.

10. What are the range, the mode, the mean,
and the median of the data? 3, 18, 16.75, 17

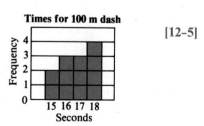

Times for 100 m dash

Seconds

Self-Test answers and Extra Practice are at the back of the book.

452   *Chapter 12*

12-6 Permutations

After school, Vilma plans to go to the music store and then to the pool. She can take any one of 3 routes from school to the music store and then take either of 2 routes from the store to the pool. In how many different ways can Vilma go from school to the pool?

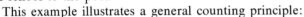

To answer, consider that for each route Vilma can take from school to the music store, she has a choice of either of 2 routes to continue from there. Thus, she has a choice of 3 × 2, or 6, possible different ways to go from school to the pool.

This example illustrates a general counting principle:

> If there are *m* ways to do one thing and *n* ways to do another, then there are *m* × *n* ways to do both things.

In mathematics, an arrangement of a group of things in a particular order is called a **permutation.** The counting principle can help you count the number of different permutations of any group of items.

EXAMPLE 1 In how many different ways can you arrange the three cards shown at the right if you arrange them side by side in a row?

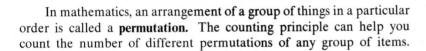

Solution Notice that there are 3 possibilities for the first card: A, B, or C. After the first card is selected, there are 2 possibilities for the second card. After the first and second cards have been selected, there is just 1 possibility for the third card.

Applying the counting principle, there are 3 × 2 × 1, or 6, possible ways to arrange the three cards.

To check, list the permutations:
A B C	B A C	C A B
A C B	B C A	C B A

Notice that the number of permutations of 3 things is 3 × 2 × 1. We can write 3! (read *3 factorial*) to represent the expression 3 × 2 × 1. In general, the number of permutations of *n* things is

$$n \times (n-1) \times (n-2) \times \cdots \times 3 \times 2 \times 1.$$

We can write this expression as *n*!.

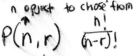

n object to chose from
$$P(n, r) \quad \frac{n!}{(n-r)!}$$
pick r of those object

Statistics and Probability **453**

Teaching Suggestions
p. 433d

Related Activities p. 433e

Reading Mathematics

Students will learn the meaning of the following mathematical terms in this lesson: *counting principle, permutation, factorial.*

The use of the word *counting* in the context of the general counting principle may cause some consternation. Students are accustomed to using the term *count* to mean list, enumerate, put in a one-to-one correspondence with a subset of the positive integers, and so on. Discuss the idea that counting is involved here, too, if by counting we mean giving the number of something.

Chalkboard Examples

Find the value of each.
1. $_5P_3$ **60**
2. $_7P_4$ **840**
3. $_8P_5$ **6720**

A supervisor initials a form with two initials.

4. How many different sets of initials are there? **676**
5. How many sets of initials have the same letter for the first and last initial? **26**
6. How many sets of initials are there in which the initials are different? **650**

Additional Answers
Self-Test A

5. mean, 13; median, 12; range, 14

6.
x	f
9	2
12	4
15	3
16	1
18	2

If we let $_nP_n$ represent the number of permutations of a group of n things when using all n things, we can write the following formula.

Formula

For the number of permutations of n things taken n at a time,

$$_nP_n = n \times (n - 1) \times (n - 2) \times \cdots \times 3 \times 2 \times 1 = n!$$

EXAMPLE 2 How many four-digit whole numbers can you write using the digits 1, 2, 3, and 4 if no digit appears more than once in each number?

Solution You need to find the number of permutations of 4 things taken 4 at a time.
Using the formula,

$$_4P_4 = 4! = 4 \times 3 \times 2 \times 1 = 24.$$

Therefore, 24 four-digit whole numbers can be written using the given digits.

Sometimes we work with arrangements that involve just a portion of the group at one time.

EXAMPLE 3 This year, 7 dogs are entered in the collie competition at the annual Ridgedale Kennel Club show. In how many different ways can first, second, and third prizes be awarded in the competition?

Solution You want to find the number of permutations of 7 things taken 3 at a time. There are 7 choices for first prize, 6 for second, and 5 for third. Thus,

$$7 \times 6 \times 5 = 210.$$

There are 210 possible ways to award the prizes.

If we let $_nP_r$ represent the number of permutations of n objects taken r at a time, we can write the following formula.

Formula

For the number of permutations of n things taken r at a time, we use the following formula carried out to r factors:

$$_nP_r = n \times (n - 1) \times (n - 2) \times \cdots$$

Using the formula in Example 3 above, we find $_7P_3 = 7 \times 6 \times 5 = 210.$

Class Exercises

Find the value of each.

1. 4! 24
2. 3! 6
3. 2! 2
4. 1! 1

5. $_5P_5$ 120
6. $_3P_3$ 6
7. $_5P_4$ 120
8. $_6P_3$ 120

Solve.

9. In wrapping a gift, you have a choice of 3 different boxes and 4 different wrapping papers. In how many different ways can you wrap the gift? 12

10. There are 3 roads from Craig to Hartsdale, 2 roads from Hartsdale to Lee, and 4 roads from Lee to Trumbull. In how many different ways can you travel from Craig to Trumbull by way of Hartsdale and Lee? 24

Use the formula to answer. Then list all of the permutations to check.

11. In how many different ways can you arrange the letters in the word CAR? 6

12. In how many different ways can you arrange the 4 cards shown at the right if you take 3 at a time and arrange them side by side? 24

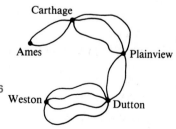

Written Exercises

Find the value of each.

A

1. 5! 120
2. 6! 720
3. 7! 5040
4. 8! 40,320

5. $_6P_6$ 720
6. $_7P_7$ 5040
7. $_8P_8$ 40,320
8. $_5P_5$ 120

9. $_6P_4$ 360
10. $_8P_4$ 1680
11. $_{43}P_3$ 74,046
12. $_{23}P_2$ 506

Problems

Exercises 1–4 refer to the map at the right. Tell how many different ways you can travel from one city to the other.

A

1. Ames to Plainview 6
2. Carthage to Dutton 6

3. Carthage to Weston 24
4. Ames to Dutton 12

Statistics and Probability **455**

Additional A Exercises

Find the value of each.

1. $_5P_2$ 20
2. $_6P_5$ 720
3. $_8P_3$ 336

A four-digit number is to be made using the digits 1, 3, 5, and 8.

4. How many numbers can be made if repeated digits are allowed? 256

5. How many numbers can be made if all digits must be different? 24

6. How many even numbers can be made if all digits must be different? 6

5. A furniture store sells couches that are available in 3 different styles, 7 different colors, and 2 different sizes. How many different couches are available? 42

6. How many different sandwiches can you make using one kind of bread, one kind of meat, and one kind of cheese with these choices? 18

> Bread: white, rye, whole wheat
> Cheese: Swiss, cheddar
> Meat: turkey, chicken, roast beef

Use a formula to solve. List the permutations to check your answer.

7. In how many different ways can you arrange the 4 books shown side by side on a shelf? 24

8. In how many different ways can Carla, Dean, and Ellen be seated in a row of 3 chairs? 6

9. How many different two-digit whole numbers can you make with the digits 1, 3, 5, and 7 if no digit appears more than once in each number? 12

10. In how many different ways can you arrange the letters in the word RING if you take the letters 3 at a time? 24

Solve.

B **11.** In how many different ways can 7 books be arranged side by side on a shelf? 5040

12. In how many different ways can 6 students stand in a row of 6? 720

13. In how many different ways can you arrange the letters in the word ANSWER if you take the letters 5 at a time? 720

14. How many different four-digit numbers can you make using the digits 1, 2, 3, 5, 7, 8, and 9 if no digit appears more than once in a number? 840

Using the digits 1, 2, 4, 5, 7, and 8, how many different three-digit numbers can you form according to each of the following rules?

C **15.** Each digit may be repeated any number of times in a number. 216

16. The numbers are even numbers and no digit appears more than once in a number. 60

17. There is a 5 in the ones' place and no digit appears more than once in a number. 20

456 *Chapter 12*

18. In how many different ways can you arrange the letters in the word ROOT? (*Hint:* Notice that two of the letters are indistinguishable.) 12

19. In how many different ways can you arrange the letters in the word NOON? 6

The diagram at the right, called a **Venn diagram,** illustrates the following statement.

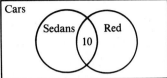

> Of 100 cars, 35 are sedans, 25 are red, and 10 are red sedans.

The rectangular region represents the number of cars. One circular region represents the number of sedans; the other represents the number of red cars. The overlapping portion of the two circular regions represents the number of cars that are red and sedans. The number of red cars that are not sedans is 25 − 10, or 15.

Draw a Venn diagram to illustrate the statement. Then answer the questions.

20. Of 240 knit caps, 110 are striped, 65 are blue, and 45 are striped and blue.
  a. How many are striped but not blue? 65
  b. How many are blue but not striped? 20
  c. How many are striped or blue (striped, or blue, or both)? 130
  d. How many are neither striped nor blue? 110

Review Exercises

Simplify.

1. $\frac{70}{5} \times \frac{1}{2}$ 7

2. $\frac{15}{12} \times \frac{36}{60}$ $\frac{3}{4}$

3. $\frac{21}{5} \times \frac{10}{14}$ 3

4. $\frac{27}{51} \times \frac{17}{3}$ 3

5. $\frac{9 \times 8}{3 \times 2}$ 12

6. $\frac{7 \times 6}{4 \times 3}$ $\frac{7}{2}$

7. $\frac{11 \times 10 \times 9}{3 \times 2 \times 1}$ 165

8. $\frac{23 \times 22 \times 21 \times 20}{4 \times 3 \times 2 \times 1}$ 8855

 Challenge

You and a friend have decided to jog through Peachtree Park. The park has five entrance gates and several paths as shown in the diagram at the right. To jog along all of the paths without covering any path more than once, through which gate would you enter? Gate 1 or Gate 4

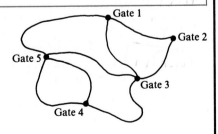

Statistics and Probability **457**

Suggested Assignments

Core
  455/2–12 even; Prob. 1–4
  456/Prob. 5–13 odd
  457/Rev. 4–8

Enriched
Day 1: 455/2–12 even
    456/Prob. 6, 8, 10;
    11–17
Day 2: 457/Prob. 18–20
    457/Rev. 4–8
    457/Challenge

Supplementary Materials

Practice Masters, p. 55

12-7 Combinations

Sometimes we select groups of objects from a larger group without regard to the order of the objects selected. Such groups in which the order is not considered are called **combinations.**

Suppose there is a group of 4 students—Jon, Lin, Meg, and Ray—who wish to go to the computer center today. If only 3 of them may go today, what are the possible combinations of these students who may be selected to go? To find any one combination, just leave out 1 student from the group of 4. The possible combinations are listed below.

Jon, Lin, Meg   Jon, Lin, Ray   Jon, Meg, Ray   Lin, Meg, Ray

The number of groups of 3 students that can be selected from a group of 4 students is 4.

Here is another way to approach the problem.

$$\begin{bmatrix} \text{number of groups} \\ \text{of 3 students you} \\ \text{can select from 4} \end{bmatrix} \times \begin{bmatrix} \text{number of ways of} \\ \text{arranging 3 stu-} \\ \text{dents in a group} \end{bmatrix} = \begin{bmatrix} \text{number of ways of} \\ \text{arranging 3 out} \\ \text{of 4 students} \end{bmatrix}$$

$$N \qquad \times \qquad _3P_3 \qquad = \qquad _4P_3$$

Solving for N, we find that

$$N = \frac{_4P_3}{_3P_3} = \frac{4 \times 3 \times 2}{3 \times 2 \times 1} = 4.$$

This formula gives us the same answer that we found by showing and counting the number of combinations of 3 students that may be selected from a group of 4 students.

EXAMPLE 1 How many combinations of 4 cards can be chosen from the cards shown at the right?

Solution Use the formula to find the number of combinations of 6 cards taken 4 at a time.

$$N = \frac{_6P_4}{_4P_4} = \frac{\overset{3}{\cancel{6}} \times 5 \times \overset{1}{\cancel{4}} \times \overset{1}{\cancel{3}}}{\underset{1}{\cancel{4}} \times \underset{1}{\cancel{3}} \times \underset{1}{\cancel{2}} \times 1} = \frac{15}{1} = 15$$

$$n C r = \frac{n!}{(n-r)! \, r!}$$

List the combinations to check.

A B C D	A B D E	A C D E	A D E F	B C E F
A B C E	A B D F	A C D F	B C D E	B D E F
A B C F	A B E F	A C E F	B C D F	C D E F

458 *Chapter 12*

In general, if we let $_nC_r$ represent the number of combinations of n things taken r at a time, we can use the following formula.

Formula

For the number of combinations of n things taken r at a time,

$$_nC_r = \frac{_nP_r}{_rP_r} = \frac{n \times (n-1) \times \cdots \text{(to } r \text{ factors)}}{r!}$$

EXAMPLE 2   Four of 7 students who have volunteered will be chosen to hand out programs at the drama club performance. How many combinations of these students can be selected?

Solution   We wish to find the number of combinations of 7 students taken 4 at a time.
Using the formula, we find

$$_7C_4 = \frac{_7P_4}{_4P_4} = \frac{7 \times 6 \times 5 \times 4}{4 \times 3 \times 2 \times 1} = \frac{35}{1} = 35.$$

Class Exercises

Find the value of each.

1. $_5C_3$ 10 **2.** $_5C_4$ 5 **3.** $_6C_2$ 15 **4.** $_7C_2$ 21 **5.** $_8C_4$ 70 **6.** $_8C_6$ 28 **7.** $_{12}C_3$ 220 **8.** $_{20}C_2$ 190

Use the formula to solve. List the combinations to check your answer.

9. How many combinations of 2 cards can be chosen from the cards shown at the right? 6

10. How many combinations of 3 letters can be chosen from the letters A, B, C, D, and E? 10

Problems

A   **1.** How many combinations of 4 books can you choose from 6 books? 15

2. How many groups of 3 types of plants can be selected from 6 types? 20

3. How many straight lines can be formed by connecting any 2 of 6 points, no 3 of which are on a straight line? 15

Statistics and Probability   **459**

Additional A Problems

1. How many sets of 3 records can you choose from 6 records? 20

2. How many teams of 4 horses can you choose from 9 horses? 126

3. A menu offers peas, beans, carrots, potatoes, and beets. Your meal includes a choice of two vegetables. How many combinations of two vegetables could you choose? 10

4. There are 6 movies in town, and you could see two on Saturday and one on Sunday. How many combinations are there of the movies you could see? 20

5. You buy 10 different books. How many combinations of 3 books can you make? 120

4. How many groups of 4 fabrics can be selected from 7 fabrics? 35

B **5.** How many ways can a class of 21 students select 2 of its members as class representatives for student government? 210

6. The school photographer wants to photograph 3 students from a club with 14 members. How many combinations can be made? 364

7. Kristen must answer 5 of 10 questions on her quiz. How many combinations of questions are possible? 252

8. Philip wishes to check 2 books out of his school library. If the library contains 800 books, in how many ways might Philip make his choice of books? 319,600

9. You have a total of 4 coins: a penny, a nickel, a dime, and a quarter. How many different amounts of money can you form using the given number of these coins?
   a. 1 coin 4 **b.** 2 coins 6 **c.** 3 coins 4 **d.** 4 coins 1 **e.** one or more coins 15

10. There are three books left in the sale rack: a book about sailing, a cookbook, and a book about baseball. How many combinations can be formed using the given number of these books?
   a. 1 book 3   **b.** 2 books 3   **c.** 3 books 1   **d.** one or more books 7

C **11.** In how many ways can a five-member committee of 3 seniors and 2 juniors be selected from a group of 14 seniors and 8 juniors? (*Hint:* Find the number of combinations of each type and determine their product.) 10,192

12. A basketball squad has 17 members. The coach has designated 3 members to play center, 6 to play guard, and 8 to play forward. How many ways can the coach select a starting team of 1 center, 2 guards, and 2 forwards? (*Hint:* See the hint in Exercise 11.) 1260

Review Exercises

Explain the meaning of each term.

1. factor   **2.** multiple   **3.** even number   **4.** odd number

5. cube   **6.** at least one   **7.** at most one   **8.** exactly one

12-8 The Probability of an Event

In a simple game, the five cards shown are turned face down and mixed so that all choices are *equally likely.*

You then draw a card. If the card is a heart, you win a prize. To find your chance of winning, notice that there are 5 possible **outcomes.** Notice, too, that 2 of the outcomes are hearts. We say that 2 of the outcomes **favor** the event of drawing a heart. The **probability,** or chance, of drawing a heart is $\frac{2}{5}$. If we let H stand for the event of drawing a heart, we may write $P(H) = \frac{2}{5}$. This statement is read as *the probability of event H is $\frac{2}{5}$.*

In general we have the following:

Formula

The probability of an event E is

$$P(E) = \frac{\text{number of outcomes favoring event } E}{\text{number of possible outcomes}}$$

for equally likely outcomes.

When all outcomes are equally likely, as in drawing one of the cards in the game described above, we say that the outcomes occur *at random,* or *randomly.*

In this chapter, we shall often refer to *experiments* such as drawing cards, drawing marbles from a bag, or rolling game cubes. We shall always assume that the outcomes of these experiments occur at random. When we refer to spinners like the one shown at the right, we shall always assume that the pointer stops at random but not on a division line.

Often it is helpful to list all possible outcomes of an experiment. We could show the possible outcomes for the spinner shown above by using letters to represent the colors and by writing the following:

$$R1 \qquad B2 \qquad W3$$
$$R6 \qquad B5 \qquad W4$$

Statistics and Probability **461**

Teaching Suggestions
p. 433f

Related Activities p. 433f

Reading Mathematics

Students will learn the meaning of the following mathematical terms in this lesson: *outcome, favor, probability, random, impossible, certain.*
In mathematics, some words have different meanings from their ordinary usage, but some words such as *certain* and *impossible* mean the same as they do in ordinary language.

A coin purse contains 3 pennies, 5 nickels, and 2 dimes. You take a coin out at random.

1. What is the probability that it is a nickel? $\frac{1}{2}$

2. What is the probability that it is a dime? $\frac{1}{5}$

3. What is the probability that it is worth less than 10¢? $\frac{4}{5}$

4. What is the probability that it is not a penny? $\frac{7}{10}$

5. What is the probability that it is a quarter? 0

EXAMPLE 1 Find the probability that the pointer of the spinner shown on the preceding page stops on a wedge of the type described.

  a. even-numbered   **b.** odd-numbered
  c. red   **d.** not red
  e. even-numbered *and* red   **f.** green
  g. not green

Solution The number of possible outcomes is 6.

  a. $P(\text{even-numbered}) = \frac{3}{6} = \frac{1}{2}$

  b. $P(\text{odd-numbered}) = \frac{3}{6} = \frac{1}{2}$

  c. $P(\text{red}) = \frac{2}{6} = \frac{1}{3}$

  d. $P(\text{not red}) = \frac{4}{6} = \frac{2}{3}$

  e. $P(\text{even-numbered and red}) = \frac{1}{6}$

  f. $P(\text{green}) = \frac{0}{6} = 0$

  g. $P(\text{not green}) = \frac{6}{6} = 1$

The events in parts (f) and (g) of the example illustrate these facts:

> The probability of an impossible event is 0.
> The probability of a certain event is 1.

Sometimes it is useful to picture the possible outcomes of an experiment. Consider the experiment of rolling the two game cubes that are shown at the right. One cube is blue, one cube is red. The numbers 1 through 6 are printed on each cube, one number per face. An outcome can be represented by an ordered pair of numbers. The array at the right shows the 36 possible outcomes when the two cubes are rolled. The encircled dot stands for the outcome of a 5 on the top face of the red cube and a 3 on the top face of the blue cube, or the ordered pair (5, 3).

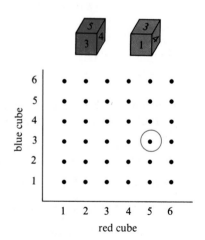

EXAMPLE 2 Two game cubes are rolled.
a. Find the probability that one cube *or* the other cube shows a 5 (that is, that the number 5 is on the top face of either or both cubes).
b. Find the probability that the sum of the top faces is 5.

Solution First, make a sketch to show the possible outcomes. Then circle the event.

a.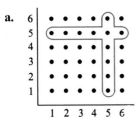

$$P(a\ 5) = \frac{11}{36}$$

b.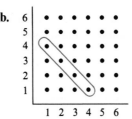

$$P(\text{sum} = 5) = \frac{4}{36} = \frac{1}{9}$$

Problem Solving Reminder
Sometimes *making a sketch* can help you solve a problem. In Example 2, above, picturing an outcome as the graph of an ordered pair simplifies the problem.

Class Exercises

Two red, one white, and three blue marbles are put into a bag. Find each probability for a marble chosen at random.

1. $P(\text{red})$ $\frac{1}{3}$

2. $P(\text{white})$ $\frac{1}{6}$

3. $P(\text{blue})$ $\frac{1}{2}$

4. $P(\text{green})$ 0

5. $P(\text{not green})$ 1

6. $P(\text{red or white})$ $\frac{1}{2}$

7. $P(\text{white or blue})$ $\frac{2}{3}$

8. $P(\text{red or blue})$ $\frac{5}{6}$

Exercises 9–12 refer to the spinner at the right. Find the probability that the pointer stops on a wedge of the type described.

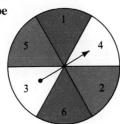

9. numbered with a factor of 6 $\frac{2}{3}$

10. numbered with a multiple of 3 $\frac{1}{3}$

11. even-numbered or blue $\frac{2}{3}$

12. even-numbered and blue $\frac{1}{6}$

Statistics and Probability **463**

Find the probability that the pointer stops on a wedge of the type described.

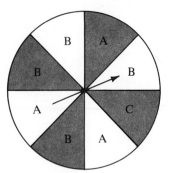

1. red $\frac{1}{2}$

2. B $\frac{1}{2}$

3. blue $\frac{1}{4}$

4. C $\frac{1}{8}$

5. blue or B $\frac{5}{8}$

6. red and A $\frac{1}{8}$

Written Exercises

Find the probability of each roll if you use a single game cube.

A **1.** a 5 $\frac{1}{6}$

2. an odd number $\frac{1}{2}$

3. a number less than 5 $\frac{2}{3}$

4. a number greater than 3 $\frac{1}{2}$

5. a 7 0

6. a number less than 7 1

Each of the 20 cards shown at the right has a letter, a number, and a color. Each card is equally likely to be drawn. Find each probability.

7. $P(C)$ $\frac{1}{4}$

8. $P(A)$ $\frac{1}{4}$

9. $P(1)$ $\frac{1}{5}$

10. $P(2)$ $\frac{1}{5}$

11. $P(\text{red})$ $\frac{1}{2}$

12. $P(\text{blue})$ $\frac{1}{2}$

13. $P(\text{not A})$ $\frac{3}{4}$

14. $P(\text{not D})$ $\frac{3}{4}$

15. $P(1 \text{ or } 2)$ $\frac{2}{5}$

16. $P(1, 2, 3, \text{ or } 4)$ $\frac{4}{5}$

17. $P(\text{neither 1 nor 2})$ $\frac{3}{5}$

18. $P(\text{not 1, or 2, or 3, or 4})$ $\frac{1}{5}$

Exercises 19–28 refer to the spinner below. Find the probability that the pointer stops on a wedge of the type described.

19. red $\frac{1}{3}$

20. white or blue $\frac{2}{3}$

21. numbered with a factor of 12 $\frac{1}{2}$

22. even-numbered $\frac{1}{2}$

23. numbered with a multiple of 3 $\frac{1}{3}$

24. numbered with a multiple of 4 $\frac{1}{4}$

25. odd-numbered or red $\frac{2}{3}$

26. odd-numbered and red $\frac{1}{6}$

27. red and a factor of 6 $\frac{1}{12}$

28. blue and a multiple of 5 0

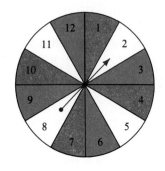

Two game cubes are rolled. Find the probability that this sum shows.

B **29.** 7 $\frac{1}{6}$

30. 12 $\frac{1}{36}$

31. 3 $\frac{1}{18}$

32. 9 $\frac{1}{9}$ $\frac{4}{9}$

33. 7 or 11 $\frac{2}{9}$

34. 2 or 12 $\frac{1}{18}$

35. less than 7 $\frac{5}{12}$

36. 6, 7, or 8

For Exercises 37 and 38, use a *tree diagram* to picture the possible outcomes of the random experiment.

EXAMPLE   Two coins are tossed. Find the probability of obtaining at least one head.

Solution   Let H stand for heads and T stand for tails.

First Coin	Second Coin	Outcomes

H
   H ——————— H, H
   T ——————— H, T

T
   H ——————— T, H
   T ——————— T, T

There are 4 possible outcomes. Three of the outcomes have one or more heads.

$$P(\text{at least one H}) = \frac{3}{4}$$

37. You have two bags of marbles, each of which holds one blue marble, one red marble, and one green marble. You choose one marble at random from each bag. Find the probability of obtaining the following.
    a. two red marbles $\frac{1}{9}$ **b.** at least one blue marble $\frac{5}{9}$ **c.** no green marbles $\frac{4}{9}$
    d. at most one green marble $\frac{8}{9}$ **e.** exactly one red marble $\frac{4}{9}$

38. Three coins are tossed. Find the probability of obtaining the following.
    a. at least two heads $\frac{1}{2}$ **b.** three heads $\frac{1}{8}$ **c.** no heads $\frac{1}{8}$
    d. at most two tails $\frac{7}{8}$ **e.** exactly one head $\frac{3}{8}$

C 39. You have one penny, one nickel, one dime, and one quarter in your pocket. You select two coins at random. What is the probability that you have taken at least 25¢ from your pocket? $\frac{1}{2}$

Review Exercises

Evaluate each expression using the given values of the variable.

$1 - x$

   1. $x = 1$ 0   **2.** $x = \frac{1}{2}$ $\frac{1}{2}$ **3.** $x = \frac{2}{3}$ $\frac{1}{3}$ **4.** $x = -\frac{2}{1}$

$\dfrac{x}{1 - x}$

   5. $x = \frac{1}{3}$ $\frac{1}{2}$ **6.** $x = \frac{2}{3}$ 2   **7.** $x = \frac{3}{7}$ $\frac{3}{4}$ **8.** $x = \frac{4}{7}$ $\frac{4}{3}$

Statistics and Probability   **465**

Suggested Assignments

Core
  464/1–35 odd
  465/37
  465/Rev. 1–4

Enriched
  464/8–28 even; 29–36
  465/38, 39
  465/Rev. 1–4

Supplementary Materials

Practice Masters, p. 56

Teaching Suggestions
p. 433f

Related Activities p. 433g

Reading Mathematics

Students will learn the meaning of the following mathematical terms in this lesson: *odds in favor, odds against.*
    Students with an interest in sports may know something about odds. If so, ask them to explain how odds are used to rate the likelihood of a given athlete's or team's winning.

Chalkboard Examples

A jar contains 3 red beans, 3 white beans, and 2 brown beans.

1. How many beans are not red? 5

2. How many beans are there altogether? 8

3. A bean is chosen at random. Find the probability that the bean is
    a. red $\frac{3}{8}$
    b. not red $\frac{5}{8}$
    c. red or brown $\frac{5}{8}$

4. A bean is chosen at random. Find the odds in favor of the bean being
    a. red 3 to 5
    b. white 3 to 5
    c. brown 1 to 3
    d. not red 5 to 3

12-9 Odds in Favor and Odds Against

EXAMPLE 1   A game is played with the spinner shown at the right. To win the game, the pointer must stop on a wedge that shows a prime number. Find each probability.
a. You win.   **b.** You do not win.

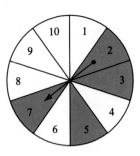

Solution   There are 10 possible outcomes.
               For you to win, the pointer must stop on
               2, 3, 5, or 7. Therefore:

   a. $P(\text{win}) = \frac{4}{10} = \frac{2}{5}$

   b. $P(\text{not win}) = \frac{6}{10} = \frac{3}{5}$

Example 1 illustrates this general fact:

> If the probability that an event occurs is p, then the probability that the event does not occur is $1 - p$.

   In Example 1 there are 4 ways of winning and 6 ways of not winning. We therefore say:

a. The *odds in favor* of winning are 4 to 6, or 2 to 3.

b. The *odds against* winning are 6 to 4, or 3 to 2.

> ### *Formula*
> If the probability that an event occurs is p (where $p \neq 0$ and $p \neq 1$), then:
>
>   Odds in favor of the event $= \dfrac{p}{1 - p}$
>
>   Odds against the event $= \dfrac{1 - p}{p}$

   Odds are usually expressed in the form "x to y," where x and y are integers having no common factor.

466   *Chapter 12*

EXAMPLE 2   Find the odds (a) in favor of and (b) against rolling a sum of 6 with two game cubes.

Solution   From the array of possible outcomes, we see that:

$$P(\text{sum} = 6) = \frac{5}{36} = p$$

$$P(\text{sum} \neq 6) = 1 - p = 1 - \frac{5}{36} = \frac{31}{36}$$

a. Odds in favor $= \dfrac{p}{1-p}$

$$\frac{\frac{5}{36}}{\frac{31}{36}} = \frac{5}{36} \div \frac{31}{36} = \frac{5}{36} \times \frac{36}{31} = \frac{5}{31}$$

Odds in favor are 5 to 31.

b. Odds against are 31 to 5.

EXAMPLE 3   The chance of rain tomorrow is 40%. What are the odds against its raining?

Solution   The probability of rain is $p = 40\% = 0.4$.

Odds against rain $= \dfrac{1-p}{p} = \dfrac{1-0.4}{0.4} = \dfrac{0.6}{0.4} = \dfrac{3}{2}$

Odds against rain are 3 to 2.

Class Exercises

1. The chance of rain tomorrow is 20%. Find the odds against rain. 4 to 1

2. Find the odds against rolling a 4 with one game cube. 5 to 1

Exercises 3–6 refer to the spinner at the right. Find the odds (a) in favor of and (b) against the pointer stopping on a wedge of the type described.

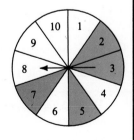

3. an odd number 1 to 1; 1 to 1   **4.** a multiple of 3 3 to 7; 7 to 3

5. a factor of 10 2 to 3; 3 to 2   **6.** a number less than 7 3 to 2; 2 to 3

7. The odds are 1 to 1 that an event will occur. What is the probability that the event will occur? $\frac{1}{2}$

8. The probability that an event will occur is $\frac{1}{2}$. What are the odds against the event? 1 to 1

Statistics and Probability   **467**

A collector has 12 pennies marked D, 5 marked S, and 3 that are not marked with a letter. A penny is picked at random from the collection. Find the odds (a) in favor, and (b) against, picking a penny of the type described.

1. D 3 to 2, 2 to 3
2. S 1 to 3, 3 to 1
3. unmarked 3 to 17, 17 to 3
4. not S 3 to 1, 1 to 3
5. not D 2 to 3, 3 to 2
6. S or D 17 to 3, 3 to 17

Written Exercises

Exercises 1–6 refer to a bag containing 6 red, 2 white, and 4 blue marbles. Find the odds in favor of drawing a marble of the type described.

A

1. red 1 to 1
2. white 1 to 5
3. blue 1 to 2
4. white or blue 1 to 1
5. blue or red 5 to 1
6. red or white 2 to 1

7. The chance of rain tomorrow is 60%. What are the odds against rain? 2 to 3

8. The probability that the Lions football team will win the next game is 0.6. What are the odds that it will win? 3 to 2

9. The Student Union Party has a 30% chance of winning in the next school election. What are the odds against its winning? 7 to 3

In Exercises 10–15 a card has been drawn at random from the 20 cards that are shown. Find the odds against drawing a card of the type described.

10. an A 3 to 1
11. a blue card 1 to 1
12. a red card 1 to 1
13. a C 3 to 1
14. a 1, 2, or 3 2 to 3
15. B2, B3, B4, or B5 4 to 1

Two game cubes are rolled. Find the odds against obtaining the sum described.

16. 7 5 to 1
17. 11 17 to 1
18. 7 or 11 7 to 2
19. 2 or 12 17 to 1
20. greater than 7 7 to 5
21. less than 6 13 to 5

B

22. **a.** even 1 to 1   **b.** odd 1 to 1

23. **a.** divisible by 3 2 to 1   **b.** not divisible by 3 1 to 2

The two game cubes are rolled again. Find the odds in favor of the event described.

24. Exactly one 5 shows. 5 to 13
25. At least one 5 shows. 11 to 25
26. Two even numbers show. 1 to 3
27. At least one odd number shows. 3 to 1

C **28.** The odds in favor of the Melodies winning the music competition are 5 to 3. What is the probability that the Melodies will win? $\frac{5}{8}$

29. The odds in favor of drawing a red marble at random from a bag of marbles are 1 to 8. What is the probability of drawing a red marble? $\frac{1}{9}$

Review Exercises

Perform the indicated operations. Simplify.

1. $\frac{5}{6} + \frac{7}{12} - \frac{11}{24}$ $\frac{23}{24}$ **2.** $\frac{7}{8} + \frac{15}{16} - \frac{7}{24}$ $1\frac{25}{48}$ **3.** $\frac{11}{20} + \frac{9}{10} - \frac{8}{15}$ $\frac{11}{12}$ **4.** $\frac{5}{9} + \frac{25}{27} - \frac{71}{81}$ $\frac{49}{81}$

5. $\frac{17}{18} - \frac{2}{3} + \frac{5}{12}$ $\frac{25}{36}$ **6.** $\frac{37}{40} - \frac{41}{60} + \frac{11}{12}$ $1\frac{19}{120}$ **7.** $\frac{11}{14} - \frac{17}{28} + \frac{9}{49}$ $\frac{71}{196}$ **8.** $\frac{7}{9} - \frac{5}{12} + \frac{13}{18}$ $1\frac{1}{12}$

 | **Computer Byte**

If we toss a coin, there are two possible outcomes—a head or a tail. If these two outcomes are equally likely, then the probability of each is $\frac{1}{2}$. Does this mean that if we toss a coin 10 times, we will get 5 heads and 5 tails? (Not necessarily.)

The following program will simulate tossing a coin. The program is based on a list of "random numbers" that are decimals between 0 and 1. (Usage of the RND function varies. Check this program with the manual for the computer that you are using, and make any necessary changes.)

```
10   PRINT "HOW MANY TOSSES";
20   INPUT N
30   LET H = 0
40   FOR I = 1 to N
50   LET A = RND (1)
60   IF A < .5 THEN 90
70   PRINT TAB( 6);"TAIL"
80   GOTO 110
90   LET H = H + 1
100   PRINT "HEAD"
110   NEXT I
120   PRINT
130   PRINT "H = ";H; TAB( 10);"T = ";N - H;
140   PRINT  TAB( 20);"H/N = ";H/N
150   END
```

1. Run the program 10 times for N = 25.
   a. For how many runs was $0.45 < H/N < 0.55$? Answers may vary.
   b. What percent was this?

Statistics and Probability   **469**

Suggested Assignments

Core
  468/1–23
  469/Rev. 2–8 even
  469/Computer Byte

Enriched
Day 1: 468/1–21 odd; 22–27
Day 2: 469/28, 29
     469/Rev. 3–8
     469/Computer Byte

Supplementary Materials

Practice Masters, p. 56

Teaching Suggestions
p. 433g

Related Activities p. 433h

Reading Mathematics

Students will learn the meaning of the following mathematical term in this lesson:
mutually exclusive.

Chalkboard Examples

Two game cubes are tossed.
One is red, the other green.
Are events *A* and *B* mutually
exclusive?

1. *A:* The total is even.
   B: The total is odd. **Yes**

2. *A:* The green cube shows
   2.
   B: The total is 8. **No**

3. *A:* The red cube shows 6.
   B: The total is 6. **Yes**

4. *A:* The green cube shows
   3.
   B: The red cube shows
   4. **No**

A and *B* are mutually exclusive events. Complete.

5. $P(A \text{ and } B) = \underline{}$ **0**

6. If $P(A) = \frac{1}{5}$ and

   $P(A \text{ or } B) = \frac{7}{10}$, then

   $P(B) = \underline{}$. **$\frac{1}{2}$**

7. If $P(A) = P(B) = \frac{3}{8}$, then

   $P(A \text{ or } B) = \underline{}$. **$\frac{3}{4}$**

12-10 Mutually Exclusive Events

The pointer shown at the right stops at random but not on a
division line. Consider the following events.

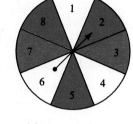

   R: The pointer stops on a red wedge.

   B: The pointer stops on a blue wedge.

   O: The pointer stops on an odd-numbered wedge.

   E: The pointer stops on an even-numbered wedge.

   Events *R* and *B* cannot both occur at once. Such events are said to
be **mutually exclusive.** Notice that events *B* and *E* are *not* mutually
exclusive because they both occur when the pointer stops on a blue
wedge that is even-numbered.

   In the spinner above, five of the eight wedges are colored red or
blue. Therefore,

$$P(R \text{ or } B) = \frac{5}{8}.$$

Notice that

$$P(R) = \frac{1}{4}, \ P(B) = \frac{3}{8}, \text{ and } P(R) + P(B) = \frac{1}{4} + \frac{3}{8} = \frac{5}{8}.$$

Thus, $P(R \text{ or } B) = P(R) + P(B)$.

If *A* and *B* are mutually exclusive events, then

$$P(A \text{ or } B) = P(A) + P(B)$$

EXAMPLE The probability that a randomly chosen car is green is 0.15 and that it
is red is 0.25.
a. Find the probability that the next car you see will be red or green.
b. Find the odds against its being red or green.

Solution **a.** The events described are mutually exclusive. Thus,

$$P(\text{red or green}) = P(\text{red}) + P(\text{green})$$
$$= 0.25 + 0.15 = 0.40$$

The probability that the next car will be red or green is 40%.

b. Odds against red or green $= \frac{1 - 0.40}{0.40} = \frac{0.6}{0.4} = \frac{3}{2}$

The odds against the next car's being red or green are 3 to 2.

470 *Chapter 12*

Class Exercises

Are events *A* and *B* mutually exclusive?

1. You take a test. **Yes**
   A: You pass it.
   B: You fail it.

2. You take a test. **No**
   A: You score less than 9.
   B: You score more than 6.

3. Two coins are tossed. **Yes**
   A: Two heads result.
   B: Two tails result.

4. Two game cubes are rolled. **Yes**
   A: The sum is 5.
   B: A 5 shows on one cube.

5. Two game cubes are rolled. **Yes**
   A: Cubes show the same number.
   B: The sum is 7.

6. Two game cubes are rolled. **No**
   A: Cubes show the same number.
   B: The sum is 8.

***A* and *B* are mutually exclusive events. Find *P(A or B)*.**

7. $P(A) = \frac{1}{4}$, $P(B) = \frac{3}{8}$ $\frac{5}{8}$

8. $P(A) = 0.2$, $P(B) = 0.5$ **0.7**

9. $P(A) = \frac{1}{2}$ and $P(B) = \frac{2}{3}$. Are *A* and *B* mutually exclusive events? **No**

Written Exercises

Solve. *A* and *B* are mutually exclusive events.

A   **1.** $P(A) = \frac{1}{5}$, $P(B) = \frac{2}{3}$. Find $P(A \text{ or } B)$. $\frac{13}{15}$

2. $P(A) = 0.32$, $P(B) = 0.45$. Find $P(A \text{ or } B)$. **0.77**

3. $P(A) = 0.4$, $P(A \text{ or } B) = 0.7$. Find $P(B)$. **0.3**

4. $P(B) = \frac{1}{3}$, $P(A \text{ or } B) = \frac{3}{4}$. Find $P(A)$. $\frac{5}{12}$

In Exercises 5–10, find the probability that the pointer stops on a wedge of the type described.

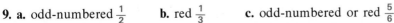

5. a. red $\frac{1}{3}$ **b.** white $\frac{1}{2}$ **c.** red or white $\frac{5}{6}$

6. a. blue $\frac{1}{6}$ **b.** red $\frac{1}{3}$ **c.** blue or red $\frac{1}{2}$

7. a. blue $\frac{1}{6}$ **b.** not blue $\frac{5}{6}$

8. a. white $\frac{1}{2}$ **b.** not white $\frac{1}{2}$

9. a. odd-numbered $\frac{1}{2}$ **b.** red $\frac{1}{3}$ **c.** odd-numbered or red $\frac{5}{6}$

10. a. odd-numbered $\frac{1}{2}$ **b.** blue $\frac{1}{6}$ **c.** odd-numbered or blue $\frac{2}{3}$

Statistics and Probability   **471**

Additional A Exercises

A and *B* are mutually exclusive events. Complete.

1. If $P(A) = \frac{1}{4}$ and $P(B) = \frac{1}{2}$, then $P(A \text{ or } B) = \underline{\quad?\quad}$. $\frac{3}{4}$

2. If $P(A \text{ or } B) = 0.83$ and $P(B) = 0.59$, then $P(A) = \underline{\quad?\quad}$. **0.24**

3. If $P(A) = P(B)$ and $P(A \text{ or } B) = 0.48$, then $P(B) = \underline{\quad?\quad}$. **0.24**

4. If $P(A) = P(B) = \frac{5}{12}$, then $P(A \text{ or } B) = \underline{\quad?\quad}$. $\frac{5}{6}$

Exercises 11–15 refer to the cards at the right. Find the probability that a card drawn at random is of the type described.

A 1	A 2	A 3	A 4	A 5
B 1	B 2	B 3	B 4	B 5
C 1	C 2	C 3	C 4	C 5
D 1	D 2	D 3	D 4	D 5

11. **a.** a 5 $\frac{1}{5}$ **b.** less than 3 $\frac{2}{5}$
   c. a 5 or less than 3 $\frac{3}{5}$

12. **a.** a 2 $\frac{1}{5}$ **b.** greater than 3 $\frac{2}{5}$
   c. a 2 or greater than 3 $\frac{3}{5}$

13. **a.** a D $\frac{1}{4}$ **b.** a red card greater than 2 $\frac{3}{10}$
   c. a D or a red card greater than 2 $\frac{11}{20}$

14. **a.** a B $\frac{1}{4}$ **b.** a blue card greater than 3 $\frac{1}{5}$
   c. a B or a blue card greater than 3 $\frac{9}{20}$

15. **a.** a C $\frac{1}{4}$ **b.** a red card less than 4 $\frac{3}{10}$
   c. a C or a red card less than 4 $\frac{11}{20}$

Two game cubes are rolled. Find the probability of the event described.

B 16. **a.** The sum is 5. $\frac{1}{9}$
   b. A 5 shows. $\frac{11}{36}$
   c. Neither is the sum 5 nor does a 5 show. $\frac{7}{12}$

17. **a.** The sum is 4. $\frac{1}{12}$
   b. A 6 shows. $\frac{11}{36}$
   c. Neither is the sum 4 nor does a 6 show. $\frac{11}{18}$

18. **a.** The sum is 9. $\frac{1}{9}$
   b. The roll is a double (for example, ⬜3⬜ ⬜3⬜). $\frac{1}{6}$
   c. The sum is 9 or a double is rolled. $\frac{5}{18}$

19. **a.** The sum is 7. $\frac{1}{6}$
   b. The roll is a double. $\frac{1}{6}$
   c. The sum is 7 or a double is rolled. $\frac{1}{3}$

20. Joe's batting average (the probability of his getting a hit) is 0.350. What are the odds against his getting a hit? 13 to 7

21. The probability of Jan's team winning the next softball game is 55%. Find the odds that the team will lose. 9 to 11

C 22. The probability that the next soup ordered will be chicken is 0.45; that it will be tomato is 0.35. What are the odds against its being chicken or tomato? 1 to 4

23. At West High School the probability that a randomly chosen student is a senior is 0.20. The probability that the student is a junior is 0.25. Find the odds against the student's being a junior or senior.
   11 to 9

472   *Chapter 12*

A sightseer at Breathless Gorge dropped his sandwich from a gondola. The object fell at the rate of 9.8 meters per second (m/s) after the first second, 19.6 m/s after the second second, and 29.4 m/s after the third second. How fast will the sandwich be falling at 4 s? **39.2 m/s**

A card is drawn. Find the probability of drawing the kind of card described.

Self-Test B

1. In how many different ways can you arrange 4 boxes side by side on a shelf? **24** [12-6]

2. How many different three-digit numbers can you make with the digits 1, 2, 3, 4, and 5 if no digit appears more than once in each number? **60**

3. How many combinations of 3 letters can be chosen from the letters A, B, C, D, and E? **10** [12-7]

4. In how many ways can a committee of 2 people be selected from a group of 15 people? **105**

Find the probability that the pointer on the spinner shown at the right stops on a wedge of the type described.

5. 3 $\frac{1}{8}$ 6. odd-numbered $\frac{1}{2}$ [12-8]

7. red $\frac{1}{4}$ 8. a number less than 9 **1**

9. What are the odds in favor of the pointer on the spinner shown stopping on a wedge with a number greater than 6? **1 to 3** [12-9]

10. What are the odds against the pointer on the spinner shown stopping on a blue wedge? **3 to 1**

11. The probability of snow next week is 75%. What are the odds in favor of snow? **3 to 1**

12. Events *A* and *B* are mutually exclusive. $P(A) = \frac{5}{12}$. $P(B) = \frac{1}{6}$. Find $P(A \text{ or } B)$. $\frac{7}{12}$ [12-10]

13. Events *A* and *B* are mutually exclusive. $P(A) = 0.5$. $P(A \text{ or } B) = 0.7$. Find $P(B)$. **0.2**

5. blue $\frac{1}{2}$

6. red $\frac{1}{2}$

7. not a star $\frac{2}{3}$

8. star $\frac{1}{3}$

9. What are the odds in favor of drawing a blue triangle from the cards above? **1 to 5**

10. What are the odds against drawing a star? **2 to 1**

11. Events *A* and *B* are mutually exclusive. $P(A) = 0.45$. $P(A \text{ or } B) = 0.8$. Find $P(B)$. **0.35**

Self-Test answers and Extra Practice are at the back of the book.

Statistics and Probability **473**

Suggested Assignments

Core
Day 1: 471/1–10
        472/11–16
Day 2: 472/18, 20
        473/Self-Test B

Enriched
Day 1: 471/2–10 even
        472/12, 14; 16–23
Day 2: 473/Challenge
        473/Self-Test B

Supplementary Materials

Practice Masters, p. 56
Test 12B, pp. 81–82

Enrichment Note

To describe a set of data, we use two kinds of statistics: those that measure central tendency, such as the mean and median, and those that measure dispersion, or spread. A measure of each kind is necessary for an adequate characterization of the data.

As the examples on page 474 show, widely different data sets can have the same mean and range. In fact, the range is of such limited use that it is seldom considered to be of real interest.

To provide a more useful measure of dispersion, we are led to the progressively more useful and sophisticated measures called deviation, variance, and standard deviation. Each of these statistics was derived as a means of expressing the difference, on the average, of the individual data values and the average, or mean, value.

The deviation is not a useful approach to describing dispersion. Because positive and negative values can counter each other, a widely dispersed set of data can have a deceptively small total deviation. No such problem exists with the variance. Since deviations are squared, there is no cancelling of positive and negative deviations. A new problem arises, however, because the units of the variance are not consistent with those of the original data. The standard deviation is found by taking the square root of the variance; thus we return to the same unit used with the original data.

If students study statistics later, they will find that the mean and the standard deviation are the two statistics

(Continue on next page.)

Standard Deviation

For many purposes the *range* of a set of data is a poor measure of its spread. Consider, for example, the frequency distributions and histograms below for the mass in kilograms of various rocks found by three groups of rock collectors.

Group A		Group B		Group C	
Mass (kg)	Frequency	Mass (kg)	Frequency	Mass (kg)	Frequency
1	4	1	1	1	1
3	1	3	3	3	2
7	1	5	2	5	4
9	4	7	3	7	2
		9	1	9	1

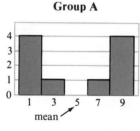

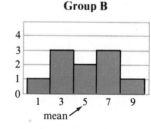

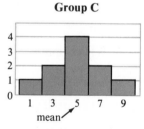

Each distribution has a range of 8. But a glance at each histogram reveals that distribution A is more spread out around its center, or mean, than are distributions B and C.

A more useful measure of the spread of a distribution is the **deviation** from the mean. Suppose a bowler has scores of 198, 210, and 156. The mean score is 188. The table at the right shows how much each score varies, or *deviates*, from the mean.

Score	Deviation
198	+10
210	+22
156	−32

The **variance** and **standard deviation** are two commonly used measures of how data are scattered around the mean. The variance is com-

474 *Chapter 12*

puted by squaring each deviation from the mean, adding these squares, and dividing the sum by the number of entries in the distribution. The standard deviation is found by computing the positive square root of the variance. The standard deviation is a more useful statistic than the variance because comparisons are being made of common units. For example, when data are given in meters, the variance will be in square meters, but the standard deviation will be in meters.

The table below shows the calculation of the variance and standard deviation for each frequency distribution on the preceding page. In each case, x is the mass and m is the mean, which is 5. Notice that the more a distribution is spread out from its mean, the larger its standard deviation.

Group A			Group B			Group C		
	deviation			deviation			deviation	
x	$(x - m)$	$(x - m)^2$	x	$(x - m)$	$(x - m)^2$	x	$(x - m)$	$(x - m)^2$
1	−4	16	1	−4	16	1	−4	16
1	−4	16	3	−2	4	3	−2	4
1	−4	16	3	−2	4	3	−2	4
1	−4	16	3	−2	4	5	0	0
3	−2	4	5	0	0	5	0	0
7	2	4	5	0	0	5	0	0
9	4	16	7	2	4	5	0	0
9	4	16	7	2	4	7	2	4
9	4	16	7	2	4	7	2	4
9	4	16	9	4	16	9	4	16
		136 kg²			56 kg²			48 kg²

variance $= \frac{136}{10} = 13.6$ kg²   variance $= \frac{56}{10} = 5.6$ kg²   variance $= \frac{48}{10} = 4.8$ kg²

standard
deviation $= \sqrt{13.6}$
≈ 3.7 kg

standard
deviation $= \sqrt{5.6}$
≈ 2.4 kg

standard
deviation $= \sqrt{4.8}$
≈ 2.2 kg

Find (a) the mean, (b) the deviation, (c) the variance, and (d) the standard deviation of the given data. Use the table on page 508, or approximate the square root to the nearest hundredth by interpolation.

1. From a sample of four dairy cows, a farmer recorded the following yields for one day: 11 gal, 13 gal, 9 gal, and 15 gal.
   a. 12 gal   b. −1, 1, −3, 3   c. 5 gal²   d. 2.24 gal
2. In a survey of local stores, the following prices were quoted for a World watch: $34, $27, $41, and $38.
   a. $35   b. −1, −8, 6, 3   c. $27.5 dollars²   d. $5.24
3. The fuel efficiency ratings of five new cars were 20, 19, 20, 22, and 33 mi/gal.   a. 22.8 mi/gal   b. −2.8, −3.8, −2.8, −0.8, 10.2
   c. 26.96 (mi/gal)²   d. 5.19 mi/gal

Statistics and Probability **475**

most frequently used to describe data. In fact, for a normal distribution (a bell curve) the mean and standard deviation together give a complete characterization of the data.

Rather than squaring the deviations we could use their absolute values. The mean of these absolute values is called the average deviation. It is much less widely used than the standard deviation in advanced work.

Students are sometimes intimidated by the elaborate calculations needed to figure a standard deviation. This would be an excellent place to suggest the use of a calculator or computer. The calculations may be arduous, but the procedure, or algorithm, is straightforward. We repeat the same sequence of operations over and over. This makes the standard deviation a prime candidate for a computer program in BASIC; this should be within the ability of an able student.

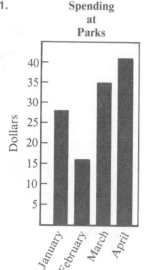
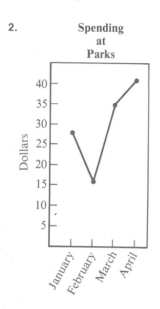
Chapter Review

Complete.
Refer to the bar graph for Exercises 1-3.

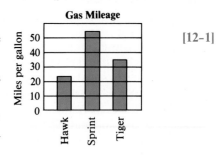

Gas Mileage

1. The car with the best gas mileage is the
_____?_____ . Sprint   [12-1]

2. The Tiger gets approximately __?__ miles
per gallon. 35

3. If we join the midpoints of the tops of the
bars in the bar graph, we obtain a ____?____
graph. broken-line

4. To show on a circle graph that 25% of a team is in the seventh grade,   [12-2]
you would use a wedge of a circle that has an angle measure of __?__
degrees. 90

Use the data 65, 67, 67, 69, 70, 73 for Exercises 5-9.

5. The range is __?__ . 8   **6.** The median is __?__ . 68   [12-3]

7. The mean is __?__ . 68.5   **8.** The mode is __?__ . 67   [12-4]

9. The frequency of 67 is __?__ . 2

Refer to the frequency table for Exercises 10 and 11.

10. If you drew a histogram   [12-5]
for the data, the tallest bar
would represent __?__ . 60¢

11. The range of the data is
__?__ . 3

Cost of a Quart of Milk			
Price	59¢	60¢	61¢	62¢
Frequency	4	5	2	1

True or false?

12. You can arrange the letters in the word DRAW in 4 different ways if   [12-6]
you take the letters 3 at a time. False

13. A group of 3 people can be selected from 8 people in 56 ways. True   [12-7]

14. When a single game cube is rolled, the probability that the roll   [12-8]
shows a number greater than 3 is $\frac{1}{2}$. True

15. The odds in favor of rolling a 2 with a single game cube are 1 to 5. True   [12-9]

16. The probability of rolling a 3 or a 6 with a single game cube is $\frac{1}{3}$. True   [12-10]

476 *Chapter 12*

Chapter Test

Refer to the bar graph for Exercises 1 and 2.

Boiling Points

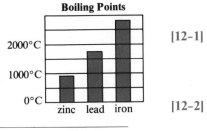

1. Give the approximate boiling points of the three elements. zinc: 900°C; lead: 1750°C; iron: 2800°C   [12–1]

2. Draw a broken-line graph for the data. Check students' graphs.

3. Draw a pictograph for the data below. Check students' graphs.   [12–2]

Number of Shares of Stock Sold

1980	1,546,000	1981	2,341,000
1982	3,995,000	1983	4,784,000

4. Find the mean, the median, and the range of 28, 14, 19, 24, 30.   [12–3]
   23, 24, 16

Refer to the frequency table for Exercises 5–7.

Number of Minutes	Frequency
155	2
158	3
159	1
162	1
163	1
166	2
167	3
168	5

5. Give the mean, the median, the range, and the mode of the data. Round the mean to the nearest tenth.   [12–4]
   163.4, 166, 13, 168

6. Draw a histogram for the data. Check students' graphs.   [12–5]

7. Draw a frequency polygon for the data. Check students' graphs.

Solve.

8. In how many different ways can 3 people sit in a row of 5 seats? 60   [12–6]

9. How many combinations of 3 colors can you choose from 7 colors? 35   [12–7]

Exercises 10–13 refer to the spinner shown below at the right. Find the probability that the pointer will stop on a wedge of the type described.

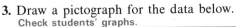

10. blue $\frac{1}{6}$ 11. green 0   [12–8]

12. odd-numbered and red $\frac{1}{3}$

13. What are the odds in favor of the pointer stopping on a red wedge? 1 to 2   [12–9]

14. Events A and B are mutually exclusive. $P(A) = \frac{1}{3}$. $P(B) = \frac{5}{12}$.   [12–10]
    Find $P(A \text{ or } B)$. $\frac{3}{4}$

Statistics and Probability   **477**

Supplementary Materials
Chapter 12 Test, pp. 83–84

3.   **Spending at Parks**

$ = $5.00

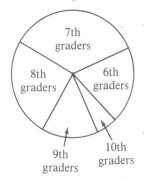

4.   **Kingswood Basketball League**

Review for Retention

1. A parallelogram has length 7 cm and width 4.5 cm. Find the perimeter. **23 cm**

2. Give the measures of the complement and the supplement of $\angle A$ if $m\angle A = 9°$. **81°, 171°**

3. A circle has radius 1.5 m. Find the circumference. Use $\pi \approx 3.14$. **9.42 m**

4. If $\triangle ABC \cong \triangle XYZ$, then $\overline{AC} \cong \underline{\ ?\ }$. $\overline{XZ}$

5. 2500 m = $\underline{\ ?\ }$ km **2.5**

Give the coordinates of the given points. Name the points for the ordered pairs.

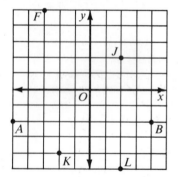

6. A $(-5, -2)$
7. $(-3, 5)$ F
8. J $(2, 2)$
9. L $(2, -5)$
10. $(4, -2)$ B
11. $(-2, -4)$ K

Cumulative Review (Chapters 1–12)

Exercises

Simplify.

1. $5.4 + (7 \times 6.3)$ **49.5**

2. $\dfrac{16 + 9}{32 + 8}$ $\dfrac{5}{8}$

3. $13(9.2 \div 16)$ **7.475**

4. $4x - y + xy + 3y$ $4x + xy + 2y$

5. $2m + 2n - m + n$ $m + 3n$

6. $3p^2(p + 5)$ $3p^3 + 15p^2$

Perform the indicated operation. Write the answer as a proper fraction in lowest terms or as a mixed number in simple form.

7. $\dfrac{3}{5} + \dfrac{4}{7}$ $1\dfrac{6}{35}$

8. $\dfrac{8}{11} - \dfrac{1}{3}$ $\dfrac{13}{33}$

9. $\dfrac{3}{4} \times \dfrac{7}{8}$ $\dfrac{21}{32}$

10. $-1\dfrac{1}{2} \div -2\dfrac{1}{2}$ $\dfrac{3}{5}$

Solve.

11. $6x = -4 + (-18)$ $-3\dfrac{2}{3}$

12. $-3 - 7 = x + 1$ -11

13. $x(4 - 2) = 40$ **20**

14. $x + (-9) > -2$
All the numbers greater than 7.

15. $4 + (-12) \le x - 6$
All the numbers greater than or equal to -2.

16. $11 - x > 0$
All the numbers less than 11.

Find the radius of a circle with the given circumference. Use $\pi \approx \dfrac{22}{7}$.

17. $C = 264$ **42**

18. $C = 343.2$ **54.6**

19. $C = 83.6$ **13.3**

20. $C = 897.6$ **142.8**

Solve.

21. What is 39% of 120? **46.8**

22. What is 125% of 89? **111.25**

23. What percent of 60 is 12? **20%**

24. What percent of 75 is 35? $46\dfrac{2}{3}\%$

25. 18 is 50% of what number? **36**

26. 35 is 8% of what number? **437.5**

Use a straight-line graph to complete the ordered pairs, then find the slope.

27. $A(7, 0)$, $B(5, 1)$, $C(-1, ?)$, $D(?, 7)$ 4 -7
slope = $-\dfrac{1}{2}$

28. $A(0, 0)$, $B(2, 1)$, $C(4, ?)$, $D(?, 3)$ 2   6
slope = $\dfrac{1}{2}$

Find the perimeter and the area of the polygon described.

29. A rectangle with sides 136.5 m and 97.5 m **468 m; 13,308.75 m²**

30. A parallelogram with base 15 cm, one side 7 cm, and height 6 cm **44 cm; 90 cm²**

31. A triangle with base 63 m, sides 51 m and 30 m, and height 24 m **144 m; 756 m²**

Is the triangle with sides of the given lengths a right triangle?

32. 12, 16, 20 **Yes**

33. 4, 6, 9 **No**

34. 9, 12, 15 **Yes**

478   *Chapter 12*

Problems

Problem Solving Reminders

Here are some problem solving reminders that may help you solve some of the problems on this page.

- Some steps in your plan may not involve operations.
- Consider whether a chart will help to organize information.
- Check by using rounding to find an estimated answer.

Solve.

1. Rosalie has 2 ten-dollar bills. She would like to buy a book for $6.95, some puzzles for a total cost of $12.50, and birthday cards for a total cost of $3.60. Does she have enough money? No

2. A faucet leaks at the rate of $\frac{1}{4}$ cup of water per hour. How much water will leak in 24 hours? 6 c

3. A Rosebud rocking chair can be purchased for $245.70 in a furniture store or for $189 at a factory store. What is the percent of markup for the furniture store? 30%

4. In order for two elements to combine, the sum of their valence numbers must be equal to 0. One atom of carbon has a valence number of 4, and one atom of fluorine has a valence number of -1. How many atoms of fluorine are needed to combine with 1 atom of carbon? 4 atoms

5. Find the length of a diagonal of a square if each side of the square has a length of 7 cm. Round to the nearest tenth. 9.9 cm

6. Two cyclists depart at the same time from the same point, traveling in opposite directions. One cyclist travels at a speed of 14 mi/h, while the other cyclist travels at a speed of 16 mi/h. How long must the cyclists travel to be at least 135 mi apart? $4\frac{1}{2}$ h

7. Find the area of a rectangular yard that has one side of length 12 m and perimeter 54 m. 180 m²

8. You can buy whole chickens at Sal's Market for $1.09/lb. For an additional $.25/lb, the butcher will cut up the chicken and remove the bones. If chicken is sold in tenths of a pound, how much boneless chicken can be purchased for $7.50? 5.6 lb

9. A rectangular painting is 5 ft wide and has an area of 15 ft². The frame around the painting is 3 in. wide. What are the dimensions of the framed painting? $5\frac{1}{2}$ ft × $3\frac{1}{2}$ ft

Statistics and Probability **479**

a. Solve the equation for y in terms of x.
b. Find solutions of the equation for the given values of x: $-5, 2, 8$.

12. $5x + y = 15$
$y = 15 - 5x$;
40, 5, -25

13. $-7x + y = 3$
$y = 3 + 7x$;
$-32, 17, 59$

14. $2x = 1 - y$
$y = 1 - 2x$;
11, $-3, -15$

Solve. Give your answer to the nearest tenth.

15. Use the divide-and-average method to approximate $\sqrt{40}$. 6.3

16. Use interpolation and the table on page 508 to approximate $\sqrt{27.5}$. 5.2

17. Use the divide-and-average method to approximate $\sqrt{11}$. 3.3

18. Use interpolation and the table on page 508 to approximate $\sqrt{77.8}$. 8.8

Is the triangle with sides of the given lengths a right triangle?

19. 5, 11, 13 No

20. 8, 15, 17 Yes

21. 6, 7, 9 No

22. 10, 24, 26 Yes

Give answers in terms of radicals with the radical in the numerator.

23. A leg of a 45° right triangle has a length of 17. How long is the hypotenuse? $17\sqrt{2}$

24. In a 30°–60° right triangle, the shorter leg has a length of 11. How long is the hypotenuse? 22

25. In a 30°–60° right triangle, the hypotenuse has a length of 12. How long is the longer leg? $6\sqrt{3}$

Skill Review

Addition

```
  236
    4
  108
+  57
  405


  14.71
   3.009
+ 291.681
  309.400
```

Add.

1. $\begin{array}{r} 84 \\ +\ 15 \\ \hline 99 \end{array}$ **2.** $\begin{array}{r} 46 \\ +\ 32 \\ \hline 78 \end{array}$ **3.** $\begin{array}{r} 25 \\ +\ 18 \\ \hline 43 \end{array}$ **4.** $\begin{array}{r} 59 \\ +\ 16 \\ \hline 75 \end{array}$

5. $\begin{array}{r} 26 \\ +\ 95 \\ \hline 121 \end{array}$ **6.** $\begin{array}{r} 79 \\ +\ 56 \\ \hline 135 \end{array}$ **7.** $\begin{array}{r} 653 \\ +\ 88 \\ \hline 741 \end{array}$ **8.** $\begin{array}{r} 296 \\ +\ 35 \\ \hline 331 \end{array}$

9. $\begin{array}{r} 8.7 \\ +\ 0.5 \\ \hline 9.2 \end{array}$ **10.** $\begin{array}{r} 0.36 \\ +\ 2.44 \\ \hline 2.8 \end{array}$ **11.** $\begin{array}{r} 299.1 \\ +\ 68.33 \\ \hline 367.43 \end{array}$ **12.** $\begin{array}{r} 933.068 \\ +\ 724.3997 \\ \hline 1657.4677 \end{array}$

13. $\begin{array}{r} 5.4 \\ 12.137 \\ 1.25 \\ +\ 306.49 \\ \hline 325.277 \end{array}$ **14.** $\begin{array}{r} 1.6256 \\ 6.006 \\ 9.36 \\ +\ 1.49 \\ \hline 18.4816 \end{array}$ **15.** $\begin{array}{r} 24.603 \\ 18.4 \\ 2.9 \\ +\ 0.216 \\ \hline 46.119 \end{array}$ **16.** $\begin{array}{r} 911.34 \\ 0.52 \\ 26.1 \\ +\ 83.192 \\ \hline 1021.152 \end{array}$

17. 257 + 631 888   **18.** 463 + 451 914   **19.** 358 + 164 522

20. 10.4 + 3.25 13.65   **21.** 19.6 + 0.462 20.062 **22.** 4.78 + 31.1 35.88

23. 5.176 + 2.98 8.156   **24.** 67.4 + 45.93 113.33 **25.** 19.71 + 2.388 22.098

26. 27.0564 + 281.4 308.4564   **27.** 3.51032 + 14.99 18.50032

28. 6.8 + 37.51 + 108.2 152.51   **29.** 89.71 + 5.5 + 0.62 95.83

30. 5326 + 703 + 9427 + 8 15,464   **31.** 1027 + 349 + 8 + 12 1396

32. 16.24 + 5.6 + 18.09 + 6.7 46.63   **33.** 2.55 + 0.34 + 0.42 + 3.57 6.88

34. 61.476 + 14.1 + 0.59 + 366 442.166   **35.** 90.072 + 32.4 + 24 + 8.6 155.072

36. 115 + 20 + 9 + 7603 7747   **37.** 70 + 1328 + 94 + 5 1497

38. 193.7 + 4.08 + 11.5 + 1.9026 211.1826   **39.** 0.428 + 83.7 + 6.999 + 7.06 98.187

40. 29 + 72 + 604 + 396 1101   **41.** 785 + 120 + 7 + 653 1565

42. 356 + 9 + 12 + 2301 2678   **43.** 6 + 24 + 315 + 1409 1754

44. 37.7 + 0.6 + 6.834 + 16 61.134   **45.** 1165 + 0.08 + 17.1 + 94.028 1276.208

46. 570.2 + 74.4 + 6.553 + 9.2 660.353   **47.** 7.8118 + 27.6 + 5.302 + 14 54.7138

Skill Review

Subtraction

```
  630
- 249
  381
```

```
  300.710
-  46.008
  254.702
```

Subtract.

1.
```
  64
- 51
  13
```
2.
```
  98
- 37
  61
```
3.
```
  56
- 30
  26
```
4.
```
  79
- 42
  37
```

5.
```
  896
- 241
  655
```
6.
```
  613
- 402
  211
```
7.
```
  978
- 365
  613
```
8.
```
  784
- 463
  321
```

9.
```
  18.636
- 13.435
   5.201
```
10.
```
  67.86
- 54.22
  13.64
```
11.
```
  27.954
- 16.21
  11.744
```
12.
```
  46.5822
- 24.001
  22.5812
```

13.
```
  8.434
- 6.297
  2.137
```
14.
```
  35.061
-  9.875
  25.186
```
15.
```
  6.952
- 5.06
  1.892
```
16.
```
  583.86
- 279.9
  303.96
```

17.
```
  453
-  17.46
  435.54
```
18.
```
  55.7
-  3.9
  51.8
```
19.
```
  0.081
- 0.007
  0.074
```
20.
```
  2.0056
- 0.918
  1.0876
```

21. 57 − 32 25

22. 86 − 45 41

23. 98 − 36 62

24. 49 − 26 23

25. 78 − 34 44

26. 76 − 65 11

27. 85 − 37 48

28. 42 − 29 13

29. 90 − 57 33

30. 94.7 − 39 55.7

31. 48.08 − 7.95 40.13

32. 279.5 − 33.7 245.8

33. 64.08 − 7.05 57.03

34. 605.01 − 31.23 573.78

35. 0.072 − 0.009 0.063

36. 1314 − 197 1117

37. 6240 − 3078 3162

38. 8521 − 2364 6157

39. 7017 − 3468 3549

40. 4320 − 2006 2314

41. 9481 − 2556 6925

42. 22.916 − 17.4 5.516

43. 25.006 − 3.98 21.026

44. 518.2 − 327.41 190.79

45. 2.7736 − 0.1531 2.6205

46. 800.6 − 315 485.6

47. 0.9001 − 0.035 0.8651

48. 207.001 − 44.62 162.381

49. 91.003 − 17.6 73.403

50. 23,025 − 18,769 4256

51. 55,317 − 40,769 14,548

Skill Review

Multiplication

476
×15
———
2380
476
———
7140

341.6 1 place
×0.27 2 places
———
23912
6832
———
92.232 3 places

Multiply.

1. 13
×2
——
26

2. 21
×4
——
84

3. 53
×3
——
159

4. 64
×2
——
128

5. 47
×3
——
141

6. 16
×5
——
80

7. 90
×4
——
360

8. 34
×6
——
204

9. 84
×12
——
1008

10. 63
×23
——
1449

11. 71
×65
——
4615

12. 40
×31
——
1240

13. 785
×1.2
——
942

14. 6.61
×3
——
19.83

15. 808
×17.2
——
13,897.6

16. 22.5
×8.9
——
200.25

17. 89.06
×0.5
——
44.53

18. 37.5
×0.28
——
10.5

19. 212.8
×0.67
——
142.576

20. 93.65
×4.11
——
384.9015

21. 20 × 30 600

22. 60 × 50 3000

23. 10 × 90 900

24. 50 × 700 35,000

25. 900 × 80 72,000

26. 600 × 80 48,000

27. 3400 × 200 680,000

28. 400 × 1500 600,000

29. 300 × 470 141,000

30. 18 × 345 6210

31. 563 × 27 15,201

32. 99 × 198 19,602

33. 314 × 16 5024

34. 408 × 70 28,560

35. 923 × 60 55,380

36. 11.6 × 38.51 446.716

37. 47.3 × 6.05 286.165

38. 86.9 × 121.75 10,580.075

39. 36.91 × 0.51 18.8241

40. 8.05 × 0.003 0.02415

41. 20.35 × 3.7 75.295

42. 854.6 × 2.19 1871.574

43. 41.6 × 212.5 8840

44. 5129.36 × 0.008 41.03488

45. 85.004 × 93.11 7914.7224

46. 9.8413 × 16.55 162.873515

47. 3.7509 × 0.031 0.1162779

48. 83.751 × 98.230 8226.86073

49. 251 × 0.0074 1.8574

50. 326.11 × 7.001 2283.09611

51. 0.8612 × 0.0101 0.00869812

Skill Review

Division

```
    12.51
6.8)85.068
    68
    170
    136
    346
    340
     68
     68
      0
```

Divide.

1. $5\overline{)85}$ → 17

2. $8\overline{)96}$ → 12

3. $2\overline{)92}$ → 46

4. $13\overline{)273}$ → 21

5. $32\overline{)512}$ → 16

6. $17\overline{)714}$ → 42

7. $4\overline{)140.8}$ → 35.2

8. $7\overline{)160.3}$ → 22.9

9. $18\overline{)13.68}$ → 0.76

10. $5.06\overline{)480.7}$ → 95

11. $3.8\overline{)59.66}$ → 15.7

12. $8.1\overline{)423.63}$ → 52.3

Divide. Round to the nearest tenth if necessary.

13. $8\overline{)86}$ → 10.8

14. $6\overline{)50}$ → 8.3

15. $4\overline{)63}$ → 15.8

16. $49\overline{)172}$ → 3.5

17. $32\overline{)424}$ → 13.3

18. $26\overline{)817}$ → 31.4

19. $7.3\overline{)4001}$ → 548.1

20. $6.9\overline{)117}$ → 17.0

21. $0.56\overline{)27.8}$ → 49.6

To round a quotient to a particular place, divide to one place beyond the place specified and then round.

```
      22.988
2.71)62.30000
     54 2
      8 10
      5 42
      2 680
      2 439
        2410
        2168
        2420
        2168
         252
```

Rounded to the nearest hundredth the quotient is 22.99.

Divide. Round to the nearest hundredth if necessary.

22. $315 \div 9$ 35

23. $513 \div 7$ 73.29

24. $536 \div 8$ 67

25. $405 \div 5$ 81

26. $341 \div 6$ 56.83

27. $11 \div 4$ 2.75

28. $3775 \div 15.6$ 241.99

29. $6.3 \div 2.4$ 2.63

30. $11.9 \div 4.6$ 2.59

31. $276 \div 37.5$ 7.36

32. $88.01 \div 0.6$ 146.68

33. $764 \div 0.4$ 1910

34. $21.6 \div 28$ 0.77

35. $12.75 \div 51$ 0.25

36. $1066 \div 27$ 39.48

37. $17,063 \div 33$ 517.06

38. $24,474 \div 60$ 407.9

39. $19,412 \div 0.15$ 129,413.33

40. $1.0472 \div 0.66$ 1.59

41. $565.28 \div 11.8$ 47.91

42. $47.611 \div 0.4$ 119.03

43. $29,919 \div 56$ 534.27

44. $15,960 \div 38$ 420

45. $23,674 \div 77$ 307.45

46. $11,500 \div 25$ 460

47. $21,984 \div 36$ 610.67

48. $87,048 \div 403$ 216

49. $186.22 \div 0.038$ 4900.53

50. $28,400 \div 75$ 378.67

51. $1234.5 \div 67$ 18.43

52. $8.7553 \div 0.47$ 18.63

53. $96.14 \div 0.026$ 3697.69

54. $0.054 \div 1.86$ 0.03

55. $0.0269 \div 4.001$ 0.01

56. $365.4 \div 74.1$ 4.93

57. $11.99 \div 0.121$ 99.09

Extra Practice: Chapter 1

Simplify the numerical expression.

1. $44.23 - 1.6$ 42.63

2. 83×6 498

3. $4.80 \div 30$ 0.16

4. $74 + 116$ 190

Evaluate the expression when $d = 6$ and $y = 4$.

5. $y - 3$ 1

6. $d + d$ 12

7. $2y \times 3$ 24

8. $y + d + 2$ 12

Simplify the numerical expression.

9. $18 \div (2 \times 3) + 6$ 9

10. $5 \times (5 - 2) \div 3$ 5

11. $\dfrac{8 - 2 \times 3}{(6 - 4)(5 + 1)}$ $\frac{1}{6}$

Evaluate the expression when $x = 4.2$ and $y = 9$.

12. $4(x + y)$ 52.8

13. $5y - x$ 40.8

14. $(y - x)(x + y)$ 63.36

Evaluate the expression when $a = 5$ and $b = 10$.

15. $3a - \dfrac{a}{5}$ 14

16. $a(b - 2) \div 3$ $13\frac{1}{3}$

17. $\dfrac{ab - 20}{a + b}$ 2

Evaluate.

18. 3^4 81

19. 13^2 169

20. 25^3 15,625

21. 34^2 1156

22. 17^3 4913

23. 7^5 16,807

24. 30^3 27,000

25. 9^4 6561

Multiply.

26. $9^2 \times 3^4$ 6561

27. $10^3 \times 2^4$ 16,000

28. $7^3 \times 13^2$ 57,967

29. $15^3 \times 4^5$ 3,456,000

30. $6^3 \times 100^2$ 2,160,000

31. $4^3 \times 1^5$ 64

32. $2^5 \times 11^3$ 42,592

33. $3^3 \times 2^6$ 1728

Write the decimal in expanded form.

34. 734

35. 516.21

36. 0.024

37. 25.2

38. 2138

39. 91.9

40. 0.38

41. 307.009

Write as a decimal.

42. 18 and 21 hundredths 18.21

43. 5 and 4 thousandths 5.004

44. 242 and 6 tenths 242.6

45. 9 and 9 ten-thousandths 9.0009

46. 85 thousandths 0.085

47. 6 ten-thousandths 0.0006

Round to the place specified.

48. hundreds; 871.21 900

49. tenths; 113.93 113.9

50. thousandths; 1.00414 1.004

484 *Extra Practice*

51. hundredths; 0.0577 0.06   **52.** tens; 382.45 380   **53.** hundredths; 45.552 45.55

54. thousandths; 3.4279 3.428   **55.** hundreds; 84 100   **56.** tenths; 74.991 75.0

What value of the variable makes the statement true?

57. $7.4 \times n = 1.84 \times 7.4$ 1.84   **58.** $6.81 = r + 6.81$ 0

59. $8.726z = z$ 0   **60.** $3.4(5.12 + 9.4) = (5.12 + 9.4)p$ 3.4

61. $(79 \times k) + (79 \times 4) = 79 \times 12$ 8   **62.** $a \times 24.5 = 24.5$ 1

Solve for the given replacement set.

63. $q + 9 = 17$; $\{8, 9, 10\}$ 8   **64.** $b - 12 = 35$; $\{45, 46, 47\}$ 47

65. $x \div 14 = 8$; $\{110, 112, 114\}$ 112   **66.** $53 + m = 66$; $\{13, 15, 17\}$ 13

67. $8f = 56$; $\{5, 6, 7\}$ 7   **68.** $17t = 102$; $\{7, 8, 9\}$ no solution

69. $2g - 8 = 14$; $\{10, 11, 12\}$ 11   **70.** $4(a + 6) = 36$; $\{1, 2, 3\}$ 3

Use inverse operations to solve.

71. $k + 16 = 28$ 12   **72.** $n \div 6 = 122$ 732   **73.** $7p = 217$ 31   **74.** $p - 11 = 41$ 52

75. $m \div 12 = 204$ 2448   **76.** $17 + z = 53$ 36   **77.** $6m = 240$ 40   **78.** $a - 35 = 41$ 76

Solve, using the five-step plan.

79. Recently, Ken ran a 400 m race in 52.3 s. This was 0.2 s slower than the school record. What is the school record? 52.1 s

80. On July 1, Kay had $542.07 in her savings account. On September 1, she had $671.82 in her account. How much did she save between July 1 and September 1? $129.75

81. A machine produces 3 plastic parts each minute that it runs. If the machine runs for 7 h, how many parts will it produce? 1260 parts

82. Exercise World is buying 4 new exercise bicycles for $129.95 each and 6 exercise mats for $47.85 each. What is the total cost? $806.90

Solve and check.

83. John owes Tom $18. John earns $5 an hour and already has $3. How long must John work to earn enough to pay Tom back? 3 h

84. Rosa sells newspapers at the bus stop. If each paper costs $.25, how many must Rosa sell to take in $10? 40 papers

Extra Practice   **485**

Extra Practice: Chapter 2

Express as an integer.

1. $|^-3|$ 3   **2.** $|5|$ 5   **3.** $|1|$ 1   **4.** $|0|$ 0   **5.** $|^-6|$ 6

6. $|4|$ 4   **7.** $|^-2|$ 2   **8.** $|^-7|$ 7   **9.** $|9|$ 9   **10.** $|^-8|$ 8

Graph the number and its opposite on the same number line. Check students' graphs.

11. 6   **12.** $^-9$ **13.** 8   **14.** 5   **15.** $^-1$

Write the integers in order from least to greatest.

16. 0, 4, $^-4$, 3, $^-3$ $^-4, ^-3, 0, 3, 4$

17. 5, 0, $^-2$, $^-8$, 6 $^-8, ^-2, 0, 5, 6$

18. 7, $^-3$, $^-2$, 1, 9 $^-3, ^-2, 1, 7, 9$

19. $^-1$, 3, $^-7$, 5, $^-4$ $^-7, ^-4, ^-1, 3, 5$

20. $^-6$, $^-7$, 0, $^-5$, $^-2$ $^-7, ^-6, ^-5, ^-2, 0$

21. $^-4$, 5, 4, $^-5$, 0 $^-5, ^-4, 0, 4, 5$

Replace __?__ **with =, >, or < to make a true statement.**

22. 31 __?__ 61 <   **23.** 18×4 __?__ 82 <   **24.** 47 __?__ $49 - 9$ >

List the integers that can replace x to make the statement true.

25. $|x| = 5$ $^-5, 5$ **26.** $|x| = 2$ $^-2, 2$ **27.** $|x| = 0$ 0

28. $|x| = 4$ $^-4, 4$ **29.** $|x| \leq 6$ $^-6, ^-5, ^-4, \ldots, 4, 5, 6$ **30.** $|x| \leq 3$ $^-3, ^-2, ^-1, \ldots, 3$

Graph the numbers in each exercise on the same number line. Check students' graphs.

31. 1, $^-1.5$, 0, $^-2$ **32.** $^-2$, $^-4$, 2.5, $^-3.5$ **33.** 3, 1.2, $^-2.4$, $^-5$

34. 7.6, $^-6.7$, 6, $^-7$ **35.** 1, 1.5, $^-2$, 2.5   **36.** 2, $^-1.8$, $^-2.1$, 0

Draw an arrow to represent the decimal number described. Check students' diagrams.

37. The number 5, with starting point $^-4$

38. The number $^-8$, with starting point 6

39. The number 6, with starting point $^-5$

40. The number $^-6$, with starting point 3

Find the sum.

41. $2.7 + 7.2$ 9.9   **42.** $^-4.9 + ^-7.6$ -12.5 **43.** $^-2.25 + 2.25$ 0

44. $^-3.8 + ^-3.8$ -7.6 **45.** $^-148 + ^-256$ -404 **46.** $6.1 + ^-2.3$ 3.8

47. $^-0.6 + ^-2.3$ -2.9 **48.** $18.12 + 1.66$ 19.78   **49.** $^-5.2 + 2.9$ -2.3

50. $^-2.8 + ^-3.9$ -6.7 **51.** $1.9 + 19$ 20.9   **52.** $^-14.75 + 9.94$ -4.81

Find the difference.

53. $30.5 - 18$ 12.5   **54.** $16 - 24.3$ −8.3   **55.** $10.6 - 11.2$ −0.6

56. $16.2 - (-7)$ 23.2   **57.** $5 - (-15.3)$ 20.3   **58.** $18 - (-9.7)$ 27.7

59. $-8.3 - 5.2$ −13.5   **60.** $-7 - 14.6$ −21.6   **61.** $-12.3 - 8$ −20.3

62. $43.4 - (-136)$ 179.4   **63.** $-3 - (-8.2)$ 5.2   **64.** $-12.9 - (-4.5)$ −8.4

Evaluate when $x = -3.2$ and $y = -5.7$.

65. $-y$ 5.7   **66.** $-x$ 3.2   **67.** $-|x|$ −3.2

68. $-|y|$ −5.7   **69.** $y - x$ −2.5   **70.** $-x - y$ 8.9

71. $x - (-y)$ −8.9   **72.** $-x - (-y)$ −2.5   **73.** $-y - (-x)$ 2.5

Find the quotient.

74. $-15.5 \div 0.5$ −31   **75.** $-16.4 \div 4$ −4.1   **76.** $-150 \div 7.5$ −20

77. $36.6 \div -0.06$ −610   **78.** $38 \div -0.4$ −95   **79.** $8.19 \div (-9)$ −0.91

80. $-3.038 \div (-7)$ 0.434   **81.** $-63.7 \div (-0.007)$ 9100   **82.** $-246 \div (-0.6)$ 410

83. $-0.003 \div (1)$ −0.003   **84.** $0 \div (-0.85)$ 0   **85.** $-0.9 \div (-1.8)$ 0.5

Find the product.

86. $2.4(-1.2)$ −2.88   **87.** $-1.4(3.4)$ −4.76   **88.** $4.5(-1.7)$ −7.65

89. $-8.2(-6.1)$ 50.02   **90.** $-4.3(-3.4)$ 14.62   **91.** $-6.2(-5.3)$ 32.86

92. $-2.15(1.15)$ −2.4725   **93.** $3.14(-8.1)$ −25.434   **94.** $-5.22(8.11)$ −42.3342

95. $4.25(-3.14)$ −13.345   **96.** $1.11(-1.11)$ −1.2321   **97.** $-6.75(2.32)$ −15.66

Evaluate the expression if $a = 4$, $b = 2$, and $c = 6$.

98. $5c^3$ 1080   **99.** $(4b)^3$ 512   **100.** $2ab^4$ 128   **101.** $2a^3$ 128

102. $3(ab)^2$ 192   **103.** $(3c)^b$ 324   **104.** $a^2 - b^4$ 0   **105.** c^2a 144

Write the expression without exponents.

106. 7^{-3} $\frac{1}{343}$ **107.** $(-4)^{-2}$ $\frac{1}{16}$ **108.** 2^{-5} $\frac{1}{32}$ **109.** $(-6)^{-4}$ $\frac{1}{1296}$ **110.** 8^{-1} $\frac{1}{8}$

111. $(-9)^{-2}$ $\frac{1}{81}$ **112.** 5^{-4} $\frac{1}{625}$ **113.** $(-1)^{-7}$ −1   **114.** 3^{-6} $\frac{1}{729}$ **115.** $(-5)^{-3}$

116. $8^5 \times 8^{-7}$ $\frac{1}{64}$ **117.** $10^4 \times 10^{-3}$ 10   **118.** $5^9 \times 5^{-9}$ 1   **119.** $4^{-2} \times 4^0$

120. $9^{17} \times 9^{-17}$ 1   **121.** $3^{-6} \times 3^4$ $\frac{1}{9}$ **122.** $6^{-2} \times 6^5$ 216   **123.** $2^{10} \times 2^{-8}$

Extra Practice   **487**

1. 1, 2, 3, 6
2. 1, 7
3. 1, 2, 5, 10
4. 1, 13
5. 1, 3, 5, 15
6. 1, 2, 3, 6, 9, 18
7. 1, 41
8. 1, 2, 3, 6, 7, 14, 21, 42
9. 1, 2, 4, 13, 26, 52
10. 1, 2, 4, 7, 8, 14, 28, 56
11. 1, 59
12. 1, 2, 4, 8, 16, 32, 64

Extra Practice: Chapter 3

List all the factors of each number.

1. 6	**2.** 7	**3.** 10	**4.** 13	**5.** 15	**6.** 18
7. 41	**8.** 42	**9.** 52	**10.** 56	**11.** 59	**12.** 64

Which of the numbers 2, 3, 4, 5, 9, and 10 are factors of the given number?

13. 155 5   **14.** 168 2, 3, 4   **15.** 189 3, 9   **16.** 210 2, 3, 5, 10   **17.** 272 2, 4   **18.** 305 5

19. 1080 2, 3, 4, 5, 9, 10   **20.** 1100 2, 4, 5, 10   **21.** 1260 2, 3, 4, 5, 9, 10   **22.** 1362 2, 3   **23.** 1423 none   **24.** 1485 3, 5, 9

Determine whether each number is prime or composite. If the number is composite, give the prime factorization.

25. 10 2×5 **26.** 34 2×17 **27.** 54 2×3^3 **28.** 41 prime   **29.** 30 $2 \times 3 \times 5$ **30.** 18 2×3^2

Write as a proper fraction in lowest terms or as a mixed number in simple form.

31. $\frac{15}{45}$ $\frac{1}{3}$ **32.** $-\frac{22}{64}$ $-\frac{11}{32}$ **33.** $\frac{7}{5}$ $1\frac{2}{5}$ **34.** $\frac{180}{240}$ $\frac{3}{4}$

35. $-\frac{144}{96}$ $-1\frac{1}{2}$ **36.** $-\frac{58}{12}$ $-4\frac{5}{6}$ **37.** $\frac{75}{125}$ $\frac{3}{5}$ **38.** $\frac{-145}{95}$ $-1\frac{10}{19}$

39. $\frac{14}{-8}$ $-1\frac{3}{4}$ **40.** $\frac{32}{28}$ $1\frac{1}{7}$ **41.** $\frac{-63}{81}$ $-\frac{7}{9}$ **42.** $-\frac{48}{54}$ $-\frac{8}{9}$

Complete.

43. $\frac{1}{4} + \frac{1}{4} + \frac{1}{4} + \frac{1}{4} = \underline{\ ?\ }$ 1   **44.** $\underline{\ ?\ } \times \frac{1}{3} = -\frac{2}{3}$ -2

45. $5 \times \underline{\ ?\ } = -1$ $-\frac{1}{5}$ **46.** $\frac{3}{10} = 3 \div \underline{\ ?\ }$ 10

47. $\left(-\frac{1}{7}\right) + \left(-\frac{1}{7}\right) = \underline{\ ?\ }$ $-\frac{2}{7}$ **48.** $4 \times \underline{\ ?\ } = \frac{4}{9}$ $\frac{1}{9}$

49. $\frac{2}{5} = \frac{?}{20}$ 8   **50.** $\frac{-8}{9} = \frac{?}{27}$ -24 **51.** $-\frac{12}{30} = -\frac{2}{?}$ 5

52. $\frac{20}{-36} = \frac{?}{-9}$ 5   **53.** $3 = \frac{12}{?}$ 4   **54.** $-4 = \frac{-28}{?}$ 7

Write as an improper fraction.

55. $5\frac{2}{3}$ $\frac{17}{3}$ **56.** $3\frac{4}{5}$ $\frac{19}{5}$ **57.** $-4\frac{3}{10}$ $-\frac{43}{10}$ **58.** $-15\frac{1}{6}$ $-\frac{91}{6}$

59. $-7\frac{1}{8}$ $-\frac{57}{8}$ **60.** $9\frac{3}{25}$ $\frac{228}{25}$ **61.** $6\frac{1}{4}$ $\frac{25}{4}$ **62.** $-5\frac{11}{12}$ $-\frac{71}{12}$

488 *Extra Practice*

Write the set of fractions as equivalent fractions with the least common denominator (LCD).

63. $\frac{5}{6}$, $\frac{3}{8}$ $\frac{20}{24}$, $\frac{9}{24}$ **64.** $\frac{4}{5}$, $-\frac{3}{10}$ $\frac{8}{10}$, $-\frac{3}{10}$ **65.** $\frac{4}{8}$, $\frac{5}{12}$ $\frac{12}{24}$, $\frac{10}{24}$

66. $-\frac{8}{15}$, $-\frac{7}{20}$ $-\frac{32}{60}$, $-\frac{21}{60}$ **67.** $-\frac{11}{28}$, $\frac{17}{42}$ $-\frac{33}{84}$, $\frac{34}{84}$ **68.** $\frac{7}{30}$, $\frac{19}{70}$ $\frac{49}{210}$, $\frac{57}{210}$

Add or subtract. Write the answer as a proper fraction in lowest terms or as a mixed number in simple form.

69. $\frac{5}{13} + \frac{4}{13}$ $\frac{9}{13}$ **70.** $-\frac{7}{8} - \frac{5}{8}$ $-1\frac{1}{2}$ **71.** $\frac{5}{12} - \frac{1}{12}$ $\frac{1}{3}$

72. $\frac{5}{9} + \left(-\frac{1}{4}\right)$ $\frac{11}{36}$ **73.** $-\frac{9}{14} - \frac{5}{32}$ $-\frac{179}{224}$ **74.** $\frac{3}{7} - \left(-\frac{4}{5}\right)$ $1\frac{8}{35}$

75. $-4\frac{1}{12} + 2\frac{4}{5}$ $-1\frac{17}{60}$ **76.** $5\frac{2}{3} - 2\frac{5}{8}$ $3\frac{1}{24}$ **77.** $-3\frac{7}{12} + 7\frac{5}{16}$

78. $2\frac{3}{7} - \left(-4\frac{5}{6}\right)$ $7\frac{11}{42}$ **79.** $-1\frac{3}{28} + \left(-4\frac{10}{21}\right)$ $-5\frac{7}{12}$ **80.** $-15\frac{1}{2} - \left(-8\frac{3}{4}\right)$ $-6\frac{3}{4}$

Multiply or divide. Write the answer as a proper fraction in lowest terms or as a mixed number in simple form.

81. $-\frac{3}{4} \times \frac{4}{5}$ $-\frac{3}{5}$ **82.** $\frac{21}{56} \times \frac{20}{25}$ $\frac{3}{10}$ **83.** $\frac{7}{8} \times \left(-\frac{4}{7}\right)$ $-\frac{1}{2}$

84. $6\frac{3}{4} \times \left(-1\frac{1}{3}\right)$ -9 **85.** $-2\frac{5}{8} \times \left(-\frac{16}{19}\right)$ $2\frac{4}{19}$ **86.** $-4\frac{2}{7} \times 2\frac{1}{4}$ $-9\frac{9}{14}$

87. $\frac{4}{9} \div \frac{2}{9}$ 2 **88.** $-\frac{3}{8} \div \left(-\frac{5}{16}\right)$ $1\frac{1}{5}$ **89.** $-\frac{8}{15} \div \left(-2\frac{2}{7}\right)$

90. $-3\frac{3}{5} \div \left(2\frac{4}{15}\right)$ $-1\frac{10}{17}$ **91.** $-\frac{5}{6} \div 4\frac{1}{2}$ $-\frac{5}{27}$ **92.** $3\frac{5}{9} \div (-32)$ $-\frac{1}{9}$

Write as a terminating or repeating decimal. Use a bar to show a repeating decimal.

93. $\frac{3}{8}$ 0.375 **94.** $\frac{3}{5}$ 0.6 **95.** $\frac{21}{22}$ $0.9\overline{54}$ -0.3125 **96.** $-\frac{5}{16}$

97. $\frac{1}{6}$ $0.1\overline{6}$ **98.** $-\frac{5}{9}$ $-0.\overline{5}$ **99.** $-\frac{8}{15}$ $-0.5\overline{3}$ **100.** $-\frac{161}{189}$

101. $\frac{287}{385}$ $0.7\overline{45}$ **102.** $3\frac{5}{12}$ $3.41\overline{6}$ **103.** $-2\frac{3}{11}$ $-2.\overline{27}$ **104.** $4\frac{1}{18}$ $4.0\overline{5}$

Write as a proper fraction in lowest terms or as a mixed number in simple form.

$-3\frac{1}{40}$

105. 0.6 $\frac{3}{5}$ **106.** -0.04 $-\frac{1}{25}$ **107.** 1.34 $1\frac{17}{50}$ **108.** -4.22 $-4\frac{11}{50}$ **109.** -3.025

$-2\frac{1}{6}$

110. $0.\overline{6}$ $\frac{2}{3}$ **111.** $-2.\overline{09}$ $-2\frac{1}{11}$ **112.** $1.\overline{7}$ $1\frac{7}{9}$ **113.** $8.2121\ldots$ $8\frac{7}{33}$ **114.** $-2.1666\ldots$

Extra Practice   **489**

Extra Practice: Chapter 4

Use transformations to solve each equation. Write down all the steps.

1. $r + 30 = 80$ 50

2. $31 + d = 47$ 16

3. $\frac{1}{4}b = \frac{3}{4}$ 3

4. $x - 21 = 19$ 40

5. $79 - a = 17$ 62

6. $14 + 12 = 17 + a$ 9

7. $1.23 = 1.50 - a$ 0.27

8. $\frac{7}{8} + a = 4$ $3\frac{1}{8}$

9. $13t = 52$ 4

10. $84 = 14k$ 6

11. $\frac{n}{6} = 12$ 72

12. $15 = \frac{x}{3}$ 45

13. $28 = 7v$ 4

14. $3 = \frac{p}{3}$ 9

15. $\frac{t}{7} = 5(3 + 4)$ 245

16. $9 = \frac{x}{10}$ 90

17. $\frac{1}{7} = \frac{3}{7}k$ $\frac{1}{3}$

18. $\frac{12}{5}c = \frac{3}{10}$ $\frac{1}{8}$

19. $0.25a = 1.0$ 4

20. $1.7 = 1.7x$ 1

21. $\frac{5}{9} = \frac{12}{5}k$ $\frac{25}{108}$

22. $1.25 = 0.6f$ $2.08\overline{3}$

23. $6.25n = 1.25$ 0.2

24. $\frac{11}{15} = \frac{3}{5}y$ $1\frac{2}{9}$

25. $\frac{p}{6} - 12 = 3$ 90

26. $72 = \frac{p}{3} + 3$ 207

27. $3.6x - 2.5 = 15.5$ 5

28. $1.24 - 1.2m = 1.0$ 0.2

29. $17 = 5y - 3$ 4

30. $\frac{8}{3} = \frac{2}{5}v - \frac{1}{3}$ $7\frac{1}{2}$

31. $\frac{m}{3} = \frac{1}{3}(6 + 12)$ 18

32. $2x - 3 = 15 - 6$ 6

Write a variable expression for the word phrase.

33. The difference when a number t is subtracted from eighteen $18 - t$

34. Five added to the product of a number x and nine $5 + 9x$

35. Forty divided by a number m, decreased by sixteen $\frac{40}{m} - 16$

36. The remainder when a number q is subtracted from two hundred $200 - q$

37. Eleven more than three times a number y $3y + 11$

38. The sum of a number r and six, divided by twelve $\frac{r + 6}{12}$

Write an equation for each word sentence.

39. The product of six and a number n is fifty-four. $6n = 54$

40. Twelve less than two times a number n is seventy. $2n - 12 = 70$

41. The sum of a number n and nineteen is sixty-one. $n + 19 = 61$

Choose a variable and write an equation for each problem.

42. The altitude of the Dead Sea is 1296 ft below sea level. How much greater is the altitude of Death Valley, California, at 282 ft below sea level? $n = -282 - (-1296)$

43. An astronaut enters a space capsule 1 hr 40 min before launch time. How long has the astronaut been in the capsule 2 h 32 min after the launch? $n = 152 - (-100)$

44. The Torrance baseball team scored 10 runs in the first 3 innings. Gardena scored 2 in the first and 5 in the fourth. If Torrence does not score again, how many more runs does Gardena need to win? $2 + 5 + n = 10 + 11$

Write an equation for each problem. Solve the equation using the five-step method. Check your answer.

45. Mercury melts at 38.87° below 0°C and boils at 356.9°C. What is the difference between these temperatures? 395.77°C

46. Yolanda rode the bus from a point 53 blocks south of Carroll Avenue to a point 41 blocks north of Carroll Avenue. How many blocks did she travel? 94 blocks

47. John sailed for 7 hours on Swan Lake. If he sailed for two more hours than he fished, how long did he fish? 5 h

48. In a local election 1584 people voted. The winner received 122 votes more than the loser. How many votes did each candidate receive? winner: 853 votes; loser: 731 votes

49. It takes Fritz 55 min to commute to and from work. The ride home takes 7 min less than the ride to work. How long does it take each way? 31 min to work; 24 min home

50. Ann swam a total of 78 laps on Monday and Tuesday. She swam 12 more laps on Tuesday than on Monday. How far did she swim each day? Monday: 33 laps; Tuesday: 45 laps

Extra Practice: *Chapter 5*

Draw a sketch to illustrate each of the following. Check students' drawings.

1. Three points on a line
2. Two intersecting lines
3. Three noncollinear points
4. Two intersecting planes
5. Two rays with a common endpoint, *A*
6. Two segments with a common endpoint, *B*

Complete.

7. 10 km = __?__ m 10,000   8. 0.27 km = __?__ m 270   9. 9 m = __?__ cm 900

10. 0.5 km = __?__ m 500   11. 77 m = __?__ cm 7700   12. 175 mm = __?__ m 0.175

13. 1500 m = __?__ km 1.5   14. 81 cm = __?__ mm 810   15. 0.1575 km = __?__ m 157.5

16. 900 mm = __?__ m = __?__ cm 0.9, 90   17. 2 m = __?__ cm = __?__ mm 200, 2000

18. If the sum of the measures of two angles is 180°, the angles are __?__. supplementary

19. A small square is often used to indicate a(n) __?__ angle. right

20. Perpendicular lines form __?__° angles. 90

21. The __?__ is the common endpoint of two rays that form an angle. vertex

22. If m∠*A* = 40°, the complement of ∠*A* measures __?__°. 50

23. A(n) __?__ angle has a measure between 90° and 180°. obtuse

24. A triangle with at least two sides congruent is called a(n) __?__ triangle. isosceles

25. Triangles can be classified by their __?__ or their __?__. sides; angles

26. The sum of the measures of the angles of a triangle is __?__°. 180

27. A(n) __?__ triangle has two perpendicular sides. right

28. The sum of the lengths of any two sides of a triangle is __?__ than the length of the third side. greater

29. A triangle with three congruent sides is called a(n) __?__ triangle. equilateral

30. A triangle with all its angles less than 90° is called a(n) __?__ triangle. acute

True or false?

31. A regular polygon has all the sides equal. True

32. All the angles of a rectangle have a measure of 90°. True

33. A trapezoid always has one pair of congruent sides. False

34. The opposite sides of a parallelogram are congruent. True

35. Only two sides of a rhombus are congruent. False

36. A square with a perimeter of 24 cm has 4 sides that measure 6 cm. True

37. A regular decagon, 5 cm on a side, has a perimeter of 50 cm. True

Solve. Use $\pi \approx 3.14$ and round answers to three digits.

38. The radius of a circle is 30 cm. Find the diameter. 60 cm

39. The radius of a circle is 56 mm. Find the circumference. 352 mm

40. The diameter of a circle is 3 m. Find the circumference. 9.42 m

41. The diameter of a circle is 16 mm. Find the circumference. 50.2 mm

42. The circumference of a circle is 20 m. Find the diameter. 6.37 m

43. The circumference of a circle is 25.8 m. Find the radius. 4.11 m

Complete the statements about the pair of congruent figures.

44. $\overline{KL} \cong$ _?_ $\overline{RQ}$ **45.** $\overline{NK} \cong$ _?_ $\overline{SR}$

46. $\overline{LM} \cong$ _?_ $\overline{QP}$ **47.** $\overline{SP} \cong$ _?_ $\overline{NM}$

48. $\angle N \cong$ _?_ $\angle S$ **49.** $\angle S \cong$ _?_ $\angle N$

50. $\angle L \cong$ _?_ $\angle Q$ **51.** $\angle Q \cong$ _?_ $\angle L$

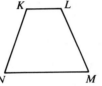
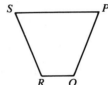

Are the triangles in each pair congruent? If so, name the triangles that are congruent and explain why they are congruent.

52.   no

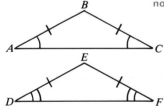

53. $\triangle CAB \cong \triangle DAB$; SSS

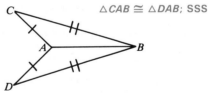

Use a compass and a straightedge to make each construction.   Check students' papers.

54. Draw a segment AB. Construct the perpendicular bisector.

55. Draw an acute angle ABC. Construct $\overrightarrow{BX}$ so that it bisects $\angle ABC$.

56. Construct an angle congruent to $\angle ABC$ of Exercise 55.

Extra Practice: Chapter 6

Express each ratio as a fraction in lowest terms.

1. $\dfrac{10 \text{ min}}{1 \text{ h}}$ $\dfrac{1}{6}$

2. $\dfrac{6 \text{ cm}}{2 \text{ m}}$ $\dfrac{3}{100}$

3. $\dfrac{250 \text{ mL}}{2 \text{ L}}$ $\dfrac{1}{8}$

4. $\dfrac{6 \text{ kg}}{600 \text{ g}}$ $\dfrac{10}{1}$

5. $\dfrac{7 \text{ days}}{4 \text{ weeks}}$ $\dfrac{1}{4}$

6. $\dfrac{3 \text{ h}}{45 \text{ min}}$ $\dfrac{4}{1}$

7. $\dfrac{15 \text{ mm}}{5 \text{ cm}}$ $\dfrac{3}{10}$

8. $\dfrac{60 \text{ cm}}{150 \text{ mm}}$ $\dfrac{4}{1}$

Solve. Express each ratio in lowest terms.

9. A student walked 25 km in 4 h. What was the average speed in kilometers per hour? 6.25 km/h

10. A special typewriter has 46 keys. Of these 46 keys, 26 are used for letters of the alphabet. What is the ratio of the number of keys not used for letters to the total number of keys? $\dfrac{10}{23}$

Solve.

11. In order to make 4 servings, a recipe calls for 3 eggs to be used. How many eggs will be needed to make 32 servings? 24 eggs

12. Charlie runs 5 mi in 37 min. If he could maintain the same speed, how long would it take him to run 15 mi? 1 h 51 min

13. A dozen apples cost $1.80. What is the unit price? 15¢

14. A car travels 234 km in 4.5 h. What is the car's average speed? 52 km/h

15. $\dfrac{19}{20} = \dfrac{n}{10}$ 9.5

16. $\dfrac{8}{48} = \dfrac{n}{4}$ $\dfrac{2}{3}$

17. $\dfrac{4}{13} = \dfrac{12}{n}$ 39

18. $\dfrac{n}{27} = \dfrac{12}{81}$ 4

19. $\dfrac{40}{n} = \dfrac{5}{9}$ 72

20. $\dfrac{n}{64} = \dfrac{12}{8}$ 96

21. $\dfrac{100}{40} = \dfrac{20}{n}$ 8

22. $\dfrac{7}{3} = \dfrac{n}{18}$ 42

23. Joe bought 4 shock absorbers for the price of 3 at a clearance sale. He paid a total of $39. How much would the 4 shock absorbers cost at their regular price? $52

24. Billie runs 4 km in 25 min. How long will it take to run 10,000 m? 1 h 2.5 min

25. A supermarket sells 12 oranges for $1.30. How much would 18 oranges cost at the same rate? $1.95

A map has a scale of 1 cm : 8 km. What actual distance does each map length represent?

26. 8 cm   64 km

27. 5.5 cm   44 km

28. 3 cm   24 km

29. 7.9 cm   63.2 km

30. 3.75 cm   30 km

31. 10.2 cm   81.6 km

32. 6.25 cm   50 km

33. 15.25 cm   122 km

Express as a fraction in lowest terms or as a mixed number in simple form.

34. 5% $\frac{1}{20}$ **35.** 10% $\frac{1}{10}$ **36.** 72% $\frac{18}{25}$ **37.** 39% $\frac{39}{100}$ **38.** 2% $\frac{1}{50}$

39. 27% $\frac{27}{100}$ **40.** 25% $\frac{1}{4}$ **41.** 200% 2 **42.** 163% $1\frac{63}{100}$ **43.** 215% $2\frac{3}{20}$

Express as a percent.

44. $\frac{3}{4}$ 75% **45.** $\frac{1}{10}$ 10% **46.** $\frac{3}{5}$ 60% **47.** $\frac{1}{8}$ $12\frac{1}{2}$% **48.** 7 700%

49. $\frac{7}{16}$ $43\frac{3}{4}$% **50.** $\frac{43}{20}$ 215% **51.** $\frac{36}{25}$ 144% **52.** $\frac{23}{4}$ 575% **53.** $\frac{22}{5}$ 440%

Express each percent as a decimal.

54. 15% 0.15 **55.** 71% 0.71 **56.** 5% 0.05 **57.** 15.2% 0.152 **58.** 98% 0.98

59. 2.4% 0.024 **60.** 7.5% 0.075 **61.** 625% 6.25 **62.** 0.42% 0.0042 **63.** 200% 2

Express each decimal as a percent.

64. 0.45 45% **65.** 0.23 23% **66.** 1.33 133% **67.** 0.05 5% **68.** 12.5 1250%

69. 0.0025 0.25% **70.** 10.2 1020% **71.** 0.53 53% **72.** 0.008 0.8% **73.** 0.125 12.5%

Express each fraction as a decimal, then as a percent.

74. $\frac{2}{5}$ 0.4; 40% **75.** $\frac{1}{4}$ 0.25; 25% **76.** $\frac{7}{10}$ 0.7; 70% **77.** $\frac{5}{8}$ 0.625; 62.5% **78.** $\frac{1}{16}$ 0.0625; 6.25%

79. $1\frac{3}{8}$ 1.375; 137.5% **80.** $\frac{5}{16}$ 0.3125; 31.25% **81.** $8\frac{3}{4}$ 8.75; 875% **82.** $\frac{13}{16}$ 0.8125; 81.25% **83.** $5\frac{1}{5}$ 5.2; 520%

Answer each question by writing an equation and solving it. Round to the nearest tenth of a percent if necessary.

84. 12% of 50 is what number? 6

85. 110% of 99 is what number? 108.9

86. What percent of 81 is 27? 33.3%

87. 85% of what number is 425? 500

88. 15% of $30 is how much? $4.50

89. What percent of 250 is 75? 30%

90. What percent of 256 is 32? 12.5%

91. 60% of what number is 144? 240

92. 5% of 1000 is what number? 50

93. 140% of what number is 35? 25

94. 18% of $85 is how much? $15.30

95. What percent of 825 is 25? 3.0%

96. 30% of what number is 23.7? 79

97. 6% of what number is 3.48? 58

98. What percent of 325 is 65? 20%

99. 12% of 408 is what number? 48.96

Extra Practice: *Chapter 7*

Find the percent increase or decrease from the first number to the second. Round to the nearest tenth of a percent if necessary.

1. 45 to 66 46.7%   **2.** 50 to 60 20%   **3.** 140 to 84 40%   **4.** 256 to 500 95.3%

5. 15 to 75 400%   **6.** 144 to 96 33.3%   **7.** 360 to 234 35%   **8.** 196 to 49 75%

Find the new number produced when the given number is increased or decreased by the given percent.

9. 64; 25% increase 80   **10.** 80; 65% decrease 28

11. 78; 150% increase 195   **12.** 480; 35% increase 648

Solve.

13. Mervyn's is having a sale on batteries. The regular price of $2.40 is decreased by 20%. What is the sale price? $1.92

14. A bicycle that usually sells for $120 is on sale for $96. What is the percent of discount? 20%

15. Great Hikes purchases backpacks from the manufacturer at $10 each. Then the backpacks are sold at the store for $25 each. What is the percent of markup? 150%

16. If there is a sales tax of 5%, how much will it cost to buy a $57 handbag? $59.85

17. A wheelbarrow sells for $36. Next month the price will be marked up 6%. How much will the wheelbarrow cost next month? $38.16

18. A furniture store has a total income of $3600 per week and total operating costs of $3096 per week. To the nearest tenth, what percent of the income is profit? 14%

19. The Thort Company made a profit of $32,175 on sales of $371,250. To the nearest tenth, what percent of the sales was profit? 8.7%

20. Dora's commission last month was $621. Her total sales were $8280. What is her rate of commission? 7.5%

21. Foster Realty Co. charges a 6% commission for the sale of property. If a homeowner wishes to clear $130,000 after paying the commission, for how much must the home be sold? $138,297.87

22. Ivan works for salary plus commission. He earns $500 per month plus 4% commission on all sales. What sales level is needed for Ivan to earn $675 in a given month? $4375

23. Last Friday, 720 people at Data Tech drove cars to work. Of these, 585 bought gas on the way home. What percent of the drivers bought gas on the way home? Use a proportion to solve. $81\frac{1}{4}$%

24. How much does a $53.00 iron cost if it is taxed at 5%? Use a proportion to solve. $55.65

25. Jill has $525 in a savings account that pays 6% simple interest. How much will she have in the account after 1 year, if she makes no deposits or withdrawals? $556.50

26. Holly has a savings account that pays 6.5% interest, compounded monthly. If she started the account with $750 and makes no deposits or withdrawals, how much will be in the account after 3 months? $762.25

27. Phil borrowed $5000 for one year. The interest on the loan came to $689.44. To the nearest tenth, what was the interest rate? 13.8%

28. Victor had a two-year loan with a simple interest rate of 13% annually. At the end of the two years he had paid $1454.44 in interest. What was the original of Victor's loan? $5594

29. Consider a principal of $2750 earning an interest rate of 10.5%. If compounded semiannually for one year, what is the total interest earned on $2750? (If you do not have a calculator, round to the nearest penny at every step.) $296.33

30. A $600 deposit is left in an account for 9 months. If the account earns an 8% interest compounded quarterly, what is the total interest earned at the end of the 9 months? (If you do not have a calculator, round to the nearest penny at every step.) $36.72

31. Carol has 60 boxes of light bulbs. If she sells 15% of the boxes today, how many will be left? 51 boxes

32. At a pet store, fish that usually cost $1.25 each are on sale for $.75 each. What is the percent of decrease? 40%

33. A restaurant raises its price for the salad bar 20% to $1.50. What did the salad bar cost before? $1.25

34. The band concert drew an audience of 270 on Thursday. On Friday, attendance increased 30%. How many people attended on Friday? 351 people

35. The discount rate at an appliance store sale is 15%. What is the sale price of a dishwasher if the original price was $600? $510

36. Nancy Allen earns a 12% commission on her sales. Last month she earned $4800. What was the total value of her sales? $40,000

Extra Practice **497**

Extra Practice: Chapter 8

Solve.

1. $2a + 7a = 36$ 4

2. $12x - 8x = 4$ 1

3. $-10y + 12y = 1$ $\frac{1}{2}$

4. $d - 7d = -72$ 12

5. $-5t + 12t = 3$ $\frac{3}{7}$

6. $-3p - 9p = 6$ $-\frac{1}{2}$

7. $x + 3x + 6 = 8$ $\frac{1}{2}$

8. $4c + 8c - 3 = 9$ 1

9. $-n - 3 + 10n = 9$ $1\frac{1}{3}$

10. $5z + 10 - 12z = -4$ 2

11. $8 + y - 9y = -4$ $1\frac{1}{2}$

12. $d + 12 - 7d = 48$ -6

13. $4a = a + 3$ 1

14. $16p = 12 + 8p$ $1\frac{1}{2}$

15. $32 - 6x = 2x$ 4

16. $50 + t = 6t$ 10

17. $3x = -6x + 36$ 4

18. $y = 12y - 44$ 4

19. $3c + 4 = 5c + 5$ $-\frac{1}{2}$

20. $2n - 5 = 7n + 20$ -5

21. $d - 9 = 24 - 10d$ 3

22. $-x + 7 = 6x + 21$ -2

23. $3 - 4y = 13 + 2y$ $-1\frac{2}{3}$

24. $-3a + 6 = 5 - 2a$ 1

Solve.

25. At Moor's Deli, a ham sandwich and a glass of milk cost a total of $3.25. If the sandwich costs four times as much as the milk, what is the cost of each? sandwich: $2.60; milk: $.65

26. The sum of two consecutive integers is 135. What are the two integers? 67, 68

27. A 60 ft piece of rope is cut into two pieces, one three times as long as the other. What is the length of each piece? 15 ft, 45 ft

28. The perimeter of an isosceles triangle is 75 cm. If the congruent sides of the triangle are each twice as long as the remaining side, what is the length of each side? 15 cm, 30 cm, 30 cm

Replace _?_ with $<$ or $>$.

29. 15 _?_ 23 $<$

30. 57 _?_ 49 $>$

31. 35 _?_ 18 $>$

32. $7 + 11$ _?_ 31 $<$

33. 17 _?_ $12 + 4$ $>$

34. $29 - 15$ _?_ 17 $<$

Write an inequality for each word sentence.

35. Seventeen is greater than twelve. $17 > 12$

36. A number plus twelve is less than twenty-two. $n + 12 < 22$

37. Twice a number is greater than sixty-nine. $2n > 69$

38. Seven is smaller than two times five. $7 < 2 \times 5$

39. Eighty minus twenty-six is greater than two times twenty-one. $80 - 26 > 2 \times 21$

40. Thirty-three is less than six times a number. $33 < 6n$

Use transformations to solve the inequality. Write down all the steps.

41. $y + 5 \leq -17$

42. $q - 8 > 24$

43. $5\frac{1}{6} - \frac{1}{3} < k$

44. $7.8 + 4.3 \geq m$

45. $f < (17 - 3)0.5$

46. $z \leq \frac{1}{2}(25 - 7)$

47. $6e > 42$

48. $-5a \leq 45$

49. $28 < -7u$

50. $52 \geq 4x$

51. $\frac{w}{-3} > 21$

52. $\frac{c}{4} \geq 17$

53. $-11 \leq \frac{a}{5}$

54. $\frac{e}{-2} < -23$

55. $10 > \frac{v}{7}$

56. $-5x + 7 + 2x - 13 < 9$

57. $-22 \geq 10d - 4 - 3d + 12$

58. $2 > \frac{4}{5}n + 3 - \frac{1}{5}n + 6$

59. $5 + \frac{3}{7}u - 8 + \frac{2}{7}u \leq 5$

60. $-w + 8 \leq 4w - 17$

61. $-6s - 4 < s + 31$

62. $10 + \frac{2}{3}h > -\frac{5}{3}h + 6$

63. $8 - \frac{1}{6}p \geq 4 - \frac{1}{3}p$

64. $4(m + 3) \geq 48$

65. $35 < -5(x + 2)$

66. $34 < (18t - 6)\frac{1}{3}$

67. $\frac{-1}{7}(14 + 21u) \geq 7$

Solve.

68. Of all pairs of consecutive integers whose sum is greater than 250, find the pair whose sum is least. **125, 126**

69. Two cars start from the same point traveling in different directions. One car travels at a speed of 52 mi/h, and the other car travels at a speed of 48 mi/h. How long must they travel to be 300 mi apart? **3 h**

70. A purse contains 20 coins, all either quarters or dimes. If the total value of the coins is greater than $3.50, at least how many are quarters? **11 quarters**

Extra Practice **499**

Extra Practice: Chapter 9

For Exercises 1–6, give the coordinates of the point.

1. A $(-6, 2)$ **2.** B $(5, -4)$ **3.** C $(4, 4)$

4. D $(-3, -2)$ **5.** E $(-2, 4)$ **6.** F $(1, 1)$

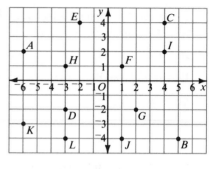

Name the point for the ordered pair.

7. $(2, -2)$ G **8.** $(-3, -4)$ L

9. $(4, 2)$ I **10.** $(-6, -3)$ K

11. $(1, -4)$ J **12.** $(-3, 1)$ H

a. Graph the given ordered pairs on a coordinate plane.
b. Connect all the points in the order listed by means of line segments to produce a closed figure.   a., b. Check students' graphs.
c. Name the figure as specifically as you can.

13. $(3, 3)$, $(3, 0)$, $(-2, 0)$, $(-5, 0)$, $(-5, 3)$, $(3, 3)$ c. rectangle

14. $(2, -2)$, $(2, -6)$, $(-2, -6)$, $(-2, -2)$, $(0, -2)$, $(2, -2)$ c. square

15. $(1, 5)$, $(-2, 2)$, $(-5, -1)$, $(0, -1)$, $(6, -1)$, $(1, 5)$ c. triangle

16. $(0, 7)$, $(3, 5)$, $(2, 2)$, $(-2, 2)$, $(-3, 5)$, $(0, 7)$ c. pentagon

17. $(7, -4)$, $(4, -1)$, $(2, 1)$, $(1, 2)$, $(1, -4)$, $(7, -4)$ c. isosceles right triangle

Tell whether the ordered pair is a solution of the given equation.

$-x + 2y = 4$
18. $(4, 0)$ No   **19.** $(-4, 0)$ Yes   **20.** $(2, 3)$ Yes   No
                                                              21. $(-2, 3)$

$x + 3y = 6$
22. $(0, 2)$ Yes   **23.** $(6, 0)$ Yes   **24.** $(2, 1)$ No   Yes
                                                              25. $(3, 1)$

$2x + y = 5$
26. $(3, 1)$ No   **27.** $(2, 1)$ Yes   **28.** $(1, 3)$ Yes   Yes
                                                              29. $(0, 5)$

a. Solve the equation for y in terms of x.
b. Find the solutions of the equation for the given values of x.

30. $2x + y = 8$ $y = -2x + 8$; $(-1, 10)$,
     values of x: $-1, 0, 1$ $(0, 8)$, $(1, 6)$

31. $y - 3x = 4$ $y = 3x + 4$; $(-5, -11)$,
     values of x: $-5, 0, 5$ $(0, 4)$, $(5, 19)$

32. $-x + y = 1$ $y = x + 1$; $(-1, 0)$,
     values of x: $-1, \frac{1}{2}, 2$ $\left(\frac{1}{2}, 1\frac{1}{2}\right)$, $(2, 3)$

33. $3x - 2y = -6$ $y = \frac{3}{2}x + 3$; $(-2, 0)$,
     values of x: $-2, 0, 2$ $(0, 3)$, $(2, 6)$

34. $2x + y = 6$ $y = -2x + 6$; (0, 6),
 values of x: 0, 3, 1 (3, 0), (1, 4)

35. $x - y = 3$ $y = x - 3$; (6, 3),
 values of x: 6, -1, -3 $(-1, -4)$,
 $(-3, -6)$

Graph the equation on a coordinate plane. Use a separate set of axes for each equation. Check students' graphs.

36. $2x + y = 4$ **37.** $x - 3y = -3$ **38.** $x + 2y = -4$

39. $3x + 4y = 12$ **40.** $2x + 5y = 10$ **41.** $-x + y = -1$

42. $x + y = 2$ **43.** $3x - y = 3$ **44.** $4x - 2y = 3$

45. $2x = y - 2$ **46.** $y = x - 3$ **47.** $-3x + 4y = 12$

Use a graph to solve the system. Do the lines intersect, coincide, or are they parallel?

Intersect at $(-2, 2)$

48. $x - y = -2$ Intersect   **49.** $x - y = 6$ Intersect   **50.** $2x + y = -2$
 $2x + y = 5$ at (1, 3) $2x + y = 0$ at (2, -4) $x - y = -4$

51. $2x + y = 2$ Parallel   **52.** $6x + 3y = 6$ Coincide   **53.** $3x + y = -6$
 $2x + y = -3$ $2x + y = 2$ $2x - y = 1$
                                                                     Intersect at $(-1, -3)$

54. A parking lot attendant charges $3 for the first hour and $1 for each extra hour after that. Write an equation that relates the total cost of parking (y) to the number of extra hours a car is parked (x). Graph the equation. What is the slope of the graph? From your graph determine how much it would cost to park a car for 5 h after the initial hour. $y = x + 3$; check students' graphs; slope $= 1$; $8

55. The initial charge for a phone call to Jonesboro is 25¢ for the first 3 min. After that the charge is 5¢ for every additional minute. Write an equation that relates the total cost of a phone call (y) to the number of additional minutes on the phone (x). Graph the equation. What is the slope of the graph? From the graph determine the cost of a call requiring 7 min beyond the initial 3. $y = 5x + 25$; check students' graphs; slope $= 5$; 60¢

56. The temperature in a town rose at a constant rate from 5 A.M. to 12 noon. At 9 A.M. the temperature was 17°C. At 11 A.M. the temperature was 21°C. Use this information to draw a graph and determine what the temperature was at 5 A.M. and at 12 noon.
 Check students' graphs; 9°C at 5 A.M., 23°C at 12 noon

Graph the inequality. Check students' graphs.

57. $x + 2y < 4$ **58.** $2x - y < 1$ **59.** $6x + y \geq 7$

60. $-x + 3y < 0$ **61.** $2x + y \geq 1$ **62.** $3x + y \leq -2$

Extra Practice **501**

Extra Practice: Chapter 10

Find the area and perimeter of a rectangle with the given dimensions.

1. 100 m by 50 m
5000 m²; 300 m

2. 27 mm by 13 mm
351 mm²; 80 mm

3. 125 cm by 61 cm
7625 cm²; 372 cm

4. If a rectangle has a width of 57 km and an area of 3648 km², what is
(a) the length and (b) the perimeter? **a.** 64 km **b.** 242 km

Find the area of a parallelogram with the given dimensions.

5. $b = 12$ cm, $h = 11$ cm
132 cm²

6. $b = 105$ m, $h = 28$ m
2940 m²

7. $b = 17$ km, $h = 7$ km
119 km²

8. If a parallelogram has a height of 13 cm and an area of 201.5 cm²,
what is the base? 15.5 cm

Find the area of each polygon.

717.5 m²

9. Triangle: base 23 cm, height 7 cm 80.5 cm²
10. Triangle: base 35 m, height 41 m

11. Trapezoid: bases 11.5 m and 6.5 m, height 15 m 135 m²

12. If a triangle has a height of 113 cm and an area of 4576.5 cm², what
is the base? 81 cm

13. If a trapezoid has an area of 531 mm² and bases of 32.1 mm and
21 mm, what is the height? 20 mm

Solve. Use $\pi \approx 3.14$ and round the answer to three digits.

14. A circle has a radius of 42 cm. What is the area? 5540 cm²

15. A circle has a diameter of 22 m. What is the area? 380 m²

16. A circle has an area of $12\frac{4}{7}$ ft². What is the diameter? 4 ft

17. A circle has a radius of 56 m. What is the area? 9850 m²

Copy each figure and show on your drawing any lines or points of symmetry.

18.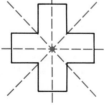

19.

20.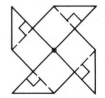

21. A prism with height 5 m has base area 173 m². Find the volume. 865 m³

22. Find the volume of a cylinder with height 82 cm and base area 50 cm². 4100 cm³

23. A right triangle with legs 15 mm and 7 mm is the base of a prism with height 24 mm. Find the volume of the prism. 1260 mm³

24. Find the volume of a cylinder with height 300 cm and diameter 15 cm. 53,000 cm³

25. The volume of a triangular prism is 2340 cm³. Find the height of the prism if the base area is 78 cm². 30 cm

26. A cone with base area 234 mm² is 82 mm high. Find its volume and its capacity in liters. 0.0064 L   6400 mm³

27. A pyramid with height 52 cm has a rectangular base measuring 12 cm by 17 cm. Find the volume. 3536 cm³

28. The base of a cone has diameter 70 cm. If the height of the cone is 120 cm, what is the volume? 154,000 cm³

For Exercises 29–32, find (a) the lateral surface area and (b) the total surface area of the figure described.

29. A prism of height 15 cm whose bases are right triangles with sides 15 cm, 36 cm, and 39 cm a. 1350 cm² b. 1890 cm²

30. A cylinder with radius 4 cm and height 11 cm a. 276 cm² b. 377 cm²

31. A cube with edges that are 15 cm a. 900 cm² b. 1350 cm²

32. A rectangular prism of height 27 cm and base 15 cm by 12 cm
a. 1458 cm² b. 1818 cm²

For Exercises 33–36, leave your answers in terms of π.

33. Find the surface area of a sphere with radius 18 cm. 1296π cm²

34. Find the volume of a sphere with diameter 30 cm. 4500π cm³

35. Find the radius of a sphere whose surface area is 576π m². 12 m

36. Find the volume of a sphere whose radius is 16 cm. 5461$\frac{1}{3}\pi$ cm³

37. If the mass of 1 L of gasoline is 0.66 kg, what is the mass of 4 L?
2.64 kg

38. Each edge of a cube of steel measures 12 cm. Find the mass of the cube if the mass of 1 cm³ of steel is 7.82 g. 13,512.96 g

39. A rectangular prism of aluminum is 15 cm long, 7 cm wide, and 30 cm high. Find the mass of the prism if the mass of 1 cm³ of aluminum is 2.708 g. 8530.2 g

Extra Practice: Chapter 11

If the given symbol names an integer, state the integer. If not, name the two consecutive integers between which the number lies.

1. $\sqrt{9}$ 3
2. $\sqrt{39}$ 6, 7
3. $-\sqrt{27}$ −6, −5
4. $\sqrt{10}$ 3, 4
5. $\sqrt{17}$ 4, 5
6. $\sqrt{5}$ 2, 3
7. $\sqrt{81}$ 9
8. $-\sqrt{12}$ −4, −3
9. $\sqrt{60}$ 7, 8
10. $-\sqrt{78}$ −9, −8
11. $\sqrt{25}$ 5
12. $\sqrt{19}$ 4, 5
13. $\sqrt{16}$ 4
14. $\sqrt{43}$ 6, 7
15. $\sqrt{84}$ 9, 10
16. $\sqrt{64}$ 8

Approximate to the tenths' place, using the divide-and-average method.

17. $\sqrt{24}$ 4.9
18. $\sqrt{30}$ 5.5
19. $\sqrt{92}$ 9.6
20. $\sqrt{74}$ 8.6
21. $\sqrt{51}$ 7.1
22. $\sqrt{29}$ 5.4
23. $\sqrt{10}$ 3.2
24. $\sqrt{86}$ 9.2
25. $\sqrt{37}$ 6.1
26. $\sqrt{80}$ 8.9
27. $\sqrt{5.6}$ 2.4
28. $\sqrt{9.8}$ 3.1

For Exercises 29–53, refer to the table on page 508.
Approximate the square root to the nearest hundredth.

29. $\sqrt{8}$ 2.83
30. $\sqrt{19}$ 4.36
31. $\sqrt{5}$ 2.24
32. $\sqrt{11}$ 3.32
33. $\sqrt{24}$ 4.90
34. $\sqrt{52}$ 7.21
35. $\sqrt{39}$ 6.25
36. $\sqrt{2}$ 1.41
37. $\sqrt{31}$ 5.57
38. $2\sqrt{18}$ 8.49
39. $\sqrt{58}$ 7.62
40. $5\sqrt{45}$ 33.54

Approximate the square root to the nearest hundredth by interpolation.

41. $\sqrt{15.8}$ 3.97
42. $\sqrt{6.3}$ 2.51
43. $\sqrt{21.4}$ 4.63
44. $\sqrt{83.6}$ 9.14

State whether or not a triangle with sides of the given lengths is a right triangle.

45. 2, 3, 4 No
46. 3, 4, 5 Yes
47. 10, 20, 24 No
48. 8, 15, 17 Yes
49. 10, 12, 15 No
50. 6, 8, 10 Yes
51. 30, 40, 50 Yes
52. 7, 9, 12 No
53. 12, 16, 20 Yes

A right triangle has sides of lengths a, b, and c, with c the length of the hypotenuse. Find the length of the missing side. If necessary, use the table on page 508 for the square root values and round answers to the nearest hundredth.

54. $a = 5$, $b = 8$ 9.43
55. $a = 4$, $b = 5$ 6.40
56. $a = 3$, $c = 5$ 4
57. $b = 12$, $c = 15$ 9
58. $b = 15$, $c = 17$ 8
59. $a = 7$, $b = 7$ 9.90

504 *Extra Practice*

60. $a = 6$, $c = 10$ 8 **61.** $b = 8$, $c = 17$ 15 **62.** $a = 13$, $c = 14$
5.20

Find the lengths marked x and y. In each exercise, the triangles are similar.

63.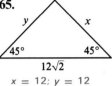

$x = 20$ $y = 40$

64.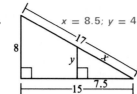

$x = 8.5$; $y = 4$

Find the lengths marked x and y in the triangle. Give your answer in terms of radicals when radicals occur.

65.

$12\sqrt{2}$

$x = 12$; $y = 12$

66.

$x = 5\sqrt{3}$; $y = 10$

67.

$10\sqrt{3}$

$x = 20$; $y = 10$

68.

$45°$ $45°$ 6

$x = 6$; $y = 6\sqrt{2}$

Rewrite the expression in lowest terms with the radical in the numerator.

69. $\dfrac{2}{\sqrt{3}}$ $\dfrac{2\sqrt{3}}{3}$

70. $\dfrac{5}{\sqrt{x}}$ $\dfrac{5\sqrt{x}}{x}$

71. $\dfrac{x}{\sqrt{2a}}$ $\dfrac{x\sqrt{2a}}{2a}$

72. $\dfrac{7}{\sqrt{4}}$
$\dfrac{7}{2}$, or $3\dfrac{1}{2}$

Use the diagram to name each ratio.

73. $\tan A$ $\dfrac{x}{y}$

74. $\sin A$ $\dfrac{x}{z}$

75. $\cos A$ $\dfrac{y}{z}$

76. $\tan B$ $\dfrac{y}{x}$

77. $\cos B$ $\dfrac{x}{z}$

78. $\sin B$ $\dfrac{y}{z}$

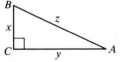

For Exercises 79–88, use the tables on pages 508 and 509. Find $\sin A$, $\cos A$, and $\tan A$ for the given measure of $\angle A$.

79. $27°$ **80.** $68°$ **81.** $89°$ **82.** $5°$

Find the measure of $\angle A$ to the nearest degree.

83. $\sin A = 0.436$ 26° **84.** $\cos A = 0.224$ 77° **85.** $\tan A = 1.35$
53°

Refer to the diagram at the right.

86. Find the value of x. $x = 5$

87. Find $\angle D$ to the nearest degree. 23°

88. Find $\angle E$ to the nearest degree. 67°

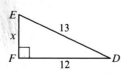

Extra Practice **505**

11.

x	f
8	1
9	2
10	4
11	3
12	3
14	1
16	1

12.

x	f
5	1
7	3
8	2
9	2
10	2
11	2
12	2

13.

x	f
1	3
2	5
3	3
4	3
5	4

14.

x	f
15	2
16	3
17	3
18	2

Extra Practice: *Chapter 12*

Illustrate. Check students' graphs.

1. Make a broken-line graph and a bar graph to illustrate the given data.

Class Typing Speed

Words per minute	20	19	18	17	16	15	14
Number of students	1	5	1	12	6	4	1

2. During the baseball season, Tom hit 16 home runs, Fred hit 12, Jamie hit 10, Dale hit 6, and Corey hit 6. Illustrate the data using both a pictograph and a circle graph.

Find the mean, the median, and the range of each set of data.

3. 2, 4, 5, 8, 8, 10, 12 7, 8, 10

4. 6, 7, 7, 9, 11, 12, 12, 16 10, 10, 10

5. 1, 2, 3, 3, 3, 4, 4, 7, 8, 9 4.4, 3.5, 8

6. 310, 220, 300, 300, 240, 220, 300 270, 300, 90

7. 210, 250, 190, 180, 155 197, 190, 95

8. 1.4, 1.7, 2.7, 1.9, 2.1, 2.2 2, 2, 1.3

9. 8000, 6000, 3000, 8000, 7000, 1000 5500, 6500, 7000

10. 1.9, 2.1, 2.1, 1.7, 1.5, 2.1, 1.5, 1.9 1.85, 1.9, 0.6

Make a frequency table for the given data. Then find the mean, the median, the range, and the mode.

11. 8, 9, 10, 11, 9, 12, 12, 16, 12, 14, 11, 10, 10, 11, 10 11, 11, 8, 10

12. 9, 7, 9, 12, 10, 11, 5, 8, 8, 7, 12, 7, 11, 10 9, 9, 7, 7

13. 4, 2, 1, 2, 4, 2, 5, 1, 3, 3, 4, 3, 5, 2, 1, 2, 5, 5 3, 3, 4, 2

14. 16, 17, 15, 16, 17, 18, 18, 16, 15, 17 16.5, 16.5, 3, 16 and 17

Make a table, and arrange the data listed below into the following intervals: 4.5–34.5, 34.5–64.5, 64.5–94.5. Then use the table to make a histogram and a frequency polygon.

15. 64 91 86 23 67

16 42 63 25 46

44 88 48 67 86

68 25 46 86 67

52 25 67 32 86

x	f
4.5–34.5	6
34.5–64.5	8
64.5–94.5	11

16. 61 84 88 8 17

23 27 46 10 23

65 42 65 46 65

23 35 46 27 46

5 42 27 46 84

x	f
4.5–34.5	10
34.5–64.5	9
64.5–94.5	6

506 *Extra Practice*

Find the value of each.

17. 6! 720 **18.** 3! 6 **19.** 10! 3,628,800 **20.** 2! 2 **21.** $\frac{120}{5!}$

22. In how many different ways can you arrange the letters in the word DIRECT if you take the letters 3 at a time? 120

23. $_4C_2$ 6 **24.** $_{10}C_3$ 120 **25.** $_6C_3$ 20 **26.** $_{12}C_2$ 66 **27.** $_{10}C_5$ $\frac{252}{}$

28. How many combinations of 3 fish can you choose from 7 fish? 35

29. There are 52 basketball teams entered in a tournament. How many combinations can make it to the final game? 1326

A bag contains 3 green, 2 blue, 1 red, and 1 white marble. Find the probability for a marble chosen at random.

30. P(green) $\frac{3}{7}$ **31.** P(not green) $\frac{4}{7}$ **32.** P(yellow) 0

33. P(not yellow) 1 **34.** P(green or red) $\frac{4}{7}$ **35.** P(red, white, or green) $\frac{5}{7}$

Kate has 24 albums: 4 by the Deltas, 6 by the Squares, 6 by the Tuscon Band, 3 by Eliot Smith, 3 by the Marks, and 2 by the Deep River Quartet. She selects one at random.

36. Find the odds in favor of selecting a record by the following.
  a. the Marks **b.** the Deep River Quartet **c.** the Squares
  1 to 7 1 to 11 1 to 3
37. Find the odds against selecting a record by the following.
  a. Eliot Smith **b.** the Tuscon Band **c.** the Squares
  7 to 1 3 to 1 3 to 1

Two game cubes are rolled. Find the probability of each.

38. a. The cubes show the same number. $\frac{1}{6}$ **39. a.** The difference is 1. $\frac{5}{18}$
  b. The sum is 3. $\frac{1}{18}$ **b.** The sum is 12. $\frac{1}{36}$
  c. The cubes show the same number **c.** The difference is 1 or the sum is
  or the sum is 3. $\frac{2}{9}$ 12. $\frac{11}{36}$

40. $P(A) = 0.40$, $P(B) = 0.60$, $P(A$ and $B) = 0.24$. Find $P(A$ or $B)$. 0.76

41. Find the probability that a month, chosen at random, begins with the letter J or has 30 days. $\frac{1}{2}$

42. $P(A) = 0.25$, $P(B) = 0.20$, $P(A$ and $B) = 0.05$. Find $P(A$ or $B)$. 0.40

43. Two game cubes are rolled. Find the probability of each event.
  a. The cubes show the same number. $\frac{1}{6}$
  b. The sum is 8. $\frac{5}{36}$
  c. The cubes show the same number and the sum is 8. $\frac{1}{36}$
  d. The cubes show the same number or the sum is 8. $\frac{5}{18}$

Extra Practice **507**

Table of Square Roots of Integers from 1 to 100

Number	Positive Square Root	Number	Positive Square Root	Number	Positive Square Root	Number	Positive Square Root
N	$\sqrt{N}$	N	$\sqrt{N}$	N	$\sqrt{N}$	N	$\sqrt{N}$
1	1	26	5.099	51	7.141	76	8.718
2	1.414	27	5.196	52	7.211	77	8.775
3	1.732	28	5.292	53	7.280	78	8.832
4	2	29	5.385	54	7.348	79	8.888
5	2.236	30	5.477	55	7.416	80	8.944
6	2.449	31	5.568	56	7.483	81	9
7	2.646	32	5.657	57	7.550	82	9.055
8	2.828	33	5.745	58	7.616	83	9.110
9	3	34	5.831	59	7.681	84	9.165
10	3.162	35	5.916	60	7.746	85	9.220
11	3.317	36	6	61	7.810	86	9.274
12	3.464	37	6.083	62	7.874	87	9.327
13	3.606	38	6.164	63	7.937	88	9.381
14	3.742	39	6.245	64	8	89	9.434
15	3.873	40	6.325	65	8.062	90	9.487
16	4	41	6.403	66	8.124	91	9.539
17	4.123	42	6.481	67	8.185	92	9.592
18	4.243	43	6.557	68	8.246	93	9.644
19	4.359	44	6.633	69	8.307	94	9.695
20	4.472	45	6.708	70	8.367	95	9.747
21	4.583	46	6.782	71	8.426	96	9.798
22	4.690	47	6.856	72	8.485	97	9.849
23	4.796	48	6.928	73	8.544	98	9.899
24	4.899	49	7	74	8.602	99	9.950
25	5	50	7.071	75	8.660	100	10

Exact square roots are shown in red. For the others, rational approximations are given correct to three decimal places.

Table of Trigonometric Ratios

Angle	Sine	Cosine	Tangent	Angle	Sine	Cosine	Tangent
1°	.0175	.9998	.0175	46°	.7193	.6947	1.0355
2°	.0349	.9994	.0349	47°	.7314	.6820	1.0724
3°	.0523	.9986	.0524	48°	.7431	.6691	1.1106
4°	.0698	.9976	.0699	49°	.7547	.6561	1.1504
5°	.0872	.9962	.0875	50°	.7660	.6428	1.1918
6°	.1045	.9945	.1051	51°	.7771	.6293	1.2349
7°	.1219	.9925	.1228	52°	.7880	.6157	1.2799
8°	.1392	.9903	.1405	53°	.7986	.6018	1.3270
9°	.1564	.9877	.1584	54°	.8090	.5878	1.3764
10°	.1736	.9848	.1763	55°	.8192	.5736	1.4281
11°	.1908	.9816	.1944	56°	.8290	.5592	1.4826
12°	.2079	.9781	.2126	57°	.8387	.5446	1.5399
13°	.2250	.9744	.2309	58°	.8480	.5299	1.6003
14°	.2419	.9703	.2493	59°	.8572	.5150	1.6643
15°	.2588	.9659	.2679	60°	.8660	.5000	1.7321
16°	.2756	.9613	.2867	61°	.8746	.4848	1.8040
17°	.2924	.9563	.3057	62°	.8829	.4695	1.8807
18°	.3090	.9511	.3249	63°	.8910	.4540	1.9626
19°	.3256	.9455	.3443	64°	.8988	.4384	2.0503
20°	.3420	.9397	.3640	65°	.9063	.4226	2.1445
21°	.3584	.9336	.3839	66°	.9135	.4067	2.2460
22°	.3746	.9272	.4040	67°	.9205	.3907	2.3559
23°	.3907	.9205	.4245	68°	.9272	.3746	2.4751
24°	.4067	.9135	.4452	69°	.9336	.3584	2.6051
25°	.4226	.9063	.4663	70°	.9397	.3420	2.7475
26°	.4384	.8988	.4877	71°	.9455	.3256	2.9042
27°	.4540	.8910	.5095	72°	.9511	.3090	3.0777
28°	.4695	.8829	.5317	73°	.9563	.2924	3.2709
29°	.4848	.8746	.5543	74°	.9613	.2756	3.4874
30°	.5000	.8660	.5774	75°	.9659	.2588	3.7321
31°	.5150	.8572	.6009	76°	.9703	.2419	4.0108
32°	.5299	.8480	.6249	77°	.9744	.2250	4.3315
33°	.5446	.8387	.6494	78°	.9781	.2079	4.7046
34°	.5592	.8290	.6745	79°	.9816	.1908	5.1446
35°	.5736	.8192	.7002	80°	.9848	.1736	5.6713
36°	.5878	.8090	.7265	81°	.9877	.1564	6.3138
37°	.6018	.7986	.7536	82°	.9903	.1392	7.1154
38°	.6157	.7880	.7813	83°	.9925	.1219	8.1443
39°	.6293	.7771	.8098	84°	.9945	.1045	9.5144
40°	.6428	.7660	.8391	85°	.9962	.0872	11.4301
41°	.6561	.7547	.8693	86°	.9976	.0698	14.3007
42°	.6691	.7431	.9004	87°	.9986	.0523	19.0811
43°	.6820	.7314	.9325	88°	.9994	.0349	28.6363
44°	.6947	.7193	.9657	89°	.9998	.0175	57.2900
45°	.7071	.7071	1.0000	90°	1.0000	.0000	Undefined

Summary of Formulas

Circumference

$C = \pi d$

$C = 2\pi r$

Area

Rectangle: $A = lw$

Triangle: $A = \frac{1}{2}bh$

Parallelogram: $A = bh$

Trapezoid: $A = \frac{1}{2}(b_1 + b_2)h$

Circle: $A = \pi r^2$

Volume

Prism: $V = Bh$

Cylinder: $V = \pi r^2 h$

Pyramid: $V = \frac{1}{3}Bh$

Cone: $V = \frac{1}{3}\pi r^2 h$

Sphere: $V = \frac{4}{3}\pi r^3$

Lateral Area

Prism: lateral area = perimeter of base $\times$ height

Cylinder: lateral area = $2\pi rh$

Surface Area

Prism: total surface area = lateral area + area of bases

Cylinder: total surface area = $2\pi rh + 2\pi r^2$

Sphere: $A = 4\pi r^2$

Mass

Mass = Density $\times$ Volume

Distance

distance = rate $\times$ time

Percentage

percentage = rate $\times$ base

Interest

Interest = Principal $\times$ rate $\times$ time

APPENDIX A: *Estimation*

Sometimes solving a problem involves long and repetitive calculations. To avoid doing these, it is often possible to use **estimation.** We *estimate* when we need to find only an approximate answer to a problem or to test the reasonableness of the calculated answer. For example, suppose that we want to find the total number of rainy days this summer, and it rained 7 days in June, 12 days in July, and 9 days in August. To find the sum we approximate each number. Notice that the numbers all *cluster* around, or are close to, 10. Thus the sum is about $10 + 10 + 10$, or 30. There were approximately 30 rainy days this summer.

Estimation strategies that are frequently used include *rounding, clustering, front-end estimation,* and choosing *compatible numbers.* The example above illustrates the use of *clustering* in estimation. The **clustering** method is appropriate to use when finding a sum in which the addends are all close to the same number.

EXAMPLE 1   Estimate the total grocery bill for the following items.
$2.19, $1.88, $1.79, $2.31, $1.74, $1.98, $2.08, $2.26

Solution   Each item costs about $2.00.
The total grocery bill will be close to $8 \times \$2.00$, or $16.00.

Front-end estimation helps us to add or subtract numbers quickly. Determine the highest place value shown for the given numbers. Add or subtract all the digits in that place value. Then adjust the answer by calculating with the digits in the next highest place value.

EXAMPLE 2   Fabric remnants are on sale for $.50 per yard. One bundle has 3 pieces of fabric, all having the same width but with lengths $1\frac{2}{3}$ yd, $1\frac{5}{8}$ yd, and 1 yd. About how much does the bundle cost?

Solution   When working with fractions, first add the whole numbers.

$$
\begin{array}{r}
1\frac{2}{3} \\
1\frac{5}{8} \\
+\ 1 \\
\hline
3
\end{array}
$$

Then compensate for the fractions. Both $\frac{2}{3}$ and $\frac{5}{8}$ are close to $\frac{1}{2}$ so that the sum $\frac{2}{3} + \frac{5}{8}$ is about equal to the sum $\frac{1}{2} + \frac{1}{2}$, or 1. Thus the bundle contains around $3 + 1$, or 4, yards. Since each yard costs $.50, the bundle costs about $4 \times \$.50$, or $2.00.

Rounding is a common way of estimating. Refer to pages 14–15 for a detailed explanation of rounding. When rounding more than one number in order to estimate an answer, round each number to its highest place value to allow for fast computation.

EXAMPLE 3   Denise Crosby earns a salary of $214.33 each week. Deductions of $20.28 for federal income tax, $7.94 for state income tax, and $14.61 for Social Security are taken from her pay. About how much money does Denise take home each week?

Solution   Round each deduction and then add the deductions.
Round $20.28 to $20, $7.94 to $8, and $14.61 to $10.

$$20 + 8 + 10 = 38$$

The total deductions are close to $38.

Subtract the total from the salary.
Round $214.33 to $200 and $38 to $40.

$$200 - 40 = 160$$

Denise takes home about $160 each week.

Choosing **compatible numbers** makes solving multiplication and division problems simpler. Select numbers that are easy to multiply or divide and that are close to the actual numbers.

EXAMPLE 4   A recent survey shows that about 23% of a class will vote for Bill Donnway for class treasurer. If 768 students vote, about how many can be expected to vote for Bill?

Solution   Find an estimate for 23% of 768. First change the percent to one that is close to 23% and that can be converted easily to a fraction. 23% is about 25%, or $\frac{1}{4}$. Then choose a number close to 768 that has 4 as a factor. Pick 800.

$$23\% \text{ of } 768 \longrightarrow \frac{1}{4} \times 800 = 200$$

About 200 students will vote for Bill Donnway.

Exercises

Select the best estimate.

A   **1.** 0.16 + 2.34 + 9.5

   a. 0.12   **b.** 1.2   **c.** 12   **d.** 120

2. 4.01 × 8.2

   a. 0.32   **b.** 3.2   **c.** 12   **d.** 32

Select the best estimate.

3. 72,197 − 38,846

    a. 300   **b.** 3000   **(c.)** 30,000   **d.** 300,000

4. 4213 ÷ 6.7

    a. 0.6   **b.** 6.0   **c.** 60   **(d.)** 600

B   **5.** 489.233 + 256.1 + 133.26

    a. 90   **(b.)** 900   **c.** 9000   **d.** 90,000

6. $\dfrac{7}{16} \times 6104$

    a. 30   **b.** 300   **(c.)** 3000   **d.** 30,000

7. 18% of 3477

    a. 0.7   **b.** 7   **c.** 70   **(d.)** 700

8. $\dfrac{7}{12} + \dfrac{4}{10}$

    (a.) 1   **b.** 2   **c.** 11   **d.** 22

C   **9.** $32.14 ÷ 0.78

    a. $.04   **b.** $4   **(c.)** $40   **d.** $400

10. 0.04 + 0.0006 + 1.009

    a. 0.019   **b.** 0.05   **c.** 0.1   **(d.)** 1

Problems

Estimate each answer.   Answers may vary. Accept reasonable answers.

A   **1.** Garth takes $1\frac{7}{12}$ hours to ride his bicycle to the lake. He rides around the lake in $2\frac{2}{3}$ hours. About how much more time does he take to ride around the lake than to the lake?   **1 hour**

    2. What is the greatest number of cassette tapes costing $6.45 each that Carolyn can buy with $20.00?   **3 tapes**

B   **3.** The digits in the product of 3.008 × 2.79 are 839232. Where should the decimal point be placed?   **8.39232**

    4. At Parts Inc. 0.023 of the parts built are defective. About how many of the 4140 parts built in an average day are defective?   **100 parts**

C   **5.** A $489.66 VCR is on sale for 18% off. Approximately what is the sale price?   **$400**

    6. To get the most for his money, should Adam buy 60 vitamins for $6.82 or 90 of the same vitamins for $8.85?   **90 vitamins for $8.85**

APPENDIX B: *Stem-and-Leaf Plots*

Like a frequency distribution, a **stem-and-leaf plot** is a method of displaying data. Consider the following centimeter heights of plants in a laboratory experiment:

25   16   32   28   25   11   29   17   43   24   37   33   30

In order to create a stem-and-leaf plot, you first draw a vertical line and list the tens' digits from least to greatest to the left of the line. These are the "stems."

```
1 |
2 |
3 |
4 |
```

Next, list the units' digit for each item of data to the right of its corresponding stem. These are the "leaves."

```
1 | 6, 1, 7
2 | 5, 8, 5, 9, 4
3 | 2, 7, 3, 0
4 | 3
```

Finally, rewrite your diagram with the leaves listed from least to greatest, reading from left to right. This is the finished stem-and-leaf plot.

```
1 | 1, 6, 7
2 | 4, 5, 5, 8, 9
3 | 0, 2, 3, 7
4 | 3
```

EXAMPLE   Construct a stem-and-leaf plot for the following test scores:

75   83   72   56   92   74   87   88   91   76   74   80

Solution

```
5 | 6
6 |
7 | 2, 4, 4, 5, 6
8 | 0, 3, 7, 8
9 | 1, 2
```

Note that the stem 6 is included for completeness, even though no scores require that stem.

Class Exercises

1. List the data items from which the stem-and-leaf plot shown at the right was constructed.

   4, 12, 13, 13, 17, 22, 25, 26, 34, 37, 45, 49, 49

```
0 | 4
1 | 2, 3, 3, 7
2 | 2, 5, 6
3 | 4, 7
4 | 5, 9, 9
```

Use the following data for Exercises 2 and 3:

54   65   76   83   47   62   76   89   77   88   71   80

2. List the stems for this set of data. 4, 5, 6, 7, 8

3. List the leaves for the stems 7 and 8. 7: 1, 6, 6, 7; 8: 0, 3, 8, 9

4. What are the advantages of a stem-and-leaf plot over a frequency distribution? What are the disadvantages? Answers may vary. For example: The stem-and-leaf plot retains all the information and presents it visually, but it may take up more space than a frequency distribution.

Written Exercises

Construct a stem-and-leaf plot for each set of data. Check students' plots.

A   **1.** 22, 14, 14, 25, 27, 31, 35, 29, 18

2. 54, 40, 41, 32, 55, 57, 58, 58, 36, 43

3. 62, 65, 43, 44, 44, 44, 50, 53, 72, 67

4. 81, 85, 70, 76, 92, 65, 97, 85, 87, 53, 66

5. 7, 23, 27, 24, 9, 5, 13, 16, 5, 30, 2, 12, 10

6. 45, 37, 28, 22, 45, 56, 25, 28, 37, 40, 42, 48

7. 92, 90, 58, 87, 56, 77, 91, 53, 53, 91, 95, 84

8. 11, 19, 5, 33, 9, 7, 5, 35, 16, 44, 5, 46, 41

B   **9.** Numbers of customers at a car wash on different days:
46, 42, 45, 36, 57, 72, 54, 32, 30, 44, 73, 31, 45, 53

10. Numbers of seeds out of samples of 50 that germinated:
42, 35, 31, 30, 9, 28, 27, 37, 35, 30, 41, 22, 25, 8, 33

11. Point totals for a basketball team in successive games:
87, 94, 82, 78, 95, 91, 87, 83, 101, 83, 82, 77, 80, 102, 75

12. Daily patient counts at a health clinic:
47, 39, 32, 32, 58, 63, 55, 67, 52, 44, 37, 50, 40, 71, 50

C   **13.** Consider the following standardized test scores:
570, 650, 780, 460, 550, 530, 580, 610, 720, 640, 490, 520, 480

How would you alter the rule for constructing a stem-and-leaf plot so that these data could be best displayed? Construct a stem-and-leaf plot according to your rule. Since the data are all multiples of 10, disregard the last digit and use the hundreds' digits as stems and the tens' digits as leaves.

APPENDIX C: Box-and-Whisker Plots

A **box-and-whisker plot** is a method of displaying data that gives a quick picture of the distribution of the data items. Consider the data below, which are scores on a job aptitude test whose maximum score is 100.

56 48 66 72 37 62 49 37 29 83 74 55 47 48 52 57 45

To make a box-and-whisker plot, first put the data items in increasing order, reading from left to right.

29 37 37 44 46 48 48 49 52 55 56 57 62 66 72 74 83

Next, find the three numbers that split the data into four equal-sized parts. The second of these numbers will be the median. In this example, the median is 52. The other two numbers, called the **first quartile** and the **third quartile,** are, respectively, the medians of the lower and upper halves of the data, not including the median.

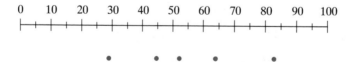

lower half			upper half

29 37 37 44 46 48 48 49 52 55 56 57 62 66 72 74 83

first quartile: median: third quartile:

$$\frac{44 + 46}{2} = 45 \qquad\qquad 52 \qquad\qquad \frac{62 + 66}{2} = 64$$

Draw a number line that includes all the *possible* data values. Underneath the line, mark with dots the boundaries of the range, the median, and the two quartiles.

0   10   20   30   40   50   60   70   80   90   100

Finally, using the dots as a guide, draw a "box" around the middle half of the range, a vertical line through the median, and "whiskers" out to the two ends of the range.

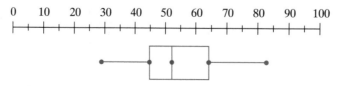

0   10   20   30   40   50   60   70   80   90   100

Class Exercises

Exercises 1–4 refer to the box-and-whisker plot below.

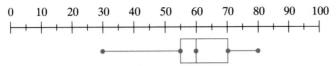

1. What is the range of the data? What is the median of the data? 50; 60

2. What are the first and third quartiles? 55, 70

3. Name the interval into which the middle half of the data falls. 55–70

4. Name the interval that contains the quarter of the data in which the data items are *most concentrated*. 55–60

Written Exercises
Check that students' plots are defined by the five points (lower extreme, first quartile, median, third quartile, upper extreme).

Construct a box-and-whisker plot for each set of data.

A 1. 18, 32, 35, 37, 45, 50, 53, 55, 60, 75, 80 18, 35, 50, 60, 80

2. 36, 38, 40, 45, 46, 55, 57, 60, 70, 77, 82 36, 40, 55, 70, 82

3. 6.6, 5.4, 8.3, 9.2, 9.0, 7.4, 8.2, 5.8, 6.3, 6.5 5.4, 6.3, 7.0, 8.3, 9.2

4. 114, 128, 105, 122, 130, 136, 118, 110, 129, 140 105, 114, 125, 130, 140

For each pair of sets of data construct two box-and-whisker plots using a common number line.

B 5. Monthly rainfall (in inches): A: 0.7, 1.5, 2.3, 3.5, 4.9
B: 1.4, 2.3, 3.7, 4.7, 7.2

Antrim: 2.5, 2.0, 4.9, 3.4, 2.1, 1.6, 1.3, 0.7, 1.4, 3.6, 3.5, 3.5

Brewster: 3.2, 4.1, 5.5, 7.2, 3.6, 2.1, 1.5, 1.4, 2.5, 3.8, 5.0, 4.4

6. Scores on a math test (out of 100): 1: 56, 74, 81, 92, 98
2: 48, 68, 81, 86, 92

Class 1: 92, 86, 74, 56, 82, 85, 78, 94, 95, 98, 80, 72, 63, 77

Class 2: 82, 84, 83, 48, 56, 64, 72, 90, 88, 86, 80, 79, 68, 92

Construct a set of data that would give rise to each box-and-whisker plot. Answers may vary. Examples are shown.

C 7.

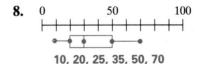

20, 40, 50, 55, 62, 65, 80

8. 0   50   100

10, 20, 25, 35, 50, 70

Glossary

Absolute value (p. 46) The distance from 0 to the graph of a number on the number line.

Acute angle (p. 174) An angle with measure between 0° and 90°.

Acute triangle (p. 179) A triangle with three acute angles.

Angle (p. 173) A figure formed by two rays with a common endpoint.

Annual rate of interest (p. 262) A percent of the principal figured on a yearly basis.

Arc (p. 198) A part of a circle.

Area (p. 346) Amount of surface, measured in square units.

Bar graph (p. 434) A graph in which the length of each bar is proportional to the number it represents.

Base of a geometric figure (pp. 346, 351, 352, 364) A selected side or face.

Base, numerical (p. 9) A number that is raised to some power. In 5^2, 5 is the base.

Bisector (p. 198) The line dividing a geometric figure into two congruent parts.

Broken-line graph (p. 434) A graph made by joining successive plotted points.

Capacity (p. 365) A measure of the volume of a container.

Center (pp. 188, 378) The point that is equidistant from all points on a circle or a sphere.

Chord (p. 188) A segment joining two points on a circle.

Circle (p. 188) A plane figure composed of all points measuring the same distance from a given point in the plane.

Circle graph (p. 260) A graph that uses the area of a circle to represent a sum of data. The area is divided into segments proportional to the data.

Circumference (p. 188) The perimeter of a circle.

Collinear points (p. 164) Two or more points that lie on the same line.

Combination (p. 458) An arrangement of a group of things in which order does not matter.

Common denominator (p. 100) A common multiple used as the denominator of two or more fractions that are equivalent to the given fractions.

Common factor (p. 97) A number that is a factor of two or more numbers.

Common multiple (p. 100) A number that is a multiple of two or more numbers.

Compass (p. 188) A tool used to draw a circle.

Complementary angles (p. 174) Two angles whose measures have a sum of 90°.

Cone (p. 369) A closed figure formed by a circular region and a curved surface that come to a point.

Congruent figures (pp. 192, 360) Figures that have the same size and shape.

Coordinate (p. 14) The number paired with a point on the number line.

Coordinate plane (p. 310) A plane marked with two perpendicular number lines, used to graph ordered pairs of numbers.

Corresponding angles (p. 192) The angles at matching vertices of congruent figures.

Cosine of an angle (p. 416) If $\angle A$ is one of the acute angles in a right triangle, the cosine of $\angle A$ is the ratio of the length of the side adjacent to $\angle A$ to the length of the hypotenuse.

Counting numbers (p. 89) The set of numbers 1, 2, 3, 4 . . . .

Cross-multiplying (p. 217) A method for solving and checking proportions.

Cube (p. 364) A rectangular prism having square faces.

Cube root of a number (p. 426) One of the three equal factors of a number.

Cylinder (p. 365) A geometric solid having two parallel bases that are congruent and one curved surface joining the bases.

Data (p. 434) Numerical information.

Decimal system (p. 13) The place-value numeration system that uses 10 as a base.

Degree (p. 173) Unit of angle measure.

Density (p. 382) The mass per unit volume of a substance.

Diameter (pp. 188, 378) A chord that contains the center of a circle or a sphere. Also, the length of such a chord.

Dimensions (p. 346) Length, width and height of a space figure.

Endpoint (p. 164) The point at the end of a line segment or ray.

Equation (p. 23) A mathematical sentence with an equals sign to indicate that two expressions name the same number.

Equilateral triangle (p. 179) A triangle in which all sides are congruent.

Equivalent equations (p. 130) Equations that have the same solution.

Equivalent fractions (p. 96) Fractions that name the same number.

Equivalent inequalities (p. 293) Inequalities that have the same solutions.

Evaluate an expression (p. 3) To replace variables in an expression with specified values and then complete the indicated arithmetic.

Expanded form (p. 13) The method of representing a number as the sum of products of each digit and powers of 10.

Even number (p. 84) Any multiple of 2.

Exponent (p. 9) A number indicating how many times the base is used as a factor.

Extremes of a proportion (p. 218) The first and last terms of a proportion.

Factor (p. 9) Any of two or more whole numbers that are multiplied to form a product.

Fraction (p. 97) An indicated quotient, for example $\frac{2}{5}$. The denominator, 5 in the example, tells the number of equal parts into which the whole has been divided. The numerator, 2, tells how many of these parts are being considered.

Frequency distribution (p. 446) A table that pairs each item in a set of data with its frequency.

Frequency polygon (p. 450) A line graph of frequencies connected to the horizontal axis at each end to form a polygon.

Function (p. 317) A set of ordered pairs in which no two different ordered pairs have the same x-coordinate.

Geometric construction (p. 198) A geometric drawing for which only a compass and a straightedge may be used.

Graph of an equation (p. 320) The line consisting of all points whose coordinates satisfy the equation.

Graph of a number (p. 14) The point on the number line paired with the number.

Graphs *See* Bar graph, Broken-line graph, Circle graph, Histogram, Pictograph.

Greatest common factor (GCF) (p. 97) The greatest whole number that is a factor of two or more given whole numbers.

Grouping symbols (p. 5) Symbols such as parentheses, ( ), and brackets, [ ], that are used to group expressions.

Height (p. 346) The perpendicular distance between the bases of a geometric figure. In triangles, cones, and pyramids, the perpendicular distance from the base to the opposite vertex.

Histogram (p. 450) A bar graph that shows a frequency distribution.

Hypotenuse (p. 402) The side opposite the right angle in a right triangle.

Identity elements (p. 19) 0 is the identity element for addition, because it can be added to any number without changing the value of the number. 1 is the identity element for multiplication, because it may be multiplied by any number without changing the value of the number.

Improper fraction (p. 98) A positive fraction whose numerator is greater than or equal to its denominator, or the opposite of such a fraction.

Inequality (p. 47) A mathematical sentence formed by placing an inequality sign between two expressions.

Inscribed polygon (p. 189) A polygon that has all of its vertices on the circle.

Integers (p. 46) The whole numbers and their opposites: . . . , -2, -1, 0, 1, 2, ...

Interest (p. 262) The amount of money paid for the use of money.

Interpolation (p. 399) A method of approximation.

Inverse operations (p. 26) Operations that undo each other. Addition and subtraction are inverse operations, as are multiplication and division.

Irrational number (p. 119) All real numbers that are not rational.

Isosceles triangle (p. 179) A triangle with at least two sides congruent.

Lateral area (p. 373) The surface area of a solid, not including the bases.

Least common denominator (LCD) (p. 100) The least common multiple of two or more denominators.

Least common multiple (LCM) (p. 100) The least number that is a multiple of two or more nonzero numbers.

Legs of a right triangle (p. 402) The two sides forming the right angle.

Like terms (p. 282) Terms in which the variable parts are the same.

Line (p. 164) A figure determined by two points and extending in both directions without end.

Line segment (p. 164) Two points on a line and all the points between them.

Linear equation in two variables (p. 321) An equation with two variables that can be written in the form $ax + by = c$, where a and b are both not 0.

Lowest terms (p. 97) A fraction is in lowest terms when the numerator and the denominator have no common factor but 1.

Mass (p. 382) The measure of the amount of matter an object contains.

Mean (p. 443) The value found by dividing the sum of a group of numbers by the number of numbers in the group. Also called *average*.

Means of a proportion (p. 218) The second and third terms of a proportion.

Median (p. 443) The number that falls in the middle when data are listed from least to greatest. If the number of data is even, the median is the mean of the two middle items.

Midpoint (p. 169) The point of a segment that divides it into two congruent segments.

Mixed number (p. 98) A whole number plus a proper fraction.

Mode (p. 447) The number that occurs most often in a set of data.

Multiple (p. 84) A product of a given number and any whole number.

Mutually exclusive events (p. 470) Events that cannot both occur at the same time.

Noncollinear points (p. 164) Points not on the same line.

Number line (p. 14) A line on which consecutive integers are assigned to equally spaced points on the line in increasing order from left to right.

Number sentence (p. 23) An equation or inequality indicating the relationship between two mathematical expressions.

Numerical coefficient (p. 3) In an expression such as $3ab$, the number 3 is the numerical coefficient of ab.

Numerical expression (p. 2) An expression that names a number, such as $2 + 3$.

Obtuse angle (p. 174) An angle with measure between $90°$ and $180°$.

Obtuse triangle (p. 179) A triangle that has one obtuse angle.

Odd number (p. 84) A whole number that is not a multiple of 2.

Odds of an event (p. 466) A ratio that compares the probability of an event occurring and the probability of the event not occurring.

Open sentence (p. 23) A mathematical sentence that contains one or more variables.

Opposites (p. 46) A pair of numbers such as -4 and 4.

Ordered pair of numbers (p. 312) A pair of numbers whose order is important.

Origin (pp. 14, 312) The graph of zero on a number line, or (0, 0) in a rectangular coordinate plane.

Outcome (p. 461) The result of an event.

Parallel lines (p. 165) Lines in the same plane that do not intersect.

Parallel planes (p. 165) Planes that do not intersect.

Parallelogram (p. 183) A quadrilateral with both pairs of opposite sides parallel.

Percent (p. 227) A ratio of a number to 100, shown by the symbol %.

Percent of change (p. 246) The amount of change divided by the original amount.

Perfect square (p. 394) A number whose square root is an integer.

Perimeter (p. 184) The distance around a plane figure.

Permutation (p. 453) An arrangement of a group of things in a particular order.

Perpendicular bisector (p. 198) The line that is perpendicular to a segment at its midpoint.

Perpendicular lines (p. 173) Two lines that intersect to form 90° angles.

Pi (p. 188) The ratio of the circumference of a circle to its diameter.

Pictograph (p. 438) A form of bar graph with the bars replaced by rows or columns of symbols.

Plane (p. 165) A flat surface extending infinitely in all directions.

Point (p. 164) The simplest figure in geometry representing an exact location.

Polygon (p. 183) A closed plane figure made up of line segments.

Polyhedron (p. 364) A three-dimensional figure formed of polygonal parts of planes.

Power of a number (pp. 9, 70) A product in which all the factors, except 1, are the same. For example, $2^3 = 2 \times 2 \times 2 = 8$, so 8 is the third power of 2.

Prime factorization (p. 90) An expression showing a positive integer as the product of prime factors.

Prime number (p. 89) A whole number greater than 1 that has only two whole number factors, itself and 1.

Principal (p. 262) An amount of money on which interest is paid.

Prism (p. 364) A polyhedron that has two parallel, congruent faces called bases. The other faces are parallelograms.

Probability (p. 461) The ratio of the number of outcomes favoring an event to the total number of possible outcomes.

Proper fraction (p. 98) A positive fraction whose numerator is less than its denominator, or the opposite of such a fraction.

Proportion (p. 217) An equation stating that two ratios are equal.

Protractor (p. 173) A device used to measure angles.

Pyramid (p. 369) A polyhedron that has a polygonal base and three or more triangular faces.

Quadrilateral (p. 183) A polygon with four sides.

Radical (p. 412) An expression such as $\sqrt{5}$ or $\sqrt{a}$; the radical sign symbol used to denote the square root of a number.

Radius (pp. 188, 356) A line segment joining any point on a circle or sphere to the center. Also, the length of that segment.

Random variable (p. 461) A variable whose value is determined by the outcome of a random experiment.

Range (p. 443) The difference between the greatest and the least numbers in a set of data.

Rate (p. 214) A ratio that compares quantities of different kinds of units.

Ratio (p. 210) An indicated quotient of two numbers.

Ray (p. 164) A part of a line with one endpoint.

Real number (p. 119) Any number that is either a rational number or an irrational number.

Reciprocals (p. 113) Two numbers whose product is 1.

Rectangle (p. 184) A quadrilateral with four right angles.

Regular polygon (p. 183) A polygon in which all sides are congruent and all angles are congruent.

Relatively prime numbers (p. 97) Two or more numbers that have no common factor but 1.

Replacement set (p. 23) The given set of numbers that a variable may represent.

Rhombus (p. 184) A parallelogram in which all sides are congruent.

Right angle (p. 174) An angle with measure 90°.

Right triangle (p. 179) A triangle with a right angle.

Rigid motions (p. 193) Motions such as rotation, translation, and reflection, used to move a figure to a new position without changing its shape or size.

Rounding (p. 14) A method of approximating a number.

Scalene triangle (p. 179) A triangle with no two sides congruent.

Scientific notation (p. 76) A method of expressing a number as the product of a power of 10 and a number between 1 and 10.

Segment (p. 164) *See* line segment.

Semicircle (p. 188) Half of a circle.

Sides of an equation (p. 23) The mathematical expressions to the right and to the left of the equals sign.

Sides of a figure (pp. 178, 183, 212) The rays that form an angle or the segments that form a polygon.

Similar figures (p. 196) Figures that have the same shape but not necessarily the same size.

Simple form (p. 106) A mixed number is in simple form if its fractional part is expressed in lowest terms.

Simplify an expression (p. 2) To replace an expression with its simplest name.

Sine of an angle (p. 416) If $\angle A$ is an acute angle of a right triangle, the sine of $\angle A$ is the ratio of the length of the side opposite $\angle A$ to the length of the hypotenuse.

Skew lines (p. 166) Two nonparallel lines that do not intersect.

Slope of a line (p. 328) The steepness of a line; that is, the ratio of the change in the y-coordinate to the change in the x-coordinate when moving from one point on a line to another point.

Solid (p. 364) An enclosed region of space bounded by planes.

Solution (pp. 23, 130) A value of a variable that makes an equation or inequality a true sentence.

Solving a right triangle (p. 420) The process of finding the measures of the sides and angles of a right triangle.

Sphere (p. 378) A figure in space made up of all points equidistant from a given point.

Square (p. 184) A rectangle with all four sides congruent.

Square root of a number (p. 394) One of the two equal factors of the number.

Statistical measures (p. 443) Measures including the range, mean, median, and mode used to analyze numerical data.

Supplementary angles (p. 174) Two angles whose measures have a sum of 180°.

Surface area (p. 373) The total area of a solid.

Symmetric (p. 360) A figure is symmetric with respect to a line if it can be folded on that line so that every point on one side coincides exactly with a point on the other side. A figure is symmetric with respect to a point O if for each point A on the figure there is a point B on the figure for which O is the midpoint of AB.

System of equations (p. 324) A set of two or more equations in the same variables.

Tangent of an angle (p. 416) If $\angle A$ is an acute angle of a right triangle, the tangent of $\angle A$ is the ratio of the length of the side opposite $\angle A$ to the length of the side adjacent to $\angle A$.

Terms of an expression (p. 3) The parts of a mathematical expression that are separated by a $+$ sign.

Terms of a proportion (p. 217) The numbers in a proportion.

Transformation (pp. 130, 282) Rewriting an equation or inequality as an equivalent equation or inequality.

Trapezoid (p. 183) A quadrilateral with exactly one pair of parallel sides.

Triangle (p. 178) A polygon with three sides.

Trigonometric ratios (p. 416) Any of the sine, cosine, or tangent ratios.

Value of a variable (p. 2) Any number that a variable represents.

Variable (p. 2) A symbol used to represent one or more numbers.

Variable expression (p. 2) A mathematical expression that contains a variable.

Vertex of an angle (p. 173) The common endpoint of two intersecting rays.

Vertex of a polygon or polyhedron (p. 178) The point at which two sides of a polygon or three or more edges of a polyhedron intersect.

Volume (p. 364) A measure of the space occupied by a solid.

x-axis (p. 312) The horizontal number line on a coordinate plane.

x-coordinate (p. 312) The first number in an ordered pair of numbers that designates the location of a point on the coordinate plane. Also called the *abscissa*.

y-axis (p. 312) The vertical number line on a coordinate plane.

y-coordinate (p. 312) The second number in an ordered pair of numbers that designates the location of a point on the coordinate plane. Also called the *ordinate*.

Index

Profit, 254
Programs in BASIC, 122
  for determining probability, 469
  for finding averages, 449
  for finding lowest common multiple, 121
  for plotting linear equations, 338
  to produce Pythagorean triple, 425
Programming languages, 39, 122
  See also BASIC
Proper fraction, 98
Properties, 18
  addition and subtraction, 19, 282
    of zero, 19
  associative, 18
  commutative, 18, 63, 282
  for decimals, 118, 119
  distributive, 20, 282
  of 45° right triangles, 411
  multiplication and division, 19, 282
    of one, 19
    of zero, 19
  for positive and negative fractions, 92–93, 103, 118, 119
  of proportions, 218
  of straight line, 328
  of 30–60 degree right triangles, 412
Proportions, 208, 217, 220
  of lengths and widths, 224
  and percent, 257, 260
  in problem solving, 257
  property of, 218
  in scale drawings, 224
Protractor, 173
Pyramids, 344, 369
PYTHAGORAS, 402
Pythagorean Theorem, 402, 411
  converse of, 402
Pythagorean triple, 404

Quadrants I–IV, 313
Quadrilateral, 183
Quantities, graphing relationships between, 328–329
Quotients, 67

Radical, 412
Radius, 188, 356, 378
Random outcomes, of probability, 461
Range, 443, 474
Rates, 214, 257
  of interest, 262
  See also Ratios
Rational numbers, 82, 94, 113, 118–119, 397
Ratio(s), 208, 210
  the Golden Ratio, 239
  percent, 227
  in proportions, 217
  and rates, 214
  scale, 224
  slope as, 328
  of sides in a triangle, 406
  trigonometric, 416
Ray, 164, 199
Reading Mathematics, vii, 3, 60, 71, 111, 132, 144, 184, 268, 288, 312, 357, 370, 378, 399, 408, 446
Real number line. See Number line
Real numbers, 119, 397
Reciprocals, 113, 136
Rectangle, 184, 239, 346
Rectangular coordinate system, 312
  See also coordinate plane
Reflection, 194
Relatively prime, 97
Repeating decimal, 117, 118
Replacement set, 23, 130
Research activity, 275, 305
Review Exercises, 4, 8, 12, 17, 25, 32, 53, 58, 66, 69, 72, 88, 91, 95, 99, 133, 135, 146, 151, 168, 172, 182, 187, 191, 197, 213, 216, 219, 223, 230, 233, 249, 253, 256, 266, 284, 292, 296, 300, 315, 319, 327, 333, 350, 355, 359, 368, 372, 377, 381, 395, 401, 410, 415, 419, 437, 442, 445, 448, 457, 460, 465, 469
  See also Chapter Review, Cumulative Review
Rhombus, 184
Right angle, 174
Right triangles, 179, 352, 402, 407
  isosceles, 411

solving, 420
Rigid motions, 193–194
Root(s), 394, 396, 399, 426
  square, 394, 396, 399
Rotation, 194
Rounding to whole numbers, 14
  in estimation, 511, 512
Rulers, metric, 169
Rules
  for divisibility, 85–86
  for exponents and powers of ten, 9, 70, 73
  for fractions
    adding and subtracting, 103, 106
    dividing, 113
    multiplying, 109
  for order of operations, 6
  for percentage
    expressing a fraction as a percent, 227, 232
    expressing a percent as a fraction, 228
    expressing a percent as a decimal, 231
    expressing a decimal as a percent, 231
  for positive and negative numbers, 54, 55, 59, 63, 64, 67
  for rounding decimal numbers, 14
  for scientific notation, 76
  See also Properties and Formulas
RUN command, 123, 203, 338

Scale, 46, 208, 224
  drawings, 224
Scientific notation, 76, 203
Segment, 164
  congruent, 169
  diagonal, 183
  radius, 188, 378
  of a sphere, 378
Self-Test A, 22, 62, 102, 142, 177, 226, 261, 290, 323, 363, 405, 452, 473
Self-Test B, 37, 75, 121, 155, 201, 237, 273, 303, 337, 385, 424, 473
  See also Chapter Review, Cumulative Review, Review Exercises

Credits

Answers to Selected Exercises

1 Introduction to Algebra

PAGE 4 WRITTEN EXERCISES 1. 48
3. 105 **5.** 14.15 **7.** 4.5 **9.** 25 **11.** 4 **13.** 12
15. 27 **17.** 2 **19.** 47 **21.** 26 **23.** 512 **25.** 9
27. 24 **29.** 2.5 **31.** 112.5 **33.** 680.805
35. 3.15 **37.** 2

PAGE 4 REVIEW EXERCISES 1. 51.87
3. 45.93 **5.** 0.27 **7.** 6.3

PAGES 7–8 WRITTEN EXERCISES 1. 92
3. 51 **5.** 2 **7.** 126 **9.** 7 **11.** 36 **13.** 10
15. 70 **17.** 36 **19.** 196 **21.** 3 **23.** 1512
25. 91 **27.** 84 **29.** 0.5 **31.** 4.1 **33.** 5827.248
35. 14.6 **37.** $2x \times (y - 4) + 2x$
or $2x \times y - (4 + 2)x$
39. $x \times [y + (z \div 3 + 1)] - z$

PAGE 8 REVIEW EXERCISES 1. 5 **3.** 6
5. 3 **7.** 168

PAGE 8 CALCULATOR KEY-IN 1. 288
3. 16.5 **5.** 6048

PAGES 11–12 WRITTEN EXERCISES 1. 5^6
3. 8^9 **5.** 7^7 **7.** 4^6 **9.** 10^1 **11.** 10^6
13. 1,000,000 **15.** 10,000 **17.** 16 **19.** 256
21. 400 **23.** 3375 **25.** 6400 **27.** 256 **29.** 1296
31. 4096 **33.** 125 **35.** 169 **37.** 400
39. 1,680,700 **41.** 0 **43.** 961 **45.** 256
47. 6912 **49.** 72,000 **51.** 0 **53.** 27 **55.** 90,000
57. 27 **59.** 218 **61.** 25 **63.** 225 **65.** 3375
67. 16

PAGE 12 REVIEW EXERCISES 1. 60 **3.** 57
5. 30 **7.** 24

PAGES 16–17 WRITTEN EXERCISES
1. $(3 \times 10) + 8$ **3.** $(8 \times 1000) + (9 \times 10) + 1$
5. $(4 \times 0.1) + (7 \times 0.01)$
7. $(6 \times 0.01) + (3 \times 0.001)$
9. $(1 \times 0.1) + (8 \times 0.01) + (7 \times 0.001)$
11. 54.57 **13.** 9002.146 **15.** 7.43 **17.** 19.005
19. 0.0048 **21.** 6.025 **23.** 30 **25.** 290 **27.** 650
29. 160 **31.** 72.46 **33.** 0.06 **35.** 0.01 **37.** 18.17
39. 0.001 **41.** 401.090 **43.** 250.341
45. 8.100 **47.** $(5 \times 10^3) + (2 \times 10^2) + (8 \times 10^1)$
49. $(1 \times 10^2) + (8 \times 10^1) +$

$$(3 \times 10^0) + \left(8 \times \frac{1}{10^2}\right)$$

51. $\left(9 \times \frac{1}{10^2}\right) + \left(1 \times \frac{1}{10^3}\right)$

53. $(7 \times 10^0) + \left(4 \times \frac{1}{10^1}\right) + \left(8 \times \frac{1}{10^2}\right) +$

$$\left(2 \times \frac{1}{10^3}\right)$$

55. $(2 \times 10^2) + (4 \times 10^0) + \left(5 \times \frac{1}{10^1}\right)$

57. $(3 \times 10^1) + (8 \times 10^0) + \left(3 \times \frac{1}{10^3}\right)$ **59.** b
61. a **63.** b **65.** c

PAGE 17 REVIEW EXERCISES 1. 9.4
3. 960 **5.** 60 **7.** 14.8

PAGES 21–22 WRITTEN EXERCISES
1. 14.6; associative **3.** 14.24; distributive
5. 18.97; commutative and associative
7. 0.21; commutative and associative
9. False **11.** True **13.** $n = 0$ **15.** $t = 3.2$
17. $w = 0$ **19.** $g = 15.9$ **21.** $n = 3$
23. $d = 1565$ **25.** $t = 0$ **27.** 3.88 **29.** 400
31. 900 **33.** 32 For exercises 35 and 37,
answers will vary. An example is given.
35. $a = 2, b = 3, c = 4$
37. $a = 2, b = 4, c = 6$

PAGE 22 SELF-TEST A 1. 46 **2.** 15 **3.** 168
4. 9 **5.** 4 **6.** 6 **7.** 16 **8.** 512 **9.** 9
10. 100,000 **11.** 100,000 **12.** 80 **13.** 3.18
14. 300 **15.** 102 **16.** 93 **17.** 21 **18.** 67.96

PAGES 24–25 WRITTEN EXERCISES
1. True **3.** False **5.** False **7.** True **9.** True
11. True **13.** 29 **15.** 8 **17.** No solution
19. No solution **21.** 1518 **23.** 1.26 **25.** 11
27. 12 **29.** 9 **31.** 2 **33.** No solution **35.** 4
For exercises 37 and 39, answers will vary. An
example is given. **37.** $3x + 5 = 35$
39. $(x + 20) \div 6 - 10 = 10$ **41.** $+, -$
43. $+, \div$ **45.** $\div, -, \times$ **47.** $-, +, \div$

PAGE 25 REVIEW EXERCISES 1. 11.67
3. 27.14 **5.** 7.337 **7.** 2.84

PAGE 28 WRITTEN EXERCISES
1. $x = 15 - 8$; 7 **3.** $f = 74 - 38$; 36
5. $y = 14 + 9$; 23 **7.** $b = 32 + 25$; 57
9. $c = 27 \div 3$; 9 **11.** $m = 108 \div 9$; 12
13. $n = 9 \times 6$; 54 **15.** $g = 7 \times 16$; 112
17. $a = 17 - 17$; 0 **19.** $n = 42 \div 14$; 3
21. $h = 297 \times 11$; 3267 **23.** $d = 110 + 87$; 197
25. $q = 465 \div 31$; 15 **27.** $p = 358 - 208$; 150
29. $c = 536 - 511$; 25 **31.** $g = 401 + 19$; 420
33. $x = 31.9 - 1.6$; 30.3 **35.** $c = 2.56 \div 1.6$;
1.6 **37.** 6 **39.** 7 **41.** 13 **43.** 17 **45.** 24

47. 120 **49.** 0.54 **51.** 3.3 **53.** 12.84
55. ×, + **57.** ×, − **59.** ÷, +

PAGE 28 REVIEW EXERCISES **1.** 2 **3.** 52
5. 60 **7.** 31

PAGES 31–32 PROBLEMS **1.** 11.65 m
3. $41,520 **5.** $7.20 **7.** 936 people **9.** $1596
11. $4.25

PAGE 32 REVIEW EXERCISES **1.** 340
3. 175 **5.** 500 **7.** 400

PAGES 35–37 PROBLEMS **1.** $113.70
3. $24.79 **5.** 22 bonus points **7.** smaller:
4263 square ft; larger: 16,620 square ft
9. 41 points **11.** $488.25 **13.** 12,948 shares
15. $3.90

PAGE 37 SELF-TEST B **1.** 29 **2.** 8 **3.** No
solution **4.** 3 **5.** 44 **6.** 16 **7.** 9 **8.** $114.15
9. 49 passengers **10.** $182.24

PAGE 40 CHAPTER REVIEW **1.** F **3.** A
5. D **7.** False **9.** True **11.** True **13.** False
15. False **17.** False **19.** False **21.** d

PAGE 42 CUMULATIVE REVIEW
EXERCISES **1.** 809 **3.** 3.1 **5.** 351.9 **7.** 27
9. 25 **11.** 2 **13.** 43 **15.** 16.5 **17.** 6 **19.** 27
21. 64 **23.** 15,625 **25.** a **27.** a **29.** False
31. False **33.** 7 **35.** 3 **37.** 19 **39.** 2 **41.** 13
43. 2

PAGE 43 CUMULATIVE REVIEW
PROBLEMS **1.** $3010 **3.** $42.95 **5.** $20
7. $17

2 Positive and Negative Numbers
PAGES 48–49 WRITTEN EXERCISES

11. > **13.** > **15.** > **17.** > **19.** <
21. > **23.** > **25.** > **27.** <
29. 18 < 32 < 46, or 46 > 32 > 18
31. 103 < 130 < 310, or 310 > 130 > 103
33. 689 < 698 < 986, or 986 > 698 > 689

35. 3 **37.** 0 **39.** 9 **41.** 8 **43.** ⁻15, ⁻2, 0, 6
45. ⁻12, ⁻8, ⁻1, 1, 7 **47.** ⁻14, ⁻10, 4, 8, 14
49. ⁻6.4, ⁻2.7, 0.6, 3:1
51. 6, ⁻6

53. 4, ⁻4

55. 0

57. ⁻1, 0, 1

59. ⁻4, ⁻3, ⁻2, ⁻1, 0, 1, 2, 3, 4

61. ⁻7, ⁻6, ⁻5, ⁻4, ⁻3, 3, 4, 5, 6, 7

63. positive **65.** No number has a negative
absolute value.

PAGE 49 REVIEW EXERCISES

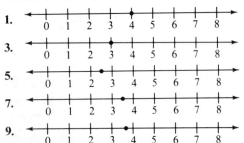

PAGES 52–53 WRITTEN EXERCISES

11.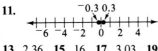

13. 2.36 **15.** 16 **17.** 3.03 **19.** $<$ **21.** $<$
23. $<$ **25.** $>$ **27.** $<$ **29.** $^-8$, $^-7.6$, $^-1.75$,
6.03, 6.3 **31.** $^-100.5$, $^-46.8$, $^-2.1$, $^-2$, 3.11
33. $^-3.3$, $^-0.33$, $^-0.3$, 30.3, 33
35.

37.

39.

41. 4.1, $^-4.1$ **43.** 26.3, $^-26.3$ **45.** 1.19, $^-1.19$
47. $^-4.5$ **49.** $^-12$ **50.** 8.25 **51. a.** 4, 3, 2, 1, 0,
$^-1$, $^-2$, $^-3$, $^-4$
b.

53. a. $^-5$, $^-4$, $^-3$, $^-2$, $^-1$, 0, 1, 2, 3, 4, 5
b.

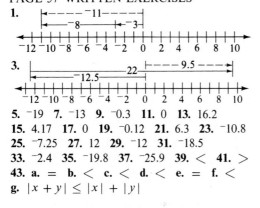

PAGE 53 REVIEW EXERCISES 1. 11.14;
distributive **3.** 27.18; multiplicative property
of one **5.** 132.3; distributive **7.** 1075;
commutative and associative **9.** 0;
multiplicative property of zero

PAGE 57 WRITTEN EXERCISES
1.

3.

5. $^-19$ **7.** $^-13$ **9.** $^-0.3$ **11.** 0 **13.** 16.2
15. 4.17 **17.** 0 **19.** $^-0.12$ **21.** 6.3 **23.** $^-10.8$
25. $^-7.25$ **27.** 12 **29.** $^-12$ **31.** $^-18.5$
33. $^-2.4$ **35.** $^-19.8$ **37.** $^-25.9$ **39.** $<$ **41.** $>$
43. a. $=$ **b.** $<$ **c.** $<$ **d.** $<$ **e.** $=$ **f.** $<$
g. $|x + y| \leq |x| + |y|$

PAGE 58 PROBLEMS 1. $^-7 + 13 + ^-3$;
3°C **3.** 3.5 + $^-11$ + 2; lost; 5.5 yd lost
5. $^-4.30 + 2.50 + 2.60$; gain

PAGE 58 REVIEW EXERCISES 1. 156.1
3. 64.9 **5.** 44.89 **7.** 4.2 **9.** 285

PAGES 60-61 WRITTEN EXERCISES
1. 7 + (-19) **3.** 6.2 + 8.3 **5.** -12 **7.** 14.5
9. -6 **11.** -27 **13.** 42 **15.** 15 **17.** -43
19. 20 **21.** 44 **23.** -1.1 **25.** 2.2 **27.** -24.6
29. -24.6 **31.** 3.37 **33.** 24.8 **35.** -41.3
37. 1.8 **39.** 4.5 **41.** -6.2 **43.** 1.7 **45.** 10.7
47. -10.7 **49.** 1.7 **51.** 8 **53.** 8 **55.** -19
57. -18 **59.** 7 **61.** -8 **63. a.** $=$ **b.** $>$
c. $>$ **d.** $>$ **e.** $|x - y| \geq |x| - |y|$

PAGES 61-62 PROBLEMS 1. $-3 - (-11)$;
8°C change **3.** 1266 $-$ 1455; 229 m
5. 18.75 $-$ 1.00 $-$ 1.75 $-$ 1.50; $14.50
7. 78 $-$ 5.8 $-$ 7.5 $-$ 12; 52.7 cm **9.** $44.22

PAGE 62 SELF-TEST A 1. $<$ **2.** $>$ **3.** $<$
4. $=$ **5.** $=$ **6.** $^-54$, $^-4.52$, $^-0.25$, 0, 5.4
7. $^-7.3$, $^-3.79$, $^-0.37$, $^-0.09$, 37 **8.** 33 **9.** 0
10. $^-1.44$ **11.** 35 **12.** 0 **13.** -36 **14.** 11.6
15. -11.6 **16.** -11.6

PAGES 65-66 WRITTEN EXERCISES
1. 27 **3.** -56 **5.** 96 **7.** 0 **9.** -12
11. 5.1 **13.** -2.9 **15.** 15.4 **17.** -5 **19.** 459
21. -66.69 **23.** 0 **25.** 3.42 **27.** -111.24
29. 37.875 **31.** 61.38 **33.** -1.054 **35.** 0
37. 361.9 **39.** -40.81 **41.** -8.2 **43.** -100
45. -2 **47.** -2 **49.** 0 **51.** 2 **53.** -30
55. 0

PAGE 66 REVIEW EXERCISES 1. 56
3. 154 **5.** 13 **7.** 26

PAGE 66 CALCULATOR KEY-IN 8192

PAGES 68-69 WRITTEN EXERCISES
1. -6 **3.** 3 **5.** 0 **7.** -12 **9.** -7.5 **11.** 3.6
13. -35 **15.** -5.3 **17.** 8 **19.** 0 **21.** -0.5
23. -9.5 **25.** -2.2 **27.** 13.8 **29.** 0.1545
31. -6.3 **33.** 4.7 **35.** -1.85 **37.** -3.2
39. 0.625 **41.** -4.2 **43.** -1.2 **45.** -2
47. -72 **49.** -8

PAGE 69 REVIEW EXERCISES 1. 49
3. 784 **5.** 112 **7.** 1 **9.** 37

PAGE 69 CALCULATOR KEY-IN 1. 1.1
3. -28.201 **5.** 5101.015

PAGES 71-72 WRITTEN EXERCISES
1. 64 **3.** 100 **5.** 14 **7.** 225 **9.** 1 **11.** 3^2
13. 9^2 **15.** $(16 \times 4)^2$ **17.** 2^7 **19.** 10^5 **21.** n^{11}
23. 100 **25.** 81 **27.** 576 **29.** 1 **31.** 1875

33. 225 **35.** 1 **37.** 1000 **39.** 96 **41.** 52
43. 4 **45.** $\frac{1}{8}$ **47.** 1

PAGE 72 REVIEW EXERCISES **1.** −2
3. 2 **5.** 12 **7.** 1

PAGE 72 CALCULATOR KEY-IN **1.** 56,
56 **3.** 3243, 3243 $\qquad$ $a^2 - b^2$, $(a + b)(a - b)$

PAGE 74 WRITTEN EXERCISES **1.** $-\frac{1}{32}$
3. $\frac{1}{1000}$ **5.** 1 **7.** $\frac{1}{25}$ **9.** $\frac{1}{64}$ **11.** $\frac{1}{49}$ **13.** 1
15. $\frac{1}{27}$ **17.** $\frac{1}{256}$ **19.** $-\frac{1}{8}$ **21.** 1 **23.** −3
25. 5 **27.** −2 **29.** −2 **31.** 8 **33.** 0 **35.** 1
37. −4 **39.** −3 **41.** $\frac{1}{x^5}$ **43.** $\frac{1}{a^5}$ **45.** $\frac{1}{w^8}$

PAGE 75 SELF-TEST B **1.** −47.46
2. −136.68 **3.** 378 **4.** −11 **5.** −31 **6.** 8
7. 8 **8.** 225 **9.** 1296 **10.** $\frac{1}{16}$ **11.** $-\frac{1}{216}$
12. $\frac{1}{343}$ **13.** $\frac{1}{81}$

PAGES 76–77 ENRICHMENT
1. 5.798×10^3 **3.** 8.915673×10^6 **5.** 1.75
7. 5.01×10^{-2} **9.** 3790 **11.** 301,000
13. 0.056 **15.** 0.0000000399 **17.** 7.4×10^{-4}
19. 1.5×10^{11}

PAGE 78 CHAPTER REVIEW **1.** < **3.** >
5. = **7.** < **9.** > **11.** > **13.** False
15. True **17.** True **19.** False **21.** True
23. False **25.** False **27.** True **29.** True
31. True **33.** True **35.** True **37.** c **39.** d
41. d

PAGES 80–81 CUMULATIVE REVIEW
EXERCISES **1.** 6 **3.** 180 **5.** 3 **7.** 17
9. True **11.** True **13.** False **15.** False
17. True **19.** ⁻6.18 **21.** −8 **23.** 4.3
25. −0.12 **27.** −9 **29.** −1.6 **31.** 4.009
33. 7700 **35.** 909.1 **37.** 103.6 **39.** 10^{10} or
10,000,000,000 **41.** 64 **43.** 6 **45.** 100
47. −20, −7, 0, 6, 12, 15 **49.** −5, −3, 0, 1, 7,
9

PAGE 81 CUMULATIVE REVIEW
PROBLEMS **1.** $59.46 **3.** 4 times **5.** Deli
Delights

3 Rational Numbers

PAGES 87–88 WRITTEN EXERCISES **1.** 1,
2, 3, 6, 7, 14, 21, 42 **3.** 1, 2, 4, 8, 16, 32 **5.** 1,
2, 4, 7, 8, 14, 28, 56 **7.** 1, 2, 3, 4, 6, 7, 12, 14,
21, 28, 42, 84 **9.** 1, 41 **11.** 2, 3, 4 **13.** 3, 5
15. 3, 9 **17.** 2, 3, 4, 5, 10 **19.** none

21. a. yes **b.** no **c.** no **23. a.** yes **b.** yes
c. yes **25. a.** yes **b.** yes **c.** yes **27.** 4
29. 5 **31.** 9 **33.** if number represented by last
three digits is a multiple of 8 **35.** if last two
digits are 00, 25, 50, or 75

PAGE 88 REVIEW EXERCISES **1.** <
3. > **5.** < **7.** >

PAGE 91 WRITTEN EXERCISES
1. composite **3.** composite **5.** composite
7. prime **9.** composite **11.** composite
13. $2^2 \cdot 3$ **15.** $2^3 \cdot 3$ **17.** $3 \cdot 13$ **19.** $2 \cdot 3 \cdot 11$
21. $2 \cdot 3^3$ **23.** $2^2 \cdot 3 \cdot 7$ **25.** $2^2 \cdot 7^2$
27. $2^2 \cdot 7 \cdot 11$ **29.** $2 \cdot 3 \cdot 19$ **31.** All other even
numbers are divisible by 2. **33.** All prime
numbers greater than 2 are odd numbers. The
sum of two odd numbers is an even number.
35. 1, 3, 7, 9 **37.** 1001; the three digit number

PAGE 91 REVIEW EXERCISES **1.** 2
3. −1 **5.** 240 **7.** 2

PAGE 94–95 WRITTEN EXERCISES
1.
3.
5.
7. $\frac{-1}{2}$, $\frac{1}{-2}$ **9.** $\frac{1}{-11}$, $-\frac{1}{11}$ **11.** $\frac{-2}{9}$, $-\frac{2}{9}$
13. $\frac{-13}{6}$, $\frac{13}{-6}$ **15.** $\frac{-3}{4}$, $\frac{3}{-4}$ **17.** 6 **19.** $\frac{1}{4}$
21. 3 **23.** −3 **25.** $-\frac{7}{8}$ **27.** −1 **29.** $-\frac{1}{3}$
31. −3 **33.** −9 **35.** $\frac{7}{6}$ **37.** $\frac{3}{7}$ **39.** $-\frac{1}{9}$
41. $-\frac{2}{7}$ **43.** $-\frac{3}{8}$

PAGE 95 REVIEW EXERCISES **1.** 3, 4, 8,
18, 36 **3.** 1, 5, 6, 10, 15, 30, 45 **5.** 6, x

PAGE 99 WRITTEN EXERCISES **1.** 4
3. 5 **5.** 7 **7.** 3 **9.** 125 **11.** $\frac{3}{5}$ **13.** $2\frac{3}{4}$
15. $-\frac{1}{9}$ **17.** $-5\frac{2}{3}$ **19.** $-\frac{2}{5}$ **21.** $10\frac{5}{12}$
23. $-6\frac{1}{13}$ **25.** $-42\frac{6}{7}$ **27.** $\frac{17}{8}$ **29.** $\frac{99}{16}$
31. $-\frac{35}{8}$ **33.** $-\frac{49}{3}$ **35.** $-\frac{83}{10}$ **37.** 3 **39.** −1
41. 0 **43.** 24 **45.** $\frac{b}{5}$ **47.** $\frac{d}{e}$ **49.** $\frac{n}{3}$ **51.** $\frac{v}{3u}$

PAGE 99 REVIEW EXERCISES 1. 49
3. 1296 5. 1 7. 5184 9. 243

PAGES 101–102 WRITTEN EXERCISES

1. $\frac{4}{12}, \frac{1}{12}$ 3. $\frac{6}{8}, \frac{5}{8}$ 5. $\frac{6}{27}, -\frac{1}{27}$ 7. $\frac{70}{147}, \frac{6}{147}$

9. $-\frac{20}{30}, \frac{7}{30}$ 11. $\frac{16}{300}, \frac{21}{300}$ 13. $-\frac{48}{112}, -\frac{7}{112}$

15. $\frac{35}{294}, \frac{30}{294}$ 17. $\frac{70}{80}, \frac{25}{80}, \frac{42}{80}$ 19. $\frac{108}{252}, \frac{441}{252},$

$\frac{112}{252}$ 21. $\frac{2}{130}, \frac{78}{130}, \frac{45}{130}$ 23. $-\frac{60}{72}, \frac{16}{72}, -\frac{63}{72}$

25. $\frac{2a}{6}, \frac{b}{6}$ 27. $\frac{20h}{500}, \frac{5h}{500}, \frac{4h}{500}$ 29. $\frac{3}{3c}, \frac{2}{3c}$

31. $\frac{3yz}{xyz}, \frac{xz}{xyz}, \frac{5xy}{xyz}$ 33. $<$ 35. $<$ 37. $>$

PAGE 102 SELF-TEST A 1. 2, 3, 4, 9 2. 3,
9 3. 2, 3, 4, 5, 9, 10 4. none 5. composite;
$2^2 \cdot 3^3$ 6. prime 7. composite; $3 \cdot 29$

8. prime 9. $-\frac{1}{3}$ 10. $\frac{7}{9}$ 11. $\frac{2}{-3}$ 12. $\frac{1}{4}$

13. $-2\frac{2}{5}$ 14. $\frac{16}{21}$ 15. $-1\frac{23}{48}$ 16. $4\frac{1}{4}$ 17. $\frac{11}{5}$

18. $-\frac{11}{3}$ 19. $\frac{94}{15}$ 20. $\frac{19}{12}$ 21. $-\frac{69}{8}$ 22. $\frac{28}{40},$

$\frac{35}{40}$ 23. $-\frac{30}{147}, \frac{14}{147}$ 24. $\frac{27}{450}, \frac{12}{450}$ 25. $-\frac{16}{30},$

$-\frac{1}{30}$

PAGES 104–105 WRITTEN EXERCISES

1. $\frac{2}{3}$ 3. $-\frac{4}{17}$ 5. 0 7. $-\frac{11}{5}$ 9. $\frac{16}{21}$ 11. $\frac{7}{2}$

13. $-\frac{3}{8}$ 15. $-\frac{51}{10}$ 17. $\frac{287}{156}$ 19. $-\frac{41}{72}$

21. $\frac{7}{12}$ 23. $\frac{3}{5}$ 25. $-\frac{17}{18}$ 27. $\frac{19}{12}$ 29. $\frac{1}{10}$

PAGE 105 REVIEW EXERCISES 1. $1\frac{3}{8}$

3. $3\frac{2}{7}$ 5. $5\frac{11}{12}$ 7. $9\frac{4}{13}$

PAGES 107–108 WRITTEN EXERCISES

1. $8\frac{4}{5}$ 3. $\frac{10}{11}$ 5. $6\frac{2}{3}$ 7. $-20\frac{1}{7}$ 9. $3\frac{5}{6}$

11. $2\frac{1}{2}$ 13. $-2\frac{5}{24}$ 15. $-3\frac{17}{30}$ 17. $5\frac{3}{4}$

19. $-3\frac{7}{8}$ 21. $11\frac{2}{3}$ 23. $-19\frac{1}{5}$ 25. $9\frac{11}{12}$

27. $-8\frac{1}{4}$ 29. $-8\frac{2}{7}$ 31. 4 33. $\frac{2}{15}$ 35. $\frac{1}{4}$

PAGE 108 PROBLEMS 1. $14\frac{11}{16}$ yd 3. $\frac{5}{6}$ mi

5. $1\frac{5}{8}$ in. 7. right : $1\frac{5}{16}$ in.; bottom : $\frac{11}{16}$ in.

PAGE 108 REVIEW EXERCISES 1. $\frac{2}{-7}$

3. $\frac{5}{-9}$ 5. $-\frac{1}{7}$ 7. 4 9. 3

PAGES 111–112 WRITTEN EXERCISES

1. 7 3. -2 5. $\frac{1}{28}$ 7. $-\frac{1}{60}$ 9. $\frac{10}{27}$ 11. $-\frac{1}{4}$

13. $-\frac{2}{27}$ 15. $\frac{5}{8}$ 17. 0 19. $\frac{15}{64}$ 21. 1

23. $43\frac{11}{12}$ 25. $-22\frac{1}{7}$ 27. $3\frac{10}{27}$ 29. $\frac{1}{24}$

31. $\frac{1}{72}$ 33. $-4\frac{1}{2}$ 35. $6n$ 37. $-\frac{y}{2}$ 39. $\frac{2}{5}$

41. 3

PAGE 112 REVIEW EXERCISES 1. 60

3. -36 5. 8 7. $-3\frac{1}{9}$

PAGE 115 WRITTEN EXERCISES 1. $\frac{2}{3}$

3. 25 5. $\frac{25}{72}$ 7. $3\frac{8}{9}$ 9. 6 11. $5\frac{1}{5}$ 13. $-\frac{9}{16}$

15. 7 17. $5\frac{23}{64}$ 19. -2 21. -9 23. $\frac{1}{3}$

25. $-\frac{1}{2}$

PAGES 115–116 PROBLEMS 1. $\frac{1}{19}$

3. \$7,500 5. \$4 per hour 7. \$6.50 9. $\frac{1}{6}$ of

the class 11. $\frac{3}{20}$ of the workers

PAGE 116 REVIEW EXERCISES
1. $n = 240 - 135$; 105 3. $y = 156 \div 4$; 39
5. $x = 432 \div 12$; 36 7. $m = 418 \div 38$; 11

PAGE 120 WRITTEN EXERCISES 1. 0.25
3. $0.\overline{2}$ 5. 0.9 7. $-0.\overline{6}$ 9. -0.375
11. -0.12 13. 1.1 15. $0.58\overline{3}$ 17. $0.2\overline{6}$

19. $-1.3\overline{8}$ 21. 0.15 23. $3.\overline{285714}$ 25. $\frac{1}{20}$

27. $-\frac{3}{5}$ 29. $2\frac{7}{100}$ 31. $5\frac{1}{8}$ 33. $-1\frac{3}{8}$

35. $12\frac{5}{8}$ 37. $\frac{9}{40}$ 39. $-1\frac{413}{500}$ 41. $-\frac{5}{9}$

43. $-1\frac{1}{90}$ 45. $\frac{5}{33}$ 47. $\frac{35}{99}$ 49. $-1\frac{4}{33}$

51. $2\frac{121}{900}$ 53. $\frac{41}{333}$ 55. rational 57. rational
59. $3.0, 3.00\overline{9}, 3.0\overline{9}, 3.1$ 61. a. 1 b. $=$

63. a. $-1\frac{1}{4}$ b. $=$

PAGE 121 SELF-TEST B **1.** $\frac{7}{12}$ **2.** $-\frac{21}{30}$
3. $-\frac{2}{15}$ **4.** $22\frac{4}{9}$ **5.** $-10\frac{1}{24}$ **6.** $17\frac{3}{8}$ **7.** $3\frac{3}{4}$
8. $-\frac{1}{24}$ **9.** $-8\frac{1}{7}$ **10.** $1\frac{1}{2}$ **11.** $-\frac{1}{8}$
12. $-4\frac{1}{2}$ **13.** 0.625 **14.** $0.\overline{18}$ **15.** -0.0125
16. $1.1\overline{6}$ **17.** $\frac{7}{8}$ **18.** $1\frac{2}{3}$ **19.** $-2\frac{213}{1000}$ **20.** $\frac{7}{30}$

PAGE 121 COMPUTER BYTE **1.** 300
3. 510 **5.** 2640

PAGE 123 ENRICHMENT **1.** Answers will vary.

PAGE 124 CHAPTER REVIEW **1.** 4, 6, 8, 12, 24 **3.** c **5.** False **7.** True **9.** False
11. False **13.** F **15.** G **17.** K **19.** L **21.** I
23. J

PAGE 126 CUMULATIVE REVIEW
EXERCISES **1.** 58 **3.** 7 **5.** 5 **7.** 12
9. 225 **11.** 8 **13.** 25 **15.** 250
17. $75.70 > 75.40 > 75.06$
19. $0.33 > 0.30 > 0.03$ **21.** $-7, 7$ **23.** $-5,$
$-6, -7$ and so on; also 5, 6, 7, and so on
25. $-5, 5$ **27.** $-32, -33, -34, -35, -36,$
$-37, -38, -39, 32, 33, 34, 35, 36, 37, 38, 39$
29. 18 **31.** 12 **33.** -4 **35.** $-\frac{4}{5}$ **37.** $\frac{2}{5}$
39. $-\frac{10}{7}$ **41.** $-\frac{2}{7}$ **43.** $\frac{2}{5}$ **45.** $-5\frac{5}{8}$
47. $8\frac{23}{136}$

PAGE 127 CUMULATIVE REVIEW
PROBLEMS **1.** $196.88 **3.** No **5.** $787.50
7. $444.75

Chapter 4 Solving Equations

PAGE 133 WRITTEN EXERCISES **1.** 12
3. -1 **5.** -4 **7.** 23 **9.** 17 **11.** 7 **13.** 12
15. 6 **17.** 8 **19.** $-\frac{2}{5}$ **21.** $3\frac{2}{3}$ **23.** 1.1
25. 0.253 **27.** 1.196 **29.** $9\frac{3}{4}$ **31.** $2\frac{7}{12}$
33. 0.358 **35.** $3\frac{4}{5}$ **37.** 1.73

PAGE 133 REVIEW EXERCISES **1.** 5 **3.** 3
5. 9

PAGE 135 WRITTEN EXERCISES **1.** 15
3. 18 **5.** 6 **7.** 54 **9.** -84 **11.** 28 **13.** 5
15. -10 **17.** 91 **19.** 11 **21.** $7\frac{1}{2}$ **23.** -221

25. -252 **27.** $-\frac{5}{6}$ **29.** $9\frac{2}{3}$ **31.** 364 **33.** 247
35. $\frac{2}{19}$ **37.** $10\frac{1}{2}$

PAGE 135 REVIEW EXERCISES **1.** $\frac{3}{14}$
3. $\frac{2}{15}$ **5.** $3\frac{1}{19}$

PAGE 138 WRITTEN EXERCISES **1.** 88
3. 20 **5.** -1.5 **7.** -24 **9.** 60 **11.** 19.5
13. 18 **15.** 20 **17.** -30 **19.** -49.5 **21.** $13\frac{1}{2}$
23. $10\frac{1}{2}$ **25.** 6.5 **27.** -0.8 **29.** $-\frac{1}{9}$ **31.** $-\frac{5}{6}$
33. 7.595 **35.** 0.02148 **37.** 5.7 **39.** 15.6
41. 3.3

PAGE 138 REVIEW EXERCISES **1.** 30
3. 55 **5.** 103 **7.** 17 **9.** 19

PAGE 138 CALCULATOR KEY-IN **1.** 0.3
3. 2.7203791 **5.** 3.3807

PAGES 141–142 WRITTEN EXERCISES
1. 11 **3.** 7 **5.** 11 **7.** 10 **9.** 3 **11.** 80
13. 30 **15.** 55 **17.** 24 **19.** $4\frac{1}{3}$ **21.** $22\frac{1}{2}$
23. $7\frac{1}{2}$ **25.** $3\frac{1}{3}$ **27.** $1\frac{7}{9}$ **29.** $1\frac{17}{21}$ **31.** $4\frac{3}{7}$ **33.** $\frac{1}{4}$
35. $\frac{25}{66}$ **37.** $\frac{5}{11}$ **39.** $\frac{2}{15}$ **41.** 27

PAGE 142 SELF-TEST A **1.** -24 **2.** 10
3. 9 **4.** 56 **5.** -13 **6.** -68 **7.** 17 **8.** -33
9. 150 **10.** $-2\frac{4}{13}$ **11.** -80 **12.** -1.74
13. $27\frac{1}{2}$ **14.** 120 **15.** 6 **16.** -3

PAGE 142 CALCULATOR KEY-IN 852

PAGES 145–146 WRITTEN EXERCISES
1. $8b$ **3.** $53 - d$ **5.** $30 + t$ **7.** $g + 9$
9. $78 - m$ **11.** $n + 19$ **13.** $d \div 11$
15. $12 - z$ **17.** $11t + 15$ **19.** $91(m + n)$
21. $r \div (83 - 10)$ **23.** $c[(12 + 9) + 3]$
25. $(60 + 40 + 10) \div d$ **27.** $b + 3$ **29.** $x + 6$
31. $25q$ **33.** $x \div 60$ **35.** $x - 10$

PAGE 146 REVIEW EXERCISES **1.** 27
3. 576 **5.** -15 **7.** 19

PAGE 148 WRITTEN EXERCISES
1. $5d = 20$ **3.** $3w - 7 = 8$ **5.** $5 \div r = 42$
7. $n - 1 = 5$ **9.** $2n \div 3 = 15$
11. $(4 + x) \div 2 = 34$ **13.** $59 - x = 3 + 2x$
15. $(x - 5) \div 3 = 2$

PAGE 148 REVIEW EXERCISES **1.** $n - 4$
3. $n \div 7$ **5.** $40 - n$ **7.** $2n$

PAGES 150–151 PROBLEMS **1.** $9n = 1170$
3. $18n = 13.50$ **5.** $144 - n = 116$
7. $n = (12 + 18) - 19$ **9.** $2000 + n = 2650$

11. $\frac{4}{5}n = 180$ **13.** $2n - 30 = 20$ **15.** $\frac{1}{9}n = 5$

PAGE 151 REVIEW EXERCISES
1. $n - 8 = 43$ **3.** $n + 14 = 70$
5. $n - 17 = 34$

PAGES 154–155 PROBLEMS **1.** 250 lb
3. 480 books **5.** 24 shirts **7.** 25 people
9. 150 lb **11.** 24 gal

PAGE 155 SELF-TEST B **1.** $12x$ **2.** $60 - d$
3. d **4.** c **5.** a **6.** $21n = 189$
7. $n - 450 = 1845$ **8.** 412 tennis balls

PAGE 157 ENRICHMENT **1.** 3 **3.** 3
5. 2; 7

PAGE 158 CHAPTER REVIEW **1.** 20
3. divide **5.** a **7.** c **9.** b **11.** b

PAGE 160 CUMULATIVE REVIEW
EXERCISES **1.** 5 **3.** 5 **5.** -1 **7.** 32
9. 16 **11.** $<$ **13.** $<$ **15.** $<$ **17.** $>$
19. $x = 8$ **21.** $x = -20$ **23.** $x = -18.5$
25. $x = 5$ **27.** $x = -12$ **29.** $-3\frac{7}{12}$ **31.** $-1\frac{3}{8}$
33. $1\frac{3}{20}$ **35.** -21 **37.** $-\frac{1}{9}$ **39.** $3\frac{11}{48}$ **41.** 20
43. 24 **45.** -14 **47.** 0.75 **49.** 11 **51.** -6

PAGE 161 CUMULATIVE REVIEW
PROBLEMS **1.** $2.97 **3.** 220,000 readers
5. $418.50 **7.** $656.38 **9.** 100 inquiries

5 Geometric Figures

PAGES 167–168 WRITTEN EXERCISES
1. $\overrightarrow{YX}$ **3.** $\overrightarrow{PQ}$ **5.** $\overleftrightarrow{XY}, \overleftrightarrow{XZ}, \overrightarrow{XY}, \overrightarrow{YX}$ **7.** S, P,
O or T, Q, O **9.** $\overrightarrow{PS}, \overrightarrow{PO}, \overrightarrow{PQ}$ **11.** $\overrightarrow{ST}$ and
$\overrightarrow{PQ}$ **13.** Answers may vary; for example, $\overrightarrow{PS}$
and $\overrightarrow{OT}$ **15.** Answers may vary; for example,
$\overrightarrow{OS}$ and $\overrightarrow{OT}$ **17.** $\overrightarrow{OS}$ **19.** $\overrightarrow{OP}, \overrightarrow{OQ}, \overrightarrow{OS}, \overrightarrow{OT}$
21. Answers may vary; for example, $\overrightarrow{AX}$ and
$\overleftrightarrow{XY}$; X **23.** Answers may vary; for example,
$\overleftrightarrow{XW}$ and $\overleftrightarrow{AD}$, plane XWD **25.** true **27.** false
29. false **31.** true **33.** one **35.** Two
nonparallel lines in a plane must intersect, and
their intersection is a point.

PAGE 168 REVIEW EXERCISES **1.** 2.9
3. 4.6 **5.** 3.0 **7.** 9.3

PAGES 171–172 WRITTEN EXERCISES
1. a. 8 cm **b.** 80 mm **3. a.** 9 cm **b.** 92 mm
5. a. 8 cm **b.** 82 mm **7.** $\overline{AE}$ and $\overline{PT}$; $\overline{VZ}$ and
$\overline{GJ}$ **9.** 450; 4500 **11.** 2.5, 2500 **13.** 60; 6000

15. 2 **17.** 0.625 **19.** 4500 **21.** 3.74 m by
5.2 m **23.** 4.675 m by 7.05 m **25.** 27 mm
27. 65 cm **29.** 2.1875 **31.** 35

PAGE 172 REVIEW EXERCISES **1.** 90
3. 40 **5.** 140 **7.** 105 **9.** 65

PAGES 175–177 WRITTEN EXERCISES
1. **3.**

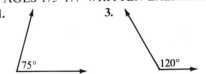

5. 50°; acute **7.** 140°; obtuse **9.** 47°; 137°
11. 45° **13.** 19°; 161°
15. **17.**

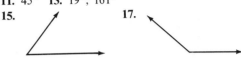

19. $\overleftrightarrow{BC}$ and $\overleftrightarrow{AB}$; $\overleftrightarrow{AD}$ and $\overleftrightarrow{AB}$ **21.** $\angle CED$ and
$\angle DEA$; $\angle CEB$ and $\angle AEB$
23. **25.** 90°

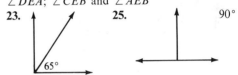

27. true **29.** $m\angle 1 = m\angle 3 = 60°$,
$m\angle 2 = m\angle 4 = 120°$

PAGE 177 SELF-TEST A **1.**

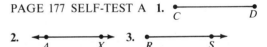

2. **3.**

4. Answers may vary; for example, $\overleftrightarrow{XW}$ and
$\overleftrightarrow{YZ}$ **5.** Answers may vary; for example, plane
WXY and plane DAB **6.** Answers may vary;
for example, $\overleftrightarrow{BC}$ and $\overleftrightarrow{ZC}$ **7.** Answers may
vary; for example, plane DCB and plane
ZCD **8.** 4 **9.** 0.87 **10.** 0.785 **11.** 10.9
12. MB; $\overline{MB}$ **13.** 90° **14.** congruent **15.** is
perpendicular to **16.** acute **17.** 48 **18.** 73

PAGES 181–182 WRITTEN EXERCISES
1. 80° **3.** 90° **5.** isosceles **7.** equilateral
9. isosceles, obtuse **11.** scalene, acute
13. $\triangle ACB, \triangle DEC, \triangle DEA$ **15.** $\triangle BDC$
17. a. **b.** **19.** 60°

21. 15° **23.** 42°, 42°
25. They are congruent.
27. a. 13 **b.** 3 **31.** The
medians intersect in one point.

PAGE 182 REVIEW EXERCISES **1.** 15.08
3. 15.52 **5.** 20.33 **7.** 21.873 **9.** 24.768

PAGES 185–187 WRITTEN EXERCISES
1. pentagon **3.** hexagon **5.** triangle **7.** square
9. 14.1 **11.** 312 cm **13.** 72.6 mm **15.** 1356 m
17. 108° **19.** 2.56 m **21.** 12 m **23.** 3
25.   **27.** 22

29. a 360° **b.** 1440° **c.** 360° **d.** 1080°
31. 5

PAGE 187 REVIEW EXERCISES **1.** 22.4
3. 49 **5.** 10.9 **7.** 44.8

PAGES 190–191 WRITTEN EXERCISES
1. 25.1 cm **3.** 2830 mm **5.** 134 m **7.** 90.1 m
9. 143 km **11.** 199 m **13.** 1.59 mm
15. 3 74 km **17.** 2.79 cm **19.** 40,074 km
21. 47.1 km **23.** 94.2 m **25.** 35.7 **27.** 41.4
29. 22.7 **31.** $S = \frac{\pi d}{2}$ **33.** Draw a circle and

label three points A, B, C on the circle. Let
point D be a point not on the circle.
Quadrilateral $ABCD$ cannot be inscribed in the
circle **35.** An angle inscribed in a semicircle is
a right angle.

PAGE 191 REVIEW EXERCISES **1.** 18
3. 27 **5.** 8 **7.** 14

PAGES 196–197 WRITTEN EXERCISES
1. c **3.** SSS **5.** rotation or reflection **7.** a
rotation, two reflections, or a translation and a
reflection **9.** $\triangle GHK \cong \triangle FHK$; SAS
11. a. $\angle N$ **b.** $\angle Y$ **c.** $\overline{NS}$ **d.** $\overline{RL}$ **13. a.** $\overline{FG}$
b. $\overline{EH}$ **c.** $\angle EFG$ **d.** $\overline{CD}$ **15.** no

PAGE 197 REVIEW EXERCISES **1.** 7
3. 11 **5.** 72 **7.** 4

PAGE 197 CALCULATOR KEY-IN
1. 3.1604938 **3.** 3.141$\overline{6}$ **5.** 3.1416 The closest
approximation is $\frac{355}{113}$.

PAGES 200–201 WRITTEN EXERCISES
1.   **5.**

  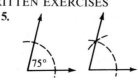

7. The perpendicular bisector appears to
pass through the vertex of the angle
formed by the two congruent sides. **9.** yes
11.   **13.** yes

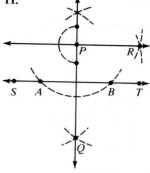

PAGE 201 SELF-TEST B **1.** equilateral
2. 180 **3.** 3 **4.** octagon **5.** parallelogram
6. 33 cm **7.** 100 cm **8.** true **9.** false
10. $\overline{FG}$, J, IJF
11.   **12.**

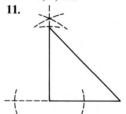 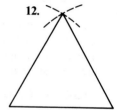

PAGE 203 ENRICHMENT **1.** 57,960,000
3. 149,730,000 **5.** 12 **7.** 32,186,000,000
9.
```
10  FOR I=1 TO 5
20  PRINT "HOW MANY HOURS";
30  INPUT T
40  LET R=760
50  PRINT "DISTANCE TRAVELED"
60  PRINT "IS ";R*T;" MILES."
70  NEXT I
80  END
```

PAGE 204 CHAPTER REVIEW **1.** collinear
points **3.** midpoint **5.** false **7.** true
9. false **11.** d **13.** c
15.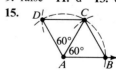

$\triangle ABC$ is
equilateral, thus
$\angle CAB = 60°$.
$\triangle ABC \cong DAC$,
thus $\angle DAC = 60°$,
$\angle DAB = 120°$.

PAGE 206 CUMULATIVE REVIEW
EXERCISES **1.** 8 **3.** 7 **5.** 12 **7.** −19

9. 9 **11.** 45 **13.** 14 **15.** $-18\frac{3}{4}$ **17.** 72
19. 24 **21.** 30 **23.** 15 **25.** $\frac{4}{5}$ **27.** $-\frac{1}{9}$ **29.** $\frac{2}{3}$
31. 0.4 **33.** 0.4375 **35.** $-0.2\overline{7}$ **37.** $\frac{7}{100}$ **39.** 2
41. $-1\frac{8}{33}$ **43.** true

PAGE 207 CUMULATIVE REVIEW
PROBLEMS **1.** $31.11 **3.** $124 **5.** 52 m
7. 127 boxes **9.** 22 m

6 Ratio, Proportion, and Percent

PAGES 211–212 WRITTEN EXERCISES
1. a. $\frac{5}{7}$ **b.** $\frac{5}{12}$ **c.** $\frac{12}{7}$ **3. a.** $\frac{9}{4}$ **b.** $\frac{9}{13}$ **c.** $\frac{13}{4}$
5. $\frac{3}{8}$ **7.** $\frac{2}{7}$ **9.** $\frac{15}{4}$ **11. a.** $\frac{5}{26}$ **b.** $\frac{21}{26}$ **c.** $\frac{26}{5}$
13. a. $\frac{1}{3}$ **b.** $\frac{2}{1}$ **c.** $\frac{3}{2}$ **15.** $\frac{3}{5}$ **17.** $\frac{14}{9}$

PAGES 212–213 PROBLEMS **1.** $\frac{80}{3}$
3. $62\frac{1}{2}$ lb/ft^3 **5.** $\frac{11}{2}$ **7. a.** 2:5 **b.** 2:5 **c.** $\frac{2}{5}$
9. $\frac{3}{7}$ **11.** $\frac{5}{18}$

PAGE 213 REVIEW EXERCISES **1.** 9 **3.** 9
5. 5 **7.** 12

PAGES 215–216 PROBLEMS **1.** 17¢ **3.** $16
5. $5.25 **7.** 195 km **9.** 240 km **11.** Best
Brand Pear Tomatoes **13.** Sparkle Window
Cleaner **15.** 5 gal **17.** 62 km/h; 74 km/h

PAGE 216 REVIEW EXERCISES **1.** 20 cm
3. 84 cm **5.** 142.4 m **7.** 57.4 m **9.** 49.44 cm

PAGE 219 WRITTEN EXERCISES **1.** 4
3. 56 **5.** 35 **7.** 60 **9.** 72 **11.** 45 **13.** $7\frac{1}{2}$
15. $8\frac{1}{2}$ **17.** 10 **19.** 12 **21.** 20 **23.** 15
25. $5\frac{3}{5}$ **27.** $4\frac{1}{2}$ **29.** $\frac{1}{3}$ **31.** $\frac{4}{1}$

PAGE 219 REVIEW EXERCISES **1.** $13\frac{1}{3}$
3. $22\frac{7}{9}$ **5.** $8\frac{11}{18}$ **7.** $43\frac{1}{2}$ **9.** $60\frac{3}{10}$

PAGES 221–223 PROBLEMS **1. a.** 880 km
b. 14 h **3. a.** $3.75 **b.** 28 oranges
5. a. 5.3 cm^3 **b.** 337.5 cm^3 **7.** $1.20 **9.** 8 cans
11. $11\frac{1}{4}$ oz; $10\frac{2}{3}$ servings **13.** 6 min
15. 12 wins **17.** 12 vests **19.** $1333\frac{1}{3}$ ft^2
21. 6955 votes for; 2782 votes against
23. 76,800 km

PAGE 223 REVIEW EXERCISES **1.** $\frac{200\ \text{cm}}{15\ \text{cm}}$

3. $\frac{30\ \text{ft}}{5\ \text{ft}}$ **5.** $\frac{2000\ \text{m}}{450\ \text{m}}$ **7.** $\frac{36\ \text{in.}}{20\ \text{in.}}$

PAGE 223 CALCULATOR KEY-IN
1. 1.4925373 **3.** 3.9385584 **5.** 0.208982

PAGES 225–226 WRITTEN EXERCISES
1. 1104 in. **3.** 576 in. **5.** 960 in. **7. a.** 2 cm

b. 800 km **9. a.** 10.5 cm **b.** 4200 km
11. a. 3 cm **b.** 1200 km **13.** 400 km
15. 1,384,300 km **17.** 139,700 km

PAGE 226 SELF-TEST A **1.** $\frac{3}{2}$ **2.** $\frac{17}{9}$ **3.** $\frac{2}{11}$
4. $1.15 **5.** $.61 **6.** 2 **7.** 4 **8.** 135 **9.** $.67
10. $110 **11.** 1 in. **12.** 1 cm:16 cm

PAGE 229 WRITTEN EXERCISES **1.** $\frac{3}{4}$
3. $\frac{9}{20}$ **5.** $\frac{3}{25}$ **7.** $1\frac{1}{4}$ **9.** $\frac{31}{200}$ **11.** $\frac{43}{400}$ **13.** 80%
15. 30% **17.** 48% **19.** 62% **21.** 220%
23. 102% **25.** $87\frac{1}{2}$% **27.** $\frac{1}{2}$% **29.** $\frac{3}{4}$%
31. $302\frac{1}{2}$% **33.** $\frac{1}{6}$ **35.** $\frac{5}{12}$

PAGE 230 PROBLEMS **1.** 38% **3.** 60%
5. 5% **7.** $62\frac{1}{2}$ **9.** 10%; 70%; 80%

PAGE 230 REVIEW EXERCISES **1.** 0.45
3. 0.275 **5.** 0.04 **7.** $0.\overline{72}$ **9.** $0.57\overline{3}$

PAGE 233 WRITTEN EXERCISES **1.** 0.93
3. 1.14 **5.** 2.6 **7.** 0.495 **9.** 0.006 **11.** 0.0005
13. 59% **15.** 9% **17.** 260% **19.** 1283%
21. 0.7% **23.** 8.67% **25.** 0.375; 37.5%
27. 0.006; 0.6% **29.** 1.625; 162.5% **31.** 0.5875;
58.8% **33.** $0.708\overline{3}$; 70.8% **35.** 0.2857143;
28.6% **37.** $16\frac{2}{3}$% **39.** $88\frac{8}{9}$% **41.** $83\frac{1}{3}$%

PAGE 233 REVIEW EXERCISES **1.** 2.95
3. 15.438 **5.** 23.8576

PAGES 235–236 WRITTEN EXERCISES
1. 40% **3.** 270 **5.** 1300 **7.** 5.4 **9.** 83.3%
11. 104.5 **13.** 87 **15.** 0.896 **17.** 114.3%
19. 224 **21.** 54 **23.** 252

PAGES 236–237 PROBLEMS **1.** $12.50
3. $77.5% **5.** 10% **7.** 11.5% **9.** 4 billion
11. a. 10% **b.** 40%

PAGE 237 SELF-TEST B **1.** $\frac{27}{100}$ **2.** $\frac{83}{100}$
3. $1\frac{16}{25}$ **4.** $2\frac{9}{10}$ **5.** 5% **6.** 37.5% **7.** 400%
8. 325% **9.** 0.45 **10.** 0.78 **11.** 3.48
12. 0.008 **13.** 64% **14.** 81% **15.** 785%
16. 6.8% **17.** 25% **18.** 205% **19.** 11 **20.** 120

PAGE 239 ENRICHMENT **1.** 3, 21, 144, and
987 are divisible by 3; 5, 55, and 610 are
divisible by 5. **3.** The new pattern consists of
every other Fibonacci number, starting with 3.
5. The new pattern consists of every other
Fibonacci number, starting with 5.

PAGE 240 CHAPTER REVIEW **1. a 3.** b
5. c **7.** a **9.** b **11.** c **13.** e **15.** b **17.** c

PAGE 242 CUMULATIVE REVIEW
EXERCISES **1.** 5 **3.** 2 **5.** 6 **7.** 3 **9.** 4
11. 36 **13.** false **15.** false **17.** $\frac{10}{15}, \frac{3}{15}$
19. $-\frac{3}{24}, \frac{8}{24}$ **21.** $\frac{24}{60}, \frac{10}{60}, \frac{15}{60}$ **23.** 5 **25.** 3
27. 16 **29.** 1 **31.** 64 **33.** $2\frac{7}{13}$ **35.** rhombus
37. diameter

PAGE 243 CUMULATIVE REVIEW
PROBLEMS **1.** $79.38 **3.** 23,500 ft
5. 1230 lb **7.** l: 15 m; w: 5 m **9.** $616.13

7 Percents and Problem Solving

PAGES 247–248 WRITTEN EXERCISES
1. 15% **3.** 40% **5.** 82.5% **7.** 46.9% **9.** 0.8%
11. 27.5% **13.** 132 **15.** 57.2 **17.** 205.8
19. 124.5 **21.** 60 **23.** 336 **25.** 338.8 **27.** 64
29. 120

PAGES 248–249 PROBLEMS **1.** 1,134
employees **3.** 25% **5.** 7511 books **7.** 16.7%
9. 246 homes **11.** $1.25

PAGE 249 REVIEW EXERCISES **1.** 9.72
3. 17 **5.** 520 **7.** 220.5 **9.** 0.04

PAGES 252–253 PROBLEMS **1.** $67.15
3. 14% discount **5.** $26.46 **7.** $30 **9.** 25%
markup **11.** $12.50 **13.** 72% of the original
price **15.** The final prices will be equal.

PAGE 253 REVIEW EXERCISES **1.** radius
3. diameter

PAGES 255–256 PROBLEMS **1.** $129
3. $978 **5.** $10,900 **7.** $64,893.62
9. $58,510.64 **11.** $7,380 **13.** $4,250

PAGE 256 REVIEW EXERCISES **1.** 10
3. 6 **5.** 128 **7.** 0.4

PAGE 259 WRITTEN EXERCISES **1.** 5.12
3. 80% **5.** 40

PAGES 259–261 PROBLEMS **1.** 82.5%
3. 49 books **5.** $34.80; $27.84 **7.** $36.50
9. a. 108° **b.** $3.6 million
11. b. food $450; clothing $270; housing $540;
medical $180; other $360
13. b. salaries $489,600;
maintenance/repair $54,400; books/supplies
$34,000; recreation $34,000; after-school
programs $34,000; teacher training $34,000

PAGE 261 SELF-TEST A **1.** 25% **2.** 35%
3. 23% **4.** $103.70 **5.** 30% discount

6. $6,360 **7.** $72,688 **8.** 437.4 **9.** 80% **10.** 75
violations

PAGES 264–265 WRITTEN EXERCISES
1. $384; $1664 **3.** $745.20; $3505.20 **5.** $1692;
$7332 **7.** $5550.60; $11,930.60 **9.** 14%
11. 8.5% **13.** 16% **15.** $\frac{1}{2}$ yr **17.** $4450
19. $6720 **21.** $1850 **23.** $102.12

PAGES 265–266 PROBLEMS **1.** $577.50
3. $96.25 **5.** 7.5% **7.** 8 yr

PAGE 266 REVIEW EXERCISES **1.** 0.375
3. 0.05 **5.** 1.496 **7.** 0.833 **9.** 2.396

PAGE 266 CALCULATOR KEY-IN **1.** 16
3. 48% **5.** $86.\overline{6}$%

PAGES 268–269 WRITTEN EXERCISES
1. $7056 **3.** $1560.60 **5.** $3149.28
7. $2137.84 **9.** $3975.35 **11.** $9724.05
13. $7.70 **15.** 9 mo

PAGE 269 PROBLEMS **1.** $1852.20 **3.** 12%
simple interest will earn more. **5.** 13.2%

PAGES 271–273 PROBLEMS **1.** $2.50
3. $21,942 **5.** $165 **7.** $7000 **9.** $56,400
11. 10%

PAGE 273 SELF-TEST B **1.** $10,000
2. 14% **3.** $3,149.28 **4.** 9 mo **5.** $2,169.65

PAGE 275 ENRICHMENT **1.** 125.86; 162.75;
20.00 **3.** 249.75; 323.80; 35.00 **5.** 665.61;
676.09; 90.00

PAGE 276 CHAPTER REVIEW **1.** 25%
3. 95 **5.** c **7.** true **9.** c

PAGE 278 CUMULATIVE REVIEW
EXERCISES **1.** 8 **3.** 7 **5.** 12 **7.** −19
9. 9 **11.** 45 **13.** −7, −2.5, −2.2, 0, 3, 6.4
15. −8.4, −3, −1.6, −1.0, 0.5 **17.** True
19. True **21.** True **23.** $\frac{6}{9}, \frac{5}{9}$ **25.** $-\frac{88}{33}, \frac{27}{33}$
27. $\frac{28}{12}, \frac{9}{12}$ **29.** $\frac{68}{128}, -\frac{3}{128}$ **31.** 12 **33.** 180
35. 63 **37.** rotation and translation; ASA
39. rotation and translation; SSS

PAGE 279 CUMULATIVE REVIEW
PROBLEMS **1.** 15 cm **3.** 4.4 km **5.** up $4\frac{5}{8}$
points **7.** 58.125 L **9.** 10 students

8 Equations and Inequalities

PAGES 283–284 WRITTEN EXERCISES
1. $2m$ **3.** $-7c$ **5.** $c - 5$ **7.** $-7y + 77$

9. $-4a - 30$ **11.** $6x - 14$ **13.** $\frac{1}{2}$ **15.** 9
17. $-1\frac{1}{4}$ **19.** 5 **21.** $-\frac{1}{2}$ **23.** -1 **25.** $\frac{1}{2}$
27. -1 **29.** $2\frac{1}{2}$ **31.** 1 **33.** -1 **35.** 6
37. $-\frac{3}{4}$ **39.** $-1\frac{2}{3}$ **41.** $1\frac{1}{2}$ **43.** 5 **45.** -3
47. -14

PAGE 284 REVIEW EXERCISES **1.** 1
3. 15 **5.** 12 **7.** $10\frac{1}{2}$ **9.** 4

PAGE 286 WRITTEN EXERCISES **1.** 5
3. 7 **5.** -6 **7.** $-\frac{1}{2}$ **9.** -4 **11.** $-\frac{3}{5}$ **13.** 4
15. $-2\frac{1}{2}$ **17.** 3 **19.** 1 **21.** $\frac{1}{3}$ **23.** 6 **25.** 1
27. -3 **29.** $-8\frac{1}{2}$ **31.** -16 **33.** $6\frac{2}{3}$ **35.** 80

PAGE 286 REVIEW EXERCISES **1.** 4 **3.** 6
5. 12 **7.** 24

PAGES 288–289 PROBLEMS **1.** 16 ft, 24 ft
3. 35 min, 45 min **5.** 10 cm, 20 cm, 20 cm
7. 74 points **9.** 34 ft **11.** 10 yr **13.** 1000 m

PAGE 290 SELF-TEST A **1.** 4 **2.** $-\frac{1}{2}$
3. -2 **4.** 2 **5.** -6 **6.** $\frac{1}{5}$ **7.** 16 **8.** -9
9. 5 **10.** -4 **11.** -2 **12.** 2 **13.** -4 **14.** $\frac{7}{9}$
15. -11 **16.** $7\frac{1}{2}$ **17.** 20 ft **18.** 106

PAGE 291–292 WRITTEN EXERCISES
1. $12 < 22$ **3.** $6 > 0$ **5.** $0 < 8 < 10$
7.

11. $6 > t$ **13.** $p > q$ **15.** $10d < 5n$
17. $6 < 2n < 8$ **19.** $x < a < y$
21. $2 < 6 < 10 < 20 < 50$ **23.** $a < 5 < 8 < b$

PAGE 292 REVIEW EXERCISES **1.** 5 **3.** 5
5. 9 **7.** 77

PAGES 295–296 WRITTEN EXERCISES All
the numbers: **1.** less than 12 **3.** greater than
42 **5.** less than 3 **7.** greater than or equal
to 20 **9.** less than -18 **11.** less than 7
13. less than -7 **15.** less than or equal to 12
17. less than or equal to 15 **19.** less than
-26 **21.** less than or equal to 60 **23.** less
than or equal to -11 **25.** less than -168
27. greater than 21.3 **29.** less than $5\frac{3}{7}$
31. less than or equal to -3.87 **33.** less than
or equal to 47 **35.** less than or equal to -10.8
37. greater than or equal to 3 **39.** greater
than 21 **41.** greater than -4.1 **43.** less than
or equal to -92.4 **45.** greater than $22\frac{13}{15}$
47. greater than or equal to -9 **49.** greater
than $\frac{1}{5}$ **51.** less than -1.7

PAGE 296 REVIEW EXERCISES **1.** -2.6,
-1.4, 1.2, 3.2 **3.** -12.2, -12.09, -11.2, 12,
112 **5.** -30.05, -5.3, -5.03, 0.35, 3.05
7. -2.89, -2.8, 2.089, 2.89, 28.9

PAGES 299–300 WRITTEN EXERCISES All
the numbers: **1.** less than -6

3. greater than or equal to -9

5. less than -30

7. greater than or equal to -42

9. greater than $5\frac{2}{5}$ **11.** greater than or equal to
-10 **13.** greater than 2 **15.** greater than or
equal to 3 **17.** greater than -4 **19.** less than
or equal to 5 **21.** less than 8 **23.** less than or
equal to $-3\frac{1}{13}$ **25.** less than or equal to -3
27. greater than 1 **29.** less than or equal
to -2 **31.** greater than 15 **33.** less than 2
35. greater than 24 **37.** less than -7.2
39. greater than or equal to -10.3

PAGE 300 REVIEW EXERCISES **1.** $n + 9$
3. $n - 16$ **5.** $n + 3$ **7.** $\frac{n}{5}$

PAGES 302–303 PROBLEMS **1.** 36, 37
3. 4 hr **5.** $22,714.29 **7.** 3, 4, 5 **9.** 400
employees **11.** 51 checks

PAGE 303 SELF-TEST B **1.** $a < b$
2. $35 > 4z$ All the numbers: **3.** less than or
equal to 28 **4.** greater than 3 **5.** greater
or equal to 7 **6.** greater than $4\frac{2}{3}$ **7.** greater
than -14 **8.** greater than 5 **9.** less than 2
10. greater than 2 **11.** less than or equal to 0
12. greater than or equal to -6 **13.** 74, 75

PAGE 306 CHAPTER REVIEW **1.** False
3. True **5.** True **7.** False **9.** b **11.** c
13. D **15.** B **17.** E **19.** G **21.** b

PAGE 308 CUMULATIVE REVIEW
EXERCISES **1.** -5 **3.** 18 **5.** 2 **7.** 2 **9.** 4
11. 64 **13.** 3 **15.** 7 **17.** 5 **19.** 4 **21.** $-\frac{1}{4}$
23. 3 **25.** $\frac{4}{8}$, $\frac{7}{8}$ **27.** $\frac{4}{20}$, $\frac{15}{20}$ **29.** $\frac{8}{12}$, $\frac{3}{12}$, $\frac{5}{12}$
31. skew **33.** diameter **35.** vertex **37.** $91\frac{2}{3}\%$
39. 200

PAGE 309 CUMULATIVE REVIEW
PROBLEMS **1.** $79.38 **3.** 23,500 ft
5. 1230 lb **7.** 52 cm **9.** $616.13

9 The Coordinate Plane

PAGES 314–315 WRITTEN EXERCISES
1. $(-5, -5)$ **3.** $(5, 1)$ **5.** $(-3, -2)$
7. $(-1, 4)$ **9.** I **11.** V **13.** D **15.** W **17.** M
19. c. rectangle **21. c.** parallelogram
23. b. $(-5, 1)$, $(-2, -2)$, $(2, -2)$, $(2, 1)$
d. Translation **25. b.** $(-2, 3)$, $(2, 3)$, $(4, 1)$,
$(4, -1)$, $(1, 1)$, $(-1, 1)$, $(-4, -1)$, $(-4, 1)$
d. Translation **27. b.** $(-6, 5)$, $(-2, 1)$, $(-9, 3)$
d. Reflection

PAGE 315 REVIEW EXERCISES **1.** 8
3. 27 **5.** -5 **7.** -15

PAGES 318–319 WRITTEN EXERCISES
1. Yes **3.** Yes **5.** No **7.** No **9.** No **11.** No
13. Yes **15.** Yes **17.** $y = -2x + 7$
19. $y = 4x + 16$ **21.** $y = \frac{2}{3}x - 2$
23. a. $y = x + 7$ **b.** $(2, 9)$, $(-5, 2)$, $(7, 14)$
25. a. $y = \frac{1}{2}x + 5$ **b.** $(4, 7)$, $(0, 5)$, $(6, 8)$
27. a. $y = -\frac{1}{4}x + 5$ **b.** $(4, 4)$, $(-8, 7)$, $(0, 5)$
29. a. $y = \frac{3}{2}x - 3$ **b.** $(4, 3)$, $(-2, -6)$,
$(-8, -15)$ **31. a.** $y = \frac{1}{2}x + \frac{5}{2}$ **b.** $(3, 4)$, $(5, 5)$,
$(-1, 2)$ **33. a.** $y = \frac{5}{2}x + 3$ **b.** $(2, 8)$, $(1, 5\frac{1}{2})$,
$(-3, -4\frac{1}{2})$ In Exercises 35–43, answers will
vary. Examples are given. **35.** $(-1, 0)$, $(0, -1)$,
$(1, -2)$ **37.** $(-1, 1)$, $(0, 0)$, $(1, -1)$
39. $(-1, 0)$, $(0, 5)$, $(1, 10)$ **41.** $(-3, -6)$,
$(0, -4)$, $(3, -2)$ **43.** $(-1, 4)$, $(0, 6)$, $(1, 8)$
45. $x + y = 0$ **47.** $x + y = -3$

PAGE 319 REVIEW EXERCISES **1.** 3
3. 28 **5.** 3 **7.** -56 **9.** -4

PAGES 321–323 WRITTEN EXERCISES
1.

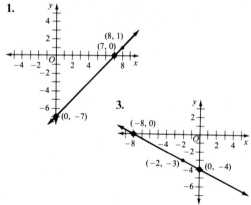

3.

5.–33. Each graph is a straight line through the
points listed: **5.** $(0, 10)$, $(1, 8)$, $(5, 0)$ **7.** $(0, 0)$,
$(1, 1)$, $(2, 2)$ **9.** $(-2, -1)$, $(0, 0)$ **11.** $(0, -6)$,
$(6, 0)$ **13.** $(-3, 0)$, $(0, -3)$ **15.** $(0, 4)$, $(1, 0)$
17. $(-2, 0)$, $(0, 6)$ **19.** $(-8, 0)$, $(0, 2)$
21. $(-4, 0)$, $(0, 3)$ **23.** $(-\frac{5}{2}, 0)$, $(0, 1)$
25. $(0, 6)$, $(6, 0)$ **27.** $(0, -6)$, $(2, 0)$ **29.** $(-12, 0)$, $(0, 6)$
31. $(0, -\frac{1}{2})$, $(\frac{1}{3}, 0)$ **33.** $(0, -8)$, $(6, 0)$
35. **37.**

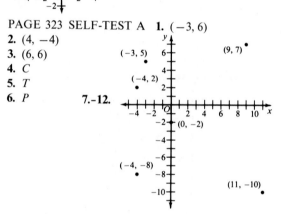

39. **47.** $-\frac{3}{4}$

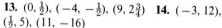

PAGE 323 SELF-TEST A **1.** $(-3, 6)$
2. $(4, -4)$
3. $(6, 6)$
4. C
5. T
6. P **7.–12.**

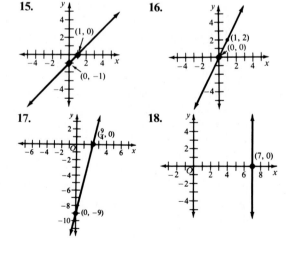

13. $(0, \frac{1}{2})$, $(-4, -\frac{1}{2})$, $(9, 2\frac{3}{4})$ **14.** $(-3, 12)$,
$(\frac{1}{2}, 5)$, $(11, -16)$
15. **16.**

17. **18.**

544 *Answers*

PAGES 326–327 WRITTEN EXERCISES
1. Intersect **3.** Parallel **5.** Coincide
7. Parallel **9.** Intersect **11.** Coincide
13. Intersect **15.** Parallel **17.** Intersect **19.** 2

PAGE 327 REVIEW EXERCISES **1.** $1\frac{1}{8}$
3. $\frac{7}{8}$ **5.** $\frac{4}{5}$ **7.** $\frac{1}{13}$

PAGE 327 CALCULATOR KEY-IN
$13,107.20

PAGES 331–333 PROBLEMS **1.** $\frac{3}{2}$ **3.** 4°C
5. 245 mi **7. a.** $y = 4.5x + 2$ **c.** 7 lb
9. a. $y = \frac{7}{12}x + \frac{1}{6}$ **c.** $10\frac{2}{3}$ min **11.** 5.5 s

PAGE 333 REVIEW EXERCISES All the
numbers: **1.** greater than $1\frac{1}{3}$ **3.** greater than or
equal to -1 **5.** less than or equal to 0
7. greater than or equal to -1 **9.** greater
than 41

PAGE 333 CALCULATOR KEY-IN 1; 121;
12,321; 1,234,321; 123,454,321; and so on.

PAGES 336–337 WRITTEN EXERCISES
1. $y = -3x - 6$ **3.** $y = x - 2$
5. $y = -x + 3$
7.

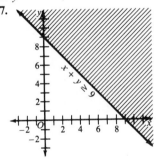

9. Solid line through $(-1, 0)$ and $(0, 2)$, shaded
region at left above line **11.** Solid line
through $(0, 4)$ and $(2, 0)$, shaded region at right
above line **13.** Solid line through $(-\frac{5}{2}, 0)$ and
$(0, 5)$, shaded region at left above line
15. Dashed line through $(0, -\frac{1}{3})$ and $(\frac{1}{2}, 0)$,
shaded region at left above line **17.** Solid line
through $(0, 8)$ parallel to x-axis, shaded region
below line **19.** Solid line through $(-1, 0)$ and
$(0, -1)$, shaded region at left below line.
21. Solid line through $(-3, 0)$ parallel to y-
axis, shaded region to left of line. **23.** Dashed
line through $(-\frac{5}{2}, 0)$ and $(0, 5)$, shaded region
at right below line **25.** $x < 4$ **27.** $y \geq -3$

PAGE 337 SELF-TEST B **1.** intersect
2. coincide **3.** parallel **4.** 4 wk

5.

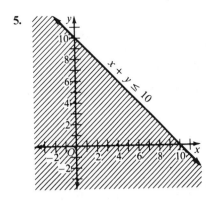

6.

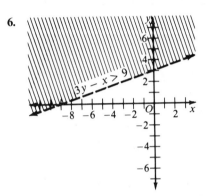

7.

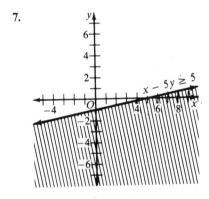

PAGES 338–339 ENRICHMENT
1. $y = 0.5x + 1.32$ **3.** 2.9 kg
5. $y = -3.3x + 20.8$ **a.** 15.85°C **b.** 6.3 h
7. $y = 0.59x + 7.39$; $10,930; $11,520

PAGE 340 CHAPTER REVIEW **1.** False
3. True **5.** C **7.** B **9.** Straight line through
$(0, 0)$ and $(1, -1)$ **11.** Straight line through
$(0, 2)$ and $(-1, 0)$ **13.** C **15.** constant
17. dashed

PAGE 342 CUMULATIVE REVIEW
EXERCISES **1.** 5*b* **3.** *y* + *z* − 12
5. 3*p* + 7 **7.** 288.01 **9.** 100.76 **11.** 4.8911
13. 554.09 **15.** 3.0088 **17.** −425.0612
19. −8.174 **21.** $-\frac{3}{14}$ **23.** $1\frac{1}{8}$ **25.** $-4\frac{47}{50}$
27. $t = -\frac{3}{4}(\frac{1}{5});\ -\frac{3}{20}$ **29.** *x* + 12 > 2*x*; the
solutions are all the numbers less than 12
31. 20.7 m **33.** 1.6 **35.** 42 **37.** no **39.** yes

PAGE 343 CUMULATIVE REVIEW
PROBLEMS **1.** $84.88 **3.** 7.5 times
5. $9799; $10,038 **7.** 44.1% **9.** 0.5 kW·h

10 Areas and Volumes

PAGES 348–349 WRITTEN EXERCISES
1. 1050 cm²; 130 cm **3.** 2665 km²; 212 km
5. 4416 mm²; 280 mm **7.** 2490.67 km²;
205.6 km **9.** perimeter: 40; area: 93.75
11. length: 80; perimeter: 250 **13.** width: 0.4;
area: 3.44 **15.** 74 **17.** 0.5 **19.** 4 **21.** 37
square units **23.** 30 square units **25.** 72
square units

PAGE 350 PROBLEMS **1.** 24 m²
3. a. 720 ft² **b.** $1080 **5.** 15 m **7.** 2025 m²

PAGE 350 REVIEW EXERCISES **1.** 28
3. 1.04 **5.** 40 **7.** 0.078

PAGES 354–355 WRITTEN EXERCISES
1. 67.34 m² **3.** 2127.5 cm² **5.** 290 mm²
7. 1830 km² **9.** 44.4 cm² **11.** 24 cm **13.** 4 m
15. 8 mm **17.** 15 **19.** The base and the height
are the same for each triangle. **21.** 450 cm²;
450 cm² **23.** 9 : 1; 3 : 1

PAGE 355 REVIEW EXERCISES **1.** 75
3. 6.76 **5.** 292 **7.** 1.33 **9.** 4868

PAGES 358–359 WRITTEN EXERCISES
1. 78.5 km² **3.** 0.283 m² **5.** $9\frac{5}{8}$ square units
7. 100π m² **9.** 4π square units **11.** 10 m
13. 2 cm **15.** 4π **17.** $31\frac{1}{2}π$ cm²

19. (25π − 50)m² **21.** $A = \dfrac{C^2}{4π}$

PAGE 359 PROBLEMS **1.** $1100 **3.** 314 m²
5. 462 cm² **7.** $\frac{100}{157}$

PAGE 359 REVIEW EXERCISES **1.** 16
3. 9 **5.** 18 **7.** 15

PAGES 362–363 WRITTEN EXERCISES
1.

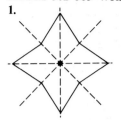

3.

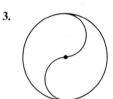

5.

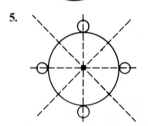

7. 84 m² **9.** 50π square units **11.** 135
square units **13.** 16 square units
15. (200 + 50π)cm²

PAGE 363 SELF-TEST A **1.** 273 cm²
2. 84 m² **3.** 72 cm² **4.** 36 m² **5.** 707 mm²
6. 616 cm² **7.**   **8.** 28 square
units

PAGES 366–368 WRITTEN EXERCISES
1. 90 cubic units **3.** 108 cubic units **5.** 22,608
cubic units **7.** 514 cubic units **9.** 50 L
11. 6330 L **13.** 4π; 3 **15.** 5; 4 **17.** 3; 9π
19. 60 cubic units **21. a.** quadrupled
b. halved **c.** doubled **23.** 3

PAGE 368 PROBLEMS **1.** 96 L
3. 7070 cm³ **5.** 1.62 cm

PAGE 368 REVIEW EXERCISES **1.** 32
3. 0.845 **5.** 1256 **7.** 10; −10

PAGES 371–372 WRITTEN EXERCISES
1. 72 cubic units **3.** 301 cubic units **5.** 56 cubic units **7.** 0.16 L **9.** 1000 L **11.** 10 **13.** 6 **15.** 3 **17.** 15 **19.** 3 **21.** 18

PAGE 372 PROBLEMS **1.** 2,590,000 m³ **3.** 14,700 cm³

PAGE 372 REVIEW EXERCISES **1.** 36 m **3.** 105 cm **5.** 51.2 km **7.** 580.8 km

PAGES 375–377 WRITTEN EXERCISES
1. 5700 cm² **3.** 14.56 m² **5.** 1660 cm²; 2560 cm² **7.** 226 square units; 283 square units **9.** 360 square units; 468 square units **11.** 30 cubic units; 72 square units **13.** 5 cm **15.** 6 **17.** 72 m²; 120 m² **19.** $n - 2$

PAGE 377 REVIEW EXERCISES **1.** 6 **3.** 105 **5.** 35 **7.** 38

PAGES 379–381 WRITTEN EXERCISES
1. 36π square units; 36π cubic units **3.** 144π square units; 288π cubic units **5.** 400π square units; $\frac{4000}{3}\pi$ cubic units **7.** $\frac{16}{3}\pi$ cubic units **9.** 9.68π square units **11.** 51.84π square units; 62.208π cubic units **13.** 9 units; 324π square units **15.** 8 units; $\frac{2048}{3}\pi$ cubic units **17.** 324π cubic units **19.** The Earth's volume is about 49.3 times that of the moon. **21. a.** $2:3$ **b.** $2:3$ **c.** $2:3$

PAGE 381 REVIEW EXERCISES **1.** 2.1 **3.** 0.64 **5.** 3.5 **7.** 810

PAGE 381 CALCULATOR KEY-IN
1. About 126 times greater

PAGES 383–384 WRITTEN EXERCISES
1. 6300 **3.** 4300 **5.** 810 g **7.** 34 kg **9.** 460 t **11.** 180 g **13.** 33.1 g **15.** 72.7 g **17.** 7460 kg

PAGES 384–385 PROBLEMS **1.** 13.3 kg **3.** 81.1 g **5.** 3.91 t

PAGE 385 SELF-TEST B **1.** 41.8 **2.** 27,200 **3.** 9248; 9.248 **4.** 0.314 m³ **5.** 1200 m³ **6.** 10,800 cm³ **7. a.** 98 square units **b.** 122 square units **8. a.** 94.2 square units **b.** 251 square units **9. a.** 3024 square units **b.** 3672 square units **10. a.** 1296π cm² **b.** 7776π cm³ **11. a.** 144π m² **b.** 288π m³ **12.** 8240 g **13.** 181.76 g

PAGE 387 ENRICHMENT **1.** New York

3. Rio de Janeiro **5.** Moscow **7.** Casablanca **9.** 40°N, 105°W **11.** 55°N, 0° **13.** 15°N, 15°W **15.** 65°N, 165°W

PAGE 388 CHAPTER REVIEW **1.** b **3.** c **5.** d **7.** 3864 cm³ **9.** 45.2 cubic units **11.** 168; 266 **13.** 2300; 18400 **15.** 60.48 kg

PAGES 390–391 CUMULATIVE REVIEW EXERCISES **1.** 5 **3.** 10 **5.** 12.5 **7.** -22.5 **9.** $\frac{37}{12}$, or $3\frac{1}{12}$ **11.** $\frac{2}{5}$ **13.** $\frac{52}{3}$, or $17\frac{1}{3}$ **15.** $-\frac{37}{4}$, or $-9\frac{1}{4}$ **17.** All the numbers greater than 3 **19.** All the numbers less than or equal to 40 **21.** All the numbers greater than or equal to 9 **23.** 7 **25.** 21 **27.** 45°; 45° **29.** 8.1 **31.** 24% **33.** 63,200 **35.** $y = 18 - 4x$ **37.** $y = x - 8\frac{1}{3}$ **39.** $y = \frac{20}{x}$ **41.** 196π cm² **43.** 15625π km² **45.** $3,258,025\pi$ cm² **47.** 256π square units; $\frac{2048}{3}\pi$ cubic units **49.** 5184π square units; $62,208\pi$ cubic units

PAGE 391 CUMULATIVE REVIEW PROBLEMS **1.** 1929 stories **3.** 25 m **5.** $\frac{1}{4}$ **7.** 5%

11 Applying Algebra to Right Triangles
PAGE 395 WRITTEN EXERCISES **1.** 6 and 7 **3.** -4 **5.** 1 **7.** -6 **9.** 7 and 8 **11.** 5 and 6 **13.** 3 and 4 **15.** 1 and 2 **17.** 3 **19.** 4 and 5 **21.** 9 **23.** $>$ **25.** $<$ **27.** $=$ **29.** $>$ **31.** 81 **33.** 11

PAGE 395 REVIEW EXERCISES **1.** 6.57 **3.** 8.67 **5.** 11.95 **7.** 0.13

PAGE 398 WRITTEN EXERCISES **1.** 3.3 **3.** 5.7 **5.** 2.8 **7.** 5.1 **9.** 7.5 **11.** 9.5 **13.** 2.3 **15.** 3.0 **17.** 2.9 **19.** 1.9 **21.** 12.3 **23.** 26.5 **25.** 3.9 **27.** 8.4 **29.** 0.6 **31.** 0.2 **33.** 1.41 **35.** 2.23

PAGE 398 REVIEW EXERCISES **1.** 58 **3.** 6.72 **5.** 3.89 **7.** 93.57

PAGE 398 CALCULATOR KEY-IN **1. a.** 1 **b.** 10 **c.** 100 **3. a.** 8.3666002 **b.** 83.666002 **c.** 836.66002 **5. a.** 0.73484692 **b.** 7.3484692 **c.** 73.484692

PAGES 400–401 WRITTEN EXERCISES **1.** 8.06 **3.** 7.48 **5.** 9.85 **7.** 64.03 **9.** 0.87 **11.** 22.25 **13.** 26.15 **15.** 59.40 **17.** 12.57 **19.** 0.37 **21.** 0.43 **23.** 2.43 **25.** 9.03

27. 2.95 **29.** 7.13 **31.** 27.15 **33.** 22.36
35. 19.49 **37.** 58.91

PAGE 401 PROBLEMS **1.** 9.22 m **3.** $21
5. 3.87 cm **7.** 5.92 m

PAGE 401 REVIEW EXERCISES **1.** 0.81
3. 0.0036 **5.** 13.69 **7.** 590.49

PAGE 404 WRITTEN EXERCISES **1.** 289
3. 400 **5.** Yes **7.** Yes **9.** Yes **11.** Yes
13. No **15.** $c = 10$ **17.** $a = 3.32$
19. $c = 11.40$ **21.** $b = 70$ **23.** $a = 27$, $b = 36$,
$c = 45$

PAGES 404–405 PROBLEMS **1.** 108.2 km
3. 55.7 m **5.** 7.1 cm **7.** 17.3

PAGE 405 SELF-TEST A **1.** 7 and 8
2. -9 **3.** 8 **4.** 7 **5.** 9.3 **6.** 4.2 **7.** 7.1
8. 3.1 **9.** 2.4 **10.** $c = 5$ **11.** $a = 28$
12. $b = 16$

PAGES 409–410 WRITTEN EXERCISES
1. RQ **3.** 9 **5.** 104° **7.** 25 **9.** 65°; 65°
11. $x = 5$, $y = 9$ **13.** $x = 27$, $y = 25$
15. $x = 46\frac{2}{7}$, $y = 14$ **17.** 180 cm **19. a.** 18
b. 18 **21.** $\angle CDA \cong \angle BCA$; $\angle A \cong \angle A$; so
$\angle B \cong \angle DCA$ **23.** Yes; angles congruent,
sides proportional **25.** Not necessarily; the
lengths of the sides may differ.

PAGE 410 REVIEW EXERCISES **1.** 519
3. 1562 **5.** 2.2454 **7.** 4.878 **9.** 3741.36

PAGES 413–414 WRITTEN EXERCISES
1. $\frac{3\sqrt{10}}{5}$ **3.** $\sqrt{3}$ **5.** $\frac{2\sqrt{x}}{x}$ **7.** $x = 3.2$, $y = 5.5$
9. $x = 7.4$, $y = 8.6$ **11.** $x = 3.2$, $y = 4.5$
13. $2\sqrt{2}$ **15.** $5\sqrt{3}$; $10\sqrt{3}$ **17.** $AB = 5.4$
19. $BC = 6.0$ **21.** $BC = 1.7y$ **23.** $x = 6$,
$y = 3$

PAGES 414–415 PROBLEMS **1.** 8.7 m
3. 20 m **5.** 56.6 cm **7.** 40; 28.3 **9. a.** 0.9 r
units **b.** 0.4 r² units² **11.** 5.2 m

PAGE 415 REVIEW EXERCISES **1.** 1.25
3. $0.\overline{2}$ **5.** 1.1 **7.** $0.1\overline{6}$

PAGES 418–419 WRITTEN EXERCISES
1. $\sin A = \frac{3}{5}$; $\cos A = \frac{4}{5}$; $\tan A = \frac{3}{4}$; $\sin B = \frac{4}{5}$;
$\cos B = \frac{3}{5}$; $\tan B = \frac{4}{3}$ **3.** $\sin A = \frac{39}{89}$;
$\cos A = \frac{80}{89}$; $\tan A = \frac{39}{80}$; $\sin B = \frac{80}{89}$; $\cos B = \frac{39}{89}$;
$\tan B = \frac{80}{39}$ **5.** $\sin A = \frac{a}{c}$; $\cos A = \frac{b}{c}$;

$\tan A = \frac{a}{b}$; $\sin B = \frac{b}{c}$; $\cos B = \frac{a}{c}$; $\tan B = \frac{b}{a}$
7. $x = 5$; $\tan A = \frac{5}{12}$ **9.** $x = \sqrt{21}$;
$\sin A = \frac{\sqrt{21}}{11}$ **11.** $x = 24$; $\cos A = \frac{12}{13}$
13. a. $\frac{\sqrt{3}}{2}$; 0.866 **b.** $\frac{1}{2}$; 0.500 **c.** $\sqrt{3}$; 1.732
15. a. 6.4 **b.** 2.7 **c.** 0.4 **17. a.** 3.8 **b.** 8.2
c. 0.5

PAGE 419 REVIEW EXERCISES **1.** b
3. a **5.** b **7.** b

PAGE 422 WRITTEN EXERCISES
1. 0.4226; 0.9063; 0.4663 **3.** 0.9994; 0.0349;
28.6363 **5.** 0.6293; 0.7771; 0.8098 **7.** 0.9613;
0.2756; 3.4874 **9.** 0.6428; 0.7660; 0.8391
11. 0.9063; 0.4226; 2.1445 **13.** 81° **15.** 1°
17. 76° **19.** 30° **21.** 60° **23.** 6 **25.** 58°
27. 25° **29.** 70° **31.** $c = 9.4$, m $\angle A = 32°$,
m $\angle B = 58°$ **33.** $a = 9.5$, $b = 3.1$,
m $\angle B = 18°$ **35.** $a = 8.1$, m $\angle A = 64°$,
m $\angle B = 26°$ **37.** $a = 41.3$, $c = 43.9$,
m $\angle A = 70°$ **39.** $a = 19.2$, $c = 22.6$,
m $\angle B = 32°$

PAGES 423–424 PROBLEMS **1.** 42.0 m
3. 11° **5. a.** 42.5 m **b.** 10.7 m **7.** 39° **9.** 67°

PAGE 424 SELF-TEST B **1.** $\sim$ **2.** $\frac{TN}{TY}$

3. 7.5 **4.** = **5.** 6 cm **6.** $4\sqrt{3}$; $8\sqrt{3}$ **7.** $\frac{p}{q}$

8. $\frac{r}{q}$ **9.** $\frac{p}{r}$ **10.** m $\angle P = 60°$, m $\angle R = 30°$,
$p = 5.2$ **11.** $p = 23.5$, $q = 24.1$, m $\angle R = 12°$
12. $q = 8.7$, $r = 3.4$, m $\angle P = 67°$
13. $r = 20.1$, $p = 13.1$, m $\angle P = 33°$

PAGE 425 COMPUTER BYTE **1.** 3, 4, 5
3. 5, 12, 13 **5.** Output: THERE IS NO SUCH
TRIPLE.

PAGE 427 ENRICHMENT **1.** 3 **3.** 2 **5.** 4
7. There is no square root because a is
negative and n is even. **9.** -10 **11.** 5
13. $\sqrt{36} = 6$ **15.** $\sqrt[3]{64} = 4$ **17.** $\sqrt[4]{16} = 2$
19. $\sqrt[4]{81} = 3$ Calculator Activity
1. 2.1544347 **3.** 2.1867241 **5.** 1.4953488
7. About 9.4203395 π

PAGE 428 CHAPTER REVIEW **1.** 2
3. 5.35 **5.** 4.899 and 5 **7.** False **9.** False
11. F **13.** 45° **15.** $7\sqrt{2}$ **17.** A **19.** D **21.** F

PAGES 430–431 CUMULATIVE REVIEW
EXERCISES **1.** $\frac{10}{27}$ **3.** 3300 **5.** $-3\frac{1}{3}$
7. -100 **9.** 0 **11.** -200 **13.** 2.5 **15.** -1
17. $>$ **19.** $<$ **21.** 38 **23.** 2.5 **25.** $7\frac{1}{3}$ **27.** 8
29. 12 **31.** $5\frac{3}{5}$ **33.** 11.6 ft **35.** 4 **37.** 10
39.

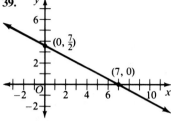

41.

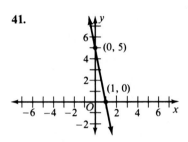

43. 55.5π **45.** $\dfrac{5\sqrt{2}}{2}$ **47.** $2\sqrt{n}$

PAGE 431 CUMULATIVE REVIEW
PROBLEMS **1.** 40 dimes, 49 nickels, 52
quarters **3.** $22.50 **5.** $2.17 **7.** 52 in. by
52 in.

12 Statistics and Probability

PAGES 436–437 WRITTEN EXERCISES
1. 100 million persons **3.** approx. 400 million
5. 23%
7.

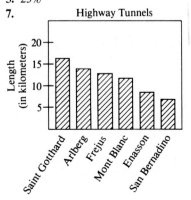

11.

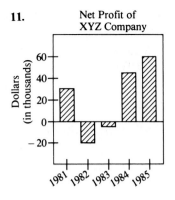

PAGE 437 REVIEW EXERCISES **1.** 282
3. 354 **5.** 135 **7.** 131.4

PAGES 440–442 WRITTEN EXERCISES
1.

$\frac{1}{4}$	90°
$\frac{3}{10}$	108°
$\frac{1}{5}$	72°
$\frac{1}{4}$	90°
240 1	360°

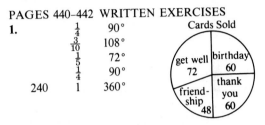

3. Surface of Earth **5.** Number of Cars Rented

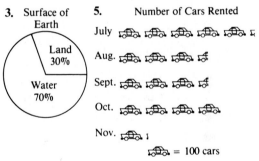

9. People Living in U.S.

15. a. Distribution of Library Grant

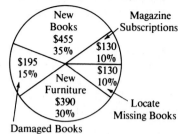

b.   Distribution of Library Grant

= $100

Magazine Subscriptions   New Books   Repair Damaged Books   New Furniture   Locate Missing Books

PAGE 442 REVIEW EXERCISES 1. 0.84, 2.6, 3, 4, 7 **3.** −6, −5, $3\frac{1}{2}$, $4\frac{1}{4}$, 7 **5.** −12, −10, −9, −6, −2 **7.** 0.09, 0.9, 1.09, 1.1

PAGES 444–445 WRITTEN EXERCISES
1. 24; 23; 12 **3.** 16; 15; 19 **5.** 55.5; 55.5; 24
7. 3.2; 3.4; 0.9 **9.** −1; −2; 8 **11.** 0.3; 0.2; 2.1 **13.** −2°, −1°, 19° **15.** 16 **17.** 16
19. 94 **21.** It is increased by 5.

PAGE 445 REVIEW EXERCISES 1. 6.1
3. 14.8 **5.** 14 **7.** 3

PAGES 447–448 WRITTEN EXERCISES
1. 4; 6.95; 7; 7 **3.** 20; 10; 10; 5 **5.** 6; 16.75; 17; 16 and 17

7.

x	f	
8	2	range = 8
6	1	mean = 3.9
5	4	median = 4
4	5	mode = 4
3	2	
1	3	
0	1	

9.

x	f	
20	6	range = 6
19	7	mean = 18.1
18	8	median = 18
17	5	mode = 18
16	2	
15	1	
14	1	

11.

x	f	
103	2	range = 6
102	2	mean = 100.4
101	6	median = 100
100	9	mode = 100
99	3	
97	1	

13. 72

PAGE 448 REVIEW EXERCISES 1. The average of a set of data. **3.** The number from a set of data which occurs most often. **5.** An integer not evenly divisible by 2. **7.** A number greater than 1 whose only factors are 1 and itself.

PAGE 449 COMPUTER BYTE 1. $18.\overline{3}$
3. $578.1\overline{6}$ **5.** approx. 4494.13042 **7.** 489,439.2

PAGES 451–452 WRITTEN EXERCISES
1. 15 **3.** 1 **5.** 9 **7.** 20 **9.** 34
11.

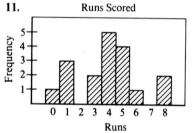

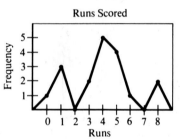

17.

x	f
10–15	3
15–20	3
20–25	5
25–30	4
30–35	5
35–40	4
40–45	6

PAGE 452 SELF-TEST A
1.

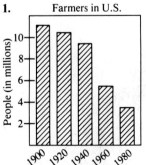

2.

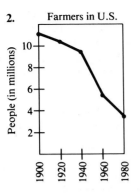

Farmers in U.S.

3. Farmers in United States

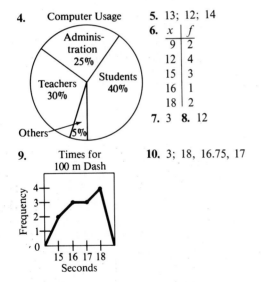

🚶 = 1,000,000 people

4. Computer Usage

5. 13; 12; 14

6.

x	f
9	2
12	4
15	3
16	1
18	2

7. 3 **8.** 12

9. Times for 100 m Dash

10. 3; 18, 16.75, 17

PAGE 455 WRITTEN EXERCISES **1.** 120
3. 5040 **5.** 720 **7.** 40,320 **9.** 360 **11.** 74,046

PAGES 455–457 PROBLEMS **1.** 6 **3.** 24
5. 42 **7.** 24 **9.** 12 **11.** 5040 **13.** 720
15. 216 **17.** 20 **19.** 6

PAGE 457 REVIEW EXERCISES **1.** 7 **3.** 3
5. 12 **7.** 165

PAGES 459–460 PROBLEMS **1.** 15 **3.** 15
5. 210 **7.** 252 **9. a.** 4 **b.** 6 **c.** 4 **d.** 1
e. 15 **11.** 10,192

PAGE 460 REVIEW EXERCISES **1.** Any of
two or more whole numbers that are multiplied
to form a product. **3.** Any whole numbers that
is divisible by 2. **5.** The product of a number
by itself 3 times. **7.** One or less

PAGES 464–465 WRITTEN EXERCISES
1. $\frac{1}{6}$ **3.** $\frac{2}{3}$ **5.** 0 **7.** $\frac{1}{4}$ **9.** $\frac{1}{5}$ **11.** $\frac{1}{2}$ **13.** $\frac{3}{4}$
15. $\frac{2}{5}$ **17.** $\frac{3}{5}$ **19.** $\frac{1}{3}$ **21.** $\frac{1}{2}$ **23.** $\frac{1}{3}$ **25.** $\frac{2}{3}$ **27.** $\frac{1}{12}$
29. $\frac{1}{6}$ **31.** $\frac{1}{18}$ **33.** $\frac{2}{9}$ **35.** $\frac{5}{12}$ **37. a.** $\frac{1}{9}$ **b.** $\frac{5}{9}$
c. $\frac{4}{9}$ **d.** $\frac{8}{9}$ **e.** $\frac{4}{9}$ **39.** $\frac{1}{2}$

PAGE 465 REVIEW EXERCISES **1.** 0 **3.** $\frac{1}{3}$
5. $\frac{1}{2}$ **7.** $\frac{3}{4}$

PAGES 468–469 WRITTEN EXERCISES
1. 1 to 1 **3.** 1 to 2 **5.** 5 to 1 **7.** 2 to 3 **9.** 7
to 3 **11.** 1 to 1 **13.** 3 to 1 **15.** 4 to 1 **17.** 17
to 1 **19.** 17 to 1 **21.** 13 to 5 **23. a.** 2 to 1
b. 1 to 2 **25.** 11 to 25 **27.** 3 to 1 **29.** $\frac{1}{9}$

PAGE 469 REVIEW EXERCISES **1.** $\frac{23}{24}$
3. $\frac{11}{12}$ **5.** $\frac{25}{36}$ **7.** $\frac{71}{196}$

PAGE 469 COMPUTER BYTE **1.** Answers
may vary; 1

PAGES 471–472 WRITTEN EXERCISES
1. $\frac{13}{15}$ **3.** 0.3 **5. a.** $\frac{1}{3}$ **b.** $\frac{1}{2}$ **c.** $\frac{5}{6}$ **7. a.** $\frac{1}{6}$ **b.** $\frac{5}{6}$
9. a. $\frac{1}{2}$ **b.** $\frac{1}{3}$ **c.** $\frac{5}{6}$ **11. a.** $\frac{1}{5}$ **b.** $\frac{2}{5}$ **c.** $\frac{3}{5}$
13. a. $\frac{1}{4}$ **b.** $\frac{3}{10}$ **c.** $\frac{11}{20}$ **15. a.** $\frac{1}{4}$ **b.** $\frac{3}{10}$ **c.** $\frac{2}{5}$
17. a. $\frac{1}{12}$ **b.** $\frac{11}{36}$ **c.** $\frac{11}{18}$ **19. a.** $\frac{1}{6}$ **b.** $\frac{1}{6}$ **c.** $\frac{1}{3}$
21. 9 to 11 **23.** 11 to 9

PAGE 473 SELF-TEST B **1.** 24 **2.** 120 **3.** 10
4. 210 **5.** $\frac{1}{8}$ **6.** $\frac{1}{2}$ **7.** $\frac{1}{4}$ **8.** 1 **9.** 1 to 3
10. 1 to 3 **11.** 3 to 1 **12.** $\frac{7}{12}$ **13.** 0.2

PAGE 475 ENRICHMENT **1. a.** 12 gal
b. -1, 1, -3, 3 **c.** 5 gal² **d.** 2.24 gal
3. a. 22.8 mi/gal **b.** -2.8, -3.8, -2.8, -0.8,
10.2 **c.** 26.96 mi/gal² **d.** 5.19 mi/gal

PAGE 476 CHAPTER REVIEW **1.** Sprint
3. broken line **5.** 8 **7.** 68.5 **9.** 2 **11.** 3
13. True **15.** True

PAGE 478 CUMULATIVE REVIEW
EXERCISES **1.** 49.5 **3.** 7.475 **5.** $m + 3n$
7. $1\frac{6}{35}$ **9.** $\frac{21}{32}$ **11.** $-3\frac{2}{3}$ **13.** 20 **15.** All the
numbers greater than or equal to -2 **17.** 42
19. 13.3 **21.** 46.8 **23.** 20% **25.** 36

Answers **551**

27. $C(-1, 4)$; $D(-7, 7)$; $m = -\frac{1}{2}$
29. $P = 468$ m; $A = 13308.75$ m^2
31. $P = 144$ m; $A = 756$ m^2 **33.** no

PAGE 479 CUMULATIVE REVIEW
PROBLEMS **1.** No **3.** 30% **5.** 9.9 cm
7. 180 m^2 **9.** $5\frac{1}{2}$ ft $\times$ $3\frac{1}{2}$ ft

Skill Review

PAGE 480 ADDITION **1.** 99 **3.** 43 **5.** 121
7. 741 **9.** 9.2 **11.** 367.43 **13.** 325.277
15. 46.119 **17.** 888 **19.** 522 **21.** 20.062
23. 8.156 **25.** 22.098 **27.** 18.50032 **29.** 95.83
31. 1396 **33.** 6.88 **35.** 155.072 **37.** 1497
39. 98.187 **41.** 1565 **43.** 1754 **45.** 1276.208
47. 54.7138

PAGE 481 SUBTRACTION **1.** 13 **3.** 26
5. 655 **7.** 613 **9.** 5.201 **11.** 11.744
13. 2.137 **15.** 1.892 **17.** 435.54 **19.** 0.074
21. 25 **23.** 62 **25.** 44 **27.** 48 **29.** 33
31. 40.13 **33.** 57.03 **35.** 0.063 **37.** 3162
39. 3549 **41.** 6925 **43.** 21.026 **45.** 2.6205
47. 0.8651 **49.** 73.403 **51.** 14,548

PAGE 482 MULTIPLICATION **1.** 26
3. 159 **5.** 141 **7.** 360 **9.** 1008 **11.** 4615
13. 942 **15.** 13,897.6 **17.** 44.53 **19.** 142.576
21. 600 **23.** 900 **25.** 72,000 **27.** 680,000
29. 141,000 **31.** 15,201 **33.** 5024 **35.** 55,380
37. 286.165 **39.** 18.8241 **41.** 75.295
43. 8840 **45.** 7914.7224 **47.** 0.1162779
49. 1.8574 **51.** 0.00869812

PAGE 483 DIVISION **1.** 17 **3.** 46 **5.** 16
7. 35.2 **9.** 0.76 **11.** 15.7 **13.** 10.8 **15.** 15.8
17. 13.3 **19.** 548.1 **21.** 49.6 **23.** 73.29
25. 81 **27.** 2.75 **29.** 2.63 **31.** 7.36 **33.** 1910
35. 0.25 **37.** 517.06 **39.** 129,413.33
41. 47.91 **43.** 534.27 **45.** 307.45 **47.** 610.67
49. 4900.53 **51.** 18.43 **53.** 3697.69 **55.** 0.01
57. 99.09

Extra Practice

PAGES 484–485 CHAPTER 1 **1.** 42.63
3. 0.16 **5.** 1 **7.** 24 **9.** 9 **11.** $\frac{1}{6}$ **13.** 40.8
15. 14 **17.** 2 **19.** 169 **21.** 1156 **23.** 16,807
25. 6561 **27.** 16,000 **29.** 3,456,000 **31.** 64
33. 1728 **35.** $(5 \times 10^2) + (1 \times 10^1) +$

$(6 \times 10^0) + \left(2 \times \frac{1}{10^1}\right) + \left(1 \times \frac{1}{10^2}\right)$

37. $(2 \times 10^1) + (5 \times 10^0) + \left(2 \times \frac{1}{10^1}\right)$

39. $(9 \times 10^1) + (1 \times 10^0) + \left(9 \times \frac{1}{10^1}\right)$

41. $(3 \times 10^2) + (0 + 10^1) + (7 \times 10^0) +$

$\left(0 \times \frac{1}{10^1}\right) + \left(0 \times \frac{1}{10^2}\right) + \left(9 \times \frac{1}{10^3}\right)$ **43.** 5.004
45. 9.0009 **47.** 0.0006 **49.** 113.9 **51.** 0.06
53. 45.55 **55.** 100 **57.** 1.84 **59.** 0 **61.** 8
63. 8 **65.** 112 **67.** 7 **69.** 11 **71.** 12 **73.** 31
75. 2448 **77.** 40 **79.** 52.1 s **81.** 1260 parts
83. 3 h

PAGES 486–487 CHAPTER 2 **1.** 3 **3.** 1
5. 6 **7.** 2 **9.** 9

11.

13.

15.

17. $^-8$, $^-2$, 0, 5, 6 **19.** $^-7$, $^-4$, $^-1$, 3, 5 **21.** $^-5$,
$^-4$, 0, 4, 5 **23.** $<$ **25.** 5, $^-5$ **27.** 0 **29.** 6, 5,
4, 3, 2, 1, 0, $^-1$, $^-2$, $^-3$, $^-4$, $^-5$, $^-6$
41. 9.9 **43.** 0 **45.** $^-404$ **47.** $^-2.9$ **49.** $^-2.3$
51. 20.9 **53.** 12.5 **55.** -0.6 **57.** 20.3
59. -13.5 **61.** -20.3 **63.** 5.2 **65.** 5.7
67. -3.2 **69.** -2.5 **71.** -8.9 **73.** 2.5
75. -4.1 **77.** -610 **79.** -0.91 **81.** 9100
83. -0.003 **85.** 0.5 **87.** -4.76 **89.** 50.02
91. 32.86 **93.** -25.434 **95.** -13.345
97. -15.66 **99.** 512 **101.** 128 **103.** 324
105. 144 **107.** $\frac{1}{16}$ **109.** $\frac{1}{1296}$ **111.** $\frac{1}{81}$
113. -1 **115.** $-\frac{1}{125}$ **117.** 10 **119.** $\frac{1}{16}$ **121.** $\frac{1}{9}$
123. 4

PAGES 488–489 CHAPTER 3 **1.** 1, 2, 3, 6
3. 1, 2, 5, 10 **5.** 1, 3, 5, 15 **7.** 1, 41 **9.** 1, 2,
4, 13, 26, 52 **11.** 1, 59 **13.** 5 **15.** 3, 9
17. 2, 4 **19.** 2, 3, 4, 5, 9, 10 **21.** 2, 3, 4, 5, 9,
10 **23.** none **25.** 2×5 **27.** 2×3^3
29. $2 \times 3 \times 5$ **31.** $\frac{1}{3}$ **33.** $1\frac{2}{5}$ **35.** $-1\frac{1}{2}$ **37.** $\frac{3}{5}$
39. $-1\frac{3}{4}$ **41.** $-\frac{7}{9}$ **43.** 1 **45.** $-\frac{1}{5}$ **47.** $-\frac{2}{7}$
49. 8 **51.** 5 **53.** 4 **55.** $\frac{17}{3}$ **57.** $-\frac{43}{10}$
59. $-\frac{57}{8}$ **61.** $\frac{25}{4}$ **63.** $\frac{20}{24}, \frac{9}{24}$ **65.** $\frac{12}{24}, \frac{10}{24}$
67. $-\frac{33}{84}, \frac{34}{84}$ **69.** $\frac{9}{13}$ **71.** $\frac{1}{3}$ **73.** $-\frac{179}{224}$
75. $-1\frac{17}{60}$ **77.** $3\frac{35}{48}$ **79.** $-5\frac{7}{12}$ **81.** $-\frac{3}{5}$
83. $-\frac{1}{2}$ **85.** $2\frac{4}{19}$ **87.** 2 **89.** $\frac{7}{30}$ **91.** $-\frac{5}{27}$
93. 0.375 **95.** $0.9\overline{54}$ **97.** $0.1\overline{6}$ **99.** $-0.5\overline{3}$
101. $0.7\overline{45}$ **103.** $-2.\overline{27}$ **105.** $\frac{3}{5}$ **107.** $1\frac{17}{50}$
109. $-3\frac{1}{40}$ **111.** $-2\frac{1}{11}$ **113.** $8\frac{7}{33}$

PAGES 490–491 CHAPTER 4 **1.** 50 **3.** 3
5. 62 **7.** 0.27 **9.** 4 **11.** 72 **13.** 4 **15.** 245
17. $\frac{1}{3}$ **19.** 4 **21.** $\frac{25}{108}$ **23.** 0.2 **25.** 90 **27.** 5
29. 4 **31.** 18 **33.** $18 - t$ **35.** $\frac{40}{m} - 16$
37. $3y + 11$ **39.** $6n = 54$ **41.** $n + 19 = 61$
43. $n = 152 - (-100)$ **45.** 395.77°C **47.** 5 h
49. 31 min to work; 24 min home

PAGES 492–493 CHAPTER 5
1. 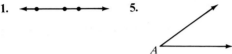 **5.**

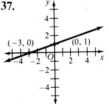

7. 10,000 **9.** 900 **11.** 7,700 **13.** 1.5 **15.** 157.5
17. 200; 2000 **19.** right **21.** vertex **23.** obtuse
25. sides, angles **27.** right **29.** equilateral
31. True **33.** False **35.** False **37.** True
39. 352 mm **41.** 50.2 mm **43.** 4.11 m
45. $\overline{SR}$ **47.** $\overline{NM}$ **49.** $\angle N$ **51.** $\angle L$
53. $\triangle CAB \cong \triangle DAB$; SSS
55.

PAGES 494–495 CHAPTER 6 **1.** $\frac{1}{6}$ **3.** $\frac{1}{8}$
5. $\frac{1}{4}$ **7.** $\frac{3}{10}$ **9.** 6.25 km/h **11.** 24 eggs
13. 15¢ **15.** 9.5 **17.** 39 **19.** 72 **21.** 8
23. $52 **25.** $1.95 **27.** 44 km **29.** 63.2 km
31. 81.6 km **33.** 122 km **35.** $\frac{1}{10}$ **37.** $\frac{39}{100}$
39. $\frac{27}{100}$ **41.** 2 **43.** $2\frac{3}{20}$ **45.** 10% **47.** $12\frac{1}{2}$%
49. $43\frac{3}{4}$% **51.** 144% **53.** 440% **55.** 0.71
57. 0.152 **59.** 0.024 **61.** 6.25 **63.** 2 **65.** 23%
67. 5% **69.** 0.25% **71.** 53% **73.** 12.5%
75. 0.25; 25% **77.** 0.625; 62.5% **79.** 1.375;
137.5% **81.** 8.75; 875% **83.** 5.2; 520%
85. 108.9 **87.** 500 **89.** 30% **91.** 240
93. 25 **95.** 3.0% **97.** 58 **99.** 48.96

PAGES 496–497 CHAPTER 7 **1.** 46.7%
3. 40% **5.** 400% **7.** 35% **9.** 80 **11.** 195
13. $1.92 **15.** 150% **17.** $38.16 **19.** 8.7%
21. $138,297.87 **23.** $81\frac{1}{4}$% **25.** $556.50
27. 13.8% **29.** $296.33 **31.** 51 boxes
33. $1.25 **35.** $510

PAGES 498–499 CHAPTER 8 **1.** 4 **3.** $\frac{1}{2}$
5. $\frac{3}{7}$ **7.** $\frac{1}{2}$ **9.** $1\frac{1}{3}$ **11.** $1\frac{1}{2}$ **13.** 1 **15.** 4 **17.** 4
19. $-\frac{1}{2}$ **21.** 3 **23.** $-1\frac{2}{3}$ **25.** sandwich: $2.60,
milk: $0.65 **27.** 15 ft, 45 ft **29.** $<$ **31.** $>$
33. $>$ **35.** $17 > 12$ **37.** $2n > 69$
39. $80 - 26 > 2(21)$ All the numbers: **41.** less
than or equal to -22 **43.** greater than $4\frac{5}{6}$
45. less than 7 **47.** greater than 7 **49.** less
than -4 **51.** less than -63 **53.** greater than
or equal to -55 **55.** less than 70 **57.** less
than or equal to $-4\frac{2}{7}$ **59.** less than or equal
to $11\frac{1}{5}$ **61.** greater than -5 **63.** greater than
or equal to -24 **65.** less than -9 **67.** less
than or equal to -3 **69.** 3 h

PAGES 500–501 CHAPTER 9 **1.** $(-6, 2)$
3. $(4, 4)$ **5.** $(-2, 4)$ **7.** G **9.** I **11.** J
13. **c.** rectangle **15.** **c.** triangle
17. **c.** right triangle
19. yes **21.** no **23.** yes **25.** yes **27.** yes
29. yes **31. a.** $y = 3x + 4$ **b.** $(-5, -11)$,
$(0, 4)$, $(5, 19)$ **33. a.** $y = \frac{3}{2}x + 3$ **b.** $(-2, 0)$,
$(0, 3)$, $(2, 6)$ **35. a.** $y = x - 3$ **b.** $(6, 3)$,
$(-1, -4)$, $(-3, -6)$
37.

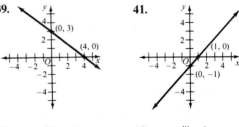

39. 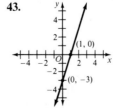 **41.**

43. 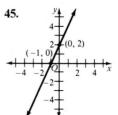 **45.**

47.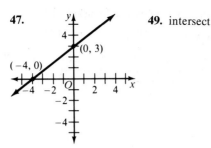

49. intersect

51. parallel **53.** intersect **55.** $y = 5x + 25$; slope is 5; 60¢

57. 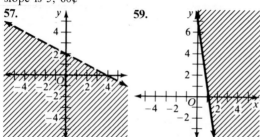 **59.**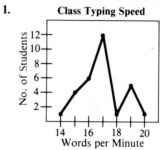

61.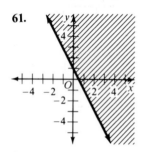

PAGES 502–503 CHAPTER 10 **1.** 5000 m², 300 m **3.** 7625 cm², 372 cm **5.** 132 cm²
7. 119 km² **9.** 80.5 cm **11.** 135 m
13. 20 mm **15.** 380 m² **17.** 9850 m²
19.   **21.** 865 m³

23. 1260 mm³ **25.** 30 cm **27.** 3536 cm³
29. a. 1350 cm² **b.** 1890 cm² **31. a.** 900 cm²
b. 1350 cm² **33.** 1296π cm² **35.** 12 m
37. 2.64 kg **39.** 8530.2 g

PAGES 504–505 CHAPTER 11 **1.** 3 **3.** -6,
-5 **5.** 4, 5 **7.** 9 **9.** 7, 8 **11.** 5 **13.** 4
15. 9, 10 **17.** 4.9 **19.** 9.6 **21.** 7.1 **23.** 3.2
25. 6.1 **27.** 2.4 **29.** 2.83 **31.** 2.24 **33.** 4.90
35. 6.25 **37.** 5.57 **39.** 7.62 **41.** 3.97
43. 4.63 **45.** no **47.** no **49.** no **51.** yes

53. yes **55.** 6.40 **57.** 9 **59.** 9.90 **61.** 15
63. $x = 20$, $y = 40$ **65.** $x = 12$, $y = 12$
67. $x = 20$, $y = 10$ **69.** $\dfrac{2\sqrt{3}}{3}$ **71.** $\dfrac{x\sqrt{2a}}{2a}$

73. $\dfrac{x}{y}$ **75.** $\dfrac{y}{z}$ **77.** $\dfrac{x}{z}$ **79.** 0.4540, 0.8910,
0.5095 **81.** 0.9998, 0.0175, 57.2900 **83.** 26°
85. 53° **87.** 23°

PAGES 506–507 CHAPTER 12
1.

Class Typing Speed

No. of Students / Words per Minute

3. mean: 7; median: 8; range: 10 **5.** mean:
4.4; median: 3.5; range: 8 **7.** mean: 197;
median: 190; range: 95 **9.** mean: 5500;
median: 6500; range: 7000

11.

x	f
8	1
9	2
10	4
11	3
12	3
13	0
14	1
15	0
16	1

mean: 11; median: 11; range: 8; mode: 10

13.

x	f
1	3
2	5
3	3
4	3
5	4

mean: 3; median: 3; range: 4; mode: 2

15.

x	f
4.5–34.5	6
34.5–64.5	8
64.5–94.3	11

17. 720 **19.** 3,628,800 **21.** 120 **23.** 6 **25.** 20
27. 252 **29.** 1,326 **31.** $\frac{4}{7}$ **33.** 1 **35.** $\frac{5}{7}$
37. a. 7 to 1 **b.** 3 to 1 **c.** 3 to 1 **39. a.** $\frac{5}{18}$
b. $\frac{1}{36}$ **c.** $\frac{11}{36}$ **41.** $\frac{1}{2}$ **43. a.** $\frac{1}{6}$ **b.** $\frac{5}{36}$ **c.** $\frac{1}{36}$ **d.** $\frac{5}{18}$

Appendix A • Estimation

PAGES 512–513   EXERCISES   **1.** c
3. c   **5.** b   **7.** d   **9.** c
PAGE 513   PROBLEMS   **1.** 1 hour
3. after the 8   **5.** $400

Appendix B • Stem-and-Leaf Plots

PAGE 515   WRITTEN EXERCISES

1. 1 | 4, 4, 8   **3.** 4 | 3, 4, 4, 4
2 | 2, 5, 7, 9   5 | 0, 3
3 | 1, 5   6 | 2, 5, 7
                        7 | 2

5. 0 | 2, 5, 5, 7, 9   **7.** 5 | 3, 3, 6, 8
1 | 0, 2, 3, 6   6 |
2 | 3, 4, 7   7 | 7
3 | 0   8 | 4, 7
                         9 | 0, 1, 1, 2, 5

9. Car Wash Customers   **11.** Basketball Point Totals
3 | 0, 1, 2, 6   7 | 5, 7, 8
4 | 2, 4, 5, 5, 6   8 | 0, 2, 2, 3, 3, 7, 7
5 | 3, 4, 7   9 | 1, 4, 5
6 | 10 | 1, 2
7 | 2, 3

13. Since the data are all   4 | 6, 8, 9
multiples of ten, disregard   5 | 2, 3, 5, 7, 8
the last digit and use the   6 | 1, 4, 5
hundreds' digits as stems   7 | 2, 8
and the tens' digits as leaves.

Appendix C • Box-and-Whisker Plots

PAGE 517   WRITTEN EXERCISES

1.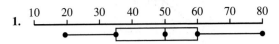

3.

5.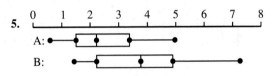

7. Example: 20, 40, 50, 55, 62, 65, 80

555